THAI-ENGLISH
STUDENT'S DICTIONARY

THAI-ENGLISH STUDENT'S DICTIONARY

Compiled by

MARY R. HAAS

With the assistance of

George V. Grekoff   Ruchira C. Mendiones
Waiwit Buddhari   Joseph R. Cooke
Soren C. Egerod

STANFORD UNIVERSITY PRESS
STANFORD, CALIFORNIA

This work was developed pursuant to a contract
between the United States Office of Education and the
University of California, Berkeley, and is published
with permission of the United States Office of Education.

Stanford University Press
Stanford, California
Copyright © 1964 by Mary R. Haas
Printed in the United States of America
ISBN 0-8047-0567-4
Original printing 1964
Last figure below indicates year of this printing:
15 14 13 12 11 10 09 08 07

PREFACE

The principal aim of this dictionary is to provide a convenient reference work for the English-speaking student of Thai. Existing Thai-English dictionaries--at least those prepared within the last two decades--are invariably geared to meet the needs of the Thai-speaking student of English, since that is the market they are intended to reach. But such dictionaries fail in certain crucial respects to satisfy the legitimate needs of the American student. In particular it has been noticed that: (1) They fail to provide a scientifically accurate and up-to-date guide to the pronunciation of Thai words. (2) They neglect to distinguish important levels of usage, e.g., vulgar, common, elegant, colloquial, literary, etc., which are well known to Thai speakers but are impossible for the culturally-unoriented American student to figure out. (3) They lack many important idioms, compounds, and other specialized combinations of words. (4) Examples, when given, are more likely to be chosen to clarify the peculiarities of English than those of Thai.

The present dictionary contains the following types of information with each of its entries: (1) The traditional Thai spelling as shown in the official Thai monolingual dictionary (the Thai Ministry of Education, Bangkok, 1950). (2) A carefully worked out phonemic transcription using Roman letters. (3) An abbreviation designating the word class, where pertinent. (4) The level of usage, both social and technical, where pertinent. (5) The English definition or equivalent. (6) Many synonyms and antonyms. (7) Examples showing a variety of uses, when the definition alone is insufficient. The dictionary also contains some special kinds of entries which are missing from many dictionaries. Among these are: (1) Most of the common place names of Thailand, including abbreviated and colloquial (but not dialectal) place names and also most of the common foreign place names likely to be found in newspapers. (2) Common abbreviations of titles, organizations, dates, and the like that are frequently encountered in newspapers.

Although this dictionary has been prepared especially to meet the needs of the American student who wishes to read Thai newspapers and other Thai source materials, the Thai student of English will also find much useful information in this dictionary. The reason for this is that we have tried very hard to find the best and most natural English translation for as many words as possible. The numerous subentries and examples will also often be of interest to the Thai student as well as the American student.

The Thai-English Student's Dictionary is one of two dictionaries being compiled at present by those engaged in work on the Thai Dictionary Project. The other, larger dictionary will be entitled Modern Thai-English Dictionary. Materials for the master file have been gleaned from the context of modern periodicals, newspapers, government reports, and advanced textbooks on literature, history, and the sciences. Idiomatic and colloquial usages have been collected from novels and short stories and from examples supplied by educated native speakers. The Student's Dictionary contains selected items from the master file. Particular attention has been paid to items likely to be found in standard prose source materials, including the daily newspapers. The foundations of analysis and description of Thai that are needed for the compilation of a dictionary were worked out by the editor during the course of many years of research. The special needs of American students have become familiar through several years (1947-60) of teaching Thai in the Department of Oriental Languages, University of California, Berkeley. Since 1953 teaching duties have been primarily devoted to courses in general linguistics in the Department of Linguistics, but from time to time Thai has been used as a demonstration language in a field methods course. In 1956-57 the problems of intonation at terminal points and of stress within the rhythm group were given special emphasis in such a course.

All of the assistants aided materially in the compilation of the Student's Dictionary, though mostly at different stages of the work and for differing periods of time. The responsibility of combing the master files to find the selections they considered important was assumed in succession, by Dr. Soren C. Egerod (now of the University of Copenhagen), Dr. Waiwit Buddhari (now of Chulalongkorn University), and Dr. Ruchira Chinnapongse Mendiones. Dr. Buddhari and Dr. Mendiones have also provided many illustrative examples and have served as models for the normal pronunciation or pronunciations shown in romanized phonemic transcription included with each entry. Dr. Mendiones has further served as consultant in regard to many definitions and has assisted in the overall editing. Mr. George V. Grekoff (now of the University of Washington) carried out instructions for maintaining overall consistency in editing and for the cross checking of references, in so far as there was time for this. He also cooperated in working out details of format and layout and undertook the first proofreading as the offset typing proceeded up to August, 1962. Since then the cross checking and proofreading have been done by Mr. Joseph R. Cooke. The writing of all of the front matter, many grammatical comments, notes, and definitions, and finally another overall proofreading fell to the editor.

The extensive master file could not have been accumulated without the assistance of a great many educated speakers of Thai. In particular we wish to express our indebtedness to the following: Miss Boonchom Chaikosi, Mr. Banvech Chantrasmi, Dr. Vichien Diloksambandh, Dr. Phaitoon Ingkasuwan, Mr. Niphon Kantasewi, M. R. W. Sobhak Kasemsanta, Miss Pensri Kiangsiri, Miss Punnee Kiangsiri, Mr. Ratana Oonyawongse, Dr. Kaw Swasdi Panish, Mr. Chamnan Pradithavanis, Mr. Somprasongk Prathnadi, Mr. Suchat Pusavat, Miss Krisna Tantranon, and Miss Charuwan Thirawat. A number of linguistics research assistants also assisted materially in the compilation of the master files, especially at all levels of the cross-referencing process, including the typing of phonetics and English onto slips and also in proofreading and filing the slips as they were typed. Those who helped in this capacity at different times are Dr. Roy A. Miller (now of Yale University), Dr. David DeCamp (now of the University of Texas), Dr. Karl V. Teeter (now of Harvard University), Dr. Wick R. Miller (now of the University of Utah), and Dr. Catherine A. Callaghan. Of especially great importance has been the excellent work of two Thai typists, Mrs. Sarapee Oonyawongse, who typed many thousands of slips for the master file, and Mrs. Boonsiri Donom, who continued the typing of slips and also typed the prefinal manuscript and the offset copy for the present dictionary.

The Thai Dictionary Project was begun in 1951 under the auspices of the Institute of East Asiatic Studies (since 1955 subsumed under the Institute of International Studies) of the University of California, Berkeley. Up until June 15, 1960, most of the funds for the support of this research came out of the research funds of the Institute. In 1956-57, and again in 1958-59, the American Council of Learned Societies provided two grants specifically earmarked for work on the Student's Dictionary. Since June 15, 1960, the continuing work on both dictionaries has been provided for under a government contract (U.S. Office of Education, Language Development, Department of Health, Education, and Welfare). An IBM Executive typewriter with Heritage type was especially selected to blend with the only available IBM Thai typewriter. The typewriters were purchased during the time the Project was being supported by the Institute. The editor and her assistants acknowledge the various kinds of financial aid and assistance from all of these quarters with deep gratitude.

M. R. H.

September, 1963.

Berkeley, California.

PREFACE TO THE SECOND PRINTING

We have taken the occasion of the second printing to remove a few errors that have been discovered by us or brought to our attention by friends. The corrections cover the page references in the introductory sections as well as a few mistakes in cross reference, spelling, or transcription scattered throughout the volume. Owners of copies of the first printing are reminded that most of the corrections are minor or easily detectable by the user. The only exception is that ก฻ was misspelled everywhere as ก฻ . This correction has been made on p. 2, col. I, 1. 36 and in the following subentries together with their cross references throughout the book.

M. R. H.

September, 1964.

Berkeley, California.

CONTENTS

Dictionary Order of Vowel or Vowel + Consonant Symbols   x

Brief Description of Thai   xi

     I.   Phonemes   xi

     II.   Derivation   xv

     III.   Syntax   xx

Some References on the Thai Language   xxiii

Explanatory Notes   xxiv

     The Main Entry   xxiv

     Subentries and Examples   xxvii

     Transliteration   xxvii

List of Abbreviations and Labels   xxviii

THAI-ENGLISH DICTIONARY   1-638

ก	k	1	ณ	n	161	ร	r	438
ข	kh	46	ด	d	161	ฤ	ry	471
ค	kh	72	ต	t	180	ฤๅ	ryy	472
ฆ	kh	102	ถ	th	212	ล	l	472
ง	ŋ	102	ท	th	222	ฦ	ly	498
จ	c	108	ธ	th	252	ฦๅ	lyy	498
ฉ	ch	129	น	n	254	ว	w	498
ช	ch	135	บ	b	279	ศ	s	512
ซ	s	155	ป	p	289	ษ	s	516
ฌ	ch	159	ผ	ph	336	ส	s	516
ญ	j	159	ฝ	f	349	ห	h	554
ฎ	d	160	พ	ph	354	ฬ	l	600
ฏ	t	160	ฟ	f	381	อ	?	600
ฐ	th	160	ภ	ph	386	ฮ	h	637
ฑ	th	160	ม	m	391			
ฒ	th	161	ย	j	423			

DICTIONARY ORDER OF VOWEL + CONSONANT SYMBOLS

Symbol + no cons.	Symbol + cons.	Value		Examples
Zero	. . .	-a(ʔ)	ศิลป	sǐnlápàʔ⁄, sǐnlápaɔ arts
. . .	Zero	-o-	คน	khon⁄ person
Zero	. . .	-ɔɔ	บริษัท	bɔɔrisàd⁄ company
-ร	. . .	-ɔɔn	นคร	nakhɔɔn⁄ city
-รร	. . .	-an	บรรดา	bandaa⁄ all
. . .	-รร/	-a-	ธรรม	tham⁄ dharma
. . .	-ว/	-ua	ส่วน	sŭan⁄ garden
-อ	Same	-ɔɔ	ขอ	khɔ̌ɔ⁄ to ask for, ของ khɔ̌ɔŋ⁄ thing
-ะ	. . .	-a(ʔ)	ปะ	pàʔ⁄ to patch, กระดูก kradùug⁄ bone
. . .	-ั/	-a-	วัน	wan⁄ day
-ัว	. . .	-ua	หัว	hŭa⁄ head
-า	Same	-aa	มา	maa⁄ to come, บ้าน bâan⁄ house
-ำ	. . .	-am	ทำ	tham⁄ to do, make
-ิ	Same	-i(ʔ)	ติ	tìʔ⁄ to criticize, หิน hǐn⁄ stone
-ี	Same	-ii	สี	sǐi⁄ color, หีบ hìib⁄ box
-ึ	Same	-y(ʔ)	ตึ	tỳʔ⁄ faintly, ถึง thy̌ŋ⁄ to reach
. . .	-ื	-yy-	คืน	khyyn⁄ night
-ือ	. . .	-yy	มือ	myy⁄ hand
-ุ	Same	-u(ʔ)	บุ	bùʔ⁄ to line, ถุง thŭŋ⁄ sack, bag
-ู	Same	-uu	ดู	duu⁄ to look, ถูก thùug⁄ to be right
เ-	Same	-ee	เท	thee⁄ to pour, เพลง phleeŋ⁄ song
. . .	เ-็/	-e-	เต็ม	tem⁄ to be full
เ-ย	. . .	-əəj	เนย	nəəj⁄ butter
เ-อ	. . .	-əə	เธอ	thəə⁄ you
เ-อะ	. . .	-əʔ	เยอะ	jə́ʔ⁄ a whole lot
เ-ะ	. . .	-eʔ	เตะ	tèʔ⁄ to kick
เ-า	. . .	-aw	เรา	raw⁄ we
เ-าะ	. . .	-ɔʔ	เคาะ	khɔ́ʔ⁄ to knock
. . .	เ-ิ/	-əə-	เดิน	dəən⁄ to walk
เ-ีย	Same	-ia	เมีย	mia⁄ wife, เสียง sǐaŋ⁄ sound
เ-ียะ	. . .	-iaʔ	เผียะ	phìaʔ⁄ sound of a slap, bang
เ-ือ	Same	-ya	เสือ	sy̌a⁄ tiger, เหนื่อย ny̌aj⁄ to be tired
แ-	Same	-ɛɛ	แม่	mɛ̂ɛ⁄ mother, แปด pὲɛd⁄ eight
. . .	แ-็/	-ɛ-	แข็ง	khɛ̌ŋ⁄ to be hard
แ-ะ	. . .	-ɛʔ	แพะ	phɛ́ʔ⁄ goat
โ-	Same	-oo	โต	too⁄ to be big
โ-ะ	. . .	-oʔ	โต๊ะ	tóʔ⁄ table
ใ-	. . .	-aj	ใน	naj⁄ in
ไ-	. . .	-aj	ไป	paj⁄ to go

In arranging the order of words in a Thai dictionary consonants always take precedence over vowels. Symbols which are sometimes read as consonants, sometimes as vowels, are alphabetized as consonants. The chart above shows the dictionary order of all common symbols having a vowel or vowel + consonant reading. Any intervening initial or final consonant symbols will fall in their proper alphabetical order.

BRIEF DESCRIPTION OF THAI

The minimum words of the Thai language are predominately monosyllabic, but unanalyzable polysyllabic words also occur. Besides consonants and vowels, each syllable has one of five phonemically differentiated tones. Morphology is restricted to derivation since the language makes no use of inflection. In syntax the order of words is usually quite rigid though minor variations are occasionally permissible. Thai is like English in that the typical sentence contains subject, verb and object, in that order. But Thai attributive constructions differ from those of English in that the head must always precede the attribute. Additional features of Thai are described in the following paragraphs under the headings Phonemes, Derivation, and Syntax.

I. PHONEMES

CONSONANTS:		Bilabial	Dental	Palatal	Velar	Glottal
Stops:	Vd. Unasp.	b	d		-g	
	Vl. Unasp.	p-	t-	c-	k-	ʔ
	Vl. Asp.	ph-	th-	ch-	kh-	
Spirants:	Vl. Unasp.	f-	s-			h-
Sonorants:	Vd. Semivowels	w		j		
	Vd. Nasals	m	n		ŋ	
	Vd. Lateral		l-			
	Vd. Trill or Retroflex		r-			

Examples of Consonants

บิน bin/ to fly, สิบ sìb/ ten, ดิน din/ earth, เห็ด hèd/ mushroom, นก nóg/ bird. ไป paj/ to go, ตาย taaj/ to die, จริง ciŋ/ to be true, กิน kin/ to eat, อิ่ม ʔìm/ to be full, แกะ kɛʔ/ sheep.
ผ่าน phàan/ to pass, ไทย thaj/ Thai, ช้าง cháaŋ/ elephant, ฆ่า khâa/ to kill.
ฟ้า fáa/ sky, ซื้อ sýy/ to buy, ห้า hâa/ five.
หมา mǎa/ dog, ตาม taam/ to follow, นา naa/ field, ร้าน ráan/ store, งู ŋuu/ snake, ฟัง faŋ/ to listen.
ลิง liŋ/ monkey, รู้ rúu/ to know.
Rare Anglicized finals: เอ็ช. ʔéch/ (the letter) H, เอ็ฟ. ʔéf/ F, ออฟฟิศ ʔɔ́ffís/ office (also ʔɔ́ffíd/), เลนซ์ lens/ lens (also len/), ฟุตบอลล์ fúdbɔɔl/ football (also fúdbɔn/).

VOWELS:	Front Unrounded	Central	Back Rounded
High	i, ii, ia	y, yy, ya	u, uu, ua
Mid	e, ee	ə, əə	o, oo
Low	ɛ, ɛɛ	a, aa	ɔ, ɔɔ

Examples of Vowels

ติ tì?⁄ to criticize, ลิ้น lín⁄ tongue, มี mii⁄ to have; there is, มีด mîid⁄ knife, เลีย lia⁄
to lick, เสียง sĭaŋ⁄ sound, (vocal) noise, tone (of the spoken language).

เตะ tè?⁄ to kick, เล่น lên⁄ to play, เท thee⁄ to pour out, เหตุ hèed⁄ reason.

แพะ phέ?⁄ goat, แข็ง khɛ̆ŋ⁄ to be hard, แม่ mɛ̂ɛ⁄ mother, แพง phɛɛŋ⁄ to be expensive.

คร่ำ khrý?⁄ to be old-fashioned, หนึ่ง nỳŋ⁄ one, มือ myy⁄ hand, พื้น phýyn⁄ floor, เสือ sўa⁄
tiger, เมือง myaŋ⁄ town.

เยอะ jэ́?⁄ to be a whole lot, เงิน ŋən⁄ silver, money, เซ่อ sэ̂ə⁄ to be foolish, เนย nəəj⁄
butter.

คะ khá⁄ yes! (w. sp.), ปะ pà?⁄ to patch, พัด phád⁄ to blow, มา maa⁄ to come, หลาน
lăan⁄ grandchild, niece, nephew.

ดุ dù?⁄ to be fierce, หุง hŭŋ⁄ to cook (rice), หมู mŭu⁄ pig, ขูด khùud⁄ to scrape, หัว hŭa⁄
head, ควร khuan⁄ ought to.

โต๊ะ tó?⁄ table, อด ?òd⁄ to starve, โหล lŏo⁄ dozen, โลก lôog⁄ world.

เพราะ phrэ́?⁄ because, ส่อง sэ̀ŋ⁄ to shine, ห่อ hэ̀э⁄ package, สอง sэ̆эŋ⁄ two.

TONES (in nonterminal position).

| Middle | Low | Falling | High | Rising |

NOTE: The middle tone is shown by no mark, the low tone by (`), the falling tone by (^), the
high tone by (´), and the rising tone by (˘). Thai grammarians call the middle tone the "common"
tone and refer to the low, falling, high, and rising tones as the 1st, 2nd, 3rd, and 4th tones respectively. This is in reference to the tones as sounds, not as written symbols.

Examples of tones

นา naa⁄ field, น้อยหน่า nɔ́ɔjnàa⁄ custard apple, หน้า nâa⁄ face, น้า náa⁄ maternal uncle
or aunt (yg.), หนา nǎa⁄ to be thick.

เผ็ด phèd⁄ to be hot (peppery), เพชร phéd⁄ diamond, หมาก màag⁄ areca, มาก mâag⁄ to
be much. Rare: เถอะ thə?⁄ [sic] imperative particle, คะ khá⁄ yes (w. sp.), ชิชะ
chíchá⁄ interjection of contempt.

EMPHATIC TONES. Any of the five tones can be accompanied by the phoneme of emphasis. This is indicated by placing an exclamation point (!) in front of the syllable receiving this
treatment. Such tones are uttered at a higher pitch level than their corresponding normal tones
and also have a somewhat "screechy" quality. They occur in exclamatory utterances. A high
emphatic tone may replace any one of the five normal tones in emphatic repetitive expressions.

Examples of Emphatic Tones

อุ๊ยตาย !ʔújtaaj′↓ exclamation expressing dismay, ช่วยด้วย chûaj!dûaj′↓ Help! (an urgent
call), ถุย !thŭj′ imitative of a sound uttered to spurn someone. Emphatic repetitive expressions: ดิ๊ดี !díidii′ Very good! ร้อนๆ !rɔ́ɔnrɔ́ɔn′ Frightfully hot! ยากยาก !jâagjâag′
Terribly difficult! อิ๊มอิ่ม !ʔímʔìm′ Awfully full! เค็มเค็ม !khémkhem′ Terribly salty!

STRESS. This is marked by a heavy acute (′) placed after any syllable which is uttered
with full strength. All unmarked syllables are "reduced" in strength, i.e. are considerably
shortened and weakened. The stress is not necessarily always placed on the same syllable.
Sometimes the difference is simply a matter of free variation (or individual variation) but at
other times it implies a different connotation for the phrase. Each rhythm group has at least
one stressed syllable. There is no spacing between the syllables of a single rhythm group, but
when more than two stressed syllables occur within a rhythm group, a hyphen is used to indicate
a slightly lesser amount of cohesion.

Examples of Stress

ภาษา phaasǎa′ language; นาวี naa′wii′ navy; ไม่ดี mâjdii′ not good, bad; เมื่อคืนนี้ mŷaɔ
khyyn′níi′ last night; จะไปบ้าน capajbâan′ will go home; เดือนมีนาคม dyanmiinaa′khom′
March; ไม่เป็นตัวเป็นตน mâjpentua′penton′ to be unformed, amorphous; ผู้โฆษณา phûukhôoɔ
sanaa′ advertiser; ไกลตาไกลใจ klaj′taa′-klaj′caj′ out of sight, out of mind.
ชาวบ้านร้านตลาด chaawbâan′-ráan′talàad′ the whole neighborhood.

TERMINALS. There are three terminal markers to indicate the intonation of a phrase
or sentence: the raised high in which the whole utterance is raised in pitch (↑), the sustained in
which there is little if any drop in pitch before pause (→), and the falling or dropping intonation
(↓). These markers are rarely needed in a dictionary since complete utterances are entered
only in the case of a few fixed phrases or in the illustrative material needed for some of the
entries.

Examples of Terminals

เอ๊ะ ยังไม่ไปโรงเรียนเรอะ !ʔé′→ jaŋmâjpaj′rooŋrian′rə́↑ Haven't (you) gone to school yet?
คอยจนแล้วจนรอด khɔɔj′-conléɛw′conrɔ́ɔd′→ (We) waited and waited (but he didn't come).
เราจะไปไหนก็ได้ rawcapajnǎj′kɔ̂dâaj′↓ We can go anywhere we like.

Permitted Initials

Every syllable must begin in a consonant, but not more than two consonants are permitted here. All single consonants shown in the chart on page xi with the exception of /-g/ may
occur in initial position. Initial clusters begin in /p, t, k, ph, th, kh/ followed by /l, r, w/, but
/t, th/ are followed only by /r/ and /w/ follows only /k, kh/.

CONSONANT CLUSTERS:

	p	t	k	ph	th	kh
l	pl		kl	phl		khl
r	pr	tr	kr	phr	thr	khr
w			kw			khw

Examples of Consonant Clusters

ปลา plaa′ fish, กลาง klaaŋ′ middle, เพลง phleeŋ′ song, คลอง khlɔɔŋ′ canal.

แปรง prɛɛŋ′ brush, ตรง troŋ′ to be straight, กรง kroŋ′ cage, พรม phrom′ rug, ทฤษฎี

thrísadii′ theory, ครู khruu′ teacher. The /tr/ cluster is relatively rare; /thr/ is

extremely rare, perhaps limited to the example quoted.

กว่า kwàa′ (more) than, ขวาน khwǎan′ ax.

Permitted Finals

The term "final" is used here in a special sense meaning the vowel plus the tone plus the final consonant if any. In other words it includes everything except the initial consonant or consonant cluster. Thai permitted finals are divided into two main types, (1) smooth and (2) stopped or abrupt, as described below.

TYPE I. SMOOTH FINALS (ON ALL FIVE TONES)

1. Doubled vowel or vowel cluster.
2. Short vowel, doubled vowel or vowel cluster + /m, n, ŋ/.
3. Short front vowel, doubled front vowel or /ia/ + /w/.
4. Short back vowel, doubled back vowel or /ua/ + /j/. Also /ya/ + /j/ and very rarely /y/ or /yy/ + /j/.
5. Mid and low central vowels /ə, əə, a, aa/ + /j/ or /w/.

TYPE II. STOPPED OR SHORT FINALS (ON LOW, FALLING, HIGH, AND MID TONES)

6. Short vowel + /b, d, g, ʔ/ on low or high tone, rarely falling tone. Very rarely short vowel + /ʔ/ on mid tone. Occasionally short vowel on high or falling tone; or frequently on mid tone except before pause.
7. Doubled vowel or vowel cluster + /b, d, g/ on low or falling tone. Very rarely on high tone.
8. Vowel cluster + /ʔ/ on low or high tone, but this is extremely rare.

Examples of Permitted Finals

1. มี mii′ to have, เท thee′ to pour out, แม่ mɛ̂ɛ′ mother, ซื้อ sýy′ to buy, เซ่อ sə̂ə′ to be foolish, ผ่า phàa′ to cut, slice, หมู mǔu′ pig, โหล lǒo′ dozen, พ่อ phɔ̂ɔ′ father, เมีย mia′ wife, เมื่อ mŷa′ when, ผัว phǔa′ husband.

2. พิมพ์ phim′ to print, เห็น hěn′ to see, ซึ่ง sŷŋ′ which, ลง loŋ′ to descend. คีม khiim′ tongs, พื้น phýyn′ floor, ของ khɔ̌ɔŋ′ thing. เยี่ยม jîam′ to visit, เพื่อน phŷan′ friend, ลวง luaŋ′ to deceive.

3. หิว hǐw′ to be hungry, เร็ว rew′ to be fast, เลว leew′ to be bad, เลี้ยว líaw′ to turn.

4. คุย khuj′ to chat, โดย dooj′ by, คอย khɔɔj′ to wait, สวย sǔaj′ to be pretty, เหนื่อย nŷaj′ to be tired. Rare: ฮึ, ฮึ !hýj′, !hýyj′ not so!

5. ไม่ไปไม่เปย mâjpaj′/mâjpəj′ won't go, เนย nəəj′ butter, ไปเร็วไปเร็ว pajrew′/pajrəw′ go fast! ไปเที่ยวไปเที่ยว pajthîaw′/pajthə̂əw′ to go around. เรา raw′ we, ราว raaw′ about, เหล้า lâw′ liquor, หนาว nǎaw′ to be cold, ใส sǎj′ to be clear, สาย sǎaj′ line.

6. ขับ khàb′ to drive, คับ kháb′ to be tight; เผ็ด phèd′ to be hot (peppery); เพชร phéd′ diamond; ผัก phàg′ greens, พัก phág′ to rest; แกะ kὲʔ′ sheep, แพะ phέʔ′ goat. Rare: จั๊ก cág′ colloq. (rain) to fall. Very rare: เถอะ thəʔ′ imperative particle. Short vowel without final stop: ยิชยะ chíchá′ interjection of contempt, ค่ะ khâ′ yes! (w. sp.), พิกล phîkon′ to be strange, peculiar, สถิติ sathìtìʔ′ statistics, วนศาสตร wanasàad′ forestry, แต่ละประเทศ tɛlaprathêed′ every single country.

7. หีบ hìib′ box, ลูบ lûub′ to stroke; เหตุ hèed′ reason, เพศ phêed′ sex; หมาก màag′ areca (nut), มาก mâag′ to be much. Rare: โน๊ด nóod′ note [f. Eng.]

8. Rare: ผัวะเผียะ,พวัะเพี้ยะ phùaʔphìaʔ′, phúaʔphíaʔ′ imit. of the sound of beating, slapping, cracking, ตามเดี๊ยะ taamdìaʔ′ to follow closely, เจี๊ยะ cíaʔ′ slang to eat.

II. DERIVATION

The derivational processes used are compounding and reduplication, the former affecting verbs and nouns, the latter affecting verbs and imitative words.

Compounding

Common types of compounding resulting in verbs are listed and illustrated below:

1. Verb + noun: VERB

เข้าใจ khâwcaj′ to understand: เข้า to enter + ใจ heart, spirit, mind.

ดีใจ diicaj′ to be glad (to be heart-good): ดี to be good + ใจ.

ตั้งใจ tâŋcaj′ to intend (to be heart-set): ตั้ง to set, place + ใจ.

ตั้งหน้า tâŋnâa′ colloq. to be determined, intent: ตั้ง + หน้า face.

2. Noun + verb: VERB

ใจดี cajdii′ to be good-natured (good-hearted) ใจ + ดี.

ใจเย็น cajjen′ to be patient, cool-headed: ใจ + เย็น to be cool.

ใจกว้าง cajkwâaŋ′ to be generous: ใจ + กว้าง to be wide.

ใจร้อน cajróɔn′ to be impatient, hot-headed: ใจ + ร้อน to be hot.

หูเบา hŭubaw′ to be credulous (light-eared): หู ear + เบา to be light (in weight).

ใจเบา cajbaw′ to be gullible (light-minded): ใจ + เบา.

หัวแข็ง hŭakhĕŋ′ to be obstinate, hard-headed: หัว head + แข็ง to be hard.

ปากหวาน pàagwăan′ to be suave, smooth-tongued: ปาก mouth + หวาน to be sweet.

คอหวาน khɔɔwăan′ to have a sweet tooth (be sweet-necked): คอ neck + หวาน.

3. Verb + verb (coordinate compound): VERB

หุงต้ม hŭŋtôm′ to cook (general term): หุง to cook (rice) + ต้ม to be boil (food).

สวยงาม sŭajŋaam′ to be beautiful: สวย to be pretty + งาม to be beautiful.

เปลี่ยนแปลง plìanplɛɛŋ′ to alter: เปลี่ยน to change + แปลง to change, transform.

ขนส่ง khŏnsòŋ′ to transport: ขน to carry back and forth + ส่ง to send.

เปรี้ยวหวาน prîawwăan′ to be sweet and sour: เปรี้ยว to be sour + หวาน to be sweet.

ติดตั้ง tìdtâŋ′ to install: ติด to connect, stick (to) + ตั้ง to set, place.

Important types of compounding resulting in nouns include the following;

1. Noun + verb (head + attribute): NOUN

ของกิน khɔ̌ɔŋkin⁄ eatables, foodstuff: ของ thing, stuff + กิน to eat.

น้ำแข็ง námkhɛ̌ŋ⁄ ice: น้ำ water + แข็ง to be hard.

เงินสด ŋənsòd⁄ cash: เงิน money, silver + สด to be fresh.

เสื้อคลุม sŷakhlum⁄ overcoat: เสื้อ coat + คลุม to cover over.

ผู้พิมพ์ phûuphim⁄ publisher, printer: ผู้ person, one who + พิมพ์ to print.

ช่างพิมพ์ châaŋphim⁄ printer: ช่าง artisan, smith (bound stem, see pp. 142-3) + พิมพ์.

ข่าวลือ khàawlyy⁄ rumor: ข่าว news + ลือ to be rumored.

โรงซ่อม rooŋsɔ̂ɔm⁄ repair shop: โรง building, structure (see p. 469) + ซ่อม to mend.

ที่แขวน thîikhwɛ̌ɛn⁄ peg or hook for hanging things: ที่ place + แขวน to hang.

คำนำ khamnam⁄ preface (leading word): คำ word (see pp. 89-90) + นำ to lead.

ความโกรธ khwaamkròod⁄ anger: ความ state, condition (see pp. 81-2) + โกรธ to be angry.

ความร้อน khwaamrɔ́ɔn⁄ heat: ความ + ร้อน to be hot.

การวิ่ง kaanwîŋ⁄ running, the act of running: การ activity, -ing (see p. 29, mng. 3 and notes) + วิ่ง to run.

2. Noun + verb with object (head + attribute): NOUN

คนขายตั๋ว khonkhǎajtǔa⁄ ticket seller (ticket-selling person): คน person, -er (see pp. 73-4) + ขายตั๋ว to sell tickets: ขาย to sell, ตั๋ว ticket.

ช่างตัดผม châaŋ⁄tàdphǒm⁄ barber (hair-cutting person): ช่าง artisan, smith (see pp. 142-3) + ตัดผม to cut hair: ตัด to cut, ผม hair of the head.

ที่เขี่ยบุหรี่ thîikhìa⁄burìi⁄ ash tray (cigarette-flicking place): ที่ place + เขี่ยบุหรี่ to flick (off ashes from) a cigarette: เขี่ย to flick, บุหรี่ cigarette.

เครื่องซักผ้า khrŷaŋságphâa⁄ washer, washing machine (clothes-washing apparatus): เครื่อง gear, apparatus, implement (see pp. 97-8) + ซักผ้า to wash cloth: ซัก to wash, ผ้า cloth.

3. Noun + noun (head + attribute): NOUN

รถไฟ ródfaj⁄ train: รถ vehicle, car + ไฟ fire.

ไฟฟ้า fajfáa⁄ electricity: ไฟ fire + ฟ้า fáa⁄ sky.

ขนตา khǒntaa⁄ eyelashes: ขน hair (except of the head) + ตา eye.

การเมือง kaanmyaŋ⁄ politics (country affairs): การ affairs of, matters of (see p. 29, mng. 2) + เมือง country (nation); town.

เครื่องมือ khrŷaŋmyy⁄ tool: เครื่อง apparatus, implement (see pp. 97-8) + มือ hand.

คนกระเป๋า khonkrapǎw⁄ fare collector (purse-person): คน person, -er (see pp. 73-4) + กระเป๋า purse.

ช่างทอง châaŋthɔɔŋ⁄ goldsmith: ช่าง artisan, smith (see pp. 142-3) + ทอง gold.

ชาวเมือง chaawmyaŋ⁄ native, native inhabitant; townspeople: ชาว inhabitant of, dweller in (see pp. 146-7) + เมือง country (nation); town.

4. Noun + noun (coordinate compound): NOUN

พ่อแม่ phɔ̂ɔmɛ̂ɛ/ parents: พ่อ father + แม่ mother.

พี่น้อง phîinɔ́ɔŋ/ brothers and sisters: พี่ older sibling + น้อง younger sibling.

ผัวเมีย phŭamia/ married couple: ผัว husband + เมีย wife.

ลูกหลาน lûuglǎan/ descendants: ลูก child + หลาน grandchild.

ปู่ย่าตายาย pùujâa/taajaaj/ ancestors: ปู่ย่า paternal grandparents (ปู่ paternal grandfather, ย่า paternal grandmother) + ตายาย maternal grandparents (ตา maternal
grandfather, ยาย maternal grandmother). This example is a secondary coordinate
cpd. pleasingly welded together by the rhyme that exists between the second part of
the first primary coordinate and the first part of the second primary coordinate.

แขนขา khɛ̌ɛnkhǎa/ (the four) limbs: แขน arm + ขา leg.

เสื้อผ้า sŷaphâa/ clothing: เสื้อ coat, upper garment + ผ้า cloth, lower garment.

วัวควาย wuakhwaaj/ livestock (in general): วัว cattle + ควาย water buffalo.

เป็ดไก่ pèdkàj/ barnyard fowl (collectively): เป็ด duck + ไก่ chicken.

มีดพร้า mîidphráa/ knives (of all kinds): มีด knife + พร้า jungle knife, kris.

เรือแพ ryaphɛɛ/ watercraft: เรือ boat + แพ raft, houseboat.

ภาษีอากร phaasǐi/ʔaakɔɔn/ (all kinds of) government revenue: ภาษี taxes + อากร
revenue.

Elaborate Expressions

Elaborate expressions are usually colloquial but a few are considered elegant. They
are frequently based on compounds of the types illustrated above and are expanded by repeating
a part of the compound and adding a new part, by inserting a syllable for the sake of rhyme, or
by inserting a syllable which has some vague semantic relation to one of the original parts.
Most of these expressions are made up of four parts. The semirepeated expressions have the
same item as the first and third or as the second and fourth part. The expressions that are
characterized by rhyme always show internal rhyme (i.e. the rhyming of adjacent syllables)
between the second and third parts. The rhyming part is the one in second position and may
be an item which (1) has no meaning and therefore functions only as a rhyme, (2) has a meaning
inconsistent with the rest of the expression and again functions only as a rhyme, or (3) has a
meaning of greater or less consistency with the rest of the expression and also rhymes. Those
expressions which insert a part which has a vague semantic relation to one of the parts of the
original expression often place it in second or fourth position. A variety of examples are shown
below.

หยิบเล็กหยิบน้อย jìblég/jìbnɔ́ɔj/ elab. colloq. to pilfer: หยิบ to pick up, take up (in
the hand), เล็กน้อย a little bit: เล็ก to be little, small, น้อย to be little, lesser.
The word หยิบ is repeated and its second occurrence splits the coordinate
เล็กน้อย.

รวบหัวรวบหาง rûabhǔa/rûabhǎaŋ/ idiom. to gather everything together; to sum
everything up: รวบ to gather together, หัว head, หาง tail.

ร้อนอกร้อนใจ rɔ́ɔnʔòg/rɔ́ɔncaj/ elab. colloq. to be worried, anxious: ร้อนใจ to be
worried, anxious: ร้อน to be hot, ใจ heart, spirit, mind. The word อก chest
is often paired with ใจ in expressions like this, but ร้อนอก is not used alone.

เดือดเนื้อร้อนใจ dɏadnɏa/rɔ́ɔncaj/ elab. colloq. to worry, be upset. Cf. เดือดร้อน
dɏadrɔɔn/ to worry, feel anxious: เดือด to boil (of water), ร้อน to be hot, and
ร้อนใจ to be worried, anxious (as in the preceding example). เนื้อ flesh, meat
is added for balance and because of its vague semantic relation to ใจ.

ลืมหูลืมตา lyymhŭu/lyymtaa/ elab. colloq. to open one's eyes to what is going on
around one. Cf. ลืมตา lyymtaa/ to open the eyes: ลืม to open (eyes only), ตา eye.
หู ear is often paired with ตา eye because of its vague semantic relation.

หูป่าตาเถื่อน hŭupàa/taathɏan/ elab. colloq. to be ignorant of what is going on. Here
หู ear and ตา eye are paired as above, and ป่า forest and เถื่อน forest are
likewise paired. The expression is welded together by the rhyming of ป่า and ตา.

หุงหาอาหาร hŭŋhǎa/ʔaahǎan/ elab. eleg. to cook, prepare food: หุง to cook (rice),
หา to look for, อาหาร eleg. food. หา rhymes with the first part of อาหาร.

เก็บหอมรอมริบ kèbhɔ̌ɔm/rɔɔmríb/ elab. colloq. to save up: เก็บ to pick up, collect, หอม (no mng., for rhyme only), รอม to save, ริบ (no mng.).

ผู้หลักผู้ใหญ่ phûulàg/phûujàj/ elab. colloq. (one's) superiors, elders. Cf. ผู้ใหญ่
phûujàj/ superior, elder; adult: ผู้ person (in cpds.), ใหญ่ to be great. The expression is elaborated by repeating ผู้ and adding หลัก basis, principle, the latter word having at best only a vague semantic connection with the whole expression.

น้ำหูน้ำตา tears, occurring in the phrase น้ำหูน้ำตาไหล námhŭu/námtaa/-lǎj/ elab.
colloq. to cry, shed tears. Cf. น้ำตา námtaa/ tears: น้ำ water, ตา eye.
The word น้ำ is repeated and หู ear is paired with ตา to form the elaboration.

หมูเห็ดเป็ดไก่ mŭuhèd/pèdkàj/ colloq. meats of various kinds: หมู pig, เห็ด (inserted to rhyme with เป็ด ; otherwise means "mushroom"), เป็ด duck, ไก่
chicken.

Reduplication

Simple reduplication is used to form many imitative words, such as แค้กๆ khégkhég/
imit. of the sound of coughing, แฉ่งๆ chèŋchèŋ/ imit. of a clattering sound. There are also
other kinds of reduplication including several interesting types of ablauting reduplication. Some
of these are listed and illustrated below.

1. A back vowel alternates with its corresponding front vowel:

u and i: ยุ่งยิ่ง jûŋjîŋ/ to be confused, confusing, entangled (cf. ยุ่ง idem); จู้จี้ cûucîi/ to
be fussy, particular; ซุบซิบ súbsíb/ to whisper; งัวเงีย ŋuaŋia/ to feel drowsy.

o and e: โซเซ soosee/ to stagger; โหรงเหรง rǒoŋrěeŋ/ to be sparse, few; โพล้เพล้ phlóɔ⊃
phlée/ twilight; โยกเยก jôogjêeg/ to oscillate (cf. โยก idem).

ɔ and ɛ: ง่อนแง่น ŋɔ̂nŋɛ̂n/ to be loose (as a tooth), wobbly; จ้อกแจ้ก cɔ̂gcɛ̂g/ to be noisy, loud
(as a crowd); งอแง ŋɔɔŋɛɛ/ to be fussy, childish.

2. Any vowel may alternate with a:

i and a: ชิชะ chíchá′ interjection of contempt; ชิงชัง chiŋchaŋ′ to hate, abhor, detest (cf. ชัง to hate, detest); วี๊ดว๊าด wíidwáad′ to scream, screech (of women).

ia and aa: เกรียวกราว kriawkraaw′ noisy, noisily.

e and a: เปล่งปลั่ง plèŋplàŋ′ to glow (with health), be radiant (of looks); เคว้งคว้าง khwéeŋ-khwáaŋ′ to be adrift; aimlessly; เก้งก้าง kêeŋkâaŋ′ to be gangly, awkward.

ɛ and a: แพรวพราว phrɛɛwphraaw′ (or พราวแพรว) to glitter; แกรกกราก krɛ̀ɛgkràag′ imit. of a rustling sound.

y and a: พึมพัม phympham′ mutteringly; จึงจำ ŋymŋam′ in murmurs; อึดอัด ʔy̌dʔàd′ to feel constricted, hemmed in; อึดอาด ʔy̌dʔàad′ to be slow, inert.

ya and aa: เหนื่อยหน่าย nỳajnàaj′ listlessly (cf. เหนื่อย nỳaj′ to be tired).

ə and a: เงอะงะ ŋə́ʔŋá′ to be awkward, maladroit, inept; เหนอะหนะ nə̀ʔnà′ to be sticky; เซ่อซ่า sə̂əsâa′ colloq. to be foolish, stupid, blundering; เรื่อร่า rə̂ərâa′ intrusively.

u and a: ผลุนผลัน phlǔnphlǎn′ hastily, precipitately; รุงรัง ruŋraŋ′ to be untidy, messy; ซู่ซ่า sûusâa′ roaringly (of water); มูมมาม muummaam′ to be slovenly in manner of eating

ua and aa: พรวดพราด phrûadphrâad′ abruptly, precipitately (cf. พรวด idem).

o and a: โปรยปราย proojpraaj′ to scatter, sow, disseminate; โชยชาย choojchaaj′ to blow gently (of the wind); โครกคราก khrôogkhrâag′ imit. sound of snoring, heavy breathing.

ɔ and a: หมองหมาง mɔ̌ɔŋmǎaŋ′ sadly, lamentingly.

3. There are also other miscellaneous vowel alternations:

a and e: ฮาเฮ haahee′ imit. sound of hearty laughter. Also เฮฮา.

a and ɛ: คลางแคลง khlaaŋkhlɛɛŋ′ to feel suspicious, have doubts.

i and ɛ: ยิ้มแย้ม jímjɛ́ɛm′ to be bright and smiling. Also แย้มยิ้ม.

ə and ɛ: เยอะแยะ jə́ʔjɛ́′ to be plentiful, a lot of, a multitude of (cf. แยะ and เยอะ idem); เฉอะแฉะ chə̀ʔchɛ̀′ to be wet, slushy.

o and ɔ: ตรมตรอม tromtrɔɔm′ sadly, forlornly. Also ตรอมตรม.

ə and ɔ: เออออ ʔəəʔɔɔ′ colloq. to agree.

4. A change in vowel quantity with or without a change in vowel quality:

Short vowel and same vowel doubled: ปู๊ดๆ púdpúud′, ป๊อดๆ pɔ́dpɔ́ɔd′, แป๊ดๆ pɛ́dpɛ́ɛd′ imit. sound of car horn honking. (The short vowel is not reflected in the Thai spelling.)

Short vowel and different vowel doubled: วังเวง waŋweeŋ′ to be lonely and desolate; อิดออด ʔìdʔɔ̀ɔd′ to demonstrate unwillingness or half-heartedness; อุ้ยอ้าย ʔûjʔâaj′ to be ponderous and slow-moving; สุรุ่ยสุร่าย surûjsurâaj′ to be a spendthrift, wasteful; ยุ่มย่าม jûmjâam′ meddlesomely; ลนลาน lonlaan′ excitedly and precipitately.

5. A change in tone is always accompanied by other changes:

Short vowel and same or different vowel doubled, plus change in tone: กระแดะกระแด๋ kradɛ̀ʔ- kradɛ̌ɛ′ to be forward, bold (of a woman); กระซิบกระซาบ krasíb′krasâab′ to whisper (cf. กระซิบ idem). วับวาบ wábwâab′ to flicker, flickeringly.

III. SYNTAX

The typical sentence contains subject, verb, object, in that order, e.g.

เขาซื้อเนื้อ kháw^{1}sýy^{2}nýa^3↓ He^1 buys^2 meat.^{3}

However, certain types of subjectless sentences are also used, e.g.

มีคนมากที่นี่ mii^{1}khon^{2}mâag^3-thîinîi^4↓ There are^1 lots of^3 people^2 here.^{4}

Pronouns are generally omitted if they are implied in the linguistic or situational context, e.g.

ไปไหน paj^{1}nǎj^2↓ Where^2 are (you) going^1? (said upon meeting a friend).

The nucleus of the predicate is usually a verb, as shown in the examples above, but there is an important type of verbless predication in which a demonstrative pronoun occupies either the subject or predicate position, e.g.

นี่หนังสือของใคร nîi^{1}naŋsўy^{2}khɔɔŋ^{3}khraj^4↓ Whose (of^{3}whom^4) book^2 (is) this^1?

นั่นอะไร nân^{1}ʔaraj^2↓ What^2('s) that^1?

ใครนี่นะ khraj^{1}nîi^{2}nâ?^{3}↓ Now^3 who^1('s) this^2?

Obligatory categories of tense and number do not exist, and a sentence like ม้าวิ่งเร็ว máa^1‿ wîŋ^{2}rew^3↓ may mean "The horse^1 runs^2 fast,^{3}" "The horses run fast," "Horses run fast," or "The horse(s) ran fast." But time and number may be shown by special words when needed.

The word classes are nouns (N), numerals (Nm), classifiers (C), demonstrative adjectives (dA), interrogative-indefinite adjectives (iA), demonstrative pronouns (dP), interrogative-indefinite pronouns (iP), personal pronouns (P), verbs (V), adverb-auxiliaries (AA), prepositions (Pp), conjunctions (Cj), particles (Pt), and exclamatives (E). Before illustrating some of these classes, it is important to point out that words corresponding to adjectives and adverbs in English are true verbs in Thai. Consequently a word like ดี dii^1 means "is good; good; well" and is used in the following ways: (1) as the nucleus of a predication, e.g.

วันนี้อากาศดี wanníi^1 ʔaakàad^2-dii^3↓ The weather^2 is fine^3 today.^{1}

(2) as the modifier of a noun, e.g.

เขาเป็นคนดี kháw^{1}pen^{2}khon^{3}dii^4↓ He^1 is^2 a good^4 person.^{3}

(3) as the modifier of another verb, e.g.

เขาพูดภาษาไทยได้ดี kháw^{1}phûud^{2}phaasǎathaj^{3}dâj^{4}dii^5↓ He^{1}can^{4}speak^{2}Thai^{3}well.^{5}

Nouns may be used alone or serve as the head in noun-phrases containing head plus attribute, in that order. The attribute may be simple, e.g. another noun, a personal pronoun, a verb, or a demonstrative adjective. However, it is often complex, e.g. a preposition + noun or pronoun, a numeral +classifier, a classifier + verb, a classifier + demons. or interrog.-indef. adjective, a numeral + classifier + demons. or interrog.-indef. adjective, a verb + classifier + demonstrative adjective, a relative clause, or a classifier + relative clause. A few examples:

พ่อผม phɔɔ^{1}phǒm^2 (noun, personal pronoun) my (m. sp.)^2 father.^{1}

คนดี khon^{1}dii^2 (noun, verb) a good^2 person.^{1}

ส้มนี้ sôm^{1}nîi^2 [nîi sic] (noun, demons. adj.) this^2 orange.^{1}

แม่ของเขา mɛɛ^{1}khɔɔŋ^{2}kháw^3 (noun, prepos., pers. pron.) his (of^2 him^3) mother.^{1}

นักเรียนสามคน nágrian^1-sǎam^{2}khon^3 (noun, num.,clf.) three^{2,3} students.^{1}

นักเรียนคนนี้ nágrian$'^1$khon^{2}níi$'^3$ (noun, clf., demons. adj.) this^{2,3} student.^{1}

นักเรียนคนไหน nágrian$'^1$khon^{2}nǎj$'^3$ (noun.,clf.,interrog.-indef. adj.) which^{2,3} student.^{1}

นักเรียนสามคนนี้ nágrian$'^1$-sǎam$'^2$khon^{3}níi^4 (noun, num.,clf., demons. adj.) these^{3,4} three^{2,3} students.^{1}

ผู้หญิงสวยสามคนนี้ phûujɪ̆ŋ$'^1$sǔaj$'^2$-sǎam$'^3$khon^{4}níi$'^5$ (noun, verb, num.,clf., demons. adj.) these^{4,5} three^{3,4} pretty^2 women.^{1}

ผู้หญิงที่ซื้อของ phûujɪ̆ŋ$'^1$-thîi^{2}sýy$'^3$khɔ̆ɔŋ$'^4$ (noun + rel. cl.) women^1 who^2 shop.^{3,4}

The principal uses of numerals, classifiers, and demonstrative and interrogative-indefinite adjectives are illustrated above. It is important to observe that the choice of classifier is determined by the noun-head. Thus คน khon$'$ is the ordinary classifier for people: ตัว tua$'$ for animals (and also for tables, chairs, playing cards); ลำ lam$'$ for boats; คัน khan$'$ for vehicles (except carts); เล่ม lêm$'$ for sharp-pointed objects, such as knives, and for carts, books, etc.; and many others. In addition to the types of classifiers just mentioned there are also classifiers denoting times or occasions, periods of time, units of money and other types of measurement. These are often used in attributive phrases without expressed noun-head, e.g.

คราวนี้ khraaw^{1}níi$'^2$ (clf., demons. adj.) this^2 time^1 (occasion).

สองวัน sɔ̆ɔŋ^{1}wan$'^2$ (num.,clf.) two^1 days.^{2}

ห้าบาทห้าสิบสตางค์ hâa^{1}bàad$'^2$-hâasìb$'^3$sataŋ$'^4$ (num., clf.; num., clf.) five^1 bahts^2 (and) fifty^3 satangs.^{4} เงิน ŋən$'$ "money" may be placed first as noun-head.

Personal pronouns may be substituted for nouns but they are not followed by as many types of attributes. Such pronouns are differentiated not only for person and sometimes number but also for relative social status and occasionally for sex. Deferential first person terms differentiated for sex are ผม phǒm$'$ I (m. sp.) and ดิฉัน dichán$'$ I (w. sp.). Pronouns differentiated on the status level often have paired terms for "I" and "you", e.g.

ผม phǒm$'$ I (m. sp.) or ดิฉัน dichán$'$ I (w. sp.) paired with คุณ khun$'$ you. These are deferential terms used among equals or when speaking to superiors.

ฉัน chán$'$ I (m. or w. sp.) paired with เธอ thəə$'$ you. Used when speaking to intimates or inferiors, hence often to children.

กัน kan$'$ I (m. sp. to m.) paired with แก kɛɛ$'$ you. Used among intimates of the same sex, otherwise insulting.

Third person pronouns are also differentiated for social status, rarely for number, and still more rarely for sex. Some of the most common of these are the following:

แก kɛɛ$'$ he, she, they. Common respectful term.

เขา kháw$'$ he, she, they. General term.

มัน man$'$ he, she, it, they. A derogatory term when used of people, the common term when speaking of animals (and occasionally of things; see p. 397).

หล่อน lɔ̀n$'$ she. Of frequent use in the written language.

There is also a first person plural pronoun เรา raw$'$ used as the common term for "we." In addition it is sometimes used to mean "I" when speaking to oneself or to intimates and inferiors.

Most kinship terms also have as one of their uses a pronominal one. Thus พ่อ phɔ́ɔ′ "father" may be used to mean "you, he, Father" (sp. to or of one's father) or "I, Father" (father sp. to child); see p. 366. Similar extensions of usage characterize แม่ mɛ̂ɛ′ mother, p. 410; พี่ phîi′ older sibling, p. 372; น้อง nɔ́ɔŋ′ younger sibling, p. 257, and many others.

Verbs have two main functions, in one of which they are called "primary verbs" (V), in the other "secondary verbs" (sV). Primary verbs function as the nucleus of a predication and are translated by English verbs. Secondary verbs, on the other hand, resemble English adverbs if intransitive, English prepositions if transitive. Examples:

น้ำลง náam′[1] loŋ′[2]↓ The water[1] recedes.[2] (ลง to descend, recede, prim. v.)

นั่งลงเถอะ nâŋ′[1] loŋ′[2] thəʔ′[3]↓ Sit[1] down![2,3] (นั่ง to sit, prim. v.; ลง down, sec. v.)

เขาเป็นครู kháw[1] pen[2] khruu′[3]↓ He[1] is[2] a teacher.[3] (เป็น to be ..., prim. v.)

เขากินไข่เป็นอาหารเช้า kháw[1] kin[2] khàj′[3] pen[4] ʔaahǎancháaw′[5]↓ He[1] eats[2] eggs[3] for[4] breakfast.[5] (กิน to eat ..., prim. v.; เป็น for, as ..., sec. v.)

Adverb-auxiliaries are a class of words, some of which are translated by English auxiliary verbs and others by English adverbs. All belong to a single class in Thai and are identified as such by their fixed position with respect to the subject (which they follow) and to the nuclear verb (which they precede), e.g. ต้อง tɔ̂ŋ′ "must" in

เขาต้องไปบ้าน kháw[1] tɔ̂ŋ′[2] paj[3] bâan′[4]↓ He[1] must[2] go[3] home.[4]

Other important adverb-auxiliaries include the following: จะ caʔ "shall, will," ควร khuan′ or ควรจะ khuan′caʔ "ought to," เห็นจะ hěncaʔ "seemingly, seems to," ไม่ mâj′, mâjɔ "not," ยัง jaŋ′ "still, yet," จึง cyŋ′ "consequently." More than one adverb-auxiliary may be used in the same sentence and in this event their relative order is fixed. Examples:

เขาจะไม่ไปบ้าน kháw[1] ca[2] mâj′[3] paj[4] bâan′[5]↓ He[1] will[2] not[3] go[4] home.[5]

เขายังอยู่บ้าน kháw[1] jaŋ[2] jùu′[3] bâan′[4]↓ He[1] is[3] still[2] at home.[4]

เขายังไม่ไปบ้าน kháw′[1] jaŋ[2] mâj′[3] paj[4] bâan′[5]↓ He[1] hasn't[3] gone[4] home[5] yet.[2]

Conjunctions are used to connect sentences or clauses and they precede everything else:

เมื่อเขาไปบ้าน mŷa[1] kháw′[2] paj[3] bâan′[4]→ when[1] he[2] went[3] home.[4]

ถ้าผมไม่อยู่บ้าน thâa[1] phǒm′[2] mâj[3] jùu[4] bâan′[5]→ if[1] I[2] am[4] not[3] at home.[5]

Particles are sentence-ending words and fall into two classes, those indicating mode and those connoting the social status and sometimes the sex of the speaker. Modal particles include question, imperative, and other particles (first two examples below). Status particles include ครับ khráb′ (deferential m. sp.), คะ khâ′, คะ khá′ (deferential w. sp.), and จ๊ะ câ′, จ๋ะ cá′ (m. or w. sp. to intimates or inferiors, including children). Status particles always follow other particles, e.g.

เขาไปบ้านแล้วหรือครับ kháw[1] paj[2] bâan′[3] lɛ́ɛw[4] rý[5] khráb′[6]↓ Has[4] he[1] gone[2] home[3,5]?[6]

ตื่นเถอะ tỳyn′[1] thəʔ′[2]↓ Wake up[1]![2] (เถอะ imperative part.)

ขอบคุณค่ะ khɔ̀ɔbkhun′[1] khâ′[2]↓ Thanks[1] (w. sp.)[2].

เธอขอบดูหนังไหมจ๊ะ thəə′[1] chɔ̂ɔb′[2] duu[3] nǎŋ′[4]-mâj[5] cá′[6]↓ Do you[1] like[2] to see[3] movies[4,5]?[6] (ไหม question part., จ๊ะ status part. used with intimates, children).

SOME REFERENCES ON THE THAI LANGUAGE

TEXTBOOKS AND DICTIONARIES

Bhaopichitr, Dr. Kamol. Modern English-Thai Dictionary. Bangkok, B. E. 2492
(1949). 819 pp.

-----. Modern Thai-English Dictionary. Bangkok, B. E. 2498 (1955). 765 pp.

Haas, Mary R. Thai Reader. American Council of Learned Societies, Washington, D. C.,
1954. Pp. 1-215.

-----. Thai Vocabulary. American Council of Learned Societies, Washington, D. C.,
1955. Pp. 217-589.

-----. The Thai System of Writing. American Council of Learned Societies, Washington, D. C., 1956. 115 pp.

Haas, Mary R., and Heng R. Subhanka. Spoken Thai, Books I and II. Henry Holt and Co.,
New York, 1946-48. 701 pp.

Jamsai, M. L. Manich. English-Thai Dictionary. 8th printing, Bangkok, B. E. 2490
(1947). 610 pp.

-----. Thai-English Dictionary. 3rd rev. ed., Bangkok, 1949. 692 pp.

McFarland, G. B. Thai-English Dictionary. Stanford University Press, second printing, 1954. 1019 pp.

Phloyphrom, Plang. Pru's Standard Thai-English Dictionary. Bangkok, 1955.
1774 pp.

Sreshthaputra, So, ed. The New Model English-Thai Dictionary. Bangkok, 1940.
3 vols., 4000 pp.

Thai-Thai Dictionary. Ministry of Education, Bangkok, B. E. 2493 (1950). 1057 pp.

ARTICLES AND MONOGRAPHS

Abramson, Arthur S. The Vowels and Tones of Standard Thai: Acoustical
Measurements and Experiments. Publication Twenty of the Indiana University
Research Center in Anthropology, Folklore, and Linguistics. Bloomington, 1962.

Egerod, Soren. "Swatow Loan Words in Siamese." Acta Orientalia, vol. XXIII (1958-59),
pp. 137-156.

Fowler, Murray, and Tasniya Isarasena. The Total Distribution of the Sounds of
Siamese. University of Wisconsin Press, Madison, 1952. 8 pp. + 4 microcards.

Haas, Mary R. "Techniques of Intensifying in Thai." Word, vol. II (1946), pp. 125-130.

-----. "Types of Reduplication in Thai." Studies in Linguistics, vol. I (1942), no. 1,
pp. 1-6.

-----. "The Use of Numeral Classifiers in Thai. "Language, vol. XVIII (1942), pp. 201-205.

Henderson, Eugenie J. A. "Prosodies in Siamese: a Study in Synthesis." Asia Major n.s.,
vol. I (1949).

Noss, Richard B. Thai Reference Grammar. Washington, D. C. 1964.

EXPLANATORY NOTES

The materials of this dictionary have been arranged, in so far as practicable, in accordance with the convenient principle adopted in The American College Dictionary (Random House, Inc., New York, latest printing, 1963). This means that all items are in one alphabetical list: regular vocabulary items, abbreviations, names of people, place names, and foreign words. This is even more important in a Thai dictionary than in an English dictionary, since the Thai writing system uses no capital letters or any other device to set off names of people and places from ordinary words. Furthermore some abbreviations are signalled by a period (not otherwise used in Thai writing) but other abbreviations are not so signalled.

The Main Entry

The material included with each main entry will include at the maximum the following kinds of information:

1. the main entry word in traditional Thai spelling.
2. the phonemic rendition of the actual pronunciation of the word.
3. the abbreviation designating the word class.
4. the restrictive label.
5. the meaning or meanings in English.
6. run-on entries without phonemic rendition but including meaning.
7. the origin of certain types of borrowed terms.
8. variant spellings.
9. synonyms, antonyms, and words compared or distinguished.
10. notes.

A more detailed description of the nature of these features is provided in the following paragraphs.

1. The main entry word.

The main entry word is written in traditional Thai letters and placed at the left, a little further to the left than the usual line of text. The spelling shown is that given in the official Thai monolingual dictionary (the Ministry of Education, Bangkok, 1950).

Separate entries are made for all words which, even though spelled in exactly the same way, are of unrelated derivation. In such cases each entry word is followed by a Thai numeral, e.g. ๑ (1), ๒ (2), ๓ (3), ๔ (4), etc. See ขัน ๑, ขัน ๒, ขัน ๓, ขัน ๔, p. 55. Moreover, in some cases words related in derivation have such divergent meanings that a separation is desirable in order to keep the subentries and examples of the separate meanings together, e.g. ผม ๑ hair of the head, and ผม ๒ I (def. m. sp.), p. 337.

If a main entry is followed immediately by a comma the material that follows in Thai writing is an equivalent term. If a dash (--) is used it means that the whole of the main entry is to be read for the dash. Example:

กระดาก,--ใจ kradàag´, kradàagcaj´ V 1. to be shy, bashful. [Etc., p. 7]

Sometimes an entry is followed by material in parentheses. For nouns this is the classifier or classifiers, e.g. ขอ ๑ (ตัว,อัน) khɔ̌ɔ/ (tua/, ʔan/) N hook (p.51). For verbs it is a
preposition, secondary verb, or other word, with which the verb is usually associated. Example:

แข่ง(กับ) khɛ̀ŋ/(kaɔ) V to compete (with). P. 70.

Whenever possible the translation of the parenthesized material is also placed in parentheses,
as in the example just given.

2. The phonemic rendition.

The phonemic rendition shows the actual pronunciation of the word according to the system described on pp. xi-xv. Sometimes this pronunciation is unexpected in terms of the spelling
of the word, i.e. the reading fails to conform in one or more respects to the rules of the Thai
system of writing. The phonemic rendition is then followed by an asterisk in order (1) to call attention to the unusual pronunciation and (2) to indicate that the pronunciation shown is not a typographical error. Since a number of quite common words have unexpected pronunciations, the asterisk is used only when the word appears as a main entry and is not repeated in
subentries, examples, or cross references. When in doubt consult the main entry. Examples:

แถว thɛ̌w/* (where one might expect thɛ̌ɛw/) line, row. P. 221.

ประโยชน์ prajòod/* (where one might expect prajôod/) advantage, usefulness. P.306.

หนังสือ naŋsy̌y/* (where one might expect nǎŋsy̌y/) book. P. 557.

Sometimes two or more pronunciations are shown, all except one of which is unexpected. In this
case no asterisk is used since it is clear that not all pronunciations can be regular. Examples:

กับ ๑ kàb/, kaɔ with. P. 26.

เขา ๔ khǎw/, kháw/ he, she, they. P. 66.

Sometimes different pronunciations are associated with different meanings or uses. This is
shown by parenthetical numbers before each pronunciation which in turn are keyed to the numbered meanings, as in the following example:

เสีย (1-3) sǐa/, sǐa; (4) sía, sá V 1. to lose [etc.]. 2. to waste [etc.]. 3. to break
down [etc.]. sV 4. sec. vb. indicating a hortative [etc.]. P 547.

3. The abbreviation designating the word class.

The abbreviations used for the word classes are AA (adverb-auxiliary), C (classifier),
Cj (conjunction), dA (demonstrative adjective), dP (demonstrative pronoun), E (exclamative),
iA (interrogative-indefinite adjective), iP (interrogative-indefinite pronoun), N (noun), Nm (numeral), nN (name noun), P (personal pronoun), pN (place name), Pp (preposition), Pt (particle),
qM (modifier of a quantifier), rcP (reciprocal pronoun), rM (restricted modifier), sV (secondary
verb), T (title, usually with the given name), V (verb). Some of these are illustrated on pp. xix-xxi.
If the entry word is used in more than one word class the appropriate abbreviation precedes each
definition where it is needed. Example:

ขะโมย (คน) khamooj/ (khon/) N 1. thief. V 2. to steal, pilfer. P. 48.

4. The restrictive label.

The restrictive label indicates the levels of usage, both social and technical. This is
shown in expanded type. Social and literary restrictions include the following: a r c h a i c,

colloq. (colloquial), com. (common), def. (deferential), derog. (derogatory), eleg. (elegant), epithet, euphem. (euphemism), expl. (expletive), fig. (figurative), idiom. (idiomatic), illit. (illiterate), lit. (literary), obs. (obsolete), obsolesc. (obsolescent), roy. (royal), sacer. (sacerdotal), slang, vulg. (vulgar), writ. (written). Technical labels are those found in most dictionaries. See List of Abbreviations and Labels.

  5. The meaning or meanings in English.

  The separate meanings are numbered. If a new word class designation is needed it precedes the number; if a new restrictive label is needed it follows the number. Example:

> ตก tòg′ V 1. to drop, fall; to fall (straight) down (from, into, onto). 2. to fall off, drop off, decrease, diminish. 3. to droop (as ears, tail). 4. to set (of the sun, moon). 5. to set in (as afternoon). 6. hort. to set (of fruit, pods, seed). 7. eleg. to lay (eggs). 8. colloq. to come to (such and such an amount), be approximately, come close to. 9. to fade (of colors). sV 10. down, through (completive sense); conclusively. →Dist. 1. ล้ม, หกล้ม. →Ant. 1. ลุก. 2,4. ขึ้น. 3. ขี้. [P. 180.]

  6. Run-on entries.

  Run-on entries are commonly used derivatives. They show the deriving element in Thai writing immediately followed (or preceded) by a dash (--). The dash stands for the whole of the main entry (or subentry) form. Only the meaning of the run-on entry is shown and, if needed, the restrictive label. The phonemic rendition, word class designation, and classifier are omitted. This information can be secured by referring to the place in the dictionary where the deriving element is listed as a main entry. The most common deriving elements shown in run-on entries are the following: การ -ing (mng. 3, p. 29), คน -er, person (mng. 2, p. 73), ความ -ness (mng. 3, pp. 81-82), เครื่อง -er, apparatus (mng. 3, p. 97), ช่าง -er, -smith (mng. 2, p. 142), ต้น plant, tree (mng. 4, p. 182), ผู้ -er (mng. 3, p. 344), อย่าง in ... a manner, -ly (mng. 2, p. 604). Example:

> พิมพ์ phim′ V to print, imprint. การ-- printing; publishing. ผู้-- publisher; printer. ช่าง-- printer. P. 371.

  7. The origin of certain types of borrowed terms.

  Words known to be recent borrowings from Chinese, English, French, Portuguese, Vietnamese, etc., are so marked. Many very old borrowings from Chinese are not so marked, partly because there is some disagreement among scholars as to whether they are loanwords or genetically related words. No attempt was made to identify the Pali and Sanskrit loanwords or to distinguish those which were borrowed directly from those which came into Thai through Cambodian as an intermediary language. Many of these words bear the restrictive labels of eleg. or lit., but are not otherwise marked. Therefore this dictionary is not, and is not intended to be, an etymological dictionary in any sense of that term.

  8. Variant spellings.

  If there are any variant spellings these are shown. Each variant spelling also occurs in its proper alphabetical position as a main entry but is not followed by anything other than a

reference to the more usual spelling. Some words were until quite recently spelled in a somewhat different fashion. This "former spelling" is signalled by the abbreviation "FS."

9. Synonyms, antonyms, and words compared or distinguished.

Synonyms, antonyms, and words compared or distinguished are keyed to the numbered
definitions by numbers which precede the synonym, antonym, etc. See the examples shown with
ตก tòg′ under 5. above. Thus →Dist. 1. ลม, หกลม means that mng. 1 of ตก is to be distinguished from the meaning of ลม and หกลม even though the English gloss overlaps.

10. Notes.

A note (NOTE) is added whenever there is a special comment to be made in regard to
the spelling, pronunciation, or grammatical function of the entry word. Long notes often appear
in smaller than ordinary type. All material appearing in smaller type is to be considered a note
whether so labelled or not. In this category are many special lists of items, e.g. Names of Some
Departments (p. 4), Names of the Ministries (p. 9), Kings of the Chakri Dynasty (p. 114), Names
of the Planets (p. 166), Names of the Twelve Cyclical Years (p. 320), etc. There are many notes
describing grammatical function followed by examples. These are scattered throughout the dictionary, e.g. การ (p. 29), ความ (p. 81), จะ (p. 112), ทำ (p. 237), นัก ๑ (p. 259).

Subentries and Examples

Subentries are derivatives or expressions based on the main entry. The Thai spelling
of each subentry is placed at the first indentation to the left. Examples are also placed at the
first indentation to the left but are always preceded by a circle (o). Subentries are shown in
strict alphabetical order, but examples are placed in an order keyed to the definitions or grammatical comments that precede them. Sometimes it is necessary to show a derivative of a subentry. These secondary derivatives are, like examples, preceded by a circle (o). Subentries
or examples under secondary derivatives are preceded by a double circle (oo).

Transliteration

Thai place names are written in the so-called "general" system of transliteration
worked out by the Royal Institute of Thailand as described in the beginning pages of "Notifica-
tion of the Royal Institute concerning the transcription of Thai characters into Roman" (Journal
of the Thailand Society, vol. 33, part 1, pp. 49-65, 1941). Whenever there is another common
romanized spelling, it is shown in parentheses after the transliteration. A sample entry showing
the Thai spelling, the phonemic writing, the transliteration and another common romanized spelling is:

แม่โขง mɛ̂ɛkhǒoŋ′ pN 1. the Maekhong (Mekong) River [etc.].

Occasionally a special Thai term best left untranslated (or used as an alternate to the translation) is also transliterated in accordance with the same system, e.g.

จังหวัด caŋwàd′ N čhangwat, i.e. township (an administrative unit).

LIST OF ABBREVIATIONS AND LABELS

◡	(1) replaces a hyphen in entries in which the phonemics carries over to a new line. (2) indicates the word is in close transition with whatever follows, e.g. kɔ◡, p. 1.
*	sic. Indicates a given unexpected pron. is correct. So marked in main entry only.
AA	adverb-auxiliary; pp. xx and xxii.
Abbrev.	abbreviation, the abbreviated form is.
account.	accounting.
A. D.	Christian era. To obtain the corresponding year of the Buddhist era, add 543.
addr.	address, addressing.
adv. -aux.	adverb-auxiliary.
aero.	aerodynamics.
Am. Eng.	American English.
anat.	anatomy.
Ant.	antonym.
archaic	archaic term.
arith.	arithmetic.
astron.	astronomy.
bank.	banking term.
B. E.	Buddhist era. To obtain the corresponding year of the Christian era subtract 543.
bot.	botany.
boxing	boxing term.
Brit. Eng.	British English.
Bur.	Burmese.
C	classifier; pp. xx and xxi.
Camb.	Cambodian.
Cf.	compare, esp. etymologically.
chem.	chemistry.
Chin.	Chinese.
Cj	conjunction; pp. xx and xxii.
clf.	classifier; clfs., classifiers.
coll.	collective, collectively.
colloq.	colloquial term.
com.	common term, as opposed to colloq., eleg., roy., sacer., slang, vulg.
Comp.	compare, ref. to terms related in mng.or use and of the same or diff. status level.
conv. f.	converted from, e.g. กำเนิด kamnɔ̀əd′ is conv. f. เกิด kɔ̀əd′ by the addition of

	-°า-น- -amn-.
cpd.	compound; cpds., compounds.
cpl.	coupled (with).
cross ref.	cross reference. Also cross refer.
dA	demonstrative adjective; p. xx.
def.	deferential speech.
derog.	derogatory term.
dial.	dialectal, i.e. not Bangkok Thai.
Dist.	distinguish, used esp. when the gloss obscures an important Thai semantic diff.
dP	demonstrative pronoun; p. xx.
E	east, eastern.
E	exclamative; p. xx.
econ.	economics.
elab.	elaborate; p. xvii.
elect.	electricity.
eleg.	elegant term. See com.
Eng.	English.
epithet	epithet.
eq.	an equal in rank or status.
eq. to	equivalent to. Also equiv. to.
esp.	especially.
euphem.	euphemism, euphemistic term.
ex.	example(s).
excl.	exclamative, exclamation.
expl.	expletive.
Eur.	European, used when the specific source for a borrowed term is unknown, esp. of terms of international currency.
f.	from (borrowed from), e.g. [f. Chin.]
fig.	figurative. Also figur.
finance	financial term.
Fr.	French.
FS.	former spelling, e.g. ปะนิด FS. See ชนิด.
geog.	geographical.
geom.	geometry.
gov.	government.
gram.	grammar, grammatical term.
Hind.	Hindi.
hort.	horticulture.
iA	interrogative-indefinite adj. ; pp. xx, xxi.
idem	the same in meaning as the preceding.

idiom.	idiom, idiomatic.		psych.	psychology.
illit.	illiterate, i.e. in the speech of the uneducated.		Pt	particle; pp. xx and xxii.
imit.	imitative or onomatopoetic.		qM	modifier of a quantifier.
indef.	indefinite.		radio	radio or wireless term.
inf.	inferior, one who is an inferior in status.		rcP	reciprocal pronoun.
int.	intimate, one who is an intimate.		ref.	referring, reference. Also refer.
intens.	intensifier.		reg.	regard, regarding.
iP	interrogative-indefinite pronoun; p. xx,		restricted	of restricted use in this mng.
Japan.	Japanese.		rM	restricted modifier.
joc.	jocular.		roy.	royal speech, used in addressing or
juris.	jurisprudence.			speaking about royalty.
law	law, legal term.		rP	relative pronoun.
lit.	literary. Also, literally.		S	south, southern.
m.	man, men; m. sp., man speaking.		sacer.	sacerdotal speech (Buddhist usage).
Mal.	Malay.		SE	southeast, southeastern.
math.	mathematics.		sec. vb.	secondary verb.
meas.	measurement, measured.		sew.	sewing term.
med.	medicine.		slang	a slang expression.
milit.	military.		smthg.	something.
mng.	meaning, e.g. mng. 1. meaning 1.		sp.	speaking; sp. to eq., speaking to an equal,
mus.	music.			to inf., to an inferior, etc.
N	north, northern.		special.	specialized meaning or usage.
N	noun; pp. xx and xxi.		sport.	sports term.
NE	northeast, northeastern.		sq.	square, in measurements.
Nm	numeral, numerative; pp. xx and xxi.		sup.	superior, one who is a superior.
n. mod.	noun modifier, n. in modifying position.		sV	secondary verb; p. xxii.
nN	name noun, i.e. names of people, groups,		SW	southwest, southwestern.
	organizations, etc. Contrast pN.			synonym.
num.	numeral, numerative.		T	title, usually one used with the given
NW	northwest, northwestern.			name.
obs.	obsolete.		tech.	technical, technology.
obsolesc.	obsolescent term.		theatr.	theatrical term.
occ.	occasionally.		tr. f.	translated from (a loan translation).
Opp.	opposite.		unspec.	unspecified.
P	pronoun; pp. xx and xxi.		V	verb; pp. xx and xxii.
part.	particle.		Var.	variant.
pathol.	pathology.		vb.	verb.
phys.	physics.		Viet.	Vietnamese.
pN	place name, i.e. names of cities, countries,		vulg.	vulgar speech. See com.
	rivers, museums, temples, wats, etc.		W	west, western.
polit.	politics.		w.	woman, women; w. sp., woman speaking.
Port.	Portuguese.		writ.	written language, writing.
Pp	preposition; pp. xx and xxi.		yg.	younger.
pron.	pronunciation.		zool.	zoology.

THAI-ENGLISH
STUDENT'S DICTIONARY

ก

ก kɔɔ′ MIDDLE consonant. Pronounced k initially, g finally.

ก. Abbrev. for กรัม gram.

ก็ ๑ kɔ̂ɔ AA then, consequently, also, too. Often not translated in English.

o ถ้าคุณอยากมาด้วย ก็มา thâakhunjàag′maadûaj′→ kɔ̂maa′↓ If you want to come along, then come.

o จะไปไหนก็ลำบาก capajnǎj′kɔ̂lambàag′ (it's) hard to go anywhere (e.g. in the rain).

o ไม่ช้าก็เร็ว mâjcháa′kɔ̂rew′ sooner or later.

o ไม่มากก็น้อย mâjmâag′kɔ̂nɔ́ɔj′ whether many or few, much or little; if not a (whole) lot, then (at least) some.

o ยิ่งนอนก็ยิ่งขี้เกียจ jîŋ′nɔɔn′-kɔ̂jîŋ′khîiklad′↓ The more you sleep, the lazier you become.

ก็ดี kɔ̂dii′ "is (are) fine too." Often used correlatively, as in the 3rd example.

o ก็ดีเหมือนกัน kɔ̂dii′mǔankan′↓ okay, fine (it's all right with me).

o กลับบ้านเสียก็ดี klàbbâan′sǐakɔ̂dii′↓ Might as well go home.

o จะเป็นการช่วยทางทรัพย์ก็ดี หรือจะเป็นการช่วยทางกำลังก็ดี ผู้รับย่อมยินดีรับทั้งนั้น capenkaan′cchûaj′thaaŋsáb′-kɔ̂dii′→ rýycapenkaanchûaj′cthaaŋkamlaŋ′-kɔ̂dii′→ phûuráb′jɔ̂mjindiiráb′-tháŋnán′↓ Whether it be financial assistance or physical assistance, the recipient will welcome either.

ก็ได้ kɔ̂dâaj′ (postposed, with ได้ as sec. vb.) can also; may; (it) is all right (to).

o เราจะไปไหนก็ได้ rawcapajnǎj′kɔ̂dâaj′↓ We can go anywhere we like.

o อะไรก็ได้ ʔaraj′kɔ̂dâaj′↓ Anything will do. Anything whatever.

ก็ตาม kɔ̂taam′ 1. is of no consequence, of no moment; 1st example. 2. no matter (who, which, what, etc.), hence (who)ever, (which)ever, (what)ever, etc.; 2nd and 3rd examples. NOTE. The complementary clause following ก็ตาม often ends in ทั้งนั้น; see 1st example.

o เขาจะเป็นหมอหรือเป็นนักวิทยาศาสตร์ก็ตาม

ฉันดีใจทั้งนั้น kháwcapenmɔɔ′rýypennágwíd-thajaasàad′ kɔ̂taam′→ chándiicaj′tháŋnán′↓ (Whether) he becomes a doctor or a scientist is of no consequence; I'll be happy either way.

o ใครก็ตาม khraj′kɔ̂taam′ no matter who, whoever, anybody.

o บ้านเมืองใดก็ตาม bâanmyaŋdaj′kɔ̂taam′ no matter which country (it is), whichever country it is.

o แม้(ว่า...)จะ...ก็ตาม (แต่)... mέε′(wâa-...)ca-...kɔ̂taam′→ (tἒɛ-)... Even though (such and such might occur), still (such and such would be the case). Notwithstanding (such and such), still (such and such is the case).

oo แม้จะมีอุปสรรคบ้างก็ตาม แต่ประเทศชาติของเรา จะเจริญวัฒนา mέε′camii′ʔùbpasàg′bâaŋ′ kɔ̂taam′→ tἒɛprathêed′châad′khɔ̌ŋraw′ cacaroən′wádthanaa′↓ Even though there may be some obstacles, still our country will advance and progress.

o อย่างไรก็ตาม jàaŋraj′kɔ̂taam′ however, at any rate. →Also อย่างไรก็ดี.

ก็ตามแต่. See ตามแต่ under ตาม ๑.

ก็ตามที. See ตามที under ตาม ๑.

ก็มี kɔ̂mii′ "is (are) found too."

o เพื่อน ๆ เราที่ไม่ดีก็มี ที่ดีก็มี phɯ̂anphɯan′raw′ thîimâjdii′kɔ̂mii′→ thîidii′kɔ̂mii′↓ Among our friends there are some who are bad and some who are good.

o บางคนที่ไม่ทำดีก็มี baaŋkhon′ thîimâjthamdii′c kɔ̂mii′↓ There are, to be sure, some people who do ill.

o กินเวลาเดือนครึ่งก็มี สองเดือนก็มี kinweelaa′c dyankhrɯ̂ŋ′-kɔ̂mii′→ sɔ̌ɔŋdyan′kɔ̂mii′↓ Sometimes it takes one and a half months, sometimes two months.

ก็แล้วกัน kɔ̂lέɛw′kan 1. mildly hortatory expression: let's, you might (do such and such). Often indicates indifference: go ahead and (do such and such; it would be all the same to me). 2. that's it, that's all there is to it.

ก็แล้วไป kɔ̂lέɛw′paj↓ Then let it go, leave it at that.

แล้ว(...)ก็... lέɛw(...)kɔ̂... and then.

o แล้วเขาก็มา lέɛwkháw′kɔ̂maa′ and then he came.

o แล้วก็หยุด lɛ́ɛwkɔ̂jùd′ and then (he) stopped.

ก็ ๒ in ละก็ lakɔ̂ɔ′ Pt 1. particle sometimes used at the end of a conditional clause, often with the force of a mild entreaty. 2. particle used at the end of the subject of a predication, in a corroborative sense: "you know," "after all," etc. →Also written ละก่อ. →See under ละ ๔.

กก. Abbrev. for กิโลกรัม kilogram.

กก ๑ kòg′ V 1. to cuddle up against; to throw an arm over. 2. to sit or lie on (so as to cover); (a hen) to set.

กก ๒ kòg′ N 1. the base, the portion of an organ at or near its point of attachment. 2. the major part or fragment (as of a rice grain).

กก ๓,หญ้า-- (ต้น) kòg′, jâakòg′ (tôn′) N sedge, rush, reed.

กก ๔ in แม่น้ำกก mɛ̂ɛnáamkòg′ pN the Kok river.

กก kóg′ C 1. group, party, faction. N 2. idem. Rarely used as a noun; when so used, its clf. is (กก). [f. Chin.] →Syn. See พวก.

ก.ข.ค. kɔɔkhɔ̌ɔkhɔɔ′ the ABC's.

ก.ค. Abbrev. for กรกฎาคม July.

กง ๑ koŋ′ N 1. wheel. 2. circle.

กง ๒ in กงการ koŋkaan′ N colloq. affair, business.

กง kóŋ′ C 1. measure of volume (about one-eighth of a cup). V 2. slang to drink or sip an alcoholic beverage. [f. Chin.]

กง (คน) kòŋ′ (khon′) N grandfather. [f. Chin.]

กงสี (กงสี) koŋsǐi′ (koŋsǐi′) N company, organization, group. [f. Chin.]

กงสุล (คน,นาย) koŋsǔn′ (khon′, naaj′) N consul. [f. Eur.]

สถานกงสุล (แห่ง) sathǎan′koŋsǔn′ (hɛ̀ŋ′) N consulate.

กฎ (ข้อ) kòd′ (khɔ̂ɔ′) N rule, regulation, law.

กฎเกณฑ์ kòdkeen′ N rule (as of conduct), regulation.

กฎจราจร kòd′caraacɔɔn′ N traffic laws.

กฎธรรมชาติ kòd′thammachâad′ N law(s) of nature.

กฎบัตร (ฉบับ) kòdbàd′ (chabàb′) N charter (as of the United Nations).

กฎมนเทียรบาล kòd′monthianbaan′ N laws per-

taining to royalty.

กฎหมาย (ฉบับ,มาตรา) kòdmǎaj′ (chabàb′, mâadɔtraa′) N law. นัก-- legal authority.

o กฎหมายนานาประเทศ kòdmǎaj′-naanaa′praɔtheed′ N international law.

o กฎหมายแพ่ง kòdmǎaj′phɛ̂ŋ′ N civil law.

o กฎหมายระหว่างประเทศ kòdmǎaj′-ráwàaŋ′ɔprathêed′ N international law.

o กฎหมายอาญา kòdmǎaj′ʔaajaa′ N criminal law.

o ชอบด้วยกฎหมาย chɔ̂ɔb′dûajkòdmǎaj′ to be lawful, legitimate.

o ตามกฎหมาย taam′kòdmǎaj′ 1. to be legal, according to the law. 2. legally.

o ทำผิดกฎหมาย thamphìd′kòdmǎaj′ to break the law.

o นอกกฎหมาย nɔ̂ɔg′kòdmǎaj′ 1. to be unlawful, illegal, illegitimate. 2. illegally.

o ผิดกฎหมาย phìd′kòdmǎaj′ 1. to be illegal, unlawful, against the law. 2. illegally.

กฎอัยการศึก kòd′ʔajjakaansɤ̀g′ N martial law.

กฐิน kathǐn′ N 1. annual festival, following the rainy season, during which new robes are presented to the monks. 2. the robes so presented (see below).

ผ้ากฐิน phâakathǐn′ N yellow robe presented to a priest during the กฐิน festival.

กด ๑ kòd′ V to press, press on (something), push.

กดกระดิ่ง kòd′kradìŋ′ to ring the bell.

กดขี่ kòdkhìi′ V to oppress, tyrannize.

กดดัน kòd′dan′ V 1. to press. 2. to oppress. ความ-- pressure; oppression.

กดราคา kòd′raakhaa′ V to underprice.

กด ๒ in ปลากด (ตัว) plaakòd′ (tua′) N catfish (Tachysurus).

กตัญญู katanjuu′ V 1. to be grateful. N 2. gratitude.

กติกา (ข้อ) kàtikaa′ (khɔ̂ɔ′) N rule, regulation (as in sports).

กติกาสัญญา (ฉบับ) kàtikaa′sǎnjaa′ (chabàb′) N agreement, pact.

องค์การกติกาแอตแลนติคเหนือ ʔoŋkaan′-kàtikaa′ɔʔɛ̀dlɛɛn′tìgnɤ̌a′* North Atlantic Treaty Organization.

ก.ท. ๑ kɔɔthɔɔ′. Abbrev. for กรุงเทพฯ Bangkok.

ก.ท. ๒ kɔɔthɔɔ′. Abbrev. for ก่อนเที่ยง "before

noon"; hence, A. M.

ก้น(แต่) kɔ̂n/(tɛɛɔ) V to be thinking only of, to have one's mind constantly on.

ก้น (ก้น) kôn/ (kôn/) N 1. the bottom (of anything). 2. the rear, bottom (of a person or animal). →Syn. 2. ตูด vulg., ทวารหนัก eleg.

ก้นบึ้ง kônbŷŋ/ N the bottom way down; way down at the bottom.

นอนก้น nɔɔnkôn/ V to settle on the bottom, precipitate.

ยุงก้นปล่อง (ตัว) juŋ/kônplɔ̀ŋ/ (tua/) N anopheles mosquito.

หัวหกก้นขวิด hǔahòg/kônkhwìd/ sV colloq. gallivanting about, on the go.

กนก. See กระหนก.

กบ ๑ kòb/ V to be filled, to be full.

กบ ๒ (ตัว) kòb/ (tua/) N 1. frog. 2. carpenter's plane.

กบไสไม้ (ตัว) kòb/sǎjmáaj/ (tua/) N carpenter's plane.

ขี้กบ (ชิ้น) khîikòb/ (chín/) N wood shavings.

ไสกบ sǎjkòb/ V to plane.

กบฏ kabòd/ V 1. to rebel. N 2. rebellion. 3. a rebel. การ-- revolt, insurrection, rebellion, revolution. คน-- rebel, insurgent. →Also ขบถ.

ทำกบฏ tham/kabòd/ V to rebel, revolt, stage a revolution.

เป็นกบฏ pen/kabòd/ V to rebel, mutiny, commit treason.

พวกกบฏ (คน,พวก) phûagkabòd/ (khon/, phûag/) N rebels, the rebel faction.

กบาล kabaan/ N vulg. the head. Sometimes used among intimates without offense; often has a humorous connotation. [f. Camb.]

ก.พ. ๑ kɔɔphɔɔ/. Abbrev. for คณะกรรมการข้าราช การพลเรือน Civil Service Commission.

ก.พ. ๒ Abbrev. for กุมภาพันธ์ February.

กม. Abbrev. for กิโลเมตร kilometer.

ก.ม. Abbrev.for กฎหมาย law. Sometimes also for kilometer; see กม. above.

กม kôm/ V 1. to bend (over), stoop. 2. to bow (the head).

กมกราน kômkraan/ V to prostrate oneself.

กมลง kôm/loŋ/ V to bend down.

กมหน้า kômnâa/ V 1. to bow the head. 2. to knuckle down (and do something).

ก.ย. Abbrev. for กันยายน September.

กร (กร) kɔɔn/ (kɔɔn/) N roy. hand, arm.

ต่อกร tɔ̀ɔ/kɔɔn/ V lit. to fight. →Syn. ต่อสู้ com.

กรกฎ. Abbrev. for กรกฎาคม July.

กรกฎาคม karágkadaa/khom/ N July. เดือน-- idem. →The names of all the months are listed under เดือน.

กรง (กรง,ลูก) kroŋ/ (kroŋ/, lûug/) N 1. cage. 2. (prison) cell.

ลูกกรง (ด้าน,อัน,ซี่) lûugkroŋ/ N 1. balustrade, railing (dâan/, ʔan/). 2. the sides of a cage or pen (i.e. one having upright bars)(dâan/). 3. bar of a balustrade, cage, pen (sîi/); in this sense, usually ซี่ลูกกรง.

กรณฑ์ (อัน) kron/ (ʔan/) N math. root.

กรณี (กรณี) karanii/ (karanii/), kɔɔ- N 1. case, incident. 2. circumstances, causes. →Also spelled กรณีย์. NOTE. The spelling กรณีย์ is considered to be incorrect for this word. It is nevertheless commonly used.

o ในกรณีเช่นนั้น najkaranii/chênnán/ in such a case.

กรณีพิพาท karanii/phíphâad/ N dispute, controversy.

พันธกรณี phanthá?/karanii/ N obligation.

วงการลันทัดกรณี woŋkaan/-sǎnthád/karanii/ well-informed circles, sources.

กรณีย์. See note under กรณี.

กรณียกิจ kɔɔraniijakìd/ N work that should be done; necessary matters, duties.

กรด (ชนิด) kròd/ (chaníd/) N acid.

กรดกำมะถัน kròd/kammathǎn/ N sulfuric acid.

กรดเกลือ kròd/klya/ N hydrochloric acid.

กรดดินประสิว kròd/dinprasǐw/ N nitric acid.

น้ำกรด námkròd/ N acid (solution).

สภาพกรด saphâab/kròd/ N acidity.

กรน kron/ V to snore.

กรม (กรม) krom/, krommaɔ (krom/) N 1. department (subdivision of a ministry), bureau; see list on page 4. T 2. rare an element in conferred titles for royalty. →See 1. กระทรวง.

NAMES OF SOME DEPARTMENTS

กรมการขนส่ง kromkaan'khŏnsòŋ' Department of Transportation.

กรมการค้าต่างประเทศ krom'-kaankháa'tàaŋɔprathêed' Department of Foreign Trade.

กรมการค้าภายใน krom'-kaankháa'phaajnaj' Department of Domestic Trade.

กรมการประมง kromkaan'pramoŋ' Department of Fisheries.

กรมการแพทย์ **krom**'kaanphêɛd' Medical Department.

กรมการ**ศาสนา kromkaan**'sàadsanǎa' Department of Religious Affairs.

กรมเกษตร **kromkasèed** Department of Agriculture.

กรมคลัง kromkhlaŋ' Treasury Department.

กรมควบคุมการค้า krom'-khûabkhum'kaankháa' Department of Trade Control.

กรมโฆษณาการ krom'khôodsanaakaan' Department of Publicity (now abandoned). →See กรม ประชาสัมพันธ์.

กรมเจ้าท่า krom'câwthâa' Harbor Department.

กรมชลประทาน krom'chonprathaan' Irrigation Department.

กรมตำรวจ krom'tamrùad' Police Department.

กรมที่ดิน krom'thîidin' Department of Lands.

กรมบัญชีกลาง krom'banchiiklaaŋ' Comptroller-General Department.

กรมประชาศึกษา krom'-prachaa'sỳgsǎa' Department of Public Schools.

กรมประชาสงเคราะห์ krom'-prachaa'sŏŋkhrɔ́ʔ' Public Welfare Department.

กรมประชาสัมพันธ์ krom'-prachaa'sǎmphan' Public Relations Department. →Formerly กรมโฆษณาการ.

กรมปศุสัตว์และสัตว์พาหนะ krom'pasusàd' lɛsàd'ɔphaahanáʔ' Animal Husbandry Department.

กรมป่าไม้ krompàamáaj' Forestry Department.

กรมไปรษณีย์โทรเลข krom'-prajsanii'thooralêeg' Post and Telegraph Department.

กรมพลศึกษา krom'phalásỳgsǎa' Physical Education Department.

กรมพิธีการ krom'-phíthii'kaan' Protocol Department.

กรมมหาดไทย krom'mahàadthaj' Department of the Interior, a department of the Ministry of the Interior.

กรมโยธาเทศบาล krom'-joothaa'thêedsabaan' Department of Public Works.

กรมรถไฟ kromródfaj' State Railways Organization.

กรมราชทัณฑ์ krom'râadchathan' Penitentiary Department.

กรมโรงงานอุตสาหกรรม krom'-rooŋŋaan'ʔùdɔsǎahakam' Department of Factories.

กรมเลขาธิการคณะรัฐมนตรี krom'-leekhǎathíkaan'ɔkhanárádthamontrii' Department of the Secretary-General to the Council of Ministers.

กรมโลหกิจ krom'loohakìd' Department of Mines.

กรมวิทยาศาสตร์ krom'wídthajaasàad' Science Department.

กรมศิลปากร krom'sǐnlápaakɔɔn' Department of Fine Arts.

กรมศุลกากร krom'sǔnlákaakɔɔn' Department of Customs.

กรมเศรษฐการ krom'sèedthakaan' Department of Economic Affairs.

กรมส่งเสริมการค้า krom'-sòŋsɤ̌ɤm'kaankháa' Department of Commercial Enterprise Promotion.

กรมสรรพสามิต krom'sǎnphasǎamíd' Excise Department.

กรมสรรพากร krom'sǎnphaakɔɔn' Revenue Department.

กรมสหกรณ์ krom'sahàkɔɔn' Department of Cooperatives.

กรมสาธารณสุข krom'sǎathaaranásùg' Department of Public Health.

กรมสามัญศึกษา krom'-sǎaman'sỳgsǎa' Department of Elementary Education. →Formerly the Department of General Education. →See cross reference.

กรมอัยการ krom'ʔajjakaan' Department of Public Prosecution.

กรมอาชีวศึกษา krom'-ʔaachiiwá'sỳgsǎa' Department of Vocational Education.

กรมอุตุนิยมวิทยา krom'-ʔùtùníjom'wídthajaa' Meteorological Department.

กรมการ (คณะ,ชุด,คน) krommakaan' N 1. administrative staff of the local government (khaɔná?', chúd'). 2. an official of the local government (khon'). →Chiefly in compounds.

o กรมการจังหวัด krommakaan'caŋwàd' N 1. the administrative staff of a čhangwat. 2. a provincial official who is a member of this staff.

o กรมการอำเภอ krommakaan'ʔamphəə' N 1. the administrative staff of an amphoe. 2. a district official who is a member of this staff.

กรมทหาร (กรม) kromthahǎan' (krom') N milit. regiment.

กรมหมื่น krommamỳyn' T rare a conferred title for royalty.

เจ้ากรม (คน) câwkrom' (khon') N the head of a department.

กรมธรรม์ (ใบ,ฉบับ) krommathan' (baj', chabàb') N lit. loan contract.

กรมธรรม์ประกันภัย krommathan'-prakan'phaj' N lit. insurance policy.

กรรไกร (เล่ม) kankraj/ (lêm/) N eleg. scissors.
→Variant forms are กรรไตร, กันไกร, กันไตร.
→Syn. ตะไกร com.

ขากรรไกร (ข้าง) khăakankraj/ (khâaŋ/) N the
jaws.

กรรตุการก kantùkaa/róg/ N gram. nominative
case.

กรรตุวาจก kantùwaa/còg/ N gram. active voice.

กรรไตร kantraj/. Variant of กรรไกร.

กรรม (อย่าง) kam/ (jàaŋ/) N 1. deeds. 2. sin.
3. misfortune, karma. 4. gram. object of a
verb.

ก่อกรรมทำเข็ญ kɔ̀ɔkam/thamkhěn/ V elab.
colloq. to cause trouble, do evil, commit
crimes.

จองเวรจองกรรม(ต่อ) cɔɔŋ/ween/-cɔɔŋ/kam/=
(tɔ̀ɔ=) V 1. to hold a grudge (against). 2. to
seek revenge.

เจ้ากรรม câwkam/ V 1. to be unlucky, unfortunate. sV 2. darned. E 3. Darn it all! (mild
swear word).

ตามบุญตามกรรม taambun/taamkam/ letting nature take its course, leaving it to fate.

ถึงแก่กรรม thŷŋ/kɛ̀ɛkam/ eleg. to pass away,
die. →Syn. ตาย com.

นิติกรรม nítìkam/ N law. juristic act, legal act.

บาปกรรม bàab/kam/ N 1. sin. V 2. to be sinful.

ผลกรรม phŏnlakam/ N retribution (for one's
evil deeds).

รับกรรม ráb/kam/ V to receive a punishment
or penalty.

เวรกรรม ween/kam/ N 1. fate, misfortune (as
a result of karma). E 2. excl. expressing
one's feelings toward some misfortune, ill fate,
bad luck.

กรรมกร (คน) kammakɔɔn/ (khon/) N 1. laborer,
worker. 2. unskilled labor.

กรรมการ (คน, คณะ, ชุด) kammakaan/ N 1. committee member (khon/). 2. committee, commission (khaná?/, chúd/).

คณะกรรมการ (คณะ, ชุด) khanákammakaan/
(khaná?/, chúd/) N committee, commission.

กรรมการก kammakaa/róg/ N gram. accusative
case.

กรรมพันธุ์ kammaphan/ N heredity.

โรคกรรมพันธุ์ (อย่าง, ชนิด) rôog/kammaphan/
(jàaŋ/, chaníd/) N hereditary disease.

กรรมวาจก kammawaa/còg/ N gram. passive voice.

กรรมวิธี kammawíthii/ N 1. ceremonial procedure.
2. tech. process.

กรรมสิทธิ์ kammasìd/ N 1. ownership. 2. monopoly.
3. right, copyright.

กรรมาธิการ, คณะ-- kammaa/thíkaan/, khanákam=
maa/thíkaan/ N committee; commission.

กรวด (ก้อน, เม็ด) krùad/ (kɔ̂ɔn/, méd/) N pebbles,
gravel.

ก้อนกรวด (ก้อน) kɔ̂ɔnkrùad/ (kɔ̂ɔn/) N small
stones, pebbles, gravel.

กรวย (กรวย, อัน) kruaj/ (kruaj/, ?an/) N funnel,
cone.

กรอ krɔɔ/ V to spin (thread, yarn).

กรอด้าย krɔɔdâaj/ V 1. to wind a skein of thread
or yarn onto a spool. 2. to wind thread or yarn
into a skein.

กรอฟัน krɔɔfan/ V to drill a tooth.

กรอก krɔ̀ɔg/ V 1. to fill with; to pour into. 2. to
fill, fill out, fill in (a blank form, an application).
→Also ตรอก.

พูดกรอกหู(ว่า) phûud/krɔ̀ɔghŭu/(wâa/) 1. to talk
into a person's ear. 2. to drop a hint or make
a complaint which is intended for the ears of a
particular person present.

กรอง krɔɔŋ/ V to filter, strain. การ-- chem.
filtration. เครื่อง-- filter.

ร้อยกรอง rɔ́ɔjkrɔɔŋ/ V 1. to string, thread. 2.
to compose verse. N 3. verse.

สิ่งกรอง sìŋkrɔɔŋ/ N chem. filtrate.

กร่อน krɔ̀n/* V to be worn away, eroded.

กรอบ ๑ (กรอบ, อัน) krɔ̀ɔb/ (krɔ̀ɔb/, ?an/) N frame.

กรอบ ๒ krɔ̀ɔb/ V to be crisp.

กรอบแกรบ krɔ̀ɔbkrɛ̀ɛb/ imit. a crackling sound.

หมี่กรอบ mìikrɔ̀ɔb/ N crisp fried noodles (with
pork or meat)(a Thai dish).

กรอบ ๓ in จนกรอบ con/krɔ̀ɔb/ V colloq. to be
extremely poor.

กรอม krɔɔm/ V (cloth) to hang down to, cover.

๐ นุ่งกระโปรงกรอมเท้า nûŋkraprooŋ/-krɔɔm/=
tháaw/ to wear a floor-length skirt, to wear a

If item is not found under กระ-, see กะ-, ข-.

skirt so that it covers the feet.

○ ผ้าปูโต๊ะกรอมพื้น phâapuutó?'-krɔɔm'phýyn' the tablecloth hangs down to the floor.

กร่อย krɔ̀j'* V 1. to be flat, tasteless, brackish.

  2. to be uninteresting, dull.

กระ ๑ krà?' N spots, freckles.

ตกกระ tògkrà?' V to be freckled.

กระ ๒ (แผ่น,ตัว) krà?' (phɛ̀n', tua') N 1. scale of the hawksbill turtle, used to make combs, knife handles, eyeglass frames, etc. (phɛ̀n').

  2. short for เต่ากระ.

เต่ากระ (ตัว) tàwkrà?' (tua') N hawksbill, a kind of spotted sea turtle.

กระ- kracɔ. Frequent initial syllable, often inter- changeable with กะ- kacɔ, sometimes with ข- khacɔ. Look under these latter spellings for items not found below.

กระจก (บาน,แผ่น) kracòg' N 1. mirror (baan').

  2. plate of glass, e.g. a window-pane (phɛ̀n').

  3. lens (phɛ̀n'). →Comp. 3. แว่น.

  กระจกขยาย (อัน,บาน) kracòg'khajǎaj' N 1. magnifying glass (?an'). 2. magnifying mirror (?an', baan').

  กระจกเงา (แผ่น,บาน) kracòg'ŋaw' (phɛ̀n', baan') N mirror.

  กระจกตา (อัน) kracòg'taa' (?an') N anat. cornea.

  กระจกนูน (แผ่น,บาน) kracòg'nuun' N 1. con- vex mirror (phɛ̀n', baan'). 2. convex lens (phɛ̀n').

  กระจกฝ้า (แผ่น,บาน) kracòg'fâa' (phɛ̀n', baan') N frosted glass, opaque glass.

  กระจกเว้า (แผ่น,บาน) kracòg'wáw' N 1. con- cave mirror (phɛ̀n', baan'). 2. concave lens (phɛ̀n').

  กระจกหน้า (แผ่น,บาน) kracòg'nâa' N 1. wind- shield (phɛ̀n'). Short for กระจกหน้ารถ. 2. lens of a headlight, floodlight, etc. (phɛ̀n'). 3. front mirror (baan').

  กระจกหน้ารถ (แผ่น) kracòg'nâa'-ród' (phɛ̀n') N windshield. →Also กระจกหน้า.

  กระจกหลัง (บาน) kracòg'lǎŋ' (baan') N rear- view mirror.

  กระจกหลังรถ (แผ่น) kracòg'lǎŋ'-ród' (phɛ̀n')

N rear window (of a car).

  ส่องกระจก sɔ̀ŋkracòg' V 1. to look into a mirror. 2. to look through a lens.

กระจง (ตัว) kracoŋ' (tua') N chevrotain (small deerlike ruminant).

กระจอก in นกกระจอก (ตัว) nógkracɔ̀ɔg' (tua') N sparrow.

  นกกระจอกเทศ (ตัว) nógkracɔ̀ɔg'thêed' (tua') N ostrich.

กระจ้อยร่อย kracɔ̀j'rɔ̂j'* V to be tiny.

กระจัด kracàd' V 1. to scatter, disperse. 2. to drive out. 3. to be scattered, dispersed.

  การ-- scattering, expulsion; phys. displace- ment.

  กระจัดกระจาย kracàd'kracaaj' V to be scattered.

กระจับ (ตัว) kracàb' (tua') N variety of water chestnut (Trapa bicornis, T. bispinosa).

กระจ่า (อัน) kracàa' (?an') N a shallow coconut- shell ladle with a wooden handle.

กระจ่าง kracàaŋ' V to be clear, bright.

กระจาด (ใบ) kracàad' (baj') N a deep tray or basket made of bamboo or rattan.

กระจาบ in นกกระจาบ (ตัว) nógkracàab' (tua') N rice bird, weaverbird (Ploceidae and other families).

กระจาย kracaaj' V to scatter, spread, broadcast.

  กระจายเสียง kracaajsĭaŋ' V to broadcast (on the radio).

  ○ วิทยุกระจายเสียง wídthajú?'/kracaajsĭaŋ' N radio broadcast.

  ฟุ้งกระจาย fúŋ'kracaaj' V phys. to diffuse.

กระจิบ in นกกระจิบ (ตัว) nógkracìb' (tua') N general name for various families of small birds, e.g. warblers (Sylviidae), etc.

กระจุก kracùg' C 1. bunch, clump, tuft. 2. lump, mass. N 3. idem. Rarely used as a noun; when so used, its clf. is (กระจุก).

  เป็นกระจุก penkracùg' 1. in bunches, bunched together, bunched up. 2. in a mass, in lumps.

กระจุกกระจิก kracùg'kracìg' V to be trifling, in- significant, petty.

กระจุ๋มกระจิ๋ม kracǔm'kracǐm' V to be delicate, lovely.

กระโจน kracoon' V to plunge, leap, jump (at).

If item is not found under กระ-, see กะ-,ข-.

→Also โจน.

กระโจม (หลัง) kracoom′ (lǎŋ′) N 1. tent, pavilion. V 2. (clothing) to cover.

กระโจมไฟ (หลัง, แห่ง) kracoomfaj′ (lǎŋ′, hɛ̀ŋ′)
N lighthouse.

กระฉอก krachɔ̀ɔg′ V (liquid) to spill, splash out.

กระฉับกระเฉง krachàb′krachěeŋ′ V to be active,
lively.

กระชอน (อัน, กระชอน) krachɔɔn′ (ʔan′, krachɔɔn′)
N strainer, sieve (for straining liquids).

กระชั้น krachán′ V to be very close to, in close
succession with, on the heels of.

กระชับ kracháb′ V 1. to be tight, tight-fitting. 2.
to be stringent. 3. to tighten, fasten firmly,
draw or pull tightly together. 4. to make stringent.

กระชาก krachâag′ V 1. to drag off (as by the arm),
drag off by force. 2. to jerk away, to yank.

ฉุดกระชาก chùd′krachâag′ V to drag, drag off
by force.

กระชาย krachaaj′ N a kind of herb whose roots
are used in cooking (e.g. Kaempferia pandurata).
ต้น-- (ต้น) the plant.

กระชุ (ลูก, ใบ) krachúʔ′ (lûug′, baj′) N a deep
bamboo basket for holding cotton, charcoal, etc.

กระชุ่มกระชวย krachûm′krachuaj′ V to be vigorous, spry, robust.

กระเช้า (ใบ) kracháw′ (baj′) N a basket of bamboo or rattan used especially for flowers or
fruit.

กระแชง (ผืน) krachɛɛŋ′ (phɰ̌ɰn′) N removable
convex roofing sheet for boat transporting grain.
Often made of thatch.

กระโชก(เอา, เอากับ, ให้) krachôog′(ʔaw′, ʔawɔ
kaɔ, hâj′, hâjɔ) V 1. to be abrupt and forcefully emphatic (in manner, esp. in speech).
2. to be abrupt with, to treat brusquely. 3.
(a dog) to bark, bark at.

กระโชกกระชาก krachôog′krachâag′. See mngs.
1 and 2 under กระโชก.

กระโชกโฮกฮาก krachôog′hôoghâag′ V to be
harsh, rough, crude, brusque (in manner, esp.
in speech).

พัดกระโชก phád′krachôog′ V (the wind) to blow

hard, blow in gusts.

กระซิก in หัวเราะต่อกระซิก hǔarɔ́ʔ′-tɔ̀ɔ′krasíg′
to giggle, to laugh merrily.

กระซิบ krasíb′ V to whisper. →Syn. ซุบซิบ.

กระซิบกระซาบ(กัน) krasíb′krasâab′(kan′) V
to be whispering (to each other). →Syn. ซุบซิบ.

กระเซ็น krasen′ V (a liquid) to splash, be splashed.

กระเซ้า krasáw′ V to tease.

กระเซิง as in เป็นกระเซิง penkrasəəŋ′ (the hair)
to stand out from the head, stick out in all directions (as when mussed, windblown, too thick,
too curly).

กระดก kradòg′ V to move one end up or down, as
a lever.

กระด้ง (ใบ, ลูก) kradôŋ′ (baj′, lûug′) N a large,
flat, round tray, made of bamboo.

กระดอง (กระดอง) kradɔɔŋ′ (kradɔɔŋ′) N carapace,
shell (of crustaceans).

กระดอน kradɔɔn′ V to bounce, bounce up, ricochet.

กระดาก, --ใจ, --อาย kradàag′, kradàagcaj′, kraɔ
dàagʔaaj′ V 1. to be shy, bashful. 2. to be
ashamed. ความ-- bashfulness, shyness.

กระด่าง. See กระด่ำกระด่าง.

กระด้าง kradâaŋ′ V 1. to be hard, rigid, unbending,
unyielding. 2. to be hard (of water). 3. to be
obstinate, unyielding (of people). 4. to be harsh,
coarse, crude. →Syn. 1. แข็ง. →Ant. See
นิ่ม.

กระด้างกระเดื่อง kradâaŋ′kradɯ̀aŋ′ V 1. to be
rebellious. 2. to be unyielding.

กระดาน (แผ่น) kradaan′ (phɛ̀n′) N 1. board. C
2. clf. for a game (i.e. a single contest) of chess,
of checkers. 3. clf. for a chessboard.

กระดานชนวน (แผ่น) kradaanchanuan′ (phɛ̀n′)
N slate (for writing on).

กระดานดำ (แผ่น) kradaandam′ (phɛ̀n′) N blackboard.

o แปรงลบกระดานดำ (อัน) prɛɛŋ′lóbkradaandam′
(ʔan′) N blackboard eraser.

กระดานเล่นคลื่น (แผ่น) kradaan′lênkhlɰ̂ɰn′ (phɛ̀n′)
N surfboard.

กระดานหก (แผ่น, ที่, อัน) kradaanhòg′ (phɛ̀n′, thîi′,
ʔan′) N seesaw.

กระดานหมากรุก (กระดาน, แผ่น) kradaanmàagrúg′

(kradaan′, phɛ̀n′) N chessboard.

ฝากระดาน (แผ่น) fǎakradaan′ (phɛ̀n′) N wooden
　　wall, wooden partition of a room.

หน้ากระดาน nâakradaan′ N milit. rank, line.

o เรียงหน้ากระดาน riaŋ′nâakradaan′ V milit.
　　to fall in, form troops in line.

กระดาษ (แผ่น, ปึก, ริม, รีม, กล่อง, ม้วน) kradàad′
　　N paper (phɛ̀n′ for a sheet; pỳg′ for a stack;
　　rim′, riim′ for a ream; klɔ̀ŋ′ for a box, as of
　　stationery; múan′ for a roll). [f. Port.]

กระดาษกรอง kradàadkrɔɔŋ′ N chem. filter
　　paper.

กระดาษก๊อปปี้ kradàadkɔ́bpîi′ N carbon paper.
　　[ก๊อปปี้ f. Eng. copy]

กระดาษแก้ว kradàadkɛ̂ɛw′ N 1. cellophane. 2.
　　tracing paper.

กระดาษเขียนจดหมาย kradàadkhǐancòdmǎaj′ N
　　writing paper, stationery.

กระดาษแข็ง kradàadkhɛ̌ŋ′ N cardboard, card
　　paper, stiff paper.

กระดาษชำระ kradàadchamrá?′ N eleg. toilet
　　paper. →Syn. See next entry.

กระดาษเช็ดก้น kradàad′chédkôn′ N com. toilet
　　paper. NOTE. This term is used among inti-
　　mates only; otherwise elegant terms such as
　　กระดาษชำระ, กระดาษอนามัย are used.

กระดาษซับ kradàadsáb′ N blotter, blotting paper.

กระดาษดีบุก kradàaddiibùg′ N tin foil.

กระดาษทราย kradàadsaaj′ N sandpaper.

กระดาษฟาง kradàadfaaŋ′ N an absorbent straw
　　paper made by the Chinese, used chiefly as
　　toilet paper.

กระดาษอนามัย kradàad′-?anaa′maj′ N eleg.
　　toilet paper. →Syn. กระดาษเช็ดก้น com.

กระดาษอัดสำเนา kradàad′-?àd′sǎmnaw′ N 1.
　　carbon paper. 2. (mimeograph) stencil paper,
　　any duplicating paper.

หน้ากระดาษ (หน้ากระดาษ, หน้า) nâakradàad′
　　(nâakradàad′, nâa′) N 1. page (of a book, news-
　　paper, letter). C 2. page, pages (ref. to the
　　length of written materials such as letters, au-
　　thors' manuscripts, etc.).

กระด่ำกระด่าง kradam′kradàaŋ′ V to be discolored.

กระดิก kradìg′ V to wag, wiggle, move, motion.

กระดิกหาง kradìg′hǎaŋ′ to wag the tail.

กระดุกกระดิก kradùg′kradìg′ V to wiggle, fidget,
　　squirm.

กระดิ่ง (ใบ) kradìŋ′ (baj′) N 1. small bell, usually
　　one rung by hand. 2. doorbell.

กระดี่ in ปลากระดี่ (ตัว) plaakradìi′ (tua′) N
　　gourami (esp. Trichogaster), a kind of small
　　fresh-water fish.

กระดึบ kradɯ̀yb′ V to crawl, move very slowly.

กระดุกกระดิก. See under กระดิก.

กระดุม, ลูก-- (เม็ด) kradum′, lûugkradum′ (méd′)
　　N button. →Also ดุม, ลูกดุม.

กลัดกระดุม klàd′kradum′ V to button.

รังกระดุม (รัง) raŋkradum′ (raŋ′) N buttonhole.
　　→Also รังดุม.

กระดูก (อัน, ชิ้น) kradùug′ (?an′, chín′) N 1. bone
　　(of person, animal, but not of fish). V slang
　　2. (a problem) to be difficult, hard. 3. to be
　　stingy. →Dist. 1. ก้าง ๑.

กระดูกสันหลัง kradùug′sǎnlǎŋ′ N vertebra, back-
　　bone, spine.

กระดูกไหปลาร้า kradùug′-hǎj′plaaráa′ N the
　　clavicle, collarbone.

กระดูกอ่อน kradùug′?ɔ̀ɔn′ N cartilage. โรค--
　　rickets.

เข้ากระดูกดำ khâwkradùug′dam′ to be deep-seated,
　　ingrained, firmly entrenched. อย่าง-- deeply,
　　in the extreme, extremely (esp. of hating).

โครงกระดูก (อัน) khrooŋkradùug′ (?an′) N
　　skeleton.

แช่งชักหักกระดูก chɛ̂ɛŋchág′hàgkradùug′ V to
　　curse vehemently.

ฝังในกระดูก fǎŋ′najkradùug′ V to become a habit,
　　be deeply ingrained.

กระเด็น, --ไป kraden′, kraden′paj′ V 1. to glance
　　off, bounce off, fly off, splash. 2. to be thrown
　　off. 3. to throw off, fling aside, knock aside.

กระเดียด ๑ kradìad′ V to carry against the hip or
　　the waist (as a basket).

กระเดียด ๒, --จะ kradìad′, kradìad′ca⊃ AA be
　　disposed toward, tend to be; rather, somewhat.

o เขากระเดียดจะเป็นคนขี้โมโห kháwkradìad′-
　　capenkhon′khîimoohǒo′ He tends to be a hot-
　　tempered man.

กระเดือก kradỳag′ V to swallow forcibly, with
effort.

  ลูกกระเดือก (ลูก) lûugkradỳag′ (lûug′) N the
Adam's apple.

กระเดื่อง See กระด้างกระเดื่อง under กระด้าง.

กระโดง (อัน) kradooŋ′ (ʔan′) N mast.

  เส้ากระโดง (เส้า) sǎwkradooŋ′ (sǎw′) N mast.

กระโดด kradòod′ V 1. to jump, leap. 2. to hop.
→Also โดด ๑.

  กระโดดน้ำ kradòodnáam′ V to jump into the
water.

  กระโดดโลดเต้น kradòod′-lôod′tên′ V to hop
and skip about (merrily, as children do).

  กระโดดสะพาน kradòod′saphaan′ V to jump off
a bridge.

กระได (กระได) kradaj′ (kradaj′) N com. 1.
stairs, stairway. 2. ladder. →Syn. บันได
eleg.

กระต๊อบ (หลัง) kratɔ́ɔb′ (lǎŋ′) N shack, hut.

กระตั้ว in นกกระตั้ว (ตัว) nógkratûa′ (tua′) N
cockatoo (Kakatoë). [กระตั้ว f. Mal.]

กระต๊าก kratáag′ imit. hen's cackle.

กระต่าย (ตัว) kratàaj′ (tua′) N 1. rabbit, hare.
2. a coconut grater, in its primitive form consisting of a small bench with a toothed metallic
blade attached to one end.

  หูกระต่าย (อัน, หู) hǔukratàaj′ (ʔan′, hǔu′) N
1. bow tie. 2. bowknot.

กระติก (ใบ) kratìg′ (baj′) N 1. jug (for water).
2. canteen. 3. thermos bottle.

กระตือรือร้น kratyy′ryyrón′ V to be anxious, enthusiastic, eager, hasty, in a rush.

กระตุก kratùg′ V to pull suddenly, to pull with
jerks, to jerk.

กระตุ้น kratûn′ V 1. to hit, strike. 2. to stimulate,
incite. 3. to urge, encourage. การ-- phys.
impulse.

กระเต็น in นกกระเต็น (ตัว) nógkraten′ (tua′)
N kingfisher (Alcedinidae).

กระเตื้อง, --ขึ้น kratŷaŋ′, kratŷaŋ′khŷn′ V to improve, get better.

กระโตกกระตาก kratòog′kratàag′ V colloq. to
make a noise about something (which ought to
be kept quiet); to spill the beans. →Comp.

กระต๊าก.

กระถาง (ใบ) krathǎaŋ′ (baj′) N 1. earthen flower-
pot. 2. metal pot for burning incense sticks.

กระโถน (ใบ) krathǒon′ (baj′) N spittoon.

กระทง ๑ krathoŋ′ C 1. a count (in an indictment).
2. a section, clause (of a text).

  กระทงความ krathoŋ′khwaam′ N 1. sense, meaning. 2. an aspect of a matter.

  o หมดถ้อยกระทงความ mòd′thɔ́j′-krathoŋ′khwaam′
exhaustively, in every detail.

กระทง ๒ (ใบ) krathoŋ′ (baj′) N small fruit tray
made of banana leaves, paper, etc.

กระทบ krathób′ V 1. to strike, strike against, bump
against, collide with. 2. to touch on. 3. to concern, affect. การ-- clash, collision; impact.

  กระทบกระเทียบ krathób′krathîab′ V to insinuate,
be sarcastic.

  กระทบกระเทือน krathób′krathyan′ V 1. to affect,
stir, move, shake, have an impact on. 2. to be
shaken. ความ-- effect, influence, impact.

  กระทบถึง krathób′thŷŋⸯ to touch on, concern, affect.

  o พูดกระทบถึง phûud′krathób′-thŷŋⸯ to speak
insinuatingly about, insinuate (something) about.

กระทรวง (กระทรวง) krasuaŋ′ (krasuaŋ′) N ministry (of the government). NOTE. The hierar-
chical structure of the Thai government is as
follows: กระทรวง ministry; กรม department
(within a ministry); กอง division (of a department); แผนก subdivision (of a division). →See
also ทบวง.

NAMES OF THE MINISTRIES
  กระทรวงกลาโหม krasuaŋ′kalaahǒom′ Ministry
of Defense.

  กระทรวงการคลัง krasuaŋ′kaankhlaŋ′ Ministry
of Finance. Short form: กระทรวงคลัง.

  กระทรวงการต่างประเทศ krasuaŋ′-kaan′tàaŋⸯ
prathêed′ Ministry of Foreign Affairs. Short
form: กระทรวงต่างประเทศ.

  กระทรวงการสาธารณสุข krasuaŋ′-kaan′sǎa′thaaⸯ
ranásùg′ Ministry of Public Health. Short
form: กระทรวงสาธารณสุข.

  กระทรวงการอุตสาหกรรม krasuaŋ′-kaan′ʔùdsǎaⸯ
hàkam′ Ministry of Industry. Short form:
กระทรวงอุตสาหกรรม.

  กระทรวงเกษตร, กระทรวงเกษตราธิการ krasuaŋ′ⸯ
kaseed′, krasuaŋ′kaseed′traathíkaan′ Ministry
of Agriculture.

กระทรวงคมนาคม krasuaŋ'khommanaa'khom'
Ministry of Communication.

กระทรวงคลัง krasuaŋ'khlaŋ'. Short form of
กระทรวงการคลัง, Ministry of Finance.

กระทรวงต่างประเทศ krasuaŋ'tàaŋprathêed'.
Short form of กระทรวงการต่างประเทศ,
Ministry of Foreign Affairs.

กระทรวงพาณิชย์ krasuaŋ'phaaníd' Ministry of
Commerce (now abandoned).

กระทรวงมหาดไทย krasuaŋ'mahàadthaj' Ministry
of the Interior.

กระทรวงยุติธรรม krasuaŋ'júdtitham' Ministry
of Justice.

กระทรวงวัฒนธรรม krasuaŋ'wádthanátham' Ministry of Culture (now abandoned).

กระทรวงศึกษาธิการ krasuaŋ'sỳgsăa'thíkaan'
Ministry of Education.

กระทรวงเศรษฐการ krasuaŋ'sèed'thakaan'
Ministry of Economics.

กระทรวงสหกรณ์ krasuaŋ'sahàkɔɔn' Ministry
of Cooperatives.

กระทรวงสาธารณสุข krasuaŋ'săa'thaaranásòg'.
Short form of กระทรวงการสาธารณสุข,
Ministry of Public Health.

กระทรวงอุตสาหกรรม krasuaŋ'?ùdsăa'hàkam'.
Short form of กระทรวงการอุตสาหกรรม,
Ministry of Industry.

เจ้ากระทรวง (คน) câwkrasuaŋ' (khon') N minister, head of a ministry.

ปลัดกระทรวง (นาย,คน) palàd'krasuaŋ' (naaj',
khon') N undersecretary (of a ministry).

o รองปลัดกระทรวง (นาย,คน) rɔɔŋ'-palàd'ɔ
krasuaŋ' (naaj',khon') N deputy undersecretary (of a ministry).

กระท้อน ๑ (ใบ,ลูก,ผล) krathɔɔn' (baj',lûug',
phòn') N fruit of the sandorica. ต้น-- (ต้น)
the sandorica tree (Sandoricum indicum).

กระท้อน ๒ krathɔɔn' V 1. to reflect. 2. to rebound.

กระท้อนกระแท่น krathɔn'krathɛn'* V to be incoherent.

กระท่อม (หลัง) krathɔ̂m'*(lăŋ') N hut, cottage.

กระทั่ง krathâŋ' Cj 1. until. Pp 2. to, up to, until.
→Normally in combinations like the following.

จนกระทั่ง conkrathâŋ' Cj 1. until. Pp 2. to, up
to, until.

แม้กระทั่ง mɛ́ɛkrathâŋ' Cj 1. even when. Pp 2. even.

กระทัด in กระทัดรัด krathádrád' V 1. to be well-
proportioned and somewhat small in size; to be
compact. 2. to be short and to the point. 3.
to be well-fitting.

กระทันหัน krathanhăn' V to be sudden, abrupt.
อย่าง--,โดย-- abruptly.

กระทาชาย (นาย,คน) krathaa'chaaj' (naaj',khon')
N archaic a man.

กระทำ kratham' V eleg., lit. to perform, to do.
การ-- deed, act, action; behavior (i.e. physical behavior of a material). →Syn. ทำ com.

o การประชุมนี้จะกระทำกันที่กรุงเทพ ฯ kaanpraɔ
chum'níi cakrathamkan'thîikruŋthêeb'↓ They
will hold (i.e. conduct) this meeting in Bangkok.

กระทำการค้า kratham'kaankháa' to do business.

กระทำผิด kratham'phìd' to do wrong, make a
mistake.

กระทำภัตตกิจ kratham'phádtakìd' eleg. sacer.
to eat. →Syn. See กิน com.

กระทำลัตย์ kratham'sàd' V eleg. to vow.

กระทิง ๑, วัว-- (ตัว) krathiŋ', wuakrathiŋ' (tua')
N gaur (Bos gaurus), a kind of wild ox.

กระทิง ๒ in ปลากระทิง (ตัว) plaakrathiŋ' (tua')
N a kind of fresh-water fish (Mastocembelidae).

กระทืบ krathŷyb' V to stamp with the foot.

กระทุง in นกกระทุง (ตัว) nógkrathuŋ' (tua') N
pelican (Pelecanidae).

กระทุ้ง krathúŋ' V 1. to poke, push, knock against
with a long object. 2. to nudge. 3. colloq.
to push, encourage someone to do something.

กระทุ่ม ๑ in ต้นกระทุ่ม (ต้น) tônkrathûm' (tôn')
N a kind of tree (usually Rubiaceae). ดอก--
(ดอก) blossom of this tree.

กระทุ่ม ๒ in กระทุ่มน้ำ krathûm'náam' V to paddle,
splash (with hands and feet, while swimming).

กระทู้,--ถาม (ข้อ,เรื่อง,กระทู้) krathúu', krathúuɔ
thăam' (khɔ̆ɔ', rŷaŋ',krathúu') N question posed
in a legislative body (in parliamentary practice).

กระเทย (คน,ตัว) krathəəj' N hermaphrodite (khon'
for persons; tua' for animals).

กระเทเร่ in เอียงกระเทเร่ ?iaŋ'krathêerêe' V
to tilt to one side.

กระเทห์ in เล่ห์กระเทห์ lêe'krathêe' N trick,
deceit, cunning.

o ทำเล่ห์กระเทห์ thamlêe'krathêe' to act cunningly, practise deceit or intrigue.

กระเทียบ. See กระทบกระเทียบ.

กระเทียม (หัว,กลีบ) krathiam' N garlic (hŭa' for

the bulb; klìib⁄ for cloves). ต้น-- (ต้น)
the garlic plant. ใบ-- (ใบ) garlic leaf.

หัวเดียวกระเทียมลีบ hǔa⁄diaw⁄-krathiam⁄lîib⁄
V idiom. to have no friends or relations, to
be alone in the world.

กระเทือน krathyan⁄ V to shake, vibrate, move.

กระทบกระเทือน krathób⁄krathyan⁄ V 1. to affect,
stir, move, shake, have an impact on. 2. to be
shaken.

กระเทือนใจ krathyancaj⁄ V to hurt someone's
feelings, to hurt (someone).

กระแทก krathᵉᵉg⁄ V to hit, strike smartly, forcibly; to bump against, collide (with).

กระแทกเท้า krathᵉᵉg⁄tháaw⁄ to stamp the feet.

กระแทกประตู krathᵉᵉg⁄pratuu⁄ to slam the door.

กระแทกเสียง (กับ,ใส่) krathᵉᵉg⁄sǐaŋ⁄ (kaɔ,
sàj⁄) to speak sharply (to), snap (at) (with
raised voice).

กระแท่น. See กระท่อนกระแท่น.

กระแทะ (เล่ม) krathᵉʔ⁄ (lêm⁄) N a small ox-
cart.

กระนั้น kranán⁄ 1. so, thus, like that. 2. nevertheless, even so (in this sense usually preceded
by แต่,ถึง ; see below).

แต่กระนั้น tᵉᵉkranán⁄ but nevertheless, but even
so.

ถ้ากระนั้น tháakranán⁄ if so, in such a case.

ถึงกระนั้น thÿŋkranán⁄ even so, nevertheless, in
spite of that.

แม้กระนั้น mᵉᵉkranán⁄ however, yet.

กระนี้ kraníi⁄ so, in this way, like this.

กระบวน (กระบวน) krabuan⁄ (krabuan⁄) N 1. procession, line, train (of moving persons, animals, vehicles). 2. in the matter of, as regards
(short for ในกระบวน). 3. artfulness, eva-
siveness; see 1st example. C 4. clf. for processions, lines, trains. 5. procedure, method,
strategy, technique. →Also in mng. 5 ขบวน.
NOTE. In ref. to trains ขบวน is the usual form.

○ เขามีกระบวนมากจริง kháwmiikrabuan⁄-mâag⁄ɔ
ciŋ⁄ She sure hedges a lot: "has a great deal
of artfulness."

○ แห่กระบวนนี้ยาวมาก hᵉᵉ⁄krabuanníi⁄ jaawɔ
mâag⁄ this procession is very long.

○ โดยกระบวนนี้ dooj⁄krabuanníi⁄ by this technique, tactic.

กระบวนการ krabuankaan⁄ N 1. procedure. 2.
administration. 3. movement (as in "liberation
movement"). 4. tech. process.

○ กระบวนการยุติธรรม krabuankaan⁄júdtitham⁄
the judicial administration (collectively, viz.,
the courts, the police, various government
departments).

○ กระบวนการกู้ชาติ krabuankaan⁄-kûu⁄châad⁄
the liberation movement.

○ กระบวนการไฮโดรลิสิส krabuankaan⁄hajdroo⁄ɔ
lisìs⁄ chem. the process of hydrolysis.

กระบวนรถ krabuanród⁄ N 1. procession of vehicles. 2. railroad train. →In mng. 2 usually
ขบวนรถ.

กระบวนเรือรบ krabuan⁄ryarób⁄ N naval fleet.

กระบวนแห่ krabuanhᵉᵉ⁄ N procession, parade.

กระบิดกระบวน krabìd⁄krabuan⁄ V to hedge,
manifest reluctance in an artful way. ทำ--
idem.

ในกระบวน najkrabuan⁄ 1. in the matter of, as
regards. 2. of, among.

○ ในกระบวนแก้ตัว เป็นที่หนึ่ง najkrabuankᵉᵉ⁄tua⁄
penthîinÿŋ⁄↓ In the matter of making excuses,
you are first rate!

เป็นกระบวน penkrabuan⁄ 1. in a procession, in
formation. 2. colloq. in great numbers.

กระบวย (อัน,ลูก,ใบ) krabuaj⁄ (ʔan⁄,lûug⁄,baj⁄)
N a deep coconut-shell ladle with a long handle,
used for dipping water.

กระบอก (กระบอก) krabɔɔg⁄ (krabɔɔg⁄) N 1. cylinder. C 2. clf. for cylindrical objects, e.g.
gun; also for an eye socket.

กระบอกตา krabɔɔgtaa⁄ N eye socket.

กระบอกปืน krabɔɔgpyyn⁄ N gun barrel.

กระบอกสูบ krabɔɔgsùub⁄ N cylinder (of an engine).

ปลากระบอก (ตัว) plaakrabɔɔg⁄ (tua⁄) N sea
mullet (Mugilidae).

ปากกระบอก (ปาก) pàagkrabɔɔg⁄ (pàag⁄) N
muzzle (of firearms).

หุ่นกระบอก (ตัว) hùnkrabɔɔg⁄ (tua⁄) N marionette,
puppet.

กระบอง (อัน) krabɔɔŋ⁄ (ʔan⁄) N club, staff, stick.

If item is not found under กระ-, see กะ-,ข-.

กระบะ (ใบ) krabà?/ (baj/) N 1. small wooden
　　tray. 2. hand truck, handcart.
　รถกระบะ (คัน) ród/krabà?/ (khan/) N hand
　　truck, handcart.
กระบาน krabaan/. See กบาล.
กระบาย (ลูก,ใบ) krabaaj/ (baj/,lûug/) N small
　　bamboo basket, bamboo dish (with unreinforced
　　edge).
กระบาล krabaan/. See กบาล.
กระบิด in กระบิดกระบวน krabìd/krabuan/ V to
　　hedge, manifest reluctance in an artful way.
　　ทำ-- idem.
กระบี่ ๑ (อัน) krabìi/ (?an/) N 1. sword. 2. bay-
　　onet.
กระบี่ ๒ krabìi/ pN Krabi (in S Thailand).
กระบือ (ตัว) krabyy/ (tua/) N eleg. water buf-
　　falo. [f.Camb.] →Syn. ควาย com.
กระบุง (ใบ) krabuŋ/ (baj/) N a bushel basket with
　　a square bottom and a circular opening.
กระเบน in ปลากระเบน (ตัว) plaakrabeen/ (tua/)
　　N ray, skate.
กระเบียด krabìad/ C a unit of length equal to one
　　quarter of an inch. →See นิ้ว.
　กระเบียดนิ้ว krabìad/níw/ C one quarter of an
　　inch.
　๐ ทุก ๆ กระเบียดนิ้ว thúgthúg/krabìadníw/ each
　　and every minor detail, each and every little bit.
กระเบื้อง (แผ่น) krabŷaŋ/ (phèn/) N tile.
　กระเบื้องเคลือบ krabŷaŋkhlŷab/ N enameled
　　tile, glazed tile.
กระปริบกระปรอย kraprìb/kraprooj/ V to be light
　　and intermittent, to occur a little at a time.
กระปรี้กระเปร่า kraprîi/kapràw/ V to be active,
　　sprightly.
กระป๋อง (ใบ) krapɔ̌ŋ/*(baj/) N 1. tin can. 2. pail.
　　C 3. clf. for things packed in tin cans.
　กระป๋องน้ำ (ใบ,ลูก) krapɔ̌ŋnáam/ (baj/,lûug/)
　　N water bucket, pail.
　เครื่องกระป๋อง (กระป๋อง) khrŷaŋkrapɔ̌ŋ/ (kraɔ
　　pɔ̌ŋ/) N canned goods, canned food.
　ปลากระป๋อง (ตัว,กระป๋อง) plaakrapɔ̌ŋ/ N
　　canned fish (tua/ for fish that is canned; kraɔ
　　pɔ̌ŋ/ for a can of canned fish).
　นมกระป๋อง (กระป๋อง) nomkrapɔ̌ŋ/ (krapɔ̌ŋ/)

N canned milk.
กระปุก (ลูก,ใบ) krapùg/ (lûug/,baj/) N piggy bank
　　(a small pot or jar with a small slit opening).
กระเป๋า (กระเป๋า,ใบ) krapǎw/ (krapǎw/,baj/) N
　　1. pocket. 2. pocketbook, purse. คน-- fare
　　collector on public conveyances.
　กระเป๋าเดินทาง (ใบ,ลูก) krapǎwdəənthaaŋ/
　　(baj/,lûug/) N 1. traveling bag. 2. suitcase.
　กระเป๋าถือ (ใบ,ลูก) krapǎwthŷy/ (baj/,lûug/)
　　N handbag, pocketbook.
　กระเป๋ารั่ว krapǎwrûa/ V colloq. to be broke.
　กระเป๋าหนัก krapǎwnàg/ V colloq. to be rich,
　　have loads of money.
　กระเป๋าหิ้ว (ใบ,ลูก) krapǎwhîw/ (baj/,lûug/)
　　N 1. carrying bag, carrying case. 2. handbag,
　　pocketbook (having handles).
กระเปาะ (กระเปาะ) krapɔ̀?/ (krapɔ̀?/) N 1.
　　(glass) bulb. 2. bot. receptacle (part of a flower).
　　3. base on which a precious stone is mounted.
กระโปก in ลูกกระโปก (ลูก) lûugkrapòog/ (lûug/)
　　N com.,vulg. testicles. →Syn. ลูกอัณฑะ
　　eleg., ไข่ colloq.,euphem.
กระโปรง (ตัว,อัน) kraprooŋ/ N 1. skirt (tua/).
　　2. hood of an automobile (?an/).
　กระโปรงชั้นใน kraprooŋ/chánnaj/ N slip (a
　　woman's undergarment).
กระผม kraphǒm/ P eleg.def. m. sp. I, me.
　　→Syn. See ผม.
　เกล้ากระผม klâawkraphǒm/ P elab.eleg.def.
　　m. sp. I, me.
กระพริบ,--ตา kraphríb/, kraphríb/taa/ V to blink,
　　blink the eyes. →Also พริบตา.
กระพือ kraphyy/ V 1. to flap, flutter, shake. 2.
　　to spread out, diffuse.
กระพุ่ม,--มือ kraphûm/, kraphûm/myy/ V to hold
　　the hands together at the chest, palm to palm,
　　as a sign of respect (as when listening to a ser-
　　mon, or in salutation). →Comp. ไหว้. →Syn.
　　พนม,ประณม.
กระเพาะ (กระเพาะ,ลูก,ใบ) kraphɔ́?/ (kraphɔ́?/,
　　lûug/,baj/) N stomach.
　กระเพาะขี้ kraphɔ́?/khîi/ N com.,vulg. bowel,
　　rectum.
　กระเพาะปัสสาวะ kraphɔ́?/pàdsǎawá?/ N eleg.

If item is not found under กระ-, see กะ-,ข-.

urinary bladder.

กระเพาะอาหาร kraphɔ́?/ʔaahǎan/ N stomach.

กระเพื่อม kraphŷam/ V 1. to throb, oscillate. 2. to ripple (of water). 3. to move with a fluctuating, wave-like motion.

กระมัง kramaŋ/ Pt most likely, like as not. Often best rendered in English as: "I suppose that...; could it be that...?"

  o หนูเป็นคนที่นี่กระมัง nǔu/ penkhon/thîinîi/ kra⊃maŋ/↓ I suppose that you're a native of these parts.

กระยา krajaa/ N eleg., lit. food, provisions.

กระรอก (ตัว) krarɔ̂ɔg/ (tua/) N squirrel.

กระไร kraraj/ what; how.

  o ขั้งกระไรเลย châŋ/krarajləəj/↓ How could he! How come?(expressing reproach, indignation).

  o ดีกระไร dii/kraraj/ How good!

  o ดูจะกระไรอยู่ duu/cakraraj/-jùu↓ That looks rather odd (funny, inappropriate)!

กระวนกระวาย krawon/krawaaj/ V to be restless, uneasy, perturbed.

กระวาน (ลูก) krawaan/ (lûug/) N cardamom. The seed is used as an ingredient in curry. ต้น-- (ต้น) the cardamom plant.

กระวีกระวาด krawii/krawâad/ V 1. to hurry, be in a hurry. sV 2. briskly, in lively fashion.

กระษาปณ์ krasàab/ N eleg. money.
  โรงกระษาปณ์ rooŋkrasàab/ (rooŋ/) N mint (i.e. where money is coined).

กระสอบ (ใบ) krasɔ̀ɔb/ (baj/) N (gunny) sack, bag.
  กระสอบป่าน krasɔ̀ɔb/pàan/ N gunny sack, jute bag.

กระสับกระส่าย krasàb/krasàaj/ V to be nervous, restless, ill-at-ease.

กระสา in นกกระสา (ตัว) nógkrasǎa/ (tua/) N heron (Ardeidae).

กระสาย,น้ำ-- krasǎaj/, námkrasǎaj/ N a liquid additive used in the preparation of medicines.
  ยักกระสาย jágkrasǎaj/ V slang 1. to change the topic. 2. to change the method, the approach.

กระสุน (นัด,ลูก) krasǔn/ (nád/,lûug/) N 1. bullet, shot, pellet, projectile. 2. cartridge. 3. ammunition.

กระสุนปืน krasǔn/pyyn/ N 1. bullet, shell. 2. cartridge. เครื่อง-- firearms and ammunition.

กระสุนปืนใหญ่ krasǔn/pyynjàj/ N artillery shell, projectile.

ลูกกระสุน (นัด,ลูก) lûugkrasǔn/ (nád/,lûug/) N 1. bullet, shot, pellet, projectile. 2. cartridge.

กระสูบ in ปลากระสูบ (ตัว) plaakrasùub/ (tua/) N a kind of fresh-water fish (Hampala macrolepidota).

กระแส (กระแส) krasɛ̌ɛ/ (krasɛ̌ɛ/) N 1. current, flow, circulation. 2. course, way. →Sometimes spelled กระแส่.

  o ข่าวกระแสต่าง ๆ khàaw/-krasɛ̌ɛ/tàaŋtàaŋ/ news from various sources or channels.

กระแสเงิน krasɛ̌ɛ/ŋən/ N 1. monetary currency. 2. circulation of money, flow of money.

กระแสน้ำ krasɛ̌ɛ/náam/ N 1. a current of water. 2. the course of a stream.

กระแสพระราชดำรัส krasɛ̌ɛ/phrárâadchadamràd/ N roy. speech (made by the king).

กระแสไฟฟ้า krasɛ̌ɛ/fajfáa/ N electric current.

กระแสโลหิต krasɛ̌ɛ/loohìd/ N circulation of the blood.

กระหนก,ลาย-- (ลาย) kranòg/, laajkranòg/ (laaj/) N generic term for a kind of decorative pattern characteristic of Thai art. →Also spelled กนก and pronounced kanòg/.

กระหนาบ kranàab/ V 1. to flank. 2. colloq. to bawl out. →Also ขนาบ.
  ตีกระหนาบ tiikranàab/ V to attack from both sides.

กระหน่ำ kranàm/ V 1. to hit, strike, shoot repeatedly. sV 2. repeatedly.
  ตีกระหน่ำ tii/kranàm/ V to beat, attack repeatedly.

กระหม่อม (กระหม่อม) kramɔ̀m/*(kramɔ̀m/) N 1. the top of the head. P 2. eleg. def. m. sp. I, me. Used in addressing high-ranking royalty and the Supreme Patriarch. Pt 3. eleg. def. m. sp. particle used at the end of statements addressed to high-ranking royalty and to the Supreme Patriarch. →Cf. 2. หม่อมฉัน w. sp. 3. เพคะ w. sp. →Cf. ผม.

กระหมิบ kramìb/ V to constrict. →Usually ขมิบ. Also see following entry.

กระหมุบกระหมิบ kramùb/kramìb/ V to move the lips,

work the mouth silently.

กระหย่ง krajòŋ′ V to stand on tiptoe. →Also
กระโหย่ง, โขย่ง.
เดินกระหย่งเท้า dəən′-krajòŋ′tháaw′ to tiptoe,
walk on tiptoe.

กระหยิ่ม krajìm′ V to be happy, satisfied, proud.

กระหาย krahǎaj′ V 1. to be thirsty. 2. to desire,
to wish for. ความ-- thirst; strong desire.
กระหายน้ำ krahǎaj′náam′ V to be thirsty.

กระหึม, กระหึ่ม krahǔm′, krah ่ym′ V 1. to roar, be
roaring. N 2. roar.

กระหืดกระหอบ krah ่yd′krahɔ̀ɔb′ V to be out of
breath, to pant.

กระเหม็ดกระแหม่ kramèd′kramɛ̀ɛ′ V to be thrifty,
frugal, economizing. ความ-- thriftiness.

กระโห้ in ปลากระโห้ (ตัว) plaakrahôo′ (tua′)
N a kind of fresh-water fish (Catlocarpio siamensis).

กระโหย่ง krajòoŋ′ V to stand on tiptoe.

กระออมกระแอม kra?ɔ̌m′kra?ɛ̌m′ V to hem and
haw.

กระอัก kra?àg′ V to cough up (e.g. blood).
กระอักกระอ่วน kra?àg′kra?ùan′ V to hesitate,
waver, feel ill at ease.

กระแอม kra?ɛm′ V imit. to utter "ahem!" (to
attract attention or to clear the throat).

กรัง kraŋ′ V to be stuck together (by adhesion, in
a dried mass).
เสบียงกรัง sabiaŋ′kraŋ′ N dried food supply.

กรัม kram′ C gram. Abbreviated ก. [f. Eur.]

กราก ๑ kràag′ rM intensifier used with แห้ง
"dry."

กราก ๒ kràag′ V to walk hastily, scurry, dash,
rush (up to).

กราด ๑ in กราดเกรี้ยว kràadkrîaw′ V 1. to be
furious. 2. to scold angrily. 3. to treat unsparingly. →Also เกรี้ยวกราด.

กราด ๒ kràad′ V 1. to scatter. 2. to be scattered.
sV 3. all around, at random.
มองกราด mɔɔŋ′kràad′ V to look around.

กราน kraan′ V to prostrate oneself (in doing obeisance). →Chiefly in compounds.
o ก้มกราน kômkraan′ V to prostrate oneself.
ยืนกราน jyyn′kraan′ V 1. to stand firm, remain

unyielding. 2. to insist.

กร้าน krâan′ V to be hard, rough, coarse, weathered.

กราบ ๑ kràab′ V to prostrate oneself (in obeisance).
The palms are pressed together and the hands
rest on the floor; the forehead rests against the
hands.
กราบทูล kràabthuun′ V to address highranking
royalty.
กราบเท้า kràabtháaw′ V 1. to prostrate oneself
at someone's feet (as a sign of very high respect).
2. a term used in the salutation of a letter to
show respect (followed by the title of the addressee); more commonly กราบเรียน (see
below).
o กราบเท้าคุณพ่อที่เคารพอย่างสูง kràabtháaw′ɔ
khunphɔ̂ɔ′-thîikhawrób′jàaŋsǔuŋ′ (I) salute
(my) most highly respected father.
กราบบังคมทูล kràab′-baŋkhom′thuun′ V roy.
to address the king or queen.
กราบเรียน kràabrian′ V 1. elab. eleg. to inform,
tell (sp. to sup.). 2. a term of respect used in
the salutation of a letter (followed by the name
of the addressee). Currently preferred to กราบ
เท้า in mng. 2.
กราบลา kràablaa′ V to take leave of (one's elders
or superiors). This is usually done by prostrating oneself.

กราบ ๒, --เรือ (กราบ,ข้าง) kràab′, kràabrya′
(kràab′, khâaŋ′) N gunwale.

กราม (ซี่) kraam′ (sîi′) N molar.
ขบกราม khòbkraam′ to grit one's teeth (as when
angry).

กราย kraaj′ V 1. to pass closely, come close to.
2. to move slowly, leisurely, ostentatiously.
กรีดกราย krìidkraaj′ V 1. to swing the arms
slowly attempting to look gracious, elegant while
walking; to put on airs. 2. to shun work, avoid
effort in work. sV 3. ostentatiously.
เยื้องกราย jýaŋkraaj′ V to walk slowly and grace-
fully, walk with an air (mostly of women).

กร้าว krâaw′ V to be tough, harsh.
เสียงกร้าว sǐaŋkrâaw′ N a tough, harsh voice.

กร้ำ kram′ V to tolerate, suffer, experience.

กริ่ง ๑ (อัน) kriŋ′ (?an′) N 1. bell, buzzer.

If item is not found under กระ-, see กะ-, ข-.

2. ring, buzz.

กริ๋ง ๒. See entries below.

  กริ๋งเกรง kriŋkreeŋ/ V to suspect, fear (that).

  กริ๋งใจ kriŋcaj/ V to suspect, to have a hunch, have misgivings.

กริช (อัน) krìd/ (?an/) N Malay dagger, kris. [f. Malay]

กริบ krìb/ rM intensifier used with คม "sharp," เงียบ "quiet."

กริ่ม in ยิ้มกริ่ม jímkrìm/ to be smiling happily, beaming.

กริยา (คำ) kàrijaa/, krìjaa/ (kham/) N 1. verb. 2. behavior, manners. คำ-- verb. NOTE. In mng. 2 more commonly กิริยา.

  กริยาวิเศษณ์ (คำ) kàrijaa/wísèed/ (kham/) N adverb. คำ-- idem.

กริ้ว krîw/ V roy. to be angry, angered. →Syn. โกรธ com.

กรีฑา kriithaa/ N sports events, athletic events. →Comp. กีฬา.

  กรีฑาสถาน (แห่ง) kriithaa/sathǎan/ (hɛ̀ŋ/) N sports arena, stadium.

กรีด ๑ krìid/ V to cut, slash, scratch.

  กรีดกราย krìidkraaj/ V 1. to swing the arms slowly attempting to look gracious, elegant while walking; to put on airs. 2. to shun work, avoid effort in work. sV 3. ostentatiously.

กรีด ๒, กรี๊ด krìid/, kríid/ V to scream, shriek.

กรีธา kriithaa/ V 1. to mobilize. 2. to maneuver, move (an army).

กรุ krù?/ V to line (a container)(with paper, straw, etc.).

กรุง (กรุง) kruŋ/ (kruŋ/) N metropolis, city.

  กรุงเก่า kruŋkàw/ pN common name of อยุธยา Ayuthaya (the old capital).

  กรุงเทพ ฯ kruŋthêeb/ pN Krungthep, the common name of Bangkok. →Short for the official name, a portion of which is given below. →Also พระนคร.

  o กรุงเทพพระมหานคร บวรรัตนโกสินทร์ มหิน-
ทรายุธยา มหาดิลกภพนพรัตน์ ราชธานีบุรีรมย์
อุดมสันติสุข kruŋthêeb/-phrámahǎa/nákhɔɔn/
bɔwɔɔn/-rádtanákoo/sǐn/ mahǐn/tharaa/-júd⊃
thajaa/ mahǎa/dilòg/-phíphób/nób/pharád/

råad/chathaa/nii/-burii/rom/ ?ùdom/sǎntisùg/ pN (the principal portion of) the official name of Bangkok.

  กรุงรัตนโกสินทร์ kruŋ/rádtanákoo/sǐn/ pN Ratanakosin, a formal name for Bangkok.

  กรุงลอนดอน kruŋ/lɔɔndɔɔn/ pN London.

  ชาวกรุง (คน) chaawkruŋ/ (khon/) N city people.

กรุณา karunaa/ V 1. to be kind, merciful. 2. be so kind as to, please (do such and such). ความ-- compassion, kindness, mercy, mercifulness.

  กรุณาปรานี karunaa/praanii/ V to be kind, merciful, kindhearted. →Also spelled -ปราณี.

  ทรงพระกรุณาโปรดเกล้าฯ soŋ/phrákarunaa/-prôod/klâaw/ roy. by royal decree.

  พระมหากรุณาธิคุณ phrámahǎa/karunaa/thikhun/ N roy. kindness and grace.

กรุ่น krùn/ V 1. to be smoldering. 2. to be odorous.

กรู kruu/ V to run up together in crowds, to throng.

กฤษฎีกา in พระราชกฤษฎีกา (ฉบับ) phráråad/⊃ chakrìdsadiikaa/ (chabàb/) N royal decree.

กล. Abbrev. for กิโลลิตร kiloliter.

กล (แบบ, อย่าง, อัน) kon/, konɔ, konlaɔ (bɛ̀ɛb/, jàaŋ/, ?an/) N trick. Often occurs as a bound form meaning "mechanical device; trick." เครื่อง-- machine. ช่าง-- (see below).

  กลไก konkaj/ N mechanism.

  กลจักร (เครื่อง) konlacàg/ (khrŷaŋ/) N engine.

  กลมารยา (อย่าง) kon/maanjaa/ (jàaŋ/) N trick, artifice, deception.

  กลเม็ด (อย่าง) konlaméd/ (jàaŋ/) N trick.

  กลยุทธ (แบบ, อย่าง) konlajúd/ (bɛ̀ɛb/, jàaŋ/) N 1. eleg. tactics, strategy; stratagem. 2. colloq. trick.

  กลศาสตร์ konlasàad/ N mechanics (the science).

  ชอบกล chɔ̂ɔbkon/ V to be out of the ordinary, funny, strange, peculiar.

  ช่างกล (คน) châaŋkon/ (khon/) N mechanic. การ-- mechanics.

  ปืนกล pyynkon/ N machine gun.

  เรือกลไฟ ryakonfaj/ N steamship, steamer.

  แรงกล rɛɛŋkon/ N mechanical power.

  วิทยากล wídthajaakon/ N magic.

  เสียกล sǐa/kon/ V to be tricked, outsmarted.

  แสดงกล sadɛɛŋkon/ V eleg. to do tricks,

perform stunts. →Syn. เล่นกล com.

กลบ klòb′ V 1. to cover with earth, fill up with earth, bury. 2. to shut, to hide.

  กลบเกลื่อน klòbklỳan′ V to cover up (a blunder).

  เอาทรายกลบตัว ?awsaaj′-klòb′tua′ V to bury oneself in sand.

กลม klom′ V to be round (as a circle, sphere, cylinder, etc.).

  กลมกล่อม klomklɔ̀m′ V to be well-blended, smooth, pleasing (of flavors).

  กลมกลืน klomklyyn′ V 1. to mix well, blend well. 2. to be well-mixed, well-blended.

  กลมเกลียว klomkliaw′ V to be harmonious, united; to get along well (together).

  กอดกันกลม kɔ̀ɔd′kanklom′ V to embrace each other tightly, to hug (each other).

  วงกลม (วง) woŋklom′ (woŋ′) N circle.

กลวง kluaŋ′ V to be hollow.

กล้วย ๑ (ลูก,ใบ,ผล,หวี,เครือ) klûaj′ N banana (lûug′, baj′, phǒn′ for the fruit; wǐi′ for a hand; khrya′ for a bunch). ต้น-- (ต้น) the banana tree.

  กล้วยแขก (ชิ้น) klûajkhɛ̀ɛg′ (chín′) N banana slices, dipped in batter and fried.

  กล้วยเชื่อม (ชิ้น,ลูก,ใบ,ผล) klûajchŷam′ (chín′, lûug′, baj′, phǒn′) N glazed banana, a kind of dessert.

  กล้วยตาก (ลูก,ใบ) klûajtàag′ (lûug′, baj′) N dehydrated banana (dried in the sun).

  กล้วยปิ้ง (ลูก,ใบ) klûajpîŋ′ (lûug′, baj′) N roasted banana.

  กล้วยหอม (ลูก,ใบ,ผล) klûajhɔ̌ɔm′ (lûug′, baj′, phǒn′) N banana (fragrant variety).

  เครือกล้วย (เครือ) khryaklûaj′ (khrya′) a bunch of bananas.

  ดงกล้วย doŋklûaj′ N banana plantation.

  หวีกล้วย (หวี) wǐiklûaj′ (wǐi′) N a hand of bananas.

กล้วย ๒ in กล้วยไม้ (ดอก) klûajmáaj′ (dɔ̀ɔg′) N orchid. ต้น-- (ต้น) the orchid (plant).

  o ดอกกล้วยไม้ (ดอก) dɔ̀ɔgklûajmáaj′ (dɔ̀ɔg′) N orchid (the flower).

กลอก klɔ̂ɔg′ V to turn, roll (e.g. one's eyes).

  กลับกลอก klàbklɔ̂ɔg′ V 1. to go back on one's

word, renege. 2. to be undependable, unreliable.

กลอง (ใบ,ลูก) klɔɔŋ′ (baj′, lûug′) N drum..

กล่อง (ใบ) klɔ̀ŋ′*(baj′) N 1. small box, case (e.g. case for eyeglasses). C 2. clf. for specific kinds of such containers. 3. clf. for things in such containers; hence, box of (paper clips, straight pins, etc.).

กล้อง (กล้อง,อัน) klɔ̂ŋ′*(klɔ̂ŋ′, ?an′) N 1. pipe. 2. camera, binoculars. C 2. clf. for tube-like objects.

  กล้องจุลทรรศน์ (กล้อง) klɔ̂ŋ′cunlathád′ (klɔ̂ŋ′) N microscope.

  กล้องถ่ายรูป (กล้อง,อัน) klɔ̂ŋ′thàajrûub′ (klɔ̂ŋ′, ?an′) N camera.

  กล้องโทรทัศน์ (กล้อง) klɔ̂ŋ′thoorathád′ (klɔ̂ŋ′) N telescope.

  กล้องยาสูบ (อัน) klɔ̂ŋ′jaasùub′ (?an′) N tobacco pipe.

  กล้องส่องทางไกล (กล้อง,อัน) klɔ̂ŋ′sɔ̀ŋthaaŋklaj′ (klɔ̂ŋ′, ?an′) N 1. binoculars. 2. spyglass.

  ลำกล้อง (อัน) lamklɔ̂ŋ′ (?an′) N 1. gun barrel. 2. hollow tube such as a pipe stem.

  สูบกล้อง sùubklɔ̂ŋ′ V to smoke a pipe, puff on a pipe, draw on a pipe.

กลอน ๑ (อัน,กลอน) klɔɔn′ (?an′, klɔɔn′) N bolt, latch.

  ถอดกลอน thɔ̀ɔdklɔɔn′ V to unbolt, unlatch (a door, window).

  ลงกลอน loŋklɔɔn′ V to bolt, latch (a door, window). →Also ลั่นกลอน,ใส่กลอน.

กลอน ๒ (บท) klɔɔn′ (bòd′) N a kind of Thai verse form.

  บทกลอน (บท) bòdklɔɔn′ (bòd′) N a verse or poem in the verse form of the กลอน.

กลอน ๓ in ลูกกลอน (ลูก) lûugklɔɔn′ (lûug′) N bolus, a wet lump or tablet of freshly prepared medicine.

กล่อม klɔ̀m′* V to sing lullabies to, lull to sleep.

  กลมกล่อม klomklɔ̀m′ V to be well-blended, smooth, pleasing (of flavors, odors).

  กล่อมใจ klɔ̀mcaj′ V to lull, soothe, calm (the heart, the feelings).

  กล่อมหอ klɔ̀mhɔ̌ɔ′ V to serenade the bride and groom on their wedding night.

เกลี้ยกล่อม klîaklɔ̂m/ V to persuade, talk someone into doing something.

ขับกล่อม khàbklɔ̂m/ V to sing lullabies, to lull
to sleep.

เพลงกล่อมลูก (เพลง) phleeŋ/klɔ̂mlûug/ (phleeŋ/)
N cradlesong.

กล่อมแกล่ม klɔ̂mklɛ̂m/* V 1. to mumble, speak indistinctly. sV 2. incompletely (of chewing). 3.
indistinctly (of speaking).

กลัก (กล๊ก) klàg/ (klàg/) N 1. small case, tele-
scoping box (like a match box). C 2. clf. for
things in such containers; hence, box of
(matches, gummed labels, etc.).

กลัด klàd/ V 1. to button. 2. to pin (together).

กลัดกระดุม klàd/kradum/ V to button.

กลัดกลุ้ม,--ใจ klàdklûm/, klàdklûmcaj/ V to
feel depressed.

เข็มกลัด (อัน) khěmklàd/ (ʔan/) N 1. safety pin.
2. pin, brooch.

กลั่น klàn/ V to distill, extract.

กลั่นตัว klàntua/ V to condense.

กลั่นน้ำมัน klàn/námman/ to refine crude oil.

การ-- oil-refining.

ต้มกลั่น tômklàn/ V to distill.

น้ำกลั่น námklàn/ N distilled water.

กลั้น klân/ V 1. to restrain, suppress, hold back,
inhibit (regular bodily functions, expressions
of emotion). 2. to refrain from (performing
a bodily function, expressing emotion).

กลั้นใจ klâncaj/ to hold one's breath.

กลั้นสะอื้นไว้ klânsaʔŷn/wáj/ to hold back the
sobs.

กลับ klàb/ V 1. to turn back, go back, return. 2.
to turn to the opposite, turn over, turn upside
down, turn inside out. sV 3. in return. AA
4. still (contrariwise), contrary to expectation.

กลับกลอก klàbklɔ̀ɔg/ V 1. to go back on one's
word, renege. 2. to be undependable, unreliable. ความ-- unreliability, fickleness.

กลับกลายเป็น klàbklaaj/penɔ to turn into, become
(contrary to expectation).

กลับกับ klàb/kaɔ to be the reverse of, the opposite of.

กลับไข่ klàbkhàj/ 1. (a hen) to turn her eggs.

2. to turn eggs over (in the pan).

กลับคำ klàbkham/ V to go back on one's word.

กลับคืน klàbkhyyn/ V 1. to return, go back. 2.
to restore. 3. to get back, recover. sV 4. back.

กลับใจ klàbcaj/ V 1. to change one's mind, to
turn over a new leaf, have a change of heart.
2. to be converted (to a religion).

กลับตัว klàbtua/ V to reform oneself, turn over
a new leaf. →Also กลับเนื้อกลับตัว.

กลับตาลปัตร klàb/taalapàd/ idiom. 1. to make
a reversal, a switch. 2. to change one's mind.
3. to go back on one's word.

กลับเนื้อกลับตัว klàbnýa/klàbtua/ V elab. colloq.
to charge one's conduct, to reform oneself.

กลับเป็น klàb/penɔ 1. to turn out to be (contrary
to expectation). 2. to return to (a former state),
become (such and such) again.

กลับไป klàbpaj/ V to go back, return thither.

กลับไปกลับมา klàbpaj/klàbmaa/ V 1. to change
back and forth again and again. 2. to be unreliable.
sV 3. back and forth.

กลับมา klàbmaa/ V to come back, return hither.

ขากลับ khǎaklàb/ the return trip, (on) the way back.

มุมกลับ mumklàb/ N 1. reflex angle. 2. antithesis.

o คิดในมุมกลับ khíd/najmumklàb/ idiom. 1. to
take or consider an antithetic point of view.
2. conversely.

ลากลับ laaklàb/ V to take one's leave, say good-by
(when departing to return home, return to work,
etc.).

หักกลับ hàgklàb/ V to turn, bend back; to bend
the other way.

หันกลับ hǎnklàb/ to turn back, turn around.

กลัว klua/ V to fear, be afraid of. ความ-- fear.

น่ากลัว nâaklua/, nâa/klua/ V to be frightening,
scary, dreadful, fearful, horrible, terrifying,
terrible.

น่ากลัวน่ากลัว nâa!klúa/nâaklua/ V colloq. to
be very scary, extremely frightening, dreadful.

หวาดกลัว wàad/klua/ V to be scared, frightened.

กลั้ว klûa/ V 1. to gargle. 2. to mix, blend.

กลั้วคอ klûakhɔɔ/ V to gargle (the throat).

กล้า ๑ (ต้น) klâa/ (tôn/) N young rice plant (for
transplanting).

ตกกล้า tògklâa′ V to sow germinated rice grain. →Syn. ทอดกล้า.

กล้า ๒ klâa′ V 1. to dare, venture; to be brave enough to, bold enough to. 2. to be strong, powerful.

กล้าแข็ง klâakhěŋ′ V to be brave, strong.

กล้าหาญ klâahǎan′ V to be brave, bold, courageous. ความ-- bravery.

แข็งกล้า khěŋklâa′ V 1. to be hard (of metal, esp. steel). 2. to be brave.

ใจกล้า cajklâa′ V to be bold, brave, venturesome.

แดดกล้า dὲεdklâa′ the sunlight is strong.

ปากกล้า pàagklâa′ V 1. to use bold words, strong words. 2. to be fresh (in talking).

พัดกล้า phád′klâa′ V to blow strong.

เหล็กกล้า lὲgklâa′ N steel.

กลาก in ขี้กลาก khîiklâag′ N ringworm (skin disease) (tinea).

กลาง klaaŋ′ N 1. center, middle. When preceding another noun this is usually translated "at, in, in the middle of." 2. (as n.mod.) central, middle, center. คน-- (see below).

กลางคน as in วัยกลางคน waj′klaaŋkhon′ 1. middle age (of people). Among the Thai approx. 35-50 years of age. 2. (as n.mod.) middle-aged. →Also อายุกลางคน →Comp. ชรา.

กลางคัน klaaŋkhan′ in the middle, before it was finished (of an interrupted action, event).

กลางคืน klaaŋkhyyn′ at night, in the night.

o เวลากลางคืน weelaa′klaaŋkhyyn′ at night, in the nighttime. ใน-- idem.

กลางแจ้ง klaaŋcὲεŋ′ outdoors, in the open, in the open air.

กลางดึก klaaŋdỳg′ late at night, in the deep of the night.

กลางถนน klaaŋthanǒn′ in the street, in the middle of the street. ที่-- idem.

กลางบ้าน klaaŋbâan′ idiom. local, pertaining to old-fashioned village folklore.

กลางปี klaaŋpii′ mid-year, in the middle part of the year.

กลางฟ้า klaaŋfáa′ in the sky, in the middle of the sky.

กลางเมือง klaaŋmyaŋ′ 1. in public, in the open. 2. public, civil, internal (within the country).

o สงครามกลางเมือง (ครั้ง) sǒŋkhraam′klaaŋɔ myaŋ′ (khráŋ′) civil war.

กลางวัน klaaŋwan′ in the daytime, by day.

o กลางวันแสก ๆ klaaŋwan′sὲεgsὲεg′ in broad daylight.

กลางหาว klaaŋhǎaw′ under the skies, in the open air.

กึ่งกลาง kỳŋklaaŋ′ N 1. center, middle. 2. central, middle, center (as n.mod.).

คนกลาง (คน) khonklaaŋ′ (khon′) N 1. the middle one (in a group). 2. middleman; mediator, arbitrator. 3. one who is neutral.

ครึ่ง ๆ กลาง ๆ khrŷŋkhrŷŋ′klaaŋklaaŋ′ partially, halfway, half-done.

ใจกลาง cajklaaŋ′ N core, central part.

ตรงกลาง troŋklaaŋ′ in the middle, at the center.

ปานกลาง paanklaaŋ′ 1. moderately, in a moderate degree. 2. moderate; average.

เป็นกลาง penklaaŋ′ 1. to be neutral (in a controversy). 2. elect. to be neutral, not charged. ความ-- neutrality.

ภาคกลาง phâagklaaŋ′ N 1. the central part (of a country, a geographical area). 2. central.

ศูนย์กลาง (แห่ง) sǔunklaaŋ′ (hὲŋ′) N center (as in "industrial center").

ส่วนกลาง (ส่วน) sùanklaaŋ′ (sùan′) N 1. the central part. 2. central.

อักษรกลาง (ตัว) ʔàgsɔ̌ɔnklaaŋ′ (tua′) N a MIDDLE consonant.

กลาด in เกลื่อนกลาด klỳanklàad′ V to be scattered all over, dispersed.

กล้าม,--เนื้อ (มัด,ชิ้น) klâam′, klâamnýa′ (mád′, chín′) N muscle.

กลาย klaaj′ V 1. to change, transform, convert. 2. to be changed, transformed, converted.

กลายเป็น klaajpenɔ 1. to change, turn into. 2. to be changed, converted into. 3. to become. 4. to turn out to be.

o กลายเป็นไอ klaajpenʔaj′ to become steam, vaporize, evaporate.

ปีกลาย piiklaaj′ last year (i.e. during the preceding year). →Also เมื่อ--.

กล่าว klàaw/ V com. 1. to say, declare, mention. 2. to be mentioned. คำ-- a saying. →Syn. 1. ปรารภ eleg.

กล่าวขวัญ(ถึง) klàawkhwǎn/(thy̌ŋɔ) to speak (of), talk (about), mention.

กล่าวคือ klàawkhyy/ that is; namely.

กล่าวโดยย่อ klàaw/doojjɔ̀ɔ/ briefly speaking.

กล่าวถึง klàawthy̌ŋɔ to talk about.

กล่าวเท็จ klàawthéd/ V eleg. to lie, tell lies, speak falsely. →Syn. See โกหก com.

กล่าวโทษ klàawthôod/ V to blame, accuse, charge (with).

กล่าวว่า klàawwâa/ V to say, declare that.

กล่าวหา klàawhǎa/ V to accuse, charge, allege. คำ-- accusation, charge.

ดังกล่าว daŋklàaw/ as mentioned, as stated; (the) aforementioned.

ที่กล่าวนี้ thîiklàaw/nîi/ which are spoken of here.

บอกกล่าว bɔ̀ɔgklàaw/ V to apprise, inform, mention, notify, send a notice.

ยกมากล่าว jóg/maaklàaw/ V to quote, cite, mention.

ว่ากล่าว wâa/klàaw/ V to advise, admonish, reprove.

กลาโหม in กระทรวงกลาโหม krasuaŋ/kalaahǒom/ Ministry of Defense.

กลิ้ง klîŋ/ V to roll (of itself).

ลูกกลิ้ง (ลูก,อัน) lûugklîŋ/ (lûug/,ʔan/) N roller (for compacting, pulverizing, printing, etc.).

กลิ่น (กลิ่น) klìn/ (klìn/) N odor, scent, smell.

กลิ่นฉุย klìnchǔj/ V to be odorous (penetrating and sudden, as the odor of strong fumes).

กลิ่นตัว klìntua/ N body odor.

ดับกลิ่น dàb/klìn/ lit. V to deodorize.

ได้กลิ่น dâjklìn/ V to scent, smell, catch the scent (of).

หมดกลิ่น mòdklìn/ V to become odorless, lose (its) odor.

กลีบ (กลีบ) klìib/ (klìib/) N 1. petal. 2. leaflike object. C 3. section (e.g. of an orange, mangosteen).

กลึง klyŋ/ V to lathe.

กลืน klyyn/ V 1. to swallow. 2. to match in color. 3. idiom. to endure.

กลมกลืน klomklyyn/ V 1. to mix, blend well.

2. to be well-mixed, blended.

กลืนแสง klyyns̀ɛɛŋ/ V to absorb light.

ดูดกลืน dùud/klyyn/ V to absorb.

กลุ่ม klùm/ C 1. cluster, aggregation; group; bloc. 2. ball (of thread).

กลุ่มดาว klùmdaaw/ N constellation (of stars).

กลุ่มประเทศ klùmprathêed/ N 1. group of nations. 2. bloc, coalition.

จับกลุ่ม càbklùm/ V to gather, assemble, crowd around, form a group.

ด้ายกลุ่ม (กลุ่ม) dâajklùm/ (klùm/) N thread commercially wound into a ball.

ประเทศกลุ่มคอมมิวนิสต์ prathêed/klùmkhɔɔmmiwɔ níd/ the communist bloc of nations.

เป็นกลุ่มเป็นก้อน penklùm/penkɔ̂ɔn/ all in one piece, in one lump, all nicely together.

o รวมเงินเป็นกลุ่มเป็นก้อน ruamŋ̀ən/-penklùm/ɔ penkɔ̂ɔn/ to gather the money (from different sources) into one lump sum.

รวมกลุ่ม ruamklùm/ V to form a group, gather into a group, assemble.

กลุ้ม klûm/ V 1. to be darkened, gloomy. 2. to worry, be worried.

กลัดกลุ้ม,--ใจ klàdklûm/, klàdklûmcaj/ V to feel depressed.

กลุ้มอกกลุ้มใจ klûmʔòg/klûmcaj/ V elab. colloq. to worry, be downcast, depressed. →Also กลุ้มใจ colloq.

แก้กลุ้ม kɛ̂ɛklûm/ V to ease one's mind, overcome or relieve one's anxiety.

กวด kùad/ V to chase, pursue, attempt to overtake.

กวดขัน kùadkhǎn/ V 1. to be strict. 2. to be strict (with).

กวดตาม kùadtaam/, kùad/taamɔ V colloq. to run after.

กวดวิชา kùadwíchaa/ V 1. to be tutored, coached, taught (in order to make up a deficiency in one's studies). 2. to tutor, coach, teach (in order to help someone make up a deficiency). In mng.2 usually followed by ให้.

กวน kuan/ V 1. to stir, stir up. 2. to trouble, bother, disturb.

กวนใจ kuancaj/ V to disturb, bother, agitate.

o น่ากวนใจ nâa/kuancaj/ V to be annoying,

irritating.

กวนประสาท kuan'prasàad' V to get on one's nerves; to drive one crazy.

ก่อกวน kɔ̀ɔ'kuan' V 1. to agitate, stir up. 2. to bother, annoy.

รบกวน róbkuan' V to bother, trouble, annoy, vex.

ก๋วยเตี๋ยว, ก๊วยเตี๋ยว kúajtĭaw', kŭajtĭaw' N Chinese noodles.

กวัก, --มือ kwàg', kwàgmyy' V to beckon (to), summon (a person) by waving one's hand (palm downward).

o เขากวักมือให้ฉันมา kháwkwàg'myy'-hâjchán⊃ maa' He motioned to me to come over.

กวักมือเรียก kwàgmyy'rîag' V to summon, call (someone) over (by beckoning with one's hand).

กวัด kwàd' V to swing, sway. Chiefly in compounds.

กวัดแกว่ง kwàdkwὲŋ' V 1. to swing, brandish. 2. to oscillate, swing.

กวัดไกว kwàdkwaj' V to swing, sway.

กวัดหาง kwàdhăaŋ' V to wag the tail.

กวา in แตงกวา (ใบ, ลูก, ผล) tɛɛŋkwaa' (baj', lûug', phŏn') N cucumber.

กว่า kwàa', kwàa⊃ sV 1. more (to a greater degree), -er (often followed by กัน); more than, -er than. N 2. colloq. (and a) remainder. In this sense, กว่า usually follows a clf, and may be translated "over, more than; after (a specified time)"; 4th example. Cj 3. by the time that, before. In this sense often followed by จะ; 5th example. →Syn. 2. เศษ eleg.

o ดีกว่า diikwàa', dii'kwàa⊃ to be better, better than.

o ดีกว่า...นิดหน่อย dii'kwàa⊃...nídnɔ̀ɔj' a little bit better than.

o ดีกว่าเป็นกอง dii'kwàapenkɔɔŋ' to be much better.

o ๕ ไมล์กว่า hâamajkwàa' over five miles (but less than six).

o กว่าจะตกถึงมือผู้รับ kwàacatòg'-thŷŋmyy'phûu⊃ ráb' by the time (or before) it gets to the recipient.

กว่าๆ kwàakwàa' colloq. (and a) small fraction; hence, somewhat more than, slightly more than, just a little more than, just over, just after.

→Syn. เศษๆ.

o ๕ ไมล์กว่าๆ hâamajkwàakwàa' just over five miles.

กว่าเพื่อน kwàaphŷan' colloq. the most (thus and so), the ...-est (of those being compared). →Comp. ที่สุด.

o สวยกว่าเพื่อน sŭajkwàaphŷan' to be the most beautiful one of all, more beautiful than any of the others.

เกินกว่า kəən'kwàa⊃ beyond, far more than; far too; far too much.

จนกว่า(...)จะ conkwàa'(...)ca⊃ right up until, until the time that.

มากกว่า (1) mâag'kwàa'; (2) mâag'kwàa⊃ 1. more, -er. 2. more than, -er than.

ยิ่งกว่านั้น jîŋ'kwàanán' moreover.

เหลือบ่ากว่าแรง lŷabàa'kwàarɛɛŋ' elab. colloq. to be more than one can do, take on, shoulder.

กวาง (ตัว) kwaaŋ' (tua') N deer.

เขากวาง (เขา, ข้าง) khăwkwaaŋ' (khăw', khâaŋ') N antlers.

กว้าง kwâaŋ' V to be broad, wide. ความ-- breadth, width. →Ant. แคบ.

กว้างขวาง kwâaŋkhwăaŋ' V 1. to be roomy, spacious, vast, extensive. 2. to be well-known, popular (of persons). อย่าง-- extensively.

กว้างใหญ่ kwâaŋjàj' V to be large, wide, extensive.

ใจกว้าง cajkwâaŋ' V to be generous, magnanimous.

กวางตุ้ง kwaaŋtûŋ' pN Canton.

กวาด kwàad' V to sweep.

กวาดต้อน kwàadtɔ̂ɔn' V to herd.

กวาดบ้าน kwàadbâan' to sweep the house.

กวาดล้าง kwàadláaŋ' V 1. to clean out, wipe out. 2. fig. to purge, eliminate, kill off.

กวาดสายตา kwàad'săajtaa' to sweep (with one's gaze).

ปัดกวาดบ้าน pàdkwàad'bâan' V to clean house, i.e. to dust and sweep.

ไม้กวาด (ด้าม, อัน) májkwàad' (dâam', ?an') N broom.

ลูกกวาด (ก้อน, เม็ด) lûugkwàad' (kɔ̂ɔn', méd') N candy, esp. bonbons, hard candies.

กว้าน kwâan' V to haul in; to take great quantities of.

กว้านซื้อ kwâansýy' V to corner the market (by

buying up in large quantities).

กวี (คน) kawii′ (khon′) N poet. นัก-- poet.

  กวีนิพนธ์ (เรื่อง) kawii′níphon′ (rŷaŋ′) N poetry.

  จินตกวี (คน) cintakawii′ (khon′) N poet.

  บทกวี bòdkawii′ N poetry. This includes all
    kinds of verse forms, viz. โคลง,ฉันท์,กาพย์,
    กลอน.

กษัตริย์ (องค์,พระองค์) kasàd′ (ʔoŋ′, phrá′oŋ′) N
  king, monarch.

  พระมหากษัตริย์ (องค์,พระองค์) phrámahǎa′kaɔ
    sàd′ (ʔoŋ′, phrá′oŋ′) N king: "great king."

กสิกร (คน) kàsikɔɔn′ (khon′) N eleg. farmer,
  agriculturist. →Syn. ชาวนา com.

กสิกรรม kàsikam′ N agriculture. การ-- idem.

  ประเทศกสิกรรม prathêed′kàsikam′ N agricul-
    tural country.

กอ kɔɔ′ C clump (of growing plants, trees).

  กอไผ่ (กอ) kɔɔphàj′ (kɔɔ′) N a clump of bam-
    boo.

ก่อ kɔɔ′ V 1. to build, construct. 2. to start, create,
  originate. →Dist. ทำ.

  ก่อกรรมทำเข็ญ kɔɔkam′thamkhěn′ V elab.
    colloq. to cause trouble, do evil, commit
    crimes.

  ก่อกวน kɔɔkuan′ V 1. to agitate, stir up. 2. to
    bother, annoy.

  ก่อการ kɔɔkaan′ V to instigate (an affair, a
    disturbance). ผู้-- rebel, revolutionary.

  ก่อการปฏิวัติ kɔɔkaan′pàtiwád′ to instigate a revo-
    lution.

  ก่อการร้าย kɔɔkaan′ráaj′ to make trouble, cause
    violence.

  o พวกก่อการร้าย phûagkɔɔkaan′ráaj′ N trouble-
    makers, gangsters, saboteurs.

  ก่อกำเนิด kɔɔ′kamnə̀əd′ V to originate, initiate,
    give birth (to).

  ก่อกู้ kɔɔ′kûu′ V to restore, bring back, build up.

  ก่อ(...)ขึ้น kɔɔ(...)khŷn′ to start, initiate.

  ก่อไฟ kɔɔfaj′ V to start a fire, build a fire.

  ก่อเรื่อง kɔɔrŷaŋ′ V to start trouble, cause
    trouble.

  ก่อวินาศกรรม kɔɔ′wínâadsakam′ V to engage in
    sabotage, cause destruction. ผู้-- saboteur.

  ก่อสร้าง kɔɔsâaŋ′ V to build, construct. ช่าง--

builder.

  o สถานที่ก่อสร้าง sathǎanthîikɔɔsâaŋ′ N construc-
    tion site.

  ก่อหวอด kɔɔwɔɔd′ V to start, cause (trouble,
    mischief).

  ก่อให้เกิด kɔɔ′hâjkə̀əd′ V to cause, give rise to.

  ก่ออิฐ kɔɔʔìd′ to lay bricks.

ก้อ. See ละก้อ under ละ ๔.

ก๊อก ๑ (อัน) kɔ́g′*(ʔan′) N faucet, spigot, tap, cock.
  [f. Eng. cock]

  ก๊อกน้ำ (อัน) kɔ́gnáam′ (ʔan′) N water-tap, faucet.

  น้ำก๊อก námkɔ́g′ N tap water.

ก๊อก ๒ in ไม้ก๊อก májkɔ́g′* N 1. cork (the material).
  2. a cork (stopper). [f. Eng. cork]

กอง (กอง) kɔɔŋ′ (kɔɔŋ′) N 1. troop, force. 2.
  pile, heap. 3. division (i.e. a subdivision of a
  กรม ; see note under กระทรวง). C 4. idem.
  V 5. to pile up. 6. to be piled up, lie in a heap.

  กองโจร (กอง) kɔɔŋcoon′ (kɔɔŋ′) N 1. robber
    gang. 2. guerrilla band.

  กองตำรวจ (กอง) kɔɔŋtamrùad′ (kɔɔŋ′) N police
    force.

  กองทหาร (กอง) kɔɔŋthahǎan′ (kɔɔŋ′) N troops,
    forces, army.

  กองทัพ (กองทัพ) kɔɔŋtháb′ (kɔɔŋtháb′) N 1. the
    armed forces (of a country). 2. an army, force;
    troops, forces.

  o กองทัพบก kɔɔŋtháb′bòg′ N army, military land
    forces. →Abbrev. ทบ.

  o กองทัพเรือ kɔɔŋtháb′rya′ N navy, naval forces.
    →Abbrev. ทร.

  o กองทัพอากาศ kɔɔŋtháb′ʔaakàad′ N air force.
    →Abbrev. ทอ.

  กองบังคับการ (กอง,แห่ง) kɔɔŋ′-baŋkháb′kaan′
    (kɔɔŋ′, hὲŋ′) N milit. general headquarters.

  กองบัญชาการ (กอง,แห่ง) kɔɔŋ′banchaakaan′
    (kɔɔŋ′, hὲŋ′) N milit. headquarters.

  กองพล (กอง,กองพล) kɔɔŋphon′ (kɔɔŋ′, kɔɔŋphon′)
    N milit. division.

  o กองพลน้อย kɔɔŋphonnɔ́ɔj′ N brigade.

  o กองพลใหญ่ kɔɔŋphonjàj′ N division.

  กองพัน (กอง,กองพัน) kɔɔŋphan′ (kɔɔŋ′, kɔɔŋphan′)
    N battalion.

  กองไฟ (กอง) kɔɔŋfaj′ (kɔɔŋ′) N bonfire.

กองยานยนต์ (กอง) kɔɔŋjaanjon′ (kɔɔŋ′) N 1. department of vehicles. 2. milit. motorized unit.

กองรถรบ (กอง) kɔɔŋródrób′ (kɔɔŋ′) N armored unit.

กองร้อย (กอง, กองร้อย) kɔɔŋrɔ́ɔj′ (kɔɔŋ′, kɔɔŋ= rɔ́ɔj′) N milit. company.

กองเรือรบ (กอง) kɔɔŋryaròb′ (kɔɔŋ′) N fleet (of warships).

กอง(...)ไว้ kɔɔŋ′(...)wáj′ V to heap, pile (something) up.

กองสัญญาน (กอง) kɔɔŋsǎnjaan′ (kɔɔŋ′) N signal corps.

กองหนุน (กอง) kɔɔŋnǔn′ (kɔɔŋ′) N the military reserves.

ทอยกอง thɔɔjkɔɔŋ′ N a kind of gambling game in which players throw coins at a stack of cards or coins which serve as the stake.

เป็นกอง penkɔɔŋ′ colloq. much, a lot, a heap, heaps, abundantly.

o ดีกว่าเป็นกอง dii′kwàapenkɔɔŋ′ to be much better, a lot better.

o เขามีเงินตั้งเป็นกอง kháwmiiŋən′tâŋpenkɔɔŋ′↓ He has a heap of money.

เป็นกองส่องกอง penkɔɔŋ′sɔ̌ɔŋkɔɔŋ′ elab. colloq. a lot, a whole lot, heaps; a lot of, a whole lot of, heaps of.

o เงินเป็นกองส่องกอง ŋən′-penkɔɔŋ′sɔ̌ɔŋkɔɔŋ′ lots of money, heaps of money.

เป็นก่ายเป็นกอง penkàaj′penkɔɔŋ′ elab. colloq. a lot, a whole lot, heaps; a lot of, a whole lot of, heaps of.

มากมายก่ายกอง mâagmaaj′kàajkɔɔŋ′ elab. colloq. so much, so many, a whole lot, a great deal.

ก้อง kɔ̂ŋ′* V 1. to echo, to resound. 2. to be loud, noisy.

กึกก้อง kỳgkɔ̂ŋ′ idem.

เสียงก้อง sǐaŋkɔ̂ŋ′ N echo.

กอด kɔ̀ɔd′ V com. 1. to embrace, hug. 2. to caress. →Syn. ตระกอง eleg.

กอดจูบลูบคลำ kɔ̀ɔd′cùub′-lûub′khlam′ V colloq. to pet, to neck.

กอดรัด kɔ̀ɔd′rád′ V to embrace, hug.

กอดอก kɔ̀ɔd′ɔ̀g′ V to fold one's arms over the chest.

สวมกอด sǔamkɔ̀ɔd′ V to embrace.

ก่อน kɔ̀ɔn′ sV 1. previous. 2. first (before doing something else). Sometimes best translated "for a while"; 2nd example. Cj 3. before. Pp 4. before.

o เมื่ออาทิตย์ก่อน mŷaʔaathíd′kɔ̀ɔn′ last week.

o กินข้าวก่อนซิ kinkhâaw′kɔ̀ɔnsî′↓ Have some food first (i.e. before you do anything else).

o ขอยืมก่อนนะ khɔ̌ɔjyym′kɔ̀ɔnná′↓ May I borrow it a while (i.e. before you use it again)?

o แปรงฟันก่อนเข้านอน prɛɛŋfan′kɔ̀ɔnkhâwnɔɔn′↓ Brush your teeth before going to bed.

ก่อน ๆ kɔ̀ɔnkɔ̀ɔn′ past, previous (implying plurality in the noun). →See ปี--, วัน-- below.

ก่อนจะ kɔ̀ɔn′ca= before (doing such and such).

ก่อนที่จะ kɔ̀ɔn′thîica= before (doing such and such).

ก่อนเที่ยง kɔ̀ɔnthîaŋ′ A.M., before noon. →Abbrev. ก.ท.

ก่อนเพื่อน kɔ̀ɔnphŷan′ colloq. first, before other things, before anyone else.

ก่อนเวลา kɔ̀ɔnweelaa′ early, ahead of time.

ก่อนหน้า kɔ̀ɔnnâa′ before, previously, prior to.

ก่อนอื่น kɔ̀ɔnʔỳyn′ first of all, before anything else.

ครั้งก่อน khráŋkɔ̀ɔn′ last time, the time before; previously, formerly.

คราวก่อน khraawkɔ̀ɔn′ the time before, on the last occasion.

ชาติก่อน châadkɔ̀ɔn′ (one's) previous life, existence.

เดือนก่อน dyankɔ̀ɔn′ last month.

แต่ก่อน tɛ̀kɔ̀ɔn′, takɔ̀ɔn′* in the past, in former times, previously.

ประเดี๋ยวก่อน pradǐawkɔ̀ɔn′ (for) a moment; just a minute.

ปีก่อน piikɔ̀ɔn′ last year.

ปีก่อน ๆ pii′kɔ̀ɔnkɔ̀ɔn′ the past years.

ไปก่อน pajkɔ̀ɔn′ V 1. to walk ahead, go ahead. sV 2. for the time being, temporarily, ahead of time, in advance.

มาก่อน maakɔ̀ɔn′ before, in the past.

เมื่อก่อน mŷakɔ̀ɔn′ before, previously.

ลาก่อน laakɔ̀ɔn′ good-bye. Used only by one who is leaving, departing.

วันก่อน wankɔɔn/ the other day.

วันก่อน ๆ wan/kɔɔnkɔɔn/ the previous days.

สมัยก่อน samǎj/kɔɔn/ formerly, in the old days, in former times.

เสียก่อน sǐakɔɔn/ first, beforehand, in advance.

ก่อน kɔɔn/ C 1. lump. 2. clf. for lumpy objects, e.g. rocks, lumps of clay or sugar, cubes of sugar, chunks or hunks of coal or charcoal, bricks, broken bricks, cakes of soap, clouds, and figuratively, sums of money.

ก่อนกรวด kɔɔnkrùad/ N small stones, pebbles, gravel.

ก่อนดิน kɔɔndin/ N a clod of earth.

ก่อนเลือด kɔɔnlɯ̂ad/ N blood clot.

ก่อนหิน kɔɔnhǐn/ N a rock (of any size).

เป็นก่อน penkɔɔn/ 1. to be lumpy, to form lumps. 2. in lumps.

o เป็นกลุ่มเป็นก่อน penklùm/penkɔɔn/ elab. colloq. to be all in one piece, in one lump, all nicely together.

oo รวมเงินเป็นกลุ่มเป็นก่อน ruamŋɤn/-penklùm/ɔ penkɔɔn/ to gather the money (from different sources) into one lump sum.

กอบ ๑ kɔɔb/ V to scoop up (with the hands), take up handfuls.

กอบกู้ kɔɔb/kûu/ V to restore, redeem, save.

กอบโกย kɔɔbkooj/ V to gather in, scoop together (in large amounts).

เป็นกอบเป็นกำ penkɔɔb/penkam/ elab. colloq. 1. to be solid, substantial, productive, effective, with tangible results. 2. solidly, substantially, as a steady thing, as a staple. →Syn. เป็นล่ำเป็นสัน.

กอบ ๒. Variant spelling of กอปร.

ก๊อปปี้ in กระดาษก๊อปปี้ kradàad/kɔ́bpîi/* N carbon paper. [f. Eng. copy]

กอปร(ด้วย) kɔɔb/(dûajɔ) V to consist of, comprise. →Also spelled กอบ. →Syn. ประกอบ.

ก้อย ๑ (นิ้ว) kɔ̂j/*(níw/) N the little finger.

เกี่ยวก้อย(กัน) kìawkɔ̂j/(kan) V to hook each other's little fingers (of lovers, or of intimate friends of the same sex, esp. w.).

o เดินเกี่ยวก้อย dɤɤn/kìawkɔ̂j/ V to walk with little fingers hooked. Cf. Eng. "walk arm in

arm."

นิ้วก้อย (นิ้ว) níwkɔ̂j/ (níw/) N the little finger.

ก้อย ๒ kɔ̂j/* N tails (the reverse of a coin).

โยนหัวโยนก้อย joonhǔa/joonkɔ̂j/ V to flip a coin.

กะ ๑ (กะ) kà?/ (kà?/) N colloq. round, period, shift.

กะ ๒ kà?/ V to estimate, guess, calculate.

กะการ kà?/kaan/ V to work out a plan, to plan.

กะ ๓ kaɔ with. →Variant of กับ ๑.

o ยังกะ jaŋkaɔ like, as if.

o ระหว่าง...กะ... rawàaŋɔ...kaɔ... between (such and such a place or time) and (another place or time).

กะ ๔ kaɔ to, for. →Variant of แก่ ๓.

o มีกะใจ miikacaj/ colloq. 1. to have the will, the spirit (to do something). 2. to be thoughtful, considerate of others; to be kind enough to, considerate enough to.

กะ- kaɔ. Frequent initial syllable, often interchangeable with กระ- kraɔ, sometimes with ข- khaɔ. Look under these latter spellings for items not found below.

กะแช่ kachɛ̂ɛ/ N liquor made from the sap of a palm.

กะทะ (ใบ) kathá?/ (baj/) N frying pan, skillet.

กะทิ kathí?/ N coconut cream (the liquid squeezed from the grated meat of a ripe coconut; used as a cooking ingredient).

น้ำกะทิ námkathí?/ N coconut cream.

หัวกะทิ hǔakathí?/ N 1. concentrated coconut cream, obtained when the coconut meat is pressed the first time. 2. figur. the cream, i.e. the best part (of anything).

หางกะทิ hǎaŋkathí?/ N dilute coconut cream, obtained after the coconut meat has been pressed repeatedly.

กะเทาะ kathɔ́?/ V 1. to flake, chip off, be chipped. 2. to crack, shell (nuts, seeds).

กะแท้ in แมงกะแท้ (ตัว) mɛŋkathɛ́ɛ/* N a kind of bug, known for its distinctive odor when crushed (Pentatomidae).

กะบัง (อัน) kabaŋ/ (?an/) N weir, a dam combined with an underwater fish trap.

กะบิ kabì?/ C a chunk, a lump (of anything).

กะปิ kapì?/ N shrimp paste.

If item is not found under กะ- see กระ-, ข-.

กะโผลกกะเผลก kaphlòog/kaphlêeg/ V 1. to limp.
　　sV 2. with a limp.

กะพง. See entries below.
　ปลากะพง (ตัว) plaakaphoŋ/ (tua/) N a general
　　name for marine fish of the perch and bass
　　families.
　หอยกะพง (ตัว) hɔ̌jkaphoŋ/* (tua/) N a kind of
　　sea mussel (Modiola senhauseni).

กะพรุน in แมงกะพรุน (ตัว) meŋkaphrun/* (tua/)
　　N jellyfish (Medusae).

กะพัน in คงกะพัน khoŋkaphan/ V to be invulnerable.

กะรัง in ปลากะรัง (ตัว) plaakaraŋ/ (tua/) N
　　grouper, a salt-water fish (Epenephelus).

กะรุ่งกะริ่ง karûŋ/kariŋ/ V 1. to be ragged, in
　　tatters, in shreds. sV 2. in tatters, in shreds.

กะเรี่ยกะราด karîa/karâad/ V to be scattered,
　　strewn about.
　ยิ้มกะเรี่ยกะราด jím/-karîa/karâad/ to smile
　　wryly and sheepishly, with embarrassment,
　　confusion.

กะล่อน kalɔ̂n/* V 1. to be a glib talker. 2. to be
　　deceitful, unreliable.

กะละมัง (ใบ,ลูก) kalamaŋ/ (baj/, lûug/) N en-
　　ameled bowl or basin.

กะลา (ใบ,ลูก) kalaa/ (baj/, lûug/) N 1. hard
　　shell of the coconut. 2. a half of a coconut
　　shell, used as a bowl.

กะลาสี (คน) kalaasǐi/ (khon/) N sailor, seaman.
　　→Dist. ทหารเรือ.

กะโล่ (ใบ) kalôo/ (baj/) N a large, flat round
　　tray of bamboo, coated with dammar to make
　　it waterproof.
　หมวกกะโล่ (ใบ) mùagkalôo/ (baj/) N sun
　　helmet.

กะหรี่,แกง-- karìi/, keeŋkarìi/ N Indian curry.
　　[f. Tamil] →Also เกอหรี่ kəərìi/.

กะหล่ำดอก (ดอก,หัว) kalàm/dɔ̀ɔg/ (dɔ̀ɔg/, hǔa/)
　　N cauliflower. ต้น-- (ต้น) the cauliflower
　　plant.

กะหล่ำปลี (หัว) kalàm/plii/ (hǔa/) N cabbage.
　　ต้น-- (ต้น) the cabbage plant.

กะเหรี่ยง karìaŋ/ N Karen, the Karens.

กะโหลก (กะโหลก) kalòog/ (kalòog/) N 1. skull.
　　2. hard shell of the coconut, used as a cup.

กะโหลกมะพร้าว (ลูก,ใบ) kalòog/maphráaw/
　　(lûug/, baj/) N hard shell of the coconut, the
　　endocarp.

กะโหลกศีรษะ (ใบ,กะโหลก) kalòog/sǐisà?/ (baj/,
　　kalòog/) N anat. skull.

หัวกะโหลก (ใบ,หัว) hǔakalòog/ (baj/, hǔa/) N
　　N skull.

กัก kàg/ V 1. to confine, restrict, detain, shut in,
　　shut up. 2. to store, stock, accumulate.

กักกัน kàgkan/ V 1. to confine, restrict, detain,
　　shut in, shut up. 2. to store, stock, accumulate.
　　การ-- confinement.
　o ค่ายกักกัน (ค่าย,แห่ง) khâaj/kàgkan/ (khâaj/,
　　hèŋ/) N concentration camp.

กักตุน kàgtun/ V to hoard. การ-- hoarding.
　　[ตุน f. Chin.]

ค่ายกักเชลย (ค่าย) khâaj/kàgchaləəj/ (khâaj/)
　　N prisoner-of-war camp.

กั๊ก. See entries below. [f. Chin.]
　สี่กั๊ก (แห่ง) sìikág/ (hèŋ/) N crossroads, inter-
　　section.
　เสื้อกั๊ก (ตัว) sŷakág/ (tua/) N vest, waistcoat.

กักขฬะ kàg/khalà?/ V to be hard, rough, cruel, vile,
　　vulgar.

กังขา kaŋkhǎa/ V 1. lit., eleg. to doubt, have doubts,
　　be skeptical. N 2. doubt, skepticism. ความ--
　　doubt, skepticism.

กังวล kaŋwon/ V to worry, be concerned, anxious.
　　ความ-- worry.

กังวาน kaŋwaan/ V 1. to be resonant, sonorous.
　　N 2. resonance, sonority.

กังหัน (อัน) kaŋhǎn/ (?an/) N 1. windmill. 2. weather
　　vane. 3. pinwheel (child's toy). →Also จังหัน

กัญชา kanchaa/ N hashish, marijuana, i.e. Indian
　　hemp (Cannabis sativa).

กัณฑ์ kan/ C 1. chapter, section (of a religious text).
　　2. sermon.

กัด kàd/ V 1. to bite. 2. (a snake) to strike. 3. to
　　corrode, eat away (by chemical action).
　กัดกัน kàd/kan/ V to fight (of animals).
　กัดปลา kàdplaa/ V 1. to have a fishfight. N 2.
　　a fishfight.
　กัดฟัน kàdfan/ V 1. to gnash one's teeth. 2.
　　colloq. to grin and bear (it), be patient.

ถูก...กัด thùugɔ...kàd′ to be bitten by (something).

ปลากัด (ตัว) plaakàd′ (tua′) N Siamese fighting
fish (Betta).

กัน ๑ kan′ rcP 1. each other, one another, mutually,
together. 2. severally (imparting a distributive
sense to the verb). Often not rendered explicitly in English.

o คุยกัน khuj′kan to chat, converse with one
another.

o ไปถามกันเถอะ pajthǎam′kanthə?′ Let's go ask.

o เป็นปัญหาที่ขบกันไม่แตก penpanhǎa′-thîikhòb′ɔ
kanmâjtɛɛg′ It's a problem they can't solve,
a problem that can't be solved.

o เงินหมดเพราะมีคนขอกันมากเหลือเกิน ŋən′ɔ
mòd′→phrɔmiikhon′-khɔɔ′kanmâag′-lɯ̌akəən′↓
The money is all used up, because so very
many people have (each, severally) asked for
some.

o ต่างเงียบกันไปครู่หนึ่ง tàaŋ′-ŋîabkanpajkhrûu′ɔ
nyŋ↓ Each remained silent for a moment.

กระทำกัน kratham′kanɔ to be done, accomplished,
effectuated; (a conference) to be held, conducted.

กล่าวกันว่า klàaw′kanwâa′ it is said that; they
say that.

กันและกัน kan′lɛkan′ each other, one another
(often preceded by ต่อ, ซึ่ง, แห่ง) .

เข้าใจกันว่า khâwcaj′kanwâa′ it is understood
that.

จบกัน còb′kan↓ That's the end of it all! No use
continuing! (expression of despair).

ช่วยกันเอง chûaj′kan?eeŋ′ to help each other
out, help themselves out.

ด้วยกัน dûajkan′ 1. together. 2. altogether, all
told, in all. 3. along, together with (them, us,
etc.). →See cross reference.

ดีกัน dii′kan to be reconciled, to make up.

เดียวกัน diaw′kan the same.

ตัดกัน tàd′kan 1. to intersect. 2. to contrast
with one another.

ต่างกัน tàaŋ′kan to differ, be different, be separate (i.e. from each other).

เป็นที่ทราบกันว่า penthîisâab′kanwâa′ it is known
that.

พากัน phaa′kanɔ AA adv. -aux. indicating con-
certed action, simultaneous and indentical action
by the members of a group.

o พากันหัวเราะ phaa′kanhǔarɔ?′ everybody
laughed (together).

เลิกกัน lə̂əg′kan V colloq. 1. to be separated,
divorced. 2. to break off a friendship, break
off dealings with each other. 3. that's all; we've
finished (common phrase ending a telephone
conversation).

แล้วกัน ๑. See entries below.

o ก็แล้วกัน kɔlɛɛw′kan 1. mildly hortatory expression: let's, you might (do such and such).
Often indicates indifference: go ahead and (do
such and such; it would be all the same to me).
2. that's it, that's all there is to it.

o เป็นแล้วกัน penlɛɛw′kan that's settled; that
does it; that's all (i.e. we've finished what we
had to say).

แล้วกัน ๒ lɛɛw′kan↓ E exclamative indicating
surprise and disappointment.

เหมือนกัน mw̌ankan′ 1. to be similar, alike, the
same. 2. also, too, likewise. 3. either (with
negative expressions). →See cross reference.

อะไรกัน ?arajkan′↓ What's up? Something's up.
→See cross reference.

กัน ๒ kan′ P I, me (m. sp. to intimate m.; otherwise
derogatory). Paired with แก "you."

กันเอง kan?eeŋ′ I myself; me myself.

กัน ๓ in กันเอง kan?eeŋ′ N 1. an intimate, an equal.
2. intimate, familiar, informal. คน-- an acquaintance, an intimate, an equal. อย่าง--
informally; in a friendly, intimate manner.
NOTE. Distinguish the sequence กันเอง in
expressions like ช่วยกันเอง under กัน ๑,
where it has the sense of "mutually themselves
(ourselves)." Distinguish also กันเอง "I myself"
under กัน ๒.

o "ฉัน"ใช้สำหรับกันเอง chán′ chájsǎmràbkan?eeŋ′↓
The pronoun "ฉัน" is used with intimates.

เป็นกันเอง pen′kan?eeŋ′ to be intimate, familiar,
informal; to feel at home.

กัน ๔ kan′ V 1. to prevent, ward off, protect from.
2. to bar, shield, cut off, obstruct.

กันชน (อัน) kanchon/ (ʔan/) N 1. buffer. 2. bumper (as of automobile).

คุ้มกัน khúmkan/ V to protect, guard against.

o เรือคุ้มกัน (ลำ) rya/khúmkan/ (lam/) N convoy, armed ship used as an escort.

ที่กันภัย (แห่ง, ที่) thîi/kanphaj/ (hὲŋ/, thîi/) N shelter.

o ที่กันภัยทางอากาศ thîi/kanphaj/-thaaŋʔaakàad/ N air-raid shelter.

ป้องกัน pɔ̂ŋkan/* V 1. to protect, defend. 2. to take a preventive measure. การ-- defense, protection; prevention (of disease, crime).

ผ้ากันเปื้อน (ผืน) phâakanpɣ̂an/ (phɣ̆yn/) N apron.

ยากันเชื้อโรค jaakan/chýarôog/ N antiseptic.

กัน ๕ kan/ V to shave, remove hair.

กั้น kân/ V 1. to cut off (by coming between), to shut off, bar, block. 2. to shelter, cover. 3. to be cut off, sheltered (from, by).

กั้นรั้ว kânrúa/ V to put up a fence.

สกัดกั้น sakàd/kân/ V to block the way, obstruct the advance.

กันไกร (เล่ม) kankraj/ (lêm/) N scissors. Variant of กรรไกร.

กันดาร kandaan/ V 1. to be barren, arid. 2. to be lacking in.

กันดารน้ำ kandaan/náam/ to lack water, be short of water.

ทุรกันดาร thúrákandaan/ V to be extremely arid, barren, waste (e.g. land).

กันไตร (เล่ม) kantraj/ (lêm/) N scissors. Variant of กรรไกร.

กัน. Abbrev. for กันยายน September.

กันยายน kanjaa/jon/ N September. เดือน-- idem. →The names of all the months are listed under เดือน.

กับ ๑ kàb/, kaɔ with (in the sense of "accompanying"), together with, accompanied by. Other renditions are shown in the examples which follow. NOTE. Since กับ is usually pronounced kaɔ, it will be so transcribed throughout this dictionary. Cf. กะ ๓, a variant written form which reflects the usual pronunciation.

o การค้ากับต่างประเทศ kaankháa/katàaŋprathêed/ trade with foreign countries.

o ของนั้นต้องวางกับดิน khɔ̌ɔŋ/nán/ tɔ̂ŋwaaŋ/kadin/↓ Those things have to be set on the ground.

o เขาทำตาเขียวกับสามีหล่อน kháwtham/taakhǐaw/-kasǎa/miilɔ̀ɔn/↓ She glared angrily at her husband.

o ตากับยาย taa/kajaaj/ maternal grandparents ("grandfather and grandmother").

o ตำแหน่งผู้นำตกอยู่กับ... tamnὲŋ/phûunam/ tòg/ɔ jùukaɔ ... The leadership fell to (so and so).

o หายวับไปกับตา hǎaj/wáb/-pajkataa/↓ It disappeared from sight.

o อวดลูกแมวกับน้า ʔùad/lûugmɛɛw/-kanáa/↓ She showed the kitten to her aunt.

กลับกับ klàb/kaɔ to be the reverse of, the opposite of.

กับข้าว kakhâaw/ "with rice." →Dist. กับข้าว under กับ ๒.

กับทั้ง kàbtháŋ/* and also, and in addition, together with, withal. →Also กับทั้ง...ด้วย.

เข้ากับ khâw/kaɔ to side with.

คล้ายกับ(ว่า) khláaj/ka(wâa/) as if, as though.

ตรงกับ troŋ/kaɔ to correspond exactly to.

ถึงกับ thɣ̌ŋ/kaɔ so (e.g. sick) that; so as, to the point that, until.

o เจ็บถึงกับลุกไม่ขึ้น cèb/-thɣ̌ŋkalúg/mâjkhɣ̂n/ to be so sick that one can't get up.

เท่ากับ thâw/kaɔ to be the same as, to equal, be equal to, be equivalent to; as...as.

ยังกับ jaŋkaɔ colloq. like, as if. Variant of อย่างกับ.

ระหว่าง...กับ... rawàaŋɔ ...kaɔ ... between (such and such a place or time) and (another place or time).

รับกับ ráb/kaɔ V 1. to match. 2. to be in line with. 3. to become, be becoming to (someone).

อยู่กับที่ jùukathîi/ 1. to stay put; to be fixed, still, firm, stationary. 2. firmly, rooted to the ground.

o ยืนอยู่กับที่ jyyn/jùukathîi/ 1. to stand pat, stand firm (resist). 2. to stand in one place.

อยู่กับเหย้าเฝ้ากับเรือน jùukajâw/fâwkaryan/ to stay at home and look after things (considered a good quality for a woman).

กับ ๒ kàb/ N food. Short for the following entries. NOTE. Probably related to กับ ๑.

กับแกล้ม kàbklɛ̂ɛm/ N food eaten with alcoholic

drinks.

กับข้าว kàbkhâaw/ N 1. food that is eaten with
rice. 2. dishes (in the sense of foods). →Dist.
กับข้าว under กับ ๑.

o ทำกับข้าว thamkàbkhâaw/ V com. to cook.
คน-- a cook. →Syn. ปรุงอาหาร eleg.

กับ ๓ (อัน) kàb/ (ʔan/) N trap, snare.

o ดักกับไว้ dàgkàb/wáj/ to set out a trap.

กับป์ in ชั่วกับป์ชั่วกัลป์ chûakàb/chûakan/ forever,
for all time, eternally. →See also กัลป์.

กัมปนาท kampanâad/ N loud, thundering noise.

กัมพูชา kam/phuuchaa/ N lit. Cambodia; Cambodian. →Syn. เขมร com.

ประเทศกัมพูชา prathêed/-kam/phuuchaa/ pN
eleg.,lit. Cambodia.

กัมมันตภาพ kamman/taphâab/ N phys., chem.
activity; radioactivity.

o กัมมันตภาพรังสี kamman/taphâab/-raŋsǐi/ N
radioactivity.

กัมมันตรังสี kamman/taraŋsǐi/ radioactive.

กัลกัตตา,กัลกัตตา kallákàtaa/, kanlákàtaa/, kan/kàdɔ
taa, kanlákàdtaa/ pN Calcutta. เมือง-- idem.

กัลป์ in ชั่วกับป์ชั่วกัลป์ chûakàb/chûakan/ forever,
for all time, eternally. →See also กับป์.

กัวลาลัมเปอร์ kualaalampəə/ pN Kuala Lumpur, capital of the Federation of Malaya. เมือง-- idem.

กา ๑ (ตัว) kaa/ (tua/) N writ.com. crow.
→Also อีกา com.

กาๆ kaa/kaa/ imit. "caw caw" (the cry of the
crow).

กาฝาก (ต้น) kaafàag/ (tôn/) N 1. a kind of
parasitic climbing plant. 2. a parasite, one
who lives at the expense of others.

ปากกา (ด้าม,ตัว,ปาก) pàagkaa/ N 1. pen
(dâam/). 2. pen-point (tua/); short for ตัว
ปากกา. 3. crow's beak (pàag/).

o ตัวปากกา (ตัว) tua/pàagkaa/ (tua/) N pen-
point.

ปีกกา pìigkaa/ N 1. the flank (of a military
force). 2. any shape resembling a "V" (remi-
niscent of a crow in flight). 3. brace, braces,
i.e. the typographical characters { }.

อีกา (ตัว) ʔiikaa/ (tua/) N com. crow.

กา ๒ (ลูก,ใบ) kaa/ (lûug/, baj/) N teakettle; pot

with spout. →Also กาต้มน้ำ,กาน้ำ kaa/tômɔ
náam/, kaanáam/.

กา ๓ kaa/ V to mark with +, x, or a check.

o ถ้าผิดก็ช่วยกาให้ที thâaphìd/→kɔchûajkaa/hâjthii/↓
If there is an error, please mark it, "x" it.

สภากาชาด saphaakaachâad/ N the Red Cross.

กาก kàag/ N refuse, leavings, residue, dregs, dross,
roughage.

กากน้ำตาล kàagnámtaan/ N molasses.

กากมะพร้าว kàagmaphráaw/ N coconut meat
residue, i.e. the unusable residue left after the
meat has been grated and pressed.

หน้ากาก (หน้ากาก,อัน) nâakàag/ (nâakàag/,ʔan/)
N mask, hood, cover.

กากบาท (อัน) kaakabàad/ (ʔan/) N the plus sign
(+); the multiplication sign (×); any "x" mark.
→Sometimes written กากบาด.

เครื่องหมายกากบาท (อัน) khrŷaŋmǎaj/kaakabàad/
N a cross, an "x" mark, a plus mark, i.e. any
mark with crossing lines (including the fourth
tonal marker).

ไม้กากบาท (อัน) májkaakabàad/ (ʔan/) N the
fourth tonal marker (˘). →Syn. ไม้จัตวา,
เครื่องหมายกากบาท.

กากี in สีกากี sǐikaakii/ N khaki color. [f. Hind.]

กาง kaaŋ/ V to spread out, stretch out, hang out.

กางมุ้ง kaaŋmúŋ/ V to hang up a mosquito net.

ขอกาง khɔɔ/kaaŋ/ sV (with) elbows out (as when
walking with an air of determination). Generally
used with เดิน.

ท้องกาง thɔɔŋkaaŋ/ V 1. to have a full belly, a
belly bulging with food or water. sV 2. with a
full belly. →Dist. ท้องขึ้น.

ก้าง ๑ (อัน,ชิ้น) kâaŋ/ (ʔan/,chín/) N bone (of a
fish). →Dist. กระดูก.

ก้างปลา (อัน,ชิ้น) kâaŋplaa/ (ʔan/,chín/) N
fish bone.

ก้าง ๒. See เก้งก้าง.

กางเกง (ตัว) kaaŋkeeŋ/ (tua/) N pants, trousers.

กางเกง(ชั้น)ใน (ตัว) kaaŋkeeŋnaj/, kaaŋkeeŋ/ɔ
chánnaj/ (tua/) N shorts, underpants; panties.

เสื้อกางเกง (ชุด) sŷa/kaaŋkeeŋ/ (chúd/) N 1.
suit of clothes (for a man). 2. any ensemble
of clothes that includes pants, e.g. blouse and

slacks for ladies, night clothes for children.

กางเขน (อัน) kaaŋkhěen′ (ʔan′) N cross.

　นกกางเขน (ตัว) nógkaaŋkhěen′ (tua′) N dyal, or magpie robin (Copsychus saularis).

　ไม้กางเขน (อัน) májkaaŋkhěen′ (ʔan′) N cross.

กาจ kàad′ V to be wicked, brave, bold.

　เก่งกาจ kèŋkàad′ V to be bold, brave, fearless.

　ร้ายกาจ ráajkàad′ V 1. to be fierce, cruel, harsh, severe. 2. to be wicked.

กาซ, ก๊าซ káad′, káas′ N gas, i.e. gaseous substance. [f. Eng.] →Also แกส. →Dist. กาส.

กาญจนบุรี kaancanáburii′ pN Kančhanaburi, a township in central Thailand west of Bangkok.

กาด. See ผักกาด under ผัก.

กาน kaan′ V 1. to trim, prune. 2. to girdle (a tree).

ก้าน (ก้าน) kâan′ (kâan′) N 1. stem, stalk, petiole. 2. midrib of a leaf or of a pinnate leaflet. C 3. clf. for twigs, for small pieces of wood or bamboo, for match sticks.

　ก้านมะพร้าว (ก้าน) kâanmaphráaw′ (kâan′) N midrib of a pinnate leaflet of the coconut palm. →Dist. ทางมะพร้าว under ทาง ๒.

　ก้านสูบ (อัน) kâansùub′ (ʔan′) N piston rod.

　หน่วยก้าน nùajkâan′ N bearing, manner, manners, breeding.

กานพลู kaanphluu′ N clove. ดอก-- (ดอก) flower of the clove tree. ต้น-- (ต้น) the clove tree.

กาบ (กาบ) kàab′ (kàab′) N 1. bract, spathe. 2. fragment (of coconut husk).

　กาบกล้วย kàabklûaj′ N fibrous layer on the trunk of a banana tree.

　กาบมะพร้าว kàabmaphráaw′ N 1. coir. 2. fragment of coconut husk.

　กาบอ้อย kàabʔɔ̂j′ N the sheath of a sugar cane leaf.

กาบ ๆ káabkáab′ imit. "quack! quack!" (the quacking of a duck).

กาพย์ (บท) kàab′ (bòd′) N a kind of Thai verse form.

กาแฟ kaafɛɛ′ N coffee. [f. Eur.]

　กาแฟผง kaafɛɛphǒŋ′ N instant coffee.

　กาแฟเย็น kaafɛɛjen′ N iced coffee.

　ร้านกาแฟ ráankaafɛɛ′ N coffee shop.

กาม kaam′, kaam′maɔ N sexual desire.

กามคุณ kaam′makhun′ N 1. sexual desire. 2. sensuality.

กามโรค kaam′marôog′ N eleg., tech. venereal disease. เป็น-- to have a venereal disease.

น้ำกาม námkaam′ N semen, spermatic fluid. →Syn. น้ำอสุจิ.

ก้าม (ก้าม) kâam′ (kâam′) N claw, pincer (of lobster or crab).

　ต้นก้ามปู (ต้น) tônkâampuu′ (tôn′) N 1. rain tree (Enterolobium saman). 2. the East Indian walnut (Albizzia lebbeck). →Syn. ต้นจามจุรี.

　วางก้าม waaŋkâam′ V idiom. to act big.

กาย ๑ kaaj′, kaajɔ, kaajaɔ N body. →Chiefly in cpds.

กายกรรม kaajjakam′ N gymnastics.

กายบริหาร kaajbɔɔrihǎan′ N (bodily) exercise.

กายสิทธิ์ kaajjasìd′ N 1. magic; miraculous power. 2. (as n. mod.) magic, miraculous.

กำลังกาย kamlaŋkaaj′ N 1. physical strength. 2. energy.

o ออกกำลังกาย ʔɔ̀ɔg′kamlaŋkaaj′ to exercise (one's body).

เครื่องประดับกาย khrŷaŋpradàb′kaaj′ N eleg. ornament (to be worn on the body).

เจียมกาย ciamkaaj′ V eleg. to be humble, modest, unassuming; to know one's place (and not go beyond it).

แต่งกาย tɛ̀ŋkaaj′ V eleg. to dress.

ทางกาย thaaŋkaaj′ 1. physical, bodily. 2. physically.

ทุกข์กาย thúgkaaj′ V to suffer (physically). ความ-- physical suffering.

ร่างกาย (ร่าง) râaŋkaaj′ (râaŋ′) N body (the usual body-part term).

เรือนกาย ryankaaj′ N eleg. the (human) body, form.

สุขกาย sùgkaaj′ V 1. to be healthy, in good health. 2. to be physically well off.

กาย ๒ in เกียกกาย kìagkaaj′ N milit. commissary.

ก่าย kàaj′ V 1. to be resting one's limb on. 2. to be resting on, leaning on, lying across (used of limbs of the body, sometimes also of long, thin objects such as sticks, rifles).

o นอนก่ายหน้าผาก nɔɔnkàaj′nâaphàag′ to lie with

one's arm on the forehead.

o วางก่ายกัน waaŋkàaj/kan to lay (long objects) across each other, one over the other (but not parallel to each other).

o เอามือก่ายหน้าผาก ʔawmyykàaj/nâaphàag/ to rest one's arm on the forehead.

ก้าวก่าย kâawkàaj/ V 1. to infringe, intrude upon. 2. to extend over into.

o ก้าวก่ายธุระ kâawkàaj/thúrá?/ to be officious, interfere in the affairs of others.

เป็นก่ายเป็นกอง penkàaj/penkɔɔŋ/ elab. colloq. a lot (of), a whole lot (of), heaps (of).

มากมายก่ายกอง mâagmaaj/kàajkɔɔŋ/ elab. colloq. so much, so many, a lot, a great deal.

การ kaan/ N 1. work, affair(s), matter(s); 1st and 2nd examples. 2. bound element placed before nouns to form noun derivatives meaning "affairs of..., matters of..."; 3rd-4th examples and 1st note. 3. bound element placed before active verbs to form noun derivatives signifying "act of (doing thus and so)"; 5th example and 2nd note. 4. bound final element in compounds of Sanskrit origin; 6th example. นัก-- messenger. →Sometimes การ is confused with การณ q.v. →See ความ-- (Note 3).

o ในการนี้ najkaan/níi/ in this matter.

o เป็นการยาก penkaan/jâag/ is a difficult matter; with difficulty.

o การเมือง kaanmyaŋ/ politics: "affairs of the state."

o การบ้าน kaanbâan/ housework; household affairs; (student's) homework.

o การรบ kaanrób/ (the) fighting, (a) battle: "act of fighting."

o กรรมการ kammakaan/ committee, commission.

NOTE 1. As a bound element before nouns การ often corresponds in meaning to such English suffixes as -ery (cookery), -y (diplomacy), -ics (politics), among others. Sometimes, however, the English noun has no specific element corresponding to การ (e.g. finance, medicine).

การครัว kaankhrua/ cookery.

การทูต kaanthûud/ diplomacy.

การเศรษฐกิจ kaansèed/thakìd/ economy; economic affairs.

การช่างไม้ kaanchâaŋmáaj/ carpentry.

การทหาร kaanthahǎan/ soldiery; military affairs.

การป่าไม้ kaanpàamáaj/ forestry.

การเมือง kaanmyaŋ/ politics.

การคลัง kaankhlaŋ/ finance; financial matters.

การแพทย์ kaanphêed/ medicine (as a subject of study, a scientific field); medical matters.

NOTE 2. When placed before active verbs to form noun derivatives, การ can almost always be rendered in English by the suffix -ing. Several other suffixes are often also appropriate, some of these being -tion, -sion (navigation; aggression), -al (trial), -ance, -ence (assistance; conference), -ment (management). The Thai derivative can sometimes also be translated by an English noun in which there is no specific element corresponding to การ (e.g. attack, debate, banquet).

การจัดการ kaancàdkaan/ management (in the sense of "managing").

การโจมตี kaancoomtii/ attack, assault, raid.

การช่วยเหลือ kaanchûajlỹa/ helping out, assisting; assistance, aid.

การตรวจ kaantrùad/ examination, inspection, investigation.

การโต้วาที kaantôo/waathii/ debate.

การบิน kaanbin/ flying; aviation.

การประชุม kaanprachum/ meeting, conference, session.

การรักษา kaanrágsǎa/ care, maintenance, preservation; cure, remedy.

การเลี้ยง kaanlíaŋ/ feast, banquet; feeding, taking care of.

NOTE 3. Most derivatives based on การ are listed only under the nouns or verbs from which they are derived. Thus, to find การกระทบ, look under กระทบ. Classifiers used with derivatives based on การ are usually one of the following, depending upon appropriateness: ครั้ง, นัด for a specific event; อย่าง, ชนิด for a type of activity or state. These classifiers are therefore omitted in the entries below except where a special distinction needs to be made.

กงการ koŋkaan/ N colloq. affair, business.

กรมการ (คณะ,ชุด,คน) krommakaan/ N 1. administrative staff of the local government (khaɔ ná?/, chúd/). 2. an official of the local government (khon/). →Chiefly in compounds. →See cross reference.

กรรมการ (คน,คณะ,ชุด) kammakaan/ N 1. committee member (khon/). 2. committee, commission (khaná?/, chúd/).

กระบวนการ (กระบวน) krabuankaan/ (krabuan/)

N 1. procedure; administration. 2. movement (as in "liberation movement"). 3. t e c h. process.

ก่อการ kɔ̀ɔkaan/ V to instigate (an affair, a disturbance).

กะการ kà?/kaan/ V to work out a plan, to plan.

การกบฏ (ครั้ง) kaankabòd/ (khráŋ/) N revolt, insurrection, rebellion, revolution.

การกระทำ kaankratham/ N 1. deed, act, action. 2. behavior (i.e. physical behavior of a material).

การกสิกรรม kaankàsikam/ N agriculture.

การกิน kaankin/ N 1. eating. 2. s l a n g corruption.

การเข้าใจ kaankhâwcaj/ N understanding, comprehension.

การเข้าใจผิด kaankhâwcajphìd/ N misunderstanding.

การคมนาคม kaankhommanaakhom/ N communication.

การค้า kaankháa/ N 1. business, trade, commerce. 2. trading.

o ภาษีการค้า phaasǐi/kaankháa/ N business tax.

o หอการค้า hɔ̌ɔ/kaankháa/ N chamber of commerce.

การงาน kaanŋaan/ N work (in general). →Also งานการ.

การเงิน kaanŋən/ N money matters, finance, financial affairs; (as n. mod.) financial.

o ภาวะการเงิน phaawá?/kaanŋən/ N financial condition, financial situation.

การจราจร kaancaraa/cɔɔn/ N traffic.

การจลาจล kaancalaa/con/ N unrest, disorder, rebellion.

การจารกรรม kaancaarakam/ N espionage, spying.

การโดยสาร kaandoojsǎan/ N 1. traveling (in a vehicle). 2. taking (a vehicle).

การต่อสู้ kaantɔ̀ɔsûu/ N fight, struggle, battle.

การต่างประเทศ kaantàaŋpratheêd/ N foreign affairs.

การทำมาหากิน kaanthammaa/hǎakin/ N 1. making a living, earning a living. 2. occupation, livelihood.

การทำเหมืองแร่ kaantham/mǔaŋrɛ́ɛ/ N ore-mining.

การที่ kaan/thîi⊃ 1. the fact that, the fact being that.

o การที่เรามีอาณาเขตจดทะเล ทำให้เราได้โภคทรัพย์หลายอย่างจากทะเล kaan/-thîirawmii?aanaa⊃ khèed/còdthalee/→ thamhâjrawdâajphôogkhasáb/⊃ lǎajjàaŋ/-càagthalee/↓ The fact that we have boundaries along the sea makes it possible for us to obtain many kinds of provisions from the sea.

การที่จะ kaan/thîica⊃ in order to, for (doing thus and so). →See cross reference.

การบ้าน kaanbâan/ N 1. housework. 2. household affairs, domestic affairs. 3. homework (of students). [3. tr. f. Eng.]

การประปา kaanprapaa/ N (city) water supply.

การเป็นไป kaanpenpaj/ N getting along, how one gets along; relationship (between), interaction (between).

การมาเรียน kaanmaarian/ N attendance (in school).

การยืดหยุ่น kaanjɯ̂ydjùn/ N p h y s. elasticity.

การศึกษา kaansɯ̀gsǎa/ N education. นัก-- educator.

การสร้าง kaansâaŋ/ N construction, building (i.e. the activity).

การสอน kaansɔ̌ɔn/ N teaching.

กำกับการ kamkàb/kaan/ V to be in control, in charge of things. ผู้-- director, head, the person in charge of things.

กำหนดการ kamnòd/kaan/ N program, schedule of events (of a ceremony, festival).

กิจการ kìdcakaan/ N work, activity, business.

โครงการ khrooŋkaan/ N plan, project, program. →Also -การณ์ FS.

โฆษณาการ khôosanaakaan/, khôodsa⊃ N 1. advertisement. 2. publicity.

งานการ ŋaan/kaan/ N work (in general). →Also การงาน.

จัดการ càdkaan/ 1. to make arrangements; to take care of, manage (things); to deal with, handle (situations). 2. c o l l o q. to fix, polish off, take care of.

เจ้ากี้เจ้าการ câwkîi/câwkaan/ V to be a busybody,

a meddler (used esp. of one who takes on a responsibility, obligation or function of his own accord, at the same time involving others in the obligation without their knowledge or consent).

ใช้การได้ chájkaan′dâaj 1. to be in working condition, useable. 2. That's good! (said in praise). 3. It worked!

ดำเนินการ damnəən′kaan′ V 1. to carry on the work; to conduct, run (e.g. a business); to manage things. 2. to operate, be in operation, be in action.

ได้การ dâjkaan′ V 1. to be successful. 2. to be workable. 3. It works!

ตรวจการ trùadkaan′ V to inspect things, carry out an inspection.

ต้องการ tôŋkaan′ V 1. to want, need, require. AA 2. want to, wish to. ความ-- need, needs, requirements.

ตัวการ (คน) tuakaan′ (khon′) N 1. the culprit. 2. the principal (in an action). 3. a ringleader.

ตุลาการ (คน,นาย) tùlaa′kaan′ (khon′, naaj′) N judge.

ทางการ thaaŋkaan′ N 1. official source, government source. 2. (as n. mod.) official.

ทำการ thamkaan′ V to work, do work.

ธุระการ (อย่าง) thúrá?′kaan′ (jàaŋ′) N 1. practical matters (of an administrative nature). 2. (as n. mod.) administrative.

ในการ najkaan′ 1. in (such and such a) matter, (such and such) matters. 2. in the matter of, in matters of.

บงการ boŋkaan′ V to direct things, give commands, give orders.

บรรณาธิการ (คน) bannaa′thíkaan′ (khon′) N editor.

บริการ bɔɔrikaan′ N 1. service. V 2. to serve, assist.

บังคับการ baŋkháb′kaan′ V to command, be in command.

บัญชาการ banchaa′kaan′ V to command, be in command.

ปฏิบัติการ pàtibàd′kaan′ V to conduct matters, do things; to perform, operate, execute, carry out. การ-- operation, action.

o ห้องปฏิบัติการ (ห้อง) hɔ̂ŋ′-pàtibàd′kaan′ (hɔ̂ŋ′) N laboratory.

ประจำการ pracamkaan′ V to be on duty.

ประวัติการ prawàd′kaan′ N history, chronicle of events. →Sometimes spelled -การณ.

ป่วยการ pùajkaan′ V to be no use, in vain, for nothing.

o ค่าป่วยการ khâapùajkaan′ N idiom. fee, service charge, commission.

เป็นการ penkaan′ to be successful, effective; to have succeeded.

o เป็นงานเป็นการ penŋaan′penkaan′ elab. colloq. to be systematic, business-like.

เป็นการจริงจัง penkaan′ciŋcaŋ′ 1. to be earnest, to be an earnest matter. 2. earnestly, with all one's heart.

เผด็จการ phadèd′kaan′ V to exercise absolute control, be dictatorial.

แผนการ (อย่าง,อัน) phɛ̌ɛnkaan′ (jàaŋ′, ?an′) N plan, project, scheme. →Often incorrectly spelled -การณ.

ยุทธการ (ครั้ง) júdthakaan′ (khráŋ′) N 1. military operation. 2. battle.

ระเบียบการ (ฉบับ,เล่ม) rabìabkaan′ (chabàb′, lêm′) N 1. (printed) information (e.g. about the policies and general nature of a club, school, society, institution). 2. schedule, prospectus.

รักษาการ rágsǎakaan′ V to be on guard, on duty, in charge.

ราชการ (อย่าง) râadchakaan′ (jàaŋ′) N 1. government service. 2. a government job.

รายการ (รายการ) raajkaan′ (raajkaan′) N 1. list, list of items. 2. item (in a list of items).

วงการ (วง) woŋkaan′ (woŋ′) N 1. circle(s) (as in "government circles"). 2. field, realm.

ว่าการ wâakaan′ V 1. to direct things, administer. 2. to be in charge.

วิชาการ wíchaa′kaan′ N 1. knowledge. 2. technology. 3. (as n. mod.) academic, theoretical, technical. นัก-- scholar.

วิทยาการ wídthajaakaan′ N science, knowledge.

วิธีการ (อย่าง,วิธี) wíthii′kaan′ (jàaŋ′, wíthii′) N method, procedure.

สั่งการ sàŋ′kaan′ V to give orders, instructions.

หลักการ (หลักการ) làgkaan′ (làgkaan′) N principle.

ให้การ hâjkaan′ V to give testimony, testify.

องค์การ (องค์การ) ʔoŋkaan′ (ʔoŋkaan′) N organization.

อัยการ (คน,นาย) ʔajjakaan′ (khon′, naaj′) N prosecutor.

อำนวยการ ʔamnuajkaan′ V to direct things, conduct (the) affairs.

เอาการ(อยู่) ʔawkaan′(jùu′) V colloq. 1. to be quite a thing; (that's) quite a thing. sV 2. mighty, pretty, quite, rather.

เอาการเอางาน ʔawkaan′/ʔawŋaan′ V to take one's work seriously, be in earnest about one's work.

การก (การก,ชนิด) kaa′róg′ (kaa′róg′, chaníd′) N gram. case.

กรรตุการก kaantùkaa′róg′ N nominative case.

กรรมการก kammakaa′róg′ N accusative case.

การณ์ kaan′ N situation, circumstance, events. Normally a final element in compound nouns which are mostly of Sanskrit origin, but in a few expressions it is an independent word. →Often confused with การ.

โครงการณ์. See โครงการ.

แถลงการณ์ (ฉบับ) thalɛ̌ɛŋ′kaan′ (chabàb′) N official announcement, pronouncement, bulletin, communique. ผู้-- spokesman.

ประวัติการณ์ prawàd′kaan′ N (the) record, events worth recording. →Sometimes spelled -การ.

ปรากฏการณ์ praakòd′kaan′ N phenomenon.

แผนการณ์. See แผนการ.

พฤติการณ์ phrýdtikaan′ N course of events, circumstances.

มองการณ์ไกล mɔɔŋkaanklaj′ to be farsighted (have foresight), to foresee an incident or situation.

รู้เท่าไม่ถึงการณ์ rúu′thâw′-mâjthŷŋkaan′ to be blind to the situation, be unable to see what someone is up to.

สถานการณ์ sathǎanákaan′ N condition; situation.

สังเกตการณ์ sǎŋkèed′kaan′ V to observe.

เหตุการณ์ (อย่าง) hèedkaan′ (jàaŋ′) N 1. incident, event. 2. circumstances, situation.

การ์ด (แผ่น,ใบ) káad′* (phɛ̀n′, baj′) N card. [f. Eng.]

การ์ดชื่อ káadchŷy′ N colloq. calling card. Now usually นามบัตร.

การ์ตูน (เรื่อง) kaatuun′ (rŷaŋ′) N cartoon. [f. Eng.]

นักเขียนการ์ตูน (คน) nágkhǐan′kaatuun′ (khon′) cartoonist.

การบูร kaarabuun′ N camphor.

การันต์ kaaran′ N com. the cancellation sign ( ) used in the Thai writing system. →Syn. ไม้ทัณฑฆาต eleg.

การาจี kaaraacii′ pN Karachi, capital of Pakistan.

กาล kaan, kaalá?′, kaalaɔ N 1. time, period, era. 2. gram. tense.

กาลเทศะ kaalá?′theesà?′ N the time and place, the occasion.

กาลโน้น kaalanóon′ a long time ago.

เก่าเกินกาล kàw′kəənkaan′ to be out-of-date, antiquated.

เฉพาะกาล chaphɔ́?′kaan′ temporary.

โบราณกาล booraan′nakaan′ N lit. ancient times, former times, antiquity.

พุทธกาล phúdthakaan′ N 1. the time of the Buddha. 2. the Buddhist era.

รัชชกาล rádchakaan′ N 1. reign. 2. the reign of.

ฤดูกาล rýduu′kaan′ N season, time.

กาว kaaw′ N glue.

แป้งกาว pɛ̂ɛŋkaaw′ N (library) paste (commercial).

ก้าว (ก้าว) kâaw′ (kâaw′) N 1. step. 2. pace (approximate linear measure). V 3. to step, take a step.

ก้าวก่าย kâawkàaj′ V 1. to infringe, intrude upon. 2. to extend over into.

o ก้าวก่ายธุระ kâawkàaj′thúrá?′ to be officious, interfere in the affairs of others.

ก้าวขา kâawkhǎa′ V to step, step forward.

ก้าวพลาด kâawphlâad′ V 1. to misstep, miss one's footing. 2. to miscalculate, misjudge.

ก้าวร้าว kâawráaw′ V 1. to show disrespect. sV 2. disrespectfully, abusively.

ก้าวหน้า kâawnâa′ V 1. to step ahead, go forward. 2. to progress, advance, develop. การ-- progress, progressing; math. progression. ความ-- progress, advancement.

o เจริญก้าวหน้า carəən′kâawnâa′ V to progress.

เขย่งเก็งกอยก้าวกระโดด khajèŋkeŋkɔɔjkâaw/ɔ
kraddòod/ N hop-step-and-jump, an athletic
sport.

ก๊าส in น้ำมันก๊าส námman/káad/ N kerosene.
[ก๊าส f. Eng.] →Dist. กาซ,ก๊าซ,แกส,แก๊ส.

กาไหล่ kaalàj/ V 1. to plate (with metal). 2. to be
plated.

กาฬ kaan/, kaala⊃ V 1. to be black. 2. to be
deathly, death-like.

กาฬโรค kaalarôog/ N plague.

เหงื่อกาฬ ŋỳakaan/ N (a) cold sweat (as from
fright).

กำ kam/ V 1. to hold tightly in the hand, grasp,
clench. C 2. handful (as of sand), bunch (as
of vegetables).

กำปั้น (อัน) kampân/ (ʔan/) N fist.

กำมือ kammyy/ V 1. to clench the hand. N 2.
grip, clutch, clutches. C 3. handful (as of sand).

กำหมัด kammàd/ V 1. to clench one's fist. N
2. fist.

เต็มกำ,--มือ tem/kam/, tem/kammyy/ 1. (in
the amount of) a handful. 2. with one's hand
or hands full.

ก่ำ kàm/ rM intensifier used with แดง "red,"
สุก "ripe."

ก้ำ in ก้ำกึ่ง (กัน) kâmkỳŋ/(kan/) V 1. to be half
(this) and half (that). 2. to be about the same
(as each other). sV 3. about equally.

ก้ำกวม kamkuam/ V to be vague, ambiguous,
unclear.

กำกับ kamkàb/ V 1. to direct, control. 2. to accompany, go with (as a caption or legend accompanying an illustration). ผู้-- (see below).

กำกับการ kamkàb/kaan/ V to be in control, in
charge of things. ผู้-- director, head, the person in charge.

ผู้กำกับ (คน,นาย) phûukamkàb/ (khon/, naaj/)
N 1. director. 2. colloq. chief of police.

o ผู้กำกับการตำรวจ phûukamkàb/kaantamrùad/
N (district or provincial) chief of police.

o ผู้กำกับการแสดง phûukamkàb/kaansadεεŋ/
N stage director, film director.

กำจัด kamcàd/ V 1. to expel, drive away. 2. to
eliminate, get rid of. 3. to extinguish. →Syn.

ขจัด writ.

กำชับ kamcháb/ V to insist firmly, urge emphatically
and persistently.

กำดัด kamdàd/ V to be young, youthful, adolescent
(of a girl).

กำนัน (คน,นาย) kamnan/ (khon/, naaj/) N elder,
headman of a ตำบล (a political district).

กำนัล ๑ kamnan/ V to give a present.

กำนัล ๒ as in นางกำนัล (คน) naaŋkamnan/ (khon/)
N personal maid of a queen or princess.

กำเนิด kamnəəd/* N 1. birth. 2. origin. V eleg.
3. to be born. 4. to be produced. [conv. f. เกิด]

ก่อกำเนิด kɔ̀ɔ/kamnəəd/ V to originate, initiate,
give birth (to).

เครื่อง(ให้)กำเนิดไฟฟ้า (เครื่อง) khrŷaŋ(hâj)⊃
kamnəəd/fajfáa/ (khrŷaŋ/) N electric generator.

ถือกำเนิด thỹy/kamnəəd/ V to be born, originated,
initiated, produced.

ทรงกำเนิด soŋ/kamnəəd/ V roy. to be born.

มาแต่กำเนิด maatὲεkamnəəd/ from birth.

กำบัง kambaŋ/ V 1. to obstruct. 2. to shield, shelter.
N 3. shelter.

กำปั่น ๑,เรือ-- (ลำ) kampàn/, ryakampàn/ (lam/)
N ship, merchant ship.

กำปั่น ๒ (ใบ,ลูก) kampàn/ (baj/, lûug/) N safe
(as for money, valuables).

กำพร้า kamphráa/ V 1. to be bereaved of (one's
parent or parents). N 2. orphan. 3. epidermis;
short for หนัง-- below. คน-- orphan.

เด็กกำพร้า (คน) dὲgkamphráa/ (khon/) N orphan.

หนังกำพร้า nǎŋkamphráa/ N epidermis.

กำแพง (กำแพง) kamphεεŋ/ (kamphεεŋ/) N com.
wall (surrounding a town, a temple). →Syn.
ปราการ eleg.

กำมะถัน kammathǎn/ N sulfur.

กรดกำมะถัน kròd/kammathǎn/ N sulfuric acid.

กำมะลอ kammalɔɔ/ imitation, false, phony.

กำมะหยี่ kammajìi/ N velvet.

กำยาน kamjaan/ N 1. a kind of incense. 2. benzoin.

กำยำ kamjam/ V to be strong, muscular.

กำราบ kamrâab/* V to subdue.

กำเริบ kamrə̂əb/ V 1. to get worse, become more
intense (esp. of disease). 2. colloq. to become
more aggressive, demanding, presumptuous.

กำเริบเสิบสาน kamrə̂əb'sə̀əbsǎan' V elab.
c o l l o q. to become impudent, insolent, more
aggressive, demanding, presumptuous.

กำไร kamraj' V 1. to profit, gain, have as profit.
N 2. profit, gain.

กำไรสุทธิ kamraj'sùdthí?' N net profit.

ผลกำไร phǒn'kamraj' N profit, gain.

กำลัง ๑ kamlaŋ' N 1. strength, force, power, energy. 2. m a t h. power.

กำลังกาย kamlaŋkaaj' N physical strength, bodily strength, energy.

o ออกกำลังกาย ?ɔ̀ɔgkamlaŋkaaj' to exercise
(one's body).

กำลังงาน kamlaŋŋaan' N 1. power. 2. phys.
energy.

กำลังใจ kamlaŋcaj' N will power, will, spirit.

o หมดกำลังใจ mòd'kamlaŋcaj' to lose heart,
be discouraged.

กำลังดัน kamlaŋdan' N pressure.

กำลังตำรวจ kamlaŋtamrùad' N the strength of
a police force.

กำลังทหาร kamlaŋthahǎan' N military manpower.

กำลังทางอากาศ kamlaŋthaaŋ?aakàad' N milit.
air power.

กำลังปรมาณู kamlaŋparamaanuu' N atomic
power.

กำลังไฟฟ้า kamlaŋfajfáa' N electric power.

กำลังม้า kamlaŋmáa' C horsepower. [tr.f.Eng.]
→ S y n. แรงม้า.

กำลังเรือรบ kamlaŋryarób' N naval power,
naval strength.

กำลังแรง kamlaŋrɛɛŋ' N power.

กำลังวังชา kamlaŋwaŋchaa' N bodily strength.

กำลังสอง kamlaŋsɔ̌ɔŋ' N m a t h. square, the
second power. Often best translated "squared,"
"to the second power."

o ยกกำลังสอง jóg'kamlaŋsɔ̌ɔŋ' 1. to square,
raise to the second power. 2. to be squared.

กำลังหนุน kamlaŋnǔn' N reserve force, supporting force.

เต็มกำลัง tem'kamlaŋ' as hard as possible, with
all one's might.

ถอยกำลัง thɔ̌j'kamlaŋ' to be weakened.

เป็นกำลัง pen'kamlaŋ' c o l l o q. very much, considerably, extremely.

ยกกำลัง jóg'kamlaŋ' 1. to mobilize, raise a (military) force. 2. m a t h. to raise, be raised to
the (stated) power; see example.

o ยกกำลังสอง jóg'kamlaŋsɔ̌ɔŋ' 1. to square,
raise to the second power. 2. to be squared.

หมดกำลัง mòd'kamlaŋ' to be exhausted, all in.

ออกกำลัง ?ɔ̀ɔg'kamlaŋ' 1. to exercise, take exercise. 2. to exert strength, put forth physical
effort.

อ่อนกำลัง, --ลง ?ɔ̀ɔn'kamlaŋ', ?ɔ̀ɔn'kamlaŋ'loŋ to
be weakened, get softened up, become less intense.

กำลัง ๒ kamlaŋ' AA progressive adv.-aux. indicating
action going on or state prevailing at a given time.

o กำลังวิ่ง kamlaŋwîŋ' is, are running.

o กำลังร้อน kamlaŋrɔ́ɔn'↓ It's hot! (right now).

กำลังจะ kamlaŋca' AA be about to, be on the
point of, on the verge of.

o กำลังจะตายมิตายแหล่ kamlaŋcataaj' mítaaj'lɛ̀ɛ'
to be on the point of dying, to be on the verge of
death.

กำลัง...อยู่ kamlaŋɔ ...jùu to be in the process
of (doing such and such).

o กำลังทำอะไรอยู่ kamlaŋtham?araj'jùu↓ What
are you doing?

o ขณะที่กำลังอ่านอยู่นั้น khànà?'-thîikamlaŋ?àan'ɔ
jùunán' while he was (in the midst of) reading.

กำไล (คู่,วง,ข้าง,ขอน) kamlaj' N bangle, clasp-
less bracelet, anklet (khûu' for a pair; woŋ',
khâaŋ', khɔ̌ɔn' for one of a pair).

กำหนด kamnòd' N 1. limit (of time). 2. schedule.
V 3. to limit; to set, stipulate, schedule, fix
(a time). 4. to be limited; to be set, stipulated,
fixed, scheduled.

กำหนดการ kamnòdkaan' N program, schedule
of events (of a ceremony, festival).

กำหนดจะ kamnòd'caɔ 1. to plan to. 2. to be
scheduled to, due to.

กำหนด(...)ไว้ (1) kamnòd'(...)wáj'; (2) kamɔ
nòd'wáj' 1. to fix, stipulate (something). 2.
to be fixed, stipulated (as by law).

ถึงกำหนด thy̌ŋ'kamnòd' to reach the appointed
time, deadline, limit; it is time (e.g. to go to bed).

กำหนัด kamnàd′ N 1. joy, excitement. V 2. to be
excited (sexually).

กำแหง kamhɛ̌ɛŋ′ V colloq. 1. to be bold, foolhardy. 2. to dare, have the nerve to. 3. to be
arrogant.

กิ่ง (กิ่ง) kìŋ′ (kìŋ′) N 1. twig, branch. C 2.
branch (as of knowledge).

  กิ่งไม้ (กิ่ง) kìŋmáaj′ (kìŋ′) N twig, branch
  (of plant or tree).

  กิ่งอำเภอ (กิ่ง) kìŋ′ʔamphəə′ (kìŋ′) N a branch
  of an amphoe (an administrative district).

  เขากิ่ง (เขา) khǎwkìŋ′ (khǎw′) N antler.

  แตกกิ่ง tɛ̀ɛgkìŋ′ V to branch out.

กิ้งก่า (ตัว) kîŋkàa′ (tua′) N tree lizard, chame-
leon.

กิจ kìd′, kìdcaɔ, kìdɔ N work, activity, business.
→Chiefly in compounds.

  กิจการ (อย่าง) kìdcakaan′, kìdkaan′ (jàaŋ′)
  N work, activity, business.

  กิจวัตร (อย่าง) kìdcawád′ (jàaŋ′) N routine,
  routine matter.

  ภารกิจ phaa′rákìd′ N work to be done, task,
  duty, responsibility.

  เศรษฐกิจ sèedthakìd′ N economy, economic
  affairs. การ-- idem.

  o ระบอบเศรษฐกิจ rabɔ̀ɔb′sèedthakìd′ N economic system.

กิตติ as in กิตติศัพท์ kìdtisàb′ N 1. rumor, news.
2. renown.

กิตติมศักดิ์ kìtim′masàg′ N (as n. mod.) honorary.

  ปริญญากิตติมศักดิ์ parin′jaa′kìtim′masàg′ N honorary degree.

กิน kin′ V com. 1. to eat, consume, take (food,
drink, medicine). 2. to take (bribes, cuts).
3. to win (in a game). การ-- eating; slang
corruption. →Syn. 1. เสวย roy., รับประ-
ทาน, บริโภค eleg., กระทำภัตตกิจ eleg.
sacer., ฉัน com.sacer., เจี๊ยะ slang,
ยัด, แดก vulg.

  กำลังกิน kamlaŋkin′ 1. is, are eating. 2. ripe,
  just right for eating.

  กินกัน kin′kan 1. to eat (together). 2. to fit, suit
  one another, be well suited for each other.

  o มีสายตาไม่กินกัน miisǎajtaa′-mâjkin′kan (they)

don't like each other's looks, don't get along.

  o เราลงมือกินกันเถอะ rawloŋmɯɯkin′kanthə?′↓
  Let's start eating.

กินข้าว kinkhâaw′ V com. to eat (esp. with reference to eating one's meal) →Comp. กินอาหาร
com. →Syn. รับประทานข้าว eleg. ฉันจังหัน
sacer.

กินข้าวกินปลา kinkhâaw′kinplaa′ V colloq. to
eat (a meal).

กินความ kinkhwaam′ V to include, cover (in
meaning).

  o กินความถึง kinkhwaam′thɯ̌ŋ′ to touch on, refer
  to, include.

กินใจ kincaj′ V 1. to be wary (of). 2. to be deeply
moving (as a story, movie).

กินดิบ kindìb′ V 1. to eat raw or while still unripe.
2. colloq. to win easily, win hands down.

กินได้ kindâaj′ V 1. to be able to eat. 2. to have
an appetite. 3. to be edible. 4. can be served,
eaten.

กินแถว kinthɛ̌ɛw′ colloq. 1. (to do something)
right on down the line, going through an entire
row or series. 2. to scoop the pool, sweep the
board.

กินที่ kinthîi′ to take up room, space.

กินนอน kinnɔɔn′ V 1. to eat and sleep (at a certain
place, esp. when done habitually, frequently, or
for a period of time). sV 2. used as the equivalent of Eng. "boarding," as in the following examples.

  o นักเรียนกินนอน (คน) nágrian′kinnɔɔn′ (khon′)
  N boarding-school student.

  o โรงเรียนกินนอน (แห่ง, โรงเรียน) rooŋrian′ɔ
  kinnɔɔn′ (hɛ̀ŋ′, rooŋrian′) N boarding school.

กินน้ำลึก kinnám′lýg′ to require a deep waterway
(as a big ship).

กินไพ่ kinphâj′ V to win at cards.

กินเมือง kinmyaŋ′ V to rule, govern (a subject
city or state).

กินไม่เข้า kin′mâjkhâw′ 1. can't eat (it), can't
get (it) down. 2. inedible.

กินยา kinjaa′ to take medicine.

กินเลือดกินเนื้อ kinlŷad′kinnýa′ V colloq.,figur.
to eat (someone) up alive (because of anger).

กินเวลา kin'weelaa' 1. to take time. 2. to take up (a given amount of time). 3. to last (a given time).

กินสินบน kin'sǐnbon' to accept bribes.

กินหมาก kinmàag' V to chew betel.

กินแหนง kinnɛ̌ɛŋ' V to be mistrustful, suspicious (of).

กินอยู่ kinjùu' V to room and board (with).

o ค่ากินอยู่ khâakinjùu' N living expenses, esp. room and board.

o ให้กินอยู่ hâjkinjùu' to provide room and board.

กินอาหาร kin'ʔaahǎan' V com. to eat. Used of eating in general, including both snacks and regular meals. →Comp. กินข้าว. →Syn. รับประทานอาหาร eleg.

ของกิน (อย่าง) khɔ̌ɔŋkin' (jàaŋ') N foodstuff, edibles, things to eat. →Comp. ของใช้ "things to use."

ค่ากิน khâakin' food expenses; food (as an item of expense), the cost of food.

นั่งกินนอนกิน nâŋ'kin'-nɔɔn'kin' V to lead an easy life.

น่ากิน nâakin', nâa'kin' V to be tasty-looking.

น้ำกิน náamkin' N drinking water, water for drinking.

มีอันจะกิน mii?an'cakin' to be well-off, well-to-do.

สลากกินแบ่ง (ฉบับ,ใบ) salàag'kinbèŋ' (chabàb', baj') N eleg. lottery ticket. →Syn. ลอต เตอรี่, ตั๋วลอตเตอรี่ com., หวยเบอร์ colloq.

หวัดกิน wàd'kin' V colloq. to catch cold, have a cold.

หากิน hǎakin' 1. to make a living, earn a living. 2. to look for food.

o ทำมาหากิน thammaa'hǎakin' V to earn a living. การ-- making a living, earning a living; occupation, livelihood.

o ผู้หญิงหากิน (คน) phûujǐŋ'hǎakin' (khon') N prostitute, street-walker.

ให้(...)กิน hâj(...)kin' V to feed, provide with food.

อยู่กินด้วยกัน jùukin'dûajkan' to live together, cohabit (man and woman, husband and wife).

อยู่ง่ายกินง่าย jùuŋâaj'kinŋâaj' to be easy to

please (with regard to living and eating accommodations).

อยู่ดีกินดี jùudii'kindii' to live and eat well, have a fair standard of living.

กิริยา kìrijaa' N behavior, manners. →Comp. กริยา.

กิริยาไม่ดี kìrijaa'mâjdii' bad manners.

คำกิริยา (คำ) kham'kìrijaa' (kham') N gram. verb. →More commonly คำกริยา.

จริตกิริยา carìd'kìrijaa' N (personal) way, manner (esp. of w.).

ทำกิริยา tham'kìrijaa' 1. to act, perform an action, go through a motion. 2. chem. to react.

เสียกิริยา sǐa'kìrijaa' V to show bad manners, be unmannerly, impolite.

กิเลศ,กิเลส kìlèed' N lust, unbridled desires.

กิโล kiloo' C kilo (i.e. kilogram, kilometer).

กิโลกรัม kilookram' C kilogram. [f. Eur.]

กิโลเมตร kilooméd' C kilometer. [f. Eur.]

กิโลลิตร kiloolíd' C kiloliter. [f. Eur.]

กิ่ว kìw' V to be constricted, narrow.

ท้องกิ่ว thɔ́ɔŋ'kìw' slang to have an empty stomach, be very hungry.

กิฬา kilaa'. Variant form of กีฬา.

กี่ ๑ (หลัง) kìi' (lǎŋ') N loom.

กี่ ๒ kìi' Nm 1. how many. 2. how many? Must be followed by a clf. except in a few special expressions; 1st subentry.

กี่มากน้อย kìimâagnɔ́ɔj' colloq. how much, how many. ไม่-- not so much, not so many.

กี่โมง kìimooŋ' at what time.

o กี่โมงแล้วครับ kìimooŋ'lɛ́ɛwkhráb'↓ m. sp. What time is it?

กี่วัน kìiwan' how many days.

กี่หน kìihǒn' how many times.

ไม่กี่ mâjkìi⊃ not many.

o ต่อมาไม่กี่วัน tɔ̀ɔmaa'mâjkìiwan' not many days later.

o ไม่กี่มากน้อย mâjkìimâagnɔ́ɔj' colloq. not so much, not so many.

กี้ ๑ kíi' 1. just now. C 2. a previous occasion.

เมื่อกี้ mŷakíi' just now, just a moment ago.

เมื่อกี้นี้ mŷakíiníi' idem.

กี้ ๒ in เจ้ากี้เจ้าการ câwkíi'câwkaan' V to be a

busybody, a meddler; used esp. of one who takes on a responsibility, obligation or function of his own accord, at the same time involving others in the obligation without their knowledge or consent.

กี๊ kíi'. Variant form of กี้ ๑.

กีด klid' V to obstruct, interfere, hinder, object.

  กีดกัน klidkan' idem.

  กีดขวาง klidkhwǎaŋ' V to be in the way of, to bar (the way), obstruct. เครื่อง-- barrier.

กีบ (กีบ) klib' (klib') N hoof.

  กีบผ่า klibphàa' N cloven hoof.

กีฬา (อย่าง,ประเภท) kiilaa' (jàaŋ', praphêed') N (athletic) sport, sports. การ-- athletics, athletic sport(s). นัก-- athlete. →Also กิฬา. →Comp. กรีฑา.

  ดูกีฬา duu'kiilaa' to watch a game.

  เล่นกีฬา lên'kiilaa' V to play (athletic games).

  สนามกีฬา (แห่ง) sanǎamkiilaa' (hὲŋ') N 1. stadium. 2. playing field, sports field.

กึก ๑. See entries below.

  ชะงักกึก chaŋág'kỳg' V to stop suddenly, stop short.

  หยุดกึก jùdkỳg' idem.

กึก ๒ in กึกก้อง kỳgkɔ́ŋ'* V to echo, to resound; to be very loud, noisy.

กึ่ง kỳŋ' N half, middle.

  ก้ำกึ่ง (กัน) kâmkỳŋ' (kan') V 1. to be half (this) and half (that). 2. to be about the same (as each other). sV 3. about equally.

  กึ่งกลาง kỳŋklaaŋ' N 1. center, middle. 2. (as n. mod.) central, middle, center.

  กึ่งทรงกลม (ซีก) kỳŋ'soŋklom' (sîig') N eleg. hemisphere.

  กึ่งราชการ kỳŋ'râadchakaam' semi-official.

กุ kù?' V colloq. 1. to be groundless, false, fake. 2. to fake, make up.

กุ๊ก ๆ kúgkúg' imit. "cluck, cluck" (the clucking of a hen).

กุ้ง (ตัว) kûŋ' (tua') N crustacean, i.e. shrimp, prawn, lobster.

  กุ้งก้ามกราม kûŋkâamkraam' N a large variety of prawns.

  กุ้งฝอย kûŋfɔ̌j' N a small variety of shrimps.

กุญแจ (ลูก,ดอก,อัน) kuncɛɛ' N 1. lock, padlock (lûug', dɔ̀ɔg'). 2. key (dɔ̀ɔg'). 3. wrench (?an').

  กุญแจมือ (ข้าง,คู่) kuncɛɛmyy' (khâaŋ', khûu') N handcuffs.

  เขี่ยกุญแจ khìa'kuncɛɛ' to pick a lock (e.g. with a wire).

  ไขกุญแจ khǎj'kuncɛɛ' V to unlock (a lock), to turn the key (in order to unlock).

  แม่กุญแจ (ลูก,ดอก) mɛ̂ɛkuncɛɛ' (lûug', dɔ̀ɔg') N padlock, lock.

  ลั่นกุญแจ lânkuncɛɛ' V to lock.

  ลูกกุญแจ (ดอก) lûugkuncɛɛ' (dɔ̀ɔg') N key.

  ใส่กุญแจ sàjkuncɛɛ' V to lock.

กุฏฐัง kùdthǎŋ' N leprosy. โรค-- idem.

กุด kùd' V 1. to be shortened. 2. to be amputated.

กุดัง (หลัง,โรง) kudaŋ' (lǎŋ', rooŋ') N warehouse, godown. [f. Malay] →Also โกดัง.

  รถกุดัง (คัน) ród'kudaŋ' (khan') N (motor) truck.

กุน kun' (Year of the) Pig. →The complete list of the cyclical years is given under ปี.

กุน kún' V sew. to bind (with a binding). [f. Chin.]

กุม kum' V to seize, hold.

  กุมตัว kumtua' V to arrest, detain.

  จับกุม càbkum' V to arrest.

  รัดกุม rádkum' V 1. to fit well (of clothes). 2. to be airtight, i.e. without any loopholes (e.g. of rules).

กุมภ. Abbrev. for กุมภาพันธ์ February.

กุมภาพันธ์ kumphaa'phan' N February. เดือน-- idem. →The names of all the months are listed under เดือน.

กุมาร (องค์) kumaan' (?oŋ') N roy. boy.

กุเลา in ปลากุเลา (ตัว) plaakulaw' (tua') N a kind of salt water fish.

กุศล kusǒn', kusǒnlá⊃ N good deeds, merits. การ-- charity.

กุหลาบ kulàab' N rose. ดอก-- (ดอก) rose (the flower). ต้น-- (ต้น) rosebush.

กู kuu' P sp. to inf. I, me. Rude word, paired with มึง "you."

กู่ kùu' V to halloo, shout, call out (esp. when searching for someone).

  กู่หา kùu'hǎa' V to call out (in search of someone).

กู้ kûu' V 1. to redeem, salvage. 2. to borrow

(money at interest).

ก่อกู้ kɔɔ'kûu' V to restore, bring back, build up.

กอบกู้ kɔɔb'kûu' V to restore, redeem, save.

กู้ชาติ as in กระบวนการกู้ชาติ krabuankaan'-kûuchâad' liberation movement.

กู้หน้า kûu'nâa' V to save face.

ขอกู้ khɔɔkûu' V eleg. to borrow (at interest).

เงินกู้ ŋənkûu' N loan.

ให้(...)กู้ hâj(...)kûu' V to loan, lend (to some-one)(at interest).

กูล in เกื้อกูล kɣakuun' V eleg. to aid, support.

เก kee' V 1. to be twisted, distorted, slanted; to be disfigured, lame. 2. colloq. to play truant (from school or duty).

ขาเก khǎakee' V to have a twisted leg (as from paralysis).

เก๊ kée' V colloq. to be false, counterfeit. [f. Chin.] →Syn. เทียม, ปลอม com., ไม่แท้ lit.

เก๋ kěe' V to be chic, gay, smart-looking.

เกกมะเหรก kèegmarèeg' V to be knavish, roguish, wayward. →Cf. เกเร.

เกกมะเหรกเกเร kèegmarèeg'keeree' idem.

เก็ง keŋ' V to guess, conjecture, speculate.

เก่ง kèŋ'* V 1. to be expert (in doing something), be good at (doing something). sV 2. expertly.

o เขาเก่งทางการครัว kháwkèŋ'-thaaŋ'kaanɔ khrua'↓ She's good at cooking.

o เล่นเต็นนิสเก่ง lên'tennid'-kèŋ' V to play tennis well, expertly.

เก่งกาจ kèŋkàad' V to be bold, brave, fearless.

อวดเก่ง ʔùadkèŋ' V to act as though one is able to do something without trying; hence, to think oneself smart, to talk big, to brag.

เก้ง (ตัว) kêeŋ' (tua') N writ. com. barking deer. →Also อีเก้ง com.

เก๋ง (หลัง) kěŋ'*(lǎŋ') N 1. the hood or covering of a boat or car. 2. a building with a Chinese temple-style roof. [f. Chin.]

รถเก๋ง (คัน) ródkěŋ' (khan') N sedan (car).

เก็งกอย in เขย่งเก็งกอยก้าวกระโดด khajèŋkeŋɔ kɔɔjkâaw'kradòod' N hop-step-and-jump, an athletic sport.

เก้งก้าง kêeŋ'kâaŋ' V to be gangly, gangling, awk-ward, clumsy.

เกณฑ์ ๑ keen' N 1. standard. 2. fixed point or line. 3. limit.

หลักเกณฑ์ làgkeen' N rule, principle.

อยู่ในเกณฑ์ jùunajkeen' 1. to be within the limits of, in the area of. 2. to be in a state of.

เกณฑ์ ๒ keen' V 1. to force, compel. 2. to draft, conscript; to levy (troops).

เกณฑ์จ้าง keen'câaŋ' V to conscript for labor (with pay).

ถูกเกณฑ์ทหาร thùugkeen'thahǎan' V to be drafted.

หมายเกณฑ์ (ใบ,ฉบับ) mǎajkeen' (baj', chabàb') N conscription notice.

เกด in ลูกเกด (เม็ด) lûugkèed' (méd') N colloq. raisin.

เก็บ kèb' V 1. to pick up, collect, gather. 2. to keep, to store; to confine. 3. slang to get rid of, to silence.

เก็บเกี่ยว kèbklaw' V to harvest.

o ฤดูเก็บเกี่ยว rýduu'kèbklaw N harvest, har-vesttime.

เก็บงำ kèbŋam' V to hide, conceal (something).

เก็บเงิน kèbŋən' to collect money. คน-- cashier, bill collector.

เก็บ(...)เงียบ kèb(...)ŋîab' to keep (something) in secret.

เก็บได้ kèbdâaj' V to pick up (something lost or discarded by others).

เก็บตัว kèbtua' V 1. to confine, place (someone) in confinement. 2. slang to get rid of, do away with (someone). 3. to be shut in, withdrawn (in personality).

เก็บภาษี kèb'phaasǐi' to collect a tax or duty. การ-- taxation, taxing, the collection of taxes or duties. คน-- tax collector.

เก็บเล็กผสมน้อย kèb'lég'-phasǒm'nɔɔj' elab. colloq. to save up little by little.

เก็บ(...)ไว้ kèb(...)wáj' V to put up, store up, put away, keep (something).

เก็บสำรับ kèb'sǎmráb' V to clear (the table); to put up the (food) tray.

เก็บหอมรอมริบ kèbhɔɔm'rɔɔmríb' V colloq. to save up.

เกี่ยวเก็บ klawkèb' V to harvest.

คนเก็บเงิน (คน) khon/kèbŋən/ (khon/) N 1.
cashier. 2. bill collector.

คนเก็บตั๋ว (คน) khon/kèbtŭa/ (khon/) N ticket
collector.

นำเก็บ nam/kèb/ V to put into storage.

เมียเก็บ (คน) miakèb/ (khon/) N mistress;
illicit wife; secret minor wife or concubine.
→Syn. เมียลับ.

โรงเก็บ rooŋkèb/ N storehouse.

โรงเก็บรถ (โรง) rooŋ/kèbród/ (rooŋ/) N
garage.

ฤดูเก็บ rýduu/kèb/ N harvest, harvesttime.

หมากเก็บ màagkèb/ N jackstones.

ห้องเก็บของ (ห้อง) hɔ̂ŋ/kèbkhɔ̌ŋ/ (hɔ̂ŋ/) N
storeroom.

เกม (อย่าง) keem/ (jàaŋ/) N game. [f. Eng.]

เกย, --แหง kəəj/, kəəjhɛ̀ɛŋ/ V to run aground.

เกรง kreeŋ/ V to be in awe of, to fear.

กริ่งเกรง krìŋkreeŋ/ V to suspect, be afraid
(that).

เกรงขาม kreeŋkhǎam/ V to be in awe of, to
fear, to revere.

เกรงใจ kreeŋcaj/ V to have consideration for;
to be reluctant to impose (upon).

ยำเกรง jamkreeŋ/ V to respect, be in awe of.

หวั่นเกรง wànkreeŋ/ V to be afraid of, apprehensive of.

หวาดเกรง wàadkreeŋ/ V to be afraid, to fear.

เกร็ง kreŋ/ V 1. to stiffen, harden. 2. to be rigid.

เกร็ด krèd/ N 1. embellishments, frills (added to
a story). 2. fragments, bits, minor matters.

เกราะ (ชุด) krɔ̀ʔ/ (chúd/) N 1. armor. 2. suit
of armor.

รถเกราะ (คัน) ródkrɔ̀ʔ/ (khan/) N milit. 1.
tank. 2. armored car.

เกริ่น krə̀n/* V to inform in advance, to forewarn.

เกรียงไกร kriaŋkraj/ V to be powerful, superior.
ความ-- power, supremacy.

เกรียน krian/ V to be (very) short (esp. of hair).

เกรียม ๑ kriam/ V to be parched, scorched, sun-
burnt, singed.

เหี้ยมเกรียม hîamkriam/ V to be unmerciful,
unrelenting.

เกรียม ๒ kriam/. Variant of เตรียม.

เกรียวกราว kriawkraaw/ V to be noisy, make a
din, make a commotion, a tumult.

เกรี้ยวกราด krîawkràad/ V 1. to be furious. 2. to
scold angrily; to treat unsparingly.

เกเร keeree/ V to be knavish, roguish, wayward.
→See เกกมะเหรก.

เกล็ด (เกล็ด,อัน) klèd/ (klèd/,ʔan/) N 1. scale
(as of fish); flake. 2. sew. tuck, dart. V 3.
to crack (grain, as a bird).

ขอดเกล็ด khɔ̀od/klèd/ to scale (a fish).

จีบเกล็ด cìb/klèd/ V sew. to make darts.

ตีเกล็ด tii/klèd/ sew. to make a tuck, to tuck.

เป็นเกล็ด penklèd/ to be scaly.

เกลอ (คน) kləə/ (khon/) N colloq. pal, friend,
comrade. →Syn. เพื่อน com., มิตร eleg.

เกลอแก้ว kləəkɛ̂ɛw/ N (one's) best pal; good pal,
very intimate friend.

เพื่อนเกลอ (คน) phŷankləə/ (khon/) N close
friend, pal.

เกลา klaw/ V to smooth, trim, polish.

เกลี้ยงเกลา klîaŋklaw/ V to be smooth; to be
neat and clean, unblemished.

เกล้า klâaw/* N 1. roy. head. V 2. com. to roll
or tie up the hair in a bun. →Syn. 1. See หัว.

เกล้ากระผม klâawkraphŏm/ P elab. eleg. def.
m. sp. I, me. →Syn. See ผม com.

เกล้าผม klâawphŏm/ V to tie up the hair in a bun.

ทูนหัวทูนเกล้า thuun/hŭa/-thuun/klâaw/ V elab.
colloq. to adore, idolize.

ผู้บังเกิดเกล้า phûubaŋkə̀ɤd/klâaw/ N eleg.
parents. →Syn. พ่อแม่ com.

เกลี่ย klìa/ V to smooth off, level down.

ไกล่เกลี่ย klàjklìa/ V to settle matters; to mediate, arbitrate.

เกลี้ย in เกลี้ยกล่อม klîaklɔ̂m/ V to persuade, talk
someone into doing something.

เกลี้ยง klîaŋ/ V 1. to be smooth, clean. 2. colloq.
to be used up, exhausted, all gone, cleaned out.

o ข้าวเกลี้ยงจาน khâaw/klîaŋcaan/ The plate is
clean (because the rice has been eaten).

เกลี้ยงเกลา klîaŋklaw/ V 1. to be smooth. 2.
to be neat and clean, unblemished.

เกลียด klìad/ V to hate, detest.

เกลียดชัง klìadchaŋ/ V to hate, detest, despise

(hate strongly).

จงเกลียดจงชัง　coŋklìad/coŋchaŋ/　V　e l a b.
c o l l o q. to hate and hold a grudge against
(someone).

น่าเกลียด　nâaklìad/, nâa/klìad/　V　to be ugly,
unsightly.

เกลียว　kliaw/　V 1. to be twisted. N 2. twisted
string. 3. spiral thread (of a screw), helical
groove.

กลมเกลียว　klomkliaw/　V to be harmonious,
united; to get along well (together).

เกลียวสัมพันธ์　kliaw/sǎmphan/　N the bonds of a
relationship.

เป็นเกลียว　penkliaw/　1. in a coil-like form.
2. in a twisting, spiraling fashion.

o ตัวเป็นเกลียว　tua/penkliaw/　i d i o m. very
hard, busily (of working).

ลงเกลียวกัน　loŋkliaw/kan/ V　i d i o m. to get along
together.

เกลือ　klya/　N 1. common salt. 2. a chemical salt.

กรดเกลือ　kròd/klya/　N hydrochloric acid.

เกลือกรด　klyakròd/　N acid salt.

เกลือจืด　klyacỳyd/　N gypsum.

เกลือด่าง　klyadàaŋ/　N basic salt.

ดีเกลือ　diiklya/　N Epsom salt.

เกลือก　klỳag/　V 1. to roll, be rolling (in something). 2. to wallow.

เกลื่อน　klỳan/　V 1. to be abundant, luxuriant. 2. to
be found all over the place, scattered all over.

กลบเกลื่อน　klòbklỳan/　V to cover up (a blunder).

เกลื่อนกลาด　klỳanklàad/　V to be scattered all
over, dispersed.

เกลื่อนไปหมด　klỳan/pajmòd/　to be scattered all
over in large numbers.

เกลื้อน　klỳan/　N chloasma, a skin disease characterized by yellowish-brown spots. โรค-- i d e m.

เกวียน　(เล่ม)　kwian/ (lêm/)　N 1. cart, wagon.
C 2. a unit of capacity, equiv. to 2000 liters.

เกษตร　kasèed/, kasèed/traʒ　N land, cultivated
land. Chiefly in compounds.　การ-- agriculture, agricultural work.

เกษตรกร　(คน)　kasèed/trakɔɔn/ (khon/)　N
agriculturist, farmer.

เกษตรกรรม　kasèed/trakam/, kasèed/kam/　N

agriculture (esp. as a field of study).

เกษตรศาสตร์　kasèed/sàad/　N agriculture (as a
science).

เกษตราธิการ　kasèed/traathíkaan/　N agricultural
supervision.

เกษม　kasěem/　V to be happy, delighted, cheerful.

เกษร　FS. See เกสร.

เกสร　(อัน)　keesɔ̌ɔn/ (ʔan/)　N　b o t. 1. general
term for stamen and pistil. 2. pollen. →Also
เกษร FS.

ละอองเกสร　(เม็ด)　laʔɔɔŋ/keesɔ̌ɔn/ (méd/)　N
b o t. pollen, pollen grain.

เก้อ　kə̂ə/　V to get disappointed, be hurt and embarrassed by having one's anticipations unfulfilled.

แก้เก้อ　kɛ̂ɛkə̂ə/　V to cover up one's embarrassment (by laughing or by changing the subject).

เกอหรี่, แกง--　kəərlì/, kɛɛŋkəərlì/　N Indian curry.
→Also กะหรี่ karlì/.

เกะกะ　kèʔkàʔ/　V to be obstructive, disorderly.

เกา　kaw/　V to scratch (oneself)(with one's fingers).

เก่า　kàw/　V 1. to be old (of non-living things). 2.
to be old, i.e. former (of both living and non-
living things). →D i s t. แก่ ๑, ชรา, เฒ่า.

กรุงเก่า　kruŋkàw/　pN common name of อยุธยา
Ayuthaya (the old capital).

เก่าเกินกาล　kàw/kəənkaan/　to be out-of-date,
antiquated.

เก่าแก่　kàwkɛ̀ɛ/　V to be old, of long standing.

ของเก่า　(อย่าง, ชิ้น)　khɔ̌ɔŋkàw/ (jàaŋ/, chín/)
N antique.

เพื่อนเก่า　(คน)　phỳankàw/ (khon/)　N an old
friend, former friend.

มือเก่า　(คน, มือ)　myykàw/ (khon/, myy/)　N
i d i o m. an old hand (at some activity). →A n t.
มือใหม่.

หัวเก่า　(คน)　hǔakàw/　V 1. to be conservative, traditional, old-fashioned. N 2. (a) conservative (khon/).

เก้า　(๙)　kâaw/*　Nm nine. →S y n. นพ l i t.

เก้าสิบ　(๙๐)　kâawsìb/　Nm ninety.

สิบเก้า　(๑๙)　sìbkâaw/　Nm nineteen.

เกาลัด　(เม็ด, ลูก)　kawlád/ (méd/, lûug/)　N chestnut.

เกาหลี　kawlǐi/　pN Korea.

เก้าอี้　(ตัว)　kâwʔîi/ (tua/)　N chair.

เก้าอี้นวม　(ตัว)　kâwʔîinuam/ (tua/)　N overstuffed

chair.

นั่งเก้าอี้ naŋ'kâw?îi/ V 1. to be seated, take a chair. 2. c o l l o q. to take a position in, have a seat in, take an office.

เกาะ ๑ (เกาะ) kɔ?/ (kɔ?/) N island.

เกาะชะวา kɔ?/chawaa/ pN Island of Java.

เกาะลังกา kɔ?/laŋkaa/ pN Island of Ceylon.

เกาะฮาวาย kɔ?/haawaaj/ pN Hawaiian Islands. [ฮาวาย f. Eng.]

หมู่เกาะ (หมู่, หมู่เกาะ) mùukɔ?/ (mùu/, mùukɔ?/) N a group of islands, archipelago.

เกาะ ๒ kɔ?/ V 1. to cling, perch. 2. to cling to.

เกิด kə̀əd/ V c o m. 1. to be born. 2. to arise, occur, happen, take place. 2. to originate, give rise to. คน-- births (persons born, cases of birth). ความ-- birth. →S y n. บังเกิด e l e g.

ก่อให้เกิด kɔ̀ɔ/hâjkə̀əd/ V to cause, give rise to.

เกิดขึ้น kə̀əd/khŷn/ V 1. to occur. 2. to start up, break out, develop.

เกิดความคิด kə̀əd/khwaamkhíd/ to get an idea.

เกิดประโยชน์ kə̀əd/prajòod/ to be advantageous, beneficial, useful; to be of benefit, do (some) good.

เกิดมา (1) kə̀əd/maa/; (2) kə̀əd/maac V 1. to be born, to have been born. 2. c o l l o q. to happen to (e.g. get sick).

เกิดมี kə̀əd/miic V 1. to happen that; there happened to be. 2. to arise, occur, exist. 3. to happen to have.

o อาจจะเกิดมีขึ้นได้ ?àadcakə̀əd/mii/-khŷndâaj/ may occur, might occur.

เกิดลูกหลาน kə̀əd/lûuglǎan/ to have descendants.

ตามมีตามเกิด taammii/taamkə̀əd/ according to one's means, as one can afford.

ทำให้เกิด thamhâjkə̀əd/ to cause, produce, give rise to.

บ่อเกิด (แห่ง) bɔ̀ɔkə̀əd/ (hɛ̀ŋ/) N source, origin, place of origin; birthplace (e.g. of a custom).

บ้านเกิด (แห่ง) bâankə̀əd/ (hɛ̀ŋ/) N birthplace.

ปีเกิด piikə̀əd/ N year of birth.

แรกเกิด rɛ̂ɛg/kə̀əd/ newborn.

วันเกิด (วัน) wankə̀əd/ (wan/) N birthday.

เกิน kəən/ V to exceed, be in excess of.

เก่าเกินกาล kàw/kəənkaan/ to be out-of-date,

antiquated.

เกินกว่า kəən/kwàac beyond, far more than; far too, far too much.

เกินคาด kəənkhâad/ beyond expectation.

เกินไป kəənpaj/ excessively, too.

o จนเกินไป conkəən/paj/ excessively, far too.

o มากเกินไป mâag/kəənpaj/ too much; much too (e.g. hot).

o ร้อนเกินไป rɔ́ɔn/kəənpaj/ (it) is too hot.

มากเกินควร mâag/kəənkhuan/ 1. more than is good, proper. 2. much too (e.g. big, etc.).

ไม่เกิน mâjkəən/ not to exceed, not more than, no more than.

ล่วงเกิน lûaŋkəən/ to trespass against, offend, show disrespect to (someone).

เหลือเกิน lǔakəən/, lýakəən/ very, extremely, exceedingly.

o ช่างเหลือเกิน châŋ/lýakəən/ V 1. to be extraordinary, terrific. 2. to be awful, terrible.

เกีย. See เกียร์.

เกียกกาย kìagkaaj/ N milit. commissary.

เกี่ยง kìaŋ/ V to argue over, disagree as to who will do it (put it up to the other person).

เกี่ยงราคา kìaŋ/raakhaa/ to argue over the price.

เกียจ. See entries below.

เกียจคร้าน kìadkhráan/ V e l e g. to be lazy.

ขี้เกียจ khîikìad/ V c o l l o q. to be lazy.

รังเกียจ raŋkìad/ V to dislike, to mind.

เกียร์ (เกียร์) kia/ (kia/) N gear. [f. Eng.] →Also written เกีย.

เข้าเกียร์ khâwkia/ to put in gear, engage the gears.

เปลี่ยนเกียร์ plìankia/ to shift gears.

เกียรติ kìad/, kìadtic N honor.

เกียรติยศ kìadtijód/ N honor, prestige.

เกียรติศักดิ์ kìadtisàg/ N prestige.

เป็นเกียรติ, เพื่อ-- penkìad/, phŷapenkìad/ as an honor; in honor (of).

ผู้มีเกียรติ (ท่าน) phûumiikìad/ (thân/) N honorable person (i.e. one with rank, distinction).

เสื่อมเกียรติ sỳamkìad/ V to be disgraced, degraded.

เกี่ยว ๑ kìaw/ V to hook, hitch.

เกี่ยวก้อย(กัน) kìawkɔ̂j/(kan) V to hook each other's little fingers (of lovers or intimate friends of the same sex, esp. w.).

o เดินเกี่ยวก้อย dəən'klawkɔ̂j V to walk with little fingers hooked. Cf. Eng. "walk arm in arm."

เกี่ยว ๒ klaw' V 1. to cut (as with a sickle). 2. to harvest, reap.

เก็บเกี่ยว kèbklaw' V to harvest.

o ฤดูเก็บเกี่ยว rýduu'kèbklaw' N harvest, harvesttime, harvesting season.

เกี่ยวเก็บ klawkèb' V to harvest.

เกี่ยว ๓ (กับ,ด้วย) klaw'(kaɔ, dûajɔ) V to concern, be related (to), concerned (with).

เกี่ยวข้อง(กับ) klawkhɔ̂ŋ'(kaɔ) V 1. to be related (to). 2. to have dealings (with), have to do (with).

เกี่ยวดอง klawdɔɔŋ' V to be related (of kindred).

เกี่ยวพัน klawphan' V to be related (to). การ-- relation, connection.

คาบเกี่ยว khâabklaw' V to overlap, be overlapping, extend over (into).

ไม่เกี่ยว mâjklaw' 1. not to be concerned, not to concern. 2. to be unrelated.

ยุ่งเกี่ยว(กับ) jûŋklaw'(kaɔ) V to associate with, get involved with.

เกี้ยว kîaw' V to court, woo, seduce.

เกี้ยวพาราสี kîawphaa'raasǐi' V elab. colloq. to court, woo; to make love to.

เกี๊ยว (ชาม,ตัว) kíaw' (chaam', tua') N wonton (Chinese ravioli). [f. Chin.]

เกียวโต kiawtoo' pN Kyoto. [f. Japan.]

เกี๊ยะ (ข้าง,คู่) kía?' N Chinese wooden slippers (khâaŋ' for one of a pair; khûu' for a pair). [f. Chin.]

เกื้อ kɣa' V eleg. to help.

เกื้อกูล kɣakuun' V eleg. to aid, support.

เกือก (ข้าง,คู่) kɣag' N com. shoes (khâaŋ' for one of a pair; khûu' for a pair). →Syn. รอง เท้า eleg.

เกือกม้า (อัน,ข้าง) kɣagmáa' (ʔan', khâaŋ') N horseshoe.

ยาขัดเกือก jaakhàdkɣag' N shoe polish.

เกือบ kɣab' qM 1. almost, nearly, about. AA 2. almost, nearly, on the verge of. →Syn. 1. ร่วม. 2. จวน, แทบ, ปาง ๒.

o เกือบทุกคน kɣab'thúgkhon' almost every person.

o เขาก็เกือบไป kháwkɔ̀kɣab'paj↓ He almost (e.g. got hit) too.

เกือบจะ kɣabcaɔ AA almost, nearly, on the verge of.

เกือบ(จะ)ไม่ kɣab(ca)mâjɔ AA hardly, scarcely.

o เกือบจะไม่ไปแล้วซี kɣabcamâjpaj'lɛ́ɛwsii↓ (I) almost didn't go.

o ดูเกือบจะไม่ออก duukɣab'camâjʔɔ̀ɔg' (one) can hardly make (it) out, can hardly distinguish (them); (it) can hardly be made out.

แก kɛɛ' P com. 1. he, him, she, her, they, them. 2. you (m. sp. to int. m., or w. sp. to int. w.; otherwise derogatory except among persons of low social status). Paired with กัน ๒, ฉัน "I, me."

พี่แก phîikɛɛ' colloq. he, that fellow; she, that lady.

แก ๑ kɛɛ' V 1. to be old, aged (of living things, e.g. people, animals, plants). 2. to be ripe, mature (of fruit). 3. to be dark (of colors). 4. to be strong, concentrated (of coffee, tea, and other liquids). 5. to be an old hand at, be accustomed to. คน-- old person. →Dist. 1. เก่า. →Syn. 1. ชรา, เฒ่า.

กรดแก่ kròdkɛɛ' N chem. concentrated acid.

เก่าแก่ kàwkɛɛ' V to be old, of long standing.

แก่งอม kɛɛ'ŋɔɔm' V to be overripe.

แก่ตัว kɛɛtua' V to age.

แก่หง่อม kɛɛŋɔ̀m' V to be very old (of people).

คนเฒ่าคนแก่ khonthâw'khonkɛɛ' N elab. colloq. old people, elderly people, the aged.

ครรภ์แก่ khan'kɛɛ' V eleg. 1. to be at full pregnancy. N 2. full pregnancy. →Syn. ท้องแก่ com.

เฒ่าแก่ (คน) thâwkɛɛ' (khon') N 1. a go-between who arranges a marriage. 2. an aged, wealthy Chinese man.

เต็มแก่ temkɛɛ' in the highest degree, extremely, exceedingly.

o หิวข้าวเต็มแก่ hǐwkhâaw'temkɛɛ' to be exceedingly hungry.

สาวแก่ (คน) sǎawkɛɛ' (khon') N spinster, old maid.

หญิงแก่ (คน) jǐŋkɛɛ' (khon') N eleg. old woman.

→Syn. ยายแก com.

แก้ ๒ kɛ̂ɛ´ AA too much.

o แก้พูด kɛ̂ɛ´phûud´ to talk too much.

แก่ ๓ kɛ̀ɛɔ, kɛ̀ɔ, kaɔ to (with indirect object), for.
NOTE. (1) The pronunciation kaɔ is often reflected in the orthography; see กะ ๔. (2)
Subentries in which variant pronunciations of
แก่ are indicated give the usual pronunciation
first.

ได้แก่ dâajkɛ̀ɛɔ, -kaɔ 1. to consist of, include, be
(followed by one item or a list of items). 2. such
as, namely, consisting of. 3. (a prize) to go to
(someone). →See cross ref. →Comp. 1, 2. คือ.

ถึงแก่กรรม thŷŋ´kɛ̀ɛkam´ eleg. to pass away,
die. →Syn. ตาย com.

แน่นแก่ใจ nɛ̂ɛ´kɛ̀caj´ to be confident.

เป็นไทยแก่ตัว penthaj´kɛ̀tua´ to be independent.

เป็นอิสระแก่กัน penʔìdsarà?´kɛ̀ɛkan´ to be independent of one another.

มีแก่ใจ mii´kacaj´, -kɛ̀ɛ- 1. to have the will,
the spirit (to do something). 2. to be kind
enough to, considerate enough to. 3. to be
thoughtful, considerate of others. ความ--
will, spirit; considerateness, thoughtfulness.

รู้แก่ใจ rúu´kacaj´, -kɛ̀ɛ- to know full well, to
be fully aware.

ละอายแก่ใจ lá?aaj´kacaj´, -kɛ̀ɛ- to be ashamed.

สาแก่ใจ sǎa´kacaj´, -kɛ̀ɛ- to feel satisfied, to do
something to one's heart's content (esp. when
getting the better of somebody, when giving him
what he deserves).

เห็นแก่ hěn´kɛ̀ɔ to look out for, think (only) of.

o เพื่อเห็นแก่ phɣ̂ahěn´kɛ̀ɔ for the sake of.

o มิเห็นแก่ míhěn´kɛ̀ɔ without thinking of, without regard to, without regard for.

o เห็นแก่ได้ hěn´kɛ̀dâaj´ to be acquisitive, covetous. →Syn. โลภ.

o เห็นแก่ตัว hěn´kɛ̀tua´ to think only of oneself,
be selfish.

o เห็นแก่หน้า hěn´kɛ̀nâa´ to be partial, prejudiced.

เหมาะแก่ mɔ̀?´kɛ̀ɔ, -kaɔ to be suited to.

ให้แก่ hâjkɛ̀ɔ, -kaɔ to, for.

ให้(. . .)แก่ hâj(. . .)kɛ̀ɔ, -kaɔ to give (some-

thing) to (someone).

อายแก่ใจ ʔaaj´kacaj´, -kɛ̀ɛ- to be ashamed.

แก้ kɛ̂ɛ´ V 1. to untie, undo, unwrap. 2. to undo,
take off (clothes). 3. to undo (an error), correct,
revise, alter. 4. to mend, repair. 5. to solve.
6. to remedy, relieve (an illness). 7. to explain
away, make an excuse. เครื่อง-- remedy, cure.

แก้กลุ้ม kɛ̂ɛklûm´ V to ease one's mind, overcome
or relieve one's anxiety.

แก้เก้อ kɛ̂ɛkə̂ə´ V to cover up one's embarrassment (by laughing or by changing the subject).

แก้ขัด kɛ̂ɛkhàd´ V 1. to serve the purpose temporarily (as a means of relief), to tide one over.
2. to relieve one's soreness (as by massage).

แก้ไข kɛ̂ɛkhǎj´ V to correct, emend, amend, improve, revise, resolve (a bad situation).

แก้แค้น kɛ̂ɛkhɛ́ɛn´ V to take revenge.

แก้(. . .)ตก kɛ̂ɛ´(. . .)tòg´ 1. to be able to solve,
to solve successfully. 2. to be solvable.

o แก้ไม่ตก kɛ̂ɛ´mâjtòg´ can't solve (it), can't
figure (it) out; can't be solved, is unsolvable.

แก้ตัว kɛ̂ɛtua´ V 1. to make up for one's losses
or errors. 2. to find an excuse, make false
excuses.

o เรียนแก้ตัว rian´kɛ̂ɛtua´ to repeat a class or
course (because of previous failure).

แก้ปัญหา kɛ̂ɛ´panhǎa´ V to solve a problem, solve
a riddle.

แก้ผ้า kɛ̂ɛphâa´ V 1. to undress, disrobe, strip.
2. to be naked.

แก้เผ็ด kɛ̂ɛphèd´ V to get back at (someone).

แก้ฝัน kɛ̂ɛfǎn´ V to interpret a dream.

แก้มือ kɛ̂ɛ´myy´ V to ask for a return match, a
chance to make up for one's loss.

แก้ลำ kɛ̂ɛ´lam´ V to retaliate.

แก้หน้า kɛ̂ɛ´nâa´ V to save face.

แก้(. . .)หาย kɛ̂ɛ´(. . .)hǎaj´ 1. to cure. 2. to
correct, reform. 3. to be curable.

o แก้ไม่หาย kɛ̂ɛ´mâjhǎaj´ to be incurable, incorrigible; incorrigibly.

ขูดแก้ khùud´kɛ̂ɛ´ V to scrape off (the error),
make a correction by scraping.

ทางแก้ (ทาง) thaaŋkɛ̂ɛ´ (thaaŋ´) N solution;
remedy.

ยาแก้บิด (ขนาน) jaakɛ̂ɛbìd/ (khanǎan/) N medicine for dysentery.

แกง kɛɛŋ/ N curry, curried food. เครื่อง-- the spices and seasoning used in making curries.

แกงกะหรี่,แกงเกอหรี่ kɛɛŋkarìi/, kɛɛŋkəərìi/ N Indian curry.

แกงไก่ kɛɛŋkàj/ N chicken curry.

แกงจืด kɛɛŋcỳyd/ N mildly seasoned soup.

แกงเผ็ด kɛɛŋphèd/ N hot curry.

แกงส้ม kɛɛŋsôm/ N a sour soup made with tamarind paste.

ข้าวแกง khâawkɛɛŋ/ N rice and curry eaten as a complete meal.

แก่ง ๑ (แก่ง,แห่ง) kɛ̀ŋ/*(kɛ̀ŋ/,hɛ̀ŋ/) N rapids.

แก่ง ๒ in แก่งแย่ง kɛ̀ŋjɛ̂ɛŋ/* V to engage in rivalry, vie (with); to be at odds (with), at loggerheads (with).

แกโซลีน,น้ำมัน-- kɛɛsooliin/, námman/kɛɛsooliin/ N gasoline. [f. Eng.] →Also แก๊สโซลีน kɛ́dɔsooliin/.

แกน ๑ (แกน) kɛɛn/ (kɛɛn/) N axis.

ฝ่ายแกน fàajkɛɛn/ N the Axis, the Axis side.

แกน ๒ in แกน ๆ kɛɛnkɛɛn/ unwillingly, halfheartedly.

แก่น kɛ̀n/* N 1. core, center, nucleus. 2. heart of a tree.

แก่นสาร kɛ̀nsǎan/ N essence, essentials, substance.

o เป็นแก่นสาร penkɛ̀n/sǎan/ V 1. to be essential, substantial, solid. 2. to make sense.

ไม้แก่น májkɛ̀n/ N 1. a hardwood tree. 2. hardwood.

แกบ. Variant spelling of แก๊ป ๑,๒.

แก๊ป ๑, หมวก-- (ใบ) kɛ́b/, mùagkɛ́b/*(baj/) N cap (for the head). [f. Eng.]

แก๊ป ๒ (อัน) kɛ́b/*(ʔan/) N percussion cap. [f. Eng.]

แกม kɛɛm/ V to be mixed with, mingled with.

แก้ม (แก้ม,ข้าง) kɛ̂ɛm/ (kɛ̂ɛm/,khâaŋ/) N com. cheek. →Syn. ปราง lit., eleg.

แกร่ง krɛ̀ŋ/* V to be strong, solid.

แกร็น krɛn/ V to be stunted, dwarfed.

แกรบ. See กรอบแกรบ under กรอบ ๒.

แกร่ว krɛ̀w/* V to pass the time idly, hang around

(implying an element of impatience or ennui).

แกล้ง klɛ̂ɛŋ/ V 1. to make a show (of doing something), make a pretense. 2. to do on purpose. 3. to tease, annoy.

แกลบ (อัน,ชิ้น) klɛ̀b/ (ʔan/, chín/) N husk of rice, chaff.

แกล้ม ๑ klɛ̂ɛm/ N snacks, appetizers taken with or between drinks.

แกล้ม ๒. See กล่อมแกล้ม.

แกลลอน kɛɛlɔɔn/ N gallon. [f. Eng.]

แกล้ว in แกล้วกล้า klɛ̂ɛwklâa/ V to be brave, bold, courageous.

แกว in รู้แกว rúukɛɛw/ to have an inkling, a notion.

แก้ว kɛ̂ɛw/ N 1. crystal; glass. 2. a precious, indispensable organ or component. 3. the best of its kind. เครื่อง-- glassware.

กระดาษแก้ว (แผ่น) kradàadkɛ̂ɛw/ (phɛ̀n/) N transparent paper.

เกลอแก้ว kləə/kɛ̂ɛw/ N colloq. (one's) best pal; good pal, very intimate friend.

แก้วตา kɛ̂ɛwtaa/ N 1. anat. crystalline lens of the eye. 2. idiom. the beloved, precious one, the apple of one's eye.

o แก้วตาดำ kɛ̂ɛwtaadam/ N iris (of the eye).

แก้วน้ำ (ใบ) kɛ̂ɛwnáam/ (baj/) N water glass, tumbler.

แก้วหู kɛ̂ɛwhǔu/ N eardrum.

แก้วเหล้า (ใบ) kɛ̂ɛwlâw/ (baj/) N glass for liquor (e.g. cocktail glass, liqueur glass, etc.).

ตัวแก้ว (ตัว) tuakɛ̂ɛw/ (tua/) N (non-hairy) caterpillar, larva of butterfly or moth. →Dist. บุ้ง.

ถ้วยแก้ว (ใบ) thûajkɛ̂ɛw/ (baj/) N glass (for drinking), tumbler.

นกแก้ว (ตัว) nógkɛ̂ɛw/ (tua/) N parrot.

ร้อยแก้ว rɔ́ɔjkɛ̂ɛw/ N prose.

รากแก้ว (ราก) râagkɛ̂ɛw/ (râag/) N taproot.

หมอบราบคาบแก้ว mɔ̀ɔbrâab/khâabkɛ̂ɛw/ elab. colloq. to give in, surrender, yield completely.

เอาแก้ว as in ถามเอาแก้วอะไร thǎam/-ʔawɔkɛ̂ɛw/ʔaraj/↓ idiom. Why in the world (do you, should I, etc.) ask?

แกว่ง kwɛ̀ŋ/* V to swing.

กวัดแกว่ง kwàdkwɛ̀ŋ/ V 1. to swing, brandish. 2. to oscillate, swing.

แกส, แก๊ส kɛ́ɛd′, kɛ́ɛs′ N gas, i.e. gaseous substance. [f. Eng.] →Also กาซ. →Dist. ก๊าส.

แก๊สโซลีน kɛ́dsooliin′ N gasoline. →Also แกโซลีน.

แกะ ๑ (ตัว) kɛ̀ʔ′ (tua′) N sheep.

ขนแกะ khŏnkɛ̀ʔ′ N wool, lamb's wool.

เด็กเลี้ยงแกะ (คน) dèg′líaŋkɛ̀ʔ′ (khon′) N 1. shepherd boy. 2. one who cries wolf.

ลูกแกะ (ตัว) lûugkɛ̀ʔ′ (tua′) N lamb.

แกะ ๒ kɛ̀ʔ′ V 1. to carve, carve out, etch. 2. to be carved. 3. to pick out, remove (tiny objects with the tip of the finger).

แกะสลัก kɛ̀ʔ′salàg′ V to carve.

ช่างแกะ (คน) châaŋkɛ̀ʔ′ (khon′) N sculptor, carver.

โก้ kôo′ V colloq. to be grand, elegant, beautiful, smart, all dressed up.

โก้ ๆ kôokôo′ sV grandly, elegantly, smartly, in a chic manner.

เล่นโก้ ๆ lên′kôokôo′ for fun, for the fun of it.

โกโก้ kookôo′ N cocoa, chocolate. [f. Eng.]

โกง kooŋ′ V 1. to be bent, crooked. 2. to cheat, chisel, deceive, take unfair advantage of others; to defraud, swindle. 3. to try to get out of a commitment, avoid one's duties or obligations. ผู้-- a cheat, a swindler. →Syn. 1, 2. คด. →Comp. 2. ฉ้อ.

ฉ้อโกง chɔ́ɔkooŋ′ V to cheat, defraud, swindle.

หลังโกง lǎŋkooŋ′ V 1. to have a crooked back (as from a deformity). 2. to be round-shouldered, stooped over; to have one's shoulders slouched over.

โก่ง kòoŋ′ V 1. to bend upward, to arch. 2. to arch (the neck).

โก่งราคา kòoŋ′raakhaa′ to raise the price; to maintain a high price.

โก่งศร kòoŋ′sɔ̌ɔn′ to draw a bow.

ทำหลังโก่ง thamlǎŋ′kòoŋ′ to arch the back (as a cat).

โกฏิ kòod′ Nm, C ten million. →Also สิบล้าน.

โกดัง (หลัง, โรง) koodaŋ′ (lǎŋ′, rooŋ′) N warehouse, godown. [f. Malay.] →Also กุดัง.

รถโกดัง (คัน) ród′koodaŋ′ (khan′) N (motor) truck.

โกน koon′ V to shave (beard, hair).

โกนหนวด koonnùad′ V to shave (literally, shave the beard).

มีดโกน (เล่ม) mîidkoon′ (lêm′) N razor.

o ใบมีดโกน baj′mîidkoon′ (baj′) N razor blade.

โกเบ koobee′ pN Kobe. [f. Japan.]

โกย kooj′ V 1. to scoop together. 2. to scamper, run quickly.

กอบโกย kɔ̀ɔbkooj′ V to gather in, scoop together (in large amounts).

โกรก kròog′ V 1. to blow gently (of the wind). 2. to be breezy, windy; to be open, airy, exposed to the breeze.

โกร่ง (ใบ) kròoŋ′ (baj′) N apothecary's mortar.

โกรธ kròod′ V com. to be angry. ความ-- (see below). →Syn. กริ้ว roy., ฉุน, โมโห com.

โกรธขึ้ง kròod′khʉ̂ŋ′ V to be angry.

โกรธจิด ๆ kròod′-taŋìd′taŋìd′ somewhat angered, a little angry.

ความโกรธ khwaamkròod′ N anger. →Syn. โทสะ eleg., โมโห, ความโมโห com.

โกร๋น krɔ̌ɔn′ V to be sparse, thin (of hair on the head).

โกโรโกโส kooroo′koosǒo′ V to be dilapidated.

โกลก in แม่น้ำโกลก mɛ̂ɛnáamkoológ′ pN the Kolok River.

โกลาหล koolaahǒn′ N 1. disturbance, tumult, confusion, melee. V 2. to be tumultuous, turbulent. ความ-- tumult, turbulence.

โกศ (โกศ, ลูก, ใบ) kòod′ (kòod′, lûug′, baj′) N urn.

โกหก koohòg′ V com. to tell a lie. →Syn. ปด, กล่าวเท็จ, พูดเท็จ eleg., พูดไม่จริง com.

โกหกพกลม koohòg′phóglom′ V elab. colloq. to tell a lie.

ขี้โกหก khîikoohòg′ V com. to be given to lying, prevarication. →Syn. ขี้ปด eleg.

ใกล้ klâj′ V 1. to be near, close, nearby. 2. to be close to. →Ant. ไกล.

ใกล้ ๆ klâjklâj′ quite close, near.

ใกล้(...)เข้า klâj′(...)khâw to approach, to near, come near.

ใกล้เคียง klâjkhiaŋ′ V to be close, near, nearby, neighboring.

o ใกล้เคียงกับ klâjkhiaŋ′kac to be close to; to be nearly as much as.

o เพื่อนบ้านใกล้เคียง phɯ̂anbâan'klâjkhiaŋ' N neighbor.

ใกล้แค่ klâj'khɛ̂ɛ' 1. to be as near as. 2. to be near (such and such).

ใกล้ชิด klâjchíd' V to be near, close, intimate.

ใกล้หูใกล้ตา klâjhǔu'klâjtaa' elab. colloq. nearby, close to home, right under someone's nose, close to (and therefore subject to) the observation or supervision of (someone). →Opp. ไกลหูไกลตา.

เข้าใกล้ khâwklâj' V to come near, get close.

เดี๋ยวใกล้เดี๋ยวไกล dǐawklâj'dǐawklaj' now nearby, now far away.

ระยะใกล้ rajá?'klâj' short distance; short range.

ไก (ไก) kaj' (kaj') N trigger.

กลไก konkaj' (chín', ?an') N mechanism.

ไกปืน (ไก) kajpyyn' (kaj') N trigger (of a gun).

ลั่นไก lân'kaj' V 1. to pull the trigger. 2. (a gun) to go off.

ลับไก sàb'kaj' V to pull the trigger.

ไก่ (ตัว) kàj' (tua') N 1. chicken. 2. class term for fowl.

แกงไก่ kɛɛŋkàj' N chicken curry.

ไก่เขี่ย kàj'khìa' (a) chicken (is) scratching (the ground). This expression is frequently used with reference to poor handwriting, as in the example below.

o ลายมือยังกะไก่เขี่ย laajmyy'jaŋka?kàjkhìa' the handwriting is sloppy.

ไก่งวง kàjŋuaŋ' N turkey.

ไก่แจ้ kàjcɛ̂ɛ' N bantam chicken.

ไก่ชน kàjchon' N fighting cock.

ไก่บ้าน kàjbâan' N domestic fowl.

ไก่ป่า kàjpàa' N wild fowl.

ไก่ฟ้า kàjfáa' N pheasant.

ไก่สาว kàjsǎaw' N pullet.

ไก่อ่อน (คน) kàj?ɔ̀ɔn' (khon') N colloq. a naive, inexperienced person, a greenhorn.

ชนไก่ (หน, ครั้ง) chonkàj' (hǒn', khráŋ') N 1. cockfight. V 2. to have a cockfight.

เดือยไก่ (อัน) dyajkàj' (?an') N spur of a cock.

แต่ไก่โห่ tɛkàjhòo' colloq. at cockcrow, at early dawn; so early.

เป็ดไก่ (ตัว) pèd'kàj' (tua') N barnyard fowl.

o หมูเห็ดเป็ดไก่ mǔuhèd'pèdkàj' N colloq. meats of various kinds.

แม่ไก่ (ตัว) mɛ̂ɛkàj' (tua') N hen.

ลิ้นไก่ línkàj' N uvula.

ลูกไก่ (ตัว) lûugkàj' (tua') N chick, baby chicken.

เล้าไก่ láwkàj' N chicken coop.

ไก๊ in ทำไก๊ thamkàj' V to feign ignorance or innocence; to play dumb.

ไกร in เกรียงไกร kriaŋkraj' V to be powerful, superior.

ไกล klaj' V to be far, distant. →Ant. ใกล้.

กระโดดไกล kradòod'klaj' N broad jump.

ไกลเชียวอยู่ klaj'khǒo'juu↓ It's quite far.

ไกลตาไกลใจ klaj'taa'-klaj'caj' "out of sight, out of mind."

ไกลลิบลับ klaj'líbláb' V to be very far, distant.

ไกลหูไกลตา klajhǔu'klajtaa' elab. colloq. distant, far off, far from (the supervision or observation of someone). →Opp. ใกล้หูใกล้ตา.

เดี๋ยวใกล้เดี๋ยวไกล dǐawklâj'dǐawklaj' now nearby, now far away.

ตะวันออกไกล tawan?ɔ̀ɔg'klaj' the Far East.

มองการณ์ไกล mɔɔŋkaanklaj' to be farsighted (have foresight), to foresee an incident or situation.

ระยะไกล rajá?'klaj' long distance; long range.

แสนไกล, ไกล-- sɛ̌ɛn'klaj', klaj'sɛ̌ɛnklaj' V to be very far away.

ห่างไกล hàaŋklaj' to be far, far away.

ไกล่ in ไกล่เกลี่ย klàjklìa' V to settle matters; to mediate, arbitrate. ผู้-- mediator, arbitrator.

o ข้อไกล่เกลี่ย (ข้อ) khɔ̂ɔ'klàjklìa' (khɔ̂ɔ') N point of mediation, point of arbitration.

ไกว kwaj' V to rock, swing, sway.

กวัดไกว kwàdkwaj' idem.

ข

ข khɔ̌ɔ' HIGH consonant. Pronounced kh initially, g finally.

ข- khaɔ. Frequent initial syllable, sometimes interchangeable with กระ- kraɔ and กะ- kaɔ, e.g. ขบวน, กระบวน, or กะบวน "procession, train."

ขจัด khacàd′ V w r i t. to get rid of, dispose of, do away with, put an end to, eliminate. →S y n. กำจัด c o m.

ขจี khacii′ V 1. to be lovely, soft. rM 2. intensifier used with เขียว "green."

ขณะ khanà?′ C time, the while, moment, instant.

  ขณะที่ khanà?′thîic while.

  o ขณะที่กำลัง...อยู่นั่น khanà?′-thîikamlaŋ... jùunán′ while (he) was (in the midst of) doing (such and such). (ขณะ is a clf. with intervening relative clause followed by นั่น).

  ขณะนั้น khanà?′nán′ at that time.

  ขณะนี้ khanà?′níi′ at this time, at present.

  ขณะเมื่อ khanà?′mŷa′ while, when, at the moment when.

  ชั่วขณะ chûakhanà?′ for a while, for a moment, temporarily.

ขด khòd′ V 1. to coil, roll into a coil. sV 2. curled up. C 3. coil, ring.

  ขดลวด (ขด) khòdlûad′ (khòd′) N 1. a coil of wire. 2. e l e c t. coil.

  นอนขด nɔɔn′khòd′ to lie curled up.

ขน ๑ (เส้น, ขน, อัน) khŏn′ N 1. fur, hair (except of the head) (sên′). 2. feathers; (hog) bristles; (porcupine) quills (khŏn′, ?an′). →D i s t. ผม ๑.

  ขนแกะ khŏnkɛ?′ N wool, lamb's wool.

  ขนไก่ khŏnkàj′ N chicken feathers.

  ขนคิ้ว khŏnkhíw′ N eyebrow hairs.

  ขนตา khŏntaa′ N eyelashes.

  ขนลุก khŏn′lúg′ V to have the hair standing on end (as when frightened).

  ขนอ่อน khŏn?ɔɔn′ N down (soft under feathers); fuzz (body hair).

  ขนอุย khŏn?uj′ N down (first soft feathering).

ขน ๒ khŏn′ V to carry (from one place to another), transfer.

  ขนลงจาก khŏn′loŋcàagc to unload from.

  ขนส่ง khŏnsòŋ′ V to transport. การ-- transporting, transportation.

  คนขนของ (คน) khonkhŏnkhɔɔŋ′ (khon′) N porter.

ขน khôn′ V to be thick, concentrated (of liquid).

ขนแค้น, ยากจน-- khônkhɛɛn′, jâagcon′khônkhɛɛn′ V to be poor, hard up, needy, impoverished.

เข้มขน khêmkhôn′ V to be concentrated, thick.

ทำให้ขน tham′hâjkhôn′ to thicken, condense (a liquid).

นมขน nomkhôn′ N condensed milk.

ขนด (ขนด) khanòd′ (khanòd′) N 1. coils (of a snake). 2. the base of a snake's tail.

  ขนดหาง khanòd′hăaŋ′ N the base of a snake's tail.

ขนบ khanòb′ N pattern, model. Chiefly in compounds.

  ขนบธรรมเนียม (อย่าง, แบบ) khanòb′thamniam′ (jàaŋ′, bɛ̀ɛb′) N custom, manners, tradition.

ขนม (อย่าง) khanŏm′ (jàaŋ′) N general term for sweet dainties, candied foods, puddings, pastries, etc. Chiefly in compounds.

  ขนมเข่ง (เข่ง, คู่) khanŏmkhèŋ′ (khèŋ′, khûu′) N Chinese pastry in the shape of a basket. Often sold in pairs, hence clf. คู่.

  ขนมจีน (จับ, หัว) khanŏmciin′ (càb′, hŭa′) N Thai vermicelli, which comes in bunches.

  ขนมปัง (แผ่น, ชิ้น, ปอนด์) khanŏmpaŋ′ N bread (phɛ̀n′ for a slice; chín′ for a piece; pɔɔn′ for a loaf). [paŋ: f. Port.]

  ขนมปังปิ้ง (แผ่น, ชิ้น) khanŏmpaŋpîŋ′ (phɛ̀n′, chín′) N toast, i.e. toasted bread.

  ขนมเปียกปูน (ชิ้น) khanŏmpîagpuun′ (chín′) N a stiff, dark gray pudding, cut in diamond-shaped pieces.

  ขนมหวาน (อย่าง) khanŏmwăan′ (jàaŋ′) N heavily sweetened or candied food, e.g. confections, sweetmeats.

ขนัด khanàd′ C 1. garden plot, orchard lot. 2. row, cluster (esp. of trees).

ขนาด (ขนาด) khanàad′ (khanàad′) N 1. size, dimension, magnitude; extent, degree; as...as. C 2. i d e m.

  ขนาดกลาง khanàad′klaaŋ′ (a) medium size; medium-sized, middle-sized.

  ขนาดเท่าคน khanàad′thâwkhon′ the size of a person.

  มีขนาดเท่า ๆ (กับ) miikhanàad′thâwthâw′(kac) to be of the same size as.

  เล็กขนาด lég′khanàad′ to be as small as.

If item is not found under ข-, see กะ-, กระ-.

หลายขนาด lǎajkhanàad′ (of) many sizes.

ขนาน ๑ khanǎan′ C 1. clf. for kinds of medicine.
2. amount.

ขนานใหญ่ khanǎan′jàj′ colloq. on a grand scale,
in a big way.

ขนาน ๒ (กัน, กับ) khanǎan′(kan′, kaɔ) V to be
parallel (to).

เส้นขนาน (เส้น, คู่) sên′khanǎan′ N 1. a parallel line (sên′ for individual lines; khûu′ for
pairs). 2. geog. a parallel of latitude.

ขนาน ๓ in ขนานนาม khanǎan′naam′ eleg. to
name, give a name; to call.

ขนาบ khanàab′. See กระหนาบ.

ขนุน (ลูก, ใบ, ผล) khanǔn′ (lûug′, baj′, phǒn′) N
jackfruit. ต้น-- (ต้น) jackfruit tree.

ขบ ๑ khòb′ V 1. to bite on, to crack with the teeth.
2. to decide (an issue). 3. to solve, crack (a
riddle).

ขบกราม khòb′kraam′ to grit one's teeth (as when
angry).

ขบคิด khòb′khíd′ V to crack, solve (a problem).

ขบไม่แตก khòb′mâjtɛ̀ɛg′ 1. can't solve (it); can't
be solved, unsolvable.

ขบ ๒ in ขบขัน khòbkhǎn′ V to be funny, humorous,
comical, amusing.

ขบถ khabòd′. See กบฏ.

ขบวน khabuan′ C clf. for processions, lines,
trains. →See กระบวน.

ขม khǒm′ V to be bitter (in taste).

ขมขื่น khǒmkhỳyn′ 1. to feel bitter, embittered.
2. to be bitter (in taste). 3. to be hard to bear,
bitter. ความ-- bitterness.

ขื่นขม khỳyn′khǒm′ V to be bitter.

ข่ม khòm′ V 1. to press, press down. 2. to oppress, suppress.

ข่มขวัญ khòmkhwǎn′ V to terrorize, threaten,
attempt to coerce by fear.

ข่มขี่ khòmkhìi′ V to oppress, tyrannize.

ข่มขืน khòmkhỳyn′ V 1. to rape. 2. to coerce.

ข่มขู่ khòmkhùu′ V to threaten, intimidate.

ข่มหมู่ khòmmùu′ V slang to browbeat a weaker
or inferior person, to bully.

ข่มเหง khòmhěeŋ′ V to bully, browbeat, abuse,
mistreat, persecute.

ขมวด khamùad′ V 1. to twist and tie (sewing-thread,
the hair, etc.). C 2. a twist (of hair or anything
twisted in this fashion).

ขมวดคิ้ว khamùad′khíw′ to knit the brow, frown.

ขมอง (ขมอง) khamɔ̌ɔŋ′ (khamɔ̌ɔŋ′) N brain.
Usually the same as สมอง, which is a more
modern term.

ขมักเขม้น FS. See ขะมักเขม้น.

ขมัน. See ขมีขมัน.

ขมับ (ข้าง) khamàb′ (khâaŋ′) N temple (of the
head).

ขมัว. See ขมุกขมัว.

ขมา khamaa′/* N eleg. pardon.

ขมิ้น (หัว, แง่ง) khamîn′ (hǔa′, ŋɛ̂ŋ′) N turmeric
(the plant and its derivatives). The clf. hǔa′
is used for the rhizome, ŋɛ̂ŋ′ for the branches
of the rhizome. ต้น-- (ต้น) the turmeric
plant.

ขมิบ khamìb′ V to constrict. See also ขมุบขมิบ.

ขมีขมัน khamǐi′khamǎn′ V 1. to hustle, rush, hurry.
sV 2. fast, energetically.

ขมุกขมัว khamùg′khamǔa′ V 1. to be nearly dark,
twilight. 2. to be hazy (of weather).

ขมุบขมิบ khamùb′khamìb′ V (one's lips) to be moving slightly.

o ทำปากขมุบขมิบ thampàag′-khamùb′khamìb′
to work the mouth silently.

ขโมย (คน) khamooj′/*(khon′) N 1. thief. V 2. to
steal, pilfer. →Also ขะโมย FS. →Dist. 1.
โจร. →Syn. 2. ลัก.

o ลักเล็กขโมยน้อย lág′lég′-khamooj′nɔ́ɔj′ V
elab. colloq. to pilfer.

ขยะ ๑, --มูลฝอย khajà?′, khajà?′muunfɔ̌ɔj′ N waste,
garbage, refuse, trash, litter.

ถังขยะ (ใบ) thǎŋkhajà?′ (baj′) N garbage pail,
garbage can.

ขยะ ๒ in ขยะแขยง khajà?′khajɛ̌ɛŋ′ V to feel
disgust, repugnance, loathing.

น่าขยะแขยง nâa′-khajà?′khajɛ̌ɛŋ′ V to be disgusting, repulsive, repugnant, loathsome.

ขยัก khajàg′ V 1. colloq. to save (money for a
better use); to keep back some (for future use).
C 2. interval, span (of time); sitting.

ขยัน, --ขันแข็ง khajǎn′, khajǎn′khǎnkhɛ̌ŋ′ V to be

diligent, industrious, assiduous. ความ-- diligence, industriousness, application.

ขยันขยอ FS. See ขะยันขะยอ, คะยันคะยอ.

ขยับ khajàb′ V to move slightly, shift, adjust, change position.

ขยับเขยื้อน khajàb′khajŷan′ V to shift slightly, budge, move.

ขยาด khajàad′ V to be afraid of, in fear of (esp. because of previous experience).

ขยาย khajǎaj′ V 1. to expand, enlarge, magnify, dilate. 2. to disclose, reveal, divulge.

กระจกขยาย (อัน) kracòg′khajǎaj′ (?an′) N 1. magnifying glass. 2. magnifying mirror.

ขยายความลับ khajǎaj′khwaamláb′ to reveal a secret.

ขยายตัว khajǎaj′tua′ to expand, become expanded (e.g. because of heat).

ขยายส่วน khajǎaj′sùan′ to enlarge proportionately (e.g. in drawing a map).

ขยายเสียง khajǎaj′sǐaŋ′ to amplify (sound). เครื่อง-- amplifier.

แว่นขยาย (อัน) wɛ̂n′khajǎaj′ (?an′) N magnifying lens, reading glass.

ขยำ khajǎm′ V to squeeze with the hand, crumple up in the hand, knead or mix with the hands.

ขย้ำ khajâm′ V to pounce, pounce and seize; to seize ravenously (as a dog a bone).

ขยิก. See ขยุกขยิก.

ขยิบ khajìb′ V to wink. See also ขยุบขยิบ.

ขยิบตา, ขยิบหู-- khajìb′taa′, khajìb′hǔu′-khaɔ jìb′taa′ V elab. colloq. to wink, signal by a wink.

ขยี้ khajîi′ V 1. to rub hard with the hands, to scrub. 2. to squeeze, crush (by rubbing).

ขยี้ตา khajîi′taa′ to rub one's eyes.

ขยุกขยิก khajùg′khajìg′ V 1. to squirm, wriggle, fidget. 2. (handwriting) to be unsteady, squiggly, scribbled.

ขยุบ, --ขยิบ khajùb′, khajùb′khajìb′ V 1. to squirm, wriggle, fidget, make a slight movement. 2. to flick (the eyelids when dust gets into the eyes). 3. to get a prickly sensation (of the skin).

o ปากคันขยุบขยิบ pàag′khan′-khajùb′khajìb′

colloq. to feel very much like saying something; to have an itch to say something.

ขยุบ ๆ khajùb′khajùb′ sV with a throbbing movement or sensation.

ขรม kharǒm′, khrǒm′ V 1. to be loud, noisy, boisterous. sV 2. loudly, noisily.

ขระ. See ขรุขระ.

ขรึม khrŷm′ V to be solemn, grave.

เคร่งขรึม khrêŋkhrŷm′ V to be serious, solemn.

ขรุขระ khrù?khrà?′ V to be bumpy, rough, uneven (of a surface, e.g. a street).

ขลัก. See ขลุกขลัก ๑,๒.

ขลัง khlǎŋ′ V to have supernatural powers, to be miraculous, magical.

ขลับ khlàb′ rM intensifier used with ดำ "black" and มัน ๑ "oily," adding or emphasizing the meaning of "glossy."

ขลาด khlàad′ V to be cowardly, timid.

ขี้ขลาด khîikhlàad′ V colloq. to be given to being cowardly, timid, timorous.

ขลุก (อยู่กับ) khlùg′(jùukaɔ) V to be very occupied (with), absorbed (in), tied up (with).

ขลุกขลัก ๑ khlùg′khlàg′ V to meet with difficulty, have a hard time (doing something).

ขลุกขลัก ๒ khlùgkhlàg′ V 1. to rattle. sV 2. with a rattling or clattering sound.

ขลุกขลุ่ย khlùgkhlùj′ V 1. to be occupied (with), in companionship (with). sV 2. colloq. comfortably, easily, cosily.

ขลุม in ตีขลุม tii′khlǔm′ colloq. to take advantage of the situation or of appearances (e.g. let it be believed that one is the owner of what is actually borrowed jewelry).

ขลุ่ย (อัน) khlùj′ (?an′) N flute.

เป็นปี่เป็นขลุ่ย penpìi′penkhlùj′ harmoniously, in united fashion.

ขวด (ใบ) khùad′ (baj′) N 1. bottle, flask (generally made of glass). C 2. clf. for things in bottles.

o น้ำหวานสองขวด námwǎan′sɔ̌ɔŋkhùad′ two bottles of pop.

ขวดปักดอกไม้ (ใบ) khùad′pàgdɔ̀ɔgmáaj′ (baj′) N flower vase.

ขวดโหล (ใบ) khùadlǒo′ (baj′) N widemouthed jar with glass stopper.

ขวนขวาย khwŏnkhwǎaj′, khŭankhwǎaj′ V to be active, energetic in finding something to do (esp. in order to better one's status or position). Also ขวายขวน.

ขวน khùan′ V to scratch, scratch on (with claws, nails, thorns, etc.). →Syn. ตะกุย.

ขีดขวน khìid′khùan′ V to scratch, mark with a sharp object.

ขวบ khùab′ C years of age (for children up to 12 or 13 years of age; after that ปี is used).

o อายุห้าขวบ ?aajú?′/hâakhùab′ (he) is five years old.

ขวย khŭaj′ V to feel bashful, shy, embarrassed. ความ-- bashfulness, shyness, embarrassment.

แก้ขวย kɛ̂ɛkhŭaj′ to cover one's embarrassment.

ขวยเขิน khŭajkhə̆ən′ V to feel bashful, shy, embarrassed, self-conscious (often esp. of women). ความ-- feeling of embarrassment, self-consciousness.

ขวยใจ khŭajcaj′ V to feel shame; to feel embarrassed, mortified, shamed. ความ-- embarrassment, shame.

ขวักไขว่ khwàgkhwàj′ V 1. to move or act pell-mell, helter-skelter. sV 2. pell-mell, helter-skelter, to and fro, hither and thither, at random.

ขวัญ (ขวัญ) khwǎn′ (khwǎn′) N 1. the whorl of hair on top of the head. 2. (one's) guardian spirit, psyche. 3. spirits, morale.

กล่าวขวัญ (ถึง) klàawkhwǎn′(thy̆ŋɔ) to speak (of), talk (about), mention.

ข่มขวัญ khòmkhwǎn′ V to terrorize, threaten, attempt to coerce by fear.

ขวัญดี khwǎndii′ V to be in good spirits; to have good morale.

ขวัญตา khwǎntaa′ N 1. a pleasure or treat to the eye. 2. sweetheart, darling (used of a woman or child). P 3. you (expressing endearment when speaking to a woman or child).

ขวัญบิน khwǎnbin′ V idiom. to be startled, terrified, frightened, scared. →Syn. ตกใจ.

ขวัญเสีย, เสียขวัญ khwǎnsĭa′, sĭakhwǎn′ V 1. to lose one's fighting spirit. 2. to get scared.

ขวัญหนี khwǎnnĭi′ V to be startled, frightened.

ขวัญหนีดีฝ่อ khwǎnnĭi′diifɔ̀ɔ′ V elab. colloq.

to be startled, frightened; to be scared out of one's wits.

ขวัญหาย khwǎnhăaj′ V to be startled, frightened.

ขวัญอ่อน khwǎn?ɔ̀ɔn′ V 1. to be timorous, easily frightened. N 2. (usually คน--) an easily frightened person, used esp. of children, women.

ของขวัญ (อย่าง, ชิ้น, อัน) khɔ̆ɔŋkhwǎn′ (jàaŋ′, chín′, ?an′) N gift, present (given on the occasion of a birthday, anniversary, etc.).

ขู่ขวัญ khùu′khwǎn′ V to terrorize, threaten, intimidate, attempt to coerce by fear.

ทำขวัญ thamkhwǎn′ V 1. to perform a ceremony in order to encourage and strengthen. 2. to make compensation for injury done (to another).

o ค่าทำขวัญ khâa′thamkhwǎn′ N compensation, indemnity (for personal injury or damage).

รับขวัญ rábkhwǎn′ V colloq. to caress, kiss.

เรียกขวัญ rîagkhwǎn′ V to call (back) the protecting spirit.

ขวั้น. See ควั่น.

ขวับ khwàb′ sV abruptly, suddenly.

หันขวับ hănkhwàb′ to turn suddenly.

ขวา khwǎa′ sV right, to the right (opp. of left). →Opp. ซ้าย.

ชกขวา chógkhwǎa′ boxing to deliver a blow with the right.

ถนัดขวา thanàd′khwǎa′ V to be right-handed.

ทางขวามือ thaaŋkhwǎa′myy′ to the right, on the right.

มือขวา myykhwǎa′ N 1. the right hand. 2. idiom. (one's) right-hand man. 3. something one is good at, something that is second nature to one.

เลี้ยวขวา líawkhwǎa′ to turn right.

ขวาก (อัน) khwàag′ (?an′) N spikes, barbs (metal or wood), esp. for use in making snares.

ขวาง khwǎaŋ′ V to lie across, bar (the way), obstruct, thwart.

กว้างขวาง kwâaŋkhwǎaŋ′ V 1. to be roomy, spacious, vast, extensive. 2. to be well-known, popular (of persons). อย่าง-- extensively.

กีดขวาง kìidkhwǎaŋ′ V to be in the way of, to bar (the way), obstruct. เครื่อง-- barrier, obstacle.

ขวางทาง khwǎaŋthaaŋ′ V to block the way, bar the way.

ขวางโลก khwǎaŋlôog′ V to do things in opposition to what other people usually do. Cf. Eng. "crosswise with the world."

ขวางหู khwǎaŋhǔu′ V to offend the ears, be offensive to listen to.

ขัดขวาง khàdkhwǎaŋ′ V to interfere, get in the way, obstruct, block, restrain.

ตามขวาง taamkhwǎaŋ′ across, crosswise, transverse.

ขว้าง khwâaŋ′ V to throw, hurl, cast, fling.

ขว้างปา khwâaŋ′paa′ V to throw, hurl (at).

ทิ้งขว้าง thíŋ′khwâaŋ′ V to throw aside, discard, neglect (things); to forsake, desert, abandon (a person).

ขวาน (เล่ม) khwǎan′ (lêm′) N axe, hatchet.

ขวายขวน. See ขวนขวาย.

ขวิด khwìd′ V to gore, attack with the horns.

หัวหกก้นขวิด hǔahòg′kônkhwìd′ sV colloq. gallivanting about, on the go.

ขอ ๑ (ตัว, อัน) khɔ̌ɔ′ (tua′, ʔan′) N hook.

ขอแขวนเสื้อ (อัน) khɔ̌ɔkhwɛ̌ɛnsŷa′ (ʔan′) N coat hook.

ตะขอ, ตาขอ (ตัว, อัน) takhɔ̌ɔ′, taakhɔ̌ɔ′ (tua′, ʔan′) N 1. hook (as of a hook-and-eye). 2. a long-handled hook.

ไม้ขอ (อัน) májkhɔ̌ɔ′ (ʔan′) N hook with a wooden handle.

ขอ ๒ khɔ̌ɔ′, khɔ̌ɔɔ V 1. com. to ask for, beg, request. →Syn. ขอประทาน def., ขอพระราชทาน roy. 2. may I have (such and such). AA 3. let me, may I.

o ขอน้ำหน่อย khɔ̌ɔnám′nɔ̀j↓ May I have some water? Give me some water.

o ขอดูหน่อย khɔ̌ɔduu′nɔ̀j↓ Let me look at it.

ขอกู้ khɔ̌ɔkûu′ V eleg. to borrow (at interest).

ขอตัว khɔ̌ɔtua′ V to excuse oneself (with respect to an invitation, performing a service, etc.), to beg off.

ขอทาน khɔ̌ɔthaan′ V 1. to beg, ask for alms. N 2. short for คน-- beggar.

ขอที khɔ̌ɔ′thii, khɔ̌ɔthii′ See ขอเสียที.

ขอโทษ khɔ̌ɔthôod′ V 1. to apologize. 2. Excuse me! Beg pardon! →Syn. ขอประทานโทษ eleg. def., ทานโทษ colloq.

o คำขอโทษ (ข้อ) kham′khɔ̌ɔthôod′ (khɔ̌ɔ′) N apology, excuse.

ขอโทษขอโพย khɔ̌ɔthôod′khɔ̌ɔphooj′ V elab. colloq. to apologize.

ขอประทาน khɔ̌ɔprathaan′ V def., sp. to sup. to beg, request. →Syn. See ขอ com.

o ขอประทานโทษ khɔ̌ɔprathaanthôod′ eleg. def. Kindly pardon me! Kindly excuse me! →Syn. See ขอโทษ com.

o ขอประทานเสนอ khɔ̌ɔprathaan′sanɔ̌ə′ eleg. def. I respectfully submit (this matter for your consideration). Used esp. in official correspondence.

ขอพระราชทาน khɔ̌ɔphrárâadchathaan′ V roy. to beg, request. →Syn. See ขอ com.

o ขอพระราชทานอภัยโทษ khɔ̌ɔphrárâadchathaan′ʔaphajjathôod′ 1. roy. to ask for amnesty (for prisoners). 2. May your highness excuse me!

ขอร้อง khɔ̌ɔrɔ́ɔŋ′ V to request, implore, entreat, beseech.

o คำขอร้อง (ฉบับ, ข้อ, อย่าง) kham′khɔ̌ɔrɔ́ɔŋ′ N 1. (written) petition (chabàb′). 2. request (for help)(khɔ̌ɔ′, jàaŋ′).

ขอรับ khɔ̌ɔráb′ Pt eleg.def. m. sp. 1. particle used as the final element of statements and questions. 2. Yes (in answer to a question). 3. particle placed after name or kin term to address or call the attention of someone. 4. Yes? (as a reply when called or spoken to). For examples, see ครับ. →Syn. ครับ def. m. sp.

ขอรับอนุญาต khɔ̌ɔráb′ʔánújâad′, khɔ̌ɔ′-ráb′ʔánúɔjâad′ to apply for permission.

ขอแรง khɔ̌ɔrɛɛŋ′ to ask (someone) to lend a hand, ask for assistance (in doing work).

ขอษมา, -สมา khɔ̌ɔsamaa′ V to ask forgiveness, apologize.

ขอเสียที khɔ̌ɔ′sǐathii′↓ Please don't, just this once! (requesting that something be stopped).

ขอแสดงความยินดีด้วย khɔ̌ɔsadɛɛŋkhwaamjindii′dûaj↓ Congratulations! Accept my congratulations!

ขอให้ khɔ̌ɔhâjɔ. See examples below.

o ขอให้ดูตัวอย่างอันนั้น khɔ̌ɔhâjduu'-tuajàaŋ'/ʔanɔ nán'↓ Let's look at that example.

o ขอให้ทราบไว้ด้วย khɔ̌ɔhâjsâab'wájdûaj'↓ Will you please bear that in mind!

o ขอให้เรารู้จักเป็นเพื่อนกันดีกว่า khɔ̌ɔhâjraw'- rúucàg'penphŷan'-kandiikwàa'↓ Let us rather know each other as friends.

ขออนุญาต khɔ̌ɔʔànújâad' to ask permission, seek permission (to).

o ขออนุญาตไปด้วยคน khɔ̌ɔʔànújâad'pajdûajkhon'↓ Permit me to go along.

ขออนุมัติ khɔ̌ɔʔànumád' eleg. to seek approval, permission, approbation. Used chiefly in official correspondence.

ขออภัย khɔ̌ɔʔaphaj' to apologize.

ขี้ขอ khîikhɔ̌ɔ' V colloq. to have a habit of asking for things.

คำขอ (ขอ) khamkhɔ̌ɔ' (khɔ̌ɔ') N request.

ร้องขอ rɔ́ɔŋ'khɔ̌ɔ' V 1. to cry for (e.g. help). 2. to beg for, request.

วอนขอ wɔɔn'khɔ̌ɔ' V to plead, beg (for).

สู่ขอ sùu'khɔ̌ɔ' V to ask for a girl's hand in marriage (usually through an intermediary).

ข้อ (ข้อ) khɔ̂ɔ' (khɔ̂ɔ') N 1. joint, node. C 2. clf. for joints. 3. clf. for points (in a discussion, argument), items. →Syn. 3. ประการ eleg.

ข้อกล่าวหา (ข้อ,กระทง) khɔ̂ɔ'klàawhǎa' (khɔ̂ɔ', krathoŋ') N accusation, charge.

ข้อกาง khɔ̂ɔ'kaaŋ' sV (with) elbows out (as when walking with an air of determination). Chiefly used with เดิน.

ข้อไกล่เกลี่ย (ข้อ) khɔ̂ɔ'klàjklìa' (khɔ̂ɔ') N point of mediation, point of arbitration.

ข้อขัดข้อง (ข้อ) khɔ̂ɔ'khàdkhɔ̂ŋ' (khɔ̂ɔ') N objection.

ข้อเขียน (อย่าง,วิชา) khɔ̂ɔkhǐan' (jàaŋ', wíchaa') N written examination (as opposed to oral).

ข้อไข (ข้อ) khɔ̂ɔkhǎj' (khɔ̂ɔ') N solution (to a riddle, a math. problem).

ข้อความ (ข้อ,ตอน) khɔ̂ɔkhwaam' (khɔ̂ɔ', tɔɔn') N 1. item, point (of discourse, inquiry). 2. passage (from an article, etc.). 3. text (as of

speech, letter), statement, account.

ข้อคิด (ข้อ) khɔ̂ɔkhíd' (khɔ̂ɔ') N idea, point worth considering, something to think about.

ข้อซักถาม (ข้อ) khɔ̂ɔ'ságthǎam' (khɔ̂ɔ') N question (esp. in an official interrogation).

ข้อตกลง (ข้อ) khɔ̂ɔ'tògloŋ' (khɔ̂ɔ') N agreement, settlement; points of agreement.

ข้อต่อ (ข้อ,แห่ง) khɔ̂ɔtɔ̀ɔ' (khɔ̂ɔ', hὲŋ') N joint, connection.

ข้อตีน (ข้อ,ข้าง) khɔ̂ɔtiin' (khɔ̂ɔ', khâaŋ') N com. ankle. →Syn. ข้อเท้า eleg.

ข้อโต้แย้ง (ข้อ) khɔ̂ɔ'tôojɛ́ɛŋ' (khɔ̂ɔ') N point of dispute, argument.

ข้อเท็จจริง (ข้อ) khɔ̂ɔ'thédciŋ' (khɔ̂ɔ') N facts, evidence, the facts of the matter.

ข้อเท้า (ข้อ,ข้าง) khɔ̂ɔtháaw' (khɔ̂ɔ', khâaŋ') N eleg. ankle. →Syn. ข้อตีน com.

ข้อนิ้ว (ข้อ) khɔ̂ɔníw' (khɔ̂ɔ') N knuckle.

ข้อบกพร่อง (ข้อ,ประการ) khɔ̂ɔ'bògphrɔ̂ŋ' (khɔ̂ɔ', prakaan') N weakness, fault, defect, flaw.

ข้อบังคับ (ข้อ) khɔ̂ɔ'baŋkháb' (khɔ̂ɔ') N rule, regulation.

ข้อปฏิบัติ (ข้อ) khɔ̂ɔ'pàtibàd' (khɔ̂ɔ') N 1. procedure, practice. 2. obligation (e.g. toward a friend).

ข้อผูกพัน (ข้อ) khɔ̂ɔ'phùugphan' (khɔ̂ɔ') N obligation, binding condition; restriction, strings (attached to a deal).

ข้อผูกมัด (ข้อ) khɔ̂ɔ'phùugmád' (khɔ̂ɔ') idem.

ข้อพิสูจน์ (ข้อ) khɔ̂ɔ'phísùud' (khɔ̂ɔ') N proof.

ข้อมือ (ข้อ,ข้อมือ,ข้าง) khɔ̂ɔmyy' (khɔ̂ɔ', khɔ̂ɔɔ myy', khâaŋ') N wrist. →Cf. ข้อไม้ข้อมือ.

ข้อแม้ (ข้อ) khɔ̂ɔmɛ́ɛ' (khɔ̂ɔ') N stipulation, condition.

ข้อไม้ข้อมือ (ข้อ,ข้าง) khɔ̂ɔmáaj'khɔ̂ɔmyy' (khɔ̂ɔ', khâaŋ') N elab. colloq. wrist. →Cf. ข้อมือ.

ข้อเรียกร้อง (ข้อ) khɔ̂ɔ'rîagrɔ́ɔŋ' (khɔ̂ɔ') N demand, request.

ข้อศอก (ข้อศอก,ข้าง) khɔ̂ɔsɔ̀ɔg' (khɔ̂ɔsɔ̀ɔg', khâaŋ') N elbow.

ข้อสงสัย (ข้อ) khɔ̂ɔ'sǒŋsǎj' (khɔ̂ɔ') N point of doubt, doubtful point.

ข้อสอบ (ข้อ) khɔ̂ɔsɔ̀ɔb' (khɔ̂ɔ') N examination questions.

ข้อสังเกต (ข้อ) khɔ̂ɔ'sǎŋkèed' (khɔ̂ɔ') N observation, item or comment based on observation.

ข้อเสนอ (ข้อ) khɔ̂ɔsanəə' (khɔ̂ɔ') N proposal,
offer, proposition.

ข้อหา (ข้อ,กระทง) khɔ̂ɔhǎa' (khɔ̂ɔ', krathoŋ')
N accusation, charge.

ข้ออ้าง (ข้อ) khɔ̂ɔ'ʔâaŋ' (khɔ̂ɔ') N 1. justification. 2. supporting statement, citation, reference (to an authority).

เป็นข้อใหญ่ penkhɔ̂ɔ'jàj' mainly, chiefly.

ฟาดข้อ (กับ) fâadkhɔ̂ɔ'(kaʔ) V slang to argue,
fight (with).

ส่วนข้อที่ว่า sùankhɔ̂ɔ'thîiwâa' as to the point
that, as for the case in which.

หัวข้อ (หัวข้อ) hǔakhɔ̂ɔ' (hǔakhɔ̂ɔ') N 1. topic,
subject (as of debate). 2. heading, outline.

ของ (อย่าง) (1) khɔ̌ɔŋ' (jàaŋ'); (2,3) khɔ̌ɔŋ‿ N
1. thing, something, article, goods, stuff, material, substance, possession. 2. initial element in certain noun derivatives. Pp 3. of,
owned by, belonging to. In meaning 3, ของ is
often best rendered, together with the noun or
pronoun following it, by an English adjective
or possessive, as in การเศรษฐกิจของชาติ
kaansèed'thakìd'khɔ̌ɔŋchâad' the national
economy, and ประเทศของเรา prathêed'ʔ‿
khɔ̌ɔŋraw' our country. NOTE. Many of the
following derivatives take the clfs. อย่าง
"kind, sort," ชิ้น "piece," or อัน, a general
clf.; these clfs. are omitted below.

ของกลาง khɔ̌ɔŋklaaŋ' N 1. a material object
whose ownership is disputed before the authorities or in court. 2. the physical evidence (as
stolen goods).

ของกิน khɔ̌ɔŋkin' N foodstuff, edibles, things
to eat. →Comp. ของใช้.

ของเก่า khɔ̌ɔŋkàw' N antique.

ของขวัญ khɔ̌ɔŋkhwǎn' N gift, present (given on
the occasion of a birthday, anniversary, etc.).

ของแข็ง khɔ̌ɔŋkhɛ̌ŋ' N solid.

ของคาว khɔ̌ɔŋkhaaw' N dish of the main course
prepared of meat or fish. Contrast ของหวาน.

ของจำเป็น khɔ̌ɔŋcampen' N necessities.

ของชำ khɔ̌ɔŋcham' N dry foodstuff, food suscep-

tible of storage (as dried, pickled, bottled, and
canned foods). →Also ของแห้ง. →Opp. ของสด.

ของใช้ khɔ̌ɔŋcháj' N useful articles, things to
use, utensils. →Comp. ของกิน "things to
eat." →Syn. เครื่องอุปโภค eleg.

ของตน khɔ̌ɔŋton' one's own.

ของเถื่อน (อย่าง) khɔ̌ɔŋthỳan' (jàaŋ') N smuggled goods, contraband, bootleg goods.

ของธรรมดา khɔ̌ɔŋ'thammadaa' N the usual,
ordinary, natural thing.

ของฝาก khɔ̌ɔŋfàag' N 1. something entrusted to
one person to be delivered to another person.
2. something brought as a gift for one's hostess
or her family.

ของมัน khɔ̌ɔŋman' its, of it.

ของมัน ๆ khɔ̌ɔŋ'manman' N fatty, oily substance
or thing.

ของลับ (อัน) khɔ̌ɔŋláb' (ʔan') N genitalia, private parts.

ของเล่น khɔ̌ɔŋlên' N toy, plaything.

ของว่าง khɔ̌ɔŋwâaŋ' N snack.

ของส่วน khɔ̌ɔŋsaŋùan' N euphem. bust, breasts.
→Syn. นม com.

ของสด khɔ̌ɔŋsòd' N fresh, raw foods (of any kind).
→Opp. ของชำ,ของแห้ง.

ของสดของคาว khɔ̌ɔŋsòd'khɔ̌ɔŋkhaaw' N fresh,
raw foods (often esp. raw meats).

ของเสีย,ของเสีย ๆ khɔ̌ɔŋsǐa', khɔ̌ɔŋ'sǐasǐa'
N waste matter, things that are bad, not usable,
deteriorated, worn out, damaged.

ของเสียหาย khɔ̌ɔŋ'sǐahǎaj' N 1. damaged things.
2. things that are bad or objectionable to do.

ของหวาน khɔ̌ɔŋwǎan' N dessert, sweetstuff.

ของเหลว khɔ̌ɔŋlěew' N liquid. →Dist. ของไหล.

ของเหลวไหล khɔ̌ɔŋlěewlǎj' N nonsense.

ของแห้ง khɔ̌ɔŋhɛ̂ɛŋ' N dry foodstuff, food susceptible of storage. →Also ของชำ. →Opp. ของสด.

ของให้ khɔ̌ɔŋhâj' N gift, present.

ของไหล khɔ̌ɔŋlǎj' N fluid. →Dist. ของเหลว.

ขายของ khǎajkhɔ̌ɔŋ' V to sell, sell things.

ข้าวของ (สิ่ง,อย่าง,ชิ้น,อัน) khâawkhɔ̌ɔŋ' (sìŋ',
jàaŋ', chín', ʔan') N belongings, things, possessions; equipment, gear.

เจ้าของ (คน) câwkhɔ̌ɔŋ' (khon') N owner,

proprietor.

ซื้อของ sýykhɔɔŋ′ V to shop, buy things.

สิ่งของ (สิ่ง,อย่าง,ชิ้น,อัน) sìŋkhɔɔŋ′ (sìŋ′, jàaŋ′,chín′,ʔan′) N things.

ห่อของ (ห่อ) (1) hɔɔkhɔɔŋ′ (hɔɔ′); (2) hɔɔ′khɔɔŋ′ N 1. package. V 2. to wrap, wrap things.

ของ ๑ (ใบ,ลูก) khɔŋ′*(baj′,lûug′) N creel, fish basket made of rattan or bamboo.

ของ ๒. See entries below.

เกี่ยวของ (กับ) klawkhɔŋ′(kaɔ) V to be related (to); to have dealings (with), have to do (with).

ของใจ khɔŋcaj′ V to be in doubt (about), dubious (about), unclear in one's mind (about). ความ-- dubiousness.

ขัดของ khàdkhɔŋ′ V to object, have objections; to dissent.

ขุ่นของใจ khùnkhɔŋcaj′ V to be moody, in a bad mood.

ขอด ๑ khɔɔd′ V to scrape off, remove; to scrape the bottom (of a container).

ขอดเกล็ด khɔɔd′klèd′ to scale (a fish).

ขอดค่อน,ค่อนขอด khɔɔdkhɔɔn′, khɔɔnkhɔɔd′ V to criticize, make slurring remarks, ridicule, revile. การ-- ridiculing, criticizing.

ขอดหม้อ khɔɔd′mɔɔ′ to scrape the bottom of the pot.

o ข้าวขอดหม้อ khâaw′khɔɔdmɔɔ′ the rice in the pot is running low.

ขอด ๒ khɔɔd′ V to knot.

ขอน,--ไม้ (ท่อน) khɔɔn′, khɔɔnmáaj′ (thɔɔn′) N log, section of unhewn timber.

ขอน. See คอน ๑.

ขอนแก่น khɔɔnkɛ̀n′* pN Khɔnkæn, a township in NE Thailand.

ขอบ ๑ (ขอบ) khɔɔb′ (khɔɔb′) N edge, rim, margin.

ขอบเขต (อัน) khɔɔbkhèed′ (ʔan′) N limit, boundary, confines.

ขอบจักรวาฬ khɔɔb′càgkrawaan′ N eleg. horizon. →Syn. ขอบฟ้า com.

ขอบถนน (ขอบ) khɔɔb′thanɔn′ (khɔɔb′) N curb (along the edge of a street).

ขอบทะเล (ด้าน,แห่ง) khɔɔb′thalee′ (dâan′,hɛ̀ŋ′) N the edge of the sea; the horizon of the sea.

ขอบฟ้า khɔɔbfáa′ N com. horizon. →Syn. ขอบจักรวาฬ eleg.

ขอบ ๒. See entries below.

ขอบคุณ khɔɔbkhun′ eleg. 1. Thank you! V 2. to thank. ความ-- thanks, gratitude.

ขอบใจ khɔɔbcaj′ com.,colloq. 1. Thank you! Thanks! V 2. to thank.

ขอบพระคุณ khɔɔbphrákhun′ eleg. def. 1. Thank you! V 2. to thank.

ขอม khɔɔm′ N lit. Cambodia; Cambodian. This term is used in historical chronicles. See the modern term เขมร.

ขะมักเขม้น khamàg′khamên′, khamág′khamên′ V to be serious, determined, earnest, energetic. ขมักเขม้น FS.

ขะโมย FS. See ขโมย.

ขะยั้นขะยอ khaján′khajɔɔ′ V to urge, press, pressure. ขยั้นขยอ FS. Also written คะยั้นคะยอ.

ขัง ๑ khàŋ′ V 1. to shut up, pen up, confine, detain, cage, jail. 2. to be confined, to be caught (as water in a hole).

คุมขัง khumkhàŋ′ V to jail, imprison, detain in custody.

ต้องขัง tɔ̂ŋkhàŋ′ V to be imprisoned.

ห้องขัง (ห้อง) hɔ̂ŋkhàŋ′ (hɔ̂ŋ′) N cell, detention cell.

ขัง ๒. See ขึ้งขัง.

ขัด ๑ khàd′ V 1. to obstruct, hinder, interrupt, interfere (with). 2. to oppose, resist, object, refuse, disagree (with), conflict (with). 3. to fasten, latch. 4. to cross, extend across and over, be woven, interlaced. 5. (an animal) to be injured, crippled. 6. (one's bones) to feel sore, broken.

แก้ขัด kɛ̂ɛkhàd′ V 1. to serve the purpose temporarily (as a means of relief), to tide one over. 2. to relieve one's soreness (as by massage).

ขัดกับ khàd′kaɔ to conflict with, be contradictory to, disagree with.

ขัดขวาง khàdkhwǎaŋ′ V to interfere, get in the way, hinder, obstruct, block, restrain.

ขัดของ khàdkhɔŋ′ V to object, have objections; to dissent. ความ-- objection, dissension.

o ข้อขัดของ (ข้อ) khɔ̂ɔ′khàdkhɔŋ′ (khɔ̂ɔ′) N

objection.

o เหตุขัดข้อง (เหตุ) hèed'khàdkhɔ̌ŋ' (hèed') N obstacle, hindrance, interference, handicap.

ขัดขึน khàd'khy̌n' V to interrupt, break in, butt in.

ขัดขืน khàdkhy̌yn' V to disobey, to violate (a law).

ขัดคอ khàdkhɔɔ' V 1. to interrupt, break in repeatedly (as while someone is speaking). 2. to gainsay, disagree.

ขัดเคือง khàdkhyaŋ' V to feel angry, be angered, provoked.

ขัดจังหวะ khàd'caŋwàʔ' V 1. to interrupt, intervene. 2. to break in in the middle of. 3. to be interspersed (as trees dotting the landscape).

ขัดใจ khàdcaj' V 1. to annoy, to get in the way. 2. to be contrary, contradictory. 3. to be annoyed, irritated.

ขัดตา khàdtaa' V to be somewhat disturbing in appearance, not pleasing to the eye.

ขัดแย้ง(กัน) khàdjɛ́ɛŋ'(kan') V to be in conflict, to disagree (with one another), contradict (one another).

ขัดสน khàdsǒn' V 1. to lack, be short of, be in need of. 2. to be poor, in want, needy.

ขัดสมาธิ,-ธิ์ khàdsamàad' V to sit with knees apart and legs crossed under (usually on the floor).

ขัดหู,ฟัง-- khàdhǔu', faŋ'khàdhǔu' V to be displeasing to the ear, jarring, not sound right.

เข็มขัด (สาย,เส้น) khěmkhàd' (sǎaj', sên') N belt.

เมื่อยขัด my̌aj'khàd' V to feel stiff and sore.

ขัด ๒ khàd' V 1. to rub (against), scrub. 2. to polish, shine.

ขัดถู khàd'thǔu' V to burnish, furbish, polish up.

ขัดมัน khàdman' V to be polished, shiny, glossy.

ขัดสี khàd'sǐi' V 1. to scrub. 2. to polish. การ-- friction; abrasion.

ขัน ๑ khǎn' V 1. to tighten by turning or twisting. 2. to force oneself to try something (against great odds), to make a diligent or daring effort.

o ขันก๊อก khǎnkɔ́g' to turn the faucet off.

กวดขัน kùadkhǎn' V to be strict (with).

ขันแข็ง,แข็งขัน khǎnkhɛ̌ŋ', khɛ̌ŋkhǎn' V to be diligent, industrious; to do things assiduously,

wholeheartedly.

o ขยันขันแข็ง khajǎn'khǎnkhɛ̌ŋ' V to be diligent, industrious, assiduous.

แข่งขัน khɛ̀ŋkhǎn' V to compete.

คับขัน khábkhǎn' V 1. to be in a tight spot, in a critical situation. 2. to be of a critical, emergency nature.

ขัน ๒ (ใบ,ลูก) khǎn' (baj', lûug') N bowl, basin.

ขัน ๓ khǎn' V 1. to crow. 2. to coo.

ขันจ้อ khǎn'cɔ̂ɔ' to crow, coo incessantly.

ขัน ๔ khǎn' V 1. to find (it) amusing, be amused by. 2. to be funny, amusing, ridiculous, absurd.

o ขันดีนะ khǎn'diiná'↓ Isn't that amusing! Isn't it ridiculous! Isn't that absurd!

o เขาขันกันใหญ่ kháwkhǎn'kanjàj'↓ They all laughed heartily.

o เธอขันคำพูดของเขา thəə'-khǎn'khamphûud'ᴐ khɔ̌ɔŋkháw'↓ She was amused by his words.

ขบขัน khòbkhǎn' V to be funny, humorous, comical, amusing.

น่าขัน nâa'khǎn', nâakhǎn' V to be funny, comical, amusing, ridiculous.

ขั้น khân' C step (of ladder, stairs); step (in a procedure); rank, level; stage (of development).

เป็นขั้น ๆ pen'khânkhân' step by step, in stages.

ขันธ์ in ดับขันธ์ dàbkhǎn' V lit. to die (of Buddha).

ขับ ๑ khàb' V 1. to drive, operate (a vehicle). 2. to drive (a herd). 3. to drive away, chase away. 4. to secrete (excrete). 5. to tease. คน-- driver, chauffeur, pilot. ผู้-- eleg. idem.

ขับขี่ khàbkhìi' V to drive, operate a vehicle. ผู้-- operator, driver (of a vehicle).

o ใบขับขี่ (ใบ) bajkhàbkhìi' (baj') N operator's license, driver's license.

ขับเคี่ยว khàbkhîaw' V to drive or exert (oneself) vigorously, relentlessly.

ขับต้อน khàb'tɔ̂ɔn' V to drive, herd, urge on.

ขับรถ khàbród' to drive a car. คน-- driver, chauffeur.

ขับไล่ khàblâj' V to drive away, chase away, repel.

o เครื่องบินขับไล่ (เครื่อง) khrŷaŋbin'khàblâj' (khrŷaŋ') N pursuit plane, fighter plane.

ขับ ๒ khàb' V to sing, recite. →Chiefly in cpds.

ขับกล่อม khàbklɔ̂m′ V to sing lullabies, to lull to sleep.

ขับเพลง khàbphleeŋ′ V to sing, sing a song.

ขับร้อง khàbrɔ́ɔŋ′ V to sing.

เพลงขับ (เพลง) phleeŋ′khàb′ (phleeŋ′) N song.

ขับ ๓ in ขับขัน. See คับขัน.

ขัย in อายุขัย ?aajúʔkhăj′ N life span.

ขั้ว (ขั้ว) khûa′ (khûa′) N 1. pole (of the earth, of a magnet). 2. connecting point, e.g. point where stem is attached to fruit.

o แถบขั้วโลก thɛ̀ɛb′khûalôog′ the polar regions.

ขั้วใต้ khûatâaj′ N 1. south pole (of a magnet). 2. geog. South Pole.

ขั้วเหนือ khûanŷa′ N 1. north pole (of a magnet). 2. geog. North Pole.

ต้นขั้ว (ใบ) tônkhûa′ (baj′) N stub (as of a check), counterfoil (Brit.).

หัวขั้ว (อัน, หัวขั้ว) hŭakhûa′ (?an′, hŭakhûa′) N point where the stem is attached to a fruit.

ขา ๑ (ข้าง, ขา) khăa′ (khâaŋ′, khăa′) N 1. leg (of the body, of a piece of furniture, of a journey). 2. member (of an informal group, coterie). C 3. clf. for a player (e.g. of cards); for each part of a structurally connected pair, triad, etc., as the blades of a pair of scissors, the legs of a pair of pants, the legs of a tripod.

o ขาหลัง (ขา) khăalăŋ′ (khăa′) N hind legs.

o ขาไป khăapaj′ the trip going; (on) the way to, (on) the way there.

o ขาไพ่ ๔ ขา khăaphâj′-sìi′khăa′ four card players.

o กรรไกรขาเดียว kankraj′khăadiaw′ a single-bladed scissors.

ขากรรไกร (ข้าง) khăakankraj′ (khâaŋ′) N the jaws.

ขากลับ khăaklàb′ the return trip; (on) the way back.

ขาเก khăakee′ V to have a twisted leg (as from paralysis).

ขาข้างเดียว khăa′khâaŋdiaw′ one-legged.

ขาเข้า khăakhâw′ (on) the way in, incoming.

o สินค้าขาเข้า (อย่าง, ชนิด) sĭnkháa′khăakhâw′ (jàaŋ′, chaníd′) imports.

ขาแข็ง, แข็งขา (ข้าง, ขา) khăa′khɛ̌ŋ′, khɛ̌ŋkhăa′

(khâaŋ′, khăa′) N colloq. legs.

ขาประจำ (คน) khăapracam′ (khon′) N colloq. steady customer, regular customer.

ขาไพ่ (ขา, คน) khăaphâj′ (khăa′, khon′) N card player.

ขาหัก khăahàg′ V to have a broken leg.

ขาอ่อน (ข้าง) khăaʔɔ̀ɔn′ (khâaŋ′) N thigh.

แขนขา (ข้าง) khɛ̌ɛnkhăa′ (khâaŋ′) N arms and legs, limbs.

คู่ขา (คน) khûukhăa′ (khon′) N partner.

สามขา (อัน) săamkhăa′ (?an′) N tripod.

หว่างขา wàaŋkhăa′ N space between the legs.

โอ่งต่อขา ?òoŋ′tɔ̀ɔkhăa′ colloq. to be very fat (of people): "jar with legs."

ขา ๒ khăa′ Pt def. 1. element used by women and children after a name, title, or kin term to address someone, or call someone's attention. 2. Yes. (as a reply when called or spoken to). →Syn. จ๋า ๑ com.

ข่า (แง่ง, หัว) khàa′ (ŋɛ̂ŋ′, hŭa′) galangal (Alpinia sp.), an aromatic rhizome used in cookery and medicine.

ข้า ๑ (คน) khâa′ (khon′) N servant, attendant, slave. ข้า ๒, q.v., is a secondary meaning.

ข้าราชการ (คน, นาย) khâarâadchakaan′ (khon′, naaj′) N government official.

o ข้าราชการ(ฝ่าย)ทหาร khâarâadchakaan′(fàaj)⊂ thahăan′ N employees of the military services (as opposed to those of the civil service).

o ข้าราชการ(ฝ่าย)ปกครอง khâarâadchakaan′⊂ (fàaj)pògkhrɔɔŋ′ N government official (esp. an administrative or law enforcement official).

o ข้าราชการ(ฝ่าย)พลเรือน khâarâadchakaan′⊂ (fàaj)phonlaryan′ civilian government employees.

คณะกรรมการ-- khaná?′kammakaan′-khâarâad⊂ chakaan′(fàaj)phonlaryan′ N Civil Service Commission.

ข้าหลวง (คน, นาย) khâalŭaŋ′ (khon′, naaj′) N 1. royal servant, esp. female, a lady in waiting. 2. governor (as of a čhangwat); commissioner.

o ข้าหลวงประจำจังหวัด (นาย, คน) khâalŭaŋ′- pracam′caŋwàd′ (naaj′, khon′) N former designation for the governor of a čhangwat; see ผู้ว่าราชการจังหวัด.

o ข้าหลวงภาค (นาย,คน) khǎalǔaŋ'phâag'
(naaj',khon') N former designation for the
governor of a region; see ผู้ว่าราชการภาค.

o ข้าหลวงใหญ่ (นาย,คน) khǎalǔaŋ'jàj' (naaj',
khon') N high commissioner, governor general.

ขี้ข้า (คน) khîikhâa' (khon') N colloq. slave.

ข้า ๒ khâa' P 1. sp. to inf. or int. I, me. Paired
with เอ็ง "you." 2. lit. I, me. Sometimes
paired with ท่าน "you" (ref. to a person of status), or with เจ้า "you" (ref. to an inferior).
→See 1. ข้า ๑.

ข้าพเจ้า,ข้าฯ khâaphacâw' P eleg. I, me.
Used esp. by public speakers and writers.
Paired with ท่าน "you."

ข้า ๓. See ข้าศึก.

ขาก khàag' V to hawk up and spit out (phlegm).

ข้าง,ลูก-- (ลูก) khàaŋ', lûugkhàaŋ' (lûug') N
top (the toy).

ข้าง khâaŋ', khâŋ⌐ C 1. side; also used for one of
a pair, such as an arm, leg, shoe, tusk, fender.
Pp 2. by the side of, beside. →Comp. 1. ภาย.

o ขาข้างเดียว khǎa'khâŋdiaw' one-legged, (with)
one leg.

o ข้างละห้าคน khâŋlahâa'khon' five persons on
each side.

o ข้างหน้าต่าง khâŋnâatàaŋ' at, beside a window.

ข้าง ๆ khâŋkhâaŋ' beside, on the sides of.

ข้างขึ้น khâŋkhŷn' (period of) the waxing moon.

ข้างเคียง khâŋkhiaŋ' nearby, by the side of,
adjacent, close. คน-- intimate person, close
associate.

ข้างต้น khâŋtôn' at the beginning, at the outset;
used esp. in phrases like ดังกล่าวมาแล้วข้างต้น
daŋklàaw'maalέεw'-khâaŋtôn' "as already
stated at the beginning."

ข้างนอก khâŋnɔ̂ɔg' outside, (the) outside.

ข้างน้อย khâŋnɔ́ɔj' the minority (esp. in voting).

ข้างใน khâŋnaj' inside, (the) inside.

ข้างบน khâŋbon' upper part, above, on top, upstairs. →Ant. ข้างล่าง.

ข้างมาก khâŋmâag' the majority (esp. in voting).

o เสียงข้างมาก sǐaŋ'khâŋmâag' the majority
vote. →Ant. เสียงข้างน้อย.

ข้างแรม khâŋrεεm' (period of) the waning moon.

ข้างล่าง khâŋlâaŋ' lower part, below, down below,
downstairs. →Ant. ข้างบน.

ข้างหน้า khâŋnâa' 1. in front, ahead; in front of.
2. future, in the future.

ข้างหลัง khâŋlǎŋ' in back, behind.

เข้าข้าง khâwkhâaŋ' to side with, sympathize with.

ค่อนข้าง (จะ) khɔ̂nkhâaŋ(caʔ) AA inclined to be,
rather, more or less, on the side of, somewhat.

เคียงข้าง khiaŋkhâaŋ' side by side.

รอบข้าง rɔ̂ɔbkhâaŋ' on all sides, all around.

สีข้าง (ข้าง) sǐikhâaŋ' (khâaŋ') N side (of the
body).

ขาด khàad' V 1. to lack. 2. to be lacking, be missing (from). 3. to be torn, worn out (of clothing).
4. to be broken, separated (from), severed
(from). 5. to finish; to be final. sV 6. off;
completely, absolutely.

o ขาดความรู้ khàad'khwaamrúu' to lack knowledge.

o ขาดโรงเรียน khàad'rooŋrian' to miss school.

o เสื้อขาดแล้ว sŷa'khàadlέεw'↓ (My) coat is torn
(ref. to a new coat), is worn out (ref. to an old one).

o พูดยังไม่ทันขาดคำ phûud'-jaŋmâjthankhàad'⌐
kham' had not yet finished talking.

o แทะ(...)ขาด thέʔ'(...)khàad' to gnaw off,
gnaw loose.

o หายขาด hǎajkhàad' to recover completely,
be completely cured.

ขาดแคลน khàadkhlεεn' V to lack, be short of,
have a shortage of. ความ-- lack, shortage.

ขาดใจ khàadcaj' V to die, expire.

ขาดตกบกพร่อง khàadtòg'bògphrɔ̂ŋ' V to be deficient, defective, wanting; to fall short.

ขาดตลาด khàad'talàad' V (a commodity) to be
scarce, out of stock.

ขาดตัว khàadtua' V (the price) to be fixed, definite,
rock-bottom (esp. in bargaining).

ขาดทุน khàadthun' V 1. to lose money, sustain
losses (in business). 2. to be at a disadvantage.

ขาดมือ khàad'myy' V to be wanting, in short
supply, out of stock; (the supply of something)
to run out.

ขาดเรียน khàadrian' V to be absent from school,
miss school, cut classes.

ขาดวิ่น khàadwîn′ V to be torn raggedly.

ขาดเสียมิได้ khàad′sĭamídâaj′ to be indispensable.

ขาดเหลือ khàadlɯ̌a′ V to be lacking (in), short (of).

คำขาด (ฉบับ,ข้อ) khamkhàad′ (chabàb′,khɔ̂ɔ′) N ultimatum.

เฉียบขาด chìabkhàad′ V to be resolute (of a person), irrevocable (of an order), absolute.

ชี้ขาด chíi′khàad′ V to make a final decision.

เด็ดขาด dèdkhàad′ V 1. to be decisive. 2. to be resolute, firm. 3. to be absolute, without exception. sV 4. definitely, absolutely. 5. decidedly, unquestionably, very, extremely.

ตัดขาด tàdkhàad′ V to separate, sever, break off, cut off.

เป็นอันขาด pen?ankhàad′ definitely, decidedly, positively, absolutely, under any circumstances. Used in negative or prohibitive constructions.

o อย่า...เป็นอันขาด jàa...pen?ankhàad′ do not (do so and so) under any circumstances; (you) are absolutely not to (do such and such).

oo อย่าข้ามถนนคนเดียวเป็นอันขาด jàakhâam′thaɔnǒn′-khondiaw′pen?ankhàad′, Don't you ever under any circumstance cross the street alone.

ผูกขาด phùugkhàad′ V to monopolize. การ-- monopoly.

ฝนขาดเม็ดแล้ว fǒn′-khàadméd′lɛ́ɛw↓ It has stopped raining.

มิได้ขาด mídâjkhàad′ incessantly, regularly, constantly, unfailingly.

ไม่ขาด mâjkhàad′ 1. without a break, continuously. 2. can't be severed.

o ตัดไม่ขาด tàd′mâjkhàad′ can't cut it off.

โรคขาดอาหาร rôog′khàad?aahǎan′ N malnutrition, undernourishment.

ขาน khǎan′ V to call out; to call (the roll).

ขานรับ khǎan′ráb′ V to answer (a call); to call in reply.

โจษขาน côod′khǎan′ V 1. to talk loudly. 2. to spread the word around.

ขาม khǎam′ V to be in awe of, to fear, dread.

เกรงขาม kreeŋ′khǎam′ to be in awe of, to fear, to revere.

ข้าม khâam′ V to cross, cross over, step over, skip.

ข้ามถนน khâamthanǒn′ to cross the street.

ข้ามหน้า khâamnâa′ V 1. to bypass (someone), go over the head (of). 2. to disrespectfully ignore the presence (of).

ตรง(กัน)ข้าม troŋ(kan)khâam′ 1. to be opposite, the opposite of, contrary (to). 2. on the contrary, conversely. 3. to be right across from each other.

มองข้าม mɔɔŋkhâam′ V to overlook, disregard.

อ่าน(...)ข้าม ๆ ?àan′/(...)khâamkhâam′ to skim, read (something) by skimming.

ขาย khǎaj′ V com. to sell. คน-- salesperson, seller, vendor; also ผู้--. →Syn. จำหน่าย eleg.

ขายของ khǎajkhɔ̌ɔŋ′ V to sell, sell things. คน-- salesperson, seller, vendor.

o ร้านขายของ ráan′khǎajkhɔ̌ɔŋ′ N store, shop.

ขายชาติ khǎajchâad′ V to betray one's country, commit treason. คน-- traitor.

ขายเชื่อ khǎajchɯ̂a′ V to sell on credit.

ขายดิบขายดี khǎajdìb′khǎajdii′ V elab. colloq. to have good sales; to sell well.

ขายตั๋ว khǎajtǔa′ V to sell tickets. คน-- ticket seller.

ขายทอดตลาด khǎajthɔ̂ɔd′talàad′ to sell at auction.

ขายปลีก khǎajplìig′ V to retail.

ขายส่ง khǎajsòŋ′ V to wholesale (i.e. sell in quantity to a distributor).

o ราคาขายส่ง raakhaa′khǎajsòŋ′ wholesale price.

ขายหน้า khǎajnâa′ V to be disgraced, shamed.

ขายเหมา khǎajmǎw′ V to sell in bulk, to wholesale (i.e. without allowing selection of individual or choice pieces).

ค้าขาย kháakhǎaj′ V to engage in trade, buy and sell. การ-- business, trade, commerce.

ซื้อขาย sɯ́y′khǎaj′ V to trade, engage in commerce.

เร่ขาย rêe′khǎaj′ V to peddle.

ข่าย (อัน) khàaj′ (?an′) N 1. net. 2. limit, scope, range, sphere, category.

ข่ายบังคับ khàaj′baŋkháb′ N jurisdiction.

ตาข่าย (ตาข่าย,อัน,ผืน) taakhàaj′ (taakhàaj′, ?an′,phɯ̌yn′) N 1. netting, meshwork. 2. net (for ensnaring birds; for badminton, soccer, etc.). Also written ตะข่าย.

○ ถุงตาข่าย (ใบ) thŭŋ'taakhàaj' (baj') N net (in the form of a bag, as a butterfly net).

ขาล khăan' N (Year of the) Tiger. →The complete list of the cyclical years is given under ปี.

ขาว ๑ khăaw' V to be white.

ขาวจ๊วก khăawcúag' to be real white, chalk white.

ขาวจ๊วะ khăawcúaʔ' idem.

ขาวโพลง khăawphlooŋ' to be white all over, solid white.

ขาวโร่ khăawrôo' to be distinctly white, strikingly white.

ไข่ขาว khàjkhăaw' N egg white, albumen.

ตาขาว (1) taakhăaw'; (2) taa'khăaw' N 1. white of the eye. V 2. to be cowardly.

ทองขาว thɔɔŋkhăaw' N 1. white gold. 2. platinum.

ทองคำขาว thɔɔŋkhamkhăaw' N 1. platinum. 2. white gold.

ปูนขาว puunkhăaw' N lime.

ผ้าขาวบาง (ผืน) phâakhăawbaaŋ' (phɨ̌yn') N cheesecloth, gauze.

สีขาว sǐikhăaw' N 1. white, the color white. V 2. to be white.

ขาว ๒ in ผ้าขาวม้า (ผืน) phâakhawmáa'* (phɨ̌yn') N a long strip of patterned cloth used by men for various purposes (e.g. as a towel, loincloth, sash, or covering for the head).

ข่าว (ชิ้น, เรื่อง) khàaw' (chín', rɨ̂aŋ') N news. คน-- reporter.

ข่าวกระแสต่าง ๆ khàaw'-krasɛ̌ɛ'tàaŋtàaŋ' news from various sources or channels.

ข่าวคราว (ชิ้น) khàawkhraaw' (chín') N news (esp. one's personal news), tidings.

ข่าวโฆษณา khàaw'khôodsanaa' propaganda.

ข่าวทางการ khàaw'thaaŋkaan' official news.

ข่าวพาดหัว khàaw'phâadhǔa' headline news.

ข่าวล่า khàawlâa' late news.

○ ข่าวล่าที่สุด khàawlâa'thîisùd' the latest news.

ข่าวลือ (เรื่อง) khàawlyy' (rɨ̂aŋ') N rumor.

ข่าวเล่าลือ (เรื่อง) khàaw'lâwlyy' (rɨ̂aŋ') N rumor.

ข่าวสาร (ชิ้น, เรื่อง, อย่าง) khàawsăan' (chín',

rɨ̂aŋ', jàaŋ') N news.

○ สำนักข่าวสารอเมริกัน sămnág'-khàawsăan'ɔ ʔameerikan' U.S. Information Service.

ได้ข่าว(ว่า) dâjkhàaw'(wâaɔ) to hear (that), hear the news (of).

นักวิจารณ์ข่าว (คน) nágwícaan'khàaw' (khon') N news commentator.

ผู้ส่งข่าว (คน) phûusòŋkhàaw' (khon') N correspondent (for a newspaper).

ผู้สื่อข่าว (คน) phûusɨ̀ykhàaw' (khon') N newspaper reporter.

ภาพข่าว (ภาพ) phâabkhàaw' (phâab') N news pictures.

รายงานข่าว (กระแส, สาย, ฉบับ) (1) raajŋaanɔ khàaw' (krasɛ̌ɛ', săaj', chabàb'); (2) raajŋaan'ɔ khàaw' N 1. news report. V 2. to report news.

ลงข่าว loŋkhàaw' to publish the news.

สรุปข่าว sarùb'khàaw' V 1. to give a news summary. N 2. news summary.

เสนอข่าว sanǝǝ'khàaw' to present the news.

หัวข่าว (เรื่อง) hǔakhàaw' (rɨ̂aŋ') N news headline.

เหยี่ยวข่าว (คน) jìawkhàaw' (khon') N slang news reporter. [prob. tr. f. Eng. newshawk]

ข้าว khâaw', khâawɔ N rice. Also used in compounds designating cereal grains.

กับข้าว kàbkhâaw' N 1. food that is eaten with rice. 2. dishes (in the sense of foods). Often shortened to กับ. →See กับ ๒.

○ ทำกับข้าว thamkàbkhâaw' V to cook. คน-- cook.

กินข้าว kinkhâaw' V com. to eat (esp. to eat one's meal). →Comp. กินอาหาร. →Syn. รับประทานข้าว eleg., ฉันจังหัน sacer.

ข้าวแกง khâawkɛɛŋ' N rice with curry, eaten as a complete meal.

ข้าวของ (อย่าง, สิ่ง, ชิ้น, อัน) khâawkhɔ̌ɔŋ' (jàaŋ', sìŋ', chín', ʔan') N belongings, things, possessions; equipment, gear.

ข้าวเจ้า khâawcâaw' N nonglutinous rice. Also spelled ข้าวจ้าว. →Opp. ข้าวเหนียว.

○ แป้งข้าวจ้าว pɛ̂ŋ'khâawcâaw' N rice flour.

ข้าวต้ม khâawtôm' N rice boiled to soupy consistency, rice porridge.

ข้าวตอก khâawtɔ̀ɔg/ N popped rice, puffed rice.

ข้าวตัง khâawtaŋ/ N crisp cooked rice crust that
sticks to the bottom of the pot. (Eaten like
crackers when fried.)

ข้าวเบา khâawbaw/ N a rapidly maturing variety
of rice. →Opp. ข้าวหนัก.

ข้าวปลา, --อาหาร khâaw/plaa/, khâawplaa/ʔaaɔ
hăan/ N elab. colloq. food.

ข้าวเปลือก khâawplỳag/ N paddy, unhusked rice.

ข้าวผัด khâawphàd/ N fried rice.

ข้าวโพด (ฝัก,ดอก) khâawphôod/ (fàg/, dɔ̀ɔg/)
N corn, i.e. maize. Sometimes incorrectly
spelled ข้าวโภชน์. ต้น--(ต้น) corn (the plant).

ข้าวฟ่าง khâawfâaŋ/ N millet.

ข้าวยากหมากแพง khâawjâag/màagphɛɛŋ/ elab.
colloq. famine or hard times to exist, food
to be scarce.

ข้าวเย็น (มื้อ) khâawjen/ N 1. leftover cooked
rice, cold rice. 2. special. evening meal,
dinner (mýy/).

ข้าวสวย khâawsŭaj/ N boiled or steamed rice
(in which each grain is nicely separate).

ข้าวสาร khâawsăan/ N raw, husked rice.
→Opp. ข้าวสุก.

ข้าวสาลี khâawsăalii/* N wheat.

ข้าวสุก khâawsùg/ N boiled rice, cooked rice.
→Opp. ข้าวสาร.

ข้าวหนัก khâawnàg/ N a slowly maturing variety
of rice. →Opp. ข้าวเบา.

ข้าวเหนียว khâawnĭaw/ N glutinous rice.
→Opp. ข้าวเจ้า.

ปลายข้าว plaajkhâaw/ N broken milled rice
(used as animal feed).

รวงข้าว (รวง) ruaŋkhâaw/ (ruaŋ/) N rice ears.

หิวข้าว hĭwkhâaw/ V to be hungry.

หุงข้าว hŭŋkhâaw/ V to cook rice.

ข้าวแฝ่ khâwfɛ̀ɛ/* N colloq. coffee. The standard
word is กาแฟ kaafɛɛ/.

ข้าวหนม khâwnŏm/* N colloq. sweet foods.
The standard word is ขนม khanŏm.

ข้าศึก (คน) khâasỳg/ (khon/) N com. enemy.
→Syn. ปรปักษ์ eleg., ศัตรู com.

ขำ khăm/ V 1. to be funny, amusing. 2. to be
amused. 3. (a person) to be attractive (in

appearance).

นึกขำในใจ nýgkhăm/najcaj/ to be inwardly amused.

ขิง (หัว,แง่ง) khĭŋ/ (hŭa/, ŋɛ̂ŋ/) N ginger (hŭa/ for
the rhizome; ŋɛ̂ŋ/ for the branches of the rhizome). ต้น-- (ต้น) the ginger plant.

ถึงพริกถึงขิง thỳŋphríg/thỳŋkhĭŋ/ V elab.
colloq. 1. to be really hot, peppery, spicy
(of food). 2. to be racy, piquant (of conversation). อย่าง-- special. hotly, heatedly (of
arguing, debating).

ยุ่งขิง jûŋkhĭŋ/ V colloq. 1. to be highly involved, complicated, confusing. 2. to have
dealings (with), have to do (with).

ขี่ khìi/ V to ride; to drive.

กดขี่ kòdkhìi/ V to oppress, tyrannize.

ข่มขี่ khòmkhìi/ V to oppress, tyrannize.

ขับขี่ khàbkhìi/ V to drive, operate (a vehicle).

ขี่จักรยาน khìi/càgkrajaan/ V to ride a bicycle.

ขี้ ๑ khîi/ N 1. com.,vulg. excrement, dung,
droppings, excretion. 2. com. dregs, dirt,
ashes, residue. V 3. com.,vulg. to defecate.
→Syn. 1,3. อุจจาระ eleg., ทุ่ง ๒ colloq.

ขี้กบ (ชิ้น) khîikòb/ (chín/) N wood shavings.

ขี้กลาก khîiklâag/ N ringworm (tinea).

ขี้ไก่ (ก้อน) khîikàj/ (kɔ̂ɔn/) N com. fowl excrement.

ขี้ขยะ (กอง) khîikhajà?/ (kɔɔŋ/) N colloq.
waste, refuse, rubbish.

ขี้ข้า (คน) khîikhâa/ (khon/) N colloq. slave.

ขี้เขม่า khîikhamàw/ N colloq. soot, lampblack;
carbon deposit (as in car engine).

ขี้คร้อก khîikhrɔ̂ɔg/ N derog.,colloq. slave
(an appellation).

ขี้ครั่ง khîikhrâŋ/ N colloq. sticklac, i.e. lac
in its natural state before being refined for use.

ขี้ควาย khîikhwaaj/ N com. buffalo dung.

ขี้โคลน khîikhloon/ N colloq. mud.

ขี้ไคล khîikhlaj/ N colloq. scurf.

ขี้ตะกอน khîitakɔɔn/ N colloq. precipitate,
sediment, silt.

ขี้ตะไบเหล็ก khîitabajlèg/ iron filings.

ขี้ตา (ก้อน) khîitaa/ (kɔ̂ɔn/) N matter (in the eye).

ขี้ไต้ khîitâaj/ N punk, a composition of resin and
rotten wood used as tinder.

ขี้เถ้า khîithâw′ N ashes.

ขี้บุหรี่ khîiburìi′ N cigarette ashes.

ขี้ปะติ๋ว khîipatǐw′ V colloq. to be little, small
(in value), trifling, insignificant.

ขี้ปาก khîipàag′ N colloq. 1. gossip, idle talk.
2. the parroting of another's words. 3. a victim of gossip.

ขี้เป๋ khîipěe′ V colloq. to be bad, of poor
quality.

ขี้ผึ้ง khîiphûŋ′ N wax, beeswax.

ขี้ฟัน khîifan′ N com. decaying food particles
between the teeth.

ขี้มูก khîimûug′ N com.,vulg. snot. →Syn.
น้ำมูก eleg.

ขี้มูลฝอย khîimuunfɔ̌j′ N colloq. rubbish, refuse, litter.

ขี้ยา khîijaa′ N residuum (of opium). See also
under ขี้ ๒.

ขี้รังแค khîiraŋkhɛɛ′ N com. dandruff. →Syn.
ขี้หัว colloq.

ขี้ริ้ว khîiríw′ V colloq. to have no looks at
all, be plain and homely, unattractive (used of
people).

o หน้าตาขี้ริ้ว nâataa′khîiríw′ idem.

o ผ้าขี้ริ้ว (ผืน) phâakhiiríw′* (phǔyn′) N
colloq. rag.

ขี้เรื้อน khîirýan′ N colloq. leprosy.

o เป็นขี้เรื้อน pen′khîirýan′ to have leprosy,
be a leper.

ขี้เลื่อย khîilŷaj′ N sawdust.

ขี้วัว khîiwua′ N com. dung of cattle, cow ma-
nure.

ขี้สนิม khîisanìm′ N colloq. rust.

ขี้หนู khîinǔu′ N mouse or rat droppings. →See
also examples below.

o ขนมขี้หนู khanǒm′khîinǔu′ N a kind of sweet
food.

o พริกขี้หนู phrígkhîinǔu′ N bird pepper, a tiny,
very hot variety of chili.

ขี้หัว khîihǔa′ N colloq. 1. dandruff. 2. dirt (such
as collects on a comb). →Syn. 1. ขี้รังแค com.

ขี้หู khîihǔu′ N earwax.

ขี้- ๒ khîi⊂. Bound stem meaning "characterized
by, given to." Placed before verbs or nouns to

form verb derivatives. →Dist. เจ้า-๓,ช่าง ๒.

ขี้เกียจ khîikìad′ V com. to be lazy. →Syn.
เกียจคร้าน eleg.

ขี้โกง khîikooŋ′ V to be given to cheating, taking
advantage of others, trying to get out of obligations.

ขี้โกหก khîikoohòg′ V com. to be given to lying,
telling lies. →Syn. ขี้ปด eleg.

ขี้ขลาด khîikhlàad′ V colloq. to be given to
being cowardly, timid, timorous.

ขี้ขอ khîikhɔ̌ɔ′ V colloq. to have a habit of
asking for things.

ขี้คุก khîikhúg′ V colloq. to be a jailbird.

ขี้ตืด khîitỳyd′ V colloq. to be stingy. →Syn.
ตระหนี่ eleg., ขี้เหนียว com.

ขี้ตื่น khîitỳyn′ V colloq. to be easily excited
or alarmed.

ขี้ถัง khîithǎŋ′ V colloq. to be all that is bad
(of people).

ขี้เทือก khîithŷag′ V colloq. to be muddy, full
of mud or dirt.

ขี้บ่น khîibòn′ V colloq. to be given to complaining, grumbling; to be a complainer, grumbler.

ขี้ปด khîipòd′ V eleg. to be given to lying,
prevarication. →Syn. ขี้โกหก com.

o ขี้ปดมดเท็จ khîipòd′-mód′théd′ V elab. eleg.
to tell a lie, prevaricate.

ขี้เมา khîimaw′ V 1. to be given to drunkenness,
to be a drunkard; to be habitually drunk. 2. to
be given to motion sickness. ความ-- drunkenness. คน-- a drunkard; contrasts with คนเมา
one who is drunk (at a given time).

ขี้ยา (คน) khîijaa′ V 1. to be addicted to opium.
N 2. an opium addict (khon′). See also under
ขี้ ๑.

ขี้ร้อน khîirɔ́ɔn′ V to be sensitive to hot weather.

ขี้โรค khîirôog′ V to be sickly, unhealthy.

ขี้ลืม khîilyym′ V to be forgetful.

ขี้เล่น khîilên′ V to be playful.

ขี้สงสัย khîisǒŋsǎj′ V to be skeptical, given to
skepticism.

ขี้สงสาร khîisǒŋsǎan′ V to be overly sympathetic,
readily sympathetic, compassionate.

ขี้หนาว khîinǎaw′ V to be sensitive to cold weather.

ขี้หลง, --ขี้ลืม khîiloŋ/, khîilǒŋ/khîilyym/ V
    e l a b. c o l l o q. to be forgetful, absent-minded.
ขี้หวงแหน khîihǔaŋhěɛn/ V to be possessive.
ขี้หึง khîihẙŋ/ V to be jealous, given to jealousy
    (of husband and wife; of lovers).
ขี้เหนียว khîinǐaw/ V c o l l o q. to be stingy.
    →S y n. ตระหนี่ elĕg., ขี้ตึ๊ด c o l l o q.
ขี้อวด khîi?ùad/ V to be boastful, given to brag-
    ging.
ขี้อ้อน khîi?ɔɔn/ V to be given to crying.
ขี้อาย khîi?aaj/ V to be shy, bashful.
ขี้เอาถ่าน khîi?awthàan/ V to be diligent, indus-
    trious.
ขีด (ขีด) khìid/ (khìid/) N 1. line; dash (typo-
    graphical symbol). 2. limit. V 3. to draw,
    scratch (lines), mark, score (with lines).
ขีดขวน khìidkhǔan/ V to scratch, mark with a
    sharp object.
ขีดเขียน khìidkhǐan/ V to write.
ขีดฆ่า khìidkhâa/ V to scratch out, cross out,
    strike out.
ขีดคู่นย์ (ขีด) khìidsǔun/ (khìid/) N zero line,
    zero point; rest point (of a balance).
ขีดเส้นใต้ khìid/sêntâaj/ to underline, under-
    score.
ไม้ขีด, --ไฟ (อัน, ก้าน, กลัก) májkhìid/, májɔ
    khìidfaj/ N match, matchstick (?an/, kâan/
    for individual matches; klàg/ for boxes).
o ขีดไม้ขีดไฟ khìid/májkhìidfaj/ V to strike a
    match.
รอยขีด (รอย) rɔɔjkhìid/ (rɔɔj/) N scratch.
ขึง khẙŋ/ V 1. to stretch, to stretch taut, stretch
    out. 2. to string (as a tennis racket).
ขึงขัง khẙŋkhǎŋ/ V to be vigorous, serious,
    energetic.
ขึ้ง, --โกรธ khẙŋ/, khẙŋ/krôod/ V to be angry.
ขึ้น ๑ khẙn/ V 1. to rise, grow. 2. to board, climb,
    mount, get on. 3. to ascend (a throne), enter
    upon (a new reign, a new year). 4. to raise,
    lift up. sV 5. up; more, increasingly, get . . .
    -er. →A n t. ลง. →S y n. 3. เถลิง elĕg.
ขาขึ้น khǎakhẙn/ N the upstream trip, the north-
    bound trip; (on) the way up.
ข้างขึ้น khâaŋkhẙn/ (period of) the waxing moon.

ขึ้นเงา khẙnŋaw/ V to be glossy, lustrous.
ขึ้นเงิน khẙnŋɔn/ V to redeem for cash.
ขึ้นจากเรือ khẙncàagrya/ to step ashore, disem-
    bark.
ขึ้นใจ. See entries below.
o จำขึ้นใจ cam/khẙncaj/ to learn by heart.
o จำได้ขึ้นใจ camdâaj/khẙncaj/ 1. to remember
    vividly. 2. to learn by heart.
ขึ้นช้าง khẙncháaŋ/ V 1. to mount an elephant.
    2. to be mounted on an elephant.
ขึ้นชื่อ khẙnchʉy/ V c o l l o q. 1. to be famous,
    well-known, popular, have a reputation. 2. to
    be mentioned or talked about often.
ขึ้นเช็ค khẙnchég/ V to cash a check. [เช็ค f. Eng.]
ขึ้นต้น khẙntôn/ V to begin, commence.
ขึ้นทะเบียน khẙn/thabian/ V to register for some-
    thing, be registered, get (one's name) on a reg-
    ister. Usually for military service and for auto-
    mobiles.
ขึ้นนั่งเมือง khẙnnâŋ/myaŋ/ c o l l o q. to become
    the ruler of a country.
ขึ้นบก khẙnbòg/ V to land, go ashore.
o ยก. . .ขึ้นบก jóg/. . .khẙnbòg/ to land (e.g.
    troops), put ashore.
ขึ้นบัญชี khẙn/banchii/ V to be registered, listed,
    entered in a list.
ขึ้นปีใหม่ khẙn/piimàj/ to start a new year.
o งานขึ้นปีใหม่ ŋaan/khẙnpiimàj/ New Year fes-
    tival.
o วันขึ้นปีใหม่ wan/khẙnpiimàj/ New Year's Day.
ขึ้นไป khẙnpaj/ V 1. to go up. sV 2. up, upward;
    onward; increasingly.
o ยิ่ง ๆ ขึ้นไป jîŋjîŋ/khẙnpaj/ better and better,
    more and more, progressively, increasingly.
ขึ้นมา khẙnmaa/ V 1. to come up, rise. 2. to
    grow, increase. sV 3. up, upward; onward;
    increasingly.
o ตลอดขึ้นมาจนถึง talɔɔd/-khẙnmaa/conthẙŋɔ
    all the way up to.
ขึ้นรถ khẙnród/ V to take, board, get on a train
    or bus; to take, get in a car.
ขึ้นรา khẙnraa/ V to get mildewed, moldy.
ขึ้นราคา khẙnraakhaa/ V to raise the price.
ขึ้นลง khẙnloŋ/ V 1. to fluctuate, rise and fall;

เขน ๑ (อัน) khěen/ (?an/) N a round shield.

เขน ๒ in กางเขน (อัน) kaaŋkhěen/ (?an/) N cross.

เข็น khěn/ V to push; to move forward by pushing and pulling.

    เข็น(...)ไม่ไป khěn(...)mâjpaj/ 1. can't budge (something); (it) won't budge. 2. (a person) to be unteachable, dumb.

    รถเข็น (คัน) ródkhěn/ (khan/) N pushcart, buggy (esp. baby buggy).

เข่น khèn/* V to beat hard.

    เข่นเขี้ยว khènkhîaw/ V to gnash the teeth, grind the teeth (in anger).

เข็ม (เล่ม,อัน) khěm/ (lêm/, ?an/) N 1. needle, pin. 2. hand (of a clock).

    เข็มกลัด (อัน) khěmklàd/ (?an/) N 1. safety pin. 2. pin, brooch.

    o เข็มกลัดซ่อนปลาย (อัน) khěmklàd/sɔ̂ɔnplaaj/ (?an/) N safety pin.

    เข็มขัด (สาย,เส้น) khěmkhàd/ (sǎaj/, sên/) N belt.

    o หัวเข็มขัด (หัว,อัน) hǔakhěmkhàd/ (hǔa/, ?an/) N buckle.

    เข็มชั่วโมง (อัน) khěm/chûamooŋ/ (?an/) N hour hand (of clock or watch).

    เข็มชี้ khěmchíi/ N pointer, indicator.

    เข็มทิศ (อัน) khěmthíd/ (?an/) N compass.

    เข็มนาที (อัน) khěm/naathii/ (?an/) N minute hand (of clock or watch).

    เข็มยาว (อัน) khěmjaaw/ (?an/) N idem.

    เข็มเย็บผ้า (เล่ม) khěm/jébphâa/ (lêm/) N sewing needle.

    เข็มสั้น (อัน) khěmsân/ (?an/) N hour hand.

    เข็มหมุด (เล่ม,ตัว) khěmmùd/ (lêm/, tua/) N pin.

    เข้าด้ายเข้าเข็ม khâwdâaj/khâwkhěm/ V idiom. to be crucial, decisive.

    ต้นเข็ม (ต้น) tônkhěm/ (tôn/) N a shrub or tree of the genera Ixora, Pavetta, or Duperrea.

    ตั้งเข็ม tâŋ/khěm/ V idiom. to form a purpose.

    ปลาเข็ม (ตัว) plaakhěm/ (tua/) N needlefish, fish of the Belonidae family.

เข้ม khêm/* V 1. to be intense, strong, concentrated. 2. to be deep, dark (of colors).

    เข้มข้น khêmkhôn/ V to be concentrated, thick.

    เข้มแข็ง khêmkhěŋ/ V 1. to be strong, powerful, vigorous, ardent. sV 2. sedulously, hard and persistently (as of working). ความ-- strength, power, ardor.

    เข้มงวด khêmŋûad/ V 1. to be strict, rigid. 2. to curb.

เข้มิ้ง khamě̂ŋ/ rM used with จ้อง "gaze," มอง "look" in the sense of "fixedly, rigidly."

เขม่น khamèn/* V 1. (muscles) to twitch. 2. slang to find irritating, be irritated by; to be irritating, get on one's nerves.

    o ผมเขม่นหมอนั่นมาก phǒm/-khamèn/mɔ̌ɔ/-nânɔ maag/↓ I'm quite irritated by that fellow.

    o หมอนี่เขม่นจริง mɔ̌ɔnîi/khamèn/ciŋ/↓ This guy really gets on my nerves.

เขม้น ๑ khamên/* V to stare (at).

    เขม้นมอง khamên/mɔɔŋ/ V 1. to stare at, gaze at. 2. to look at (something) closely, fixedly.

เขม้น ๒ in ขะมักเขม้น khamàg/khamên/, khamág/ɔ khamên/ V to be serious, determined, earnest, energetic.

เขมร khaměen/ N com. Cambodia; Cambodian, Khmer. →Syn. กัมพูชา lit.

    ประเทศเขมร prathêed/khaměen/ pN eleg. Cambodia.

เขม่า khamàw/ N colloq. soot, lampblack; carbon deposit (as in car engine). →Also ขี้--.

เขย khɔ̌ɔj/ N a male relative by marriage who is the husband of a blood relative within a given family. The term designates a man as an in-law of his wife's blood relatives. Generally combined with kinship terms. →Opp. สะใภ้.

    น้องเขย (คน) nɔ́ɔŋkhɔ̌ɔj/ (khon/) N brother-in-law who is the husband of one's younger sister.

    พี่เขย (คน) phîikhɔ̌ɔj/ (khon/) N brother-in-law who is the husband of one's older sister.

    ลูกเขย (คน) lûugkhɔ̌ɔj/ (khon/) N son-in-law.

    หลานเขย (คน) lǎankhɔ̌ɔj/ (khon/) N the husband of one's niece or granddaughter.

เขยก,โขยก-- khajèeg/, khajòog/khajèeg/ V 1. to limp, hobble (in walking). 2. to wobble (as a table).

เขย่ง khajèŋ/* V 1. to tiptoe, stand on tiptoe. 2. to

hop on one leg.

เขย่งเก็งกอยก้าวกระโดด khajèŋkeŋkɔɔjkâaw′ɔ
kradòod′ N hop-step-and-jump, an athletic
sport.

เขย่า khajàw′ V to shake.

เขย่าขวัญ khajàw′khwǎn′ V 1. to threaten. 2.
to frighten, shake profoundly.

เขยิบ khajə̀b′* V 1. to shift, move over. 2. to better one's position, move up.

เขยื้อน,ขยับ-- khajýan′, khajàb′khajýan′ V to shift
slightly, budge, move.

เขละ khlè?′ V 1. to be thick and coarse in consistency, gooey. sV 2. in disorderly array.

เขละ ๆ khlè?khlè?′ idem. เขละ mng. 1.

เขลา khlǎw′ V to be stupid, ignorant. ความ--
stupidity.

เขว khwěe′ V to go awry (as one's plans), be
amiss.

ไขว้เขว khwâjkhwěe′ V to be confused, mixed
up, disorganized.

เขา ๑ (ลูก) khǎw′ (lûug′) N mountain, hill.

ช่องเขา (ช่อง) chɔ̂ŋkhǎw′ (chɔ̂ŋ′) N mountain
pass.

ชาวเขาชาวดอย (คน) chaawkhǎw′chaawdɔɔj′
(khon′) N elab. colloq. mountain people.

เชิงเขา (แห่ง) chəəŋkhǎw′ (hèŋ′) N eleg.
foothills, the foot of a hill. →Syn. ตีนเขา
com.

ตีนเขา (แห่ง) tiinkhǎw′ (hèŋ′) N com. foothills, the foot of a hill. →Syn. เชิงเขา eleg.

ทิวเขา (ทิว) thiwkhǎw′ (thiw′) N mountain
range.

เทือกเขา (เทือก) thŷagkhǎw′ (thŷag′) N mountain range, mountain chain.

พืดเขา (พืด) phŷyd′khǎw′ (phŷyd′) N mountain
range, mountain chain.

ภูเขา (ลูก) phuukhǎw′ (lûug′) N mountain.

o เป็นภูเขา pen′phuukhǎw′ to be mountainous.

ยอดเขา (ยอด) jɔ̂ɔdkhǎw′ (jɔ̂ɔd′) N mountain
top, peak, pinnacle.

หว่างเขา (แห่ง) wàaŋkhǎw′ (hèŋ′) N valley,
esp. cultivatable depression between mountains.

หุบเขา (แห่ง) hùbkhǎw′ (hèŋ′) N valley.

เขา ๒ (เขา,ข้าง,อัน) khǎw′ N 1. horn (of an

animal)(khǎw′, khâaŋ′). 2. wind instrument,
horn (for blowing signals)(?an′).

เขากวาง (เขา,ข้าง) khǎwkwaaŋ′ (khǎw′, khâaŋ′)
N antlers.

เขากิ่ง (เขา) khǎwkìŋ′ (khǎw′) N antler.

เขา ๓ in นกเขา (ตัว) nógkhǎw′ (tua′) N dove,
turtledove.

เขา ๔ khǎw′, kháw′ P com. 1. he, him, she, her,
they, them (also used for indef. reference). Used
only of people. 2. colloq. I, me. →Dist. 1.
มัน ๓. →Syn. 1. ท่าน eleg. defer. NOTE.
Pronounced khǎw′ only in careful or emphatic
speech; normally kháw′.

o เขารู้หรอกน่า kháwrúu′rɔ̀gnâa↓ colloq.
I know (about it already).

o เขาเล่ากันว่า kháwlâw′kanwâa′ people are
saying (such and such).

พวกเขา phûagkháw′ N they, them, the others.
→Opp. พวกเรา.

เข่า (ข้าง,เข่า) khàw′ (khâaŋ′, khàw′) N knee.

คุกเข่า khúgkhàw′ V to kneel.

หัวเข่า (ข้าง) hǔakhàw′ (khâaŋ′) N knee.

เข้า ๑ FS. See ข้าว.

เข้าของ. See ข้าวของ.

เข้า ๒ khâw′, khâwɔ V 1. to enter. 2. to insert,
fit, put on. 3. to sympathize, side (with). 4.
to join. 5. to come into contact (with). sV 6.
in, into, to. 7. increasingly, up. As secondary
verb often best ommitted in the English translation. See also ไม่เข้า below. →Ant. ออก.

ใกล้(...)เข้า klâj(...)khâw′ to approach, come
near, come up close.

o เมื่อใกล้ค่ำเข้า mŷaklâjkhâm′khâw′ when it is
approaching nightfall.

ขาเข้า khǎakhâw′ (on) the way in, incoming.

เข้ากระดูกดำ khâwkradùug′dam′ to be deep-seated,
ingrained, firmly entrenched. อย่าง-- deeply,
extremely, in the extreme.

เข้ากัน khâw′kan 1. to match (as colors); to
blend together. 2. to side with each other.

เข้ากับ khâw′kaɔ to side with.

เข้าเกียร์ khâwkia′ to put in gear, engage the
gears.

เข้าใกล้ khâwklâj′ V to come near, get close.

เข้าข้าง khâwkhâaŋ′ to side with, sympathize with.

เข้าแข่งขัน khâw′khèŋkhǎn′ to enter the competition. คน-- competitor, contestant.

เข้าคิว khâwkhiw′ V to queue up. [คิว f. Eng.]

เข้าใครออกใคร khâwkhraj′ʔɔ̀ɔgkhraj′ colloq. to be partial, to favor one and not the other.

o ไม่เข้าใครออกใคร mâjkhâwkhraj′ʔɔ̀ɔgkhraj′ to be neutral, impartial.

เข้าโจมตี khâwcoom′tii′ V to attack, assault, strike.

เข้าใจ khâwcaj′ V to understand. การ-- (act of) understanding, comprehension. ความ-- (state of) understanding, comprehension.

o เข้าใจกันว่า khâwcaj′kanwâa′ it is understood that, it is commonly understood that.

o เข้าใจผิด khâwcajphìd′ V to misunderstand, mistake. การ-- (act of) misunderstanding. ความ-- (state of) misunderstanding.

o เข้าใจว่า khâwcaj′wâa′ 1. to understand that, be under the impression that. 2. (it) is understood that.

o เข้าใจสอน khâwcaj′sɔ̌ɔn′ to teach expertly, with know-how.

o เป็นที่เข้าใจ(ว่า) penthîi′khâwcaj′(wâa′) it is understood (that), it is a known fact (that).

เข้าชุดเข้ารอย khâwchúd′khâwrɔɔj′ V elab. colloq. to fit (in with a set, a series), to match.

เข้าด้ายเข้าเข็ม khâwdâaj′khâwkhěm′ V idiom. to be crucial, decisive.

o ตกฐานะเข้าด้ายเข้าเข็ม tòg′thǎaná?′-khâwɔ dâaj′/khâwkhěm′ to get into a tight spot, a critical situation.

เข้าตาจน khâwtaa′con′ colloq. to be in a fix, to be having a hard time.

เข้าไต้เข้าไฟ khâwtâaj′khâwfaj′ V elab. colloq. to be getting dark, be twilight.

เข้าที khâwthii′ V 1. to be appropriate; to sound all right, look all right, seem all right. 2. to be pleasant in appearance, attractive.

เข้านอน khâwnɔɔn′ V to retire, go to bed.

เข้าเนื้อ (1) khâwnýa′; (2) khâw′nýa′ V 1. idiom. to lose (opp. of gain). 2. to penetrate into the

flesh (as an ointment), into the meat (as seasoning).

เข้าป่าเข้าดง khâwpàa′khâwdoŋ′ V elab. colloq. to go off into the jungle (used esp. in a fig. sense, i.e. to get away from it all).

เข้าปิ้ง khâwpîŋ′ V idiom. to be in hot water, in a tight spot.

เข้าเป็นสมาชิก khâwpen′samaachíg′ to become a member of, to join (an organization).

เข้าไป khâwpaj′ V 1. to go in. 2. to join, enter (an organization). sV 3. in.

เข้าเฝ้า khâwfâw′ V to have an audience with (a royal person).

เข้าพบ khâwphób′ V to call on, make a (formal) call.

เข้าพรรษา khâwphansǎa′ to be in the Buddhist Lent (in the rainy season).

เข้ามา khâwmaa′ V 1. to come in. sV 2. in.

เข้าเมือง khâwmyaŋ′ V to be immigrant; to immigrate; to enter a country or town. คน-- immigrant, entrant into a country or town.

o ด่านเข้าเมือง (ด่าน) dàankhâwmyaŋ′ (dàan′) N immigration office, post (at the point of entry).

เข้ายาม khâwjaam′ V to be on duty (as a guard, night watchman).

เข้ายึด khâwjýd′ V to capture, seize, occupy.

เข้าร่วม khâwrûam′ V to join; to participate (in).

เข้ารับตำแหน่ง khâwráb′tamnèŋ′ to assume an official position, take office.

เข้ารับมือกับ khâw′rábmyy′-kaɔ to get into a fight with.

เข้ารูป khâwrûub′ V 1. to fit in (with), conform (to). 2. to be fitted, form-fitting (as a dress). 3. to form, take shape.

เข้าใส่ khâwsàj′ sV at, toward.

o กระโจนเข้าใส่ kracoon′khâwsàj′ to leap up at.

เข้าหน้า khâw′nâa′ V 1. to face, confront. 2. to meet with, be friends with. 3. to arrange pages in proper order, insert pages.

เข้าหา khâwhǎa′ V 1. to go see (someone about something). 2. to give oneself up, turn oneself in. sV 3. to, toward.

o ขีดเข้าหาตัว khìid′-khâwhǎa′tua′ to strike (a match) toward oneself.

o เข้าหากัน khâwhǎa′kan′ at each other, towards each other; together.

เข้าหุ้น khâwhûn′ V to go into partnership, team up.

เข้าออก khâw′ʔɔ̀ɔg′ V 1. to go in and out. sV 2. in and out.

ตกดึกเข้า tògdɤ̀g′khâw to get to be late (at night).

ตรงเข้าไล่ troŋ′khâwlâj′ to set out to chase, start in chasing.

ถูก(...)เข้า thùug′(...)khâw to come in contact with, be exposed to (e.g. heat).

ทดน้ำเข้านา thódnáam′khâwnaa′ to irrigate a field.

ทางเข้า (ทาง) thaaŋkhâw′ (thaaŋ′) N 1. a way in. 2. entrance, entry way, inlet. →Ant. ทาง ออก.

ผีเข้าผีออก phǐikhâw′phǐiʔɔ̀ɔg′ V 1. idiom. to be characterized by changing one's mind suddenly, without apparent or adequate motive. 2. to be changing, fluctuating, inconsistent.

ผูกติดกันเข้า phûug′-tìd′kankhâw to tie up together.

พบ(...)เข้า phób′(...)khâw to encounter, meet up with, run into.

ไม่เข้า. See entries below.

o กินไม่เข้า kin′mâjkhâw′ can't eat (it), can't get (it) down; to be inedible.

o ดันไม่เข้า dan′mâjkhâw′ can't push (it) in, can't push (it) together.

o ปิดไม่เข้า pìd′mâjkhâw′ can't close it; (it) won't close.

o ใส่ไม่เข้า sàj′mâjkhâw′ can't put it in or on; (it) won't go in, go on.

ไม่เข้าเรื่อง mâjkhâwrɤ̂aŋ′ to be irrelevant, impertinent, nonsensical.

เร็วเข้า rew′khâw↓ Hurry up!

สินค้าเข้า sǐnkháa′khâw′ N import.

เห็น(...)เข้า hěn′(...)khâw′ to catch sight of.

เขิน ๑ khɤ̌ən′ V to be lacking (in some essential), be amiss, incongruous, out of keeping.

o ประโยคนี้ฟังเขินชอบกล prajòog′níi′ faŋ′-khɤ̌ən′chɔ̂ɔbkon′↓ This sentence sounds strangely lacking, i.e. sounds forced.

ขวยเขิน khǔajkhɤ̌ən′ V to feel bashful, shy, em-

barrassed, self-conscious (often esp. of women).

เคอะเขิน khɤ́ʔkhɤ̌ən′ V to be stiff, unnatural, out of place, awkward.

เขิน ๒ khɤ̌ən′ V to be shallow (because of silt and sediment, e.g. a canal).

โขดเขิน khòod′khɤ̌ən′ N mound, hill.

ตื้นเขิน tɤ̂yn′khɤ̌ən′ V to be shallow, become shallow (e.g. of a canal getting filled with sediment.

เขิน ๓ in เครื่องเขิน (ชิ้น) khrɤ̂aŋkhɤ̌ən′ (chín′) N lacquerware.

เขี่ย khìa′ V 1. to flick, flick off (e.g. ashes from cigarette), remove, dislodge. 2. to scratch (as a chicken). 3. to scrape away (e.g. food scraps into the garbage can).

เขี่ยกุญแจ khìa′kuncɛɛ′ to pick a lock (e.g. with wire).

ถูกเขี่ย thùugkhìa′ slang to be transferred, removed, gotten out of the way.

ที่เขี่ยบุหรี่ (อัน,ที่) thîikhìa′burìi′ (ʔan′,thîi′) N ash tray.

เขียง (อัน,แผ่น) khǐaŋ′ (ʔan′,phèn′) N chopping block, cutting board.

เขียด (ตัว) khìad′ (tua′) N a small green frog.

เขียน khǐan′ V to write, draw. นัก-- writer, author.

ข้อเขียน (อย่าง,วิชา) khɔ̂ɔkhǐan′ (jàaŋ′,wíchaa′) N written examination (as opposed to oral).

ขีดเขียน khìid′khǐan′ V to write.

เขียนถึง khǐan′thɤ̌ŋɔ V 1. to write about. 2. to write to.

เขียนหนังสือ khǐan′naŋsɤ̌y′ V to write.

เขียนหวัด khǐanwàd′ V to scribble, write hastily.

เครื่องเขียน (อย่าง,ชิ้น) khrɤ̂aŋkhǐan′ (jàaŋ′, chín′) N stationery, writing supplies.

ช่างเขียน (คน) châaŋkhǐan′ (khon′) N artist, painter, draftsman.

ภาพเขียน (ภาพ) phâabkhǐan′ (phâab′) N a drawing (as opposed to a painting or photograph).

วาดเขียน wâadkhǐan′ V to draw. นัก-- artist.

เขียว khǐaw′ V to be green.

เขียวจี๋ khǐawkhacii′ to be a light, bright green (e.g. the color of grass or leaves).

เขียวชอุ่ม khǐawchaʔùm′ to be bright green, fresh

and green (of vegetation).

เขียวแปร๊ khĭawprέε′ to be very green.

เขียวแปร๊ด khĭawpréd′ to be a bright, dazzling
green.

เขียวสด khĭawsòd′ to be bright green.

เขียวอี๋ khĭaw?ĭi′ to be deep green.

เขียวอื๋อ khĭaw?ўy′ to be deep green.

ดำเขียว damkhĭaw′ 1. to be greenish-black,
green-tinged black. 2. to be "black and blue,"
in the following entry.

o ฟกช้ำดำเขียว fógchám′damkhĭaw′ colloq.
to be bruised black and blue.

ตาเขียว taa′khĭaw′ V 1. to have an angry look
in the eyes. 2. to have a black eye (i.e. a
bruised eye).

สีเขียว sĭikhĭaw′ N 1. green, the color green.
V 2. to be green.

สุดหล้าฟ้าเขียว sùdlâa′fáakhĭaw′ elab. colloq.
very far away, beyond the horizon.

เสียงเขียว sĭaŋ′khĭaw′ V 1. to have an angry
voice. sV 2. in an angry voice.

หน้าเขียว nâa′khĭaw′ V to look sick; to turn pale
(as when sick or exhausted).

เหม็นเขียว mĕnkhĭaw′ V to smell bad. Acc. to
some speakers, to have an odor like that of
crushed green leaves.

เขี้ยว (ขี้) khîaw′ (sîi′) N fang, canine tooth,
eyetooth.

เข็ดเขี้ยว khèdkhîaw′ V to dread (to do something), to be afraid, esp. because of a previous
bad experience.

เข่นเขี้ยว khènkhîaw′ V to gnash the teeth,
grind the teeth (in anger).

ถอดเขี้ยวถอดงา thɔ̀ɔdkhîaw′thɔ̀ɔdŋaa′ idiom.
(a person) to become gentle, subdued, peaceful,
no longer vicious or cross: "to remove one's
fangs and tusks."

มันเขี้ยว man′khîaw′ V "to feel like biting (into
something)." Used, for instance, when seeing
the temptingly chubby cheeks of a child.

เขื่อง khỳaŋ′ V to be rather big (for its kind).

o วาจาอันเขื่องโข waa′caa′-?ankhỳaŋ′khŏo′
big talk, boasting.

เขื่อน (เขื่อน) khỳan′ (khỳan′) N dam, dike, em-

bankment, levee, barrage, breakwater. →Comp.
ทำนบ.

แข khĕε′ N lit. moon. →Syn. เดือน.

แขก (คน,ท่าน) khὲεg′ (khon′,thân′) N 1. guest,
visitor. 2. person from India, Pakistan, the
Middle East, Africa, Malaya, Java. Often refers
particularly to an Indian (from India) when used
alone.

กล้วยแขก (ชิ้น) klûajkhὲεg′ (chín′) N banana
slices, dipped in batter and fried.

แขกดำ (คน) khὲεgdam′ (khon′) N 1. Indian with
a very dark complexion. 2. Negro.

แขกมะลายู (คน) khὲεg′malaajuu′ (khon′) N
Malayan, a person from Malaya.

แขกเมือง (คน,ท่าน) khὲεgmyaŋ′ (khon′,thân′)
N an official foreign visitor.

แขกยาม (คน) khὲεgjaam′ (khon′) Indian watchman.

แขกเหรื่อ (คน,ท่าน) khὲεg′rỳa′ (khon′,thân′)
N elab. colloq. guest.

แขกอินเดีย (คน) khὲεg′-?india′ (khon′) N
Indian, a person from India.

รับแขก rábkhὲεg′ V to receive, welcome, entertain guests or visitors.

o ห้องรับแขก (ห้อง) hɔ̂ŋ′rábkhὲεg′ (hɔ̂ŋ′) N
living room.

ลงแขก loŋkhὲεg′ V idiom. to hold a bee, get
the help of one's neighbors on a given day, esp.
for transplanting or harvesting rice.

แข็ง khĕŋ′ V 1. to be hard, firm, strong, stiff. sV
2. well, ably, firmly. →Syn. กระด้าง. →Ant.
See นิ่ม.

o ผมยังว่ายน้ำไม่แข็ง phŏm′ jaŋwâajnáam′mâjɔ
khĕŋ′ I can't swim very well yet.

กระดาษแข็ง (แผ่น) kradàad′khĕŋ′ (phὲn′) N
cardboard, card paper, stiff paper.

กล้าแข็ง klâakhĕŋ′ V to be brave, strong.

ของแข็ง khɔ̆ɔŋkhĕŋ′ N solid.

เข้มแข็ง khêmkhĕŋ′ V 1. to be strong, powerful,
vigorous, ardent. sV 2. sedulously, hard and
persistently (as of working).

แข็งกล้า khĕŋklâa′ V 1. to be hard (of metal,
esp. steel). 2. to be brave.

แข็งขัน,ขันแข็ง khĕŋkhăn′, khănkhĕŋ′ V to be

diligent, industrious; to do things assiduously, wholeheartedly.

แข็งขึ้น khěŋ'khŷn' to get harder, firmer.

แข็งใจ khěŋcaj' V to summon up one's courage, steel oneself (to do something).

แข็งตัว khěŋtua' V to harden, solidify, set, freeze (of itself).

แข็งแรง khěŋrɛɛŋ' V to be strong, powerful, solid (i.e. not weak, flimsy).

ใจแข็ง cajkhěŋ' V to be hard-hearted, unyielding.

แดดแข็ง dɛ̀ɛd'khěŋ' the sunlight is strong.

น้ำแข็ง (ก้อน) námkhěŋ' (kɔɔn') N ice.

เนยแข็ง nəəjkhěŋ' N cheese.

ปากแข็ง pàag'khěŋ' V 1. to be argumentative. 2. to be unwilling to tell or admit, to be tight-lipped.

เยือกแข็ง jŷag'khěŋ' V to freeze solid.

เสียงแข็ง sĭaŋ'khěŋ' V to be stern, firm, confident (in one's manner of speaking).

หัวแข็ง hŭakhěŋ' V to be obstinate, hard-headed.

แข่ง (กับ) khèŋ'(kaɔ)* V to compete (with).

แข่งขัน khèŋkhǎn' V to compete. การ-- competition, contest, game, match.

o การสอบแข่งขัน kaansɔ̀ɔb'khèŋkhǎn' N competitive examination.

o เข้าแข่งขัน khâw'khèŋkhǎn' to enter the competition. คน-- competitor, contestant.

o คู่แข่งขัน (คน) khûu'khèŋkhǎn' (khon') N competitor, rival.

แข่งม้า (ครั้ง, นัด, เที่ยว) (1) khèŋ'máa'; (2) khèŋmáa' 1. to race on horseback; to participate in horse racing. N 2. the races, horse races, horse racing (khráŋ', nád'); a (horse) race (thîaw'). การ-- horse racing.

คู่แข่ง (คน) khûukhèŋ' (khon') N competitor, rival.

ม้าแข่ง (ตัว) máakhèŋ' (tua') N race horse.

วิ่งแข่ง wîŋkhèŋ' V to race.

แข่ง (ข้าง) khèŋ'*(khâaŋ') N shin.

แข่งขา, ขาแข่ง (ข้าง, ขา) khèŋ'khǎa', khǎa'khèŋ' (khâaŋ', khǎa') N colloq. legs.

ลำแข่ง lamkhèŋ' N 1. idiom. personal effort, endeavor. 2. shin (rarely used in this meaning;

see following entry).

หน้าแข้ง (ข้าง) nâakhɛ̂ŋ' (khâaŋ') N shin.

แขน (แขน, ข้าง) khɛ̌ɛn' (khɛ̌ɛn', khâaŋ') N 1. arm. 2. sleeve. 3. chem. bond. C 4. a linear measure: an arm's length.

o เสื้อแขนกุด sŷa'khɛ̌ɛnkùd' sleeveless blouse.

แขนขา (ข้าง) khɛ̌ɛnkhǎa' (khâaŋ') N arms and legs, limbs.

วงแขน woŋkhɛ̌ɛn' N embrace, encircling arms.

หน้าแขน (ข้าง) nâa'khɛ̌ɛn' (khâaŋ') N "the front of the arm," i.e. the inner part of the forearm, and the forward part of the upper arm.

แขนง (แขนง) khanɛ̌ɛŋ' (khanɛ̌ɛŋ') N branch, twig.

แขยัก ๆ khajɛ̀g'khajɛ̀g' sV bit by bit with difficulty (of climbing).

แขยง ๑ in ปลาแขยง plaakhajɛ̌ɛŋ' N catfish.

แขยง ๒ in ขยะแขยง khajà?'khajɛ̌ɛŋ' V to feel disgust, repugnance, loathing.

แขวง (แขวง) khwɛ̌ɛŋ' (khwɛ̌ɛŋ') N district, region, subdivision of a province.

ศาลแขวง (ศาล) sǎan'khwɛ̌ɛŋ' (sǎan') N district court.

แขวน khwɛ̌ɛn' V to hang, suspend.

แขวนนวม khwɛ̌ɛnnuam' idiom. to quit boxing: "to hang up the boxing gloves."

ไม้แขวนเสื้อ (อัน) májkhwɛ̌ɛnsŷa' (?an') N coat hanger.

โข khǒo' V 1. to be plenty, much, many. sV 2. quite, very.

o ไกลโขอยู่ klaj'khǒo'-jùu↓ It's quite far.

โขก khôog' V to knock, rap, knock against, poke at.

โขง in แม่โขง mɛ̂ɛkhǒoŋ' pN 1. the Mækhong (Mekong) River, which forms a part of the border between Thailand and nations to the E. N 2. the brand name of a liquor made in Bangkok. →Also 1. แม่น้ำโขง.

โข่ง ๑ khòoŋ' V 1. to be stupid, ignorant, silly. 2. to be big and awkward.

โข่ง ๒ in หอยโข่ง (ตัว) hɔ̌jkhòoŋ' (tua') N a kind of snail.

โขด (โขด) khòod' (khòod') N knoll, mound. →Syn. โคก, เนิน.

โขดเขิน khòod'khə̌ən' idem.

โขน (โรง, ตัว) khǒon' N 1. a type of Thai drama.

2. the theater in which this type of drama is played (rooŋ′). 3. actors or actresses of this type of drama (tua′).

โขมง khamǒoŋ′ rM used with ควัน "smoke," คุย "talk," to mean "in large amounts, profusely."

โขยก,--เขยก khajòog′, khajòog/khajèeg′ V 1. to limp, hobble (in walking). 2. to wobble (as a table).

โขยง (โขยง) khajǒoŋ′ (khajǒoŋ′) N 1. group (of people), party, company. 2. kin.

โขย่ง khajòoŋ′ V to stand on tiptoe. →Also กระ- หย่ง,กระโหย่ง.
เดินโขย่งเท้า dəən′khajòoŋtháaw′ to tiptoe, walk on tiptoe.

โขลก khlòog′ V to pound, crush to a pulp. →Syn. ตำ.

โขลง khlǒoŋ′ C herd (of elephants).

ไข ๑ khǎj′ N 1. fat, grease. 2. marrow.
ไขมัน khǎjman′ N fat.
ไขสันหลัง khǎjsǎnlǎŋ′ N spinal cord.
o ไข้ไขสันหลัง khâj′khǎjsǎnlǎŋ′ N polio.
เทียนไข (เล่ม,แท่ง) thiankhǎj′ (lêm′, thêŋ′) N tallow candle.

ไข ๒ khǎj′ V to unlock, open by unlocking.
แก้ไข kɛ̂ɛkhǎj′ V to correct, emend, amend, improve, revise, resolve (a bad situation).
ข้อไข (ข้อ) khɔ̌ɔkhǎj′ (khɔ̌ɔ′) N solution (to a riddle, a mathematics problem).
ไขก๊อก khǎjkɔ́g′ V 1. to turn the faucet on. 2. slang to urinate. [ก๊อก f. Eng. cock]
ไขกุญแจ khǎjkuncɛɛ′ V to unlock (a lock), to turn the key (in order to unlock).
ไขควง (อัน) khǎjkhuaŋ′ (ʔan′) N screwdriver.
ไขความ khǎjkhwaam′ V to interpret; to uncover, disclose (the meaning).
ไขนาฬิกา khǎjnaalikaa′ to wind one's watch, wind the clock.
เงื่อนไข (ข้อ) ŋɣ̂ankhǎj′ (khɔ̌ɔ′) N condition, stipulation, proviso.

ไข่ (ใบ,ฟอง,ลูก) khàj′ (baj′, fɔɔŋ′, lûug′) N 1. egg. 2. anat.,bot. ovum, ovule. 3. colloq., euphem. testicles. V 4. to lay eggs, produce eggs. →Syn. 3. ลูกอัณฑะ eleg.
ไข่ขาว khàjkhǎaw′ N egg white, albumen.

ไข่ดก khàj′dòg′ V (fowls) to lay eggs abundantly.
ไข่ดาว khàjdaaw′ N fried egg.
ไข่แดง khàjdɛɛŋ′ N egg yolk.
o เป็นไข่แดง pen′khàjdɛɛŋ′ idiom. to be in the middle (e.g. of a group, crowd).
ไข่ต้ม khàjtôm′ N hard-boiled egg.
ไข่ปอก khàjpɔ̀ɔg′ N boiled eggs (with shell removed).
ไข่มุก (เม็ด,สาย) khàjmúg′ N 1. pearl (méd′). 2. (a string of) pearls (sǎaj′). →Also ไข่มุกด์.
ไข่ลวก khàjlûag′ N soft-boiled egg.
ไข่ไว้ khàj′wáj′ to lay eggs (and leave them).
ไข่หวาน khàjwǎan′ N eggs prepared in light syrup, a kind of Thai sweet.
ตกไข่ tògkhàj′ V eleg. to lay eggs. →Syn. See ออกไข่ com.
ที่ไข่ (ที่) thîikhàj′ (thîi′) N breeding place, place where eggs are laid.
ฟักไข่ fág′khàj′ V to hatch (eggs).
รังไข่ raŋkhàj′ N anat. ovary.
วางไข่ waaŋkhàj′ V eleg. to lay eggs. →Syn. See ออกไข่ com.
ออกไข่ ʔɔ̀ɔgkhàj′ V com. to lay eggs. →Syn. ตกฟอง lit.,eleg., วางไข่,ตกไข่ eleg.

ไข้ (อย่าง,ชนิด) khâj′ (jàaŋ′, chaníd′) N fever, illness (characterized by fever). คน-- sick person, patient.
ไข้ไขสันหลัง khâj′khǎjsǎnlǎŋ′ N polio.
ไข้คอตีบ khâj′khɔɔtìib′ N diphtheria.
ไข้จับสั่น khâjcabsàn′ N eleg. malaria, malarial fever. →Syn. ไข้ป่า colloq.
o เป็นไข้จับสั่น penkhâj′càbsàn′ to have malaria.
ไข้เจ็บ khâj′cèb′ N sickness. Chiefly in compounds. ความ-- sickness, illness.
o โรคภัยไข้เจ็บ (อย่าง,ชนิด) rôogphaj′khâjcèb′ (jàaŋ′, chaníd′) N disease, sickness.
ไข้ทรพิษ khâjthɔɔraphíd′ N eleg. smallpox. Also โรคทรพิษ. →Syn. ฝีดาษ com.
ไข้ป่า khâjpàa′ N colloq. malaria. →Syn. ไข้จับสั่น eleg.
ไข้รากสาดน้อย khâjrâagsàad′nɔ́ɔj′ N typhoid. Also โรค--.
ไข้รากสาดใหญ่ khâjrâagsàad′jàj′ N typhus. Also โรค--.

ไข้สุกใส khâj′sùgsǎj′ N eleg. chicken pox.
→Syn. อีสุกอีใส colloq.

ไข้หวัด khâjwàd′ N fever due to a common cold.

o ไข้หวัดใหญ่ khâjwàd′jàj′ N influenza.

ไข้เหลือง khâjlν̌aŋ′ N yellow fever.

จับไข้ càbkhâj′ V to have a fever.

เจ็บไข้,--ได้ป่วย cèbkhâj′, cèbkhâj′dâjpùaj′ V
eleb. eleg. to get sick, be sick. ความ--
sickness.

ป่วยไข้ pùaj′khâj′ V eleg. to be sick, ill.
การ-- being sick; sickness, illness.

เป็นไข้,ป่วย-- penkhâj′, pùaj′penkhâj′ V to
have a fever, be feverish, ill with a fever.

ฝากผีฝากไข้(กับ) fàagphǐi′fàagkhâj′-(kaɔ) elab.
colloq.,idiom. to ask (someone) to take care
of one's body in the event of sickness or death.

ฟื้นไข้ fν́yn′khâj′ V to recover, recuperate.

ไขว่. See entries below.

ขวักไขว่ khwàgkhwàj′ V 1. to move or act pell-
mell, helter-skelter. sV 2. pell-mell, helter-
skelter, to and fro, hither and thither, at random.

ไขว่คว้า khwàjkhwáa′ V to reach for, to grasp
at, to try desperately to get hold of (as a drowning person).

ไขว่ห้าง khwàjhâaŋ′ V 1. to have one's legs
crossed. sV 2. cross-legged, with legs
crossed.

o นั่งไขว่ห้าง nâŋ′khwàjhâaŋ′ to sit cross-legged.

ไขว้ khwâj′ V 1. to cross. 2. to be twisted,
crossed.

ไขว้เขว khwâjkhwěe′ V to be confused, mixed
up, disorganized. ความ-- misunderstanding,
confusion.

ค

ค khɔɔ′ LOW consonant. Pronounced kh initially,
g finally.

คง ๑ khoŋɔ AA surely, sure to, bound to; most
likely, probably.

o คุณคงชอบ khun′khoŋchɔɔb′↓ You're sure to
like it. You'll probably like it.

o เขาคงเป็นอะไรไป kháwkhoŋpen′ʔaraj′-paj′↓
Something must have happened to him.

o นั่นคงแพง nân′ khoŋphɛɛŋ′↓ That's sure to be
expensive. That must be expensive.

คงจะ khoŋcaɔ AA surely, sure to, bound to;
will surely, would surely; most likely will,
probably will.

คง(จะ)ไม่ khoŋ′(ca)mâjɔ surely (will) not, probably (will) not, unlikely to.

ยังคง jaŋkhoŋɔ, jaŋkhoŋ′ still, yet.

o ยังคงปรากฏมี jaŋkhoŋ′praakòdmii′ there still
appears to be, apparently there still is.

คง ๒ khoŋ V 1. to endure, remain, persist. 2.
to be enduring, lasting, steadfast.

คงกระพัน,คงกะพัน khoŋkraphan′, khoŋkaphan′
V to be invulnerable.

คงแก่เรียน khoŋkarian′ V to be learned, erudite.

คงทน khoŋ′thon′ V to be resistant, durable.

คงที่ khoŋthîi′ V to be constant, invariable.

คงเส้นคงวา khoŋsên′khoŋwaa′ V elab. colloq.
to be consistent.

เงินคงคลัง ŋon′khoŋkhlaŋ′ N treasury reserves.

มั่นคง mânkhoŋ′ V to be steadfast, stable, firm
(as in purpose), secure.

o คณะมนตรีความมั่นคง khanámontrii′khwaamɔ
mânkhoŋ′ N Security Council.

คง ๓ in แม่น้ำคง mɛ̂ɛnáamkhoŋ′ pN the Salween
River.

คงคา khoŋkhaa′ N lit. 1. river, sea, the waters.
2. short for แม่คงคา.

แม่คงคา mɛ̂ɛkhoŋkhaa′ N lit. the goddess of
the waters.

แม่น้ำคงคา mɛ̂ɛnáamkhoŋkhaa′ pN the Ganges
River.

คณนา khananaa′ V to count, calculate.

คณะ (คณะ) khaná?′, khanáɔ (khaná?′) N 1. (special) group, body; organization, team; party
(e.g. "political party"). C 2. idem.

คณะกรรมการ (คณะ,ชุด) khanákammakaan′
(khaná?′, chúd′) N committee; commission.

o คณะกรรมการข้าราชการพลเรือน khanákammaɔ
kaan′-khâarâadchakaan′phonlaryan′ N Civil
Service Commission.

คณะกรรมาธิการ khanákammaa′thíkaan′ N committee; commission.

คณะชาติ khaná?/châad/ nationalist; of the nationalist faction.

o จีนคณะชาติ ciin/-khaná?/châad/ Chinese Nationalist.

คณะเทศมนตรี (คณะ) khaná?/-thêedsamontrii/ (khaná?/) N city council, municipal council.

คณะมนตรีความมั่นคง (คณะ) khanámontrii/ɔ khwaammânkhoŋ/ (khaná?/) N Security Council.

คณะรัฐมนตรี (คณะ) khaná?/rádthamontrii/ (khaɔ ná?/) N (the) cabinet, council of ministers.

คณิต khaníd/, khaníd/taɔ N mathematics. Chiefly in compounds. →Cf. คำนวณ.

คณิตศาสตร์ khaníd/tasàad/ N mathematics.

พีชคณิต phíd/chakhaníd/ N algebra.

เรขาคณิต reekhǎa/khaníd/ N geometry.

เลขคณิต lêeg/khaníd/ N arithmetic.

คด ๑ khód/ V 1. to bend. 2. to be crooked (both literally and figuratively). →Syn. โกง. →Ant. ตรง.

คดเคี้ยว khódkhíaw/ V to be winding (as a road).

คิดคด(ต่อ) khídkhód/(tɔɔ) V to plan to betray.

ใจคด cajkhód/ V to be crooked, dishonest.

คด ๒ khód/ V to dip up, dish up (cooked rice).

คดข้าว khódkhâaw/ to dip up (cooked) rice.

คดี khadii/ N 1. case, charge (legal). 2. lit. story, account. 3. lit. way, course. Often found as the last element in words of Sanskrit origin.

คดีอาญา (คดี) khadii/?aajaa/ (khadii/) N criminal case.

ต้องคดี tɔŋ/khadii/ V to be accused, be under accusation or prosecution.

วรรณคดี (เรื่อง, เล่ม) wan/nakhadii/ (rŷaŋ/, lêm/) N literature.

สารคดี (เรื่อง, บท) sǎa/rakhadii/ (rŷaŋ/, bòd/) N (written) article, account (non-fiction).

อรรถคดี ?àd/thakhadii/ N law case.

คติ (ข้อ, บท) khatì?/ (khɔɔ/, bòd/) N 1. moral precept, ethical teaching; hence sometimes motto, maxim. 2. way, course.

มโนคติ manoo/khatì?/ N lit. idea, thought.

คทา (อัน) khathaa/ (?an/) N eleg. mace, club.

คน ๑ (คน) khon/ (khon/) N com. 1. person.

---

2. element placed before verbs to form agent nouns, hence often equiv. to -er; sometimes similarly placed before nouns. C 3. clf. for human beings. →Syn. 1. ชน eleg. 2, 3. ผู้ eleg. →See also 2. ช่าง ๑, นัก ๑, นาย, นาง, ผู้, พ่อ, แม่, เด็ก.

o คนขายตั๋ว khonkhǎajtǔa/ N ticket-seller: "one who sells tickets."

o คนครัว khonkhrua/ N cook: "kitchen-person."

o คนงาน khonŋaan/ N (unskilled) worker, workman, laborer: "work-person."

o ขออนุญาตไปด้วยคน khɔɔ/?ànújâad/pajdûajkhon/‖ Permit (me) to go along. Here คน is a clf. (and short for คนหนึ่ง); hence the literal meaning is "Permit-go-also-one-person."

NOTE. (1) Most words in which คน is used as an agentive are listed under the appropriate verb or noun only. Hence to find คนเก็บภาษี, look under เก็บ. (2) All nouns based on คน take คน as their classifier unless otherwise marked, and (คน) is therefore omitted.

กลางคน klaaŋkhon/ See under กลาง.

คนกระเป๋า khonkrapǎw/ N fare collector on public conveyances.

คนกลาง khonklaaŋ/ N 1. the middle one (in a group). 2. middleman, mediator, arbitrator. 3. one who is neutral.

คนกันเอง khonkan?eeŋ/ N an acquaintance, an intimate, an equal.

คนเกิด khonkə̀əd/ N births (i.e. cases of birth).

คนขายชาติ khonkhǎajchâad/ N traitor.

คนข่าว khonkhàaw/ N reporter.

คนขี้เมา khon/khîimaw/ N drunkard. Contrast คนเมา one who is drunk (at the moment).

คนไข้ khonkhâj/ N sick person, patient.

คนใช้ khoncháj/ N 1. servant. 2. the user.

o เด็กคนใช้ dègkhoncháj/ N servant boy, servant girl.

คนเฒ่าคนแก่ khonthâw/khonkɛ̀ɛ/ N elab. colloq. old people, elderly people.

คนเดินโต๊ะ khondəəntó?/ N waiter.

คนเดียว khondiaw/ alone, unaccompanied, by oneself (referring to a person).

คนใด (1) khondaj/ (2) khon/daj/ 1. any (person),

e.g. ทหารคนใด thahǎan′khondaj′ any soldier.

2. anyone, anyone who, whoever.

คนตาย khontaaj′ N deaths (i.e. cases of death, persons dead).

คนทั้งหลาย khontháŋlǎaj′ everyone, everybody, people in general.

คนทั่วไป khonthûapaj′ N people in general, the public.

คนไทย khonthaj′ N Thai person.

คนนอก khonnɔ̂ɔg′ N an outsider.

คนใน khonnaj′ N an insider.

คนเปรี้ยว khonprîaw′ N idiom. a flirt (woman).

คนเรา khon′raw′ N we people, we humans.

คนละ khonlaɔ 1. per person, a person; 1st example. 2. different, each different, each its own, each one's own; examples 2-5. In the second meaning the expression does not nesessarily have any reference to people.

o ให้หนังสือคนละเล่ม hâjnaŋsɣ̌y′khonlalêm′↓ Give each one (person) a book! Give a book per person!

o คนละเรื่อง khonlarɣ̂aŋ′ a different matter, problem, story; as in นั่นมันคนละเรื่อง nân′mankhonlarɣ̂aŋ′↓ That's a different problem.

o ผ้าสองผืนนี่คนละสี phâa′sɔ̌ɔŋphɣ̌yn′-nîi′ khonɔlasǐi′↓ These two pieces of cloth are of different colors.

o ต่างคนต่างก็มีทรรศนะคนละอย่าง tàaŋkhon′tàaŋkɔ̂mii′-thád′saná?′khonlajàaŋ′↓ Each separate person has a different viewpoint.

o คนละไม้คนละมือ khonlamáaj′khonlamyy′ elab. colloq. each a hand, as in ช่วยกัน-- chûaj′ɔ kan′-khonlamáaj′khonlamyy′ each one gives a helping hand.

ทุกคน thúgkhon′ everyone, everybody.

บางคน baaŋkhon′ com. someone, some (referring to people), some people. →Syn. บางท่าน eleg.

เป็นผู้เป็นคน penphûu′penkhon′ V elab. colloq. to be presentable, like a normal human.

ผู้คน (คน) phûukhon′ (khon′) N people.

ภาษาคน phaasǎakhon′ N human speech.

แรงคน rɛɛŋkhon′ N manpower.

เสียคน sǐakhon′ to lose one's integrity, to become a bad person.

คน ๒ khon′ V to stir (a liquid), stir up (ingredients).

o คนกาแฟ khon′kaafɛɛ′ to stir (one's) coffee.

ค้น khón′ V to search (for), seek.

ค้นคว้า khónkhwáa′ V 1. to search (for). 2. to do research. การ-- research. ผู้-- researcher, (scientific) investigator.

o ทำการค้นคว้า thamkaan′khónkhwáa′ to do research.

ค้นพบ khónphób′ V to find out; to discover.

ค้นหา khónhǎa′ V to search for, look for.

ตรวจค้น trùad′khón′ V to search (e.g. a person or place for concealed objects).

หมายค้น (ใบ, ฉะบับ) mǎajkhón′ (baj′, chabàb′) N search warrant.

คบ ๑ khób′ V to associate with, be friends with.

คบค้า(กับ) khóbkháa′(kaɔ) V to associate (with), be friends (with).

คบคิด(กับ) khóbkhíd′(kaɔ) V to conspire.

คบชู้สู่ชาย khóbchúu′-sùu′chaaj′ V (a woman) to have a lover or lovers, have men.

คบหา(กับ) khóbhǎa′(kaɔ) V to associate (with).

คบ ๒ (อัน) khób′ (ʔan′) N torch.

คบเพลิง (อัน) khóbphlɣɣŋ′ (ʔan′) N torch.

คม khom′ V 1. to be sharp (of edged objects, of claws). 2. to be shrewd, sharp. N 3. sharp edge. →Dist. แหลม "sharp-pointed." →Ant. 1. ทื่อ.

คมกริบ khomkríb′ V to be razor-sharp.

คมคาย khomkhaaj′ V 1. to be attractive and bright-looking. 2. to be witty.

คมสัน khomsǎn′ V to have clean-cut features, be handsome (referring to men).

ตาคม taa′khom′ 1. to be bright-eyed. 2. idiom. to have sharp eyes, be a keen observer.

แหลมคม lɛ̌ɛm′khom′ V 1. to be sharp and pointed. 2. idiom. to be quick-witted, clever, smart.

คมนาคม khommanaa′khom′ N communication. →Also การ--.

ครก (ใบ, ลูก) khróg′ (baj′, lûug′) N mortar (a grinding bowl).

ปืนครก (กระบอก) pyynkhróg′ (krabɔ̀ɔg′) N milit. mortar. [tr.f. Eng.]

ครบ khrób′ V 1. to complete. 2. to be complete

(generally of a stipulated quantity, a set, a cycle).

o ผมยังซื้อของไม่ครบเลย phǒm'-jaŋsýykhɔ̌ɔŋ'-mâjkhrób'ləəj↓ I haven't bought everything (I need) yet.

o มีสลึงพึงบรรจบให้ครบบาท mii'salŷŋ' phyŋ'ɔ bancòb' hâjkhrób'bàad'↓ If you have a quarter, you should save it until you complete a baht.

ครบถ้วน khróbthûan' V to be complete, full, entire.

ค.ร.ม. khɔɔrɔɔmɔɔ'. Abbrev. for คณะรัฐมนตรี khaná?'rádthamontrii' the cabinet (of ministers of state). →Also said as khaná?'rɔɔmɔɔɔ tɔɔ'.

ครรภ์ khan' N 1. eleg. womb. 2. pregnancy. →Syn. 1. มดลูก com. 2. ท้อง com.

ครรภ์แก่ khan'kὲὲ' V eleg. 1. to be in full pregnancy. N 2. full pregnancy. →Syn. ท้อง แก่ com.

ตั้งครรภ์ tâŋkhan' V eleg. 1. to conceive, be in early pregnancy. 2. to be pregnant. →Syn. ตั้งท้อง com.

ทรงครรภ์ soŋkhan' V roy. to be enceinte, pregnant. →Syn. see มีท้อง.

ผดุงครรภ์ phaduŋ'khan' V 1. eleg. to render care and treatment during pregnancy and childbirth. N 2. eleg. midwife. →Syn. 2. หมอ ตำแย colloq.

o แพทย์ผดุงครรภ์ (คน) phɛ̂ɛd'-phaduŋ'khan' (khon') N eleg. obstetrician.

ฝากครรภ์(กับ) fàagkhan'(kaɔ) V eleg. to have prenatal care (at).

มีครรภ์ miikhan' V eleg. to be pregnant. →Syn. มีท้อง com.

ครวญ ๑ khruan' V 1. to groan, moan, lament. 2. slang to croon (as a popular singer).

ครวญคราง khruankhraaŋ' V to moan and groan (in prolonged distress).

คร่ำครวญ khrâmkhruan' V to lament, to sob and moan.

โอดครวญ ʔòodkhruan' V 1. to lament, moan, cry. 2. slang to squawk, complain.

ครวญ ๒ in ใคร่ครวญ khrâjkhruan' V to contemplate, consider carefully.

ครหา kharahǎa' V 1. censure; to blame. 2. to slander.

ครอก ๑ (ครอก) khrɔɔg' (khrɔɔg') N litter, brood.

ขี้ครอก khîikhrɔɔg' N derog., colloq. slave (an appellation).

ครอก ๒ in ครอก ๆ khrɔɔgkhrɔɔg' imit. the sound of snoring, of gargling, of a monkey scolding.

ครอง khrɔɔŋ' V 1. to rule, rule over. 2. sacer. to wear, put on.

ครองชีพ khrɔɔŋ'chîib' V to make a living. การ-- living, making a living.

o ค่าครองชีพ khâa'khrɔɔŋchîib' N cost of living.

o มาตรฐานการครองชีพ mâad'trathǎan'kaanɔ khrɔɔŋchîib' N standard of living.

ครองตน khrɔɔŋ'ton' to live the life (of, e.g. bachelor, hermit, etc.).

ครองตัว khrɔɔŋ'tua' idem.

ครองแผ่นดิน khrɔɔŋ'phɛ̀ndin' V to reign.

ครองราชสมบัติ khrɔɔŋ'râadchasǒmbàd' to reign.

ครอบครอง khrɔ̂ɔbkhrɔɔŋ' V 1. to govern, control. 2. to take possession of, occupy.

คุ้มครอง khúmkhrɔɔŋ' V to protect, give protection to, watch over.

คู่ครอง (คน) khûukhrɔɔŋ' (khon') N spouse, mate. →Syn. คู่เคียง.

ปกครอง pògkhrɔɔŋ' V to rule, govern. See cross-reference.

ยึดครอง jýdkhrɔɔŋ' V to occupy, take possession of (by force).

ครอบ khrɔ̂ɔb' V to cover up.

ครอบครอง khrɔ̂ɔbkhrɔɔŋ' V 1. to govern, control. 2. to take possession of, occupy.

ครอบครัว (ครอบครัว) khrɔ̂ɔbkhrua' (khrɔ̂ɔbkhrua') N family.

ครอบงำ khrɔ̂ɔbŋam' V 1. to shelter, shield, cover. 2. to overwhelm, overpower (of emotion, temptation, etc.).

ฝาครอบ (ใบ) fǎakhrɔ̂ɔb' (baj') N cover, dish cover (used to keep out insects).

ครอม khrɔ̂ɔm' V 1. to bridge, put across, put over. 2. to impose, superimpose, put one over the other. 3. to be astride, to straddle, bridge.

ครั่ง khrâŋ' N sealing wax; lacquer.

ขี้ครั่ง khîikhrâŋ' N colloq. sticklac, i.e. lac in

its natural state before being refined for use.

ตัวครั่ง (ตัว) tuakhrâŋ′ (tua′) N scale-insect (the lac-producing insect).

ครั้ง khráŋ′ C 1. time, instance. 2. clf. for an event, incident, occurrence. 3. at the time of, at the time when. →Syn. 1, 2. See คราว.

o ชนะครั้งใหญ่ chaná?′khráŋjàj′ a great victory.

o สองครั้ง sɔ̌ɔŋkhráŋ′ two times, twice.

ครั้งก่อน khráŋkɔ̀ɔn′ last time, the time before; previously, formerly.

ครั้งคราว, เป็น-- khráŋ′khraaw′, penkhráŋ′ɔ khraaw′ at intervals, on occasion.

ครั้งแรก khráŋrɛ̂ɛg′ the first time.

o ในครั้งแรก najkhráŋrɛ̂ɛg′ in the first place, the first time.

o เป็นครั้งแรก penkhráŋrɛ̂ɛg′ for the first time.

ครั้งแล้วครั้งเล่า khráŋ′lɛ́ɛw′-khráŋ′lâw′ time and again.

ครั้งหนึ่ง khráŋŋnʉ̀ŋ′, khráŋ′nʉŋ 1. one time, once. 2. once upon a time.

o ครั้งหนึ่งยังมี khráŋŋnʉ̀ŋ′jaŋmiiɔ once there was... (beginning a story).

ครั้งใหญ่ khráŋjàj′ a great event.

ทุกครั้ง thúgkhráŋ′ every time.

บางครั้ง baaŋkhráŋ′ sometimes.

บางครั้งบางคราว baaŋkhráŋ′baaŋkhraaw′ elab. colloq. from time to time, now and then, sometimes, occasionally, once in a while.

เป็นครั้งเป็นคราว penkhráŋ′penkhraaw′ elab. colloq. occasionally.

เป็นหลายครั้ง penlǎaj′khráŋ′ many times, on many occasions.

เมื่อครั้ง(ที่) mʉ̂akhráŋ′(thîiɔ) when, at the time (in the past) when.

หลายครั้งหลายครา lǎajkhráŋ′lǎajkhraa′ elab. eleg. several times, many a time.

หลายครั้งหลายหน lǎajkhráŋ′lǎajhǒn′ elab. eleg. several times, many a time.

ครัด. See เคร่งครัด.

ครั่น in ความครั่น khraamkhran′ much, very.

ครั่น khrân′ V to feel feverish; to get chilled.

ครั่นคร้าม khrânkhráam′ V to be afraid, scared.

ครั่นตัว khrântua′ V to feel hot and cold, as the first symptoms of a fever.

ครั่นเนื้อครั่นตัว khrânnýa′khrântua′ V elab. colloq. idem.

ครั้น khrán′ Cj when.

ครั้นแล้ว khránlɛ́ɛw′ and then, then.

ครับ khráb′ Pt def. m. sp. 1. particle used as the final element of statements and questions; 1st and 2nd examples. 2. Yes (in answer to a question); 3rd example. 3. particle placed after name, title or kin term to address or call the attention of someone; 4th example. 4. Yes? (as a reply when called or spoken to); 5th example. →Syn. ขอรับ eleg. def. m. sp. →Cf. คะ, ค่ะ, ขา def. w. sp. →See also the variant ฮะ ๑.

o ขอโทษครับ khɔ̌ɔthôod′khráb′↓ Excuse me.

o วันนี้อากาศดีนะครับ wanníi′ ?aakàad′dii′-naɔ khráb′↓ It's a fine day, isn't it?

o ครับ khráb′↓ Yes, (it is).

o คุณมานิตครับ khunmaaníd′khráb′↓ Manid?

o ครับ khráb′↓ Yes?

ครัว (ห้อง, ครัว) khrua′ N 1. kitchen (hɔ̂ŋ′, khrua′). 2. family (khrua′). การ-- cookery, cooking. คน-- cook.

ครอบครัว (ครอบครัว) khrɔ̂ɔbkhrua′ (khrɔ̂ɔbɔ khrua′) N family.

ครัวเรือน (ครัวเรือน) khruaryan′ (khruaryan′) N family; household.

เครื่องครัว (เครื่อง, อย่าง, ชะนิด) khrŷaŋkhrua′ (khrŷaŋ′, jàaŋ′, chaníd′) N kitchen utensils.

ทำครัว thamkhrua′ V to do the cooking; to cook, prepare food.

พ่อครัว (คน) phɔ̂ɔkhrua′ (khon′) N cook (male).

แม่ครัว (คน) mɛ̂ɛkhrua′ (khon′) N cook (female).

สวนครัว (แห่ง, สวน) sǔankhrua′ (hɛ̀ŋ′, sǔan′) N kitchen garden, vegetable garden.

ห้องครัว (ห้อง) hɔ̂ŋkhrua′ (hɔ̂ŋ′) N kitchen.

ครา khraa′ C eleg. time, occasion. →Syn. See คราว.

หลายครั้งหลายครา lǎajkhráŋ′lǎajkhraa′ elab. eleg. several times, many a time.

คร่า ๑ khrâa′ V 1. to carry off by force, abduct. 2. to ruin, destroy.

คร่า ๒. See คร่าคร่า.

คราก ๑ khrâag′ V to be overstretched, overexpanded, stretched out of shape.

คราก ๒. See โครกคราก.

คราง khraaŋ′ V 1. to moan, groan. 2. to hum.

  ครวญคราง khruankhraaŋ′ V to moan and groan (in prolonged distress).

คราด (อัน) khrâad′ (ʔan′) N 1. rake; harrow; currycomb. V 2. to rake; to curry.

คร้าน(ต่อ,กับ) khráan′ (tɔ̀ɔ′, kaɔ) V to have no desire or inclination (to do something); to be apathetic (about); to be tired (of), fed up (with).

  เกียจคร้าน klàdkhráan′ V eleg. to be lazy.
  →Syn. ขี้เกียจ com.

คราบ (คราบ) khrâab′ (khrâab′) N 1. slough, cast-off skin. 2. deposit, incrustation; dirt (on one's skin). 3. perspiration stains. 4. scum, slimy residue.

  เต็มคราบ temkhrâab′ idiom., colloq. to the fullest extent, to one's full satisfaction. Used of filling the stomach.

  ลอกคราบ lɔ̂ɔgkhrâab′ V 1. to molt, slough. 2. slang to strip (someone) of clothing.

คราม ๑ khraam′ N 1. indigo (the substance). 2. bluing.

  ต้นคราม (ต้น) tônkhraam′ (tôn′) N indigo (the plant).

  ลายคราม (ชิ้น) laajkhraam′ (chín′) N china having a design in indigo. Usually refers to antique Thai (Siamese) ware. →Also เครื่อง--.

  สีคราม sĭikhraam′ N 1. indigo, the color indigo. V 2. to be indigo-colored.

คราม ๒. See โครมคราม.

คร้าม khráam′ V to be timid, afraid.

  ครั่นคร้าม khrânkhráam′ V to be afraid, scared.

ครามครัน khraamkhran′ much, very.

คราว khraaw′ C time, occasion. →Syn. ครั้ง,หน, ที com., ตั้ง colloq., ครา eleg.

  o ปีละแปดคราว piilapὲɛd′khraaw′ eight times a year.

  ข่าวคราว khàawkhraaw′ N news (esp. one's personal news), tidings.

  ครั้งคราว khráŋ′khraaw′ at intervals; on occasion.

  คราวก่อน khraawkɔ̀ɔn′ the time before, on the last occasion.

  คราวละ khraawlaɔ each time.

คราวหน้า khraawnâa′ next time, on the next occasion.

คราวหนึ่ง khraaw′nyŋ once, one time, on one occasion.

คราวหลัง khraawlăŋ′ next time, on the next occasion.

ชั่วคราว chûakhraaw′ temporarily, for the time being; temporary.

ทุกคราว thúgkhraaw′ every time.

บางครั้งบางคราว baaŋkhráŋ′baaŋkhraaw′ elab. colloq. from time to time, now and then, sometimes, occasionally, once in a while.

บางคราว baaŋkhraaw′ sometimes.

เป็นครั้งเป็นคราว penkhráŋ′penkhraaw′ occasionally.

เป็นคราว ๆ pen′khraawkhraaw′ at intervals, at times.

เมื่อคราว mŷakhraaw′ at the time when.

คราว ๆ khrâawkhrâaw′ sV briefly, sketchily, in rough outline. →Also อย่าง--.

  o พูดอย่างคราว ๆ phûud′jàaŋkhrâawkhrâaw′ roughly speaking.

คร่ำ khram′ N refuse water, sewer water. →Also น้ำ-- námkhram′.

คร่ำ ๑. See the entries below.

  คร่ำคร่า khrâmkhrâa′ V to be very old and shabby, worn out by age.

  คร่ำคร่ี khrâmkhrý?′ V to be too old (for use; in age).

คร่ำ ๒ in คร่ำครวญ khrâmkhruan′ V to lament, to sob and moan.

คร่ำ ๓ in คร่ำเคร่ง (ต่อ,ใน) khrâmkhrêŋ′ (tɔ̀ɔɔ, najɔ) V to be absorbed, engrossed (in); to be intent (on something); to be hard at it.

คริสต์,คริสต์- khríd′, khríd′taɔ, khrís′ɔ, khrí′saɔ N Christ. [f. Eur.]

  คริสต์จักร,คริสต์- khrí′sacàg′, khrís′càg′ N 1. Christendom. 2. church, the church.

  คริสต์ศักราช khríd′tasàgkaràad′, khríd′sàgkaraad′ the Christian era. →Abbrev. ค.ศ. →Also คริสต์ศก khríd′tasòg′ lit.

  คริสต์ศาสนา khríd′tasàadsanăa′, khríd′sàadsanăa′ N Christianity.

คริสต์มาส,คริสต์- khrí′samâad′ Christmas. [f. Eng.]

คริสตัง khrís'taŋ', khrí'sataŋ' N Christian (usually Roman Catholic). [f. Port.]

คริสเตียน khrís'tian', khrí'satian' N Christian (usually Protestant). [f. Eng.]

ครีบ (ครีบ,อัน) khrîib' (khrîib',ʔan') N fin.

ครีม khriim' N cream. [f. Eng.]

ครี้ khrý? V to be old, old-fashioned.
   คร่ำครี้ khrâmkhrý? V to be too old.

คริก. See entries below.
   คริกคริ้น khrýgkhrýyn' V to be merry, hilarious, full of fun.
   คริกโครม khrýgkhroom' V to be noisy, boisterous, clamorous.

ครึ่ง khrŷŋ' Nm half. →Comp. เศษ.
   o กาแฟครึ่งถ้วย kaafɛɛ'khrŷŋthûaj' half a cup of coffee.
   ครึ่งๆกลางๆ khrŷŋkhrŷŋ'klaaŋklaaŋ' partially, half-way, half-done.
   ครึ่งต่อครึ่ง khrŷŋ'tɔɔkhrŷŋ' half and half, fifty-fifty, (in) equal (parts).
   ครึ่งหนึ่ง khrŷŋ'nyŋ one half.
   เดือนครึ่ง dyan'khrŷŋ' a month and a half.
   เท่าครึ่ง,หนึ่ง-- thâw'khrŷŋ', nŷŋthâw'khrŷŋ' one and a half times (as much, as big, etc.).
   o สองเท่าครึ่ง sɔ̌ɔŋ'thâwkhrŷŋ' two and a half times (as much, as big, etc.).

ครึ้ม ๑ khrým' V to be cloudy, overcast, shady, gloomy.
   ครึ้มฟ้าครึ้มฝน khrýmfáa'khrýmfǒn' V elab. colloq. to be very cloudy, be overcast, to look like rain. →Also ครึ้มฝน.
   มืดครึ้ม mŷydkhrým' V to be overcast, cloudy; to be overshadowed, darkened.
   ร่มครึ้ม rôm'khrým' V to be nice and shady, cool and shady.

ครึ้ม ๒ khrým' V 1. colloq. to be strange, unusual (of behavior); see example. 2. to be in high spirits.
   o วันนี้เขาเกิดครึ้มอะไรขึ้นมา wanníi' kháwkɤ̀ɤdǝ khrým'/ʔaraj'-khŷnmaa'⌇ What has come over him today?
   ครึ้มใจ khrýmcaj' V to be in high spirits, highly pleased and bursting with happiness.

ครืน,ครืน ๆ khryyn', khryynkhryyn' imit. 1. the rumbling of thunder, the sound of a heavy body tumbling down. 2. the sound of laughter.

ครืน. See entries below.
   ครึกครืน khrýgkhrýyn' V to be merry, hilarious, full of fun.
   ครืนเครง khrýynkhreeŋ' idem.

ครือ khryy' V to fit, be of proper size or shape.
   ครือกัน khryy'kan to be about the same, just the same.

ครุ ๑ (ใบ,ลูก) khrú? (baj',lûug') N a water pail woven of bamboo and made tight by calking.

ครุ ๒ kharú? V 1. to be hard, heavy. 2. to be stressed, accentuated.

ครุฑ (ตัว) khrúd' (tua') N the Garuda, a mythical bird.

ครุ่น. See entries below.
   ครุ่นคิด khrûn'khíd' V to brood, to meditate persistently (about).
   ครุ่นนึก,นึกครุ่น khrûn'nýg', nýg'khrûn' V to keep thinking.

ครุมเครือ khrumkhrya' V to be ambiguous, unclear, indistinct. See also คลุม.

ครู (คน) khruu' (khon') N 1. teacher (general term). T 2. title placed before first name of a teacher. P 3. I, me, Teacher (teacher sp.); you, he, him, she, her, Teacher (sp. to or about a teacher). →Dist. อาจารย์ teacher who has a degree. →Syn. คุณครู def.
   ครูใหญ่ khruujàj' N headmaster, headmistress, principal.
   คุณครู khunkhruu' P def. 1. you, he, him, she, her, Teacher (sp. to or about a teacher). T 2. title placed before first name of a teacher.
   ชั้นครู chánkhruu' masterful, first-rate.
   วิชาครู wíchaakhruu' N education (as a subject of study).

ครู่ khrûu' C moment. →Syn. ประเดี๋ยว,เดี๋ยว.
   ครู่หนึ่ง,ครู่เดียว khrûu'nyŋ, khrûu'diaw' (for) a moment.
   ครู่ใหญ่,ครู่ใหญ่ ๆ khrûu'jàj', khrûu'jàjjàj' (for) a long moment, a long while.
   ชั่วครู่ chûakhrûu' (for) a moment.

ครูด khrûud' V to scratch, scrape against, rub against.

คลอ ๑ khlɔɔ′ V 1. to accompany (as piano with voice). sV 2. side by side.

เดินคลอเคลีย dəən′khlɔɔkhlia′ to walk side by side, close together.

คลอ ๒ khlɔɔ′ V (tears) to well up, moisten (the eyes).

○ น้ำตาคลอตา námtaa′-khlɔɔ′taa′ (her) eyes were wet with tears; tears moistened (her) eyes.

คลอง (คลอง,ล้าย) khlɔɔŋ′ (khlɔɔŋ′, săaj′) N canal, watercourse.

ลำคลอง (ล้าย) lamkhlɔɔŋ′ (săaj′) N canal.

คลอง khlɔ̂ŋ′* V to be active, nimble, fluent. ความ-- fluency (of speech), skill, expertness, proficiency.

คล่องแคล่ว,แคล่วคล่อง khlɔ̂ŋ′khlɛ̂w′, khlɛ̂w′khlɔ̂ŋ′ V 1. to be skillful, clever, nimble, agile. 2. to be fast (in doing things). 3. to be fluent (in speech).

พูดคล่อง phûudkhlɔ̂ŋ′ V to speak fluently, smoothly, in a facile manner.

คล้อง ๑ khlɔ́ɔŋ′ V 1. to rope, lasso, snare (esp. elephants). 2. to wear loosely (e.g. a scarf).

คล้อง ๒ khlɔ́ɔŋ′ V 1. to rhyme. 2. to be in harmony.

คล้องจอง(กับ) khlɔ́ɔŋcɔɔŋ′(kaɔ) V to rhyme, harmonize (with).

สอดคล้อง(กับ) sɔ̀ɔd′khlɔ́ɔŋ′-(kaɔ) V to be in line (with), in agreement (with).

คลอด khlɔ̂ɔd′ V eleg. to bear, to give birth.

คลอดบุตร khlɔ̂ɔdbùd′ V eleg. to bear a child, to give birth. การ-- childbirth, delivery.

→Syn. คลอดลูก eleg., ออกลูก com.

คลอดลูก khlɔ̂ɔdlûug′ idem.

ช่องคลอด (ช่อง) chɔ̂ŋkhlɔ̂ɔd′(chɔ̂ŋ′) N vagina.

คลอน,--แคลน khlɔɔn′, khlɔɔnkhlɛɛn′ V to be loose, shaky, unstable, unsteady.

คล้อย khlɔ́ɔj′ V 1. to be moving away, moving past. 2. to be inclined, disposed (toward).

○ เขาพึ่งคล้อยไป kháwphŷŋkhlɔ́ɔj′paj he has just passed (out of sight).

○ คล้อยตามด้วย khlɔ́ɔjtaam′dûaj′ (I) go along with (that), agree, am inclined toward (that).

คล้อยหลัง khlɔ́ɔj′lăŋ′ 1. to pass by, move past,

move out of sight. 2. to turn one's back.

บ่ายคล้อย bàaj′khlɔ́ɔj′ the late afternoon.

คละ khlá?′ V to be assorted, mixed.

คลั่ก khlâg′ V colloq. to be present in large numbers, to be numerous.

คลัง (แห่ง,คลัง) khlaŋ′ (hèŋ′, khlaŋ′) N treasury, storehouse. Chiefly in compounds. การ-- finance, financial matters.

กรมคลัง kromkhlaŋ′ Treasury Department.

คลังพัสดุ (แห่ง) khlaŋ′phádsadù?′ (hèŋ′) N storehouse.

คลังออมสิน (แห่ง) khlaŋ′?ɔɔmsĭn′ (hèŋ′) N (Thai) government savings bank.

เงินคงคลัง ŋən′khoŋkhlaŋ′ N treasury reserves.

คลั่ง khlâŋ′ V to be delirious; to talk in one's sleep or in fever.

คลั่งไคล้ khlâŋkhláj′ V to be crazed; to be mad about, infatuated with.

คลุ้มคลั่ง khlúm′khlâŋ′ V to be delirious, crazed.

คุ้มคลั่ง khúm′khlâŋ′ V 1. to lose one's temper. 2. to be mad, insane.

บ้าคลั่ง bâa′khlâŋ′ V to be mad, insane.

คลับคล้ายคลับคลา khlábkhláaj′khlábkhlaa′ sV elab. colloq. not for sure; vaguely, indistinctly.

คลา in คลาคล่ำ khlaa′khlâm′ V 1. to be loaded with, full of, replete with. 2. to be crowded, packed.

คลางแคลง,--ใจ khlaaŋkhlɛɛŋ′, khlaaŋkhlɛɛŋ′caj′ V to feel suspicious, have doubts. ความ-- suspicion, doubt, skepticism.

คลาด khlâad′ V to miss, fail to join.

คลาดเคลื่อน khlâadkhlŷan′ V to deviate, be off, be different (from the original). ความ-- deviation, discrepancy, error.

คลาดแคล้ว,แคล้วคลาด khlâadkhlέɛw′, khlέɛwɔ khlâad′ V 1. to miss, fail to meet. 2. to escape (from).

คลาดจาก khlâad′càagɔ 1. to be separated from. 2. to be out of (e.g. sight).

คลาน khlaan′ V to crawl (on the belly, or on hands and knees)(of larger animals, man, worms). →Dist. เลื้อย,ไต่.

ลุ่มลุกคลุกคลาน lômlúg′khlúgkhlaan′ V elab. colloq. to fall down and scramble up again and again.

ลัตว์เลื้อยคลาน (ตัว) sàd'lýajkhlaan' (tua') N reptile.

คลาย khlaaj' V 1. to lessen, diminish, abate. 2. to loosen, unravel, unroll. 3. to be loosend, unraveled, unrolled.

o เขาคลายความกังวลแล้ว kháwkhlaaj'khwaamɔ kaŋwon'-lɛ́ɛw' He has been relieved of his worries.

o สถานการณ์คลายความตึงเครียด sathǎanákaan'- khlaaj'khwaamtyŋkhrîad'॒ The situation is growing less tense: "is diminishing in tension."

คลี่คลาย khlîikhlaaj' V 1. to unwind, untangle, unroll. 2. to spread out, expand, progress, develop. ความ-- development.

คล้าย khláaj' V to resemble, look like. →Syn. เหมือน,ละม้าย,คล้ายคลึง.

คล้ายกับ(ว่า) khláaj'ka(wâa') as if, as though.

คล้ายคลึง khláajkhlyŋ' V to be similar, alike; to resemble.

o ละม้ายคล้ายคลึง lamáaj'khláajkhlyŋ' to resemble; to look alike.

วันคล้ายวันเกิด wan'khláajwankɤ̀ɤd' N eleg. birthday.

คล้ำ khlam' V 1. to grope. 2. to feel, feel of (something). 3. to probe (as a doctor).

ลูบคล้ำ lûub'khlam' V to caress, fondle, stroke gently, pet.

o กอดจูบลูบคล้ำ kɔ̀ɔd'cùub'-lûub'khlam' V colloq. to pet, to neck.

คล่ำ khlâm' V to be abundant, a lot.

คลาคล่ำ khlaa'khlâm' V 1. to be loaded with, full of, replete with. 2. to be crowded, packed.

คล้ำ khlám' V 1. to be dark, swarthy (of complexion). 2. to be darkened.

ผิวคล้ำ phǐwkhlám' N 1. dark, colored skin. V 2. to be dark-skinned.

สีคล้ำ sǐikhlám' N 1. a dark color. V 2. to be dark (in color). 3. to be swarthy, dark-complexioned.

คลี่ . See คลุกคลี่ .

คลี่ khlîi' V to unfold, unroll.

คลี่คลาย khlîikhlaaj' V 1. to unwind, untangle, unroll. 2. to spread out, expand, progress,

develop. ความ-- development.

คลึง ๑ khlyŋ' V 1. to roll (something into a ball). 2. to massage with a circular motion.

คลึงเคล้น khlyŋkhlén' V to caress, fondle (esp. the breast).

คลึง ๒. See คล้ายคลึง.

คลื่น (ลูก) khlŷn' (lûug') N wave. →Syn. ลอน.

คลื่นยาว khlŷnjaaw' N radio long wave.

คลื่นสั้น khlŷnsân' N radio short wave.

คลื่นเสียง khlŷnsǐaŋ' N sound wave.

คลื่นใส้ khlŷnsâj', khlŷn'sâj' V 1. to feel nauseated (literally). 2. colloq. to feel a loathing, repugnance, disgust; to feel revolted, nauseated.

o น่าคลื่นใส้ nâakhlŷn'sâj' V (something) to make one's stomach turn; to be nauseating, loathsome.

ช่วงคลื่น chûaŋkhlŷn' N wave length.

เมาคลื่น mawkhlŷn' V to be seasick.

คลุก khlúg' V 1. to mix together; to stir in; to turn over, roll (as a banana in sugar, in order to coat). 2. to be mixed, mixed with; to be rolled, turned over. 3. to be absorbed in, engrossed in. 4. (a cat) to circle and rub against one's legs.

o ล้มลุกคลุกคลาน lómlúg'khlúgkhlaan' V elab. colloq. to fall down and scramble up again and again.

คลุกคลี khlúgkhlii' V to mix (with), to mingle (with).

คลุ้ง khlúŋ' V to spread (as fumes, smoke); (the odor, smoke) to fill (e.g. the house).

o กลิ่นคลุ้งไปทั้งบ้าน klìn'khlúŋ'pajtháŋbâan'॒ The odor fills the house.

คลุม khlum' V to cover up, cover over.

คลุมเครือ khlumkhrya' V to be ambiguous, unclear, indistinct. →Also ครุมเครือ.

คลุมถุงชน khlum'thǔŋchon' V idiom. to marry off (an individual, a couple) without the mates seeing or knowing each other beforehand.

ปกคลุม pògkhlum' V to cover, be covered.

ผ้าคลุมที่นอน (ผืน) phâakhlum'thîinɔɔn' (phǔyn') N bedspread.

เสื้อคลุม (ตัว) sŷakhlum' (tua') N overcoat, topcoat, jacket.

คลุ้ม in คลุ้มคลั่ง khlúmkhlâŋ' V to be delirious,

crazed.

ควง khuaŋ′ V 1. to twirl. 2. c o l l o q. to date, go

    on a date (with a friend of the opposite sex).

   เดินควง dəən′khuaŋ′ V c o l l o q. to walk arm

    in arm (with); to walk with (one's date).

   ตะปูควง (ตัว) tapuu′khuaŋ′ (tua′) N screw.

ควบ ๑ khûab′ V 1. to combine, blend, merge. 2.

    to twist together. 3. to join, link.

   ควบคุม khûabkhum′ V 1. to control, supervise,

    place under supervision. 2. to detain. ความ- -

    control. ผู้- - supervisor; chaperon.

   ควบแน่น khûabnɛ̂n′ V t e c h. to condense.

   ควบไปด้วย (1) khûab′pajdûajɔ; (2) khûab′pajdûaj′

    1. to couple with; to be coupled with. sV 2.

    besides, in addition, at the same time.

   ส่วนควบ sùankhûab′ N component part.

ควบ ๒ khûab′ V to ride fast, gallop.

   ควบม้า khûabmáa′ V to gallop a horse.

   วิ่งควบ wîŋkhûab′ V to gallop.

ควร (1) khuan′; (2) khuanɔ V 1. to be meet, proper.

    AA 2. ought to, should. →S y n. 2. น่าจะ.

   o เรื่องควรรู้ rŷaŋ′khuanrúu′ things (or stories)

    worth knowing: "things (one) ought to know."

   ควรค่าแก่ khuankhâa′kɛ̀ɛɔ V to be worthy of, to

    deserve.

   ควรจะ khuancaɔ AA ought to, should. →S y n.

    น่าจะ.

   ตามควร taamkhuan′ V 1. to be as it should be;

    to be meet, proper. sV 2. as (one sees) fit;

    as befits, as is befitting (to).

   พอควร phɔɔkhuan′ fairly, moderately, reasonably.

   มากเกินควร mâag′kəənkhuan′ 1. more than is

    good, more than is proper. 2. much too (e.g.

    big, etc.).

   ไม่ควร (จะ) mâjkhuan(ca)ɔ ought not, should not.

   สมควร sŏmkhuan′ V to be suitable, appropriate.

   เห็นควร hěnkhuan′ V to deem it proper to, to see

    fit to.

   อันควร ʔankhuan′ suitable, proper.

ควัก khwág′ V to take out (from container, pocket),

    scoop out, spoon out (from deep container).

ควัน khwan′ N smoke, fumes.

   ควันโขมง khwan′khamŏoŋ′ billowing smoke,

    smoke issuing forth in billows.

ควันไฟ khwanfaj′ N smoke.

   ทันควัน thankhwan′ i d i o m. immediately, right

    away, suddenly.

   เป็นควัน penkhwan′ V 1. to be smoky. sV 2.

    i d i o m. eagerly, energetically; promptly.

ควั่น khwân′ V to cut, cut off (by making an incision

    around the circumference of a cylindrical object).

    →Sometimes confused with ฟั่น ๑ to twist (to-

    gether).

   ควั่นอ้อย khwân?ɔ̂ɔj′ V to cut sugar cane into

    short pieces (by making circular incisions).

   อ้อยควั่น (ขอ) ?ɔ̂ɔjkhwân′ (khɔ̂ɔ′) N sugar cane

    cut into short pieces (ready to eat).

ควา khwáa′ V to snatch, grab, reach for.

   ไขว่ควา khwàjkhwáa′ V to reach for, grasp at,

    try desperately to get hold of (as a drowning

    person).

   ค้นควา khónkhwáa′ V 1. to search (for). 2. to

    do research. การ- - research. ผู้- - re-

    searcher, (scientific) investigator.

   ควาหมับ khwáa′màb′ c o l l o q. to grasp quickly

    and firmly.

ควาง khwáaŋ′ V to be adrift, floating aimlessly;

    to be in aimless, random motion.

   เคว้งควาง khwéeŋkhwáaŋ′ V 1. to drift, be adrift.

    sV 2. adrift, aimlessly, randomly.

ความ khwaan′ V to rummage, feel around.

   ความหา khwaan′hǎa′ to rummage around, feel

    around in search of (something).

ควาน khwáan′ V to core (e.g. an apple), to pit (e.g.

    a plum), i.e. to take out (something) from the

    inside.

ความ khwaam′ N 1. the sense, the substance, the

    gist (of a matter, an account, etc.); 1st and 2nd

    example. 2. (legal) case, lawsuit; 3rd example.

    3. -ness, -ity, etc., a bound element; see notes

    1-3; concerning classifiers, see note 4.

   o จำกัดความ camkàd′khwaam′ V to define (the

    sense of something), give a definition: "delimit

    the sense."

   o ย่อความ jɔ̂ɔkhwaam′ V to condense, prepare

    an abstract, a digest: "summarize the sense."

   o สู้ความ sûu′khwaam′ V to fight a lawsuit.

NOTE 1. The most frequent use of ความ is
as a bound element placed in front of verbs to
form abstract nouns expressing a state or quality. It is usually rendered in English by such
suffixes as -ness, -ity, -th, -ment, -ance (-ence),
-(t)ion, -(t)ude, -ure, -y, -ery, -ship, -dom, -ing,
and the like. For -ing, see also note 3. No
suffix is required if the English abstract noun
is identical with the verb (hope; to hope). Most
nouns based on ความ are listed only under
the verbs from which they are derived. Thus
to find ความผิด, look under ผิด. The following examples are a sample selected for study
and are arranged according to the English suffixes just mentioned.

ความดี khwaamdii′ goodness, virtue: ดี to be
good.

ความสว่าง khwaamsawàaŋ′ brightness, brilliance:
สว่าง to be bright.

ความฉลาด khwaamchalàad′ cleverness, intelligence, sagacity: ฉลาด to be clever, intelligent, sagacious.

ความสามารถ khwaamsǎamâad′ ability: สามารถ
to be able.

ความเติบโต khwaamtə̀əbtoo′ growth: เติบโต
to grow.

ความตื่นเต้น khwaamtỳyntên′ excitement: ตื่นเต้น
to be excited.

ความสำคัญ khwaamsǎmkhan′ importance, significance: สำคัญ to be important, significant.

ความพอใจ khwaamphɔɔcaj′ satisfaction, contentment: พอใจ to be satisfied, content.

ความสูง khwaamsǔuŋ′ altitude, height, tallness:
สูง to be high, tall.

ความกดดัน khwaamkòddan′ pressure; figur.
oppression: กดดัน to press, oppress.

ความซื่อสัตย์ khwaamsŷysàd′ honesty: ซื่อสัตย์
to be honest.

ความกล้าหาญ khwaamklâahǎan′ bravery: กล้า
หาญ to be brave.

ความยากจน khwaamjâagcon′ hardship, poverty:
ยากจน to be hard up, poor.

ความเบื่อหน่าย khwaambỳanàaj′ boredom: เบื่อ
หน่าย to be bored, tired of (something).

ความประพฤติ khwaampraphrýd′ behavior, conduct: ประพฤติ to behave.

ความรู้ khwaamrúu′ knowledge: รู้ to know.

ความสำเร็จ khwaamsǎmrèd′ success: สำเร็จ
to succeed.

ความหวัง khwaamwǎŋ′ hope: หวัง to hope.

ความคิด khwaamkhíd′ thought, thoughts, thinking:
คิด to think.

NOTE 2. As a bound element, ความ can also
be placed before the negative ไม่ and its following verb.

ความไม่พอ khwaammâjphɔɔ′ insufficiency.

ความไม่พอใจ khwaammâjphɔɔcaj′ dissatisfaction,

displeasure.

ความไม่สงบ khwaammâjsaŋòb′ unrest, disquietude.

NOTE 3. A few verbs can be preceded by การ
when they have an active meaning and by ความ
when they have a nonactive or intransitive meaning; 1st and 2nd examples. Moreover, some
verbs can be preceded by either การ or ความ
without necessarily requiring a different English
rendition. In these instances a distinction which
is explicit in Thai is implicit in English; 3rd
and 4th examples. This remains true even though
some added confusion results from the fact that
ความ (as well as การ) is sometimes translated by the suffix -ing in English.

การฝัน kaanfǎn′ dreaming; ความฝัน khwaamfǎn′
(a) dream.

การเห็น kaanhěn′ (act of) seeing; ความเห็น
khwaamhěn′ idea, opinion.

การก้าวหน้า kaankâawnâa′ progress, i.e. progressing; ความก้าวหน้า khwaamkâawnâa′
progress, i.e. advancement.

การเจ็บป่วย kaancèbpùaj′ sickness, i.e. an occurrence of being sick; ความเจ็บป่วย khwaam′ɔ
cèbpùaj′ sickness, i.e. state of being sick.

NOTE 4. For the most part abstract nouns are
used in situations which do not require a classifier; 1st example. When a classifier is needed
it is usually one of those meaning "kind, sort,
variety," e.g. อย่าง, ชนิด, เช่น, and ประการ
eleg., or occasionally อัน, a general clf.,
and แบบ "type, model"; 2nd, 3rd and 4th examples. These classifiers are therefore always
omitted in entries for abstract nouns unless some
special distinction needs to be made.

จะต้องอยู่ในความควบคุมของรัฐบาล catɔ̂ŋjùu′-najɔ
khwaamkhûabkhum/khɔ̌ɔŋrádthabaan′↓ (It) will
have to be under the control of the government.

ความคิดเช่นนี้เป็นความเขลา khwaamkhíd′chênɔ
níi′ penkhwaamkhlǎw′↓ Such thinking is stupid:
"Thinking of this sort is stupidity."

ความจริงอย่างสูง ๔ ประการ khwaamciŋ′jàaŋɔ
sǔuŋ′-sìiprakaan′ the four sublime truths
(of Buddhism).

ด้วยความคิดอันหลักแหลม dûajkhwaamkhíd′/ʔanɔ
làglɛ̌ɛm′ by shrewd thought, by sharp thinking.

กระทงความ krathoŋ′khwaam′ N sense, meaning;
aspect of a matter.

กินความ kinkhwaam′ V to include, cover (in meaning).

กินความถึง kinkhwaam′th̷ỹŋɔ to touch on, refer
to, include.

ข้อความ (ข้อ, ตอน) khɔ̂ɔkhwaam′ (khɔ̂ɔ′, tɔɔn′)

N 1. item, point (of discourse, inquiry). 2. passage (from an article, etc.). 3. text (as of speech, letter), account, statement.

ไขความ khǎjkhwaam′ V to interpret; to uncover, disclose (the meaning).

คู่ความ (คน, คู่) khûukhwaam′ (khon′, khûu′) N one or both of the parties to a legal case, i.e. the plaintiff and/or the defendant.

จำกัดความ camkàd′khwaam′ V to define (the sense), give a definition. See cross reference.

แจ้งความ (เรื่อง, ฉบับ) cɛ̂ɛŋkhwaam′ (rŷaŋ′, chabàb′) N 1. advertisement, public notice. V 2. to report; to inform, give information.

ใจความ cajkhwaam′ N the meaning, gist, essence; subject matter. →Syn. เนื้อความ.

ได้ความ dâjkhwaam′ V 1. to make sense. 2. to ascertain (that), gather (that), hear (that).

o ไม่ได้ความ (1, 2) mâjdâjkhwaam′; (3) mâj′dâjɔ khwaam′↓ 1. to be nonsense, make no sense. 2. nonsensically, senselessly. 3. Nonsense! It doesn't make sense!

ตีความ tii′khwaam′ V to explain, interpret, define (as a law).

ถ้อยความ thɔ̂j′khwaam′ N lawsuit.

ทนายความ (คน) thanaajkhwaam′ (khon′) N lawyer, attorney, counselor; (Brit.) barrister, solicitor.

ท้าวความถึง tháaw′khwaam′-thy̌ŋɔ to refer to.

นอกความ nɔ̂ɔg′khwaam′ V to be beside the point.

เนื้อความ nýakhwaam′ N essence of a matter; the content (as of a book); subject matter. →Syn. ใจความ.

บทความ (บท, เรื่อง) bòdkhwaam′ (bòd′, rŷaŋ′) N an article (in a newspaper, magazine, etc.).

เบิกความ bə̀əg′khwaam′ V to testify.

เป็นความ penkhwaam′ V to be involved in a lawsuit.

ย่อความ (เรื่อง, บท) jɔ̂ɔkhwaam′ (rŷaŋ′, bòd′) V 1. to condense, prepare an abstract, a digest. N 2. digest, abstract.

รวมความ ruamkhwaam′ V to sum up, summarize. See cross reference.

เรียงความ (เรื่อง, บท) riaŋkhwaam′ (rŷaŋ′, bòd′)

N 1. essay. V 2. to write an essay.

ลูกความ (คน) lûugkhwaam′ (khon′) N litigant.

ว่าความ wâakhwaam′ V to litigate; to plead a case in court.

สรุปความ sarùb′khwaam′ V 1. to sum up, summarize, conclude. N 2. conclusion.

สู้ความ sûu′khwaam′ V to fight a lawsuit.

เสริมความ sə̌əmkhwaam′ V to overstate, exaggerate.

หมอความ (คน) mɔ̌ɔkhwaam′ (khon′) N colloq. lawyer. →Also หมอถ้อยหมอความ elab. colloq.

หมายความ(ว่า) mǎajkhwaam′(wâa) V to mean (that). See cross reference.

หาความ(ใส่) hǎakhwaam′(sàjɔ) V to make an allegation, accusation (against).

ควาย (ตัว) khwaaj′ (tua′) N com. water buffalo. →Syn. กระบือ eleg.

ควายป่า (ตัว) khwaajpàa′ (tua′) N wild buffalo.

วัวควาย (ตัว) wuakhwaaj′ (tua′) N cattle, livestock (in general).

คว่ำ khwâm′ V 1. to turn over, turn upside down, capsize. 2. to be turned over, upside down. 3. to be face down in a prone position.

คว่ำบาตร khwâmbàad′ V 1. idiom. to turn down; to disapprove of, reject. 2. to excommunicate.

ใจหายใจคว่ำ cajhǎaj′cajkhwâm′ V to be stunned with fear, get scared out of one's wits.

ล้มคว่ำ lómkhwâm′ V to fall face down.

ควินิน, ยา-- khwinin′, jaakhwinin′ N quinine. [f. Eng.]

ค.ศ. khɔɔsɔ̌ɔ′ A. D. (the Christian era). Abbrev. for คริสต์ศักราช.

คห- in คหบดี (คน) kháhà?′bodii′ (khon′) N wealthy man.

คอ (คอ) khɔɔ′ (khɔɔ′) N neck.

กลั้วคอ klûakhɔɔ′ V to gargle (the throat).

ขัดคอ khàdkhɔɔ′ V 1. to interrupt, break in repeatedly (as while someone is speaking). 2. to gainsay, disagree.

คอคอด (แห่ง) khɔɔkhɔ̂d′ (hɛ̀ŋ′) N isthmus.

คอตก khɔɔtòg′ V 1. to drop the head (with sadness, disappointment). sV 2. (with) drooping head, crestfallen.

คอต่อ khɔɔtɔɔ′ N nape.

คอบุหรี่ (คน) khɔɔ′burìi′ (khon′) N idiom.
a heavy smoker.

คอแบะ khɔɔbɛ?′ having lapels (e.g. a coat).

คอพอก khɔɔphɔɔg′ V to have a goiter.

คอสุรา (คน) khɔɔ′suraa′ (khon′) N eleg. a
person used to drinking, a heavy drinker.

คอเสื้อ (อัน) khɔɔsŷa′ (?an′) N 1. collar (of
a shirt, coat, etc.). 2. neck (of a garment).

คอหวาน khɔɔwǎan′ to have a sweet tooth.

คอหอย (คอหอย) khɔɔhɔ̌j′ (khɔɔhɔ̌j′) N colloq.
throat.

คอเหล้า (คน) khɔɔlâw′ (khon′) N a person used
to drinking, a heavy drinker.

ใจคอ cajkhɔɔ′ N 1. disposition, mood. 2. character (people only).

o นิสัยใจคอ nísǎj′cajkhɔɔ′ N disposition,
temperament.

ได้ลงคอ dâjloŋkhɔɔ′ to be unfeeling enough to.

o ลูกฆ่าพ่อได้ลงคอ lûug′khâaphɔ̂ɔ′-dâjloŋkhɔɔ′↓
The son killed his father in cold blood.

o คุณนี่ช่างทำได้ลงคอนะ khun′nîi→chaŋtham′dâjↄ
loŋkhɔɔ′-ná↓ How could you have the heart to
do this?

ติดคอ tìdkhɔɔ′ V to be stuck, lodged in the throat
(as a fish bone).

ถูกคอ(กัน) thùugkhɔɔ′(kan′) V colloq. to get
along well (with one another) because of compatible tastes and interests.

บีบคอ bìibkhɔɔ′ V to strangle (someone).

ฝืดคอ fŷydkhɔɔ′ V 1. to experience difficulty in
swallowing (as because of dryness of one's
throat). 2. to be hard to swallow (as dry bread).

ยืดคอ jŷyd′khɔɔ′ V to stretch the neck, crane
one's neck.

ลงคอ ๑. See entry below.

o หวัดลงคอ wàd′loŋkhɔɔ′ to have a sore throat,
a cold with phlegm.

ลงคอ ๒. See ได้ลงคอ above.

ลอยคอ lɔɔjkhɔɔ′ to float with the head above
water.

ลำคอ (ลำคอ) lamkhɔɔ′ (lamkhɔɔ′) N throat.

เอียงคอ ?iaŋkhɔɔ′ V to cock one's head (e.g.
in order to listen).

คอก (คอก) khɔ̂ɔg′ (khɔ̂ɔg′) N enclosure, pen, sty

(for animals); stable, cowbarn.

คอกหมู (คอก) khɔ̂ɔgmǔu′ (khɔ̂ɔg′) N pigsty.

หญ้าปากคอก jâa′pàagkhɔ̂ɔg′ idiom. easy, obvious;
commonplace, ordinary, so familiar as to remain
unnoticed: "grass (by) the barn door."

คอด khɔ̂ɔd′ V 1. to be narrowed, constricted. 2.
to be worn away.

คอคอด (แห่ง) khɔɔkhɔ̂ɔd′ (hɛ̀ŋ′) N isthmus.

คอน (คอน) khɔɔn′ (khɔɔn′) N perch, roost.

ค่อน ๑ khɔ̂ɔn′, khɔ̂n′ V to criticize, make slurring
remarks, ridicule, revile.

ค่อนขอด, ขอดค่อน khɔ̂nkhɔ̂ɔd′, khɔ̂ɔdkhɔ̂ɔn′ idem.
การ-- ridiculing, criticizing.

ค่อนแคะ khɔ̂nkhɛ́?′ to criticize, pick at.

ค่อน ๒ khɔ̂ɔn′, khɔ̂nↄ V 1. to be inclined towards,
tend toward. 2. to be on the full side, over half,
more than half.

o เป็นค่อนหม้อ penkhɔ̂n′mɔ̂ɔ′ There's plenty
more in the pot (i.e. it is well over half full).

ค่อนข้าง(จะ) khɔ̂nkhâaŋ′(caↄ) AA inclined to
be, rather, more or less, on the side of, somewhat.

o ค่อนข้างสวย khɔ̂nkhâaŋsǔaj′ rather pretty, on
the pretty side.

ค้อน ๑ (อัน) khɔ́ɔn′ (?an′) N hammer.

ค้อน ๒ khɔ́ɔn′ V to glance sidewise (coquettishly,
with friendly disapproval, or angrily). Used esp.
of women.

คอนกรีต khonkrìid′ N concrete. [f. Eng.]

คอบ in รอบคอบ rɔ̂ɔbkhɔ̂ɔb′ V to be careful, circumspect, cautious.

ค่อม in หลังค่อม lǎŋkhɔ̂ɔm′ V 1. to be hunchbacked.
2. to be roundshouldered, stooped over; to have
one's shoulders slouched over.

ค้อม khɔ́ɔm′ V to bend, stoop.

อ้อมค้อม ?ɔ̂ɔmkhɔ́ɔm′ V to be indirect, roundabout.

o พูดอ้อมค้อม phûud′?ɔ̂ɔmkhɔ́ɔm′ to speak evasively, to beat around the bush.

คอมมิวนิสต์ khɔɔmmiwnís′, -níd′ N communism;
communist. [f. Eng.]

จีนคอมมิวนิสต์ ciin′khɔmmiwnís′ N Communist
China; Chinese communist.

คอย khɔɔj′ V 1. to wait, wait for, await. AA 2.
keep (...-ing). →Syn. 1. รอ,ท่า. See also

คอยจะ.

o คอยดุ khɔɔjdù?ʔ/ keep(s) scolding (someone).

o คอยระวัง khɔɔjrawaŋ/ keep watching out, keep on the alert.

คอยจะ khɔɔjcaɔ AA waiting (for an opportunity) to, interested (solely) in. →Syn. จ้องจะ.

o คอยจะกินท่าเดียว khɔɔjcakin/thâadiaw/↓ (He's) waiting solely (for an opportunity) to eat, is interested solely (in getting) to eat.

คอยท่า khɔɔjthâa/ V to wait for, await.

รอคอย rɔɔkhɔɔj/ V to wait, wait for.

หอคอย (หอ,หลัง) hɔɔkhɔɔj/ (hɔɔ/, lǎŋ/) N watchtower.

ค่อย khɔj/ AA 1. gradually, little by little, with care. sV 2. gently, softly, low (of sound).

o อากาศค่อยเย็นลง ʔaakàad/-khɔjjen/loŋ The air gradually cools off.

o พูดค่อยเกินไป phûud/khɔjkəənpaj/ to speak too low, too softly.

ค่อย ๆ khɔjkhɔj/ idem ค่อย.

o ค่อย ๆ เดิน khɔjkhɔjdəən/ walk carefully (so as not to fall), walk slowly.

o เดินค่อย ๆ dəən/khɔjkhɔj/ to walk softly, noiselessly.

o ค่อย ๆ หน่อย khɔjkhɔj/nɔɔj/ a bit (more) gently! a little softly!

ค่อยเป็นค่อยไป khɔjpen/khɔjpaj/ to learn or acquire ability little by little, in due time.

ค่อยยังชั่ว khɔjjaŋchûa/ 1. to get better, feel better. 2. not so bad.

ไม่ค่อย mâjkhɔjɔ AA colloq. scarcely, hardly, not quite, not very. →Syn. ไม่สู้ ๒.

o ไม่ค่อยดี mâjkhɔjdii/ not very good: "hardly good."

o ไม่ค่อยเคยเห็นช้าง mâjkhɔjkhəəjhěncháaŋ/↓ (They) scarcely ever see an elephant.

คอรัปชั่น khɔɔráb/chân/ N corruption. [f. Eng.]

คะ khá/ Pt def. w. sp. 1. particle used as the final element in questions; 1st example. 2. final particle used after other particles which contain the idea of urging, suggesting, intimating (e.g. นะ, กระมัง), and occasionally of requesting or emphasizing (e.g. ปี); 2nd, 3rd, 4th, and 5th examples. 3. particle placed after

name, title, or kin term to address or to call the attention of someone; 6th example. 4. Yes? (as a reply when called or spoken to). →Syn. เจ้าคะ eleg. def. w. sp. →Cf. ครับ def. m. sp. →See also คะ, ขา ๒, and also the variant ฮะ ๑.

o กี่โมงแล้วคะ kìimooŋ/lɛɛwkhá↓ What time is it?

o คอยเดี๋ยวนะคะ khɔɔjdǐaw/nákhá↓ Wait a moment!

o อยู่ในห้องนั้นกระมังคะ jùunajhɔŋnán/kramaŋ/ɔ khá↓ (He's) probably in that room.

o เชิญนั่งซิคะ chəənnâŋ/sikhá↓ Have a seat!

o นั่นซิคะ nân/sikhá↓ That's it!

o คุณนายคะ khunnaaj/khá↓ Madame!

เจ้าคะ câwkhá/ Pt eleg. def. w. sp. Particle used in the ways described for คะ above. →Cf. ขอรับ eleg. def. m. sp.

เพคะ phekhá/ Pt eleg. def. w. sp. final particle used in addressing royalty and the Supreme Patriarch. →See กระหม่อม.

ค่ะ khâ/ Pt def. w. sp. 1. particle used at the end of statements and commands; 1st and 2nd examples. 2. Yes (in answer to a question); 3rd example. →Cf. ครับ def. m. sp. →Syn. เจ้าค่ะ eleg. def. w. sp.

o เขามาแล้วค่ะ kháwmaa/lɛɛwkhâ↓ He's already come.

o เข้ามาเถอะค่ะ khâwmaa/thəkhâ↓ Come in!

o เสร็จหรือยัง ค่ะเสร็จแล้ว sèd/rýjaŋ/↓ khâ/→ sèdlɛɛw/↓ Finished? Yes, (I've) finished.

เจ้าค่ะ câwkhâ/ Pt eleg. def. w. sp. Particle used in the ways described for ค่ะ above. →Cf. ขอรับ eleg. def. m. sp.

คะนอง khanɔɔŋ/ V to be high-spirited, exuberant, reckless.

ฟ้าคะนอง fáa/khanɔɔŋ/ N eleg. 1. thunder; thunderstorm. 2. it thunders.

คะนึง(ถึง) khanyŋ/(thŷŋɔ) V to think (about), contemplate.

คะเน khanee/ V to estimate; to guess.

คาดคะเน khâadkhanee/ V to speculate, guess.

คะแนน (คะแนน) khanɛɛn/ (khanɛɛn/) N 1. mark(s), point(s), grade, score. 2. vote.

คะแนนเสียง (คะแนน) khanɛɛnsǐaŋ/ (khanɛɛn/)

N vote, ballot.

ลงคะแนน loŋ'khanɛɛn' 1. to cast a vote, ballot.
2. to write down, record the score.

หักคะแนน hàg'khanɛɛn' to reduce the score or
grade, deduct from the score, take points off.

o ถูกหักคะแนน thùughàg'khanɛɛn' to take a deduction in one's score or grade; to lose points.

คะมำ khamam' V to fall forwards.

คะเมน in หักคะเมน hògkhameen' V 1. to turn a
somersault. 2. to tumble, fall down.

คะยั้นคะยอ khaján'khajɔɔ' V to urge, press, pressure. Also written ขะยั้นขะยอ.

คั่ง khâŋ' V to be congested, crowded, jammed.

คั่งค้าง khâŋkháaŋ' V 1. to be overdue. 2. to be
in a bottleneck, be piled up (and awaiting action);
to be pigeonholed.

คับคั่ง khábkhâŋ' V 1. to be crowded. 2. to be
dense, thick (of population).

มั่งคั่ง mâŋkhâŋ' V to be rich, wealthy.

คัด ๑ khád' V 1. to choose, select, pick out. 2. to
be choice, select, picked. 3. to copy. 4. to
excerpt. 5. to letter (as in penmanship).

คัดค้าน khádkháan' V to object (to), oppose.

คัดลอก,ลอกคัด khád'lɔɔg', lɔɔg'khád' V to copy,
imitate.

คัดเลือก khádlɣag' V to select, sort out, pick out.

คัดหัวเรือ khád'hŭarya' to steer or guide a boat
by pushing against the prow with a paddle.

คัดออก khád?ɔɔg' V to weed out, eliminate by
sorting out.

คัด ๒ khád' V to clog (up), be stuffed, clogged,
congested.

คัดจมูก khád'camùg' to have a stuffed nose.

คัดนม,นมคัด khád'nom', nomkhád' 1. (breasts)
to be congested with milk. 2. to have a conges-
tion in the breasts, mastitis.

คัน ๑ khan' C 1. clf. for long-handled objects
(spoons, forks, umbrellas, fishing rods, plows).
2. clf. for vehicles other than carts.

กลางคัน klaaŋkhan' in the middle, before it was
finished (of an interrupted action, event).

คันชั่ง (คัน) khanchâŋ' (khan') N 1. balance,
scales. 2. beam, transverse bar of a balance.

คันนา (คันนา) khannaa' (khannaa') N dike,

earthen embankment enclosing a paddy field.

คันน้ำมัน (อัน) khannámman' (?an') N accelerator
(of a car).

คันเบ็ด (คัน) khanbèd' (khan') N a fishing rod.

คันศร (คัน) khansɔɔn' (khan') N bow (the weapon).

คัน ๒ khan' V to itch, be itchy.

คันปาก khanpàag' colloq. to be itching to say
something.

คันมือ khanmyy' colloq. to be itching to do something (with the hands).

ปากคัน pàag'khan' to be loose-tongued.

คั้น khân' V to separate, interpose, divide.

คั้น khán' V to squeeze, press (so as to extract,
e.g. juice).

คั้นเอา(...)ออก khán'-?aw(...)?ɔɔg' to squeeze
(juice, etc.) out.

คาดคั้น khâadkhán' V to press for; to constrain.

บีบคั้น bìib'khán' V 1. to compress, crush, squeeze
out. 2. idiom. to oppress.

คันธุลี khanthulii' pN Khanthuli (located in Phatthalung
čhangwat in S Thailand.

คับ kháb' V 1. to be tight, tight-fitting, tightly packed.
2. (contents) to pack, be packed tightly into (a
container); to jam, crowd (a place). →Syn. แน่น.

คับขัน khábkhăn' V 1. to be in a tight spot, in a
critical situation. 2. to be of a critical, emergency nature.

o ตาคับขัน taa'khábkhăn' a critical moment.

o ภาวะคับขัน phaawá?'khábkhăn' a state of crisis
or emergency.

o เหตุการณ์คับขัน hèedkaan'khábkhăn' emergency,
crisis.

คับคั่ง khábkhâŋ' V 1. to be crowded. 2. to be
dense, thick (of population).

คับแค้น khábkhéɛn' V to be impoverished, hard-
pressed, in distress.

คับแคบ khábkhɛ̂ɛb' V to be narrow, cramped
(of space).

คับใจ khábcaj' V to feel distressed, uneasy,
apprehensive.

คัมภีร์ (เล่ม) khamphii' (lêm') N 1. sacred book,
scripture. 2. Bible.

คั่ว khûa' V to parch, roast.

มะพร้าวคั่ว maphráaw'khûa' roasted coconut meat.

คา ๑ khaa′ V 1. to be lodged in, remain imbedded,
    be stuck (to, on, etc.). 2. to be left unifinished,
    remain partly done. N 3. shackle for a pris-
    oner's neck.

  คาที่ khaathîi′ on the spot, instantly.
  ○ ตายคาที่ taaj′khaathîi′ to die on the spot.
  คามือ khaamyy′ in the act, red-handed.
  ○ จับได้คามือ càb′dâaj′-khaa′myy′ to catch in
    the act, catch red-handed.

คา ๒, หญ้า-- (ต้น) khaa′, jâakhaa′ (tôn′) N cogon,
    a tall, coarse grass used for thatching (Impe-
    rata cylindrica). Also other related species of
    grass.

  ปายคา (ปายคา) chaajkhaa′ (chaajkhaa′) N
    eaves.
  หลังคา (หลังคา) lǎŋkhaa′ (lǎŋkhaa′) N roof.

ค่า ๑ khâa′ N fee, cost, price, value.

  ค่ากิน khâakin′ N food expenses; food (as an
    expense item), the cost of food.
  ค่ากินอยู่ khâakinjùu′ N living expenses, esp.
    room and board.
  ค่าขนส่ง khâakhǒnsòŋ′ N cost of transportation.
  ค่าครองชีพ khâakhrɔɔŋchîib′ N cost of living.
  ค่าจ้าง khâacâaŋ′ N wage, wages, pay.
  ค่าชดเชย khâachódchəəj′ N compensation (for
    work done, for property damage).
  ค่าเช่า khâachâw′ N the rent, rental fee.
  ค่าใช้จ่าย khâachájcàaj′ N expenses.
  ค่าใช้สอย khâachájsɔɔj′ N expenses.
  ค่าดู khâaduu′ N admission fee (to a theater,
    wrestling match, etc.).
  ค่าโดยสาร khâadoojsǎan′ N fare, cost of pas-
    sage
  ค่าไถ่ khâathàj′ N ransom; cost of redemption.
  ค่าทำขวัญ khâathamkhwǎn′ N compensation,
    indemnity (for personal injury or damage).
  ค่าที่ khâathîi′ the price of a piece of land, of a
    lot. →For an unrelated mng. see ค่าที่ under
    ค่า ๒.
  ค่าธรรมเนียม khâathamniam′ N fee, fees.
  ค่าน้ำค่าไฟ khâanáam′khâafaj′ N cost of utilities
    (e.g. water and electricity).
  ค่าบำรุง khâabamruŋ′ N subscription, member-
    ship fee, dues.

ค่าปรับไหม khâapràbmǎj′ N fine, penalty.
ค่าป่วยการ khâapùajkaan′ N idiom. fee, service
    charge, commission.
ค่าผ่านประตู khâaphàan′pratuu′ N admission
    charge, gate fee.
ค่ารถ khâaród′ N fare, carfare.
ค่าระวาง khâarawaaŋ′ N freight charges.
○ ค่าระวางบรรทุก khâarawaaŋ′banthúg′ N ship-
    ping charge, freightage.
ค่าแรงงาน khâarɛɛŋŋaan′ N wages, pay (for
    labor).
ค่าเสียหาย khâasǐahǎaj′ N the damages, the loss,
    the amount of the loss.
ค่าอยู่ khâajùu′ N lodging (as an expense item),
    the cost of lodging.
คุณค่า khunkhâa′ N value.
มีค่า miikhâa′ to be valuable, precious.
มูลค่า muun′khâa′ N value, price.
ไร้ค่า ráj′khâa′ to be valueless, worthless.
ล้นค่า lón′khâa′ eleg. to be invaluable, priceless.
เสื่อมค่า sỳamkhâa′ to devaluate, depreciate.
    การ-- devaluation, depreciation.
หาค่าบ่มิได้ hǎakhâa′bɔ̀mídâaj′ lit. to be invalu-
    able, priceless.
หาค่ามิได้ hǎakhâa′mídâaj′ eleg. to be invaluable.

ค่า ๒ in ค่าที่ khâa′thîi′ because, owing tò the fact
    that, on account of the fact that.

ค้า kháa′ V to do business (in), trade (in), sell,
    engage in trade. การ-- business, trade, com-
    merce; trading.

  คบค้า(กับ) khóbkháa′(kaɔ) V to associate (with),
    be friends (with).
  ค้าขาย kháakhǎaj′ V to engage in trade, buy and
    sell. การ-- business, trade, commerce.
  ○ ไปมาค้าขาย pajmaa′kháakhǎaj′ to engage in
    trade, travel about on commercial business.
  ○ เรือค้าขาย (ลำ) rya′kháakhǎaj′ (lam′) N
    cargo ship.
  พ่อค้า (คน) phɔ̂ɔkháa′ (khon′) N merchant,
    trader, tradesman, shopkeeper.
  แม่ค้า (คน) mɛ̂ɛkháa′ (khon′) N merchant
    (woman), shopkeeper, market woman, street
    vendor.
  ร้านค้า (ร้าน) ráankháa′ (ráan′) N store.

ลูกค้า (คน) lûugkháa⁄ (khon⁄) N customer.

สินค้า (อย่าง,ชนิด) sǐnkháa⁄ (jàaŋ⁄, chaníd⁄) N products, produce, commodities, merchandise, goods, cargo, freight. See cross reference.

คาง (คาง) khaaŋ⁄ (khaaŋ⁄) N chin, jaw.

คางเหลือง khaaŋ⁄lʉ̌aŋ⁄ slang critically injured, near dead.

สี่เหลี่ยมคางหมู (รูป) sìilìam⁄khaaŋmǔu⁄ (rûub⁄) N geom. trapezoid.

ค่าง (ตัว)khàaŋ⁄ (tua⁄) N langur, a kind of monkey.

ค้าง (อัน,ค้าง) kháaŋ⁄ (ʔan⁄, kháaŋ⁄) N 1. prop, pole (to support plants, e.g. beanpole). V 2. to remain; to lodge, be stuck, attached. 3. to remain over, be unfinished, pending. 4. to be behind in (one's payments), to be owing.

ค้างค้าง kháŋkháaŋ⁄ V 1. to be overdue. 2. to be in a bottleneck, be piled up (and awaiting action). 3. to be pigeonholed.

ค้างคืน kháaŋkhyyn⁄ com. to stay overnight, spend the night (in a place). →Syn. แรมคืน. eleg.

ค้างเติ่ง kháaŋtə̀ŋ⁄ V colloq. to be left unfinished, to be held up (until another time). 2. to be left in the lurch.

ค้างถั่ว (อัน,ค้าง) kháaŋthùa⁄ (ʔan⁄, kháaŋ⁄) N beanpole.

ค้างแรม kháaŋrɛɛm⁄ V to stay overnight, spend the night.

ค้างไว้ kháaŋ⁄wáj⁄ V 1. to remain, be left. 2. to be left unfinished, partly done. 3. to be in debt, be owing.

○ อ่านค้างไว้ ʔàankháaŋ⁄wáj⁄ to have left the reading unfinished, to leave off reading.

ตกค้าง tògkháaŋ⁄ V to be left over, left behind.

ติดค้าง tìdkháaŋ⁄ V 1. to be in debt, be owing. 2. to be stuck, lodged (in something).

น้ำค้าง námkháaŋ⁄ N dew.

คางคก (ตัว) khaaŋkhóg⁄ (tua⁄) N toad.

ค้างคาว (ตัว) kháaŋkhaaw⁄ (tua⁄) N bat (mammal).

คาด ๑ khâad⁄ V to put around, to tie around, to belt, to strap.

คาดคั้น khâadkhán⁄ V to press for; to constrain.

คาด ๒ khâad⁄ V to anticipate, expect, guess, speculate.

เกินคาด kəənkhâad⁄ beyond expectation.

คาดกันว่า khâad⁄kanwâa⁄ it is speculated that.

คาดคะเน khâadkhanee⁄ V to speculate, guess. การ-- making a guess, speculating. ความ-- guess, speculation.

คาดโทษ khâadthôod⁄ V to set a penalty for the next recurrence of a violation for which at the given moment punishment has been withheld.

คาดหมาย khâadmǎaj⁄ V to expect, anticipate.

คาดหวัง khâadwǎŋ⁄ V to expect, anticipate.

ผิดคาด phìdkhâad⁄ V 1. to be contrary to expectation, disappointing. 2. to be disappointed (in expectations).

คาถา (บท) khaathǎa⁄ (bòd⁄) N 1. magic spell, magic words. 2. stanza (in certain verse forms).

คาน (อัน) khaan⁄ (ʔan⁄) N 1. a horizontal beam, pole or stick used as a support. 2. lever. 3. beam (of a balance).

คานดีด khaandìid⁄ N lever.

ไม้คาน (อัน) májkhaan⁄ (ʔan⁄) N a bamboo pole used for carrying loads on the shoulder.

ค้าน kháan⁄ V to oppose, contradict, be contradictory to.

คัดค้าน khádkháan⁄ V to object (to), oppose.

ฝ่ายค้าน fàajkháan⁄ N 1. negative side (in debate). 2. the opposition (in politics).

คานาดา khaanaadaa⁄ pN Canada. [f. Eng.]

คาบ ๑ khâab⁄ C period, cycle (of time).

หนังสือพิมพ์รายคาบ (ฉบับ) naŋsʉ̌yphim⁄raajkhâab⁄ (chabàb⁄) N periodical.

คาบ ๒ khâab⁄ V to hold, seize, clamp (in the teeth, in the beak).

คาบกล้อง khâabklɔ̂ŋ⁄ to hold a pipe in one's mouth.

คาบกัน khâab⁄kan to overlap, partially coincide.

คาบเกี่ยว khâabkìaw⁄ V to overlap, be overlapping, extend over (into).

คาบสมุทร (แห่ง,คาบสมุทร) khâab⁄samùd⁄ (hɛ̀ŋ⁄, khâab⁄samùd⁄) N geog. peninsula.

คาบเส้น khâabsên⁄ to be situated on the border line.

หมอบราบคาบแก้ว mɔ̀ɔbrâab⁄khâabkɛ̂ɛw⁄ elab. colloq. to give in, surrender, yield completely.

คาบ ๓ in ราบคาบ râabkhâab⁄ V to be peaceful,

tranquil; to be subdued.

คาม in คุกคาม khúgkhaam′ V to threaten, loom
  menacingly.

คาย ๑ khaaj′ V 1. to spit out. 2. to give off (e.g.
  steam). 3. to secrete.

คาย ๒ khaaj′ V to be rough (to the touch).

  คมคาย khomkhaaj′ V 1. to be attractive and
    bright-looking. 2. to be witty.

  แยบคาย jɛ̂ɛbkhaaj′ V 1. to be ingenious, skillful,
    clever. 2. to be right, appropriate, wise.

  หยาบคาย jàabkhaaj′ V to be crude, coarse, vul-
    gar, unmannerly (in speech or action).

ค่าย (ค่าย) khâaj′ (khâaj′) N 1. camp (e.g. army
  camp). 2. stockade.

  ค่ายกักกัน, - -ชีวิต (ค่าย,แห่ง) khâajkàgkan′,
    khâajkàgkanchiiwíd′ (khâaj′, hèŋ′) N concen-
    tration camp.

  ค่ายกักเชลย (ค่าย) khâajkàg′chaləəj′ (khâaj′)
    N prisoner-of-war camp.

  ค่ายทหารบก (ค่าย) khâajthahăanbòg′ (khâaj′)
    N army camp.

คารม khaarom′ N eloquent talk; apt language.

คารวะ khaarawá?′ N eleg. respect. →Syn.
  ความเคารพ.

คาว ๑ khaaw′ V to be fishy (in smell).

  ของคาว (อย่าง,จาน) khɔ̌ɔŋkhaaw′ (jàaŋ′, caan′)
    N dish of the main course prepared of meat
    or fish. Contrast ของหวาน "dessert."

  ของสดของคาว khɔ̌ɔŋsòd′khɔ̌ɔŋkhaaw′ N fresh,
    raw foods (often esp. raw meats).

  เหม็นคาว mĕnkhaaw′ to stink, smell foully of
    raw meat, blood, fish.

คาว ๒ in ค้างคาว (ตัว) kháaŋkhaaw′ (tua′) N
  bat (mammal).

คำ ๑ kham′ N "gold." Chiefly in compounds.
  →Syn. ทอง.

  ทองคำ (แท่ง,ก้อน) thɔɔŋkham′ (thɛ̂ŋ′, kɔ̂ɔn′)
    N gold; yellow gold.

คำ ๒ (คำ) kham′ (kham′) N 1. word, words,
  (oral) speech. C 2. mouthful, bite. 3. clf.
  for an utterance, a word. →Syn. ถ้อย.

NOTE 1. คำ is frequently placed in front of
verbs of speaking, saying, asking, etc., to form
noun derivatives. It is usually rendered in English by such suffixes as -tion, -ment, -ance
(-ence), -ing, etc., or by no suffix if the English
noun is identical with the verb. In spite of such
renditions, คำ is in no sense a substitute for
ความ. On the contrary, คำ is required when
the noun has reference to words or to what is
uttered in words. Most verb-based nouns
formed by using คำ are listed only under the
verbs from which they are derived. Thus to
find คำตอบ, look under ตอบ. The following
examples are a sample selected for study.
They are arranged according to the English
suffixes just mentioned.

คำชี้แจง kham′chíɛɛŋ′ explanation.
คำย่อ khamjɔ̂ɔ′ abbreviation.
คำแถลง kham′thalɛ̌ɛŋ′ declaration. statement,
  announcement.
คำพูด kham′phûud′ spoken word, utterance.
คำกล่าว kham′klàaw′ a saying.
คำด่า kham′dàa′ cursing, abuse (in words).
คำสอน kham′sɔ̌ɔn′ (a) teaching, doctrine.
คำบ่น kham′bòn′ complaint.
คำขาด kham′khàad′ ultimatum.
คำสัญญา kham′sǎnjaa′ promise.
คำวิงวอน kham′wiŋwɔɔn′ plea, supplication.
คำยินยอม kham′jinjɔɔm′ consent.

NOTE 2. คำ can also be placed in front of
nouns to form a new noun derivative. Terms
for the parts of speech are formed in this way;
see คำกริยา,คำคุณศัพท์.

NOTE 3. Wherever ฉบับ is indicated as the
classifier, or one of the classifiers, in the following entries, it is to be remembered that a
written item is referred to.

กลับคำ klàbkham′ V to go back on one's word.

คำกริยา (คำ) kham′kàrijaa′, -krì- (kham′) N
  gram. verb. →Also คำกิริยา.

คำกริยาวิเศษณ์ (คำ) kham′-kàrijaa′wisèed′
  (kham′) N gram. adverb.

คำกล่าว (ข้อ,บท) khamklàaw′ (khɔ̂ɔ′, bòd′) N
  a saying.

คำกล่าวหา (ข้อ,ประการ,คำ) kham′klàawhǎa′
  (khɔ̂ɔ′, prakaan′, kham′) N accusation, charge.

คำกิริยา (คำ) kham′kirijaa′ (kham′) N gram.
  verb. →Usually คำกริยา.

คำขอโทษ (ข้อ,ประการ) kham′khɔ̌ɔthôod′ (khɔ̂ɔ′,
  prakaan′) N apology, excuse.

คำขอร้อง (ข้อ,ฉบับ) kham′khɔ̌ɔrɔ́ɔŋ′ (khɔ̂ɔ′, cha-
  bàb′) N petition; request (for help).

คำขาด (ข้อ,ฉบับ) khamkhàad′ (khɔ̂ɔ′, chabàb′)

N ultimatum.

คำคุณศัพท์ (คำ) kham′khunnasàb′ (kham′) N
g r a m. adjective.

คำจำกัดความ (อย่าง) kham′-camkàd′khwaam′
(jàaŋ′) N the definition (of a word).

คำชี้แจง (ข้อ,ประการ) kham′chíicεεŋ (khɔ̌ɔ′,
prakaan′) N explanation.

คำเชิญ (คำ,ฉบับ) khamchəən′ (kham′, chabàb′)
N 1. invitation. 2. request.

คำด่า (คำ) khamdàa′ (kham′) N abuse (in
words), cursing.

คำดุด่า (คำ) kham′dù?dàa′ (kham′) N a scolding, (words of) abuse.

คำดูถูก (คำ,ข้อ) kham′duuthùug′ (kham′, khɔ̌ɔ′)
N an insult.

คำตอบ (คำตอบ) khamtɔ̀ɔb′ (khamtɔ̀ɔb′) N
answer, reply.

คำตาย (คำ) khamtaaj′ (kham′) N dead syllable
(in the Thai system of writing), i.e. a syllable
ending in a short vowel or a stop consonant.
→Opp. คำเป็น.

คำติเตียน kham′tì?tian′ N criticism (disapproval).

คำถาม (ข้อ,คำถาม) khamthǎam′ (khɔ̌ɔ′, khamɔ
thǎam′) N question.

o เครื่องหมายคำถาม khrŷaŋmǎaj′khamthǎam′
the question mark.

คำแถลง (ข้อ,ประการ) kham′thalɛ̌ɛŋ′ (khɔ̌ɔ′,
prakaan′) N declaration, statement, announcement.

คำทำนาย (ข้อ,ประการ) kham′thamnaaj′ (khɔ̌ɔ′,
prakaan′) N a prophecy.

คำนาม (คำ) khamnaam′ (kham′) N noun.

คำนำ (บท) khamnam′ (bòd′) N preface, fore-
word. →Dist. บทนำ.

คำแนะนำ (ข้อ,ประการ) kham′nέ?nam′ (khɔ̌ɔ′,
prakaan′) N advice, suggestion, instruction.

คำบ่น (ข้อ,ประการ) khambòn′ (khɔ̌ɔ′, prakaan′)
N complaint.

คำบอก (คำบอก) khambɔ̀ɔg′ (khambɔ̀ɔg′) N
dictation (in class).

คำบอกเล่า (อย่าง) kham′bɔ̀ɔglâw′ (jàaŋ′) N
the spoken word, word (of mouth).

คำบัญชาการ (ข้อ,ประการ) kham′banchaakaan′
(khɔ̌ɔ′, prakaan′) N order, command.

คำปฏิญาณ (ข้อ,ประการ) kham′patìjaan′ (khɔ̌ɔ′,
prakaan′) N promise, vow.

คำประกาศ (ข้อ,ฉบับ,อย่าง) kham′prakàad′
(khɔ̌ɔ′, chabàb′, jàaŋ′) N announcement.

คำประท้วง (ข้อ,ฉบับ,ประการ) kham′prathúaŋ′
(khɔ̌ɔ′, chabàb′, prakaan′) N protest.

คำประพันธ์ (บท) kham′praphan′ (bòd′) N poetry,
writing (esp. poetry, but also prose).

คำปราศรัย kham′praasǎj′ N cordial speech or
address.

คำเป็น (คำ) khampen′ (kham′) N live syllable
(in the Thai orthography), i.e. a syllable ending
in a long vowel or a sonorant. →Opp. คำตาย.

คำแปล (อย่าง) khamplεε′ (jàaŋ′) N translation,
meaning.

คำผรุสวาท (คำ) kham′-pharùd′sawâad′ (kham′)
e l e g. N abusive words, vulgar words, curses,
obscene language.

คำพยากรณ์ (ข้อ,ประการ,อย่าง) kham′phajaaɔ
kɔɔn′ (khɔ̌ɔ′, prakaan′, jàaŋ′) N forecast, prediction, prophecy.

คำพิพากษา (อย่าง) kham′phíphâagsǎa′ (jàaŋ′)
N verdict, decision.

คำพูด (คำ) khamphûud′ (kham′) N spoken word,
utterance.

o รักษาคำพูด rágsǎa′khamphûud′ to keep one's
word.

คำฟ้อง (ข้อ,ประการ,อย่าง) khamfɔ́ɔŋ′ (khɔ̌ɔ′,
prakaan′, jàaŋ′) N accusation, charge.

คำมั่นสัญญา (ข้อ,ประการ) khammân′sǎnjaa′ (khɔ̌ɔ′,
prakaan′) N promise, pledge.

คำย่อ (คำ) khamjɔ̀ɔ′ (kham′) N abbreviation.

คำยินยอม (ข้อ,ประการ) kham′jinjɔɔm′ (khɔ̌ɔ′,
prakaan′) N consent.

คำร้อง (ข้อ,ฉบับ) khamrɔ́ɔŋ′ (khɔ̌ɔ′, chabàb′)
N petition.

คำเล่าลือ (เรื่อง,ประการ,อย่าง) kham′lâwlyy′
(rŷaŋ′, prakaan′, jàaŋ′) N rumor.

คำวิงวอน (ข้อ,ฉบับ,อย่าง,ประการ) kham′wiŋɔ
wɔɔn′ (khɔ̌ɔ′, chabàb′, jàaŋ′, prakaan′) N supplication, plea.

คำวิจารณ์ (ข้อ,อย่าง,ประการ) kham′wícaan′
(khɔ̌ɔ′, jàaŋ′, prakaan′) N commentary, criticism.

คำวิเศษณ์ (คำ) kham/wísèed/ (kham/) N adjective, adverb.

คำสบถ (คำ) kham/sabòd/ (kham/) N swear word.

คำสอน (ข้อ,อย่าง,ประการ,ชนิด) khamsɔ̌ɔn/ (khɔ̌ɔ/, jàaŋ/, prakaan/, chaníd/) doctrine, teaching.

คำสั่ง (ข้อ,อย่าง,ประการ) khamsàŋ/ (khɔ̌ɔ/, jàaŋ/, prakaan/) N order, command, instruction(s).

คำสั่งสอน (ข้อ,อย่าง,ประการ,ชนิด) kham/sàŋᴐsɔ̌ɔn/ (khɔ̌ɔ/, jàaŋ/, prakaan/, chaníd/) N teaching, counsel, precept.

คำสัญญา (ข้อ,ฉบับ,ประการ) kham/sǎnjaa/ (khɔ̌ɔ/, chabàb/, prakaan/) N promise.

คำสุภาษิต (บท) kham/-suphaa/sìd/ (bòd/) N proverb.

คำหยาบ (คำ) khamjàab/ (kham/) N vulgar word(s), vulgar speech.

คำให้การ (ข้อ,ฉบับ,อย่าง,ประการ) kham/hâjᴐkaan/ (khɔ̌ɔ/, chabàb/, jàaŋ/, prakaan/) N testimony.

คำให้พร (ข้อ,ฉบับ,ประการ) kham/hâjphɔɔn/ (khɔ̌ɔ/, chabàb/, prakaan/) N blessing, greeting.

คำอธิบาย (ข้อ,บท,อย่าง,ประการ,ชนิด) kham/ᴐʔàthíbaaj/ (khɔ̌ɔ/, bòd/, jàaŋ/, prakaan/, chaníd/) N explanation.

คำอธิษฐาน (บท,อย่าง) kham/ʔàthídthǎan/ (bòd/, jàaŋ/) N prayer; wish.

คำอุจาดลามก (คำ) kham/-ʔucàad/laamóg/ (kham/) N obscene word; an obscenity.

คืนคำ khyyn/kham/ V to retract; to revoke one's promise.

ชัดถ้อยชัดคำ chádthɔ̂j/chádkham/ sV elab. colloq. clearly, distinctly, articulately.

ถ้อยคำ (คำ) thɔ̂jkham/ (kham/) N words, expression, speech.

ปากคำ (ปากคำ,อย่าง) pàagkham/ (pàagkham/, jàaŋ/) N 1. spoken word, words. 2. testimony, statement.

o ต่อปากคำ tɔ̀ɔ/pàagkham/ 1. to talk back, argue back and forth. 2. to have words (with someone).

o ให้ปากคำ hâjpàag/kham/ to testify, give testi-

mony, make a statement.

พูดคำตอบคำ phûud/kham/-tɔ̀ɔb/kham/ to say scarcely anything and only when asked, be taciturn.

ลั่นคำ lân/kham/ 1. to say, speak, declare. 2. to commit oneself, give one's word. →Syn. ลั่นปาก com., ลั่นวาจา eleg.

ค่ำ khâm/ N 1. dusk, nightfall, evening. C 2. day of the (waxing or waning) moon. V 3. to be dusk, dark.

ค่ำ ๆ khâmkhâm/ at night, of nights.

ค่ำลง khâm/loŋ/ 1. to become dark. 2. at dusk.

ตอนค่ำ tɔɔnkhâm/ (in the) evening, (at) night. →Syn. เวลาค่ำ.

มื้อค่ำ (มื้อ) mýykhâm/ (mýy/) N dinner, evening meal.

ยามค่ำ jaamkhâm/ 1. evenings, in the evening. N 2. evening (from sunset to midnight).

ย่ำค่ำ jâmkhâm/ 6 P.M.

วันขึ้น ๑ ค่ำ wankhŷn/nỳŋkhâm/ the first day of the waxing moon.

วันยังค่ำ wan/jaŋkhâm/ from morn till night, all day long.

วันยังค่ำคืนยังรุ่ง wan/jaŋkhâm/-khyyn/jaŋrûŋ/ colloq. all day and all night.

วันแรม ๑ ค่ำ wanrɛɛm/nỳŋkhâm/ the first day of the waning moon.

เวลาค่ำ weelaakhâm/ (in the) evening, (at) night. →Syn. ตอนค่ำ.

หัวค่ำ hǔakhâm/ dusk, early evening.

หามรุ่งหามค่ำ hǎamrûŋ/hǎamkhâm/ colloq. all day and all night; day and night.

อาหารค่ำ ʔaahǎankhâm/ N dinner, the evening meal.

ค้ำ khám/ V to support, hold up, prop up.

ค้ำจุน khámcun/ V to support, prop up.

ค้ำประกัน khám/prakan/ V to guarantee. การ-- guarantee. ผู้-- guarantor.

คำนวณ khamnuan/ V 1. to calculate; to estimate. N 2. mathematics (used in a loose sense). →Cf. 2. คณิต.

วิชาคำนวณ wíchaa/khamnuan/ N mathematics.

คำนับ khamnáb/ V to salute.

คำนึง (ถึง) khamnyŋ/(thy̌ŋᴐ) V lit., eleg. to think

(of), take into consideration.

คำรน khamron/ V lit. to roar, resound.

ฟ้าคำรน fáa/khamron/ lit., eleg. it thunders.

คำรบ khamrób/ C time, round, turn.

o กล่าวเป็นคำรบที่สอง klàaw/-penkhamrób/thîi‿
sɔ̌ɔŋ/ to say (something) for the second time.

คำราม khamraam/ V to roar, growl.

คิด khíd/ V to think, figure, calculate. ความ‑‑
(see below). →Syn. นึก.

ขบคิด khòb/khíd/ V to crack, solve (a problem).

ข้อคิด (ข้อ) khɔ̂ɔkhíd/ (khɔ̂ɔ/) N idea, point
worth considering, something to think about.

คบคิด(กับ) khóbkhíd/(ka‿) V to conspire.

ครุ่นคิด khrûnkhíd/ V to brood, meditate persistently (about).

ความคิด khwaamkhíd/ N thought, thoughts, idea;
thinking.

o ไร้ความคิด ráj/khwaamkhíd/ to be unthinking,
not using one's head.

ความนึกคิด khwaamnýgkhíd/ N thinking.

คิดคด(ต่อ) khídkhód/(tɔ̀ɔ/) V to plan to betray.

คิดดู khídduu/ V to think over, ponder, deliberate.

คิดตก khíd/tòg/ to have solved (a thinking problem), have gotten over (a life problem).

คิดถึง khídthÿŋ/ to think of, to miss.

o โดยความคิดถึง doojkhwaam/khídthÿŋ/ with
thoughts of you. Used as the complimentary
close of a letter to a friend.

คิดในมุมกลับ khíd/najmumklàb/ idiom. 1. to
take or consider an antithetic point of view.
2. conversely.

คิดเป็น khíd/pen‿ to be figured in (such and
such a kind of money, currency).

คิดเป็นอื่น khíd/pen?ÿÿn/ colloq. to think otherwise, have one's own opinion, take (it) to mean
something else.

คิดไป khíd/paj/ to think about it; when one thinks
about it.

คิดมิชอบ khíd/míchɔ̂ɔb/ to have evil intentions,
have unrighteous thoughts.

คิดมิดีมิร้าย khíd/-mídii/míráaj/ elab. eleg.
to have evil intentions.

คิดไม่ออก khíd/mâj?ɔ̀ɔg/ cannot figure (it) out,
cannot solve (it).

คิดร้าย khídráaj/ to intend to do harm, to plot
against.

คิดเลข khídlêeg/ to calculate, compute. เครื่อง‑‑
adding machine, calculating machine, computer.

คิดว่า khídwâa/ to think that.

คิดเห็น khídhěn/ V to think, to deem. ความ‑‑
opinion, idea.

o คุณคิดเห็นอย่างไร khun/-khídhěn/jàaŋraj/↓
What do you think? What is your opinion?

คิดออก khíd?ɔ̀ɔg/ V to figure out, solve.

คิดอ่าน khíd?àan/ V to use one's head (esp. in
bettering one's situation), to think, plan.

ช่างนึกช่างคิด châŋnýg/châŋkhíd/ V elab.
colloq. to be good at thinking, full of ideas.

ได้คิด dâjkhíd/ to realize, become aware of, regain
one's senses.

นั่งคิดนอนคิด nâŋ/khíd/-nɔɔn/khíd/ V to think
unceasingly.

ยั้งคิด jáŋkhíd/ V to ponder, pause to think.

ลองคิดดู lɔɔŋ/khídduu/, lɔɔŋkhíd/-duu‿ to think
(it) over.

ลูกคิด (อัน) lûugkhíd/ (?an/) N abacus.

o ดีดลูกคิด dìid/lûugkhíd/ 1. to figure or calculate
with an abacus. 2. colloq. to figure the angles.

หวนคิด hǔankhíd/ to think back, recall.

คิว. khiw/ the English letter "Q." [f. Eng.]

คิว khiw/ N queue, line. [f. Eng.]

เข้าคิว khâwkhiw/ V to queue up.

คิ้ว (คิ้ว) khíw/ (khíw/) N eyebrow.

ขมวดคิ้ว khamùad/khíw/ to knit the brow, frown.

ยักคิ้ว jágkhíw/ to flutter the eyebrows (indicating
assent or acknowledgment, or as when a man
flirts with a woman).

เลิกคิ้ว lə̂əgkhíw/ to raise the eyebrows (in surprise).

คี่ khîi/ N (as n. mod.) odd (opp. of even). →Opp. คู่.

คู่คี่ khûukhîi/ N 1. odd or even. V 2. to be about
even, equal. See cross reference.

เลขคี่ (จำนวน, ตัว) lêegkhîi/ (camnuan/, tua/)
N odd number. →Opp. เลขคู่.

คีบ khîib/ V to grip, take up (with forceps, chopsticks, etc.).

ปากคีบ (อัน) pàagkhîib/ (?an/) N forceps.

คีม (อัน) khiim/ (?an/) N pincers, tongs, pliers.

คึก khýg′ V to be in high spirits.

คึกคัก khýgkhák′ V to be animated, in high spirits (of persons), lively (of places).

คืน ๑ khyyn′ C night.

กลางคืน klaaŋkhyyn′ at night, in the night.

ค้างคืน kháaŋkhyyn′ com. to stay overnight, spend the night (in a place). →Syn. แรมคืน. eleg.

คืนนี้ khyynníi′ tonight.

คืนยังรุ่ง khyyn′jaŋrûŋ′ the whole night through, all night long.

o วันยังค่ำคืนยังรุ่ง wanjaŋkhâm′khyynjaŋrûŋ′ colloq. all day and all night.

คืนวันเพ็ญ khyyn′wanphen′ night of the full moon.

คืนวาน khyyn′waan′ the night before last.

o เมื่อคืนวาน,--นี้ mŷakhyyn′waan′, mŷakhyyn′ɔ waanníi′ the night before last.

ทั้งคืน tháŋkhyyn′ all night, the whole night.

ทุกคืน thúgkhyyn′ every night.

ทุกคืนวัน thúgkhyyn′wan′ night and day, by night and by day.

เที่ยงคืน thîaŋkhyyn′ midnight.

เมื่อคืน,--นี้ mŷakhyyn′, mŷakhyyn′níi′ last night.

แรมคืน rɛɛmkhyyn′ V eleg. to spend the night. →Syn. ค้างคืน com.

วันดีคืนดี wandii′khyyndii′ colloq. one fine day, on a certain day.

หายวันหายคืน hăajwan′hăajkhyyn′ elab. colloq. to recover quickly (from sickness); to improve (in health) from day to day.

คืน ๒ khyyn′ V to return (what is lost, borrowed).

กลับคืน klàbkhyyn′ V 1. to return, go back. 2. to restore. 3. to get back, recover. sV 4. back.

คืนคำ khyyn′kham′ V to retract, revoke one's promise.

คืนดี khyyn′dii′ to be reconciled.

ได้(...)คืน dâj(...)khyyn′ to get (such and such) back, regain (such and such).

เรียก(...)คืน rîag(...)khyyn′ to recall, revoke.

เอาคืน ?awkhyyn′ to take back; to win back.

คืบ khŷyb′ C 1. a span, i.e. a unit of linear measure, from the tip of the thumb to the tip of the middle finger when the hand is spread out.

V 2. to crawl (as a measuring worm); to inch forward.

คืบหน้า khŷybnâa′ V to progress, advance.

คือ khyy′ V to be (as follows, as defined); namely. →Syn. ได้แก่.

o กำลังสองของสองคือสี่ kamlaŋsɔɔŋ′khɔ̌ɔŋsɔɔŋ′- khyysìi′ the square of two is four.

กล่าวคือ klàawkhyy′ that is; namely.

คือว่า khyywâa′ that is, that is to say.

คุ khú?′ to smolder.

คุก ๑ (แห่ง,คุก) khúg′ (hὲŋ′, khúg′) N prison, jail.

ขี้คุก khîikhúg′ V colloq. to be a jailbird.

จำคุก camkhúg′ V to jail, imprison.

แหกคุก hὲεg′khúg′ V to break out of jail, break jail.

คุก ๒ in คุกเข่า khúgkhàw′ V to kneel.

คุก ๓ in คุกคาม khúgkhaam′ V to threaten, loom menacingly.

คุ้ง (คุ้ง) khúŋ′ (khúŋ′) N bend of a watercourse.

เป็นคุ้งเป็นแคว penkhúŋ′penkhwεε′ idiom., elab. colloq. lengthily, at great length (as in telling a story).

คุณ ๑ khun′, khunnaɔ N com. good, virtue, value, quality. →Syn. พระคุณ eleg. NOTE. คุณ ๒ is related but specialized in meaning.

ขอบคุณ khɔ̀ɔbkhun′ eleg. 1. Thank you! Thanks! V 2. to thank. ความ-- thanks, gratitude.

คุณความดี khun′khwaamdii′ N good, goodness, virtue.

o ประกอบคุณความดี prakɔ̀ɔb′-khun′khwaamdii′ to do good.

คุณค่า khunkhâa′ N value.

คุณธรรม khunnatham′ N 1. moral principles. 2. virtue, goodness.

คุณประโยชน์ khun′prajòod′* N usefulness, utility, value, beneficialness, advantageousness.

คุณพระช่วย khunphrá?′chûaj′↓ Oh, my goodness! (used esp. by w.; calling on the virtues of Buddha).

คุณพระศรีรัตนไตร khun′-phrásǐi′rád′tanatraj′ N the virtues of the Three Gems (of Buddhism, viz. the Buddha, his teaching, and his disciples).

คุณภาพ khunnaphâab′ N quality.

คุณลักษณะ khun′nalág′sanà?′ N quality, qualities, attributes (of a desirable nature).

คุณวุฒิ khunnawúd'thíʔ/ N qualification, competence.

o ทรงคุณวุฒิ soŋ'-khunnawúd'thíʔ/ V eleg.
to be qualified, competent, have the necessary
qualifications.

คุณศัพท์, คำ-- (คำ) khunnasàb', kham'khunnasàb'
(kham') N g r a m. adjective.

คุณสมบัติ khun'sŏmbàd', khunnasŏmbàd' N quality,
property.

แทนคุณ thɛɛn'khun' to repay a kindness to.

เป็นคุณ penkhun' 1. to be good, beneficial. 2.
for the benefit of.

พระคุณ phrákhun' N eleg. beneficence, benevolence. →Syn. คุณ ๑ c o m.

o ขอบพระคุณ khɔ̀ɔb'phrákhun' eleg. def. 1.
Thank you! V 2. to thank.

มีคุณ miikhun' to be beneficial, useful, good; to
have value, be of value.

ให้คุณ hâjkhun' V to do good, be beneficial, useful.

คุณ ๒ khun' P 1. dəf., c o m. you; paired with ผม
def. m. sp. "I, me," ดิฉัน def. w. sp. "I, me."
T 2. def. title used before the first names of
both men and women; sometimes translated
"Mr., Mrs., Miss" but usually best left untranslated in English. 3. title used before certain
relationship terms as พ่อ "father," แม่ "mother." →Related to คุณ ๑. →Comp. เจ้า ๒.
→Syn. ท่าน eleg. def.

คุณครู khunkhruu' P eleg. 1. you; he, him, she,
her; Teacher (sp. to or of a teacher). T 2. title
placed before first name of a teacher.

คุณนาย khunnaaj' P 1. you (sp. to the wife of
any government official up to the rank of พระ).
T 2. title placed before the first name of such
a lady. N 3. def. madame, lady (in reference
to one's employer).

คุณพ่อ khunphɔ̂ɔ' P eleg. 1. you; he, him;
Father (sp. to or of one's father). N 2. father
(of someone).

คุณแม่ khunmɛ̂ɛ' eleg. P 1. you; she, her;
Mother (sp. to or of one's mother). N 2.
mother (of someone).

คุณหญิง khunjǐŋ P 1. you; she, her (sp. to or of

the wife of a man in the conferred rank of
พระยา, or the wife of a premier or outstanding
minister). T 2. title placed before the first
name of such a lady. Hence "Lady --," "Madame --." →See เจ้าคุณ below.

คุณหนู khunnǔu' P def. 1. you; he, him, she, her
(sp. to or of a child; esp. used by servants of
the household). T 2. title placed before the name
of a child; hence "Master --," "Miss --."

เจ้าคุณ câwkhun' P 1. you; he, him (sp. to or of
a man in the conferred ranks of พระยา and
เจ้าพระยา). 2. you; she, her (sp. to or of
high-ranking ladies of the court). T 3. title
placed before the first names of persons described
in 1 and 2. →See คุณหญิง above for wife of
พระยา.

คุด, --คู้ khúd', khúdkhúu' V to crouch, cower.

คุดทะราด, โรค-- khúdtharâad', rôog'khúdtharâad'
N yaws, frambesia.

คุ้น(กับ) khún'(kaɔ) V 1. to get used (to), be accustomed (to), be intimate, familiar (with). 2. to
be tame.

คุ้นเคย(กับ) khúnkhəəj'(kaɔ) V to be well acquainted, familiar (with); to be habituated (to).
ความ-- acquaintance (with), familiarity (with).
ผู้-- acquaintance (person).

คุ้นหู khúnhǔu' V to sound familiar, be familiar
to the ear.

รู้จักมักคุ้น rúucàg'mágkhún' V elab. colloq.
to be acquainted (with), know personally.

คุม khum' V to take care of, watch over, take charge
of. ผู้-- warden, prison guard; warder, keeper,
one who has custody (of a detained person).

คนคุมเครื่อง khon'khumkhrŷaŋ' N the operator
of a machine.

ควบคุม khûabkhum' V 1. to control, supervise,
place under supervision. 2. to detain. ความ--
control. ผู้-- supervisor, chaperon.

คุมกัน khum'kanɔ to get together, gather, unite.

คุมขัง khumkhǎŋ' V to jail, imprison, detain in
custody.

คุมแค้น khumkhɛ́ɛn' V to harbor resentment
(toward).

เครื่องคุมอากาศ (เครื่อง) khrŷaŋkhum'ʔaakàad'

(khrŷaŋ′) N air-conditioner.

คุ้ม ๑ khúm′ V to protect.

  คุ้มกัน khúmkan′ V to protect, guard against.

  ○ เรือคุ้มกัน (ลำ) rya′khúmkan′ (lam′) N convoy, armed ship used as an escort.

  คุ้มครอง khúmkhrɔɔŋ′ V to protect, give protection to, watch over.

คุ้ม ๒ khúm′ V to be worth.

  คุ้มค่า khúmkhâa′ V to be worth while, worth
the expense.

คุ้ม ๓. See entries below.

  คุ้มคลั่ง khúmkhlâŋ′ V 1. to lose one's temper.
2. to be mad, insane.

  คุ้มดีคุ้มร้าย khúmdii′khúmráaj′ V elab. colloq.
1. to be alternately sane and insane. 2. to be
half crazy, mentally unhinged. 3. to be erratic,
changeable in temper.

คุย khuj′ V 1. com. to chat, talk, converse. 2.
colloq. to brag, boast. →Syn. 1. สนทนา
eleg.

  คุยกัน khuj′kan′ to chat, converse (with one another).

  คุยโขมง khuj′khamŏoŋ′ to talk or boast loudly,
profusely.

  คุยจ๋อ khujcɔ̆ɔ′ 1. to talk on and on, incessantly.
2. to talk eloquently.

  คุยโต khujtoo′ V colloq. to boast, talk big.

  ช่างคุย châŋkhuj′ V to be chatty, full of chatter.

คุ้ย khúj′ V to dig (with claws, as a dog), scratch
the ground (as a chicken).

คู (คู) khuu′ (khuu′) N small canal, ditch, moat.

  เหลี่ยมคู lìam′khuu′ N idiom. deceit, cunning.

  ○ มีเหลี่ยมมีคู miilìam′miikhuu′ idiom., elab.
colloq. to be sly, cunning, crafty.

คู่ khûu′ C 1. clf. for pairs (of anything), couples.
2. (as n. mod.) even (opp. of odd). V 3. to be
paired with. →Opp. 2. คี่.

  คู่แข่ง,--ขัน (คน) khûukhὲŋ′, khûukhὲŋkhǎn′
(khon′) N competitor, rival.

  คู่ครอง (คน) khûukhrɔɔŋ′ (khon′) N spouse,
mate. →Syn. คู่เคียง.

  คู่ความ (คน,คู่) khûukhwaam′ (khon′, khûu′) N
one or both of the parties to a legal case, i.e.
the plaintiff and/or the defendant.

คู่คี่ khûukhîi′ N 1. odd or even. V 2. to be about
even, equal.

  ○ เขามาคู่คี่กัน kháwmaa′khûukhîi′-kan↓ They
came out even (were evenly matched).

  ○ เล่นคู่คี่ lên′khûukhîi′ to play an odd-or-even
guessing game.

คู่เคียง (คน) khûukhiaŋ′ (khon′) N spouse, mate.
  →Syn. คู่ครอง.

คู่ใจ khûucaj′ (as n. mod.) faithful, trusted.

  ○ เพื่อนคู่ใจ phŷan′khûucaj′ N trusted friend,
bosom companion.

คู่ต่อสู้ (คน) khûu′tɔ̀ɔsûu′ (khon′) N (two) oppo-
nents, antagonists; (one's) opponent.

คู่บ้านคู่เมือง khûubâan′khûumyaŋ′ N elab. (as
n. mod.) national, characteristic of the nation
as a whole.

  ○ ช้างเป็นสัตว์คู่บ้านคู่เมืองของไทย cháaŋ′ pen⊃
sàd′-khûubâan′khûumyaŋ′-khɔ̆ɔŋthaj↓ The
elephant is the national animal of the Thai.

คู่บ่าวสาว (คู่) khûu′bàawsǎaw′ (khûu′) N the
bride and groom.

คู่ผัวตัวเมีย (คู่) khûuphǔa′tuamia′ (khûu′) N
elab. colloq. husband and wife. →Syn.
ผัวเมีย com.

คู่มือ (เล่ม) khûumyy′ (lêm′) N 1. handbook,
manual. 2. always at hand (see example).

  ○ ปืนคู่มือ pyyn′khûumyy′ one's favorite gun, the
gun one always takes along.

  ○ หนังสือคู่มือ (เล่ม) naŋsy̆y′khûumyy′ (lêm′)
N handbook, manual.

คู่รัก (คน) khûurág′ (khon′) N lovers, sweethearts; (one's) sweetheart.

คู่หมั้น (คน) khûumân′ (khon′) N fiancé, fiancée,
(one's) betrothed.

คู่หู (คน) khûuhǔu′ (khon′) N 1. (an) intimate,
(one's) trusted companion. 2. (as n. mod.)
intimate, trusted, faithful.

  ○ เพื่อนคู่หู phŷan′khûuhǔu′ intimate friend, bosom
companion.

เคียงคู่ khiaŋkhûu′ two abreast, side by side.

จับคู่ càbkhûu′ V to pair off, form a pair (with),
take a partner.

ทั้งคู่ tháŋkhûu′ both.

เลขคู่ lêegkhûu′ N even number (i.e. not odd).

→Opp. เลขคี่.

อักษรคู่ ʔàgsɔ̌ɔnkhûu′ N the paired consonants in the Thai system of writing. See cross reference. →Opp. อักษรเดี่ยว.

คู้ khúu′ V to bend.

คูณ khuun′ V math. to multiply. การ-- math. multiplication.

     ตัวคูณ tuakhuun′ N math. multiplier.

     ทวีคูณ thawii′khuun′ eleg. twofold, double, multiplied by two.

     สูตรคูณ sùudkhuun′ N mulitiplication table.

คูหา (คูหา) khuuhǎa′ (khuuhǎa′) N eleg. 1. cave, cavern. 2. booth (e.g. election booth). 3. space between pillars (in a building). →Syn. 1. ถ้ำ com.

เค . khee′ the English letter "K." [f. Eng.]

เค้น khén′* V to squeeze, press. ความ-- phys. stress.

     เค้นหัวเราะ khén′hǔarɔ́ʔ′ to force out a laugh.

เค็ม khem′ V to be salty, salted. คน-- (see below). ความ-- saltiness.

     คนเค็ม khonkhem′ N idiom. a person who drives a hard bargain, an unfair bargain, who exacts full payment in kind (for debts owed, injuries inflicted, etc.).

     น้ำเค็ม námkhem′ N salt water. →Opp. น้ำจืด.

     หน้าเค็ม nâa′khem′ to have the face of one who is คนเค็ม (see above).

เคมี kheemii′ N chemistry. [f. Eur.]

     เคมีภัณฑ์ (อย่าง,ชนิด) kheemii′phan′ (jàaŋ′, chaníd′) N chemicals.

     เครื่องเคมี khrɯ̂aŋkheemii′ N chemicals.

     ชีวเคมี chii′wakheemii′ N biochemistry.

     สารเคมี sǎan′kheemii′ N chemicals.

เคย ๑ khəəj′ N a kind of tiny shrimp. Usually in:

     กุ้งเคย (ตัว) kûŋkhəəj′ (tua′) N a kind of tiny shrimp.

     น้ำเคย námkhəəj′ N sauce made out of this kind of shrimp.

เคย ๒ khəəj′ V 1. to be familiar, accustomed. AA 2. ever, at some (one) time. 3. used to. 4. is accustomed to.

o เคยแต่อ่านเรื่องการเที่ยวที่นั่น แต่ไม่เคยไป khəəjtɛ̀ɛʔàanrɯ̂aŋ′-kaanthîaw′thîinân′→tɛ̀ɛɔ

māj khəəj′paj′↓ (I) have been accustomed only to read about going there, but (I)'ve never gone.

คุ้นเคย(กับ) khúnkhəəj′ (kàɔ) V to be well acquainted, familiar (with); to be habituated (to).

เคยจมูก khəəj′camùug′ V to smell familiar.

เคยชิน khəəjchin′ V to be familiar (with), accustomed (to). ความ-- familiarity, habit.

เคยตัว khəəjtua′ to be in the habit of, get into the habit of.

เคยหู khəəjhǔu′ V to sound familiar, be familiar to the ear.

เช่นเคย chênkhəəj′ as usual.

ตามเคย taamkhəəj′ as usual.

ไม่ค่อยเคยเห็น mājkhɔ̂jkhəəjhěn′ scarcely ever see.

ไม่เคย mājkhəəj′ AA never (e.g. "have never done").

ไม่เคยเลย mājkhəəj′ləəj′ never before.

อย่างเคย jàaŋkhəəj′ as usual.

เครง in ครื้นเครง khrɯ́ynkhreeŋ′ V to be merry hilarious, full of fun.

เคร่ง khrêŋ′* V 1. to be strict, rigorously observant of precepts, rules. 2. to be devout.

     คร่ำเคร่ง(ต่อ,ใน) khrâmkhrêŋ′ (tɔ̀ɔ, najɔ) V to be absorbed, engrossed (in); to be intent (on something); to be hard at it.

     เคร่งขรึม khrêŋkhrɯ̌m′ V to be serious, solemn.

     เคร่งครัด khrêŋkhrád′ V idem เคร่ง.

     เคร่งเครียด khrêŋkhrîad′ V to be serious (in appearance), grave, gloomy. ความ-- seriousness, solemnity.

เครดิต khredìd′* N credit. [f. Eng.]

เครา ๑ khraw′ N beard, whiskers.

     หนวดเครา nùadkhraw′ N beard (including the mustache).

เครา ๒ in เครื่องเครา khrɯ̂aŋkhraw′ N thing, things, equipment, paraphernalia.

เคราะห์ khrɔ́ʔ′ N luck (often more particularly "bad luck"), fortune, fate.

     เคราะห์ดี khrɔ́ʔ′dii′ V 1. to be fortunate, lucky. 2. fortunately, luckily, it's fortunate (that).

     เคราะห์ร้าย khrɔ́ʔ′ráaj′ V 1. to be unfortunate, unlucky. 2. unfortunately, unluckily, it's unfortunate (that).

ดาวเคราะห์,ดาวพระเคราะห์ (ดวง) daawkhrɔ́ʔ/, daawphrákhrɔ́ʔ/ (duaŋ/) N planet.

พ้นเคราะห์ phónkhrɔ́ʔ/ to be free from misfortune or bad luck.

สงเคราะห์ sǒŋkhrɔ́ʔ/ V to show kindness to, to help, assist.

เครียด khrîad/ V to be tense, strained, stern.

เคร่งเครียด khrêŋkhrîad/ V to be serious (in appearance), grave, gloomy.

ตึงเครียด tyŋ/khrîad/ V 1. to be tense, strained (as a situation). 2. to be stern (as of the face). ความ-- tension.

เครือ ๑ khrya/ N 1. bunch (of bananas). C 2. idem. 3. family, kindred, lineage.

เครือกล้วย (เครือ) khryaklûaj/ (khrya/) a bunch of bananas.

เครือจักรภพอังกฤษ khrya/-càgkraphób/ʔaŋkrìd/ the British Commonwealth.

เครือญาติ khryajâad/ N lineage, family tree; kindred.

ตกเครือ tòg/khrya/ a bunch of bananas to set.

ในเครือเดียวกัน najkhrya/diawkan/ to be akin (to), related (to), of the same lineage.

ว่านเครือ wâan/khrya/ N lineage, family; kindred.

เครือ ๒ khrya/ N creeper, creeping plant, vine.

เครือ ๓ khrya/ V 1. to be indistinct, blurred. 2. to be faint and trembling (of the voice).

ครุมเครือ,คลุมเครือ khrumkhrya/, khlumkhrya/ V to be ambiguous, unclear, indisdinct.

แหบเครือ hὲɛb/khrya/ V to be hoarse and trembly (of the voice, esp. of the elderly or the sick).

เครื่อง (เครื่อง) (1,2) khrŷaŋ/ (khrŷaŋ); (3) khrŷaŋ꞊ N 1. gear, apparatus, complex machinery, engine. C 2. clf. for many noun derivatives based on เครื่อง, see note 3 below. 3. a bound element used to form noun derivatives; see notes 1 and 2. →Comp. -ภัณฑ์ tech.

NOTE 1. เครื่อง is very productively used as a bound element placed in front of either nouns or verbs to form new noun derivatives. In this use it has the sense of "gear, apparatus, device, contrivance, preparation (concoction), ware, goods, implement, implementation, instrument, paraphernalia." The English suffixes -er, -or

(as used with names of objects, e.g. projector) and -ery (e.g. machinery) are also frequent translations of this word. Most nouns based on เครื่อง are listed only under the nouns or verbs from which they are derived. Thus to find เครื่องกรอง look under กรอง. The following examples are a sample selected for study. The first six are based on verbs, the last six on nouns.

เครื่องเขียน khrŷaŋkhǐan/ stationery, writing supplies: "writing paraphernalia."

เครื่องฉายหนัง khrŷaŋchǎajnǎŋ/ motion picture projector: "movie-showing instrument."

เครื่องตกแต่ง khrŷaŋtògtὲŋ/ decorations, ornaments: "decorating paraphernalia."

เครื่องพ่น khrŷaŋphôn/ sprayer: "spraying apparatus."

เครื่องดื่ม khrŷaŋdỳym/ beverage, drink: "drinking preparation (i.e. preparation to be drunk)."

เครื่องหลับนอน khrŷaŋlàbnɔɔn/ bedding: "sleeping gear."

เครื่องแก้ว khrŷaŋkὲεw/ glassware: "glass ware."

เครื่องครัว khrŷaŋkhrua/ kitchen utensils: "kitchen implements."

เครื่องเคมี khrŷaŋkhee/mii/ chemicals: "chemistry preparation(s)."

เครื่องแกง khrŷaŋkεεŋ/ the spices and seasoning used in making curry: "curry preparation."

เครื่องโทรศัพท์ khrŷaŋthoorasàb/ telephone: "telephone-instrument."

เครื่องยาง khrŷaŋjaaŋ/ rubber goods: "rubber goods."

NOTE 2. A few words based on เครื่อง have counterparts based on ของ. The difference in meaning is usually slight, but those based on เครื่อง may imply that a greater degree of intricacy or complexity is involved. A few examples are explained below.

ของเล่น khɔ̌ɔŋlên/ toy(s), plaything(s); เครื่องเล่น khrŷaŋlên/ toy(s), including elaborate toys, such as tricycles, and playground equipment, such as swings, slides, etc.

ของกิน khɔ̌ɔŋkin/ foodstuff, things to eat; เครื่องกิน khrŷaŋkin/ food, provisions.

ของแต่งตัว khɔ̌ɔŋ/tὲŋtua/ things to wear (including ornaments); เครื่องแต่งตัว khrŷaŋtὲŋtua/ apparel, attire, finery, (complete) wardrobe.

NOTE 3. Classifiers used with derivatives based on เครื่อง are usually one of the following, depending on appropriateness: เครื่อง, for objects intricately bound together; ชุด, for sets or suits; ชิ้น, for a piece, particularly a piece out of a set; อย่าง,ชนิด,สิ่ง (eleg.), for a kind or sort; อัน, as a general clf. for units; or occasionally some other classifiers. Examples:

เครื่องชั่ง (เครื่อง) khrŷaŋchâŋ/ (khrŷaŋ/) scales,

balance.

เครื่องแบบ (ชุด) khrŷaŋbὲɛb′ (chúd′) uniform.

เครื่องเงิน (ชุด,ชิ้น) khrŷaŋŋən′ (chúd′, a set; chín′, a piece) silverware.

เครื่องปรุง (อย่าง,ชนิด) khrŷaŋpruŋ′ (jàaŋ′, chaníd′) ingredients.

เครื่องไฟฟ้า (อย่าง,ชนิด,อัน) khrŷaŋfajfáa′ (jàaŋ′, chaníd′ for kinds; ʔan′ for units) electrical appliance(s).

เครื่องหมาย (อัน) khrŷaŋmǎaj′ (ʔan′) sign, mark, symbol, signal.

เครื่องแปลง (ตัว) khrŷaŋplɛɛŋ′ (tua′) elect. transformer.

เครื่องกระป๋อง (กระป๋อง) khrŷaŋkrapɔ̌ŋ′ (kracɔpɔ̌ŋ′) N canned goods, canned food.

เครื่องคุมอากาศ (เครื่อง) khrŷaŋkhum′ʔaakàad′ (khrŷaŋ′ N air-conditioner.

เครื่องเครา (อย่าง,สิ่ง) khrŷaŋkhraw′ (jàaŋ′, sìŋ′) N thing(s), equipment, paraphernalia.

เครื่องจักร (เครื่อง,ชนิด) khrŷaŋcàg′ (khrŷaŋ′, chaníd′) N machinery; engine, machine.

○ เครื่องจักรไอน้ำ (เครื่อง) khrŷaŋcàg′ʔajnáam′ (khrŷaŋ′) N steam engine.

เครื่องตอบแทน khrŷaŋtɔ̀ɔbthɛɛn′ N (a) reciprocation.

เครื่องไทยทาน (อย่าง) khrŷaŋthajjathaan′ (jàaŋ′) N alms.

เครื่องใน (ชิ้น) khrŷaŋnaj′ (chín′) N internal body organs.

เครื่องบำเรอ (อย่าง) khrŷaŋbamrəə′ (jàaŋ′) N entertainment.

เครื่องพิสูจน์ khrŷaŋphísùud′ N proof, material proof.

เครื่องมือ (อย่าง,ชิ้น,อัน) khrŷaŋmyy′ (jàaŋ′, chín′,ʔan′) N tool, device, instrument, apparatus, equipment.

เครื่องไม้เครื่องมือ (อย่าง,ชิ้น,อัน) khrŷaŋmáaj′ɔkhrŷaŋmyy′ (jàaŋ′,chín′,ʔan′) N elab. colloq. implements, tools.

เครื่องยศ (ชิ้น,อัน) khrŷaŋjód′ (chín′,ʔan′) N insignia of rank.

เครื่องยา (ชนิด,อย่าง,ขนาน) khrŷaŋjaa′ (chacníd′, jàaŋ′, khanǎan′) N medicine, drug; ingredient (of a drug).

เครื่องสาย (ชิ้น) khrŷaŋsǎaj′ (chín′) N music stringed instrument.

เครื่องสำอาง (อย่าง,ชนิด) khrŷaŋsǎmʔaaŋ′

(jàaŋ′,chaníd′) N cosmetics.

เครื่องหมาย (อัน) khrŷaŋmǎaj′ (ʔan′) N sign, mark, symbol, signal. →See cross reference.

เครื่องอะหลั่ย, เครื่องอาหลั่ย khrŷaŋʔalàj′, khrŷaŋɔʔaalàj′ N spare parts, replacement parts.

ช่างเครื่อง (คน,นาย) châaŋkhrŷaŋ′ (khon′,naaj′) N 1. mechanic; machinist. 2. engineer (operator of an engine).

ทรงเครื่อง soŋkhrŷaŋ′ V 1. roy. to be dressed in regalia, armor, etc.; to be decorated. 2. com. to be over-dressed; to have more (ingredients, trimming, money, etc.) than necessary.

น้ำมันหยอดเครื่อง (กระป๋อง,อย่าง) námman′jɔ̀ɔdɔkhrŷaŋ′ (krapɔ̌ŋ′,jàaŋ′) N lubricating oil, motor oil.

เป็นเครื่องตอบแทน penkhrŷaŋ′tɔ̀ɔbthɛɛn′ in return, as a reciprocation, in retaliation.

ห้องเครื่อง (ห้อง) hɔ̂ŋkhrŷaŋ′ (hɔ̂ŋ′) N engine room.

เคล็ด ๑ khléd′ N (refined) means, tactic, technique.

เคล็ดลับ khlédláb′ N secret means, secret technique.

เคล็ด ๒ khléd′ V to be sprained, get sprained.

เคลน. See คลึงเคลน.

เคล้า khláw′ V 1. to mix, blend. 2. (a cat) to rub against (the legs).

เคล้าเคลีย khláwkhlia′ V to stay close around, rub against (as a child with its mother, young people in love, etc.).

เสียดเคล้า sìad′khláw′ V to rub and press (against)(as a cat against the legs).

เคลิบ. See เคลิบเคลิ้ม under เคลิ้ม.

เคลิ้ม khlə́əm′ V to doze, to be half-asleep, be in a dreamy state.

เคลิบเคลิ้ม khlə̀əbkhlə́əm′ V to be carried away, enraptured; to be in a state of reverie.

เคลิ้มฝัน khlə́əmfǎn′ V to dream, forget oneself.

เคลีย. See entries below.

เคล้าเคลีย khláwkhlia′ V to stay close around, rub against (as a child with its mother, young people in love, etc.).

เดินคลอเคลีย dəən′khlɔɔkhlia′ to walk side by side, close together.

เคลื่อน khlŷan′ V to move, shift. การ-- movement,

moving.

คลาดเคลื่อน khlâadkhlŷan′ V to deviate, be off,
be different (from the original).

เคลื่อนที่ khlŷanthîi′ V 1. to move. 2. to be
mobile. 3. to be out of place; to be dislocated.
การ-- phys. motion. →Cf. 3. เป็นที่.

เคลื่อนไหว khlŷanwǎj′ V to move, move about.
การ-- movement, activity, moving. ความ--
movement, motion.

เคลือบ khlŷab′ V to enamel, glaze, plate, coat.

เคลือบแคลง khlŷabkhlɛɛŋ′ V to be in doubt,
(feel) suspicious, doubtful.

เคลือบแฝง khlŷabfɛ̌ɛŋ′ V to be hidden, concealed,
unclear, ambiguous.

หม้อเคลือบ (ใบ, ลูก) mɔ̂ɔkhlŷab′ (baj′, lûug′)
N enamelled pot.

เคว้ง in เคว้งคว้าง khwéeŋkhwáaŋ′ V 1. to drift,
be adrift. sV 2. adrift, aimlessly, randomly.

เคอะ, เคอะ ๆ khɔ́ʔ′, khɔ́ʔkhɔ́ʔ′ V to be stiff,
unnatural, out of place, awkward.

o ท่าทางเคอะ ๆ thâathaaŋ′khɔ́ʔkhɔ́ʔ′ (their)
manners are out of place, stiff (e.g. of country
people in town).

เคอะเขิน khɔ́ʔkhɔ̌ən′ idem. เคอะ.

เค้า kháw′ N trace, imprint, stamp (as of ancestry);
vestige; outline.

เค้าเงื่อน (ข้อ) kháwŋŷan′ (khɔ̂ɔ′) N clue.

เค้ามูล kháwmuun′ N primary source.

เค้าเรื่อง kháwrŷaŋ′ N outline, scheme, plot of
a story.

เค้าหน้า kháwnâa′ N the look of the face, facial
appearance, facial expression.

จับเค้า càbkháw′ V to get the idea; to detect.

ต้นเค้า tônkháw′ N prototype.

ตั้งเค้า tâŋkháw′ V to show (its) first signs.

o ฝนตั้งเค้า fǒn′tâŋkháw′ it looks like rain, it
is getting ready to rain.

นกเค้าแมว (ตัว) nógkháwmɛɛw′ (tua′) N a kind
of owl: "bird with the look of a cat."

มีเค้า miikháw′ to show a trace, a vestige (of).

เคารพ khawrób′ V to show respect, pay reverence.
ความ-- respect. →Syn. นับถือ com.

ทำความเคารพ thamkhwaam′khawrób′ V to
salute, pay respect to.

รูปเคารพ rûub′khawrób′ N idol, image of worship.

เคาะ khɔ́ʔ′ V to knock, tap; to knock at, on.

เคียง khiaŋ′ V to be side by side, on the same level,
close beside, near.

ใกล้เคียง klâjkhiaŋ′ V to be close, near, nearby,
neighboring.

o ใกล้เคียงกับ klâjkhiaŋ′kàɔ 1. to be close to.
2. to be nearly as much as.

o เพื่อนบ้านใกล้เคียง phŷanbâan′klâjkhiaŋ′ N
neighbor.

ข้างเคียง khâaŋkhiaŋ′ nearby, by the side of,
adjacent, close. คน-- intimate person, close
associate.

คู่เคียง (คน) khûukhiaŋ′ (khon′) N spouse, mate.
→Syn. คู่ครอง.

เคียงข้าง khiaŋkhâaŋ′ side by side.

เคียงคู่ khiaŋkhûu′ two abreast, (two) side by
side.

เคียงบ่าเคียงไหล่ khiaŋbàa′khiaŋlàj′ idiom.,
elab. colloq. 1. shoulder to shoulder. 2.
on the same level.

เคียด khîad′ V to be angry.

เคียดแค้น khîadkhɛ́ɛn′ V to be angry, harbor
feelings of anger.

เคียว (เล่ม) khiaw′ (lêm′) N sickle.

เคี่ยว khîaw′ V to boil down.

ขับเคี่ยว khàbkhîaw′ V to drive or exert (oneself)
vigorously, relentlessly.

เคี่ยวเข็ญ khîawkhěn′ V to force, urge repeatedly.

เคี้ยว khíaw′ V to chew.

คดเคี้ยว khódkhíaw′ V to be winding (as a road).

เคี้ยวเอื้อง khíawʔŷaŋ′ V to chew the cud, ruminate.

เคือง khyaŋ′ V 1. to be annoyed, irritated, peeved,
angry. N 2. anger. การ-- (act of) being angry,
getting angry. ความ-- anger.

ขัดเคือง khàdkhyaŋ′ V to feel angry, be angered,
provoked.

เคืองใจ khyaŋcaj′ V 1. to be angry, provoked.
N 2. anger.

ฝืดเคือง fŷydkhyaŋ′ V 1. to be poor, hard up.
2. to be scarce, meager. 3. to be difficult and
frustrating; to have rough going. อย่าง-- poorly,
in poverty, in an impoverished manner.

แค่ khɛ̂ɛ′ point, level (which has been reached, attained); as far as, up to (such and such a point).

ใกล้แค่ klâj′khɛ̂ɛɔ 1. to be as near as. 2. to be
near (such and such).

แค่นั้น khɛ̂ɛ′-nán′, khɛɛnán′ up to that point, that
far, that much, to that extent.

แค่ไหน khɛɛnǎj′ up to which point, how far, how
much, to what extent.

ถึงแค่นี้ thɯ̌ŋkhɛ̂ɛ′níi′ up to this point, to this
extent.

เพียงแค่ phiaŋkhɛ̂ɛ′ only as far as, only to the
point of.

สูงแค่เอว sǔuŋ′khɛ̂ɛ?ew′ to be waist-high.

แคก ๆ khɛ́gkhɛ́g′* imit. the sound of coughing.

แคน (อัน) khɛɛn′ (?an′) N mouth organ. Used by
people in N and NE Thailand.

แค้น khɛ̂n′* V 1. to force (oneself) to, to feel
obliged to. sV 2. forcedly.

แค้น khɛ́ɛn′ V to feel resentful, harbor feelings of
anger. ความ-- injured feelings, resentment.

แก้แค้น kɛ̂ɛkhɛ́ɛn′ V to take revenge.

ขันแค้น khɔ̂n′khɛ́ɛn′ V to be poor, hard up,
needy, impoverished.

คับแค้น khábkhɛ́ɛn′ V to be impoverished, hard-
pressed, in distress.

คุมแค้น khumkhɛ́ɛn′ V to harbor resentment
(toward).

เคียดแค้น khîadkhɛ́ɛn′ V to be angry, harbor
feelings of anger.

แค้นใจ khɛ́ɛn′caj′ V to harbor feelings of anger.

เดือดแค้น dɯ̀adkhɛ́ɛn′ V to be furious, boiling
mad (at), very angry (with).

ยากแค้น jâag′khɛ́ɛn′ V to be impoverished.

แร้นแค้น rɛ́ɛnkhɛ́ɛn′ V to be poverty-stricken,
needy.

ล้างแค้น láaŋ′khɛ́ɛn′ V to get rid of one's resentment (usually by taking revenge).

แคบ khɛ̂ɛb′ V to be narrow. →Ant. กว้าง.

คับแคบ khábkhɛ̂ɛb′ V to be narrow, cramped
(of space).

ใจแคบ cajkhɛ̂ɛb′ V to be narrow-minded, selfish,
lacking in generosity.

ช่องแคบ (ช่อง, แห่ง) chɔ̂ŋkhɛ̂ɛb′ (chɔ̂ŋ′, hɛ̀ŋ′)
N 1. strait; channel. 2. (mountain) pass.

แคม (แคม) khɛɛm′ (khɛɛm′) N 1. edge (esp. of a
boat). 2. fig. margin.

แคร่ (แคร่) khrɛ̂ɛ′ (khrɛ̂ɛ′) N 1. litter; a bed or
small platform floored with bamboo slats. 2.
the carriage of a typewriter.

แคร่หาม (แคร่) khrɛ̂ɛhǎam′ (khrɛ̂ɛ′) N litter,
palanquin.

แครง in หอยแครง (ตัว) hɔ̌jkhrɛɛŋ′ (tua′) N
cockle.

แคระ khrɛ́?′ V to be dwarfed, stunted.

แคลง. See entries below.

คลางแคลง, --ใจ khlaaŋkhlɛɛŋ′, khlaaŋkhlɛɛŋcaj′
V to feel suspicious, have doubts.

เคลือบแคลง khlŷabkhlɛɛŋ′ V to be in doubt,
(feel) suspicious, doubtful.

แคลงใจ khlɛɛŋcaj′ V to feel suspicious, have
doubts.

แคลน. See entries below.

ขาดแคลน khàadkhlɛɛn′ V to lack, be short of,
have a shortage of.

คลอนแคลน khlɔɔnkhlɛɛn′ V to be loose, shaky,
unstable, unsteady.

ดูแคลน duukhlɛɛn′ V to disdain, despise. ความ--
contempt.

แคล่ว in แคล่วคล่อง khlɛ̂wkhlɔ̂ŋ′* V 1. to be skillful,
clever, nimble, agile. 2. to be fast (in doing
things). 3. to be fluent (in speech). →Also
คล่องแคล่ว.

แคล้ว khlɛ́ɛw′ V 1. to miss, fail to meet. 2. to
escape (from).

แคล้วคลาด khlɛ́ɛwkhlâad′ idem. →Also คลาดแคล้ว.

แคว (แคว) khwɛɛ′ (khwɛɛ′) N tributary, branch
of a river.

เป็นคุ้งเป็นแคว penkhúŋ′penkhwɛɛ′ idiom., elab.
colloq. lengthily, at great length (as in telling
a story).

แคว้น (แคว้น) khwɛ́ɛn′ (khwɛ́ɛn′) N district, region,
territory, province, state.

แว่นแคว้น (แว่นแคว้น) wɛ̂nkhwɛ́ɛn′ (wɛ̂nkhwɛ́ɛn′)
N territory, province, state.

แคะ khɛ́?′ V to pick out, pry out, take out.

คอนแคะ khɔ̂nkhɛ́?′ V to criticize, pick at.

โค (ตัว) khoo′ (tua′) N eleg. cow, bull, ox; cattle.
→Syn. วัว com.

โคจร khoocɔɔn′ V to travel (of celestial bodies).

o วงโคจร (วง) woŋ′khoocɔɔn′ (woŋ′) N orbit.

โคบาล (คน) khoobaan′ (khon′) N eleg. cowherd, cowboy.

โคก (โคก) khôog′ (khôog′) N mound, knoll.
→Syn. โขด, เนิน.

โค่ง khôoŋ′ V to be oversized.

o นักเรียนโค่ง nágriankhôoŋ′ joc. biggest student or oldest student (in the class).

โค้ง khóoŋ′ V to be bent, curved (as a line).
ความ-- curvature.

หัวโค้ง (แห่ง) hŭakhóoŋ′ (hèŋ′) N curve (as in
a road).

โคน (โคน) khoon′ (khoon′) N base (as of tree).

ถอนรากถอนโคน thɔ̆ɔnrâag′thɔ̆ɔnkhoon′) V 1.
elab. colloq. to pull out by the roots. 2. fig.
to destroy, extirpate.

โค่น khôon′ V 1. to cut down; to fell. 2. to overthrow. 3. to fall down.

โคม (ดวง) khoom′ (duaŋ′) N lantern.

โคมไฟ (ดวง) khoomfaj′ (duaŋ′) N lantern,
lamp.

โคมลอย in ข่าว-- khàaw′khoomlɔɔj′ N unfounded rumor, unsubstantiated news.

โครก,--คราก khrôog′, khrôogkhrâag′ imit. the
sound of snoring, of heavy breathing, of wind
in the stomach or intestines.

ชักโครก (ที่) chágkhrôog′ V 1. to flush the
toilet. N 2. flush-toilet (thîi′).

โครง (โครง) khrooŋ′ (khrooŋ′) N 1. frame (as
of a window, kite). 2. skeleton.

โครงกระดูก khrooŋkradùug′ N skeleton.

โครงการ khrooŋkaan′ N plan, project, program.
→Also -การณ์ FS.

o วางโครงการ waaŋ′khrooŋkaan′ to lay plans.

โครงเรื่อง khrooŋrŷaŋ′ N plot, outline, structure (of a story).

โครงสร้าง khrooŋsâaŋ′ N structure, arrangement of constituents.

ซี่โครง (ซี่) sîikhrooŋ′ (sîi′) N ribs.

โคร่ง khrôoŋ′ V to be huge.

โครม,--คราม khroom′, khroomkhraam′ imit.
the sound of heavy objects crashing to the
ground.

ครึกโครม khrýgkhroom′ V to be noisy, boisterous,
clamorous.

โคราช khoorâad′ pN Khorat, colloquial name for
นครราชสีมา Nakhǫn Ratsima, a township in
NE Thailand.

โคลง ๑ (บท) khlooŋ′ (bòd′) N a kind of Thai
verse form.

โคลง ๒ khlooŋ′ V to rock, shake; to be unsteady;
(a boat) to roll, toss about.

โคลน khloon′ N mud.

ขี้โคลน khîikhloon′ N colloq. mud.

น้ำโคลน námkhloon′ N muddy water.

บังโคลน (ข้าง) baŋkhloon′ (khâaŋ′) N fender
(of car), mudguard (of car, bicycle).

เป็นโคลน penkhloon′ to be muddy.

ใคร khraj′ iP 1. who? 2. someone, anyone.

เข้าใครออกใคร khâwkhraj′/ʔɔ̀ɔgkhraj′ colloq.
to be partial, to favor one and not the other.

o ไม่เข้าใครออกใคร mâjkhâwkhraj′/ʔɔ̀ɔgkhraj′
colloq. to be neutral, impartial.

ใครก็ตาม khraj′kɔ̂taam′ anybody, whoever.

ใครคนหนึ่ง khraj′khonnyŋ′ somebody, someone.

ใคร ๆ khrajkhraj′ anyone, everyone, everybody.

ใครต่อใคร khraj′tɔ̀ɔkhraj′ person after person,
anyone, almost everyone. Used when the speaker
cannot, or does not wish to specify names.

ใคร...ไหม khrajɔ...máj is there anyone
who...?

ใครอื่น khraj?ỳyn′ somebody else.

ทีใครก็ทีมัน thii′khraj′-kɔ̂thii′man′⌋ When it's a
fellow's turn, why then, it's his turn!

ไม่มีใคร mâjmiikhraj′ there is no one.

ใคร่ khrâj′ V 1. to wish, have desires (used only
in compounds). AA 2. wish to, desire.

ความใคร่ khwaamkhrâj′ N 1. desire. 2. sexual
desire.

ใคร่จะ khrâjcaɔ AA wish to, would like to.

ไม่ใคร่ mâjkhrâjɔ AA scarcely.

รักใคร่(กัน) rágkhrâj′(kan) V to love, be fond of
(one another).

ใคร่ครวญ khrâjkhruan′ V to contemplate, consider
carefully.

ไคล, ขี้-- khlaj′, khîikhlaj′ N scurf.

ไคล้. See คลั่งไคล้.

ฆ

ฆ khɔɔ/ LOW consonant. Pronounced kh initially,
g finally. This letter is very rare.

ฆราวาส (คน) kharaawâad/ (khon/) N eleg.
layman (in the religious sense, i.e. one who is
not a priest).

ฆ้อง (ใบ) khɔ́ɔŋ/ (baj/) N gong.

ฆ่า khâa/ V 1. to kill, execute, destroy. 2. to cross
out, strike out. คน-- murderer. →Syn. 1.
สำเร็จโทษ,ประหารชีวิต eleg.

ขีดฆ่า khìid/khâa/ V to scratch out, cross out,
strike out.

ฆ่าฟัน khâa/fan/ V to kill, slay. การ-- killing,
slaying, slaughter (of people).

ฆ่าเวลา khâa/weelaa/ V to kill time.

ยาฆ่าตัวแมลง jaakhâa/tuamalɛɛŋ/ insecticide.

ฆาต khâad/, khâadta⊃ N destruction, liquidation.
Chiefly in compounds.

ฆาตกรรม khâadtakam/ N murder.

เพชฌฆาต (คน) phédchakhâad/ (khon/) N executioner.

เฆี่ยน khîan/ V to beat, whip.

โฆษก (นาย,คน) khoosòg/ (naaj/, khon/) N announcer, spokesman.

โฆษณา khôosanaa/, khôodsanaa/* V 1. to advertise,
publicize. N 2. advertisement. การ--,ผู้--
(see below).

การโฆษณา (เรื่อง) kaankhôosanaa/ (rŷaŋ/) N
1. advertisement; publicity. 2. propaganda.

โฆษณาการ khôosanaakaan/ N advertisement;
publicity.

o กรมโฆษณาการ krom/khôosanaakaan/ N
Department of Publicity (now abandoned). →See
กรมประชาสัมพันธ์.

โฆษณาชวนเชื่อ khôosanaa/chuanchŷa/ N 1. propaganda. V 2. to propagandize.

ผู้โฆษณา (คน) phûukhôosanaa/ (khon/) N advertiser.

แผนกโฆษณา phanɛ̀ɛg/khôosanaa/ N advertising
division or department.

ง

ง ŋɔɔ/ LOW consonant. Pronounced ŋ both initially
and finally.

งก ŋóg/ V 1. to be greedy. 2. to be nervous, shaking,
shaky.

งกงัน, งันงก ŋógŋan/, ŋanŋóg/ V to be trembling
(with excitement), out of control (of oneself).

งกเงิน ŋóg/ŋən/ V to be avaricious, greedy for
money.

งง ŋoŋ/ V 1. to be dazed, dizzy, stupefied, stunned.
2. to be puzzled, perplexed, confused, addled.

งงงวย, งวยงง ŋoŋŋuaj/, ŋuajŋoŋ/ V to be astonished, perplexed, stunned.

o พิศวงงงงวย phísawŏŋ/ŋoŋŋuaj/ V to be dumbfounded, bewildered, perplexed.

งงงัน ŋoŋŋan/ V to be bewildered, stunned.

งุนงง ŋunŋoŋ/ V to be dazed, bewildered, perplexed.

งด ๑ ŋód/ V 1. to stop, halt, cancel. 2. to be stopped,
canceled.

งดเลิก ŋódlə̂əg/ V 1. to cancel, dissolve. 2. to
be canceled, dissolved.

งดเว้น ŋódwén/ to refrain (from), abstain (from).

งด(...)ไว้ ŋód/(...)wáj⊃ V to postpone (something), put (something) aside for the time being.

ให้งด hâjŋód/ to order to stop.

งด ๒ in งดงาม ŋódŋaam/ V to be pretty, beautiful,
splendid. ความ-- beauty.

งบ. See entries below.

งบดุล ŋóbdun/ N 1. balance sheet. 2. the balance.

งบบัญชี ŋóbbanchii/ V 1. to close an account. 2.
to calculate the balance in an account.

งบประมาณ (งบประมาณ) ŋóbpramaan/ (ŋóbpra⊃
maan/) N budget.

งม ŋom/ V 1. to grope in the water for; to dive for.
2. fig. to fumble; to plod along (in ignorance
of the true situation).

งมงาย ŋomŋaaj/ V 1. to be foolish, stupid, mentally sluggish. 2. to be absorbed in beyond reason, foolishly wrapped up in.

งมโง่ ŋomŋôo/ V to be foolish, stupid.

งวง (งวง) ŋuaŋ′ (ŋuaŋ′) N 1. trunk, proboscis. 2. spadix, fruit-bearing stem (as of a coconut palm).

ไก่งวง (ตัว) kàjŋuaŋ′ (tua′) N turkey.

งวงช้าง (งวง) ŋuaŋcháaŋ′ (ŋuaŋ′) N trunk of the elephant.

งวงผึ้ง (งวง) ŋuaŋphŷŋ′ (ŋuaŋ′) N proboscis or sucking organ of the bee.

งวงมะพร้าว (งวง) ŋuaŋmaphráaw′ (ŋuaŋ′) N spadix of the coconut palm.

งวงหอยทาก (งวง) ŋuaŋhɔ̌jthâag′ (ŋuaŋ′) N protruding eye stalk of the land snail.

งวง ŋûaŋ′ V to be sleepy, drowsy.

งวงนอน ŋûaŋnɔɔn′ V to be sleepy, drowsy.

งวด ๑ ŋûad′ C 1. occasion, time, period. 2. installment (of a payment).

เป็นงวด ๆ penŋûadŋûad′ in installments, periodically.

งวด ๒ ŋûad′ V 1. to dry out, dry up. 2. to be depleted (of supplies, merchandise, stock).

เข้มงวด khêmŋûad′ V 1. to be strict, rigid. 2. to curb.

งวน (อยู่กับ) ŋûan′(jùukaʔ) V to be busy (with), absorbed (in).

งวย in งวยงง, งงงวย ŋuajŋoŋ′, ŋoŋŋuaj′ V to be astonished, perplexed, stunned.

งอ ŋɔɔ′ V 1. to bend, fold, curl. 2. to be crooked, bent, curled. →Dist. ลอน, หยิก.

งอแง ŋɔɔŋɛɛ′ V 1. to be fussy, childish. 2. to cry, pout (like a child).

หน้างอ nâa′ŋɔɔ′ to have an angry face, look sullen.

หัวเราะงอ, --หาย hǔarɔ́ʔ′ŋɔɔ′, hǔarɔ́ʔ′ŋɔɔhǎaj′ colloq. to double up with (violent) laughter.

งอ ŋɔ́ɔ′ V to humble oneself in order to conciliate.

งอนงอ ŋɔɔnŋɔ́ɔ′ V to try to humor, assuage, be nice to an offended person (in order to make up with him).

งอก ŋɔ̂ɔg′ V 1. to sprout, bud. 2. to grow, increase, multiply (esp. of plants). C 3. sprout, plumule, bud.

งอกงาม ŋɔ̂ɔgŋaam′ V to grow, develop, thrive (of plants).

งอกเงย ŋɔ̂ɔgŋəəj′ V to grow, develop, increase,

multiply (of profits, interest; of plants).

ถั่วงอก (ต้น) thùaŋɔ̂ɔg′ (tôn′) N bean sprouts.

หินงอก hǐnŋɔ̂ɔg′ N stalagmite.

งอง in งองแงง ŋɔ̌ŋŋɛ̌ŋ′* V to scrap, quarrel.

งอดแงด ŋɔ̌dŋɛ̌d′* V 1. to be angry, ill-tempered. 2. to pout.

งอน ŋɔɔn′ V 1. to bend, curve; to curve upwards (as the elephant's tusk). 2. to pout, show displeasure (esp. of women, children); to feign displeasure, pout coquettishly (of women).

งอนงอ ŋɔɔnŋɔ́ɔ′ V to try to humor, assuage, be nice to an offended or sulking person (in order to make up with him).

งอนแงน ŋɔ̌nŋɛ̌n′* V to be loose and shaky (as a loose tooth); to be unfirm, unsteady, wobbly, tottering.

งอบ (ใบ) ŋɔ̀ɔb′ (baj′) N a kind of hat made of palm leaves and bamboo, worn by farmers.

งอม ŋɔɔm′ V 1. to be overripe. sV 2. idiom. very much, greatly.

งอมแงม ŋɔɔmŋɛɛm′ sV utterly, extremely, beyond recovery.

สุกงอม sùg′ŋɔɔm′ V to be overripe.

งอย ŋɔ̌j′* V to be lame.

งอยเปลี้ย ŋɔ̌jplîa′ V to be lame.

เป็นงอย penŋɔ̌j′ V to be lame.

งะ. See เงอะงะ.

งั่ง in อ้ายงั่ง ʔâjŋâŋ′* derog. epithet (you) fool!

งัด ŋád′ V to pry up, force up, raise with a lever.

งัน ŋan′ V to be silent, remain silent, be stunned.

งงงัน ŋoŋŋan′ V to be bewildered, stunned.

งันงก, งกงัน ŋanŋóg′, ŋógŋan′ V to be trembling (with excitement), out of control (of one's self).

นิ่งงัน nîŋ′ŋan′ V to be silent, speechless.

งั้น ŋán′ colloq. like that. →Short for ยังงั้น, อย่างงั้น. →See อย่างนั้น.

o งั้นนะซีเล่า ŋán′nasiilâw′ That's it. That's the point. That's why....

o งั้นหรือ ŋán′rý↓, -rɔ̌′-, -rɔ̌ə′- Is that so? Is that it? →See หรือ.

ม่ายงั้น, ไม่งั้น mâajŋán′, mâjŋán′ colloq. otherwise, or else, if not. →Short for ไม่อย่างงั้น.

งับ ŋáb′ V 1. to snap, snap at, nip. 2. to clamp. 3. to close, shut.

งัว (ตัว) ŋua′ (tua′) N ox. Variant of วัว, q.v.

จัวเจีย ŋuaŋia/ V to feel sleepy, drowsy, not fully
awake.

งา ๑ (เม็ด) ŋaa/ (méd/) N sesame. ต้น-- (ต้น)
sesame (the plant).

น้ำมันงา námman/ŋaa/ N sesame oil.

งา ๒ (ข้าง, งา) ŋaa/ N 1. tusk (of the elephant)
(khâaŋ/, ŋaa/). 2. ivory.

งาช้าง ŋaacháaŋ/ N 1. ivory. 2. elephant tusk.

ช้างงา (ตัว, เชือก) cháaŋŋaa/ (tua/, chŷag/) N
tusker, tusked elephant.

ถอดเขี้ยวถอดงา thɔ̀ɔdkhîaw/thɔ̀ɔdŋaa/ idiom.
(a person) to become gentle, subdued, peaceful,
be no longer vicious or cross; "to remove one's
fangs and tusks."

งา ŋâa/ V to be ajar. Sometimes also short for
เงื้องา.

เงื้องา ŋýaŋâa/ V to raise (the hand, a weapon)
in a threatening gesture; to gesture menacingly
(by raising the hand, preparing to strike).

งาง ŋáaŋ/ V to pull out, pull back.

งาน ŋaan/ N 1. work, task, job. 2. ceremony,
festival, affair. C 3. unit of agricultural work
in terms of area of land to be worked, approx.
400 sq. meters. การ-- work (in general).
คน-- (unskilled) worker, workman, laborer.

> NOTE. งาน as a noun can take any of several
> classifiers, e.g. ชิ้น chín/ for a specific task,
> อย่าง jàaŋ/ for kind of work, ด้าน dâan/ for
> an aspect or field of work, ครั้ง, หน khráŋ/,
> hŏn/ for a festivity.

กำลังงาน kamlaŋŋaan/ N 1. power. 2. phys.
energy.

งานก่อสร้าง ŋaankɔ̀ɔsâaŋ/ N construction work.

งานการ ŋaankaan/ N work (in general). →Also
การงาน.

งานขึ้นปีใหม่ ŋaan/khŷnpiimàj/ New Year festival.

งานฉลอง ŋaanchalɔ̌ɔŋ/ N festival, celebration.

งานเฉลิม ŋaanchalə̌əm/ N 1. celebration (of a
state or royal function). 2. the celebration of
the king's birthday.

งานด้านปกครอง ŋaandâan/pògkhrɔɔŋ/ the administrative aspect of the work, the administration.

งานบ้าน ŋaanbâan/ N housework, household
chores.

งานเบ็ดเตล็ด ŋaan/bèdtalèd/ odd jobs.

งานปีใหม่ ŋaanpiimàj/ N New Year festival.

งานพระเมรุ ŋaan/phrámeen/ N roy. cremation
ceremony.

งานพิธี ŋaanphíthii/ N ceremony.

งานรื่นเริง ŋaanrŷynrəəŋ/ N party, festivity, a
gathering for entertainment.

งานลีลาศ ŋaanliilâad/ N dancing party, dance.

งานวัด ŋaanwád/ N a fair held within the Buddhist
temple grounds.

งานวิจัย ŋaanwícaj/ N research work.

งานศพ ŋaansòb/ N funeral.

งานอดิเรก ŋaan/ʔàdirèeg/* N hobby.

ดำเนินงาน damnəən/ŋaan/ V 1. to carry on the
work. 2. to execute, carry out. 3. to manage,
administer.

ดูงาน duuŋaan/ V to observe, observe the operation (e.g. of a system), observe (something) in
operation.

ได้งานทำ dâjŋaan/tham/ 1. to get a job. 2. to
have a job.

แต่งงาน tèŋŋaan/ V 1. to get married, be married.
2. to marry off. การ-- marrying, marriage.

o แต่งงานกับ tèŋŋaan/kaɔ to marry, get married
to.

ทำงาน thamŋaan/ V to work, do work. คน--
worker.

นายงาน (คน) naajŋaan/ (khon/) N person in
charge of a project, supervisor.

บริหารงาน bɔɔrihǎan/ŋaan/ V to administer,
execute.

ประสานงาน prasǎan/ŋaan/ V to coordinate the
work (e.g. of different departments).

เป็นงานเป็นการ penŋaan/penkaan/ V elab.
colloq. to be systematic, business-like.

พนักงาน (คน, นาย) phanágŋaan/ (khon/, naaj/)
N 1. employee, worker, person responsible for
a task. 2. duty, responsibility.

o เจ้าพนักงาน (คน, นาย) câwphanágŋaan/ (khon/,
naaj/) N official, person in charge.

พลังงาน phalaŋŋaan/ N energy.

รายงาน (ฉบับ) raajŋaan/ (chabàb/) N 1. report.
V 2. to report.

แรงงาน rɛɛŋŋaan/ N labor, work.

o ค่าแรงงาน khâarɛɛŋŋaan/ N wages, pay (for labor).

โรงงาน (โรง, แห่ง) rooŋŋaan/ (rooŋ/, hɛ̀ŋ/) N factory, workshop, plant.

ไร้งาน ráj/ŋaan/ V to be unemployed, out of a job, out of work. ความ-- unemployment.

เล่นงาน lênŋaan/ V 1. colloq. to hit, strike, attack, hurt. 2. to scold. 3. to take serious measures against.

วงงาน woŋŋaan/ N sphere of activity, field of work.

ว่างงาน wâaŋŋaan/ V 1. to be unoccupied, have leisure. 2. to have run out of work, finished the work at hand. 3. to be unemployed. คน-- unemployed person; unoccupied person.

สำนักงาน (แห่ง) sămnákŋaan/ (hɛ̀ŋ/) N office.

หยุดงาน jùdŋaan/ 1. to stop working. 2. to take a vacation. 3. to absent oneself from work. 4. to go on strike.

เอาการเอางาน ʔawkaan/ʔawŋaan/ V elab. colloq. to take one's work seriously, to be in earnest about one's work.

งาน. See งุ่นงาน.

งาม ŋaam/ V 1. to be beautiful. 2. (plants) to thrive, flourish. sV 3. beautifully, nicely (esp. referring to the growth of plants). ความ-- beauty. →Syn. 1. สวย.

o ข้าวขึ้นงาม khâaw/khŷnŋaam/↓ The rice is growing nicely.

o ปลูกอะไรก็ไม่งาม plùug/ʔaraj/-kɔ̂mâjŋaam/ No matter what you plant (there), it won't thrive.

งดงาม ŋódŋaam/ V to be pretty, beautiful, splendid.

งอกงาม ŋɔ̂ɔgŋaam/ V to grow, develop, thrive (of plants).

งามผาด ŋaamphàad/ V to appear beautiful at first glimpse, to be superficially beautiful (mostly of women).

งามพิศ ŋaamphíd/ V to appear increasingly beautiful upon contemplation, to be profoundly beautiful (mostly of women).

โฉมงาม (คน) chǒomŋaam/ (khon/) N beautiful girl, a beauty.

ราคางาม raakhaa/ŋaam/ a good price, an attrac-

tive price.

ฤกษ์งามยามดี rɤ̂ɤgŋaam/jaamdii/ N elab. colloq. auspicious time.

สง่างาม saŋàa/ŋaam/ V to be stately, handsome and dignified, grand, majestic.

สวยงาม sǔajŋaam/ V to be beautiful. ความ-- beauty.

เห็นดีเห็นงาม hěndii/hěnŋaam/ V elab. colloq. 1. to approve. 2. to agree.

งาม ๑ (ง่าม) ŋâam/ (ŋâam/) N fork (as of a tree).

ง่ามมือ ŋâammyy/ N the region between two fingers.

เป็นง่าม penŋâam/ to be forked.

ง่าม ๒. See งุ่มง่าม.

ง่าย. See งมง่าย.

ง่าย ŋâaj/ V 1. to be simple, easy. sV 2. easily.

ง่าย ๆ ŋâajŋâaj/ V 1. to be simple, very easy. sV 2. plainly, unceremoniously. 3. easily.

o พูดง่าย ๆ phûud/ŋâajŋâaj/ 1. plainly speaking. 2. briefly speaking, in short. 3. generally speaking.

ง่ายดาย ŋâajdaaj/ V 1. to be easy, very easy, simple. sV 2. easily, simply.

ใจง่าย cajŋâaj/ V (a woman) to be cheap, easy to get, free with her affections.

โดยง่าย doojŋâaj/ with ease, easily.

มักง่าย mágŋâaj/ V to be careless, heedless, sloppy, slovenly.

ว่าง่าย wâaŋâaj/ V to be obedient, tractable.

ว่านอนสอนง่าย wâanɔɔn/sɔ̌ɔnŋâaj/ V elab. colloq. to be tractable, easily led, compliant, obedient.

อยู่ง่ายกินง่าย jùuŋâaj/kinŋâaj/ colloq. to be easy to please (with regard to food and accommodations).

ง้าว ๑, ขอ-- (อัน) ŋáaw/, khɔ̌ɔŋáaw/ (ʔan/) N a pike with curved blade.

ง้าว ๒ ŋáaw/ imit. the yowling, caterwauling of a cat. →Dist. เหมียว.

งำ ŋam/ V to conceal, hide, protect, preserve.

เก็บงำ kèbŋam/ V to hide, conceal (something).

ครอบงำ khrɔ̂ɔbŋam/ V 1. to shelter, shield, cover. 2. to overwhelm, overpower (of emotion, temptation, etc.).

เงื่อนงำ ŋŷanŋam/ N 1. clue, key to a solution.
2. hidden point, catch.

ซ่อนงำ sɔɔn/ŋam/ V to conceal.

จ๊ำ ŋâm/ imit. the sound of a dog chomping his
food.

จ๋ำ ŋám/ V to jut out.

จิบ. See จุบจิบ.

จิ้ว (โรง) ŋíw/ (rooŋ/) N Chinese play.

จี้ ŋíi/ colloq. like this. Short for ยังจี้, อย่างจี้.
→See อย่างนี้.

จีบ ŋîib/ C 1. clf.for a nap. V 2. to take a nap.

จึมจ่ำ ŋymŋam/ sV by murmuring, muttering, mum-
bling, in murmurs, mutteringly.

พูดจึมจ่ำ phûud/ŋymŋam/ to murmur, mutter,
mumble.

จุนงง ŋunŋoŋ/ V to be dazed, bewildered, perplexed.

จุนง่าน ŋunŋâan/ V to be upset, restless, irritated,
angered.

จุบจิบ ŋúbŋíb/ V 1. to behave or perform surreptitiously. sV 2. surreptitiously.

จุ้ม ŋúm/ V to be curved, bent downward, hooked
(like the beak of a parrot).

จุ้มง่าม ŋûmŋâam/ V 1. to be clumsy, awkward.
sV 2. clumsily, sluggishly.

จู (ตัว) ŋuu/ (tua/) N snake.

จูเขียว (ตัว) ŋuukhĭaw/ (tua/) N a common
green anake.

จู ๆ ปลา ๆ ŋuuŋuu/plaaplaa/ a little bit, bits
and pieces (of knowledge).

จูเหลือม (ตัว) ŋuulўam/ (tua/) N python.

จูเห่า (ตัว) ŋuuhàw/ (tua/) N cobra.

เงน. See โงนเงน under โงน.

เงย ŋəəj/ V to raise, lift (one's head, face).

งอกเงย ŋɔ̀ɔgŋəəj/ V to grow, develop, increase,
multiply (of profits, interest; of plants).

เงยหน้า ŋəəjnâa/ V to look up; to raise one's
head, lift up one's face.

มุมเงย mumŋəəj/ N angle of elevation.

เงอะงะ ŋə́ʔŋáʔ/ V to be awkward, maladroit, inept.

เงา (เงา) ŋaw/ (ŋaw/) N image, reflection,
shadow.

กระจกเงา (บาน,แผ่น) kracòg/ŋaw/ (baan/,
phɛ̀n/) N mirror.

ขึ้นเงา khŷnŋaw/ V to be glossy, lustrous.

เงา ๆ ŋawŋaw/ N a fleeting image.

o เห็นแต่เงา ๆ hěn/tɛ̀ɛŋawŋaw/ to catch but a
glimpse (of).

เงามืด ŋawmŷyd/ N silhouette, dark shadow.

ขัดเงา chágŋaw/ V 1. to shine, polish. 2. to be
shiny, glossy.

o น้ำมันขัดเงา námman/chágŋaw/ N varnish.

เป็นเงา penŋaw/ to be glossy, shiny.

เป็นเงาตามตัว penŋaw/-taam/tua/ "as one's
shadow follows one's body": a simile for an
inevitable consequence. Cf. Eng. "as night
follows day."

เง่า ๑ ŋâw/ N 1. ancestor. 2. base or underground
portion of a plant stem or tree trunk. →Some-
times also เหง้า.

รากเง่า râagŋâw/ N 1. root. 2. origin, source.

เง่า ๒. See โง่เง่า.

เงาะ ๑ (ใบ,ลูก,ผล) ŋɔ́ʔ/ (baj/, lûug/, phŏn/) N
rambutan, a kind of red fruit covered with soft
spines or hairs (Nephelium lapaceum (Sapin-
daceae)).

เงาะ ๒ (คน) ŋɔ́ʔ/ (khon/) N Negrito, Semang.
Derived from เงาะ ๑.

หัวเงาะ hŭaŋɔ́ʔ/ 1. curly hair, kinky hair. 2.
Negrito mask.

เงิน ŋən/* N 1. silver. 2. money. The clf. ก้อน
is used for a sum of money. การ-- (see below).
→Syn. ทรัพย์ eleg. →Often coupled with ทอง
"gold."

กระแสเงิน krasɛ̆ɛ/ŋən/ N 1. monetary currency.
2. circulation or flow of money.

การเงิน kaanŋən/ N 1. money matters, finance,
financial affair(s). 2. (as n. mod.) financial.

o ภาวะการเงิน phaawá/ʔkaanŋən/ N financial
situation.

ขึ้นเงิน khŷnŋən/ to redeem for cash.

คนเก็บเงิน (คน) khon/kèbŋen/ (khon/) N cashier,
bill collector.

เครื่องเงิน (ชิ้น,ชุด) khrŷaŋŋən/ (chín/,chúd/)
N silverware, articles of silver.

จกเงิน ŋóg/ŋən/ to be avaricious, greedy for
money.

เงินกู้ ŋənkûu/ N loan.

เงินคงคลัง ŋən'khoŋkhlaŋ' N treasury reserves.

เงิน ๆ ทอง ๆ ŋənŋən'thɔɔŋthɔɔŋ' N colloq. finances, money. →See also เงินทอง.

o เรื่องเงิน ๆ ทอง ๆ rŷaŋ'-ŋənŋən'thɔɔŋthɔɔŋ' N colloq. money matters, financial matters.

เงินเดือน ŋəndyan' N monthly salary.

เงินแดง ŋəndɛɛŋ' N counterfeit money.

เงินได้ ŋəndâaj' N income.

o ภาษีเงินได้ phaasĭi'ŋəndâaj' N income tax.

เงินต้น ŋəntôn' N finance principal, capital sum.

เงินตรา ŋəntraa' N minted currency.

เงินทอง ŋən'thɔɔŋ' N 1. gold and silver. 2. colloq. money. →See also เงิน ๆ ทอง ๆ above.

เงินทอน ŋənthɔɔn' N change (money returned).

เงินทุน ŋənthun' N capital (money in an investment).

เงินปันผล ŋən'panphŏn' dividend (given to a shareholder).

เงินผ่อน ŋənphɔ̀ɔn' N installment.

เงินฝาก ŋənfàag' N money on deposit.

o บัญชีเงินฝาก banchii'ŋənfàag' N bank account.

เงินเพิ่มพิเศษ ŋənphə̂əm'phísèed' N special auxiliary allowance for employees (in addition to the regular salary).

เงินมัดจำ ŋən'mádcam' N deposit (down payment).

เงินสด ŋənsòd' N cash.

เงินหมุนเวียน ŋən'mŭnwian' N currency (money in actual use, in circulation).

ช่างเงิน (คน) châaŋŋən' (khon') N silversmith.

บ่อเงิน (บ่อ) bɔ̀ɔŋən' (bɔ̀ɔ') N silver mine.

เบิกเงิน bə̀əg'ŋən' V to withdraw money (as from the bank).

o ใบเบิกเงิน (ใบ) baj'bə̀əgŋən' (baj') N bank. withdrawal slip.

ปลาเงินปลาทอง plaaŋən'plaathɔɔŋ' N small carp with gold and silver coloring.

ฝากเงิน fàag'ŋən' to deposit money (in the bank).

o ใบฝากเงิน (ใบ) baj'fàagŋən' (baj') N bank. deposit slip.

o สมุดฝากเงิน (เล่ม) samùd'fàagŋən' (lêm') N bankbook, passbook.

ร้อนเงิน rɔɔn'ŋən' V to be in desperate need of money.

เลี่ยมเงิน lîamŋən' V 1. to plate, cover, be plated, covered with a thin sheet of silver. 2. to enframe, be enframed with a thin strip of silver.

หาเงิน hăaŋən' V to earn money, earn a living.

o หาเงินหาทอง hăaŋən'hăathɔɔŋ' elab. colloq. idem.

เงี่ย in งัวเงี่ย ŋuaŋia' V to feel sleepy, drowsy, not fully awake.

เงี่ย in เงี่ยหูฟัง ŋîahŭu'faŋ' to cock the ears, i.e. try hard to listen.

เงี่ยง (เงี่ยง) ŋîaŋ' (ŋîaŋ') N hook; barb.

เงี่ยน ŋîan' V 1. to lust, be desirous (sexually). 2. to have a craving for (narcotics).

เงียบ ŋîab' V to be quiet, still, silent, soundless.

เก็บ(...)เงียบ kèb(...)ŋîab' to keep (something) in secret.

เงียบกริบ ŋîabkrìb' to be completely soundless.

เงียบ ๆ ŋîabŋîab' 1. silent, quiet, taciturn. 2. silently, quietly, in silence.

เงียบฉิบ ŋîab'chìb' to be very silent, not let oneself be heard from at all.

เงียบเขียบ ŋîabchîab' to be dead silent.

เงียบลง ŋîab'loŋ' to quiet down.

เงียบเหงา ŋîabŋăw' V to be silent and lonely.

เงี้ยว ŋîaw' N Shan. →Syn. ฉาน.

เงื้อ ŋŷa' V to raise (the hand, a weapon) in a threatening gesture; to gesture menacingly (by raising the hand, preparing to strike).

เงื้อง่า ŋŷaŋâa' idem.

เงื้อมือ ŋŷa'myy' to raise the hand (in order to strike).

เงือก (ตัว) ŋŷag' (tua') N 1. mermaid. 2. dugong, an aquatic mammal (Dugong).

เงื่อน (เงื่อน,ประการ) ŋŷan' N 1. knot (ŋŷan'). 2. joint (ŋŷan'). 3. hint, clue (prakaan').

เค้าเงื่อน (ข้อ) kháwŋŷan' (khɔ̂ɔ') N clue.

เงื่อนไข (ข้อ) ŋŷankhâj' (khɔ̂ɔ') N condition, stipulation, proviso.

o ยอมแพ้โดยไม่มีเงื่อนไข jɔɔmphɛɛ'-doojmâjmii'ŋŷankhâj' to surrender unconditionally.

เงื่อนงำ ŋŷanŋam' N 1. clue, key to a solution. 2. hidden point, catch.

เจิ่ม. See entries below.

เจิ่มผา (แห่ง) ŋýamphǎa′ (hὲŋ′) N precipice, overhanging rock, projecting cliff.

เจิ่มมือ ŋýammyy′ N idiom. control, clutches, power, hands.

o อยู่ในเจิ่มมือของ jùunajŋýammyy′khɔ̌ɔŋɔ to be in the clutches of.

แง ŋɛɛ′ 1. imit. the sound of a baby crying. V 2. colloq. to cry.

งอแง ŋɔɔŋɛɛ′ V 1. to be fussy, childish. 2. to cry, pout (like a child).

แง่ (แง่) ŋε̂ε′ (ŋε̂ε′) N 1. angle. 2. point of view.

มองในแง่ร้าย mɔɔŋ′najŋε̂ε′ráaj′ to look at something from a pessimistic viewpoint.

แง่ง ๑ ŋε̂ŋ′* C branch of a rhizome, e.g. of ginger, turmeric, galangal, etc.

แง่ง ๒ ŋε̂ŋ′* 1. imit. the snarling of a dog. V 2. to snarl, growl.

งองแง่ง ŋɔŋŋε̂ŋ′ V to scrap, quarrel.

แง่น. See งอนแง่น.

แง่ม. See งอมแง่ม.

แง้ม ŋέεm′ V 1. to open slightly. 2. to be ajar.

แงะ ŋέʔ′ V to pry, pry open.

โง่ ŋôo′ V to be stupid, foolish. ความ-- stupidity.

งมโง่ ŋomŋôo′ V to be stupid, foolish.

โง่เง่า ŋôoŋâw′ V to be utterly stupid.

โง่บรม,บรมโง่ ŋôo′bɔɔrom′, bɔɔrom′maŋôo′ V colloq. to be utterly stupid, abysmally ignorant. ความ-- utter stupidity, ignorance.

โง้ง ŋóoŋ′ V to be arched; to be long and curved.

โง่น in โง่นเง่น ŋoonŋeen′ V to be tottering, unsteady.

โง้น ŋóon′ colloq. like that; that way, of that sort. →Short for ยังโง้น,อย่างโง้น. →See อย่าง โน้น.

ไง ŋaj′ colloq. 1. how?, what?, in what way? 2. how, what, in what way, in whatever way. 3. odd, strange, not quite right, unacceptable. →Short for ยังไง,อย่างไง. →See อย่างไร.

จ

จ cɔɔ′ MIDDLE consonant. Pronounced c initially,

d finally.

จง ๑ coŋ′ AA lit.,eleg. imperative and hortatory adv. -aux: "let's; come on (and); go (and)." May also be used by sup. to inf.

o ขอให้คุณจงลบโชคดีเถิด khɔ̌ɔhâjkhun′coŋsòbɔ chôogdii′-thə̀əd↓ May you have good luck!

o พวกเราจงช่วยกันเถิด phûagraw coŋchûaj′kanɔ thə̀əd↓ Let's all pitch in!

จง ๒. See entries below.

จงเกลียดจงชัง coŋklîad′coŋchaŋ′ V to hate and hold a grudge against (someone), to hate and bear ill will (toward someone).

จงใจ coŋcaj′ AA intend to, intentionally, deliberately.

o จงใจฆ่าเขา coŋcajkhâa′kháw′ intend to kill, kill intentionally, deliberately.

o จงใจทำ coŋcajtham′ to do (something) intentionally.

จงรัก,--ภักดี(ต่อ) coŋrág′, coŋrág′phágdii′(tɔ̀ɔɔ) V to be loyal, faithful (to).

จง ๓ in เจาะจง cɔ̀ʔcoŋ′ V 1. to pick out, single out; to specify, be specific about. 2. to be specific, precise.

จงอาง,งู-- (ตัว) coŋ?aaŋ′, ŋuu′coŋ?aaŋ′ N king cobra.

จด ๑ còd′ V to touch on, adjoin, abut. →Syn. จรด eleg.

จดจ่อ(อยู่กับ) còdcɔ̀ɔ′(jùukaɔ) V to concentrate (on), to pay close attention (to).

จับจด càbcòd′ V to be desultory (in doing work).

จด ๒ còd′ V to mark, note, jot down, record.

จดจำ còdcam′ V to retain, fix in one's mind.

จดทะเบียน còd′thabian′ V to register (intr.), be registered. การ-- registration.

จดหมาย (ฉบับ) còdmǎaj′ (chabàb′) N letter (epistle). →Abbrev. จ.ม.

o จดหมายลงทะเบียน còdmǎaj′loŋthabian′ N registered mail.

o จดหมายเวียน còdmǎajwian′ N circular.

o จดหมายเหตุ còdmǎajhèed′ N written account, record (as of events), document.

จด ๓. See entries below.

จดจ้อง còdcɔ̂ŋ′ V to pause, hesitate (because of indecision or mental block; often staring fixedly at something). →See จ้อง ๑.

หมดจด mòdcòd′ V 1. to be flawless, spotless, clean, neat. sV 2. spotlessly, neatly.

จตุ- càtuɔ, càtù?′. Combining form meaning "four," as in the entries below. See also จัตุ- .

จตุบาท càtubàad′ lit., eleg. quadruped (adj.). →Syn. สี่เท้า eleg.

จตุปัจจัย càtù?′pàdcaj′ N the four requisites for maintaining the comfort of a Buddhist priest, viz., food, shelter, clothing and drugs.

จตุรัส. See จัตุรัส under จัตุ-.

จตุสดมภ์ càtùsadom′ N the four-way administrative organization of the government, in use as late as the early Bangkok period. Known also as เวียง, วัง, คลัง, นา wiaŋ′→waŋ′→khlaŋ′→naa′ "state, palace, treasury, and farmland (administration)."

จน ๑ con′ V 1. to be poor, hard up, impoverished, in distress. 2. to be at an impasse, stuck, up against it. ความ-- poverty. คน-- poor person, poor people, the poor. →Cf. จำนน. →Ant. รวย.

เขาตาจน khâwtaa′con′ colloq. to be in a fix, to be having a hard time.

จนกรอบ con′krɔ̀ɔb′ V colloq. to be extremely poor.

จนใจ con′caj′ V colloq. 1. to be unable to think of a way. 2. It can't be helped.

จนตรอก con′trɔ̀ɔg′ V idiom. to be at an impasse, have no way out.

จนแต้ม con′tɛ̂ɛm′ V to be checked, blocked, cornered, brought to an impasse.

จนปัญญา con′panjaa′ V colloq. to be at one's wit's end, to have run out of ideas (in trying to figure something out).

จนมุม con′mum′ V idiom. to be cornered, trapped, at bay.

ยากจน jâagcon′ V to be poor, poverty-stricken. ความ-- poverty. คน-- poor people, poor person.

ยากดีมีจน jâagdii′-mii′con′ elab. colloq. (whether) rich or poor.

จน ๒ con′ Cj 1. until, till; so (e.g. sweet) that. Pp 2. until, till. →Syn. ตราบเท้า eleg.

○ เขาคอยจนฝนหาย kháwkhɔɔj′-confǒn′hǎaj′↓ He waited till it stopped raining.

○ เขาคอยตั้งแต่เช้าจนเที่ยง kháwkhɔɔj′-tâŋtɛɛ⊃ cháaw′conthîaŋ′↓ He waited from morning till noon.

○ หวานจนแสบคอ wǎan′-consɛ̀ɛb′khɔɔ′ so sweet that it stings the throat.

จนกระทั่ง conkrathâŋ′ Cj 1. until. Pp 2. to, up to, until. →Syn. ตราบเท้า eleg.

จนกว่า(...)จะ conkwàa′(...) caɔ right up until, until the time that.

จนเกินไป conkəən′paj excessively, far too.

จนได้ condâaj′ 1. until (one) obtains (something), succeeds. 2. anyway (in spite of opposition or prohibition).

จนตลอด contalɔ̀ɔd′ Pp all the way through, throughout.

จนตาย contaaj′ till death.

จนติดปาก contìd′pàag′ as a regular thing, constantly, habitually (of a person's verbal habits).

จนถึง conthǔŋ⊃ Pp up until, as far as, to the point of.

จนแล้วจนรอด conlɛ́ɛw′conrɔ̂ɔd′ colloq. on and on, over and over.

○ คอยจนแล้วจนรอด khɔɔj′-conlɛ́ɛw′conrɔ̂ɔd′→ (we) waited and waited (but he didn't come).

จนสุดกำลัง consùd′kamlaŋ′ with all one's strength, to the utmost of one's strength.

จวบจน cùab′con′ Pp until. In rare use also a conjunction.

ตลอดจน talɔ̀ɔd′conɔ Pp including, (extending) all the way to; even to (what is specified).

จบ còb′ V 1. to finish, end, be ended. sV 2. finish (doing something by coming to the end); to the end, through (see examples below). C 3. round, cycle, time. →Dist. 2. เสร็จ. →Comp. 1, 2. สิ้น, หมด.

○ ยังเล่าไม่จบ jaŋlâw′mâjcòb′↓ (I) have not yet finished telling (about it).

○ อ่านหนังสือจบ ?àan′naŋsy̌y′-còb′ finish reading the book, read the book through.

จบกัน còb′kan↓ That's the end of it all! No use continuing! (expression of despair).

จบลง còb′loŋ′ V to end, be concluded.

จุดจบ cùdcòb′ N the end, the end-point.

ตอนจบ tɔɔncòb′ N the ending (of book, play), the finale.

ไม่รู้จบ mâjrúu′còb′ 1. unending, endless; recurring (decimal). 2. endlessly, without end.

จ.ม. Abbrev. for จดหมาย letter.

จม com′ V 1. to sink. 2. to be submerged, buried, embedded. 3. to be unproductive, dead (of investment).

o มีงานจม miiŋaan′com′ to be up to one's ears in work.

จมดิน comdin′ V to be embedded, buried (in the ground).

จมน้ำ comnáam′ V to sink (into water).

o จมน้ำตาย comnáam′taaj′ to drown, get drowned, die by drowning.

จมเบ้า com′bâw′ slang to be glued to one's place, remain in one's place for an inordinately long period.

จมไปเลย com′pajləəj′ slang very; so very much.

จมมิด com′míd′ V 1. to be entirely submerged. 2. to penetrate completely (as a knife blade into the flesh).

ล้มจม lômcom′ V 1. to go bankrupt. 2. to collapse, fall (as a government).

จมูก (จมูก) camùug′ (camùug′) N nose; snout.

ขื่อจมูก khŷycamùug′ N the nasal septum.

รูจมูก (รู) ruucamùug′ (ruu′) N nostril.

จร cɔɔn′, cɔɔnᴐ, cɔɔraᴐ V lit. to go, wander, move about. คน-- (see below).

คนจร (คน) khoncɔɔn′ (khon′) N 1. itinerant, traveler, wanderer. 2. temporary guest (in a hotel).

คนจรจัด (คน) khoncɔɔncàd′, khoncɔɔracàd′ (khon′) N vagrant, vagabond, homeless wanderer.

โคจร khoocɔɔn′ V to travel (of celestial bodies).

วงจร (วง) woŋcɔɔn′ (woŋ′) N elect. circuit.

จรเข้. See จระเข้.

จรด caròd′ V eleg. to touch, reach, join, abut. →Syn. จด ① com.

o จากคีรษะจรดปลายเท้า càagsǐisà?′-caròd′ᴐ plaajtháaw′ from head to foot.

จรรยา canjaa′ N 1. etiquette. 2. ethics.

จรรยาแพทย์ canjaaphɛ̂ɛd′ N medical ethics.

เสียจรรยา sǐa′canjaa′ to go against etiquette, to violate rules of proper conduct, ethics, good manners.

จรรโลง canlooŋ′ V eleg. to support, sustain, maintain.

จรวด (ลูก) carùad′ (lûug′) N rocket.

เครื่องบินจรวด (เครื่อง,ลำ) khrŷaŋbin′carùad′ (khrŷaŋ′,lam′) N jet plane.

จระเข้ (ตัว) cɔɔrakhêe′ (tua′) N crocodile.

จราจร caraa′cɔɔn′ N 1. traffic; usually การ--, except in compounds. 2. traffic patrolman; short for ตำรวจ-- below. การ-- traffic.

กฎจราจร (ข้อ) kòd′-caraa′cɔɔn′ (khɔ̂ɔ′) N traffic laws.

ตำรวจจราจร (คน,นาย) tamrùad′-caraa′cɔɔn′ (khon′,naaj′) N traffic patrolman, traffic cop; the traffic police.

ทางจราจร thaaŋ′-caraa′cɔɔn′ N traffic lane.

จริง ciŋ′ V com. 1. to be true, real. sV 2. truly, truthfully. ความ-- (see below). →Ant. เท็จ eleg.

ความจริง (ประการ) khwaamciŋ′ (prakaan′) N 1. truth; the facts; in fact, in reality. 2. (a) truth (e.g. of Buddhism).

o มีมูลความจริง miimuun′khwaamciŋ′ to have a factual basis; there is an element of truth.

จริง ๆ ciŋciŋ′ sV really, very.

จริงจัง ciŋcaŋ′ V 1. to be serious, earnest. sV 2. seriously, earnestly. อย่าง-- really, seriously, truthfully.

o เป็นการจริงจัง penkaan′ciŋcaŋ′ to be earnest, an earnest matter; earnestly, with all one's heart.

จริงใจ ciŋcaj′ V to be sincere, heartfelt. ความ-- sincerity.

o ไม่จริงใจ mâjciŋcaj′ V to be insincere.

จริงอยู่(ที่) ciŋ′jùu′-(thîiᴐ) it's true (that); actually, in fact.

ใจจริง cajciŋ′ N (one's) true feelings, frank thoughts. อย่าง-- frankly, candidly.

ดีจริง,ดีจริง ๆ dii′ciŋ↓, dii′ciŋciŋ′↓ That's fine! How nice!

เท็จจริง as in ข้อเท็จจริง khɔ̂ɔ′thédciŋ′ N facts,

evidence, the facts of the matter: "points false and true."

เท่าตัวจริง thâw′tuaciŋ′ life-size, actual size.

แท้จริง thɛ́ɛ′ciŋ′ V to be real, genuine, actual.

เป็นจริง penciŋ′ to come true, be realized; to materialize (as a dream, a plan). ความ-- the actual facts; (in) actuality.

พูดไม่จริง phûud′mâjciŋ′ V com. to tell an untruth. →Syn. See โกหก.

เสียจริง sĭaciŋ′ colloq. really, so very (much).

o เกลียดเสียจริง klìad′sĭaciŋ′ (I) really hate it, hate it so very much.

เห็นจริง hĕnciŋ′ V to be convinced.

o รู้แจ้งเห็นจริง rúucɛ̂ɛŋ′hĕnciŋ′ V elab. colloq. to perceive and understand clearly.

o ให้เห็นจริง hâjhĕn′ciŋ′ convincingly.

อันที่จริง ʔan′thîiciŋ′ in fact, as a matter of fact (followed by a clause).

เอาจริง ʔawciŋ′ V to be serious, earnest; to take things seriously.

จริต carìd′ N 1. conduct, behavior. 2. affectation, mannerism, airs.

จริตกิริยา carìd′kìrijaa′ N (personal) way, manner (esp. of women).

วิกลจริต wíkon′carìd′ to be insane.

เสียจริต sĭa′carìd′ 1. to lose one's mind. 2. to be insane. คน-- insane person.

จเร (นาย,คน) caree′ (naaj′, khon′) N inspector.

จเรตำรวจ (นาย,คน) caree′tamrùad′ (naaj′, khon′) N police inspector.

จลาจล (ครั้ง,หน) calaa′con′ (khráŋ′, hŏn′) N unrest, disorder, rebellion. การ-- idem.

จ.ว. Abbrev. for จังหวัด čhangwat, province.

จวก cúag′ rM intensifier used with ขาว "white."

จวง cūaŋ′ V to plunge (into with full force).

จวน ๑ (หลัง) cuan′ (lăŋ′) N official residence of the governor of a province.

จวน ๒ cuan′ AA almost, nearly, on the verge of. Used also as a verb in some special expressions, e.g. จวนตัว below. →Syn. เกือบ,แทบ, ปาง ๒.

จวนจะ cuancaɔ AA idem.

จวนเจียน cuancian′ AA idem.

จวนตัว cuantua′ something to be imminent, on the verge of overtaking one (as when one is pursued by an enemy, confronted by an urgent issue).

จวบ in จวบจน cùab′con′ Pp until. In rare use also a conjunction.

จ.ศ. cɔɔsɔ̆ɔ′. Abbrev. for จุลศักราช cun′lasàgkaɔ ràad′ the Thai minor era, beginning March 21, 633 A.D.

จอ ๑ cɔɔ′ N (Year of the) Dog. →The complete list of the cyclical years is given under ปี.

จอ ๒,--หนัง (จอ) cɔɔ′, cɔɔnăŋ′ (cɔɔ′) N screen (for shadow play, movies).

จ่อ cɔ̀ɔ′ V 1. to point (at), hold close (to). sV 2. to, toward, up to, close to, against.

o เอามีดจ่อออก ʔawmîid′-cɔ̀ɔ′ʔɔ̀g′ hold a knife against (someone's) chest.

จดจ่อ(อยู่กับ) còdcɔ̀ɔ′(jùukaɔ) V to concentrate (on), to pay close attention (to).

จ๊อ cɔ́ɔ′ rM modifier used with verbs of uttering e.g. ขัน ๓ "crow," คุย "chat," พูด "talk," เล่า "tell," in the sense of "on and on, incessantly; eloquently."

จอก ๑ (ใบ) cɔ̀ɔg′ (baj′) N a small cup or glass.

จอก ๒ (ต้น) cɔ̀ɔg′ (tôn′) N water-lettuce, a floating plant (Araceae).

จอก in ลูกจอก (คน) lûugcɔ̀ɔg′ (khon′) N slang subordinate; low ranking employee, member of the lower ranks.

จอกแจก,--จอแจ cɔ̀gcɛ̂g′, cɔ̂gcɛ̂g′cɔɔcɛɛ′* V 1. to be noisy, loud (as a large crowd). sV 2. noisily, loudly.

จอง cɔɔŋ′ V to reserve, make a reservation.

จองจำ cɔɔŋcam′ V to imprison (with fetters).

จองตั๋ว cɔɔŋtŭa′ to reserve a ticket, make a reservation.

จองเวร,--จองกรรม(ต่อ) cɔɔŋween′, cɔɔŋween′ɔ cɔɔŋkam′(tɔ̀ɔɔ) V 1. to hold a grudge (against). 2. to seek revenge. →Syn. อาฆาต.

จับจอง càbcɔɔŋ′ V to lay claim to (a piece of nonpossessed land), preempt.

จ้อง cɔ̂ŋ′* V 1. to gaze at, stare at, gaze, stare. V 2. to be waiting, watching, biding one's time. AA 3. waiting (for an opportunity) to, interested (solely) in. →See 3. จ้องจะ.

จดจ้อง còdcɔ̂ŋ′ V to pause, hesitate (because of

indecision or mental block).

จองเขม็ง cɔ̌ŋ'khamĕŋ' to stare fixedly (at).

จองจะ cɔ̌ŋ'caɔ AA waiting (for an opportunity) to, interested (solely) in. →Syn. คอยจะ.

o พวกนี้จองจะกินท่าเดียวแหละ phûagníi' cɔ̌ŋ'ɔ cakin'-thâadiaw'lɛ̀?↓ These people are interested solely in (getting) to eat.

จองดู cɔ̌ŋduu' V to stare at.

จอง(...)เป่ง cɔ̌ŋ(...)pěŋ' V to stare, stare right at.

จองมอง cɔ̌ŋmɔɔŋ' V to stare at.

จอง cɔ̌ŋ'* V slang to be cowardly, a coward.

คนจอง (คน) khoncɔ̌ŋ' (khon') N a coward.

จอง ๆ cɔ̌ŋcɔ̌ŋ' sV slavishly.

หน้าตาจอง nâataacɔ̌ŋ' (with) a submissive expression, being quiet and looking dumb.

จองหอง cɔŋhɔ̌ŋ'* to be haughty, unduly proud, vain.

จอแจ cɔɔcɛɛ' V to be crowded, congested, in confusion.

จอกแจกจอแจ cɔ̀gcɛ̂g'cɔɔcɛɛ' V 1. to be noisy, loud (as a large crowd). sV 2. noisily, loudly.

จอด cɔ̀ɔd' V 1. to stop, to park (a car), moor (a boat). 2. slang to die, be killed.

ที่จอดรถ (แห่ง,ที่) thîi'cɔ̀ɔdród' (hɛ̀ŋ',thîi') N parking space; parking lot.

จอน in จอนหู (ข้าง) cɔɔnhǔu' (khâaŋ') N 1. sideburns. 2. lock of hair growing from in front of a woman's ear, and worn tucked up behind it.

จอน in ล่อนจอน lɔ̂ncɔɔn'* V to be nude, naked, bare.

จอบ (เล่ม) cɔ̀ɔb' (lêm') N hoe.

จอม cɔɔm' highest, supreme; head of. Chiefly in compounds.

จอมปลวก (ลูก) cɔɔmplùag' (lûug') N termite hill.

จอมเผด็จการ (คน) cɔɔm'phadèd'kaan' (khon') N dictator.

จอมพล (นาย,คน) cɔɔmphon' (naaj',khon') N 1. field marshal. T 2. Field Marshal --.

จอมพลเรือ (นาย,คน) cɔɔmphonrya' (naaj',khon') N 1. admiral of the fleet. T 2. Admiral --.

จอมราช cɔɔmrâad' N king.

เจ้าจอม câwcɔɔm' N 1. a lesser concubine of the king. 2. a rank for lesser concubines.

T 3. title placed in front of the first name of a lesser concubine. →See ล่นม.

เจ้าจอมเข่อ câwcɔɔm'sə̀ə' colloq. a big fool.

จอม cɔ̌m'* V to park, moor, land.

จอย ๑ cɔ̌j'* V to be sad, hopeless, discouraged (ref. to facial expression); to look sick, spiritless, pepless.

หน้าจอย nâa'cɔ̌j' to look sad, sick, spiritless.

จอย ๒ cɔ̌j'* rM intensifier used with หวาน "sweet," เหลือง "yellow."

จะ cà?', caɔ AA 1. will, shall; would, should. 2. to (in the Eng.infinitive). Used in ref. to future or unrealized events. See also Note 2 under ที่ ๒.

NOTE. จะ is commonly used together with other adverb-auxiliaries. In such instances, a fixed relative order is observed. Certain adverb-auxiliaries must follow but not precede จะ, e.g. จะต้อง catɔ̂ŋ' "will have to," จะไม่ camâj' "will not" (where ไม่ is not in turn followed by another adverb-auxiliary). Most adverb-auxiliaries, however, must precede จะ, which is then usually best rendered by the English infinitive marker "to," e.g. ควรจะ "ought to." Other such sequences are found under กำลัง,เกือบ,คง,ควร,ใคร่,จวน,จึง,ชัก,ดู, ต้องการ, ติด,ถึง,แทบ,น่า,พอ,เพิ่ง,มัก,ไม่สู้ เห็น,ย่อม,สมควร,แสน,อยาก,ออก,อาจ.

o ก่อนจะเข้านอน kɔ̀ɔn'cakhâwnɔɔn' before going to bed.

o จะทำอย่างไร catham'jàaŋraj' 1. what's to be done, what one should do; what shall (one) do? 2. no matter what (one) does.

o จะเป็นไรไป capen'rajpaj↓ It doesn't matter.

o มีอันจะกิน mii?an'cakin' to be well off, well-to-do.

o ยินดีที่จะทำ jindii'thîicatham' to be glad to do.

o เราจะไปไหนก็ได้ rawcapajnǎj'kɔ̂dâaj↓ We can go anywhere we like.

จะ câ' Pt sp. to inf. or int. 1. the final particle of statements and certain commands; 1st and 2nd examples. 2. Yes (in answer to a question); 3rd example. Used when sp. to servants, children, intimates. →Cf. ครับ def. m. sp., ค่ะ def. w. sp.

o ดีแล้วจะ diiłɛ́ɛw'câ'↓, dii'łɛ́ɛwcâ'↓ That's fine!

o เชิญเถอะจะ chəən'thəcâ'↓ Go ahead!

o จะทานแล้ว cà→thaanlέεw↓ Yes, (I)'ve eaten.

จะ cá⁄ Pt sp. to inf. or int. 1. the final particle
in questions; 1st example. 2. the final particle
after other particles which are used to urge,
suggest, or intimate (e.g. นะ, กระมัง), and
occasionally after one used for request or
emphasis (e.g. ปี); 2nd example. 3. particle
placed after name, title, or kin term to address
or to call the attention of someone; 3rd example.
Used when sp. to servants, children, intimates.
→Cf. ครับ def. m. sp., คะ def. w. sp. See
also จ๊ะ and จ๋า ๑.

o ชอบไหมจ๊ะ chɔ̂ɔb⁄májcá⁄↓ Do (you) like it?

o กินซิจ๊ะ kin⁄sicá?↓ Eat. Go ahead and eat.

o แม่ผันจ๊ะ mêεphǎn⁄cá⁄↓ Phan! (calling her).

จะงอย (อัน, จะงอย) caŋɔɔj⁄ (?an⁄, caŋɔɔj⁄) N
hooked end.

จะแจ้ง cà?⁄cɛ̂εŋ⁄ V to be clear, distinct (of what
is seen or heard). sV 2. clearly, distinctly.
→Cf. แจ้ง.

จะละเม็ด. Sometimes spelled จาละเม็ด, จาระเม็ด.
See entries below.

ไข่จะละเม็ด (ฟอง, ลูก, ใบ) khàj⁄caalaméd⁄*
(fɔɔŋ⁄, lûug⁄, baj⁄) N eggs of the green turtle.
This large sea turtle is called เต่าตนุ.

ปลาจะละเม็ด (ตัว) plaa⁄caalaméd⁄* (tua⁄) N
butterfish, an edible marine fish (Stromateus).

จัก ๑ càg⁄. Literary variant of จะ.

จัก ๒ càg⁄ V to split; to jag, notch (usually more
than once).

-จักสาน. See entries below.

o การจักสาน kaancàgsǎan⁄ N making of wickerwork, making of woven or plaited articles, such
as mats, screens, baskets.

o ช่างจักสาน (คน) châaŋcàgsǎan⁄ (khon⁄) N
wickerworker.

เป็นจัก ๆ pencàgcàg⁄ to be toothed, notched,
serrated, jagged. →Dist. เป็นแฉก. →Syn.
เป็นฟัน, เป็นหยัก.

จัก ๓ in รู้จัก rúucàg⁄ V 1. to be acquainted with,
to know (a person). 2. to know how (to do
something).

จัก càg⁄ C com. clf. for a shower, a rainfall.
→Syn. ห่า eleg.

ตกจั๊กใหญ่ tòg⁄cágjàj⁄ colloq. (rain) to pour
heavily.

จักจั่น (ตัว) cágkacàn⁄* (tua⁄) N cicada.

จักจี้, จั๊กจี้ cágkacîi⁄* V to be ticklish. →See also จี้.

จักร (อัน) càg⁄ (?an⁄) N 1. wheel; discus. 2.
discus rimmed with sharp teeth (now used as an
emblem of the Thai army). 3. machine (esp.
in compounds). →Comp. 1. จักรี. NOTE.
จักร càgkraɔ also appears as the prior member in numerous compounds of Sanskrit origin.
Such compounds are treated as separate dictionary entries.

กลจักร (เครื่อง) konlacàg⁄ (khrŷaŋ⁄) N engine.

เครื่องจักร (เครื่อง) khrŷaŋcàg⁄ (khrŷaŋ⁄) N
machinery, engine, machine.

จักรเย็บผ้า (คัน, เครื่อง, หลัง) càg⁄jébphâa⁄
(khan⁄, khrŷaŋ⁄, lǎŋ⁄) N sewing machine.

ฝีจักร fǐicàg⁄ N speed, velocity (of any thing propelled by an engine).

รถจักร (คัน) ródcàg⁄ (khan⁄) N locomotive.

จักรพรรดิ (องค์) càgkraphád⁄ (?oŋ⁄) N 1. emperor.
T 2. Emperor --.

จักรพรรดินิยม càgkraphád⁄níjom⁄ N imperialism.

o พระเจ้าจักรพรรดิ phrácâwcàgkraphád⁄ N 1.
emperor. 2. the emperor of (e.g. Japan).

สมเด็จพระมหาจักรพรรดิ (องค์) sǒmdèd⁄-phráɔ
mahǎa⁄càgkraphád⁄ (?oŋ⁄) N roy. emperor.

จักรภพ càgkraphób⁄ N empire.

o เครือจักรภพอังกฤษ khrya⁄-càgkraphób⁄?aŋkrìd⁄
the British Commonwealth.

จักรยาน, รถ-- (คัน) càgkrajaan⁄, ród⁄càgkrajaan⁄
(khan⁄) N cycle (as a bicycle).

จักรยานยนต์ (คัน) càgkrajaan⁄jon⁄ (khan⁄) N
motorcycle.

จักรวรรดิ (จักรวรรดิ) càgkrawàd⁄* (càgkrawàd⁄)
N empire.

จักรวรรดิญี่ปุ่น càgkrawàd⁄jîipùn⁄ N the Japanese
empire.

จักรวรรดินิยม càgkrawàd⁄níjom⁄ N imperialism.

จักรวาล càgkrawaan⁄ N the universe.

ขอบจักรวาล khɔ̂ɔb⁄càgkrawaan⁄ N eleg. horizon.
→Syn. ขอบฟ้า com.

สุริยจักรวาล sùrijá?⁄càgkrawaan⁄ N the solar
system.

จักรี càg′krii′ N 1. king, monarch: "one possessing the wheel." nN 2. Chakri, name of the present dynasty. →See 1. จักร. NOTE. The names of the kings of this dynasty are listed below. Expanded print indicates the popular shortened form of the name.

KINGS OF THE CHAKRI DYNASTY

พระบาทสมเด็จพระพุทธยอดฟ้าจุฬาโลก phrábàad′ɔ sɔ̌mdèd′-phráphúdthajɔ̂ɔd′fáa′ - culaa′- lôog′ King Rama I (1782-1809).

พระบาทสมเด็จพระพุทธเลิศหล้านภาลัย phrábàad′ɔ sɔ̌mdèd′-phráphúdthalɤ̂ɔd′lâa′ - náphaalaj′ King Rama II (1809-1824).

พระบาทสมเด็จพระนั่งเกล้าเจ้าอยู่หัว phrábàad′ɔ sɔ̌mdèd′-phránâŋ′klâaw′-câaw′jùuhǔa′ King Rama III (1824-1851).

พระบาทสมเด็จพระจอมเกล้าเจ้าอยู่หัว phrábàad′ɔ sɔ̌mdèd′-phrácɔɔm′klâaw′- câaw′jùuhǔa′ King Rama IV (1851-1868).

พระบาทสมเด็จพระจุลจอมเกล้าเจ้าอยู่หัว phrábàad′ɔ sɔ̌mdèd′-phrácunlacɔɔm′klâaw′-câawjùuɔ hǔa′ King Rama V, King Chulalongkɔn (Chula- longkorn)(1868-1910). See จุฬาลงกรณ.

พระบาทสมเด็จพระมงกุฎเกล้าเจ้าอยู่หัว phrábàad′ɔ sɔ̌mdèd′-phrámoŋkùd′klâaw′-câaw′jùuhǔa′ King Rama VI, King Wachirawut (Vajiravudh) (1910-1925).

พระบาทสมเด็จพระปกเกล้าเจ้าอยู่หัว phrábàad′ɔ sɔ̌mdèd′-phrápòg′klâaw′-câaw′jùuhǔa′ King Rama VII, King Prachathipok (1925-1934).

พระบาทสมเด็จพระปรเมนทรมหาอานันทมหิดล phráɔ bàad′sɔ̌mdèd′-phrápɔrameen′tharámahǎa′-ʔaaɔ nan′thámahìdon′ King Rama VIII, King Anan (Ananda)(1934-1946), popularly known as phráɔ câwjùuhǔa′-ʔaanan′thamahìdon′.

พระบาทสมเด็จพระเจ้าอยู่หัวภูมิพลอดุลเดช phráɔ bàad′sɔ̌mdèd′-phrácâwjùuhǔa′-phuumíɔ phon′-ʔadun′dèed′ King Rama IX, King Phumi- phon (Phumiphol), the present King of Thailand (1946-).

จัง caŋ′ sV colloq. very much, a great deal, ex- tremely. Probably ablaut variant of จริง.

  o ถูกจัง thùug′caŋ′ to be dirt cheap, extremely cheap.

  จริงจัง ciŋcaŋ′ V 1. to be serious, earnest. sV 2. seriously, earnestly. อย่าง-- really, se- riously, truthfully.

จังงัง caŋŋaŋ′ V to be stupefied, stunned, astounded.

จังหวะ (จังหวะ) caŋwà?′ (caŋwà?′) N a beat (as in music), timing interval, rhythm.

  ขัดจังหวะ khàd′caŋwà?′ V 1. to interrupt, inter-

vene; to break in in the middle of. 2. to be interspersed (as trees dotting the landscape).

จังหวัด caŋwàd′ N čhangwat, i.e. township (an ad- ministrative unit). NOTE (1) Thailand is divided into over seventy จังหวัด. These are subdivided first into อำเภอ "amphoe," then again into ตำบล "tambon," and occasionally still further into หมู่บ้าน "village." (2) In this dictionary names of จังหวัด are glossed: "township in..."

ต่างจังหวัด tàaŋ′caŋwàd′ out-of-town, provincial: "a different čhangwat." Normally used to refer to sections of a country outside of its capital.

จังหัน ๑ caŋhǎn′ N com. sacer. food, rice, meal, repast. Used with ฉัน ๓.

จังหัน ๒ caŋhǎn′. See กังหัน.

จัญไร canraj′ V to be bad, mean, evil, wicked.

จัด ๑ càd′ V 1. to arrange, prepare, put in order. 2. to manage.

  o จัดอาหาร càd′ʔaahǎan′ to prepare food.

  จัดการ càdkaan′ 1. to make arrangements, to take care of, manage (things), to deal with, handle (situations). 2. colloq. to fix, polish off, take care of. การ-- management, managing. คน-- person in charge (usually temporarily). ผู้-- manager.

  o จัดการกับลูก càdkaan′kalûug′ to attend to a child, take care of a child.

  o จัดการเรื่องการแย่งกันขึ้นลงรถประจำทาง càdɔ kaan′-rɤ̂aŋkaanjɛ̂ɛŋ′kan-khɤ̂n′loŋ′-ródpracamɔ thaaŋ′ to deal with the (problem of) scrambling to get on and off buses.

  o จัดการให้ลูกกินนม càdkaan′-hâjlûug′kinnom′ to arrange for the child to have his milk.

  o ผมจะต้องไปจัดการกับนายคนนั้นเสียที phǒm′- catɔ̂ŋpajcàdkaan′kanaajkhonnán′-síathii↓ I'll have to go and fix that guy.

จัด(...)ขึ้น càd(...)khɤ̂n′ to arrange, set up, establish.

จัดแจง càdcɛɛŋ′ V 1. to arrange, prepare. AA 2. make oneself ready to, prepare to (do some- thing).

จัดแจงจะ càdcɛɛŋcaɔ AA prepare to (do some- thing).

จัดตั้ง càdtâŋ′ V to set up, establish, form.

จัดสรร càdsǎn/ V to allocate, set aside for a specific purpose, apportion.

จัดสร้าง càdsâaŋ/ V to build, construct.

จัดหา càdhǎa/ V to secure, provide, (try to) find.

o จัดหาเงินให้ càdhǎa/-ŋən/hâj/ to provide money for (someone or some purpose).

รื้อจัด rýy/càd/ V to rearrange.

จัด ๒ càd/ V 1. to be hard, strong, intense, extreme. sV 2. extremely.

o เค็มจัด khemcàd/ V to be very salty.

o ปากจัด pàagcàd/ V to have a sharp tongue, be sharp-tongued, sarcastic, given to giving a tongue-lashing.

o ลมจัด lom/càd/ 1. to be windy. 2. the wind is strong.

o ลมพัดจัด lomphád/càd/ the wind is blowing hard.

จัดจ้าน càdcâan/ V to be sarcastic, sharp-tongued, outspoken, bold (in speech).

จัดเจน, เจนจัด(ต่อ,กับ,ใน) càdceen/, ceencàd/ (tɔ̀ɔ, kà, najɔ) V to be experienced, skillful, well-versed (in). ความ-- experience.

จัดวา càdtawaa/ Nm restricted four. See following examples. →Cf. สี่.

ชั้นจัดวา chán/càdtawaa/ the fourth (and lowest) rank in civil service.

นายพลจัดวา (นาย,คน) naajphon/càdtawaa/ (naaj/,khon/) N 1. brigadier general. T 2. Brigadier General --.

ไม้จัดวา májcàdtawaa/ N the fourth tonal marker (̌) of the Thai writing system. →Syn. ไม้ กากบาท. →Dist. เสียงจัดวา "rising tone."

จัตุ- Combining form meaning "four," used chiefly in the expression given below; elsewhere จตุ-.

จัตุรัส (รูป) càdturàd/ (rûub/) N square. →Also written จตุรัส.

จัน in ดอกจัน (ดอก) dɔ̀ɔgcan/ (dɔ̀ɔg/) N 1. asterisk. 2. asterisk-like mark on a cobra's hood.

จันทน์ can/ N sandalwood and other fragrant woods (Santalaceae).

จันทน์เทศ canthêed/ N nutmeg. ต้น-- (ต้น) nutmeg tree.

ต้นจันทน์ (ต้น) tôncan/ (tôn/) N 1. sandalwood tree. 2. nutmeg tree; short for ต้นจันทน์เทศ.

จันทบุรี can/tháburii/ pN Čhanthaburi (Chantaburi), a township in C Thailand, SE of Bangkok.

จันทร์ (ดวง) can/ (duaŋ/) N 1. the moon. 2. astron. satellite, moon. 3. short for วัน--. →Also 1,2. ดวง--, พระ--.

จันทรคราส (คราส) canthakhrâad, cantharakhrâad/ (khráŋ/) N lunar eclipse.

วันจันทร์ wancan/ N Monday. →The days of the week are listed under วัน.

จับ càb/ V 1. to grasp, catch, catch hold (of), seize, arrest; to cling, hold on (to). C 2. bunch (as of vermicelli (see ขนมจีน), or of noodle-like shreds of egg yolk (see ฝอยทอง)).

ไข้จับสั่น khâj/càbsàn/ N eleg. malaria, malarial fever. →Syn. ไข้ป่า colloq.

จับกลุ่ม càbklùm/ V to gather, assemble, crowd around, form a group.

จับกัน càb/kan/ to gather together, stick together, combine (intr.).

จับกุม càbkum/ V to arrest.

o ถูกจับกุม thùug/càbkum/ to be arrested, get arrested.

จับไข้ càbkhâj/ V to have a fever.

จับคู่ càbkhûu/ V to pair off, form a pair (with), take a partner.

จับเค้า càb/kháw/ V to get the idea; to detect.

จับจด càbcòd/ V to be desultory (in doing work).

จับจอง càbcɔɔŋ/ V to lay claim to (a piece of nonpossessed land), preempt.

จับจ่าย, --ใช้สอย càbcàaj/, càbcàaj/chájsɔ̌ɔj/ V elab. colloq. to spend, expend.

จับใจ càbcaj/ V to capture one's imagination; to captivate, impress.

o น่าจับใจ nâa/càbcaj/ V to be captivating, impressive.

จับชีพจร càb/chîibphacɔɔn/ to take the pulse.

จับต้อง càb/tɔ̂ŋ/ V to hold, to touch with the hands.

จับตัว càbtua/ V to catch, capture, arrest a person (as a criminal, a prisoner of war).

จับตา càbtaa/ V 1. to watch closely, keep an eye on. 2. to be eye-catching, striking.

o งามจับตา ŋaam/càbtaa/ to be strikingly beautiful.

o จับตาดูเขา càbtaa′-duu′kháw to keep an eye
　on him.

o จับตามอง càbtaa′mɔɔŋ′ to keep an eye on, to
　fix one's eyes on.

จับตาย càb′taaj′ V to take dead: "capture dead."
　→Ant. จับเป็น.

จับบทอีกแล้ว càbbòd′ʔìiglɛ́ɛw colloq. to bring
　up (that) subject again; to start up again.

จับปลา càbplaa′ V to fish. การ-- fishing.

จับเป็น càb′pen′ V to catch alive, take alive.
　→Ant. จับตาย.

จับมือ càbmyy′ V 1. to shake hands. 2. to hold
　hands, clasp hands. 3. to grasp (someone's)
　hands.

จับมือถือแขน càbmyy′-thy̌ykhɛ̌ɛn′ elab. colloq.
　1. to hold hands. 2. to hold by the arm.

จับไม้จับมือ càbmáaj′càbmyy′ V elab. colloq.
　1. to shake hands. 2. to hold hands.

จับรถ càbród′ to catch a bus or any other kind
　of vehicle. [tr. f. Eng.] →See ขึ้นรถ.

จับระบำ càb′rabam′ V to dance (in reference to
　a group performance on the stage).

จับสลาก càb′salàag′ to draw lots.

ลมจับ lomcàb′ colloq. to faint, collapse.

หมายจับ (ฉบับ) mǎajcàb′ (chabàb′) N warrant
　of arrest.

จั่ว (อัน) cùa′ (ʔan′) N gable.

จั๊วะ cúaʔ′ rM intensifier used with ขาว "white."

จา in พูดจา phûudcaa′ V colloq. to speak.

จา ๑ càa′ N 1. leader, head, chief. 2. petty offi-
　cer (navy). 3. noncommissioned officer (army,
　air force, police). T 4. title placed before the
　first name of a petty officer, noncommissioned
　officer.

จ่าจังหวัด càa′caŋwàd′ N lieutenant governor
　of a čhangwat.

จ่านายสิบ càa′naajsìb′ N 1. sergeant major.
　T 2. Sergeant Major --.

จ่าศาล (คน) càasǎan′ (khon′) N court clerk.

จ่าเอก càaʔèeg′ N 1. first petty officer. T 2.
　title placed before first name of same.

พันจ่า phancàa′ N 1. warrant officer. T 2.
　title placed before first name of same.

จา ๒ in จ่าหน้า càanâa′ V 1. to address, provide

with a heading. 2. to write down, put down (a
　name). 3. to be addressed to (followed by ถึง).

จ้า cáa′ V 1. to be bright, strong (of light, color,
　sound). rM 2. modifier used with แดด "sun-
　shine", สว่าง "bright", ส่อง "shine", ร้อง
　"cry", เหลือง "yellow". See also เจิดจ้า.

จ๋า ๑ cǎa′ Pt com. sp. to inf. or int. 1. particle
　placed after name, title, or kin term to address
　or to call the attention of someone. 2. Yes?
　(as a reply when called or spoken to). Used
　when sp. to servants, children, intimates.
　Similar to จ๊ะ, mng. 3, but tends to imply
　greater tenderness of feeling. →Cf. ครับ def.
　m. sp.. ขา def. w. sp.

แม่ผันจ๋า mɛ̂ɛphǎn′cǎa′↓ Phan! (calling her).

จ๋า ๒ cǎa′ rM intensifier meaning "very, ultra"
　used with ใหม่ "new," ฝรั่ง "occidental."

จาก ๑ (ต้น, ตับ) càag′ N 1. nipa palm (Nipa
　fruticans) (tôn′). 2. a thatch of nipa palm leaves
　(tàb′).

จาก ๒ (ไป, มา) càag′(paj′, maa′) V 1. to leave,
　depart, go away. Pp 2. from, since.

จากกัน càag′kan to separate (mutually), leave
　(one another).

จากนั้น càagnán′ after that.

ต่อจากนั้น tɔ̀ɔ′càagnán′ from then on.

ถัดจากนั้น thàd′càagnán′ next to that.

นอกจาก nɔ̀ɔg′càagɔ 1. besides, outside of, aside
　from. 2. except, other than, excluding, beyond.

o นอกจากว่า nɔ̀ɔgcàagwâa′ 1. unless. 2. pro-
　vided that.

เนื่องจาก nŷaŋ′càagɔ owing to, on account of,
　due to; owing to the fact that, because of the fact,
　since.

หลังจาก lǎŋ′càagɔ after.

จาง caaŋ′ V 1. to fade (away). 2. to be faded (of
　color), diluted.

เจือจาง cyacaaŋ′ V 1. to dilute. 2. to be dilute,
　diluted.

เจื่อนจาง cỳancaaŋ′ V 1. to become tasteless,
　insipid. 2. to become thin, diluted. 3. to
　vanish, fade, evaporate.

ทำให้(...)จาง tham′hâj(...)caaŋ′ to dilute
　(something), fade (something).

โรคโลหิตจาง rôog'-loohìd'caaŋ' N anemia.

จ้าง câaŋ' V to hire, employ.

เกณฑ์จ้าง keen'câaŋ' V to conscript for labor (with pay).

ค่าจ้าง khâacâaŋ' N wage, wages, pay.

นายจ้าง (คน) naajcâaŋ' (khon') N employer; boss.

รับจ้าง rábcâaŋ' V to take employment; to hire (oneself) out. คน-- employee.

เรือจ้าง (ลำ) ryacâaŋ' (lam') N sampan (taxi boat propelled by oar).

ลูกจ้าง (คน) lûugcâaŋ' (khon') N hireling, employee.

ว่าจ้าง wâacâaŋ' V to hire, employ, engage.

สินจ้าง sǐncâaŋ' N remuneration.

จาน ๑ (ใบ) caan' (baj') N plate, dish.

จานบิน (ลำ) caanbin' (lam') N flying saucer.

จานผี (ลำ) caanphǐi' (lam') idem.

จานรอง (ใบ) caanrɔɔŋ' (baj') N saucer.

จานเสียง (แผ่น) caansǐaŋ' (phèn') N phonograph record. More commonly แผ่นเสียง.

จาน ๒ in เจือจาน cyacaan' V to share.

จ้าน. See entries below.

จัดจ้าน càdcâan' V 1. to be sarcastic, sharp-tongued, outspoken, bold (in speech).

จุ้นจ้าน cûncâan' V 1. to be meddlesome. 2. to be obstructive.

จาม ๑ caam' V to sneeze.

จาม ๒ caam' V to strike with all one's force, esp. with a heavy weapon, ax.

จามจุรี in ต้นจามจุรี (ต้น) tôncaam'curii' (tôn') N 1. the East Indian walnut (Albizzia lebbeck). 2. the rain tree (Enterolobium saman). →Syn. ต้นก้ามปู.

จ่าย càaj' V 1. to spend, pay, disburse. 2. to distribute (e.g. electrical power). →Cf. จำ-หน่าย.

จับจ่าย, --ใช้สอย càbcàaj', càbcàaj'chájsɔɔj' V elab. colloq. to spend, expend.

จ่ายเงิน càajŋɤn' 1. to pay. 2. to spend money.

จ่ายตลาด càajtalàad' V to do one's daily shopping, buy the groceries.

ใช้จ่าย chájcàaj' V to spend, expend.

o ค่าใช้จ่าย khâa'chájcàaj' N expenses, expend-

itures.

รายจ่าย raajcàaj' N expenditures, expenses.

จาร-. Bound form meaning "spy."

จารกรรม caarakam' N eleg. espionage, spying. →Also การ--

จารชน (คน) caarachon' (khon') N eleg. secret agent, spy, intelligence officer.

จาระไน caaranaj' V to explain in full detail, elucidate.

จาระบี caarabii' N a kind of heavy lubricating grease.

จาระเม็ด. See จะละเม็ด.

จาริก caa'ríg' V to travel, wander (often in reference to the Buddha).

จารีต (อย่าง) caa'rîid' (jàaŋ') N custom, common practice, convention, tradition.

จารีตประเพณี (อย่าง) caa'rîid'praphee'nii' (jàaŋ') N custom, tradition.

จารึก caa'rýg' V 1. to engrave (on stone, metal or wood). 2. to write (on anything).

จาละเม็ด. See จะละเม็ด.

จ้าละหวั่น câalawàn' sV in a disorderly manner, chaotically.

จ้าว. See เจ้า ๑. In many instances เจ้า is pronounced câaw' and is therefore sometimes spelled จ้าว.

จำ cam' V 1. to confine, contain, retain. 2. to remember; to memorize. AA 3. have to, be compelled to. การ-- remembering. ความ-- memory. →Cf. 1. จำนำ.

จดจำ còdcam' V to retain, fix in one's mind.

จองจำ cɔɔŋcam' V to imprison (with fetters).

จำขึ้นใจ cam'khŷncaj' to learn by heart.

จำคุก camkhúg' V to jail, imprison.

จำจะต้อง cam'catɔ̂ŋ' AA will have to, (it) will be necessary to.

จำใจ camcaj' AA force (oneself to do something), be forced (to do something against one's will).

จำได้ camdâaj' V to remember, recognize, be able to recall.

o จำได้ขึ้นใจ camdâaj'khŷncaj' 1. to learn by heart. 2. to remember vividly.

จำต้อง cam'tɔ̂ŋⵀ AA have to, be needed to,

be compelled to.

จำเป็น campen/ V to be necessary. ความ-- necessity (e.g. force of circumstances), necessitation. →Dist. ความ-- f. ของ-- below.

o ของจำเป็น (สิ่ง,อย่าง) khɔ̌ɔŋcampen/ (sìŋ/, jàaŋ/) N necessities.

o จำเป็นต้อง campen/tɔ̂ŋ AA be forced to, compelled to; must, have to; it is necessary to.

จำไว้ (1, 2) cam/wáj/; (3) cam/wáj↓ V 1. to confine, lock up, put away. 2. to fix in one's mind. 3. Remember that!

ทรงจำ soŋcam/ V eleg. to remember, have memory of, esp. in ความ-- a memory, memories.

ท่องจำ thɔ̂ŋcam/ V to memorize, learn by rote.

ทั้งจำทั้งปรับ tháŋcam/tháŋpràb/ both fine and imprisonment: "both to imprison and to fine."

มัดจำ (จำนวน) mádcam/ (camnuan/) N deposit (given as security, as down payment).

เรือนจำ (แห่ง) ryancam/ (hὲŋ/) N jail, prison.

จ้ำ câm/ V slang 1. to hurry. sV 2. hurriedly, repeatedly, in rapid succession.

o เดินจ้ำ dəən/câm/ to walk hurriedly.

จำกัด camkàd/ V 1. to limit, define; to be limited, defined. 2. Ltd.

ข้อจำกัด (ข้อ) khɔ̂ɔcamkàd/ (khɔ̂ɔ/) N restriction, limitation.

จำกัดความ camkàd/khwaam/ V to define (the sense), give a definition.

o คำจำกัดความ (ประการ,อย่าง) kham/-camɔ kàd/khwaam/ (prakaan/, jàaŋ/) N the definition (of a word).

จำเจ camcee/ V 1. to be repetitious, tiresome, monotonous. sV 2. repeatedly, repetitiously.

จ้ำ ๆ เจ ๆ camcam/ceecee/ sV repeatedly.

จำเดิม camdəəm/ from the beginning, originally. →Cf. เดิม.

จำเดิมแต่ camdəəm/-tὲὲ since, since the time (of).

o จำเดิมแต่เกิดมา camdəəm/-tὲὲkə̀əd/maa/ since birth.

จำนง camnoŋ/ V to desire, wish. ความ-- desire, wish, intention.

เจตจำนง cèed/camnoŋ/ N aim, purpose, intention, determination.

จำนน camnon/ V to be defeated. [conv.f. จน ๑]

ยอมจำนน jɔɔm/camnon/ V to surrender, give in, admit defeat.

จำนวน camnuan/ C quantity, number, amount.

จำนวนร้อยละ (. . .) (1) camnuan/-rɔ́ɔj/lá?/; (2) camnuan/-rɔ́ɔj/laɔ... N 1. percentage. 2. (so and so much) percent.

o จำนวนร้อยละสิบ camnuan/-rɔ́ɔj/lasìb/ ten percent.

เป็นจำนวน pencamnuan/ in the amount (of), in amount.

ยอดจำนวน jɔ̂ɔd/camnuan/ N the total number; the total.

จำนอง camnɔɔŋ/ V to mortgage. การ-- mortgage. ผู้-- mortgagor.

ผู้รับจำนอง (คน) phûuráb/camnɔɔŋ/ (khon/) N mortgagee.

จำนำ camnam/ V 1. to pawn. 2. to mortgage. [conv.f. จำ]

เจ้าจำนำ (เจ้า,คน,ราย) câwcamnam/ N 1. establishment which one regularly patronizes or sells to (câw/). 2. steady customer (an individual)(khon/, raaj/).

ตัวจำนำ (คน) tuacamnam/ (khon/) N hostage.

โรงจำนำ, โรงรับจำนำ (โรง) rooŋ/camnam/, rooŋráb/camnam/ (rooŋ/) N pawnshop.

จำแนก camnɛ̂ɛg/ V eleg. 1. to divide, separate. 2. to be divided, separated. [conv.f. แจก] →Syn. แยก com.

จำพวก camphûag/ C group, type, species (as of animals, plants). →Cf. พวก.

จำเพาะ camphɔ́?/ V to be special, particular, specific. →Cf. เฉพาะ.

จำม่ำ câmmâm/ rM intens. used with อ้วน "fat."

จำเริญ camrəən/ V to progress, develop, grow, thrive, prosper. [conv.f. เจริญ]

จำลอง camlɔɔŋ/ V to imitate, copy, reproduce, model.

รูปจำลอง (รูป) rûubcamlɔɔŋ/ (rûub/) N miniature, scale model.

จำเลย (คน,ฝ่าย) camləəj/ (khon/, fàaj/) N 1. defendant. 2. the accused.

จำหน่าย camnàaj/ V eleg. 1. to sell, be sold.

2. to distribute. [conv.f. จ่าย] →Syn. 1. ขาย
com.

พิมพ์(...)จำหน่าย phim′(...)camnàaj′ V to
publish (for sale). ผู้-- publisher.

จำหลัก camlàg′ V to carve (wood, stone), chase
(metal). →Cf. ฉลัก, สลัก.

จำอวด (คณะ) camˀùad′ (khanáˀ′) N a comical
show, a farce.

ตัวจำอวด (ตัว) tuacamˀùad′ (tua′) N comical
actor, buffoon.

จิก ๑ cìg′ V 1. to peck (of a bird). 2. to nose-dive.
3. slang to snatch, swipe.

จิก ๒. See จุกจิก.

จิ้งจก (ตัว) cîŋcòg′ (tua′) N house lizard.

จิ้งจอก cîŋcɔɔg′. See entries below.

สุนัขจิ้งจอก (ตัว) sunág′cîŋcɔɔg′(tua′) N eleg.
fox.

หมาจิ้งจอก (ตัว) mǎacîŋcɔɔg′ (tua′) N com.
fox, jackal.

จิงโจ้ (ตัว) ciŋcôo′ (tua′) N kangaroo.

จิ้งหรีด (ตัว) cîŋrìid′ (tua′) N cricket.

จิต (จิต) cìd′, cìdtaɔ, cìdɔ N mind, heart, soul,
spirit. →Also spelled จิตต์. →Syn. See ใจ.

จิตใจ cìdcaj′ N mind; mind and spirit, heart
and soul; feeling, sentiment.

o ด้วยจิตใจชื่นบาน dûajcìdcaj′-chŷyn′baan′ with
cheery heart, feelings of gladness.

จิตแพทย์ (นาย,คน) cìdtaphɛ̂ɛd′ (naaj′, khon′)
N tech. psychiatrist.

จิตวิทยา cìdtawídthajaa′ N psychology.

ดวงจิต (ดวง) duaŋcìd′ (duaŋ′) N mind, soul.

ทางจิต thaaŋcìd′ mental; mentally.

มิตรจิต mídtracìd′ N friendliness.

เมตตาจิต mêedtaacìd′ N kindheartedness.

ไมตรีจิต majtriicìd′ N spirit of friendship.

โรคจิต (ชนิด) rôogcìd′ (chaníd′) N mental
disease.

สองจิตสองใจ sɔ̌ɔŋcìd′sɔ̌ɔŋcaj′ elab. colloq.
to be of two minds (about something), be undecided; to hesitate.

จิตต์. See จิต.

จิตร- cìdtraɔ, cìdtaɔ. Combining form referring
to "painting, drawing."

จิตรกร (คน) cìdtrakɔɔn′, cìdtakɔɔn′ N eleg.

artist, painter.

จิตรกรรม cìdtrakam′, cìdtakam′ N eleg. 1.
(the act, the art of) painting, drawing. 2. a
painting, a drawing.

จินต- cin′taɔ. Combining form referring to "thinking, meditation."

จินตกวี (คน) cin′takawii′ (khon′) N poet.

จินตนาการ cin′tanaa′kaan′ N 1. thinking, meditation. V 2. to think, meditate.

จิบ cìb′ V to sip, take a little bit at a time.

จิปาถะ cìpaa′thàˀ′ sundry, of all kinds.

o ของจิปาถะ khɔ̌ɔŋ′cìpaa′thàˀ′ sundries, things
of all kinds.

จิ้ม cîm′ V 1. to dip into. 2. to spear (for the
purpose of picking up, as with a fork, a toothpick).
→Cf. จุ่ม.

o เอากล้วยจิ้มน้ำตาล ˀawklûaj′-cîm′námtaan′↓
Dip the banana into the sugar: "Take the banana
(and) dip into sugar."

จิ้มฟัน cîmfan′ to pick the teeth.

o ไม้จิ้มฟัน (อัน) májcîmfan′ (ˀan′) N toothpick.

น้ำจิ้ม námcîm′ N 1. sauce, dip (i.e. a sauce or
preparation into which food is dipped).

จิ้มลิ้ม cîmlím′ V to be lovely, attractive.

จิ๋ว cǐw′ V to be tiny.

รุ่นจิ๋ว rûncǐw′ in the class of small things, of
the tiny variety, midget.

เล็กจิ๋ว légcǐw′ to be extremely tiny.

จี. cii′ the English letter "G." [f. Eng.] →Also ยี.

จี่ in รู้จักมักจี่ rúucàg′mágcìi′ V elab. colloq.
to be acquainted (with), know personally.

จี้ ๑ cîi′ V 1. to poke, tickle. 2. to point at. 3. to
point out, emphasize (by repeatedly pointing
out). 4. to prod, exhort. 5. slang to hold up
(rob).

o ถูกจี้ thùugcîi′ to get held up, be the victim of
a holdup.

จี้ไช cîi′chaj′ V slang to prod (figuratively),
keep insisting.

จี้เล่น cîi′sên′ V slang to make someone laugh;
to provoke laughter.

จี้(ให้)ถูกเล่น cîi′-hâjthùug′sên′, cîi′-thùug′sên′
fig., colloq. to hit the right spot, touch the
right chord (for successfully evoking a desired

response).

นักจี้ (คน) nágcîi/ (khon/) N slang a hold up
man.

บ้าจี้ bâacîi/ V to be extremely ticklish.

จี้ ๒ (อัน) cîi/ (?an/) N pendant of a necklace.

จี่ cîi/ rM intensifier used with ด่วน "urgent,"
ร้อน "hot (in temperature)," เผ็ด "hot (in
taste)," เร็ว "fast," วิ่ง "run."

จี๊ด cíid/ rM intensifier used with เปรี้ยว "sour."

จีน cìin/ N eleg. China, the Chinese. →Syn.
เจ๊ก com.

ขนมจีน (จับ,หัว) khanŏmciin/ (càb/, hŭa/) N
Thai vermicelli, which comes in bunches.

คนจีน (คน) khonciin/ (khon/) N eleg. a
Chinese.

จีนคณะชาติ ciin/-khaná?/châad/ N Chinese
Nationalist.

จีนคอมมิวนิสต์ ciin/khɔmmiwnís/, -níd/ N 1.
Communist China. 2. Chinese Communist(s).

จีนแดง ciindɛɛŋ/ N 1. Red China. 2. the
Chinese Red(s), the Red Chinese.

ชาวจีน (คน) chaawciin/ (khon/) N a Chinese,
the Chinese.

เด็กเจ๊กเด็กจีน (คน) dègcég/dègciin/ (khon/)
N elab. colloq. Chinese children.

ประเทศจีน (ประเทศ) pratheedciin/ (pratheed/)
N eleg. China. →Syn. เมืองจีน com.

ภาษาจีน (ภาษา) phaasǎaciin/ (phaasǎa/) N
Chinese (the language).

เมืองจีน (เมือง,แห่ง) myaŋciin/ N com. 1.
China (myaŋ/). 2. Chinatown (as a part of
another city)(hὲŋ/). →Syn. 1. ประเทศจีน
eleg.

จีบ cìib/ N 1. pleat. V 2. to pleat, gather in folds.
3. slang to try to gain the favor of, to woo.

จีบเกล็ด cìib/klèd/ V sew. to make darts.

จีรัง ciiraŋ/ V eleg. to last long, endure.

จีวร (ผืน) ciiwɔɔn/ (phŭyn/) N the robe of a
Buddhist priest.

จึง cyŋ/ AA eleg. so, then, as a consequence.
→Syn. ถึง colloq.

o อากาศดีเขาจึงอยากเดินเล่น ?aakàad/dii/→
kháwcyŋjàag/dəənlên/↓ The weather's nice,
so he wants to go for a walk.

จึงจะ cyŋcaɔ AA eleg. so that, in order to.
→Syn. ถึงจะ colloq.

o คุณต้องอ่านจึงจะรู้ khuntɔ̂ŋ?àan/→cyŋcarúu/↓
You have to read it, so you will know.

จืด cὺyd/ V 1. to be fresh (of water). 2. to be un-
seasoned, insipid, flat in taste. คน-- idiom.
a passive, unimposing, unassuming person.

แกงจืด kɛɛŋcὺyd/ N mildly seasoned soup.

จืดตา cὺyd/taa/ V to be colorless, dull, dull-
looking, drab, uninteresting.

จืดไป (1) cὺyd/paj/; (2) cὺyd/paj↓ V 1. to fade
away. 2. (it's) too insipid!

ใจจืด cajcὺyd/ V to be unsympathetic, unresponsive, unthoughtful.

ดินจืด dincὺyd/ N depleted soil.

น้ำจืด námcὺyd/ N fresh water. →Opp. น้ำเค็ม.

จุ cù?/ V 1. to have (such and such) a capacity,
hold (such and such an amount). 2. to be ample.
sV 3. amply, in large amounts. ความ-- capacity. →Cf. บรรจุ,ประจุ.

o กินจุ kincù?/ to eat heartily. คน-- a hearty
eater, big eater.

จุใจ cù?/caj/ to be satisfying. →Syn. สมใจ.

จุ, จุย, จุ๊ย cú?/. Variant spellings for an exclamation normally pronounced as a click, though a
spelling pronunciation is often used when reading
from a text.

จุ ๆ cú?cú?/ "tut, tut!", "tch, tch!" (the suction
click). Frequently used as a mild rebuke, especially to enjoin silence; also used to indicate
that one is moved, affected.

จุปาก cú?pàag/ V to tut, go "tch, tch!"

จุก (อัน,จุก) cùg/ (?an/, cùg/) N 1. stopper (of
bottle). 2. topknot; short for หัวจุก (see below).
3. colicky pain. V 4. to stop up, shut. 5. to
suffer from colic.

จุกขวด (จุก) cùgkhùad/ (cùg/) N stopper (for
bottle).

จุกไม้ก๊อก (จุก) cùg/májkɔ́g/ (cùg/) N cork
(for bottle).

หัวจุก (อัน,จุก) hŭacùg/ (?an/, cùg/) N 1. topknot.
2. certain things or parts resembling a topknot
in form or in location, e.g. the tip of an onion
bulb, the knob on a jar cover.

จุกจิก cùgcìg′ V 1. to be petty, trifling. 2. to annoy, bother (pettily, as children do).

ของจุกจิก (สิ่ง,อย่าง) khɔ̌ɔŋ′cùgcìg′ (sìŋ′, jàaŋ′) N knickknacks, little things.

จู้จี้จุกจิก cûucîi′cùgcìg′ V to be fussy, unreasonably particular.

เข้าขี้จุกจิก sâwsîi′cùgcìg′ V to wheedle, coax repeatedly, keep harping on something, nag.

เรื่องจุกจิก rŷaŋ′cùgcìg′ N trivial matter, petty matter, trifle.

จุด ๑ (จุด) cùd′ (cùd′) N 1. spot, speck, dot, point. 2. the decimal point, the point used to separate hours and minutes in expressions of time. 3. a point on a scale, in a continuum. V 4. to dot. →Also 4. ใส่จุด.

จุดจบ cùdcòb′ N the end, the ending-point.

จุดเดือด cùddỳad′ N boiling point.

จุดประสงค์ (ประการ,อย่าง) cùd′prasǒŋ′ (prackaan′, jàaŋ′) N purpose, goal.

จุดรวม (แห่ง,จุด) cùdruam′ (hὲŋ′, cùd′) N center, hub (figurative sense).

จุดลูกน้ำ cùd′lûugnáam′ N colloq. the comma.

จุดศูนย์กลาง (แห่ง) cùd′sǔunklaaŋ′ (hὲŋ′) N the center, center point.

จุดสำคัญ cùd′sǎmkhan′ 1. important point. 2. strategic position.

จุดหมาย (ที่,แห่ง,อัน,จุด) cùdmǎaj′ (thîi′, hὲŋ′, ʔan′, cùd′) N destination, goal, aim, end.

เป็นจุด ๆ pencùdcùd′ 1. to be dotted, full of dots. 2. point by point (with เป็น as sec. vb.).

จุด ๒ cùd′ V to light, kindle, ignite. →Syn. ตาม ๒.

จุดบุหรี่ cùd′burìi′ V to light a cigarette.

o ที่จุดบุหรี่ (อัน) thîicùd′burìi′ (ʔan′) N cigarette lighter.

จุดไฟ cùdfaj′ to light a fire, set afire.

o จุดไฟไม่ติด cùdfaj′mâjtìd′ 1. to be nonignitable (e.g. wet wood). 2. to be unable to light a fire.

จุน cun′ V to support, prop up. Chiefly in fol. cpd.

ค้ำจุน khámcun′ V to support, prop up.

จุนจ้าน cûncâan′ V 1. to be meddlesome. 2. to be obstructive.

จุ่ม cùm′ V to dip into, immerse (briefly) in (a liquid). →Cf. จิ้ม.

จุมพิต cumphíd′ V lit., eleg. to kiss. →Syn. จูบ com.

จุ๊ย. See จุ.

จุล-. Bound form meaning "small, little." Also used to translate "micro-."

จุลชีพ (ตัว) cunlachîib′ (tua′) N microbe. [tr. f. Eur.]

จุลทรรศน์, จุลทัศน์ cunlathád′. See entries below.

o กล้องจุลทัศน์ (กล้อง) klɔ̂ŋ′cunlathád′ (klɔ̂ŋ′) N microscope.

o ขนาดจุลทัศน์ khanàad′cunlathád′ microscopic size; microscopic.

จุลศักราช cun′lasàgkaràad′ N the Thai minor era, beginning March 21, 638 A.D. →Abbrev. จ.ศ.

จุลอินทรีย์ (ตัว) cun′laʔinsii′ (tua′) N microorganism. [tr. f. Eur.]

จุลินทรีย์ (ตัว) culin′sii′ (tua′) N microorganism. [tr. f. Eur.]

จุฬา in ว่าวจุฬา (ตัว) wâwculaa′ (tua′) N starshaped kite (called the male). →Cf. ว่าวปักเป้า. →Cf. also จุฬา in the next two entries.

จุฬาฯ culaa′. Short for จุฬาลงกรณ์มหาวิทยาลัย. Sometimes also written จุฬา.

จุฬาลงกรณ์ culaaloŋkɔɔn′ pN 1. Chulalongkɔn, pre-coronation name of King Rama V of the present Chakri dynasty. →See จักรี. 2. Short for entry below.

จุฬาลงกรณ์มหาวิทยาลัย culaaloŋkɔɔn′mahǎawídthajaalaj′ pN Chulalongkɔn University.

จู่ cùu′ V to move suddenly (taking by surprise).

o จู่เข้าไป cùu′khâwpaj′ to rush in, enter precipitately (taking by surprise).

จู่ ๆ cùucùu′ sV suddenly, unexpectedly, all of a sudden.

จู่โจม cùucoom′ V to attack suddenly, by surprise.

จูง cuuŋ′ V to lead (by the hand).

จูงใจ cuuŋcaj′ V to influence (the mind or thinking), induce, persuade.

จูงมือ cuuŋmyy′ V to lead by the hand.

ชักจูง chágcuuŋ′ V to urge, persuade, induce, incite.

จู้จี้, --จุกจิก cûucîi′, cûucîi′cùgcìg′ V to be fussy, unreasonably particular.

จูบ cùub′ V com. to kiss. →Syn. จุมพิต eleg.

กอดจูบลูบคลำ kɔ̀ɔd/cùub/-lûub/khlam/ V
colloq. to pet, to neck.

เจ. cee/ the English letter "J." [f. Eng.]

เจ๊ก (คน) cég/*(khon/) N com. a Chinese.
[f. Chin.] →Syn. จีน eleg.

เจ๊กตื่นไฟ cég/tỳynfaj/ "a Chinese excited over
a fire," a simile used to describe an easily
excitable person.

เด็กเจ๊กเด็กจีน (คน) dègcég/dègciin/ (khon/)
N elab. colloq. Chinese children.

รถเจ๊ก (คัน) ródcég/ (khan/) N rickshaw.

เจ๋ง céŋ/* V slang to lose. [f. Chin.]

เจ็ด cèd/ Nm seven.

เจ็ดสิบ cèd/sìb/ Nm seventy.

ชั่วเจ็ดที ดีเจ็ดหน chûa/cèdthii→dii/cèdhǒn/ good
luck is intermingled with bad: "bad for seven
times, good for seven times."

สิบเจ็ด sìbcèd/ Nm seventeen.

เจดีย์ (องค์) ceedii/ (ʔoŋ/) N pagoda, stupa, a
memorial edifice with or without relics preserved inside. →Also พระ-- .

เจต- . Bound form meaning "mind, thought."

เจตจำนง cèed/camnoŋ/ N eleg. aim, purpose,
intention, determination.

เจตนา cèed/tanaa/ N eleg. 1. intention, will,
purpose, design. V 2. to intend to, mean (to).

o เขาไม่มีเจตนาที่จะทำร้ายคุณ kháwmâjmiiceed/ɔ
tanaa/-thîicathamráaj/khun/ He doesn't mean
to do you any harm.

เจตนารมณ์ cèed/tanaarom/ N eleg. intention,
purpose, design.

เจน ๑ (ต่อ,กับ,ใน) ceen/(tɔ̀ɔɔ, kaɔ, najɔ) V to
be used (to), experienced (in).

เจนจัด,จัดเจน(ต่อ,กับ,ใน) ceencàd/, càdceen/ɔ
(tɔ̀ɔɔ, kaɔ, najɔ) V to be experienced, skillful,
well-versed (in). ความ-- experience.

เจน ๒ in ชัดเจน chádceen/ V to be plain, clear,
distinct, explicit.

เจนีวา,เจนิวา ceeniiwaa/, ceeniwaa/, ceeni(i)wâa/
pN Geneva. [f. Eng.]

เจ็บ cèb/ V 1. to be sick, hurt, be in pain. 2. to
hurt, be sore, painful. คน-- patient. ความ--
pain. →Syn. ปวด .

ไข้เจ็บ khâj/cèb/ N sickness. Chiefly in com-

pounds. See cross reference.

เจ็บไข้,--ได้ป่วย cèbkhâj/, cèbkhâj/dâjpùaj/ V
elab. eleg. to get sick, be sick. ความ--
sickness.

เจ็บใจ cèbcaj/ V to feel hurt, have one's feelings
hurt. ความ-- resentment, a sense of injury
or insult.

เจ็บช้ำ,--น้ำใจ cèbchám/, cèbchám/námcaj/ V
elab. colloq. to feel hurt, have one's feelings
hurt.

เจ็บตจิด ๆ cèb/-taŋìd/taŋìd/ hurting a little.

เจ็บตัว cèbtua/ to hurt oneself, get hurt.

เจ็บปวด cèbpùad/ V 1. to be painful, to hurt. 2.
to be in pain. ความ-- pain, painfulness.

เจ็บป่วย,ป่วยเจ็บ cèbpùaj/, pùajcèb/ V to be sick,
ill. การ-- sickness, illness. ความ-- sickness, illness. ผู้-- a patient.

บาดเจ็บ bàadcèb/ V 1. to get hurt, be injured,
wounded. N 2. injury, wound.

โรคภัยไข้เจ็บ (อย่าง,ชนิด) rôogphaj/khâjcèb/
(jàaŋ/, chaníd/) N elab. colloq. disease,
sickness.

ล้มเจ็บ lómcèb/ V to fall sick.

หายเจ็บ hǎajcèb/ V to recover, get well.

เจรจา(กับ) ceenracaa/, ceeracaa/(kaɔ) V eleg.
to discuss, talk over, confer (particularly in
reference to business or technical matters),
negotiate. การ-- talk, conference; negotiation.

เจรจาหว่านล้อม ceeracaa/wàanlɔ́ɔm/ to talk
someone into doing or accepting something in
a roundabout way.

เจริญ carəən/ V 1. to progress, advance, develop,
grow, thrive, prosper. 2. fig. to pursue, cultivate, promote (in certain expressions only).
ความ-- progress, advancement; civilization.
→Cf. จำเริญ. →Syn. 1. เฟื่อง,รุ่งเรือง com.,
วัฒนา eleg.

เจริญก้าวหน้า carəən/kâawnâa/ V to progress.

เจริญงอกงาม carəən/ŋɔ̀ɔgŋaam/ V to thrive,
grow well (of plants).

เจริญตาเจริญใจ carəən/taa/-carəən/caj/ V elab.
colloq. to be esthetically pleasing.

เจริญเติบโต carəən/tə̀əbtoo/ V to grow, progress.
ความ-- the progress and growth.

เจริญพระพุทธมนต์ carəən/phráphúd/thamon/ V
    s a c e r. (a priest) to chant, recite sacred
    verses.

เจริญพระราชไมตรี(กับ) carəən/phráràadchamajɔ
    trii/(kaɔ) V (a kingdom) to maintain diplo-
    matic relations, cultivate friendly relations
    (with).

เจริญรอย carəən/rɔɔj/ f i g. to follow. The noun
    in this construction may be expanded by other
    nouns, e.g. เจริญรอยพระยุคลบาท carəən/
    rɔɔj/-phrájúkhon/bàad/ V r o y. (a commoner)
    to follow in the king's footsteps.

เจริญรุ่งเรือง carəən/rûŋryaŋ/ V to prosper,
    be civilized. ความ-- prosperity and civiliza-
    tion.

เจริญวัย carəən/waj/ V to grow up.

เจริญอาหาร carəən/ʔaahǎan/ V e l e g. 1. to
    have a great appetite. 2. (an appetizer, apéritif,
    etc.) to stimulate the appetite.

เจอ cəə/ V to meet, encounter. →Cf. เจอะ.

เจ่อ cə̀ə/ V to swell, be swollen (esp. lips or mouth).

เจอ in เพ้อเจอ phə́əcəə/ V to ramble, speak
    without making much sense.

เจ๋อ cə̌ə/ V c o l l o q. to intrude, butt in.

เจอะ cə̀ʔ/ V to meet, encounter. →Cf. เจอ.

เจ้า ๑ (องค์,คน) câaw/, câwɔ, câawɔ N 1. prince,
    ruler, holy being (ʔoŋ/). 2. s l a n g guy, fellow,
    gal (khon/). C 3. clf. for a selling enterprise as
    identified with the occupation of its owner, as
    in Eng. "the baker (or the baker's)." T 4. title
    placed before the first name of a child, or of
    an inferior.

กรมเจ้าท่า krom/câwthâa/ Harbor Department.

เจ้ากรม (คน) câwkrom/ (khon/) N the head of
    a department.

เจ้ากระทรวง (คน) câawkrasuaŋ/ (khon/) N
    minister, head of a ministry.

เจ้าของ (คน) câwkhɔ̌ɔŋ/ (khon/) N owner, pro-
    prietor.

o เจ้าของเดิม câwkhɔ̌ɔŋ/dəəm/ the original
    owner.

o เจ้าของบ้าน (คน) câwkhɔ̌ɔŋ/bâan/ (khon/) N
    landlord, landlady, house-owner; host, hostess.

o เจ้าของร้าน (คน) câwkhɔ̌ɔŋ/ráan/ (khon/) N

storekeeper, proprietor of a store.

เจ้าคณะ (รูป) câawkhaná?/ (rûub/) N s a c e r.
    a Buddhist priest who is head of all priests in
    a certain defined area (e.g. in a čhangwat).

เจ้าคุณ câwkhun/ P 1. you, he, him (sp. to or of a
    man in the conferred ranks of พระยา and
    เจ้าพระยา). 2. you, she, her (sp. to or of high-
    ranking ladies of the court). T 3. title placed
    before the first names of persons described in
    1 and 2. →See คุณหญิง for wife of พระยา.

เจ้าจอม câwcɔɔm/ N 1. a lesser concubine of
    the king. 2. a rank for lesser concubines. T
    3. title placed in front of the first name of a
    lesser concubine. →See สนม.

เจ้าจอมเชื่อ câwcɔɔm/sə̂ə/ c o l l o q. A big fool!

เจ้าจำนำ (เจ้า,คน,ราย) câwcamnam/ N 1.
    an establishment which one regularly patronizes
    or sells to (câw/). 2. steady customer (an indi-
    vidual) (khon/, raaj/).

เจ้าชาย (องค์) câwchaaj/ (ʔoŋ/) N prince.

เจ้าตัว câwtua/ N the person in question. Often
    rendered by "he himself," "she herself," etc.

เจ้านาย (องค์,คน,ท่าน) câawnaaj/ N 1. royal
    personage, royalty, member of the royal family
    (ʔoŋ/). 2. c o l l o q. boss, chief (khon/, thân/).
    →D i s t. ขุนนาง.

เจ้าบ่าว (คน) câwbàaw/ (khon/) N bridegroom.

เจ้าป่า (องค์) câawpàa/ (ʔoŋ/) N spirit guardian
    of a forest.

เจ้าพนักงาน (คน,นาย) câwphanágŋaan/ (khon/,
    naaj/) N official, person in charge.

เจ้าพระยา (ท่าน,คน) câwphrajaa/ (thân/, khon/)
    N 1. term for the highest rank of conferred
    nobility. →See ขุนนาง. T 2. title placed in
    front of the honorific name conferred with the
    rank. →See เจ้าคุณ for term of address.

o แม่น้ำเจ้าพระยา mɛ̂ɛnáamcâwphrajaa/ pN the
    Čhaophraya (Chao Phya) R., at whose mouth
    Bangkok is situated. NOTE. Generally called
    "Menam" (from the Thai word for "river") in
    books in English about Thailand.

เจ้าฟ้า,สมเด็จ-- (องค์) câawfáa/, câwfáa/, sɔ̌mɔ
    dèd/câwfáa/ (ʔoŋ/) N prince of the highest rank,
    i.e. the son of the king born by the queen.

T 2. Prince --. →Cf. พระองค์เจ้า.

o เจ้าฟ้าหญิง (องค์) câwfáajǐŋ/ (ʔoŋ/) N 1. princess of the highest rank, i.e. daughter of the king born by the queen. T 2. Princess --.

เจ้าภาพ (คน) câwphâab/ (khon/) N host, hostess.

เจ้ามือ (คน) câwmyy/ (khon/) N 1. the dealer (in card games), the banker (in gambling games). 2. the one who treats.

เจ้าเมือง (คน,องค์) câwmyaŋ/ (khon/,ʔoŋ/) N ruler of a city or country (ʔoŋ/, if royal).

เจ้าสาว (คน) câwsǎaw/ (khon/) N bride.

เจ้าหญิง (องค์) câwjǐŋ/ (ʔoŋ/) N 1. princess. Used of foreign princesses, or of any Thai princess down to the level of หม่อมเจ้า. T 2. Princess --. Used with the names of foreign princesses.

เจ้าหน้าที่ (คน,นาย) câwnâathîi/ (khon/, naaj/) N official, officer, authorized person, staff member.

o เจ้าหน้าที่ตำรวจ câwnâathîi/tamrùad/ N police officer, constable; the police.

o เจ้าหน้าที่เทศบาล câwnâathîi/thêedsabaan/ N municipal officers, city officials.

เจ้าหนี้ (คน) câwnîi/ (khon/) N creditor.

เจ้าหล่อน câwlɔ̀n/ P she, her.

เจ้าอาวาส (องค์) câaw/ʔaawâad/ (ʔoŋ/) N abbot of a Buddhist monastery.

เทพเจ้า (องค์) thêebphacâaw/ (ʔoŋ/) N a god, a deity.

พระเจ้า (องค์) phrácâaw/, phrácâwɔ (ʔoŋ/) N 1. God (esp. of a monotheistic religion). 2. ruler, king, lord, god; used in certain compounds only. T 3. King --. 4. an element occurring in various royal and religious titles. →See cross reference.

พระองค์เจ้า (องค์) phrá/ʔoŋ/câaw/ (ʔoŋ/) N 1. roy. prince, a son of the king born by a lesser concubine. T 2. Prince --. →Cf. เจ้าฟ้า.

หม่อมเจ้า (องค์) mɔ̀mcâaw/ (ʔoŋ/) N 1. a prince or princess in the grandchild generation of royal descent, or one who is treated as such. T 2. Prince --, Princess --. →Abbrev. ม.จ.

เจ้า ๒ câw/ P sp. to inf. you. Paired with ข้า ๒

"I, me." →Comp. คุณ ๒.

พวกเจ้า phûagcâw/ you people, you folks (superior speaking to group or crowd).

เจ้า- ๓. Bound stem meaning "characterized by, given to." Placed before verbs or nouns to form verb derivatives. →Cf. ขี้- ๒,ช่าง ๒.

เจ้ากรรม câwkam/ V 1. to be unlucky, unfortunate. sV 2. darned. E 3. Darn it all! (mild swear word).

เจ้ากี้เจ้าการ câwkîi/câwkaan/ V to be a busybody, a meddler (used esp. of one who takes on a responsibility, obligation or function of his own accord, at the same time involving others in the obligation without their knowledge or consent).

เจ้าชู้ câwchúu/ V to be flirtatious, be a flirt (of either sex); to be a "wolf" (of a man). คน-- a flirt.

o ทำเจ้าชู้ tham/câwchúu/ to act like a flirt, like a "wolf."

เจ้าเนื้อ câwnýa/ V to be fat, plump, chubby (used esp. of children). คน-- fatty, fatso.

เจ้าเล่ห์ câwlêe/ V to be crooked, dishonest, tricky (of people).

เจ้าอารมณ์ câw/ʔaarom/ V to be temperamental, given to changes of mood.

เจ้า ๔. See entries below.

เจ้าคะ câwkhá/ Pt eleg. def. w. sp. particle used in the ways described for คะ, q.v. →Dist. ขอรับ eleg. def. m. sp.

เจ้าคะ câwkhâ/ Pt eleg. def. w. sp. particle used in the ways described for ค่ะ, q.v. →Dist. ขอรับ eleg. def. m. sp.

เจ้า ๕ in ข้าวเจ้า khâawcâaw/* N nonglutinous rice. →Opp. ข้าวเหนียว.

เจาะ cɔ̀ʔ/ V to puncture, bore, make a hole, punch a hole.

เจาะจง cɔ̀ʔcoŋ/ V 1. to pick out, single out; to specify, be specific about. 2. to be specific, precise.

เจาะรู cɔ̀ʔ/ruu/ to make a hole (by puncturing, boring, digging).

พอเหมาะพอเจาะ phɔɔmɔ̀ʔ/phɔɔcɔ̀ʔ/ V elab. colloq. to be just right, fit exactly.

เหมาะเจาะ mɔ̀ʔ/cɔ̀ʔ/ V to fit perfectly, be just

right.

เจิ่ง cɔ̀əŋ', cə̀ŋ' V to flood.

เจิด in เจิดจ้า cə̀ədcâa' V to be brilliant.

เจิม cəəm' V to anoint, consecrate.

เจียด cìad' V to use only a tiny portion of, to
spare a little (of).

  เจียดเวลา cìad'weelaa' to take a bit of time
off, spare a little time (for some purpose).

เจียน ๑ cian' V to cut, trim.

เจียน ๒ cian' AA almost, nearly. Short for
จวนเจียน.

  จวนเจียน cuancian' AA almost, nearly. →Syn.
จวน, เกือบ, แทบ.

เจี๊ยบ ๑ cíab' imit. chirp, cheep, peep (of chick).

  ลูกเจี๊ยบ (ตัว) lûugcíab' (tua') N chick.

เจี๊ยบ ๒ cíab' rM intens. used with เย็น "cold,"
สมัย "times," หวาน "sweet," ใหม่ "new."

เจียม ciam' V to be humble, self-effacing.

  เจียมกาย ciamkaaj' V eleg. to be humble,
modest, unassuming; to know one's place (and
not go beyond it). ความ-- modesty.

  เจียมใจ ciamcaj' V to be humble, modest, self-
effacing, unassuming.

  เจียมตัว ciamtua' V to be humble, modest, unassuming. ความ-- modesty.

เจียระไน ciaranaj' V 1. to cut diamonds, jewels,
crystal. 2. (diamonds, etc.) to be fashioned,
cut.

เจียว ciaw' V 1. to render fat. 2. to fry in oil
(e.g. minced garlic, onions, eggs).

  ไข่เจียว khàjciaw' N omelet.

เจี้ยว in เต้าเจี้ยว tâwcîaw' N bean paste, miso,
a salty condiment made of soy beans. [f. Chin.].

เจี๊ยะ cía?' V slang to eat (something). [f. Chin.]
→Syn. กิน com.

  แปะเจี๊ยะ. See under แปะ.

เจือ cya' V 1. to mix, mingle, dilute. 2. to be
mixed, mingled.

  เจือจาง cyacaaŋ' V 1. to dilute. 2. to be dilute,
diluted.

  เจือจาน cyacaan' V to share.

  โลหะเจือ loohà?'cya' N alloy.

เจื่อน cỳan' V to be embarrassed, discountenanced,
(one's face) to fall.

เจื่อนจาง cỳancaaŋ' V 1. to become tasteless,
insipid. 2. to become thin, diluted. 3. to vanish,
fade, evaporate.

เจื้อย cŷaj' V 1. to be flowing, continuous (of sound,
esp. the voice). sV 2. flowingly.

  เรื่อยเจื้อย rŷajcŷaj' on and on, continuously.

  หวานเจื้อย wǎancŷaj' to be melodious, dulcet,
mellifluous.

แจ ๑ cɛɛ' sV colloq. closely.

แจ ๒. See จอแจ.

แจ cɛ̌ɛ' V to be stunted, stubby, stumpy.

  ไก่แจ้ (ตัว) kàjcɛ̌ɛ' (tua') N bantam chicken.

แจ้ cɛ̌ɛ' V 1. to be intense (of sunlight). rM 2.
intensifier used with แดง "red."

แจก cɛ̀ɛg' V to distribute, hand out, give out, pass
out, issue. →Comp. จำแนก.

  แจกจ่าย cɛ̀ɛgcàaj' V to distribute.

  แจกแจง cɛ̀ɛgcɛɛŋ' V to analyze, explain part by
part.

  แจกแว่น cɛ̀ɛgwɛ̀n' V slang to give (someone)
a black eye.

  แจกหมาก cɛ̀ɛgmàag' V slang to punch (someone) in the mouth.

แจก. See จอกแจก.

แจกัน (ใบ) cɛɛkan' (baj') N vase.

แจง cɛɛŋ' V to explain. Chiefly in compounds.

  จัดแจง càdcɛɛŋ' V 1. to arrange, prepare. AA
2. make oneself ready to, prepare to (do something) (also followed by จะ).

  แจกแจง cɛ̀ɛgcɛɛŋ' V to analyze, explain part by
part.

  ชี้แจง chíicɛɛŋ' V to explain, make clear.

แจ้ง cɛ̂ɛŋ' V 1. to tell, inform, report, make known.
2. to be clear, unobscured. →Comp. จะแจ้ง.

  กลางแจ้ง klaaŋcɛ̂ɛŋ' outdoors, in the open, in the
open air.

  แจ้งความ (เรื่อง, ฉะบับ) cɛ̂ɛŋkhwaam' (rŷaŋ',
chabàb') N 1. advertisement; public notice.
V 2. to report, inform, give information. 3.
to advertise. ผู้-- informer.

  แจ้งชัด, ชัดแจ้ง cɛ̂ɛŋchád', chádcɛ̂ɛŋ' V to be
clear, distinct. อย่าง-- clearly.

  โจ่งแจ้ง cɔ̀oŋcɛ̂ɛŋ' sV clearly, openly, flagrantly.

  ทุ่งแจ้ง (ทุ่ง, แห่ง) thûŋcɛ̂ɛŋ' (thûŋ', hɛ̀ŋ') N open

field, meadow, clearing.

รู้แจ้งเห็นจริง rúucɛɛŋ'hĕnciŋ' V elab.colloq. to perceive and understand clearly.

แจด cɛɛd' rM intensifier used with แดง "red," เปรี้ยว "sour."

แจ่ม cɛ̀m' V to be clear, bright, unobscured. Chiefly in compounds.

   แจ่มแจ้ง cɛ̀mcɛ̂ɛŋ' V to be clear (in meaning).

   แจ่มชัด cɛ̀mchád' V to be clear (in meaning).

   แจ่มใส cɛ̀msăj' V 1. to be clear, fine (of the weather). 2. to be bright, cheerful (of expression).

แจว (แจว) cɛɛw' (cɛɛw') N 1. oar. V 2. to oar, row. 3. slang to flee, take off.

แจ๋ว cɛ̆w'* V to be melodious, pleasing to the ear.

แจ๋ว cɛ̆w'* V to be clear, bright (of eyes, voice).

   แจ๋วแหวว cɛ̆wwĕw' V to be bright, shining, crystal clear (of eyes).

   ชัดแจ๋ว chád'cɛ̆w' V colloq. to be very clear.

โจ๋. See จิงโจ้.

โจ่ง in โจ่งแจ้ง còoŋcɛɛŋ' sV clearly, openly, flagrantly.

โจทก์ (คน) còod' (khon') N prosecutor; plaintiff.

โจทย์ (ข้อ) còod' (khɔɔ') N arithmetical problem. NOTE. โจทย์ sometimes occurs as a misspelling for โจทก์ immediately above.

โจน coon' V to plunge, leap, jump. Shortened form of กระโจน.

   โลดโผนโจนทะยาน lôodphŏon'-coon'thajaan' V elab. colloq. to be exciting, thrilling, adventurous.

โจม coom' V to move suddenly, rush forward. Chiefly in the following derivatives.

   จู่โจม cùucoom' V to attack suddenly, by surprise.

   โจมตี coomtii' V to attack, assault, raid. การ-- attack, assault, raid.

โจร (คน) coon', coonᵓ, coonraᵓ (khon') N armed bandit, robber. →Dist. ขโมย.

   กองโจร (กอง) kɔɔŋcoon' (kɔɔŋ') N 1. robber gang. 2. guerrilla band.

   โจรกรรม coonrakam' N robbery, theft.

   โจรสลัด coonsalàd' (khon') N pirate.

โจษ còod' V 1. to be rumored. 2. to spread the word around.

ใจ (ใจ) caj' (caj') N heart, mind, spirit (in the figurative sense). Commonly used in combination with verbs or with other nouns. →Syn. จิต,จิตใจ com., มโน eleg. →Often coupled with เนื้อ or อก in semirepeated expressions or split expressions; see examples under เนื้อ, and อก.

กล่อมใจ klɔ̀mcaj' V to lull, soothe, calm (the heart, the feelings).

กลั้นใจ klâncaj' V to hold one's breath.

กลับใจ klàbcaj' V 1. to change one's mind, to turn over a new leaf, have a change of heart. 2. to be converted (to a religion).

กลุ้มใจ,กลุ้มอก-- klûmcaj', klûmʔòg'klûmcaj' V elab. colloq. to worry, be downcast, depressed.

กำลังใจ kamlaŋcaj' N will power, will, spirit.

o หมดกำลังใจ mòd'kamlaŋcaj' to lose heart, be discouraged.

กินใจ kincaj' V 1. to be wary (of). 2. to be deeply moving (as a story, movie).

เกรงใจ kreeŋcaj' V to have consideration for; to be reluctant to impose (upon).

ไกลตาไกลใจ klaj'taa'-klaj'caj' out of sight, out of mind.

ขวยใจ khŭajcaj' V to feel shame; to feel embarrassed, mortified, shamed.

ข้องใจ khɔ̂ŋcaj' V to be in doubt (about), dubious (about), unclear in one's mind (about).

ขอบใจ khɔ̀obcaj' com. 1. Thanks. Thank you! V 2. to thank (someone). →Syn. ขอบคุณ eleg.

ขัดใจ khàdcaj' V 1. to annoy, get in the way. 2. to be contrary, contradictory. 3. to be annoyed, irritated.

ขาดใจ khàadcaj' V to die, expire.

ขุ่นใจ khùncaj' V to be depressed, perturbed, gloomy.

เข็ญใจ khĕncaj' V to be destitute, impoverished.

เข้าใจ khâwcaj' V to understand. การ-- (act of) understanding, comprehension. ความ-- (state of) understanding, comprehension.

แข็งใจ khĕŋcaj' V to summon up one's courage, steel oneself (to do something).

ครึ้มใจ khrý́mcaj′ V to be highly pleased and bursting with happiness.

ความในใจ khwaam′najcaj′ what is on one's mind, in one's heart.

คับใจ khábcaj′ V to feel distressed, uneasy, apprehensive.

คู่ใจ khûucaj′ (as n. mod.) faithful, trusted.

o เพื่อนคู่ใจ phɯ̂an′khûucaj′ trusted friend, bosom companion.

เคืองใจ khyaŋcaj′ N 1. anger. V 2. to be angry, provoked.

แคลงใจ khlɛɛŋcaj′ V to feel suspicious, have doubts.

จงใจ coŋcaj′ AA intend to, intentionally, deliberately.

จนใจ con′caj′ V colloq. 1. to be unable to think of a way. 2. It can't be helped.

จริงใจ ciŋcaj′ V to be sincere, heartfelt. ความ-- sincerity.

จับใจ càbcaj′ V to capture one's imagination; to captivate, impress.

จำขึ้นใจ cam′khŷncaj′ to learn by heart.

จำใจ camcaj′ AA force (oneself to do smthg.), be forced (to do smthg. against one's will).

จิตใจ cìdcaj′ N mind; mind and spirit, heart and soul; feeling, sentiment. →Syn. see ใจ.

จูงใจ cuuŋcaj′ V to influence (the mind or thinking), induce, persuade.

เจ็บใจ cèbcaj′ V to feel hurt, have one's feelings hurt.

ใจกล้า cajklâa′ V to be bold, brave, venturesome.

ใจกลาง cajklaaŋ′ N core, central part.

ใจกว้าง cajkwâaŋ′ V to be generous, magnanimous.

ใจแข็ง cajkhɛ̌ŋ′ V to be hard-hearted, unyielding.

ใจคด cajkhód′ V to be crooked, dishonest.

ใจความ cajkhwaam′ N 1. the meaning, gist, essence. 2. subject matter. →Syn. เนื้อความ.

ใจคอ cajkhɔɔ′ N disposition, mood; character (of people only).

o นิสัยใจคอ nísǎj′cajkhɔɔ′ N disposition.

ใจแคบ cajkhɛ̂ɛb′ V to be narrow-minded, selfish, lacking in generosity.

ใจง่าย cajŋâaj′ V (a woman) to be cheap, easy to get, free with her affections.

ใจจริง cajciŋ′ N (one's) true feelings, frank thoughts. อย่าง-- frankly, candidly.

ใจจืด cajcɯ̀yd′ V to be unsympathetic, unresponsive, unthoughtful.

ใจขึ้น cajchýyn′ V 1. to be cheerful, carefree. 2. to be relieved.

ใจดำ cajdam′ V to be merciless, mean, selfish, unsympathetic, unscrupulous. คน-- blackguard.

ใจดี cajdii′ V to be good-natured, kindhearted. ความ-- kindheartedness, good-naturedness.

ใจเด็ด cajdèd′ V to be resolute, bold, determined.

ใจเดียว cajdiaw′ V to be faithful, constant (esp. in love).

ใจต่ำ cajtàm′ V to be base, vile.

ใจเต้น cajtên′ V 1. to be excited, to have one's heart pounding. sV 2. (with) pounding heart.

ใจแตก cajtɛ̀ɛg′ V 1. to be self-indulgent and unrestrained, spoiled. 2. to develop a passion for (e.g. gambling).

ใจทราม cajsaam′ V to be base, vile, immoral.

ใจน้อย cajnɔ́ɔj′ V to be touchy, sensitive, easily offended.

ใจบุญ cajbun′ V 1. to be generous, charitable. 2. to be pious.

ใจเบา cajbaw′ V to be easily influenced, easily swayed; to be credulous, gullible.

ใจป้ำ cajpâm′ V 1. to be generous, stouthearted, willing to take a risk. 2. to be resolute, determined. →Syn. 2. เด็ดเดี่ยว.

ใจฝ่อ cajfɔ̀ɔ′ V to be frightened, have one's heart shrink with fear.

ใจมา. See entries below.

o ใจมาขึ้นเป็นกอง caj′-maa′khŷnpenkɔɔŋ′ to take heart, be heartened, recover (as from fright).

o ใจมาตั้งกระบุง caj′-maa′tâŋkrabuŋ′ idem.

ใจเย็น cajjen′ V to be calm, steady, cool-headed, imperturbable. →Opp. ใจร้อน.

ใจร้อน cajrɔ́ɔn′ V 1. to be hasty, impetuous. 2. to be burning with impatience, anxious (e.g. to get something done). →Opp. ใจเย็น.

ใจเร็ว cajrew′ V to be hasty, impetuous, impulsive. ความ-- hastiness, rashness.

ใจลอย cajlɔɔj′ V to be absent-minded, have one's mind wander.

ใจสั่น cajsàn′ V to be frightened, have one's heart quiver with fear.

ใจเสาะ cajsɔ́ʔ′ V 1. to be afraid to face something unpleasant, feel scared, be unnerved. 2. to be unable to take it (as when teased or annoyed).

ใจเสีย cajsĭa′ V to lose heart, be disheartened, dismayed.

ใจหดหู่ cajhòdhùu′ V to be downhearted, despondent, heartsick.

ใจหวิว cajwĭw′ V to feel dizzy or faint, be giddy, have a dizzy spell.

ใจหายใจคว่ำ,ใจหาย cajhǎaj′cajkhwâm′, cajhǎaj′ V elab. colloq. to be stunned with fear, get scared out of one's wits.

o น่าใจหาย nâa′cajhǎaj′ V to be shocking, frightful, frightening.

ใจหายวาบ cajhǎaj′wâab′ V to be shocked, stunned with fear.

ใจอ่อน caj?ɔ̀ɔn′ V to be yielding, soft-hearted, easily influenced, easily touched.

ชอบใจ chɔ̂ɔbcaj′ V 1. to be pleased, happy, amused. 2. to be satisfied, gratified. →Syn. ถูกใจ,พอใจ.

ชื่นใจ chŷyncaj′ V 1. to please, delight. 2. to be pleased, delighted. 3. to be pleasant, charming, refreshing. 4. colloq. to kiss, hug (a loved one, in order to refresh, satisfy oneself). N 5. sweetheart (used by lovers, by parents to children). →See also 1-4. ชื่นอกชื่นใจ.

ดวงใจ (ดวง,คน) duaŋcaj′ N 1. the heart (duaŋ′). 2. sweetheart (khon′). 3. sweetheart, beloved (used as a term of endearment).

ด้วยใจ dûajcaj′ with one's heart, sincerely.

ดั่งใจ daŋcaj′ as one wishes, as one has in mind, as desired.

ดีใจ diicaj′ V to be happy, glad.

ดีอกดีใจ dii?òg′diicaj′ V elab. colloq. to be happy, glad.

ตกใจ tògcaj′ V com. to get frightened, scared, to take fright. →Syn. ตระหนก eleg., ตุ๊ก-กะใจ colloq., ขวัญบิน idiom.

ตั้งใจ tâŋcaj′ V 1./to intend. AA 2. intend to.

ตามใจ taamcaj′ V 1. to humor, please, yield to the wishes (of). 2. to do as one pleases.

ถอนใจ thɔ̌ɔncaj′ V to sigh, heave a sigh.

ถึงใจ thy̌ŋcaj′ V colloq. 1. to gratify, satisfy; to hit the spot (for someone). sV 2. to the utmost, in the highest degree, extremely, satisfyingly, pleasingly.

ถูกใจ thùugcaj′ V 1. to please; to be satisfactory, pleasing, appealing; to be to one's liking, to one's taste. 2. to get along well (with), be compatible. →Syn. พอใจ,ชอบใจ.

ทันใจ thancaj′ fast, fast enough, immediately.

นอกใจ nɔ̂ɔgcaj′ V to be unfaithful (of husband or wife); to be unfaithful to.

น้อยใจ nɔ́ɔjcaj′ V to feel slighted, feel inferior, feel neglected (by others).

น้ำใจ námcaj′ N 1. heart (for doing something), spirit, feelings. 2. good will, good feelings, thoughtfulness.

เป็นใจ(กับ) pencaj′(kaʔ) V to connive (with), be secretly accessory, be an accomplice (of) (e.g. in wrongdoing). →See also รู้เห็น--.

ผิดใจ phìd′caj′ V to have a falling out, to be sore (at).

ใฝ่ใจ(ใน) fàjcaj′ (najʔ) V to be interested (in), absorbed (in), to pay close attention (to).

พอใจ phɔɔcaj′ V to be satisfied. ความ-- satisfaction, contentment. →Syn. ชอบใจ,ถูกใจ.

o ไม่พอใจ mâjphɔɔcaj′ to be dissatisfied, displeased. ความ-- dissatisfaction, displeasure.

ภูมิใจ(ใน) phuumcaj′ (najʔ) V 1. to be proud (of). 2. to have a sense of accomplishment.

มีแก่ใจ miikɛɛcaj′, miikacaj′ 1. to have the desire, the will, the courage (to do something). 2. to be thoughtful, considerate of others. 3. to be kind enough, considerate enough to. →Also มีกะใจ.

มีใจเป็นธรรม miicaj′pentham′ to have a sense of justice.

เย็นใจ jencaj′ V to be unworried, calm, relaxed, composed. →Opp. ร้อนใจ.

ร้อนใจ rɔ́ɔncaj′ V to be worried, anxious, perturbed. →Opp. เย็นใจ.

รู้แก่ใจ rúu'kὲεcaj/ to know full well, to be fully
    aware.

ไว้วางใจ wájwaaŋcaj/ V to trust, have faith in.

สนใจ sŏncaj/ V to be interested (in), absorbed
    (in).

สองจิตสองใจ sɔ̌ɔŋcìd'sɔ̌ɔŋcaj/ elab. colloq.
    to be of two minds (about something), be unde-
    cided; to hesitate.

สองใจ sɔ̌ɔŋcaj/ V idiom. to be unfaithful, to
    have two loves.

สิ้นใจ sîncaj/ V to die.

เสียใจ sĭacaj/ V to be sorry, feel sorry, feel
    badly.

หดหู่ใจ hòdhùucaj/ V to be downhearted, de-
    spondent, heartsick.

หนักใจ nàgcaj/ V to be depressed, heavy-hearted,
    anxious; to have a weight upon one's mind, a
    burden upon one's heart.

หัวใจ (หัวใจ) hŭacaj/ (hŭacaj/) N the heart
    (organ of the body).

o โรคหัวใจ rôog'hŭacaj/ N heart disease.

หายใจ hăajcaj/ V to breathe.

o ลมหายใจ lom'hăajcaj/ N breath.

เห็นใจ hĕncaj/ V 1. to sympathize (with), be
    sympathetic (toward). 2. to see someone's
    true nature or feelings.

อย่างใจ jàaŋcaj/ according to one's wishes.

อ่อนใจ(กับ,ใน) ʔɔ̀ɔncaj/ (kaɔ, najɔ) V to
    feel weary (of), discouraged (about).

อัดใจ ʔàdcaj/ V 1. to hold one's breath. 2. to
    be depressed (in spirits).

เอาใจ ʔawcaj/ V to please, humor, try to please,
    be indulgent (toward).

เอาใจใส่ ʔaw'cajsàj/ to take an interest in, pay
    attention to.

เอาแต่ใจตน ʔaw'-tὲcaj'ton/ to be self-centered,
    consider only one's own interests or wishes.

ไจ caj/ C skein.

ฉ

ฉ chɔ̌ɔ/ HIGH consonant. Pronounced ch initially;
    not used as a final consonant.

ฉก chòg/ V 1. to snatch, grab. 2. to strike (as a
    snake).

ฉกรรจ์ chakan/ V 1. to be strong, severe, grave,
    extreme. 2. to be fierce, cruel. 3. to be able-
    bodied, adult (of a man 18-30 yrs. old).

    ข้อกล่าวหาฉกรรจ์ khɔ̂ɔklàawhăa'chakan/ a serious
        charge.

    ชายฉกรรจ์ (คน) chaajchakan/ (khon/) N able-
        bodied, adult man (approx. 18-30 yrs. old).

    ร้ายฉกรรจ์ ráaj'chakan/ V 1. to be strong, fierce,
        cruel, bad. sV 2. extremely, very.

    วัยฉกรรจ์ wajchakan/ N youth, young adulthood.

ฉกาจ chakàad/ V to be bold, brave, daring, fierce,
    ferocious.

ฉงน chaŋŏn/ V 1. to be puzzled, perplexed, confused.
    2. to be uncertain, in doubt, skeptical.

    ฉงนใจ chaŋŏn'caj/ V to be puzzled, bewildered.
        ความ-- bewilderment.

    ฉงนฉงาย chaŋŏn'chaŋăj/ V to be puzzled, per-
        plexed.

ฉงาย. See ฉงนฉงาย above.

ฉนวน (อย่าง,แห่ง) chanŭan/ N 1. insulator (jàaŋ/).
    2. a screened-off passageway or walk for ladies
    of the court (hὲŋ/).

ฉนาก in ปลาฉนาก (ตัว) plaachanàag/ (tua/) N
    sawfish (Pristis).

ฉบับ chabàb/ C clf. for an issue, edition (as of a
    newspaper), a copy (as of a book), letters (epis-
    ties), documents, banknotes, lottery tickets.
    →Also ฉะบับ FS. NOTE. As a clf. for bank-
    notes and lottery tickets, ใบ may also be used.

    ต้นฉบับ (ฉบับ) tônchabàb/ (chabàb/) N original
        manuscript, source document.

    แบบฉบับ (อัน,อย่าง) bὲεb'chabàb/ (ʔan/, jàaŋ/)
        N pattern, example, model, style (esp. what is
        traditionally accepted as worthy of imitation).

ฉมวก (อัน) chamùag/ (ʔan/) N a three-pronged
    fish spear, trident.

ฉล. See ฉอฉล.

ฉลอง chalɔ̌ɔŋ/ V to celebrate. การ-- festival,
    celebration.

o ฉลองวันเกิด chalɔ̌ɔŋ'wankə̀əd/ to celebrate a
    birthday.

งานฉลอง (ครั้ง) ŋaanchalɔ̌ɔŋ/ (khráŋ/) N festival,

celebration.

เฉลิมฉลอง chalə̆əm/chalɔ̆ɔŋ/ V to commemorate, celebrate. การ-- commemoration.

ฉลัก chalàg/ V 1. to carve (wood, stone). 2. to
chase (metal). →Also จำหลัก, สลัก. →Comp.
ลัก.

ฉลาก (ใบ, แผ่น) chalàag/ (baj/, phὲn/) N 1. label
(esp. for drugs, medicines). 2. lot (as a ticket
in a lottery). →Also สลาก.

ฉลากกินแบ่ง (ฉบับ, ใบ) chalàag/kinbὲŋ/ (chaɔ
bàb/, baj/) N lottery ticket.

ฉลาด, เฉลียว-- chalàad/, chalǐaw/chalàad/ V to
be clever, bright, smart, intelligent, keen,
sagacious. ความ-- cleverness, intelligence,
sagacity.

ฉลาดแต่ไม่เฉลียว chalàad/→tὲεmâjchalǐaw/
(she's) smart, but unsuspecting, not wise to the
true situation.

ชาญฉลาด chaanchalàad/ V to be ingenious.

ฉลาม, ปลา-- (ตัว) chalǎam/, plaachalǎam/ (tua/)
N shark.

ฉลุ chalù?/ V 1. to perforate, make an intricate
pattern on a scroll by perforation and sawing.
2. to be perforated.

ฉลู chalǔu/ N (Year of the) Ox. →The complete
list of the cyclical years is given under ปี.

ฉวย ๑ chǔaj/ V to snatch, grab, seize (esp. suddenly or with a quick motion).

ฉวยโอกาศ chǔaj?ookàad/ to seize the opportunity.
ผู้--, นัก-- opportunist.

ฉาบฉวย chàabchǔaj/ sV cursory, cursorily;
casual, casually; in a slapdash, slipshod manner.

ฉวย ๒ (ว่า) chǔaj/(wâaɔ) Cj if, in case.

o ฉวยว่าคุณไม่สบาย chǔaj/-wâakhun/mâjsabaaj/
in case you get sick.

ถ้าฉวย thâachǔaj/ Cj if, if by chance.

ฉวัดเฉวียน chawàd/chawǐan/ V 1. to swoop or dart
about (in the air), to fly rapidly and haphazardly
about with turning, wheeling motions. 2. fig.
to dash around (of a person or vehicle).

ฉวี chawǐi/ N 1. skin. 2. complexion.

ฉอ chɔɔ/ V to defraud, cheat, swindle. →Comp.
โกง.

ฉอโกง chɔɔkooŋ/ idem.

ฉอฉล chɔɔchǒn/ idem.

ฉอด ๆ, ฉอด chɔɔdchɔ̂ɔd/, chɔ̂ɔd/ rM modifier used
with พูด "speak" in the sense of "incessantly,
fluently, volubly."

ฉอเลาะ chɔɔlɔ́?/ V 1. to coo, talk fondly, amorously
(used particularly of w. sp. to boy-friend or
husband). 2. to speak cajolingly.

o ฉอเลาะกัน chɔɔlɔ́?/kan to bill and coo (of a
loving couple).

ฉอุ่ม cha?ùm/. See ช่อุ่ม.

ฉะ chà?/ V 1. colloq. to hit, attack. 2. to strike
(with a sword or knife). 3. to fight, quarrel (of
people). 4. slang to eat.

ฉะฉาน chà?chǎan/ V 1. to be clear, distinct (of
speech). sV 2. clearly, distinctly. →Cf. ฉาน.

ฉะเชิงเทรา chà?chəəŋsaw/ pN Chachoengsao, a
township E of Bangkok.

ฉะนั้น chanán/ so, therefore; like that. →Comp.
เช่นนั้น.

เพราะฉะนั้น phrɔ́chanán/ Cj therefore.

มิฉะนั้น míchanán/ Cj otherwise.

o คุณต้องแน่ใจ มิฉะนั้นอย่าพูด khuntɔ̂ŋnὲε/caj/→
míchanán/ jàaphûud/↓ You must be certain;
otherwise don't speak.

o หรือมิฉะนั้น rɣ̆y/míchanán/ or else.

ฉะนี้ chaníi/ like this, such as this. →Comp. เช่นนี้.

o ด้วยประการฉะนี้ dûajprakaan/chaníi/ lit. in
this manner, for this reason.

o ปานฉะนี้ paanchaníi/ like this, to this extent,
this much.

ฉะบับ FS. See ฉบับ.

ฉะเพาะ FS. See เฉพาะ.

ฉะออน ๑ cha?ɔ̌ɔn/* V to implore, wheedle, cajole.

ฉะออน ๒ cha?ɔ̌ɔn/* V to be slender, slim (of the
figure).

ฉัตร (คัน) chàd/, chàd/traɔ (khan/) N tiered
umbrella (emblem of royalty).

ฉัตรมงคล chàd/tramoŋkhon/ N celebration of
Coronation Day.

ฉัน ๑ chǎn/, chán/ P sp. to int. or inf. I, me.
Often paired with เธอ "you"; in narration paired
with ท่าน "you."

ดิฉัน dichǎn/, dichán/ P def. w. sp. I, me.
Equivalent to ผม def. m. sp. "I, me." Often

paired with คุณ "you."

ฉัน ๒ chăn′ like, as. Often functions as a limited
 type of clf. followed by ใด, นั้น, etc. Sometimes used together with อย่าง.

o เขาทำผมฉันใด ผมก็ทำเขาฉันนั้น kháwtham⊃
 phŏm′chăndaj′→ phŏm′-kɔ̆thamkháw′chănnán′↓
 Whatever he does to me, I'll do to him likewise.

o ฉันมิตร chănmíd′ like friends, as friends,
 friendly.

ฉัน ๓ chăn′ V com. sacer. to eat (in general).
 →Syn. See กิน com.

 ฉันจังหัน chăn′caŋhăn′ sacer. to eat (food),
 partake of a repast. →Syn. กินข้าว com.

ฉัน ๔. See เฉิดฉัน.

ฉันท์ ๑ (บท) chăn′ (bòd′) N a kind of Thai poem
 with definite metrical rules based on one of the
 forms of ancient Indian versification.

ฉันท์ ๒. See เอกฉันท์ under เอก.

ฉับ ๑ chàb′ quickly, suddenly, instantly. Chiefly
 in compounds.

 ฉับพลัน chàbphlan′ instantly, promptly, at once,
 abruptly. โดย--, ใน--, อย่าง-- idem.

 ฉับไว chàbwaj′ quickly, instantly; promptly.

ฉับ ๒ chàb′ imit. an abrupt sound, as the clash
 of cymbals; a loud clacking sound.

ฉา, ฉา ๆ chàa′, chàachàa′ imit. expression
 describing such sounds as the splashing of a
 waterfall, water, rain; the swooshing of a strong
 wind; the sizzling of frying food; the intoning
 of a chorus singing; etc.

 โฉวฉา chŏochàa′ V colloq. to be widely talked
 about (used of people).

ฉาก ๑ (ฉาก) chàag′ (chàag′) N 1. curtain, scene,
 scenery. 2. act (of a show or play). 3. screen
 for dividing rooms, partition.

 ฉากตา chàagtaa′ N anat. retina.

 เปิดฉาก pɔ̀ɔdchàag′ 1. to raise the curtain (on
 a scene). 2. fig. to open (a conversation), to
 begin, launch (a war or other activity).

 หลังฉาก lăŋchàag′ N 1. backstage, behind the
 scenes. 2. the inside story or account, the
 real picture, the real underlying facts. NOTE.
 When used of people, this usually implies a
 shameful, hidden way of life which belies the

public image.

 ออกฉาก ?ɔ̀ɔgchàag′ 1. to appear on the stage.
 2. fig. to appear on the scene, to resume one's
 activities (after an absence).

ฉาก ๒, ไม้-- (อัน) chàag′, májchàag′ (?an′) N
 carpenter's or draftsman's square (L- or T-
 shaped).

 ได้ฉาก dâjchàag′ V tech. to be perpendicular,
 normal.

 มุมฉาก (มุม) mumchàag′ (mum′) N right angle;
 (as n. mod.) right-angled.

ฉาง (ฉาง, หลัง) chàaŋ′ (chàaŋ′, lăŋ′) N 1. barn,
 storehouse (for rice), storage bin, Thai silo.
 C 2. clf. for same.

ฉาง chàaŋ′ 1. imit. the sound of clanking of metal
 objects, the clashing of cymbals. rM 2. intensifier used with ดัง "loud."

ฉาด chàad′ 1. imit. the sound of slapping, clapping,
 of striking together. C 2. clf. for a slap.

 o ตบฉาด tòb′chàad′ to slap hard.

 o ตบฉาดหนึ่ง tòb′chàad′nyŋ to slap once.

ฉาดฉาน chàadchăan′ sV distinctly, clearly, fluently
 (of speech).

ฉาน chăan′ V 1. to scatter. rM 2. intensifier
 meaning "bright, radiant," used with แดง "red,"
 แสง "light." →Comp. ฉะฉาน.

 แตกฉาน tɛ̀ɛgchăan′ V 1. to scatter, disperse.
 2. to be scattered, dispersed, fragmented. sV
 3. thoroughly, explicitly, in every detail.

ฉาบ ๑ (อัน, คู่) chàab′ N large type of cymbal
 approximately 6-12 inches in diameter (?an′
 for one; khûu′ for a pair). →See also ฉิ่ง.

ฉาบ ๒ chàab′ V 1. to paint, coat, whitewash. 2.
 to be coated.

ฉาบ ๓ in ฉาบฉวย chàabchŭaj′ sV cursory, cursorily; casual, casually; in a slapdash, slipshod
 manner. อย่าง-- cursorily, casually, in a
 slapdash manner.

ฉาย chăaj′ V 1. to show, project (on a screen).
 2. to shine (as the sun). 3. to reflect. 4.
 slang to show off.

 o เดือนฉาย dyanchăaj′ lit. the moon is shining.

 ฉายเฉิด, เฉิดฉาย chăajchɵ̀ɵd′, chɵ̀ɵdchăaj′ V
 to be radiant, bright and gay (of persons); to be

attractive.

ฉายหนัง chǎajnǎŋ′ to show a movie. เครื่อง-- motion picture projector.

ฉุยฉาย chǔjchǎaj′ V 1. to be ostentatious (in manner), foppish. sV 2. ostentatiously, gaily.

ไฟฉาย (กระบอก, ดวง) fajchǎaj′ (krabɔ̀ɔg′, duaŋ′) N flashlight, searchlight, spotlight.

รูปฉาย (แผ่น, ใบ) rûubchǎaj′ (phɛ̀n′, baj′) N photograph.

ฉายา (ฉายา, ใบ, อย่าง) chǎajaa′ N 1. shade, shadow, image, projection. 2. photographic portrait (baj′). 3. the Pali name of a priest (chǎajaa′, jàaŋ′). 4. colloq. epithet.

ฉาว. See entries below.

ฉาวโฉ่, โฉ่ฉาว chǎawchòo′, chòochǎaw′ sV widely and unfavorably (of being talked about), notoriously.

อื้อฉาว ?ŷychǎaw′ V 1. to be talked of a lot, to be spread far and wide. sV 2. a lot, widely, far and wide.

ฉ่ำ in ฉ่ำแฉะ chǎmchɛ̀?′ V 1. to be damp, wet, slushy (as rain-soaked earth). 2. slang to be lethargic, inert.

ฉ่ำ chàm′ V to be juicy, wet, damp, moist, humid.

หวานฉ่ำ wǎanchàm′ V 1. to be sweet and juicy (as a pineapple). 2. colloq. to be honeyed (of a person's eyes, speech).

ฉ่ำฉา in ไม้ฉ่ำฉา májchàmchǎa′ N deal, wood of pine and other conifers.

ฉิ่ง (อัน, คู่) chìŋ′ N small cup-shaped cymbal appr. 2.5 inches in diameter (ʔan′ for one; khûu′ for a pair). →See also ฉาบ.

ฉิบ (1) chìb′, chíb′, !chíb′; (2, 3) chíb′ rM 1. intensifier used with เงียบ, เสีย, หายไป (see examples). sV 2. darned, damned (in the sense of very, exceptionally). E 3. m. sp. Damn! Darn! NOTE. In mngs. 2 and 3 ฉิบ is short for ฉิบหาย, and is generally avoided by women and by men in the presence of women.

o เงียบฉิบ ŋîab/chíb′ very silent; very quietly.

o เสียฉิบ síachíb′, sía!chíb′, síachìb′ too (e.g. easily). Here ฉิบ intensifies the completive sense of the sec. vb. เสีย. See the following example.

oo ให้เขากินไปเสียฉิบ hâj/kháwkin/pajsía!chíb′↓ (We) let him win too easily!

o หายไปฉิบเขียว hǎaj/pajchíb/chiaw↓, -!chíb′- (He) disappeared completely!

o เร็วฉิบ rew/chíb′ damn(ed) quick, very quickly. →Short for เร็วฉิบหาย.

ฉิบหาย chìbhǎaj′, chíbhǎaj′, !chíbhǎaj′ V 1. to perish, be utterly ruined, destroyed. sV 2. m. sp. damned, darned (in the sense of very, extremely). E 3. m. sp. Damn! Darn! →Also 2, 3. ฉิบ. →Syn. 1. See วอดวาย. NOTE. In mngs. 2 and 3 used by men sp. to men who are intimates; otherwise insulting.

o ฉิบหายแล้วเรา chíbhǎaj/lɛ́ɛwraw′↓ We are ruined!

o ดีฉิบหาย dii′/!chíbhǎaj′ darned good, damn(ed) good.

ฉิว, ฉิว ๆ chǐw′, chǐwchǐw′ V 1. to be angry, indignant, peeved. rM 2. modifier used with พัด "blow," แล่น "sail," วิ่ง "run," in the sense of smoothly and swiftly, uninterruptedly.

ฉี่ chìi′ 1 imit. a sizzling sound. V 2. colloq. to urinate (esp. to or of a child). rM 3. intensifier used with ร้อน "hot (in temperature)," occasionally with เผ็ด "hot (in taste)."

หูฉี่ hǔuchìi′ colloq. extreme, extremely: "ear-sizzling."

o แพงหูฉี่ phɛɛŋ/hǔuchìi′ to be extremely expensive.

ฉีก chìig′ V 1. to tear, rip. 2. to get torn, ripped.

ฉีก(...)ออก chìig(...)?ɔ̀ɔg′ 1. to tear open, tear out. 2. to get torn open, torn out.

สมุดฉีก (เล่ม) samùd/chìig′ (lêm′) N scratch pad, writing tablet (with leaves which can be torn out).

ฉีด chìid′ V to inject, inoculate.

ฉีดยา chìidjaa′ V 1. to inject medicine, inoculate. 2. to get an injection, a shot.

ยาฉีด (หลอด, ขนาน) jaachìid′ N medicine for injection (lɔ̀ɔd′ for tubes; khanǎan′ for kinds, varieties).

ฉุ chù?′ V to be fat, flabby.

ฉุก chùg′ V to happen suddenly, precipitately, unexpectedly.

ฉุกเฉิน chùgchɘɘn′ V to be exigent, of an emergency nature, in a state of critical disorder.

o ภาวะฉุกเฉิน phaawá?′chùgchɘɘn′ N emergency, state of emergency.

o เหตุฉุกเฉิน hèed′chùgchɘɘn′ N emergency.

ฉุกละหุก chùglahùg′ V to be in confusion, disorder (because of haste, unpreparedness).

ฉุด chùd′ V to drag, pull, haul, abduct.

ฉุดกระชาก chùd′krachâag′ V to drag, drag off by force.

ฉุน chŭn′ V com. 1. to be angry, get angry, be angered, enraged, furious. 2. to be strong (of odors), pungent (as the odor of strong tobacco). →Syn. 1. โกรธ, โมโห com., กริ้ว roy.

ฉุนตจิด ๆ chŭn′-taŋìd′taŋìd′ somewhat angered, a little angry.

ฉุนเฉียว, เฉียวฉุน chŭnchĭaw′, chĭawchŭn′ V to be hot-tempered, quick-tempered, easily angered.

ฉุย ๑ chŭj′ V 1. to be wafted quickly in large quantity (of smoke and odor only). rM 2. intensifier used esp. with หอม "fragrant," เหม็น "stink" to express both rapidity of diffusion and strength of the odor.

กลิ่นฉุย klìnchŭj′ to be odorous (penetrating and sudden, as the odor of strong fumes).

หอมฉุย hɔɔmchŭj′ 1. to have a strong and pleasant lingering odor. 2. to be exceedingly pleasant, sweet (in odor).

ฉุย ๒ in ฉุยฉาย chŭjchâaj′ N 1. a posture of the Thai classical dance. 2. type of music for the Thai classical dance. V 3. to be ostentatious, foppish (in manner). sV 4. ostentatiously, gaily.

o เดินฉุยฉาย dəən′chŭjchâaj′ colloq. to strut, walk ostentatiously (as a fop, a dandy).

ฉู chùu′ rM intensifier used with เหม็น "stink."

ฉูด in ฉูดฉาด chùudchàad′ V to be vivid, loud, gaudy, flashy (of colors, of clothing). →Ant. เรียบ ๆ.

เฉ chĕe′ V to be aslant, not straight; to deviate, diverge, be out of line.

เฉ่ง chèŋ′/* V colloq. to pay, settle up (an account).

เฉด chèed′ V colloq. to chase away, drive off,

expel.

เฉพาะ chaphɔ?′ V 1. to be specific, peculiar to. sV 2. particularly, especially, exclusively. →Comp. จำเพาะ.

เฉพาะกาล chaphɔ?′kaan′ temporary.

เฉพาะหน้า chaphɔ?′nâa′ confronting, at hand, immediate.

o งานเฉพาะหน้า ŋaan′-chaphɔ?′nâa′ work or business at hand.

เฉพาะอย่างยิ่ง chaphɔ?′-jàaŋjîŋ′ in particular, especially. โดย-- idem.

โดยเฉพาะ doojchaphɔ?′ especially, particularly, in particular.

ตัวเฉพาะ (ตัว) tuachaphɔ?′ (tua′) N math. 1. prime number. 2. (as n. mod.) prime.

เฉย, เฉย ๆ chɘɘj′, chɘɘjchɘɘj′ V 1. to be impassive, indifferent, unperturbed. 2. to be passive, quiet, still, calm. 3. to be indifferent to, ignore (followed by ต่อ, กับ).

o ทำเฉยเสีย thamchɘɘj′sía keep (something) quiet, say nothing more about (it).

o ให้เฉย ๆ hâj′chɘɘjchɘɘj′ to give without expecting to be repaid.

เฉยเมย chɘɘjməəj′ V to be indifferent, passive.

เพิกเฉย(ต่อ, กับ) phəəgchɘɘj′(tɔɔ, ka⊃) V to ignore, neglect, pay no attention (to).

หน้าเฉยตาเฉย nâachɘɘj′taachɘɘj′ elab. colloq. with dead-pan expression, i.e. looking expressionless and as if nothing has happened. อย่าง-- idem.

เฉลย chalɘɘj′ V to answer (a challenge or accusation), give an answer, solve (a problem or puzzle).

เฉลิม chalɘɘm′ V 1. to add to, increase, extend. 2. to celebrate. 3. to be excellent.

งานเฉลิม ŋaanchalɘɘm′ N 1. celebration (of state or royal function). 2. the celebration of the king's birthday.

เฉลิมฉลอง chalɘɘm′chalɔɔŋ′ V to commemorate, celebrate. การ-- commemoration.

เฉลิมพระชนมพรรษา chalɘɘm′-phráchon′phansăa′ to celebrate the king's birthday.

o วันเฉลิมพระชนมพรรษา wanchalɘɘm′-phráchon′⊃ phansăa′ N anniversary of the king's birthday.

วันเฉลิม wanchalɘɘm′ N day of celebration; the

king's birthday (abbrev. for the last entry
above).

เฉลี่ย challìa′ V 1. to average, distribute evenly.
2. to divide, share equally. 3. to be average,
mean. →Syn. 1. ถัว colloq.

o ความร้อนเฉลี่ย khwaamrɔ́ɔn′challìa′ the average temperature.

คิดเฉลี่ย khídchallìa′ V to take the average; on
the average.

เฉลี่ยเจือจาน challìacyacaan′ V to share, distribute evenly.

ส่วนเฉลี่ย sùanchallìa′ N eleg. 1. the average.
2. share, portion.

เฉลียง ๑ (เฉลียง) challĭaŋ′ (challĭaŋ′) N veranda,
porch.

เฉลียง ๒ challĭaŋ′ sV diagonal, diagonally, on the
bias, cater-cornered. →Comp. เฉียง.

o ผ้าเฉลียง phâachallĭaŋ′ (a piece of) cloth (cut)
on the bias.

เฉลียว,--ใจ challĭaw′, challĭawcaj′ V to have a
flash of realization; to have an inkling; to have
it occur to one.

ฉลาดแต่ไม่เฉลียว chalàad′→tὲɛmâjchallĭaw′
(she's) smart, but unsuspecting, not wise to the
true situation.

เฉลียวฉลาด challĭaw′chalàad′ V to be clever,
bright, smart, intelligent, keen, sagacious.
ความ-- cleverness, intelligence, sagacity.

เฉวียน. See ฉวัดเฉวียน.

เฉอะ,--แฉะ chɔ̀ʔ′, chɔ̀ʔchὲʔ′ V to be slushy,
wet, damp. →See แฉะ.

เฉา chăw′ V 1. to wilt, wither, shrivel up. 2. to
be wilted, withered.

เฉาะ chɔ́ʔ′ V 1. to chop. 2. to break open (as a
coconut).

เฉิด chə̀əd′ magnificent, magnificently. Chiefly in
compounds.

เฉิดฉัน chə̀ədchăn′ sV pretty, elegant, beautiful.

เฉิดฉาย,ฉายเฉิด chə̀ədchăaj′, chăajchə̀əd′ V
to be radiant, bright and gay; to be attractive.

เฉิน in ฉุกเฉิน chùgchə̀ən′ V to be exigent, of an
emergency nature, critical.

เฉียง chĭaŋ′ V 1. to be oblique, aslant, deflected,
inclined, diagonal. 2. to bend, deflect, slant,

incline, turn (toward). →Comp. เฉลียง ๒.

o เฉียงไปทางตะวันออก chĭaŋ′-pajthaaŋtawan′ɔ
ʔɔ́ɔg′ (turning) a little to the east.

o เดินเฉียง dəənchĭaŋ′ 1. to walk diagonally.
2. to proceed out of the normal course or path.

o ตะวันตกเฉียงใต้ tawan′tòg′-chĭaŋtâaj′ southwest, southwestern.

เฉียด chĭad′ V to pass too close, very close; to
just miss, almost graze.

o ลูกปืนเฉียดหัว lûugpyyn′chĭadhŭa′ the bullet
just missed (somebody's) head.

เฉียบ ๑. See entries below. →Comp. เฉียบ ๒.

เฉียบขาด chĭabkhàad′ V to be resolute (of a
person), irrevocable (of an order), absolute.
อย่าง-- absolutely, strictly, decisively.

เฉียบแหลม chĭablἔɛm′ V to be keen, sharp,
shrewd (of people).

เฉียบ ๒ chĭab′ rM intensifier used with เย็น
"cold." →Comp. เขี้ยบ, เฉียบ ๑.

เฉียว in เฉียวฉุน,ฉุนเฉียว chĭawchŭn′, chŭnchĭaw′
V to be hot-tempered, quick-tempered, easily
angered.

เฉี่ยว chĭaw′ V 1. to swoop down upon. 2. to snatch,
snatch away suddenly. 3. to pass swiftly, suddenly, at close quarters (as a car passing a person or another car too closely). rM 4. viva-
ciously, flashingly, strikingly; used esp. with
ตาคม "bright-eyed," สวย "pretty."

เฉือน chŭan′ V 1. to cut off, slice off. 2. slang
to edge out (in a contest).

เฉื่อย,เฉื่อย ๆ chŭaj′, chŭajchŭaj′ V 1. to be slow,
inert, leisurely. sV 2. in leisurely fashion.
3. steadily but gently, lazily (of a breeze blowing).
ความ-- inertia, inactivity.

เฉื่อยชา chŭajchaa′ V to be inert, inactive.

เฉื่อยช้า chŭajcháa′ V 1. to be slow. sV 2. slowly.

แฉ,แฉโพย chὲɛ′, chὲɛphooj′ V colloq. to reveal,
disclose (a secret).

แฉก chὲɛg′ C jag, shred, strip, one of a series of
projections, often pointed, of a deeply notched
periphery, as of a fringe.

เป็นแฉก penchὲɛg′ to be fringed, deeply serrated,
jagged. →Dist. เป็นจักๆ, เป็นฟัน, เป็นหยัก.

เป็นสองแฉก pensɔ̌ɔŋ′chὲɛg′ to be bifurcated,

swallow-tailed.

แสง ๑ chèŋ/* rM modifier used with ยิ้ม "to

smile," in the sense of "broadly, happily."

แสง ๒ in แสง ๆ chèŋchèŋ/* imit. a clattering

sound.

แฉลบ chalɛ̀ɛb/ V to move, slide, fly, be blown along

in a tilted position, or in a direction slanted

from the perpendicular (e.g. of a plane banking,

a ship heeling); to slice (e.g. meat) slantwise.

แฉลบตัด chalɛ̀ɛb/tàd/ V to tilt (bank, or heel,

etc.) and cut across.

แฉล่ม chalɛ̂m/* V to be beautiful, pretty, attractive,

lovely (esp. of the face).

แฉะ chɛ̀?/ V 1. to be damp, wet, slushy (as rain-

soaked earth). 2. slang to be lethargic, inert.

ฉ่ำแฉะ chǎmchɛ̀?/ idem.

เฉอะแฉะ chɔ̀?chɛ̀?/ V to be slushy, wet, damp.

ขึ้นแฉะ chýynchɛ̀?/ V to be damp, wet (as

weather on a rainy day).

เปียกแฉะ pìagchɛ̀?/ V to be wet, watery.

o ปากเปียกปากแฉะ pàagpìag/pàagchɛ̀?/ V

elab. colloq., idiom. to talk oneself blue

in the face, i.e. to keep telling, instructing,

advising, admonishing.

โฉ. Implies being "widespread" and "unpleasant."

See entries below. →See also ฉู.

โฉ่ฉาว, ฉาวโฉ่ chòochǎaw/, chǎawchòo/ sV

widely and unfavorably (of being talked about),

notoriously.

เหม็นโฉ่ měnchòo/ to smell very bad, stink badly.

โฉด, --เขลา chòod/, chòodkhlǎw/ V to be foolish,

stupid.

โฉนด (ใบ, ฉบับ) chanòod/ (baj/, chabàb/) N title

deed for a piece of land.

โฉบ chòob/ V to swoop down on, swoop down on

and snatch away.

โฉม chǒom/ N appearance, look, figure, shape.

โฉมงาม (คน) chǒomŋaam/ (khon/) N beautiful

girl, a beauty.

โฉมหน้า chǒomnâa/ N face, facial features,

countenance.

o บ่ายโฉมหน้า bàaj/chǒomnâa/ to head toward,

change one's course, turn away.

รูปโฉม rûubchǒom/ N figure, shape, appearance,

build.

โฉลก chalòog/ N luck, fortune.

โฉว in โฉวฉา chǒowchàa/ V colloq. to be widely

talked about (used of people).

ไฉน, เหตุ-- chanǎj/, hèedchanǎj/ how, why, for what

reason.

ช

ช chɔɔ/ LOW consonant. Pronounced ch initially,

d finally. The sound ch as an initial low conso-

nant is also very rarely written with ฌ.

ชก chóg/ V to box, punch (with fist).

ชกขวา chógkhwǎa/ to deliver a blow with the

right (in boxing).

ชกต่อย chógtɔ̀j/ V to box, fight with fists.

ชกมวย chógmuaj/ V to box (usually in ref. to

professional boxing).

ชง choŋ/ V to steep, infuse, make (tea or coffee),

prepare (condensed milk by mixing in hot water).

ชงชา choŋchaa/ V to make tea.

ชงนม choŋnom/ V to prepare condensed milk

(by adding hot water).

ชฎา (ชฎา,หัว) chadaa/ (chadaa/, hǔa/) N 1.

theatrical high-pinnacled headdress or crown

(worn by actor or actress). 2. woman's hairdo

of similar shape.

ชด. Chiefly in compounds.

ชดช้อย chódchɔ́ɔj/ V to be gentle, soft, graceful

in manner (used of women).

ชดเชย chódchəəj/ V to replace what is lost, to

compensate.

o ค่าชดเชย khâachódchəəj/ N compensation,

(for work done, for property damage).

ชดใช้ chódcháj/ V to reimburse, repay, pay (for

amount of loss or damage).

ชตา. See ชะตา.

ชน ๑ chon/ V 1. to collide, bump into, run into,

butt, hit. 2. to fight (of certain animals, esp.

cocks, bulls). 3. to pit (e.g. cocks against each

other). 4. to complete (a round or cycle).

o ถูกรถยนต์ชน thùugródjon/chon/ to get hit by

a car.

การชนกัน kaanchon′kan′ N collision.

ไก่ชน (ตัว) kàjchon′ (tua′) N fighting cock.

คลุมถุงชน khlum′thǔŋchon′ V idiom. to marry off (an individual, a couple) without the mates knowing or seeing each other beforehand.

ชนไก่ (บ่อน, ครั้ง, หน) chonkàj′ N 1. cockfight (bɔ̀n′ in ref. to the place; hǒn′, khráŋ′ in ref. to time, occasion). V 2. to have a cockfight.

ชนช้าง choncháaŋ′ V to fight on elephantback. Both rider and elephant engage in combat.

ชน ๒ chon′, chonɔ, chonnaɔ N eleg. person, people. Chiefly in compounds. →Syn. คน com.

กลุ่มชน (กลุ่ม) klùmchon′ (klùm′) N public gathering, crowd.

ชนชาติไทย (คน) chonchâadthaj′ (khon′) N people of Thai nationality.

ชนชาวอังกฤษ (คน) chonchaaw′ʔaŋkrìd′ (khon′) N the British people, Englishmen.

ชนต่างด้าว (คน) chon′tàaŋdâaw′ (khon′) N aliens.

ชนบท (แห่ง) chonnabòd′ (hèŋ′) N eleg. 1. the country, rural area. 2. (as n. mod.) rural. →Syn. บ้านนอก colloq.

ประชาชน (คน) prachaachon′ (khon′) N the public, the populace.

ชนม chon′. Sometimes used in lit. or roy. words to connote "birth; life." →Also ชนม์ FS.

พระชนมพรรษา phráchon′phansǎa′ N roy. age. →Syn. อายุ com.

วายชนม waajchon′ V lit. to die. →Syn. See ตาย.

ชนวน (แผ่น, เล่น, สาย) chanuan′ N 1. slate (phèn′). 2. fuse, primer (sên′, sǎaj′).

กระดานชนวน (แผ่น) kradaanchanuan′ (phèn′) N slate (for writing on, such as is used by the schoolchild).

เป็นชนวน penchanuan′ to lead to; to cause; to be the prime cause.

หินชนวน (แผ่น) hǐn′chanuan′ (phèn′) N slate (the rock).

ชนะ chaná?′ V 1. to win, win out. 2. to defeat, beat, conquer, overcome. คน-- winner, victor.

ชนะใจ chaná?′caj′ V to win the love of, the trust of; to capture the heart of.

ชนะใจตัวเอง chaná?′caj′-tuaʔeeŋ′ to overcome desire, temptation.

ชัยชนะ (ครั้ง) chajchaná?′ (khráŋ′) N victory.

เอาชนะ ʔawchaná?′ V to strive to win, win out, overcome.

ชนิด chaníd′ C kind, type, variety, description, sort, species. →Syn. อย่าง com., ประการ, ประเภท, สถาน eleg.

o นานาชนิด naa′naa′chaníd′ various kinds, of all sorts, of every description.

ชบา (ดอก) chabaa′ (dɔ̀ɔg′) N hibiscus (the flower). ต้น-- (ต้น) hibiscus (the plant).

ชม chom′ V 1. to admire, look at with pleasure. 2. to praise. 3. eleg. to look at, view. การ-- admiration, praise. →Syn. 3. ดู com.

ชมชื่น, ชื่นชม chomchŷyn′, chŷynchom′ V to admire, be delighted (with), pleased (with).

ชมเชย chomchəəj′ V to admire, praise, compliment.

o คำชมเชย kham′chomchəəj′ N word(s) of praise, compliment.

o รางวัลชมเชย raaŋwan′chomchəəj′ N honorable mention.

ชมนกชมไม้ chomnóg′chommáaj′ elab. colloq. to admire the scenery, enjoy the beauty of nature.

ชม(...)เปาะ chom′(...)pɔ̀?′ to praise again and again.

เชยชม chəəjchom′ V 1. to admire, praise. 2. to fondle, caress tenderly.

ติชม tì?′chom′ V to find fault with, criticize (finding both good and bad points).

น่าชม nâa′chom′, nâachom′ V 1. to be praise-worthy, admirable. 2. eleg. to be interesting to see, look at. →Syn. 2. น่าดู com.

ชมด in ชมดชม้อย chamód′chamɔ́ɔj′ attractively shy in manner (of women).

ชมพู chomphuu′. Short for สี-- when สี is implicit in the context.

สีชมพู sǐichomphuu′ N 1. pink (the color). V 2. to be pink, pink-colored.

ชมพู่ (ใบ, ลูก, ผล) chomphûu′ (baj′, lûug′, phǒn′) N rose-apple (the fruit). ต้น-- (ต้น) rose-apple tree (Myrtaceae).

ชมรม (ชมรม,แห่ง) chomrom/ N 1. gathering, party (of people)(chomrom/). 2. meeting-place (hὲŋ/).

ชม้อย chamɔ́ɔj/ V to look down or away coyly, shyly, bashfully (of a woman).

ชมดชม้อย chamód/chamɔ́ɔj/ sV attractively shy in manner (of a woman).

ชม้อยชม้าย chamɔ́ɔj/chamáaj/ V to look down and glance back again in a shyly flirtatious manner.

ชม้าย chamáaj/ V to glance sidewise (of a woman).

o ทำตาชม้าย thamtaa/chamáaj/ to cast a side-long glance.

ชโย chajoo/ E 1. bravo! hurrah! V 2. to hail with bravos, say "bravo!" →See also ไชโย.

ชรา charaa/ V eleg. 1. to be old, aged (of people). N 2. (old) age, senility; also ความ--. คน-- old person; old people, the aged. →Comp. 2. วัยกลางคน,อายุกลางคน. →Dist. เก่า. →Syn. 1. เฒ่า,แก่ ๑ com.

ชราภาพ charaa/phâab/ N lit. (old) age.

วัยชรา waj/charaa/ N old age, period of old age.

ชล chon/, chonɔ, chonlaɔ N eleg. water. Chiefly in compounds.

ชลบุรี chon/burii/ N Chonburi (Jolburi), a township on the E coast of the Gulf of Thailand. →Syn. เมืองชล colloq.

ชลประทาน chonprathaan/, chonlaprathaan/ N irrigation, irrigating. →Also การ--.

ชลมารค chonlamâag/ N watercourse.

เมืองชล myaŋchon/ N colloq. Chonburi. →Syn. ชลบุรี.

ช่วง chûaŋ/ C span, extent; interval.

o วิ่งช่วงยาว wîŋ/chûaŋjaaw/ to run with long strides.

ช่วงคลื่น chûaŋkhlŷyn/ N phys. wave length.

ช่วงเวลา chûaŋweelaa/ N spell, period of time.

เช่าช่วง châwchûaŋ/ V to take a sublease.

รับช่วง rábchûaŋ/ V to inherit, take over, receive something which has been passed on and is to be harbored or used and often passed on again (e.g. a tradition, a business, used clothing, a subcontract).

ชวด ๑ chûad/ AA not get (to do something), lose

the chance (to do something). →Syn. อด colloq.

o นายมาเราเลยชวดไปกินเลี้ยง naaj/maa/→ rawɔ ləəjchûad/pajkinlíaŋ/ The boss came (back) (and) we lost our chance to go for a feed.

ชวด ๒ chûad/ N (Year of the) Rat. →The complete list of the cyclical years is given under ปี.

ชวด ๓ chûad/ N colloq. great-grandparent (on either side). →Also ทวด.

ชวน chuan/ V to urge, persuade, ask, invite (to do something).

o ที่ชวนชม thîichuanchom/ which invites (one's) admiration.

โฆษณาชวนเชื่อ khôosanaa/chuanchŷa/ N 1. propaganda. V 2. to propagandize.

ชวนหัว (เรื่อง) chuanhŭa/ (rŷaŋ/) N 1. humorous story, anecdote, comedy. V 2. to be amusing, comical.

ชักชวน chágchuan/ V to induce, persuade, urge (to do something).

ช่วย chûaj/ V to help, assist; to rescue. การ-- assistance; rescue. ผู้-- assistant, helper; rescuer. NOTE. ช่วย often implies asking a favor, hence may sometimes be translated "please."

o ช่วยส่งสะบู่มาให้ผมที chûajsòŋsabùu/-maahâj/ɔ phŏmthii/ Please hand me the soap!

คุณพระช่วย khunphrá?/chûaj/ Oh, my goodness! (used esp. by women).

ช่วยกัน chûaj/kan to help each other, everyone to help. See examples.

o ช่วยกันคนละไม้คนละมือ chûaj/kan-khonlamáaj/ɔ khonlamyy/ colloq. each one gives a helping hand.

o พวกเราจงช่วยกันเถิด phûagraw/ coŋchûaj/kanɔ thòəd/ Let's all pitch in!

ช่วยชีวิต chûaj/chiiwíd/ V to save (someone's) life.

ช่วยด้วย chûaj/!dûaj/ Help! (an urgent call).

ช่วยเหลือ chûajlŷa/ V to help out, assist, give help. การ-- assisting, assistance. ความ-- assistance, aid.

รัฐมนตรีช่วยว่าการ (คน,ท่าน) rádthamontrii/ɔ chûajwâakaan/ (khon/, thân/) N deputy minister (of the government).

เอาใจช่วย ʔawcaj′chûaj′ V to give moral support (to), root (for).

ช่วเลข chawalêeg′ N shorthand. การ-- stenography. นัก-- stenographer.

ชวา chawaa′ pN Java.

ชวาลา (ดวง) chawaa′laa′ (duaŋ′) N (oil) lamp, torch.

ช่อ chɔɔ′ C cluster, bunch (as of fruit, flowers).

ช่อดอกไม้ (ช่อ) chɔɔ′dɔɔgmáaj′ (chɔɔ′) N bouquet, corsage.

ชอก in ชอกช้ำ, ช้ำชอก chɔɔgchám′, chámchɔɔg′ V to be bruised.

ช็อค, ช้อค chɔ́g′ V to be shocked. [f. Eng.]

ช็อค (แท่ง) chɔ́g′*(thɛ̂ŋ′) N chalk. →Also ชอล์ก. [f. Eng.]

ชอง in ช่ำชอง châmchɔɔŋ′ V to be expert, skillful, proficient.

ช่อง (ช่อง) chɔ̂ŋ′*(chɔ̂ŋ′) N 1. opening, hole (through something), cavity, space, gap. 2. fig. opportunity, opening.

ช่องกุญแจ (ช่อง) chɔ̂ŋkuncɛɛ′ (chɔ̂ŋ′) N keyhole.

ช่องขายตั๋ว (ช่อง) chɔ̂ŋkhǎajtǔa′ (chɔ̂ŋ′) N ticket window.

ช่องเขา (ช่อง) chɔ̂ŋkhǎw′ (chɔ̂ŋ′) N mountain pass.

ช่องคลอด (ช่อง) chɔ̂ŋkhlɔ̂ɔd′ (chɔ̂ŋ′) N eleg. vagina, birth canal.

ช่องแคบ (ช่อง, แห่ง) chɔ̂ŋkhɛ̂ɛb′ (chɔ̂ŋ′, hɛ̀ŋ′) N 1. strait. 2. channel. 3. (mountain) pass.

ช่องท้อง chɔ̂ŋthɔ́ɔŋ′ N abdominal cavity.

ช่องทาง (ทาง) chɔ̂ŋthaaŋ′ (thaaŋ′) N 1. way, means. 2. chance, opportunity.

ช่องไฟ (ช่อง) chɔ̂ŋfaj′ (chɔ̂ŋ′) N idiom. spaces between letters or words.

ช่องมอง chɔ̂ŋmɔɔŋ′ N peephole, small window.

ช่องว่าง (ช่อง, แห่ง) chɔ̂ŋwâaŋ′ (chɔ̂ŋ′, hɛ̀ŋ′) N 1. a vacant or unoccupied space or room. 2. gap. 3. blank space (as on an application).

ชี้ช่อง chíi′chɔ̂ŋ′. Short for ชี้ช่องทาง.

ชี้ช่องทาง chíi′chɔ̂ŋthaaŋ′ to point the way, guide, counsel, advise.

บ้านช่อง bâanchɔ̂ŋ′ N colloq. home, house.

ชอน chɔɔn′ V to bore, dig, burrow (in a winding or zigzag fashion).

ช่อน in ปลาช่อน (ตัว) plaachɔ̂ɔn′ (tua′) N 1. serpenthead, a kind of fresh water fish. 2. euphem. penis.

ช้อน (คัน) chɔ́ɔn′ (khan′) V 1. to scoop, dip up, skim. 2. to bend, curve (esp. upwards). N 3. spoon. 4. long-handled fish net, dip net.

ช้อน(...)ขึ้น chɔ́ɔn′(...)khŷn′ 1. to lift up (e.g. the head of a person who has fainted). 2. to bend, curve upwards (as the horns of a buffalo).

ช้อนช่อม chɔ́ɔnsɔ̂ɔm′ N "spoon and fork," i.e. silverware, consisting of fork and spoon. Cf. Eng. "knife and fork."

ชอบ chɔ̂ɔb′ V 1. to like, be fond of. 2. to like (to do something). 3. to be pleased, satisfied. 4. to be right, appropriate. การ-- (see below). ความ-- merit; favor (with someone).

การชอบ kaanchɔ̂ɔb′ N 1. the right thing, what conforms to certain rules or standards. 2. fondness (for doing something, expressed by a following verb).

o การชอบกิน kaanchɔ̂ɔbkin′ (someone's) fondness for eating.

ชอบกล chɔ̂ɔbkon′ V to be out of the ordinary, funny, strange, peculiar.

o ดูชอบกล duu′chɔ̂ɔbkon′ to seem out of the ordinary, funny, strange, peculiar.

o ดูชอบกลดี duu′chɔ̂ɔbkon′-dii′ to seem right, sound good.

o ดูไม่ชอบกล duu′mâjchɔ̂ɔbkon′ to seem inappropriate, funny, strange, peculiar.

ชอบใจ chɔ̂ɔbcaj′ V 1. to be pleased, happy, amused. 2. to be satisfied, gratified. →Syn. พอใจ, ถูกใจ.

ชอบด้วย chɔ̂ɔb′dûajɔ to agree with, be in accordance with.

o ชอบด้วยกฎหมาย chɔ̂ɔb′dûajkòdmǎaj′ to be lawful, legitimate.

ชอบที่จะ chɔ̂ɔb′thîicaɔ ought to.

ชอบธรรม chɔ̂ɔb′tham′ V to be righteous, just, honest.

ชอบนักชอบหนา chɔ̂ɔbnág′chɔ̂ɔbnǎa′ V elab. colloq. to favor highly, to like very much.

ชอบพอ chɔ̂ɔbphɔɔ′ V to be fond of, to love.

มิชอบ míchɔ̂ɔb′ to be wrong, illegal, inappropriate, bad, dishonest.

o คิดมิชอบ khíd′míchɔ̂ɔb′ to have evil intentions, have unrighteous thoughts.

o ในทางมิชอบ najthaaŋ′míchɔ̂ɔb′ in an unlawful manner, illegally.

ไม่ชอบ mâjchɔ̂ɔb′ 1. to dislike, be displeased. 2. to be inappropriate, improper, out of keeping (with).

o ไม่ชอบด้วยกฎหมาย mâjchɔ̂ɔb′dûajkòdmǎaj′ to be against the law, unlawful, illegal.

o ไม่ชอบที่จะ mâjchɔ̂ɔb′thîicaɔ ought not, should not.

รับผิดชอบ rábphìdchɔ̂ɔb′ V to be responsible (for). ความ-- responsibility.

เห็นดีเห็นชอบ(กับ) hěndii′hěnchɔ̂ɔb′(kaɔ) V elab. colloq. to agree (with), approve, be in favor (of). ความ-- approval. →Also เห็นชอบ, เห็นดี.

เห็นผิดเป็นชอบ hěnphìd′penchɔ̂ɔb′ to mistake wrong for right, bad for good.

ช้อย. See entries below.

ปดช้อย chódchɔ́ɔj′ V to be gentle, soft, graceful in manner (used of women).

แช่มช้อย chɛ̂mchɔ́ɔj′ V to be beautiful, cute, charming.

ชอล์ก (แท่ง) chɔ́g′*(thɛ̂ŋ′) N chalk. [f. Eng.] →Also ช้อค.

ช่อุ่ม ๑ chaʔùm′ rM modifier used with เขียว "green" in the sense of "bright, fresh" (of vegetation only). →Sometimes also ฉอุ่ม.

ช่อุ่ม ๒ chaʔùm′ V to be dark, cloudy, overcast.

ชะ ๑ cháʔ′ V to rinse, to wash away.

ชะล้าง cháʔláaŋ′ V to rinse, wash away.

ชะ ๒, ชะ ๆ chá′, cháchá′↑ E excl. indicating reproach, anger, contempt.

ชะง่อน chaŋɔ̀n′* N overhanging rock.

ชะงัก chaŋág′ V to stop abruptly.

ชะงักงึก chaŋág′ŋʉ̀g′ V to stop suddenly, stop short.

ติดชะงัก tìd′chaŋág′ V to be stuck, get stuck.

ชะงัด chaŋád′ V to be effective, sure, certain.

ชะเง้อ chaŋə́ə′ V to stretch one's neck out to see.

ชะแง้ chaŋɛ́ɛ′ V to stretch one's neck out to see.

ชะโงก chaŋôog′ V to poke (one's head) out, lean out.

o ชะโงกหน้าต่าง chaŋôog′nâatàaŋ′ to thrust (one's head) in or out of a window.

ชะตา chataa′ N fate, destiny. →Also ชตา, ชาตา.

ชะตาตกต่ำ chataa′tògtàm′ to fall on bad days; one's star to have fallen; to have bad luck; to meet an unfavorable fate.

ถูกชะตา thùugchataa′ V (a person) to appeal to one on first sight, strike one as just right, "click" with one, arouse a feeling of natural empathy with one.

ชะนวน FS. See ชนวน.

ชะนะ FS. See ชนะ.

ชะนิด FS. See ชนิด.

ชะนี (ตัว)chanii′ (tua′) N gibbon.

ชะบา FS. See ชบา.

ชะมด (ตัว) chamód′ (tua′) N civet cat.

ชะมอย FS. See ชมอย.

ชะมัด,--ญาติ chamád′ chamád′jâad′ colloq. very, extremely.

ชะมาย FS. See ชมาย.

ชะรอย charɔɔj′ Cj probably; perhaps, maybe.

ชะลอ chalɔɔ′ V to slow down.

ชะลอม (ใบ) chalɔɔm′ (baj′) N a kind of bamboo basket used for fruit. It has loose strips on top which can be opened widely or tied shut.

ชะลูด in สูงชะลูด sǔuŋ′chalûud′ V to be very tall and thin (as a flagpole).

ชะเลย FS. See เชลย.

ชะแลง (อัน) chalɛɛŋ′ (ʔan′) N crowbar.

ชัก ๑ chág′ V 1. to pull, draw out, pull at. 2. to have spasms, convulsions. คน-- (see below). →Syn. 1. ดึง.

คนชัก khonchág′ N spastic (person); one who is having spasms, convulsions.

ชักโครก (ที่, อัน) chágkhrôog′ V 1. to flush (the toilet). N 2. flush-toilet (thîi′, ʔan′).

ชักเงา chágŋaw′ V 1. to shine, polish. 2. to be shiny, glossy.

o น้ำมันชักเงา námman′chágŋaw′ N varnish.

ชักจูง chágcuuŋ′ V to urge, persuade, induce, incite.

ชักชวน chágchuan′ V to induce, persuade, urge (to do something).

For items not found under ชะ-, see ช- followed by the appropriate consonant.

ชักช้า chágcháa′ V to be slow, to hesitate, to delay. →Syn. ร่ำไร.

ชักแด็ก ๆ chág′dɛ̀gdɛ̀g′ to have violent convulsions, muscular spasms.

ชักตัวอย่าง chág′tuajàaŋ′ to give an example.

ชักธง chágthoŋ′ to raise the flag.

ชักนำ chágnam′ V 1. to lead. 2. to persuade, induce.

o ขดชักนำ khòd′chágnam′ elect. induction coil.

ชักปีกกา chág′plìgkaa′ to form a flank defense.

ชักใย chágjaj′ to form threads, spin a web or cocoon (as spiders, silkworms).

ชักรูป chágrûub′ colloq. to take a picture, to photograph.

ชักว่าว chágwâw′ to fly a kite.

ชักหน้าไม่ถึงหลัง chág′nâa′-mâjthyŋlăŋ′ idiom. can't make ends meet.

โรคชัก rôogchág′ N colloq. disease characterized by convulsions.

ลิ้นชัก (ลิ้นชัก) línchág′ (línchág′) N drawer.

ชัก ๒, ชักจะ chágɔ, chágcaɔ AA tend to, be inclined to, (start) getting, be starting to get. →Syn. ถอน ๒.

o วันนี้อากาศชักจะร้อน wanníi′ ʔaakàad′chágɔ carɔ́ɔn↓ It tends to be hot today.

o ฉันชักจะหิวแล้วละ chán′ chágcahǐw′lɛ́ɛwla?↓ I'm starting to get hungry.

ชัง chaŋ′ V to hate, detest.

เกลียดชัง klìadchaŋ′ V to hate, detest, despise (hate strongly). ความ-- hatred.

จงเกลียดจงชัง coŋklìad′coŋchaŋ′ V elab. colloq. to hate and hold a grudge against (someone).

ชิงชัง chiŋchaŋ′ to hate, abhor, detest, loathe.

นึกชังในใจ nýgchaŋ′najcaj′ to harbor feelings of hatred.

เลือกที่รักมักที่ชัง lŷag′thîirág′-mág′thîichaŋ′ elab. colloq. to show partiality, show favoritism; to be partial in one's likes and dislikes.

ชั่ง ๑ châŋ′ V to weigh. เครื่อง-- (see below).

คันชั่ง (คัน) khanchâŋ′ (khan′) N 1. balance, scales. 2. beam, transverse bar of a balance.

เครื่องชั่ง (เครื่อง, อัน, คัน) khrŷaŋchâŋ′ (khrŷaŋ′, ʔan′, khan′) N scales, balance.

ชั่งใจ châŋcaj′ V to weigh in the mind, consider.

ชั่งหลวง châŋlŭaŋ′ C a unit of weight equivalent to 600 grams.

ตาชั่ง (คัน, อัน) taachâŋ′ (khan′, ʔan′) N colloq. scales, balance.

มาตราชั่ง mâadtraa′châŋ′ N system of weight measurement.

ชั่ง ๒ châŋ′ C a former monetary unit equivalent to 80 baht.

ชั่ง ๓ châŋ′ See ช่าง ๒,๓.

ชัฏ in ป่าชัฏ pàa′chád′ N dense jungle, deep forest.

ชัด chád′ V to be plain, clear, distinct.

แจ่มชัด cɛ̀mchád′ V to be clear (in meaning).

ชัดเจน chádceen′ V to be plain, clear, distinct, explicit.

ชัดแจ้ง, แจ้งชัด chádcɛ̂ɛŋ′, cɛ̂ɛŋchád′ V to be clear, distinct. อย่าง-- clearly.

ชัดแจ๋ว chád′cɛ̌w′ V colloq. to be very clear.

ชัด ๆ chádchád′ clearly, obviously, apparently.

ชัดถ้อยชัดคำ chádthɔ̂j′chádkham′ elab. colloq. clearly, distinctly, articulately.

แน่ชัด nɛ̂ɛchád′ V 1. to be certain, definite, sure. sV 2. surely, clearly.

เป็นที่เห็นชัด penthîi′hěnchád′ it is evident (that).

ฟังไม่ชัด faŋ′mâjchád′ 1. to be unclear, indistinct (of sound). 2. to be unable to hear clearly.

ชัน ๑ (ก้อน) chan′ (kɔ̂ɔn′) N dammar.

ชัน ๒ chan′ V to be steep.

ตั้งชัน tâŋ′chan′ V (hair, fur) to stand on end, be on end.

ชั้น chán′ N 1. stage, level, layer, stratum, class (in school; in accomodations), rank, grade; shelf; floor, story. C 2. idem. →Syn. อันดับ.

ชั้นครู chánkhruu′ masterful, first-rate.

ชั้นจัตวา cháncàdtawaa′ the fourth (and lowest) rank in civil service.

ชั้นเชิง, เชิงชั้น (อย่าง) chánchəəŋ′, chəəŋchán′ (jàaŋ′) N tactics, strategy, stratagem, trick.

ชั้นต้น chántôn′ beginning stage, beginning level, lower level.

o ในชั้นต้น najchántôn′ at first, at the beginning stage.

ชั้นตรี chántrii′ the third rank (from the top) in civil service.

ชั้นเตรียม chántriam′ pre-elementary level (of education).

ชั้นโท chánthoo′ the second rank (from the top) in civil service.

ชั้นนอก chánnɔ̂ɔg′ the outside, the outer layer.

o เสื้อชั้นนอก (ตัว) sŷachánnɔ̂ɔg′ (tua′) N coat.

ชั้นนำ chánnam′ leading, outstanding.

ชั้นใน chánnaj′ the inside, the inner layer.

o กางเกงชั้นใน (ตัว) kaaŋkeeŋ′chánnaj′ (tua′) N shorts, underpants; panties.

o กระโปรงชั้นใน kraprooŋ′chánnaj′ N slip, woman's undergarment.

o เสื้อชั้นใน (ตัว) sŷachánnaj′ (tua′) N undershirt, man's undergarment; vest; slip, woman's undergarment.

ชั้นบน chánbon′ upstairs, upper story, upper layer, upper shelf.

ชั้นประถม chán′prathǒm′ N elementary grades, grade school level.

o โรงเรียนชั้นประถม (แห่ง, โรงเรียน) rooŋrian′-chán′prathǒm′ (hèŋ′, rooŋrian′) N elementary school, grade school.

ชั้นผู้ใหญ่ chán′phûujàj′ senior, high-ranking.

ชั้นมัธยม chán′mádthajom′ secondary school level.

o ชั้นมัธยมตอนปลาย chán′-mádthajom′tɔɔnplaaj′ senior high school level.

o ชั้นมัธยมบริบูรณ์ chán′-mádthajom′bɔɔribuun′ N the final year of secondary schools.

ชั้นเยี่ยม chánjîam′ top grade, first class, best.

ชั้นแรก chánrɛ̂ɛg′ (at) first; the first step, shelf, class, stage etc.

o ในชั้นแรก najchánrɛ̂ɛg′ at first, at the beginning stage.

ชั้นล่าง chánlâaŋ′ downstairs, lower story, lower layer, lower shelf.

ชั้นสอง chánsɔ̌ɔŋ′ second class (accomodations); the second story, level, stage, etc.

ชั้นสาม chánsǎam′ third class (accomodations); the third story, level, stage, etc.

ชั้นหนึ่ง chánnỳŋ′ first class (accomodations).

ชั้นหลัง chánlǎŋ′ the later generation.

o ในชั้นหลัง najchánlǎŋ′ later, in a later period.

ชั้นอ๋อง chán?ɔ̌ŋ′ colloq. top, of the best quality, outstanding.

ชั้นเอก chán?èeg′ the first (highest) rank in civil service.

ซ้ำชั้น sámchán′ to repeat a class (in school), take a course over.

ในชั้นต้น. See under ชั้นต้น above.

เป็นชั้น ๆ penchánchán′ in layers, ranks, grades, classes.

ชันสูตร channasùud′ V to examine, test.

o ชันสูตรศพ channasùud′sòb′ to perform an autopsy.

ชัย chaj′, chajɔ, chajjaɔ N victory.

ชัยชนะ (ครั้ง, อย่าง) chajchaná?′ (khráŋ′, jàaŋ′) N victory.

o ได้ชัยชนะ dâajchajchaná?′ to gain a victory, to win (a war).

ชิงชัย chiŋchaj′ V 1. to fight (competitively). 2. to compete for victory (as in a battle).

มีชัย mii′chaj′ V lit. to be victorious, win.

ชัยนาท chajnâad′ pN Chainat, a township in C Thailand.

ชั่ว ๑ chûa′ V to be bad, vile, wicked. ความ-- vice(s), evil(s). →Syn. เลว. →Ant. ดี.

ค่อยยังชั่ว khɔ̂jjaŋchûa′ 1. to get better, feel better. 2. not so bad.

ใจชั่ว cajchûa′ V to be bad (at heart).

ชั่วช้า chûacháa′ V to be bad, evil, vile, base.

ผู้หญิงคนชั่ว (คน) phûujǐŋ′khonchûa′ (khon′) N a prostitute.

ชั่ว ๒ chûa′ C time span, period, duration.

ชั่วกัปป์ชั่วกัลป์ chûakàb′chûakan′ elab. colloq. forever, for all time, eternally.

ชั่วขณะ chûakhanà?′ for a while, for a moment, temporarily.

ชั่วคราว chûakhraaw′ temporarily, for the time being; temporary.

o เป็นการชั่วคราว penkaan′chûakhraaw′ 1. to be temporary, to be a temporary matter. 2. temporarily, as a temporary thing.

ชั่วครู่ chûakhrûu′ (for) a moment.

ชั่วนาตาปี chûanaa′taapii′ elab. colloq. year in and year out, for ever.

ชั่วฟ้าดินสลาย chûafáa′dinsalǎaj′ elab. colloq. idiom. forever, till doomsday. →Also ชั่วฟ้าดิน.

ชั่วโมง chûamooŋ′ C hour.

o เข็มชั่วโมง (อัน) khěm′chûamooŋ′ (?an′) N hour hand (of a clock).

o สามชั่วโมง sǎam'chûamooŋ' (for) three hours.

ชั่วระยะ chûarajá?/ interval of space or time.

ชั่วระยะเวลา chûarajá?'weelaa' (for) a period of, (for) an interval (of time) of.

ชั่วลูกชั่วหลาน chûalûug'chûalǎan' generation after generation. →Cf. ลูกหลาน.

ชั่วแล่น chûalɛ̂n' colloq. (for) a brief moment, momentarily; momentary.

ชั่วเวลา chûaweelaa' for, in the time of; for, in a period of.

o ชั่วเวลาสองชั่วโมง chûaweelaa'sɔ̌ɔŋchûamooŋ' for two hours; in two hours.

o ชั่วเวลาอีกไม่ช้า chûaweelaa'?ìigmâjcháa' it won't be long now (until something takes place).

ชั่วแว็บเดียว chûawɛ́b'diaw' (for) a split second.

ไม่ชั่วแต่ mâjchûatɛ̀ɛ⊃ not only, it is not only.

ชา ๑ chaa' N tea (leaves).

ชาเย็น chaajen' N iced tea.

น้ำชา námchaa' N tea (the liquid).

ใบชา bajchaa' N tea leaves.

ชา ๒ chaa' V to be numb.

เฉื่อยชา chỳajchaa' V to be inert, inactive.

ชาเย็น chaa'jen' V to be cold, indifferent, unfeeling, cool (toward someone). ความ-- coolness, coldness (of behavior).

มึนชา mynchaa' to be cold (in disposition).

เย็นชา jen'chaa' V 1. to be cold, unresponsive, unfeeling, cool (e.g. toward someone). 2. to be numb from cold.

เหน็บชา nèbchaa' V 1. to be numb. 2. to have beriberi. N 3. beriberi; short for โรค--.

o โรคเหน็บชา rôog'nèbchaa' N beriberi.

ชา ๓ in ลือชา lyychaa' to be well-known, widely spoken of.

ช้า ๑ cháa' V 1. to be slow, late, delayed (in arriving). sV 2. slowly. ความ-- slowness, lateness. อย่าง-- at the latest. →Dist. ล้าย ๒. →Syn. นาน, เนิ่น. →Ant. เร็ว. →Sometimes coupled with นาน "long (of time)."

เฉื่อยช้า chỳajcháa' V 1. to be slow. sV 2. slowly.

ชักช้า chágcháa' V to be slow, to hesitate, delay. →Syn. ร่ำไร.

ช้า ๆ cháacháa' sV slowly, more slowly.

ช้านาน cháanaan' V to be long (of time).

ช้าลง cháa'loŋ V to get slower, slow down, slow up.

ช้าเสียแล้ว cháa'síalɛ́ɛw' cháa'sálɛ́ɛw' it's too late.

เชื่องช้า chŷaŋcháa' V to be slow, sluggish.

แช่มช้า chɛ̂mcháa' V to be slow and graceful.

มิช้ามินาน mícháa'mínaan' writ. not long (afterwards), soon (afterwards).

ไม่ช้า mâjcháa' soon, in a short time, shortly. →Also ใน--.

o ไม่ช้าก็เร็ว mâjcháa'kɔ̂rew' sooner or later.

o ไม่ช้าไม่นาน mâjcháa'mâjnaan' by and by.

o อยู่มาไม่ช้า jùumaa'mâjcháa' writ. not long afterwards.

รอช้า rɔɔcháa' V to hesitate, delay.

ล่าช้า lâacháa' V 1. to be tardy, late. 2. to be slow. ความ-- tardiness, lateness.

ช้า ๒. See entries below.

ชั่วช้า chûacháa' V to be bad, evil, vile, base.

ต่ำช้า tàmcháa' V to be depraved, morally bad.

หยาบช้า jàabcháa' V to be rude, vulgar (in words, behavior).

ช้า ๓ in ป่าช้า (แห่ง) pàacháa' (hὲŋ') N cemetery.

ช่าง ๑ (คน) châaŋ', châaŋ⊃ (khon') N 1. artisan, specialist, expert, master. 2. bound stem meaning "artisan, smith" placed before verbs or nouns to form noun derivatives. V 3. to be skilled. การ-- (see below). →See also 2. คน ๑.

NOTE 1. ช่าง is freely used as a bound stem meaning "artisan, smith" placed before nouns or verbs to form noun derivatives; 1st and 2nd examples. Common English translations are -smith ("goldsmith") and the agentives -er ("photographer") and -ist ("artist"); 1st, 2nd and 3rd examples.

o ช่างทอง châaŋthɔɔŋ' goldsmith: "smith (in) gold."

o ช่างพิมพ์ châaŋphim' printer: "artisan (who) prints."

o ช่างเขียน châaŋkhǐan' artist, painter, draftsman: "artisan, craftsman (who) writes, draws."

NOTE 2. ช่าง is not equivalent to คน and ผู้ when used as agentive, since ช่าง implies skill and craftsmanship, but the three stems are occasionally used in similar circumstances, with or without some slight difference in meaning; see examples.

- ช่างตัดผม châaŋtàdphŏm/ barber. คนตัดผม khontàdphŏm/ idem.
- ช่างพิมพ์ châaŋphim/ printer. ผู้พิมพ์ phûuɔphim/ publisher, printer.

NOTE 3. All noun derivatives based on ช่าง take คน as their clf. and (คน) is therefore omitted in all subentries coming in this category.

การช่าง kaanchâaŋ/ N 1. craft, skilled work. 2. engineering, construction (as a science).

ช่างกล châaŋkon/ N mechanic. การ-- mechanics.

- นายช่างกล naajchâaŋkon/ N mechanical engineer.

ช่างก่อสร้าง châaŋkɔ̀ɔsâaŋ/ N builder.

ช่างแก้นาฬิกา châaŋkɛ̂ɛ/naalikaa/ N watch-repairman.

ช่างแกะ châaŋkɛ̀ʔ/ N sculptor, carver.

ช่างเขียน châaŋkhǐan/ N painter (artist), draftsman.

ช่างเครื่อง châaŋkhrŷaŋ/ N 1. mechanic, machinist. 2. engineer (operator of an engine).

ช่างเครื่องยนตร์ châaŋkhrŷaŋjon/ N machinist, mechanic.

ช่างจักสาน châaŋcàgsǎan/ N wickerworker.

ช่างซ่อม châaŋsɔ̂ɔm/ N repairman.

ช่างตัดผม châaŋdàdphŏm/ N hairdresser.

ช่างต่อเรือ châaŋtɔ̀ɔrya/ N boatbuilder, shipbuilder.

ช่างตัดผม châaŋtàdphŏm/ N barber.

ช่างตัดเสื้อ châaŋtàdsŷa/ N tailor, dressmaker.

ช่างถ่ายรูป châaŋthàajrûub/ N photographer.

ช่างทอผ้า châaŋthɔɔphâa/ N weaver.

ช่างทอง châaŋthɔɔŋ/ N goldsmith.

ช่างทาสี châaŋthaasǐi/ N painter (workman).

ช่างทำเครื่องเงิน châaŋtham/khrŷaŋŋən/ N silversmith.

ช่างปั้น châaŋpân/ N modeller (one who molds clay).

ช่างฝีมือ châaŋfǐimyy/ N skilled craftsman.

ช่างพิมพ์ châaŋphim/ N printer.

ช่างเพชร châaŋphéd/ N jeweler.

ช่างฟิต châaŋfíd/ N mechanic. [ฟิต f. Eng. "fit"]

ช่างไฟฟ้า châaŋfajfáa/ N electrician.

ช่างภาพ châaŋphâab/ N photographer, camera-

man.

ช่างไม้ châaŋmáaj/ N carpenter. การ-- carpentry.

ช่างยนตร์ châaŋjon/ N mechanical engineer.

ช่างย้อมผ้า châaŋjɔ́ɔmphâa/ N dyer.

ช่างโลหะ châaŋloohàʔ/ N metalworker.

ช่างสลัก châaŋsalàg/ N sculptor.

ช่างแสง usually in โรงช่างแสง rooŋchâaŋsɛ̌ɛŋ/ N arsenal.

ช่างหัดใหม่ châaŋhàdmàj/ N apprentice.

ช่างเหล็ก châaŋlèg/ N blacksmith.

ช่างอากาศ châaŋʔaakàad/ N airplane mechanic.

ทหารช่าง thahǎanchâaŋ/ N 1. corps of engineers. 2. military technician, military engineer.

นายช่าง (คน) naajchâaŋ/ (khon/) N 1. craftsman, artisan. 2. short for นายช่างกล or other derivative beginning with นายช่าง.

ช่าง ๒ châŋɔ* AA 1. very, so, awfully, terribly, terrifically. Used especially with descriptive verbs; 1st, 2nd, and 3rd examples. 2. bound stem meaning "given to, good at, full of," placed before verbs to form new verb derivatives. Also sometimes corresponds to the English suffixes -y, -ative, -ant, -ive; 4th, 5th, and 6th examples. →Cf. ขี้- ๒, เจ้า- ๓.

- เขาช่างสวยเสียจริง ๆ kháwchâŋsǔaj/síacinciŋ/↓ She's very beautiful, really beautiful.
- ช่างขี้เกียจเสียจริง ๆ châŋkhîikìad/síacinciŋ/↓ How terribly lazy!
- ช่างน่าตื่นเต้นเสียเหลือเกิน châŋnâa/tỳyntên/-síalýakəən/↓ How terrifically exciting!
- ช่างคุย châŋkhuj/ to be chatty, full of chatter.
- ช่างพูด châŋphûud/ V to be talkative, full of talk.
- ช่างสังเกต châŋsǎŋkèed/ V to be observant, perceptive.

ช่างกระไรเลย châŋ/krarajləəj/ How could he! How come? (expressing reproach, indignation).

ช่างคิด châŋkhíd/ to be given to thinking, be full of ideas.

- เขาช่างคิดจริงนะ kháwchâŋkhíd/ciŋná/↓ He's really good at thinking.
- เขาเป็นคนช่างคิด kháwpenkhon/châŋkhíd/↓ He is a person given to thinking, a person who uses his brain.

ช่างเถียง châŋthǐaŋ′ V to be good at arguing, argumentative.

ช่างนึกช่างคิด châŋnýg′châŋkhíd′ elab. colloq. to be good at thinking, be full of ideas.

ช่างพูดช่างคุย châŋphûud′châŋkhuj′ V elab. colloq. to be talkative and full of chatter.

ช่างมี...เสียจริง ๆ châŋmiiɔ...sǐaciŋciŋ′ there certainly are...

ช่างเหลือเกิน châŋ′lýakəən′ V 1. to be extraordinary, terrific. 2. to be awful, terrible.

ช่าง ๓ châŋ′* V 1. to let (it) go, let (it) alone, let (it) be. 2. to be unconcerned, not to care.

o ลูกเต้าจะเป็นอย่างไรก็ช่าง lûugtâw′capenjàaŋɔ raj′→kɔchâŋ′↓ (she) doesn't care what will become of (her) children.

ช่างเขาปะไร châŋ′kháwparaj↓ Let them (do such and such)! It makes no difference what they do!

ช่างเถอะ châŋthə?′↓ Never mind! Forget it! Who cares?

ช่างเป็นไร, -ปะไร châŋ′penraj↓, châŋ′paraj↓ Let it be. Let it go. I don't care. I don't care what happens (to it, to him).

ช่างมัน, --ปะไร, --เป็นไร châŋman↓, châŋ′man↓, châŋ′manparaj′↓ châŋ′manpenraj↓ Let it be. Let it go. I don't care about him, about it. I don't care what happens to him, to it.

ช่างหัวมันปะไร châŋhǔa′manparaj↓ colloq. I couldn't care less what happens to it. I don't give a darn what happens to him.

ช้าง (เชือก,ตัว) cháaŋ′ N elephant (chýag′ eleg.; tua′ com.).

ขุนช้างขุนแผน. See under ขุน.

งวงช้าง (งวง) ŋuaŋcháaŋ′ (ŋuaŋ′) N trunk of the elephant.

งาช้าง (อัน,ข้าง) ŋaacháaŋ′ N 1. ivory. 2. elephant tusk (?an′, khâaŋ′).

ชนช้าง choncháaŋ′ V to fight on elephantback. Both rider and elephant engage in combat.

ช้างงา cháaŋŋaa′ N tusker, tusked elephant.

ช้างต้น cháaŋtôn′ N the traditional State Elephant, the king's personal elephant.

ช้างเถื่อน cháaŋthŷan′ N wild elephant.

ช้างเท้าหลัง cháaŋtháawlǎŋ′ N "the hind legs of

the elephant," a simile used to describe one who is a follower.

ช้างเผือก cháaŋphỳag′ N white (albino) elephant.

o ทางช้างเผือก thaaŋcháaŋphỳag′ N the Milky Way.

ช้างพลาย cháaŋphlaaj′ N bull elephant.

ช้างพัง cháaŋphaŋ′ N cow elephant.

ช้างสาร cháaŋsǎan′ N elephant, esp. a large, powerful one.

ช้างสีดอ cháaŋsǐidɔɔ′ N a tuskless bull elephant.

หูช้าง (บาน) hǔucháaŋ′ (baan′) N side wing windows on an automobile: "elephant's ears."

ชาญ. See entries below. →Cf. ชำนาญ.

กล้าหาญชาญชัย klâahǎan′chaanchaj′ V to be bold, brave, courageous.

ชาญฉลาด chaanchalàad′ V to be ingenious.

เชี่ยวชาญ chîawchaan′ V to be experienced skillfull, expert.

ชาด châad′ N annatto; rouge.

สภากาชาด saphaakaachâad′ N the Red Cross.

ชาตา. See ชะตา.

ชาติ ๑ (ชาติ) châad′ (châad′) N nation, nationality, race.

ขายชาติ khǎajchâad′ V to betray one's country, commit treason.

คณะชาติ khaná?′/châad′ nationalist, of the nationalist faction.

ชาติไทย châadthaj′ N Thai nationality; the Thai nation.

o ชนชาติไทย (คน) chonchâadthaj′ (khon′) N people of Thai nationality.

ชาตินิยม châad′níjom′ nationalistic. นัก-- nationalist.

o พรรคชาตินิยม phágchâad′níjom′ N nationalist party.

o ลัทธิชาตินิยม ládthí?′-châad′níjom′ N nationalism.

ชาติผิวขาว châad′phǐwkhǎaw′ N the white race.

ชาติผิวดำ châad′phǐwdam′ N the black race.

ชาติผิวเหลือง châad′phǐwlɰ̌aŋ′ N the yellow race.

เชื้อชาติ (เชื้อชาติ) chýachâad′ (chýachâad′) N race, nationality. →Dist. สัญชาติ.

o สัญชาติอเมริกัน เชื้อชาติไทย sǎnchâad′?ameeɔ rikan′→chýachâad′thaj′ (of) American citizenship, Thai nationality.

ต่างชาติ tàaŋchâad′ foreign, of another nationality. คน-- foreigner, esp. a person of another
race.

ต่างชาติต่างภาษา tàaŋchâad′tàaŋphaasǎa′ e l a b.
c o l l o q. (of) different nationality and speech.

ธงชาติ (ผืน) thoŋchâad′ (phǔyn′) N national
flag.

นานาชาติ naanaa′châad′ 1. va rious peoples,
nations. 2. (as n. mod.) international.

ประจำชาติ pracamchâad′ national, characteristic of a nation.

o ธงประจำชาติ (ผืน) thoŋ′pracamchâad′
(phǔyn′) N national flag.

ประเทศชาติ prathêedchâad′ N country, nation.

แปลงชาติ plɛɛŋchâad′ V to become naturalized,
change one's citizenship.

พฤกษชาติ phrýg′sachâad′ N plant, vegetable
kingdom.

พี่น้องร่วมชาติ phîinɔ́ɔŋ′rûamchâad′ (one's) fellow citizens.

เพลงชาติ (เพลง) phleeŋchâad′ (phleeŋ′) N
national anthem.

มนุษยชาติ manúd′sajachâad′ N mankind.

ระหว่างชาติ rawàaŋchâad′ international.

วันชาติ wanchâad′ N National Day.

เศรษฐกิจของชาติ sèedthakìd′khɔ̌ɔŋchâad′ the
national economy.

สัญชาติ sǎnchâad′ N l a w citizenship. →Dist.
เชื้อชาติ.

o สัญชาติอเมริกัน เชื้อชาติไทย sǎnchâad′ʔameeɔ
rikan′→chýachâad′thaj′ (of) American citizenship, Thai nationality.

สันนิบาตชาติ sǎnníbàad′châad′ N the League of
Nations.

องค์การสหประชาชาติ ʔoŋkaan′sahàprachaachâad′
N the United Nations Organization (UN, UNO).

โอนชาติ ʔoonchâad′ to become naturalized, to
change one's citizenship.

โอนเป็นของชาติ ʔoon′penkhɔ̌ɔŋchâad′ to nationalize.

ชาติ ๒ (ชาติ) châad′ (châad′) N (a) life.

ชาติก่อน châadkɔ̀ɔn′ (one's) previous life, existence.

ตลอดชาติ talɔ̀ɔdchâad′ all (one's) life.

ตาปีตาชาติ taapii′taachâad′ i d i o m. year in and
year out.

ชาติ ๓ in รสชาติ ródchâad′ N taste, flavor.

ชาติ ๔ in ธรรมชาติ thammachâad′ N nature.

ชาน ๑ (ชาน) chaan′ (chaan′) N 1. platform, porch
(without roof). 2. environs. Chiefly in compounds.

ชานชาลา (ชานชาลา, แห่ง) chaanchaalaa′, (chaanɔ
chaalaa′, hɛ̀ŋ′) N (railroad) station platform.

ชานชาลาสถานี (ชานชาลา, แห่ง) chaanchaalaa′ɔ
sathǎanii′ (chaanchaalaa′, hɛ̀ŋ′) i d e m.

ชานบ้าน (ชาน) chaanbâan′ (chaan′) N the premises (around a house).

ชานบ้านชานเรือน chaanbâan′chaanryan′ e l a b.
c o l l o q. the premises.

ชานเมือง (แห่ง) chaanmyaŋ′ (hɛ̀ŋ′) N outskirts,
environs of a city. →Dist. ชายเมือง.

ชานสถานี (ชาน, แห่ง) chaansathǎanii′ (chaan′,
hɛ̀ŋ′) N outer edge of a station.

นอกชาน (นอกชาน, แห่ง) nɔ̂ɔgchaan′ (nɔ̂ɔgchaan′,
hɛ̀ŋ′) N (uncovered) porch, open patio (adjoining
the house).

ชาน ๒ chaan′ N Shan. [prob. f. Eng.] →Syn. เงี้ยว.

ชาม (ใบ, ลูก) chaam′ (baj′, lûug′) N 1. bowl, dish.
C 2. bowl, as a measure of quantity.

ถ้วยชาม (ใบ, ลูก) thûajchaam′ (baj′, lûug′) N
the dishes, dishware.

o ตู้ถ้วยชาม (ตู้, ใบ) tûu′thûajchaam′ (tûu′, baj′)
N cupboard.

ชาย ๑ (คน) chaaj′ (khon′) N c o m. 1. man. 2.
male (of people only). →Chiefly in compounds.
→Opp. หญิง. →Dist. 2. ตัวผู้ male (of animals). →Syn. บุรุษ. NOTE. The usual term
for "man" is ผู้ชาย, as below, but in special
cases ชาย occurs alone, as in the following
example.

o ทั้งหญิงและชาย tháŋjĭŋ′-lɛchaaj′ both men and
women.

กระทาชาย (นาย, คน) krathaa′chaaj′ (naaj′, khon′)
N a man. An old word, used only jokingly.

คบชู้สู่ชาย khóbchúu′-sùu′chaaj′ V (a woman) to
have a lover or lovers, have men.

ความเป็นชาย khwaampenchaaj′ N masculinity.

เจ้าชาย (องค์) câwchaaj/ (²oŋ/) N prince.

ชายฉกรรจ์ (คน) chaajchakan/ (khon/) N able-
bodied adult man (approx. 18-30 yrs. old).

ชายโสด (คน) chaajsòod/ (khon/) N bachelor.

ชายหนุ่ม (คน) chaajnùm/ (khon/) N young man,
a youth.

น้องชาย (คน) nɔ́ɔŋchaaj/ (khon/) N 1. younger
brother. 2. slang m. sp. (younger) partner,
bud, buddy (in addressing someone).

บุตรชาย (คน) bùdchaaj/ (khon/) N eleg. son,
male child. →Syn. ลูกชาย com.

ผู้ชาย (คน) phûuchaaj/ (khon/) N 1. man. 2.
male (of people).

○ เด็กผู้ชาย (คน) dègphûuchaaj/, -phuu- (khon/)
boy, lad. →Also เด็กชาย.

ฝ่ายชาย fàajchaaj/ N 1. the man's side. 2.
men's, male.

พี่ชาย (คน) phîichaaj/ (khon/) N 1. older
brother. 2. slang m. sp. (older) partner,
bud, buddy (in addressing someone).

เพศชาย phêedchaaj/ N male sex; masculine
gender.

เพื่อนชาย (คน) phɯ̂anchaaj/ (khon/) N male
friend.

ลูกชาย (คน) lûugchaaj/ (khon/) N son. →Syn.
บุตรชาย eleg.

หลานชาย (คน) lǎanchaaj/ (khon/) N grandson,
nephew.

ชาย ๒ (ชาย, แห่ง) chaaj/ (chaaj/, hɛ̀ŋ/) N 1. edge,
rim, border, periphery. 2. at the edge of, beside, near, along. V 3. to saunter by, saunter
up.

ชายคา (ชายคา) chaajkhaa/ (chaajkhaa/) N
eaves.

ชายแดน (แห่ง) chaajdɛɛn/ (hɛ̀ŋ/) N border,
frontier.

ชายตา chaajtaa/ V to glance sidewise.

ชายทะเล (แห่ง) chaajthalee/ (hɛ̀ŋ/) N seashore.

ชายฝั่ง (แห่ง) chaajfàŋ/ (hɛ̀ŋ/) N coast, shore;
bank, edge (of river).

ชายเมือง (แห่ง) chaajmyaŋ/ (hɛ̀ŋ/) N the edge
of town, i.e. the inside edge of a city or town.
→Dist. ชานเมือง.

ชายหาด (ชายหาด, แห่ง) chaajhàad/ (chaajhàad/,

hɛ̀ŋ/) N beach.

ลอยชาย lɔɔjchaaj/ V 1. to saunter along (e.g.
when speed is needed). sV 2. saunteringly.

ชาย ๓ chaaj/ V to decline, be in descent (of the
afternoon sun).

ชาย ๔ chaaj/ V to blow gently (of the wind).
โชยชาย choojchaaj/ V idem.

ช่าย in ไม่ช่าย. Variant of ไม่ใช่, used to represent a long-drawn-out pronunciation of the second syllable.

ชายา, พระ-- chaajaa/, phráchaajaa/ N roy. wife,
consort.

ชาลา (ชาลา, แห่ง) chaalaa/ (chaalaa/, hɛ̀ŋ/) N
platform (for a railroad station, or between two
palace buildings; normally not for a house).

ชานชาลา, ชานชาลาสถานี (ชานชาลา, แห่ง) chaanᴐ
chaalaa/, chaanchaalaa/sathǎanii/ (chaanchalaa/,
hɛ̀ŋ/) N (railroad) station platform.

ชาว-. Bound stem meaning "inhabitant of, dweller
in," and placed in front of nouns to form noun
derivatives. NOTE. All nouns in the subentries
below take คน as their clf. unless otherwise
marked and (คน) is therefore omitted.

ชนชาวอังกฤษ chonchaaw/²aŋkrìd/ N the British
people, Englishmen.

ชาวกรรมกร chaawkammakɔɔn/ N laborers,
workers.

ชาวกรุง chaawkruŋ/ N city people.

ชาวเกาะ chaawkɔ́²/ N islanders.

ชาวเขาชาวดอย chaawkhǎw/chaawdɔɔj/ N elab.
colloq. mountain people. →Also ชาวเขา.

ชาวคณะ chaawkhaná²/ N members of a group,
of an association.

ชาวจีน chaawciin/ N a Chinese; the Chinese.

ชาวตลาด chaawtalàad/ N an unrefined, common
person.

ชาวตะวันตก chaawtawantòg/ N Occidental, Westerner.

ชาวตะวันออก chaawtawan²ɔ́ɔg/ N Oriental, Easterner.

ชาวต่างประเทศ chaawtàaŋprathêed/ N foreigner.

ชาวไทย chaawthaj/ N a Thai; the Thai.

ชาวนา chaawnaa/ N farmer, rice farmer.

ชาวบ้าน chaawbâan/ N 1. villager, commoner,

the common folk. 2. neighbor.

ชาวบ้านร้านตลาด chaawbâan'-ráan'talàad' N
elab. colloq. the whole neighborhood.

ชาวบูรพา chaawbuuraphaa' N eleg., lit. Easterner, Oriental.

ชาวประมง chaawpramoŋ' N fisherman.

ชาวป่า chaawpàa' N a person living in the wilds,
e.g. a hunter.

ชาวพระนคร chaawphránákhɔɔn' N an inhabitant
of Bangkok, the Bangkokians.

ชาวพื้นเมือง chaawphýynmyaŋ' N native, native
inhabitant.

ชาวเมือง chaawmyaŋ' N 1. native, native inhabitant. 2. townspeople.

ชาวยุโรป chaawjúròob' N a European.

ชาวเรือ chaawrya' N seafarer.

ชาวไร่ชาวนา chaawrâj'chaawnaa' N elab.
colloq. farmers. →See ไร่นา.

ชาวโลก chaawlôog' N inhabitants of the earth.

ชาวสวน chaawsŭan' N gardener (e.g. truck gardener), orchardist.

ชาวเหนือ chaawnʉ̌a' N Northerner.

ชำ ๑ cham' V hort. to start a slip, a cutting, by
soaking temporarily in a pot before planting.

ชำ ๒. See entries below.

ของชำ khɔ̌ɔŋcham' N dry foodstuff, food susceptible of storage. →Also ของแห้ง.

ร้านชำ (ร้าน) ráancham' (ráan') N grocery
store. In Thailand this is normally a store
which sells dry or storable foodstuff only.

ช่ำ châm' V to be satisfied, gratified, full.

o คุยกันอย่างช่ำใจ khuj'-kanjàaŋchâm'caj'
chatted to (their) heart's content.

o เสียช่ำไปเลย síachâm'pajləəj' to one's full
satisfaction.

ช้ำ chám' V to be bruised.

เจ็บช้ำ,--น้ำใจ cèbchám', cèbchám'námcaj' V
to feel hurt, have one's feelings hurt.

ช้อกช้ำ,ช้ำช้อก chɔ́ɔgchám', chámchɔ́ɔg' V to be
bruised.

ช้ำใจ chámcaj' V to feel hurt.

ฟกช้ำ fógchám' V to be bruised, bruised and
swollen.

ช่ำชอง châmchɔɔŋ' V to be expert, skillful, profi-

cient.

ชำนาญ chamnaan' V to be skillful, expert in, experienced in. ความ-- experience, expertise.
ผู้-- an expert. [conv. f. ชาญ]

ชำนิชำนาญ chamní?'chamnaan' V to be skillful.

ชำนิ,--ชำนาญ chamní?', chamní?'chamnaan' V to
be skillful, experienced in.

ชำระ chamrá?' V 1. to rinse, purify, cleanse, clear
up. 2. to pay.

กระดาษชำระ (ม้วน,แผ่น) kradàad'chamrá?'
(múan', phèn') N toilet paper (múan' for a roll;
phèn' for a sheet).

ชำระดอกเบี้ย chamrá?'dɔɔgbîa' to pay interest.

ชำระหนี้ chamrá?'nîi' to pay a debt.

ผ่อนชำระหนี้ phɔ̀ɔn'-chamrá?'nîi' to pay a debt
in installments.

ชำรุด chamrúd' V to be damaged, become damaged,
get out of order, be defective. →Comp. ทรุด.

ชำเรา chamraw' V to rape.

ชำแรก chamrɛ̂ɛg' V to penetrate. →Comp. แทรก,
แซก.

ชำเลือง chamlyaŋ' V to glance sidewise.

ชำแหละ chamlɛ̀?' V to cut, slice (esp. meat).

ชิ chí?', chí' E excl. of contempt, hatred, anger.

ชิง ๑ chiŋ' V 1. to snatch away (from another).
2. to contest for. 3. to compete, vie.

ชิงชัย chiŋchaj' V 1. to fight (competitively).
2. to compete for victory (as in a battle).

ชิงตำแหน่ง chiŋtamnèŋ' V to compete for a title
(as in sports).

ตีชิง tii'chiŋ' V to assault and rob (someone).

ชิง ๒ in ชิงชัง chiŋchaŋ' V to hate, abhor, detest,
loathe.

ชิงช้า (อัน) chiŋcháa' (?an') N swing (for swinging).

ชิด chíd' V to be close, near, nearby.

ใกล้ชิด klâjchíd' V to be near, close, intimate.

มิดชิด mídchíd' completely, entirely, closely,
tightly (covered, wrapped, hidden). อย่าง--
idem.

ชิน ๑ chin' N lead (mineral).

ชิน ๒ chin' V to be used to (it), get used to (it).

เคยชิน khəəjchin' V to be familar (with), accustomed (to). ความ-- familiarity, habit.

ชิ้น chín' C 1. piece (of anything whole), hence clf.

for pieces of clothing, furniture, bread, meat, bones, work (a specific task), etc. N 2. slang lover, sweetheart.

เป็นชิ้นเป็นอัน penchín/penʔan/ V elab. colloq. to be a good, solid piece; to be well organized, well constructed. อย่าง-- well, solidly.

ชิ้นปลามัน chín/plaaman/ colloq. the best part of things, the juiciest, most desirable portion.

ชินโต in คำสนาชินโต sàadsanǎa/chintoo/ N Shinto.

ชิม chim/ V to taste, to take a taste of, to sample. →Syn. ลิ้ม.

ชี ๑ (รูป) chii/ (rûub/) N ascetic (of either sex).
ชีต้น (องค์,รูป) chiitôn/ (ʔoŋ/, rûub/) N (Buddhist) priest.
นางชี (คน) naaŋchii/ (khon/) N eleg. nun. →Syn. See แม่ชี com.
แม่ชี mêɛchii/ N nun. →Syn. ยายชี,นางชี.

ชี ๒ in ผักชี (ต้น) phàgchii/ (tôn/) N coriander.

ชี ๓ in ฝาชี (อัน,ฝา) fǎachii/ (ʔan/,fǎa/) N a mesh cover placed over a dish of food as protection against flies and other insects. It is usually conical in shape and made of wire, bamboo, or rattan.

ชี ๔ in แม่น้ำชี mêɛnáamchii/ pN the Chi (Ji) River, a tributary of the Mun R. in NE Thailand.

ชี้ chíi/ V to point, point at, point out.
เข็มชี้ (อัน) khěmchíi/ (ʔan/) N pointer, indicator.
ชี้ขาด chíi/khàad/ V to make a final decision.
ชี้แจง chíiceɛŋ/ V to explain, make clear.
o คำชี้แจง (ข้อ) kham/chíiceɛŋ/ (khɔ́ɔ/) explanation.
ชี้ช่อง chíichɔ̂ŋ/ V to point the way, to guide, counsel, advise.
o ชี้ช่องทาง chíi/chɔ̂ŋthaaŋ/ idem.
ชี้ตัว chíi/tua/ V to identify, point at (a person).
ชี้มือ chíimyy/ V colloq. to point, point one's finger. →Also ชี้ไม้-- elab. colloq.
ชี้หน้า chíi/nâa/ V 1. to shake one's finger at (in reproach). 2. to point right at (e. g. the culprit).
นิ้วชี้ (นิ้ว) níwchíi/ (níw/) N index finger, forefinger.
ไม่รู้ไม่ชี้ mâjrúu/mâjchíi/ elab. colloq. 1. to

pay no attention; to refuse to listen. 2. to refuse to be answerable for the consequences (e.g. after a warning has been ignored).

ชีพ chîib/, chîibpha⊃ N restricted life. →Usually ชีวิต. →See also อาชีพ.
ครองชีพ khrɔɔŋchîib/ V to make a living.
เครื่องชูชีพ (เครื่อง,ชุด,อัน) khrŷaŋchuuchîib/ (khrŷaŋ/, chúd/,ʔan/) N life preserver.
จุลชีพ (ตัว) cunlachîib/ (tua/) N microbe. [trans. f. Eng.]
ชีพจร chîibphacɔɔn/ N pulse, heartbeat.
o จับชีพจร càb/chîibphacɔɔn/ to take the pulse.
ดับชีพ dàbchîib/ V 1. eleg. to die. sV 2. dead. 3. colloq. awfully, murderously. →For examples see cross reference.
มิจฉาชีพ mídchǎa/chîib/ N illegal or wrong means of making a living.
ร่มชูชีพ (ผืน) rôm/chuuchîib/ (phɯ̌yn/) N parachute.
เลี้ยงชีพ,หา-- líaŋchîib/, hǎa/líaŋchîib/ V to make a living.
สิ้นชีพ sînchîib/ V to die.

ชีว-,ชีวะ-. Bound form mng. "life"; translates "bio-."
ชีวเคมี chii/wákhee/mii/ N biochemistry.
ชีวประวัติ chii/wáprawàd/ N life history, biography.
ชีววิทยา chii/wáwídthajaa/ N biology.
ชีวา in มีชีวิตชีวา miichiiwíd/chiiwaa/ elab. colloq. to be lively, spirited, animated.
ชีวิต (ชีวิต) chiiwíd/ (chiiwíd/) N life.
ค่ายกักกันชีวิต (ค่าย,แห่ง) khâajkàgkan/chiiwíd/ (khâaj/,hɛ̀ŋ/) N concentration camp.
ชีวิตครอบครัว chiiwíd/khrɔ̂ɔbkhrua/ N family life.
ชีวิตชีวา in มีชีวิตชีวา miichiiwíd/chiiwaa/ elab. colloq. to be lively, spirited, animated.
ชีวิตวิวาห์ chiiwíd/wíwaa/ N married life.
ใช้ชีวิต(อย่าง,ให้) chájchiiwíd/ to live one's life, spend one's life (as, like such and such, in such and such a manner (jàaŋ/); for such and such a purpose (hâj/).
เด็ดชีวิต dèd/chiiwíd/ V lit.,eleg. to kill.
ประกันชีวิต prakan/chiiwíd/ V 1. to insure one's life. N 2. life insurance.
ประหารชีวิต prahǎan/chiiwíd/ V eleg. 1. to execute, put to death. 2. to be executed. →Syn.

1. See ฆ่า c o m.

มีชีวิต miichiiwíd′ V 1. to be alive, be living.
2. c o l l o q. to be lively. →Ant. 1. ตาย.

○ สิ่ง(ที่)มีชีวิต sìŋ′-(thîi)mii′chiiwíd′ living
things.

ล้างชีวิต láaŋ′chiiwíd′ V to kill, destroy.
ไว้ชีวิต wáj′chiiwíd′ V to spare the life (of).
สิ้นชีวิต sîn′chiiwíd′ V to die.
เสียชีวิต sĭa′chiiwíd′ V to lose one's life, to die.
เห็นชีวิต hěn′chiiwíd′ V to have seen life, be
experienced about life or living.
เอาชีวิต ʔaw′chiiwíd′ V to take a life, to kill.
เอาชีวิตรอด ʔawchiiwíd′rɔɔd′ to save one's own
life.

ชืด chŷyd′ V to be tasteless.
เย็นชืด jenchŷyd′ V to be stone cold, cold and
tasteless (of food which should be served hot).

ชื่น chŷyn′ V 1. to be glad, cheerful, happy, pleased.
2. to be pleasant, charming.
ชื่นใจ chŷyncaj′ V 1. c o m. to please, delight.
2. to be pleased, delighted. 3. to be pleasant,
charming, refreshing. 4. c o l l o q. to kiss, hug
(a loved one, in order to refresh, satisfy oneself). N 5. sweetheart (used by lovers, by
parents to children). →Also 1-4. ชื่นอกชื่นใจ.
ชื่นชม,ชมชื่น chŷynchom′, chomchŷyn′ V admire,
be delighted (with), pleased (with).
ชื่นบาน chŷynbaan′ V to be cheerful, happy.
ความ-- pleasure, delight, happiness.
ชื่นอกชื่นใจ chŷynʔòg′chŷyncaj′. See mngs. 1-4
under ชื่นใจ above.
ชุ่มชื่น chûmchŷyn′ V 1. to be happy, joyful. 2.
to be pleasant, refreshing.
แช่มชื่น chɛ̂mchŷyn′ V to be pleasant, cheerful,
joyful.
สดชื่น sòdchŷyn′ V to be fresh, lively, cheerful.
ชื้น chŷyn′ V to be damp, moist, humid. ความ--
humidity.
ใจชื้น cajchŷyn′ V to be cheerful, carefree; to
be relieved.
ชื้นแฉะ chŷynchɛ̀ʔ′ V to be damp, wet (as weather on a rainy day).
ชื่อ (ชื่อ) chŷy′ (chŷy′) N c o m. 1. name. V 2.
to be named. →Syn. 1. นาม eleg.

การ์ดชื่อ (แผ่น,ใบ) káadchŷy′ (phɛ̀n′, baj′) N
colloq. calling card. →Now usually นามบัตร.
[การ์ด f. Eng.]
ขึ้นชื่อ khŷnchŷy′ V c o l l o q. 1. to be famous,
well-known, popular, have a reputation. 2. to be
mentioned or talked about often.
ชื่อตัว (ชื่อ) chŷytua′ (chŷy′) first name, given
name.
ชื่อเล่น (ชื่อ) chŷylên′ (chŷy′) N nickname.
ชื่อสกุล (ชื่อ) chŷysakun′ (chŷy′) N family name,
surname. →Usually นามสกุล.
ชื่อเสียง chŷysĭaŋ′ N fame, reputation, name.
○ มีชื่อเสียง miichŷysĭaŋ′ to be well known, famous, famed.
เซ็นชื่อ senchŷy′ V to sign, sign one's name.
→Syn. ลงชื่อ com., เซ็นนาม,ลงนาม eleg.
ได้ชื่อ(ว่า) dâjchŷy′(wâa′) V 1. to get the name
of, be called, named. 2. to have gained the name
(of), hence to be considered, regarded as.
ตั้งชื่อ(ให้) tâŋchŷy′(hâjɔ) V to name, give a
name (to).
ฝากชื่อ fàagchŷy′ i d i o m. to leave a good name
behind for oneself.
มีชื่อ miichŷy′ to be well known, famous, famed.
มีชื่อโด่งดัง miichŷy′-dòŋ′daŋ′ c o m. to be widely
known, renowned. →Syn. มีนามโด่งดัง eleg.
รายชื่อ raajchŷy′ N list of names, roll, register.
→Syn. รายนาม eleg.
เรียกชื่อ rîagchŷy′ V 1. to call the name (of).
2. to call the roll.
ลงชื่อ loŋchŷy′ V to sign, sign one's name.
ลือชื่อ lyychŷy′ V 1. (people, everyone) to talk
about (it), spread (it) around. 2. to be famous,
widely spoken of. →Also เลื่องชื่อลือนาม.
เสียชื่อ sĭachŷy′ V to spoil one's reputation, lose
one's (its) good name.
ชุก chúg′ V to be abundant.
ชุกชุม chúgchum′ V 1. to be plentiful, abundant.
sV 2. plentifully, in abundance (esp. animals).
ฝนชุก,ฝนตกชุก fŏnchúg′, fŏntòg′chúg′ it's raining
a lot; it rains a lot, there's lots of rain.
ชุด chúd′ C clf. for a suit (e.g. of clothing), suite
(of furniture), set (e.g. of ornaments, glassware,
books), deck (of cards); for a committee, cabinet

(of ministers); for a team.

o คณะรัฐมนตรีชุดสงคราม khanárádthamontrii′ɔ chúd′sŏŋkhraam′ war-time cabinet.

o ชุดราตรี (ชุด) chúd′raatrii′ (chúd′) N evening dress, evening wear (for both men and women).

o ชุดเหย้า chúdjâw′ N home team.

เข้าชุดเข้ารอย khâwchúd′khâwrɔɔj′ V elab. colloq. to fit (in with a set, a series), to match.

ชุน chun′ V to darn (mend).

ชุบ chúb′ V 1. to dip, be dipped in. 2. to plate (metal), to gild. 3. to quench (steel), harden (steel) by quenching.

ชุบชีวิต chúb′chiiwíd′ V to brighten (one's) life.

ชุบตัว chúbtua′ V 1. to dip, immerse oneself in liquid. 2. to bathe oneself by taking a fast dip. 3. to immerse oneself in magical water in order to acquire supernatural powers or to improve oneself. 4. to acquire prestige in one's own society by visiting a prestige area (e.g. by going abroad). 5. to restore oneself to good standing.

ชุบทอง chúbthɔɔŋ′ V to gild.

ชุบน้ำ chúbnáam′ V to moisten with water, dip into water.

ชุบย้อม chúbjɔɔm′ V to enliven, give new vigor to.

ชุบเลี้ยง chúblíaŋ′ V to foster, raise, rear (esp. children who are not one's own).

ชุบให้มีชีวิต chúb′hâjmiichiiwíd′ to bring to life, animate.

ชุม chum′ V 1. to be abundant, plentiful. C 2. clf. for an ensemble of flutes. →Cf. ชุมนุม, ประชุม.

ชุกชุม chúgchum′ V 1. to be plentiful, abundant. sV 2. plentifully, in abundance (esp. animals).

ชุมชน (กลุ่ม) chumchon′ (klùm′) N an assemblage of people.

ชุมทาง (แห่ง) chumthaaŋ′ (hèŋ′) N road junction, crossroads.

ชุมทางรถไฟ (แห่ง) chumthaaŋ′ródfaj′ (hèŋ′) N railroad junction.

ชุมพล in ที่ชุมพล (แห่ง) thîi′chumphon′ (hèŋ′) N assembly point for troops.

ชุ่ม chûm′ V to be wet, soaked, moist, damp.

ชุ่มชื่น chûmchŷyn′ V 1. to be happy, joyful. 2. to be pleasant, refreshing.

ชุ่มชื้น chûmchýyn′ V to be wet, soaked, moist, damp.

ชุ่มโชก chûmchôog′ V to be soaking wet, drenched.

ชุมนุม chumnum′ V 1. to gather together, assemble, congregate, concentrate (in one place). C 2. (political) party, group; collection; assembly, gathering. →Cf. ชุม.

การชุมนุมทหาร kaanchumnum′thahǎan′ N troop concentration.

ชุมนุมชน (กลุ่ม, ชุมนุม) chumnumchon′ (klùm′, chumnum′) N a concentration of people.

o แหล่งชุมนุมชน lèŋ′chumnumchon′ congested area, populous area.

ชุมนุมเรื่องสั้น chumnum′rŷaŋsân′ N an anthology of short stories.

ที่ชุมนุมทหาร (แห่ง) thîi′-chumnum′thahǎan′ (hèŋ′) N assembly point for troops.

ร่วมชุมนุม rûam′chumnum′ V to congregate, gather together.

ชุมพร chumphɔɔn′ pN Chumphɔn, a township in S Thailand.

ชุ่ย, ชุ่ยๆ chûj′, chûjchûj′ V 1. to be of poor grade. sV 2. of poor grade, untidily, sloppily, carelessly, haphazardly, cursorily.

ชุลมุน chunlamun′ V 1. to mill around (as a crowd). sV 2. helter-skelter, pell-mell, in confusion. ความ-- commotion, confusion.

ชู chuu′ V to raise, lift, elevate, boost.

เครื่องชูชีพ (เครื่อง, อัน, ชุด) khrŷaŋchuuchîib′ (khrŷaŋ′, ʔan′, chúd′) N life preserver.

ชูกำลัง chuu′kamlaŋ′ V to be invigorating, bracing, strengthening.

ชูคอ chuu′khɔɔ′ V to hold one's head proudly erect.

ชูรส chuuród′ V to bring out, enhance the flavor.

เชิดชู chəədchuu′ V to lift up, raise, boost, glorify.

น้ำส้มสายชู námsôm′sǎajchuu′ N vinegar.

ร่มชูชีพ (ผืน) rôm′chuuchîib′ (phǔyn′) N parachute.

ชู้ (คน) chúu′ (khon′) N adulterer, paramour, lover (usually ref. to a man; used when extra-marital relations involve a married woman).

คบชู้สู่ชาย khóbchúu/-sùu/chaaj/ V (a woman)
to have a lover or lovers, to have men.

เจ้าชู้ câwchúu/ V to be flirtatious, be a flirt
(of either sex); to be a "wolf" (of a man). คน--
flirt.

o ทำเจ้าชู้ tham/câwchúu/ to act like a flirt,
like a "wolf."

เป็นชู้ penchúu/ V to be adulterous (usually ref.
to a man).

มีชู้ miichúu/ V (a married woman) to be adulterous, have a lover.

เล่นชู้ lênchúu/ V (a woman) to commit adultery.

เช็ค ๑ (ใบ) chég/ (baj/) N check. [f. Eng.]

ขึ้นเช็ค khŷnchég/ V to cash a check.

เช็ค ๒ chég/ [f. Eng.] See entries below.

เครื่องหมายเช็ค khrŷaŋmǎajchég/ N a check
mark.

เช็คเอาไว้ chég/?awwáj/ V to check (something)
off, make check marks (next to something).

เช้ง chéeŋ V colloq. to be beautiful, attractive.

เช้งวับ chéeŋ/wáb/ to be very beautiful.

เช็ด chéd/ V 1. to wipe, wipe off (so as to clean).
2. to wipe away (tears). →Dist. ปัด,ปาด.

ที่เช็ดเท้า (ผืน) thîi/chédtháaw/ (phǔyn/) N
door mat.

ผ้าเช็ดตัว (ผืน) phâachédtua/ (phǔyn/) N towel,
bath towel.

เช่น chên/* for instance, such as, like. Often functions as a limited type of clf. meaning "way,
manner," as in เช่นนั้น, เช่นนี้ below.

เช่นเคย chênkhəəj/ as usual.

เช่นเดียวกับ chêndiaw/kaɔ 1. the same as. 2.
in the same way as.

เช่นนั้น chênnán/ like that, (in) that way. →Comp.
ฉะนั้น

เช่นนี้ chênníi/ like this, (in) this way. →Comp.
ฉะนี้.

เช่น...เป็นต้น chên/...pentôn/ for example,
such as... for example. NOTE. This expression is used to encompass a list of whatever is
being exemplified. เช่น introduces the list and
เป็นต้น follows it: "such as (เช่น) apples,
oranges, and bananas, for example (เป็นต้น)."

เช่นว่า chênwâa/ as mentioned.

อาทิเช่น ?aathí?/chên/ notably (such and such
persons). NOTE. This expression is placed in
front of a list of names, with the name of the
most important person given first.

เชย ๑ chəəj/ V 1. to touch gently, lovingly, chuck
(under the chin). sV 2. gently (of the wind blowing). 3. slang to be behind the times, unfash-
ionable, silly, stupid.

ชมเชย chomchəəj/ V to admire, praise, compliment.

เชยชม chəəjchom/ V 1. to admire, praise. 2.
to fondle, caress tenderly.

เชย ๒ in ชดเชย chódchəəj/ V to replace what is
lost, to compensate.

เชลย (คน) chaləəj/ (khon/) N captive, prisoner
(of war). →Also ชะเลย FS.

ค่ายกักเชลย (ค่าย,แห่ง) khâajkàg/chaləəj/ (khâaj/,
hὲŋ/) N prisoner-of-war camp.

เชลยศึก (คน) chaləəjsỳg/ (khon/) N captive,
prisoner of war.

เชษฐบุรุษ chêed/thaburùd/ N eleg. a great statesman.

เช่า châw/ V to rent, i.e. to take (property) on a
rental basis.

ค่าเช่า khâachâw/ N the rent, the rental fee.

เช่าช่วง châwchûaŋ/ V to take a sublease.

เช่าซื้อ châwsýy/ V to buy on the installment plan,
to buy as one rents.

รถเช่า (คัน) ródchâw/ (khan/) N 1. taxi. 2.
rented car.

ให้เช่า hâjchâw/ V 1. to let, rent out. 2. to be
for rent.

เช้า cháaw/* C 1. morning, early morning. V 2.
to be morning, early morning. 3. to be early
(with respect to some expected or appointed time
in the morning). sV 4. early (in the morning).
→Opp. สาย ๒.

o เช้าแล้วละ cháaw/lέεwla?↓ It's morning.

เช้าตรู่ cháawtrùu/ N the early morning, dawn;
very early (in the morning).

o ยามเช้าตรู่ jaam/cháawtrùu/ N the early morning; early in the morning. ใน-- in the early
morning.

เช้านี้ cháaw/níi/ this morning.

เช้า สาย บ่าย เย็น ก็ได้ cháaw/ sǎaj/ bàaj/ jen/
kɔ̂dâaj/ any time during the day: "early morning, late morning, afternoon, evening."

เช้ามืด cháawmŷyd/ N the very early morning
(while still dark).

ตอนเช้า tɔɔncháaw/ in the morning.

ตื่นเช้า tỳyncháaw/ to get up early.

แต่เช้า tɛ̀ɛcháaw/ early in the morning.

ทุกเช้า thúgcháaw/ every morning.

เมื่อเช้า mŷacháaw/ this morning (prior to present).

โมงเช้า mooŋcháaw/ colloq. 7 A.M., seven
o'clock in the morning.

รุ่งเช้า rûŋcháaw/ at daybreak.

เวลาเช้า weelaacháaw/ N morning; in the morning. ใน-- in the morning.

หาเช้ากินค่ำ hǎacháaw/kinkhâm/ V idiom. to
live from hand to mouth.

อาหารเช้า (มื้อ) ʔaahǎancháaw/ (mýy/) N
eleg. breakfast.

เชาวน์ chaw/ N intelligence; quick wit.

เชิง ๑ chəəŋ/ N 1. eleg. manner, way; technique;
-wise (e.g. "businesswise"); line (of procedure,
action). C 2. idem. →Cf. ด้าน ๑.

ชั้นเชิง, เชิงชั้น (อย่าง) chánchəəŋ/, chəəŋchán/
(jàaŋ/) N tactics, strategy, stratagem, trick.

เชิงซ้อน chəəŋsɔ́ɔn/ "complex" as in สารประกอบ
เชิงซ้อน sǎanprakɔ̀ɔb/chəəŋsɔ́ɔn/ chem.
complex compound.

ในเชิงค้า najchəəŋ/kháa/ along the lines of doing
business, in the business line, businesswise.

ในเชิงรำ najchəəŋ/ram/ in the technique of
dancing, in the dancing line.

เป็นเชิงล้พยอก penchəəŋ/sàbphajɔ̀ɔg/ in a teasing
manner, teasingly.

ไม่เชิง mâjchəəŋ/ not exactly, not quite.

สิ้นเชิง sînchəəŋ/ completely, totally, entirely.
อย่าง-- idem.

เชิง ๒ chəəŋ/ N foot, base, lower end, foundation.

กระดูกเชิงกราน kradùug/chəəŋkraan/ N anat.
pelvis.

เชิงกราน chəəŋkraan/ N 1. portable earthenware
fireplace for cooking. 2. short for กระดูก--.

เชิงเขา (แห่ง) chəəŋkhǎw/ (hɛ̀ŋ/) N eleg.

foothills, the foot of a hill. →Syn. ตีนเขา com.

เชิงเทียน (อัน) chəəŋthian/ (ʔan/) N candlestick.

เชิงบันได chəəŋbandaj/ N foot of the stairs.

เชิญ chəən/ V 1. to invite. AA 2. please (do such
and such), come and (do such and such). →Syn.
นิมนต์ sacer.

o เชิญเข้ามา chəən/khâwmaa/↓ Please come in!

o เชิญ...ซิ chəən/...sí, chəən/...sî go ahead
and (do such and such), come on and (do such and
such), won't you please (do such and such), etc.

o เชิญทางนี้ chəən/thaaŋníi/↓ This way, please.

คำเชิญ (คำ, ฉบับ) khamchəən/ (kham/, chabàb/)
N 1. invitation. 2. request.

เชื้อเชิญ chýachəən/ V to invite.

เชิด chə̂əd/ V 1. to lift, raise, elevate, exalt. 2.
to be lifted, raised. 3. to activate, control,
direct, esp. from behind the scenes.

เชิดชู chə̂ədchuu/ V to lift up, raise, boost, glorify.

เชิดหน้าชูตา chə̂ədnâa/chuutaa/ V elab. colloq.
to enhance the prestige (of).

เชิดหุ่น chə̂ədhùn/ V to make a puppet perform.

พาเงินเชิด phaaŋən/chə̂əd/ slang to steal money,
lift money, run off with money.

เชิ้ต,เชิ๊ต,เชิร์ต,เสื้อ-- (ตัว) chə́əd/, sŷachə́əd/
(tua/) N shirt. [f. Eng.]

เชียงราย chiaŋraaj/ pN Chiangrai, a township in
N Thailand.

เชียงใหม่ chiaŋmàj/ pN Chiangmai, the principal
township in N Thailand.

เชียบ chîab/ rM intensifier used with เงียบ "silent."

เชี่ยบ chîab/ rM intensifier used with เย็น "cold."
→Cf. เฉียบ ๒.

เชียร์ chia/ V to cheer, cheer on, applaud, encourage.
[f. Eng. "cheer"]

เชียว chiaw/ colloq. really, very, indeed. →Con-
traction of ทีเดียว thiidiaw/. NOTE. This expression is emphatic in meaning, and is often
best rendered by an emphatic intonation in
English.

o ต้องวิ่งเชียว tɔ̂ŋwîŋ/chiaw↓ You really have to
run!

o ออกไปเดี๋ยวนี้เชียว ʔɔ̀ɔgpajdǐawníi/chiaw↓ Go
on out, right away!

เชี่ยว ๑ chîaw/ V to be strong, swift, rapid (of

current of water).

เขี่ยว ๒ in เขี่ยวชาญ chîawchaan′ V to be experienced, skillful, expert. ผู้-- an expert.

เชื่อ chŷa′ V 1. to believe, believe in. 2. to buy on
credit, short for ซื้อเชื่อ.

ขายเชื่อ khǎajchŷa′ V to sell on credit.

โฆษณาชวนเชื่อ khôosanaa′chuanchŷa′ N 1.
propaganda. V 2. to propagandize.

เชื่อกันว่า chŷa′kanwâa′ it is believed that.

เชื่อใจ chŷacaj′ V to trust.

เชื่อถือ chŷathŷy′ V to believe (in), have faith
(in). ความ-- trust, faith. →Syn. เลื่อมใส,
ศรัทธา.

เชื่อถือได้ chŷathŷy′dâaj′ to be reliable, trustworthy.

เชื่อฟัง chŷafaŋ′ V to heed, pay attention (to),
obey.

เชื่อมั่น chŷamân′ V to believe firmly. ความ--
confidence, conviction, firm belief.

ซื้อเชื่อ sýychŷa′ V to buy on credit.

น่าเชื่อ nâachŷa′ V 1. to be convincing, believable. 2. to be realistic (as a novel).

o ไม่น่าเชื่อ mâjnâachŷa′ V to be unbelievable,
incredible.

เหลือเชื่อ lɣachŷa′ V to be unbelievable, incredible, fantastic.

เชื้อ ๑ chŷa′ N family line.

เชื้อชาติ (เชื้อชาติ,เหล่า) chŷachâad′ (chŷaɔ
châad′, lâw′) N race, nationality. →Dist.
สัญชาติ.

เชื้อสาย chýasǎaj′ N lineage, family, descendants.

เชื้อ ๒ chýa′ N 1. germ, bacteria. 2. enzyme,
ferment, leaven. In compounds often "agent;
essence."

เชื้อเพลิง chýaphlǝǝŋ′ N tech. fuel, combustible substance.

o น้ำมันเชื้อเพลิง námman′chýaphlǝǝŋ′ N fuel
oil.

เชื้อไฟ chýafaj′ N fuel, combustible substance,
kindling.

เชื้อโรค (ชนิด) chýarôog′ (chaníd′) N germ,
microbe, bacteria.

เชื้อหมัก chýamàg′ N yeast.

หมักเชื้อ màgchýa′ V 1. to ferment. N 2. bacte-
rial or fungous culture.

เชื้อ ๓ in เชื้อเชิญ chýachǝǝn′ V to invite.

เชือก (เส้น) chŷag′ (sên′) N 1. rope, cord. C 2.
eleg. clf. for elephants, esp. elephants in cap-
tivity.

เชื่อง chŷaŋ′ V to be tame, docile, domesticated.

เชื่องช้า chŷaŋcháa′ V to be slow, sluggish.

เลี้ยงไม่เชื่อง líaŋ′mâjchŷaŋ′ V to be untameable.

เชือด chŷad′ V to cut forcefully, cut with a sawing
motion (using a knife or similar implement),
to slit (i.e. an animal's throat).

เชือน chyan′ V to dawdle, loiter.

แชเชือน chɛɛchyan′ V to be slow, negligent,
dawdling.

เชื่อม ๑ chŷam′ V 1. to join. 2. to cement. 3. to
solder, vulcanize, weld.

เชื่อมต่อ chŷam′tɔ̀ɔ′ V to connect, join.

ตัวเชื่อม tuachŷam′ N binder, joining agent.

เชื่อม ๒ chŷam′ V to feel drowsy, lethargic.

เชื่อมซึม chŷamsym′ V idem.

เชื่อม ๓ chŷam′ V 1. to candy, cook in thick syrup.
2. to be candied.

กล้วยเชื่อม (ชิ้น,ลูก,ใบ,ผล) klûajchŷam′ (chín′,
lûug′, baj′, phǒn′) N glazed banana, a kind of
dessert.

น้ำเชื่อม námchŷam′ N syrup.

แช chɛɛ′ V to dawdle, loiter.

แชเชือน chɛɛchyan′ V to be slow, negligent,
dawdling.

แช่ chɛ̂ɛ′ V to soak, immerse, steep.

แช่เย็น chɛ̂ɛ′jen′ V to put on ice.

o งานแช่เย็น ŋaan′-chɛ̂ɛ′jen′ the work remains
cold and untouched, is shelved (sarcastic).

ตู้แช่ (ตู้) tûuchɛ̂ɛ′ (tûu′) N freezer.

แช็ก chɛ́g′ imit., in ไฟแช็ก fajchɛ́g′ N colloq.
(cigarette) lighter.

แช่ง,สาป-- chɛ̂ɛŋ′, sàabchɛ̂ɛŋ′ V to curse, invoke
curses (upon); to revile.

แช็ด chɛ́d′ rM intensifier used with แดง "red."

แช่ม chɛ̂m′*. See entries below.

แช่มช้อย chɛ̂mchɔ́ɔj′ V to be beautiful, cute,
charming.

แช่มช้า chɛ̂mcháa′ V to be slow and graceful.

แช่มชื่น chɛ̂mchɥ̂yn′ V to be pleasant, cheerful, joyful.

แชมเปี้ยน chɛmpîan′* N champion. [f. Eng.]

โชก chôog′ V to be soaking wet.

ชุ่มโชก chûmchôog′ V to be soaking wet, drenched.

โชกโชน chôogchoon′ V to be thoroughly wet, drenched. อย่าง-- colloq. extensively.

เปียกโชก pìagchôog′ V to be sopping wet, drenched.

ฝนตกโชก fŏntòg′chôog′ it's pouring, raining in bucketsful.

โชค (อย่าง) chôog′ (jàaŋ′) N fortune, luck, merit.

โชคดี,สบ-- chôogdii′, sòb′chôogdii′ V to have good luck, to be lucky.

ถือโชคถือลาง thɥ̌ychôog′thɥ̌ylaaŋ′ V elab. colloq. to be superstitious.

มีโชค miichôog′ V to have good luck, to be lucky.

เสี่ยงโชค sìaŋchôog′ V to take a chance, try one's luck.

โชย,พัด-- chooj′, phádchooj′ V to blow gently (of the wind). →Comp. ฉาย ๔.

โชยฉาย choojchaaj′ idem.

ใช่ (1) châj′, châjɔ; (2) châj′↓ V 1. to be so, to be it, be the one (meant, intended). 2. That's it! That's so! Yes!

ใช่ไหม châjmáj′↓, châj′máj↓ expression used to convert a statement into a yes-or-no question.

o เขามาแล้วใช่ไหม? kháwmaaléɛw′→châjmáj′↓ He has come, hasn't he?

o ไม่ถูกใช่ไหม? mâjthùug′→châjmáj′↓ It's not correct, is it?

โดยใช่เหตุ doojchâjhèed′ unnecessarily, for no reason.

มิใช่ míchâj′ idem ไม่ใช่ below.

ไม่ใช่ (1) mâjchâjɔ, mâjchâj′; (2) mâjchâj′↓ 1. is not, are not, am not. 2. No, it's not! No!

o นี่ไม่ใช่ดินสอ nîi′ mâjchâj′dinsɔɔ′ This is not a pencil.

o ไม่ใช่เล่น mâjchâjlên′ colloq. quite.

o ไม่ใช่หรือ mâjchâjrɥ́y↓, mâjchâj′rɥ́y′↓ isn't it? aren't you? don't you?

ใช้ cháj′ V 1. to use, spend, expend. 2. to make

use of, employ. 3. to order, send (someone to do something). 4. to be used (to do something). การ-- use, using, expending. คน-- (see below).

ของใช้ (อย่าง) khɔɔŋcháj′ (jàaŋ′) N useful articles, things to use, utensils. →Comp. ของกิน "things to eat."

คนใช้ (คน) khonchɔj′ (khon′) N 1. servant. 2. the user.

o เด็กคนใช้ (คน) dègkhonchɔj′ (khon′) N servant boy, servant girl.

เครื่องใช้ (อย่าง) khrɥ̂aŋcháj′ (jàaŋ′) N utensils, appliances, equipment.

ชดใช้ chódcháj′ V to reimburse, repay, pay (for amount of loss or damage).

ใช้การได้ chájkaan′dâaj′ V 1. to be in working condition, usable. 2. that's good! (said in praise). 3. It worked!

ใช้จ่าย chájcàaj′ V to spend, expend.

o ค่าใช้จ่าย khâachájcàaj′ N expenses.

ใช้ชีวิต(อย่าง,ให้) chájchiiwíd′ to live one's life, spend one's life (as, like such and such, in such and such a manner (jàaŋ′); for such and such a purpose (hâj′)).

ใช้ได้ chájdâaj′ V to be serviceable, usable, fair, (all) right, valid.

ใช้ทำ chájtham′ to be used to make (something).

ใช้ใบ chájbâj′ V to communicate by signs, gestures; to signal.

ใช้ลูกไม้ chájlûugmáaj′ to play tricks.

ใช้เวลาเดินประมาณหกชั่วโมง chájweelaadəən′-pramaan′hògchûamooŋ′ it takes about six hours traveling time, about six hours to go (there) (e.g. by train).

ใช้สอย chájsɔ̌ɔj′ V to expend, use, make use of.

o ค่าใช้สอย khâachájsɔ̌ɔj′ N expense.

o จับจ่ายใช้สอย càbcàaj′chájsɔ̌ɔj′ V elab. colloq. to spend, expend.

o อาศัยใช้สอย ʔaasǎj′chájsɔ̌ɔj′ V 1. to utilize, use. 2. to use (something belonging to another, through his courtesy). 3. to depend on (someone to do errands, etc.).

ใช้หนี้ chájnîi′ to pay the debt.

นำมาใช้ nam′maacháj′ to introduce, bring into use.

บังคับใช้ baŋkháb′cháj′ V to enforce (a law).

ประกาศใช้ prakàad′cháj′ V to proclaim, declare (to be law), to promulgate (a decree, law).

ผ่อนใช้ phɔɔn′cháj′ V to pay by installments.

พอใช้ phɔɔcháj′ V to be adequate, passable, fair.

o ดีพอใช้ dii′phɔɔcháj′ fairly good; passably good.

มีใช้ miicháj′ V 1. to have for use, have available. 2. to be in use, in operation (e.g. machines), in force (e.g. rules).

รับใช้ rábcháj′ V 1. to serve. 2. to be a servant. คน-- servant, a person who attends the wants of another.

สาวใช้ (คน) săawcháj′ (khon′) N maidservant.

ไช chaj′ V to bore, pierce, bore through.

จี้ไช(ให้) cîi′chaj′(hâj′) V slang to prod (figuratively), keep insisting.

ไชยภูมิ chajjaphuum′ pN Chaiyaphum, a township in NE Thailand.

ไชยา chajjaa′ pN Chaiya, an amphoe in S Thailand.

ไชโย chajjoo′ E 1. bravo! hurrah! V 2. to hail with bravos, say "bravo!" →See also ชโย.

ซ

ซ sɔɔ′ LOW consonant. Pronounced s initially, not used as a final consonant. The sound s as an initial low consonant is occasionally also written by means of the combination ทร-.

ซก. Abbrev. for เซนติกรัม centigram.

ซด sód′ V to sip drawing in the breath.

ซน,ซุก-- son′, súgson′ V to be naughty, mischievous.

ซ่น (ซ่น) sôn′ (sôn′) N heel (of the foot). →Also spelled ส้น, q.v. for additional entries.

ซบ sób′ V to rest (one's head or face on something).

ซบเซา sóbsaw′ V to be drowsy, dull, listless, dejected.

ซบหน้า sóbnâa′ V to rest one's head (on one's arms or on the table, so that the face is hidden).

บัดซบ bàdsób′ V to be idiotic, stupid, foolish.

ซม. Abbrev. for เซนติเมตร centimeter.

ซม som′ V to be in a stupor.

ซล. Abbrev. for เซนติลิตร centiliter.

ซวด in ซวดทรง sûadsoŋ′ N eleg. shape, form, contour, figure. →Also written ทรวดทรง.

ซวน,--เซ suan′, suansee′ V to stagger, reel.

ซวย suaj′ V slang to have bad luck, be accursed. [f. Chin.]

ซอ (คัน) sɔɔ′ (khan′) N a Thai stringed instrument; a violin, fiddle.

ซอด้วง sɔɔdûaŋ′ N a treble stringed instrument.

ซออู้ sɔɔ′ûu′ N an alto stringed instrument.

สีซอ sĭisɔɔ′ V to play a stringed instrument.

ซอก sɔ̀ɔg′ N narrow space between two objects, narrow passage.

ทุกซอกทุกมุม thúgsɔ̀ɔg′thúgmum′ elab. colloq. every nook and cranny.

ซอง sɔɔŋ′ N 1. envelope, flat container or case. C 2. clf. for envelopes, for packs (of cigarettes), etc.

ซองจดหมาย (ซอง) sɔɔŋcòdmăaj′ (sɔɔŋ′) N envelope (for a letter).

ซองบุหรี่ (อัน,ซอง) sɔɔŋburìi′ (ʔan′, sɔɔŋ′) N cigarette case (ʔan′); flip-top box for cigarettes, cigarette package (of paper) (sɔɔŋ′).

ซองแว่นตา (ซอง) sɔɔŋwêntaa′ (sɔɔŋ′) N eyeglass case.

ปืนลูกซอง (กระบอก) pyyn′lûugsɔɔŋ′ (krabɔ̀ɔg′) N shotgun.

ซ่อง (ซ่อง,แห่ง) sɔ̂ŋ′/*(sɔ̂ŋ′, hèŋ′) V 1. to frequent. 2. to meet secretly. N 3. den, hangout, secret meeting place. 4. brothel.

ซ่องสุม sɔ̂ŋsŭm′ V 1. to meet, get together. 2. to meet secretly.

ซ่องโสเภณี (ซ่อง) sɔ̂ŋ′sŏopheenii′ (sɔ̂ŋ′) N brothel.

ซ่อน sɔ̂ɔn′ V to hide.

เข็มกลัดซ่อนปลาย (อัน) khĕmklàd′sɔ̂ɔnplaaj′ (ʔan′) N safety pin.

ซ่อนง่ำ sɔ̂ɔn′ŋam′ V to conceal.

ซ่อนหา sɔ̂ɔnhăa′ N hide-and-seek (children's game).

ซุกซ่อน súgsɔ̂ɔn′ V to hide, conceal.

ซ้อน sɔ́ɔn′ V 1. to put one on top of the other, pile up. 2. to overlap. 3. to be situated one over the other.

For words not found under ซ-, see ทร-.

ขับข้อน sábsɔɔn´ V to be complex, complicated, intricate, overlapping.

ช่อม ๑ (คัน) sɔ̂ɔm´, sɔ̂m´ (khan´) N fork. →Also written ส้อม.

　ช้อนช่อม chɔ́ɔnsɔ̂ɔm´ N "spoon and fork," i.e. silverware, consisting of fork and spoon. Cf. Engl. "knife and fork."

ช่อม ๒ sɔ̂ɔm´ V to mend, repair.

　ช่างช่อม (คน) châaŋsɔ̂ɔm´ (khon´) N repairman.

　ช่อมแช้ม sɔ̂ɔmsɛɛm´ V to mend, repair, restore.

　โรงช่อม (โรง) rooŋsɔ̂ɔm´ (rooŋ´) N repair shop.

ช้อม sɔ́ɔm´ V 1. to husk, pound (in a mortar). 2. to practise, drill, rehearse.

　ช้อมรบ sɔ́ɔmrób´ V to hold maneuvers. การ-- maneuvers. →Syn. ประลองยุทธ eleg.

　ล่อบช้อม sɔ̀ɔbsɔ́ɔm´ V to take or give a test, a quiz (other than a final examination).

ช้อย ๑ (ช้อย) sɔɔj´ (sɔɔj´) N lane.

ช้อย ๒ sɔɔj´ V to mince, cut, slice (into small pieces).

ชะ sá´. Shortened variant of เสีย.

　o กินชะ, กินชะขิ kin´sá↓, kinsá´↓, kin´sás↑↓ Eat (it). You'd better eat (it).

ชัก ๑ ság´ V to launder, wash (cloth only). →Dist. ล้าง "to wash (other than cloth or hair)"; ส้ระ "to wash (the hair)."

　ชักผ้า ságphâa´ V to wash clothes. คน-- wash- erman, -woman; laundryman, -woman. เครื่อง-- washer, washing machine.

　o ร้านชักผ้า (ร้าน) ráan´ságphâa´ (ráan´) N laundry (establishment).

　o โรงชักผ้า (โรง) rooŋságphâa´ (rooŋ´) N laundry (establishment).

　ชักฟอก ságfɔ̂ɔg´ V to launder, wash.

　o ผงชักฟอก phǒŋ´ságfɔ̂ɔg´ N soap powder, deter- gent powder.

　ชักรีด ságrîid´ V 1. to wash and iron, launder. 2. to clean and press.

　ชักแห้ง sághɛ̂ɛŋ´ V to be dry-cleaned.

ชัก ๒ ság´ V to question. →Dist. ถาม.

　ชักไข้ ságsáj´ V to question thoroughly.

　ชักถาม ságthǎam´ V 1. to interrogate, question, cross-examine. 2. to inquire into.

　o ข้อชักถาม (ข้อ) khɔ̂ɔ´ságthǎam´ (khɔ̂ɔ´) N question (esp. in an official interrogation).

ชัก ๓ ság´ colloq. as little as, merely, just. →Variant of สัก.

ชัง (อัน) saŋ´ (ʔan´) N 1. stubble. 2 (corn) cob. 3. fibrous covering over the meat of the jackfruit.

　ชังข้าว (อัน) saŋkhâaw´ (ʔan´) N rice stubble.

ชัด sád´ V 1. to throw, fling, hurl (e.g. a dart), cast (e.g. dice). 2. to toss, dash against (as waves with a boat). 3. to put the blame on (others), implicate. 4. to decline (of the sun).

　o ชัดแขน sádkhɛ̌ɛn´ to fling out the arms.

　ชัดเข sádsee´ V to wander, roam aimlessly.

ชับ ๑ sáb´ V to blot, absorb, soak up.

　กระดาษชับ (แผ่น) kradàadsáb´ (phèn´) N blotter.

　ชับใน (ชิ้น) sábnaj´ (chín´) N 1. lining (of clothes). 2. underwear.

ชับ ๒ in ชับข้อน sábsɔɔn´ V to be complex, compli- cated, intricate, overlapping.

ชา saa´ V to subside, abate, diminish (in force). Often followed by ลง.

ช่า in เช่อช่า sɔ̂əsâa´ V colloq. to be foolish, stupid, blundering.

ฉาก ๑ (ฉาก) sâag´ (sâag´) N corpse, carcass, (desiccated) remains, remnants. →Dist. ศพ.

　ฉากศพ (ฉาก) sâagsòb´ (sâag´) N corpse, remains (of a person).

ฉาก ๒ in ซ้ำฉาก, ซ้ำ ๆ ฉาก ๆ sámsâag´, sámɔ sám´sâagsâag´ V 1. to be recurrent. sV 2. repeatedly.

ช่าน sâan´ V 1. to scatter. 2. to be scattered.

　ฉาบช่าน sâabsâan´ V 1. to permeate, penetrate. 2. to be thoroughly absorbed.

　ฟุ้งช่าน fúŋsâan´ V 1. (one's mind or thoughts) to wander, be jumbled. sV 2. incoherently, in jumbled fashion.

　o คิดฟุ้งช่าน khíd´fúŋsâan´ to think incoherently, (one's) thoughts to be jumbled.

　โรคดีช่าน rôog´diisâan´ N jaundice.

ฉาบ sâab´ V to spread, permeate. Only in cpds.

　ฉาบช่าน sâabsâan´ V 1. to permeate, penetrate. 2. to be thoroughly absorbed.

　ฉาบชึ้ง sâabsýŋ´ V 1. to be deeply impressed, captivated. 2. to be impressive.

For words not found under ช-, see ทร-.

ฃึมฃาบ symsâab´ V 1. to permeate, penetrate.
2. to be absorbed, to soak in.

ฃ่าม in ชุ่มฃ่าม sûmsâam´ V 1. to be clumsy. sV
2. clumsily.

ฃ้าย sáaj´ sV left, to the left. →Opp. ขวา.

ถนัดฃ้าย thanàd´sáaj´ V to be lefthanded.

ทางฃ้ายมือ thaaŋsáaj´myy´ to the left, on the left.

ฝ่ายฃ้าย fàajsáaj´ N the Left, Leftists.

เลี้ยวฃ้าย líawsáaj´ to turn left.

ฃาว saaw´ V to rinse, wash (rice) before cooking.

ฃาวเสียง saawsĭaŋ´ to sound out (people's)
views or opinions (on an issue).

ฃ้ำ sám´ V 1. to repeat. sV 2. in addition, also;
again, anew; repeatedly.

กล่าวฃ้ำ(ว่า) klàawsám´(wâa´) to repeat (that).

ฃ้ำชั้น sámchán´ to repeat a class (in school),
take a course over.

ฃ้ำซาก,ฃ้ำ ๆ ซาก ๆ sámsâag´, sámsám´sâagɔ
sâag´ V 1. to be recurrent. sV 2. repeatedly.

ด้วยฃ้ำ dûajsám´ also, too, in addition, even
more.

มิหนำฃ้ำ mínămsám´ colloq. in addition, moreover, worse than that.

ฃิ sí´, sî´. Variant of ฃี.

ฃิ่ sî´. Variant of ฃี.

ฃิ่น in ผ้าฃิ่น (ผืน) phâasîn´ (phȳyn´) N a sarong-
like lower garment worn by women. →Comp.
ผ้าถุง.

ฃิบ in ชุบฃิบ súbsíb´ V to whisper. →Syn.
กระซิบ, กระซิบกระซาบ.

ฃิป (อัน) síb´ (?an´) N zipper. [f. Eng.]

ฃิเมนต์. See ซีเมนต์.

ฃี. sii´ the English letter "C." [f. Eng.]

ฃี sii´ Pt particle indicating definiteness or emphasis. →Also written ฃิ sí´, sî´, ฃิ่ sî´, ฃี่ sîi´,
สิ sì´.

๐ กินเลียฃี, กินเลียฃี kin´sîasî↓ Eat (it).

ฃี่ ๑ sîi´ N 1. bar (as of a cage), rib, tooth (of a
comb), tine (of a fork). C 2. clf. for teeth,
ribs, the teeth of a comb, the tines of a fork, etc.

ฃี่โครง (ฃี่) sîikhrooŋ´ (sîi´) N ribs.

ฃี่ ๒ sîi´. Variant of ฃี.

ฃี้ in เฃ้าฃี้ sáwsîi´ V to wheedle, coax repeatedly,
keep harping on something, nag.

ฃีก sîig´ C 1. (a) half (of a globular object, e.g. a
coconut). 2. piece, section, part.

ฃีกไม้ (ฃีก,ฃิ้น) sîigmáaj´ (sîig´, chín´) N a
piece or length of split wood, splinter.

เป็นฃีก ๆ pensîigsîig´ in pieces, into pieces.

พระจันทร์ครึ่งฃีก phrácan´khrȳŋsîig´ N half-moon.

ฃีด sîid´ V to be pale.

ฃีดเฃียว sîidsiaw´ V to be pale and wan.

ฃีดเผือด sîidphȳad´ V to be very pale, white as
a sheet.

ชุบฃีด sûubsîid´ V to be thin and pale, emaciated,
sickly.

ฃีเมนต์ in ปูนฃีเมนต์ puunsiimen´* N cement. [f. Eng.]
→Also ซีเมนต์.

ฃีอาโต sii?aatôo´* nN SEATO (Southeast Asia
Treaty Organization). [f. Eng.]

ฃึ่ง ๑ sŷŋ´ rP lit. which, that, who (as a relative
pronoun). →Syn. ที่ com.

ผู้ฃึ่ง phûusŷŋ´ one who.

ฃึ่ง ๒. See entries below.

ฃึ่งฃึ่งหน้า sŷŋsŷŋ´nâa´ directly, right to one's
face. อย่าง-- idem.

ถึงฃึ่ง thȳŋ´sŷŋɔ lit. to reach, arrive at.

นำมาฃึ่ง nam´maa´-sŷŋɔ lit., eleg. to bring,
bring in, bring about (e.g. sorrow, misfortune).

ฃึ้ง sýŋ´ V 1. to be deep, profound. 2. to impress,
captivate.

ฃาบฃึ้ง sâabsýŋ´ V 1. to be deeply impressed,
captivated. 2. to be impressive.

ฟังให้ฃึ้ง,ฟังฃึ้ง faŋ´hâjsýŋ´, faŋ´sýŋ´ to listen with
deep feeling.

ลึกฃึ้ง lýgsýŋ´ V to be profound, deeply-felt.

ฃึม ๑ sym´ V to be drowsy, sluggish.

เฃื่อมฃึม chŷamsym´ V to feel drowsy, lethargic.

ฃึมเฃา symsaw´ V to be dull, drowsy.

มึนฃึม mynsym´ V to be drowsy, dull.

ฃึม ๒ sym´ V to seep, soak in.

ฃึมฃาบ symsâab´ V 1. to permeate, penetrate.
2. to be absorbed, soak in.

ฃึมทราบ symsâab´ V colloq. to know well, know
thoroughly.

แทรกฃึม sɛ̂ɛgsym´ V to infiltrate, penetrate into,
permeate.

ปากกาหมึกฃึม (ด้าม) pàagkaa´mȳgsym´ (dâam´)

N fountain pen.

ขืน in วานขืน, --นี้ waansyyn´, waansyyn´níi´ the day before yesterday.

ซื่อ sŷy´ V to be honest, straightforward.

ซื่อตรง sŷytroŋ´ V 1. to be honest. 2. to be faithful.

ซื่อสัตย์,สัตย์ซื่อ. sŷysàd´, sàdsŷy´ V 1. to be honest. 2. to be faithful, loyal. ความ-- honesty; faithfulness, loyalty.

พาซื่อ phaasŷy´ naively, unsuspectingly.

ซื้อ sýy´ V to buy.

กว้านซื้อ kwâansýy´ V to corner the market (by buying up in large quantities).

เช่าซื้อ châwsýy´ V to buy on the installment plan, to buy as one rents.

ซื้อของ sýykhɔɔŋ´ V to shop. การ-- shopping, buying. คน-- buyer, shopper, customer.

ซื้อขาย sýykhǎaj´ V to trade, engage in commerce.

ซื้อเชื่อ sýychŷa´ V to buy on credit.

ซื้อปลีก sýyplìig´ V to buy at retail.

ซื้อหา sýyhǎa´ V to buy.

รับซื้อ rábsýy´ V to purchase.

ซุก súg´ V 1. to snuggle, press close to, cuddle up to. 2. to stuff (something) into (a small space). 3. to hide.

o เอามือซุกกระเป๋า ʔawmyy´-súg´krapǎw´ to put one's hands in one's pockets.

ซุกซน súgson´ V to be naughty, mischievous.

ซุกซ่อน súgsɔɔn´ V to hide, conceal.

หัวซุกหัวซุน hǔasúg´hǔasun´ V to rush, be in a rush. →See also following example.

o ล้มหัวซุกหัวซุน lóm´-hǔasúg´hǔasun´ V to tumble head over heels, tumble headlong.

ซุง (ต้น) suŋ´ (tôn´) N log.

ซุป súb´ N soup. [f. Eng.]

ซุบซิบ súbsíb´ V to whisper. →Syn. กระซิบ, กระซิบกระซาบ.

พูดซุบซิบ phûud´súbsíb´ 1. to whisper, talk in a low, whispering voice. 2. to gossip.

ซุ่ม sûm´ V to hide, lie in wait.

ซุ่มซ่อน sûmsɔɔn´ V to lie in ambush.

ซุ้ม (ซุ้ม) súm´ (súm´) N arbor; archway.

ซุ้มประตู súmpratuu´ N the arch over a gate.

ซุ่มซ่าม sûmsâam´ V 1. to be clumsy. sV 2. clumsily.

ซุย suj´ V to be loose, crumbly.

ซูบ sûub´ V to be thin and pale, emaciated.

ซูบซีด sûubsîid´ V to be thin and pale, emaciated, sickly.

ซูบผอม sûubphɔɔm´ V to be pale and skinny, emaciated.

เซ see´ V to stagger, be unsteady (in walking).

ซัดเซ sádsee´ V to wander, roam aimlessly.

เซหลุน ๆ see´lǔnlǔn´ to stumble and trip, stagger (as when pushed forcibly and unexpectedly).

โซเซ soosee´ V 1. to stagger, reel (as an intoxicated person). sV 2. staggeringly, unsteadily.

เซ็งแซ่ seŋsɛɛ´ V to be noisy.

เซ็ด. sêd´/* the English letter "Z." [f. Eng. zed] →Also แซ็ด.

เซ็ท ๑ séd´ C set (tennis). [f. Eng.]

เซ็ท ๒ séd´ V to set (hair). [f. Eng.]

เซ็ทผม sédphǒm´ V to set the hair, have one's hair set.

เซ็น sen´ V to sign.

เซ็นชื่อ senchŷy´ V to sign, sign one's name. →Syn. ลงชื่อ com.; เซ็นนาม,เซ็นชื่อ eleg.

เซ็นสัญญา sen´sǎnjaa´ V to sign a contract.

ลายเซ็น (อัน,แห่ง) laajsen´ (ʔan´, hὲŋ´) N signature, autograph.

เซนติกรัม,เซ็น- sentikram´/* C centigram. Abbr. ซก. [f. Eur.]

เซนติเมตร,เซ็น- sentiméed´/* C centimeter. Abbr. ซม. [f. Eur.]

เซนติลิตร,เซ็น- sentilíd´/* C centiliter. Abbr. ซล. [f. Eur.]

เซฟ (ใบ) séef´, séeb´/*(baj´) N com. a safe. [f. Eng.]

ตู้เซฟ (ตู้,ใบ) tûuséef´, -séeb´ (tûu´ baj´) N com. a safe. →Syn. ตู้นิรภัย eleg.

เซล,เซลล์ sel´, sen´, seel´ N tech. cell (biological, electrical). [f. Eng.]

เซ่อ sɘ̀ə´ V to be foolish, silly, stupid.

เซ่อซ่า sɘ̀əsâa´ V colloq. to be foolish, stupid, blundering.

เซอร์ sɘɘ´, sɘ̀ə´ the English title "Sir." [f. Eng.]

เซอะ sɘ́ʔ´/ V to be foolish, silly, stupid.

เซอูล see?uul´ pN Seoul.

For words not found under ซ-, see ทร-.

เซา saw˅ V 1. to calm down, to stop. 2. to be
  sluggish.
  ขี้เซา khîisaw˅ to be a sleepyhead.
  ซบเซา sóbsaw˅ V to be drowsy, dull, listless,
    dejected.
  ซึมเซา symsaw˅ V to be dull, drowsy.
เซ้าซี้,--จุกจิก sáwsíi˅, sáwsíi´cùgcìg˅ V to wheedle, coax repeatedly, nag, keep harping on something.
เซาะ sɔ́ʔ˅ V to erode, cut through, wear down.
เซิฟ sɔ́əb˅, sɔ̀əb˅* V to serve, wait on a table.
  [f. Eng.]
เซี่ยงไฮ้ sîaŋháj˅ pN Shanghai. [f. Chin.]
เซียว siaw˅ V to be withered, pale.
  ซีดเซียว sîidsiaw˅ V to be pale and wan.
เซื่อง sŷaŋ˅ V to be slow, inactive, lifeless.
แซ่, เซ็ง-- sɛ̂ɛ˅, seŋsɛ̂ɛ˅ V to be noisy.
แซก sɛ̂ɛg˅ See แทรก.
แซง sɛɛŋ˅ V 1. to insert. 2. to be in between; to
  intervene. 3. to overtake.
  แทรกแซง sɛ̂ɛgsɛɛŋ˅ V 1. to insert. 2. to inter-
    vene, interfere, intrude.
แซด sɛ̂d˅* V to be noisy, loud, buzzing.
แซ็ด. sɛ̂d˅* the English letter "Z." [f. Eng. zed]
  →Also เซ็ด.
แซม sɛɛm˅ V 1. to insert. 2. to be inserted, be in
  between.
  ซ่อมแซม sɔ̂ɔmsɛɛm˅ V to mend, repair, restore.
  แซมผม sɛɛmphŏm˅ V to insert in the hair (e.g.
    an ornament).
โซ ๑ soo˅ V 1. to be starving. 2. to be destitute.
  ผอมโซ phɔ̌ɔmsoo˅ V to be skinny and weak
    (because undernourished).
โซ ๒ in โซเซ soosee˅ V 1. to stagger, reel (as
  an intoxicated person). sV 2. staggeringly,
  unsteadily.
โซ่ (เส้น) sôo˅ (sên˅) N chain.
โซดา soodaa˅ N 1. soda. 2. short for น้ำโซดา
  below. [f. Eng.]
  โซดาไฟ soodaafaj˅ N colloq. caustic soda.
  น้ำโซดา námsoodaa˅ N soda water, carbonated
    water.
โซม soom˅ V 1. to soak, bathe. 2. to be drenched.
โซเวียต soowîad˅ N Soviet Russia, the Soviets.

โซเวียตรัสเซีย soowîad´rádsia˅ pN Soviet Russia.
สหภาพโซเวียต sahàphâab´soowîad˅ N the Soviet
  Union.
ไซ (ลูก, ใบ) saj˅ (lûug˅, baj˅) N a kind of fish trap,
  made of bamboo strips.
ไซ้ sáj˅ V to root, dig, probe (with beak or snout).
  ซักไซ้ ságsáj˅ V to question thoroughly.
  ไซ้ขน sájkhŏn˅ V to preen the feathers.
ไซ่ง่อน sâjŋɔ̂n˅* pN Saigon. [f. Viet.]
ไซบีเรีย sajbiiria˅ pN Siberia. [f. Eng.]

ฌ

ฌ chɔɔ˅ LOW consonant. Pronounced ch initially,
  not used as a final consonant. The letter ฌ is
  rarely used; the sound ch as an initial low consonant is usually written ช.
ฌาปนกิจ chaa´panákìd˅ N 1. cremation. V 2. to
  cremate.
  พิธีฌาปนกิจ phíthii´chaa´panákìd˅ N cremation rite.
ฌาปนสถาน (แห่ง) chaa´panásathăan˅ (hὲŋ˅) N
  crematory.

ญ

ญ jɔɔ˅ LOW consonant. Pronounced j initially,
  n finally. The sound j as an initial low consonant
  is usually written ย.
ญวน juan˅ N Vietnam, Vietnamese. Formerly
  Annam, Annamese.
  ชาวญวน (คน) chaawjuan˅ (khon˅) N a Vietnamese,
    the Vietnamese.
  ประเทศญวน (ประเทศ) prathêedjuan˅ (prathêed˅)
    N Vietnam.
  ภาษาญวน (ภาษา) phaasăajuan˅ (phaasăa˅) N
    Vietnamese (the language).
ญัตติ jádtìʔ˅ N motion, proposition, resolution
  (parliamentary procedure).
ญาณ jaan˅ N knowledge; intellect; enlightenment.
  Found chiefly as a final element in Sanskrit
  loanwords.
ญาติ (คน) ๑ jâad˅ (khon˅) N 1. relative, kin. 2.

cousin.

เครือญาติ khryajâad′ N 1. lineage, family tree.
2. kindred.

ญาติพี่น้อง (คน) jâadphîin3ɔ́ɔŋ′ (khon′) N relatives.

ญาติมิตร jâadmíd′ N 1. relatives and friends.
V 2. slang to play cards together.

ญาติโยม (คน) jâadjoom′ (khon′) N relatives.

ประเทศญาติ (ประเทศ) prathêed′jâad′ (pracɔthêed′) N related country.

เป็นญาติกัน penjâad′kan′ to be related (to each other).

ญาติ ๒ in ชะมัดญาติ chamád′jâad′ colloq. very, extremely.

ญี่ปุ่น jîipùn′ N Japan, Japanese. [f. Japanese]

จักรวรรดิญี่ปุ่น càgkrawàd′jîipùn′ N the Japanese empire.

ชาวญี่ปุ่น (คน) chaaw′jîipùn′ (khon′) N a Japanese, the Japanese.

ประเทศญี่ปุ่น (ประเทศ) prathêed′jîipùn′ (pracɔthêed′) N Japan.

ภาษาญี่ปุ่น (ภาษา) phaasăa′jîipùn′ (phaasăa′)
N Japanese (the language).

ฎ

ฎ dɔɔ′ MIDDLE consonant. Pronounced d both
initially and finally. The sound d is usually
written ด, but as a final consonant it is also
written in a number of other ways. See ด.
The letter ฎ is rarely used.

ฎีกา (ใบ, ฉะบับ) diikaa′ (baj, chabàb′) N 1. petition. V 2. to petition. ผู้-- petitioner.

ศาลฎีกา săandiikaa′ N supreme court.

ฏ

ฏ tɔɔ′ MIDDLE consonant. Pronounced t initially,
d finally. The sound t as an initial middle
consonant is usually written ต. The letter ฏ
is rare. An example of its use is the word
ปฏิบัติ pàtibàd′ "to do, act, perform."

ฐ

ฐ thɔ̌ɔ′ HIGH consonant. Pronounced th initially,
d finally. The sound th as an initial high consonant is usually written ถ. The letter ฐ is
rare. An example of a word of frequent use in
which it occurs is รัฐบาล rádthabaan′ "the
government."

ฐาน (ฐาน) thăan′ (thăan′) N 1. base, foundation.
2. basis, grounds. 3. status, capacity.

ฐานทัพ (แห่ง) thăantháb′ (hèŋ′) N military base.

ถิ่นฐาน (แห่ง) thìnthăan′ (hèŋ′) N place; place
of residence.

ภูมิฐาน phuumthăan′ V to be dignified, grand.

มูลฐาน muunthăan′ N 1. basis, foundation. 2.
(as n. mod.) basic, fundamental.

รากฐาน râagthăan′ N 1. foundation. 2. basis.
3. secure position or standing (of a person).

o มีรากฐาน miirâagthăan′ 1. to have a foundation.
2. (a person) to have a secure position or standing.

หลักฐาน làgthăan′ N 1. basis, foundation. 2.
evidence, testimony. 3. colloq. wealth.

ฐานะ thăaná?′ N status, position, condition, standing.

วิทยฐานะ wídthajá?′thăaná?′ N academic, educational standing.

ฑ

ฑ thɔɔ′ LOW consonant. Pronounced th initially,
d finally. It is also occasionally treated as a
MIDDLE consonant and pronounced d initially.
The sound th as an initial low consonant is
usually written ท. The letter ฑ is extremely
rare. Examples of words in which it occurs
are มณฑล monthon′ "monthon, a former
political division"; นาฑี naathii′ "minute";
บัณฑิต bandìd′ "pundit." The first two examples
show it treated as a LOW consonant, the last
example as a MIDDLE consonant.

ฌ

ฌ thɔɔ′ LOW consonant. Pronounced th initially,
　　d finally. The sound th as an initial consonant
　　is usually written ท. The letter ฌ is ex-
　　tremely rare. An example of a fairly frequent
　　word in which it occurs is วัฒนธรรม.

เฒ่า (คน)thâw′ (khon′) N old person, aged person.
　　A spelling เถ้า is also used. ผู้-- i d e m.
　　→Dist. เก่า. →Syn. แก่ ๑ c o m., ชรา
　　e l e g.
　　คนเฒ่าคนแก่ (คน) khonthâw′khonkɛ̀ɛ′ (khon′)
　　　N e l a b. c o l l o q. old people, elderly people.
　　เฒ่าแก่ (คน) thâwkɛ̀ɛ′ (khon′) N 1. a go-be-
　　　tween who arranges a marriage. 2. an aged,
　　　wealthy Chinese man.

ณ

ณ nɔɔ′ LOW consonant. Pronounced n both initially
　　and finally. The sound n both initially and fi-
　　nally is usually written น. Though the letter
　　ณ is extremely rare as a word-initial conso-
　　nant, it occurs in other positions in some fairly
　　common words, e.g. ขณะ, คุณ, บริเวณ.

ณ ná?ɔ, náɔ Pp 1. at, in, of (place or time). 2.
　　element in surnames, indicating relationship
　　to royalty or to former local princes who served
　　as governors of provinces.
　o ณอยุธยา ná??àjúdthajaa′ nN Na-Ayuthaya
　　　(Na-Ayuthia), an addition to the surname of per-
　　　sons who, though without royal titles, are re-
　　　lated to the Chakri line. Based on อยุธยา, a
　　　township in C Thailand and former capital of
　　　the country.
　o ณสงขลา násǒŋkhlǎa′, ná?sǒŋkhlǎa′ nN Na-
　　　Songkhla, surname of persons descended from
　　　the local prince who served as governor of
　　　Songkhla in earlier times. Based on สงขลา,
　　　a township in S Thailand.
　ณต่างประเทศ nátàaŋ′prathêed′ abroad.
　ณบัดนี้ nábàdníi′ at present, now.

เณร (รูป,องค์) neen′ (rûub′,?oŋ′) N one who
　　enters the priesthood while under the age of
　　twenty. →Also สามเณร.

ด

ด dɔɔ′ MIDDLE consonant. Pronounced d both ini-
　　tially and finally. The sound d as an initial
　　consonant is also sometimes written with ฎ
　　or ท, and as a final consonant with จ, ช, ฎ, ฏ,
　　ฐ, ฑ, ฒ, ต, ถ, ท, ธ, ศ, ษ, or ส.

ดก. Abbrev. for เดชิกรัม decigram.

ดก dòg′ V 1. to be plentiful, abundant. 2. to be
　　productive.
　　ไข่ดก khàjdòg′ V (fowls) to be productive, lay
　　　eggs abundantly.

ดคก. Abbrev. for เดคากรัม decagram.

ดง (แห่ง) doŋ′ (hὲŋ′) N forest, jungle. →Syn. ป่า.
　　เข้าป่าเข้าดง khâwpàa′khâwdoŋ′ V e l a b. c o l l o q.
　　　to go off into the jungle (used esp. in a fig. sense,
　　　i.e. to get away from it all).
　　ดงกล้วย doŋklûaj′ N banana plantation.
　　ดงดิบ,ป่า-- (แห่ง) doŋdìb′, pàa′doŋdìb′ (hὲŋ′)
　　　N tropical evergreen forest.

ดั้นดั้น,ดั้นด้น dôndân′, dândôn′ V 1. to brave the way,
　　make a way through, push forward, force one's
　　way through. 2. to venture.

ดนตรี (พวก,อย่าง) dontrii′ (phûag′, jàaŋ′) N music.
　　เครื่อง-- musical instruments. นัก-- musi-
　　cian. →Syn. ดุริยางค์ l i t., e l e g.
　　เล่นดนตรี lên′dontrii′ V to play music.

ดม dom′ V to smell, sniff.
　　ยาดม (แห่ง) jaadom′ (thὲŋ′) N 1. smelling salts.
　　　2. inhalant.

ดร. Transliteration of the English abbreviation
　　"Dr.," read as dɔ́gtɵ̂ɵ′. Used as a title for a
　　person with a Ph. D., D. Ed., etc.

ดล don′ V 1. to arrive, reach. 2. to come about.
　　2. to cause, inspire (often implying supernatural
　　means).
　　ดลบันดาล,--ใจ don′bandaan′, don′-bandaan′caj′
　　　V to cause, inspire, motivate (often implying
　　　supernatural means).

ดวง duaŋ′ C 1. clf. for certain round shapes or objects, e.g. seals, stamps, spots, stains; for sources of light, e.g. lamps, stars, the sun, the moon; for the eyes; for the soul. 2. class term for such items.

ดวงจันทร์ (ดวง) duaŋcan′ (duaŋ′) N 1. the moon. 2. a s t r o n. satellite, moon.

ดวงจิต (ดวง) duaŋcìd′ (duaŋ′) N mind, soul.

ดวงใจ (ดวง,คน) duaŋcaj′ N 1. the heart (duaŋ′). 2. sweetheart, beloved (khon′).

ดวงตรา (ดวง) duaŋtraa′ (duaŋ′) N seal.

o ดวงตราไปรษณียากร (ดวง) duaŋtraa′-prajɔ sanii′jaakɔɔn′ (duaŋ′) N postage stamp.

ดวงตา (ดวง) duaŋtaa′ (duaŋ′) N the eye.

ดวงประทีป (ดวง) duaŋprathîib′ (duaŋ′) N 1. flame. 2. light, e.g. the light from a flame, a lamp or a lantern.

ดวงไฟ (ดวง) duaŋfaj′ (duaŋ′) N 1. ball of fire. 2. a distant light or fire.

ดวงไฟฟ้า (ดวง) duaŋfajfáa′ (duaŋ′) N electric light.

ดวงวิญญาณ (ดวง) duaŋwinjaan′ (duaŋ′) N the soul.

ดวงอาทิตย์ (ดวง) duaŋ°aathíd′ (duaŋ′) N the sun.

เต็มดวง temduaŋ′ V to be full (of the moon).

o พระจันทร์เต็มดวง phrácan′temduaŋ′ the moon is full.

ดวง ๑ (ตัว) dûaŋ′ (tua′) N the grub or larva of certain beetles and weevils.

ดวง ๒ (อัน) dûaŋ′ (°an′) N a kind of trap made of bamboo, e.g. for catching mice.

ซอด้วง (คัน) sɔɔdûaŋ′ (khan′) N a Thai stringed instrument in treble key (having the shape of ดวง ๒ above).

ด่วน dùan′ V 1. to be urgent, hasty. 2. to be in haste.

ด่วนจี๋ dùancǐi′ V to be extremely urgent.

โดยด่วน doojdùan′ with urgency, with haste.

ธุระด่วน thúrá?′/dùan′ urgent business.

รถด่วน (ขบวน,คัน) róddùan′ N express train (khabuan′); express bus (khan′).

ด้วน dûan′ V 1. to cut, cut off. 2. to be cut off, amputated, cut short.

ด้วย dûaj′ Pp 1. with, by, by means of, as, because of. sV 2. also, too, as well. 3. either (with negative expressions). →Syn. 1. โดย. NOTE. ด้วย means "also, too" in the sense of "in addition." เหมือนกัน means "also, too" in the sense of "likewise, the same." A similar distinction exists for the meaning "either" in negative expressions.

o ที่เห็นได้ด้วยตา thîihěndâaj′/dûajtaa′ which can be seen with the eyes, with (one's own) eyes.

o ขอไปด้วยได้ไหม khɔ̌ɔpajdûaj′dâaj′/máj↓ Can I go too?

กอปรด้วย kɔ̀ɔb′dûajɔ to consist of.

ช่วยด้วย chûaj!dûaj′↓ Help! (an urgent call).

ชอบด้วยกฎหมาย chɔ̂ɔb′/dûajkòdmǎaj′ to be lawful, legitimate, in accordance with the law.

ด้วยกัน dûajkan′ 1. together. 2. altogether, all told, in all. 3. along, together with (them, us, etc.).

o อยู่กินด้วยกัน jùukin′/dûajkan′ to live together, cohabit (man and woman, husband and wife).

o มี ๔ จุดด้วยกัน miisìi′cùd′-dûajkan′↓ There are four points altogether.

o ทั้งหมดด้วยกัน,หมดด้วยกัน tháŋmòd′/dûajkan′, mòd′/dûajkan′ altogether, all told, all in all.

o ผมอยากจะชวนคุณไปด้วยกัน phǒmjàag′/cachuanɔ khun′pajdûajkan′↓ I'd like to invite you to go along: "together with (us)."

ด้วยใจ dûajcaj′ with one's heart, sincerely.

ด้วยซ้ำ dûajsám′ also, too, in addition, even more.

ด้วยดี dûajdii′ 1. amicably, with good feeling. 2. well, successfully, normally.

ด้วยตนเอง dûajton?eeŋ′ in person; by oneself, as oneself, personally.

ด้วยเรื่อง dûajrŷaŋ′ about, concerning, over, with regard to, in the matter of, in the case of.

ด้วยวิธี dûajwíthii′ by means of.

ด้วยเหตุนี้ dûajhèed′/níi′ therefore, for this reason, because of this.

ต้องด้วย tɔ̂ŋ′dûajɔ to conform to, concur with.

เต็มไปด้วย tem′pajdûajɔ to be full of, filled with.

เนื่องด้วย nŷaŋ′dûajɔ owing to, on account of, due to, arising from, because; owing to the fact that, because of the fact that, since.

พร้อมด้วย phrɔ́ɔm'dûajɔ together with, at one
and the same time with.

เริ่มด้วย rə̂əm'dûajɔ to begin with, to begin by
(doing such and such).

ว่าด้วย wâa'dûajɔ to be concerned with, to deal
with.

เห็นด้วย hěndûaj' to agree (with what has been
said).

ดอก ๑ dɔ̀ɔg' N 1. flower, blossom (in compounds).
C 2. clf. for flowers of all kinds, for incense
sticks, for arrows. NOTE. ดอก in mng. 1
is a class term, not a general term. The general term for "flower, blossom" is ดอกไม้.
Specific kinds of flowers are named by using the
class term followed by a specific term, e.g.
ดอกมะลิ "jasmine," ดอกฝิ่น "poppy," ดอกส้ม
"orange blossom."

กะหล่ำดอก (ดอก,หัว) kalàm'dɔ̀ɔg' (dɔ̀ɔg', hǔa')
N cauliflower.

ดอกกล้วยไม้ (ดอก) dɔ̀ɔgklûajmáaj' (dɔ̀ɔg') N
orchid (the flower).

ดอกกานพลู (ดอก) dɔ̀ɔgkaanphluu' (dɔ̀ɔg') N
flower of the clove tree.

ดอกกุหลาบ (ดอก) dɔ̀ɔgkulàab' (dɔ̀ɔg') N rose.

ดอกจัน (ดอก) dɔ̀ɔgcan' (dɔ̀ɔg') N 1. asterisk.
2. asterisk-like mark on a cobra's hood.

ดอกทอง dɔ̀ɔgthɔɔŋ' N colloq., derog. a loose
woman, prostitute. →Syn. โสเภณี eleg.

o อีดอกทอง ʔiidɔ̀ɔg'thɔɔŋ'↓ Prostitute! Bag!
(term of abuse).

ดอกบัว (ดอก)dɔ̀ɔgbua' (dɔ̀ɔg') N lotus (flower).

ดอกเบี้ย dɔ̀ɔgbîa' N finance interest.

o ดอกเบี้ยทบต้น dɔ̀ɔgbîa'thóbtôn' N finance
compound interest.

ดอกฝิ่น (ดอก) dɔ̀ɔgfìn' (dɔ̀ɔg') N poppy.

ดอกมะลิ (ดอก) dɔ̀ɔgmalíʔ' (dɔ̀ɔg') N jasmine.

ดอกไม้ (ดอก) dɔ̀ɔgmáaj' (dɔ̀ɔg') N flower,
blossom (of any kind). This is a general term;
see note in main entry.

ช่อดอกไม้ (ช่อ) chɔ̂ɔ'dɔ̀ɔgmáaj' (chɔ̂ɔ') bouquet, corsage.

o ดอกไม้เพลิง (ดอก) dɔ̀ɔgmáajphləəŋ' (dɔ̀ɔg')
N eleg. pyrotechnic display, fireworks.
→Syn. ดอกไม้ไฟ com.

o ดอกไม้ไฟ dɔ̀ɔgmáajfaj' (dɔ̀ɔg') N com. fireworks. →Syn. ดอกไม้เพลิง eleg.

o ดอกไม้แรกแย้ม dɔ̀ɔgmáaj'rɛ̂ɛgjɛ́ɛm' a flower
which is just beginning to open. Often used as
a simile for a young girl.

o น้ำดอกไม้ námdɔ̀ɔgmáaj' N 1. water scented
with flowers. 2. bot. nectar.

ดอกส้ม (ดอก) dɔ̀ɔgsôm' (dɔ̀ɔg') N orange blossom.

ดอกเห็ด (ดอก) dɔ̀ɔghèd' (dɔ̀ɔg') N mushroom.

เป็นดอก pendɔ̀ɔg' 1. to be flowered, decorated
with a floral design. 2. to be in flower.

มีดอก miidɔ̀ɔg' to be in flower. →Dist. เป็นดอก.

ออกดอก ʔɔ̀ɔgdɔ̀ɔg' V 1. to blossom. 2. to flourish,
blossom out. 3. to develop a rash (from venereal
disease).

อีดอก ʔiidɔ̀ɔg'↓ Short for อีดอกทอง ʔiidɔ̀ɔg'thɔɔŋ'
Prostitute! Bag! (term of abuse).

ดอก ๒ dɔ̀g', dɔg', dɔ̀ɔg' Pt writ. particle often
used with statements expressing negation, contradiction, or those correcting a misapprehension. Usually makes a statement milder, less
abrupt, or expresses reassurance. →Syn. หรอก
com. →See also examples under หรอก.

ดอง ๑ dɔɔŋ' V 1. to pickle. 2. to be pickled. 3.
(a liquid) to flood, soak, cover (e.g. a paddy
field) for a long time.

ผักดอง phàgdɔɔŋ' N pickled vegetable.

หมักดอง màgdɔɔŋ' V to preserve or pickle by
slow fermentation.

ดอง ๒. See entries below.

เกี่ยวดอง kìawdɔɔŋ' V to be related (of kindred).

ปรองดอง prɔɔŋ'dɔɔŋ' V 1. to reconcile. 2. to
compromise. 3. to reach an agreement, be in
agreement. 4. to get along well (with somebody).

ดอด dɔ̀ɔd' V 1. to sneak (in), be unobserved, come
unobserved.

ดอน dɔɔn' V 1. to be high (of land). N 2. highland.

ที่ดอน thîidɔɔn' N the highlands.

ดอนเมือง dɔɔnmyaŋ' pN Don Muang international
airport N of Bangkok.

ด้อม dɔ̂m'* V to steal (in), sneak (in), be stealthy
unobserved.

ดอย (ลูก) dɔɔj' (lûug') N 1. mountain. 2. Mount --.

ชาวเขาชาวดอย (คน) chaawkhǎw/chaawdɔɔj/ (khon/) N elab. colloq. mountain people.

ด้อย dɔ̂j/* V to be inferior.

ปมด้อย (อย่าง, ข้อ) pomdɔ̂j/ (jàaŋ/, khɔ̂ɔ/) N psych. inferiority complex.

ดอลล่า dɔɔlâa/, dɔnlâa/* C dollar. [f. Eng.]

ดะ dà?/ sV at random, haphazardly, indiscriminately, promiscuously.

ดัก ๑ dàg/ V 1. to set (a trap). 2. to trap, snare, catch (by means of a trap). 3. to lie in wait.

คอยดัก khɔɔjdàg/ V 1. to wait (for someone to come along his intended route). 2. to wait lying in ambush. 3. to wait in order to intercept (e.g. a radio message).

ดักกับไว้ dàgkàb/wáj/ to set out a trap.

หลุมดัก (หลุม) lǔmdàg/ (lǔm/) N pitfall (for trapping large animals).

ดัก ๒ in ดักดาน dàgdaan/ V 1. to suffer hardship for a long period of time. 2. to be in a deadlock, at a standstill.

ดักแด้ (ตัว) dàgdɛ̂ɛ/ (tua/) N chrysalis.

ดัง ๑ daŋ/ V 1. to be loud, noisy. 2. to be heard.

ดังไปทั้งป่า daŋ/pajtháŋpàa/ resounding through the whole forest.

โด่งดัง dòoŋdaŋ/ V to be famous, renowned.

ดัง ๒ daŋ/ like, as, according to. Often functions as a limited type of clf. meaning "manner, kind," as in ดังนั้น, ดังนี้ below.

ดังกล่าว daŋklàaw/ as mentioned, as stated; aforementioned.

ดังจะกล่าวต่อไปนี้ daŋcaklàaw/tɔ̀ɔpajníi/ as follows, as below.

ดังใจ daŋcaj/ as one wishes, as one has in mind, as desired.

ดังเดิม daŋdəəm/ as (it was) before, as formerly.

ดังนั้น daŋnán/ like that, in that manner; like that, of that kind; thus; hence; so.

ดังนี้ daŋníi/ like this, in this manner; like this, of this kind; thus; as follows.

o ข่าวดังนี้ khàaw/daŋníi/ news such as this.

o เป็นมาดังนี้หลายคราว penmaa/daŋníi/-lǎajə khraaw/ it happened like this many times.

ดังปรากฏ daŋpraakòd/ as has appeared, as could be seen, as is manifest, evident.

เหมือนดัง mǔandaŋ/ as, like.

ดั่ง dàŋ/. Variant form of ดัง "like, as."

ดั้ง ๑ dâŋ/ N shield, protective cover.

ดั้ง ๒ in ดั้งเดิม dâŋdəəm/ original, primitive; at the very beginning.

ดัชนี dàdchanii/ N index (finger).

ดัด dàd/ V to bend, change (forcibly).

ดัดแปลง dàdplɛɛŋ/ V to change, modify, adapt.

ดัดผม dàdphǒm/ V 1. to curl the hair. 2. to have one's hair waved, get a permanent wave.

o ช่างดัดผม (คน) châaŋdàdphǒm/ (khon/) N hairdresser.

ดัดสันดาน dàd/sǎndaan/ V to reform (a person).

o โรงเรียนดัดสันดาน rooŋrian/-dàd/sǎndaan/ N reformatory school.

ดัดให้เชื่อง dàd/hâjchŷaŋ/ 1. to tame, domesticate. 2. to be tamed.

ดัน dan/ V 1. to push. 2. to insist stubbornly, doggedly. ความ-- pressure; oppression. →Ant. ดึง.

กดดัน kòd/dan/ V to press; to oppress.

กำลังดัน kamlaŋdan/ N pressure.

ดันทุรัง dan/thuraŋ/ V to be obstinate, headstrong.

ดึงดัน dyŋdan/ V to be obstinate.

ดุดัน dù?dan/ V to be angry, furious, fierce.

ผลักดัน phlàg/dan/ V 1. to push, shove. 2. phys. to repel. 3. to put pressure on, influence.

แรงดัน rɛɛŋdan/ N pressure.

ดั้นด้น, ด้นดั้น dâandôn/, dôndân/ V 1. to brave the way, make a way through, push forward, force one's way through. 2. to venture.

ดับ dàb/ V 1. to extinguish, snuff out, put out. 2. to suppress, abolish (thoughts, emotions). 3. to abate, die out. sV 4. extremely, shockingly. ความ-- death.

ดับกลิ่น dàbklìn/ V to deodorize.

ดับขันธ์ dàbkhǎn/ V lit. to die (of the Buddha).

ดับชีพ dàbchîib/ V eleg. 1. to die. sV to death, dead. 3. colloq. awfully, murderously.

o ยิงดับชีพ jiŋ/dàbchîib/ eleg. to shoot to death.

o ร้อนดับชีพ rɔ́ɔn/dàbchîib/ colloq. to be awfully hot, murderously hot.

ดับเพลิง dàbphləəŋ/ V eleg. to put out a fire. คน-- fireman. →Syn. ดับไฟ com.

○ รถดับเพลิง (คัน) ród′dàbphləəŋ′ (khan′) N
fire engine.

ดับไฟ dàbfaj′ V c o m. 1. to put out a fire. 2.
to turn off the light. →Syn. 1. ดับเพลิง e l e g.
2. ปิดไฟ.

ดับวูบ dàbwûub′ 1. to go out, be extinguished,
snuffed out suddenly (of a flame, light). 2. to
blank out, pass out suddenly (of a person).

ดับคูนย์, ดับสูญ dàb′sŭun′ V l i t. to die out, to be
extinct.

แตกดับ tὲɛg′dàb′ V 1. to be ruined. 2. to perish.

พูดน้ำไหลไฟดับ phûud′-námlăj′fajdàb′ V c o l l o q.
to chatter away, talk a blue streak, talk rapidly
and profusely.

แพงดับไปเลย phɛɛŋ′-dàb′pajləəj′ c o l l o q.
extremely expensive.

ดับบลิว, ดับเบิลยู, ดับปลิว dàbbaliw′, dàbbliw′, dàbbəɔc
juu′, dàbbənjuu′, dàbpliw′ the English letter
"W." [f. Eng.]

ดา ๑ in ดาเข้าหา daa′khâwhăa′ to advance towards in a group, in a body.

ดา ๒ in แมงดา (ตัว, คน) mɛɛŋdaa′ N 1. king
crab or horseshoe crab (tua′). 2. water bug
(tua′). 3. s l a n g gigolo (khon′).

ด่า dàa′ V to curse, speak abusively to, scold.
คำ-- abuse (in words), cursing.

คำดุด่า kham′dù?dàa′ N a scolding, (words of)
abuse.

ด่าทอ dàathɔɔ′ V 1. to curse, revile, speak
abusively. 2. to exchange abusive or opprobrious language.

ด่าว่า dàawâa′ V speak abusively, swear at.

ด่าง ๑ dàaŋ′ V to be mottled, uneven (of color).
ดำด่าง damdàaŋ′ V to be unevenly black.

ด่าง ๒ dàaŋ′ N alkali.
เกลือด่าง (อย่าง, ชนิด) klyadàaŋ′ (jàaŋ′, chaɔ
níd′) N basic salt.

ดาด ๑ dàad′ V 1. to line, pave (with). 2. to be
lined, paved (with).

ฝีดาด fĭidàad′ N c o m. smallpox. NOTE. Commonly spelled ฝีดาษ ; see under ดาษ. →Syn.
โรคไข้ทรพิษ, ไข้ทรพิษ e l e g.

ดาด ๒. See entries below.

ดาดฟ้า (แห่ง) dàadfáa′ (hὲŋ′) N deck (of ship

or building), (sun-)deck.

หินดาด hĭndàad′ N a rock ledge.

ดาน ๑ daan′ V to be hard, compact, solid.

ดินดาน dindaan′ N the deep, hard, compact soils.

ดาน ๒ in ตักดาน dàgdaan′ V 1. to suffer hardship
for a long period of time. 2. to be in a deadlock,
at a standstill.

ด่าน (ด่าน) dàan′ (dàan′) N 1. official station or
post. 2. military post. 3. customs house. 4.
port of entry. 5. frontier town, outpost, outlying
regions. 6. border route or pass.

ด่านเข้าเมือง (ด่าน) dàankhâwmyaŋ′ (dàan′) N
immigration office, post (at the point of entry).

ด่านภาษี dàanphaasĭi′ N customs station, customs
post, customs house.

เมืองด่าน myaŋdàan′ N border town, frontier
settlement.

ด้าน ๑ dâan′ C 1. side, part (as of a room), sector
(as of a city). 2. side, line, field (of research),
direction, viewpoint, aspect. →Cf. เชิง.

○ มหาสมุทรแอตแลนติกด้านอเมริกา mahăsamùd′ɔ
?ɛdlɛɛntìg′-dâan′?ameerikaa′ the American
side of the Atlantic.

ด้านยุทธศาสตร์ dâan′júdthasàad′ the military
aspect.

ด้านหลัง dâanlăŋ′ the rear (as of a house); in the
back.

ในด้าน najdâan′ in the line of, field of.

○ ในด้านการค้า najdâan′kaankháa′ in the field
of business, on the business side.

มืดแปดด้าน mŷyd′pὲɛddâan′ i d i o m. to be in the
dark, be completely lost (when trying to figure
something out).

สี่เหลี่ยมด้านขนาน (รูป) sìilìam′dâankhanăan′
(rûub′) N parallelogram.

ด้าน ๒ dâan′ V 1. to be hard, callous, coarse,
rough. 2. to be brazen, shameless. 3. to be a
dud (of explosives).

ดื้อด้าน dŷydâan′ V to be obstinate.

หน้าด้าน nâadâan′ V to be shameless. →Syn.
หน้าหนา. →Ant. หน้าบาง.

ดาบ (เล่ม) dàb′ (lêm′) N sword.

ดาบปลายปืน (อัน) dàbplaajpyyn′ (?an′) N bayonet.

ดาบสั้น (เล่ม) dàbsân′ (lêm′) N dagger.

มีดดาบ (เล่ม) mîiddàab/ (lêm/) N sword.

ดาบส (องค์) daabòd/ (?oŋ/) N lit.,eleg. hermit.

ด้าม (ด้าม) dâam/ (dâam/) N 1. handle, hilt, holder. C 2. idem; clf. for pens.

ด้ามปากกา (ด้าม) dâam/pàagkaa/ (dâam/) N penholder.

ด้ามปืน (ด้าม) dâampyyn/ (dâam/) N gunstock.

ใหม่ถอดด้าม màj/thòɔddâam/ to be brand-new.

ดาย ๑ in ดายหญ้า daajjâa/ to mow excess or un-wanted grass or weeds; to weed.

ดาย ๒. See entries below.

ง่ายดาย ŋâajdaaj/ V 1. to be easy, very easy, simple. sV 2. easily, simply.

ดูดาย duudaaj/ V to look on without lending a hand; to remain indifferent, on the side lines.

เสียดาย sĭadaaj/ V 1. to feel sorry (about some-thing lost, or about a lost opportunity). 2. to' deplore, regret. 3. to be regrettable.

อยู่เดียวดาย jùu/diawdaaj/ to be lonely, alone.

ด้าย (เส้น,หลอด) dâaj/ (sên/,lɔɔd/) N thread; (cotton) string (used for crocheting).

กรอด้าย krɔɔdâaj/ V to wind thread or yarn into a skein; to wind a skein of thread or yarn onto a spool.

เข้าด้ายเข้าเข็ม khâwdâaj/khâwkhĕm/ V idiom. to be crucial, decisive.

ด้ายกลุ่ม (กลุ่ม) dâajklùm/ (klùm/) N thread commercially wound into a ball.

ด้ายไหม (เส้น,ไจ,หลอด) dâajmăj/ N silk thread (sên/ for strands; caj/ for skeins; lɔɔd/ for spools).

เส้นด้าย sêndâaj/ N strand of (cotton) thread.

ดารา (ดวง,คน) daaraa/ N 1. star (duaŋ/). 2. stage or motion picture star (khon/, duaŋ/).

ดาราศาสตร์ daaraasàad/ N astronomy.

ดาล in เดือดดาล dɏaddaan/ V to be furious, boil-ing mad.

ดาว (ดวง,คน) daaw/ N 1. star, planet (duaŋ/). 2. stage or motion picture star, a renowned beauty (khon/, duaŋ/).

NAMES OF THE MAJOR PLANETS (clf. ดวง)

ดาวพระเกตุ daawphrákèed/ Neptune.

ดาวพระพฤหัส,ดาวพฤหัส daaw/phráphárýhàd/, daawpháryhàd/ Jupiter.

ดาวพระพิภพ,ดาวพิภพ daaw/phráphíphób/, daaw= phíphób/ Earth. →Also ดาวโลก.

ดาวพระพุธ daawphráphúd/ Mercury.

ดาวพระยม daawphrájom/ Pluto.

ดาวพระศุกร์ daawphrásòg/ Venus.

ดาวพระเสาร์ daawphrásăw/ Saturn.

ดาวพระอังคาร daaw/phrá?aŋkhaan/ Mars.

ดาวมฤตยู daawmarýdtajuu/ Uranus.

กลุ่มดาว (กลุ่ม) klùmdaaw/ (klùm/) N constella-tion.

ไข่ดาว (ใบ,ฟอง) khàjdaaw/ (baj/,fɔɔŋ/) N fried egg.

ดาวเคราะห์ (ดวง) daawkhrɔ́?/ (duaŋ/) N planet.

ดาวเทียม (ลูก) daawthiam/ (lûug/) N artificial earth satellite.

ดาวไถ daawthăj/ N 1. Orion (the constellation). 2. slang one given to sponging off of others.

ดาวประกายพรึก (ดวง,คน) daaw/prakaajphrýg/ N 1. the morning star (duaŋ/). 2. slang a young beauty (khon/, duaŋ/). →Sometimes incor-rectly written -พฤกษ์. →Also ดาวรุ่ง. →Opp. 1. ดาวประจำเมือง.

ดาวประจำเมือง (ดวง) daaw/pracammyaŋ/ (duaŋ/) N the evening star. →Opp. ดาว ประกายพรึก,ดาวรุ่ง.

ดาวพระเคราะห์ (ดวง) daawphrákhrɔ́?/ (duaŋ/) N planet.

ดาวรุ่ง (ดวง,คน) daawrûŋ/ N 1. morning star (duaŋ/). 2. a renowned beauty (khon/, duaŋ/). →Also ดาวประกายพรึก. →Opp. ดาวประจำ เมือง.

ดาวเรือง (ดอก) daawryaŋ/ (dɔɔg/) N marigold. ต้น-- (ต้น) marigold plant.

ดาวฤกษ์ (ดวง) daawrɏɏg/ (duaŋ/) N fixed star.

ดาวโลก (ดวง) daawlôog/ (duaŋ/) N the earth.

ดาวหนัง (ดวง,คน) daawnăŋ/ (duaŋ/, khon/) N motion picture star.

ดาวหมู่ (หมู่) daawmùu/ (mùu/) N constellation.

ดาวหาง (ดวง) daawhăaŋ/ (duaŋ/) N comet.

ดาวเหนือ (ดวง) daawnɏa/ (duaŋ/) the North Star.

เสือดาว (ตัว) sɏadaaw/ (tua/) N leopard.

หอดูดาว (หอ,แห่ง) hɔɔduudaaw/ (hɔɔ/, hɛ̀ŋ/) N observatory.

ด้าว in ต่างด้าว tàaŋdâaw/ 1. foreign country. 2. (as.n.mod.) alien, foreign. →See cross ref.

ดาษ dàad′ V to be plentiful, abundantly distributed.

ดาษดื่น dàaddỳyn′ V 1. to be plentiful, widely distributed, full of. sV 2. plentifully, abundantly, commonly.

ฝีดาษ fǐidàad′ N com. smallpox. →Sometimes spelled ฝีดาด, which is considered to be etymologically correct; see under ดาด ๑. →Syn. โรคไข้ทรพิษ, ไข้ทรพิษ eleg.

o ปลูกฝีดาษ plùugfǐidàad′ V 1. to vaccinate (against smallpox). 2. to be vaccinated.

ดำ ๑ dam′ V 1. to be black. 2. to be dark.

กระดานดำ (แผ่น) kradaandam′ (phɛ̀n′) N blackboard.

เข้ากระดูกดำ khâwkradùug′dam′ idiom. 1. to be deep-seated, ingrained. 2. deeply, intensely. อย่าง-- deeply, intensely.

แขกดำ (คน) khɛ̀ɛgdam′ (khon′) N 1. Indian with a very dark complexion. 2. Negro.

ใจดำ cajdam′ V to be merciless, mean, selfish, unsympathetic, unscrupulous.

ดำขลับ damkhlàb′ to be a very glossy black.

ดำเขียว damkhǐaw′ 1. to be greenish black, green-tinged black. 2. "black and blue," as in the following entry.

o ฟกช้ำดำเขียว fógchám′damkhǐaw′ colloq. to be bruised black and blue.

ดำด่าง damdàaŋ′ V to be unevenly black.

ดำแดง damdɛɛŋ′ V to be reddish black, red-tinged black.

o สีดำแดง sǐidamdɛɛŋ′ N 1. red-tinged black, reddish black. V 2. to be reddish black.

ดำปี๋ dampǐi′ to be very black.

ดำปิ๊ด dampýd′ to be coal black, jet-black.

ดำปี๊ด dampýd′ to be coal black, jet-black.

ดำปือ dampǔy′ to be coal black, jet-black.

ดำมะเมื่อม dam′mamŷam′ to be jet-black and glossy.

ดำเย็น damjen′ N colloq. black iced coffee. →Syn. โอเลี้ยง slang.

ดินดำ dindam′ N gunpowder.

ดึกดำบรรพ์ dỳg′damban′ V to be ancient, belonging to antiquity.

เด็กตาดำ ๆ dèg′-taa′damdam′ innocent child.

ตาดำ taadam′ N anat. pupil of the eye. →Also ตุ๊กตา.

ผิวดำ phǐwdam′ N dark skin; dark skinned.

สีดำ sǐidam′ N 1. black, the color black. V 2. to be black.

เสือดำ (ตัว) sŷadam′ (tua′) N black panther.

หน้าดำหน้าแดงอยู่กับ nâadam′nâadɛɛŋ′-jùukac colloq. to be busily engaged in (e.g. work). Has the force of English "have one's nose to the grindstone."

ดำ ๒ dam′ V to dive.

ดำน้ำ damnáam′ V to dive into water.

o เรือดำน้ำ (ลำ) ryadamnáam′ (lam′) N submarine.

ดำ ๓ dam′ V to transplant (rice).

ดำนา damnaa′ V to transplant (young rice plants).

ปักดำ pàg′dam′ V to transplant (young rice plants).

ดำ in ดื่มดำ dỳymdàm′ V to feel deeply, have a deep feeling (for something, as an artist for art).

ดำเนิน damnəən′ V 1. roy. to proceed, walk, go. 2. eleg. to proceed, proceed with, continue. [conv.f. เดิน]

ดำเนินการ damnəən′kaan′ V 1. to carry on the work; to conduct, run (e.g. business); to manage things. 2. to operate, be in operation, be in action.

ดำเนินงาน damnəən′ŋaan′ V to carry on the work; to execute, carry out; to manage, administer.

ทางดำเนิน (ทาง) thaaŋdamnəən′ (thaaŋ′) N eleg. way, path, procedure.

ดำรง damroŋ′ V 1. lit., eleg. to endure, last. 2. to stand, exist. 3. to support, maintain, sustain. 4. to hold. 5. to establish. 6. to make straight. [conv.f. ตรง] →Comp. 3. ธำรง.

ดำรงตำแหน่ง damroŋ′tamnèŋ′ to hold the position of.

ดำรัส damràd′* V roy. to speak, talk. [conv.f. ตรัส] พระราชดำรัส phrárâad′chadamràd′ speech (made by the king).

ดำริ damrì?* V eleg. to contemplate, plan, consider. [conv.f. ตริ]

ดิก dìg′ sV entirely, perfectly, wholly.

o กลมดิก klom′dìg′ to be perfectly round, be a perfect circle.

o เหมือนกันดิก mўan′kandìg′ exactly the same.

ดิ่ง dìŋ′ V 1. to be straight, direct. 2. to be vertical.

สายดิ่ง (สาย) sǎajdìŋ′ (sǎaj′) N sounding line.

เส้นดิ่ง (เส้น) sêndìŋ′ (sên′) N vertical line.

ดิฉัน dichán′* P def. w. sp. I, me. Paired with คุณ "you." →Cf. ผม ๒ def. m. sp., อิฉัน illit. w. sp.

ดิถี dìthǐi′ N eleg. day, date. →Also วาระดิถี.

ดิน din′ N 1. earth, ground, soil, land. 2. (explosive) powder. →Dist. 1. บก. →Syn. 1. ธรณี eleg.

ก้อนดิน kɔ̂ɔndin′ (kɔ̂ɔn′) N a clod of earth.

จมดิน comdin′ V to be embedded, buried (in the ground).

ดินจืด dincʉ̀ʉd′ N depleted soil.

ดินดาน dindaan′ N the deep, hard, compact soils.

ดินดำ dindam′ N gunpowder.

ดินแดน (แห่ง,ผืน) dindɛɛn′ (hɛ̀ŋ′, phʉ̌yn′) N region, area, territory.

ดินทราย dinsaaj′ N sandy soil.

ดินน้ำลมไฟ din′→náam′→lom′→faj′ the four elements: earth, water, wind, and fire.

ดินปนทราย dinponsaaj′ N loam, sandy soil.

ดินประสิว dinprasǐw′ N saltpeter.

o กรดดินประสิว krɔ̀d′dinprasǐw′ N nitric acid.

ดินปืน dinpyyn′ N gunpowder.

ดินเผา dinphǎw′ N the baked or hardened clay of earthenware. เครื่อง-- earthenware.

ดินฟ้าอากาศ dinfáa′ʔaakàad′ N climate.

ดินระเบิด dinrabɤ̀ɤd′ N explosive powder.

ดินสอ (แท่ง) dinsɔ̌ɔ′ (thɛ̂ŋ′) N pencil.

ดินสอพอง dinsɔ̌ɔphɔɔŋ′ N a soft, prepared chalk, used as an after-bath powder for its cooling effect.

ดินเหนียว (ก้อน) dinnǐaw′ (kɔ̂ɔn′) N clay.

ใต้ดิน tâajdin′ underground, subterranean.

ที่ดิน (แปลง,ผืน) thîidin′ (plɛɛŋ′, phʉ̌yn′) N piece of land; lot (for a house or building).

o หอทะเบียนที่ดิน (แห่ง) hɔ̌ɔthabian′thîidin′ (hɛ̀ŋ′) N land registration office.

น้ำมันดิน námman′din′ N tar, coal tar.

แผ่นดิน (ผืน,แผ่นดิน) phɛ̀ndin′ N 1. earth, ground, land (phʉ̌yn′). 2. nation, kingdom, realm (phɛ̀ndin′). C 3. reign.

พื้นดิน phʉ́yndin′ N the ground, earth, earth-surface.

ฟ้าดิน fáa′din′ "heaven and earth."

o จนฟ้าดินสลาย confáa′dinsalǎaj′ until the end of the world.

o ชั่วฟ้าดิน,--สลาย chûafáa′din′, chûafáa′dinsalǎaj′ forever, in all eternity.

มนุษย์เดินดิน (คน) manúd′dɤɤndin′ (khon′) an ordinary human being (in the sense of not possessing supernatural powers).

ดิ้น ๑ dîn′ V to wriggle, writhe, struggle.

ดิ้นแด็ก ๆ dîn′dɛ̀gdɛ̀g′ to writhe frantically.

ดิ้นรน dînron′ V to struggle (to free oneself).

ดีดดิ้น dìid′dîn′ V to be affected, artificial (of manners).

ให้ดิ้นตายซี hâjdîn′taaj′-sì↓ idiom. 1. expression equiv. to "Cross my heart and hope to die!" 2. expression used to convey impatience at having to wait for something.

ดิ้น ๒ (สาย) dîn′ (sǎaj′) N tinsel (metallic thread for embroidery).

ดิบ dìb′ V 1. to be raw, unripe, green, uncooked. 2. to be crude, unrefined (as petroleum), unbleached (as cloth), untreated (by heat). คน-- a man who has not yet entered priesthood. →Ant. สุก.

กินดิบ kindìb′ V 1. to eat raw or while still unripe. 2. colloq. to win easily, win hands down.

ขายดิบขายดี khǎajdìb′khǎajdii′ V elab. colloq. to have good sales; to sell well.

ดงดิบ,ป่า-- (แห่ง) doŋdìb′, pàa′doŋdìb′ (hɛ̀ŋ′) N tropical evergreen forest.

ดิบ ๆ สุก ๆ dìbdìb′sùgsùg′ not well-cooked, half-cooked.

ได้ดิบได้ดี dâajdìb′dâajdii′ V elab. colloq. 1. to attain power, rank, prominence. 2. to be well-off.

น้ำดิบ námdìb′ N unboiled water. (Water must be boiled before it is safe for consumption). →Ant. น้ำสุก.

ป่าดิบ (แห่ง) pàadìb′ (hɛ̀ŋ′) N tropical evergreen forest.

ผ้าดิบ (ผืน) phâadìb′ (phʉ̌yn′) unbleached muslin.

ฝ้ายดิบ fâajdìb′ N raw cotton.

ดี. dii/ the English letter "D." [f. Eng.]

ดี ๑ dii/ V 1. to be good, fine, nice. sV 2. well, nicely; nice and (e.g. cool), quite. ความ-- goodness, virtue, good. อย่าง-- good, of good quality; well. →Ant. ชั่ว, เลว.

o เราจะไปนั่งกันที่ไหนดี rawcapajnaŋ/kanthîinǎj/-dii/↓ Where would be good place for us to go sit?

o อากาศทะเลเย็นดี ʔaakàad/thalee/-jendii/↓ The sea air is nice and cool.

ก็ดี kɔ̌dii/ "is (are) fine too." Often used correlatively; see cross reference for example.

o ก็ดีเหมือนกัน kɔ̌dii/-mɣ̌ankan↓ O.K., fine (it's all right with me).

o อย่างไรก็ดี jàaŋraj/kɔ̌dii/ even so, however, anyhow.

ขวัญดี khwǎndii/ V to be in good spirits, have good morale.

คืนดี khyyndii/ V to be reconciled.

คุ้มดีคุ้มร้าย khúmdii/khúmráaj/ V elab. colloq. 1. to be alternately sane and insane. 2. to be half crazy, touched, mentally unhinged. 3. to be erratic, changeable in temper.

เคราะห์ดี khrɔ́ʔdii/ V 1. to be fortunate, lucky. 2. fortunately, luckily, it's fortunate (that). →Opp. เคราะห์ร้าย.

ใจดี cajdii/ V to be good-natured, kindhearted.

โชคดี, ลบ-- chôogdii/, sòb/chôogdii/ V to have good luck, be lucky.

ด้วยดี dûajdii/ 1. amicably, with good feeling. 2. well, successfully, normally.

ดีกว่า diikwàa/, dii/kwàaↄ to be better, better than.

ดีกัน dii/kan to be reconciled, to make up.

ดีขึ้น dii/khɣ̂n 1. to get better, improve. 2. That's better!

ดีจริง, ดีจริง ๆ dii/ciŋ↓, dii/ciŋciŋ/↓ That's fine! How nice!

ดีใจ diicaj/ V to be glad. ความ-- gladness.

ดีละ dii/laʔ↓ Very well! O.K.! All right then! (as when indignant).

ดีแล้ว diilέεw/↓, dii/lέεw↓ That's good.

ดีอกดีใจ diiʔòg/diicaj/ V elab. colloq. to be glad, happy.

โดยดี doojdii/ amicably, good-naturedly, willingly, unhesitatingly, readily.

ถือดี thɣ̌ydii/ V 1. to be proud, haughty, arrogant, self-assertive. 2. to dare, have the audacity to.

o ถือดียังไงถึงมาว่าฉันยังงั้ thɣ̌y/dii/jaŋŋaj/-thɣ̌ŋↄmaawâa/chánjaŋŋíi↓ How dare you talk like that to me!

ปากดี pàag/dii/ V to have a loose tongue. This term is used sarcastically.

เป็นอย่างดี penjàaŋdii/ 1. quite well. 2. willingly, gladly.

เป็นอันดี penʔandii/ 1. well, very well. 2. willingly, gladly.

ผู้ดี (คน) phûudii/ (khon/) N 1. nobleman, noblewoman. 2. gentleman, gentlewoman. 3. a refined person, person of refinement.

พอดี phɔɔdii/ precisely, exactly, just right (in size, amount, etc.); just the right moment; just then, at that very moment.

มีดีมีร้าย mídii/míráaj/ V elab. eleg. to be bad, evil, harmful.

มือดี myy/dii/ V 1. idiom. to be a good hand (at some activity). N 2. a good hand, a good player. →Opp. มือเลว.

ไม่ดี mâjdii/ to be bad, not good. ความ-- badness, (the) bad.

o ลมไม่ดี lom/mâjdii/ colloq. to be in a bad mood.

ไม่ทำดี mâjtham/dii/ to be bad; not to do good.

ยากดีมีจน jâagdii/-mii/con/ elab. colloq. (whether) rich or poor.

ยินดี(ที่) jindii/ (thîiↄ) V to be glad, pleased (that). ความ-- gladness, pleasure (state of being pleased).

ไยดี in ไม่ไยดี(ต่อ) mâjjajdii/(tɔ̀ɔↄ) to be indifferent (to), pay no attention (to). Often written -ใย-.

รู้ดี rúudii/ 1. to know well. 2. to presume to know; to know better; to know it all. →In mng. 2. used sarcastically, reproachfully; see cross reference.

ฤกษ์ดี rɔ̂g/dii/ N propitious, auspicious time.

ฤกษ์งามยามดี rɔ̂gŋaam/jaamdii/ N elab. colloq. auspicious time.

ลองดี lɔɔŋ'dii/ V colloq. to put to the test (as a law, by defying it; or a person, to determine his capabilities).

ลางดี laaŋdii/ N good omen.

วันดีคืนดี wandii'khyyndii/ elab. colloq. one fine day, (on) a certain day.

สนุกดี sanùg'dii/ V 1. to be fun, amusing, entertaining. 2. to have fun, have a good time.

สบายดี sabaaj'dii/, sabaaj/dii V 1. to be well (in health), happy, contented. 2. (a place) to be comfortable. sV 3. well, comfortably.

o สบายดีหรือ sabaaj/diirý↓ How are you? (common greeting).

ลิ้นดี sîndii/ colloq. much, very, extremely.

หวังดี wǎŋdii/ V to have good wishes, intentions.

เห็นดีเห็นงาม hěndii/hěnŋaam/ V elab. eleg. to agree; to approve.

เห็นดีเห็นชอบ(กับ) hěndii/hěnchɔɔb/(kaɔ) V elab. colloq. to agree (with), approve, be in favor (of). →Also เห็นดี, เห็นชอบ.

อยู่ดีกินดี jùudii/kindii/ V to live and eat well, have a fair standard of living.

อวดดี ?ùaddii/ V 1. to be impudent, bold, insolent, impertinent. 2. to dare, i.e. have the nerve (to do such and such). →Syn. 2. ถือดี.

อารมณ์ดี ?aarom/dii/ V 1. to be in a good humor; to be agreeable, good-humored, good-natured. N 2. good humor.

ดี ๒ dii/ N gall bladder.

ขวัญหนีดีฝ่อ khwǎnnǐi/diifɔɔ/ V elab. colloq. to be startled, frightened, scared out of one's wits.

ดีเกลือ diiklya/ N Epsom salt.

น้ำดี námdii/ N bile.

โรคดีซ่าน rôog/diisâan/ N jaundice.

ดี ๓ dii/ element inserted for the sake of rhyme and alliteration in the following.

หลายปีดีดัก lǎaj/pii/-dii/dàg/ elab. colloq. many, many years.

ดี in ดีดี !díi/dii/ V to be very good, fine. Emphatic form of ดี ๆ.

ดีด dìid/ V 1. to tap on (with fingers). 2. to flick. 3. to pluck (a stringed instrument). 4. to snap (the fingers). 5. to flip. 6. to spring back.

7. to kick (e.g. jerk sidewise, of a horse).

คานดีด khaandìid/ N lever.

ดีดกลับ dìidklàb/ V to spring back.

ดีดดิ้น dìid/dîn/ V to be affected, artificial (of manners).

ดีดนิ้ว dìidníw/ V to snap one's fingers.

ดีดลูกคิด dìid/lûugkhíd/ V 1. to figure, calculate with an abacus. 2. colloq. to figure the angles.

พิมพ์ดีด phimdìid/ V 1. to type, typewrite. N 2. typing. 3. short for เครื่อง-- typewriter.

ดีบุก diibùg/ N 1. tin. 2. colloq. any alloy containing tin as a primary component.

กระดาษดีบุก kradàad/diibùg/ N tin foil.

ดีปลี diiplii/ N a kind of long pepper.

ดึก dỳg/ V to be late at night.

กลางดึก klaaŋdỳg/ late at night, in the deep of the night.

ดึกดำบรรพ์ dỳg/damban/ V to be ancient, belonging to antiquity.

ดึกดื่น dỳgdỳyn/ to be late at night.

ตกดึกเข้า tògdỳg/khâw to get to be deep in the night.

ตอนดึก tɔɔndỳg/ the dead of night; late at night.

ยามดึก jaamdỳg/ late at night.

ดึง dyŋ/ V to pull, draw, tug. ความ-- tension. →Ant. ดัน.

ดึงดัน dyŋdan/ V to be obstinate. →Syn. ดื้อ.

ดึงดูด dyŋdùud/ V to attract. ความ-- attraction, gravitation.

o ดึงดูดใจ dyŋdùud/caj/ V to appeal to, be appealing to.

ดื้อดึง dŷydyŋ/ V to be obstinate.

ดื่น dỳyn/ V to be numerous, abundant, common.

ดาษดื่น dàaddỳyn/ V 1. to be plentiful, widely distributed, full of. sV 2. plentifully, abundantly, commonly.

ดึกดื่น dỳgdỳyn/ late at night.

ดื่ม dŷym/ V to drink. เครื่อง-- beverage, drink (of any kind).

ดื่มด่ำ dŷymdàm/ V to feel deeply, have a deep feeling (for something, as an artist for art).

ดูดดื่ม dùuddŷym/ V to be absorbed (emotionally), deeply affected.

นักดื่มสุรา (คน) nágdŷym'suraa/ (khon/) N eleg. heavy drinker. →Also นักดื่ม. →Syn. นักเลง

เหล้า.

น่าดื่ม nâadỳym′ V to look good to drink, look inviting (of a drink).

ดื้อ dŷy′ V 1. to be stubborn, obstinate. 2. to be dull (of a blade). ความ-- stubbornness, obstinacy. →Syn. 1. ดึงดัน. 2. ทื่อ.

ดื้อด้าน dŷydâan′ V to be obstinate.

ดื้อดึง dŷydyŋ′ V to be obstinate.

หัวดื้อ hŭadŷy′ V to be bull-headed, stubborn, obstinate.

ดุ dù?′ V 1. to be fierce, cruel, harsh, severe, cross. 2. to scold.

คำดุด่า kham′dù?dàa′ N a scolding, (words of) abuse.

ดุดัน dù?dan′ V to be angry, furious, fierce.

ดุเดือด dù?dỳad′ V to be furious, ferocious, savage (as in fighting). อย่าง-- ferociously, viciously, savagely (as of fighting).

ดุร้าย dù?ráaj′ V to be ferocious.

ดุว่า dù?′wâa′ V to bawl out, reprimand.

ดุก,ปลา-- (ตัว) dùg′, plaadùg′ (tua′) N freshwater catfish (Siluridae).

ดุจ dùd′, dùd′caɔ Pp lit.,eleg. the same as, like, as. →Syn. อย่างกับ colloq.

○ เขารักกันดุจพี่น้อง kháwrág′kan′-dùdcaphîɔ nɔ́ɔŋ↓ They love each other like brothers.

ดุจว่า,ดุจดังว่า dùd′cawâa′, dùd′cadaŋ′-wâa′ as if.

ดุน dun′ V 1. to push, push against, shove away. 2. to raise (in relief). →Cf. ดัน.

ลายดุน laajdun′ N embossed design, design in relief.

ดุ้น dûn′ C clf. for pieces of firewood, long fragments of bone, etc.

ดุม,ลูก-- (เม็ด) dum′, lûugdum′ (méd′) N button. →Also กระดุม,ลูกกระดุม.

ดุมล้อ dumlɔ́ɔ′ N hub of a wheel.

รังดุม (รัง) raŋdum′ (raŋ′) N buttonhole. →Also รังกระดุม.

ดุ่ม,ดุ่ม ๆ dùm′, dùmdùm′ V 1. to walk intent (on getting where one is going). sV 2. looking down (while walking), intently, with a preoccupied air (of walking).

เดินดุ่ม,เดินดุ่ม ๆ dəəndùm′, dəən′dùmdùm′ to walk intent (on getting to one's destination), to walk with a preoccupied air, i.e., with head slightly lowered and without looking around.

ดุริยางค์ durijaaŋ′ N 1. lit.,eleg. music. 2. musical instrument. →Syn. 1. ดนตรี com.

วงดุริยางค์ (วง) woŋ′durijaaŋ′ (woŋ′) N orchestra.

ดุล dun′, dunɔ, dunlaɔ N balance, scales.

งบดุล ŋóbdun′ N balance sheet; the balance.

ดุลพินิจ dun′phíníd′, dunlaphíníd′ N 1. careful, impartial, prudent consideration. 2. equitable judgment.

ดุลย,ดุลย- dun′, dunjaɔ, dunlajaɔ N 1. balance, equilibrium. 2. equality, comparability. V 3. to be equal, comparable.

ดุลยภาพ dunjaphâab′ N equality, balance, equilibrium.

ดุษณีภาพ dùdsaniiphâab′ N quiet, quietness.

ดุเหว่า,นก-- (ตัว) duwàw′ nógduwàw′ (tua′) N the Malayan koel, a kind of large, black bird (Cuculinae).

ดู duu′ V 1. to look, look at. 2. to appear, seem. คน--,ผู้-- spectator, onlooker; the audience. →Syn. 1. ชม eleg.

ค่าดู khâaduu′ N admission fee (to theater, wrestling match, etc.).

คิดดู khídduu′ V to think over, ponder, deliberate.

จ้องดู cɔ̂ŋduu′ V to stare at.

ดูกีฬา duu′kiilaa′ V to watch a game.

ดูแคลน duukhlɛɛn′ V to disdain, despise.

ดูงาน duuŋaan′ V to observe, observe the operation (e.g. of a system), observe (something) in operation.

ดูจะ duu′caɔ AA to seem, look like.

○ ดูจะกระไรอยู่ duu′cakraraj′-jùu idiom. 1. to look inappropriate, funny, odd. 2. That looks rather odd!

ดูดาย duudaaj′ V to look on without lending a hand; to remain indifferent, on the side lines.

ดูถูก duuthùug′ V to insult, look down upon, show contempt for. คำ-- insult. →Syn. ดูหมิ่น.

ดูท่า duuthâa′ to look like, look as though; judging by appearance, behavior.

ดูไม่เห็น duu′mâjhĕn′ can't see (e.g. because of

darkness).

ดูไม่ออก duu/mâj˘ɔ̀ɔg/ can't tell, can't make it out (by looking).

ดูเล่น duulên/ to look at for fun, for amusement.

o เลี้ยงไว้ดูเล่น líaŋ/wájduulên/ to keep, raise (e.g. a pet) for one's pleasure in watching (it).

ดูแล duulɛɛ/ V to look after, take care of, tend, supervise. ผู้-- superintendent, overseer, caretaker, keeper.

ดูว่า duu/wâaɔ to see that, observe that.

o ดูว่า...หรือไม่ duu/wâaɔ...rýymâj/ to see whether...or not.

ดูหนัง duunǎŋ/ V to see a movie.

ดูหนังสือ duu/naŋsɣ̌y/ V to study (by oneself).

ดูหมิ่น duumìn/ V to insult, look down upon, despise. ความ-- contempt. →Syn. ดูถูก.

ดูหมิ่นถิ่นแคลน duumìn/thìnkhlɛɛn/ V elab. colloq. to look down upon someone because of his lower status (financially and socially).

ดูเห็น duuhěn/ V to be able to see.

ดูเหมือน duumɣ̌an/ (it) looks as though, seems as though.

ดูออก duu˘ɔ̀ɔg/ V to ascertain, be able to tell by looking.

ตรวจดู trùadduu/ V to go over (something) carefully, examine for, check.

น่าดู nâaduu/ V to be worth seeing, pleasant to see, look at. →Syn. น่าชม eleg.

เฝ้าดู fâwduu/ V to keep watching, keep an eye on.

พอดู phɔɔduu/ colloq. quite, noticeably, perceptibly.

o ไกลพอดู klaj/phɔɔduu/ quite far.

พิศดู phíd/duu/, phíd/saduu/ V to look at carefully.

เพ่งดู phêŋ/duu/ V to stare at, gaze at.

ฟังดู faŋ/duu/ V to sound, seem, appear.

มองดู mɔɔŋ/duu/ V to look, look at, regard.

ระลึกถึง...ดู ralɣ́g/thɣ̌ŋɔ...duu/ to reflect, think upon.

ลองคิดดู lɔɔŋ/khídduu/ V to think (it) over.

ลองดู lɔɔŋ/duu V to try, try out, try and see (what something is like).

เลี้ยงดู líaŋduu/ V 1. to raise, bring up. 2. to

take care of, look after. 3. to feast.

เลือกดู lɣ̂agduu/, lɣ̂ag/duuɔ V to select.

แลดู lɛɛduu/ V 1. to look, have the appearance. 2. to look (at).

ส่องดู sɔ̀ŋduu/ V 1. to look at (through an optical instrument or by means of a mirror). 2. to throw a light on and see. 3. to look through (an optical instrument).

หมอดู (คน) mɔ̌ɔduu/ (khon/) N fortuneteller.

แอบดู ˘ɛ̀ɛbduu/ V to peep, peek.

ดูด dùud/ V to suck, absorb.

ดูดกลิ่น dùudklyyn/ V to absorb.

ดูดดึง,ดึงดูด dùuddyŋ/, dyŋdùud/ V to attract. ความ-- attraction, gravitation.

o ดึงดูดใจ dyŋdùud/caj/ V to appeal to, be appealing to.

ดูดดื่ม dùuddɣ̀ym/ V to be absorbed (emotionally), deeply affected.

เด็ก (คน) dèg/ (khon/) N 1. child (immature person). V 2. to be a child, to be young (rare; see ยังเด็ก below). →Dist. 1. ลูก "child" (relationship term). →Opp. 1. ผู้ใหญ่.

NOTE. In some instances เด็ก is used in place of คน ๑ (mng. 2) to form agent nouns when the agent is a child. Hence it is often equiv. to -er and is placed before either verbs or nouns; 1st and 2nd examples. It is also sometimes placed in front of certain well-established agentives made by other means, e.g. คน ๑, นัก ; 3rd and 4th examples. →See คน ๑.

o เด็กเดินโต๊ะ dègdəəntó?/ (child) waiter: "table walker." Cf. คนเดินโต๊ะ waiter.

o เด็กกระเป๋า dègkrapǎw/ (child) fare collector: "purse-child." Cf. คนกระเป๋า.

o เด็กคนใช้ dègkhoncháj/ servant child: "child-servant."

o เด็กนักเรียน dègnágrian/ schoolchild: "child-student."

เด็กกระเป๋า dègkrapǎw/ N boy who collects fares on public conveyances.

เด็กกำพร้า dègkamphráa/ N orphan.

เด็กคนใช้ dègkhoncháj/ N servant boy, servant girl.

เด็กชาย dègchaaj/ N 1. boy, lad. T 2. title placed in front of the first name of a boy, esp. one of school age. →Also 1. เด็กผู้ชาย. → Opp.

เด็กหญิง .

เด็กเดินโต๊ะ dègdəəntó?/ N (child) waiter.

เด็กตาดำ ๆ dèg/taa/damdam/ innocent child.

เด็กผู้ชาย dègphûuchaaj/, -phuu- N boy, lad.
→Also เด็กชาย .

เด็กผู้หญิง dègphûujǐŋ/, -phuu- N girl, lass.
→Also เด็กหญิง .

เด็กฝาแฝด (คู่,คน) dègfǎafɛ̀ɛd/ (khûu/, khon/)
N twin children.

เด็กเลี้ยงแกะ dèglíaŋkɛ̀?/ N 1. shepherd boy.
2. one who cries wolf.

เด็กหญิง dègjǐŋ/ N 1. girl. T 2. title placed in
front of the first name of a girl, esp. of school
age. →Also 1. เด็กผู้หญิง . →Opp. เด็กชาย .

เด็กอ่อน dèg/ɔ̀ɔn/ N infant. →Syn. ทารก eleg.

ยังเด็ก(อยู่) jaŋdèg/(jùu/) is still a child, is still
young.

ลูกเด็กเล็กแดง,ลูกเล็กเด็กแดง lûugdèg/légdɛɛŋ/,
lûuglég/dègdɛɛŋ/ N elab. colloq. infants
and young children (collectively).

ศาลเด็กและเยาวชน sǎandèg/lɛjawwachon/ N
juvenile court.

เดคากรัม deekhaakram/ C decagram. Abbr. ดคก.
[f. Eur.]

เด้ง dêŋ/* V to bounce.

เดช dèed/ N power, might.

เดซิกรัม deesikram/ C decigram. Abbrev. ดก.
[f. Eur.]

เด็ด ๑ dèd/ V 1. to pluck, nip off, pinch off. 2.
to sever, snap apart.

เด็ดชีวิต dèd/chiiwíd/ V lit.,eleg. to kill.

เด็ด ๒ dèd/ V 1. to be bold, resolute, determined.
2. to be decisive. sV 3. decidedly, unquestionably.

ใจเด็ด cajdèd/ V to be bold, resolute, determined.

เด็ดขาด dèdkhàad/ V 1. to be decisive. 2. to
be resolute, firm. 3. to be absolute, without
exception. sV 4. definitely, absolutely. 5.
decidedly, unquestionably, very, extremely.

เด็ดเดี่ยว dèddìaw/ V 1. to be definite, absolute,
decided. 2. to be determined, resolute. →Syn.
ใจป้ำ .

ไม้เด็ด (ไม้) máajdèd/ (máaj/) N 1. decisive

blow. 2. decisive trick or stratagem.

เด่น dèn/* V 1. to be prominent, conspicuous, outstanding. 2. to be clear, distinct.

เด่นชัด dènchád/ V to be distinct, clear, evident,
vivid.

เด่นหรา dènrǎa/ V to be conspicuously prominent,
flaunted conspicuously.

ปมเด่น (อย่าง,ข้อ) pomdèn/ (jàaŋ/, khɔ̂ɔ/) N
psych. superiority complex.

เดา daw/ V to guess.

เดิน dəən/ V 1. to walk, proceed. 2. to run (as a
watch, clock). 3. to run (as the bowels). 4. to
run, direct, operate (a business, a motor).
→Cf. ดำเนิน .

คนเดินถนน khondəən/thanǒn/ N pedestrian.

เดินเข้ามา(ใน) dəən/khâwmaa/(naj⊃) to walk
in(to), come in(to), enter.

เดินคลอเคลีย dəən/khlɔɔkhlia/ to walk side by
side, walk close together (as of lovers).

เดินควง dəənkhuaŋ/ V colloq. to walk arm in
arm (with); to walk with (one's date).

เดินจ้ำ dəəncâm/ to walk hurriedly.

เดินฉุยฉาย dəən/chǔjchǎaj/ colloq. to strut,
walk ostentatiously.

เดินดุ่ม,-- ๆ dəəndùm/, dəən/dùmdùm/ to walk
intent (on getting to one's destination), to walk
with a preoccupied air, i.e. with head slightly
lowered and without looking around.

เดินแต้ม dəəntɛ̂ɛm/ V colloq. to maneuver,
make a tactical move (in politics, chess).

เดินโต๊ะ dəəntó?/ V to serve, wait on a table.
คน-- waiter, waitress.

o เด็กเดินโต๊ะ (คน) dègdəəntó?/ (khon/) N
(child) waiter, waitress.

o หญิงเดินโต๊ะ (คน) jǐŋdəəntó?/ (khon/) N
waitress.

เดินแถว dəənthɛ̌w/ V to march; to walk in line.

เดินทอง dəənthɔɔŋ/ V 1. to letter in gold, print
gold letters. 2. to be gold-lettered, with gold
lettering.

เดินทาง ๑ dəənthaaŋ/ V to travel, take a trip.
การ-- travel, traveling (in general). คน--,
ผู้-- traveler.

o กระเป๋าเดินทาง (ใบ,ลูก) krapǎw/dəənthaaŋ/

(baj′, lûug′) N traveling bag, suitcase.

o เดินทางโดยรถไฟ dəənthaaŋ′doojródfaj′ to
travel by train.

o ไฟฟ้าเดินทาง (อัน,กระบอก,ดวง) fajfáa′ɔ
dəənthaaŋ′ (ʔan′, krabɔ̀ɔg′, duaŋ′) N flashlight.

o หนังสือเดินทาง (ฉบับ) naŋsɏ̌y′dəənthaaŋ′
(chabàb′) N passport.

o หีบเดินทาง (ใบ) hìib′dəənthaaŋ′ (baj′) N
trunk, footlocker.

o ออกเดินทาง ʔɔ̀ɔgdəənthaaŋ′ to start out, set
out on a journey.

เดินทาง ๒ dəən′thaaŋɔ to walk by way of, along.

o เดินทางถนนใหญ่ dəən′thaaŋthanǒnjàj′ to walk
along the main roads.

เดินเท้า dəəntháaw′ V to go by foot, on foot.
คน-- person on foot, pedestrian.

เดินเท้าเปล่า dəəntháawplàaw′ to walk barefooted.

เดินบก dəənbòg′ V to walk; to travel on foot.

เดินไปเดินมา, เดินไปมา dəənpaj′dəənmaa′, dəənɔ
pajmaa′ to walk back and forth, up and down.

เดินย่ำเท้า dəən′jâmtháaw′ to march (as soldiers).

เดินรถ dəənród′ V 1. to operate a line, manage
a fleet of motor vehicles (as a bus line). 2.
to drive, operate a motor vehicle.

o ระเบียบการเดินรถ rabìab′kaandəənród′ N
1. regulations for operating vehicles, esp. a
bus line. 2. the timetable, schedule of a bus
line.

เดินรถไฟ dəənródfaj′ V to operate a railway.

เดินรี่ dəənrîi′ to walk straight (to).

เดินเรือ dəənrya′ V 1. to navigate, direct a ship
on its course. 2. to operate a shipping line.
การ-- navigation.

o บริษัทเดินเรือ bɔrisàd′dəənrya′ N shipping
company.

เดินเล่น dəənlên′ to stroll, walk for pleasure.

เดินเหิน dəənhɤ̌ɤn′ V colloq. to walk.

เดินอากาศ dəənʔaakàad′ V to go by air.
→Chiefly in compounds.

o บริษัทเดินอากาศ bɔrisàd′dəənʔaakàad′ N airlines, airline company.

ท้องเดิน thɔ́ɔŋdəən′ V 1. to have diarrhea, have

a running of the bowels. N 2. diarrhea.
→Comp. ท้องเสีย, a more general term.

ทางเดิน (ทาง,สาย) thaaŋdəən′ (thaaŋ′, sǎaj′)
N 1. path, trail. 2. f ig. channel.

มนุษย์เดินดิน (คน) manúd′dəəndin′ (khon′) N
an ordinary human being (in the sense of not
possessing supernatural powers).

ระยะเดิน rajá?′dəən′ walking distance.

เรือเดินทะเล (ลำ) ryadəən′thalee′ (lam′) N
sea-going steamer.

เรือเดินสมุทร (ลำ) ryadəən′samùd′.(lam′) N
ocean-going steamer.

ออกเดิน ʔɔ̀ɔgdəən′ V to start out, set out (to walk
somewhere).

เดิม dəəm′ N 1. (as n. mod.) former, previous,
original. 2. the origin, beginning. →Cf. จำเดิม.

ดั้งเดิม daŋdəəm′ as (it was) before, as formerly.

เดิมพัน dəəmphan′ N the bet, the stake in gambling.

o วางเดิมพัน waaŋ′dəəmphan′ V to bet, place a
bet.

ตามเดิม taamdəəm′ as before, as previously.

แต่เดิม tɛ̀ɛdəəm′ from the beginning, from the
first, formerly.

บ้านเดิม (แห่ง) bâandəəm′ (hɛ̀ŋ′) N home town,
native town.

แรกเริ่มเดิมที rɛ̂ɛgrɤ̂ɤm′dəəmthii′ elab. originally, in the beginning.

เดียง in - เดียงสา diaŋsǎa′ bound form meaning
"worldly wise, worldly wisdom," used only in
negative expressions.

ไม่เดียงสา mâjdiaŋsǎa′ to be innocent, naive
(as of a child).

ไร้เดียงสา ráj′diaŋsǎa′ to lack worldly wisdom
(as of a child).

เดียว diaw′ V 1. to be single, sole (when preceded
by a clf.). 2. to be the same (identically the
same). คน-- (see below). อย่าง-- sole,
solely, alone (see also below). →Syn. เดี่ยว,
โดด. →Sometimes coupled with หนึ่ง "one."

o อันหนึ่งอันเดียว ʔannɤ̀ŋ′/ʔandiaw′ 1. one and the
same. 2. single, united, inseparable.

คนเดียว khondiaw′ alone, unaccompanied, by oneself.

ใจเดียว cajdiaw′ V to be faithful, constant (esp. in love): "single-hearted."

ชั่วแว็บเดียว chûawέb′diaw′ (for) a split second.

เช่นเดียวกับ chêndiaw′kaɔ 1. the same as. 2. in the same way as.

เดียวกัน diawkan′ the same.

o ในขณะเดียวกันนั้น najkhanà?′-diaw′kannán′ at that very same moment.

o เป็นเนื้อเดียวกัน pennýa′diawkan′ to be homogeneous; to be well-blended, smoothly joined.

o เป็นเสียงเดียวกัน pensɪaŋ′diawkan′ in one voice, in unison.

เดียวกับ diaw′kaɔ the same as.

เดียวดาย in อยู่เดียวดาย jùu′diawdaaj′ to be lonely, alone.

เดี๋ยวเดียว dɪawdiaw′ (in) just a moment.

ทีเดียว thiidiaw′ 1. a single time. 2. at once. 3. exactly, quite, very. See cross reference.

นิดเดียว níddiaw′ 1. to be tiny. 2. a tiny bit.

แบบเดียวกับ bὲεb′diawkaɔ in the same style as, on the same pattern as, the same as.

พรวดเดียว phrûaddiaw′ all at once, in one gulp, in one fell swoop.

อย่างเดียวกับ jàaŋdiaw′kaɔ 1. the same as. 2. in the same way as.

เดี่ยว dìaw′ V to be single, sole; to be alone. →Syn. เดียว, โดด.

เด็ดเดี่ยว dèddìaw′ V 1. to be definite, absolute, decided. 2. to be determined, resolute.

เดี่ยวโดด, โดดเดี่ยว dìawdòod′, dòoddìaw′ V to be single, lone, isolated.

อักษรเดี่ยว ?àgsɔ̌ondìaw′ N 1. the set of consonant symbols which have no counterpart in another tonal class; namely, the semivowel, liquid, or nasal symbols which require a preposed ห or อ for conversion from the low tonal class to the high tonal class. 2. any member of this set. →Opp. อักษรคู่.

เดี๋ยว dǐaw′ C 1. moment. 2. in a moment; suddenly. →Also ประเดี๋ยว. →Syn. ครู่.

o ค่อย ๆ หน่อยเดี๋ยวแก้วแตกหมด khɔ̂jkhɔ̂j′nɔ̀j→ dǐawkɛ̂ɛw′-tὲεg′mòd′↓ Easy; all the glassware will be broken in a moment!

เดี๋ยวใกล้เดี๋ยวไกล dǐawklâj′dǐawklaj′ now nearby, now far away.

เดี๋ยวเดียว dǐawdiaw′ in just a moment.

เดี๋ยวนี้ dǐawníi′ now, at present, at the present time.

เดียะ dìa?′ rM modifier used with ไต่ "climb," ตรง "straight," ตาม "follow."

เดือด dỳad′ V 1. (a liquid) to boil. 2. to be boiling (mad), in a rage. →Dist. 1. ต้ม "to boil (food)".

ดุเดือด dù?dỳad′ to be furious, ferocious, savage (as in fighting).

เดือดแค้น dỳadkhέεn′ V to be furious, boiling mad (at), very angry (with).

เดือดดาล dỳaddaan′ V to be furious, boiling mad. ความ-- anger, fury.

เดือดเนื้อร้อนใจ dỳadnýa′rɔ́ɔncaj′ elab. colloq. to worry, be upset. →See เดือดร้อน.

เดือดพล่าน dỳadphlâan′ V 1. to boil vigorously. 2. colloq. to be furious, boiling mad.

เดือดร้อน dỳadrɔ́ɔn′ V 1. to be in trouble. 2. to worry, feel anxious, unhappy, upset. ความ-- trouble, worry.

เดือน ๑ (ดวง) dyan′ (duaŋ′) N 1. moon. C 2. month. →Syn. 1. แข lit.

NAMES OF THE CALENDAR MONTHS

เดือนมกราคม dyanmógkaraa′khom′ January.

เดือนกุมภาพันธ์ dyankumphaa′phan′ February.

เดือนมีนาคม dyanmiinaa′khom′ March.

เดือนเมษายน dyanmee′sǎajon′ April.

เดือนพฤษภาคม dyanphrýsaphaa′khom′ -phrýdsa- May.

เดือนมิถุนายน dyanmíthunaa′jon′ June.

เดือนกรกฎาคม dyankarágkadaa′khom′ July.

เดือนสิงหาคม dyansɪ̌ŋhǎa′khom′ August.

เดือนกันยายน dyankanjaa′jon′ September.

เดือนตุลาคม dyantulaa′khom′ October.

เดือนพฤศจิกายน dyanphrýsaclkaa′jon′, -phrýdsa- November.

เดือนธันวาคม dyanthanwaa′khom′ December.

LUNAR MONTHS

เดือนอ้าย dyan?âaj′ the first lunar month, approx. December-January.

เดือนยี่ dyanjîi′ the second lunar month.

เดือนสาม dyansǎam′ the third lunar month.

เดือนสี่ dyanslì′ the fourth lunar month; etc.

NOTE. เดือนสี่เดือนห้า dyanslì′dyanhâa′ "the fourth and fifth lunar months," around March-April and April-May, are the hot season in Thailand, while the beginning of เดือนหก dyanhòg′ "the sixth lunar month," around the end of May, more or less coincides with the beginning of the rainy season. เดือนแปด "the eighth lunar month" was repeated in specified years to bring the system back into adjustment.

เงินเดือน ŋəndyan′ N salary, monthly salary.

เดือนก่อน dyankɔɔn′ last month.

เดือนเกิด dyankəəd′ N month of birth.

เดือนฉาย dyanchǎaj′ lit. the moon is shining.

เดือนตก dyantòg′ the moon sets.

เดือนที่แล้ว dyanthîiléɛw′ last month, in the last month.

เดือนมืด dyanmŷyd′ waning moon′ →Opp. เดือน หงาย.

เดือนยี่ dyanjîi′ N the second lunar month.

เดือนหงาย dyanŋǎaj′ waxing moon. →Opp. เดือนมืด.

เดือนหน้า dyannâa′ next month.

เดือนอ้าย dyan?âaj′ N the first lunar month.

ประจำเดือน pracam′dyan′ 1. monthly. N 2. colloq. menstruation, (menstrual) period.

รายเดือน raajdyan′ monthly.

รายสองเดือน raaj′sɔɔŋdyan′ bimonthly.

แรมเดือน, เป็น-- rɛɛmdyan′, penrɛɛm′dyan′ for a month, for months.

แสงเดือน sɛɛŋdyan′ N moonlight.

เดือน ๒ in ใส้เดือน (ตัว) sâjdyan′ (tua′) N earthworm.

เดือย (อัน) dyaj′ (?an′) N 1. spur (of a cock). 2. vulg. penis.

แด่ dɛɛ′ Pp def. to, towards.

แด้ in ดักแด้ (ตัว) dàgdɛɛ′ (tua′) N chrysalis.

แดก dɛɛg′ V vulg. to eat. →Syn. See กิน com.

แดกห่า dɛɛghàa′ V vulg. to eat: "to eat the plague." →See also ยัดห่า.

แด็ก, แด็ก ๆ dɛg′, dɛgdɛg′ rM intensifier for ชัก ๑ "have spasms," ดิ้น "writhe," สั่น "shake."

แดง dɛɛŋ′ V 1. to be red. N 2. the Reds. nN 3. "Red," a nickname for children.

ไข่แดง khàjdɛɛŋ′ N egg yolk. See cross ref.

เงินแดง ŋəndɛɛŋ′ N counterfeit money.

จีนแดง ciindɛɛŋ′ N 1. Red China. 2. Chinese Red(s), the Red Chinese.

ดำแดง damdɛɛŋ′ to be reddish black, red-tinged

black.

แดงก่ำ dɛɛŋkàm′ to be bright red, intensely red.

แดงขึ้น dɛɛŋ′khŷn′ 1. to redden, get redder. 2. idiom. to be exposed, revealed.

แดงแจ๋ dɛɛŋcɛɛ′ to be intensely red.

แดงแจด dɛɛŋcéd′, dɛɛŋcéɛd′ to be quite red, very red.

แดงฉาน dɛɛŋchǎan′ to be very red, bright red.

แดงแข็ด dɛɛŋchéd′ to be bright red.

แดงแปร๊ด dɛɛŋpréd′ to be bright, dazzling red.

แดงเรื่อ dɛɛŋrŷa′ to be light red, a faint red.

แดงโร่ dɛɛŋrôo′ to be distinctly red, strikingly red.

ทองแดง thɔɔŋdɛɛŋ′ N copper.

โบแดง boodɛɛŋ′ N blue ribbon (but literally a "red ribbon" or "bow" which in Thailand symbolizes an award for the best). [โบ f. Eng.]

ป่าแดง (แห่ง) pàadɛɛŋ′ (hɛ̀ŋ′) N deciduous forest.

มดแดง (ตัว) móddɛɛŋ′ (tua′) N red ant.

ยาแดง jaadɛɛŋ′ N mercurochrome.

โรคตาแดง rôog′taadɛɛŋ′ N pathol. conjunctivitis.

ลูกเล็กเด็กแดง, ลูกเด็กเล็กแดง (คน) lûuglég′ɔ dègdɛɛŋ′, lûugdèg′légdɛɛŋ′ (khon′) N infants and young children (collectively).

สตางค์แดง (อัน) sataaŋdɛɛŋ′ (?an′) N penny (one cent coin).

สีแดง sǐidɛɛŋ′ N 1. red, the color red. V 2. to be red.

หน้าดำหน้าแดงอยู่กับ nâadam′nâadɛɛŋ′-jùukaɔ colloq. to be busily engaged in (e.g. work). Has the force of English "have one's nose to the grindstone."

หน้าแดง nâadɛɛŋ′ V to blush, be blushing.

หมูแดง mǔudɛɛŋ′ N Chinese-style barbecued pork.

อินเดียนแดง ?indiandɛɛŋ′ N American Indian. [อินเดียน f. Eng.]

แดด dɛɛd′ N sunshine, sunlight.

แดดกล้า dɛɛdklâa′ the sunlight is strong.

แดดแข็ง dɛɛdkhɛ̌ŋ′ idem.

แดดจ้า dɛɛdcâa′ the sunlight is bright.

แดดเปรี๊ยง dɛɛdprîaŋ′ the sun is merciless.

ตากแดด tàagdɛɛd′ V 1. to sun (oneself), expose

to the sun, spread out in the sun . 2. to be exposed to the sun.

นาฬิกาแดด (อัน) naalikaa'dɛ̀ɛd' (ʔan') N sun-dial.

บังแดด baŋdɛ̀ɛd' V to shield from the sun.

ผึ่งแดด phʉ̀ŋdɛ̀ɛd' V to expose to the sun, dry in the sun.

แสงแดด sɛ̌ɛŋdɛ̀ɛd' N sunlight.

อาบแดด ʔàabdɛ̀ɛd' V to take a sunbath, bask in the sunshine.

แดน dɛɛn' N 1. border, boundary. 2. land, terri-tory.

เขตแดน khèeddɛɛn' N 1. territory, area, zone. 2. boundary, border, frontier.

ชายแดน (แห่ง) chaajdɛɛn' (hɛ̀ŋ') N border, frontier.

ดินแดน (แห่ง, ผืน) dindɛɛn' (hɛ̀ŋ', phʉ̌yn') N region, area, territory.

พรมแดน phromdɛɛn' N frontier, border.

โด่ง dòoŋ' V to be high, lofty, elevated.

โด่งดัง dòoŋdaŋ' V to be famous, renowned.

โดด ๑ dòod' V to jump, leap. →Also กระโดด.

โดดร่ม dòodrôm' V 1. to make a parachute jump, bail out (of a plane). 2. slang to play truant.

โดด ๒ dòod' V to be single, lone, isolated. →Syn. เดียว, เดี่ยว.

โดดเดี่ยว dòoddìaw' V to be single, lone, iso-lated.

ลูกโดด (ลูก) lûugdòod' (lûug') N ball, bullet, slug (whatever is discharged singly).

เลขโดด lêegdòod' N digit (numerical symbol).

โดน ๑ doon' V 1. to hit, strike (with destructive effect). 2. to hit against, collide.

โดน ๒ doon' V element used in making passive constructions. →Syn. ถูก ๔. →Dist. ได้รับ eleg.

o โดนกักบริเวณ doonkàg'bɔɔriween' to be quar-antined, confined to a specified area (by some-one).

o โดนเจาะยาง dooncɔ̀ʔ/jaaŋ to get one's tire punctured (by someone).

โดย dooj' Pp writ. 1. by, with, by means of. 2. with (e.g. ease). 3. by (such and such a person, as author, agent). →Syn. 1, 2 ด้วย. 2. อย่าง

com.

NOTE. (1) When โดย is used to express means, it is usually best translated as "by"; 1st example. (2) โดย is frequently used in adverbial phrases where it is rendered in English as "with" followed by a noun (with ease, with haste) or else by the suffix -ly ("easily," "hastily"); 2nd and 3rd ex-amples. Less commonly it is translated "in"; 4th example. (3) Another frequent use is to in-troduce the author or similar agent; 5th example.

o เดินทางโดยรถไฟ dəənthaaŋ'doojródfaj' to travel by train.

o โดยง่าย doojŋâaj' with ease, easily.

o โดยเร็ว doojrew' with haste, hastily; with speed, speedily.

o โดยย่อ doojjɔ̂ɔ' in brief, briefly.

o รูปนี้ถ่ายโดยนาย ก rûubnfi' thàaj'doojnaajkɔɔ' This picture was taken by Mr. A.

โดยความคิดถึง doojkhwaam'khídthʉ̌ŋ' with thoughts of you. Used as the complimentary close of a letter to a friend.

โดยเฉพาะ, --อย่างยิ่ง doojchaphɔ́ʔ', doojchaphɔ́ʔ'ᴐ jàaŋjîŋ' in particular, particularly, especially.

โดยด่วน doojdùan' with urgency, with haste.

โดยดี doojdii' amicably, good-naturedly, willingly, unhesitatingly, readily.

โดยตรง doojtroŋ' directly.

โดยตลอด doojtalɔ̀ɔd' thoroughly; with thorough-ness.

โดยตลอดรอดฝั่ง doojtalɔ̀ɔd'rɔ̂ɔdfàŋ' elab. colloq., idiom. safe and sound.

โดยทั่วไป doojthûapaj' in general, generally.

o กล่าวโดยทั่วไป klàaw'doojthûapaj' generally speaking.

โดยทาง doojthaaŋ' 1. by way of. 2. by (such and such) means, in (such and such a) way.

โดยทางรถไฟ doojthaaŋ'ródfaj' by railway, by rail.

โดยที่...ไม่ dooj'thîᴐ...mâjᴐ without (being such and such, doing such and such); without (such and such happening) (e.g. without things falling).

โดยมาก doojmâag' by and large, for the most part, mostly.

โดยไม่ dooj'mâjᴐ without (being such and such, doing such and such).

o โดยไม่ยาก dooj'mâjjâag' without difficulty.

o โดยไม่รู้สึกตัว dooj'mâjrúusʉ̀gtua' without being

aware of it, without realizing it.

โดยรอบ doojrɔ̂ɔb′ around, all around.

โดยเรียบร้อย dooj′rîabrɔ́ɔj′ 1. in good condition, in fine shape. 2. smoothly, with smoothness.

โดยลำดับ dooj′lamdàb′ progressively, gradually.

โดยลำพัง dooj′lamphaŋ′ by oneself, alone, singlehandedly.

โดยสาร. See main entry below.

ถูกหลอกโดย thùuglɔ̀ɔg′dooj⊃ deceived by.

โดยสาร doojsǎan′ V to travel (by means of a conveyance), to take passage. การ-- traveling (in a vehicle); taking (a vehicle). คน--, ผู้-- passenger. →Cf. โดย.

ค่าโดยสาร khâadoojsǎan′ N fare, cost of passage.

โดยสารเครื่องบิน doojsǎan′khrŷaŋbin′ to travel by plane, to take a plane.

รถโดยสาร (คัน) rót′doojsǎan′ (khan′) N 1. passenger car (as opposed to freight car). 2. bus.

รถยนต์โดยสาร (คัน) rótjon′doojsǎan′ (khan′) N bus.

ใด ๑ daj′ iA 1. any, any whatsoever. 2. which? what? →Normally preceded by a classifier.

คนใด (1) khondaj′; (2) khon′daj′ 1. any (person), e.g. ทหารคนใด thahǎan′khondaj′ any soldier. 2. anyone, anyone who, whoever.

ใด ๆ dajdaj′ any (usually imparting a plural or distributive sense to the preceding word).

...ใด...หนึ่ง ...daj′/...nỳŋ′ one...or the other, either..., any... (used with clf.). →Also ...หนึ่ง...ใด.

o ใช้คำใดคำหนึ่งก็ได้ cháj′-khamdaj′khamnỳŋ′-kɔ̀dâaj′ You can use either word, any word.

เท่าใด thâwdaj′ how much, how many, however much, however many.

ประการใด prakaan′daj′ 1. what, whatever; whatsoever; how, however. 2. what? whatever?; how? however?

o หล่อนจะทำประการใด lɔ̀ncatham′-prakaan′daj′↓ Whatever will she do?

o ไม่มีมูลความจริงแต่ประการใด mâjmiimuun′-khwaamciŋ′-tὲεprakaan′daj′↓ There is no truth whatsoever (in it).

ประการใดประการหนึ่ง prakaan′daj′-prakaan′nỳŋ′ any one (of the aforementioned things).

ผู้ใด phûudaj′ eleg. 1. who, whom, anyone, anybody. 2. who? whom?

เพียงใด phiaŋdaj′ how, how much, to what extent, to what degree.

เมื่อใด mŷadaj′ 1. when? 2. when, whenever.

เหตุใด hὲεddaj′ 1. why, (for) what reason, whatever reason. 2. why? (for) what reason?

อย่างหนึ่งอย่างใด jàaŋnὲŋ′jàaŋdaj′ anything, any kind, any way (of a given number of alternatives); either thing, either kind, either way.

ใด ๒ in ทันใด thandaj′ suddenly, immediately. →Comp. ทันที.

ได้ (1) dâj′, dâaj′; (2) dâjɔ; (3) dâaj′; (4) dâaj′↓ V 1. to get, obtain, procure; to reach, attain. AA 2. get to, got to, did (indicating past time). sV 3. able to, can, could, might, may. 4. Yes. O.K. All right! (in reply to a question).

o ได้ทำ dâjtham′ did, did do.

o ทำได้ thamdâaj′↓ (He) may, can do (it).

ก็ได้ kɔ̀dâaj′ (postposed, with ได้ as sec. vb.) can also; may; (it) is all right (to).

o เราจะไปไหนก็ได้ rawcapajnǎj′kɔ̀dâaj′↓ We can go anywhere we like.

o อะไรก็ได้ ?araj′kɔ̀dâaj′↓ Anything will do. Anything whatever.

กินได้ kindâaj′ V 1. to be able to eat. 2. to have an appetite. 3. to be edible. 4. can be served, eaten.

เก็บได้ kὲbdâaj′ V to pick up (something lost or discarded by others).

เงินได้ in ภาษีเงินได้ phaasǐi′ŋəndâaj′ income tax.

จนได้ condâaj′ 1. until (one) obtains (something), succeeds. 2. anyway (in spite of opposition or prohibition).

o เขาไปจนได้ kháwpaj′condâaj′↓ He went anyway.

จะเห็นได้ว่า cahĕn′dâjwâa′ it may be seen that.

เจ็บไข้ได้ป่วย cὲbkhâj′dâjpùaj′ V elab. eleg. to get sick, be sick.

จำได้ camdâaj′ V to remember, recognize, be able to recall.

เชื่อถือได้ chŷathŷy′dâaj′ V to be reliable.

ใช้การได้ chájkaan′dâaj′ V 1. to be in working

condition, useable. 2. That's good! (said in praise). 3. It worked!

ใช้ได้ chájdâaj′ V to be serviceable, useable, fair, (all) right, valid.

ได้กลิ่น dâjklìn′ V to scent, smell, catch the scent (of).

ได้กัน dâaj′kan colloq. 1. to become intimate sexually (of lovers). 2. to become common-law husband and wife. 3. to get married.

ได้การ dâjkaan′ V 1. to be successful, workable. 2. It works!

ได้แก่ dâjkɛ̀ɛ′ 1. to consist of, include, be (followed by one item or a list of items). 2. such as, namely, consisting of. 3. (a prize) to go to (someone). →Cf. 1, 2. คือ.

o หัวหน้าครอบครัวได้แก่พ่อ. hǔanâa′khrɔ̂ɔbkhruaɔ dâjkɛ̀ɛphɔ̂ɔ↓ The head of the family is the father.

o รางวัลที่หนึ่งได้แก่นาย ก. raaŋwan′thîinỳŋ′ dâjkɛ̀ɛnaajkɔɔ↓ The first prize went to Mr. A.

ได้ข่าว(ว่า) dâjkhàaw′(wâaɔ) V to hear (that), hear the news (of).

ได้ความ dâjkhwaam′ V 1. to make sense. 2. to ascertain (that).

o ไม่ได้ความ (1,2) mâjdâjkhwaam′ (3) mâj′dâjɔ khwaam′↓ 1. to be nonsense, make no sense. 2. nonsensically, senselessly. 3. Nonsense! It doesn't make sense!

ได้คิด dâjkhíd′ 1. to realize, become aware of. 2. to regain one's senses.

ได้(...)คืน dâj(...)khyyn′ to get (such and such) back, regain (such and such).

ได้งานทำ dâjŋaan′tham′ to get a job, have a job.

ได้เงิน dâjŋən′ V to make money; to get (money).

ได้ใจ dâajcaj′ V to become overbold, be emboldened (to carry some action to excess).

ได้ชื่อ(ว่า) dâjchŷy(wâa′) V 1. to get the name of, be known (as). 2. to have gained the name of, hence to be considered, regarded as.

ได้ซิ dâaj′si Sure! Certainly!

ได้ดิบได้ดี dâajdìb′dâajdii′ V elab. colloq. 1. to attain power, rank, prominence. 2. to be well off.

ได้ทราบ dâjsâab′ V to hear of, learn of, get to

know of.

ได้ที่ dâaj′thii′ V 1. to gain the advantage (over one's opponent). 2. fig. to be on top. →Dist. ได้เปรียบ. →Ant. เสียที.

ได้เปรียบ dâjprìab′ V to have an advantage (over) have the edge (over). →Dist. ได้ที. →Ant. เสียเปรียบ.

ได้ผล dâjphǒn′ V 1. to get results. 2. (something) to be successful, effective.

ได้(...)เพิ่มเติม dâaj′(...)phəəmtəəm′ V to gain more of (such and such), get additional (such and such).

ได้(...)เพิ่มอีก dâj(...)phəəm′ʔìig′ to get (such and such) in addition.

ได้ยิน. See as separate main entry below.

ได้รับ dâjráb′ V 1. to get, obtain, receive. 2. to have received. 3. eleg. expression used to make passive or pseudo-passive constructions; see note. →Cf. ถูก ⊄, โดน.

NOTE. In some instances ได้รับ is used as the elegant substitute for ถูก ⊄; 3rd example. In other somewhat similar circumstances, ได้รับ is not only elegant but also the word choice when a favorable result ensues, whereas ถูก ⊄ and โดน tend to be used more often when an unfavorable result ensues.

o ได้รับแต่งตั้ง dâjráb′tɛ̀ŋtâŋ′ eleg. to get appointed.

o ได้รับทราบ(ว่า) dâjrábsâab′(wâa′) eleg. to have learned (that); to have received confirmation (that).

o ได้รับบาดเจ็บ dâjráb′bàadcèb′ eleg. to get injured, get wounded.

ได้ฤกษ์ dâjrə̂əg′ V to reach the auspicious moment.

ได้ลงคอ dâjloŋkhɔɔ′ to be unfeeling enough to (do such and such). →See cross reference.

ได้เวลา dâjweelaa′ V 1. to reach the time (of). 2. it's the time (to do such and such).

ได้สติ dâjsatìʔ′ V 1. to come to (oneself), regain consciousness. 2. to come to one's senses, regain one's common sense.

ได้เสีย dâaj′sĭa′ V 1. to gain and lose, gain and spend. 2. to be common-law husband and wife.

o ลอบลักได้เสีย lɔ̂ɔblág′-dâaj′sĭa′ colloq. to

live together (as man and wife) secretly.

o ส่วนได้เสีย sùandâaj'sǐa' N an interest (i.e. an involvement in gain or loss). →Also ส่วนได้ส่วนเสีย.

oo ฝ่ายที่มีส่วนได้เสีย fàaj'-thîimii'-sùandâaj'ɔsǐa' the interested party, parties.

ตีได้ tii'dâaj' V to conquer, take (e.g. a town).

ไปได้ (1) pajdâaj'↓; (2) pajdâaj', paj!dâaj' 1. (He) may, can go. 2. idiom. how can (you do such and such)! (rhetorical question with element of criticism); see example.

o ใจเสาะไปได้ cajsɔ?'/pajdâaj'↓, -paj!dâaj'- How can you be such a scaredy cat?

ผลพลอยได้(อย่าง) phǒn'phlɔɔjdâaj'(jàaŋ') N by-product.

เพื่อจะได้ (1) phŷacadâjɔ; (2) phŷacadâajɔ, -dâaj' 1. in order to, in order that, in order to get to (do something). 2. in order to get, obtain.

เพื่อจะ...ให้ได้ phŷacaɔ...hâjdâaj' in order to be able to.

มิได้ (1) mídâaj'; (2) mídâjɔ; (3) mídâaj'; (4) mídâaj'↓ eleg. 1. not get, gain, obtain, procure. 2. didn't; not get to, didn't get to. 3. cannot. 4. No! (general negative). →Syn. ไม่ได้ com.

o มิได้ขาด mídâjkhàad' incessantly; regularly.

o มิได้อะไร (1) mídâj?araj'; (2) mídâaj'/?araj' 1. is of no use. 2. (one) will not gain anything.

o หาค่ามิได้ hǎakhâa'mídâaj' eleg. to be invaluable. May be used by some speakers in the meaning "valueless."

ไม่ได้ (1) mâjdâjɔ, mâjdâaj'; (2) mâjdâjɔ; (3) mâjdâaj'; (4) mâjdâaj'↓ com. 1. not get, gain, obtain, procure. 2. didn't; not get to, didn't get to. 3. can't, cannot, unable to. 4. No! (in answer to ได้ไหม ; also used prohibitively). →See cross ref. →Syn. มิได้ eleg.

o ผมไม่ได้ไปไหน phǒm'mâjdâjpajnǎj' I didn't go anywhere.

o ผมไปไม่ได้ phǒmpaj'mâjdâaj' I can't go.

o ฟังไม่ได้ faŋ'mâjdâaj' 1. to sound awful, unpleasant; can't bear to listen (to it). 2. to sound unbelievable, unreasonable, invalid.

ไม่เสียไม่ได้ mâjsǐa'mâjdâaj' to neither lose nor

gain; to break even.

รายได้ raajdâaj' N income.

ไว้ใจได้ wájcaj'dâaj' V to be trustworthy.

สอบได้ sɔɔbdâaj' V to pass (an examination or course in school)

หาได้...ไม่ hǎa'dâjɔ...mâj' eleg. did not, has not, have not, not (often refers to past time). Equiv. to ไม่ได้ as adv.-aux.

หาได้ไม่ hǎadâaj'mâj' eleg. cannot. Equiv. to ไม่ได้ as sec. verb.

เห็นแก่ได้ hěn'kɛɛdâaj' to be acquisitive, covetous. →Syn. โลภ.

อยากได้ jàagdâaj' to desire, to wish to have.

อาจ...ได้ ?àadɔ...dâaj' might, may.

o อาจกล่าวได้ ?àadklàaw'dâajɔ it may be said.

ได้ยิน dâjjin' V to hear.

ได้ยินกับหู dâjjin'kahǔu' to hear with one's own ears.

ได้ยินได้ฟัง dâjjin'dâjfaŋ' elab. colloq. 1. to hear. 2. to have heard of.

ฟังไม่ได้ยิน faŋ'mâjdâjjin' can't hear (e.g. because of noise).

แอบได้ยิน ?ɛɛb'dâjjin' to overhear (unintentionally).

ต

ต tɔɔ' MIDDLE consonant. Pronounced t initially, d finally. The sound t as an initial middle consonant is also very rarely written with ฏ.

ตก tòg' V 1. to drop, fall; to fall (straight) down (from, into, onto). 2. to fall off, drop off, decrease, diminish. 3. to droop (as ears, tail). 4. to set (of the sun, moon). 5. to set in (as afternoon). 6. hort. to set (of fruit, pods, seed). 7. eleg. to lay (eggs). 8. colloq. to come to (such and such an amount), be approximately, come close to. 9. to fade (of colors). sV 10. down, through (completive sense); conclusively. →Dist. 1. ล้ม, หกล้ม. →Ant. 1. ลุก. 2,4. ขึ้น. 3. ชี้.

o ตกเก้าอี้ tòg' kâw?îi' to fall off (one's) chair.

o ราคาตก raakhaa'tòg' prices to fall, drop off.

o หูตก hǔu'tòg' to have drooping ears.

o เดือนตก dyan′tòg′ the moon sets.

o ตกดึก tògdỳg′ the deep of the night sets in.

o ตกรวง tògruaŋ′ ears (of rice plants) to set.

o ตกไข่ tògkhàj′ eleg. to lay eggs.

o ตกร้อยบาท tògrɔ́ɔj′bàad′ colloq. it comes to a hundred bahts.

o คิดตก khíd′tòg′ to have solved (a thinking problem), have gotten over (a life problem).

o สอบไล่ตก sɔ̀ɔblàj′tòg′ to fail in an examination.

แก(...)ตก kɛ̂ɛ′(...)tòg′ V 1. to be able to solve (something), solve successfully. 2. to be solvable.

คอตก khɔɔ′tòg′ V 1. to drop the head, have a drooping head (because of sadness, disappointment). 2. to feel dejected. sV 3. (with) drooping head, crestfallen.

ตกกระ tògkrà?′ V to be freckled.

ตกกล้า tògklâa′ V to sow germinated rice grain. →Syn. ทอดกล้า.

ตกไข่ tògkhàj′ V eleg. to lay eggs. →Syn. See ออกไข่ com.

ตกค้าง tògkháaŋ′ V to be left over, left behind.

ตกเครือ tògkhrya′ V (a bunch of bananas) to set.

ตกจักใหญ่ tòg′càgjàj′ colloq. (rain) to pour heavily.

ตกใจ tògcaj′ V com. to get frightened, scared, to take fright. ความ-- fright. →Also ตก กะใจ colloq., →Syn. ตระหนก eleg., ขวัญบิน idiom.

o เครื่องหมายตกใจ khrŷaŋmǎaj′tògcaj′ N the exclamation point. Used with exclamatives and exclamatory sentences. →Syn. อัศเจรีย์ eleg., tech.

ตกดิน tògdin′ V (the sun) to set.

ตกดึกเข้า tògdỳg′khâw′ V to get to be deep in the night.

ตกตะกอน tòg′takɔɔn′ V to precipitate. การ-- precipitation.

ตกต่ำ tògtàm′ V to drop, decline, be declining, falling low. ความ-- decline.

o เศรษฐกิจตกต่ำ sèed′thakìd′tògtàm′ N economic depression.

ตกแต่ง tògtɛ̀ŋ′ V to decorate, beautify. เครื่อง--

decorations, ornaments. NOTE. ตกแต่ง is sometimes confused with ตบแต่ง "to marry off, arrange a marriage."

ตกถึงมือ tòg′thy̌ŋmyy′ to come to the hand of, come into the possession of.

ตกบ่าย tògbàaj′ V 1. to be afternoon. 2. in the afternoon, when the afternoon sets in.

ตกปลา tògplaa′ V to fish.

ตกปาก,--ตกคำ tògpàag′, tògpàag′tògkham′ V elab. colloq. to give a verbal promise, make a verbal agreement.

ตกเป็นของ tòg′penkhɔ̌ɔŋ′ to become the property of, become (someone)'s.

ตกผลึก tòg′phalỳg′ V to crystallize, deposit crystals.

ตกฟอง tògfɔɔŋ′ V lit., eleg. to lay eggs. →Syn. See ออกไข่ com.

ตกฟาก tògfâag′ V colloq. to be born: "drop to the floor."

ตกมัน tògman′ V (an elephant) to be in must, rut.

ตกยาก tògjâag′ V to sink into poverty, become impoverished; to suffer hardship.

ตกรถ tògród′ V to miss one's bus, train, etc.

ตกรวง tògruaŋ′ V (ears of rice plants) to set.

ตกราง tògraaŋ′ V to be derailed.

ตกลง tògloŋ′ V 1. to agree (to something). 2. to fall (straight) down. การ-- agreement, settlement.

o ข้อตกลง (ข้อ) khɔ̂ɔ′tògloŋ′ (khɔ̂ɔ′) N 1. agreement, settlement. 2. points of agreement.

o ตกลงกัน tògloŋ′kan 1. to come to an agreement. 2. to be settled, agreed upon.

ตกลงใจ tògloŋcaj′ V to decide, make up one's mind ความ-- decision.

o ไม่ตกลงใจ mâjtògloŋcaj′ to be undecided, not have made up one's mind.

ตกลูก tòglûug′ V to give birth, drop young (of animals).

ตกโลหิต tòg′loohìd′ V eleg. to bleed excessively (in menstruation, in childbirth). →Syn. ตกเลือด com.

ตกหาย tòghǎaj′ V to be missing, lost (through having been dropped).

ตกอยู่(ใน,กับ,ใต้) tòg′jùu′(najɔ, kaɔ, tâjɔ).

See examples below.

o ตกอยู่ในมือ tòg'jùunajmyy' to fall into the hands (of).

o ยังตกอยู่ในประเทศเขมร jaŋtòg'-jùunajpracʉ thêed'khamĕen' still remains in, falls in Cambodia.

ตกอับ tòg°àb' V 1. (a person) to fall, sink into poverty, reach the depths of (his) downfall. 2. to be fallen.

ตะวันตก tawantòg' com. west. →Syn. ประจิม lit., eleg. →The literary and the common terms for the eight chief points of the compass are listed under ทิศ.

ตัวตก (ตัว) tuatòg' (tua') N omitted character or letter (in printing, typing).

ทำ(...)ตก tham(...)tòg' to drop (something), let (something) drop.

น้ำตก (แห่ง) námtòg' (hèŋ') N waterfall; falls.

ปลงตก ploŋtòg' V 1. to realize, become aware, come to the realization. 2. to know life (be aware of the vicissitudes of life).

ฝนตก fŏntòg' it's raining; it rains.

พลัดตก phládtòg' V to fall down, drop down.

ยิงตก jiŋtòg' V to shoot down, to drop (by shooting).

สอบไล่ตก sɔ̀ɔblâjtòg' V to fail an examination.

สีตก sĭitòg' 1. the colors fade. V 2. to have colors that fade.

o สีไม่ตก sĭi'mâjtòg' 1. the colors are fast. V 2. to be colorfast.

ตก in ตกกะใจ tóg'kacaj' V colloq. to be scared, frightened. →Var. of ตกใจ.

ตงิด ๆ taŋìd'taŋìd' rM slightly. Used with words expressing sensations such as hunger, anger, pain, e.g. หิว "hungry," โกรธ "angry," เจ็บ "hurt," etc.

ตด tòd' V com. to pass wind, break wind, fart. →Syn. ผายลม eleg.

ตน ๑ ton' N eleg. the self, oneself, one's own self. →Often coupled with ตัว. →Syn. ตัว com.

o ลืมตัวลืมตน lyymtua'lyymton' V elab. colloq. to forget oneself.

การแยกตน kaanjɛ̂ɛgton' N phys. fission.

ครองตน khrɔɔŋton' to live the life (of, e.g. a bachelor, a hermit, etc.).

ตนเอง ton°eeŋ' oneself, one's own self. More emphatic than ตน alone.

o การปกครองตนเอง kaanpògkhrɔɔŋ'ton°eeŋ' N self-government.

o ด้วยตนเอง dûajton°eeŋ' in person; by oneself, as oneself, personally.

o ตามใจตนเอง taamcaj'ton°eeŋ' to do as one likes, follow one's own wishes.

ไม่เป็นตัวเป็นตน mâjpentua'penton' to be unformed, amorphous, not to have taken shape.

ลืมตัวลืมตน lyymtua'lyymton' V to forget oneself.

วางตน waaŋton' V eleg. 1. to behave, conduct oneself. 2. to place oneself.

ตน ๒ ton' C clf. for giants, demons, hermits, ascetics, and the like.

ต้น tôn' N 1. beginning, source. 2. trunk, stalk. C 3. clf. for trees and plants of all kinds; for stalks, stems, posts, and the like. 4. class term for trees and plants of all kinds. →Ant. 1. ปลาย. NOTE. ต้น is a class term, not a general term. The general term for "tree" is ต้นไม้. Specific trees and plants are named by using the class term followed by specific terms, e.g. ต้นกล้วย "banana tree," ต้นกุหลาบ "rosebush" ต้นอ้อ "giant reed."

ข้างต้น khâŋtôn' at the beginning, at the outset.

ขึ้นต้น khŷntôn' V to begin, commence.

เงินต้น ŋəntôn' N finance principal, capital, sum.

ขั้นต้น chántôn' beginning stage, beginning level, lower level.

ชีต้น (องค์, รูป) chiitôn' (°oŋ', rûub') N (Buddhist) priest.

ต้นกล้วย (ต้น) tônklûaj' (tôn') N banana tree.

ต้นกะหล่ำดอก (ต้น) tôn'-kalàm'dɔ̀ɔg' (tôn') N the cauliflower plant.

ต้นกะหล่ำปลี (ต้น) tôn'-kalàm'plii' (tôn') N the cabbage plant.

ต้นกานพลู (ต้น) tônkaanphluu' (tôn') N clove tree.

ต้นก้ามปู (ต้น) tônkâampuu' (tôn') N 1. the rain tree (Enterolobium saman). 2. the East Indian walnut (Albizzia lebbeck). →Syn. ต้นจามจุรี.

ต้นกุหลาบ (ต้น) tônkulàab' (tôn') N rosebush.

ต้นขนุน (ต้น) tônkhanŭn/ (tôn/) the jack tree (Artocarpus integrifolia).

ต้นขั้ว (ใบ) tônkhŭa/ (baj/) N stub (as of a check), counterfoil (Brit.).

ต้นเข็ม (ต้น) tônkhĕm/ (tôn/) N a shrub or tree of the genera Ixora, Pavetta, or Duperrea.

ต้นคราม (ต้น) tônkhraam/ (tôn/) N indigo plant.

ต้นคอ tônkhɔɔ/ N nape.

ต้นคิด in คนต้นคิด (คน) khontônkhíd/ (khon/) N inventor, author, originator.

ต้นเค้า tônkháw/ N prototype.

ต้นจันทน์ (ต้น) tôncan/ (tôn/) N 1. sandalwood tree. 2. nutmeg tree, short for ต้นจันทน์เทศ.

ต้นจามจุรี (ต้น) tôncaamcurii/ (tôn/) N 1. the East Indian walnut (Albizzia lebbeck). 2. the rain tree (Enterolobium saman). →Syn. ต้นก้ามปู.

ต้นฉบับ (ฉบับ) tônchabàb/ (chabàb/) N original manuscript, source document.

ต้นตอ tôntɔɔ/ N original cause; source, origin.

ต้นตาล (ต้น) tôntaan/ (tôn/) N sugar palm, toddy palm.

ต้นไทร (ต้น) tônsaj/ (tôn/) N banyan tree (Ficus bengalensis).

ต้นน้อยหน่า (ต้น) tônnɔɔjnàa/ (tôn/) N rough-skinned custard apple tree (Annona squamosa).

ต้นน้อยโหน่ง (ต้น) tônnɔɔjnòoŋ/ (tôn/) N smooth-skinned custard apple tree (Annona reticulata).

ต้นน้ำ (แห่ง) tônnáam/ (hὲŋ/) N source of a river.

ต้นปาล์ม (ต้น) tônpaam/ (tôn/) N palm tree (general term). [ปาล์ม f. Eng.]

ต้นผักชี (ต้น) tônphàgchii/ (tôn/) N the coriander plant.

ต้นไผ่ (ต้น) tônphàj/ (tôn/) N bamboo stalk, stem.

ต้นฝรั่ง (ต้น) tônfaràŋ/ (tôn/) N the guava tree.

ต้นฝิ่น (ต้น) tônfìn/ (tôn/) N poppy plant.

ต้นพลู (ต้น) tônphluu/ (tôn/) N the betel vine.

ต้นพุทรา (ต้น) tônphúdsaa/ (tôn/) N the jujube tree.

ต้นเพลิง (แห่ง) tônphləəŋ/ (hὲŋ/) N eleg. the source of a fire. →Syn. ต้นไฟ com.

ต้นโพธิ์ (ต้น) tônphoo/ (tôn/) N pipal, bo tree (Ficus religiosa).

ต้นไฟ (แห่ง) tônfaj/ (hὲŋ/) N com. the source of a fire. →Syn. ต้นเพลิง eleg.

ต้นมะขาม (ต้น) tônmakhăam/ (tôn/) N tamarind tree (Tamarindus indica).

ต้นมะเขือ (ต้น) tônmakhўa/ (tôn/) N eggplant (the plant).

ต้นมะเขือเทศ (ต้น) tônmakhўathêed/ (tôn/) N tomato plant.

ต้นมะนาว (ต้น) tônmanaaw/ (tôn/) N lime tree, lemon tree.

ต้นมะปราง (ต้น) tônmapraaŋ/ (tôn/) N marian plum tree.

ต้นมะพร้าว (ต้น) tônmaphráaw/ (tôn/) N the coconut palm, coco palm (Cocos nucifera).

ต้นมะเฟือง (ต้น) tônmafyaŋ/ (tôn/) N carambola tree.

ต้นมะม่วง (ต้น) tônmamûaŋ/ (tôn/) N mango tree (Mangifera indica).

ต้นมะระ (ต้น) tônmará? (tôn/) N bitter melon plant.

ต้นมะละกอ (ต้น) tôn/malakɔɔ/ (tôn/) N papaya tree (Carica papaya).

ต้นมังคุด (ต้น) tôn/maŋkhúd/ (tôn/) N mangosteen tree (Garcinia mangostana).

ต้นมันเทศ (ต้น) tôn/manthêed/ (tôn/) N sweet potato plant.

ต้นมันฝรั่ง (ต้น) tôn/manfaràŋ/ (tôn/) N potato plant.

ต้นมันสำปะหลัง (ต้น) tôn/-man/sămpalăŋ/ (tôn/) N cassava plant.

ต้นมือ tôn/myy/ N idiom. the early phase or stage, the beginning.

ต้นไม้ (ต้น) tônmáaj/ (tôn/) N tree (of any kind). This is a general term; see note under main entry.

ต้นยาง (ต้น) tônjaaŋ/ (tôn/) N rubber tree, i.e. the tree from which latex is derived.

ต้นยี่โถ (ต้น) tônjîithǒo/ (tôn/) N oleander.

ต้นระกำ (ต้น) tônrakam/ (tôn/) N a type of palm which bears red, edible fruit.

ต้นละมุด (ต้น) tônlamúd/ (tôn/) N a kind of fruit tree.

ต้นสน (ต้น) tônsŏn/ (tôn/) N 1. pine tree (Pinus).

2. any closely related coniferous tree.

ต้นส้ม (ต้น) tônsôm′ (tôn′) N orange tree.

ต้นสัก (ต้น) tônsàg′ (tôn′) N the teak tree.

ต้นหน (คน) tônhŏn′ (khon′) N navigator, steersman, captain of a vessel.

ต้นหมาก (ต้น) tônmàag′ (tôn′) N areca palm.

ต้นหยี, ต้นลูกหยี (ต้น) tôn′jĭi′, tôn′lûugjĭi′ (tôn′) N a type of tree which bears a sour fruit.

ต้นเหตุ (ประการ, อย่าง) tônhèed′ (prakaan′, jàaŋ′) N cause, origin.

ต้นอ้อ (ต้น) tôn?ôɔ′ (tôn′) N giant reed.

ต้นอ้อย (ต้น) tôn?ôj′ (tôn′) N sugar cane.

ต้นอินทผลัม (ต้น) tôn′-?in′tháphalam′ N the date palm. →Also written -ผาลัม.

ตอนต้น (ตอน) tɔɔntôn′ (tɔɔn′) N 1. the beginning part. 2. at first, to begin with. →Opp. ตอนปลาย.

ตั้งต้น tâŋtôn′ V to begin, commence.

แต่ต้น tɛ̀εtôn′ from the beginning.

เบื้องต้น bŷaŋtôn′ N eleg. 1. the beginning part, elementary part. 2. at the beginning. 3. (as n. mod.) introductory, preliminary. →Opp. เบื้องปลาย.

เป็นต้น pentôn′ as a beginning. Commonly used in expressions of the type show below.

o เช่น...เป็นต้น chên′...pentôn′ for example; such as (a list of things), for example. NOTE. This expression serves to encompass a list of whatever is being exemplified; hence เช่น introduces the list and เป็นต้น follows it: "such as apples, oranges, and bananas, for example."

o ตั้งแต่วันนั้นเป็นต้นมา tâŋ′tɛ̀εwannán′-pentôn′ɔ maa′ from that day on.

o เป็นต้นว่า pentôn′wâa′ for instance.

พยัญชนะต้น (ตัว) phajanchaná?′tôn′ (tua′) N initial consonant.

ยามต้น jaamtôn′ N the first watch period, i.e. 6-9 P.M.

ยืนต้น jyyntôn′ V to remain growing, hence, to be perennial.

o พืชยืนต้น (ต้น, ชนิด) phŷyd′jyyntôn′ (tôn′, chaníd′) N perennial plant.

เริ่มต้น rə̀əmtôn′ V to begin, start, commence.

ลำต้น (ล้าต้น) lamtôn′ (lamtôn′) N trunk (of a tree).

เสมอต้นเสมอปลาย samə̌ə′tôn′-samə̌ə′plaaj′ V 1. to be consistent. sV 2. consistently.

ตนุ in เต่าตนุ (ตัว) tàw′tanù?′ (tua′) N a large green sea turtle. Its eggs are called ไข่จะละ เม็ด.

ตบ tòb′ V 1. to slap, clap, pat. 2. slang to bribe.

ตบตา tòbtaa′ V colloq. to deceive, fool the eyes (e.g. by placing the best on top).

ตบแต่ง tòbtɛ̀ŋ′ V 1. to decorate, embellish. 2. to marry off, arrange a marriage. →Comp. ตกแต่ง.

o ตบแต่งร่างกาย tòbtɛ̀ŋ′râaŋkaaj′ V to dress (oneself).

ตบปีก tòbpìig′ V to flap the wings.

ตบมือ tòbmyy′ V to clap the hands.

ตบเอา tòb′?aw′ V slang to extort. การ-- extortion.

ตม tom′ N mud, mire.

เป็นตม pentom′ V to be muddy.

ต้ม tôm′ V 1. to boil (food). 2. (food) to be boiled. 2. slang to cheat, swindle, deceive. →Dist. เดือด "(a liquid) to boil."

ข้าวต้ม khâawtôm′ N rice boiled to soupy consistency, rice porridge.

ไข่ต้ม (ฟอง) khàjtôm′ (fɔɔŋ′) N boiled egg.

ต้มกลั่น tômklàn′ V to distill.

ต้มหมู tômmŭu′ V slang to make a sucker out of someone, make a dupe of someone.

หุงต้ม hŭŋtôm′ V to cook (in general).

ต.ร. Abbrev. of ตำรวจ the police, a policeman.

ตรง troŋ′ V 1. to be straight, direct. 2. to be honest, upright. 3. to correspond, coincide, agree. 4. to be accurate, exact. sV 5. exactly, sharp (of time). 6. directly, frankly. 7. (directly) at, in, to. →Ant. 1, 2. คด.

o เวลาสี่โมงตรง weelaa′sìimooŋtroŋ′ at four o'clock sharp.

ซื่อตรง sŷytroŋ′ V 1. to be honest. 2. to be faithful (as a dog). ความ-- honesty.

โดยตรง doojtroŋ′ directly.

ตรงกลาง, ที่-- troŋklaaŋ′, thîitroŋklaaŋ′ in the middle, at the center.

If a word is not found under ตร, see กร.

ตรงกันข้าม(กับ) troŋkankhâam′(kaɔ) 1. to be opposite, the opposite of, contrary (to). 2. on the contrary, conversely. 3. to be right across from each other.

ตรงกับ troŋ′kaɔ to correspond exactly to.

ตรงข้าม(กับ) troŋkhâam(kaɔ). See ตรงกันข้าม.

ตรงเข้าไล่ troŋ′khâwlâj′ to set out to chase, start in chasing.

ตรงเดี๊ยะ troŋdìaʔ′ absolutely straight, very straight.

ตรงนั้น troŋnán′ right over there.

ตรงเป๊ง troŋpěŋ′ V 1. to be absolutely correct. 2. to be absolutely straight.

ตรงไปตรงมา troŋpaj′troŋmaa′ V colloq. 1. to be straightforward, honest, frank. sV 2. frankly, openly, straightforwardly.

ตรงรี่ troŋrîi′ V to advance directly and quickly (to).

ตรงเวลา troŋweelaa′ V to be on time, punctual.

ตรงหน้า troŋnâa′ right in front of, before.

ตามตรง taamtroŋ′ straight (of speaking), frankly.

ทางตรง thaaŋtroŋ′ N 1. the straight path, the direct way. 2. directly. →Opp. ทางอ้อม.

ที่ตรง thîitroŋɔ (directly) at, in; (right) at, in.

บอกตรง ๆ bɔɔg′troŋtroŋ′ speaking frankly, frankly, to tell the truth.

ตรม trom′ V to be sorrowful. Chiefly in compounds. →See also ตรอม.

ตรมตรอม tromtrɔɔm′ V to be melancholy, sorrowful, heartsick.

ตรวจ trùad′ V to inspect, examine, check. การ-- inspection, examination, investigation.

ตรวจการ trùadkaan′ V to inspect things, carry out an inspection. ผู้-- inspector.

ตรวจค้น trùadkhón′ V to search (e.g. a person or place for concealed objects).

ตรวจดู trùadduu′ V to go over (something) carefully, examine for, check.

ตรวจตรา trùadtraa′ V to inspect, check.

ตรวจพล trùadphon′ V to review troops.

ตรวจราชการ trùadrâadchakaan′ V to make an official inspection (of government offices, affairs).

ตรวจสอบ trùadsɔɔb′ V to check, verify.

นายตรวจ (คน) naajtrùad′ (khon′) N conductor (i.e. ticket-inspector on a train or bus).

ใบตรวจ (ฉบับ) bajtrùad′ (chabàb′) N certificate (certifying inspection).

ตรวน (เส้น) truan′ (sên′) N fetter, ankle chain (for prisoners).

ตรอก ๑ (ตรอก) trɔɔg′ (trɔɔg′) N lane, alley.

จนตรอก controɔg′ V idiom. to be at an impasse, have no way out.

ตรอก ๒ trɔɔg′ V to fill in, fill out (a blank). More commonly กรอก.

ตรอง trɔɔŋ′ V eleg. to consider, think (it) over, think carefully. →Also ตริ--, ตรึก--, ไตร่--.

ตรอม trɔɔm′ V to be sorrowful. Chiefly in compounds. →See also ตรม.

ตรมตรอม tromtrɔɔm′ V to be melancholy, sorrowful, heartsick.

ตระกอง trakɔɔŋ′ V eleg. to hug, embrace. →Syn. กอด com.

ตระการ trakaan′ eleg., lit. beautiful, appealing. Chiefly in the combination ตระการตา trakaan′ɔ taa′ eye-appealing.

ตระกูล trakuun′ N 1. family, clan, stock, tribe. 2. lineage, ancestry.

ตระเตรียม traʔtriam′ V to prepare, make ready. →See เตรียม.

ตระเวน traween′ V 1. to patrol. 2. to roam, wander about.

ตระเวนแผ่นดิน traween′phɛ̀ndin′ to roam the country, tour, travel about.

พลตระเวน (คน,นาย) phontraween′ (khon′, naaj′) N patrolman, policeman on his beat.

ลาดตระเวน lâadtraween′ V to patrol, make the rounds to inspect (a place, an installation).

o เรือลาดตระเวน (ลำ) rya′lâadtraween′ (lam′) N cruiser (a class of warship).

ตระหง่าน traŋàan′ V eleg. to be majestically tall, stately, lofty.

ตระหนก tranòg′ V eleg. to be frightened, alarmed. →Syn. See ตกใจ com.

ตระหนัก(ว่า,ถึง) tranàg′(wâa′,-thỹŋɔ) V eleg. to realize, perceive, become aware (of).

ตระหนี่ tranìi′ V eleg. to be stingy, miserly. →Syn. ขี้เหนียว com.

ตระหนี่ถี่เหนียว tranìi'thìinǐaw' V elab. eleg.
to be stingy, parsimonious.

ตระหลบ tralòb' V eleg. to diffuse (of itself), be
diffused widely (as odor, dust). →Also ตลบ
com.

ตรัง traŋ' pN Trang, a township in S Thailand.

ตรับ tràb' V eleg. to listen. Chiefly in the following expressions.

ตรับฟัง,สดับ-- tràb'faŋ', sadàb'-tràb'faŋ' V
elab. eleg. to listen (to), listen (to) carefully,
attentively.

ตรัย traj' Nm eleg. three. Of very restricted
use. →See also ตรี.

พระศรีรัตนตรัย phrásǐi'rádtanatraj' the Three
Gems (of Buddhism, viz. Buddha, his teaching,
his disciples).

ตรัส tràd' V roy. to speak, talk, say, tell. →Cf.
ดำรัส.

ตรัสรู้ tràdsarúu' V 1. sacer. to attain enlightenment (of Buddha). 2. colloq. to know.

ตรา (ตรา) traa' (traa') N brand (as indicated
by a mark, stamp, etc.), trademark, seal.

เงินตรา ŋəntraa' N minted currency.

ดวงตรา (ดวง) duaŋtraa' (duaŋ') N seal.

o ดวงตราไปรษณียากร (ดวง) duaŋtraa'-prajsac
nii'jaakɔɔn' (duaŋ') N postage stamp.

ตรวจตรา trùadtraa' V to inspect, check.

ตอกตรา(ประทับ,บน,ลงบน) tɔ̀ɔgtraa'(pratháb',
bonc, loŋbonc) V to stamp, seal. →Syn.
ประทับตรา eleg.

ตีตรา tiitraa' V to stamp. →Syn. ประทับตรา
eleg.

ประทับตรา pratháb'traa' V eleg. to stamp,
seal. →Syn. ตีตรา,ตอกตรา com.

ลายสันตราตั้ง (ฉบับ) sǎan'traatâŋ' (chabàb') N
credentials.

ตราก in ตรากตรำ tràagtram' V to endure,
undergo hardship (esp. physical hardship).

ตราบ tràab' eleg. until. Usually as in the following examples.

ตราบใด(ที่) tràab'daj'(thîic) as long as.

o ตราบใดที่(ที่)...ตราบนั้น... tràab'daj'(thîic)
...tràab'nán'... as long as...just so long...

ตราบเท่า tràab'thâw' until, till. →Syn. จน,

จนกระทั่ง.

ตรำ tram' V to endure, undergo.

ตรากตรำ tràagtram' V to endure, undergo hardship (esp. physical hardship).

ตรำฝน tramfǒn' V to be exposed to rain.

ตริ in ตริตรอง trì?trɔɔŋ' V eleg. to consider,
think (it) over, think carefully. →Also ตรึกตรอง,
ไตร่ตรอง.

ตรี trii' eleg. Nm three. Chiefly in compounds.
→Syn. สาม com. →See also ตรัย.

ชั้นตรี chántrii' the third rank (from the top) in
civil service.

นายพลตรี (นาย,คน) naajphontrii' (naaj', khon')
N 1. major general. T 2. Major General --.

ปริญญาตรี (ปริญญา) parin'jaatrii', prin'- (parinc
jaa') N bachelor's degree.

ไม้ตรี (อัน) májtrii' (?an') N the third tonal
marker (⁺) of the Thai writing system.
→Dist. เสียงตรี "high tone."

ตรึก in ตรึกตรอง trỳgtrɔɔŋ' V eleg. to consider,
think (it) over, think carefully. →Also ตริตรอง,
ไตร่ตรอง.

ตรึง tryŋ' V 1. eleg. to fasten, fix. 2. to nail down
(to the floor), pin down; to nail (to the wall), pin
up. 3. to transfix. 4. to be held in place, fixed
(to).

ตรึงใจ tryŋcaj' V eleg. to fascinate.

ตรึงตาตรึงใจ tryŋtaa'tryŋcaj' V 1. elab. eleg.
to impress deeply. 2. to be impressive, make
an unforgettable impression.

ติดตาตรึงใจ tìdtaa'tryŋcaj' V 1. elab. eleg.
to impress. 2. to be impressive.

ตรุษ trùd' N new year observances. Chiefly in compounds.

ตรุษฝรั่ง trùd'faràŋ' N occidental New Year.

ตรุษสงกรานต์ trùd'sǒŋkraan' N (Thai) New Year.

ตรู ๑ truu' V to swarm together (to), to run up
together in crowds. →More commonly กรู.

ตรู ๒ truu' V lit. to be beautiful. →Chiefly in
compounds.

ตรู่ trùu' sV very early (in the morning).

เช้าตรู่ cháawtrùu' N 1. the early morning, dawn.
2. very early (in the morning).

ตลก talòg' V 1. to be funny, comical, farcical. 2.

If a word is not found under ตร, see กร.

to joke, to clown. คน-- clown, jester.

o คนนี้ตลกจริง khonníi'-talòg'ciŋ'↓ He's a very comical fellow. He's a real card.

ตัวตลก (ตัว,คน) tuatalòg' (tua', khon') N clown, jester.

ละครตลก (เรื่อง) lakhɔɔn'talòg' (rŷaŋ') N farce, comedy.

ตลบ ๑ talòb' V to fold back, turn back, pull back.

ตลบ ๒ talòb' V to diffuse (of itself), be diffused, spread widely (as dust, odor). →Also ตระหลบ eleg.

ตลอด talɔ̂ɔd' Pp 1. through, throughout. sV 2. throughout. →Comp. ทั่ว.

จนตลอด contalɔ̂ɔd' Pp all the way through, throughout.

โดยตลอด doojtalɔ̂ɔd' thoroughly; with thoroughness.

โดยตลอดรอดฝั่ง doojtalɔ̂ɔd'rɔ̂ɔdfàŋ' elab. colloq., idiom. safe and sound.

ตลอดกาล talɔ̂ɔd'-kaan' 1. forever, indefinitely, for all time. 2. everlasting.

ตลอดขึ้นมาจนถึง talɔ̂ɔd'-khŷnmaa'conthŷŋ' all the way up to.

ตลอดคืน talɔ̂ɔd'khyyn' all night long, throughout the night.

ตลอดจน talɔ̂ɔd'conɔ Pp 1. including. 2. (extending) all the way to. 3. even to (what is specified).

ตลอดถึง talɔ̂ɔd'thŷŋɔ Pp 1. including. 2. up to and including. 3. all the way to.

ตลอดทาง talɔ̂ɔd'thaaŋ' all the way, all along the way.

ตลอดปี talɔ̂ɔd'pii' throughout the year, all the year round.

ตลอดไป talɔ̂ɔd'paj' on and on, all the time.

ตลอดรอดฝั่ง talɔ̂ɔd'rɔ̂ɔdfàŋ' idiom. all the way through.

ตลอดลงมา talɔ̂ɔd'loŋmaa' all the way down to.

ตลอดเวลา talɔ̂ɔd'weelaa' all the time.

ตลาด (แห่ง) talàad' (hὲŋ') N 1. market (place). 2. econ. market.

ขาดตลาด khàad'talàad' V (a commodity) to be scarce, out to stock.

จ่ายตลาด càajtalàad' V to buy the groceries.

ชาวตลาด (คน) chaawtalàad' (khon') N colloq. an unrefined, common person.

ชาวบ้านร้านตลาด (คน) chaawbâan'ráantalàad' (khon') N elab. colloq. the whole neighborhood.

ตลาดมืด talàad'mŷyd' N black market.

ตลาดโลก talàad'lôog' N world market.

ตลาดสด (แห่ง) talàad'sòd' (hὲŋ') N food market, market in which raw, perishable foodstuffs are sold.

ภาษาตลาด phaasăa'talàad' N the language of the common people; the unrefined speech of the market place, of the lower classes.

ตลิ่ง (ตลิ่ง) talìŋ' (talìŋ') N bank (of a river, canal). →Syn. ฝั่ง.

ตวง tuaŋ' V to measure (the volume of) (by scooping up or dipping up in a container of standard capacity). เครื่อง-- volumetric device.

ต้วมเตี้ยม tûamtîam' V 1. to be sluggish, slow. sV 2. sluggishly, very slowly.

ตวาด tawàad' V 1. to yell threateningly, scold loudly. 2. to yell at, shout at (harshly, angrily).

ตอ (ตอ) tɔɔ' (tɔɔ') N stump (of a tree).

ต้นตอ tôntɔɔ' N original cause; source, origin.

ต่อ ๑ (ตัว) tɔ̀ɔ' (tua') a kind of wasp, solitary wasp. Usually ตัวต่อ tuatɔ̀ɔ'.

ต่อ ๒ tɔ̀ɔ' V 1. to join, connect, put together, construct. 2. to continue, extend, add (on). 3. to bargain, haggle. 4. to decoy (animals). sV 5. further, on, next. 6. to, towards, against. 7. per. Cj 8. when, at the time that. →Cf. 7. ละ ๒ ; see note under ต่อปี below.

o ฝันต่อว่า făntɔ̀ɔ'wâaɔ to dream further that.

o ๓ ต่อ ๑ săam'tɔ̀ɔnŷŋ' (the odds are) three to one.

ข้อต่อ (ข้อ,แห่ง) khɔ̂ɔtɔ̀ɔ' (khɔ̂ɔ', hὲŋ') N joint, connection.

ครึ่งต่อครึ่ง khrŷŋ'tɔ̀ɔkhrŷŋ' half and half, fiftyfifty, (in) equal (parts).

คอต่อ khɔɔtɔ̀ɔ' N nape.

ใครต่อใคร khraj'tɔ̀ɔkhraj' person after person; anyone, almost everyone. Used when the speaker cannot or does not wish to specify names.

ช้างต่อ cháaŋtɔ̀ɔ' N tame elephant used as a decoy.

เชื่อมต่อ chŷam/tɔ̀ɔ/ V to connect, join.

ดีต่อ dii/tɔ̀ɔɔ V to be good to.

ตรงต่อเวลา troŋ/tɔ̀ɔweelaa/ right on time, punctually.

ต่อกร tɔ̀ɔ/kɔɔn/ V lit. to fight. →Syn. ต่อสู้ com.

ต่อจากนั้น tɔ̀ɔ/càagnán/ after that, from then on.

ต่อจากหน้า ๑ tɔ̀ɔ/càagnâanȳŋ/ continued from page one.

ต่อตา tɔ̀ɔ/taa/ V to meet the gaze (of), look (someone) in the eyes.

o โดยไม่ต่อตา dooj/-mâjtɔ̀ɔ/taa/ without meeting (his) gaze.

ต่อต้าน tɔ̀ɔtâan/ V to resist, to counter. การ-- resistance.

ต่อโทรศัพท์ tɔ̀ɔ/thoorasàb/ V to make a phone call.

ต่อปากคำ tɔ̀ɔ/pàagkham/ 1. to talk back, argue back and forth. 2. to have words (with someone).

ต่อปี tɔ̀ɔpii/ per year. →Cf. ปีละ. NOTE. Distinguish the positions of ต่อปี and ปีละ in the examples below.

o ได้เงินพันบาทต่อปี dâjŋən/phanbàad/-tɔ̀ɔpii/ gets a thousand bahts per year.

o ได้เงินปีละพันบาท dâjŋən/-piilaphan/bàad/ gets a thousand bahts annually.

ต่อไป tɔ̀ɔpaj/, tɔ̀ɔ/pajɔ, tɔ̀ɔpajɔ sV 1. next, following, later on (in time). 2. next, further on (in space). 3. on (i.e. in continuation). NOTE. This expression implies direction in time or space from the focus of interest toward a point beyond it. →Dist. ต่อมา.

o ต่อไปจะเป็นการแสดงรำวง tɔ̀ɔpaj/capenkaanɔ sadɛɛŋ/ramwoŋ/↓ Afterwards there will be some folk dancing (i.e. the Thai variety).

o ในกาลต่อไป najkaan/tɔ̀ɔpaj/ in the future, at a later time.

o ในสัปดาห์ต่อ ๆ ไป najsàbdaa/-tɔ̀ɔtɔ̀ɔ/paj/ in the following weeks.

o ต่อไปนี้ tɔ̀ɔ/pajníi/, tɔ̀ɔpajníi/ 1. from now on. 2. following, (as) follows.

o กล่าวต่อไป klàaw/tɔ̀ɔpaj/ to go on continue. (talking); to say further.

ต่อมา tɔ̀ɔ/maa/, tɔ̀ɔmaa/, tɔ̀ɔmaaɔ sV 1. next, following, later on (in time). 2. next, further on (in space). 3. on (i.e. in continuation). NOTE. This expression implies direction in time or space from a point suggested by context toward the focus of interest. →Dist. ต่อไป.

o ต่อมาเขาก็เปลี่ยนใจ tɔ̀ɔ/maa/-kháwkɔ̀plian/caj/↓ Afterwards he changed his mind.

o ต่อมาไม่กี่วัน tɔ̀ɔmaa/mâjkìiwan/ not many days later.

o ต่อมาไม่นานนัก tɔ̀ɔmaa/-mâjnaan/nág not long afterwards.

o ต่อมาอีกหน่อยหนึ่ง tɔ̀ɔmaa/-ʔlignɔ̀j/nyŋ, tɔ̀ɔɔ maaʔlignɔ̀j/nyŋ a little bit later on.

o วันต่อมา wan/tɔ̀ɔmaa/ the following day (in the past).

ต่อเมื่อ tɔ̀ɔmŷa/ 1. when, only when, at the time that. 2. until, until later when.

ต่อรอง tɔ̀ɔ/rɔɔŋ/ V to bargain, haggle.

ต่อเรือ tɔ̀ɔrya/ V to build a boat.

o ช่างต่อเรือ (คน) châaŋtɔ̀ɔrya/ (khon/) N boatbuilder, shipbuilder.

ต่อล้อต่อเถียง tɔ̀ɔlɔ̀ɔ/tɔ̀ɔthĬaŋ/ V elab. colloq. to talk back; to argue back and forth, keep arguing.

ต่อว่า tɔ̀ɔwâa/ V to come (to someone) with a grievance, express one's displeasure (to), complain (to), remonstrate (with).

ต่อว่าต่อขาน tɔ̀ɔwâa/tɔ̀ɔkhăan/ V colloq. (parties) to argue over grievances or complaints (which stand between them).

ต่อสู้ tɔ̀ɔsûu/ V com. 1. to resist, stand up against, combat, oppose. 2. to fight, battle. การ-- fight, struggle, battle. →Syn. ต่อกร lit.

o เขตต่อสู้ (เขต) khèed/tɔ̀ɔsûu/ (khèed/) N combat zone.

o คู่ต่อสู้ (คน) khûu/tɔ̀ɔsûu/ (khon/) N opponent.

o ปืนต่อสู้อากาศยาน (กระบอก) pyyn/-tɔ̀ɔsûu/-ʔaakàad/sajaan/ (krabɔ̀ɔg/) N anti-aircraft gun.

ต่อหน้า tɔ̀ɔnâa/ in the presence of, in front of, before.

ต่อให้ tɔ̀ɔ/hâjɔ 1. to give an advantage, a head start, a handicap to. 2. even given the advantage

of (such and such a provision or circumstance);
even with (such and such a person's) advantage.

ต่ออายุ tɔ̀ɔ/ʔaajú/ V 1. to renew, i.e. extend
the time (as of a passport). 2. to lengthen
one's life.

ติดต่อ(กัน,กับ) tìdtɔ̀ɔ/(kan/, kaɔ) V 1. to get in
touch (with). 2. to associate (with), be connected (with), adjoin. sV 3. without interruption, continuously, straight through (usually
with กัน).

เติมต่อ təəm/tɔ̀ɔ/ V to supplement, add.

เป็นต่อ pentɔ̀ɔ/ V to have the advantage, be leading, be in the lead (in a contest).

มากต่อมากนัก mâag/tɔ̀ɔmâag/-nág/ so much, so
many, a great deal of.

มีต่อ miitɔ̀ɔ/ (it) is continued (on page --).

o ยังมีต่อ,--ไปอีก jaŋmiitɔ̀ɔ/, jaŋmiitɔ̀ɔ/pajʔlig
1. to be continued. 2. there is still more to
come (as of a story).

สะดวกต่อการใช้ sadùag/tɔ̀ɔkaancháj/ convenient
to use.

ลำพังต่อลำพัง sɔ̌ɔŋ/tɔ̀ɔsɔ̌ɔŋ/ just the two (persons),
tête-à-tête, in privacy.

หัวเลี้ยวหัวต่อ hǔalíaw/hǔatɔ̀ɔ/ N transition,
turning point.

อะไรต่อ(มิ)อะไร ʔaraj/tɔ̀ɔ(mí)ʔaraj/ various
other things, (and) so on, (and) what not; all
kinds of things, lots of things.

อ่านต่อหน้า ๑๐๐ ʔàantɔ̀ɔ/nâarɔ́ɔj/ continued on
page 100; continue reading on page 100.

ตอก ๑ tɔ̀ɔg/ V 1. to hammer, nail, pound. 2.
slang. to hit (someone) up (e.g. for a large
donation).

ตอกตรา(ประทับ,บน,ลงบน) tɔ̀ɔgtraa/(pratháb/,
bonɔ, loŋbonɔ) V com. to stamp, seal.
→Syn. ประทับตรา eleg.

ตอกเหล้า tɔ̀ɔg/lâw/ slang to hit the bottle
(i.e. drink liquor).

ตอก ๒ (เล่น) tɔ̀ɔg/ (sên/) N bamboo strips (used
for tying or weaving).

ตอก ๓ in ข้าวตอก khâawtɔ̀ɔg/ N popped rice,
puffed rice.

ต๋อก. See entries below.

กลองต๋อก (ใบ,ลูก) klɔɔŋtɔ́g/*(baj/, lûug/) N

a small drum used to beat time.

ย่ำต๋อก jâmtɔ́g/* V colloq. to walk, hoof it (e.g.
when transportation is not available).

ตอง,ใบ-- (ใบ) tɔɔŋ/, bajtɔɔŋ/ (baj/) N banana leaf.

ไพ่ตอง (ตา,สำรับ,ใบ) phâjtɔɔŋ/ N 1. a Thai
card game (taa/). 2. the cards used in playing
the game (sǎmráb/, baj/).

ต้อง tɔ̂ŋ/* V 1. to touch, catch, get (usually in a fig.
sense). AA 2. have to, must, is to be.

o ผมต้องไปบ้าน phǒm/tɔ̂ŋpajbâan/ I have to go
home.

ของต้องพิกัด (สิ่ง,อย่าง) khɔ̌ɔŋ/tɔ̂ŋphíkàd/ (sìŋ/,
jàaŋ/) N taxable or dutiable articles.

จะต้อง catɔ̂ŋɔ AA will have to, must.

จับต้อง càbtɔ̂ŋ/ V to hold, handle, touch (with the
hands).

จำต้อง cam/tɔ̂ŋɔ AA have to, be needed to, be
compelled to.

จำเป็นต้อง campen/tɔ̂ŋɔ AA be compelled to,
forced to; must, have to; it is necessary to.

ต้องกัน tɔ̂ŋ/kan V to agree, be in agreement (of
people, of figures, etc.).

ต้องการ tɔ̂ŋkaan/ V 1. to want, need, require.
AA 2. want to, wish to. ความ-- need, needs,
requirements.

ต้องการจะ tɔ̂ŋkaan/caɔ AA want to.

ต้องขัง tɔ̂ŋkhǎŋ/ V to be imprisoned.

ต้องคดี tɔ̂ŋ/khadii/ V to be accused, be under
accusation, under prosecution.

ต้องใจ tɔ̂ŋcaj/ V 1. to please, be pleasing. 2.
to be fond of.

o ติดเนื้อต้องใจ tìdnýa/tɔ̂ŋcaj/ V to be fond of,
interested in, fascinated with (a person or thing).

ต้องด้วย tɔ̂ŋ/dûajɔ V to conform to, concur with.

ต้องตา tɔ̂ŋtaa/ V to appeal to the eye, to be attractive, eye-catching.

ต้องตาม tɔ̂ŋ/taamɔ V to agree with, be in accord
with.

ต้องนับว่า tɔ̂ŋnáb/wâaɔ is to be regarded as, must
count as.

ต้องลม tɔ̂ŋlom/ V to catch the wind, be blown by
the wind (as a weathervane, a windmill, grass).

ต้องสงสัย in the following entries.

o โดยมิต้องสงสัย dooj/-mítɔ̂ŋ/sǒŋsǎj/ lit., eleg.

without doubt.

o ผู้ต้องสงสัย (คน) phûutɔ̂ŋ'sǒŋsǎj' (khon') N
eleg. a suspect.

o อย่างไม่ต้องสงสัย jàaŋ'-mâjtɔ̂ŋ'sǒŋsǎj' com.
without doubt.

ต้องหา tɔ̂ŋhǎa' 1. to be accused. 2. to have to
seek, must seek. ผู้-- the accused, the defendant.

ต้องห้าม tɔ̂ŋhâam' to be forbidden.

o ของต้องห้าม khɔ̌ɔŋ'tɔ̂ŋhâam' N 1. forbidden
things. 2. contraband.

แตะต้อง tɛ̀ʔtɔ̂ŋ' V to touch (with the hands),
handle.

ถูกต้อง ๑ thùugtɔ̂ŋ' V to be right, correct.

ถูกต้อง ๒ thùugtɔ̂ŋ' V to touch, come into contact with.

ผู้ต้องบาดเจ็บ (คน) phûutɔ̂ŋ'bàadcèb' (khon') N
1. one who is injured. 2. the wounded.

ไม่พักต้อง mâjphág'tɔ̂ŋɔ AA does not wait, without waiting (e.g. to be invited).

ตอด tɔ̀ɔd' V to nibble (as fish on bait).

ตอน ๑ tɔɔn' V 1. to castrate. 2. hort. to propagate by layerage.

ตอน ๒ tɔɔn' C part, section (of space or time).
→Comp. ท่อน,ปั้น,ส่วน.

ตอนกลาง tɔɔnklaaŋ' N the middle part; in the
middle.

ตอนค่ำ tɔɔnkhâm' N (in the) evening, (at) night.
→Syn. เวลาค่ำ.

ตอนจบ tɔɔncòb' N the ending (of a book, a play),
the finale.

ตอนเช้า tɔɔncháaw' N 1. the morning. 2. in
the morning.

ตอนดึก tɔɔndỳg' N 1. the dead of night. 2. late
at night.

ตอนต้น tɔɔntôn' N 1. the beginning part. 2. at
first, to begin with. →Opp. ตอนปลาย.

ตอนใต้ tɔɔntâaj' N the southern part.

ตอนท้าย tɔɔntháaj' N 1. the end, the rear part.
2. at the end.

ตอนเที่ยง tɔɔnthîaŋ' N 1. noontime. 2. at
noontime.

ตอนบ่าย tɔɔnbàaj' N 1. the afternoon. 2. in the
afternoon.

ตอนปลาย tɔɔnplaaj' N 1. the end part, final part.
2. in the end, finally. →Opp. ตอนต้น.

o ชั้นมัธยมตอนปลาย chánmádthajom'tɔɔnplaaj'
senior high school level.

ตอนเย็น tɔɔnjen' N 1. the evening. 2. in the
evening. →Syn. 1. สายันห์ lit. 1,2. เวลาเย็น.
com.

ตอนแรก tɔɔnrɛ̂ɛg' N 1. the first part, the beginning part. 2. at first.

ตอนสาย tɔɔnsǎaj' N 1. the late morning. 2. in
the late morning.

ตอนหลัง tɔɔnlǎŋ' N 1. the later period. 2. later
on, afterward. 3. back part. →Ant. 1, 2. ตอน
ต้น. 3. ตอนหน้า.

ในตอนนี้ najtɔɔn'níi' at this time.

เป็นตอน ๆ pentɔɔntɔɔn' by parts.

รถตอนเดียว (คัน) ród'tɔɔndiaw' (khan') N
coupé, roadster.

ต้อน tɔ̂ɔn' V 1. to herd (along), round up. 2. to trap,
corner (by means of questions).

กวาดต้อน kwàadtɔ̂ɔn' V to herd.

ต้อนรับ tɔ̂ɔnráb' V to welcome, receive (e.g.
guests).

ตอบ ๑ tɔ̀ɔb' V 1. to answer, reply. sV 2. in answer, in response.

คำตอบ (คำตอบ,ข้อ) khamtɔ̀ɔb' (khamtɔ̀ɔb', khɔ̂ɔ')
N answer, reply.

โจมตีตอบ coom'tii'-tɔ̀ɔb' to return fire, counterattack.

ตอบแทน tɔ̀ɔbthɛɛn' V com. 1. to repay, pay back.
2. to reciprocate, retaliate. sV 3. in return,
in exchange. เครื่อง-- a reciprocation. →Syn.
1. สนอง.

ตอบรับ tɔ̀ɔbráb' V to say, answer in the affirmative; to accept.

โต้ตอบ(กัน) tôotɔ̀ɔb'(kan') V 1. to answer back
and forth, perform some action back and forth
(of conversing, exchanging letters, engaging in
musical or poetic dialogue, retaliating back and
forth, etc.). sV 2. back and forth.

พูดคำตอบคำ phûudkham'tɔ̀ɔbkham' colloq. to
say scarcely anything and only when asked, to
be taciturn.

ตอบ ๒ tɔ̀ɔb' V to be sunken, hollow (of cheeks).

→Ant. อูม.

ตอม tɔɔm′ V to fly around, swarm around (as annoying flies or insects).

ต่อม, เม็ด-- (ต่อม) tɔ̀m′, médtɔ̀m′*(tɔ̀m′) N gland.

ต่อม, ต่อม ๆ tɔ̀m′, tɔ̀mtɔ̀m′* imit. plop, plop-plop (as of the sound of something falling into the water).

ต่อย tɔ̀j′* 1. to strike. 2. (insect) to sting. 3. to break, crack open (e.g. a coconut).

ชกต่อย chógtɔ̀j′ V to box, fight with fists.

ต่อยมวย tɔ̀jmuaj′ V to box.

พูดเป็นต่อยหอย phûud′-pentɔ̀j′hɔ̌j′ 1. colloq. to chatter, jabber. 2. to be very talkative.

ตอแหล tɔɔlɛ̌ɛ′ V 1. vulg. to lie (tell falsehoods). 2. colloq. to talk a lot, chatter, babble (as a child learning to talk).

ตะ. See เป็นตุเป็นตะ.

ตะกร้อ (ลูก, ใบ, ตา) takrɔ̂ɔ′ N 1. rattan ball, used in playing takraw (lûug′, baj′). 2. takraw, a kind of Thai ball game (taa′).

ตะกรัน takran′ N scale, incrustation.

ขี้ตะกรัน khîitakran′ N sediment, precipitate.

ตะกร้า (ใบ) takrâa′ (baj′) N basket.

ตะกละ taklà?′ V to be greedy.

ตะกวด (ตัว) takùad′ (tua′) N the monitor, a large brown lizard.

ตะกอน takɔɔn′ N sediment, precipitate, silt.

→Also ขี้-- colloq.

ตกตะกอน tòg′takɔɔn′ V to precipitate. การ-- precipitation.

ตะกัก. See ตะกุกตะกัก.

ตะกั่ว takùa′ N lead (the metal).

ลูกตะกั่ว (ลูก) lûugtakùa′ (lûug′) N slang bullet, slug of lead.

ตะกาย takaaj′ V to scramble up, clamber up.

ตะกุยตะกาย takuj′takaaj′ V 1. to scramble up, scrape one's way up. 2. to rise up and scratch, climb up against, paw (as a dog).

ตะเกียกตะกาย takìag′takaaj′ V to scramble up, struggle up, scrape one's way up.

ตะกี้, ตะกี๊ takîi′, takíi′ colloq. a moment ago, just now. Normally pronounced takíi′ regardless of spelling. →Also เมื่อ--.

ตะกุกตะกัก takùg′takàg′ sV brokenly, stutteringly

(of speaking).

ตะกุย takuj′ V 1. to scratch, scrape (as with claws, nails). 2. to paw (with hooves, as a horse).

→Syn. 1. ข่วน.

ตะกุยตะกาย takuj′takaaj′ V 1. to scramble up, scrape one's way up. 2. to rise up and scratch, climb up against, paw (as a dog).

ตะเกียก in ตะเกียกตะกาย takìag′takaaj′ V to scramble up, struggle up, scrape one's way up.

ตะเกียง (ดวง) takiaŋ′ (duaŋ′) N lamp, lantern.

ตะเกียงรั้ว (ดวง) takiaŋ′rúa (duaŋ′) V lantern.

บานตะเกียง baan′takiaŋ′ colloq. a lot of.

ตะเกียบ (คู่, อัน) takìab′ (khûu′, ʔan′) N chopsticks.

ตะแกรง (อัน) takrɛɛŋ′ (ʔan′) N 1. shallow basket used as a sieve or strainer. 2. any sieve or screen for sifting, straining.

ตะโกน takoon′ V to shout, yell.

ตะไกร (เล่ม) takraj′ (lêm′) N com. scissors.

→Syn. กรรไกร eleg.

ตะขอ takhɔ̌ɔ′. See ตาขอ under ตา ๑.

ตะขาบ (ตัว) takhàab′ (tua′) N centipede.

รถตีนตะขาบ (คัน) ród′tiintakhàab′ (khan′) N caterpillar tractor.

ตะข่าย takhàaj′. See ตาข่าย under ตา ๑.

ตะเข็บ (ตะเข็บ) takhèb′ (takhèb′) N seam.

ตะครุบ takhrúb′ V to pounce on, to seize in the claws, in the hands.

ตะคิว takhiw′ N cramp.

ตะคุ่ม ๆ takhûm′takhûm′ sV indistinctly, faintly (visible).

ตะแคง takhɛɛŋ′ V to tilt to one side, lean on one side.

ตะไคร้ (ต้น, กอ) takhráj′ (tôn′, kɔɔ′) N lemon grass.

ตะบอย tabɔɔj′ V to be slow.

ตะเบ็ง tabeŋ′ V to shout, be shouting (strenuously).

o ตะเบ็งเสียงให้ดังขึ้น tabeŋsĭaŋ′-hâjdaŋ′khŷn′ to raise one's voice, make one's voice louder.

ตะไบ (อัน) tabaj′ (ʔan′) N file (the tool).

ขี้ตะไบเหล็ก khîitabaj′lèg′ iron filings.

ตะปบ tapòb′ V 1. to clap with one hand, as when trying to cover a spinning coin in a game. 2. to clap with both hands, as when trying to catch something in the air.

ตะปู (ตัว) tapuu′ (tua′) N nail (for carpentry).

If a word is not found under ตะ , see ตา.

→Also ตาปู under ตา ๑.

ตะปูควง (ตัว) tapuukhuaŋ′ (tua′) N screw.

ตะพด,ไม้-- (อัน) taphód′, májtaphód′ (ʔan′) N rod, staff, cane, walking stick (often one made of bamboo).

ตะพาบ in ตะพาบน้ำ (ตัว) taphâabnáam′ (tua′) N a soft-shelled sea turtle.

ตะเพิด taphêəd′ V to scare off, chase away by making a noise or by shouting.

ตะโพก (ข้าง) taphôog′ (khâaŋ′) N hip.

ตะโพน (ใบ) taphoon′ (baj′) N a kind of drum.

ตะเภา in หนูตะเภา (ตัว) nǔutaphaw′ (tua′) N guinea pig.

ตะราง ๑ (แห่ง) taraaŋ′ (hèŋ′) N prison.

ขี้ตะราง khîitaraaŋ′ V to be a jailbird.

ติดตะราง tìd′taraaŋ′ V to be put in jail, imprisoned.

ตะราง ๒ taraaŋ′. See ตาราง under ตา ๑.

ตะลึง,--พรึงเพริด talyŋ′, talyŋ′phryŋphrêəd′ V to be stupefied, stunned (with surprise, fright).

ตะลุง in หนังตะลุง (เรื่อง, โรง) nǎŋ′taluŋ′ N 1. shadow play (rŷaŋ′). 2. shadow play establishment (rooŋ′).

ตะลุมบอน talumbɔɔn′ at close quarters, in hand to hand combat.

ตะลุย in บุกตะลุย bùg′taluj′ V to make a lightning invasion.

ตะวัน (ดวง) tawan′ (duaŋ′) N eleg. the sun. →Syn. พระอาทิตย์ com. NOTE. Probably originally ตาวัน "eye of the day." The shortened form is now the only one in use.

ตะวันตก tawantòg′ com. west. →Syn. ประจิม lit.,eleg. →The literary and the common terms for the eight chief points of the compass are listed under ทิศ.

o ชาวตะวันตก (คน) chaawtawantòg′ (khon′) N Occidental, Westerner.

o ตะวันตกเฉียงเหนือ tawantòg′chĭaŋnŷa′ 1. the northwest. 2. northwestern.

o ทิศตะวันตก thíd′tawantòg′ N west.

ตะวันตกดิน tawan′tògdin′ the sun to set.

ตะวันออก tawanʔɔ̀ɔg′ com. east. →Syn. บุรพา lit.,eleg. →The literary and the common terms for the eight chief points of the compass

are listed under ทิศ.

o ตะวันออกกลาง tawanʔɔ̀ɔg′klaaŋ′ the middle east. [tr.f. Eng.]

o ตะวันออกไกล tawanʔɔ̀ɔg′klaj′ the Far East. [tr.f. Eng.]

o ตะวันออกเฉียงใต้ tawanʔɔ̀ɔg′chĭaŋtâaj′ 1. the southeast. 2. southeastern.

o ทิศตะวันออก thíd′tawanʔɔ̀ɔg′ N east.

ตะเหลนเป๋น talěenpěen′ rM intensifier used with ยาว "long," สูง "tall."

ตะแหลนแป๋น talěenpěn′* rM intensifier used with แบน "flat."

ตัก ๑ (ข้าง) tàg′ (khâaŋ′) N the lap.

ตัก ๒ tàg′ V to dip up (as with a dipper).

ตักเข้าไป tàg′khâwpaj′ colloq. to cost, require, take up (a stated quantity, as of money).

ตักน้ำ tàgnáam′ V to dip up water.

ตัก ๓ in ตักเตือน tàgtyan′ V to advise, caution, admonish.

ตักแตน (ตัว) tágkatɛɛn′ (tua′) N grasshopper.

ตัง ๑ in ข้าวตัง khâawtaŋ′ N rice crust that sticks to the bottom of the pot. Eaten like crackers when fried.

ตัง ๒ taŋ′. Shortened form of สตางค์, q.v.

ตั่ง (ตัว) tàŋ′ (tua′) N stool, bench.

ตั้ง ๑ tâŋ′ C 1. pile (of things). 2. colloq. time. →Syn. 2. See คราว.

ลักตั้ง sàgtâŋ′ colloq. just for (the needed) period of time.

ตั้ง ๒ tâŋ′ qM as many as, as much as, all of (a quantity). →Ant. ลัก.

o ตั้งสามชั่วโมง tâŋsǎam′chûamooŋ′ as much as three hours, all of three hours.

ตั้งกระบุง tâŋkrabuŋ′ colloq. a lot, greatly, considerably.

ตั้งบ้าน tâŋbâan′ colloq. much, a lot.

ตั้ง ๓ tâŋ′ V 1. to set, place, set up, erect, establish. 2. to settle, locate. 3. to appoint.

จัดตั้ง càdtâŋ′ V to set up, establish, form.

ตั้ง(...)ขึ้น tâŋ(...)khŷn′ to set up, establish.

ตั้งเข็ม tâŋkhěm′ V idiom. to form a purpose.

ตั้งครรภ์ tâŋkhan′ V eleg. 1. to conceive, be in early pregnancy. 2. to be pregnant. →Also ตั้งท้อง com.

ตั้งเค้า tâŋkháw/ V to show its first signs.

o ฝนตั้งเค้า fǒn/tâŋkháw/ it looks like rain, it's getting ready to rain.

ตั้งใจ tâŋcaj/ V 1. to intend. AA 2. intend to. ความ-- intention, purpose, determination, attentiveness.

o ไม่ตั้งใจฟัง mâjtâŋcaj/faŋ/ to be inattentive.

ตั้งชัน tâŋ/chan/ V (hair, fur) to stand on end, be on end.

ตั้งชื่อ(ให้) tâŋchŷy/(hâjɔ) V to name, give a name (to).

ตั้งต้น tâŋtôn/ V to begin, commence. →Syn. เริ่ม.

ตั้งแต่ tâŋtɛ̀ɛɔ Pp from (such and such a time or starting point), since.

o ตั้งแต่ง่ายที่สุดขึ้นไปถึงยากที่สุด tâŋtɛ̀ɛŋâaj/thîiɔ sùd/→khŷnpajthŷŋjâag/thîisùd/ from the eas- iest to the hardest.

o ตั้งแต่นี้ไป tâŋtɛ̀ɛníi/paj/ from now on, from this time on, henceforth.

o ตั้งแต่...เป็นต้นไป tâŋtɛ̀ɛɔ...pentôn/paj/ from (such and such a time) on (i.e. from the present toward the future); from (such and such a place) on (i.e. from a nearby point toward a distant one).

o ตั้งแต่...เป็นต้นมา tâŋtɛ̀ɛɔ..pentôn/maa/ from (such and such a time) on (i.e. from the past toward the present); from (such and such a place) on (i.e. from a distant point toward a closer one).

o ตั้งแต่พระเจ้าแผ่นดินลงมา tâŋtɛ̀ɛphrácâwphɛ̀nɔ din/loŋmaa/ from the king down.

ตั้งท้อง tâŋthɔ́ɔŋ/ V com. 1. to conceive, be in early pregnancy. 2. to be pregnant. →Also ตั้งครรภ์ eleg.

ตั้งบ้าน tâŋbâan/ to settle down.

ตั้งภูมิลำเนา tâŋphuum/mílamnaw/ V to take up residence, to settle.

ตั้งมั่น tâŋmân/ V 1. to settle down firmly; to establish oneself in a stronghold. 2. to remain firm, steadfast.

ตั้งรกราก tâŋ/rógrâag/ V to settle down perma- nently, take up residence.

ตั้งสติ tâŋ/satì?/ V to concentrate (one's mind).

ตั้งหน้าตั้งตา tâŋnâa/tâŋtaa/ V elab. colloq. to be determined (to), resolved (to), obsessed (with). →Also ตั้งหน้า colloq.

ตั้งอกตั้งใจ tâŋ?òg/tâŋcaj/ V colloq. to be intent (upon). →See ตั้งใจ.

ตั้งอยู่ tâŋ/jùuɔ V to be situated, located.

ติดตั้ง tìd/tâŋ/ V to install.

แต่งตั้ง tɛ̀ŋtâŋ/ V 1. to set (up). 2. to appoint, confer a title.

o ได้รับแต่งตั้ง dâjráb/tɛ̀ŋtâŋ/ to be appointed.

ที่ตั้ง (แห่ง) thîitâŋ/ (hɛ̀ŋ/) N location, situation.

เลือกตั้ง lŷagtâŋ/ V to choose, elect.

สาส์นตราตั้ง (ฉบับ) sǎan/traatâŋ/ (chabàb/) N credentials.

ตั้ง,ตั้ง ๆ tǎŋ/, tǎŋtǎŋ/ V slang to be rich. [f. Chin.]

ตั้งเกี๋ย taŋkǐa/ pN Tonkin. [f. Viet.]

ตัณหา (อย่าง) tanhǎa/ (jàaŋ/) N lust, desire, pas- sion.

ตัด tàd/ V to cut, sever.

ตัดกัน tàd/kan 1. to intersect. 2. to contrast with one another (as of colors).

ตัดขาด tàdkhàad/ V to separate, sever, break off, cut off.

ตัดชีวิต tàd/chiiwíd/ V lit., eleg. to kill, destroy.

ตัดถนน tàd/thanǒn/ V to build a road.

ตัดบท tàdbòd/ V to cut the discussion short; to break off a conversation, an argument (e.g. by changing the subject, by bringing the matter to a conclusion).

ตัดปัญหา tàd/panhǎa/ V to eliminate a problem.

ตัดผม tàdphǒm/ V 1. to cut the hair. 2. to get a haircut.

o ช่างตัดผม (คน) châaŋtàdphǒm/ (khon/) N barber.

o ร้านตัดผม (แห่ง) ráan/tàdphǒm/ (hɛ̀ŋ/) N barber shop.

ตัดไม้ tàdmáaj/ V to cut wood. คน-- woodcutter.

ตัดเย็บ tàd/jéb/ V to cut and sew; hence to tailor, make a dress, make a suit, etc.

ตัดรอน tàdrɔɔn/ V to cut, sever.

ตัดราคา tàd/raakhaa/ V to cut prices.

ตัดสัมพันธ์ทางการทูต tàd/-sǎmphan/thaaŋkaanthûud/ V to break off diplomatic relations.

ตัดสิน tàdsĭn′ V to decide, judge.

o ตัดสินใจ tàdsĭncaj′ V to make up one's mind.
ผู้-- judge, umpire, referee.

ตัด(. . .) เสีย tàd′(...)sía V to cut (something)
off, sever.

ตัดเสื้อ tàdsŷa′ V 1. to tailor, make a coat,
blouse, dress. 2. to have a coat, blouse, dress
made.

o ช่างตัดเสื้อ (คน) châaŋtàdsŷa′ (khon′) N
tailor.

ตัดหน้า tàdnâa′ V to cut across, cut in (in front)
(as in horse racing, traffic).

ตัดหัว tàdhŭa′ V to behead.

ผ่าตัด phàatàd′ V to operate on (surgically).
การ-- (surgical) operation, surgery.

o หมอผ่าตัด (คน) mɔ̆ɔ′phàatàd′ (khon′) N com.
surgeon. →Syn. ศัลยแพทย์ eleg.

ตัน ๑ tan′ V 1. to be stopped up, clogged up. 2.
to be solid (i.e. not hollow).

ตื้นตัน tŷyntan′ V to be choked up (e.g. with sorrow, happiness).

ถนนตัน (สาย) thanŏn′tan′ (săaj′) N a blind
street.

ไส้ตัน sâjtan′ N appendicitis.

o โรคไส้ตัน rôog′sâjtan′ N com. appendicitis.

o ไส้ตันอักเสป sâjtan′ʔàgsèeb′ N eleg. appendicitis, esp. in the acute stage. →Also ไส้ติ่ง
อักเสป.

อัดอั้นตันใจ ʔàdʔân′tancaj′ V elab. to feel
stifled, utterly helpless, depressed and heavy
at heart.

ตัน ๒ tan′ C ton. [f. Eng.]

ตับ ๑ (อัน,ชิ้น) tàb′ (ʔan′,chín′) N liver.

ตับ ๒ tàb′ C row (series of objects). →Cf. แนว,
แถว,ระนาว.

ตับจาก (ตับ) tàbcàag′ (tàb′) N a thatch of nipa
palm leaves.

เป็นตับ pentàb′ in large numbers.

ตัว tua′ N 1. self; oneself. 2. body. 3. class term
for tiny living things, such as insects, worms.
4. tech. agent. C 5. clf. for animals, fish,
insects; for tables, chairs, desks; for playing
cards, cigarettes, pen points; for articles of
clothing such as shirts, coats, dresses, trousers;
for parts, characters (in a play); for digits
(numbers), letters (of the alphabet); etc. P. 6.
colloq. you (used among intimates). →Syn.
1. ตน eleg.

กลับตัว klàbtua′ V to reform oneself, turn over
a new leaf.

กลิ่นตัว klìntua′ N body odor.

ขยายตัว khajăaj′tua′ V to expand, become expanded (e.g. because of heat).

ขอตัว khɔ̆ɔtua′ V to excuse oneself (with respect
to an invitation, performing a service, etc.),
to beg off.

เคยตัว khəəjtua′ V to be in the habit of, get into
the habit of.

จวนตัว cuantua′ V something to be imminent, on
the verge of overtaking one (as when one is pursued by an enemy, confronted by an urgent issue).

จับตัว càbtua′ V to catch, capture, arrest a person.

เจ็บตัว cèbtua′ V to hurt oneself, get hurt.

เจ้าตัว câwtua′ N the person in question. Often
rendered by "he himself," "she herself," etc.

เจียมตัว ciamtua′ V to be humble, modest, unassuming.

ตัวการ (คน) tuakaan′ (khon′) N 1. the culprit.
2. the principal (in an action). 3. ringleader.

ตัวแก้ว (ตัว) tuakɛ̂ɛw′ (tua′) N (non-hairy)
caterpillar, larva of butterfly or moth. →Dist.
บุ้ง.

ตัวเขาเอง tuakháw′ʔeeŋ′ himself.

ตัวครั่ง (ตัว) tuakhrâŋ′ (tua′) N scale-insect
(the lac-producing insect).

ตัวคูณ tuakhuun′ N math. multiplier.

ตัวจำนำ (คน) tuacamnam′ (khon′) N hostage.

ตัวเฉพาะ (ตัว) tuachaphɔ́ʔ′ (tua′) N math. 1.
prime number. 2. (as n. mod.) prime.

ตัวชา tua′chaa′ V to feel number all over.

ตัวเชื่อม (ตัว) tuachŷam′ (tua′) N binder, joining
agent.

ตัวตลก (ตัว,คน) tuatalòg′ (tua′,khon′) N clown,
jester.

ตัวตุ่น (ตัว) tuatùn′ (tua′) N 1. bamboo rat (Rhizomys). 2. mole.

ตัวแตน (ตัว) tuatɛɛn′ (tua′) N hornet.

ตัวแทน (คน,นาย) tuathɛɛn′ (khon′,naaj′) N

1. representative, agent. 2. substitute, proxy.

ตัวนำ (ตัว) tuanam′ (tua′) N tech. conductor.

ตัวประกอบ tuaprakɔ̀ɔb′ N 1. supporting character (in a play). 2. math. factor.

ตัวปะการัง (ตัว) tua′-pakaa′raŋ′ (tua′) N coral polyps.

ตัวปากกา (ตัว) tua′pàagkaa′ (tua′) N pen point.

ตัวเป็นเกลียว tua′penkliaw′ idiom. very hard, busily (of working).

ตัวเปล่า tuaplàaw′ as in คนตัวเปล่า khon′tua⊃plàaw′ N colloq. a single person, person without family ties.

ตัวผึ้ง (ตัว) tuaphŷŋ′ (tua′) N bee.

ตัวผู้ tuaphûu′ N male (of animals, insects). →Opp. ตัวเมีย female. →Dist. ชาย ๑, ผู้ชาย male (of people).

ตัวมาร (ตัว) tuamaan′ (tua′) N 1. Mara, devil, demon. 2. a person who ruins everything, an evildoer, a devil.

ตัวเมีย tuamia′ N female (of animals, insects). →Opp. ตัวผู้ male. →Dist. หญิง, ผู้หญิง female (of people).

o คู่ผัวตัวเมีย khûuphŭa′tuamia′ N colloq. husband and wife. NOTE. Here ตัว is inserted in order to provide a rhyme for ผัว. →Syn. ผัวเมีย com.

o เป็นตัวเมีย pen′tuamia′ V derog. to be a sissy, be effeminate.

o หน้าตัวเมีย nâa′tuamia′ V 1. derog. to be a sissy, be effeminate. 2. Sissy!

ตัวเมือง (ตัวเมือง) tuamyaŋ′ (tuamyaŋ′) N the city proper, esp. the business district.

ตัวแมลง (ตัว) tuamalɛɛŋ′ (tua′) N insect (of any kind).

ตัวร้อน tuarɔ́ɔn′ V to have a high (body) temperature.

ตัวโรค (ตัว) tuaroog′ (tua′) N microbe.

ตัวละคร (ตัว) tualakhɔɔn′ (tua′) N character (in a play).

ตัวเลข (ตัว) tualêeg′ (tua′) N figure, numeral (written character).

ตัวสั่น tuasàn′ V to tremble all over, shake.

ตัวแสดง (คน, ตัว) tuasadɛɛŋ′ (khon′, tua′) N 1. actor, player. 2. role, part (in a play).

ตัวหนอน (ตัว) tuanɔ̃ɔn′ (tua′) N 1. worm. 2. caterpillar (any hairless variety). →Dist. 2. บุ้ง.

ตัวหนัง (ตัว) tuanǎŋ′ (tua′) N puppet (used in the shadow play).

ตัวหนังสือ (ตัว) tuananŋš̷y′ (tua′) N com. letter (of the alphabet). →Syn. ตัวอักษร eleg.

ตัวไหม (ตัว) tuamǎj′ (tua′) N silkworm.

ตัวอย่าง (อัน, ตัวอย่าง) tuajàaŋ′ (ʔan′, tuajàaŋ′) N 1. example. 2. sample.

o ยกตัวอย่าง jóg′tuajàaŋ′ to give an example, bring up an example.

ตัวอักษร (ตัว) tuaʔàgsɔ̌ɔn′ (tua′) N eleg. letter (of the alphabet). →Syn. ตัวหนังสือ com.

ตัวเอ (ตัว) tuaʔêe′ (tua′) N colloq. the main one (person), the responsible party, the leader, the one to blame (used esp. when scolding children).

ตัวเอก (ตัว) tuaʔèeg′ (tua′) N the principal one (person); a principal character in a play, picture, etc.

ตัวเอง tuaʔeeŋ′ oneself, one's own self. More emphatic than ตัว alone.

ตายตัว taajtua′ V to be fixed (as price), stable, unalterable.

เต็มตัว temtua′ 1. all over the body, from head to toe. 2. full length (e.g. a full length photograph of someone).

ถือตัว thŷytua′ V 1. to be proud of oneself, have a high opinion of oneself. 2. to hold oneself aloof. →Ant. ถ่อมตัว.

ทั้งเนื้อทั้งตัว tháŋnýa′tháŋtua′ 1. all over (the body). 2. thoroughly. 3. to one's name (as in "not a penny to his name").

ทำตัว thamtua′ V to behave, act, make oneself (be).

เท่าตัว thâwtua′ 1. the same size or quantity (as the model), life-size. 2. as much (as the previous size, quantity, amount). See cross reference for examples.

ประจำตัว pracam′tua′ individual, private, personal, assigned to an individual.

ไม่เป็นตัวเป็นตน mâjpentua′penton′ to be unformed, amorphous, not to have taken shape.

รายตัว in เป็นรายตัว pen′raajtua′ one person at

a time, one by one, individually.

รู้ตัว rúutua/ V to be aware, conscious. ความ--
awareness, consciousness.

รู้สึกตัว rúusỳg/tua/ V 1. to come to feel, realize,
come to awareness. 2. to recover consciousness.

o โดยไม่รู้สึกตัว dooj/mâjrúusỳg/tua/ without
realizing it.

ลองตัว lɔɔŋtua/ V to try on (for size).

ลำตัว (ลำตัว) lamtua/ (lamtua/) N trunk (of the
body), torso.

ลืมตัวลืมตน lyymtua/lyymton/ V elab. colloq.
to forget oneself. →Also ลืมตัว colloq.

ลูกตัว (คน) lûugtua/ (khon/) N one's real child
(related by blood). →Dist. ลูกเลี้ยง stepchild,
adopted child.

เล่นตัว lêntua/ V to play hard to get, act as
though reluctant.

วางตัว waaŋtua/ V com. 1. to behave, conduct
oneself. 2. to place oneself.

ส่วนตัว sùantua/ private, personal, individual
(as opposed to public, collective). →Syn.
ส่วนบุคคล. →Ant. ส่วนรวม.

ส่วนตัวฉัน sùan/tuachán/ as for me; I, for my
part.

เสมอตัว samɘ̌ɘ/tua/ V to break even.

เสียตัว sǐatua/ V (a woman) to lose (her) virginity (by premarital relations).

หมดตัว mòdtua/ V to have nothing left, to be
broke. →Also หมดเนื้อ-- elab. colloq.

หลวมตัว lǔamtua/ V colloq.,idiom. to have
gotten so deeply involved (in something) that
one is unable to back out.

หาเลี้ยงตัว hǎa/líaŋtua/ V to earn a living.

หายตัว hǎajtua/ V 1. to disappear. 2. to disappear by supernatural power.

หารลงตัว hǎan/loŋtua/ to be divisible (mathema-
tically).

เห็นแก่ตัว hěn/kὲɛtua/ to think only of oneself,
be selfish.

อยู่ตัว jùutua/ V to be stable, maintain (its) form.

อวดตัว ?ùadtua/ V to boast, brag.

ออกตัว ?ɔ̀ɔgtua/ to put up excuses.

อิ่มตัว ?ìmtua/ V tech. to be saturated.

เอาตัวรอด ?awtua/rɔ̂ɔd/ 1. to save oneself, get
oneself to safety, save one's own skin. 2. to
manage to live; to make something of one's life.

ตั๋ว (ใบ) tǔa/ (baj/) N ticket. [f.Chin.]

คนเก็บตั๋ว (คน) khonkèbtǔa/ (khon/) N ticket
collector.

คนขายตั๋ว (คน) khonkhǎajtǔa/ (khon/) N ticket
seller.

ตั๋วเงิน (ใบ) tǔaŋən/ (baj/) negotiable note.

ตั๋วไปกลับ (ใบ) tǔa/pajklàb/ (baj/) N round-trip
ticket.

ตีตั๋ว tiitǔa/ V colloq. to buy a ticket.

ห้องขายตั๋ว (ห้อง) hɔ̂ŋkhǎajtǔa/ (hɔ̂ŋ/) N ticket
booth, box office.

ตา ๑ (ดวง,ตา) taa/ (duaŋ/, taa/) N 1. eye. 2.
bot. node, knot. 3. mesh (space enclosed by
threads of a net). C 4. time, moment, turn.
→Often coupled with หู "ear," and หน้า "face."
→Syn. 1. นัยน์ตา,ดวงตา,ดวงนัยน์ตา com.;
นัยนา,ดวงนัยนา,เนตร,นัยน์เนตร,ดวงนัยน์เนตร
eleg.,lit.; พระเนตร roy.

กระจกตา (อัน) kracòg/taa/ (?an/) N anat.
cornea.

กะพริบตา kaphríb/taa/ V to wink.

แก้วตา kɛ̂ɛwtaa/ N 1. anat. crystalline lens of
the eye. 2. idiom. the beloved; precious one,
the apple of one's eye.

ใกล้หูใกล้ตา klâjhǔu/klâjtaa/ elab. colloq. right
under (someone's) nose, close to (and therefore
subject to) the observation or supervision of
(someone).

ไกลตาไกลใจ klaj/taa/-klaj/caj/ "out of sight,
out of mind."

ขนตา (เส้น) khǒntaa/ (sên/) N eyelashes.

ขวัญตา khwǎntaa/ N 1. a pleasure or treat to the
eye. 2. sweetheart, darling (used of a woman or
child). P 3. you (expressing endearment when
speaking to woman or child).

ขัดตา khàd/taa/ V 1. to be somewhat disturbing
in appearance, not pleasing to the eye. 2. (It)
doesn't look right.

ขี้ตา khîitaa/ N matter in the eye.

ขึ้นหน้าขึ้นตา khŷnnâa/khŷntaa/ V elab. colloq.
to be well-known, popular, outstanding.

If a word is not found under ตา , see ตะ .

เข้าตาจน khâwtaa′con′ colloq. to be in a fix, to be having a hard time.

จับตา càbtaa′ V 1. to watch closely, keep an eye on. sV 2. eye-catching, striking.

จืดตา cỳyd′taa′ V to be colorless, drab, dull, dull-looking, uninteresting.

ฉากตา chàagtaa′ N anat. retina.

ชายตา chaajtaa′ V to glance sidewise.

เชิดหน้าชูตา chəədnâa′chuutaa′ V elab. colloq. to enhance the prestige (of).

ดวงตา (ดวง) duaŋtaa′ (duaŋ′) N the eye.

ตระการตา trakaan′taa′ eleg., lit. eye-appealing.

ตาขอ (ตัว, อัน) takhɔ̌ɔ′* (tua′, ʔan′) N 1. hook (of a hook-and-eye). 2. a long-handled hook. →Also written ตะขอ.

ตาข่าย (ตาข่าย, อัน, ผืน) takhàaj′* (takhàaj′, ʔan′, phɣ̌yn′) N 1. netting meshwork. 2. net (for ensnaring birds; for badminton, soccer, etc.). →Also written ตะข่าย.

ตาขาว (1) taakhǎaw′; (2) taa′khǎaw′ N 1. the white of the eye. V 2. to be cowardly.

ตาเข taakhěe′ V to be slightly cross-eyed.

ตาเขียว taa′khǐaw′ V 1. to have an angry look in the eye. 2. to have a black eye (i.e. a bruised eye).

ตาคม taa′khom′ V 1. to be bright-eyed. 2. idiom. to have sharp eyes, be a keen observer.

o ตาคมเฉี่ยว taa′khomchǐaw′ to have flashing eyes, to be strikingly bright-eyed.

ตาคับขัน taa′khábkhǎn′ a critical moment.

ตาชั่ง (คัน, อัน) taachâŋ′ (khan′, ʔan′) N colloq. scales, balance.

ตาดำ taadam′ N anat. pupil of the eye. →Also ตุ๊กตา.

o เด็กตาดำ ๆ dèg′-taa′damdam′ innocent child.

ตาตาราง taataraaŋ′ N 1. table (tabulation). 2. squares (as on graph paper).

o กระดาษตาตาราง (แผ่น) kradàad′taataraaŋ′ (phèn′) N 1. graph paper. 2. paper lined with squares.

ตาตุ่ม (ตาตุ่ม) tatùm′ (tatùm′)* N anklebone.

ตาบอด taabɔ̀ɔd′ V to be blind.

ตาปรือ taapryy′ V 1. to have one's eyes half-

closed with drowsiness. 2. to be dozing.

ตาปลา (เม็ด) taaplaa′ (méd′) N a corn (callous growth, as on the toe).

ตาปี taapii′ "the year round," in the following expressions.

o ชั่วนาตาปี chûanaa′taapii′ elab. colloq. year in and year out, forever.

o ตาปีตาชาติ taapii′taachâad′ elab. colloq. year in and year out.

ตาปู (ตัว) tapuu′* (tua′) N nail (for carpentry). →Also written ตะปู.

o ตาปูควง (ตัว) tapuu′khuaŋ′ (tua′) N screw.

ตาเปล่า taa′plàaw′ the naked eye.

ตาฝาด taafàad′ V to have a visual illusion, be fooled by one's visual perception.

ตาฟาง taa′faaŋ′ V to have blurred vision, to see indistinctly (e.g. because of glare, old age).

ตาราง ๑ taraaŋ′* N square (as an areal unit, e.g. square mile). →Sometimes also written ตะราง.

o ตาตาราง taataraaŋ′ N 1. table (tabulation). 2. squares (as on graph paper). →See cross reference.

o ตารางเวลา taraaŋweelaa′ N timetable.

o ๕ ตารางเมตร hâa′taraaŋméed′, -méd′ five square meters.

ตาราง ๒. See ตะราง ๑.

ตาลอย taalɔɔj′ V 1. to have vacant eyes. sV 2. with vacant eyes.

ตาลาย taalaaj′ V 1. to have blurred vision, have double or multiple vision. 2. to have a whirling sensation.

ตาเหล่ taalèe′ V to be cross-eyed, squint-eyed.

ติดตาติดใจ tìdtaa′tìdcaj′ V elab. colloq. 1. to impress, be impressive. 2. to be impressed upon one's mind, be vivid in one's mind.

ติดหูติดตา tìdhǔu′tìdtaa′ V elab. colloq. 1. to see in one's mind's eye. 2. to be vivid, striking. sV 3. vividly.

ถลึงตา thalɣ̌ŋ′taa′ V to stare (someone) down, give a stern look (showing disapproval).

ถ่างตา thàaŋtaa′ V to prop one's eyelids open, force one's eyes to stay open (as when sleepy).

ถึงตา thɣ̌ŋtaa′ V colloq. to reach (one's) turn

(to do something).

ทันตาเห็น thantaa/hěn/ 1. immediately, in time.
2. in time to see (it).

ทำตาปริบ ๆ thamtaa/prìbprìb/ V to blink the
eyes repeatedly (e.g. when stunned by defeat
or sorrow).

นัยน์ตา (ดวง) najtaa/ (duaŋ/) N eye. →Syn. ตา.

o ลูกนัยน์ตา (ดวง, ลูก) lûugnajtaa/ (duaŋ/, lûug/)
N eyeball. →Also ลูกตา.

น้ำตา námtaa/ N 1. tears, teardrops. 2. drip-
pings (e.g. of a candle).

บังตา (ผืน, บาน, ข้าง, คู่) baŋtaa/ N 1. view
breaker, i.e. either a curtain covering the window, hung from about midpoint down (phǔyn/),
or a café door (baan/). 2. eyeshade; blinker
(for a horse) (khâaŋ/, khûu/).

บางตา baaŋ/taa/ V to thin out, dwindle, fade
(in number). →Ant. หนาตา.

บาดตา bàadtaa/ V 1. to offend the eyes. 2. to
hurt one's feelings upon seeing. 3. colloq.
to be glaring, dazzling.

o สวยบาดตา sǔaj/bàadtaa/ colloq. to be
strikingly beautiful, dazzlingly beautiful.

เบิกตา, --กว้าง bə̀əgtaa/, bə̀əgtaa/kwâaŋ/ V to
open the eyes wide (as when frightened).

เป็นหูเป็นตาแทน penhǔu/pentaa/-thɛɛn/ elab.
colloq., idiom. to keep an eye on things, take
charge of things (for someone).

เปลือกตา plỳagtaa/ N eyelid.

โปร่งตา pròoŋtaa/ V 1. to be transparent. 2.
to be uncluttered.

ผิดตา phìdtaa/ V to look changed.

o ผิดหูผิดตา phìdhǔu/phìdtaa/ V elab. colloq.
to look changed; to have changed markedly in
appearance.

พรางตา phraaŋtaa/ V to camouflage.

พริบตา phríbtaa/ V 1. to blink, blink the eyes.
C 2. an instant, a wink, a twinkling. →Also 1.
กระพริบตา.

o ในพริบตา, --เดียว najphríbtaa/, naj/-phríbɔ
taa/diaw/ in the twinkling of an eye, quick as
a wink.

มอง เป็นตาเดียว mɔɔŋ/-pentaa/diaw/ (several)
to focus their eyes upon, stare at as with a

single eye, stare at simultaneously.

ม่านตา mâantaa/ N anat. iris.

มีหน้ามีตา miinâa/miitaa/ V to be in a position of
respect, esteem, deference.

ไม่วางตา mâjwaaŋtaa/ without taking (one's) eyes
off (something).

ยิบตา in สู้ยิบตา sûu/jíbtaa/ colloq. to fight or
resist until death.

โรคตาแดง rôog/taadɛɛŋ/ N pathol. conjunctivitis.

ลวงตา luaŋtaa/ V to deceive, fool the eyes.

ลับตา lábtaa/ V to be out of sight, to disappear.

ลานตา laantaa/ V colloq. to make one's eyes
spin (because of fantastically large numbers).

ลืมตา lyymtaa/ V 1. to open the eyes. 2. to have
one's eyes open. →Ant. หลับตา.

o ลืมหูลืมตา lyymhǔu/lyymtaa/ V to open one's
eyes to, become aware of what is going on around
one.

ลูกตา (ดวง, ลูก) lûugtaa/ (duaŋ/, lûug/) N anat.
eyeball. →Also ลูกนัยน์ตา.

เล่นตา lêntaa/ V to flirt with the eyes.

แว่นตา (อัน, คู่) wêntaa/ (ʔan/, khûu/) N glasses,
spectacles.

แววตา wɛɛwtaa/ N look, expression in the eye,
gleam of the eye.

สะดุดตา sadùd/taa/ V to strike the eyes, be eye-
catching, noticeable.

สายตา sǎajtaa/ N 1. sight, eyesight. 2. line
of vision.

หนาตา nǎa/taa/ V to get thick (in number, as of
a crowd). →Ant. บางตา.

หน้าตา nâataa/ N countenance.

o คนหน้าตาดี (คน) khonnâataadii/ (khon/) N
good-looking person.

หมอตา (คน) mɔ̌ɔtaa/ (khon/) N com. eye
doctor.

หมายตา mǎajtaa/ V to mark (something) with the
eyes, take notice of.

หลับตา làbtaa/ V to close the eyes. →Ant. ลืมตา.

หายหน้าหายตา hǎajnâa/hǎajtaa/ V elab. colloq.
1. to disappear. 2. to be away, out of sight, not
seen by others.

หูตาสว่าง hǔutaa/sawàaŋ/ V 1. to be wide-awake.

If a word is not found under ตา, see ตะ.

2. to be well-informed, wide-awake about what is going on.

หูป่าตาเถื่อน hŭupàa/taathŷan/ V elab. colloq. to be ignorant of what is happening.

ตา ๒ (คน) taa/ (khon/) N 1. maternal grandfather, mother's father. T 2. title used with the first names of men or boys, esp. older men.

ปู่ย่าตายาย (คน) pùujâa/taajaaj/ (khon/) N ancestors: "paternal grandparents and maternal grandparents."

พระเจ้าตา (องค์) phrácâwtaa/ (ʔoŋ/) T lit., defer. term of address for an ascetic.

พ่อตา (คน) phɔ̂ɔtaa/ (khon/) N (man's) father-in-law. →Comp. พ่อผัว (woman's) father-in-law.

อีตา ʔiitaa/ colloq. guy, fellow, mister.

o อีตาคนนั้น ʔiitaa/khonnán/ that guy, that fellow.

ตา ๓ in ตาหาก tahàag/* colloq. variant of ต่างหาก apart, separately, on the contrary. →See ต่าง ๒.

ตาก ๑ tàag/ V 1. to spread (in the sun), expose (to light, air, etc.). 2. to be exposed, dried (as in the sun).

กล้วยตาก (ใบ,ลูก) klûajtàag/ (baj/,lûug/) N dehydrated banana (dried in the sun).

ตากแดด tàagdὲὲd/ V 1. to sun (oneself), expose to the sun, spread out in the sun. 2. to be exposed to the sun.

ตากผ้า tàagphâa/ V to hang up the laundry.

ตากอากาศ tàagʔaakàad/ V to take an airing, get out in the open (as during a vacation in the country, at the seashore).

o สถานที่ตากอากาศ sathăanthîi/tàagʔaakàad/ N resort.

นอนตากยุง nɔɔn/tàagjuŋ/ to sleep exposed to mosquitoes.

ตาก ๒ tàag/ pN Tak, a township in NW Thailand.

ต่าง ๑ tàaŋ/ N packsaddle.

สัตว์ต่าง (ตัว) sàdtàaŋ/ (tua/) N pack animal.

ต่าง ๒ tàaŋ/ V 1. to be different, separate; to differ (in characteristics). In this use normally followed by กัน,กับ. sV 2. instead of, in place of, on behalf of. Nm 3. each, different. Sometimes occurs without a following clf. AA 4.

separately, individually.

o เขาต่างกันมาก kháwtàaŋ/kanmâag/ They differ greatly.

o ผ้าชนิดต่าง ๆ phâa/-chaníd/tàaŋtàaŋ/ various kinds of fabric.

o ผ้าต่างชนิด phâa/tàaŋchaníd/ a fabric of a different kind, another kind of fabric.

o อาบเหงื่อต่างน้ำ ʔàabŋỳa/tàaŋnáam/ colloq. "to bathe in sweat instead of water," a simile used to express the idea of being very hard at work.

o ต่างคนต่างก็มีทรรศนะคนละอย่าง tàaŋkhon/-tàaŋkɔmii/-thádsanáʔ/khonlajàaŋ/↓ Each separate person has a different viewpoint.

o ต่างเงียบกันไปครู่หนึ่ง tàaŋ/ŋîab/-kanpajkhrûu/ɔ nyŋ↓ Each remained silent for a moment.

ต่างกัน tàaŋ/kan/ V to differ, be different, distinct (i.e. from each other).

ต่างกับ tàaŋ/kaɔ to differ from.

ต่างคนก็ต่างใจ tàaŋkhon/kɔ̀tàaŋcaj/ Different people have different preferences. Cf. Eng. "One man's meat is another man's poison."

ต่างจังหวัด tàaŋcaŋwàd/ out-of-town, provincial: "a different changwat." Normally used to refer to sections of a country outside of its capital.

ต่างชาติ tàaŋchâad/ foreign, of another nationality. คน-- foreigner, esp. a person of another race.

o ต่างชาติต่างภาษา tàaŋchâad/tàaŋphaasăa/ elab. colloq. (of) different nationality and speech.

ต่างด้าว tàaŋdâaw/ 1. a foreign country. 2. (as n. mod.) alien, foreign. คน-- alien (esp. in the technical sense, i.e. a citizen of another country).

o ใบสำคัญต่างด้าว (ใบ,ฉบับ) baj/sămkhan/-tàaŋdâaw/ (baj/,chàbàb/) N 1. passport. 2. alien identification card.

ต่าง ๆ tàaŋtàaŋ/ different, various, sundry.

ต่าง ๆ นานา tàaŋtàaŋ/naanaa/ in various ways, in all sorts of ways, in every conceivable way; about all sorts of things; variously.

ต่างประเทศ tàaŋprathêed/ 1. a foreign country; abroad. 2. foreign. การ-- foreign affairs.

o ชาวต่างประเทศ (คน) chaawtàaŋprathêed/ (khon/) N foreigner.

o นโยบายต่างประเทศ (ประการ,อัน) nájoo/baaj/ɔ

tàaŋpratheed/ (prakaan/, ʔan/) N foreign
policy.

ต่างภาษา tàaŋphaasǎa/ a different language, a
foreign language.

ต่างเมือง tàaŋmyaŋ/ other countries, other local-
ities. คน-- N foreigner, stranger, esp. a
person from another locality.

ต่างว่า tàaŋwâac supposing, suppose, if.

ต่างหาก taaŋhàag/, taŋhàag/* 1. apart, separately.
2. on the contrary, contrary to what (you) think.
→Also ตาหาก colloq.

o ค่าส่งคิดต่างหาก khâasòŋ/-khíd/taaŋhàag/
(with) postage figured separately.

ตี้ต่าง(ว่า) tíitàaŋ/* (wâa/) colloq. suppose,
supposing.

แตกต่าง tὲɛgtàaŋ/ V to differ. ความ-- difference.

ผลต่าง phǒntàaŋ/ N difference.

ว่าต่าง wâatàaŋ/ V to act for (in a lawsuit).

ต่าง ๓. See entries below.

ต่างหู (ข้าง, คู่, อัน) tàaŋhǔu/ (khâaŋ/, khûu/, ʔan/)
N eleg. earring.

หน้าต่าง (บาน) nâatàaŋ/ (baan/) N window.

ตาน taan/ N pathol. a kind of children's disease.

ต้าน tâan/ V to resist, withstand.

ต่อต้าน tɔ̀ɔtâan/ V to resist, to counter.

ต้านทาน tâanthaan/ V to resist, withstand, afford
resistance against. การ-- resistance.
ความ-- resistance.

ตาม ๑ taam/ V 1. to follow. sV 2. following,
along (e.g. a street), around, in (e.g. the house),
according to. ผู้-- follower.

ก็ตาม kɔ̂taam/ 1. is of no consequence, of no
moment; 1st example. 2. no matter (who, which,
what, etc.), hence (who)ever, (which)ever,
(what)ever, etc.; 2nd and 3rd examples. NOTE.
The complementary clause following ก็ตาม
in mng. 1 often ends in ทั้งนั้น; see 1st example.

o เขาจะเป็นหมอหรือเป็นนักวิทยาศาสตร์ก็ตาม ฉัน
ดีใจทั้งนั้น kháwcapenmɔ̌ɔ/rýypennágwídthajaac
sàad/ kɔ̂taam/→ chándiicaj/tháŋnán/* (whether)
he becomes a doctor or a scientist is of no consequence; I'll be happy either way.

o ใครก็ตาม khraj/kɔ̂taam/ no matter who, who-

ever, anybody.

o บ้านเมืองใดก็ตาม bâanmyaŋdaj/kɔ̂taam/ no
matter which country (it is), whichever country
it is.

o แม้(ว่า...)จะ...ก็ตาม (แต่)... mɛ́ɛ/(wâa/
...)cac...kɔ̂taam/→(tὲɛc)... No matter if
(such and such occurs), still (such and such is
the case). Even though (such and such might
occur), still (such and such would be the case).
Notwithstanding (such and such), still (such and
such is the case).

oo แม้จะมีอุปสรรคบ้างก็ตาม แต่ประเทศชาติของเรา
จะเจริญวัฒนา mɛ́ɛ/camii/ʔùbpasàg/bâaŋ/ kɔ̂c
taam/→tὲɛpratheed/châad/khɔ̌ɔŋraw/ cacarəən/c
wádthanaa/↓ Even though there may be some
obstacles, still our country will advance and
progress.

o อย่างไรก็ตาม jàaŋraj/kɔ̂taam/ however, at any
rate. →Also อย่างไรก็ดี.

ก็ตามแต่. See ตามแต่ below.

ก็ตามที. See ตามที below.

กวดตาม kùadtaam/, kùad/taamc V colloq. to
run after.

ต้องตาม tɔ̂ŋ/taamc V to agree with, be in accord
with.

ตามกฎหมาย taamkòdmǎaj/ 1. to be legal, be according to the law. 2. legally.

ตามกลิ่น taamklìn/ to scent, follow the scent (of).

ตามขวาง taamkhwǎaŋ/ across, crosswise, transverse.

ตามควร taamkhuan/ V 1. to be as it should be;
to be meet, proper. sV 2. as (one sees) fit;
as befits, as is befitting (to).

ตามเคย taamkhəəj/ as usual.

ตามใจ taamcaj/ V 1. to humor, please, yield to
the wishes (of). 2. to do as one pleases.

o ตามใจคุณ taamcaj/khun/ as you wish, as you
please; whatever you wish, please.

ตามเดิม taamdəəm/ as before, as previously.

ตามเดียะ taam/dìa/ to follow closely.

ตามตรง taamtroŋ/ straight (of speaking), frankly.

ตามแต่, ก็ตามแต่ (1) taam/tὲɛc, kɔ̂taam/tὲɛc;
(2) taam/tὲɛ/↓, kɔ̂taam/tὲɛ/↓ 1. as, according
to what, in accordance with what, whatever; it

depends on what. 2. It's up to (him)! Let him! Let it go! Never mind! That depends!

o ตามแต่โอกาศจะอำนวย taam′tɛ̀ɛʔookàad′caɔ ʔamnuaj′ as opportunity permits.

o ตามแต่คุณจะเห็นควร taam′tɛ̀ɛkhun′cahĕnkhŭan′ in accordance with what you see fit.

o ตามแต่คุณจะให้ taam′tɛ̀ɛkhun′cahâj′ whatever you give.

o ตามแต่คุณจะเห็นดี taam′tɛ̀ɛkhun′cahĕndii′ in accordance with what you see fit.

o เมื่อห้ามแล้วไม่ฟัง ก็ตามแต่ mŷahâam′lɛ́ɛwmâjɔ faŋ′→ kɔ̀taam′tɛ̀ɛ′↓ (Since) he won't listen when he is forbidden (to do something), then let him (do it)!

ตามทาง (1) taamthaaŋ′; (2) taam′thaaŋɔ 1. along the way. 2. according to.

o ตามทางการ taam′thaaŋkaan′ officially.

o ตามทางค้นคว้าจากประวัติศาสตร์ taam′thaaŋɔ khónkhwáa′-càagprawàdsàad′ according to historical research.

o ตามทางที่จะไปสู่นครนั้น taamthaaŋ′-thîicapajɔ sùu′-nakhɔɔn′nán′ along the way to that city.

ตามที,ก็ตามที taam′thii′, kɔ̀taam′thii′ let it be (indicating resignation, state of being fed up with something, someone).

o ถ้าเขาอยากจะทำยังงั้น ก็ตามที thâakháwjàagɔ catham′jaŋŋán′→ kɔ̀taam′thii′↓ If he wants to do it that way, let him.

ตามที่ taam′thîiɔ 1. as (i.e. in accordance with what, that which). 2. in reference to what (that which), referring to what (that which). NOTE. When mng. 2 is implied the clause which is introduced by ที่ often has its end marked by the particle นั้น q.v.; 3rd example.

o ตามที่คุณรู้แล้ว taam′-thîikhunrúu′lɛ́ɛw′ as you already know.

o ตามที่ได้เคยปฏิบัติมาแล้ว taam′-thîidâjkhəəj′-pàtibàd′-maalɛ́ɛw′ as has previously been the practice.

o ตามที่คุณว่ามานั้น taam′-thîikhunwâa′maanán′ in reference to what you said, referring to what you said.

ตามธรรมดา taam′thammadaa′ usually, ordinarily.

ตามบ้าน taambâan′ around the house.

ตามบุญตามกรรม taambun′taamkam′ letting nature take its course, leaving it to fate.

ตามปกติ taam′pògkatìʔ′ normally, ordinarily, as usual.

ตามประสา taam′prasăa′ in the manner of, according to the ways of (e.g. a certain station in life, mode of life). →Also ตามภาษา, ตามผะสา.

o มีความสุขตามประสาเด็ก miikhwaamsùg′-taamɔ prasăa′dèg′ to be happy in the manner of a child, according to the ways of children.

ตามภาษา taam′phaasăa′ in the manner of, according to the ways of. →Also ตามประสา, ตามผะสา.

ตามมีตามเกิด taammii′taamkə̀əd′ according to one's means, as one can afford.

ตามยาว taamjaaw′ lengthwise, longitudinal.

ตามรอย taamrɔɔj′ 1. to track. 2. to imitate, follow in the footsteps (of someone).

ตามเรื่อง taamrŷaŋ′ colloq. accordingly, as the circumstances allow (or require); for the heck of it.

o แกพูดตามเรื่องไปอย่างนั้นเอง kɛɛphûud′taamɔ rŷaŋ′-pajjàaŋnán′eeŋ′↓ He said it just for the heck of it.

ตามลม taamlom′ V 1. to move leeward, move with the wind. sV 2. leeward, with the wind.

ตามลำดับ taamlamdàb′ 1. in order, in series, consecutively. 2. respectively. 3. progressively, gradually. 4. in the order of (e.g. height).

ตามลำพัง taamlamphaŋ′ alone, by oneself.

ตามสบาย taamsabaaj′ V 1. to be at ease, feel at home. sV 2. leisurely, comfortably.

ตามส่วน taamsùan′ in proportion.

ตามแหล่งที่ taamlɛ̀ŋ′thîiɔ in places where.

ตามอย่าง taamjàaŋ′ V to imitate, follow (someone's) example.

ติดตาม tìdtaam′ V 1. to follow, pursue. 2. to accompany.

ติดสอยห้อยตาม tìdsɔ̌j′hɔ̂jtaam′ V elab. colloq. to follow, accompany.

เป็นเงาตามตัว pennaw′taamtua′ "as one's shadow follows one's body," a simile for an inevitable consequence. Cf. Eng. "as night follows day."

เป็นไปตาม pen′pajtaam′ 1. to agree with, be according to, be in accordance with. 2. to be (that) way.

มองตาม mɔɔŋtaam/ V to follow (someone) with one's eyes.

ว่าตาม wâataam/ V to say after, repeat after.

ให้ไปตาม...มา hâjpajtaam/-...maa/ to send for (someone).

ตาม ๒ taam/ V to light. Chiefly in the combinations given below. →Syn. จุด.

ตามโคม taamkhoom/ V to light a lantern.

ตามไฟ taamfaj/ V to light a lamp, candle, torch.

ตาย taaj/ V 1. to die. 2. to cease, stop. 3. to be dead. 4. to be fixed, rigid, motionless (of things which are or seem to be capable of movement or adjustment). sV 5. to death, dead (as in "beat to death, strike dead"). E 6. exclamation of surprise, dismay, etc. In this last use it follows other exclamatives or occurs in combinations like ตายจริง,ตายละวา,ตาย แล้ว shown below. ความ--,คน--,ผู้-- (see below). →Syn. 1. สิ้นพระชนม์ roy., ถึงแก่ มรณภาพ sacer., ถึงแก่กรรม eleg., ม้วย lit. มอง slang. →Ant. 3-5. เป็น.

o กระโดดน้ำตาย kradòodnáam/taaj/ to jump to a watery death, commit suicide by jumping into the water.

o ยิงตาย jiŋtaaj/ to shoot to death, shoot dead.

กุญแจปากตาย kuncɛɛ/pàagtaaj/ N open end wrench (i.e. with fixed jaws).

คนตาย (คน) khontaaj/ (khon/) N 1. dead person. 2. death (i.e. cases of death, persons dead).

ความตาย khwaamtaaj/ N death. →Syn. มัจจุราช lit.

o ความเป็นความตาย khwaampen/khwaamtaaj/ N life and death.

คำตาย (คำ) khamtaaj/ (kham/) N dead syllable (in the Thai system of writing), i.e. a syllable ending in a short vowel or a stop consonant. →Opp. คำเป็น.

ฆ่าคนตาย khâa/khontaaj/ to kill, murder a person. การ-- murder, homicide.

จมน้ำตาย comnáam/taaj/ to drown, get drowned.

จับตาย càbtaaj/ V to take dead: "capture dead." →Opp. จับเป็น.

ตายจริง taaj/ciŋ/↓, taajciŋ/↓ E excl. expressing

surprise, dismay, etc.

ตายใจ taaj/caj/ V to have implicit faith in, to trust implicitly.

ตายตัว taajtua/ V to be fixed, stable, unalterable, rigid.

ตายละวา taaj/lawǎa/↓ E excl. expressing dismay.

ตายแล้ว taajléɛw/↓ E excl. expressing dismay.

ตายโหง taajhǒoŋ/ V to die a violent death.

o ให้ตายโหงตายห่า hâjtaajhǒoŋ/taajhàa/ vulg. May the plague take me! (expression used to swear that one is telling the truth).

o ให้มันตายโหงตายห่า hâjmantaajhǒoŋ/taajhàa/ vulg. May the plague take him! (a curse).

ตายตาย !táajtaaj/↓, !táaj/taaj/↓ E excl. expressing surprise, dismay, etc.

ผู้ตาย (คน) phûutaaj/ (khon/) N the deceased, the dead.

ไม้ตาย (ไม้) máajtaaj/ (máaj/) N 1. decisive blow, knock-out blow (in boxing). 2. decisive trick or stratagem.

รอดตาย rɔ̂ɔdtaaj/ V to survive, escape death.

ให้ตายซี่ hâjtaaj/sîi↓ colloq. Cross my heart and hope to die! (used to swear that one is telling the truth).

ออกจะตาย ʔɔ̀ɔgcataaj/ colloq. extremely, very much, a lot.

อุ๊ยตาย ʔújtaaj/↓, !ʔújtaaj/↓ E excl. expressing surprise, dismay, etc. Sometimes written อุ๊ย!ตาย! and pronounced !ʔúj/ taaj/↓.

ต่าย tàaj/ Variant of ไต่.

ต๊าย in ต๊ายตาย! !táajtaaj/↓, !táaj/taaj/↓ E excl. expressing surprise, dismay, etc. Sometimes written ต๊าย!ตาย! and pronounced !táaj/ taaj/↓.

ตาราง. See under ตา ๑.

ตาล (ต้น) taan/ (tôn/) N sugar palm, toddy palm. NOTE. This is the specific term. It is normally preceded by a class term such as ต้น "tree," ใบ "leaf," etc., as circumstances require.

ต้นตาล (ต้น) tôntaan/ (tôn/) N sugar palm, toddy palm (i.e. the tree).

น้ำตาล námtaan/ N sugar.

ตาลปัตร taalapàd/ N palm-leaf fan used by priests. →Sometimes incorrectly spelled ตะละปัตร.

กลับตาลปัตร klàb'taalapàd' idiom. 1. to make a reversal. 2. to change one's mind. 3. to go back on one's word.

ตำ tam' V 1. to pound (esp. in a mortar). 2. to puncture, pierce, prick (with nail, thorn, needle, or other small object). →Syn. 1. โขลก. 2. ทิ่ม, แทง.

ตำข้าว tamkhâaw' to pound rice (paddy) in a mortar (in order to remove husks and to polish it for cooking use).

ต่ำ tàm' V to be low. →Ant. สูง.

ใจต่ำ cajtàm' V to be base, vile.

ตกต่ำ tògtàm' V 1. to drop, decline. 2. to be declining, falling low. ความ-- decline.

ต่ำช้า tàmcháa' V to be depraved, morally bad.

ต่ำสุด tàm'sùd' V to be minimum, the minimum, the lowest.

ต่ำสูง tàm'sǔuŋ' "high and low." See example.

o ความเหลื่อมล้ำต่ำสูง khwaamlỳamlám'tàmsǔuŋ' N disparity, inequality.

อักษรต่ำ (ตัว) ʔàgsɔ̌ɔntàm' (tua') N a LOW consonant.

ตำนาน (เรื่อง) tamnaan' (rŷaŋ') N legend.

ตำบล (ตำบล) tambon' (tambon') N tambon, a subdivision of an amphoe (อำเภอ). More or less equivalent to a precinct. →See จังหวัด.

ตำแย in หมอตำแย (คน) mɔ̌ɔtamjεε' (khon') N colloq. midwife. →Syn. ผดุงครรภ์ eleg.

ตำรวจ (นาย, คน) tamrùad'* N policeman; the police. [conv.f. ตรวจ]

กรมตำรวจ kromtamrùad' N Police Department.

กองตำรวจ (กอง) kɔɔŋtamrùad' (kɔɔŋ') N police force.

ตำรวจจราจร (นาย, คน) tamrùad'caraacɔɔn' (naaj', khon') N 1. traffic patrolman. 2. the traffic police.

นายตำรวจ (นาย, คน) naajtamrùad' (naaj', khon') N police officer.

ผู้กำกับการตำรวจ (นาย, คน) phûukamkàb'kaanɔ tamrùad' (naaj', khon') N (district or provincial) chief of police.

พลตำรวจ (นาย, คน) phontamrùad' (naaj', khon') N 1. policeman (lowest police rank). T 2. Officer -- (ref. to a policeman).

ตำรับ (ตำรับ, เล่ม) tamràb'* (tamràb', lêm') N 1. prescription, formula (esp. medical) (tamràb'). 2. textbook, reference book, manual (of any kind) (tamràb', lêm'). →See ตำรา.

ตำรับตำรา (เล่ม) tamràb'tamraa' (lêm') N textbook.

ตำรา (ตำรา, เล่ม) tamraa' (tamraa', lêm') N 1. prescription, formula (esp. medical) (tamraa'). 2. textbook, reference book, manual (of any kind) (tamraa', lêm'). →See ตำรับ.

ตำลึง tamlyŋ' C a Thai monetary unit, equivalent to four bahts.

ตำหนิ tamnì?' V 1. to reproach, criticize, blame. N 2. defect, imperfection, flaw, blemish. [conv. f. ติ]

เป็นตำหนิ pentamnì?' V to be a defect, an imperfection, a marring feature.

มีตำหนิ miitamnì?' V to have a defect, a flaw, an identifying mark.

ตำหรับ. See ตำรับ.

ตำแหน่ง (ตำแหน่ง) tamnèŋ'*(tamnèŋ') N 1. position, rank, post. 2. place, location.

ชิงตำแหน่ง chiŋ'tamnèŋ' V to compete for a title (as in sports).

ดำรงตำแหน่ง damroŋ'tamnèŋ' V to hold the position (of).

ผู้รั้งตำแหน่ง (คน) phûuráŋ'tamnèŋ' (khon') N one acting in place of another, an acting (e.g. governor, etc.).

ติ tì?' V to criticize, blame. →Cf. ตำหนิ.

ติชม tì?'chom' V to find fault with, criticize (finding both good and bad points).

ติเตียน tì?'tian' V to criticize, reprove, express disapproval of. ความ-- disapproval, blame.

o คำติเตียน (คำ, ข้อ, ประการ) khamtì?'tian' (kham', khɔ̂ɔ', prakaan') N criticism, disapproval.

ติ่ง (ติ่ง, อัน) tìŋ' (tìŋ', ?an') N outgrowth, appendage, projection.

ไส้ติ่ง sâjtìŋ' N appendix (body part). →Cf. ไส้ตัน.

ติด tìd' V 1. to adjoin, connect. 2. to attach (to), be attached (to). 3. to stick (to), adhere (to), get stuck (to, in). 4. to be addicted to. 5. to court. 6. to kindle, ignite. 7. colloq. to owe.

ตามติด taamtìd′ V to follow closely.

ติดกระดุม tìd′kradum′ V 1. to fasten the buttons, button up. 2. to sew buttons on.

ติดกัน tìd′kan V 1. to be connected, joined together, adjoining. 2. to be of one piece.

ติดกับ ๑ tìd′kaɔ to be adjacent to, attached to.

ติดกับ ๒ tìdkàb′ V to be trapped.

ติดกาว tìdkaaw′ V to glue, stick together with glue.

ติดคอ tìdkhɔɔ′ V to be stuck, lodged in the throat (as a fish bone).

ติดค้าง tìdkháaŋ′ V 1. to be in debt, be owing. 2. to be stuck, lodged (in something).

ติดเครื่อง tìdkhrŷaŋ′ V to start up the motor.

ติดเครื่องโทรศัพท์ tìd′khrŷaŋthoorasàb′ V to install a telephone.

ติดจะ tìd′caɔ AA apt to, incline toward.

ติดใจ tìdcaj′ V to like, be fond of, take a fancy to; to be attracted, impressed (by).

ติดขะงัก tìd′chaŋág′ V to be stuck, get stuck.

ติดต่อ(กัน,กับ) tìdtɔɔ′(kan′,kaɔ) V 1. to get in touch (with). 2. to associate (with), be connected (with), adjoin. sV 3. without interruption, continuously, straight through (usually with กัน). การ-- getting in touch, contacting, communication.

o ทางติดต่อ (ทาง) thaaŋtìdtɔɔ′(thaaŋ′) N ways of communication, means of intercourse.

o โรคติดต่อ (ชนิด) rôog′tìdtɔɔ′(chaníd′) N contagious disease.

ติดตะราง tìd′taraaŋ′ V to be put in jail, imprisoned.

ติดตั้ง tìd′tâŋ′ V to install.

ติดตัว tìdtua′ sV (to have something) with one, on one's person.

ติดตาติดใจ tìdtaa′tìdcaj′ elab. colloq. V 1. to impress, be impressive. 2. to be impressed upon one's mind, be vivid in one's mind.

ติดตาม tìdtaam′ V 1. to follow, pursue. 2. to accompany. ผู้-- an aide who travels with his superior; an entourage.

ติด ๆ กัน tìdtìd′kan′ consecutively, one after another, in a row, in close succession.

ติดเนื้อต้องใจ tìdnýa′tɔ̂ŋcaj′ V to be fond of, be interested in, fascinated with.

ติดบุหรี่ tìd′burìi′ to be addicted to smoking, be a habitual smoker.

ติดปาก tìdpàag′ V to be addicted to the use of a certain word or expression.

ติดปืน tìdpyyn′ V to be armed, to carry guns (as a ship).

ติดพัน tìdphan′ V 1. to engage, occupy, concern, involve. 2. to be engaged, occupied, involved (in, with). 3. colloq. to be in love (with), to court.

o การศึกยังติดพันกันอยู่ kaansỳg′-jaŋtìdphan′kanɔ jùu′ the war is still engaging (them).

ติดไฟ tìdfaj′ V 1. to kindle, ignite a fire. 2. to be inflammable, combustible.

ติดราชการ tìd′râadchakaan′ V to be occupied with official or government duty.

ติดโรค tìdrôog′ V to contract a disease, catch a (contagious) disease.

ติดลอยห้อยตาม tìdsɔj′hɔ̂jtaam′ V elab. colloq. to follow, accompany.

ติดสินบน tìd′sǐnbon′ V 1. to bribe. 2. to give a reward for information (as the police to someone who aids in discovering the wrongdoer).

ติดสุรา tìd′suraa′ V to be addicted to alcohol, be a habitual drinker.

ติดหล่ม tìdlòm′ V to get stuck in the mud.

ติดหูติดตา tìdhǔu′tìdtaa′ V 1. to see in one's mind's eye. 2. to be vivid, striking. sV 3. vividly.

ติดอกติดใจ tìd²òg′tìdcaj′ V 1. to be attracted, impressed, fascinated (by). 2. to like, be fond of, take a fancy to.

ติดอ่าง tìd²àaŋ′ V to stammer, stutter.

ติดอาวุธเรือ tìd′²aawúd′-rya′ V to arm a ship, outfit a ship with weapons.

แนบติด nɛ̂ɛb′tìd′ V to be attached to.

ติ้ว in หมุนติ้ว mǔntíw′ V to spin very fast.

ตี tii′ V 1. to hit, beat, strike. 2. (when followed be a numeral) an hour of the morning between midnight and 6 A.M.

o ตีสอง tiisɔ̌ɔŋ′ colloq. 2 A.M. →Syn. ๒ นาฬิกา writ.

โจมตี coomtii′ to attack, raid, assault.

ตีเกล็ด tii′klèd′ V sew. to make tucks, to tuck.

ตีขลุม tii′khlǔm′ V colloq. to take advantage of the situation or of appearances (e.g. let it be believed that one is the owner of what is actually borrowed jewelry).

ตีความ tii′khwaam′ V to explain, interpret, define (as a law).

ตีชิง tii′chiŋ′ V to assault and rob (someone).

ตีได้ tii′dâaj′ V to conquer, take (e.g. a town).

ตีตรา tiitraa′ V com. to stamp (as with a seal). →Syn. ประทับตรา eleg.

ตีตั๋ว tiitǔa′ V colloq. to buy a ticket.

ตีโต้ tii′tôo′ V 1. to retaliate, make a counterattack. 2. to hit back and forth (as a tennis ball).

ตีทะเบียนรถ tiithabian′ród′ V to register a car.

ตีฝ่า tii′fàa′ V to attack and break through (the enemy's line).

ตีฝีปาก tii′fǐipàag′ V to wisecrack.

ตีพิมพ์ tii′phim′ V to print, type, publish.

o ลงตีพิมพ์ loŋtii′phim′ V to publish.

ตีราคา tiiraakhaa′ V to name the price, put a value (on), make a price estimate, appraise.

ตีสกัด tii′sakàd′ V to block, intercept (esp. in battle).

ตีสนิท tii′sanìd′ V colloq. to pretend to be acquainted (i.e. to behave like a close friend in order to obtain a favor).

ตีหน้า tiinâa′ V colloq. to put on an expression feigning (e.g. ignorance).

ตีเหล็ก tiilèg′ V to forge iron, make ironware.

ตี in ตีต่าง(ว่า) tíitàaŋ′(wâa′)* colloq. suppose, supposing.

ตีน (ตีน,ข้าง) tiin′ (tiin′,khâaŋ′) N com. foot, paw. Sometimes considered vulgar. →Syn. บาท lit., เท้า eleg., พระบาท roy.

ข้อตีน (ข้อ,ข้าง) khɔ̂ɔtiin′ (khɔ̂ɔ′,khâaŋ′) N com. ankle. →Syn. ข้อเท้า eleg.

ตีนเขา (แห่ง) tiinkhǎw′ (hèŋ′) N com. foothills, the foot of the hill. →Syn. เชิงเขา eleg.

ตีนเปล่า tiinplàaw′ barefoot, with bare feet.

นิ้วตีน (นิ้ว) níwtiin′ (níw′) N com. toe. →Syn. นิ้วเท้า eleg.

ฝีตีน fǐitiin′ N com. speed (of foot), pace.

รถตีนตะขาบ (คัน) ród′tiintakhàab′ (khan′) N caterpillar tractor.

หัวนอนปลายตีน hǔanɔɔn′plaajtiin′ N idiom. the background of a person (esp. as it relates to his social status).

ตีบ tìib′ V to be narrowed, constricted.

โรคคอตีบ rôog′khɔɔtìib′ N diphtheria.

ตี๋ tiʔ′ rM modifier meaning "faintly, slightly," used esp. with เหม็น "smell bad." →Also ตุ ๑.

ตึก (หลัง) tỳg′ (lǎŋ′) N building, esp. brick building.

ตึกระฟ้า (หลัง) tỳg′-ráʔfáa (lǎŋ′) N skyscraper.

ตึกรามบ้านช่อง tỳgraam′bâanchɔ̂ŋ′ N elab. colloq. buildings (of all kinds, collectively).

ตึก ๆ, ตึ๊ก ๆ tỳgtỳg′, tỳgtỳg′ imit. palpitation of the heart.

o ใจเต้นตึก ๆ cajtên′tỳgtỳg′ V 1. to have the heart beating with excitement. 2. the heart is pounding, palpitating. sV 3. with pounding heart, with palpitating heart.

ตึง tyŋ′ V to be tight, taut, tense, strained. ความ-- tension.

ตึงเครียด tyŋkhrîad′ V 1. to be tense, strained (as a situation). 2. to be stern (as of the face). ความ-- tension, strain.

บึงตึง bŷŋtyŋ′ V 1. to be sullen, sulky, cross. 2. to be stern.

มึนตึง myntyŋ′ V to be cold, indifferent. ความ-- indifference.

หูตึง hǔutyŋ′ V to be hard of hearing. →Dist. หูหนวก "deaf."

ตืด ๑ (ตัว) tỳyd′ (tua′) N tapeworm. →Usually ตัว--.

ตืด ๒, ขี้-- tỳyd′, khîitỳyd′ V colloq. to be stingy, tight, parsimonious. →Syn. ตระหนี่ eleg., ขี้เหนียว colloq.

ตื่น tỳyn′ V 1. to wake (of oneself). 2. to get excited, be excited about. 3. to start, become alert suddenly (as wild animals). →Dist. 1. ปลุก "to wake (someone)."

ขี้ตื่น khîitỳyn′ V colloq. to be easily excited or alarmed.

เจ๊กตื่นไฟ cég′tỳynfaj′ "a Chinese excited over a fire," a simile used to describe an easily excited person.

ตื่นขึ้น tɯ̀yn/khɯ̂n V to wake up (from sleep).

ตื่นตัว tɯ̀yntua/ V 1. to be awakened, enlightened (e.g. of a civilization). 2. colloq. to be on the alert, wide-awake.

ตื่นตาตื่นใจ tɯ̀yntaa/tɯ̀yncaj/ V elab. colloq. to be full of wonder and excitement (about something spectacular).

ตื่นเต้น tɯ̀yntên/ V to be excited, thrilled, enthusiastic. ความ-- excitement, enthusiasm.

ตื้น tɯ̂yn/ V 1. to be shallow. 2. to be superficial. 3. to be easy (of a problem). ความ-- shallowness.

ตื้นเขิน tɯ̂ynkhə̌ən/ V to be shallow, become shallow, (e.g. of a canal getting filled with sediment).

ตื้นตัน tɯ̂yntan/ V to be choked up (e.g. with sorrow, happiness).

ตื้อ tɯ̂y/ V 1. to be heavy, stuffed (of the head). rM 2. intensifier used with มืด "dark" อิ่ม "full (from eating)."

ตื๋อ tɯ̌y/ rM intensifier used with มืด "dark" วิ่ง "run."

ตุ ๑ tùʔ/ rM modifier meaning "faintly, slightly," used esp. with เหม็น "smell bad." →Also ตึ.

ตุ ๒ in เป็นตุเป็นตะ pentùʔ/pentàʔ/ to make sense, be coherent.

ตุ๊ túʔ/ rM intensifier used with อ้วน "fat, heavyset."

ตุ๊กแก (ตัว) túgkɛɛ/ (tua/) N the gecko, a large house lizard.

ตุ๊กตา (ตัว,อัน) túgkataa/ (tua/,ʔan/) N 1. doll (tua/). 2. anat. pupil of the eye (ʔan/). →Also 2. ตาดำ.

ตุน tun/ V to stock up, hoard. [f. Chin.]
กักตุน kàgtun/ V to hoard. การ-- hoarding.

ตุ่น (ตัว) tùn/ (tua/) N 1. bamboo rat (Rhizomys). 2. mole. →Usually ตัว--.

ตุ่ม (ใบ,ตุ่ม) tùm/ N 1. large earthen storage jar (baj/). 2. swelling, bump (as from a mosquito bite) (tùm/).
ตาตุ่ม (ตาตุ่ม) taatùm/ (taatùm/) N anklebone.
เป็นตุ่ม pentùm/ to have a bump on the skin (from mosquito bite or other cause).

ตุ้ม tûm/ N pendant, suspended object. →Chiefly in compounds.

ตุ้มน้ำหนัก (ลูก,ตุ้ม) tûm/námnàg/ (lûug/,tûm/) N a weight.

ตุ้มหู (ข้าง,คู่,อัน) tûmhǔu/ (khâaŋ/,khûu/,ʔan/) N earring. →Syn. ต่างหู eleg.

ลูกตุ้ม (ลูก) lûugtûm/ (lûug/) N 1. pendulum. 2. heavy pendant. 3. plummet.

ตุ้ม ๆ ต่อม ๆ tŭmtŭm/tɔ̀mtɔ̀m/* 1. imit. thump, thump-thump (as the sound of drums beating). V 2. (the heart) to thump (as from fear or suspense).

o ใจตุ้ม ๆ ต่อม ๆ caj/-tŭmtŭm/tɔ̀mtɔ̀m/ V the heart to thump from fear or suspense (as when watching a movie or play).

ตุ่ย tùj/ V 1. to be bulging, protruding, swollen, puffed up. sV 2. with cheeks bulging (as when chewing).

ตุ่ย ๆ tûjtûj/ sV with cheeks bulging (as when chewing something).

ตุรกี turakii/ pN Turkey. [f. Eng. as the word is spelled] →See เตอรกี.

ตุล. Abbrev. for ตุลาคม October.

ตุลาการ (นาย,คน) tùlaa/kaan/ (khon/,naaj/) N judge.
อำนาจตุลาการ ʔamnâad/-tùlaa/kaan/ N judicial power.

ตุลาคม tùlaa/khom/ N October. เดือน-- idem. →The names of all the months are listed under เดือน.

ตุหรัดตุเหร่ turàd/turèe/ V to wander about like a vagabond, nomad.

ตู่, ตู่เอา tùu/,tùu/ʔawɔ V 1. to claim (the ownership of something) under false pretenses. 2. to mistake, to take one (person) for another.

ตู้ (ใบ) tûu/ (baj/) N 1. class term for cupboards, cabinets, (book) cases, wardrobes, etc. C 2. clf. for such items; for things in cabinets, cases, etc. [f. Chin.]

o ตู้สองใบ tûu/sɔ̌ɔŋbaj/ two cabinets.

o หนังสือตู้นี้ naŋsɯ̌y/-tûu/níi/ this case of books.

ตู้กระจก tûu/kracòg/ N 1. glass cabinet. 2. aquarium (the glass tank).

ตู้ถ้วยชาม tûu/thûajchaam/ N cupboard, cabinet for dishes.

ตู้น้ำแข็ง tûu/námkhɛ̌ŋ/ icebox, refrigerator.

→Also ตู้เย็น.

ตู้นิรภัย tûu′níraphaj′ N eleg. a safe. →Syn.
　ตู้เซฟ com.

ตู้ไปรษณีย์ tûu′prajsanii′ N (public) mailbox (for
　sending mail).

ตู้เย็น tûujen′ N icebox, refrigerator. →Also
　ตู้น้ำแข็ง.

ตู้เสื้อผ้า tûu′sŷaphâa′ N wardrobe, bureau,
　dresser.

ตู้หนังสือ tûu′naŋsŷy′ N bookcase.

ตูด tùud′ N vulg. 1. anus. 2. bottom, rear, rump.
　→Syn. กัน com., ทวารหนัก eleg.

ตูม ๑ tuum′ V to be in bud. →Dist. บาน "be in
　bloom."

　ดอกตูม (ดอก) dɔ̀ɔgtuum′ (dɔ̀ɔg′) N flower bud.

ตูม ๒ tuum′ 1. imit. boom, as of a cannon. 2.
　imit. thump, bump, the sound of a heavy weight
　falling to the ground.

เต็ง in ไม่เต็มเต็ง mâjtemteŋ′ idiom., colloq.
　to have a screw loose, to be cracked, touched
　in the head, not all there.

เต้น tên′* V 1. to spring, jump. 2. (the heart) to
　beat, throb.

　ใจเต้น cajtên′ V 1. to be excited, to have one's
　heart pounding. sV 2. with pounding heart.

　ตื่นเต้น tỳyntên′ V to be excited, thrilled, enthu-
　siastic.

　เต้นระบำ tênrabam′ V to dance (as a solo or
　group performance).

　เต้นรำ tênram′ V to dance (ballroom dancing).
　→Comp. ฟ้อนรำ.

　o เพลงเต้นรำ (เพลง) phleeŋtênram′ (phleeŋ′)
　N dance music.

　o โรงเต้นรำ (โรง) rooŋ′tênram′ (rooŋ′) N
　dance pavilion, dance hall, ballroom.

　โลดเต้น lôodtên′ V 1. to jump up and down (with
　delight). 2. to jump about, hop.

　o กระโดดโลดเต้น kradòod′lôodtên′ V to hop
　and skip about (merrily, as children do).

　วิ่งเต้น wîŋtên′ V 1. to run and hop about (as
　children). 2. colloq. to run around busily,
　scurry around (as when trying to obtain support
　for one's purpose, or when organizing things).

เต็นท์ (หลัง, เต็นท์) tén′*(lǎŋ′, tén′) N tent. [f. Eng.]

เต็นนิส tenníd′, tennís′ N tennis. [f. Eng.]

เต็ม tem′ V 1. to be full, filled. 2. to be chock-full.
　3. to reach the limit. sV 4. in a filling amount,
　to a filling degree.

　o ที่ชายหาดมีคนเต็ม thîichaajhàad′-miikhon′tem′↓
　The beach is simply jammed (with people).

เต็มกำ, --มือ tem′kam′, tem′kammyy′ 1. (in the
　amount of) a handful. 2. with one's hand or
　hands full.

เต็มกำลัง tem′kamlaŋ′ as hard as possible, with
　all one's might.

เต็มแก่ temkὲɛ′ in the highest degree, extremely,
　exceedingly.

　o หิวข้าวเต็มแก่ hĭwkhâaw′temkὲɛ′ to be exceed-
　ingly hungry.

เต็มคราบ temkhrâab′ colloq. to the fullest ex-
　tent, to one's full satisfaction. Used of filling
　the stomach.

เต็มใจ temcaj′ V 1. to be willing. sV 2. willingly.
　ความ-- willingness.

　o ไม่เต็มใจ mâjtemcaj′ V to be reluctant, un-
　willing.

เต็มดวง temduaŋ′ V to be full (of the moon).

　o พระจันทร์เต็มดวง phrácan′temduaŋ′ the moon
　is full.

เต็มตัว temtua′ 1. all over the body, from head
　to toe. 2. full length (e.g. a full length photo-
　graph of someone).

เต็มทน temthon′ V 1. to be unable to bear (it)
　any longer. sV 2. extremely, exceedingly,
　unbearably, to the limit of one's endurance.

เต็มที temthii′ V 1. to be awful, terrible. sV 2.
　very, quite, awfully, extremely, hopelessly, badly.

เต็มที่ temthîi′ fully, to the fullest extent, to the
　full, to the utmost, extremely.

　o โตเต็มที่ too′temthîi′ full size, full grown.

เต็มประดา tempradaa′ extremely.

เต็มปาก tempàag′ idiom. freely, without qualms,
　without restraint (of speaking).

เต็มแประ temprɛ̀ʔ′ to be very full, filled to the
　limit.

เต็มไปด้วย tem′pajdûajɔ to be full of, filled with.

เต็มมือ temmyy′ to fill the hand, fill the hands;
　to be covering the hands, all over one's hands.

o ลูกบอลมีขนาดเต็มมือ lûugbɔn/ miikhanàad/-tem/myy/ the ball is of a size to fill one's hand.

o ผมนะ งานเต็มมือทุกวัน phǒmná?/ ŋaan/-tem ɔ myy/thúgwan/↓ As for me, my hands are full with work every day.

o ทรายเต็มมือเขียว saaj/temmyy/-chiaw↓ There's sand all over (your) hands!

เต็มเม็ดเต็มหน่วย temméd/temnùaj/ V 1. to be full, complete. sV 2. fully, to the utmost.

เต็มแรง temrɛɛŋ/ with full force, with all one's might.

ไม่เต็ม mâjtem/ 1. not to be full, to be unfilled. 2. short for the entries below.

o ไม่เต็มเต็ง mâjtemteŋ/ idiom., colloq. to have a screw loose, to be cracked, touched in the head, not all there.

o ไม่เต็มบาท mâjtembàad/ idiom., colloq. idem.

เตร่ trèe/ V to wander, stroll about.

เตรียม triam/ V to prepare, make ready.

ชั้นเตรียม chántriam/ preelementary level (of education).

ตระเตรียม trà?triam/ V to prepare, make ready.

เตรียมตัว triamtua/ V to prepare oneself, to get ready.

เตรียมพร้อม triamphrɔ́ɔm/ V to be prepared, on the alert, ready for action. การ-- preparedness, readiness.

เตอรกี təərakii/ pN Turkey. [f. Eng. as the word is pronounced]. →See ตุรกี.

เตอะ tə̀?/ rM intensifier used with หนา "thick."

เตะ tè?/ V 1. to kick (usually with a sharp blow, using any part of the foot other than the sole). 2. slang to tip, give a tip (e.g. to a waiter). →Dist. 1. ถีบ. →Syn. 2. ถีบ.

เตะจมูก tè?/camùug/ V colloq. (an odor) to strike the nose.

เตา (เตา) taw/ (taw/) N 1. stove. 2. furnace. 3. portable brazier. →Syn. 3. อั้งโล่.

เตาผิง tawphǐŋ/ N fireplace.

เตาเผา tawphǎw/ N 1. furnace. 2. kiln. 3. incinerator.

เตาไฟ tawfaj/ N stove (for cooking).

เตารีด (เตา, อัน) tawrîid/ (taw/, ?an/) N an iron (for pressing clothing).

เตาอบ taw?òb/ N 1. oven. 2. kiln.

เต่า (ตัว) tàw/ (tua/) N turtle, tortoise.

เต่ากระ tàwkrà?/ N hawksbill, a kind of spotted sea turtle.

เต่าตนุ tàw/tanù?/ N a large green sea turtle. Its eggs are called ไข่จะละเม็ด.

แมลงเต่า (ตัว) malɛɛŋtàw/ (tua/) N ladybug.

เต้า tâw/ N 1. breast. C 2. clf. for a breast.

เต้านม (เต้า) tâwnom/ (tâw/) N (woman's) breast.

ลูกเต้า (คน) lûugtâw/ (khon/) N (one's own) children (i.e. related by blood).

เต๋า (ลูก) tǎw/ (lûug/) N dice. [f. Chin.]

เต้าเจี้ยว tâwcîaw/ N bean paste, miso, a salty condiment made of soy beans. [f. Chin.]

เต้าหู้ tâwhûu/ N bean cake, bean curd. [f. Chin.]

เติ่ง in ค้างเติ่ง kháaŋtə̀ŋ/* V colloq. 1. to be left unfinished, to be held up (until another time). 2. to be left in the lurch.

เติบ tə̀əb/ V 1. to grow, grow big. sV 2. lavishly, plentifully.

o ใช้เติบ chájtə̀əb/ to use lavishly, extravagantly.

เติบโต tə̀əbtoo/ V to grow, grow up, develop, mature. ความ-- growth, development.

o ความเจริญเติบโต khwaamcarəən/tə̀əbtoo/ N the progress and growth, the development.

เติบใหญ่ tə̀əb/jàj/ V 1. to grow up. 2. to be grown-up.

มือเติบ myytə̀əb/ V 1. to have a lavish hand. sV 2. with a lavish hand, lavishly, liberally.

เติม təəm/ V to add on, add to, fill.

o เติมคำในช่องว่าง təəm/kham/-najchɔ̂ŋwâaŋ/ fill in the blank space (as on an application).

เติมต่อ təəm/tɔ̀ɔ/ V to supplement, add.

เพิ่มเติม phə̂əmtəəm/ V 1. to add, add to. 2. to be added, added on to.

เตี้ย tîa/ V to be short, low (in height). →Dist. สั้น "short (in length)." →Ant. สูง.

เตียง (เตียง) tiaŋ/ (tiaŋ/) N bedstead; bed, cot.

เตียงนอน (เตียง) tiaŋnɔɔn/ (tiaŋ/) N bed.

เตียน ๑ tian/ V to be clean (tidy), cleared.

เตียน ๒ in ติเตียน tì?tian/ V to criticize, reprove,

express disapproval of.

เตี๊ยม. See ต้วมเตี๊ยม.

เตือน tyan′ V to warn, remind, advise, hint to.

ตักเตือน tàgtyan′ V to advise, caution, admonish.

แต่ ๑ tɛ̀ɛ′, tɛ̀ɛɔ, tɛɔ, taɔ Cj 1. but. Pp 2. only, nothing but. AA 3. only.

o เคยแต่อ่านเรื่องการเที่ยวที่นั่น แต่ไม่เคยไป khəəjtɛ̀ʔàanrɣ̂aŋ′-kaanthîaw′thîinân′→ tɛ̀ɛɔ mâjkhəəj′paj′↓ I have only read about going there, but I've never gone.

ตามแต่, ก็-- (1) taam′tɛ̀ɛɔ, kɔ̂taam′tɛ̀ɛɔ; (2) taam′tɛ̀ɛ′↓, kɔ̂taam′tɛ̀ɛ′↓ 1. as, according to what, in accordance with what, whatever; it depends on what. 2. It's up to (him)! Let him! Let it go! Never mind! That depends! →See cross reference.

แต่(ถึง)กระนั้น tɛ̀ɛkranán′, tɛ̀ɛthɣ̌ŋ′kranán′ but nevertheless, but even so.

แต่ทว่า tɛ̀ɛthawâa′ but.

แต่ประการใด tɛ̀ɛprakaan′daj′ whatsoever, at all, of any kind, in any way.

แต่ผู้เดียว tɛ̀ɛphûudiaw′ all alone, all by oneself, solely.

แต่เพียง tɛ̀ɛphiaŋ′ nothing but, only, just.

แต่ลำพัง tɛ̀ɛlamphaŋ′ alone, by oneself.

แต่ว่า tɛ̀ɛwâa′ but.

แต่อย่างใด tɛ̀ɛjàaŋdaj′ in any way whatsoever, of any kind whatsoever, at all.

เพียงแต่ phiaŋtɛɔ only, merely.

มัวแต่ muatɛɔ to be busy with, to spend too much time (doing).

แม้แต่ mɛ́ɛtɛ̀ɛɔ, mɛ́ɛtɛɔ even, even including.

o ไม่...แม้แต่น้อย mâjɔ...mɛ́ɛtɛ̀ɛnɔ́ɔj′ not even a little bit, not in the least. →See น้อย.

ล้วนแต่ lúan′tɛɔ nothing but, all, completely.

แล้วแต่ lɛ́ɛw′tɛ̀ɛɔ (the choice) depends on, is up to, depends on whether.

o แล้วแต่คุณ lɛ́ɛw′tɛ̀ɛkhun′↓ It's up to you!

o แล้วแต่ซี่ lɛ́ɛwtɛ̀ɛ′si↓ It's up to (him)(I don't care).

ว่าแต่ wâa′tɛ̀ɛɔ V 1. to speak about (a person, matter previously mentioned). 2. to criticize (someone).

เว้นแต่,ยก-- wén′tɛ̀ɛɔ, jógwén′tɛ̀ɛɔ except,

excepting.

เสียแต่ sĭa′tɛɔ but, only (introducing an adverse reservation, restriction).

หากแต่ hàag′tɛɔ but, only.

แต่ ๒ tɛ̀ɛ′, tɛɔ, taɔ Pp from, since.

จำเดิมแต่ camdəəm′tɛ̀ɛɔ since, since the time (of).

ตั้งแต่ tâŋtɛ̀ɛɔ from (such and such a time or starting point), since.

แต่ก่อน tɛkɔ̀ɔn′, takɔ̀ɔn′ in the past, in former times, previously.

แต่เช้า tɛcháaw′ early in the morning.

แต่เดิม tɛ̀ɛdəəm′ from the beginning, from the first, formerly.

แต่ต้น tɛ̀ɛtôn′ from the beginning.

แต่นั้นมา tɛ̀ɛnán′maa′ from then on.

แต่แรก tɛ̀ɛrɛ̂ɛg′ at first, from the beginning.

แต่วัน tɛwan′ early, before the usual time, before the appointed time.

แต่วัน ๆ tɛwan′wan′ ahead of time, before the appointed time. →Also วัน ๆ.

นับแต่ náb′tɛ̀ɛɔ starting from, since.

มาแต่ maatɛ̀ɛɔ from, since.

แต่ ๓ in แต่ละ tɛlaɔ, talaɔ* each and every (one of), every single (followed by a clf.).

o แต่ละท่าน tɛlathân′ each and every one of you, each and every one of them.

o แต่ละประเทศ tɛlaprathêed′ every single country.

o แต่ละปี tɛlapii′ (in) each year.

o ไม่เว้นแต่ละวัน mâjwén′tɛlawan′ idiom. every single day, without missing a single day, day in and day out.

แตก tɛ̀ɛg′ V 1. to break (of itself), burst, split. 2. to be broken into pieces, smashed, shattered. 3. to have a break, cut, split (in the skin). →Dist. หัก.

o ปากแตก pàagtɛ̀ɛg′ V to have a cut on the lip, a split lip.

ขบไม่แตก khòb′mâjtɛ̀ɛg′ can't solve (it); can't be solved, unsolvable. Cf. Eng. "it can't be cracked."

ใจแตก cajtɛ̀ɛg′ V 1. to be self-indulgent and unrestrained, spoiled. 2. to develop a passion for (e.g. gambling).

แตกกิ่ง tɛ̀ɛg′kìŋ′ V to branch out.

แตกแขนง tὲɛg/khanɛ̌ɛŋ/ V to branch out.

แตกฉาน tὲɛgchǎan/ V 1. to scatter, disperse.
2. to be scattered, dispersed, fragmented.
sV 3. thoroughly, explicitly, in every detail.

แตกดับ tὲɛg/dàb/ V 1. to be ruined. 2. to perish.

แตกต่าง tὲɛgtàaŋ/ V to differ, be different.
ความ-- difference.

แตกใบ tὲɛg/baj/ V (a plant) to put forth leaf-
buds, leaves.

แตกปลี tὲɛg/plii/ V (a plant) to put forth its
spadix or flower cluster, (the panicle) to break
through its spathe.

แตกฟอง tὲɛg/fɔɔŋ/ V to foam, become foamy,
break into foam.

o น้ำลายแตกฟอง námlaaj/-tὲɛg/fɔɔŋ/ idiom.,
colloq. to spout forth, talk volubly. →Also
พูดจน--.

แตกแยก(กัน) tὲɛgjὲɛg/(kan/) V 1. to break up
and separate (as a group of friends), to split up.
2. to break off a friendship. 3. to be split off,
separated. การ-- separation, dissociation;
(act of) breaking off a friendship.

แตกร้าว tὲɛgráaw/ V 1. to be cracked. 2. to
split up, be divided, disunited.

แตกสตางค์ tὲɛg/sataŋ/ V to make small change.

o ขอแตกสตางค์ khɔ̌ɔtὲɛg/sataŋ/ to ask for (some)
change.

แตกสลาย tὲɛg/salǎaj/ V to go to pieces, be
ruined.

แตกหัก tὲɛg/hàg/ V 1. to be broken. 2. to be
critical, decisive, resolute. sV 3. decisively.

o ขั้นแตกหัก khân/-tὲɛg/hàg/ the stage when the
final issue is decided.

ถังแตก thǎŋtὲɛg/ V slang to be broke (have no
money).

ทำ(...)แตก tham/(...)tὲɛg/ to break, smash
(something).

ยางแตก jaaŋtὲɛg/ V to have a flat (tire), a blow-
out.

หัวแตก hǔatὲɛg/ V to have a cut on the head (on
the scalp).

แตง tɛɛŋ/ N class term for cucumbers and melons.
[f. Chin.]

แตงกวา (ใบ,ลูก,ผล) tɛɛŋkwaa/ (baj/,lûug/,

phǒn/) N cucumber.

แตงโม (ใบ,ลูก,ผล) tɛɛŋmoo/ (baj/,lûug/,phǒn/)
watermelon.

แต่ง tὲŋ/* V 1. to fix up, beautify. 2. to ornament,
decorate, adorn. 3. to compose (e.g. verse).
การ-- writing, composition. คน-- composer,
author, writer.

ตกแต่ง tògtὲŋ/ V to decorate, beautify. NOTE.
ตกแต่ง is sometimes confused with ตบแต่ง "to
marry off, arrange a marriage." See below.

ตบแต่ง tòbtὲŋ/ V 1. to decorate, embellish. 2.
to marry off, arrange a marriage.

แต่งกาย tὲŋkaaj/ V eleg. to dress. การ--
dress (i.e. mode of dress); the wearing of apparel.
เครื่อง-- clothes, clothing.

แต่งงาน tὲŋŋaan/ V 1. to get married, be married.
2. to marry off. การ-- marrying, marriage.

o แต่งงานกับ tὲŋŋaan/kaɔ to marry, get married
to.

แต่งตั้ง tὲŋtâŋ/ V 1. to set (up). 2. to appoint,
confer a title. การ-- appointing, appointment.

o ได้รับแต่งตั้ง dâjráb/tὲŋtâŋ/ to be appointed.

แต่งตัว tὲŋtua/ V to dress, get dressed, be dressed.
เครื่อง-- clothing, wearing apparel.

แต่งประโยค tὲŋ/prajòog/ V to compose sentences.

แต่งเพลง tὲŋphleeŋ/ V to write a song. นัก--
song writer.

แต่งเมีย tὲŋmia/ V colloq. to take a wife.

แต่งหน้า tὲŋnâa/ V to make up (the face).

ปรุงแต่ง pruŋ/tὲŋ/ V 1. to prepare, combine, compound, concoct. 2. to touch up, dress up, decorate.

แตด tὲɛd/ N com., vulg. clitoris.

แตน (ตัว) tɛɛn/ (tua/) N hornet. Usually ตัว--.

แต้ม tὲɛm/ V 1. to daub, smear, anoint. N 2. (a)
daub, smear. C 3. point, score (in game or
contest).

จนแต้ม contὲɛm/ V to be checked, blocked, cornered, brought to an impasse.

เดินแต้ม dəəntὲɛm/ colloq. to maneuver, make
a tactical move (in politics, chess).

ห้าแต้ม hâatὲɛm/ V 1. idiom. to commit a faux
pas, make a foolish or embarrassing mistake.
N 2. faux pas, foolish or embarrassing mistake.

แตร (อัน) trɛɛ/ (ʔan/) N horn, trumpet, bugle.

แตรวง (วง) trɛɛwoŋ/ (woŋ/) N brass band.

แตะ tɛ̀ʔ/ V to touch.

  แตะต้อง tɛ̀ʔtɔ̂ŋ/ V to touch (with the hand), to handle.

  รองเท้าแตะ (คู่, ข้าง) rɔɔŋtháawtɛ̀ʔ/ (khûu/, khâaŋ/) N slippers. ▪

โต too/ V to be big, large, mature. →Syn. ใหญ่. →Ant. เล็ก, น้อย.

  คุยโต khujtoo/ V colloq. to boast, talk big.

  เติบโต tə̀əbtoo/ V to grow, grow up, develop, mature. →Syn. เติบใหญ่.

  โตขึ้น too/khŷn/ V to grow up, get big, get bigger.

  โตเท่า too/thâwⵤ to be as big as.

  หน้าใหญ่ใจโต nâajàj/cajtoo/ V to be lavish (in entertaining friends).

  ใหญ่โต jàjtoo/ V 1. to be big, large, immense, enormous, huge. 2. to be high (in position), great, important. sV 3. in a big way, on a large scale, immensely. ความ-- immensity, hugeness, greatness.

  o เป็นใหญ่เป็นโต penjàj/pentoo/ colloq. 1. to be a big shot; to be important, of high position. 2. to have supremacy.

โต้ ๑ tôo/ V 1. to counter. sV 2. back, back and forth.

  ตีโต้ tii/tôo/ V 1. to retaliate, counterattack. 2. to hit back and forth (as in playing tennis).

  โต้ตอบ(กัน) tôotɔ̀ɔb/(kan/) V 1. to answer back and forth, perform some action back and forth (of conversing, exchanging letters, engaging in musical or poetic dialogue, retaliating back and forth, etc.). sV 2. back and forth.

  โต้เถียง tôothǐaŋ/ V 1. to argue, dispute, quarrel. 2. to contest (a point).

  โต้แย้ง tôojéɛŋ/ V 1. to argue, dispute. 2. to contradict.

  o ข้อโต้แย้ง (ข้อ) khɔ̂ɔ/tôojéɛŋ/ (khɔ̂ɔ/) N point of dispute, argument.

  โต้รุ่ง tôo/rûŋ/ 1. colloq. to stay up all night. 2. until dawn.

  โต้วาที tôo/waathii/ V 1. debate. N 2. short for การ-- debate.

โต้ ๒in มีดโต้ (เล่ม) mîidtôo/ (lêm/) N hacking knife.

โตกิโอ tookìʔoo/ pN Tokyo. [prob. f. Eng.] →See โตเกียว.

โตเกียว tookiaw/ pN Tokyo. [prob. f. Japanese] →See โตกิโอ.

โต๊ะ (ตัว) tóʔ/ (tua/) N table, desk. [f. Chin.]

  เดินโต๊ะ dəəntóʔ/ V to serve, wait on a table. คน-- waiter, waitress.

  โต๊ะเขียนหนังสือ (ตัว) tóʔ/khǐannaŋšyy/ (tua/) N writing table, desk.

  โต๊ะเครื่องแป้ง (ตัว) tóʔ/khrŷaŋpɛ̂ɛŋ/ (tua/) N dressing table, vanity (table), dresser (with mirror).

  ผ้าปูโต๊ะ (ผืน) phâapuutóʔ/ (phʉ̌yn/) N tablecloth, lunch cloth.

  ร่วมโต๊ะ rûamtóʔ/ V 1. to join someone at the table. 2. to eat together.

ใต้ tâaj/* sV com. 1. under, underneath, below. 2. south, southern, to the south, to the south of. →Opp. เหนือ. →Syn. 2. ทักษิณ lit., eleg. →The literary and the common terms for the eight chief points of the compass are listed under ทิศ.

  ขั้วใต้ khûatâaj/ N 1. south pole (of a magnet). 2. geog. the South Pole.

  ขีดเส้นใต้ khìid/sêntâaj/ to underline, underscore.

  ตะวันตกเฉียงใต้ tawantòg/chǐaŋtâaj/ the southwest.

  ตะวันออกเฉียงใต้ tawanʔɔ̀ɔg/chǐaŋtâaj/ the southeast.

  ใต้ดิน tâajdin/ underground, subterranean.

  o พวกใต้ดิน phûagtâajdin/ N underground organization.

  ใต้ถุน tâajthǔn/ N 1. the space (open or closed) under aThai house. 2. basement, cellar.

  ใต้เท้า tâajtháaw/ P eleg. defer. sp. to sup. you; your excellency.

  ใต้ฝ่าพระบาท tâajfàa/phrábàad/ P roy. you (sp. to high-ranking royalty).

  ใต้ลม tâajlom/ downwind, leeward, on the leeward side. →Ant. เหนือลม.

  ทิศใต้ thídtâaj/ N south.

  ปักษ์ใต้ pàgtâaj/ N the south, the southern part (of the country).

  ภาคใต้ phâagtâaj/ N the south, the southern part (of the country).

ภายใต้ phaajtâaj/ under underneath.

ใต้ฝุ่น tâajfùn/* N typhoon. [f. Chin., perhaps via Eng.]

ไต ๑ (ไต,ข้าง) taj/ (taj/,khâaŋ/) N 1. kidney. 2. wen.

ไต ๒ taj/ N Tai, used in names of northern Tai groups. →Comp. ไทย.

ไต่ tàj/ V 1. to crawl, creep (of insects, small creatures). 2. to climb (trees, mountains). →Dist. 1. คลาน,เลื้อย.

ไต่คู้,ไม้-- (อัน) tàjkhúu/, májtàjkhúu/ (ʔan/) N the symbol " in the Thai writing system.

ไต่เดียะ tàj/dìa?/ V to climb quickly, scamper up.

ไต่ถาม tàjthǎam/ V to inquire, make inquiries.

ไต่สวน tàjsǔan/ V to inquire into, investigate.

ไต้ (ดวง) tâaj/* (duaŋ/) N torch.

ขี้ไต้ khîitâaj/ N punk, a composition of resin and rotten wood used as tinder.

เข้าไต้เข้าไฟ khâwtâaj/khâwfaj/ V elab. colloq. to be getting dark, be twilight.

ผีพุ่งไต้ (ดวง) phǐiphûŋtâaj/ (duaŋ/) N shooting star.

ไตร traj/ Nm eleg. three. →Chiefly in compounds. →Variant spelling of ตรัย.

ไตร่ in ไตร่ตรอง tràjtrɔɔŋ/ V eleg. to consider, think (it) over, think carefully. →Also ตริตรอง, ตรึกตรอง.

ไต้หวัน tâjwǎn/ pN Taiwan (formerly called Formosa). [f. Chin.]

ถ

ถ thɔɔ/ HIGH consonant. Pronounced th initially, d finally. The sound th as an initial high consonant is also very rarely spelled with ฐ.

ถก ๑ thòg/ V to discuss.

ถกเถียง thògthǐaŋ/ V to argue, discuss.

ถก ๒ thòg/ V to roll up (sleeves), hike up, pull up (skirt, trousers). →Syn. ถลก.

ถกเขมร thòg/khaměen/ V to hike one's clothing up above the knee.

ถนน (สาย) thanǒn/ (sǎaj/) N street, road. →Syn.

See ทาง.

คนเดินถนน (คน) khondəən/thanǒn/ (khon/) N pedestrians.

ถนนหนทาง (สาย) thanǒn/hǒnthaaŋ/ (sǎaj/) N elab. colloq. roads or streets in general.

ถนนหลวง (สาย) thanǒn/lǔaŋ/ (sǎaj/) N 1. public road, public highway. pN 2. Luang Road, a street in Bangkok.

ท้องถนน thɔɔŋ/thanǒn/ N the road area, the middle of the road, the road proper (i.e. exclusive of shoulders, edges).

ปากถนน (แห่ง) pàag/thanǒn/ (hèŋ/) N entrance to a road, street.

มุมถนน (แห่ง,มุม) mum/thanǒn/ (hèŋ/, mum/) N street corner.

ริมถนน rim/thanǒn/ N roadside.

หมากลางถนน (ตัว) mǎa/klaaŋthanǒn/ (tua/) 1. stray dog. 2. slang derelict (person).

หัวถนน (แห่ง) hǔathanǒn/ (hèŋ/) N the beginning of a street.

ถนอม thanɔɔm/ V to cherish, conserve, use sparingly.

ทะนุถนอม thanú?/thanɔɔm/ V 1. elab. to care for, to cherish. 2. to treat with affection or great care.

ถนัด thanàd/ V 1. to be handy, skillful, dexterous, adroit, good at. 2. to be easy, convenient, natural (as opposed to awkward, clumsy). 3. to be clear, unobstructed. sV 4. clearly, considerably, quite, to a large extent.

ตามถนัด taam/thanàd/ according to one's ability.

ถนัดขวา thanàd/khwǎa/ V to be righthanded.

ถนัดซ้าย thanàd/sáaj/ V to be lefthanded.

ผิดถนัด phìd/thanàd/ V to be all wrong, way off, wide of the mark.

เห็นถนัด hěn/thanàd/ V to see clearly.

ใหญ่ถนัด jàj/thanàd/ V to be very big, quite large.

อย่างถนัดถนี่ jàaŋthanàd/thanìi/ elab. colloq. evidently, obviously, clearly, distinctly.

ถม thǒm/ V 1. to fill up, fill in. N 2. the niello process. เครื่อง-- niello ware.

ถมไป thǒm/paj, thǒmpaj/ to be abundant, plenty, lots.

o มีถมไป miithǒm/paj there is plenty, there is a lot.

ทับถม tháðthǒm′ V 1. to pile up. 2. i d i o m. to criticize, defame.

ถม thòm′ V to spit, spit out. →S y n. ถุย .

ถมน้ำลาย thòm′námlaaj′ V to spit.

ถมึงทึง tham:ŋ′thɯŋ′ V 1. to look sullen, sulky, very cross, forbidding. sV 2. sulkily, crossly.

ถลก thalòg′ V 1. to skin, strip off. 2. to roll up (sleeves), hike up, pull up (skirt, trousers). →S y n. 2. ถก .

ถลกหนัง thalòg′nǎŋ′ V to skin (e.g. an animal).

ถลน thalǒn′ V (the eyes) to protrude, bulge, pop.

ถล่ม thalòm′ V to collapse, cave in, tumble down.

ถลอก thalɔ̀ɔg′ V 1. to be scraped, have an abrasion. 2. to be scraped off, scratched off.

ถลัน thalǎn′ V to dash forward, rush in, rush up to.

ถลา thalǎa′ V 1. to slip and reel, to reel, stagger (as under a heavy blow, or from a strong push). 2. to skid and move sideways (as a car out of control). 3. to dash forward.

ถลำ thalǎm′ V 1. to fall, stagger forward head down. 2. to make a slip, a false step, a wrong move. 3. to trespass.

ถลึง thalɯ̌ŋ′ V to stare (sternly). Chiefly in the combination shown below.

ถลึงตา thalɯ̌ŋ′taa′ V to stare (someone) down, give a stern look (showing disapproval).

ถลุง thalǔŋ′ V 1. to smelt. 2. to hit hard (in boxing). 3. c o l l o q. to spend (money) right and left, use (money) up lavishly.

ถ่วง thùaŋ′ V 1. to hang down by weight, be weighted down. 2. to weight down. 3. to cause to sink. 4. to retard, slow down, act as a drag upon. ความ-- gravity, gravitation.

ถ่วงเวลา thùaŋweelaa′ V 1. to stall for time. 2. to waste time.

ถ้วน thûan′ V to be correct, complete (exact in amount), in a round number, even.

ครบถ้วน khróbthûan′ V to be complete, full, entire, exact in amount.

ถ้วนถี่, ถี่ถ้วน thûanthìi′, thìithûan′ V 1. to be accurate, thorough, careful, scrupulous. 2. c o l l o q. to be stingy, penny-pinching, tight.

นับไม่ถ้วน náb′mâjthûan′ countless, innumerable.

ถ้วย (ใบ) thûaj′ (baj′) N 1. cup, small bowl. C

2. clf. for cups as measures of volume.

o กาแฟสองถ้วย kaafɛɛ′sɔ̌ɔŋthûaj′ two cups of coffee.

o ถ้วยสองใบ thûaj′sɔ̌ɔŋbaj′ two cups (as containers).

จานรองถ้วย (ใบ) caan′rɔɔŋthûaj′ (baj′) N saucer.

ถ้วยแก้ว (ใบ) thûajkɛ̂ɛw′ (baj′) N glass (for drinking), tumbler.

ถ้วยชาม (ใบ, ชุด) thûajchaam′ (baj′, chúd′) N the dishes, dishware.

ถ้วยน้ำชา (ใบ) thûajnámchaa′ (baj′) N teacup.

ถวาย thawǎaj′ V r o y., s a c. to give, offer, present.

ถวายบังคม thawǎaj′baŋkhom′ V r o y. to salute (the king). →S y n. ไหว้ c o m.

ถวายพระพร thawǎaj′phráphɔɔn′ V 1. r o y. to wish well, offer a blessing. 2. the opening word of an address used by a priest when speaking to royalty. 3. yes.

ถวายพระเพลิง thawǎaj′phráphləəŋ′ V r o y. to cremate (in a royal funeral).

น้อมเกล้าฯถวาย nɔ́ɔmklâaw′thawǎaj′ V r o y. to give, offer, present (of big things) (to the king).

ถ่อ (อัน) thɔ̀ɔ′ (ʔan′) N 1. pole (for punting a boat). V 2. to pole (a boat). 3. c o l l o q. to make a special effort (e.g. in order to take a trip, go somewhere).

ถอง thɔ̌ɔŋ′ V to poke, nudge, jab with the elbow.

ถ่อง in ถ่องแท้ thɔ̀ŋthɛ́ɛ′* sV thoroughly, carefully, distinctly, clearly.

ถอด thɔ̀ɔd′ V 1. to remove, take off (as an article of clothing). 2. to dismantle, disassemble. 3. to dismiss, fire (from a position or rank).

ถอดกลอน thɔ̀ɔdklɔɔn′ V to unbolt, unlatch (a door, window).

ถอดเขี้ยวถอดงา thɔ̀ɔdkhîaw′thɔ̀ɔdŋaa′ i d i o m. (a person) to become gentle, subdued, peaceful, no longer vicious or cross: "to remove one's fangs and tusks."

ถอดด้าม in ใหม่ถอดด้าม màj′thɔ̀ɔddâam′ V i d i o m. to be brand-new.

ถอดถอน thɔ̀ɔdthɔ̌ɔn′ V to remove, dismiss (from a position).

ถอดแบบ thɔ̀ɔdbɛ̀ɛb′ V 1. to reproduce, duplicate,

copy. 2. to resemble in every minute detail. 3. to pattern after.

ถอดเป็นภาษา . . . thɔ̀ɔd/penphaasǎaɔ . . . to translate into (such and such) language.

ถอด (. . .) เสีย thɔ̀ɔd/(. . .)sía to take (something) off.

ถอด (. . .) ออก thɔ̀ɔd/(. . .)?ɔ̀ɔg/ 1. to take (something) off, remove (something). 2. to remove, dismiss, relieve (from post or duty).

ถอน ๑ thɔ̌ɔn/ V 1. to pull up (e.g. a plant). 2. to pull out, extract (e.g. tooth, nail). 3. to withdraw, retract, revoke.

ถอดถอน thɔ̀ɔdthɔ̌ɔn/ V to remove, dismiss (from a position).

ถอนคันน้ำมัน thɔ̌ɔn/khannámman/ to release the accelerator (of a car).

ถอนใจ thɔ̌ɔncaj/ V to sigh, heave a sigh.

ถอนตัว thɔ̌ɔntua/ V to withdraw (from), pull (oneself) out (of).

ถอนใบอนุญาต thɔ̌ɔn/-baj/?ànújàad/ V to revoke a license.

ถอนฟ้อง thɔ̌ɔnfɔ́ɔŋ/ V to withdraw a (legal) charge, withdraw (one's case).

ถอนฟัน thɔ̌ɔnfan/ V to pull a tooth.

ถอนรากถอนโคน thɔ̌ɔnrâag/thɔ̌ɔnkhoon/ V 1. to uproot, pull out by the roots. 2. to destroy, extirpate.

ถอนสมอ thɔ̌ɔn/samɔ̌ɔ/ V to lift anchor.

ถอนสายบัว thɔ̌ɔn/sǎajbua/ V colloq., idiom. to curtsy.

เพิกถอน phə̀əgthɔ̌ɔn/ V to revoke, annul, retract, withdraw, cancel.

รื้อถอน rýythɔ̌ɔn/ V to tear out (an installation), tear down (a house, building).

ถอน ๒ thɔ̌ɔn/ AA getting, beginning to get. →Syn. ชัก ๒.

o ถอนฉุน thɔ̌ɔnchǔn/ (he's) beginning to get angry, getting provoked.

o ชักถอนฉุน chágthɔ̌ɔn/chǔn/ idem.

ถ่อม thɔ̀m/* V 1. to humble, abase (oneself). 2. to be humble.

ถ่อมตัว thɔ̀mtua/ V 1. to humble, abase oneself. 2. to be humble, unassuming, unpretentious, modest. →Ant. ถือตัว.

ถอย thɔ̌j/* V 1. to retreat, draw back. 2. to back, back up (e.g. a car). การ- - retreat. →Dist. ท้อ.

ถอยกำลัง thɔ̌j/kamlaŋ/ to be weakened.

ถอยหลัง thɔ̌jlǎŋ/ V 1. to step back, back up. sV 2. backward, backwards, back.

ท้อถอย thɔ́ɔthɔ̌j/ V to lose courage, feel like withdrawing, be discouraged. ความ- - discouragement.

ล่าถอย lâa/thɔ̌j/ V to withdraw, draw back.

ถ่อย thɔ̀j/* V to be low, base, bad, wicked, vile. คน- - low person; (persons who are) riffraff, trash, scum.

อ้ายถ่อย, ไอ้ถ่อย ?âjthɔ̀j/↓ derog. epithet. (You) riffraff!

ถ้อย thɔ́j/* N eleg. word(s). →Chiefly in combinations. →Syn. คำ com. NOTE. Often coupled with คำ as in the 1st and 3rd entries, and sometimes coupled with ความ, as in the 2nd and 6th entries.

ชัดถ้อยชัดคำ chádthɔ́j/chádkham/ clearly, distinctly, articulately.

ถ้อยความ thɔ́jkhwaam/ N lawsuit. →See also หมอถ้อยหมอความ below.

ถ้อยคำ thɔ́jkham/ N words, wording, expressions.

ถ้อยแถลง (ฉะบับ , ครั้ง) thɔ́j/thalɛ̌ɛŋ/ (chabàb/, khráŋ/) N (official) statement, communiqué.

ถ้อยทีถ้อยอาศัยกัน thɔ́j/thii/-thɔ́j/?aasǎj/-kan V 1. to be mutually dependent on one another, be interdependent. 2. to reciprocate.

หมอถ้อยหมอความ (คน) mɔ̌ɔthɔ́j/mɔ̌ɔkhwaam/ (khon/) N elab. colloq. lawyer. →Also หมอความ colloq.

ถัก thàg/ V to knit, braid, plait, crochet.

ผมถักเปีย phǒm/thàgpia/ N pigtail hairdo.

เย็บปักถักร้อย jébpàg/thàgrɔ́ɔj/ V 1. to do needlework. N 2. needlework.

ถัง ๑ (ใบ) thǎŋ/ (baj/) N 1. bucket, pail, tub, barrel, tank. C 2. unit of capacity equivalent to 20 liters; (loosely) a bucketful, barrelful, etc.

ตัวถัง (ตัว) tuathǎŋ/ (tua/) N chassis, body (of car, bicycle, etc.).

ถังขยะ (ใบ) thǎŋkhajà?/ (baj/) N garbage can, garbage pail.

ถังแตก thăŋtὲɛg′ V slang to be broke.

ถังน้ำมัน (ถัง) thăŋnámman′ (thăŋ′) N fuel tank, gasoline tank. →Also ถังบรรจุน้ำมัน eleg.

ถังผง (ใบ) thăŋphŏŋ′ (baj′) N trash can (for litter); wastepaper basket, can.

รถถัง (คัน) ródthăŋ′ (khan′) N milit. tank.

ถัง ๒ in ขี้ถัง khîithăŋ′ V to be all that is bad (of people).

ถัด thàd′ V 1. to scoot along on the bottom (the buttocks). 2. to be next to, next after. sV 3. next, next to.

ถัดจากนั้น thàd′càagnán′ next to that.

ถัดไป thàdpaj′ next (in a series).

ถัน thăn′ N eleg. breast. →Syn. นม com.

ถัว thŭa′ V colloq. to find the average. →Syn. เฉลี่ย eleg.

ถั่ว (เม็ด, ฝัก) thùa′ (méd′, fàg′) N 1. bean, pea (méd′ for the seed; fàg′ for the pod). V 2. colloq. to be of poor quality. ต้น-- (ต้น) the bean plant; the pea plant.

ตาถั่ว taathùa′ V colloq. to be unable to see or find things even though one has good eyes.

ถั่วงอก (ต้น) thùaŋɔ̆ɔg′ (tôn′) N bean sprouts.

ถั่วฝักยาว (ฝัก) thùafàgjaaw′ (fàg′) N long-podded cowpea. ต้น-- (ต้น) long-podded cowpea plant.

ถั่วยี่สง (เม็ด) thùajîisŏŋ′ (méd′) N eleg., lit. peanut. ต้น-- (ต้น) the peanut plant. →See also ถั่วลิสง, a colloquial variant.

ถั่วลันเตา (ฝัก) thùalantaw′ (fàg′) N sugar pea, edible podded pea. ต้น-- (ต้น) the sugar pea plant.

ถั่วลิสง (เม็ด) thùalisŏŋ′ (méd′) N colloq. peanut. →Var.of ถั่วยี่สง eleg., lit.

ถั่วเหลือง (เม็ด, ฝัก) thùalўaŋ′ (méd′, fàg′) N soybean. ต้น-- (ต้น) the soybean plant.

ฝักถั่ว (ฝัก) fàgthùa′ (fàg′) N bean pod.

ถา thăa′ V 1. to swoop, move rapidly and with force. 2. to lunge.

ถาขึ้นจาก thăa′khŷncàagɔ (airplane) to take off.

ถ้า thâa′ Cj if. →Syn. หาก.

ถ้ากระนั้น thâakranán′ if so, in such a case.

ถ้าจะ thâacaɔ AA might, (it) could be, maybe.

o ถ้าจะไม่มา thâa′camâjmaa⌄ (I, he, etc.) might not come. Maybe (I, he, etc.) won't come.

o ถ้าจะว่าไป thâacawâa′paj′ one might say, one could say, so to speak, as a matter of fact.

ถ้าฉวย thâachŭaj′ Cj if, if by chance.

ถ้าแม้ thâamɛ́ɛ′ but if, if.

ถ้าหาก (ว่า) thâahàag′(wâaɔ) if, supposing that, in the event that.

ถ้าอย่างนั้น thâajàaŋnán′ in that case, in that event, if that is so, if that is the case.

ถาก thàag′ V to cut (with diagonal or almost horizontal motion), chip off lengthwise (as with an axe).

ถากถาง thàagthăaŋ′ V 1. colloq. to rub it in. 2. to criticize sarcastically, satirize.

ถาง thăaŋ′ V to clear (a forest), to cut away (grass, weeds).

แผ้วถาง phɛ̂w′thăaŋ V to clear the way (by removing weeds, obstacles).

หักร้างถางพง hàgráaŋ′thăaŋphoŋ′ V elab. colloq. 1. to clear land. 2. to clear a path (e.g. through the jungle).

ถ่าง thàaŋ′ V to part, separate, spread apart.

ถ่างตา thàaŋtaa′ V to prop one's eyelids open, force one's eyes to stay open (as when sleepy).

ถาด (ใบ) thàad′ (baj′) N tray.

ถ่าน (ท่อน, ลำ, ก้อน) thàan′ (thɔ̂ɔn′, lam′, kɔ̂ɔn′) N charcoal (thɔ̂ɔn′, lam′ for charcoal in stick form; kɔ̂ɔn′ for a chunk).

ถ่านไฟ (ก้อน) thàanfaj′ (kɔ̂ɔn′) N ember.

o ถ่านไฟเก่า thàanfajkàw′ N colloq. former lover, old flame.

ถ่านไฟฉาย (ท่อน, ก้อน) thàan′fajchăaj′ (thɔ̂ɔn′, kɔ̂ɔn′) N dry cell, battery (for flashlight). →Comp. แบตเตอรี่.

ถ่านไม้ (ก้อน) thàanmáaj′ (kɔ̂ɔn′) N charcoal obtained from wood.

ถ่านหิน (ก้อน) thàanhĭn′ (kɔ̂ɔn′) N coal.

เอาถ่าน ʔawthàan′ colloq. to be industrious.

ถาม thăam′ V 1. to ask (a question). 2. to ask, inquire of (a person). →Dist. ซัก.

กระทู้ถาม (ข้อ, เรื่อง, กระทู้) krathúu′thăam′ (khɔ̂ɔ′, rŷaŋ′, khathúu′) N question posed in a legislative body (parliamentary practice).

คำถาม (ข้อ, คำถาม) khamthăam′ (khɔ̂ɔ′, khamɔ

thǎam´) N question.

o เครื่องหมายคำถาม (อัน) khrɯ̂aŋmǎaj´khamɔ thǎam´ (ʔan´) the question mark.

ซักถาม ságthǎam´ V 1. to interrogate, question. cross-examine. 2. to inquire into. ข้อ-- a question (esp. in an official interrogation).

ไต่ถาม tàjthǎam´ V to inquire, make inquiries.

ถามไถ่ thǎamthàj´ V colloq. to inquire, ask, question.

ทูลถาม thuunthǎam´ V roy. to ask, inquire.

เรียนถาม rianthǎam´ V eleg.def. to ask, inquire.

สอบถาม sɔ̀ɔbthǎam´ V 1. to inquire into. 2. to question (somebody)(as in an investigation).

สืบถาม sɯ̌ybthǎam´ V to inquire into, make inquiries.

ถ่าย ๑ thàaj´ V 1. to let flow, evacuate, drain off. 2. to excrete, secrete. 3. to transfer (e.g. goods from one conveyance to another).

ถ่ายทอด thàajthɔ̂ɔd´ V 1. to relay. 2. to transmit, hand down (e.g. to the next generation).

ถ่ายเท thàajthee´ V 1. to provide a change of air or water, provide a through current (e.g. in order to keep air or water fresh). 2. to change a situation (by some trick or stratagem in order to evade unpleasantness).

ถ่ายแบบ thàajbɛ̀ɛb´ V to copy, make a copy (of).

ถ่ายปัสสาวะ thàajpàdsǎawá?´ V eleg. to pass urine, urinate. →Syn. เยี่ยว com.,vulg.

ถ่ายภาพ thàajphâab´ V eleg. to take pictures, to photograph. →Syn. ถ่ายรูป com.

ถ่ายภาพยนตร์ thàaj´phâabphajon´ V eleg. to take moving pictures. →Syn. ถ่ายหนัง com.

ถ่ายรูป thàajrûub´ V com. to take pictures, to photograph. →Syn. ถ่ายภาพ eleg.

o กล้องถ่ายรูป (กล้อง,อัน) klɔ̂ŋ´thàajrûub´ (klɔ̂ŋ´,ʔan´) N com. camera.

o ช่างถ่ายรูป (คน) châaŋthàajrûub´ (khon´) N com. photographer. →Syn. ช่างภาพ eleg.

ถ่ายเลือด thàajlɯ̂ad´ V to transfuse blood, have a blood transfusion. การ-- blood transfusion.

ถ่ายวิชา thàaj´wíchaa´ V to teach, to pass (one's) knowledge on, transmit knowledge.

ถ่ายหนัง thàajnǎŋ´ V com. to take moving pic-

tures. →Syn. ถ่ายภาพยนตร์ eleg.

ถ่าย(...)ออก thàaj(...)ʔɔ̀ɔg´ V 1. to excrete (something). 2. to drain off (something).

ถ่ายอุจจาระ thàajʔùdcaará?´ V eleg. to evacuate fecal matter, have a bowel movement, defecate. →Also อุจจาระ →Syn. ขี้ ๑ com.,vulg.

ภาพถ่าย (ใบ,รูป,ภาพ) phâabthàaj´ (baj´,rûub´, phâab´) N eleg. photograph, picture. →Syn. รูปถ่าย com.

ยาถ่าย (ขนาน) jaathàaj´ (khanǎan´) N purgative, laxative.

รูปถ่าย (รูป,แผ่น,ใบ) rûubthàaj´ (rûub´,phɛ̀n´, baj´) N com. photograph, picture. →Syn. ภาพถ่าย eleg.

ถ่าย ๒ thàaj´ C side. →Chiefly in the following combination.

ถ่ายเดียว thàajdiaw´ one-sided.

ถาวร thǎawɔɔn´ V eleg. to be permanent, enduring, lasting. ความ-- permanency, enduringness.

ถาวรวัตถุ (อย่าง,สิ่ง) thǎawɔɔn´wádthù´ (jàaŋ´, sìŋ´) N eleg. permanent, enduring object (as a building, a monument).

วัฒนาถาวร wádthanaa´thǎawɔɔn´ V eleg. 1. to progress, advance everlastingly; to progress and be enduring. 2. to be everlasting.

ถ้ำ (ถ้ำ,แห่ง) thâm´ (thâm´,hɛ̀ŋ´) N com. cave, tunnel. →Syn. คูหา eleg.

ถ้ำมอง (อัน) thâmmɔɔŋ´ (ʔan´) N 1. slide viewer. 2. kaleidoscope.

ถิ่น (ถิ่น,แห่ง) thìn´ (thìn´,hɛ̀ŋ´) N 1. place, location, locality, domain, domicile. C 2. place, area, section.

เจ้าของถิ่น (คน,พวก) câwkhɔ̌ɔŋthìn´ (khon´,phûag´) N natives, local inhabitants.

ดูหมิ่นถิ่นแคลน duumìn´thìnkhlɛɛn´ V elab. colloq. to look down upon someone because of his lower status.

ถิ่นฐาน (แห่ง) thìnthǎan´ (hɛ̀ŋ´) N 1. place. 2. place of residence.

ท้องถิ่น (แห่ง) thɔ́ɔŋthìn´ (hɛ̀ŋ´) area, district, locality.

o รัฐบาลท้องถิ่น rádthabaan´thɔ́ɔŋthìn´ N local government.

พลัดถิ่น phládthìn´ V to be displaced from (one's)

native land, exiled; to be outside of, removed
from (its) natural habitat.

o บุคคลพลัดถิ่น bùgkhon'phládthìn' refugee,
displaced person.

ถี thǐi' Pt emphatic particle. Variant form of ที ๒.

ถี่ thìi' V 1. to be close (in sucession), be repeated
in quick succession. 2. to be of high frequency.

ตระหนี่ถี่เหนียว tranìi'thìiniaw' V elab. eleg.
to be stingy, parsimonious. →Syn. ขี้เหนียว
com.

ถี่ถ้วน thìithûan' V 1. to be accurate, thorough,
careful, scrupulous. 2. colloq. to be stingy,
penny-pinching, tight.

ถีบ thìib' V 1. to kick, give a forceful shove with
the foot. 2. to kick, recoil (as a gun). 3. to
rise (as a kite). 4. slang to tip, give a tip
(e.g. to a waiter). →Dist. 1. เตะ. →Syn.
2, 4. เตะ.

ถีบจักรยาน thìib'càgkajaan', càgkrajaan' V to
pedal a bicycle, ride a bicycle.

ถีบตัว thìibtua' V colloq. to improve one's
character, status, etc.

รถถีบ (คัน) ródthìib' (khan') N colloq. bicycle. →Syn. รถจักรยาน eleg.

ถึง thǔŋ' V 1. to reach, get to. sV 2. to, up to
(esp. with verbs of motion). 3. of, about, concerning (esp. with verbs of talking, thinking,
etc.). 4. if it comes to the point that. AA 5.
colloq. so, then, as a consequence; see example under ถึงจะ. Cj 6. even though, even
if. →Syn. 5. จึง eleg.

o จนกว่าจะถึงโรงเรียน conkwàa'-cathǔŋ'rooŋɔ
rian' until (they) reach school.

o เดินทางไปถึงเชียงใหม่ dəənthaaŋ'-pajthǔŋ'ɔ
chiaŋmàj' to travel to Chiangmai, travel as
far as Chiengmai.

o ส่วนโทษนั้น ชาวไทยไม่พะวงถึง sùanthôod'nán'→
chaawthaj'mâjphawoŋ'thǔŋ'↓ As for the (resulting) harm, Thai people don't think about it.

กระทบถึง krathób'thǔŋɔ 1. to touch on. 2. to
concern, affect.

กล่าวถึง klàaw'thǔŋɔ to talk about.

คิดถึง khídthǔŋ', khídthǔŋɔ to think of, miss.

คุยกันถึงเรื่อง khuj'kanthǔŋrɯaŋ' to chat about,

talk about.

จนถึง conthǔŋɔ up until, as far as, to the point of.

ตลอดถึง talɔɔd'thǔŋɔ 1. including. 2. up to and
including. 3. all the way to.

ถึงกระนั้น, ถึงกะนั้น thǔŋkranán', thǔŋkanán' even
so, nevertheless, in spite of that.

ถึงกับ thǔŋkaɔ so (e.g. sick) that; so as, to the
point that, until.

o เจ็บถึงกับลุกไม่ขึ้น cèb'-thǔŋkalúg'mâjkhɯ̂n' to
be so sick that one can't get up.

ถึงการณ์ in รู้เท่าไม่ถึงการณ์ rúuthâw'mâjthǔŋkaan'
to be blind to a situation, be unable to see what
someone is up to.

ถึงกำหนด thǔŋ'kamnòd' to reach the appointed
time, deadline, limit; it is time (e.g. to go to bed).

ถึงแก่กรรม thǔŋ'kɛ̀ɛkam' eleg. to pass away,
die. →Syn. See ตาย com.

ถึงแค่นี้ thǔŋkhɛ̂ɛ'níi' colloq. to this extent, up
to this point.

ถึงจะ thǔŋcaɔ AA colloq. so, then, as a consequence. →Syn. จึงจะ eleg.

o คุณต้องไป เขาถึงจะไป khuntɔ̂ŋpaj'→ kháwthǔŋɔ
capaj'↓ You must go so he will go.

ถึง (...) จะ...ก็... thǔŋ(...)caɔ...→kɔ̂ɔ...↓
colloq. even though. See example.

o ถึงจะเก่า ก็ใช้ได้ thǔŋcakàw→kɔ̂chájdâaj'↓
Even though it is old, it can be used.

ถึงใจ thǔŋcaj' V colloq. 1. to gratify, satisfy,
hit the spot (for someone). sV 2. to the utmost,
in the highest degree, extremely, satisfyingly,
pleasingly.

o เผ็ดถึงใจ phèd'thǔŋcaj' extremely hot (peppery),
satisfyingly hot, i.e. hot in just the way one likes.

ถึงซึ่ง thǔŋ'sɯ̂ŋɔ V lit. to reach, arrive at.

ถึงตา thǔŋtaa' V colloq. to reach (one's) turn
(to do something).

ถึงที่ thǔŋthîi' V colloq. to be doomed to die.
→Short for ถึงที่ตาย thǔŋ'thîitaaj'.

ถึงพร้อม thǔŋphrɔ́ɔm' to meet or have all (requirements), attain (completeness).

ถึงพริกถึงขิง thǔŋphríg'thǔŋkhǐŋ' V elab. colloq.
1. to be really hot, peppery, spicy (of food).
2. to be racy, piquant (of conversation). อย่าง--
hotly, heatedly (of arguing, debating).

ถึงเพียงนี้ thy̆ŋphiaŋ'níi' to this extent, up to this level.

ถึงมือ thy̆ŋmyy' 1. to reach, get to. 2. to get into the hands of.

o ตกถึงมือ tòg'thy̆ŋmyy' to come to the hand of, come into the possession of.

ถึงแม้(ว่า) thy̆ŋméɛ'(wâa') although, even though.

ถึงเวร thy̆ŋween' V 1. to reach (one's) turn (to do something). 2. to be time for (a given) shift (of duty, work).

ถึงไหน thy̆ŋnǎj' to where, up to where; to what extent.

ถึงอย่างไร thy̆ŋjàaŋraj' however; anyhow.

บ่นถึง (1,2) bòn'thy̆ŋⵑ; (2) bònthy̆ŋ' 1. to complain about. 2. colloq. to talk about, mention often.

ไปถึง pajthy̆ŋ', paj'thy̆ŋⵑ, pajthy̆ŋⵑ 1. to arrive; to reach, to arrive at or in. 2. to, at, in. NOTE. Implies motion away from a contextually suggested point of reference; cf. มาถึง.

o โทรศัพท์ไปถึง thoorasàb'pajthy̆ŋⵑ to telephone (someone), call (someone) up.

มาถึง maathy̆ŋ', maa'thy̆ŋⵑ, maathy̆ŋⵑ 1. to arrive; to arrive at or in, reach. 2. to, at, in. NOTE. Implies motion towards a contextually suggested point of reference; cf. ไปถึง.

ไม่ถึง mâjthy̆ŋ' V 1. not to reach. sV 2. can't (because it's beyond reach).

o หยิบไม่ถึง jìb'mâjthy̆ŋ' can't get it, can't take it up (because it's beyond reach).

หมายถึง mǎaj'thy̆ŋⵑ to mean, have the meaning of, imply, refer to.

อ้างถึง ʔâaŋ'thy̆ŋⵑ to quote, to refer to.

เอ่ยถึง ʔə̀əjthy̆ŋ', ʔə̀əj'thy̆ŋⵑ to mention, speak of, talk about.

ถือ thy̆y' V 1. to hold, carry (in the hands). 2. to hold, uphold, profess a belief; to believe. 3. to hold (it) against (someone). 4. to regard, consider (in such and such a way). 5. to hold to a taboo (usually one relating to women's lower garments). NOTE. In mng. 5 the taboo is rather mild, and not universal. For example, a man may refuse to go under a line that holds or has held women's lower garments. In this use there is often no expressed object of ถือ.

กระเป๋าถือ (ใบ) krapǎwthy̆y'(baj') N handbag, pocketbook.

จับมือถือแขน càbmyy'thy̆ykhɛ̌ɛn' V elab. colloq. 1. to hold hands. 2. to hold by the arm.

เชื่อถือ chŷathy̆y' V to believe (in), have faith (in). ความ-- trust, faith.

ถือกันว่า thy̆y'kanwâa' 1. it is held that. 2. it is customary that. →See also ถือว่า below.

ถือกำเนิด thy̆y'kamnə̀əd' V to be born, orginated, initiated, produced.

ถือโชคถือลาง thy̆ychôog'thy̆ylaaŋ' V elab. colloq. to be superstitious. →Also ถือลาง colloq.

ถือดี thy̆ydii' V 1. to be proud, haughty, arrogant, self-assertive. 2. to dare, i.e. have the nerve (to do such and such). →Syn. 2. อวดดี.

ถือตัว thy̆ytua' V to be proud of oneself, have a high opinion of oneself, hold oneself aloof. ความ-- pride. →Ant. ถ่อมตัว.

ถือปูน thy̆ypuun' 1. to mortar (e.g. bricks). 2. to plaster.

ถือผิว thy̆yphǐw' V to practice racial discrimination. การ-- racial discrimination.

ถือพวงมาลัย thy̆y'phuaŋmaalaj' V to steer, be at the wheel, i.e. have hold of the steering wheel.

ถือว่า thy̆y'wâaⵑ to hold (the belief) that, believe that, consider that, take (it to mean) that, claim that.

o เขาถือว่าเขาเก่ง kháwthy̆y'-wâakháw'kèŋ'↓ He considers himself clever. He believes that he is smart.

ถือศาสนา thy̆y'sàasanǎa' V to profess a religion; to hold the beliefs of a religion.

ถือศีล thy̆ysǐin' V to observe religious precepts.

ถือสวน thy̆ysǔan' V to rent an orchard, rent a lot to make an orchard.

ถือสา thy̆ysǎa' V to mind (something said or done), take offense.

o ไม่ถือสา mâjthy̆ysǎa' V not to mind, take no offense.

ถือโอกาศ thy̆y'ʔookàad' V to take the opportunity.

นับถือ nábthy̆y' V 1. to respect, revere; to look up to, have respect for. 2. to profess, believe in (a religion). →Syn. เคารพ eleg.

ถุง (ใบ) thǔŋ' (baj') N bag, sack, pouch.

คลุมถุงชน khlum'thŭŋchon' V idiom.to marry off (an individual, a couple) without the mates knowing or seeing each other beforehand.

ถุงตาข่าย (ใบ) thŭŋ'takhàaj' (baj') N net (in the form of a bag, as a butterfly net).

ถุงเท้า (คู่,ข้าง) thŭŋtháaw' (khûu', khâaŋ') N socks, stockings, hose.

ถุงมือ (คู่,ข้าง) thŭŋmyy' (khûu', khâaŋ') N glove, gloves.

ผ้าถุง (ผืน) phâathŭŋ' (phŭyn') N a sarong-like lower garment worn by women. →Comp. ผ้าชิ้น.

ถุน in ใต้ถุน tâajthŭn'* N 1. the space (open or closed) under a Thai house. 2. basement, cellar.

ถุย (1) thŭj'; (2) !thŭj' V 1. to spit, spit out. E 2. imit. sound uttered to spurn someone, to show contempt. →Syn. 1. ถ่ม.

ถู thŭu' V to rub, scrub.

ขัดถู khàdthŭu' V to burnish, furbish, polish up.

ผ้าถูตัว (ผืน) phâathŭutua' (phŭyn') N wash cloth.

สบู่ถูตัว (ก้อน) sabùu'thŭutua' (kɔ̂ɔn') N toilet soap.

ถูก ๑ thùug' V to be cheap, inexpensive, low (in price). →Ant. แพง.

ดูถูก duuthùug' V to insult, look down upon, show contempt for. คำ-- insult. →Syn. ดูหมิ่น.

ถูกจัง thùug'caŋ' to be dirt cheap.

ราคาถูก raakhaa'thùug' N 1. low price. V 2. to be cheap, inexpensive, low-priced.

ถูก ๒ thùug' V to be right, correct. →Ant. ผิด.

ถูกต้อง thùugtɔ̂ŋ' V to be right, correct. →See also under ถูก ๓.

ถูกทีเดียว thùug'thiidiaw' quite right, exactly right.

ถูกแล้ว thùuglέεw' That's right!

ถูกส่วน,--ลัด thùugsùan', thùug'sùansàd' V 1. to be proportional. 2. to be of the right proportions.

ผิดถูก phìd'thùug' to be right or wrong.

ไม่ถูก mâjthùug' V 1. not to be right, to be incorrect. sV 2. incorrectly, wrong. 3. can't; see examples.

o ตัดสินใจไม่ถูก tàdsĭncaj'mâjthùug' can't make up (his) mind, can't decide.

o บอกไม่ถูก bɔ̀ɔg'mâjthùug' (I) can't say; (it's) hard to say, hard to tell.

ถูก ๓ thùug' V 1. to touch, to come in contact with. 2. to hit (as a target).

จิ้(ให้)ถูกเส้น cîi'-hâjthùug'sên', cîi'-thùug'sên' fig.,colloq. to hit the right spot, touch the right chord (for successfully evoking a desired response).

ถูก(...)เข้า thùug'(...)khâw' to come in contact with, be exposed to (e.g. heat).

ถูกคอ(กัน) thùugkhɔɔ'(kan') V colloq. to get along well (with one another) because of compatible tastes and interests.

ถูกใจ thùugcaj' V 1. to please; to be satisfactory, pleasing, appealing. 2. to be to one's liking, to one's taste. 3. to get along well (with), be compatible. →Syn. พอใจ,ชอบใจ.

ถูกประตา thùugchataa' (a person) to appeal to one on first sight, strike one as just right, "click" with one, arouse a feeling of natural empathy with one.

ถูกต้อง thùug'tɔ̂ŋ' V to touch, to come into contact with. →See also under ถูก ๒.

ถูกโรค thùugrôog' V colloq. to agree (with one's system, as food).

ถูกลอตเตอรี่ที่หนึ่ง thùuglɔ́ɔdtərîi'thîinỳŋ' V to win first prize in a lottery.

ถูกเส้นกัน thùugsên'kan to get along well (with one another) because of compatibility in behavior, character and personality.

ยิงถูก jiŋthùug' V to shoot hitting (the target).

ถูก ๔ thùug' V element used in making passive constructions. →Syn. โดน. →Dist. ได้รับ eleg. NOTE. Many passive constructions lack an expressed agent; 1st example. But if the agent is named it is placed immediately after ถูก; 2nd example.

o ศัตรูถูกกำจัดแล้ว sàdtruu'thùugkamcàd'-lέεw'↓ The enemy has been eliminated.

o วัวถูกเสือกินเสียแล้ว wua'thùugsỳa'kin'-síaɔ lέεw'↓* The cow has been eaten up by the tiger.

ถูก(...)กัด thùug(...)kàd' to be bitten (by).

ถูกเกณฑ์ทหาร thùugkeen'thahǎan' to be drafted.

ถูกขังกรงไว้ thùug'khǎŋkroŋ'-wáj' to be penned up in the cage.

ถูกเขี่ย thùugkhìa' slang to be transferred, removed, gotten out of the way.

ถูกทำโทษ thùugthamthôod' to be punished, be penalized.

ถูกทำลาย thùugthamlaaj' to be destroyed.

ถูกปราบ thùugpràab' to be subdued, subjugated, conquered. การ-- being subdued, subjugated; subjugation.

ถูกเผาไฟไป thùug'phǎwfaj/-paj' V to be burned up by fire.

ถูกภาคทัณฑ์ thùugphâagthan' eleg. to be on probation, be put on probation.

ถูกรถชน thùugród'chon' to be hit by a car.

ถูก(...)หลอก thùug(...)lɔɔg' V 1. to be fooled, tricked (by someone). 2. to be scared, frightened (e.g. by ghosts).

ถูกหักคะแนน thùughàg'khanɛɛn' to take a deduction in one's score or grade, to lose points.

เถร,เถระ (รูป,องค์) thěen', thěerá?' (rûub', ?oŋ') N senior monk, i.e. one who has been in the priesthood ten or more years.

เถล in เถลไถล thalěe'thalǎj' V colloq. 1. to dilly-dally, dawdle,fritter away (time). 2. to procrastinate, put off to the last minute.

เถลิง thalǒŋ' V eleg. to ascend (a throne), enter upon (a new reign, a new era). →Syn. ขึ้น com.

เถอะ thə?', thəɔ Pt particle used to mark an exhortation or a command. NOTE. The spelling เถอะ is used to render the usual pronunciation, which is thə?'. A more formal spelling is เถิด, q.v.

ช่างเถอะ châŋthə?'↓ Never mind! Forget it! Who cares!

เชิญเถอะ chəən'thə?'↓, chəən'thəɔ Go ahead please!

o เชิญเถอะคุณ chəən'thəkhun'↓ idem.

ไปกันเถอะ paj'kanthə?' Let's go!

เมินเสียเถอะ məən'sǐathə?' Not a chance! Never!

ไหว้พระเถอะ wâajphrá?'thə?' phrase used by older people to acknowledge the respect paid by younger people.

เอาเถอะ (1) ?awthə?'→; (2) ?aw'thə?↓ 1. Okay, ...(e.g. I'll help you). All right. So be it. Let's agree on that. 2. Get it. Take it.

เถา (เถา) thǎw' (thǎw') N 1. stems of vines or creepers. 2. creeping plant, vine. C 3. set, assortment (of crockery and certain kitchen utensils which come in graduated sizes).

เถาวัลย์ (ต้น,เถา) thǎwwan' (tôn',thǎw') N vines, climbers (in general).

เทือกเถา (เหล่า,สาย) thŷagthǎw' (làw', sǎaj') N lineage, line of descent.

ไม้เถา (ต้น) máajthǎw' (tôn') N creeper, vine, liana.

เถ้า ๑ thâw' N ashes.

ขี้เถ้า khîithâw' N colloq. ashes.

เถ้า ๒. See เผ่า.

เถาะ thɔ?' N (Year of the) Rabbit. →The complete list of the cyclical years is given under ปี.

เถิด thə̂əd', thə?' Pt particle used to mark an exhortation or a command. NOTE. The spelling pronunciation is thə̂əd', but the usual pronunciation is thə?'. This latter pronunciation is sometimes introduced in writing as เถอะ, q.v.

ลืมเสียเถิด lyym'sǐathə?' Forget it! Let's forget it.

เอาเถิด (1) ?awthə?'→; (2) ?aw'thə?↓; (3) ?awɔ thə̂əd' 1. Okay, ...(e.g. I'll help you). All right. So be it. Let's agree on that. 2. Get it. Take it. 3. a kind of tag (children's game).

เถียง thǐaŋ' V to argue, contradict, talk back to.

ต่อล้อต่อเถียง tɔɔlɔɔ'tɔɔthǐaŋ' V elab. colloq. to talk back; to argue back and forth, keep arguing.

โต้เถียง tôothǐaŋ' V 1. to argue, dispute, quarrel. 2. to contest (a point).

ถกเถียง thògthǐaŋ' V 1. to argue. 2. to discuss.

เถียงไม่ขึ้น thǐaŋ'mâjkhŷn' to be unable to win the dispute, argument; can't argue (e.g. because one's opponent is too clever, or has too high a position).

ทุ่มเถียง thûmthǐaŋ' V to argue, quarrel.

เถือ thŷa' V to cut with a knife, using a seesaw motion, to hack away (at something, e.g. as with a dull knife).

เถื่อน thỳan/ N 1. wild, desolate forest. V 2. to be savage, wild. 3. to be illegal, unauthorized, bootleg. →Sometimes coupled with ป่า "forest" which may at times be translated "wild."

ของเถื่อน (อย่าง) khɔ̌ɔŋthỳan/ (jàaŋ/) N smuggled goods, contraband, bootleg goods.

ช้างเถื่อน (เชือก) cháaŋthỳan/ (chŷag/) N wild elephant.

ป่าเถื่อน pàa/thỳan/ V to be barbaric, barbarous, savage, primitive, uncivilized. คน-- savage, barbarian; primitive, uncivilized people. อย่าง-- primitively, in an uncivilized manner.

หมอเถื่อน (คน) mɔ̌ɔthỳan/ (khon/) N quack, i.e., an unauthorized physician, doctor.

หูป่าตาเถื่อน hǔupàa/taathỳan/ V elab. colloq. to be ignorant of what is going on, of what is happening.

เหล้าเถื่อน lâwthỳan/ N bootleg liquor.

แถบ thɛ̀ɛb/ N 1. region, part, section, zone. C 2. clf. for certain long, flat, narrow shapes or objects, e.g. stripes, strips of cloth, etc.

แถบร้อน (แถบ) thɛ̀ɛbrɔ́ɔn/ (thɛ̀ɛb/) N hot region, tropical zone.

แถบอบอุ่น (แถบ) thɛ̀ɛb/ʔòbʔùn/ (thɛ̀ɛb/) N temperate zone.

เป็นแถบ ๆ penthɛ̀ɛbthɛ̀ɛb/ 1. in strips. 2. in some parts (out of many). 3. strip by strip, section by section, part by part.

ผ้าแถบ (ผืน) phâathɛ̀ɛb/ (phʉ̌yn/) N a strip of cloth used by women to wrap around the bosom (in place of all other upper garments).

แถม thɛ̌ɛm/ V 1. to add on (to) for good measure, e.g. as a bonus or lagniappe. sV 2. in addition, as lagniappe.

แถมพก thɛ̌ɛmphóg/ V 1. to give as lagniappe, give something free to a customer with the purchase of something else. 2. to give a premium.

แถลง thalɛ̌ɛŋ/ V 1. to tell, give an account of. 2. to issue a statement, announce. คำ-- declaration, statement, announcement, pronouncement. ผู้-- announcer.

o แถลงความในใจ thalɛ̌ɛŋ/khwaamnajcaj/ to reveal the secret(s) of one's heart.

ถ้อยแถลง (ฉบับ,ครั้ง) thɔ̂jthalɛ̌ɛŋ/ (chabàb/, khráŋ/) N (official) statement, communiqué.

แถลงการณ์ (ฉบับ) thalɛ̌ɛŋkaan/ (chabàb/) N official announcement, pronouncement, bulletin, communiqué. ผู้-- spokesman.

แถว thɛ̌w/* N 1. line, row. 2. section, district (of a town, place). C 3. clf. for same. →Cf. 1, 3. ตับ,แนว,ระนาว.

กินแถว kinthɛ̌w/ colloq. 1. to do something right on down the line, going through an entire row or series. 2. to scoop the pool, sweep the board.

เข้าแถว khâwthɛ̌w/ V 1. to stand in line. 2. to form a line, a queue.

เดินแถว dəənthɛ̌w/ V to walk in line, march in line.

แถวนั้น thɛ̌wnán/ 1. (in) that row. 2. (in) that section (of town). 3. around that place, that area.

เป็นแถว penthɛ̌w/ 1. in rows. 2. in large numbers.

ลูกแถว (คน) lûugthɛ̌w/ (khon/) N 1. men in the lower ranks, the rank and file (in the police force, army). 2. person standing in line (other than at the head). →Opp. หัวแถว.

ห้องแถว (หลัง,ห้อง) hɔ̂ŋthɛ̌w/ (lǎŋ/, hɔ̂ŋ/) N 1. a row of identically-constructed rooms, apartments or shops (lǎŋ/). 2. one such room, apartment or shop (hɔ̂ŋ/).

หัวแถว hǔathɛ̌w/ N person at the head of the line. →Opp. ลูกแถว.

โถ (ใบ) thǒo/ (baj/) N a kind of covered jar with a wide mouth and narrow base.

โถใส่แป้ง (ใบ) thǒo/sàjpɛ̂ɛŋ/ (baj/) N powder jar.

โถง thǒoŋ/ V to be spacious, roomy.

ห้องโถง (ห้อง) hɔ̂ŋthǒoŋ/ (hɔ̂ŋ/) N hall; large, spacious room.

โอ่โถง ʔòothǒoŋ/ V to be splendid, luxurious, magnificent.

โถม thǒom/ V to jump on, pounce on, lunge forward with force and abruptness.

ไถ (คัน) thǎj/ (khan/) N 1. plow. V 2. to plow. 3. to push forward.

ดาวไถ daawthǎj/ N 1. Orion (the constellation). 2. slang one given to sponging off others.

ไถนา thǎjnaa/ V to plow (the field).

ไถ่ thàj′ V to redeem, ransom. →Also pronounced thàaj′ in colloq. speech.

ค่าไถ่ khâathàj′ N ransom, cost of redemption.

ถามไถ่ thǎamthàj′ V to inquire, ask, question.

ไถล, เถล-- thalǎj′, thalěe′thalǎj′ V colloq. 1. to dilly-dally, dawdle, fritter away (time). 2. to procrastinate, put off to the last minute.

ท

ท thɔɔ′ LOW consonant. Pronounced th initially, d finally. The sound th as an initial low consonant is also sometimes written with ธ, or very rarely with ฑ or ฒ. The initial combination ทร- is often, but not always, pronounced s, as in ทราบ sâab′. The same combination is also pronounced thɔɔraɔ, as in ทรมาน thɔɔ- ramaan′.

ทแกล้ว in ทแกล้วทหาร (คน) thaklɛ́ɛw′thahǎan′ (khon′) N soldier, brave warrior.

ทด thód′ V 1. to raise to a higher level (as water by means of a dam). 2. to carry (a number, when adding).

ทดแทน thódthɛɛn′ V 1. to repay, do in return. 2. to replace. sV 3. as a replacement, a substitute.

ทดน้ำเข้านา thódnáam′khâwnaa′ to irrigate a field (by flooding).

ทดรอง thódrɔɔŋ′ V to lay out money in advance, pay (for something) pending reimbursement.

ทดลอง thódlɔɔŋ′ V to experiment, test, try out. การ-- experiment, test, trial.

o ห้องทดลอง (ห้อง) hɔ̂ŋ′thódlɔɔŋ′ (hɔ̂ŋ′) N laboratory.

ทดเลข thódlêeg′ V 1. arith. to carry a number (in addition). 2. to figure (on scratch paper).

o สมุดทดเลข (เล่ม) samùd′thódlêeg′ (lêm′) N scratch pad.

ทน thon′ V 1. to last, endure. 2. to bear, stand, tolerate, put up with. 3. to stand, withstand, resist (e.g. wear). 4. to be durable, lasting.

คงทน khoŋ′thon′ V to be resistant, durable.

เต็มทน temthon′ V 1. to be unable to bear (it)

any longer. sV 2. extremely, exceedingly, unbearably, to the limit of one's endurance.

ทนทาน thonthaan′ V to be enduring, lasting, durable.

ทนไฟ thonfaj′ V 1. to be fireproof, fire resistant, heat resistant. 2. to withstand fire, endure fire or heat.

ทนไม่ไหว thon′mâjwǎj′ V to be unable to stand (something).

ทนหวานอมขมกลืน thon′-wǎan?om′khǒmklyyn′ idiom. to take the bitter along with the sweet.

น้ำอดน้ำทน nám?òd′námthon′ N elab. colloq. patience, endurance.

เหลือทน lɣathon′, lɣa′thon′ V to be unbearable, intolerable.

อดทน ?òdthon′ V to be tough, enduring, patient.

ท้น thón′ V 1. to overflow. 2. to rise (as of the tide).

ทนโท่ thonthôo′ V colloq. 1. to be obvious, clear, apparent. sV 2. obviously, clearly, apparently.

o เห็นอยู่ทนโท่ hěn′jùuthonthôo′ (it) is clearly seen, is plain to see, is obvious.

ทนาย (คน) thanaaj′ (khon′) N 1. lawyer, attorney. 2. colloq. one who represents another person in some action, hence, a representative.

ทนายความ (คน) thanaajkhwaam′ (khon′) N lawyer, attorney, counselor; (Brit.) barrister, solicitor.

ทนุ FS. See ทะนุ.

ทบ. Abbrev. for กองทัพบก "army," and for ทหารบก "soldier."

ทบ thób′ V 1. to fold (in layers). C 2. fold, layer (of something folded in layers).

ดอกเบี้ยทบต้น dɔ̀ɔgbîa′thóbtôn′ N finance compound interest.

ทบทวน thóbthuan′ V 1. to go over, review. sV 2. back over, in review.

ทบทุน thóbthun′ V finance to add to the original fund or investment.

ทบวง thabuaŋ′ N 1. (government) bureau (on a par with a ministry). 2. obs. a subministry (i.e. an administrative unit comprising several departments but subordinate to a ministry). C 3. clf. for a (government) bureau.

ทบวงการเมือง thabuaŋ′kaanmyaŋ′ N a political

bureau.

ทโมน thamoon′ 1. large (of monkeys). N 2. colloq. monkey, ape (not a specific term). →Also ทะโมน FS.

ลิงทโมน (ตัว) liŋthamoon′ (tua′) N (a) big monkey. Often used as a simile to describe mischievous children.

ทยอย thajɔɔj′ V 1. to come or go in succession, in successive groups, a part at a time, a few at a time. sV 2. a little at a time, a part at a time; in successive batches, bunches, etc. →Also ทะยอย FS.

ทแยง thajɛɛŋ′ V to be diagonal. →Also ทะแยง FS.
เส้นทแยงมุม sên′thajɛɛŋmum′ N diagonal line.

ทร. Abbrev. for กองทัพเรือ "navy," and for ทหารเรือ "sailor."

ทรง ๑ (ทรง) soŋ′ (soŋ′) V 1. eleg. to hold up, maintain, keep (something) going; 1st example. 2. eleg. to remain the same, stay the same, stand still; 2nd example. 3. eleg., roy. to have, possess, be possessed of; 3rd example. 4. roy. (royalty) to perform an action, e.g. to put on (clothes), ride (a horse); see note. N 5. eleg. shape, form, figure, style; 6th example. →Syn. 3. มี com. 5. รูป, แบบ com. →See also ทรง ๒. NOTE. In mng. 4. the specific nature of the action is determined by the object which follows it, or which is suggested by the context; see 4th and 5th examples below.

o ทรงตัว soŋtua′ to balance oneself, maintain one's balance.

o อาการมีแต่ทรงกับทรุด ʔaakaan′miitɛɛsoŋ′ɔkasúd′↓ (The patient's) condition does nothing but stay the same or worsen.

o ทรงศักดิ์ soŋsàg′ eleg. to possess rank (position).

o ทรงม้า soŋmáa′ roy. 1. to be mounted on a horse. 2. to ride a horse.

o ทรงเครื่อง soŋkhrɯ̂aŋ′ roy. to be dressed in regalia, armor, etc. →See also under ทรง เครื่อง below.

o ทรงผม soŋphǒm′ eleg. style of haircut, hair style.

เครื่องทรง (อย่าง) khrɯ̂aŋsoŋ′ (jàaŋ′) N roy. garment, apparel, attire.

ทรงกลม soŋklom′ N 1. eleg. spherical shape. 2. (as n. mod.) sphere-shaped, spherical, globular.

o กึ่งทรงกลม (ซีก) kɯ̀ŋ′soŋklom′ (sîig′) N 1. eleg. hemisphere. 2. (as n. mod.) hemispherical.

o ลูกทรงกลม (ลูก) lûug′soŋklom′ (lûug′) N sphere, spherical body.

ทรงครรภ์ soŋkhan′ V roy. to be enceinte, pregnant. →Syn. See มีท้อง.

ทรงคุณวุฒิ soŋ′-khunnawúd′thíʔ′ V eleg. to be qualified, competent, have (the necessary) qualifications.

ทรงเครื่อง soŋkhrɯ̂aŋ′ V 1. roy. to be dressed in regalia, armor, etc.; to be decorated. 2. com. to be overdressed; to have more (e.g. ingredients, trimming, money) than necessary.

o แม่หม้ายทรงเครื่อง (คน) mɛ̂ɛmâaj′soŋkhrɯ̂aŋ′ (khon′) N colloq. a rich widow.

ทรงจำ in ความทรงจำ khwaam′soŋcam′ N memory, memories.

o จดหมายเหตุความทรงจำ còdmǎajhèed′khwaamɔ soŋcam′ N memoirs.

ทรงตัว soŋtua′ V to balance, support oneself. →Syn. เลี้ยงตัว.

o ทรงตัวไม่อยู่ soŋtua′mâjjùu′ to lose one's balance.

ทรงผม (ทรง, แบบ) soŋphǒm′ (soŋ′, bɛ̀ɛb′) N eleg. style of haircut, hair style.

ทรงพระราชดำรัส soŋ′phrárâad′chadamràd′ V roy. to speak, to order.

ทรงพระอักษร soŋ′phráʔàgsɔɔn′ V roy. to write.

ทรงม้า soŋmáa′ V roy. 1. to be mounted on a horse. 2. to ride a horse.

ทรงไว้ซึ่ง soŋwáj′sɯ̂ŋɔ V lit., eleg. to possess (e.g. quality, dignity).

ทรงศักดิ์ soŋsàg′ V eleg. to possess rank.

ทรวดทรง (ทรวดทรง, แบบ, อย่าง) sûadsoŋ′ (sûadɔ soŋ′, bɛ̀ɛb′, jàaŋ′) N eleg. shape, form, contour, figure, appearance. →Also spelled ช่วดทรง.

ผู้ทรงเกียรติ (ท่าน, คน) phûusoŋkìad′ (thân′, khon′) N eleg. honorable person (i.e. one with rank or distinction).

ยกทรง (ตัว) jógsoŋ′ (tua′) N brassière.

รูปทรง (แบบ,อย่าง) rûubsoŋ (bɛ̀ɛb′, jàaŋ′) N figure, shape, form, build.

เสียทรง sǐasoŋ V 1. to lose one's shape, lose its shape. 2. to spoil the shape, the look (of something).

ทรง- ๒ soŋ′, soŋɔ r o y. element placed before verbs when speaking of royalty, esp. of the king. →See also ทรง ๑. NOTE. ทรง- is normally placed in front of common verbs which have no specific royal counterpart. Although verbs which are already royal do not require the addition of ทรง-, e.g. ตรัส r o y. "to speak," some writers add ทรง- even here, e.g. ทรงตรัส r o y. "to speak."

o ขอทรงพระเจริญ khɔ̌ɔ′soŋphrácarəən′↓ Long live the King!

o พระมหากษัตริย์ทรงเป็นประมุขของประเทศ phráɔ mahǎakasàd′-soŋpenpramúg′khɔ̌ɔŋpratheêd′↓ The king is the head of the country.

ทรงพระดำเนิน soŋ′phrádamnəən′ V r o y. to walk.

ทรงมีพระโทรเลข soŋmii′phráthooralêeg′ V r o y. to send a telegram.

ทรพิษ in ไข้ทรพิษ,โรคไข้ทรพิษ khâj′thɔɔraphíd′, rôog′khâjthɔɔraphíd′ N e l e g. smallpox. →Syn. ฝีดาษ c o m.

ทรมาน thɔɔramaan′ V 1. to torture, torment. 2. to be torture, torment. การ-- torture. ความ-- suffering, distress, agony.

ทรมานด้วย thɔɔramaan′dûajɔ to suffer from (e.g. pain).

ทรยศ thɔɔrajód′ V 1. to betray. 2. to be traitorous. คน-- traitor, betrayer.

ทรรศนะ (ทรรศนะ,อย่าง) thádsaná?′/*(thádsaná?′, jàaŋ′) N e l e g. point of view, opinion. →Syn. ความเห็น c o m. →Also spelled ทัศนะ.

ทรราช (องค์,คน) thɔɔrarâad′ (?oŋ′, khon′) N l i t. e l e g. tyrant.

ทรวง suaŋ′ N e l e g. chest, breast. →Syn. อก c o m.

ทรวงอก suaŋ?òg′ N e l e g. chest, breast.

ทรวด in ทรวดทรง (ทรวดทรง,แบบ,อย่าง) sûadɔ

soŋ′ (sûadsoŋ′, bɛ̀ɛb′, jàaŋ′) N e l e g. shape, form, contour, figure, appearance. →Also spelled ซวดทรง.

ทรหด thɔɔrahòd′ V 1. to be tough, unyielding, stubborn. 2. to have great endurance.

ทรัพย์ sáb′ N e l e g. wealth, money, treasure. →Syn. เงิน,สมบัติ,สิน c o m.

ขุมทรัพย์ (ขุม,แห่ง) khǔmsáb′ N 1. treasure (often buried) (khǔm′). 2. place where treasure is found or kept (hɛ̀ŋ′).

ทรัพย์ขีด sábsǐid′ V s l a n g to become penniless, broke.

ทรัพย์ในดินสินในน้ำ sáb′najdin′-sǐn′najnáam′ e l a b. e l e g. the natural resources of earth and water: "treasure-in-the-earth, wealth-in-the-water."

ทรัพย์สมบัติ (อย่าง) sáb′sǒmbàd′ (jàaŋ′) N property, possessions, wealth.

ทรัพย์สิน (อย่าง) sábsǐn′ (jàaŋ′) N c o m. property, holdings, assets, wealth.

โภคทรัพย์ (อย่าง) phôogkhasáb′ (jàaŋ′) e l e g. resources (as in "natural resources").

มีทรัพย์ miisáb′ V to be rich, wealthy; to have money.

หลักทรัพย์ (อย่าง) làgsáb′ (jàaŋ′) N property, possessions or holdings used as security.

ทรัพยากร (อย่าง) sáb′phajaakɔɔn′ (jàaŋ′) N resources. →Cf. ทรัพย์.

ทรัพยากรธรรมชาติ (อย่าง) sáb′phajaakɔɔn′thamɔ machâad′ (jàaŋ′) N natural resources.

ทราบ sâab′ V e l e g. to know; to learn of. →Syn. รู้ c o m. NOTE. In referring to knowledge acquired by study and learning, รู้ is used, and not ทราบ.

แจ้งให้ทราบ cɛ̂ɛŋ′hâjsâab′ e l e g. to inform, let it be known.

ซึมทราบ symsâab′ V c o l l o q. to know thoroughly, know well.

เซ็นทราบ sensâab′ V to sign an acknowledgment.

ทราบว่า sâab′wâaɔ, sâabwâa′ e l e g. to know that; it was learned that.

รับทราบ rábsâab′ V 1. e l e g. to acknowledge. 2. to bear (something) in mind.

ทราม saam′ V 1. e l e g. to be low, inferior, mean,

disgraceful. 2. lit. to be young, small. →Syn.
1. เลว, ชั่ว com.

ใจทราม cajsaam′ V to be base, vile, immoral
(at heart).

ทรามวัย saamwaj′ N lit. young woman; sweetheart.

โรคจิตทราม rôog′cìdsaam′ N feeble-minded-
ness.

เลวทราม leewsaam′ V to be bad, vile.

ทราย ๑ (เม็ด, ถัง, ฯลฯ) saaj′ (méd′, thăŋ′, etc.)
N sand (méd′ for grains; thăŋ′ and others
for sand in containers or measured units).

กระดาษทราย (แผ่น) kradàadsaaj′ (phὲn′) N
sandpaper.

กลางดินกลางทราย klaaŋdin′klaaŋsaaj′ colloq.
on the ground.

ดินทราย dinsaaj′ N sandy soil.

ดินปนทราย dinponsaaj′ N loam, sandy soil.

ทะเลทราย (ทะเลทราย, แห่ง) thaleesaaj′ (thaɔ
leesaaj′, hὲŋ′) N desert.

น้ำตาลทราย námtaansaaj′ N granular sugar.

น้ำบ่อทราย nám′bɔ̀ɔsaaj′ N idiom. an inex-
haustible source of wealth, constantly productive in small amounts.

หาดทราย (แห่ง) hàadsaaj′ (hὲŋ′) N sandy
beach.

ทราย ๒, เนื้อ-- (ตัว) saaj′, nýasaaj′ (tua′) N
hog deer.

ทรุด súd′ V to sink (as a building), sag, collapse;
2. to get worse (of a patient), to worsen, deteriorate, decline. →Comp. ชำรุด.

o ทรุดตัวลงนั่ง súdtua′loŋnâŋ′ V to sink into a
chair, lower oneself into a sitting position.

ทรุดโทรม súdsoom′ V eleg. 1. to be deteriorated, worn out, in decay. 2. to be run down,
sickly.

ทรุดลง súd′loŋ V to get worse, take a turn for
the worse (of a patient).

ทฤษฎี (บท) thrísadii′ (bòd′) N theory.

ทลาย thalaaj′ V 1. to tumble down, fall (as a building, wall). 2. to tear down, pull down, demolish.
→Also ทะลาย FS.

พังทลาย phaŋ′thalaaj′ V to fall in ruins, crumble, tumble down.

ทวง thuaŋ′ V to ask for, demand (what is due); to
dun.

o ทวงเอกราช thuaŋ′ʔèegkarâad′ V to demand
independence.

ท่วง. See entries below.

ท่วงท่า thûaŋthâa′ N presence, attitude, bearing,
manner, poise.

ท่วงที thûaŋthii′ N presence, attitude, deportment,
bearing, manner.

o ท่วงทีวาจา thûaŋthii′waacaa′ N manner and
speech.

o ทันท่วงที than′thûaŋthii′ in time (with respect
to circumstances), in the nick of time.

o ทำท่วงที tham′thûaŋthii′ to put up a front.

ท้วง thúaŋ′ V 1. to direct attention to (undesirable
facts, dangers, flaws), to pick flaws in. 2. to
protest, object (as in a discussion), give a counteropinion.

ทักท้วง thágthúaŋ′ V 1. to direct attention to
(undesirable facts, dangers, flaws), to pick flaws
in. 2. to advise against, object to, express a
counteropinion.

ทวด thûad′ N great-grandparent (on either side).
→Also ช่วด colloq.

ตาทวด (คน) taathûad′ (khon′) N maternal great-
grandfather.

ทวน (เล่ม) thuan′ (lêm′) N 1. lance. V 2. to proceed against. 3. to review.

ทบทวน thóbthuan′ V1. to go over, review. sV
2. back over, in review.

ทวนคำ thuankham′ V to repeat (someone's) words.

ทวนลม thuanlom′ V to move windward, go against
the wind.

o ทำหูทวนลม thamhǔu′thuanlom′ idiom. to pretend not to hear, turn a deaf ear.

ทวน thúan′ rM intensifier used with อ้วน "fat."

อ้วนทวน ʔûanthúan′ 1. to be fat, plump, heavy,
chubby, solid. 2. to be in good health, look
healthy.

ท่วม thûam′ V to flood, inundate. →Syn. นอง.

ท่วมท้น thûamthón′ V to overflow.

น้ำท่วม náamthûam′ N 1. flood; floodwaters.

น้ำท่วมทุ่ง náam′thûamthûŋ′ N idiom. verbiage,
verboseness.

If a word is not found under ทร, see also ช.

มีหนี้สินท่วมตัว miinîisǐn′-thûam′tua′ to be deeply in debt, head over heels in debt.

ไหลท่วม lǎjthûam′ V to overflow, flow over.

ทวย thuaj′ N lit. group, the whole group, the group as a whole.

ทวยราษฎร์ thuajrâad′ N lit. people, citizenry.

ทว่า in แต่ทว่า tὲεthawâa′ but.

ทวาร thawaan′ N lit., eleg. gate, door, opening.

ทวารหนัก (ทวารหนัก) thawaannàg′ (thawaannàg′) N anat., eleg. rectum, anus. →Syn. กัน com., ตูด vulg.

ทวิ- thawíɔ lit., eleg. combining form meaning "two." →Chiefly in cpds. →Cf. ทวี, โท, ยี่, สอง.

ทวิบาท thawíbàad′ lit., eleg. biped.

ทวี thawii′ V 1. to increase (in size, quantity) (perhaps orig., to double). 2. eleg. combining form meaning "two." →Cf. ทวิ-, โท, ยี่, สอง.

ทวี(...)ขึ้น thawii′(...)khŷn′ to increase, mount.

ทวีคูณ thawii′khuun′ eleg. twofold, double, multiplied by two.

ทวีป (ทวีป) thawîib′ (thawîib′) N geog. continent.

ทศ thód′, thód′saɔ N eleg. ten, deca-. →Chiefly in compounds. →Cf. สิบ.

ทศนิยม thód′sanijom′ N 1. decimal system. 2. decimal.

ทหาร (คน) thahǎan′ (khon′) N soldier, serviceman, member of one of the armed forces.

การ-- soldiery; military affairs.

กรมทหาร (กรม) kromthahǎan′ (krom′) N regiment.

กองทหาร (กอง) kɔɔŋthahǎan′ (kɔɔŋ′) N troops, forces, army.

กำลังทหาร kamlaŋ′thahǎan′ N military manpower.

ข้าราชการ(ฝ่าย)ทหาร (คน,นาย) khâarâadchaɔkaan′(fàajɔ)thahǎan′ (khon′, naaj′) N employees of the military services (as opp. to the civil services).

ทแกล้วทหาร (คน) thaklɛ̂εw′thahǎan′ (khon′) N soldier, brave warrior.

ทหารช่าง thahǎanchâaŋ′ N military technician, military engineer; the engineers.

ทหารบก (คน) thahǎanbòg′ (khon′) N soldier, member of the army. →Abbrev. ทบ.

ทหารปืนใหญ่ (คน) thahǎan′pyynjàj′ (khon′) N artilleryman; the artillery. →Abbrev. ป.

ทหารผ่านศึก (คน,นาย) thahǎan′phàansỳg′ (khon′, naaj′) N war veteran.

ทหารม้า (คน) thahǎanmáa′ (khon′) N cavalryman; the cavalry.

ทหารยาม (คน) thahǎanjaam′ (khon′) N sentry, guard.

ทหารร่ม,--ชูชีพ (คน) thahǎanrôm′, thahǎan′rômɔchuuchîib′ (khon′) N paratrooper; paratroopers, the paratroops.

ทหารราบ (คน) thahǎanrâab′ (khon′) N infantryman; infantrymen, the infantry.

ทหารเรือ (คน) thahǎanrya′ (khon′) N sailor, member of the navy. →Dist. กะลาสี.

ทหารอากาศ (คน) thahǎan′ʔaakàad′ (khon′) N airman, member of the air force.

นายทหาร (คน,นาย) naajthahǎan′ (khon′, naaj′) N officer, (of the army or navy).

o นายทหารบก (คน,นาย) naajthahǎanbòg′ (khon′, naaj′) N army officer.

o นายทหารเรือ (คน,นาย) naajthahǎanrya′ (khon′, naaj′) N naval officer.

o นายทหารสัญญาบัตร naajthahǎan′sǎnjaabàd′ N commissioned officer.

ผู้บัญชาการทหาร (คน) phûubanchaa′kaanthahǎan′ (khon′) N commander-in-chief.

พลทหาร (คน) phonthahǎan′ (khon′) N mil. 1. private. T 2. Private --.

ราชการทหาร râadchakaan′thahǎan′ N military service.

โรงทหาร (โรง,แห่ง,หลัง) rooŋthahǎan′ (rooŋ′, hὲŋ′, lǎŋ′) N military barracks.

เสนาธิการทหาร (นาย) sěenaa′thíkaan′thahǎan′ (naaj′) N milit. chief of staff.

ทอ. Abbrev. for กองทัพอากาศ "air force," and for ทหารอากาศ "airman."

ทอ thɔɔ′ V 1. to weave. sV 2. back and forth.

ด่าทอ dàa′thɔɔ′ V 1. to curse, revile, speak abusively. 2. to exchange abusive or opprobrious language.

ทอผ้า thɔɔphâa′ to weave cloth. การ-- cloth-weaving.

o ช่างทอผ้า (คน) châaŋthɔɔphâa (khon′) N

weaver.

ทอ (ท่อ, ท่อน) thɔ̂ɔ′ (thɔ̂ɔ′, thɔ̂ɔn′) N 1. pipe (used as a conduit), tube. 2. a n a t. duct.

ท่อน้ำ thɔ̂ɔnáam′ N water pipe.

ท่อยาง thɔ̂ɔjaaŋ′ N rubber tube.

ท่ออ่อน thɔ̂ɔʔɔ̀ɔn′ N hose (i.e. rubber or other flexible type of hose).

ท้อ thɔ́ɔ′ V to be disheartened discouraged, daunted. →Dist. ถอย.

ท้อใจ thɔ́ɔcaj′ V to be discouraged, disheartened, downhearted; to lose heart. ความ-- discouragement.

ท้อถอย thɔ́ɔthɔ̌j′* V 1. to feel like giving up, withdrawing. 2. to lose courage, be discouraged, disheartened. ความ-- discouragement.

ท้อแท้ thɔ́ɔthɛ́ɛ′ V to feel dejected, downcast, in low spirits.

ย่อท้อ jɔ̂ɔthɔ́ɔ′ V 1. to lose heart, be discouraged. 2. to feel like giving up, yielding, withdrawing.

ทอง thɔɔŋ′ N gold. →S y n. คำ ①. →Often coupled with เงิน "silver."

เครื่องทอง (ชิ้น) khrɯ̂aŋthɔɔŋ′ (chín′) N articles of gold, goldware.

เครื่องทองหยอง (ชิ้น, อย่าง) khrɯ̂aŋthɔɔŋjɔ̌ɔŋ′ (chín′, jàaŋ′) N gold ornaments, gold jewelry.

เงินทอง ŋɤnthɔɔŋ′ N 1. gold and silver. 2. colloq. money.

○ เรื่องเงิน ๆ ทอง ๆ rɯ̂aŋ′-ŋɤnŋɤn′thɔɔŋthɔɔŋ′ N c o l l o q. money matters, financial matters.

ช่างทอง (คน) châaŋthɔɔŋ′ (khon′) N goldsmith.

ชุบทอง chúbthɔɔŋ′ V to gild.

ดอกทอง dɔ̀ɔgthɔɔŋ′ N c o l l o q. d e r o g. a loose woman, prostitute. →S y n. โสเภณี e l e g.

○ อีดอกทอง ʔiidɔ̀ɔg′thɔɔŋ′↓ Prostitute! Bag! (term of abuse).

เดินทอง dɤɤnthɔɔŋ′ V 1. to letter in gold, print gold letters. 2. to be gold-lettered, have gold lettering.

ทองขาว thɔɔŋkhǎaw′ N 1. white gold. 2. platinum. 3. nickel.

ทองคำ thɔɔŋkham′ N gold; yellow gold.

○ ทองคำขาว thɔɔŋkhamkhǎaw′ N 1. platinum. 2. white gold.

○ ทองคำเปลว (แผ่น) thɔɔŋkhampleew′ (phɛ̀n′)

N gold leaf.

ทองแดง thɔɔŋdɛɛŋ′ N copper.

ทองแท่ง thɔɔŋthɛ̂ŋ′* N gold bar, ingot.

ทองบรอนซ์ thɔɔŋprɔn′, thɔɔŋpɔn′* N bronze. [บรอนซ์ f. Eng.] →Also called ทองสัมฤทธิ์.

ทองใบ thɔɔŋbaj′ N gold leaf.

ทองรูปพรรณ (ชิ้น) thɔɔŋ′rûubpaphan′ (chín′) N gold made into ornaments and other articles, ornamental gold (as opposed to gold bars).

ทองสัมฤทธิ์ thɔɔŋ′sǎmríd′ N bronze. →Also called ทองบรอนซ์.

ทองเหลือง thɔɔŋlɯ̌aŋ′ N brass.

นกขุนทอง (ตัว) nógkhǔnthɔɔŋ′ (tua′) N talking myna, bird of the starling family (Sturnidae).

ปลาทอง (ตัว) plaathɔɔŋ′ (tua′) N goldfish, small carp with gold coloring. →C o m p. ปลาเงินปลาทอง.

ปิดทอง pìdthɔɔŋ′ V to cover with gold leaf, to gild.

เป็นทองแผ่นเดียวกัน penthɔɔŋ′-phɛ̀ndiaw′kan i d i o m. to be united by marriage into a single family.

เป็นทองไม่รู้ร้อน. See ทำเป็นทองไม่รู้ร้อน under ทำ.

ฝอยทอง (อัน, จับ, แผง) fɔ̌jthɔɔŋ′* (ʔan′, càb′, phɛɛŋ′) N a kind of egg-yolk confection, consisting of thin threads of yolk boiled in heavy syrup.

ฟักทอง (ใบ, ลูก, ผล) fágthɔɔŋ′ (baj′, lûug′, phǒn′) N pumpkin.

มีดทอง (เล่ม, อัน) mîidthɔɔŋ′ (lêm′, ʔan′) N brass fruit knife or paring knife. Brass is used to avoid discoloration of the fruit.

ท่อง thɔ̂ŋ′* V 1. to wade. 2. to roam around (for pleasure). 3. to recite aloud; to repeat (again and again in order to memorize). 4. to study (one's schoolwork). →S y n. เที่ยว.

ท่องขึ้นใจ thɔ̂ŋ′khɯ̂ncaj′ V to commit to memory.

ท่องจำ thɔ̂ŋcam′ V to learn by rote, memorize.

ท่องเที่ยว thɔ̂ŋthîaw′ V 1. to roam, wander. 2. to tour, travel. นัก-- tourist, traveller.

○ สำนักงานท่องเที่ยว (แห่ง) sǎmnágŋaan′thɔ̂ŋ⊃ thîaw′ (hɛ̀ŋ′) N travel bureau.

ท่องน้ำ thɔ̂ŋnáam′ V to wade.

ท่องหนังสือ thɔ̂ŋ′naŋsɯ̌ɯ′ V c o l l o q. 1. to study, do one's schoolwork. 2. to repeat (again and again in order to memorize).

ท้อง (ท้อง) thɔ́ɔŋ/ (thɔ́ɔŋ/) N com. 1. belly, stomach, abdomen. 2. bottom (of a ship, of the sea); bed (of a canal). 3. expanse (of a field, of water, of the sky); area (of water, of a road). 4. pregnancy. V com. 5. to be pregnant. →Also 5. มีท้อง. →Syn. 1. พุง. 4. ครรภ์ eleg.

o ปวดท้อง pùadthɔ́ɔŋ/ to have a stomachache, a bellyache.

o ท้องเรือ thɔ́ɔŋrya/ the bottom of a ship.

o ท้องน้ำ thɔ́ɔŋnáam/ water area, expanse of water.

o ท้องแรก thɔ́ɔŋrɛɛg/ first pregnancy.

ตั้งท้อง tâŋthɔ́ɔŋ/ V com. 1. to conceive, be in early pregnancy. 2. to be pregnant. →Syn. ตั้งครรภ์ eleg.

ท้องกาง thɔ́ɔŋkaaŋ/ V 1. to have a full belly, bulging with food or water. sV 2. with a full belly. →Dist. ท้องขึ้น.

ท้องกิ่ว thɔ́ɔŋkìw/ V slang to be very hungry.

ท้องแก่ thɔ́ɔŋkɛɛ/ V com. to be at full pregnancy. →Syn. ครรภ์แก่ eleg.

ท้องขึ้น thɔ́ɔŋkhŷn/ V 1. to be bloated. N 2. flatulence. →Dist. ท้องกาง.

ท้องเดิน thɔ́ɔŋdəən/ V 1. to have diarrhea, have a running of the bowels. N 2. diarrhea. →Comp. ท้องเสีย, a more general term.

ท้องเดียวกัน in พี่น้องท้องเดียวกัน phîinɔ́ɔŋ/-thɔ́ɔŋ/diawkan/ full brothers, sisters, brothers and sisters.

ท้องตลาด (แห่ง) thɔ́ɔŋ/talàad/ (hɛ̀ŋ/) N colloq. the market, the market place.

ท้องถนน thɔ́ɔŋ/thanǒn/ N the road area, the middle of the road, the road proper (i.e. exclusive of shoulders, edges).

ท้องถิ่น (แห่ง) thɔ́ɔŋthìn/ (hɛ̀ŋ/) N area, district, municipal area, locality.

o รัฐบาลท้องถิ่น (รัฐบาล) rádthabaan/thɔ́ɔŋthìn/ (rádthabaan/) N local government.

ท้องที่ (แห่ง) thɔ́ɔŋthîi/ (hɛ̀ŋ/) N area, district, region under the administration of a sheriff.

ท้องน่อง (ข้าง) thɔ́ɔŋnɔ̂ŋ/ (khâaŋ/) N calf (of the leg).

ท้องน้อย thɔ́ɔŋnɔ́ɔj/ N the lower abdomen; a n a t. the hypogastrium, the hypogastric region.

ท้องนา (แห่ง) thɔ́ɔŋnaa/ (hɛ̀ŋ/) N paddy field, expanse of a paddy field.

ท้องผูก thɔ́ɔŋphùug/ V to be constipated.

ท้องพระโรง thɔ́ɔŋphrárooŋ/ N throne hall.

o กระโถนท้องพระโรง (ใบ) krathǒon/thɔ́ɔŋphrá-rooŋ/ (baj/) N idiom. a scape-goat.

ท้องฟ้า thɔ́ɔŋfáa/ N the sky, the heavens.

ท้องร่วง thɔ́ɔŋrûaŋ/ V eleg. 1. to have diarrhea. N 2. diarrhea.

o โรคท้องร่วง rôog/thɔ́ɔŋrûaŋ/ N eleg. diarrhea.

ท้องร่อง (ท้องร่อง) thɔ́ɔŋrɔ̂ŋ/ (thɔ́ɔŋrɔ̂ŋ/) N irrigation ditch.

ท้องเรื่อง thɔ́ɔŋ/rŷaŋ/ N the subject matter, the essence of a story, the story itself.

ท้องไร่ (แห่ง) thɔ́ɔŋrâj/ (hɛ̀ŋ/) N field, expanse of a field.

ท้องไร่ท้องนา (แห่ง) thɔ́ɔŋrâj/thɔ́ɔŋnaa/ (hɛ̀ŋ/) N elab. colloq. fields (of all kinds).

ท้องสนามหลวง thɔ́ɔŋsanǎamlǔaŋ/ pN colloq. Phra Men (Phra Meru) Ground, the place in Bangkok where all official ceremonies are held. →Also ทุ่งพระเมรุ.

ท้องเสีย thɔ́ɔŋsǐa/ V 1. to have a disorder of the digestive tract, of the bowels; to have diarrhea. N 2. a disorder of the digestive tract, of the bowels; diarrhea. →Comp. ท้องเดิน.

o โรคท้องเสีย rôog/thɔ́ɔŋsǐa/ N colloq. diarrhea.

แน่นท้อง nɛ̂nthɔ́ɔŋ/ V to have a full feeling in the stomach (causing discomfort).

ปวดท้อง pùadthɔ́ɔŋ/ V to have a stomachache, a bellyache.

ฝีในท้อง, โรค-- fǐinajthɔ́ɔŋ/, rôog/fǐinajthɔ́ɔŋ/ N colloq. pulmonary tuberculosis. →Cf. วัณโรค.

แพ้ท้อง phɛ́ɛthɔ́ɔŋ/ V to have morning sickness (in pregnancy).

มีท้อง miithɔ́ɔŋ/ V colloq. to be in the family way, be pregnant. →Cf. อุ้มท้อง. →Syn. มีครรภ์ eleg., ทรงครรภ์ roy.

ลงท้อง loŋthɔ́ɔŋ/ V colloq. to suffer from diarrhea.

สุดท้อง sùdthɔ́ɔŋ/ last-born, youngest. Chiefly in คน--,ลูก-- the last-born child, youngest child.

หายใจไม่ทั่วท้อง hǎajcaj/mâjthûathɔ́ɔŋ/ colloq. to breathe uneasily (as in a tense situation).

อุ้มท้อง ʔûmthɔ́ɔŋ/ V 1. to be carrying a child (i.e. to be pregnant). →Cf. มีท้อง.

ทอด ๑ thɔ̂ɔd/ V 1. to fry (by the piece, e.g. a steak, a fish, an egg). 2. to be fried. →Dist. ผัด.

ทอดมัน (ชิ้น,จาน) thɔ̂ɔdman/ (chín/,caan/) N fried patty made of fish, prawns, or meat.

ทอด ๒ thɔ̂ɔd/ V 1. to cast (e.g. dice, a net). 2. to lay down. 3. hort. to send forth (shoots, spikes, etc.). C 4. section, part, stretch, relay, shift.

ขายทอดตลาด khǎajthɔ̂ɔd/talàad/ V to sell at auction.

ซัดทอด sádthɔ̂ɔd/ V to shift the blame to somebody else; to refer to somebody else as one to be blamed.

เดินทอดเดียว dəən/thɔ̂ɔddiaw/ to walk one stretch.

เดินทอดน่อง dəən/thɔ̂ɔdnɔ̂ŋ/ to walk in a leisurely manner, at a leisurely pace.

ตกทอด tògthɔ̂ɔd/ V 1. to be handed down. 2. to be passed from hand to hand.

ถ่ายทอด thàajthɔ̂ɔd/ V 1. to relay. 2. to transmit, hand down (e.g. to the next generation).

o ถ่ายทอดเสียง thàajthɔ̂ɔd/sǐaŋ/ to transmit sound by relays, to relay sound.

ทอดกฐิน thɔ̂ɔdkathǐn/ V to hold a religious ceremony in which yellow robes are presented to the priests.

ทอดกล้า thɔ̂ɔdklâa/ V to sow germinated rice grain. →Syn. ตกกล้า.

ทอดขา thɔ̂ɔdkhǎa/ V to stretch the legs.

ทอดเงา thɔ̂ɔdŋaw/ V to cast a shadow.

ทอดตัว thɔ̂ɔdtua/ V to lay oneself down, to lie down.

ทอดเต๋า thɔ̂ɔdtǎw/ V to cast, throw dice.

ทอดทิ้ง thɔ̂ɔdthíŋ/ V to neglect, abandon, desert.

ทอดพระเนตร thɔ̂ɔdphranêed/ V roy. to look, see; to cast the eyes.

ทอดสมอ thɔ̂ɔdsamɔ̌ɔ/ to cast anchor, drop anchor.

ทอดสะพาน thɔ̂ɔdsaphaan/ V idiom. to meet halfway, e.g. to encourage acquaintance with someone (as a woman encouraging a man).

ทอดแห thɔ̂ɔdhɛ̌ɛ/ V to cast a fishing net.

ทอดอาลัย thɔ̂ɔd/ʔaalaj/ V to lose hope, lose interest; to despair.

นอนทอดหุ่ย nɔɔn/thɔ̂ɔdhùj/ V colloq. to lie down completely relaxed, stretch out lazily.

เป็นทอด ๆ penthɔ̂ɔdthɔ̂ɔd/ from one to another, in succession, successively.

ทอน thɔɔn/ V 1. to give change (money). 2. to cut down, make smaller, reduce.

เงินทอน ŋənthɔɔn/ N change (money returned).

ตัดทอน tàdthɔɔn/ V to cut down, shorten.

ทอนสตางค์ thɔɔn/sataŋ/ V to give change.

ท่อน thɔ̂ɔn/ C 1. part, section, piece. 2. music. movement. →Comp. 1. ตอน,ชิ้น,ส่วน.

ท่อนไม้ thɔ̂ɔnmáaj/ N log, piece of wood.

ทอย thɔɔj/ V to pitch (e.g. a penny), to throw or toss from a low level (aiming at something).

ทอยกอง thɔɔjkɔɔŋ/ N a kind of gambling game in which players throw coins at a stack of cards or coins which serve as the stake.

ทะนง thanoŋ/ V to be proud, arrogant, haughty, overly confident. ความ-- pride, overconfidence.

ทะนาน (ใบ) thanaan/ (baj/) N 1. a measuring bowl made of a coconut shell. C 2. a formerly used unit of volume equivalent to the amount a coconut shell measure would hold. Used mostly to measure rice, beans, etc.

ทะนานหลวง thanaanlǔaŋ/ C a Thai unit of volume equivalent to one liter.

ทะนุ thanú?/ See entries below. →Also ทนุ FS.

ทะนุถนอม thanú?/thanɔ̌ɔm/ V 1. elab. to care for, to cherish. 2. to treat with affection or great care.

ทะนุบำรุง thanú?/bamruŋ/ V 1. to nourish. 2. hort. to tend (plants) with care. 3. to improve. →Also ทำนุบำรุง.

ทะเบียน thabian/ N register, registration, record.

ขึ้นทะเบียน khɯ̂n/thabian/ V to register (for something), be registered, get (one's name) on a register. Usually for military service and for automobiles.

จดทะเบียน còd'thabian/ V to register, be registered. การ-- registration.

ทะเบียนรถ thabianród/ N car registration.

o ตีทะเบียนรถ tii'thabianród/ V to register a
car.

ทะเบียนสำมะโนครัว thabian'sǎmmanoo'khrua/
N census.

นายทะเบียน (คน) naajthabian/ (khon/) N registrar, recorder.

ลงทะเบียน loŋ'thabian/ V to register, be registered.

o จดหมายลงทะเบียน còdmǎaj/-loŋ'thabian/
registered mail.

หอทะเบียนที่ดิน (แห่ง) hɔ̌ɔthabian'thîidin/ (hèŋ/)
land registration office.

ทะมัดทะแมง thamád/thamɛɛŋ/ with a business-like
manner, seriously, in a serious manner, earnestly, skillfully.

ทะมึน, ทะมื่น thamyn/, thamŷyn/ V to loom, loom
high; to be extremely high and appear gloomy,
sullen, awesome.

ทะแม่ง ๆ thamɛ̀ŋ/thamɛ̀ŋ/* V to be disagreeable,
offensive to one's senses.

ทะโมน FS. See ทโมน.

ทะยอย FS. See ทยอย.

ทะยาน thajaan/ V to jump, leap. →See also ทะเยอ
ทะยาน under ทะเยอ.

ทะยานใจ thajaancaj/ V to become overly bold,
foolhardy.

โลดโผนโจนทะยาน lôodphǒon/-coon/thajaan/
V elab. colloq. to be exciting, thrilling,
adventurous.

ทะเยอ in ทะเยอทะยาน thajəə/thajaan/ V to be
ambitious. ความ-- aspiration, ambition.

ทะแยง FS. See ทแยง.

ทะลวง thaluaŋ/ V 1. to thrust. 2. to make a hole
or passage through.

ทะลัก thalág/ V 1. to gush out, burst forth. 2. to
be forced out abruptly by pressure.

ทะลาย ๑ thalaaj/ C bunch, cluster (of coconuts,
areca nuts, etc.).

ทะลาย ๒ FS. See ทลาย.

ทะลึ่ง thalŷŋ/ V 1. to be impertinent, insolent,

fresh, forward, brash, smart-alecky. 2. to
shoot up (fast). 3. to spring up, stand up, sit up
quickly. ความ-- impertinence, insolence,
cheek.

ทะลุ thalú?/ V 1. to go through, pierce through, bore
through. 2. to be pierced through, penetrated,
bored through; to develop holes (as a cooking
pot).

ทะลุกลางปล้อง thalú?/klaaŋplɔ̂ŋ/ V idiom. to
butt in, interrupt while others are in the midst
of talking.

ทะเล (ทะเล) thalee/ (thalee/) N 1. sea. 2. (of
the) sea, marine. →Opp. บก.

o ปลาทะเล plaa'thalee/ sea fish, marine fish,
salt-water fish.

ขอบทะเล (ด้าน, แห่ง) khɔ̌ɔbthalee/ (dâan/, hèŋ/)
N the edge of the sea; the horizon of the sea.

ชายทะเล (แห่ง) chaajthalee/ (hèŋ/) N seashore.

ทะเลทราย (ทะเลทราย, แห่ง) thaleesaaj/ (thaɔ
leesaaj/, hèŋ/) N desert.

ทะเลสาบ, -ลาป (ทะเลสาบ, แห่ง) thaleesàab/
(thaleesàab/, hèŋ/) N lake.

ทะเลหลวง thaleelǔaŋ/ N a big sea.

น้ำทะเล náamthalee/ N sea water.

ปลาทะเล (ตัว) plaa'thalee/ (tua/) N sea fish,
marine fish, salt-water fish.

ฝั่งทะเล (แห่ง) fàŋ'thalee/ (hèŋ/) N 1. seashore,
seacoast, coast. 2. (as n. mod.) coastal.

โพ้นทะเล phóon'thalee/ overseas.

เรือเดินทะเล (ลำ) ryadəən'thalee/ (lam/) N
sea-going steamer, ocean liner.

ลมทะเล lom'thalee/ N sea breeze.

ลิ้นทะเล (อัน) lín'thalee/ (?an/) N cuttlebone
(used to make a powder for polishing and as
medicine).

ทะเล้น in หน้าทะเล้น nâa'thalén/* V to have a grin,
a broad grin; to be giggly. →Comp. หน้าเป็น.

ทะเลาะ thalɔ́?/ V to quarrel.

ทะเลาะวิวาท thalɔ́?/wíwâad/ to quarrel.

ทะวาย thawaaj/ N Tavoy; the Tavoy (in S Burma).

ทัก thág/ V 1. to greet, address, speak to. 2. to
make a remark, pass a remark. 3. to hint,
remind.

ทักท้วง thágthúaŋ/ V 1. to direct attention to

(undesirable facts, dangers, flaws), to pick
flaws in. 2. to advise against, object to, express a counteropinion.

ทักทาย thágthaaj′ V to greet, speak to.

ทึกทัก thýgthág′ V to jump to conclusions; to
presuppose, assume (without evidence).

ร้องทัก rɔ́ɔŋthág′ V to greet, hail, speak to
(loudly).

ทักษิณ thágsǐn′ lit., eleg. south. →Syn. ใต้ com.
→The literary and the common terms for the
eight chief points of the compass are listed
under ทิศ.

ทักษิณาวัฏ thágsinaa′wád′ lit., eleg. clockwise.
→Cf. ทักษิณ.

ทั่ง (อัน, ก้อน, แท่ง) thâŋ′ (ʔan′, kɔ̂ɔn′, thɛ̂ŋ′) N
anvil.

ทั้ง tháŋ′ qM all, all of, the whole of.

o ทั้งสอง tháŋsɔ̌ɔŋ′ both. Used with and without
a following clf.

o ทั้งสาม tháŋsǎam′ all three.

o ทั้งสี่ tháŋsìi′ all four.

กับทั้ง kàbtháŋ′ and also, and in addition, together with, withal. →Also กับทั้ง...ด้วย.

ทั้งคืน tháŋkhyyn′ all night, the whole night.

ทั้งคู่ tháŋkhûu′ both.

ทั้งตัว tháŋtua′ 1. all over (the body). 2. the
whole of (anything that takes ตัว as clf.).

ทั้ง...ทั้ง... tháŋɔ...tháŋɔ... both...and...

o ทั้งจำทั้งปรับ tháŋcam′tháŋpràb′ both fine and
imprisonment; "both to imprison and to fine."

o ทั้งแม่ทั้งลูก tháŋmɛ̂ɛ′tháŋlûug′ both mother
and child.

ทั้งที่, ทั้ง ๆ ที่ tháŋ′thîiɔ, tháŋtháŋ′thîiɔ even
though, although, in spite of, in spite of the fact
that.

ทั้งนั้น tháŋnán′, thaŋnán′ com. 1. all of them,
any of them, all or any of them, every last one;
everything, anything, everything and anything.
2. all the same, either way. →Cf. ทั้งปวง.

o ไม่ใช่ทั้งนั้น mâjchâj′tháŋnán′ neither of them,
not either of them; none of them, not any of
them.

o ที่ไหน...ทั้งนั้น thîinǎj′...tháŋnán′ any place
at all.

o เขาจะเป็นหมอหรือเป็นนักวิทยาศาสตร์ก็ตาม
ฉันดีใจทั้งนั้น kháwcapenmɔ̌ɔ′rýypennágwídthaɔ
jaasàad′-kɔ̂taam→ chándiicaj′tháŋnán′↓ (Whether)
he becomes a doctor or a scientist is of no consequence; I'll be happy either way.

ทั้งนี้ tháŋníi′ all of this, all this.

ทั้งเนื้อทั้งตัว tháŋnýa′tháŋtua′ 1. all over (the
body); thoroughly. 2. idiom. to one's name
(as in "not a penny to his name").

ทั้งปวง tháŋpuaŋ′ com. all, (of) every kind, (of)
every description. →Cf. also ทั้งนั้น, ทั้งผอง,
ทั้งเพ, ทั้งมวล, ทั้งสิ้น, ทั้งหมด, ทั้งหลาย.

o คนทั้งปวง khon′tháŋpuaŋ′ everybody.

o ท่านทั้งปวง thân′tháŋpuaŋ′ eleg. you all, all
of you.

ทั้งเป็น as in ฝังทั้งเป็น fǎŋ′tháŋpen′ to bury alive.

ทั้งผอง tháŋphɔ̌ɔŋ′ lit., eleg. all. →Cf. ทั้งปวง.

o คนทั้งผอง khon′tháŋphɔ̌ɔŋ′ lit. all people.

ทั้งเพ tháŋphee′ colloq. all (of it), the whole
thing, in (its) entirety, in toto. →Cf. ทั้งปวง.

o ไม่ใช่ทั้งเพ mâjchâj′tháŋphee′ colloq. neither
of them; none of them.

ทั้งมวล tháŋmuan′ lit., eleg. all, all (of them).
→Cf. ทั้งปวง.

ทั้ง...และ... tháŋɔ...lɛɔ... both ... and ...

o ทั้งหญิงและชาย tháŋjiŋ′lɛchaaj′ both men and
women: "women and men" (the customary order
in Thai). →Also ทั้งหญิงชาย.

ทั้งวัน tháŋwan′ all day.

ทั้งสิ้น tháŋsîn′ all, all of (it); entire(ly), total(ly).
→Cf. ทั้งปวง.

o จำนวนทั้งสิ้น camnuan′tháŋsîn′ the total amount.

o เกือบทั้งสิ้น kỳab′tháŋsîn′ almost entirely.

ทั้งหมด tháŋmòd′ com. all (of it, of them), the
whole lot. →Cf. ทั้งปวง.

ทั้งหลาย tháŋlǎaj′ all, the whole (group). →Cf.
ทั้งปวง.

o คนทั้งหลาย khon′tháŋlǎaj′ people (in general),
everyone, everybody.

o ครูทั้งหลาย khruu′tháŋlǎaj′ com. all teachers.
→Syn. บรรดาครู eleg.

o ท่านทั้งหลาย thân′tháŋlǎaj′ eleg. all of you.
Used in addressing a crowd.

o สุภาพบุรุษสตรีทั้งหลาย suphâab′-burùd′sàdtrii′-

tháŋlăaj/↓ Ladies and gentlemen! Used at the beginning of an address.

ทั้งหลายแหล่ tháŋlăajlὲε/ all.

ทั้งอาทิตย์ tháŋ?aathíd/ all week, the whole week.

พร้อมทั้ง phrɔ́ɔm/tháŋɔ together with.

รวมทั้ง ruam/tháŋɔ to include; including.

รวมทั้งหมด ruam/tháŋmòd/ altogether.

ร้อยทั้งร้อย rɔ́ɔj/tháŋrɔ́ɔj/ N colloq. 1. a hundred percent chance. 2. the whole, everybody.

ล้มทั้งยืน lóm/tháŋjyyn/ colloq. to collapse, keel over.

อีกทั้งยัง ?lig/tháŋjaŋɔ furthermore, moreover; and in addition (to that), ... still.

ทัณฑ์ than/ N eleg. punishment, penalty. →Syn. โทษ com.

โทษทัณฑ์ thôod/than/ N eleg. punishment.

ภาคทัณฑ์ phâagthan/ V eleg. to put on probation.

o ถูกภาคทัณฑ์ thùug/phâagthan/ eleg. to be on probation, be put on probation.

ไม้ทัณฑฆาต májthan/thakhâad/ N the cancellation mark (̅) used in the Thai writing system. →Syn. การันต์ com.

ลงทัณฑ์ loŋthan/ V eleg. to punish. →Syn. See ทำโทษ.

ทัด ๑ thád/ V to tuck behind the ear (as a flower, a pencil).

ทัด ๒ thád/ V to be equal (to). →Chiefly in cpds.

ทัดเทียม thádthiam/ V 1. to be equal, equivalent, on the same level. sV 2. equally, comparably. →Syn. See เท่า.

ทัด ๓ in ทัดทาน thádthaan/ V 1. to withstand, oppose, resist. 2. to advise against, warn against.

ทัน than/ V 1. to be on time, in time. 2. to overtake, catch up with, to. sV 3. in time, on time. 4. able to overtake, catch up with, to.

ทันควัน thankhwan/ idiom. immediately, right away, suddenly.

ทันใจ thancaj/ fast, fast enough.

ทันใด thandaj/ suddenly, immediately. →Comp. ทันที.

ทันตาเห็น thantaa/hěn/ 1. immediately; in time. 2. in time to see (it): "in time for the eyes to see."

ทันท่วงที than/thûaŋthii/ in time (with respect to circumstances), in the nick of time.

ทันที thanthii/ 1. prompt. 2. promptly, immediately, at once, instantly. →Comp. ทันใด.

o ทันทีทันใด thanthii/thandaj/ elab. colloq. at once, instantly, in an instant.

ทันเวลา than/weelaa/ in time.

ทันสมัย than/samăj/ up-to-date, modern.

ไม่ทัน májthan/ sV 1. not in time, not on time. 2. can't catch up with.

o ไปไม่ทันรถ paj/-májthan/ród/ to miss the car, train.

o ไม่ทันกิน májthan/kin/ colloq. too slow for use.

o ไม่ทันไร májthan/raj/ colloq. 1. only a short while later. 2. not very long ago.

o ยังไม่ทัน...ก็... jaŋmájthanɔ ...kɔ̂ɔ ... no sooner ... than ...

oo ยังไม่ทันขาดคำ เราก็... jaŋmájthankhàad/ɔ kham/→ raw/kɔ̂ɔ ... colloq. no sooner had he finished talking, than we ...

รู้ทัน rúuthan/ V to know at once what another is driving at. →Dist. รู้เท่า.

ไล่ทัน lâjthan/ V to catch up with, overtake.

ไหวทัน wăjthan/ V to be able to sense what another is up to.

ทันต์ as in ทันตแพทย์ (นาย,คน) than/taphêεd/ (naaj/, khon/) N eleg. dentist. →Syn. แพทย์ฟัน, eleg., หมอฟัน com. → ทันต์ is eq. to dent-.

ทับ ๑ tháb/ V 1. to put on top of, overlay, superimpose. 2. to run over. 3. to press. 4. colloq. (animal) to have intercourse. →Dist. ทาบ.

ทับถม thábthŏm/ V 1. to pile up. 2. idiom. to criticize, defame.

ทับศัพท์ thábsàb/ V 1. to borrow a word (from another language); to transliterate. 2. to be borrowed; to be transliterated.

นอนหลับทับสิทธิ์ nɔɔnlàb/-tháb/sìd/ V idiom. to be neglectful in exercising one's rights (as when failing to vote in an election).

ทับ ๒ (หลัง) tháb/ (lăŋ/) N dwelling place.

ทับทิม (ลูก,ใบ,ผล,เม็ด) thábthim/ N 1. pomegranate (lûug/, baj/, phŏn/). 2. ruby (méd/).

ทัพ (ทัพ) tháb/ (tháb/) N troop, army. →Chiefly in compounds.

กองทัพ (กองทัพ) kɔɔŋtháb′ (kɔɔŋtháb′) N 1. the armed forces (of a country). 2. an army, force; troop, forces.

o กองทัพบก kɔɔŋtháb′bòg′ N army. →Abbrev. ทบ.

o กองทัพเรือ kɔɔŋtháb′rya′ N navy. →Abbrev. ทร.

o กองทัพอากาศ kɔɔŋtháb′ʔaakàad′ N airforce. →Abbrev. ทอ.

ทัพบก (ทัพ) thábbòg′ (tháb′) N army, military land forces.

แม่ทัพ (คน, นาย) mɛ̂ɛtháb′ (khon′, naaj′) general, commander in chief, leader of an army.

ทัพพี (ด้าม, อัน) thábphii′ (dâam′, ʔan′) N ladle.

ทั่ว thûa′ V 1. to be all over, to be general. sV 2. thoroughly, all over. →Comp. ตลอด.

ทั่วกัน thûa′kan′ everybody, all (without omitting anyone).

ทั่วถึง thûathẙŋ′ to be all over; to reach everybody, be well-distributed.

ทั่วทุกแห่ง thûa′thúghɛ̀ŋ′ everywhere.

ทั่วประเทศ thûa′prathêed′ all over the country.

ทั่วไป, ทั่ว ๆ ไป thûapaj′, thûathûa′paj all over, in general; of the general run; general.

o คนทั่วไป khon′thûapaj′ people in general, the public.

o โดยทั่วไป doojthûapaj′ in general, generally.

oo กล่าวโดยทั่วไป klàaw′doojthûapaj′ generally speaking.

ทั่วโลก thûalôog′ all over the world; world-wide.

ฝนตกไม่ทั่วฟ้า fǒntòg′mâjthûafáa′ idiom. "it's raining here and there" (i.e. not at all points), used figuratively of an event that does not include everyone or everything (e.g. salary raises that are given to some but not to all).

หายใจไม่ทั่วท้อง hǎajcaj′mâjthûathɔ́ɔŋ′ colloq. to breathe uneasily (as in a tense situation).

ทัศน์ in ทิวทัศน์ (แห่ง) thiwthád′ (hɛ̀ŋ′) N scenery, view, landscape.

ทัศนะ (ทัศนะ, อย่าง) thádsaná?′* (thádsaná?′, jàaŋ′) N eleg. 1. point of view, opinion. 2. vision, sight. →Also spelled ทรรศนะ. →Syn. 1.

ความเห็น.

ทัศนาจร thádsanaa′cɔɔn′* V eleg. to sightsee.

ทัศนียภาพ thádsanii′japhâab′* N eleg. (natural) scenery.

ทา thaa′ V 1. to paint, smear. 2. to coat, apply, spread (on). 3. to be painted.

ทาเนย thaanəəj′ to spread butter (on), to butter.

ทาปาก thaapàag′ V to put on lipstick, apply lipstick.

ทาสี thaasǐi′ V 1. to paint, cover with paint. 2. to be painted, covered with paint. ช่าง-- painter (workman).

สีทา sǐithaa′ N paint.

ท่า ๑ (ท่า, แห่ง) thâa′ (thâa′, hɛ̀ŋ′) N 1. port, harbor. 2. pier, wharf, landing.

ท่าจีน thâaciin′ pN colloq. Thachin (Tachin), a township in C Thailand. →Also สมุทรสาคร (official name).

o แม่น้ำท่าจีน mɛ̂ɛnáamthâaciin′ pN the Thachin (Tachin) River.

ท่าเรือ (แห่ง, ท่า) thâarya′ (hɛ̀ŋ′, thâa′) N 1. harbor, port, seaport. 2. pier, wharf. →Dist. อู่เรือ.

ท่าอากาศ (แห่ง) thâaʔaakàad′ (hɛ̀ŋ′) N rare airport. [prob. tr. f. Eng.] →See สนามบิน.

เมืองท่า (เมือง) myaŋthâa′ (myaŋ′) N seaport town.

ท่า ๒ thâa′ N water. →Of restricted use. →Syn. น้ำ. →May be coupled with น้ำ as below.

ตกน้ำตกท่า tògnáam′tògthâa′ V elab. colloq. to fall into the water.

อาบน้ำอาบท่า ʔàabnáam′ʔàabthâa′ V elab. colloq. to take a bath, to shower.

ท่า ๓ thâa′ N 1. manner. C 2. posture, attitude. 3. pose (e.g. in a dance).

ดูท่า duuthâa′ V to look like, look as though; judging by appearance, behavior.

o เขาดูท่าจะเป็นคนใจดี kháwduu′thâa′-capen⊃ khon′cajdii′↓ He appears to be a good-natured person.

ท่วงท่า thûaŋthâa′ N presense, attitude, bearing, manner, poise.

ท่าเดียว thâadiaw′ 1. one pose. 2. solely, only (to . . .), nothing but (. . . -ing).

o อยากจะนั่งท่าเดียวแหละ jàagcanâŋ'thâadiaw'ɔ
lɛ?↓ (I) want <u>only</u> to sit down.

ท่าทาง thâathaaŋ' N actions, manner, mien,
bearing.

ท่าที thâa'thii' N 1. attitude, outlook. 2. indication.

o ยังไม่มีท่าที jaŋmâjmii'-thâa'thii' there is still
no indication.

ทำท่า thamthâa' V 1. to assume an attitude,
manner. 2. to act, strike a pose.

พลาดท่า phlâadthâa' V 1. to make a false step,
a wrong move, a slip. 2. by mischance, if by
mischance.

มีท่าว่า miithâa'wâaɔ there are some indications
that, it appears that.

ไม่เป็นท่า mâjpenthâa' 1. to be awkward, ungainly.
2. awkwardly, ungracefully; not in the usual
manner, not in the accepted manner.

วางท่า waaŋthâa' V to put on airs, to pose.

เห็นท่า hĕnthâa' V to get an indication of (a situation), sense a situation.

o เห็นท่าไม่ดี hĕnthâa'mâjdii' to sense a bad
situation.

ให้ท่า hâjthâa' V idiom. (a woman) to encourage
(a man's) advances; to play Cupid, encourage
or arrange for a fellow and a girl to get together.

ท่า ๔ thâa' V to wait. →Chiefly in compounds.
→Syn. คอย, รอ.

คอยท่า khɔɔjthâa' V to wait, wait for.

รอท่า rɔɔthâa' V to wait.

o โดยไม่รอท่า dooj'-mâjrɔɔ'thâa' without waiting, without hesitation.

ท้า tháa' V to challenge, dare, defy.

ท้าทาย tháathaaj' V to challenge, defy.

ทาก (ตัว) thâag' (tua') N 1. land leech. 2. garden slug.

หอยทาก (ตัว) hɔ̌jthâag' (tua') N land snail,
garden snail (Gastropoda).

ทาง ๑ (ทาง, สาย, เส้น) thaaŋ' N 1. way, path,
road, route, trail (thaaŋ', sǎaj', sên'). 2. way,
means (thaaŋ'). 3. by way of, via; toward; in,
through. C 4. clf. for roads, etc. (see mngs.
1, 2). →Syn. 1. ถนน, ลู่ com., วิถี eleg.

2. วิธี.

คนละทิศละทาง khonlathíd'lathaaŋ' elab. colloq.
each one in a different direction.

ช่องทาง (ทาง) chɔ̂ŋthaaŋ' (thaaŋ') N 1. way,
means. 2. chance, opportunity.

ชุมทาง (แห่ง) chumthaaŋ' (hɛ̀ŋ') N road junction,
crossroads.

เดินทาง ๑ dəənthaaŋ' V to travel, take a trip.
→See cross reference for examples.

เดินทาง ๒ dəən'thaaŋɔ to walk by way of, along.

o เดินทางถนนใหญ่ dəən'thaaŋthanǒnjàj' to walk
along the main roads.

โดยทาง doojthaaŋɔ 1. by way of. 2. by (such
and such) means, in (such and such a) way.

ท่าทาง thâathaaŋ' N actions, manner, mien,
bearing.

ทางกาย thaaŋkaaj' physical; physically, bodily.

ทางการ thaaŋkaan' N 1. official source, government source. 2. (as n. mod.) official.

o ข่าวทางการ khàaw'thaaŋkaan' official news.

o ตามทางการ taam'thaaŋkaan' officially.

o เป็นทางการ penthaaŋ'kaan' officially.

ทางการเมือง thaaŋkaanmyaŋ' political, politically.

o อำนาจทางการเมือง ʔamnâad'thaaŋkaanmyaŋ'
political power.

ทางไกล thaaŋklaj' N long distance.

ทางขวามือ thaaŋkhwǎamyy' to the right, on the
right.

ทางข้าม (ทาง) thaaŋkhâam' (thaaŋ') N (pedestrian) crosswalk.

ทางขึ้น (ทาง) thaaŋkhŷn' (thaaŋ') N runway
(for planes).

ทางเข้า (ทาง) thaaŋkhâw' (thaaŋ') N 1. a way
in. 2. entrance, entryway, inlet. →Opp. ทางออก.

ทางจราจร thaaŋ'caraacɔɔn' N traffic lane.

ทางจิต, ทางจิตใจ thaaŋcìd', thaaŋcìdcaj' mental,
mentally.

ทางใจ thaaŋcaj' mental, mentally.

ทางช้างเผือก thaaŋ'cháaŋphỳag' N the Milky Way.

ทางซ้ายมือ thaaŋsáajmyy' to the left, on the left.

ทางดำเนิน (ทาง) thaaŋ'damnəən' (thaaŋ') N
eleg. way, path, procedure.

ทางเดิน (ทาง, สาย, เส้น) thaaŋdəən' (thaaŋ',
sǎaj', sên') N 1. path, trail. 2. channel.

ทางตรง thaaŋtroŋ′ N 1. the straight path, the direct way. 2. directly. →Opp. ทางอ้อม.

ทางทหาร thaaŋthahǎan′ military.

ทางทิศเหนือ thaaŋthídnɯ̌a′ to the north, on the north, northward.

ทางน้ำ thaaŋnáam′ N 1. waterway. 2. by water.

ทางนี้ thaaŋníi′ this way, over this way.

ทางบก thaaŋbòg′ by land.

ทางบ้าน thaaŋbâan′ colloq. the folks at home. →Cf. ทางราชการ.

ทางไปรษณีย์ thaaŋprajsanii′ by mail.

ทางผ่าน (ทาง) thaaŋphàan′ (thaaŋ′) N passage-way.

ทางแยก (ทาง) thaaŋjɛ̀ɛg′ (thaaŋ′) N 1. side road, road or path branching off the main thoroughfare, roads branching from a fork. 2. branch line.

ทางรถไฟ (ทาง,สาย) thaaŋ′ródfaj′ (thaaŋ′, sǎaj′) N 1. railway, railroad. 2. by rail.

o โดยทางรถไฟ doojthaaŋ′ródfaj′ by railway. by rail.

ทางรถยนตร์ (สาย) thaaŋ′ródjon′ (sǎaj′) N 1. highway. 2. by automobile.

ทางร่วม (ทาง,สาย) thaaŋrûam′ (thaaŋ′, sǎaj′) N junction or merging street or highway.

ทางราชการ thaaŋrâadchakaan′ 1. official(ly). 2. colloq. the government, the authorities. →Cf. ทางบ้าน.

ทางเรือบิน (สาย) thaaŋryabin′ (sǎaj′) N 1. air route. 2. by plane, by air.

ทางลัด (ทาง) thaaŋlád′ (thaaŋ′) N short cut.

ทางวิทยาศาสตร์ thaaŋwídthajaasàad′ scientific.

ทางสัญจร (ทาง,สาย) thaaŋ′sǎncɔɔn′ (thaaŋ′, sǎaj′) N eleg. 1. thoroughfare, passageway. 2. any area traversed by pedestrian or vehicular traffic.

ทางหลวง (ทาง,สาย) thaaŋlǔaŋ′ (thaaŋ′, sǎaj′) N Royal Highways; public highways.

ทางเหนือ thaaŋnɯ̌a′ in the north.

ทางออก (ทาง) thaaŋ?ɔ̀ɔg′ (thaaŋ′) N 1. a way out. 2. exit, outlet. →Opp. ทางเข้า.

o ไม่มีทางออก mâjmii′thaaŋ?ɔ̀ɔg′ there is no way out (used both literally and figuratively).

ทางอ้อม thaaŋ?ɔ̂ɔm′ N 1. an indirect, roundabout way. 2. detour. 3. indirectly, by indirect means. →Opp. ทางตรง.

ทางอากาศ thaaŋ?aakàad′ by air.

o กำลังทางอากาศ kamlaŋ′thaaŋ?aakàad′ milit. air power.

ที่ทาง (แห่ง,ที่) thîi′thaaŋ′ (hɛ̀ŋ′, thîi′) N 1. lot (for a house or building). 2. place.

นำทาง namthaaŋ′ V to lead the way. คน--,ผู้-- guide.

แนวทาง nɛɛwthaaŋ′ N direction, trend.

ในทาง najthaaŋ′, najthaaŋ‐ 1. in (such and such) a way. 2. on the way, along the way. NOTE. In many instances this expression corresponds to English -ly; see examples.

o ในทางมิชอบ najthaaŋ′míchɔ̂ɔb′ in an unlawful manner, illegally.

o ในทางเศรษฐกิจ najthaaŋ′-sèed′thakìd′ 1. from the economic standpoint. 2. in an economical way; economically.

เป็นทาง penthaaŋ′ 1. as a way (to). 2. in the form of a line, in a line.

เปิดทาง pəədthaaŋ′ V 1. to open the way (to). 2. to yield the right of way.

มีทาง miithaaŋ′ there is a way, a means; it is possible.

o ไม่มีทาง mâjmiithaaŋ′ there is no way, no means; it is impossible.

แยกทาง jɛ̀ɛgthaaŋ′ to go separate ways.

ระยะทาง rajá?′thaaŋ′ N distance.

ริมทาง rimthaaŋ′ N wayside.

ลู่ทาง (ลู่ทาง) lûuthaaŋ′ (lûuthaaŋ′) N means, way.

วิถีทาง wíthǐi′thaaŋ′ N eleg. way, path.

สุดทาง sùdthaaŋ′ N the end of the road.

หนทาง (ทาง) hǒnthaaŋ′ (thaaŋ′) N 1. road, way. 2. means.

o หนทางแก้ไข (ทาง) hǒnthaaŋ′kɛ̂ɛkhǎj′ (thaaŋ′) N remedial means; a remedy (e.g. for a difficulty).

o หมดหนทาง mòd′hǒnthaaŋ′ to have no way, no means (to do something).

หลงทาง lǒŋthaaŋ′ to lose one's way, get lost.

ทาง ๒ (ทาง) thaaŋ′ (thaaŋ′) N 1. midrib (of the coconut palm leaf). 2. frond, leaf (of a type attached to the trunk or main stem).

ทางมะพร้าว (ทาง) thaaŋmaphráaw/ (thaaŋ/) 1. midrib of the coconut palm pinnate leaf. 2. coconut palm pinnate leaf. →Dist. ก้านมะ-พร้าว.

ทาน ๑ thaan/ N 1. alms. 2. gift, donation.

ขอทาน khɔ̌ɔthaan/ V 1. to beg, ask for alms (as a beggar). N 2. short for คน-- beggar.

พระราชทาน phrárâad/chathaan/ V roy. to give, present, grant, confer. →Syn. See ให้.

ให้ทาน hâjthaan/ to give alms.

ให้เป็นทาน hâj/penthaan/ to give as alms, give as charity.

ทาน ๒ thaan/ V 1. to resist, oppose, withstand. 2. to support. 3. to proofread, check against (the original).

ต้านทาน tâanthaan/ to resist, afford resistance against. การ-- resistance.

ทนทาน thonthaan/ V to be enduring, lasting, durable.

ทาน...อยู่ thaan/...jùu/ V to be resistant to.

ทาน ๓ thaan/ V eleg. to take (food or drink), eat, drink (something). Shortened form of รับประ-ทาน. →Syn. See กิน.

ทาน ๔ thaan/. Shortened form of ประทาน.

ทานโทษ thaanthôod/ colloq. Excuse me! Short for ขอประทานโทษ. →Syn. ขอโทษ com.

ท่าน thân/* P eleg. def. 1. you. 2. he, him, she, her, they, them. T 3. title placed in front of certain nouns indicating rank (usually in order to show additional respect). 4. title placed before the first names of, or before relationship terms referring to หม่อมเจ้า. C 5. eleg. clf. for human beings. →In mng. 1. paired with ข้าพเจ้า I, me. →Syn. 1. คุณ com. 2. เขา com.

ท่านทั้งปวง thân/tháŋpuaŋ/ eleg. you all, all of you.

ท่านทั้งหลาย thân/tháŋlǎaj/ eleg. all of you. Used in addressing a crowd.

ท่านผู้ฟังทั้งหลาย thânphûufaŋ/tháŋlǎaj/ eleg. all you who are listening, all you listeners.

ท่านผู้หญิง thânphûujǐŋ/ T eleg. def. 1. Lady --. P 2. Her Ladyship, Madame. NOTE. ท่านผู้หญิง is a title conferred upon a woman of the highest rank, e.g. the wife of the present prime minis-ter. It was formerly used of the wives of เจ้าพระยา.

บางท่าน baaŋthân/ eleg. some (referring to people); some people. →Syn. บางคน com.

พณ ฯ ท่าน phaná?/thân/ T eleg. def. 1. Honorable --. P 2. Your Excellency, His Excellency. →Used in speaking to or about high officials. NOTE. Also written ฯ พณ ฯ and พณ ฯ and sometimes incorrectly พณท่าน. The formal reading is พณหัวเจ้าท่าน phaná?/hǔaɔcâaw/-thân/.

พระท่าน phrá?/thânɔ P colloq. 1. he, him, the god, the holy being. 2. he, him, the priest.

ทาบ thâab/ V to put over, place over, lay on top (e.g. .a piece of cloth used as a patch). →Dist. ทับ.

ทาบทาม thâabthaam/ V to sound out, make discreet or indirect inquiries.

ทาม in ทาบทาม. See entry above.

ท่าม in ท่ามกลาง, ใน-- thâamklaaŋ/, najthâamklaaŋ/ in the middle of, in the midst of, amid, among.

ทาย ๑ thaaj/ V 1. to predict, prognosticate. 2. to guess. →Syn. 1. ทำนาย eleg.

เสี่ยงทาย sìaŋthaaj/ V 1. to divine, practise divination. 2. to cast lots.

ทาย ๒ thaaj/ See the following entries.

ทักทาย thágthaaj/ V to greet, speak to.

ท้าทาย tháathaaj/ V to challenge, defy.

ท้าย tháaj/ N rear, end, rear end, tail end. →Opp. หัว.

พ่วงท้าย phûaŋtháaj/ V 1. to have in tow, to pull along behind (e.g. a trailer). 2. colloq. to trail (e.g. a degree after one's name).

รั้งท้าย ráŋtháaj/ V to be the last (e.g. in line or in rank).

ลงท้าย loŋtháaj/ V 1. to be at the end. 2. to end, bring to an end, close. sV 3. finally, at last.

สุดท้าย sùdtháaj/ V to be last, final.

ให้ท้าย hâjtháaj/ V to back, support, take sides with (usually covertly).

ทายาท (คน) thaajâad/ (khon/) N eleg. heir.

รัชทายาท (องค์) rádchathaa/jâad/ (?oŋ/) N roy. royal heir, heir to the throne.

ทารก (คน) thaaróg/ (khon/) N eleg. baby, infant, child. →Syn. เด็กอ่อน com.

ทารุณ thaarun′ V eleg. to be cruel, fierce.
   ความ-- cruelty. →Syn. โหดร้าย com.
ทาส (คน) thâad′ (khon′) N slave.
   ความเป็นทาส khwaampenthâad′ N slavery,
   bondage.
ทำ tham′ V 1. to do, perform, commit. 2. to make,
   produce, manufacture. 3. to be made, produced,
   manufactured. 4. to make as if, feign, pretend.
   5. to let, make, cause (see Note 1). คน--
   maker, doer. →Dist. ก่อ .

> NOTE 1. ทำ is used as a transitivizer for a
> number of basically medio-passive verbs. In
> this use ทำ may be translated rather literally
> as "let, make, cause," but it is often simply
> implied in English through the transitive use
> of the English verb. Thus ทำจามแตก means
> "to break dishes" or, more literally, "to make
> the dishes break, cause the dishes to break."
> The noun referring to the entity being acted
> upon follows ทำ and precedes the medio-pas-
> sive verb. If no noun is used, it is understood
> from the immediately preceding context. A list
> of the most important expressions requiring
> ทำ in this use is as follows:
> ทำ(...)ตก tham′(...)tòg′ to drop (smthg.),
>   let (smthg.) drop: ตก to drop (of itself).
> ทำ(...)แตก tham′(...)tὲὲg′ to break, smash
>   (smthg.): แตก to break, get broken, get
>   smashed.
> ทำ(...)บิ่น tham′(...)bìn′ to nick, chip (the
>   edge or blade of smthg.): บิ่น to get nicked,
>   chipped.
> ทำ(...)เปื้อน tham′(...)pɤ̂an′ to soil (smthg.):
>   เปื้อน to get soiled, dirty.
> ทำ(...)ร่วง tham′(...)rûaŋ′ to make (smthg.)
>   fall off: ร่วง to fall off (as leaves).
> ทำ(...)เสีย tham′(...)sĭa′ to spoil (smthg.):
>   เสีย to get spoiled, get out of order.
> ทำ(...)หล่น tham′(...)lòn′ to make (smthg.)
>   fall off: หล่น to fall off (as leaves).
> ทำ(...)หลุด tham′(...)lùd′ to let (smthg.) slip
>   (e.g. out of one's hand): หลุด to slip (away),
>   get loose.
> ทำ(...)หก tham′(...)hòg′ to spill (smthg.):
>   หก to spill (of itself).
> ทำ(...)หัก tham′(...)hàg′ to break (smthg.)
>   (off): หัก to break off (of itself).
> ทำ(...)หาย tham′(...)hăaj′ to lose, misplace
>   (smthg.): หาย to disappear.
>
> NOTE 2. True causative expressions are made
> by means of the word ทำให้ "to cause (to do
> smthg.), make (do smthg.)"; 1st, 2nd, and 3rd
> examples. The word may also frequently cor-

respond to certain English causative suffixes,
e.g. -en (frighten), -fy, -ify (simplify), -ize
(neutralize), and others (cleanse); 1st, 4th, 5th,
and 6th examples.
o นั่นทำให้ผมตกใจ nân′ thamhâjphŏm′tὸgcaj′↓
   That frightens me. That makes me frightened.
o ทำให้ร่างกายอบอุ่น thamhâjrâaŋkaaj′′ὸb?ùn′
   to warm the body, cause the body to be warm.
o ทำให้คิดไปว่า thamhâjkhíd′pajwâa′ to make
   one think that.
o ทำให้ง่าย thamhâjŋâaj′ to simplify, make easy.
o ทำให้เป็นกลาง thamhâj′penklaaŋ′ chem. to
   neutralize.
o ทำให้สะอาด thamhâjsa?àad′ to cleanse, make
   clean.

ก่อกรรมทำเข็ญ kɔ̀ɔkam′thamkhĕn′ V elab.
   colloq. to cause trouble, do evil, commit
   crimes.
การทำเหมืองแร่ kaantham′mŭaŋrὲὲ′ N ore-mining.
ได้งานทำ dâajŋaan′tham′ 1. to get a job. 2. to
   have a job.
ทำกับข้าว thamkàbkhâaw′ V com. to cook. คน--
   cook. →Syn. ปรุงอาหาร eleg.
ทำการ thamkaan′ V to work, do work.
o ที่ทำการ (แห่ง) thîithamkaan′ (hὲŋ′) N office.
o รัศมีทำการ rádsamĭi′thamkaan′ N effective
   radius, range of operation.
ทำการค้นคว้า thamkaan′khónkhwáa′ to do research.
ทำการรบ thamkaan′rób′ to do fighting, do battle.
ทำกิริยา tham′kìrijaa′ to act, perform an action,
   go through a motion.
ทำไก๋ thamkăj′ V to feign ignorance or innocence;
   to play dumb.
ทำขวัญ thamkhwăn′ V 1. to perform a ceremony
   in order to encourage and strengthen. 2. to make
   compensation for injury done (to another).
o ค่าทำขวัญ khâa′thamkhwăn′ N compensation,
   indemnity (for personal injury or damage).
ทำครัว thamkhrua′ V to do cooking; to cook,
   prepare food.
ทำความ thamkhwaam′ V to cause or initiate something which results in bad, unpleasant, or undesirable consequences.
ทำความเคารพ thamkhwaam′khawrób′ V to salute,
   pay respect to.
ทำความผิด tham′khwaamphìd′ V 1. to commit

a crime. 2. to do wrong. →Comp. ทำผิด.

ทำความสะอาด thamkhwaam′saʔàad′ V to do the cleaning, clean (a room, house, etc.).

ทำงาน thamŋaan′ V to do work, to work. คน-- worker.

o ทำงานหนัก ๆ thamŋaan′nàgnàg′ V 1. to work hard. 2. to do hard work.

o ที่ทำงาน (แห่ง, ที่) thîithamŋaan′ (hɛ̀ŋ′, thîi′) N office, place to work.

ทำชั่ว thamchûa′ V to do evil. →Opp. ทำดี.

ทำ(. . .)ด้วย tham′(...)dûajɔ 1. to make (something) out of (something else). 2. (something) to be made out of (something else).

o ทำด้วยหิน tham′dûajhĭn′ to make of stone, be made of stone.

ทำดี thamdii′ V to do good. →Opp. ทำชั่ว.

ทำ(. . .)ตก tham(...)tòg′ to drop (something), let (something) drop. See Note 1 under ทำ.

ทำตัว thamtua′ V to behave, act, make oneself (be).

ทำตาปริบ ๆ thamtaa′prìbprìb′ V to blink the eyes repeatedly (e.g. when stunned by defeat or sorrow).

ทำตาม thamtaam′ V 1. to do accordingly, as bidden. 2. to do according to (an order, a model). 3. to imitate, copy (e.g. the actions of another).

ทำตามแบบ tham′taambɛ̀ɛb′ V to follow the pattern, imitate.

ทำตามอย่าง tham′taamjàaŋ′ V to imitate.

ทำ(. . .)แตก tham(...)tɛ̀ɛg′ to break, smash (something)(e.g. dishes). See Note 1 under ทำ.

ทำท่า thamthâa′ V 1. to assume an attitude, manner. 2. to act, strike a pose.

ทำโทษ thamthôod′ V to punish, penalize. →Syn. ลงโทษ com. ลงทัณฑ์ eleg.

o ถูกทำโทษ thùugthamthôod′ V to be punished, be penalized.

ทำนา thamnaa′ V to farm, do rice-farming. การ-- rice-farming. →Comp. ทำไร่.

ทำ(. . .)บาด as in ทำมีดบาด thammîidbàad′ to get cut by a knife, cut (oneself) on a knife: "to let a knife cut (one)."

ทำบาป thambàab′ V to commit a sin; to sin.

ทำบุญ thambun′ V perform meritorious deeds (such as the giving of alms): "to make merit."

ทำเป็นทองไม่รู้ร้อน thampenthɔɔŋ′mâjrúurɔ́ɔn′ idiom. to feign or pretend indifference; to act as though unaffected.

ทำผิด thamphìd′ V 1. to make a mistake, make an error. 2. to do wrong.: Comp. ทำความผิด.

o ทำผิดกฎหมาย thamphìd′kòdmăaj′ to break the law.

ทำมาหากิน thammaa′hăakin′ V to earn a living. การ-- making a living, earning a living; occupation, livelihood.

ทำไม. See main entry below.

ทำร้าย thamráaj′ V eleg. to do harm; to harm.

o ทำร้ายร่างกาย thamráaj′râaŋkaaj′ V to assault, cause bodily injury.

ทำไร่ thamrâj′ V to do farming, do crop-farming. →Comp. ทำนา.

ทำเล่ห์กระเท่ห์ thamlêe′krathêe′ to act cunningly, practise deceit.

ทำศึก thamsỳg′ V to make war; to war. →Syn. ทำสงคราม.

ทำสงคราม tham′sŏŋkhraam′ V to make war; to war. →Syn. ทำศึก.

ทำสวน thamsŭan′ V to do gardening, orchard work, plantation work. คน-- gardener, orchardist, plantation worker.

ทำสัญญา tham′sănjaa′ V to make a contract, an agreement.

ทำเสีย tham′sía↓ Do it!

ทำ(. . .)เสีย tham′(...)sía′ to spoil (something).

ทำเสียงดัง tham′sĭaŋdaŋ′ V to make a loud noise, to be noisy.

ทำ(. . .)หก tham′(...)hòg′ to spill (something), let (something) spill. See Note 1 under ทำ.

ทำหน้าที่ tham′nâathîi′ to do duty (for), do the duties (of), serve the function of.

ทำ(. . .)หัก tham′(...)hàg′ to break (something) off (unintentionally), cause (something) to break, break off, break apart. See Note 1 under ทำ.

ทำ(. . .)หาย tham(...)hăaj′ to lose, misplace (something). See Note 1 under ทำ.

ทำหูทวนลม thamhŭu′thuanlom′ idiom. to pretend not to hear, turn a deaf ear.

ทำให้ thamhâjɔ to cause (to do something), make (do something). See Note 2 under main entry. NOTE. This expression is distinct in meaning from ทำ(. . .)ให้(. . .) which means "to do, make (something) for (someone)."

o ทำให้เกิด thamhâjkə̀əd′ V to bring about, give rise to, produce, create, cause.

oo ทำให้เกิดการแท้งลูก thamhâjkə̀əd′-kaanthɛ́ɛŋ′ɔ lûug′ to bring about abortion.

ทำอันตราย tham/ʔantaraaj′ V to hurt, harm, injure; to do harm.

ทำเอง tham?eeŋ′ V to do, make by oneself.

วิธีทำ (วิธี) wíthii′tham′(wíthii′) N the way to do, the method of doing (something), procedure.

ทำนบ (ทำนบ,แห่ง)thamnób′ (thamnób′, hɛ̀ŋ′) N dam. →Comp. เขื่อน.

ทำนอง (ทำนอง) thamnɔɔŋ′ (thamnɔɔŋ′) N 1. melody, tune. C 2. manner, mode, way. 3. in the manner of, like.

o ในทำนองขู่ najthamnɔɔŋ′khùu′ in a threatening way.

o ในทำนองเดียวกัน(กับ) najthamnɔɔŋ′-diaw′kanɔ (kaɔ) in the same manner (as), in the same way (as).

ทำนองเพลง (ทำนอง) thamnɔɔŋ′phleeŋ′ (thamɔ nɔɔŋ′) N melody, tune.

ทำนาย thamnaaj′ V to foretell, prophesy, prognosticate. คำ-- prophecy. [conv.f. ทาย]

ทำนุ in ทำนุบำรุง thamnú?′bamruŋ′ V 1. to nourish. 2. to tend with care (as plants). 3. to improve. →Comp. ทะนุบำรุง.

ทำเนียบ (แห่ง,ทำเนียบ) thamnîab′ (hɛ̀ŋ′, thamɔ nîab′) N eleg. residence (of high government official).

ทำเนียบนายก thamnîab′naajóg′ N the prime minister's residence.

ทำเนียบรัฐบาล thamnîab′rádthabaan′ N the prime minister's office; the government office.

ทำไม thammaj′ 1. why, what for. 2. why? what for? how come? NOTE. Possibly originally from ทำไร "to do what," with assimilation of ร to ม.

ทำลาย thamlaaj′ V 1. to destroy, demolish, wipe out, ruin. 2. sport. to break (e.g. a record).

3. phys. to smash (atoms). การ-- destruction, demolition.

ทำลายสถิติ thamlaaj′sathì?tì?′ V sport. to break a record.

ทำเล (แห่ง) thamlee′ (hɛ̀ŋ′) N location.

ทิ้ง thíŋ′ V 1. to leave, desert, abandon, run away from (husband, wife). 2. to throw (away), discard, jettison. 3. to mail (letters), drop (into the mailbox). 4. to drop, release (bombs). →Often coupled with ละ.

เครื่องบินทิ้งระเบิด (ลำ) khrɣaŋbin′thíŋrabə̀əd′ (lam′) N bomber.

ทอดทิ้ง thɔɔdthíŋ′ V to neglect, abandon, desert.

ทิ้งกันลุ่ย thíŋ′kanlûj′ colloq. to leave (one's opponent) far behind; to outscore by a wide margin.

ทิ้งขว้าง thíŋ′khwâaŋ′ V 1. to throw aside, discard, neglect (things). 2. to forsake, desert, abandon (a person).

ทิ้งจดหมาย thíŋ′còdmǎaj′ V to mail a letter; (Brit.) to post a letter.

ทิ้ง(. . .)ไป thíŋ′(. . .)paj to throw (something) away, discard (something). →Dist. ทิ้ง(. . .) ไว้.

ทิ้งลูกระเบิด thíŋ′lûugrabə̀əd′ V to drop bombs, to bomb.

ทิ้ง(. . .)ไว้ thíŋ′(. . .)wáj′ V to leave (something) (in certain place). →Dist.ทิ้ง(. . .)ไป, ทิ้ง (. . .)เสีย.

ทิ้ง(. . .)เสีย thíŋ′(. . .)sía to throw (something) away. →Dist. ทิ้ง(. . .)ไว้.

ละทิ้ง lá?′thíŋ′ V to abandon, desert, neglect.

o ละทิ้งหน้าที่ lá?thíŋ′nâathîi′ to desert, be a deserter from duty (e.g. a soldier, civil servant).

สาดทิ้งเททิ้ง sàadthíŋ′theethíŋ′ V elab. colloq. to throw out.

ทิฐิ,ทิฏฐิ thídthì?′ N eleg. 1. viewpoint, opinion. 2. stubbornness, obstinacy, stubborn pride. →Also ทิษฐิ.

ทิฐิมานะ thídthì?-maaná?′ N eleg. pride and perseverance, pride spurring one to perseverance.

ทิม in ทับทิม (เม็ด,ลูก,ใบ,ผล) thábthim′ N 1. ruby (méd′). 2. pomegranate (lûug′, baj′, phǒn′).

ทิ่ม thîm′ V 1. to pierce, thrust in, stab. 2. to be

pierced. →Syn. ตำ,แทง.

ทิว (ทิว) thiw/ (thiw/) N 1. range (of mountains).
2. a distant stretch or line (of trees). →Syn. 1.
เทือก,พืด.

ทิวเขา (ทิว) thiwkhǎw/ (thiw/) N mountain
range.

ทิวทัศน์ (แห่ง) thiwthád/ (hὲŋ/) N scenery, view,
landscape.

ทิวไม้ (ทิว) thiwmáaj/ (thiw/) N a distant
stretch or line of trees, a long row of trees.

ทิศ (ทิศ) thíd/ (thíd/) N 1. direction, point of the
compass.

NAMES OF THE POINTS OF THE COMPASS
The terms for the points of the compass most often occur as noun modifiers (modifying ทิศ if no other noun
is specified). However, in simply listing the points of
the compass, no preceding noun is necessary. Also,
following จาก, the preceding noun is occasionally
omitted, as in จากตะวันออก "from the east," จากทักษิน
"from the south." Besides the above uses, ใต้ "south"
and เหนือ "north" may also occur as verb modifiers;
see ใต้, เหนือ.

	Literary Terms	Common Terms
N	อุดร ʔùdɔɔn/	เหนือ nɣǎ/
NE	อิสาน ʔìsǎan/	ตะวันออกเฉียงเหนือ tawanʔɔ̀ɔg/chɪ̀aŋnɣǎ/
E	บูรพา buuraphaa/	ตะวันออก tawanʔɔ̀ɔg/
SE	อาคเนย์ ʔaakhanee/	ตะวันออกเฉียงใต้ tawanʔɔ̀ɔg/chɪ̀aŋtâaj/
S	ทักษิน thágsɪn/	ใต้ tâaj/
SW	หรดี hɔɔradii/	ตะวันตกเฉียงใต้ tawantòg/chɪ̀aŋtâaj/
W	ประจิม pracim/	ตะวันตก tawantòg/
NW	พายัพ phaajáb/	ตะวันตกเฉียงเหนือ tawantòg/chɪ̀aŋnɣǎ/

เข็มทิศ (อัน) khěmthíd/ (ʔan/) N compass.

คนละทิศละทาง khonlathíd/lathaaŋ/ elab. colloq.
each one in a different direction.

ทิศตะวันตก thíd/tawantòg/ N west. ทาง-- to
the west, on the west, westward.

o ทิศตะวันตกเฉียงเหนือ thíd/-tawantòg/chɪ̀aŋnɣǎ/
N northwest.

ทิศตะวันออก thíd/tawanʔɔ̀ɔg/ N east. ทาง--
to the east, on the east, eastward.

ทิศใต้ (ทิศ) thídtâaj/ (thíd/) N south. ทาง--
to the south, on the south, southward.

ทิศเหนือ (ทิศ) thídnɣǎ/ (thíd/) N north. ทาง--
to the north, on the north, northward.

ทิษฐิ. See ทิฐิ.

ที. thii/ the English letter "T." [f. Eng.]

ที ๑ element occurring in special combinations

where it is used as a synonym of ท่า ๓ "manner."

เข้าที khâwthii/ V 1. to be appropriate. 2. to
sound all right, look all right, seem all right.
3. be pleasant in appearance, attractive.

ได้ที dâaj/thii/ V 1. to gain the advantage (over
one's opponent). 2. fig. to be on top. →Dist.
ได้เปรียบ. →Ant. เสียที.

ตามที,ก็ตามที taam/thii/, kɔ̂taam/thii/ let it be
(indicating resignation, state of being fed up with
something, someone). →See cross reference.

เต็มที temthii/ V 1. to be awful, terrible. sV 2.
very, quite, awfully, extremely, hopelessly, badly.

ท่วงที thûaŋthii/ N presence, attitude, deportment,
bearing, manner.

ท่าที thâa/thii/ N 1. attitude, outlook. 2. indication.

รู้ที rúuthii/ to know what is on someone's mind,
sense someone else's wishes.

เสียที sɪa/thii/ V 1. to lose the advantage to one's
opponent. 2. to lose, be defeated. →Ant. 1.
ได้ที. 2. แพ้.

ที ๒ thii/ C 1. time, instance, occasion. Pt 2. particle
of emphasis. →Syn. 1. See คราว. NOTE. Use
of ที as a particle of emphasis derives from a
shortening of สักทีหนึ่ง "just this once"; see
examples.

o หนึ่งที,ทีหนึ่ง nɣŋthii/, thii/nɣŋ/ one time, once.
NOTE. หนึ่งที is normally used in counting,
ทีหนึ่ง otherwise. See also note under main entry.

o สองที sɔ̌ɔŋthii/ two times, twice.

o สามที sǎamthii/ three times.

o ขอที khɔ̌ɔ/thii/↓, khɔ̌ɔthii/↓ colloq. Please,
just this once! (requesting that something be
stopped).

o ขอโทษที khɔ̌ɔthôod/thii/↓ Excuse me!

o ขอเสียที khɔ̌ɔ/sɪathii/↓* idem ขอที.

o เสร็จสิ้นกันไปที sèd/sɪ̂n/-kanpajthii/↓ That's
the end of that! (expression of relief).

ชั่วเจ็ดทีดีเจ็ดหน chûa/cèdthii/→dii/cèdhǒn/ "bad
for seven times, good for seven times," i.e. good
luck is intermingled with bad.

ทันที thanthii/ prompt; promptly, immediately,
at once, instantly. →Comp. ทันใด.

ทีกับ...ละก็ thii/kaᵓ...lakɔ̂ɔ/→ when it comes to,
with respect to (such and such an individual or

subject).

ที่ใครก็ที่มัน thii′khraj′-k⊃thii′man′ When it's a
  fellow's turn, why then, it's <u>his</u> turn! Cf. Eng.
  "turn about is fair play."

ที่เดียว (1) thii′diaw′; (2, 3) thiidiaw′ 1. a single
  time. 2. at once; 3rd example. 3. exactly,
  quite, very; 1st and 2nd examples. →In mng. 2
  and 3 often contracted to เที่ยว or เจี๊ยว.

o ดีที่เดียว dii′thiidiaw′ very good, quite good,
  just fine.

o ถูกที่เดียว thùug′thiidiaw′ quite right, exactly
  right.

o มาทีเดียว maa′thiidiaw↓ Come at once!
  (mother sp. to child).

ทีแรก thiirɛ̂ɛg′ 1. at first, the first time. 2. in
  the first place.

ทีไร thiiraj′ whenever, any time, whatever time.

ทีละ thiila⊃ "at a time," as in the following
  entries.

o ทีละขั้น ๒ ขั้น thiilakhân′s⊃̂⊃ŋkhân′ one or two
  steps a time.

o ทีละคน thiilakhon′ one person at a time.

o ทีละน้อย thiilan⊃́⊃j′ little by little, a little at
  a time.

ทีหลัง thiilǎŋ′ next time, later.

ทุกที thúgthii′ 1. every time, each time. 2. by
  the minute, progressively.

o ชักร้อนจัดขึ้นทุกที chágr⊃́⊃n′càd′-khŷnthúgthii′
  it's getting hotter by the minute; it's getting
  progressively hotter.

บางที baaŋthii′ sometimes, at times; perhaps;
  other times. →Syn. ลางที.

พอที phɔɔthii′↓ That's enough! Enough! Hold it!

ลางที laaŋthii′ sometimes. →Rarely used.
  →Syn. บางที.

อีกที ʔiigthii′ once more, again.

อีกทีหนึ่ง ʔiigthii′nɯŋ one more time, once more,
  again.

ที่ ๑ (ที่) thîi′ (thʔi′) N 1. place; space, room (in
  the sense of place); 1st example. 2. initial element meaning "thing where, place where," in
  certain noun derivatives; 2nd and 3rd examples.
  C 3. clf. for the above; for sinks, toilet bowls;
  4th example. Pp 4. at, in, to; 5th to 7th examples.

→Dist.1. แหล่ง. →Syn. 1. สถาน eleg., แห่ง com.

o กินที่ kinthîi′ V to take up room, space.

o ที่เขี่ยบุหรี่ (ที่,อัน) thîikhìa′burìi′ (thîi′, ʔan′)
  N ashtray.

o ที่นั่ง (ที่) thîinâŋ′ (thîi′) N seat, place to sit.

o ส้วม ๒ ที่ sûam′s⊃̌⊃ŋthîi′ two toilet bowls.

o เขาอยู่ที่บ้าน kháwjùu′thîibâan′ he is at home,
  at (his) house.

o เขาจะไปที่บ้านคุณ kháwcapaj′-thîibâan′khun′
  he will go to your house.

o เขาอยู่ที่อเมริกา kháwjùu′thîiʔameerikaa′
  he is in America.

กินที่ kinthîi′ V to take up room, space.

คงที่ khoŋthîi′ V to be constant, invariable.

คาที่ khâathîi′ on the spot, instantly.

o ตายคาที่ taaj′khaathîi′ to die on the spot.

ค่าที่ khâathîi′ the price of a piece of land, of a
  lot. →Cf. ค่าที่ under ที่ ๒.

เคลื่อนที่ khlŷanthîi′ V 1. to move. 2. to be mobile.
  3. to be out of place; to be dislocated. การ--
  phys. motion. →Cf. 3. เป็นที่.

เต็มที่ temthîi′ fully, to the fullest extent, to the
  full, to the utmost, extremely.

ท้องที่ (แห่ง) th⊃́⊃ŋthîi′ (hɛ̀ŋ′) N area, district,
  locality, region under the administration of a
  sheriff.

ที่กันภัย (แห่ง,ที่) thîi′kanphaj′ (hɛ̀ŋ′, thîi′) N
  shelter (e.g. air-raid shelter).

ที่เก็บ (แห่ง,ที่) thîikèb′ (hɛ̀ŋ′, thîi′) N storage
  place, storehouse.

ที่เกิด (แห่ง,ที่) thîikə̀əd′ (hɛ̀ŋ′, thîi′) N birthplace, source, origin.

ที่เขี่ยบุหรี่ (ที่,อัน) thîikhìa′burìi′ (thîi′, ʔan′)
  ashtray.

ที่แขวน (ที่) thîikhwɛ̌ɛn′ (thîi′) N peg, hook, place
  for hanging things.

ที่แขวนเสื้อ (ที่,อัน) thîi′khwɛ̌ɛnsŷa′ (thîi′, ʔan′)
  N coat hanger.

ที่ไข่ (ที่) thîikhàj′ (thîi′) N breeding place,
  place where eggs are laid.

ที่จอดรถ (แห่ง,ที่) thîic⊃̀⊃dród′ (hɛ̀ŋ′, thîi′) N
  1. parking space. 2. parking lot.

ที่ดอน (แห่ง,ที่) thîid⊃⊃n′ (hɛ̀ŋ′, thîi′) N the
  highlands.

ที่ดิน (แปลง, ผืน) thîidin/ (plɛɛŋ/, phɣ̌yn/) N
    piece of land, lot (for a house or building).

o หอทะเบียนที่ดิน (แห่ง) hɔ̌ɔthabian/thîidin/
    (hὲŋ/) N land registration office.

ที่ตรง thîitroŋ⊃ (directly) at, in; (right) at, in.

ที่ตั้ง (แห่ง) thîitâŋ/ (hὲŋ/) N location, situation.

ที่ทาง (แห่ง, ที่) thîi/thaaŋ/ (hὲŋ/, thîi/) N 1.
    lot (for a house or building). 2. place.

ที่ทำการ (แห่ง, ที่) thîithamkaan/ (hὲŋ/, thîi/)
    N office.

o ที่ทำการไปรษณีย์ (แห่ง) thîithamkaan/prajsaⴲ
    nii/ (hὲŋ/) N post office.

ที่ทำงาน (แห่ง, ที่) thîithamŋaan/ (hὲŋ/, thîi/) N
    office; place to work.

ที่เที่ยว (แห่ง) thîithîaw/ (hὲŋ/) N place to go,
    place to tour.

ที่นอน (ที่) thîinɔɔn/ (thîi/) N 1. mattress.
    2. berth. 3. place to sleep.

ที่นั่ง (ที่) thîinâŋ/ (thîi/) N seat, place to sit.

ที่นั่น thîinân/ there.

ที่นั่น thîinán/ at that place.

ที่นา (แห่ง) thîinaa/ (hὲŋ/) N farm, farmland.

ที่นี่ thîinîi/ here.

ที่โน่น thîinôon/ yonder, over there.

ที่บ้าน thîibâan/ at home, those at home; joc.
    one's spouse.

ที่ประกาศ (ที่) thîiprakàad/ (thîi/) N signboard,
    billboard.

ที่ประชุม (แห่ง) thîiprachum/ N 1. place of
    assembly, meeting place (hὲŋ/). 2. an assem-
    bly, gathering (of people).

ที่พัก (แห่ง, ที่) thîiphág/ (hὲŋ/, thîi/) N 1. resi-
    dence, lodging, quarters. 2. resting place.

o ที่พักแรม (แห่ง, ที่) thîi/phágrɛɛm/ (hὲŋ/, thîi/)
    N 1. a place for camping, for staying over-
    night. 2. lodgings, accommodations.

o ที่พักอาศัย thîiphág/ʔaasǎj/ N 1. residence.
    2. quarters.

ที่ทำนัก (แห่ง) thîi/phamnág/ (hὲŋ/) N 1. resi-
    dence, dwelling place. 2. place to stay.

ที่มั่น (แห่ง) thîimân/ (hὲŋ/) N fortified place,
    fortification, stronghold.

ที่มา (แห่ง) thîimaa/ (hὲŋ/) N source, origin.

ที่ราบ (แห่ง) thîirâab/ (hὲŋ/) N plain.

ที่ไร่ที่นา (แปลง) thîirâj/thîinaa/ (plɛɛŋ/) N
    field, farm. →Comp. ที่นา.

ที่ล้างหน้า (ที่) thîiláaŋnâa/ (thîi/) N washbasin.

ที่ลุ่ม (แห่ง, ที่) thîilûm/ (hὲŋ/, thîi/) N basin,
    lowland.

ที่ว่าการ (แห่ง) thîiwâakaan/ (hὲŋ/) N adminis-
    trative office (usually of the government).

ที่ว่าง (แห่ง, ที่) thîiwâaŋ/ (hὲŋ/, thîi/) N 1.
    vacancy. 2. unoccupied space, place or land.

ที่สุด thîisùd/ N the end. →Cf. ที่สุด under ที่ ๓.

o ในที่สุด najthîisùd/ in the end, at last, finally,
    eventually.

ที่หน้า thîinâaⴲ in front of.

ที่หมาย (แห่ง, ที่) thîimǎaj/ (hὲŋ/, thîi/) N 1.
    destination. 2. target (spot aimed at). 3. goal.

o ที่หมายปลายทาง (แห่ง, ที่) thîimǎaj/plaajthaaŋ/
    (hὲŋ/, thîi/) N destination.

ที่หลบภัย (แห่ง, ที่) thîilòbphaj/ (hὲŋ/, thîi/) N
    shelter (from danger).

ที่หลัง thîilǎŋⴲ in back of, behind.

ที่ไหน thîinǎj/ 1. where? 2. somewhere, anywhere.

o ที่ไหน ๆ thîi/nǎjnǎj/ anywhere, any place.

ที่อยู่ (แห่ง) thîijùu/ (hὲŋ/) N 1. living quarters,
    residence. 2. address (e.g. mailing address).

แทนที่ thɛɛnthîi/ V to replace. →Cf. แทนที่จะ
    under ที่ ๒.

เนื้อที่ nýathîi/ N 1. area. 2. space, room.

เป็นที่ penthîi/ in place (generally implying neat-
    ness, good order). →Cf. เคลื่อนที่.

o วางของให้เป็นที่ waaŋkhɔ̌ɔŋ/hâjpenthîi/ to put
    things where they belong.

o อยู่เป็นที่ jùu/penthîi/ to live at the same place
    for a long time (not moving about); (things) to
    stay in place, be in place. →Cf. อยู่กับที่ below.

แผนที่ (แผน) phɛ̌ɛnthîi/ (phɛ̌n/) N map.

ยืนที่ jyynthîi/ V 1. to be stable, stabilized. 2.
    to stay put.

สถานที่ (แห่ง) sathǎanthîi/ (hὲŋ/) N 1. place,
    site. 2. building, plant, station (place equipped
    for a particular kind of work, activity, etc.).

หน้าที่ (อย่าง) nâathîi/ (jàaŋ/) N duty.

อยู่กับที่ jùukathîi/ 1. to be fixed in place, to stay
    in place. 2. firmly rooted to the ground. →Cf.
    อยู่เป็นที่ under เป็นที่ above.

o ยืนอยู่กับที่ jyyn'jùukathîi/ 1. to stand firm
(resist). 2. to stand in one place.

อยู่ที่ jùu'thîic V 1. to depend on; (something)
to be up to (someone). 2. to live at, be at.
→See also ขึ้นอยู่(ที่) under ขึ้น ๒.

ที่ ๒ thîi/ rP which, who, that. →Syn. ซึ่ง lit.

NOTE 1. ที่ corresponds to the English relative
pronouns; hence it often needs to be translated
in special ways, viz. "(persons) who, (things)
which, (places) where, (times) when, (reasons)
why."

NOTE 2. The distinction between ที่ "which"
followed by จะ "will, would" and ที่ not so
followed requires a word of explanation in order to insure proper translation. When ที่ introduces a subordinate clause which does not
contain จะ, the predicate of this clause refers
to an event which has occurred; 1st example.
But whenever จะ occurs in the predicate of
the subordinate clause (very frequently immediately after ที่), the predicate of the subordinate clause refers to an unactualized event
(i.e. unactualized in relation to the main clause);
2nd and 3rd examples. In the first instance ที่
is left untranslated or is translated "that"; 1st
example. In the second instance, ที่ is always
left untranslated and จะ is usually translated
by the infinitive marker "to"; 2nd and 3rd examples. In addition to the type of translation already given, the predicate of a ที่-introduced
clause is often translated as a gerund, i.e., by
adding -ing to the verb stem; 4th, 5th and 6th
examples. Some Thai prepositions (or secondary verbs) can be followed by ที่- introduced
clauses, e.g. แทน "instead of" and ก่อน
"before"; 4th and 5th examples.

o ผมยินดีที่คุณมาหา phǒmjindii'thîikhunmaahǎa'↓
m. sp. I'm glad you came to see (me). I'm
glad that you came to see (me).

o ผมยินดีที่จะช่วย phǒmjindii'thîicachûaj'↓ m. sp.
I'll be glad to help you.

o เขาไม่มีเจตนาที่จะทำร้าย khǎwmâjmiicèed'c
tanaa'-thîicathamráaj'↓ He doesn't mean to
do (any) harm.

o เขามีความหวังที่จะไปยุโรป khǎwmiikhwaamc
wǎŋ'-thîicapaj'júròob'↓* He has hopes of
going to Europe. He is in hopes that he will go
to Europe.

o เขากลับบ้าน แทนที่จะไปดูหนัง khǎwklàbbâan'→
theɛn'thîicapajduunǎŋ'↓ He went home instead
of going to the movies.

o คุณต้องทำงานให้เสร็จ ก่อนที่จะกลับบ้าน khunc
tôŋthamŋaan'hâjsèd'→kɔ̀ɔn'thîicaklàbbâan'↓
You must finish (your) work before going home.

ก่อนที่จะ kɔ̀ɔn'thîicac before (doing such and such).
→See Note 2 above.

การที่ kaan'thîic the fact that, the fact being that.
→Cf. การที่จะ below and also Note 2 above.

การที่จะ kaan'thîicac to, in order to, for (doing
thus and so). →See Note 2 above, and the following
example.

o การที่จะไปไหนมาไหน ควรจะมีรถยนตร์ kaan'thîic
capajnǎj'maanǎj' khuan'camii'ródjon'↓ In order
to go anywhere you need a car. For getting around
one should have a car.

ขณะที่ khanà?'thîic while, the while that.

ค่าที่ khâa'thîic because, owing to the fact that,
on account of the fact that. →Cf. ค่าที่ under
ที่ ๑.

โดยที่...ไม่ dooj'thîic...mâjc without (being
such and such, doing such and such); without
(such and such happening; e.g. without things
falling). →See Note 2 under main entry.

ตามที่ taam'thîic 1. as, i.e. in accordance with
what (that which). 2. in reference to what (that
which), referring to what (that which). NOTE.
When mng. 2 is implied the clause which is introduced by ที่ often has its end marked by the
particle นั้น ; 2nd example.

o ตามที่คุณรู้แล้ว taam'-thîikhunrúu'léɛw' as you
already know.

o ตามที่คุณว่ามานั้น taam'-thîikhunwâa'maanán'
in reference to what you said, referring to what
you said.

ตามแหล่งที่ taamlèŋ'thîic in places where.

ทั้งที่, ทั้ง ๆ ที่ tháŋ'thîic, tháŋtháŋ'thîic even
though, although, in spite of, in spite of the fact
that.

ที่กล่าวนี้ thîiklàaw'níi' which are spoken of here.

ที่กล่าวมานี้ thîiklàaw'maaníi' which (we) have
mentioned, which has been mentioned, the aforementioned.

ที่จริง thîiciŋ' in fact, as a matter of fact.

o อันที่จริง ?anthîiciŋ' in fact, as a matter of fact.

ที่จะ. See Note 2 under main entry.

ที่แท้ thîithéɛ' actually, in fact, in truth.

ที่รัก thîirág' dear, beloved.

ที่แล้ว thîiléɛw' the previous, preceding.

o เดือนที่แล้ว dyan′thîiléɛw′ in the last month, last month.

เท่าที่ thâwthîiꞏ to the extent that, as far as, as much as.

แทนที่จะ theɛn′thîicaꞏ instead of (doing such and such). →See Note 2 under main entry. →Cf. แทนที่ under ที่ ๑.

ในอันที่จะ naj′an′thîicaꞏ in order to. →See Note 2 under main entry.

เป็นที่เข้าใจ penthîi′khâwcaj′ it is understood (that).

เป็นที่ทราบกันว่า penthîisâab′kanwâa′ it is known that.

ผู้ที่ phûu′thîiꞏ (the person) who.

ภายหลังที่ phaajlǎŋ′thîiꞏ after.

เวลาที่ weelaa′thîiꞏ when, the time when.

แสนที่จะ sɛ̌ɛn′thîicaꞏ greatly, extremely, frightfully.

o เด็กคนนี้แสนที่จะซน dègkhonníi′ sɛ̌ɛn′thîicaꞏ son′↓ This child is frightfully naughty.

เหตุที่ hèed′thîiꞏ the reason why, the reasons why.

o เพราะเหตุที่ phrɔ́hèed′thîiꞏ for the reason that, because.

ที่- ๓ thîiꞏ. Bound stem used with numerals to form ordinals, or with certain other forms to indicate position in a numbered series.

o ที่หนึ่ง thîinỳŋ′ first (in order).

o ที่สอง thîisɔ̌ɔŋ′ second.

o ที่เท่าไร thîi′thâwràj′ which one (of an ordered series); "the how-manyeth."

o ที่สุดท้าย thîi′sùdtháaj′ last.

ที่สุด thîisùd′ most, -est. →Comp. กว่าเพื่อน. →Cf. ที่สุด under ที่ ๑. NOTE. ที่สุด is often used to express what corresponds to the superlative in English (e.g. biggest, most beautiful).

o ดีที่สุด dii′thîisùd′ best, greatest.

oo อย่างดีที่สุด jàaŋdii′thîisùd′ 1. the best. 2. at best. 3. best, in the best way.

o ...ที่สุดที่จะ...ได้ ...thîisùd′thîicaꞏ...dâaj′ as...as possible.

oo เร็วที่สุดที่จะเร็วได้ rew′thîisùd′-thîicarew′ꞏ dâaj′ as fast as possible.

o มากที่สุด mâag′thîisùd′ (the) most, very most,

greatest.

oo ร้ายมากที่สุด ráajmâag′thîisùd′ (the) very most ferocious, the very worst.

บทที่สามสิบเอ็ด bòd′ thîisǎam′sìb°èd′ the 31st chapter.

วันที่ wanthîiꞏ the (such and such numbered) day, the --th. See examples.

o ลงวันที่ ๕ loŋ′wanthîihâa′ dated the fifth.

o วันที่ ๑๐ เดือนตุลาคม wanthîisìb′dyantùlaa′ꞏ khom′ the tenth of October.

ทึกทัก thýgthág′ V to jump to a conclusion; to presuppose, assume (without evidence).

ทึง. See ถมึงทึง.

ทึ่ง thŷŋ′ V to be interested (in). →Syn. สนใจ. น่าทึ่ง nâathŷŋ′ V colloq. to be interesting.

ทึ้ง thýŋ′ V to pull off, pull apart.

ทึบ thýb′ V 1. to be dense, thick (as a jungle). 2. to be opaque. 3. to be dim-witted, thick-headed, dense, dull (of mind).

ทึ่ม thŷm′ V to be foolish, simple-minded.

ทึมทึก in สาวทึมทึก (คน) sǎaw′thymthýg′ (khon′) N spinster.

ทื่อ thŷy′ to be dull (not sharp), blunt. →Dist. ทู่. →Syn. ตื้อ. →Ant. คม.

ทุก thúg′ qM every, each. NOTE. This word may be followed by a numeral plus classifier or simply by a classifier; 1st and 2nd examples. When no numeral is used, the quantity is understood to be "one," which is usually unexpressed in English also; 1st example. →Dist. ละ.

o ทุกอาทิตย์ thúg′°aathíd′ every week.

oo ทุกสองอาทิตย์ thúg′sɔ̌ɔŋ°aathíd′ every two weeks.

ทุกคน thúgkhon′ everyone, everybody.

ทุกครั้ง thúgkhráŋ′ every time.

ทุกคราว thúgkhraaw′ every time.

ทุกคืน thúgkhyyn′ every night.

ทุกซอกทุกมุม thúgsɔ̂ɔg′thúgmum′ elab. colloq. every nook and corner, every nook and cranny.

ทุกซอกเล็กมุมน้อย thúgsɔ̂ɔg′lég′-mum′nɔ́ɔj′ elab. every little nook and corner, every little nook and cranny.

ทุกที thúgthii′ 1. every time, each time. 2. every minute, by the minute, progressively.

o ใกล้เข้ามาทุกที klâj′khâwmaa′thúgthii′ is getting

closer by the minute; is getting progressively
closer.

o มากยิ่งขึ้นทุกที mâag´-jîŋkhŷn´thúgthii´ more
and more every minute; progressively more.

ทุก ๆ thúgthúg´ each and every, every.

o ทุก ๆ กระเบียดนิ้ว thúgthúg´-krabìad´níw´
each and every minor detail, each and every
little bit.

o ทุก ๆ คน thúgthúgkhon´ everybody, everyone.

ทุกปี thúgpii´ every year, each year.

ทุกวัน thúgwan´ every day.

o ทุกวันนี้ thúgwanníi´ nowadays, these days.

ทุกสิ่งทุกอย่าง thúgsìŋ´thúgjàaŋ´ everything.

ทุกหย่อมหญ้า thúgjɔ̀m´jâa´ idiom. everywhere,
all over.

ทุกหัวระแหง thúghǔa´rahɛ̌ɛŋ´ idiom. everywhere, every corner of the earth.

ทุกแห่ง thúghɛ̀ŋ´ everywhere, every place. →Also
ทุกหนทุกแห่ง.

ทุกอย่าง thúgjàaŋ´ 1. everything. 2. in every
way, in every respect, of every kind.

ทุกข์ thúg´ N sorrow, suffering, unhappiness, dis-·
tress, misery. ความ-- idem.

ทุกข์กาย thúgkaaj´ V to suffer (physically).
ความ-- physical suffering.

ทุกข์ใจ thúgcaj´ V to suffer (mentally). ความ--
mental anguish, sorrow. →Syn. โทมนัส lit.

ทุกข์ร้อน thúgrɔ́ɔn´ V to suffer, be unhappy, be
in trouble. ความ-- trouble, suffering, unhappiness, woe.

ทุกข์สุข thúgsùg´ N happiness and sorrow, the ups
and down of life. Cf. Eng. "for better or worse."

ปรับทุกข์ pràbthúg´ V to tell one's troubles.

เป็นทุกข์ penthúg´ to be dejected, worried.

o เป็นทุกข์เป็นร้อน penthúg´penrɔ́ɔn´ V elab.
colloq.to be dejected, worried, bothered (about
something). Cf. Eng. "to be hot and bothered."

ร้องทุกข์ rɔ́ɔŋthúg´ V to complain, make a complaint.

ไว้ทุกข์ wájthúg´ V to wear mourning.

ทุ่ง ๑ (ทุ่ง,แห่ง) thûŋ´ (thûŋ´,hɛ̀ŋ´) field, meadow,
open field. →Comp. นา.

ทุ่งแจ้ง (ทุ่ง,แห่ง) thûŋcɛ̂ɛŋ´ (thûŋ´,hɛ̀ŋ´) N
open field, meadow, clearing.

ทุ่งนา (แห่ง) thûŋnaa´ (hɛ̀ŋ´) N field.

ทุ่งพระเมรุ thûŋ´phrámeen´ pN the Phra Men
(Phra Meru) Ground in Bangkok. Used for special
ceremonies, including the cremation of members
of the royal family. →Also ท้องสนามหลวง
colloq.

ทุ่งราบ (แห่ง) thûŋrâab´ (hɛ̀ŋ´) N open plain
(not used of desert country).

ทุ่งหญ้า (แห่ง) thûŋjâa´ (hɛ̀ŋ´) N 1. prairie,
grassland. 2. meadow, pasture.

ลูกทุ่ง (คน) lûugthûŋ´ (khon´) N rare farmer.
Comparable to Eng. "son of the soil."

ทุ่ง ๒ thûŋ´ V 1. to pass fecal matter, evacuate the
bowels. N 2. feces. →Syn. อุจจาระ eleg.,
ขี้ ๑ com.,vulg

ไปทุ่ง pajthûŋ´ V to go to the toilet. →Syn. ถ่าย
อุจจาระ eleg.. ไปขี้ com.,vulg.

ทุจริต thúdcarìd´ V 1. to be dishonest, deceitful.
2. to cheat.

พวกทุจริต phûag´thúdcarìd´ N crooks, band of --.

ทุน thun´, thunna⊃ N 1. fund, funds, capital, investment. 2. a scholarship, a fellowship.

ขาดทุน khàadthun´ V 1. to lose money, sustain
losses (in business). 2. to be at a disadvantage.

เงินทุน ŋənthun´ N capital (money in an investment).

ทุนทรัพย์ thunnasáb´ N capital, funds (for investment).

ทุนรัฐบาล thun´rádthabaan´ N a government
scholarship.

นายทุน (คน) naajthun´ (khon´) N capitalist.

ลงทุน loŋthun´ to make an investment. การ--
investment.

o ลงทุนลงแรง loŋthun´loŋrɛɛŋ´ elab. colloq.
to put money and effort into (a project).

ทุ่น ๑ (ทุ่น) thûn´ (thûn´) N float, buoy.

ทุ่นระเบิด thûn´rabə̀əd´ N explosive underwater
mine.

o เรือทิ้งทุ่นระเบิด (ลำ) rya´-thíŋthûn´rabə̀əd´
(lam´) N mine layer.

ทุ่น ๒ thûn´ V to save (on), economize (on), cut down
on expenditure (of). NOTE. ทุ่น implies a comparison of expenditures as between alternate
courses of action.

ทุ่นเงิน thûn´ŋən´ V to save money (as by cutting

down expenses).

ทุนแรง thûn'rɛɛŋ' V to save on energy, effect an economy on energy, power, labor.

ทุบ thúb' V 1. to hammer. 2. to hit, smash (into).

ทุพพลภาพ thúbphon'laphâab' V to be disabled, incapacitated, infirm, feeble.

ทุพภิกขภัย thúbphíg'khaphaj' N eleg. famine. →Syn. ความอดอยาก com.

ทุ่ม ๑ thûm' C an hour of the night counting from 6 P. M. (as the zero hour) to midnight.

  o ทุ่มหนึ่ง thûm'nyŋ 7 P. M. →Also ทุ่ม alone, since the absence of a numeral implies "one."

  o สามทุ่ม sǎamthûm' 9 P. M.

ทุ่ม ๒ thûm' V to throw down, hurl down.

  ทุ่มเถียง thûmthǐaŋ' V to argue, quarrel.

  ทุ่มเท thûmthee' V 1. to throw, hurl. 2. to pour, pour into in great quantities. 3. to pitch in, throw one's full force (e.g. into the fray).

ทุ้ม thúm' V to be low (in tone), deep (of voice), bass.

ทุรกันดาร thúrákandaan' V to be extremely arid, barren, waste (e.g. land).

ทุรน in ทุรนทุราย thúron'thúraaj' V to manifest great pain (as by writhing, twitching, groaning).

ทุรัง in ดันทุรัง dan'thúraŋ' V to be obstinate, headstrong.

ทุเรศ thúreed' V 1. to be piteous, pitiful. 2. to be obscene.

ทุเรียน (ใบ,ลูก,ผล) thúrian' (baj', lûug', phǒn') N durian. [f. Mal.]

ทุลักทุเล thúlág'thúlee' V 1. to be difficult, hard, clumsy, awkward. 2. to be confused, in disorder. sV 3. clumsily. 4. in confusion, in disorder.

ทุเลา thúlaw' to improve (in condition; esp. of the sick).

  ทุเลาขึ้น thúlaw'khŷn to get better.

ทู in ปลาทู (ตัว) plaathuu' (tua') N a kind of mackerel (Scrombridae).

ทู่ thûu' V to be blunt, not pointed. →Dist. ทื่อ. →Ant. แหลม.

ทูต (คน,นาย) thûud' (khon', naaj') N ambassador, (foreign) minister, envoy, attaché. การ-- (see below).

  การทูต kaanthûud' N diplomacy. นัก-- diplo-

mat. ทาง-- diplomatic.

  o ความสัมพันธ์ทางการทูต khwaamsǎmphan'thaaŋɔ kaanthûud' N diplomatic relations.

ทูตทหาร (คน,นาย) thûudthahǎan' (khon', naaj') N military attaché.

ทูตสันถวไมตรี thûud'-sǎn'thawámajtrii' (naaj') N good-will ambassador.

ราชทูต (คน,นาย) râadchathûud' (khon', naaj') N royal envoy.

สถานทูต (แห่ง) sathǎanthûud' (hèŋ') N 1. legation; short for สถานอัครราชทูต. 2. embassy; short for สถานเอกอัครราชทูต.

อัครราชทูต (คน,นาย) ʔàgkharâadchathûud' (khon', naaj') N minister, esp. one who is the head of a legation.

  o เอกอัครราชทูต (คน,นาย,ท่าน) ʔèeg'ʔàgkhaɔ râadchathûud' (khon', naaj', thân') N ambassador (from a monarchy). →Dist. เอกอัคร-รัฐทูต.

อุปทูต (คน,นาย) ʔùbpathûud' (khon', naaj') N chargé d'affaires.

ทูตานุทูต (คน,นาย) thuutaa'núthûud' (khon', naaj') N diplomatic corps.

ทูน in ทูนหัว (1) thuunhǔa'; (2, 3) thuun'hǔa' V 1. to hold or place on the head (in order to carry). 2. to adore, idolize. 3. to be beloved, adored.

ทูนหัวทูนเกล้า thuunhǔa'thuunklâaw' V elab. colloq. to adore, idolize.

พ่อทูนหัว (1) phɔɔ'thuunhǔa'; (2) phɔɔthuun'hǔa' N 1. godfather. 2. a beloved boy, an adorable boy.

แม่ทูนหัว (1) mɛɛ'thuunhǔa'; (2) mɛɛthuun'hǔa' N 1. godmother. 2. a beloved girl, an adorable girl.

ทูล thuun' V roy. to speak, talk to, tell. →Syn. บอก com.

กราบทูล kràabthuun' V to address highranking royalty.

กราบบังคมทูล kràab'-baŋkhom'thuun' roy. to address the king or queen.

ทูลถาม thuunthǎam' roy. to ask, inquire.

เท thee' V 1. to pour. 2. to pour out, empty. →Sometimes coupled with ลาด to splash.

ขายดีเป็นเทน้ำเทท่า khǎaj'dii' penthee'náam'-

thee′thǎa′ i d i o m. to sell rapidly, sell like
hot cakes.

ทุ่มเท thûmthee′ V 1. to throw, hurl. 2. to pour,
pour into in great quantities. 3. to pitch in,
throw one's full force (e.g. into the fray).

สาดทิ้งเททิ้ง sàadthíŋ′theethíŋ′ V e l a b. c o l l o q.
to throw out.

ไหลมาเทมา lǎjmaa′theemaa′ V e l a b. c o l l o q.
to pour in, stream in, flow in continuously.

เทคนิค thégnìg′* N 1. technique. 2. technical.
[f. Eng.]

เท็จ théd′ V 1. e l e g. to be false, untrue; to be a
lie. N 2. a lie, a fib. →Chiefly in special combinations. →Ant. จริง c o m:

กล่าวเท็จ klàawthéd′ V e l e g. to lie, tell lies,
speak falsely. →Syn. See โกหก c o m.

เท็จจริง as in ข้อเท็จจริง khɔ̂ɔ′thédciŋ′ N facts,
the facts of the matter: "points false and true."

พูดเท็จ, เท็จพูด phûudthéd′, thédphûud′ V e l e g.
1. to tell a lie. 2. to be untrue, false. →Syn.
1. See โกหก c o m.

เทพ, เทพ-, -เทพ thêeb′, thêeb′phaɔ, ɔthêeb′ N
divine being, divinity, god. →See also เทว-,
เทวา.

กรุงเทพ ฯ kruŋthêeb′ pN Krungthep. i.e.
Bangkok.

เทพเจ้า (องค์) thêeb′phacâaw′ (ʔoŋ′) N a god,
a deity. →Syn. เทพยเจ้า.

เทพยเจ้า (องค์) thêeb′phajacâaw′ (ʔoŋ′) N a god,
a deity. →Syn. เทพเจ้า under เทพ.

เทพารักษ์ (องค์) thee′phaarág′ (ʔoŋ′) N a good
fairy, guardian fairy.

เทว-. Bound form meaning "divine beings, divinities." →See also เทพ, เทพ-, เทวา.

เทวโลก theewalôog′ N heaven, the world of the
gods. →Ant. 1. มนุษยโลก.

เทวดา (องค์) theewadaa′ (ʔoŋ′) N a god.

เทววา theewaa′ N a god, divinity. →See also เทพ,
เทว-.

เทศ, เทศ-, -เทศ (1, 2) thêed′; (3) thêed′saɔ, thêeɔ
saɔ, ɔthêed′ N 1. foreigner. In this meaning
generally opposed to ไทย in the same sentence;
see example. 2. (as n. mod.) foreign, not native
to Thailand. 3. bound form meaning "country,

town." คน-- foreigner.

o มีทั้งไทยและเทศ mii′-tháŋthaj′lɛthêed′ there
are both Thai and foreigners (there).

เครื่องเทศ (อย่าง) khrɨ̂aŋthêed′ (jàaŋ′) N spices.

จันทน์เทศ canthêed′ N nutmeg. ต้น-- (ต้น) the
nutmeg tree.

เทศบาล (เทศบาล) thêesabaan′ (thêesabaan′)
N municipality, local administration.

o เขตเทศบาล khèed′thêesabaan′ N the city
limits; municipal limit, boundary; municipal area.

o เจ้าหน้าที่เทศบาล (คน) câwnâathîi′thêesabaan′
(khon′) municipal officers.

o โยธาเทศบาล joothaa′thêesabaan′ N Public
Works.

เทศมนตรี (คน) thêesamontrii′ (khon′) N councillor (of a city or municipality).

o คณะเทศมนตรี (คณะ) khaná?′thêesamontrii′
(khaná?′) N city council, municipal council.

o นายกเทศมนตรี (นาย,คน) naajóg′thêesamonɔ
trii′ (naaj′,khon′) N mayor; president of the
city council.

ประเทศ (ประเทศ) prathêed′ (prathêed′) N
e l e g. country. →Syn. เมือง c o m.

มะเขือเทศ (ลูก,ใบ,ผล) makhˇathêed′ (lûug′,
baj′,phǒn′) N tomato. ต้น-- (ต้น) the tomato
plant.

มันเทศ (หัว) manthêed′ (hǔa′) N sweet potato.
ต้น-- (ต้น) sweet potato (the plant).

เทศน์ thêed′ V to preach. นัก-- preacher.
→Comp. เทศนา.

ฟังเทศน์ faŋthêed′ V to hear a sermon.

เทศนา thêed′sanǎa′, thêe′sanaa′* V 1. to preach.
N 2. sermon. →Comp. เทศน์.

พระธรรมเทศนา phrátham′mathêed′sanǎa′ N
Buddhist sermon, preaching.

เทศะ in กาลเทศะ kaalá?′theesà?′ N the time and
place, the occasion.

เทอม thəəm′ C term, esp. school term or semester.
[f. Eng.]

เทอะทะ thə́?′thá?′ not shapely, not streamlined,
not beautifully proportioned.

เทา thaw′ V to be gray.

สีเทา sǐithaw′ N 1. gray, the color gray. V 2.
to be gray.

เท่า thâw′ V 1. to be equal, the same (in size or quantity). C 2. clf. for a given quantity, often best rendered by "times, -fold"; see examples. →Dist. 1. เหมือน. →Syn. 1. ทัดเทียม, เทียม, เสมอ.

o ร้อยเท่า rɔ́ɔj′thâw′ a hundredfold.

o สองเท่าครึ่ง sɔ̌ɔŋthâw′khrɨ̂ŋ two and a half times (e.g. taller, as tall, smaller, as small).

o หลายเท่า lǎaj′thâw′ many times (e.g. taller, as tall, etc.).

ขนาดเท่าคน. khanàad′thâwkhon′ the size of a person.

ตราบเท่า tràab′thâw′ until; as long as.

โตเท่า... too′thâwɔ... V to be as big as.

เท่ากัน, เท่า ๆ กัน thâw′kan, thâwkan′, thâwɔ thâw′kan to be equal, the same (in size or quantity), even (in score, in capability).

o เขาสูงเท่ากัน kháwsǔuŋ′thâwkan′↓ They are equally tall.

เท่ากับ, เท่า ๆ กับ thâwkaɔ, thâwthâw′kaɔ to be the same as; to equal, be equal to, be equivalent to; as...as.

o เขาสูงเท่ากับพ่อ kháwsǔuŋ′thâwkaphɔ̂ɔ′↓ He is as tall as his father.

o ก็เท่ากับส่งเสริมให้จีนใกล้ชิดกับโซเวียต kɔthâwɔ kasɔ̀ŋsɔ̌ɔm′-hâjciin′-klâjchíd′kasoowîad′ (it) is the same as encouraging China to be closer to the Soviet Union.

o สิบกำลังสอง เท่ากับหนึ่งร้อย sìb′kamlaŋsɔ̌ɔŋ→ thâwkanŷŋrɔ́ɔj′ 10 squared equals 100.

เท่าครึ่ง, หนึ่ง-- thâw′khrɨ̂ŋ, nŷŋthâw′khrɨ̂ŋ′ one and a half times (as much, as big, etc.).

เท่าใด thâwdaj′ how much, how many.

เท่าตัว thâwtua′ 1. the same size or quantity as (the model), life-size; 1st example. 2. as much as the previous size, quantity, amount; 2nd example.

o รูปขนาดเท่าตัว rûub′-khanàad′thâwtua′ a life-sized picture.

o ได้กำไรเท่าตัว dâajkamraj′thâwtua′ to gain as much as one has invested.

o เท่าตัวจริง thâw′tuaciŋ′ life-size, actual size.

เท่าที่ thâwthîɔ to the extent that, as far as, as much as.

เท่า ๆ. See เท่ากัน, เท่ากับ.

เท่าเทียม thâwthiam′ V to equal, be equal to, be on the same level as.

เท่านั้น thâwnán′ 1. only, only that, just that. 2. that much, that many.

เท่าไร thâwràj′* 1. how much? how many? to what extent? 2. how much, how many.

o ที่เท่าไร thîi′thâwràj′ which one (of an ordered series): "the how-manyeth."

o นานเท่าไร naan′thâwràj′ how long (of time).

oo ไม่นานเท่าไร mâjnaan′thâwràj′ not very long (of time).

o ไม่เท่าไร mâjthâwràj′ not very; not much, not many.

o ไม่(...)เท่าไร, ไม่ค่อย(...)เท่าไร mâj(...) thâwràj′, mâjkhɔ̂j(...)thâwràj′ not very, not so very, not too; not very much, many; not so very much, many; not too much, many.

oo ไม่ค่อยมีคนเท่าไรหรอก mâjkhɔ̂jmiikhon′thâwɔ ràj′-rɔg there were not so very many people.

o สักเท่าไร ságthâwràj′ 1. (just) how much? (just) how many? 2. how much, how many; however much, however many. →See examples.

...สักเท่าไร(...)ก็... ságthâwràj′→ (...)kɔ... however much (many)..., still...; no matter how much (many)..., still...; no matter how (e.g. fast)..., still...

o เขาจะวิ่งเร็วสักเท่าไรก็ไม่ทัน kháwcawîŋ′rew′-ságthâwràj′-kɔmâjthan′↓ No matter how fast he runs, he won't make it.

o ไม่ว่าเขาจะรีบสักเท่าไร เขาก็ทำไม่ทัน mâjwâakháwcarîib′ɔ ságthâwràj′→ kháwkɔ̀tham′mâjthan′↓ No matter how much he hurries, he still won't get it done on time.

o ถึงเขาจะกินสักเท่าไร ก็ไม่อ้วน thɨ̌ŋkháwcakin′ságthâwràj′→ kɔmâj′ʔûan↓ No matter how much he eats, he doesn't get fat.

ไม่(...)สักเท่าไร mâj(...)ságthâwràj′ not so very; not so very much.

o ไม่ห่างจากที่นั่นสักเท่าไร mâjhàaŋ′càagthîinân′-ságthâwràj′ not so very far from there.

รู้เท่า rúu′thâw′ V to know what someone is up to, know what is behind (someone's behavior); to be on to (someone's intentions).

o รู้เท่าไม่ถึงการณ์ rúu′thâw′-mâjthɨ̌ŋkaan′ to be blind to a situation, be unable to see what someone is up to.

เท้า ๑ tháaw′* V 1. to lean on, rest on, be supported, held up. 2. to support. 3. to refer (to).

มือเท้าคาง myy′tháawkhaaŋ′ to use the hand to

support the chin, hence to rest the chin on the hand.

ไม้เท้า (อัน) májtháaw/ (ʔan/) N walking stick.

เท้า ๒ (ข้าง, เท้า) tháaw/ N eleg. foot (khâaŋ/ for either one of a pair; tháaw/ for more than two). →Syn. See ตีน.

กราบเท้า kràabtháaw/ V 1. to prostrate oneself at someone's feet (as a sign of very high respect). 2. term used in the salutation of a letter to show respect (followed by the title of the addressee).

o กราบเท้าคุณพ่อที่เคารพอย่างสูง kràabtháaw/ɔ khunphɔɔ/-thîikhawrób/jàaŋsǔuŋ/↓ (I) salute (my) most highly respected father.

ข้อเท้า (ข้อ, ข้าง) khɔ̂ɔtháaw/ (khɔ̂ɔ/, khâaŋ/) N eleg. ankle. →Syn. ข้อตีน com.

ข้างเท้าหลัง cháaŋ/tháawlǎŋ/ N 1. the hind legs of an elephant. 2. idiom. follower, one who always follows someone else.

เดินเท้า dəəntháaw/ V to go by foot, on foot. คน-- person on foot, pedestrian.

o เดินเท้าเปล่า dəən/tháawplàaw/ to walk bare-foot.

ใต้เท้า tâajtháaw/ P eleg. def. sp. to sup. you; your excellency.

เท้าหน้า (เท้า) tháawnâa/ (tháaw/) N eleg. front legs.

นิ้วเท้า (นิ้ว) níwtháaw/ (níw/) N eleg. toe. →Syn. นิ้วตีน com.

ฝ่าเท้า (ข้าง) fàatháaw/ (khâaŋ/) N eleg. sole of the foot. →Syn. ฝ่าตีน com.

ฝีเท้า fǐitháaw/ N eleg. speed (of foot), pace. →Syn. ฝีตีน com.

o เต็มฝีเท้า tem/fǐitháaw/ at full speed.

o เสียงฝีเท้า sǐaŋ/fǐitháaw/ the sound of foot-steps.

ย่ำเท้า jâmtháaw/ V to mark time (with the feet).

o เดินย่ำเท้า dəən/jâmtháaw/ to march (as soldiers).

รองเท้า (ข้าง, คู่) rɔɔŋtháaw/ N eleg. shoe, shoes (khâaŋ/ for either one of a pair; khûu/ for a pair).

รอยเท้า (รอย) rɔɔjtháaw/ (rɔɔj/) N eleg. footprints.

ส้นเท้า (ข้าง) sôntháaw/ (khâaŋ/) N eleg. heel. →Also ขึ่นเท้า. →Syn. ส้นตีน com., vulg.

สัตว์สี่เท้า (ตัว) sàd/sìitháaw/ (tua/) N eleg. quadruped.

เที่ยง thîaŋ/ N 1. noon. V 2. to be accurate, precise, steady, stable. 3. to be just (lacking in bias).

ก่อนเที่ยง kɔ̀ɔnthîaŋ/ A.M.; before noon. →Abbrev. ก.ท.

เที่ยงคืน thîaŋkhyyn/ N midnight.

เที่ยงแท้ thîaŋthée/ certain, sure. อย่าง--, โดย--, เป็น-- for certain, for sure.

เที่ยงธรรม thîaŋtham/ V to be upright, just, fair, impartial. อย่าง-- with fairness, impartially.

เที่ยงเป่ง thîaŋpěŋ/ at noon sharp.

เที่ยงวัน thîaŋwan/ M midday, noon.

เวลาเที่ยง weelaathîaŋ/ at noon.

หลังเที่ยง lǎŋthîaŋ/ P.M.; after noon. →Abbrev. ล.ท.

อาหารเที่ยง (มื้อ) ʔaahǎanthîaŋ/ (mýy/) N lunch, luncheon, midday meal.

เทียน (เล่ม) thian/ (lêm/) N candle.

เชิงเทียน (อัน) chəəŋthian/ (ʔan/) N candlestick.

เทียนขี้ผึ้ง (เล่ม, แท่ง) thian/khîiphŷŋ/ (lêm/, thêŋ/) N wax candle (made of beeswax).

เทียนไข (เล่ม, แท่ง) thiankhǎj/ (lêm/, thêŋ/) tallow candle.

ฟั่นเทียน fânthian/ V to roll wax into a candle.

แรงเทียน rɛɛŋthian/ C 1. candlepower. 2. watt.

เทียบ thîab/ V to compare; to place alongside of (esp. in order to compare).

จอดเทียบ cɔ̀ɔdthîab/ to park parallel to, pull up alongside (of).

เทียบเรือ thîabrya/ to bring a boat up alongside.

เปรียบเทียบ prìabthîab/ V to compare.

เทียม thiam/ V eleg. 1. to place on the same level. 2. to hitch up, harness, yoke. 3. to be equal, comparable to, on the same level as. 4. to be artificial, synthetic, counterfeit. →Syn. 3. See เท่า. 4. เก colloq., ไม่แท้ com.

ดาวเทียม (ดวง) daawthiam/ (duaŋ/) N artificial earth satellite.

เท่าเทียม thâwthiam/ V to equal, be equal to, be on the same level as.

เทียมแทน thiamthɛɛn/ V 1. to be a comparable

substitute for. sV 2. in place of, substituting
for.

เนยเทียม (ก้อน) nəəjthiam/ (kɔɔn/) N margarine.

ฝนเทียม fõnthiam/ N artificial rain.

ยางเทียม jaaŋthiam/ N synthetic rubber.

สูงเทียม sŭuŋ/thiam/ V to be as high as.

เทียว thiaw/ quite, exactly, very. →Contracted
form of ทีเดียว under ที ๑.   →See also
เจียว.

เที่ยว thîaw/ V 1. to roam, wander, go (from place
to place). sV 2. around (here and there for
pleasure). C 3. trip, sally, sortie, time.
→Syn. 1. ท่อง.

o สองเที่ยว sɔɔŋthîaw/ two trips (e.g. to town).

คนพาเที่ยว (คน) khonphaathîaw/ (khon/) N
escort, tourist guide.

ท่องเที่ยว thɔ̂ŋthîaw/ V 1. to roam, wander. 2.
to tour, travel. นัก-- tourist.

ที่เที่ยว (แห่ง) thîithîaw/ (hɛ̀ŋ/) N place to go,
place to tour.

เที่ยวล่อง thîawlɔ̂ŋ/ 1. on the way downstream,
on the way south. 2. the downstream trip,
south-bound trip, return trip.

ไปเที่ยว pajthîaw/ to go around (here and there
for pleasure), go out (as for an evening).

ผู้นำเที่ยว (คน) phûu/namthîaw/ (khon/) N
tourist guide.

มาเที่ยว maathîaw/ V 1. to come around (e.g.
to someone's house for a visit). 2. to come
and go around for pleasure, come on a pleasure
trip.

เทือก (เทือก) thŷag/ (thŷag/) N 1. range (as of
mountains). 2. line (as of descent). C 3. line
(in a general sense), order, sort. →Syn. 1.
ทิว, พืด.

o หรืออะไรเทือกนั้น rýyˀaraj/-thŷag/nán/ or
something along that line; or something on that
order, of that sort.

ขี้เทือก khîithŷag/ V colloq. to be muddy, full
of mud or dirt.

เทือกเขา (เทือก) thŷagkhăw/ (thŷag/) N mountain range, chain of mountains.

เทือกเถา (เหล่า, สาย) thŷagthăw/ (làw/, săaj/)
N lineage, line of descent.

แท้ ๑ thɛ́ɛ/ V 1. to be real, genuine, authentic. 2.
to be pure (e.g. in race, strain). sV 3. really,
truly, genuinely, very, very much. →Ant. 1.
ปลอม, เทียม.

ที่แท้ thîithɛ́ɛ/ actually, in fact, in truth.

เที่ยงแท้ thîaŋthɛ́ɛ/ certain, sure.

แท้จริง thɛ́ɛ/ciŋ/ V to be real, genuine, actual.

เนื้อแท้ nýa/thɛ́ɛ/ the real thing, the real sense.

พันธุ์แท้ phan/thɛ́ɛ/ N a pure strain (of plants,
animals).

ไม่แท้ mâjthɛ́ɛ/ 1. com. false, not genuine. 2.
not pure (as of metals; of races, breeds).
→Syn. 1. เก๊ colloq. เทียม eleg.

แท้ ๒ in ท้อแท้ thɔ́ɔthɛ́ɛ/ V to feel dejected, downcast, in low spirits.

แท็กซี่, รถ-- (คัน) thégsîi/, ród/thégsîi/ (khan/)
N taxi. [f. Eng.] →Also แท๊กซี่ (same pron.).

แทง thɛɛŋ/ V to pierce, stab; to stick into, put into.
→Syn. ตำ, ทิ่ม.

เสียดแทง sìadthɛɛŋ/ V to pierce, stab, sting.

แท่ง thɛ̂ŋ/* C 1. bar, ingot. 2. clf. for pencil.

แท้ง thɛ́ɛŋ/ V to miscarry, have a miscarriage,
have an (accidental) abortion.

แท้งลูก thɛ́ɛŋlûug/ idem. การ-- miscarriage,
abortion. →Dist. รีดลูก.

แทน thɛɛn/ V 1. to represent, replace, substitute
for. sV 2. in place of, in lieu of, instead of,
on behalf of, for (another). 3. instead, in place.
ผู้-- representative (in the legislature); delegate;
agent, representative.

ตอบแทน tɔ̀ɔbthɛɛn/ V 1. to repay, pay back. 2.
to reciprocate, retaliate. sV 3. in return, in
exchange.

ตัวแทน (คน, นาย) tuathɛɛn/ (khon/, naaj/) N 1.
representative, agent. 2. substitute, proxy.

ทดแทน thódthɛɛn/ V 1. to repay, do in return.
2. to replace. sV 3. as a replacement, a substitute.

เทียมแทน thiamthɛɛn/ V 1. to be a comparable
substitute for. sV 2. in place of, substituting
for.

แทนคุณ thɛɛnkhun/ V to repay a kindness to.

แทนที่ thɛɛnthîi/ V to replace. การ-- displacement.

แทนที่จะ thɛɛn'thîicaɔ instead of (doing thus and so).

รักษาการแทน rágsǎakaan'thɛɛn' to act temporarily in place of. ผู้-- acting-- (e.g. acting chairman).

แท่น (แท่น) thɛ̂n'*(thɛ̂n') N 1. dais. 2. an elevated rectangular structure used as a seat or bed.

แท่นบูชา (แท่น) thɛ̂n'buuchaa' (thɛ̂n') N altar.

แทบ thɛ̂ɛb' AA 1. almost, nearly. qM 2. almost, nearly (in this use occurs before other qM but not before Nm; see 1st example). Pp 3. close to (used only as in 2nd example). →Syn. 1. เกือบ, จวน ๒, ปาง ๒, ร่วม ๒. 2. เกือบ.

o แทบทุกคน thɛ̂ɛb'thúgkhon' almost everybody.

o แทบเท้า thɛ̂ɛbtháaw' close to the feet.

จนแทบ(จะ) conthɛ̂ɛb'(caɔ) almost to the point of; so much that (he) almost.

แทบจะ thɛ̂ɛbcaɔ AA almost, nearly.

แทรก sɛ̂ɛg' V 1. to insert between. 2. to push, squeeze through or into. 3. to permeate. 4. to be mixed (as a medicine). →Also spelled แซก. →Cf. ซำแรก.

แทรกซึม sɛ̂ɛgsym' V to infiltrate, penetrate into, permeate.

แทรกแซง sɛ̂ɛgsɛɛŋ' V 1. to insert. 2. to intervene, interfere, intrude. การ-- intervention, intrusion.

แทรกสอด sɛ̂ɛgsɔ̀ɔd' V 1. to interfere, intervene. 2. to have (something) interwoven, be threaded (with). sV 3. by inserting; interweavingly.

แทะ thέ?' V to gnaw, gnaw on, nibble on.

แทะ ..ขาด thέ?'...khàad' to gnaw off, gnaw loose.

โท thoo' Nm eleg. two. →Chiefly in compounds. →Cf. ทวิ-, ทวี, ยี่, สอง.

ชั้นโท chánthoo' the second highest rank in civil service.

นายพลโท (นาย) naajphonthoo' (naaj') N 1. lieutenant general. T 2. Lieutenant General --. →See under นาย for other similar uses of โท.

ปริญญาโท (ปริญญา) parin'jaathoo' (parin'jaa') N master's degree.

ไม้โท (อัน) májthoo' (?an') N the second tonal marker (ˇ) of the Thai writing system. NOTE. ไม้โท should be distinguished from เสียงโท. The former term refers to the written symbol, the latter to the spoken tone. ไม้โท may represent either a high tone (when it accompanies a low class consonant) or a falling tone (elsewhere). เสียงโท can only refer to the falling tone.

เสียงโท sǐaŋthoo' N gram. the falling tone. →See note under ไม้โท above.

โท่ in ทนโท่ thonthôo' V colloq. 1. to be obvious, clear, apparent. sV 2. obviously, clearly, apparently.

โทมนัส thoom'manád' lit., eleg. V 1. to feel sad, sorrowful, sorry. N 2. sorrow, sadness. →Syn. ทุกข์ใจ, เศร้าโศก com.

โทร. Abbreviation for โทรศัพท์ "telephone"; usually followed by the number.

โทร- thooraɔ bound form meaning "far, distant." →See entries below. →Cf. Eng. tele-.

โทรทัศน์ as in กล้องโทรทัศน์ (กล้อง) klɔ̂ŋ'thooraɔthád' (klɔ̂ŋ') N telescope.

โทรภาพ (เครื่อง) thooraphâab' (khrŷaŋ') N 1. television. 2. television set.

o วิทยุโทรภาพ wídthajú?'thooraphâab' idem.

โทรเลข (ฉบับ) thooraleeg' (chabàb') N 1. telegram, cablegram. V 2. to telegraph, to cable.

โทรศัพท์ (เครื่อง) thoorasàb' (khrŷaŋ') N 1. telephone. V 2. to telephone. เครื่อง-- telephone, telephone instrument.

o ต่อโทรศัพท์ tɔ̀ɔ'thoorasàb' V to make a phone call.

o โทรศัพท์ไปถึง thoorasàb'pajthŷŋ' to telephone (someone), call (someone) up.

o โทรศัพท์ไปหา thoorasàb'pajhǎa' idem.

o หูโทรศัพท์ (อัน) hǔu'thoorasàb' (?an') N telephone receiver.

โทรม soom' V 1. to deteriorate, degenerate, decline. 2. to die down (as a fire). 3. to be ruined, worn out. →Syn. 1. เสื่อม.

ทรุดโทรม súdsoom' V eleg. 1. to be deteriorated. worn out, in decay. 2. to be run down, sickly.

โทษ (อย่าง) thôod' (jàaŋ') N com. N 1. punishment, penalty. 2. harm, danger, ill effect. 3.

blame. V 4. to blame. คน-- (see below).

นัก-- prisoner, convict. →Syn. 1. ทัณฑ์ eleg.

กล่าวโทษ klàawthôod/ V to blame, accuse, charge (with).

ขอโทษ khɔ̌ɔthôod/↓ V 1. to apologize. 2. Excuse me! Beg pardon! คำ-- apology, excuse. →Syn. ขอประทานโทษ eleg. def., ทานโทษ colloq.

ขอโทษขอโพย khɔ̌ɔthôod/khɔ̌ɔphooj/ V elab. colloq. to apologize.

คนโทษ (คน) khonthôod/ (khon/) N 1. prisoner, convict. 2. the accused (not a formal legal term).

คาดโทษ khâadthôod/ V to set a penalty for the next recurrence of a violation for which at the given moment punishment has been withheld.

ถูกโทษ thùugthôod/ to be punished, penalized.

ทำโทษ thamthôod/ V to punish, penalize. →Syn. ลงโทษ com., ลงทัณฑ์ eleg.

โทษทัณฑ์ thôod/than/ N eleg. punishment.

โทษเบา thôodbaw/ N com. 1. light punishment or penalty. 2. minor offense. →Syn. ลหุโทษ eleg. →Ant. โทษหนัก.

โทษประหารชีวิต thôod/-prahǎan/chiiwíd/ N 1. the death penalty. 2. capital punishment.

โทษหนัก thôodnàg/ N com. 1. heavy punishment or penalty. 2. major offense. →Syn. มหันต- โทษ eleg. →Ant. โทษเบา.

มหันตโทษ mahǎn/tàthôod/ N eleg. 1. heavy punishment or penalty. 2. major offense. →Syn. โทษหนัก com.

มีโทษ miithôod/ V to be harmful, produce ill effects.

ยกโทษ(ให้) jógthôod/(hâjɔ) V to forgive.

ลงโทษ loŋthôod/ V 1. to punish. 2. to take disciplinary action. →Syn. See ทำโทษ.

o บทลงโทษ (ฉบับ,บท,ข้อ) bòd/loŋthôod/ (chaɔ bàb/, bòd/, khɔ̌ɔ/) N penal code.

ลหุโทษ lahù?/thôod/ eleg. N 1. light punishment or penalty. 2. minor offense, misdemeanor. →Syn. โทษเบา com.

สำเร็จโทษ sǎmrèd/thôod/ V eleg. to execute, put to death. →Syn. See ฆ่า com.

ให้โทษ hâjthôod/ V to do harm, be harmful.

ให้อภัยโทษ hâj/?aphajjathôod/ eleg. to pardon, grant amnesty (to).

โทสะ thoosà?/ N eleg. anger, rage, fury. →Syn. โทโส eleg., ความโกรธ com.

โทโส thoosǒo/ N eleg. anger, rage. →Syn. See โทสะ.

ไทย thaj/ N 1. Thai. V 2. to be free. →Comp. 1. ไต ๒.

กระทรวงมหาดไทย krasuaŋ/mahàadthaj/ Ministry of the Interior.

คนไทย (คน) khonthaj/ (khon/) N Thai person.

ชาติไทย (ชาติ) châadthaj/ (châad/) N Thai nationality; the Thai nation.

ชาวไทย (คน) chaawthaj/ (khon/) N a Thai; the Thai.

ประเทศไทย prathêedthaj/ N eleg. Thailand. →Syn. เมืองไทย com.

เป็นไทย penthaj/ 1. to be Thai. 2. to be free.

เป็นไทยแก่ตัว penthaj/kɛ̀ɛtua/ to be independent.

พริกไทย phrígthaj/ N pepper (whole or ground).

ภาษาไทย (ภาษา) phaasǎathaj/ (phaasǎa/) N the Thai language.

เมืองไทย myaŋthaj/ N com. Thailand. →Syn. ประเทศไทย eleg.

อ่าวไทย ?àawthaj/ N Gulf of Thailand.

ไทยทาน (อย่าง) thajjathaan/ (jàaŋ/) N alms. เครื่อง-- idem.

ไทร saj/ N banyan (Ficus benghalensis). ต้น-- (ต้น) tônsaj/ (tôn/) N banyan tree.

ธ

ธ thɔɔ/ LOW consonant. Pronounced th initially, d finally. The sound th as an initial low consonant is usually written ท.

ธง (ผืน) thoŋ/ (phy̌yn/) N flag, banner, pennant.

ธงประจำชาติ (ผืน) thoŋ/pracamchâad/ (phy̌yn/) N national flag. →Also ธงชาติ.

เรือธง (ลำ) ryathoŋ/ (lam/) N flagship.

ธนบัตร (ใบ,ฉบับ) thanabàd/ (baj/,chabàb/) N banknote.

ธนบุรี thon/burii/ pN Thonburi (Dhonburi), a city which lies across the river from Bangkok.

ธนาคาร (แห่ง) thanaakhaan′ (hɛ̀ŋ′) N bank.
ธนาคารชาติไทย thanaakhaan′châadthaj′ Thai
National Bank.

ธนาณัติ (ใบ) thanaa′nád′ (baj′) N (postal) money
order. การ-- money order transaction.

ธนู thanuu′ N 1. bow. 2. arrow. Chiefly in cpds.
คันธนู (คัน) khan′thanuu′ (khan′) N bow.
ลูกธนู (ดอก,ลูก) lûugthanuu′ (dɔ̀ɔg′, lûug′) N
arrow.

ธรณี thɔɔranii′ N eleg. earth, ground, soil.
→Syn. ดิน com.
ธรณีวิทยา thɔɔranii′wídthajaa′ N geology.
แม่ธรณี mɛ̂ɛ′thɔɔranii′ N goddess of the earth.

ธรรม tham′ N Buddhist teaching, righteousness,
dharma.
ชอบธรรม chɔ̂ɔb′tham′ V to be righteous, just,
honest.
เที่ยงธรรม thîaŋtham′ V to be upright, just,
fair, impartial.
เป็นธรรม pentham′ to be fair, just. ความ--
justice.
พระธรรม phrátham′ N the Dharma, the Buddhist
teachings.
พระธรรมเทศนา phrátham′mathêed′sanǎa′,
-thee′sanaa′* N eleg. Buddhist sermon,
preaching.
มนุษยธรรม manúd′sajatham′ N humanity, humaneness.
ยุติธรรม júdtitham′ N justice. V 2. to be just.
→Also ยุตติธรรม FS.
วัฒนธรรม wád′thanátham′ N culture.
อารยธรรม ʔaa′rajátham′ N civilization.

ธรรมชาติ thammachâad′ N nature.
กฎธรรมชาติ (ข้อ) kòd′thammachâad′ (khɔ̂ɔ′)
N a law of nature, laws of nature.
ขุมทรัพย์ธรรมชาติ khǔmsáb′thammachâad′ N 1.
natural resources. 2. an area of natural abundance.

ธรรมดา thammadaa′ V to be ordinary, natural,
common, usual.
กฎธรรมดา (ข้อ) kòd′thammadaa′ (khɔ̂ɔ′) N
1. a law of nature, laws of nature. 2. the way
things are, the nature of things.
ของธรรมดา (อย่าง) khɔ̌ɔŋ′thammadaa′ (jàaŋ′)

N the usual, ordinary, natural thing.
ตามธรรมดา taam′thammadaa′ usually, ordinarily,
commonly, normally.
เป็นธรรมดา penthammadaa′ 1. to be natural,
normal, usual. 2. naturally. 3. of course.
ผิดธรรมดา phìd′thammadaa′ V to be abnormal,
unusual, queer.
อย่างธรรมดา jàaŋthammadaa′ 1. as usual, in the
ordinary way. 2. of the ordinary kind.

ธรรมนูญ (ฉบับ) thammanuun′ (chabàb′) N code of
laws, charter, constitution.
ธรรมนูญองค์การสหประชาชาติ thammanuun′-ʔoŋ⊂
kaan′sahàprachaa′châad′ N United Nations
Charter.
รัฐธรรมนูญ (ฉบับ) rád′thathammanuun′ (chabàb′)
N constitution (of a state, country).

ธรรมเนียม (อย่าง,แบบ) thamniam′ (jàaŋ′, bɛ̀ɛb′)
N custom, tradition, usage.
ขนบธรรมเนียม (อย่าง,แบบ) khanòb′thamniam′
(jàaŋ′, bɛ̀ɛb′) N customs, manners, tradition.
ค่าธรรมเนียม khâa′thamniam′ N fee, fees.

ธรรมศาสตร์ thammasàad′ N 1. jurisprudence. 2.
shortened form of the entry below.
มหาวิทยาลัยธรรมศาสตร์และการเมือง mahǎa′⊂
wídthajaalaj′-thammasàad′-lɛkaan′myaŋ′
N University of Moral and Political Sciences
(in Bangkok).

ธันวาคม thanwaa′khom′ N December. เดือน--
idem. →The names of all the months are listed
under เดือน.

ธาตุ (อย่าง,ชนิด) thâad′ (jàaŋ′, chaníd′) N element.
แยกธาตุ jɛ̂ɛgthâad′ V to analyze chemically.

ธานี in ราชธานี (แห่ง) râadchathaa′nii′ (hɛ̀ŋ′) N
eleg. the capital (city). →Syn. เมืองหลวง
com.

ธาร (สาย,แห่ง) thaan′ N 1. stream, brook (sǎaj′,
hɛ̀ŋ′). 2. lit. water.
ลำธาร (สาย,แห่ง) lamthaan′ (sǎaj′, hɛ̀ŋ′) N
stream.

ธำรง thamroŋ′ V eleg. to maintain. →Comp.
ดำรง.

ธิดา (คน) thídaa′ (khon′) N eleg. daughter.
→Syn. See ลูกสาว.

ธุระ (อย่าง) thúrá?′ (jàaŋ′) N business, affairs,

errands.

ก้าวก่ายธุระ kâawkàaj/thúrá?/ to be officious,
interfere in the affairs of others.

ธุระการ (อย่าง) thúrá?/kaan/ (jàaŋ/) N 1.
practical matters (of an administrative nature).
2. (as n. mod.) administrative.

o ฝ่ายธุระการ fâaj/-thúrá?/-kaan/ 1. (on) the
practical side; the practical aspect. 2. (on)
the administrative side; the administrative aspect. →Comp. ฝ่ายวิชาการ.

ธุระกิจ (อย่าง) thúrákìd/ (jàaŋ/) N business.

ธุระปะปัง (อย่าง) thúrá?/pà?paŋ/ (jàaŋ/) N
colloq. business.

ธุระไม่ใช่ thúrá?/mâjchâj/ colloq. none of one's
business.

ธุระร้อน (อย่าง) thúrá?/rɔ́ɔn/ (jàaŋ/) N urgent
business.

มีธุระ miithúrá?/ V 1. to be busy, occupied. 2.
to have an errand (to do).

o คุณมีธุระอะไร khun/-miithúrá?/?araj/ What's
on your mind?

เสร็จธุระ sèd/thúrá?/ V to be finished with the
business at hand.

ธูป (ดอก) thûub/ (dɔ̀ɔg/) N incense, joss stick.

เธอ thəə/ P 1. sp. to intim. or inf. you. 2.
eleg. he, him, she, her. →In mng. 1 paired
with ฉัน "I, me."

น

น nɔɔ/ LOW consonant. Pronounced n both initially
and finally. The sound n as an initial low consonant is also sometimes spelled with ณ, and
as a final consonant with ญ,ณ,ร, or ล.

น. Abbrev. for นาฬิกา naalikaa/ o'clock (on the
24 hr. basis).

o ๐๒.๐๐ น. sɔ̌ɔŋ/naalikaa/ 2 A.M.

นก (ตัว,ฝูง) nóg/ (tua/, fǔuŋ/) N 1. bird (tua/
for individuals; fǔuŋ/ for flocks). 2. the cock
or hammer (of a gun). NOTE. In mng. 1 this
is both the general term and the class term.
When used as class term it is followed by a
specific term. →See Note 2 under นาง.

ขึ้นนก khʉ̂n/nóg/ to cock (a gun).

นกกระจอก nógkracɔ̀ɔg/ N sparrow.

นกกระจอกเทศ nógkracɔ̀ɔg/thêed/ N ostrich.

นกกระจาบ nógkracàab/ N rice bird, weaverbird
(Ploceidae and other families).

นกกระจิบ nógkracìb/ N general name for various
families of small birds, e.g. warblers (Sylviidae),
etc.

นกกระตั้ว nógkratûa/ N cockatoo (Kakatoë).
[กระตั้ว f. Mal.]

นกกระเต็น nógkraten/ N kingfisher (Alcedinidae).

นกกระทุง nógkrathuŋ/ N pelican (Palecanidae).

นกกระสา nógkrasǎa/ N heron (Ardeidae).

นกกางเขน nógkaaŋkhěen/ N dyal, or magpie robin.

นกแก้ว nógkɛ̂ɛw/ N parrot.

นกขุนทอง nógkhǔnthɔɔŋ/ N talking myna, bird of
the starling family (Sturnidae).

นกเขา nógkhǎw/ N turtledove, dove.

นกเค้าแมว nógkháwmɛɛw/ N a kind of owl.

นกดุเหว่า nógduwàw/ N the Malayan koel, a kind
of large black bird (Cuculinae).

นกนางนวล nógnaaŋnuan/ N sea gull.

นกนางแอ่น nógnaaŋ?èn/ N the swallow. →Syn.
นกอีแอ่น colloq. →See Note 2 under นาง.

นกเป็ดน้ำ nógpèdnáam/ N teal.

นกพิราบ nógphírâab/ N pigeon (Columbidae).

นกยูง nógjuuŋ/ N the common peafowl (Pavo
cristatus).

นกสาลิกา nógsǎalíkaa/ N the common myna.

นกหวีด (อัน) nógwìid/ (?an/) N a whistle.

นกอินทรี nóg?insii/ N eagle.

นกอีแอ่น nóg?ii?èn/ N colloq. swallow. →Syn.
นกนางแอ่น com. →See Note 2 under นาง.

นกเอี้ยง nóg?îaŋ/ N singing myna. Resembles
นกขุนทอง.

นกฮูก nóghûug/ N a kind of owl.

หลับนก làbnóg/ V idiom. to fall asleep, doze
in a sitting position.

นคร nakhɔɔn/ N city, town. NOTE. This word is
frequently used in the names of cities and town-
ships (čhangwats). It is eq. to Camb. Angkor.

นครธม nakhɔɔn/thom/ pN Angkor Thom, the
ancient capital of the Khmer.

นครนายก nakhɔɔn/naajóg/ pN Nakhɔn Nayok

(Nakorn Nayok), a township in E central Thai-land.

นครปฐม nakhɔɔn'pathǒm' pN Nakhɔn Pathom (Nakorn Patom), a township in W central Thai-land.

นครพนม nakhɔɔn'phanom' pN Nakhɔn Phanom (Nakorn Panom), a township in NE Thailand.

นครราชสีมา nakhɔɔn'râad'chasǐimaa' pN Nakhɔn Ratsima (Nakorn Rajsima), a township in NE Thailand. →Colloquial name is โคราช.

นครวัด nakhɔɔn'wád' pN Angkor Wat, ancient temple of the Khmer (in Cambodia).

นครศรีธรรมราช nakhɔɔn'-sǐi'thammarâad' pN Nakhɔn Sithamarat (Nakorn Sritamarat or Sridhamaraj), a township in S Thailand.

นครสวรรค์ nakhɔɔn'sawǎn' pN Nakhɔn Sawan (Nakorn Sawan), a township in N central Thai-land. →Colloquial name is ปากน้ำโพ.

นครโสเภณี,หญิง-- (คน) nakhɔɔn'sǒopheenii, jǐŋ'-nakhɔɔn'sǒopheenii' (khon') N courtesan, prostitute.

นครหลวง (นคร,แห่ง) nakhɔɔn'lǔaŋ' (nakhɔɔn', hɛ̀ŋ') N eleg. capital (of a country).

พระนคร phránákhɔɔn'* pN 1. Phra Nakhɔn, the township in which Bangkok is located. N 2. capital city.

o ชาวพระนคร (คน) chaaw'phránákhɔɔn' (khon') N the people of Bangkok, Bangkokians.

นนทบุรี non'tháburii' pN Nonthaburi, a township in C Thailand.

นบ in นบนอบ,นอบนบ nóbnɔ̀ɔb', nɔ̂ɔbnób' V to pay respect by pressing the palms together; to lower the body and press the palms together.

นพ nób', nóbphaɔ Nm lit. nine. →Syn. เก้า com.

ดาวนพเคราะห์ (ดวง) daaw'nóbphakhrɔ́ʔ' (duaŋ') N the nine planets.

นภา náphaa' N eleg.,lit. sky, firmament. →Syn. ฟ้า com., เวหา lit.

นม (เต้า,ข้าง,ขวด) nom' N 1. breast, udder (tâw', khâaŋ'). 2. milk (khùad' or other appro-priate container clf.). 3. any protuberance or appendage resembling a breast or nipple. →Syn. 1. ถัน eleg.

นมกระป๋อง (กระป๋อง) nomkrapɔ̌ŋ' (krapɔ̌ŋ') N canned milk.

นมข้น nomkhôn' N condensed milk.

นมผง nomphǒŋ' N powdered milk.

นมวัว nomwua' N 1. cow's milk. 2. cow's udder.

นมสด nomsòd' N 1. fresh milk. 2. evaporated milk.

o นมสดกระป๋อง nomsòd'krapɔ̌ŋ' N evaporated milk.

นมหนู nomnǔu' N 1. (carburetor) jet. 2. nipple, projection on which the gun cap is placed.

นางนม (คน) naaŋnom' (khon') N eleg. wet nurse. →Syn. แม่นม com.

น้ำนม námnom' N milk. →Usually นม mng.2.

แม่นม (คน) mɛ̂ɛnom' (khon') N com. wet nurse. →Syn. นางนม eleg.

รีดนม rîid'nom' V to milk.

วัวนม (ตัว) wuanom' (tua') N milch cow.

หย่านม jàa'nom' V to wean.

หัวนม (อัน,หัว) hǔanom' (ʔan', hǔa') N nipple.

นม ๒ in นมนาน,นานนม nomnaan', naannom' sV for a long time; long (ago). →Comp. นาน.

นมนานมาแล้ว nomnaan'maalɛ́ɛw' long, long ago.

นโยบาย (อัน) nájoo'baaj' (ʔan') N policy.

นโยบายต่างประเทศ nájoo'baaj'-tàaŋprathêed' N foreign policy.

วางนโยบาย waaŋ'-nájoo'baaj' to lay down, establish a policy.

น.ร. Abbrev. for นักเรียน student, pupil.

นรก naróg' N hell.

ห้วงนรก hûaŋ'naróg' N hell (implying vastness, depth, dreadfulness).

นราธิวาส naraa'thíwâad' pN Narathiwat, a township in S Thailand.

นวด nûad' V 1. to thresh (rice). 2. to massage, knead.

นวดข้าว nûadkhâaw' V to thresh rice.

นวดฟั้น nûad'fán' V to massage by kneading (the flesh).

บีบนวด bìib'nûad' V idem.

หมอนวด (คน) mɔ̌ɔnûad' (khon') N masseur, masseuse.

นวนิยาย (เรื่อง) náwáníjaaj' (rɯ̂aŋ') N lit. a novel. →Comp. นิยาย.

นวม (ข้าง,ผืน) nuam' N 1. padding. 2. boxing

gloves (khǎaŋ′). 3. quilt, comforter (phɣ̌yn′).

เก้าอี้นวม (ตัว) kâw?îi′nuam′ (tua′) N over-stuffed chair.

แขวนนวม khwɛ̌ɛnnuam′ V idiom. to quit box-ing: "to hang up the boxing gloves."

ผ้านวม (ผืน) phâanuam′ (phɣ̌yn′) N quilt, com-forter.

น่วม nûam′ V to be soft, flaccid, lacking firmness. →Comp. นุ่ม, นิ่ม, อ่อน. →Ant. แข็ง, กระด้าง.

นวล nuan′ V 1. to be soft-colored, cream-colored. 2. (the complexion) to be delicately beautiful; (the face) to be radiant; (the face) to be nicely powdered.

นิ่มนวล nîmnuan′ V 1. to be gentle, tender, gracious. 2. to be graceful, smooth (in action). sV 3. tenderly, graciously; smoothly, grace-fully. →Syn. นุ่มนวล.

น.ส. Abbrev. for นางสาว Miss; young lady.

นอ (อัน) nɔɔ′ (?an′) N horn (of the rhinoceros).

นอแรด (อัน) nɔɔrɛ̂ɛd′ (?an′) N rhinoceros horn.

นอก nɔ̂ɔg′ sV 1. outer external. 2. outside. 3. outside of. →Ant. ใน.

ข้างนอก khâŋnɔ̂ɔg′ outside, the outside.

คนนอก (คน) khonnɔ̂ɔg′ (khon′) N an outsider, nonmember.

นอกกฎหมาย nɔ̂ɔg′kòdmǎaj′ to be unlawful, illegal, illegitimate.

นอกความ nɔ̂ɔg′khwaam′ to be beside the point.

นอกคอก nɔ̂ɔgkhɔ̂ɔg′ V colloq. to veer off the proper or expected course (of action).

○ ลูกนอกคอก (คน) lûug′nɔ̂ɔgkhɔ̂ɔg′ (khon′) N a black sheep, a prodigal.

นอกจาก nɔ̂ɔg′càagɔ 1. besides, outside of, aside from. 2. except, other than; excluding, beyond.

○ นอกจากว่า nɔ̂ɔgcàagwâa′ 1. unless. 2. pro-vided that.

นอกใจ nɔ̂ɔg′caj′ V to be unfaithful (to) (of hus-band and wife). การ-- infidelity, being un-faithful (esp. toward one's spouse).

นอกชาน (นอกชาน, แห่ง) nɔ̂ɔgchaan′ (nɔ̂ɔgchaan′, hɛ̀ŋ′) N (uncovered) porch, open patio (adjoin-ing the house).

นอกประเด็น nɔ̂ɔg′praden′ to be irrelevant, off the subject.

นอกปัญหา nɔ̂ɔg′panhǎa′ to be beside the point.

นอกเมือง nɔ̂ɔgmyaŋ′ out-of-town.

นอกเรื่อง nɔ̂ɔgrɣ̂aŋ′ to be off the subject.

○ พูดนอกเรื่อง phûud′nɔ̂ɔgrɣ̂aŋ′ to talk irrele-vantly.

นอกลู่นอกทาง nɔ̂ɔglûu′nɔ̂ɔgthaaŋ′ elab. colloq. off the track, on the wrong track.

นอกเหนือจาก nɔ̂ɔg′nɣ̌acàagɔ over and above, aside from (that).

○ นอกเหนือจากนั้น nɔ̂ɔgnɣ̌a′càagnán′ moreover, besides that, above and beyond that.

นักเรียนนอก (คน) nágrian′nɔ̂ɔg′ (khon′) N 1. a student studying abroad. 2. one who has re-ceived his education abroad.

บ้านนอก (แห่ง) bâannɔ̂ɔg′ (hɛ̀ŋ′) N colloq. 1. the country (as opposed to the city), country-side, rural area. 2. (as n. mod.) rural, coun-trified. →Syn. ชนบท eleg. →Cf. หัวเมือง.

เปลือกนอก (เปลือก, อัน) plɣ̀agnɔ̂ɔg′ (plɣ̀ag′, ?an′) N outermost shell, e.g. epicarp (of the coconut).

ไปนอก, ไปเมืองนอก pajnɔ̂ɔg′, paj′myaŋnɔ̂ɔg′ to go abroad.

ภายนอก phaajnɔ̂ɔg′ N outside, exterior; external. การ-- external affairs.

เมืองนอก myaŋnɔ̂ɔg′ N foreign country; abroad.

เมืองนอกเมืองนา myaŋnɔ̂ɔg′myaŋnaa′ N elab. colloq. foreign country; abroad (usually the U.S.A. or in Europe).

รอบนอก rɔ̂ɔbnɔ̂ɔg′ 1. outside, outer area, periph-ery, outer part, outer layer. 2. outside (of), around the periphery (of).

ส่วนนอก sùannɔ̂ɔg′ the outer part.

เสื้อนอก (ตัว) sɣ̂anɔ̂ɔg′ (tua′) N coat, outer coat.

หัวนอก hǔanɔ̂ɔg′ colloq. a person brought up or educated abroad.

นอง nɔɔŋ′ V 1. to flood, inundate. 2. to be flooded, inundated. →Often used of flooding with other liquids besides water. →Syn. 1. ท่วม.

นองเลือด nɔɔŋ′lɣ̂ad′ V to be bloody, covered with blood, sanguinary. อย่าง-- in a bloody manner.

น้อง (ข้าง, น้อง) nɔ́ŋ′*(khǎaŋ′, nɔ́ŋ′) N calf (of the leg).

ท้องน้อง thɔ́ɔŋnɔ́ɔŋ/ N idem.

ทอดน่อง thɔ̂ɔdnôŋ/ sV in a leisurely manner, at a leisurely pace (in ref. to walking).

น่องตึง nɔ̂ŋ/tyŋ/ V to have a charley horse in the leg.

น้อง (คน) nɔ́ɔŋ/ (khon/) N com. 1. younger sibling, i.e. younger brother or sister. P 2. I, me (yg. sibling to older sibling, wife to husband, younger person to slightly older person). 3. you, he, him, she, her (sp. to or about one's yg. sibling, one's wife, a slightly younger person). T 4. title used before the first name of a yg. sibling. Comp. พี่ "older sibling."

น้องเขย (คน) nɔ́ɔŋkhɤ̌ɤj/ (khon/) N brother-in-law who is the husband of one's younger sister.

น้องชาย (คน) nɔ́ɔŋchaaj/ (khon/) N 1. younger brother. 2. slang m. sp. (younger) partner, bud, buddy (in addressing someone).

น้อง ๆ nɔ́ɔŋnɔ́ɔŋ/ 1. younger brothers and sister. 2. colloq. secondary to, inferior to, next in importance after. →Used mostly with a preceding clf.

น้องผัว (คน) nɔ́ɔŋphǔa/ (khon/) N brother- or sister-in-law of a w. in ref. to her husband's yg. brother or sister: "husband's younger sibling."

น้องเมีย (คน) nɔ́ɔŋmia/ (khon/) N brother- or sister-in-law of a m. in ref. to his wife's yg. brother or sister: "wife's younger sibling."

น้องสะไภ้ (คน) nɔ́ɔŋsapháj/ (khon/) N sister-in-law who is the wife of one's younger brother.

น้องสาว (คน) nɔ́ɔŋsǎaw/ (khon/) N younger sister.

น้องใหม่ (คน) nɔ́ɔŋmàj/ (khon/) N 1. newborn brother or sister. 2. freshman in a college or university. 3. new member.

พี่น้อง (คน) phîinɔ́ɔŋ/ (khon/) N brothers, sisters, brother and sister, brothers and sisters; cousins.

o ญาติพี่น้อง (คน) jâad/phîinɔ́ɔŋ/ (khon/) N relatives.

o พี่น้องทั้งหลาย phîinɔ́ɔŋ/tháŋlǎaj/↓ Friends! (used when making an address).

o พี่น้องร่วมชาติ phîinɔ́ɔŋ/-rûam/châad/ (one's)

fellow citizens.

ลูกน้อง (คน) lûugnɔ́ɔŋ/ (khon/) N colloq. underling, subordinate.

ลูกพี่ลูกน้อง lûugphîi/lûugnɔ́ɔŋ/ N cousins in general.

นอน ๑ nɔɔn/ V 1. to lie, recline (of animate beings or statues). sV 2. lengthwise, on its side. NOTE. Sometimes coupled with นั่ง "to sit." See นั่งคิดนอนคิด below.

กินนอน kinnɔɔn/ V 1. to eat and sleep (at a certain place, esp. when done habitually, frequently, or for a period of time). sV 2. modifier used as the equivalent of Eng. "boarding," as in the following example.

o โรงเรียนกินนอน (แห่ง, โรงเรียน) rooŋrian/ɔ kinnɔɔn/ (hɛ̀ŋ/, rooŋrian/) N boarding school.

ขี้หาวนอน khîi/hǎawnɔɔn/ to be a sleepy head.

เข้านอน khâwnɔɔn/ V to retire, go to bed.

ง่วงนอน ŋûaŋnɔɔn/ V to be sleepy, drowsy.

เตียงนอน (เตียง) tiaŋnɔɔn/ (tiaŋ/) N bed.

ที่นอน (อัน, ที่) thîinɔɔn/ (ʔan/, thîi/) N mattress.

นอนก้น nɔɔnkôn/ V to settle on the bottom, precipitate.

นอนใจ nɔɔncaj/ V to be nonchalant, unconcerned, easygoing, trusting; to take (things) easy.

นอนแบบ nɔɔnbɛ̀b/ V to lie helpless, spent (from overexhaustion, hurt, illness).

นอนแผ่ nɔɔnphɛ̀ɛ/ V to lie sprawled out, (esp. on one's back).

นอนพังพาบ nɔɔn/phaŋphâab/ V to lie flat, face down, prone.

นอนไม่หลับ nɔɔn/mâjlàb/ to be unable to sleep, to lie sleepless.

นอนลง (1) nɔɔn/loŋ/; (2) nɔɔn/loŋ↓ 1. to lie down (from sitting or standing position). 2. Lie down!

นอนหลับ nɔɔnlàb/ V to sleep, be asleep.

o นอนไม่หลับ nɔɔn/mâjlàb/ to be unable to sleep, to lie sleepless.

o นอนหลับทับสิทธิ์ nɔɔnlàb/-tháb/sìd/ idiom. to be neglectful in exercising one's rights (as when failing to vote in an election).

o นอนหลับปุ๋ย nɔɔn/làbpǔj/ to sleep soundly, sleep like a log, be fast asleep.

o นอนหลับ ๆ ตื่น ๆ nɔɔn/-làblàb/tỳyntỳyn/ to sleep fitfully.

นอนเหยียด nɔɔnjìad′ V to lie stretched out, lie down at full length.

นั่งคิดนอนคิด nâŋ′khíd′-nɔɔn′khíd′ V to think unceasingly.

บ้านเกิดเมืองนอน (แห่ง) bâankə̀əd′myaŋnɔɔn′ (hɛ̀ŋ′) N ela b. colloq. motherland, homeland.

ไปนอน pajnɔɔn′ V to retire, go to bed.

พระนอน (องค์) phrá?nɔɔn′ (?oŋ′) N a reclining Buddha (i.e. Buddha image).

ล้มตัวลงนอน lómtua′loŋnɔɔn′ V 1. to lie down, lay oneself down. 2. to flop down (as on a bed).

ล้มหมอนนอนเสื่อ lómmɔ̌ɔn′nɔɔnsɨ̀a′ V ela b. colloq. to fall sick, be brought to bed because of illness.

เวลานอน weelaanɔɔn′ N 1. bedtime, time to sleep. 2. when (one) goes to bed, while lying down, while sleeping.

ห้องนอน (ห้อง) hɔ̂ŋnɔɔn′ N bedroom.

หัวนอนปลายตีน hǔanɔɔn′plaajtiin′ N idiom. the background of a person (esp. as it relates to his social status).

หาวนอน hǎawnɔɔn′ V to be sleepy.

นอน ๒. See entries below. In this usage นอน has no independent meaning of its own, but merely serves to rhyme with สอน.

ว่านอนสอนง่าย wâanɔɔn′sɔ̌ɔnŋâaj′ ela b. colloq. 1. to be tractable, easily led, compliant, obedient.

ว่านอนสอนยาก wâanɔɔn′sɔ̌ɔnjâag′ ela b. colloq. 1. to be hard to teach, unmanageable, untractable, disobedient, unruly.

นอน ๓ in แน่นอน nɛ̂ɛnɔɔn′ V 1. to be certain, definite. sV 2. certainly, definitely, absolutely, positively, of course. การ-- certainty.

นอบ nɔ̂ɔb′ V to bend, bow. →Chiefly in compounds.

นอบนบ,นบนอบ nɔ̂ɔbnób′, nóbnɔ̂ɔb′ V to pay respect by pressing the palms together; to lower the body and press the palms together.

นอบน้อม (ต่อ) nɔ̂ɔbnɔ́ɔm′(tɔ̀ɔ=) V 1. to show respect (to). sV 2. respectfully.

น้อม nɔ́ɔm′ V to bend, bow. →Chiefly in compounds; see entries below.

น้อมใจ nɔ́ɔm′caj′ V to humble one's heart.

อ่อนน้อม(ต่อ) ?ɔ̀ɔnnɔ́ɔm′(tɔ̀ɔ=) V 1. to submit (e.g. to someone's authority). 2. to be respectful (toward), mindful (of) (e.g. one's elders).

น้อย ๑ nɔ́ɔj′ V 1. to be little, less, small, slight (in quantity). 2. to be lesser, minor, inferior. Nm 3. few (with or without a following clf.). →Comp. หน่อย. →Dist. เล็ก. →Ant. มาก, ใหญ่.

กองพลน้อย (กอง,กองพล) kɔɔŋphonnɔ́ɔj′ (kɔɔŋ′, kɔɔŋphon′) N brigade.

ข้างน้อย khâŋnɔ́ɔj′ N the minority (esp. in voting).

ใจน้อย cajnɔ́ɔj′ V to be touchy, sensitive, easily offended.

ทุกซอกเล็กมุมน้อย thúgsɔ̂ɔg′lég′-mum′nɔ́ɔj′ ela b. every little nook and corner, every little nook and cranny.

น้อยกว่า...มากนัก nɔ́ɔj′kwàa=...mâag′nág′ considerably less than, very much less than.

น้อยใจ nɔ́ɔjcaj′ V to feel slighted, feel inferior, feel neglected (by others).

น้อยเนื้อต่ำใจ nɔ́ɔjnɨ́a′tàmcaj′ V ela b. colloq. to feel slighted, feel inferior; to feel sore and resentful.

น้อยมาก nɔ́ɔjmâag′ very few, very little, very small in number.

น้อยราย nɔ́ɔj′raaj′ rare, few cases.

น้อยลง nɔ́ɔj′loŋ′ to decrease, diminish, dwindle.

น้อยหน้า nɔ́ɔjnâa′ 1. to feel inferior (to). 2. to be outdone, take second place.

ผู้น้อย (คน) phûunɔ́ɔj′ (khon′) N 1. an inferior, a junior person, a younger person. 2. the little fellow. →Opp. ผู้ใหญ่.

มักน้อย mágnɔ́ɔj′ V 1. to be content with little, be satisfied with what little one has. 2. to be unambitious. →Ant. 1. มักมาก. 2. มักใหญ่.

มากน้อย. See entries below.

o กี่มากน้อย kìimâagnɔ́ɔj′ colloq. how much, how many.

o ไม่กี่มากน้อย mâjkìi′mâagnɔ́ɔj′ colloq. not so much, not so many.

มีน้อย miinɔ́ɔj′ there is little (of something), there are few.

มีน้อยราย miinɔ́ɔj′raaj′ there are rare cases.

เมียน้อย (คน) mianɔ́ɔj′ (khon′) N com. minor

wife; second, third, or subsequent wife; concubine. →Syn. ภรรยาน้อย eleg.

ไม่น้อย mâjnɔ́ɔj′ not a little, i.e. quite, considerable.

o รุนแรงไม่น้อย runrɛɛŋ′-mâjnɔ́ɔj′ to be quite
severe.

ไม่มากก็น้อย mâjmâag′kɔ̂nɔ́ɔj′ whether many or
few, whether much or little; if not a (whole) lot,
then (at least) some.

ไม่...แม้แต่น้อย mâjɔ...mɛ́ɛtɛ̀ɛnɔ́ɔj′ not even a
little bit, not in the least.

o ไม่สวยแม้แต่น้อย mâjsǔaj′-mɛ́ɛtɛ̀ɛnɔ́ɔj′ is not
in the least beautiful.

ลักเล็กขโมยน้อย lág′lég′-khamoojnɔ́ɔj′ V elab.
colloq. to pilfer.

เล็กน้อย légnɔ́ɔj′ sV 1. a little bit. 2. little by
little. See cross reference.

o โตกว่า...เล็กน้อย too′kwàaɔ...légnɔ́ɔj′ a
little bit bigger than.

ส่วนน้อย sùannɔ́ɔj′ N minority, the small part.
คน-- the minority (of people).

หนูน้อย (คน) nǔunɔ́ɔj′ (khon′) N baby, little
fellow, small child.

อย่างน้อย jàaŋnɔ́ɔj′ at least; as a mininum.

น้อย ๒. See entries below.

น้อยหน่า (ใบ,ลูก,ผล) nɔ́ɔjnàa′ (baj′, lûug′,
phǒn′) N rough-skinned custard apple. ต้น--
(ต้น) rough-skinned custard apple tree (Annona
squamosa).

น้อยโหน่ง (ใบ,ลูก,ผล) nɔ́ɔjnòoŋ′ (baj′, lûug′,
phǒn′) N smooth-skinned custard apple.
ต้น-- (ต้น) smooth-skinned custard apple tree
(Annona reticulata).

นอรเวย์ nɔɔrawee′ pN Norway. [f. Eng.]

นะ ná′ Pt 1. particle used to make an utterance
gentler, milder (1st-3rd examples). 2. particle
indicating a mild question (4th-6th examples),
sometimes with an additional element of invitation, coaxing, suggesting (6th-7th examples).
3. part. expressing mild reproach, disappointment, criticism (8th-9th examples). →Cf. 2. the
first example under นะ ๑. NOTE. In all uses
of นะ there is an element of gentleness, mild-
ness, and in some cases this is the primary

implication; 1st-3rd examples. As a mild question นะ is often comparable to English "may I?
won't you? aren't you? isn't it? okay?" etc.;
5th-7th examples. However, in this use, นะ is
sometimes best left untranslated; 4th example.
As an expression of mild reproach, นะ is often
interposed between double occurrences of a noun
or pronoun, but the repeated segment may be
omitted without changing the meaning; 8th and
9th examples.

o ดีจริงนะ dii′ciŋná↓ How nice! Isn't that nice!
(either sincerely or sarcastically).

o ดีละนะ dii′laná↓ Very well! All right! Okay!
So that's how it is! (as in response to a disappointing action; may also express feigned disappointment).

o อย่านะ jàa′ná↓ Don't (do that). Please don't.
→Cf. 2nd example under นะ ๑.

o ใครนะ มาเคาะประตู khraj′ná maakhɔ́ʔ′pra
tuu↓ Now who could that be knocking at the door?
Who is it comes knocking at (my) door?

o วันนี้อากาศดีนะ wanníi′-ʔaakàad′dii′-ná↓ Isn't
the weather lovely today? It's fine weather today,
isn't it? It's fine day, isn't it?

o กินนะ kin′ná↓ 1. Can (I) eat (it)? (I'll) eat (one),
okay? 2. Won't (you) eat (it)? Why don't (you)
take (it)? (as when gently urging a child to take
his medicine).

o ไปด้วยกันนะ paj′dûajkan′-ná↓ Let's go together,
okay? Why don't we go together?

o เธอนะเธอ ทำไมไม่บอกให้รู้เรื่องบ้าง thəə′náɔ
thəə′ thammaj′mâjbɔɔg′-hâjrúuryaŋ′bâŋ↓ Oh,
you, why didn't you tell me?

o ชัยนะชัย ไม่เขียนถึงเราบ้างเลย chaj′náchaj′
mâjkhǐan′thy̌ŋraw′-bâŋləəj′↓ That Chaj! He
hasn't written anything to us at all.

นะ ๑ náʔ′, ná, náa′ Pt 1. particle used to express
urging, insisting, importuning (1st-3rd examples).
2. particle indicating qualified or equivocal ac-
ceptance or agreement (4th example). NOTE.
นะ and นะ are contrasted in the first example
below.

o ไปนะ paj′ná↓ Will you go? Won't you go? ไปไม่
ได้ครับ paj′mâjdâaj′-khráb′↓ No, I can't. ไปนะ

paj′nâa′↓ Oh, do go! Come on, please go!

o อย่านะ jàa′nâa↓, jàa′nâa′↓ Don't! Do stop it! (irritatedly). →Cf. 3rd example under นะ.

o มาแล้วนะ maaléɛw′nâa↓ (He) must have come.

o ทำนะทำได้ แต่กลัวไม่ดี tham′nâ?′ tham′dâaj′→ tɛ̀ɛklua′mâjdii′↓ I can do it, but I'm afraid it won't be any good.

นะ ๒ nâ?′ Pt colloq. particle marking the topic about which an immediately following comment is made.

o เงินนะ ใครๆก็อยากได้ ŋən′nâ?′→ khrajkhraj′ɔ kɔ̀jàagdâaj′↓ (Now you take) money--everybody wants to have (it).

o ส้มนี้นะ หวานดี sôm′nîi′nâ? wǎan′dii′↓, sôm′nîi′â? wǎan′dii′↓ colloq. These oranges here are nice and sweet. NOTE. In ordinary speech นี้นะ is pronounced nîi′nâ? or nîi′â?, but neither pronunciation is reflected in the orthography.

o ผู้หญิงนะ แต่งตัวช้าเสมอ phûujǐŋ′nâ? tɛ̀ŋtuaɔ cháa′samɤ̌ɤ′↓ Women (you know), always take a long time to dress.

o ที่คุณว่ามานะ ไม่จริง thîikhunwâa′maanâ′ mâjɔ ciŋ′↓ What you said is not true.

o เมื่อตอนที่คุณมาเยี่ยมนะ ฉันไม่สบาย mɤ̂atɔɔn′- thîikhun′maajîam′-nâ? chánmâjsabaaj′↓ When you come to see me I was not well. The time you come to see me I was not well.

นัก ๑ nágɔ. Bound stem meaning "expert, authority."

> NOTE 1. นัก is used to form one kind of agent noun and may be placed in front of nouns (1st-3rd examples) or verbs (4th-6th examples). Although it often refers to a person trained in a given field or activity (1st-4th examples), some uses are neutral or ironical (5th and 6th examples). The word may usually be translated by the English suffixes -er (-or), -ian, -ist (1st-5th examples). →See คน ๑.
> นักการศึกษา nágkaan′sỳgsǎa′ educator: "education expert."
> นักดนตรี nág′dontrii′ musician: "music expert."
> นักวิทยาศาสตร์ nág′wídthajaasàad′ scientist: "science expert."
> นักบิน nágbin′ aviator, pilot.
> นักท่องเที่ยว nág′thɔ̂ŋthîaw′ tourist, traveller.
> นักจี้ nágcîi′ slang hold-up man: "(rib)-tickler."

NOTE 2. All nouns based on นัก take คน as their common classifier unless otherwise marked, and (คน) is therefore omitted below. The elegant classifiers นาย (for men) and ท่าน (for persons of either sex) may be substituted for คน when an expert or authority is referred to; hence (นาย) and (ท่าน) are also omitted.

นักกฎหมาย nág′kòdmǎaj′ N legal authority.

นักกวี nág′kawii′ N poet.

นักการ nágkaan′ N messenger.

นักการทูต nág′kaanthûud′ N diplomat.

นักการพนัน nágkaan′phanan′ N gambler.

นักการเมือง nág′kaanmyaŋ′ N politician.

นักการศึกษา nágkaan′sỳgsǎa′ N educator.

นักกีฬา nág′kiilaa′ N athlete.

นักเขียน nágkhǐan′ N writer, author.

นักเขียนการ์ตูน nágkhǐan′kaatuun′ N cartoonist.

นักจี้ nágcîi′ N slang hold-up man.

นักชีววิทยา nág′chiiwáwídthajaa′ N biologist.

นักดนตรี nág′dontrii′ N musician.

นักดื่มสุรา nágdỳym′suraa′ N eleg. a heavy drinker. →Also นักดื่ม →Syn. นักเลงเหล้า colloq.

นักเต้นรำ nág′tênram′ N dancer.

นักแต่งเพลง nág′tɛ̀ŋphleeŋ′ N song writer.

นักท่องเที่ยว nág′thɔ̂ŋthîaw′ N tourist, traveller.

นักเทศน์ (คน) nágthêed′ (khon′) N preacher.

นักโทษ nágthôod′ N prisoner, convict.

นักบวช (รูป, องค์) nágbùad′ (rûub′, ?oŋ′) N ascetic, priest, hermit.

นักบิน nágbin′ N aviator, pilot.

นักบุญ nágbun′ N saint.

นักโบราณคดี nág′booraan′nakhadii′ N archeologist.

นักประพันธ์ nág′praphan′ N poet, writer, author.

นักปราชญ์ nágpràad′ wise man, learned man, philosopher, sage.

นักปาฐก nág′paathòg′ N orator, lecturer.

นักผจญภัย nág′phacon′phaj′ N adventurer.

นักพูด nágphûud′ N orator, expert speaker.

นักฟุตบอล nág′fúdbɔn′ N football player.

นักมวย nágmuaj′ N boxer.

นักแม่นปืน nág′mɛ̂npyyn′ N sharpshooter.

นักรบ nágrób′ N warrior, fighting man.

นักร้อง nágrɔ́ɔŋ′ N singer.

นักรัฐศาสตร์ nágrád′thasàad′ N political scientist.

นักเรียน nágrian′ N student, pupil.

o นักเรียนกินนอน nágrian′kinnɔɔn′ N boarding-
school student.

o นักเรียนชาย nágrianchaaj′ schoolboy, male
student.

o นักเรียนหญิง nágrianjĭŋ′ N schoolgirl, female
student, coed.

นักล้วงกระเป๋า náglúaŋ′krapăw′ N pickpocket.

นักละคร nág′lakhɔɔn′ N 1. devotee of the theater.
2. authority on drama and dramatics.

นักเลง nágleeŋ′ N 1. rogue, rascal, gambler.
2. bold person, sporting person. 3. big-hearted
person. 4. person who is an authority on something.

o นักเลงโต nágleeŋ′too′ N 1. indomitable person. 2. rogue, gangster, hoodlum, thug.

o นักเลงหนังสือ nágleeŋ′naŋsўy′ N an authority
on books.

o นักเลงหัวไม้ nágleeŋ′hŭamáaj′ N colloq.
rogue, scamp, gangster, hoodlum, tough guy.

o นักเลงเหล้า nágleeŋ′lâw′ N colloq. a heavy
drinker. →Syn. นักดื่มสุรา eleg.

นักวาดเขียน nág′wâadkhĭan′ N artist (expert in
drawing).

นักวิจารณ์ nág′wícaan′ N critic, commentator.

o นักวิจารณ์ข่าว nág′wícaan′khàaw′ N news
commentator.

นักวิทยาศาสตร์ nág′wídthajaasàad′ N scientist.

นักศึกษา nág′sўgsăa′ N student.

นักสืบ nágsўyb′ N detective.

นักหนังสือพิมพ์ nág′naŋsўyphim′ N journalist.

นัก ๒ nág′ sV so, so very; so much. →Dist. มาก.
→Syn. เหลือเกิน. NOTE. In negative phrases
(e.g. those containing ไม่ "not," อย่า "don't")
นัก is often translated (not) so very (e.g. big),
(not) too (e.g. difficult), (not) quite (e.g. satisfactory). See ไม่...นัก below.

o อยากเห็นนัก jàag′hěn′-!nág′↓ (I, m) so anxious
to see (it).

นักหนา nágnăa′ so very much, extremely. →Also
หนักหนา. NOTE. นัก and หนา are often used
in split expressions as in the following examples.

o ชอบนักชอบหนา chɔ̂ɔbnág′chɔ̂ɔbnăa′ V elab.

colloq. to favor highly, like very much.

o เป็นนักเป็นหนา pennág′pennăa′ elab.colloq.
extremely, highly, roundly, unsparingly.

มากต่อมากนัก mâag′tɔ̀ɔmâag′-nág′ so much, so
many, a great deal of.

ไม่...นัก mâj...nág′ not very, not so very (e.g.
big); not too (e.g. difficult); not quite (e.g. satisfactory).

o ไม่ใหญ่นัก mâjjàj′nág′ not very big; not too big.

o หาได้ไม่ยากนัก hăadâaj′mâjjâag′nág′ (it is)
not too difficult to find.

ยิ่งนัก jîŋnág′ exceedingly.

นั่ง naŋ′ T derog. shortened form of นาง used
for both married and unmarried women.

นั่ง nâŋ′ V 1. to sit. 2. to ride (sitting in a vehicle).
→Sometimes coupled with นอน "to lie." See
นั่งกินนอนกิน, นั่งคิดนอนคิด below.

ที่นั่ง (ที่) thîinâŋ′ (thîi′) N seat.

นั่งกินนอนกิน nâŋkin′-nɔɔnkin′ V to lead an easy
life.

นั่งเก้าอี้ nâŋ′kâwʔîi′ V 1. to be seated, take a
seat. 2. colloq. to take a position in, have a
seat in, take an office.

นั่งไขว่ห้าง nâŋ′khwàjhâaŋ′ to sit cross-legged.

นั่งคิดนอนคิด nâŋkhíd′-nɔɔnkhíd′ V to think
unceasingly.

นั่งพับเพียบ nâŋ′phábphîab′ to sit with both legs
folded back to one side.

นั่งเมือง nâŋmyaŋ′ V to govern, rule.

o ขึ้นนั่งเมือง khŷnnâŋ′myaŋ′ colloq. to become
the ruler of a country.

นั่งยอง ๆ nâŋ′jɔɔŋjɔɔŋ′ V to sit on one's heels;
to squat.

นั่งลง nâŋ′loŋ to sit down.

นั่งสามล้อ nâŋ′săamlɔ́ɔ′ to ride in a samlor, pedicab.

ผุดลุกผุดนั่ง phùdlúg′phùdnâŋ′ elab. colloq. to be
repeatedly getting up and sitting down again (e.g.
because of restlessness, impatience).

ม้านั่ง (ตัว) máanâŋ′ (tua′) N bench.

ห้องนั่งเล่น (ห้อง) hɔ̂ŋ′nâŋlên′ (hɔ̂ŋ′) N lounge
(as in hotel or school).

นัด ๑ nád′ V 1. to make an appointment, set a date,
set the time. N 2. appointment, date. C 3. shot,
round (of firing), round (of ammunition). 4. the

occasion, occurrence (of a race, a meeting).

นัดแนะ nád′nέ?′ to make an appointment, make
   arrangements (as to when, where, what, who).

นัดหมาย nád′mǎaj′ to make an appointment, set
   a time or date. การ-- appointment.

ผิดนัด phìd′nád′ to miss an appointment.

มีนัด miinád′ to have an appointment.

นัด ๒ nád′ V to sniff up, breathe (something) up
   into the nose.

นัดถุ์ in ยานัดถุ์ (ห่อ, ขวด) jaanád′ (hɔ̀ɔ′, khùad′)
   N snuff (tobacco preparation).

นั่น nân′ dP 1. that (one). 2. there. →Comp. นั้น.
   →See also นี่, โน่น.

o ดูนั่นแน่ะ duunân′nέ?↓ Look over there!

o นั่นแหละ nân′lὲ?′↓ That's it! That's the way
   it is!

o อ้ายหมอนั่น ?âjmɔɔ′nân that guy.

ที่นั่น thîinân′ there.

นั่นเอง nân?eeŋ′ "just, simply; the same, the
   same as," in various idiomatic uses; see example.

o ...เป็นม้าดี ๆ นั่นเอง ...penmáa′diidii′-nânɔ
   ?eeŋ↓ (What you saw there) is just an ordinary
   horse, just a good old horse.

นั้น nán′ dA that, those. NOTE 1. นั้น is usually
   preceded by a clf. (examples 1-3), and if no
   num. is expressed, reference is to one (item,
   group, etc.) of something (examples 2-3). But นั้น
   may appear without a preceding clf. in the sequence นั้นนะ, and the quantity, whether one or
   many, is determined by the context. นั้นนะ is
   then pronounced nânnâ?′, but there is no change
   in spelling (contrast examples 3 and 4).
   NOTE 2. Expressions introduced by ส่วน "part"
   are closed by นั้น, and ส่วน can sometimes be
   omitted (5th example). In the same way relative
   clauses introduced by ที่ may occur with or
   without a preceding clf. or noun but their close
   is clearly signalled by the presence of นั้น
   which has the force of Eng. "the" (examples
   5-7).

o ส้ม ๒ ใบนั้น sôm′-sɔ̌ɔŋbaj′nán′ those two
   oranges.

o ส้มกระจาดนั้น sôm′-kracàad′nán′ that basket

of oranges.

o ส้มใบนั้นน่ะ เล็กเกินไป sôm′bajnán′nâ? lég′ɔ
   kəən′paj↓ That orange is too small.

o ส้มนั้นน่ะ เล็กเกินไป sôm′nânnâ?′ lég′kəən′paj↓
   That orange is too small. Those oranges, they're
   too small.

o ผู้หญิงนั้น แต่งตัวช้าเสมอ phûujĭŋ′nán′ tὲŋtuaɔ
   cháa′-samǝ̌ǝ↓ (As for) women, they always take
   a long time to dress. →Also ส่วนผู้หญิงนั้น--.

o ที่คุณว่ามานั้น ไม่จริง thîikhunwâa′maanán′ mâjɔ
   ciŋ′↓ What you said is not true. "The (thing)
   that you said is not true."

o เมื่อตอนที่คุณมาเยี่ยมนั้น ฉันไม่สบาย mɯ̂atɔɔn′-
   thîikhun′maajîam′nán′ chánmâjsabaaj′ That
   time when you came to see me, I was not well.

แค่นั้น khɛ̂ɛ′nán′, khɛ̂ɛnán′ up to that point, that
   far, that much, to that extent.

เช่นนั้น chênnán′ like that.

ดังนั้น daŋnán′ like that, in that manner; like that,
   of that kind; thus, hence, so.

ตรงนั้น troŋnán′ right over there.

ทั้งนั้น tháŋnán′, thaŋnán′ 1. all of them, any of
   them, all or any of them, every last one; everything, anything, everything and anything. 2. all
   the same, either way. →Cf. ทั้งปวง.

o ไม่ใช่ทั้งนั้น mâjchâj′tháŋnán′ neither of them,
   not either of them; none of them; not any of them.

เท่านั้น thâwnán′ 1. only, only that, just that. 2.
   that much, that many.

นั้น ๆ nánnán′ such; those.

o บุคคลนั้น ๆ bùgkhon′nánnán′ such persons,
   individuals; those individuals.

นั้นเอง nán′?eeŋ′ that very, that very same.

o ในวันนั้นเอง naj′wannán′?eeŋ′ on that very day,
   on that very same day.

บัดนั้น bàd′nán′ then.

ผมเองนั้น phǒm?eeŋ′nán′ as for me.

ยิ่งกว่านั้น jîŋ′kwàanán′ moreover.

อย่างนั้น jàaŋnán′, jaŋnán′, jaŋ́nán′ like that, that
   way, of that sort. →Also ยังนั้น, ยังงั้น. →For
   examples see cross reference.

นับ náb′ V 1. to count. 2. to regard, consider
   (usually with เป็น or ว่า).

นับ...ได้ náb′...dâaj′ V 1. to be present in small

numbers: "can be counted". 2. can be regarded
(usually with ว่า).

นับตั้งแต่ náb'tâŋtὲεɔ starting from, since.

นับแต่ náb'tὲεɔ starting from, since.

นับถือ nábthўy' V com. 1. to respect, revere;
to look up to, have respect for. 2. to profess,
believe in (a religion). →Syn. เคารพ eleg.

o ที่นับถือกัน thîinábthўy'kan which is well-
regarded, accepted as a good thing.

นับเป็น (1) náb'pen'; (2) náb'penɔ 1. to know
how to count. 2. to be considered, reckoned as;
counted by (e.g. the millions).

นับไม่ถ้วน náb'mâjthûan' countless, innumerable.

นับวันแต่ nábwan'tὲεɔ day by day, as days go by.

นับว่า náb'wâaɔ to be regarded, counted as, taken
as, considered to be.

นัย naj' C 1. sense, meaning, way (of explaining).
2. hint, intimation.

o พูดเป็นนัย ๆ (ว่า) phûud'pennajnaj'-(wâa')
to hint, intimate (that).

o อีกนัยหนึ่ง ʔìignaj'nyŋ in other words; in
another sense.

นัยน์ naj', najjaɔ. See entries below. →Comp.
นัยนา.

นัยน์ตา (ดวง, ข้าง) najtaa' (duaŋ', khâaŋ') N
com. eye. →Syn. See ตา com.

o กวนนัยน์ตา kuan'najtaa' V slang to offend
one's sight.

o ดวงนัยน์ตา (ดวง) duaŋ'najtaa' (duaŋ') N
com. eye. →Syn. See ตา.

o ลูกนัยน์ตา (ลูก) lûug'najtaa' (lûug') N eyeball. →Also ลูกตา.

นัยน์เนตร (ดวง) naj'janêed' (duaŋ') N eleg.,
lit. eye. →Syn. See ตา com.

นัยนา (ดวง) naj'janaa' (duaŋ') N eleg., lit. eye.
→Comp. นัยน์. →Syn. See ตา com.

นา ๑ (แปลง, ไร่) naa' (plɛɛŋ', râj') N 1. paddy
field, rice field. 2. field, farm. ชาว-- (see
below). →Dist. ไร่. →Comp. ทุ่ง. →Some-
times coupled with ไร่, e.g. ชาวไร่ชาวนา,
ท้องไร่ท้องนา below.

o ข้าวนาเมือง khâawnaamyaŋ' N low quality rice
from plants sown broadcast.

o ข้าวนาสวน khâawnaasǔan' N high quality rice

from transplanted plants.

ชาวนา (คน) chaawnaa' (khon') N farmer, rice
farmer.

ชาวไร่ชาวนา chaawrâj'chaawnaa' farmers (of
all kinds).

ทดน้ำเข้านา thódnáam'-khâwnaa' to irrigate a
field.

ท้องนา thɔ́ɔŋnaa' N paddy field, expanse of a
paddy field.

ท้องไร่ท้องนา thɔ́ɔŋrâj'thɔ́ɔŋnaa' N elab. colloq.
fields of all kinds.

ทำนา thamnaa' to farm, do rice farming. การ--
rice farming. →Comp. ทำไร่.

ทุ่งนา (แห่ง) thûŋnaa' (hὲŋ') N field.

ปูนา (ตัว) puunaa' (tua') N field crab, a small
fresh-water crab.

เมืองนอกเมืองนา myaŋnɔ́ɔg'myaŋnaa' N elab.
colloq. foreign country, abroad (usually the
U.S.A. or in Europe).

โรงนา (โรง) rooŋnaa' (rooŋ') N farm shack,
farm shed.

ไร่นา (แปลง) râj'naa' (plɛɛŋ') N field, farm.

หน้านา nâanaa' N rice-planting season.

นา ๒ in ชั่วนาตาปี chûanaa'taapii' elab. colloq.
year in and year out, forever.

นา ๓. See นานา.

นา ๔ naa'. Variant of นะ.

o มันยากนาแกนา manjâag'naa'→kὲεnaa'↓ It's
really difficult, you see!

น่า ๑ nâa'. Variant of นะ ๑.

o ก็งั้นซิน่า kɔ̂ŋán'siinâa' that's it!

น่า ๒ nâaɔ, nâa'ɔ 1. bound stem placed in front of
verbs to make new verb derivatives. AA 2.
ought to, might like to; usually used in combination with จะ; see น่าจะ below.
NOTE. น่า in mng. 1 has such translations as
"leading to, inducing to, arousing to, attracting
to (do thus and so)"; also sometimes "interesting
(to do)" or "worth (doing)." It may sometimes
be translated as -able (1st example) or as -ing
or in other ways (2nd-5th examples). Derivatives
made by this means are frequently used with
อย่าง (3rd example).

o น่าเชื่อ nâachŷa' to be believable: เชื่อ to

believe.

o น่าอ่าน nâa?àan′ to be worth reading, interesting to read: อ่าน to read.

o อย่างน่าอ่าน jàaŋnâa/′?àan′ interestingly, in a manner worth reading.

o น่ากลัว nâaklua′ to be frightening, scary, dreadful, fearful, horrible, terrifying, terrible: กลัว to fear, be afraid.

o น่านับถือ nâa/nábthν̆y′ to be worthy of respect; to be venerable, estimable: นับถือ to respect.

น่ากลัว nâaklua′, nâa/klua′ V to be frightening, scary, dreadful, fearful, horrible, terrifying, terrible.

น่ากลัวน่ากลัว nâa!klúa/nâaklua′ V colloq. to be very scary, extremely frightening, dreadful.

น่ากวนใจ nâa/kuancaj′ V to be annoying, irritating.

น่ากิน nâakin′, nâa/kin′ V to be tasty-looking.

น่าเกลียด nâaklìad′, nâa/klìad′ V to be ugly, unsightly. ความ-- ugliness.

น่าขัน nâakhǎn′, nâa/khǎn′ V to be funny, comical, amusing, ridiculous.

น่าคิด nâa/khíd′ V to be worth thinking about.

น่าจะ nâa/caɔ AA colloq. ought to, might like to. →Syn. ควร com.

o น่าจะอ่าน nâa/ca?àan′ (you) ought to read it.

o ไม่น่าจะ mâjnâa/caɔ ought not to, should not.

oo เด็กไม่น่าจะอ่าน dèg′ mâjnâa/ca?àan′ children ought not to read it.

น่าจับใจ nâa/càbcaj′ V to be captivating, impressive.

น่าใจหาย nâa/cajhǎaj′ V to be shocking, frightful, frightening.

น่าชม nâachom′, nâa/chom′ V 1. to be admirable, praiseworthy. 2. eleg. to be delightful to look at. →Syn. 2. น่าดู com.

น่าดีใจ nâa/diicaj′ V to arouse feelings of gladness, to be delightful.

น่าดื่ม nâadν̀ym′, nâa/dν̀ym′ V to look good to drink, look inviting (of a drink).

น่าดู nâaduu′, nâa/duu′ V to be worth seeing, pleasant to see, look at. →Syn. น่าชม eleg.

o ไม่น่าดู mâjnâaduu′ to be not worth seeing, unpleasant to look at, not nice (to see, look at).

น่าทึ่ง nâathν̂ŋ′ V colloq. to be interesting.
→Syn. น่าสนใจ com.

น่านับถือ nâa/nábthν̆y′ V to be worthy of respect; to be venerable, estimable.

น่าบัดสี nâa/bàdsǐi′ V to be disgraceful, shameful.

น่าประหลาด nâa/pralàad′ V to be surprising, strange, marvelous. อย่าง-- in a strange way, mysteriously, surpisingly.

น่าพิศวง nâa/phísawoŋ′ V to be amazing, astonishing, perplexing. อย่าง-- amazingly, astonishingly, surprisingly.

น่าฟัง nâafaŋ′, nâa/faŋ′ V to be pleasant to listen to, interesting to listen to, beautiful (to hear).

น่ารัก nâarág′, nâa/rág′ V to be lovable, lovely, attractive, charming, cute. ความ-- loveliness, charm.

น่ารังเกียจ nâa/raŋkìad′ V 1. to be objectionable, repugnant, offensive. 2. to arouse aversion.

น่ารำคาญ nâa/ramkhaan′ to be annoying, disturbing.

น่ารู้ nâa/rúu′ V to be of interest, interesting, i.e. interesting to know, worth knowing.

o ข่าวน่ารู้ khàaw/nâarúu′ news of interest.

น่าวิตก nâa/wítòg′ V to be worrisome, alarming.

น่าไว้ใจ nâa/wájcaj′ V to be trustworthy.

น่าสงสัย nâa/sǒŋsǎj′ V 1. to be doubtful, suspicious, questionable. 2. to lead (one) to suspect.

น่าสงสาร (1) nâa/sǒŋsǎan′; (2) nâa/sǒŋsǎan′↓ V 1. to be pitiful, pitiable, pathetic. 2. What a pity!

น่าสนใจ nâa/sǒncaj′ V to be interesting. →Syn. น่าทึ่ง colloq.

น่าสนุก nâa/sanùg′ V to be fun.

น่าสยดสยอง nâa/-sajòd/sajɔ̌ɔŋ′ V to be horrible, dreadful.

น่าสวม nâasǔam′ V eleg. to be pretty, nice-looking, comfortable to wear (as of clothing, jewelry).

น่าเสียใจ nâa/sǐacaj′ V to be regrettable.

น่าเสียดาย (1) nâa/sǐadaaj′; (2) nâa/sǐadaaj′↓ V 1. to be regrettable. 2. What a pity! What a shame! It's too bad!

น่าอดสู nâa/?òdsǔu′ V to be shameful, disgraceful.

น่าอภิรมย์ nâa?àphírom′ V eleg. to be pleasing. enjoyable, delightful.

น่าอยู่ nâajùu′, nâa/jùu′ V to be cozy, liveable.

ความ-- coziness, liveability.

น่าอ่าน nâa?àan′, nâa/?àan′ V to be interesting to read, worth reading.

น่าเอ็นดู nâa?enduu′, nâa/?enduu′ V to be cute, lovely (as a child, pet). ความ-- loveliness.

มิน่าเล่า mínâa/lâw↓ No wonder! →Also มิน่าละ mínâa/lá ↓.

ไม่น่าเชื่อ mâjnâachŷa′ to be unbelievable.

อย่าง-- unbelievably, extraordinarily.

ไม่น่าเลย mâjnâa/!lǝ́əj′↓ It shouldn't have been like that at all! (I, he, she, etc.) shouldn't have (e.g. done that, forgotten that) at all! (implying disappointment, surprise).

น้า (คน) náa′ (khon′) N 1. younger maternal uncle or aunt, i.e. the younger brother or sister of one's mother. P 2. I, me, Uncle, Aunt (yg. maternal uncle or aunt sp. to nephew or neice); you, he, him, she, her (sp. to or of yg. maternal uncle or aunt). T 3. title placed in front of the first name of the younger maternal aunt or uncle. →Opp. อา. →Dist. ลุง,ป้า.

คุณน้า khunnáa′ P you, he, him, she, her (sp. to or of one's yg. maternal uncle or aunt).

นาก ๑ nâag′ N alloy of gold and copper.

นาก ๒ (ตัว) nâag′ (tua′) N otter.

นาค (องค์,ตัว) nâag′ N 1. man entering priesthood, postulant (?oŋ′). 2. Naga, a legendary serpent (tua′).

นาง (คน,นาง) naaŋ N 1. lady, woman (khon′, naaŋ′). 2. element placed before nouns or verbs to form female agent nouns. T 3. title placed before the first name of a married woman, hence "Mrs." 4. title used for females of birds and animals. 5. bound stem used in a few bird and animal names (not restricted to females); see Note 2. P 6. she, her. C 7. writ., eleg. clf. for ladies. →Opp. 3. นาย. →Dist. นั่ง. →See 2. คน ๑.

NOTE 1. นาง is sometimes placed before verbs or nouns to form female agent nouns, usually but not necessarily providing an elegant speech form; see examples. All nouns based on นาง take คน (or นาง writ., eleg.) as their classifier unless otherwise marked; hence (คน) and (นาง) are usually omitted below.

o นางระบำ naaŋrabam′ dancing girl: ระบำ V to dance.

o นางนม naaŋnom′ wet nurse: นม N breast; milk.

NOTE 2. In rare instances นาง occurs as a part of the common names of birds and animals; 1st-3rd examples. In even rarer instances นาง replaces อี which occurs in the corresponding colloquial names; 2nd and 3rd examples.

o นกนางนวล (ตัว) nógnaaŋnuan′ (tua′) seagull.

o นกนางแอ่น (ตัว) nógnaaŋ?ɛ̀n′ (tua′) com. swallow: นกอีแอ่น (ตัว) nóg?ii?ɛ̀n′ (tua′) colloq.

o หอยนางรม (ตัว) hɔ̌jnaaŋrom′ (tua′) com. oyster: หอยอีรม hɔ̌j?iirom′ colloq.

ขุนนาง (คน,นาย) khǔnnaaŋ (khon′, naaj′) N 1. noble, honored person (often in government service). 2. the nobility, with conferred rank. →See under ขุน. →Dist. เจ้านาย.

นางกำนัล (คน) naaŋkamnan′ (khon′) N personal maid of a queen, or of a princess.

นางชี naaŋchii′ N nun. →Syn. See แม่ชี.

นางนม naaŋnom′ N eleg. wet nurse. →Syn. แมนม com.

นางผดุงครรภ์ naaŋ/phaduŋkhan′ N eleg. midwife. →Syn. หมอตำแย colloq.

นางพญา (องค์) naaŋphajaa′ (?oŋ′) N queen.

นางพยาบาล (คน) naaŋphajabaan′ (khon′) N nurse (as in a hospital).

นางฟ้า (องค์) naaŋfáa′ (?oŋ′) N angel, fairy.

นางไม้ (องค์) naaŋmáaj′ (?oŋ′) N wood fairy, female tree spirit.

นางระบำ naaŋrabam′ N dancing girl, (woman) dancer.

นางละคร naaŋlakhɔɔn′ N actress; woman dancer, performer.

นางสาว naaŋsǎaw′ N 1. young lady, miss. T 2. title placed before the first names of unmarried women, hence "Miss." →Abbrev. น.ส.

o นางสาวไทย naaŋsǎawthaj′ Miss Thailand, i.e. the Thai beauty queen.

นางเอก naaŋ?èeg′ N 1. leading lady, heroine (as of a play). 2. colloq. wife.

นิ้วนาง (นิ้ว) níwnaaŋ′ (níw′) N ring finger.

นาฏกรรม (เรื่อง) nâad/takam′ (rŷaŋ′) N drama, play, dramatic performance.

นาที naathii′ C minute (of time). →Also spelled นาฑี.

เข็มนาที (อัน) khěm′naathii′ (ʔan′) N minute

hand (of a clock or watch).

นาน naan′ V to be long (of time). →Comp. นมนาน.

→Syn. ช้า ๑, เนิ่น. →Often coupled with

ช้า ๑ "slow."

ช้านาน cháa′naan′ V to be long (of time).

นานเท่าไร naan′thâwràj′ how long (of time).

นาน ๆ ครั้ง naannaan′khráŋ′ once in a long while.

มิช้ามินาน mícháa′mínaan′ writ. not long (after-

wards), soon (afterwards).

ไม่ช้าไม่นาน mâjcháa′mâjnaan′ soon.

ไม่นานเท่าไร mâjnaan′thâwràj′ to be not very

long (of time).

ยืนนาน jyyn′naan′ V 1. to last, endure. 2. to

live long.

อีกไม่นาน ʔìigmâjnaan′ not much longer.

นาน ๑ nâan′ pN a township in N Thailand.

แม่น้ำน่าน mɛ̂ɛnáamnâan′ pN the Mænan (Me Nan)

a tributary of the Čhaophraya River in N Thai-

land. →Also แม่น่าน.

นาน ๒. See entry below.

น่านน้ำ nâan′náam′ N territorial waters.

นานา naanaa′ Nm various, different, all. →Nor-

mally followed by a clf. →Comp. ต่าง ๆ.

นานาชนิด naanaa′chaníd′ various kinds, of all

sorts, of every description.

นานาชาติ naanaa′châad′ 1. various peoples,

nations. 2. (as n. mod.) international.

นานาประเทศ naanaa′prathêed′ 1. various

nations. 2. (as n. mod.) international.

o กฎหมายนานาประเทศ (ฉบับ,มาตรา) kòdɔ

mǎaj′-naanaa′prathêed′ (chabàb′, mâadtraa′)

N international law.

นาบ nâab′ V 1. to press down (so as to make level

or smooth); to flatten out. 2. to dry (e.g. fresh

leaves) by means of heat.

นาม (นาม) naam′ (naam′) N 1. eleg. name;

chiefly in compounds. 2. gram. noun. คำ--

noun. →Syn. 1. ชื่อ com.

เซ็นนาม sen′naam′ V to sign, sign one's name.

→Syn. See เซ็นชื่อ com.

นามบัตร (ใบ,แผ่น) naambàd′ (baj′, phὲn′) N

1. calling card. 2. business card.

นามปากกา (นาม) naam′pàagkaa′ (naam′) N

pen name.

นามแฝง (นาม) naamfἔɛŋ′ (naam′) N pseudonym,

assumed name, pen name.

นามสกุล (นามสกุล) naamsakun′ (naamsakun′)

N surname, family name, last name.

มีนามโด่งดัง miinaam′-dòoŋ′daŋ′ eleg. to be

widely known, renowned. →Syn. มีชื่อโด่งดัง

com.

มีนามอุโฆษ miinaam′ʔùkhôod′ eleg. idem.

รายนาม raajnaam′ N eleg. list of names, roll,

register. →Syn. รายชื่อ com.

o รายนามผู้แสดง raajnaam′phûusadɛɛŋ′ N the

cast (in a performance).

เรืองนาม ryaŋ′naam′ V eleg. to be famous,

renowned.

ลงนาม loŋ′naam′ V eleg. to sign, sign one's

name. →Syn. See เซ็นชื่อ com.

เลื่องชื่อลือนาม lŷaŋchŷy′lyynaam′ V 1. (people,

everyone) to talk about (it), spread (it) around.

2. to be famous, widely spoken of. →Also ลือชื่อ.

นาย (นาย,คน) naaj′ (naaj′, khon′) N 1. master,

employer, boss (man or woman). 2. element

placed before verbs or nouns to form agent nouns;

see note. T 3. title placed before the first name

of men of all ages, hence "Mr." P 4. you (used

among close friends or by mother to son, older

sibling to yg. sibling). C 5. eleg. clf. for men

of position. →See 2. คน ๑. →Opp. 3. นาง.

NOTE. นาย (mng. 2) is sometimes placed before

verbs or nouns to form agent nouns. It is usually

translated -er (-or) or -ist; 1st-3rd examples.

Ordinarily นาย refers only to men, but in its

agentive use it may sometimes refer to either

sex. In this regard it differs from its counter-

part นาง, which in its agentive use refers

only to women.

o นายจ้าง naajcâaŋ′ employer (m. or w.): จ้าง

V to hire.

o นายตรวจ naajtrùad′ (train or bus) conductor

(m. or w.): ตรวจ V to inspect.

o นายทุน naajthun′ capitalist: ทุน N capital.

คุณนาย khunnaaj′ P 1. you (sp. to the wife of any

government official up to the rank of พระ).

T 2. title used before the first name of such a

lady. N 3. def. madame, lady (in reference

to one's employer).

เจ้านาย (องค์, คน, ท่าน) câawnaaj′ N 1. royal
personage, royalty, member of the royal family
(ʔoŋ′). 2. colloq. boss, chief, superior
(khon′, thân′). →Dist. ขุนนาง.

นายงาน (คน) naajŋaan′ (khon′) N person in
charge of a project, supervisor.

นายจ้าง (คน) naajcâaŋ′ (khon′) N employer;
boss.

นายช่าง (คน) naajchâaŋ′ (khon′) N 1. craftsman, artisan. 2. short for นายช่างกล or other
derivative beginning with นายช่าง.

o นายช่างกล (คน) naajchâaŋkon′ (khon′) N
mechanical engineer.

นายตรวจ (คน) naajtrùad′ (khon′) N conductor
(i.e. ticket-inspector on a train or bus).

นายตำรวจ (นาย, คน) naajtamrùad′ (naaj′, khon′)
N police officer.

นายทหาร (นาย, คน) naajthahǎan′ (naaj′, khon′)
N officer (of the army, navy, air force).

นายทหารชั้นประทวน (นาย, คน) naajthahǎan′ɔ
chánprathuan′ (naaj′, khon′) N noncommissioned officer.

นายทหารชั้นสัญญาบัตร (นาย, คน) naajthahǎan′ɔ
chánsǎnjaabàd′ (naaj′, khon′) N commissioned
officer.

นายทหารบก (นาย, คน) naajthahǎan′bòg′ (naaj′,
khon′) N army officer.

นายทหารเรือ (นาย, คน) naajthahǎan′rya′ (naaj′,
khon′) N naval officer.

นายทหารอากาศ (นาย, คน) naajthahǎan′ʔaakàad′
(naaj′, khon′) airforce officer.

นายทะเบียน (คน) naajthabian′ (khon′) N registrar, recorder.

นายทุน (คน) naajthun′ (khon′) N capitalist.

o ระบอบนายทุน rabɔ̀ɔb′naajthun′ N eleg.
capitalism, the capitalistic system.

นายนาวา naaj′naawaa′ N naval commander
(of unspecified rank). See entries below.

o นายนาวาตรี (นาย, คน) naaj′naawaatrii′
(naaj′, khon′) N 1. lieutenant commander.
T 2. Lt. Commander --. →Also informally
นาวาตรี.

o นายนาวาโท (นาย, คน) naaj′naawaathoo′

(naaj′, khon′) N 1. commander. T 2. Commander --. →Also informally นาวาโท.

o นายนาวาเอก (นาย, คน) naaj′naawaaʔèeg′
(naaj′, khon′) N 1. captain. T 2. Captain --.
→Also informally นาวาเอก.

นายประกัน (คน) naajprakan′ (khon′) N insurer,
guarantor, bondsman.

นายพราน (คน) naajphraan′ (khon′) N hunter,
game hunter.

นายพล (นาย, คน) naajphon′ (naaj′, khon′) N 1.
general (of unspecified rank). T 2. General --.

oo นายพลแมคอาเธอร์ naajphon′még′ʔaathə̀ə′*
General McArthur.

o นายพลจัตวา (นาย, คน) naajphon′càdtawaa′
(naaj′, khon′) N 1. brigadier general. T 2.
Brigadier General --. →Also informally พลจัตวา.

o นายพลตรี (นาย, คน) naajphontrii′ (naaj′, khon′)
N 1. major general. T 2. Major General --.
→Also informally พลตรี.

o นายพลโท (นาย, คน) naajphonthoo′ (naaj′, khon′)
N 1. lieutenant general. T 2. Lt. General --.
→Also informally พลโท.

o นายพลใหญ่ (นาย, คน) naajphonjàj′ (naaj′, khon′)
N 1. supreme commander.

o นายพลเอก (นาย, คน) naajphonʔèeg′ (naaj′,
khon′) N 1. (full) general. T 2. General --.
→Also informally พลเอก.

นายพลเรือ (นาย, คน) naajphonrya′ (naaj′, khon′)
N admiral (of unspec. rank). T 2. Admiral --.

oo นายพลเรือคิง naajphonrya′khiŋ′ Admiral King.

o นายพลเรือตรี (นาย, คน) naajphon′ryatrii′
(naaj′, khon′) N 1. rear admiral. T 2. Rear
Admiral --. →Also informally พลเรือตรี.

o นายพลเรือโท (นาย, คน) naajphon′ryathoo′
(naaj′, khon′) N 1. vice-admiral. T 2. Vice-
Admiral --. →Also informally พลเรือโท.

o นายพลเรือเอก (นาย, คน) naajphon′ryaʔèeg′
(naaj′, khon′) N 1. admiral. T 2. Admiral --.
→Also informally พลเรือเอก.

นายพัน. See entries below.

o นายพันตรี (นาย, คน่) naajphantrii′ (naaj′, khon′)
N major. T 2. Major --. →Also informally
พันตรี.

o นายพันโท (นาย, คน) naajphanthoo′ (naaj′, khon′)

N 1. lieutenant colonel. T 2. Lt. Colonel --.
→Also informally พันโท.

o นายพันเอก (นาย, คน) naajphan?èeg/ (naaj/,
khon/) N 1. colonel. T 2. Colonel --. →Also
informally พันเอก.

นายแพทย์ (นาย, คน) naajphɛ̂ɛd/ (naaj/, khon/)
N eleg. (male) physician, doctor. →Syn.
หมอผู้ชาย com.

o นายแพทย์หญิง (คน) naajphɛ̂ɛd/jĭŋ (khon/)
N woman physician, doctor. →Syn. หมอผู้หญิง
com.

นายร้อย. See entries below.

o นายร้อยตรี (นาย, คน) naajrɔ́ɔjtrii/ (naaj/,
khon/) N 1. second lieutenant. T 2. (Second)
Lieutenant --. →Also informally ร้อยตรี.

o นายร้อยโท (นาย, คน) naajrɔ́ɔjthoo/ (naaj/,
khon/) N 1. first lieutenant. T 2. (First) Lieutenant --. →Also informally ร้อยโท.

o นายร้อยเอก (นาย, คน) naajrɔ́ɔj?èeg/ (naaj/,
khon/) N 1. (army) captain. T 2. Captain --.
→Also informally ร้อยเอก.

o โรงเรียนนายร้อย rooŋrian/naajrɔ́ɔj/ N cadet
academy.

นายเรือ (นาย, คน) naajrya/ (naaj/, khon/) N
captain (of a ship).

o นายเรือตรี (นาย, คน) naajryatrii/ (naaj/,
khon/) N 1. ensign. T 2. Ensign --. →Also
informally เรือตรี.

o นายเรือโท (นาย, คน) naajryathoo/ (naaj/,
khon/) N nav. 1. lieutenant junior grade.
T 2. Lieutenant --. →Also informally เรือโท.

o นายเรือเอก (นาย, คน) naajrya?èeg/ (naaj/,
khon/) N nav. 1. lieutenant senior grade.
T 2. Lieutenant --. →Also informally เรือเอก.

นายสถานี (คน) naaj/sathǎanii/ (khon/) N
station-master.

นายสิบ. See entries below.

o จ่านายสิบ càa/naajsìb/ N 1. sergeant major.
T 2. Sergeant Major --.

o นายสิบตรี (นาย, คน) naajsìb/trii/ (naaj/,
khon/) N 1. private first class. T 2. Private --.

o นายสิบโท (นาย, คน) naajsìb/thoo/ (naaj/,
khon/) N 1. corporal. T 2. Corporal --.

o นายสิบเอก (นาย, คน) naajsìb/?èeg/ (naaj/,
khon/) N 1. sergeant. T 2. Sergeant --.

นายหน้า (คน) naajnâa/ (khon/) N broker, commissioner.

นายอำเภอ (นาย, คน) naaj?amphəə/ (naaj/, khon/)
N head official of an amphoe.

นายก (คน, ท่าน) naajóg/ (khon/, thân/) N prime
official, chairman.

นายกเทศมนตรี (นาย, คน) naajóg/thêesamontrii/
(naaj/, khon/) N president of the city council;
mayor.

นายกรัฐมนตรี (ท่าน, คน) naajóg/rádthamontrii/
(thân/, khon/) N prime minister; premier.

o สำนักนายกรัฐมนตรี sǎmnág/-naajóg/rádthamon-
trii/ N Presidency of the Council of Ministers.

น้าว náaw/ V to pull and bend (something) down, back.

โน้มน้าว nóom/náaw/ V to influence (the thinking
of another).

นาวา naawaa/ N lit., eleg. boat, vessel. →Chiefly
in compounds. →Syn. เรือ com.

นายนาวาเอก (นาย, คน) naaj/naawaa?èeg/ (naaj/,
khon/) N nav. 1. captain. T 2. Captain --.
→For other ranks, see นายนาวา under นาย.

นาวาอากาศ... naawaa/?aakàad... designation
for the commissioned ranks of air force officers
in command of squadrons, wings, and groups.

นาวิกโยธิน naa/wígkajoo/thin/ N the marines.

นาวี naa/wii/ N navy.

ราชนาวี râadchanaa/wii/ N royal navy.

นาฬิกา (เรือน) naalikaa/ (ryan/) N 1. clock, watch,
timepiece. C 2. o'clock, i.e. hour of the day or
night on the 24-hour basis. →Abbrev. น.

o สิบสี่นาฬิกา, ๑๔ น. sìbsìi/naalikaa/, sìbsìi/-
nɔɔ/ 2 P.M.: "fourteen o'clock."

เข็มนาฬิกา (อัน) khěm/naalikaa/ (?an/) N the
hands of a clock or watch.

ไขนาฬิกา khǎj/naalikaa/ to wind one's watch.

ช่างแก้นาฬิกา (คน) châaŋkɛ̂ɛ/naalikaa/ (khon/)
N watch-repairman.

นาฬิกาข้อมือ (เรือน) naalikaa/khɔ̂ɔmyy/ (ryan/)
N wrist watch.

นาฬิกาแดด (อัน) naalikaa/dὲɛd/ (?an/) N sundial.

นาฬิกาปลุก (เรือน) naalikaa/plùg/ (ryan/) N
alarm clock.

หน้าปัทม์นาฬิกา (อัน) nâapàd'naalikaa' (ʔan') N
   dial (of clock, watch).

หอนาฬิกา (หอ) hɔ̌ɔ'naalikaa' (hɔ̌ɔ') N clock
   tower.

นำ nam' V 1. to lead, conduct, guide. 2. to bring,
   take, convey (in certain constructions). การ--
   leading, leadership; phys. conduction. ผู้--
   leader.

คำนำ (บท) khamnam' (bòd') N preface, fore-
   word. →Dist. บทนำ.

ชักนำ chág'nam' V 1. to lead. 2. to persuade,
   induce.

นำ(...)เข้ามาใช้ nam'(...)khâwmaacháj' to
   introduce (something), bring (something) into
   use.

นำ(...)เข้าสู่ nam'(...)khâwsùu' to lead into
   bring into.

นำทาง nam'thaaŋ' to lead the way. คน--, ผู้--
   guide, one who leads the way.

นำเที่ยว namthîaw' V to guide (on a tour, a
   pleasure trip). ผู้-- tourist guide.

นำ(...)ไป nam'(...)paj' to take, lead; to lead
   away.

นำพา nam'phaa' V to pay attention to, take an
   interest in, care for. →Chiefly in negative or
   interrogative constructions.

o ไม่นำพา mâjnam'phaa' to pay not the slightest
   attention to; to ignore (e.g. tradition, a warning).

นำ(...)มา nam'(...)maa' to bring; to lead
   (coming this way); to bring about.

o นำมาซึ่ง nam'maa'-sŷŋ'⊃ lit., eleg. to
   bring, bring in, bring about (e.g. sorrow, misfortune).

o นำมาใช้ nam'maacháj' V to bring into use,
   introduce.

นำร่อง namrɔ̂ŋ' V to pilot, navigate a ship.
   คน-- pilot, navigator (of a ship).

นำสืบ namsỳyb' law to conduct an investigation.

นำแสดงโดย namsadɛɛŋ'doojɔ writ., com.
   starring (such and such an actor, actress).

แนะนำ nɛ́ʔnam' V 1. to advise, guide. 2. to
   suggest. 3. to introduce.

บทนำ (บท) bòdnam' (bòd') N introduction,
   introductory chapter. →Dist. คำนำ.

น้ำ náam', náamɔ, námɔ N water, liquid, fluid.
   →Syn. ท่า ๒ (restricted in use).

   NOTE. (1) A number of verbs denoting activities
   associated with water normally take น้ำ as their
   fixed object; 1st example. (2) In repetitions of
   these or other expressions containing น้ำ, ท่า
   is often substituted for น้ำ; 2nd example.
   o อาบน้ำ ʔàabnáam' V to bathe, take a bath.
   o อาบน้ำอาบท่า ʔàabnáam'/ʔàabthâa' elab.
   colloq. to bathe, take a bath.

กระทุ่มน้ำ krathûm'náam' V to paddle, splash
   (with hands and feet, while swimming).

กระแสน้ำ krasɛ̌ɛ'náam' N 1. a current of water.
   2. the course of a stream.

กระหายน้ำ krahǎaj'náam' V to be thirsty.

ก๊อกน้ำ (อัน) kɔ́gnáam' (ʔan') N water-tap,
   faucet. [ก๊อก f. Eng.]

กินน้ำลึก kinnáam'lýg' to require a deep waterway
   (as a big ship).

แก้วน้ำ (ใบ) kɛ̂ɛwnáam' (baj') N water glass,
   tumbler.

ขุนน้ำขุนนาง khǔnnáam'khǔnnaaŋ' N elab. colloq.
   government officials, members of the nobility.
   →See under ขุน.

จมน้ำ comnáam' V to sink (into water).

o จมน้ำตาย comnáam'taaj' to drown, die by
   drowning.

ดำน้ำ damnáam' V to dive into water.

o เรือดำน้ำ (ลำ) rya'damnáam' (lam') N
   submarine.

ดินน้ำลมไฟ din'→náam'→lom'→faj' the four
   elements: earth, water, wind, and fire.

ตกน้ำ tògnáam' V to fall into the water.

ต้นน้ำ (แห่ง) tônnáam' (hɛ̀ŋ') N source of a river.

ทางน้ำ (สาย) thaaŋnáam' (sǎaj') N 1. waterway.
   2. by water.

น้ำกรด (อย่าง, ชนิด) námkròd' (jàaŋ', chaníd')
   N acid (solution).

น้ำกร่อย námkrɔ̀j' N brackish water.

น้ำกระสาย námkrasǎaj' N a liquid additive used
   in the preparation of medicines.

น้ำกลั่น námklàn' N distilled water.

น้ำกะทิ námkathíʔ' N coconut cream (a cooking
   ingredient derived by squeezing out the liquid
   from grated ripe coconut meat). →Cf. หัวกะทิ,

หางกะทิ.

น้ำกาม námkaam′ N semen, spermatic fluid.
→Syn. น้ำอสุจิ.

น้ำกิน náamkin′ N com. drinking water, water
for drinking.

น้ำขาว námkhǎaw′ N a kind of rice wine.

น้ำขึ้น náamkhŷn′ N flood tide. →Opp. น้ำลง.

น้ำแข็ง námkhĕŋ′ N ice.

○ ตู้น้ำแข็ง (ตู้, ใบ) tûu′námkhĕŋ′ (tûu′ baj′)
N icebox, refrigerator.

○ ใส่น้ำแข็ง sàj′námkhĕŋ′ having ice in (it), iced.

○○น้ำใส่น้ำแข็ง náam′-sàj′námkhĕŋ′ ice water.

น้ำค้าง námkháaŋ′ N dew.

น้ำเค็ม námkhem′ N salt water. →Opp. น้ำจืด.

น้ำโคลน námkhloon′ N muddy water.

น้ำเงิน in สีน้ำเงิน sǐi′námŋən′ N 1. blue, the
color blue. V 2. to be blue. →Dist. สีฟ้า.

น้ำจิ้ม námcîm′ N sauce, dip (i.e. a sauce or preparation into which food is dipped).

น้ำจืด námcỳyd′ N fresh water. →Opp. น้ำเค็ม.

น้ำใจ námcaj′ N 1. heart (for doing something),
spirit, feelings. 2. good will, good feelings,
thoughtfulness.

○ เจ็บช้ำน้ำใจ cèbchám′námcaj′ V to feel hurt,
have one's feelings hurt.

○ เสียน้ำใจ sǐa′námcaj′ V to lose heart, be
discouraged, be disheartened.

○ หนุนน้ำใจ nǔn′námcaj′ V to encourage, give
moral support to.

น้ำชา námchaa′ N tea (the liquid only).

น้ำเชื่อม námchŷam′ N syrup.

น้ำดิบ námdìb′ N unboiled water. (Water must
be boiled before it is safe for consumption.)
→Opp. น้ำสุก.

น้ำดี námdii′ N bile.

น้ำตก (แห่ง) námtòg′ (hèŋ′) N waterfall, falls.

น้ำตา námtaa′ N 1. tears, teardrops. 2. drip-
pings (e.g. of a candle).

น้ำตาล námtaan′ N sugar.

○ น้ำตาลทราย námtaansaaj′ N granulated sugar.

○ สีน้ำตาล sǐi′námtaan′ N 1. brown, the color
brown. V 2. to be brown.

น้ำท่วม náamthûam′ N flood, floodwaters.

น้ำทะเล náamthalee′ N seawater.

น้ำนม námnom′ N milk. →Also นม.

น้ำบ่อ náambɔ̀ɔ′ N well water.

น้ำบาดาล náambaadaan′ N underground water.

น้ำประปา náamprapaa′ N city water, water (as
a municipal utility).

น้ำปลา námplaa′ N fish sauce (i.e. a liquid sauce
made of fish and used as a salty seasoning in
place of salt).

น้ำผลไม้ náamphǒnlamáaj′ N eleg. fruit juice.
→Syn. น้ำลูกไม้.

น้ำผึ้ง námphŷŋ′ N honey.

น้ำฝน námfǒn′ N rain water.

น้ำพริก námphríg′ N pepper sauce, hot shrimp-
paste sauce. There are many varieties having
slightly different ingredients.

น้ำพักน้ำแรง námphág′námrɛɛŋ′ N elab. colloq.
(one's own) effort, labor; (one's) personal investment.

น้ำพุ (แห่ง) námphú?′ (hèŋ′) N fountain, spring,
water spout.

น้ำมนต์ námmon′ N holy water.

น้ำมะนาว námmanaaw′, náam⊃ N 1. lemonade,
limeade. 2. lemon juice, lime juice.

น้ำมะพร้าว náammaphráaw′ N coconut milk (i.e.
the liquid from a green coconut, a refreshing
drink). →Dist. น้ำกะทิ.

น้ำมัน námman′ N 1. oil. 2. colloq. fuel oil.
NOTE. This is both a general term and a class
term. It is followed by a specific term when a
specific kind of oil is named; subentries 2-3.

○ กลั่นน้ำมัน klàn′námman′ to refine crude oil.

○ น้ำมันก๊าส námman′káad′ N kerosene. [ก๊าส
f. Eng.]

○ น้ำมันแกโซลีน námman′kɛɛsooliin′ N gasoline.
[แกโซลีน f. Eng.]

○ น้ำมันงา námman′ŋaa′ N sesame oil.

○ น้ำมันชักเงา námman′chágŋaw′ N varnish.

○ น้ำมันเชื้อเพลิง námman′chýaphləəŋ′ N fuel oil.

○ น้ำมันดิน námman′din′ N tar, coal tar.

○ น้ำมันดิบ námman′dìb′ N crude oil.

○ น้ำมันเบนซิน námman′bensin′ N 1. benzine.
2. colloq. gasoline. [เบนซิน f. Eur.]

○ น้ำมันพืช námman′phŷyd′ N vegetable oil.

○ น้ำมันมะกอก námman′makɔ̀ɔg′ N olive oil.

o น้ำมันมะพร้าว námman'maphráaw' N coconut oil.

o น้ำมันยาง námman'jaaŋ' N dammar, resin.

o น้ำมันระกำ námman'rakam' N oil of wintergreen.

o น้ำมันแร่ námman'rɛɛ' N mineral oil.

o น้ำมันละหุ่ง námman'lahùŋ' N castor oil.

o น้ำมันสน námman'sŏn' N turpentine.

o น้ำมันใส่ผม námman'sàjphŏm' N hair tonic.

o น้ำมันหมู námman'mǔu' N lard.

o น้ำมันหยอดเครื่อง námman'jɔ̀ɔdkhrɯ̂aŋ' N lubricating oil, motor oil.

o บ่อน้ำมัน (บ่อ) bɔ̀ɔ'námman' (bɔ̀ɔ') N oil well.

o พรมน้ำมัน (ผืน,แผ่น) phrom'námman' (phɯ̌ɯn', phɛ̀n') N linoleum.

น้ำมือ námmyy' N (one's own) deed, act, action, hand, hands.

o ตายเพราะน้ำมือลูก taaj'-phrɔ́námmyy'lûug' to die by the hand of one's own son.

น้ำมูก námmûug' N eleg. nasal mucus, nasal discharge. →Syn. ขี้มูก com.,vulg.

น้ำเมา námmaw' N intoxicating beverage (usually undistilled).

น้ำย่อย námjɔ̂j' N gastric juice.

น้ำยา námjaa' N 1. com. chemical solution (nontech. term, e.g. as in "permanent wave solution"). 2. a kind of sauce made of fish, coconut cream and other ingredients and served with vermicelli.

น้ำเย็น námjen' N cold water.

น้ำร้อน námrɔ́ɔn' N hot water.

น้ำแร่ námrɛɛ' N mineral water.

น้ำลง náamloŋ' N ebb tide. →Opp. น้ำขึ้น.

น้ำลาย námlaaj' N saliva.

o ถ่มน้ำลาย thòm'námlaaj' to spit.

o น้ำลายแตกฟอง námlaaj'-tɛ̀ɛg'fɔɔŋ' idiom., colloq. to spout forth, talk volubly. →Also พูดจน--.

น้ำลูกไม้ náamlûugmáaj' N com. fruit juice. →Syn. น้ำผลไม้.

น้ำวน námwon' N whirlpool.

น้ำส้ม námsôm' N 1. vinegar. 2. orange juice. 3. orange drink, orange squash, beverage flavored with orange.

น้ำส้มคั้น námsôm'khán' N orange juice.

น้ำส้มสายชู námsôm'sǎajchuu' N vinegar. →Also น้ำส้ม.

น้ำสุก námsùg' N boiled water. →Opp. น้ำดิบ.

น้ำเสียง námsǐaŋ' N tone of voice.

น้ำใสใจจริง námsǎj'-cajciŋ' N 1. sincerity, genuineness. 2. (one's) real feelings. อย่าง-- from the bottom of one's heart.

น้ำหนัก námnàg' N 1. weight. 2. fig. weight, importance.

น้ำหน้า námnâa' N face, looks (used contemptuously).

o เกลียดน้ำหน้า klìad'námnâa' to hate the very sight of (someone), hate somebody's looks; to detest.

o สมน้ำหน้า (1) sŏm'námnâa'; (2) sŏm'námnâa'↓ 1. to get one's just deserts; to serve (somebody) right. 2. It serves (you) right!

น้ำหนึ่ง námnɯ̀ŋ' of the first water, of the highest grade, of top quality. [perh. tr. f. Eng.]

o เพชรน้ำหนึ่ง (เม็ด) phéd'námnɯ̀ŋ' (méd') N 1. diamond of the first water. 2. idiom. topnotch, i.e. the most able (person), the most beautiful (woman), the best in quality (of anything).

น้ำหมาก námmàag' N betel saliva (i.e. betel mixed with saliva, red in color).

น้ำไหลไฟดับ in the following expression.

o พูดน้ำไหลไฟดับ phûud'-náamlǎj'fajdàb' colloq. to chatter away, talk a blue streak, talk rapidly and profusely.

น้ำหวาน námwǎan' N 1. soft drink (sweetened), sweet drink. 2. flavored syrup.

น้ำหอม (อย่าง,ชนิด,ขวด,หยด) námhɔ̌ɔm' N perfume, toilet water (jàaŋ', chaníd' for kinds; khùad' for bottles; jòd' for drops). →Syn. น้ำอบ colloq.

น้ำอดน้ำทน nám?òd'námthon' N elab. colloq. patience, endurance.

น้ำอบ (อย่าง,ชนิด,ขวด,หยด) nám?òb' N colloq. perfume (jàaŋ', chaníd' for kinds; khùad' for bottles; jòd' for drops). →Syn. น้ำหอม com.

น้ำอสุจิ náam'?àsùcì?' N semen, spermatic fluid. →Syn. น้ำกาม.

บ่อน้ำ (บ่อ) bɔ̀ɔnáam' (bɔ̀ɔ') N 1. well (for water).

2. pool.

ปั้นน้ำเป็นตัว pânnáam′-pentua′ idiom. to make up a story out of whole cloth, fabricate a lie.

ปากน้ำ (แห่ง) pàagnáam′ (hɛ̀ŋ′) N 1. mouth of a river; estuary. pN 2. Paknam, a common name for Samutprakan (สมุทรปราการ), a township at the mouth of the Chaophraya R. →Also 1. ปากแม่น้ำ.

เป็นน้ำ pennáam′ V 1. to be liquid (not solid). sV 2. fluently, flowingly.

o พูด(...)เป็นน้ำ phûud′(...)pennáam′ 1. to speak (e.g. English) fluently. 2. idiom. to talk a blue streak.

ฝั่งน้ำ (ฝั่ง) fàŋ′náam′ (fàŋ′) N river bank; bank of a watercourse.

ฟองน้ำ (ลูก,ฟอง,อัน,ชิ้น,แผ่น,ๆลๆ) fɔɔŋnáam′ N 1. bubbles; foam (lûug′, fɔɔŋ′). 2. sponge (ʔan′). 3. foam rubber (ʔan′, chín′, phɛ̀n′, etc.).

แม่น้ำ (สาย) mɛ̂ɛnáam′ (sǎaj′) N river.

แมวน้ำ (ตัว) mɛɛwnáam′ (tua′) N seal; sea lion.

รดน้ำ ródnáam′ V 1. to pour water on; to water. 2. to sprinkle holy water over.

ร่องน้ำ (แห่ง,ร่อง) rɔ̂ŋnáam′ (hɛ̀ŋ′, rɔ̂ŋ′) N channel, the deeper part of a stream or waterway.

ลูกน้ำ (ตัว) lûugnáam′ (tua′) N mosquito larva.

หม้อน้ำ (หม้อ,ใบ) mɔ̂ɔnáam′ (mɔ̂ɔ′, baj′) N 1. water pot. 2. boiler. 3. water heater. 4. radiator (of a car).

ห้องน้ำ (ห้อง) hɔ̂ŋnáam′ (hɔ̂ŋ′) N bathroom.

หิวน้ำ hǐwnáam′ V to be thirsty.

อาบน้ำ ʔàabnáam′ V to bathe, take a bath, shower.

ไอน้ำ ʔajnáam′ N steam, vapor.

นิกาย níkaaj′ C sect, denomination, branch.

นิเกิล níkən′/* N nickel. [f. Eng.] →Sometimes also นิเกล níkèn′.

นิคม (นิคม,แห่ง) níkhom′ (níkhom′, hɛ̀ŋ′) N settlement, colony.

นิ่ง nîŋ′ V 1. to be still, quiet, motionless. sV 2. still, quietly.

นิ่งอึ้ง nîŋʔŷŋ′ V to be silent, speechless, dumbstruck.

แน่นิ่ง nɛ̂ɛnîŋ′ V to be unconscious.

ภาพนิ่ง phâabnîŋ′ N 1. slide (for projection), still picture. 2. shadow play figure (made of

paper or hide). Mng. 2 used esp. in the south where shadow plays are still seen.

นิจ in เป็นนิจ penníd′ constantly, regularly, always. →See also นิตย์.

นิด níd′ V to be tiny, little, small. →Chiefly in compounds.

นิดเดียว níddiaw′ 1. to be tiny. 2. a tiny bit.

นิดหน่อย nídnɔ̀j′ little, tiny, small, wee; a little bit, a wee bit. NOTE. นิด and หน่อย are often coupled in semirepeated expressions; 2nd example below.

o โตกว่า...นิดหน่อย too′kwàaɔ...nídnɔ̀j′ a little bit bigger than.

o แต้มนิดแต้มหน่อย tɛ̂ɛmníd′tɛ̂ɛmnɔ̀j′ to daub a little bit here, a little bit there.

o นิด ๆ หน่อย ๆ nídníd′nɔ̀jnɔ̀j′ trivial; a very little bit, a very tiny amount.

นิดหนึ่ง níd′nyŋ tiny; a tiny bit, a little bit.

นิตย์ See entries below. →See also นิจ.

เนืองนิตย์ nyaŋ′níd′ always, regularly, constantly.

เป็นนิตย์ penníd′ always, regularly, constantly.

นิติ-. Bound form meaning "law."

นิติกรรม nítìkam′ N law juristic act, legal act.

นิตินัย nítìnaj′ N law legal sense. โดย--,ตาม-- legally, de jure. →Opp. พฤตินัย.

นิติบัญญัติ nítìbanjàd′, nítìʔ- N law 1. legislation. 2. (as n. mod.) legislative.

o สภานิติบัญญัติ (สภา) saphaa′nítìbanjàd′ (saphaa′) N legislative body.

o อำนาจนิติบัญญัติ ʔamnâad′nítìbanjàd′ legislative power.

นิติบุคคล nítìbùgkhon′, nítìʔ- N law juristic entity.

นิติภาวะ nítìphaawá′, nítìʔ- N law legal competency.

o บรรลุนิติภาวะ banlú′nítìphaawá′ law to come of age, reach legal age, attain one's majority.

นิติศาสตร์ nítìsàad′ N eleg. law (as a subject of study).

นิทาน (เรื่อง) níthaan′ (rŷaŋ′) N fable, tale, story. →Syn. เรื่อง com., นิยาย eleg.

นินทา ninthaa′ V to gossip about, slander, blame; to criticize (someone) behind (his) back. การ--

gossip.

นิพนธ์ níphon′ V eleg. to write, compose. →Syn. แต่ง com., ประพันธ์ eleg.

พระราชนิพนธ์ (ฉบับ) phráráad′chaníphon′ (chaɔ bàb′) N roy. the writing or literary work of the king.

วิทยานิพนธ์ (เล่ม,ฉบับ) wídthajaa′níphon′ (lêm′, chabàb′) N thesis, dissertation.

นิพพาน níbphaan′ N Nirvana (used in speaking of the Buddha).

นิ่ม nîm′ V 1. to be soft, yielding (as of a comforter, tissue paper, baby's skin, etc.). sV 2. smoothly (e.g. of driving a car). →Comp. 1. นวม,นุ่ม, อ่อน. →Ant. 1. แข็ง,กระด้าง.

นิ่มนวล nîmnuan′ V 1. to be gentle, tender, gracious. 2. to be graceful, smooth (in action). sV 3. tenderly, graciously; smoothly, gracefully. →Syn. นุ่มนวล.

นุ่มนิ่ม nûmnîm′ V to be soft, yielding, gentle.

นิมนต์ nímon′ V sacer. to invite (a priest). →Syn. เชิญ com.

นิมิต (อัน) nímíd′ (ʔan′) N eleg. sign, omen.

นิยม níjom′ V 1. to prefer, favor, like, accept popularly (as a good thing). 2. to be popular, approved, favored, accepted popularly (as a good thing); to be in public demand. ความ-- preference; popularity.

จักรพรรดินิยม càgkraphád′níjom′ N imperialism.

ชาตินิยม châad′níjom′ nationalistic. นัก-- nationalist.

o พรรคชาตินิยม phág′-châad′níjom′ N nationalist party.

นิยมนิยาย. See the following entry.

o เอาเป็นนิยมนิยาย ʔaw′-penníjom′níjaaj′ colloq. to take (it) seriously, to consider (it); to count on (it).

รสนิยม ród′níjom′ N taste (perceptive judgment), liking, preference.

รัฐนิยม (ฉบับ) rádthanijom′ (chabàb′) N state convention or code of conduct (issued for the public during World War II).

นิยาย (เรื่อง) níjaaj′ (rɣaŋ′) N eleg. legend, tale, fable, story. →Syn. นิทาน,เรื่อง com.

o นวนิยาย (เรื่อง) náwáníjaaj′ (rɣaŋ′) N lit.

a novel. →Syn. เรื่องอ่านเล่น com.

นิร-. Bound stem meaning "without, not, un-."

นิรภัย níráphaj′ eleg. safe, not dangerous. →Chiefly in compounds.

o เขตนิรภัย khèed′níráphaj′ N eleg. safety zone.

o ตู้นิรภัย (ใบ) tûu′níráphaj′ (baj′) N eleg. a safe (a place for keeping valuables). →Syn. ตู้เซฟ com.

นิรันดร as in ชั่วนิรันดร chûa′níran′dɔɔn′ forever. →Also นิรันดร níran′.

นิล (เม็ด) nin′ (méd′) N 1. jet (stone). 2. any kind of black or very dark precious or semiprecious stone (including sapphire).

นิ่ว ๑ (ก้อน) nîw′ (kɔ̂n′) N gallstone, calculus.

นิ่ว ๒. See entries below.

นิ่วหน้า nîw′nâa′ V to frown, pucker up the face.

หน้านิ่ว nâa′nîw′ V to be sour-faced, frowning.

นิ้ว (นิ้ว) níw′ (níw′) N 1. digit, finger, toe. C 2. the Thai inch, roughly eight tenths of an English inch. 3. the English inch. →Also 3. นิ้วฟุต. NOTE. All nouns based on นิ้ว take นิ้ว as their classifier unless otherwise marked; hence (นิ้ว) is omitted below.

กระเบียดนิ้ว krabìad′níw′ C one quarter of an inch. →Also กระเบียด.

o ทุก ๆ กระเบียดนิ้ว thúgthúg′-krabìad′níw′ every minor detail, every little bit.

ข้อนิ้ว (ข้อ) khɔ̂ɔníw′ (khɔ̂ɔ′) N knuckle.

ดีดนิ้ว dìid′níw′ V to snap one's fingers.

นิ้วกลาง níwklaaŋ′ N middle finger.

นิ้วก้อย níwkɔ̂j′ N little finger.

นิ้วชี้ níwchíi′ N index finger, forefinger.

นิ้วตีน níwtiin′ com. toe. →Syn. นิ้วเท้า eleg.

นิ้วเท้า níwtháaw′ N eleg. toe. →Syn. นิ้วตีน com.

นิ้วนาง níwnaaŋ′ N ring finger.

นิ้วโป้,นิ้วโป้ง níwpôo′, níwpôoŋ′ N colloq. thumb. →Syn. นิ้วหัวแม่มือ com.

นิ้วฟุต níwfúd′ C inch (in the English system). →See นิ้ว. [ฟุต f. Eng.]

นิ้วมือ níwmyy′ N finger.

นิ้วหัวแม่มือ níwhŭa′mɛ̂ɛmyy′ N thumb. →Syn. นิ้วโป้,นิ้วโป้ง colloq.

ยกนิ้ว jóg′níw′ colloq. to accept (someone's)

superiority.

นิว เคลีย niwkhlia/ nuclear. →Chiefly in compounds.
[f. Eng.]

นิว เดลฮี niwdeenhii/, niwdeelhii/ pN New Delhi.
[f. Eng.]

นิวยอร์ค niwjɔɔg/* pN New York. [f. Eng.]

นิสล้ย. Var. spelling of นิสัย.

นิสัย nísǎj/ N habit, characteristic trait. →Some-
times spelled นิสล้ย.

นิสัยใจคอ nísǎj/cajkhɔɔ/ N disposition, temperament.

นิสิต (คน) nísìd/ (khon/) N eleg. university
student, college student, undergraduate (male).
→Opp. นิสิตา.

นิสิตเก่า (คน) nísìd/kàw/ (khon/) N eleg.
alumnus, alumna (of a university).

นิสิตา (คน) nísìtaa/ (khon/) N eleg. woman
college student, coed. →Opp. นิสิต.

นี่ nîi/ dP 1. this (one). 2. here. Pt 3. particle
marking an utterance as an explanation or as an
answer to a question, implying that the explanation is simply such and such (2nd example), or
that this is as much of an answer as one can
give (3rd example). →Often coupled with โน่น
(4th and 5th examples). →See also นั่น, โน่น.

o นี่ของใคร nîikhɔɔŋkhraj/ Whose is this?:
"This (is) whose?"

o ละครยังไม่เริ่มนี่จ๊ะ lakhɔɔn/ jaŋmâjrə̂əm/nîiᴐ
cá↓ The play hasn't started yet is all.

o ยังไม่เห็นมานี่คะ jaŋmâjhěnmaa/nîikhá↓ (I)
haven't <u>seen</u> (him) come yet.

o ทำโน่นทำนี่ thamnôon/thamnîi/ to do this and
that; to do this, that (and the other thing).

o จัดโน่นนิดนี่หน่อย càdnôon/níd/-nîi/nɔ̀ɔj/ to put
(things) in order, a little bit here, a little bit
there.

ที่นี่ thîinîi/ here.

นี่กี่โมงแล้ว nîi/ kìimooŋ/lɛ́ɛw/↓ What time is it?

นี่ยังไงกัน nîi/ jaŋŋaj/kan↓ What's the meaning
of this? (said on encountering something not
quite to one's liking).

นี้ nîi/ dA this, these. →See also นั้น, โน้น. →Often
coupled with โน้น; 1st example. NOTE. นี้ is
usually preceded by a clf. (2nd-4th examples),

and if no number is expressed, reference is to
one (item, pair, group, etc.) of something (3rd
and 4th examples). Occasionally นี้ may appear
without a clf. in the sequence นี้นะ, and the
quantity, whether one or more, is determined by
the context. In this case นี้นะ is pronounced
nîi/nâ?, nîinâ?/, nîi/â? (sic) but these pronunciations are not reflected in the orthography;
compare 4th and 5th examples.

o อย่างโน้นอย่างนี้ jaŋnóon/jaŋníi/ this and that;
like this and like that.

o ส้ม ๒ ใบนี้ sôm/-sɔ̌ɔŋbaj/níi/ these two oranges.

o ส้มกระจาดนี้ sôm/kracàad/níi/ this basket of
oranges.

o ส้มใบนี้นะ เล็กเกินไป sôm/bajníi/nâ? lég/ᴐ
kəən/paj↓ This orange is too small.

o ส้มนี้นะ เล็กเกินไป sôm/nîinâ?/ lég/kəən/paj↓
sômnîi/â?-* This orange is too small. These
oranges, they're too small.

คืนนี้ khyyn/níi/ tonight.

o เมื่อคืนนี้ mŷakhyyn/níi/ last night.

เช่นนี้ chênníi/ like this.

เช้านี้ cháaw/níi/ this morning.

ดังนี้ daŋníi/ like this, in this manner; like this,
of this kind; thus; as follows.

เดี๋ยวนี้ dǐawníi/ now, at present, at the present
time.

แต่ก่อนนี้ tɛkɔɔn/níi/, takɔɔn/níi/ in former times,
previously.

ทั้งนี้ tháŋníi/ all of this, all this.

บัดนี้ bàd/níi/ now, at present, at the present time.

ปานนี้ paan/níi/ to this extent, as (e.g. beautiful)
as this, like this.

o สวยปานนี้ sǔaj/paanníi/ to be as beautiful as this.

ป่านนี้ pàanníi/ by this time, by now.

พรุ่งนี้ phrûŋníi/ tomorrow.

ยังนี้ jaŋníi/ like this, this way; of this sort.
→Same as อย่างนี้.

เย็นนี้ jen/níi/ this (coming) evening, this late
afternoon.

วันนี้ wanníi/ today.

วานนี้ waan/níi/ yesterday.

หมู่นี้ mùunníi/ these days, nowadays, at present,
during this time.

อย่างนี้ jàaŋníi′, jaŋníi′, jaŋŋíi′ like this, this
way; of this sort. →Also ยังนี้,ยังงี้. →For
examples see cross reference.

นึก nýg′ V to think. ความ-- (usually ความนึกคิด,
q.v. below). →Comp. ลำนึก. →Syn. คิด.

ครุ่นนึก,นึกครุ่น khrûn′nýg′, nýg′khrûn′ V to keep
thinking.

ความนึกคิด khwaamnýgkhíd′ N thinking, thought,
thoughts.

ช่างนึกช่างคิด châaŋnýg′châaŋkhíd′ V elab.
colloq. to be good at thinking, full of ideas.

นึกขัน nýg′khǎn′ V to be amused by the thought
(of something).

o ดิฉันยังนึกขันเรื่องนั้นอยู่เลย dichán′-jaŋnýgɔ
khǎn′rɣaŋnán′jùuləəj↓ I'm still amused by the
thought of that (matter, affair,etc.).

นึกขำในใจ nýgkhǎm′najcaj′ to be inwardly
amused.

นึกครุ่น,ครุ่นนึก nýg′khrûn′, khrûn′nýg′ V to keep
thinking.

นึกฉงน nýg′chaŋǒn′ V to be puzzled, in doubt.

นึกชังในใจ nýgchaŋ′najcaj′ V to harbor a
feeling of hatred.

นึกฝัน nýg′fǎn′ V to imagine, dream (figuratively). ความ-- N dream, imagination.

o ไม่นึกไม่ฝันว่า mâjnýg′mâjfǎn′-wâaɔ (I) never
dreamed, never thought that...

นึกย้อน nýg′jɔ́ɔn′ V to think back.

นึกว่า nýg′wâaɔ, nýg′wâa′ to think that...

นึกเห็นภาพ nýg′hěnphâab′ V to picture, imagine,
visualize.

นึกอยาก nýg′jàag′ AA feel like (doing something,
e.g. taking a walk); feel like it.

นึกออก nýg′ʔɔ̀ɔg′ can remember, can recall.

o นึกไม่ออก nýg′mâjʔɔ̀ɔg′ can't think; can't
recall.

หวนนึก hǔan′nýg′ to think back, recall.

นึ่ง nŷŋ′ V 1. to steam (food), cook with steam.
2. to be steamed.

นุ่ง nûŋ′ V to dress, put on, wear (lower garment,
e.g. trousers, the phanung, etc.).

นุ่งลมห่มฟ้า nûŋlom′hòmfáa′ V elab. colloq.
to be naked, in the nude: "clothe oneself with
wind and sky."

นุ่งห่ม nûŋhòm′ V to dress, clothe oneself; to wear.
การ-- dressing. เครื่อง-- garment, clothing.

นุ่งเหลืองห่มเหลือง nûŋlɣaŋ′hòmlɣǎŋ′ to wear the
yellow robe, i.e. be in the priesthood.

ผ้านุ่ง (ผืน) phâanûŋ′ (phɣ̌yn′) N the phanung, a
lower garment made of a wide strip of cloth with
one end twisted and hitched between the legs.
Formerly worn by both sexes; now rarely seen.

นุ่น nûn′ N kapok.

ต้นนุ่น (ต้น) tônnûn′ (tôn′) kapok tree (Ceiba
pentandra).

นุ่ม nûm′ V to be soft, spongy, yielding. →Comp.
นวม,นิ่ม,อ่อน. →Ant. แข็ง,กระด้าง.

นุ่มนวล nûmnuan′ V 1. to be soft, gentle (of manner, voice). 2. to be smooth, graceful (in action,
manner). sV 3. softly, gently; smoothly, grace-
fully. →Syn. นิ่มนวล.

นุ่มนิ่ม nûmnîm′ V to be soft, yielding, gentle.

o ท่าทางนุ่มนิ่ม thâathaaŋ′nûmnîm′ gentle manner,
bearing.

อ่อนนุ่ม ʔɔ̀ɔnnûm′ V to be soft and spongy, tender.

นูน nuun′ V 1. to bulge out, curve out, be convex.
2. to swell, be swollen.

กระจกนูน (แผ่น,บาน) kracòg′nuun′ (phèn′, baan′)
N convex mirror.

นู้น nûun′ dP that, there over there, over yonder.
→Cf. โน้น.

นู้น núun′ dA that, that (one) over there. →Cf. โน้น.

เน็คไท,เน็คไท (เส้น) négthaj′ (sên′) N necktie.
[f. Eng.]

เน็ต (ผืน) néd′ (phɣ̌yn′) N net (e.g. for tennis
game). [f. Eng.]

เนตร (ดวง,ข้าง) nêed′ (duaŋ′, khâaŋ′) N lit.,
eleg. eye. →Syn. See ตา com.

พระเนตร phránêed′ roy. eye.

เนติบัณฑิต (คน) nee′tìbandìd′*(khon′) N attorney;
barrister-at-law.

เนติบัณฑิตสภา nee′tìbandìd′sàphaa′ N bar association.

เนเทอแลน neethəəlɛɛn′ pN the Netherlands. [f. Eng.]

เน้น nén′* V to stress, emphasize.

เนย nəəj′ 1. butter. 2. cheese.

เนยแข็ง nəəjkhěŋ′ N cheese.

เนยเทียม nəəjthiam′ N margarine.

เนยอ่อน nəəj?ɔɔn′ N butter.

เนรคุณ nee′rakhun′ V to be ungrateful (to).

เนรเทศ neeratheed′ V to exile, deport.

เนา naw′ V sew. 1. to baste. 2. to be basted.

เน่า nâw′ V 1. to be rotten, decayed, putrid. 2. to
decay, rot, putrify.

ไข่เน่า khàjnâw′ a rotten egg.

เน่าเปื่อย, เปื่อยเน่า nâwpỳaj′, pỳajnâw′ V to be
decomposed, rotten to the point of disintegration.

·เนิน (ลูก, แห่ง) nəən′ (lûug′, hὲŋ′) N knoll, mound.
→Syn. โคก, โขด.

เป็นเนิน pennəən′ to be hilly.

เนิ่น nə̂ən′ V 1. to be slow, tardy; to be long (of
time). 2. to pass by (of time). 3. to be early.
→Syn. 1. ช้า, นาน. 3. เร็ว.

o เวลาเนิ่นมาห้าปี weelaa′nə̂ən′-maahâa′pii′↓
Five years passed by.

แต่เนิ่น tὲnə̂ən′ early, ahead of time, in advance.

เนิ่น ๆ nə̂ənnə̂ən′ sV early, earlier.

o มาเนิ่น ๆ maa′nə̂ənnə̂ən′ to come early.

เนิบนาบ nə̂əb′nâab′ V 1. to be slow, sluggish. 2.
to be ill-fitting and untidy.

เนื้อ nýa′ N 1. meat, flesh. 2. meat, gist, substance. 3. deer (a general term). 4. anat.
tissue.

> NOTE. เนื้อ is often used as a replacement
> for ตัว in semirepeated expressions; 1st exam-
> ple. Sometimes it is used as a replacement
> for ใจ in semirepeated expressions or split
> expressions; 2nd and 3rd examples.
>
> o เจียมเนื้อเจียมตัว ciamnýa′ciamtua′ to be
> modest and unassuming: เจียมตัว idem.
>
> o ดีเนื้อดีใจ diinýa′diicaj′ V to be glad, happy,
> pleased, delighted: ดีใจ idem.
>
> o เดือดเนื้อร้อนใจ dỳadnýa′rɔɔncaj′ to worry,
> be upset, be troubled: เดือดร้อน idem.

กลับเนื้อกลับตัว klàbnýa′klàbtua′ V to change
one's conduct, to reform.

กล้ามเนื้อ (มัด, ชิ้น) klâamnýa′ (mád′, chín′) N
muscle.

กินเลือดกินเนื้อ kinlŷad′kinnýa′ colloq., fig.
to eat someone up alive (as with anger).

เข้าเนื้อ (1) khâwnýa′; (2) khâw′nýa′ V 1.
idiom. to lose (opp. of gain). 2. to penetrate
into the flesh (as an ointment), into the meat
(as seasoning).

ครั่นเนื้อครั่นตัว khrânnýa′khrântua′ V to feel hot
and cold, as the first symptoms of a fever.

เจ้าเนื้อ câwnýa′ V to be fat, plump, chubby (used
esp. of children). คน-- fatty, fatso.

เดือดเนื้อร้อนใจ dỳadnýa′rɔɔncaj′ elab. colloq.
to worry, be upset, be troubled. →See เดือดร้อน.

ติดเนื้อต้องใจ tìdnýa′tɔ̂ŋcaj′ V to be fond of, interested in, fascinated with (a person or thing).

ทั้งเนื้อทั้งตัว tháŋnýa′tháŋtua′ 1. all over (the body).
2. thoroughly. 3. idiom. to one's name (as in
"not a penny to his name").

เนื้อความ nýakhwaam′ N essence of a matter;
the content (as of a book); subject matter.
→Syn. ใจความ.

เนื้อควาย nýakhwaaj′ N buffalo meat.

เนื้อแดง nýadɛɛŋ′ N lean meat.

เนื้อทราย (ตัว) nýasaaj′ (tua′) N hog deer.

เนื้อที่ nýathîi′ N area; room (space).

เนื้อแท้ nýathέε′ N the real thing, the real sense.

เนื้อผ้า nýaphâa′ N texture of cloth.

เนื้อเพลง nýaphleeŋ′ N the words of a song, text
of a song.

เนื้อมะพร้าว nýamaphráaw′ N coconut meat.

เนื้อไม้ nýamáaj′ N wood texture; wood (exclusive
of bark).

เนื้อเรื่อง nýarŷaŋ′ N subject matter, essential
part of a story.

เนื้อวัว nýawua′ N beef.

เนื้อสัตว์ nýasàd′ N meat, flesh.

เนื้อหมู nýamŭu′ N pork.

เนื้อหา nýahăa′ N text; gist, substance.

เป็นเนื้อเดียวกัน pennýa′diawkan′ to be homogeneous; to be well-blended, smoothly joined.

ผิวเนื้อ phĭwnýa′ N complexion.

หมดเนื้อหมดตัว mòdnýa′mòdtua′ V to be penniless,
lose everything one has.

เนื้อง. See entries below.

เนื้องนิตย์ nyaŋ′níd′ always, regularly, constantly.

เนื้อง ๆ nyaŋnyaŋ′ often, unceasingly, unremittingly.

เนื้องแน่น nyaŋ′nɛ̂n′ V to be crowded, overcrowded,
congested.

เนื้อง nyaŋ′ V to be due to, connected (with), related
(to).

เนื้องจาก nyaŋ′càagɔ owing to, on account of,

due to; owing to the fact that, because of the
fact that, since.

เนื่องด้วย nyaŋ'dûajɔ owing to, on account of,
due to, arising from, because; owing to the fact
that, because of the fact that, since.

เนื่องใน nyaŋ'najɔ on the occasion of.

สืบเนื่อง sỳybnyaŋ' V 1. to pass on, be passed on,
continue. 2. to derive (from), be a consequence
(of).

o มีผลสืบเนื่อง (มาจาก) miiphŏn'-sỳybnyaŋ'ɔ
(maacàagɔ) to be a consequence (of).

หนุนเนื่อง nŭn/nyaŋ' V to bring up reinforcements (troops) in a continuous stream.

เนือย nyaj' V to be apathetic, indifferent, slow-
moving, listless.

เนือย ๆ nyajnyaj' sV apathetically, indifferently,
slowly, listlessly, uninterestingly.

เนือยลง nyaj'loŋ' V to slow down, become apathetic.

แน่ nɛɛ' V 1. to be sure, certain. 2. to be firm,
stable. 3. colloq. to be smart, sharp, good,
effective, good (at, in). sV 4. certainly, for
sure.

แน่แก่ใจ nɛɛ'kɛ̀ɛcaj' to be confident.

แน่ใจ nɛɛcaj' V 1. to be sure, certain. 2. to be
confident. อย่าง-- certainly, assuredly.

แน่ชัด nɛɛ'chád' V 1. to be certain, definite, sure.
sV 2. surely, clearly.

แน่นอน nɛɛnɔɔn' V 1. to be certain, definite.
sV 2. certainly, definitely, absolutely, positively, of course. การ-- certainty. ความ--
certainty; phys. stability.

แน่นิ่ง nɛɛ'nîŋ' V to be unconscious.

แน่วแน่ nɛ̂wnɛɛ' V 1. to be resolute, determined,
singleminded. sV 2. resolutely, unswervingly.

เป็นแน่ pennɛɛ' for a certainty, for sure.

แน่น nɛ̂n'* V 1. to be tight, tight-fitting, compact,
packed, congested, crowded. 2. (contents) to
pack, be packed tightly into (a container); to
jam, crowd (a place). sV 3. tightly, compactly.
ความ-- density, tightness, compactness.
→Syn. 1, 2. คับ.

ควบแน่น khûabnɛ̂n' V tech. to condense.

เนื่องแน่น nyaŋ'nɛ̂n' V to be crowded, over-

crowded, congested.

แน่นปิ๋ง nɛ̂n'pŷŋ' colloq. 1. to be very tight. 2.
to be firmly tied, securely tied, tied tightly.

แน่นเปลี๊ยะ nɛ̂n'plía?' V colloq. 1. to be extremely crowded, congested. 2. to be very tight,
firmly tied, tied tightly.

แน่นแฟ้น nɛ̂nféɛn' V 1. to be firm, steady, secure.
sV 2. firmly, securely. อย่าง-- firmly, securely, tightly.

แน่นหนา nɛ̂nnăa' V 1. to be strong, tightly constructed. sV 2. strongly, securely.

หนักแน่น nàgnɛ̂n' to be steady, firm.

หนาแน่น năa'nɛ̂n' V to be crowded, congested,
densely populated.

แนบ nɛ̂ɛb' V 1. to be close to, flat against; to cling
to (the body, as clothes). 2. to attach.

แนบติด nɛ̂ɛb'tìd' to be attached to.

แนบเนียน nɛ̂ɛbnian' to be a perfect fit; to be well-
fitted, well-joined.

เอาหูแนบ ?awhŭu'nɛ̂ɛb' to put one's ear against.

แนว (แนว) nɛɛw' (nɛɛw') N 1. line, row, strip.
C 2. clf. for same. →Cf. ตับ, แถว, ระนาว.

ขึ้นแนว khŷn'nɛɛw' to have welts.

แนวทาง (ทาง) nɛɛwthaaŋ' (thaaŋ') N way,
direction, trend.

แนว(ที่)ห้า (พวก, คน) nɛɛw(thîi)hâa' N idiom.
1. fifth column, spy ring (phûag'). 2. fifth columnist, spy (khon').

แนวรบ (แนว, ด้าน) nɛɛwrób' (nɛɛw', dâan') N
battle line, fighting front.

แนวหน้า nɛɛwnâa' N milit. the front, front line.

แนวหลัง nɛɛwlăŋ' N milit. the rear; rear echelon.

แน่ว nɛ̂w'* V to be direct, steadfast. sV 2. colloq.
fast, quickly.

แน่วแน่ nɛ̂wnɛɛ' V to be resolute, determined,
singleminded. sV 2. resolutely, unswervingly.

แน่วไป nɛ̂w'paj' to go straight to.

แนะ nɛ́?' V 1. to advise, guide. 2. to hint, suggest.

นัดแนะ, แนะนัด nád'nɛ́?', nɛ́?'nád' V 1. to make
an appointment, make arrangements (as to when,
where, what, and who).

แนะนำ nɛ́?nam' V 1. to advise, guide. 2. to suggest. 3. to introduce. คำ-- advice, suggestion,
instruction.

o จดหมายแนะนำตัว (ฉบับ) còdmǎaj′-nɛ́ʔnam′ɔ tua′ (chabàb′) N letter of introduction, letter of recommendation.

o แนะนำว่า nɛ́ʔnam′wâa′ to advise that, suggest that.

o แนะนำให้ nɛ́ʔnam′hâjɔ to advise to, induce to, suggest that (someone do thus and so).

o แนะนำให้รู้จัก nɛ́ʔnam′hâjrúucàg′ to introduce (someone to someone else).

แน่ะ nɛ̂ʔ′ E 1. Hey! (interjection to call attention). 2. Hey! Hi! (to greet someone). →Frequently used with a preceding demonstr. pronoun.

o ดูนั่นแน่ะ duunân′nɛ̂ʔ′ Look over there! Look at that!

o นี่แน่ะ nîi′nɛ̂ʔ′ Here! Here it is!

โน noo′ V to get a swelling, raise a lump (as from a bump on the head).

โน้ต nóod′ N 1. note, notes (taken down). 2. note, notes (musical). [f. Eng.] →Sometimes spelled โน๊ต.

จดโน้ต còd′nóod′ to record, note, take notes.

โน่น nôon′ dP that over there, that yonder. →Often coupled with นี่. →Comp. นู่น. →See also นั่น, นี่.

ทำโน่นทำนี่ thamnôon′thamnîi′ to do this and that; to do this, that (and the other thing).

ที่โน่น thîinôon′ over there, yonder.

โน้น nóon′ dA yon, that (one) over there. →Comp. นู้น. →Often coupled with นี้ (1st example). NOTE. Uses of โน้น with and without numbers and classifiers or with the particle นะ exactly parallel those of the forms นั้น and นี้ q.v.

o อย่างโน้นอย่างนี้ jàaŋnóon′jàaŋníi′ this and that; like this and like that, this way and that.

o ผู้ชายคนโน้น phûuchaaj′khonnóon′ that man over there.

อย่างโน้น jàaŋnóon′, jaŋnóon′, jaŋŋóon′ like that, that way, of that sort. →Also ยังโน้น, ยังโง้น. →Chiefly used in combinations with อย่างนี้ as in the following example; for further examples see cross reference.

โน้ม nóom′ V 1. to bend down, bend over (e.g. to pick something up). 2. to be bent over, bowed down, pulled down (as a branch loaded with fruit).

โน้มน้าว nóomnáaw′ V to influence (the thinking of another).

ใน naj′ sV 1. inner, internal. 2. in (of space, esp. enclosed space); in, at, on (of time). คน-- an insider. เครื่อง-- internal body organs. →Ant. นอก.

o ในบ้าน najbâan′ in the house.

o ในไม่ช้า najmâjcháa′ in a short time.

o ในเวลานี้ najweelaa′níi′ at this time.

o ในวันไหน najwan′nǎj′ on what day?

ข้างใน khâŋnaj′ inside, (the) inside.

ชั้นใน chánnaj′ inner layer, the inside.

o กางเกงชั้นใน (ตัว) kaaŋkeeŋ′chánnaj′ (tua′) N shorts, underpants; panties. →Also กางเกงใน.

เนื่องใน nɯ̂aŋ′najɔ on the occasion of.

ในกระบวน najkrabuan′ 1. in the matter of, as regards. 2. of, among.

ในขณะนี้ najkhanàʔ′níi′ at this time, at present; for now, for the time being.

ในคราวหน้า najkhraaw′nâa′ next time, on the next occasion.

ในใจ najcaj′ in one's head, in one's mind, on one's mind, in mind, in one's heart; inwardly, silently; see examples.

o ความในใจ khwaam′najcaj′ what is on one's mind, in one's heart.

o คิดในใจ khíd′najcaj′ 1. to figure in one's head (do mental arithmetic).· 2. to think silently, think to oneself.

o นึกขำในใจ nýgkhǎm′najcaj′ to be inwardly amused.

ในเดือนมิถุนายนหน้า najdyan′míthùnaa′jon′-nâa′ next June.

ในตอนนี้ najtɔɔn′níi′ at this time.

ในทาง najthaaŋɔ, najthaaŋ′ 1. in (such and such) a way. 2. on the way, along the way. NOTE. In many instances this expression corresponds to English -ly; see examples.

o ในทางมิชอบ najthaaŋ′míchɔɔb′ in a wrong way, illegally.

o ในทางเศรษฐกิจ najthaaŋ′-sèed′thakìd′ 1. from the economic standpoint. 2. in an economical way; economically.

ในท่ามกลาง najthâam/klaaŋ/ in the middle of, in the midst of, amidst, among.

ในที่สุด najthîisùd/ in the end, at last, finally.

ในปัจจุบัน najpàdcuban/ at present, now.

ในภายหลัง najphaaj/lǎŋ/ afterwards, later, in the future.

ในเมื่อ najmɯa/ when, in the event that.

ในไม่ช้า najmâjcháa/ in a short time, shortly, soon.

ในร่ม najrôm/ in the shade, indoors. 2. (as n. mod.) indoor.

ในระยะ najrajá?/ within (a period of time, a range of distance).

ในระหว่าง najrawàaŋ/ 1. between, among. 2. in the midst of, during.

ในราว najraaw/ about, around.

ในเร็ว ๆ นี้ najrewrew/níi/ soon, in the near future.

ในเร็ว ๆ วัน najrewrew/wan/ soon, in the very near future.

ในเรื่อง najrɯ̂aŋ/ 1. in (such and such a) case, event, matter. 2. in regard to, in the matter of, in the case of.

ในวันในพรุ่ง najwan/najphrûŋ/ colloq. in a day or two, very soon, in a short time.

ในวันหน้า najwan/nâa/ some other day (in the future), some future day.

ในวันไหน najwan/nǎj/ on what day?

ในเวลา najweelaa/ at (such and such a) time, at the time of, in, during.

o ในเวลากลางคืน najweelaa/klaaŋkhyyn/ at night.

o ในเวลานี้ najweelaa/níi/ at this time, at the present time, nowadays.

o ในเวลาหกโมง najweelaa/-hòg/mooŋ/ at six o'clock.

o ในเวลาอันรวดเร็ว najweelaa/-?anrûad/rew/ in a very short time, very quickly (of time).

ในสมัยก่อน(นี้) najsamǎj/kɔ̀ɔn(níi/) in the past, in previous times, in olden days.

ในหลวง (องค์,พระองค์) najlǔaŋ/ (?oŋ/, phrá?oŋ/) N colloq. the king (short form). →See กษัตริย์.

ในอันจะ naj?an/cà⊃ in order to, in order that.

ในโอกาศ naj?ookàad/ on the occasion of.

ภายใน phaajnaj/, phaaj/naj⊃ 1. inside, interior;

inside of, within (time or space). 2. internal. การ-- internal affair(s).

ยางใน (เส้น) jaaŋnaj/ (sên/) N inner tube (of tire).

หนองใน, โรค-- nɔ̌ɔŋnaj/, rôog/nɔ̌ɔŋnaj/ N gonorrhea.

หนึ่งในพัน nỳŋ/najphan/ 1. "one in a thousand," hence extraordinary, rare, exceptional. 2. one thousandth (i.e. the fraction).

หนึ่งในสี่ nỳŋ/najsìi/ 1. one in four, one of four. 2. one fourth.

อยู่ในมือ jùu/najmyy/ 1. to be in the hands (of), under the control (of). 2. to be at hand, on hand, in stock.

บ

บ bɔɔ/ MIDDLE consonant. Pronounced b both initially and finally. The sound b as an initial consonant is always written บ ; as a final consonant it is usually spelled with บ but sometimes also with ป,พ,ฟ, or ภ.

บ.๑ Abbrev. for บาท baht, tical.

บ.๒ Abbrev. for เครื่องบิน airplane.

บ่ bɔɔ/, bɔ⊃ AA lit., archaic, dial. not.

o หาค่าบ่มิได้ hǎakhâa/bɔ̀mídâaj/ V lit. to be invaluable, priceless.

บ.ก.๑ Abbrev. for กองบังคับการ milit. headquarters.

บ.ก.๒ Abbrev. for บรรณาธิการ editor.

บก ๑ bòg/ N 1. land (as opposed to sea). 2. (as. n. mod.) land, terrestial. →Dist. ดิน. →Opp. ทะเล.

กองทัพบก (กองทัพ) kɔɔŋtháb/bòg/ (kɔɔŋtháb/) N army, military land forces. Abbrev. ทบ.

ขึ้นบก khŷnbòg/ V 1. to land, go ashore. sV 2. ashore.

เดินบก dəənbòg/ V to walk; to travel on foot.

ทหารบก (คน) thahǎanbòg/ (khon/) N soldier.

ทางบก thaaŋbòg/ by land.

ลมบก lombòg/ N land breeze.

สัตว์บก (ตัว) sàdbòg/ (tua/) N land animal.

บก ๒ in บกพร่อง bògphrɔ̂ŋ/* V 1. to be defective,

not up to standard, deficient. 2. to be in inefficient, negligent (as of duty). ความ-- deficiency; inefficiency, negligence.

o ข้อบกพร่อง (ข้อ,ประการ) khɔ̂ɔ′bɔ̀gphrɔ̂ŋ′ (khɔ̂ɔ′, prakaan′) N weakness, fault, defect, flaw.

o ขาดตกบกพร่อง khàadtòg′bɔ̀gphrɔ̂ŋ′ V 1. to be deficient, defective, wanting. 2. to fall short.

บง in บงการ boŋkaan′ V to dictate, give commands, give orders, direct things. การ-- dictating (of orders); the dictates (of). ผู้-- dictator.

บ่ง bòŋ′ V 1. to indicate, specify, show, reveal. 2. to pick out, extract (e.g. a thorn with a needle); to pick open (e.g. an abscess). การ-- specification, specifying; extracting.

บ่งถึง bòŋ′thʉ̌ŋ′ to refer to.

บ่งเบ่ง bòŋbéŋ′* V s l a n g to make a loud noise; to be loud, noisy.

บด ๑ bòd′ V 1. to grind, pulverize, crush (as with a pestle or in a grinder). 2. to make level by means of weight (e.g. a street with a roller). เครื่อง-- grinder, grinding mechanism.

รถบดถนน (คัน) ródbòd′thanǒn′ (khan′) N steam roller.

บด ๒ bòd′ V to obstruct, obscure, shield, screen. →Chiefly in compounds.

บดบัง bòdbaŋ′ V 1. to obstruct, eclipse, obscure. 2. to be shielded, obscured.

บด ๓ in เรือบด (ลำ) ryabòd′ (lam′) N small boat (propelled by paddling or rowing).

บท (บท,เรื่อง) bòd′ (bòd′, ryaŋ′) N 1. the text, the lines (as of a song or play); subject (of an argument, discussion). C 2. clf. for chapter, lesson, verse; for proverbs, sayings, songs, etc.; for a move (in strategy).

o ลงบทชอบขึ้นมา loŋ′-bòdchɔ̂ɔb′khʉ̂nmaa′ whenever a liking arises; whenever love arises.

ตัดบท tàd′bòd′ V to cut the discussion short; to break off a conversation, an argument (e.g. by changing the subject, by bringing the matter to a conclusion).

บทกลอน (บท) bòdklɔɔn′ (bòd′) N a verse or poem in one kind of Thai verse form (the กลอน).

บทกวี bòd′kawii′ N poetry. This includes all kinds of verse forms, viz. โคลง,ฉันท์,กาพย์,กลอน.

บทความ (บท,เรื่อง) bòdkhwaam′ (bòd′, ryaŋ′) N an article (in a newspaper, magazine, etc.).

บทที่ ๑ bòd′thîinʉ̀ŋ′ 1. the first chapter, Chapter 1. 2. the first lesson, Lesson 1.

บทนำ (บท) bòdnam′ (bòd′) N introduction, introductory chapter. →Dist. คำนำ.

บทบัญญัติ (ฉบับ) bòd′banjàd′ (chabàb′) N an article (of a law, a parliamentary act, a constitution).

บทบาท bòdbàad′ N role, part (as in a play).

บทประพันธ์ (บท) bòd′praphan′ (bòd′) N a literary composition, work; a writing.

บทเพลง (บท) bòdphleeŋ′ (bòd′) N song; the text of a song.

บทเรียน (บท) bòdrian′ (bòd′) N lesson.

บทลงโทษ (บท) bòd′loŋthôod′ (bòd′) N penal code.

บอกบท bɔ̀ɔgbòd′ V t h e a t r. to prompt (e.g. an actor as to his lines).

บน ๑ bon′ sV 1. upper. 2. on upon (something); in (the sky). →Ant. ล่าง.

o บนโต๊ะ bontó?′ on the table.

o บนฟ้า bonfáa′ in the sky.

ข้างบน khâŋbon′ 1. upper part. 2. above, on top. 3. upstairs. →Opp. ข้างล่าง.

ชั้นบน chánbon′ upstairs, upper story, upper layer, upper shelf.

เบื้องบน bŷaŋbon′ 1. upper part, top. 2. above.

เป็นเบี้ยบน pen′bîabon′ i d i o m. 1. to be superior, on top. 2. to have the advantage, have the upper hand. 3. to outdo. ความ-- superiority.

บน ๒ bon′ V to make a vow (e.g. to a god).

บนบาน bonbaan′ V to pledge, make a vow (to render a gift, a service, etc. if one's desire is granted).

บ่น bòn′ V 1. to complain, grumble. 2. to say (something) repeatedly, over and over continnally.

ขี้บ่น khîibòn′ V c o l l o q. to be given to complaining, grumbling; to be a complainer, grumbler. คน-- a complainer, grumbler.

คำบ่น (ข้อ,ประการ) khambòn′ (khɔ̂ɔ′, prakaan′) N complaint.

บ่นถึง (1, 2) bòn′thʉ̌ŋ⊂; (2) bònthʉ̌ŋ′ V 1. to complain about. 2. c o l l o q. to talk about, mention often.

บ่นพึมพำ bòn′phympham′ to grumble, mutter, murmur.

บ่ม bòm′ V 1. to cure (tobacco). 2. to age (wine, wood). 3. to ripen (e.g. fruits normally picked green, as bananas, mangoes). 4. to train.

บรม bɔrom′, barom′, bɔrom′maɔ supreme, great; very, to the utmost degree.

ความบรมสุข khwaam′bɔrom′masùg′ N supreme happiness.

บรมโง่, โง่บรม bɔrom′ŋôo′, ŋôo′bɔrom′ colloq. to be utterly stupid, abysmally ignorant. ความ-- utter stupidity, ignorance.

บรมโบราณ bɔrom′booraan′ colloq. extremely ancient, very old.

บรมราชาภิเษก bɔrom′raachaa′phísèeg′ N eleg. coronation ceremony.

พระบรมมหาราชวัง (แห่ง) phráborom′mahăa′ɔ râadchawaŋ′ (hὲŋ′) N eleg. the grand palace.

พระบรมราชินี (องค์) phráborom′maraa′chinii′ (ʔoŋ′) N eleg. 1. the supreme queen, highest queen. 2. Her Majesty the Queen. →Opp. พระบาทสมเด็จพระเจ้าอยู่หัว the king.

พระบรมรูป (องค์) phráborom′marûub′ (ʔoŋ′) N eleg. picture, statue of the king.

พระบรมวงศานุวงศ์ (องค์) phráborom′mawoŋɔ săa′núwoŋ′ (ʔoŋ′) N eleg. royalty, member of the royal family.

พระบรมศพ phráborom′masòb′ N roy. corpse, body of a king. การ-- royal funeral.

บรรจง bancoŋ′ 1. to do neatly, carefully, painstakingly, delicately. 2. to be neatly, carefully, tidily done. →Also ผจง,ประจง lit.

บรรจงเขียน bancoŋ′khǐan′ to write neatly, clearly, legibly.

บรรจบ bancòb′ V eleg. 1. to put together, join. 2. to complete (as a cycle). 3. to meet, join, come together at one point. →Syn. 3. พบ com. →Cf. ประจบ ๒.

บรรจุ bancù?′ V eleg. 1. to fill, pack (a container, storage receptacle) with. 2. to load (a gun). 3. to fill (a vacant position) with, appoint. 4. to contain, hold, be filled with. 5. to store. →Cf. จุ,ประจุ.

ถังบรรจุน้ำมัน (ใบ) thăŋ′-bancù?′námman′ (baj′) eleg. oil storage tank, fuel tank. →Syn. ถัง น้ำมัน com.

บรรจุขวด bancù?′khùad′ eleg. V 1. to fill a bottle. 2. to be bottled (as in the following example).

o บรรจุขวดโดยบริษัท...จำกัด bancù?′khùad′- doojbɔɔrisàd′...camkàd′ bottled by the ... Company, Ltd.

บรรณ. Bound stem referring to "books, writings" in the following entries.

บรรณพิภพ ban′naphíphób′ N eleg. literary world, the world of literature.

บรรณาธิการ (คน) bannaa′thíkaan′ (khon′) N editor. →Often abbrev. บ.ก.

บรรณารักษ์ (คน) bannaa′rág′ (khon′) N librarian.

บรรดา bandaa′ N eleg. all, all of, the totality of. →Comp. ประดา colloq.

o บรรดาครู bandaa′khruu′ eleg. all teachers. →Syn. ครูทั้งหลาย com.

บรรดาศักดิ์ bandaasàg′ N the conferred title of rank of the nobility. See note under ขุนนาง.

บรรดาล. See บันดาล.

บรรได. See บันได.

บรรทัด (บรรทัด,อัน) banthád′ N 1. (horizontal) line, rule, ruled line (for writing on)(banthád′). 2. line (of writing, of print)(banthád′). 3. ruler (with a straight edge)(ʔan′).

บรรทัดฐาน banthád′thăan′ N convention, rule, standard, basis.

o หลักบรรทัดฐาน làg′-banthád′thăan′ N basis, foundation.

ไม้บรรทัด (อัน) máajbanthád′ (ʔan′) N ruler, straightedge.

บรรทุก banthúg′ V to load on (a truck, a ship, a train); to pack, pack on (the back of a pack animal).

ค่าระวางบรรทุก khâarawaaŋ′banthúg′ N eleg. shipping charge, freightage.

รถบรรทุก (คัน) ród′banthúg′ (khan′) N 1. eleg. truck. 2. freight car. →Syn. 1. รถกุดัง colloq.

เรือบรรทุกเครื่องบิน (ลำ) rya′-banthúg′khrŷaŋɔ bin′ (lam′) N aircraft carrier.

บรรเทา banthaw′ V 1. to relieve (e.g. suffering), alleviate, reduce. 2. (pain, pressure) to diminish, get less, lessen. 3. to get better (as when sick). 4. (a storm) to subside. 5. to give relief.

บรรเทาทุกข์ banthaw'thúg' V to relieve distress (e.g. by curing an illness, alleviating poverty).

บรรเทาเบาบาง banthaw'bawbaaŋ' V to subside, become less serious (of illness, distress, etc.).

บรรเทาลง banthaw'loŋ V to alleviate, reduce (e.g. pressure).

บรรพ,บรรพ- ban', ban'phaɔ, ban'pháɔ early, first, original.

ดึกดำบรรพ์ dỳg'damban' V to be ancient, belonging to antiquity.

บรรพกาล ban'phakaan' N lit. former times, ancient times.

บรรพบุรุษ (คน) ban'pháburùd' (khon') N eleg. ancestors, forebears, forefathers.

บรรยากาศ banjaa'kàad' N atmosphere.

บรรยาย banjaaj', banrajaaj' V 1. to describe, relate, narrate, explain. 2. to deliver (an address). การ-- narration, description; lecturing.

บรรลัย banlaj' V eleg. to die, to be destroyed, ruined, annihilated.

บรรลุ banlú?' V eleg. to arrive (at), reach, attain, accomplish, fulfill.

บรรลุถึงที่หมาย banlú?'thỹŋthîimǎaj' to reach one's destination.

บรรลุนิติภาวะ banlú?'nítìphaawá?', -nítì?phaaɔwá?' V law to come of age, reach legal age, attain one's majority.

บรรลุผล banlú?'phǒn' V to succeed, be successful, attain results.

บรรเลง banleeŋ' V eleg. to play music. →Cf. เพลง.

บรอนซ์ in ทองบรอนซ์ thɔɔŋpron'*, thɔɔŋpon'* N bronze. Also called ทองสัมฤทธิ์. [บรอนซ์ f. Eng.]

บริการ bɔɔrikaan' N 1. eleg. service. V 2. to serve, assist.

บริการน้ำ bɔɔrikaan'náam' N water service.

บริจาค,บริจจาค bɔɔricàag', bɔɔríd'càag' V eleg. to donate, contribute, give to charity.

บริบูรณ์ bɔɔribuun' V 1. to be complete, perfect,

full. 2. to be abundant, plentiful. →Syn. 2. มาก,อุดม.

ชั้นมัธยมบริบูรณ์ chán'-mádthajom'bɔɔribuun' N the final year of secondary school.

บริพาร (คน) bɔɔriphaan' (khon') N eleg. retinue; attendant.

บริภาษ bɔɔriphâad' V eleg. 1. to blame, accuse. 2. to censure, reproach.

บริโภค bɔɔriphôog' V eleg. to consume, eat. การ-- consumption. ผู้-- consumer. →Syn. กิน com.

บริมาตร bɔɔrimâad' N volume. →Also ปริมาตร.

บริวาร (คน,ดวง) bɔɔriwaan' (khon', duaŋ') N 1. followers, attendants, retinue (khon'). 2. astron. satellite (duaŋ').

ชาติบริวาร châad'bɔɔriwaan' satellite nation.

บริเวณ (บริเวณ,แห่ง) bɔɔriween' (bɔɔriween', hèŋ') N 1. area, region, environs, vicinity, grounds (around a building). 2. sector, zone. 3. compound, confines.

ยุทธบริเวณ (บริเวณ,แห่ง) júd'thabɔɔriween' (bɔɔriween', hèŋ') N milit. battle zone, war zone; theater command.

บริษัท (บริษัท,ห้อง,แห่ง,ที่) bɔɔrisàd' N 1. company, firm (bɔɔrisàd'). 2. euphem. toilet, water closet (hɔŋ', hèŋ', thîi'). →Syn. 2. ส้วม com., เวจ vulg.

บริสุทธิ์ bɔɔrisùd' V to be pure, unadulterated, virgin, innocent. ความ-- purity, pureness, virginity. อย่าง-- innocently, purely.

บริสุทธิ์ใจ bɔɔrisùd'caj' V to be open-hearted, sincere. ความ-- sincerity.

บริหาร bɔɔrihǎan' V 1. to administer, carry out, execute, put into effect; to run (something). การ-- administration; administering, running (something). ผู้-- an administrator, executive.

กายบริหาร kaaj'bɔɔrihǎan' N (bodily) exercise.

บริหารงาน bɔɔrihǎan'ŋaan' V to administer, execute. การ-- administration, administering.

อำนาจบริหาร ?amnâad'bɔɔrihǎan' administrative power, executive power.

บวก bùag' V 1. math. to add. 2. plus. 3. slang to collide.

เครื่องบวกเลข (เครื่อง) khrŷaŋ'bùaglêeg' (khrŷaŋ') N adding machine.

ผลบวก phǒnbùag′ N math. sum.

บ่วง (บ่วง) bùaŋ′ (bùaŋ′) N loop, snare, noose.
→Comp. ห่วง.

บวช bùad′ V to enter the priesthood (as a novice or as a priest), be ordained.

นักบวช (ท่าน, รูป, องค์) nágbùad′ (thân′, rûub′, ʔoŋ′) N ascetic, priest, hermit.

บ้วน bûan′ V to spit; to spit out (e.g. seeds of fruit).

บ้วนปาก bûanpàag′ V to rinse the mouth.

บวบ (ลูก) bùab′ (lûug′) N loufah gourd, sponge gourd.

บวม buam′ V 1. to swell, expand. 2. to be swollen.

ปอดบวม pɔɔdbuam′ N pneumonia. Short for โรค- -.

บอ bɔɔ′ V to be near crazy. →Dist. บ้า.

บ้าบอ bâabɔɔ′ V 1. to be half crazy, unbalanced. sV 2. awfully.

o บ้า ๆ บอ ๆ bâabâa′bɔɔbɔɔ′ colloq. 1. to be nuts, half crazy, unbalanced, off one's rocker (of people). 2. to be crazy, nonsensical, monkey business.

บ่อ (บ่อ) bɔ̀ɔ′ (bɔ̀ɔ′) N 1. well. 2. pond. 3. pit, mine. →Syn. 2. สระ ๒. 3. เหมือง.

น้ำบ่อ náambɔ̀ɔ′ N well water.

บ่อเกิด (แห่ง) bɔ̀ɔkə̀əd′ (hɛ̀ŋ′) N source, origin, place of origin; birthplace (e.g. of a custom).

บ่อเงิน (บ่อ) bɔ̀ɔŋən′ (bɔ̀ɔ′) N silver mine.

บ่อน้ำ (บ่อ) bɔ̀ɔnáam′ (bɔ̀ɔ′) N 1. well (for water). 2. pool.

บ่อน้ำมัน (บ่อ) bɔ̀ɔ′námman′ (bɔ̀ɔ′) N oil well.

บ่อน้ำร้อน (บ่อ) bɔ̀ɔnámrɔ́ɔn′ (bɔ̀ɔ′) N hot springs.

บอก bɔ̀ɔg′ V com. 1. to say (to), tell (something) (to), inform. 2. to tell, indicate. 3. to be told, spoken. →Syn. 1. เรียน eleg. 2. ทูล roy. →Dist. พูด "to talk, say."

คำบอก (ตอน, วรรค) khambɔ̀ɔg′ (tɔɔn′, wág′) N (oral) dictation (in class).

บอกกล่าว bɔ̀ɔgklàaw′ V to apprise, inform, mention, notify, send a notice.

บอกบท bɔ̀ɔgbòd′ V theatr. to prompt (an actor as to his lines).

บอกบุญ bɔ̀ɔgbun′ V to solicit contributions (for charity).

บอกใบ้ bɔ̀ɔgbâj′ V to tell by making signs (when speech is to be avoided); to give a high sign to.

บอกปัด bɔ̀ɔgpàd′ V colloq. to turn down, refuse.

บอกเปิด bɔ̀ɔgpə̀əd′ V colloq. obsolesc. to turn down, turn away, refuse.

บอกไม่ถูก bɔ̀ɔg′mâjthùug′ (I) can't say, can't tell exactly; (it's) hard to say, hard to tell.

บอกเล่า bɔ̀ɔglâw′ V to tell, relate (by word of mouth).

o คำบอกเล่า (อย่าง) kham′bɔ̀ɔglâw′ (jàaŋ′) N the spoken word, word (of mouth).

บอกเลิก bɔ̀ɔglə̂əg′ V 1. to revoke. 2. to give notice of termination (of an agreement). 3. to cancel (a subscription, membership, reservation).

บอกแล้วไหมล่ะ bɔ̀ɔglέεw′májlâ′↓ I told you so!

บ๋อง, บ๋องๆ bɔ̌ŋ′, bɔ̌ŋbɔ̌ŋ′* V colloq. to be nuts, half crazy, cracked, unbalanced.

บ๋องแบ๋ว bɔ̌ŋbέw′* V to be out of shape, queer-looking (of the face).

ทำหน้าบ๋องแบ๋ว thamnâa′bɔ̌ŋbέw′ V to make a wry face.

บอด bɔ̀ɔd′ V to be plugged, filled in (as the eye of a needle, an eyelet, or other small opening).

o ไฟบอดไปข้างหนึ่ง faj′bɔ̀ɔd′-pajkhâaŋ′nyŋ one headlight (of a car) is out.

ตาบอด taabɔ̀ɔd′ V to be blind.

บอน. Bound stem meaning "busy, restless."

ปากบอน pàagbɔɔn′ V colloq. to be a blabbermouth, tale-bearer, tattler. คน- - blabbermouth, blabber, tale-bearer, tattletale.

มือบอน myybɔɔn′ V colloq. to have mischievously busy hands.

บ่อน (แห่ง, บ่อน) bɔ̀n′ (hɛ̀ŋ′, bɔ̀n′)* N 1. place, den (often of undesirable activities, such as gambling, cockfighting, etc.). 2. gambling place.

บ่อนการพนัน (บ่อน) bɔ̀n′kaanphanan′ (bɔ̀n′) N gambling house, gambling den.

บอร์นีโอ bɔɔniiʔoo′ pN Borneo. [f. Eng.] →See บอร์นีโอ.

บอบ bɔ̀ɔb′, bɔ̀b′ V to be weak, worn out, run down.

บอบบาง bɔ̀ɔbbaaŋ′ V to be thin, frail.

บอบแบบ bɔ̀bbὲb′ V 1. to be fragile. 2. to be frail (of a person), fragile-looking.

บ๋อม bɔ̌m′* V to hit, strike, deliver a blow.

บอมบ์ (ลูก) bɔm′* (lûug′) N 1. bomb. V 2. to

bomb. [f. Eng.]

บอมเบย์ bɔmbee/* pN Bombay. [f. Eng.]

บ่อย bɔ̀j/* V to be often, frequent.

บ่อยครั้ง bɔ̀j/khráŋ/* many times, ofttimes.

บ่อย ๆ bɔ̀jbɔ̀j/* often, frequently, unceasingly, unremittingly.

บ๋อย (คน) bɔ̌j/* (khon/) N waiter, boy (servant in a public place, such as a hotel). [f. Eng.]

บอร์นีโอ,บอร์เนียว bɔɔnii?oo/, bɔɔniaw/ pN Borneo. [f. Eng.]

บอลล์ in ลูกบอลล์ lûugbɔn/, lûugbɔɔl/ N ball. [บอลล์ f. Eng.]

ปะ !bá/ E excl. expressing displeasure, dissatisfaction.

ปะหมี่ bamìi/ N Chinese egg noodles.

บัง baŋ/ V 1. to obstruct one's view. 2. to shield, veil, hide, cut off (from view).

บดบัง bòdbaŋ/ V 1. to obstruct, eclipse, obscure. 2. to be shielded, obscured.

บังโคลน (ข้าง) baŋkhloon/ (khâaŋ/) N 1. fender (of car). 2. mudguard (of car, bicycle).

บังแดด baŋdɛ̀ɛd/ V to shield from the sun.

บังตา (ผืน,บาน,ข้าง,คู่) baŋtaa/ N 1. view breaker, i.e. either a curtain covering the window, hung from about midpoint down (phʉ̌yn/), or a café door (baan/). 2. eyeshade; blinker (for a horse)(khâaŋ/, khûu/).

บังมืด baŋmʉ̂yd/ V to obstruct light.

เบียดบัง bìadbaŋ/ V to embezzle.

ปิดบัง pìdbaŋ/ V to hide, cover up, conceal, keep secret.

บั้ง (บั้ง) bâŋ/ (bâŋ/) N stripe (as on military uniform), mark.

บังเกิด baŋkə̀əd/ V eleg. 1. to originate. 2. to arise, occur, happen. 3. to be born. 4. to materialize. →Comp. เกิด com.

ทำให้บังเกิด thamhâj/baŋkə̀əd/ eleg. to cause, produce.

บังเกิดขึ้น baŋkə̀əd/khʉ̂n eleg. to occur.

บังเกิดผล baŋkə̀əd/phǒn/ V eleg. to bear fruit, yield results, be successful.

ผู้บังเกิดเกล้า phûu/-baŋkə̀əd/klâaw/ N eleg. parents.

แม่บังเกิดเกล้า (คน) mɛ̂ɛ/-baŋkə̀əd/klâaw/

(khon/) N eleg. one's real mother (as opposed to แม่เลี้ยง stepmother).

บังคม baŋkhom/ V to salute (the king or royalty).

กราบบังคมทูล kràab/-baŋkhom/thuun/ V roy. to address the king or queen.

ถวายบังคม thawǎaj/baŋkhom/ V roy. to salute (the king). →Syn. ไหว้ com.

บังควร baŋkhuan/ V to be proper, suitable, customary.

บังคับ baŋkháb/ V 1. to force, compel, coerce, require (someone to do something). 2. to command (as an officer). N 3. control, rule, authority. การ-- command; compulsion, compelling. ผู้-- short for ผู้บังคับการ (see below).

o ชนในบังคับอังกฤษ chon/-najbaŋkháb/?aŋkrìd/ British subjects; people under British rule.

ข้อบังคับ (ข้อ) khɔ̂ɔ/baŋkháb/ (khɔ̂ɔ/) N rule, regulation.

ข่ายบังคับ khàaj/baŋkháb/ N jurisdiction.

บังคับการ baŋkháb/kaan/ V to command, be in command.

o กองบังคับการ (กอง,แห่ง) kɔɔŋ/-baŋkháb/kaan/ (kɔɔŋ/, hɛ̀ŋ/) N milit. general headquarters.

o ผู้บังคับการ (คน,นาย) phûu/-baŋkháb/kaan/ (khon/, naaj/) commander (esp. in the lower echelons).

o ผู้บังคับการบิน (คน,นาย) phûu/baŋkháb/-kaanbin/ (khon/, naaj/) N air-commander.

บังคับใช้ baŋkháb/cháj/ V to enforce (a law).

บังคับบัญชา baŋkháb/banchaa/ V 1. to command, direct. 2. to keep in order. N 3. command, control, authority; short for ความ-- idem. การ-- commanding, directing. ผู้-- superior, head of an office; director.

บังคับเอา baŋkháb/?aw/ V to extort.

บีบบังคับ bìib/baŋkháb/ V to tyrannize, oppress. 2. to force, compel.

แบบบังคับ (แบบ) bɛ̀ɛb/baŋkháb/ (bɛ̀ɛb/) N rules.

บังเหียน (อัน) baŋhian/ (?an/) N bridle.

ถือบังเหียน thʉ̌y/baŋhian/ V 1. to hold the reins. 2. idiom. to keep under control, take over control (of).

สายบังเหียน (เส้น) sǎaj/baŋhian/ (sên/) N reins.

บังอาจ baŋ?àad/ AA dare to, to have the audacity to, have the nerve to (commit a daring deed, exceed propriety, etc.).

บังเอิญ baŋʔəən′ by chance, by accident, accidentally, unexpectedly; it happened that. →Also เผอิญ.

บัญชา banchaa′ N 1. order. V 2. to order.

  บังคับบัญชา baŋkháb′banchaa′ V 1. to command, direct. 2. to keep in order. N 3. command, control, authority; short for ความ-- idem. การ-- commanding, directing. ผู้-- superior, head of an office; director.

  บัญชาการ banchaakaan′ V to command, be in command. ผู้-- commander, commanding officer (esp. in the higher echelons).

  o กองบัญชาการ (กอง,แห่ง) kɔɔŋ′banchaakaan′ (kɔɔŋ′, hèŋ′) N milit. headquarters.

  o คำบัญชาการ (ข้อ,ประการ) kham′banchaa⊃ kaan′ (khɔɔ′, prakaan′) N order, command.

บัญชี (บัญชี,อย่าง) banchii′ (banchii′, jàaŋ′) N list; catalogue; account; bill. การ-- bookkeeping, accounting.

  ขึ้นบัญชี khŷn′banchii′ V to be registered, listed, entered in a list.

  งบบัญชี ŋób′banchii′ V 1. to close an account. 2. to calculate the balance in an account.

  บัญชีเงินฝาก banchii′ŋənfàag′ N bank account.

  บัญชีพัสดุ banchii′phádsadù?′ N eleg. inventory, list of articles.

  หักบัญชี hàg′banchii′ V to settle an account.

บัญญัติ (ข้อ,มาตรา) banjàd′ (khɔɔ′, màadtraa′) N 1. law, legal act, regulation. V 2. to prescribe.

  นิติบัญญัติ nítìbanjàd′, nítì?- N law 1. legislation. 2. (as n. mod.) legislative.

  บทบัญญัติ (ฉบับ) bòd′banjàd′ (chabàb′) N an article (of a law, a parliamentary act, a constitution).

  บัญญัติกฎหมาย banjàd′kòdmǎaj′ V to legislate, make laws and ordinances.

  พระราชบัญญัติ (ฉบับ) phrárâad′chabanjàd′ (cha⊃ bàb′) N law, act.

  o ร่างพระราชบัญญัติ râaŋ′phrárâad′chabanjàd′ N 1. bill, proposed legislation. V 2. to draft a bill.

บัณฑิต (คน) bandìd′* (khon′) N learned man, wise person, pundit.

เนติบัณฑิต (คน) nee′tìbandìd′ (khon′) N attorney; barrister-at-law.

มหาบัณฑิต mahǎa′bandìd′ N 1. the holder of a master's degree. 2. a master's degree.

ราชบัณฑิต (นาย) râad′chabandìd′ (naaj′) N member of the royal Academy.

บัด bàd′ C clf. for times, occasions.

  บัดนั้น bàdnán′ then.

  บัดนี้ bàdníi′ now, at present, at the present time.

  o ณบัดนี้ nábàd′níi′ 1. at this moment. 2. right away.

บัดกรี bàdkrii′ V to solder, weld.

บัดซบ bàdsób′ V to be silly, foolish, stupid, idiotic.

บัดสี bàdsǐi′ V 1. to feel ashamed, be ashamed. 2. to be shameful, disgraceful. ความ-- shame, shamefulness.

  น่าบัดสี nâa′bàdsǐi′ V to be shameful, disgraceful.

บัตร (ใบ) bàd′ (baj′) N 1. card (as for mailing). 2. ticket, coupon, ballot.

  กฎบัตร (ฉบับ) kòdbàd′ (chabàb′) N charter (as of the United Nations).

  กฎบัตรกฎหมาย kòdbàd′kòdmǎaj′ N colloq. law, ordinance.

  นามบัตร (แผ่น,ใบ) naambàd′ (phèn′, baj′) N 1. calling card. 2. business card.

  บัตรประจำตัว (ใบ) bàd′pracam′tua′ (baj′) N identification card.

  บัตรผ่านประตู (ใบ) bàdphàan′pratuu′ (baj′) N admission ticket.

  บัตรเสีย (ใบ) bàdsǐa′ (baj′) N a void ballot.

  บัตรออกเสียง bàd′?ɔɔgsǐaŋ′ N ballot.

  ประกาศนียบัตร (ใบ,ฉบับ) prakàad′sanii′jabàd′ (baj′, chabàb′) N certificate, diploma.

  ไปรษณียบัตร,-ย์- (ใบ) prajsanii′jabàd′, praj⊃ sanii′bàd′ (baj′) N postcard.

  ลงบัตร loŋbàd′ V to cast a ballot.

  หย่อนบัตร jɔ̀ɔnbàd′ V to drop a ballot (into a ballot box).

  หีบบัตร (ใบ) hìibbàd′ (baj′) N ballot box.

บั่น bàn′ V to cut up; to cut, chop to pieces.

  บั่นทอน bànthɔɔn′ V to cut down, shorten; to weaken; to hamper.

  บั่นรอน bànrɔɔn′ V 1. to degrade, weaken. 2. to destroy. 3. to cut off, break off (e.g. friendship).

บากบั่น bàagbàn/ V to persevere.

บุกบั่น bùgbàn/ V to brave the way, fight one's way (through something) courageously.

บั่น bàn/ N 1. part, section. C 2. clf. for parts, sections. →Comp. ท่อน,ตอน,ส่วน.

บั้นท้าย bântháaj/ N the last part, the last item.

บั้นปลาย bânplaaj/ N an end, the last part.

o ในบั้นปลาย najbân/plaaj/ at the end.

บั้นหลวง bânlŭaŋ/ C clf. for a Thai unit of dry measure for grain (equivalent to 1000 liters).

บั้นเอว (บั้นเอว) bân?ew/ (bân?ew/) N waist (of the body). →Comp. เอว.

บันดาล bandaan/ V to cause, produce, create (esp. by supernatural means). การ-- creation.

ดลบันดาล,--ใจ don/bandaan/, don/-bandaan/caj/ V 1. to cause, inspire, motivate (often implying supernatural means).

บันได (บันได,อัน) bandaj/ (bandaj/,?an/) N eleg. 1. stairs, stairway, step. 2. ladder. →Syn. กระได com.

บันไดรถ bandaj/ród/ N eleg. running board (of a car).

บันไดเวียน (อัน,บันได) bandaj/wian/ (?an/, banɔ daj/) N eleg. spiral staircase.

ราวบันได raaw/bandaj/ N eleg. railing (of a staircase), banister.

หัวบันได hŭabandaj/ N eleg. the head of the stairs, the top of a staircase.

บันทึก (ฉบับ) banthýg/ V 1. to record, note. N 2. record, brief, report, memorandum (chabàb/).

บันทึกเสียง banthýg/sĭaŋ/ to record sound, record the voice (esp. on tape). เครื่อง-- tape recorder.

บันเทา. See บรรเทา.

บันเทิง banthəəŋ/ V 1. to rejoice. 2. to feel glad, be joyful. 3. to have a good time. ความ-- entertainment, amusement, fun.

บันเทิงคดี (เรื่อง) banthəəŋ/khadii/ (rŷaŋ/) N an entertaining story.

บัลลังก์ (บัลลังก์) banlaŋ/ (banlaŋ/) N throne.

ราชบัลลังก์ (บัลลังก์) râad/chabanlaŋ/ (banlaŋ) N throne.

บัว bua/ N 1. lotus (any one of several varieties). 2. something resembling a lotus (e.g. in form).

ดอกบัว (ดอก) dɔɔgbua/ (dɔɔg/) N lotus flower.

ต้นบัว (ต้น) tônbua/ (tôn/) lotus plant.

สายบัว (สาย,กำ) săajbua/ N 1. stem of a variety of lotus (săaj/ for individual stems; kam/ for bunches).

บ่า ๑ bàa/ V to overflow, flow heavily. →Usually in the following entry.

ไหลบ่า lăj/bàa/ V to overflow, flow heavily.

บ่า ๒ (บ่า,ข้าง) bàa/ (bàa/,khâaŋ/) N shoulder. →Dist. ไหล่.

เคียงบ่าเคียงไหล่ khiaŋbàa/khiaŋlàj/ idiom., elab. colloq. 1. shoulder to shoulder. 2. on the same level.

เหลือบ่ากว่าแรง lŷabàa/kwàareeŋ/ elab. colloq. to be more than one can do, take on, shoulder.

บ้า bâa/ V to be crazy, mad, insane. ความ-- madness, insanity. คน-- insane person. →Dist. บอ.

บ้าคลั่ง bâa/khlâŋ/ V to be mad, insane.

บ้าจี้ bâacîi/ V to be extremely ticklish.

บ้าน้ำลาย bâa/námlaaj/ V slang to rave on and on, talk on and on; to be given to raving on and on.

บ้าบอ bâaboo/ V 1. to be half crazy, unbalanced, unhinged. sV 2. awfully.

o บ้า ๆ บอ ๆ bâabâa/boobɔɔ/ colloq. 1. to be nuts, half crazy, unbalanced, off one's rocker (of people). 2. to be crazy, nonsensical, monkey business.

บ้าบิ่น (1,2) bâa/bìn/; (3) bâabìn/ V 1. to be mad, reckless, foolhardy, rash. sV 2. recklessly, rashly. N 3. a kind of sweetmeat.

เป็นบ้า penbâa/ V 1. colloq. to be crazy, insane. sV 2. slang very, extremely, terribly.

o ร้อนเป็นบ้า rɔ́ɔn/penbâa/ V slang to be terribly hot.

ลมบ้าหมู lom/bâamŭu/ N 1. whirlwind. 2. epilepsy; short for โรค--.

o โรคลมบ้าหมู rôog/-lom/bâamŭu/ N epilepsy.

สุนัขบ้า (ตัว) sunág/bâa/ (tua/) N eleg. rabid dog. →Syn. หมาบ้า com.

อ้ายบ้า ?âjbâa↓ derog. epithet crazy guy!

บ้า !báa/ E excl. denoting contempt, dissatisfaction: "bah!"

บาก bàag/. See entries below.

บากบั่น bàagbàn′ V to try hard, persevere.

บากหน้า bàag′nâa′ V to swallow one's pride and turn to someone for help.

บาง ๑ (บาง) baaŋ′ (baaŋ′) N 1. waterway. 2. locality along a waterway.

บางกอก baaŋkɔ̀ɔg′ pN Bangkok, especially as in --น้อย baaŋkɔ̀ɔgnɔ́ɔj′, and --ใหญ่ baaŋkɔ̀ɔgɔ jàj′, names of districts in Bangkok.
NOTE. The usual name for the city of Bangkok in Thai is กรุงเทพฯ.

บางกะปิ baaŋkapì?′ pN Bangkapi, name of a district in Bangkok.

บางซื่อ baaŋsŷy′ pN name of a district in Bangkok.

บางนรา in แม่น้ำบางนรา mɛ̂ɛnáam′baaŋnaraa′ pN the Bangnara River, in S Thailand.

บางปะกง in แม่น้ำบางปะกง mɛ̂ɛnáam′baaŋpakoŋ′ pN the Bangpakong River, in C Thailand.

บางแสน baaŋsɛ̌ɛn′ pN Bangsæn, a beach resort along the Gulf of Thailand a few miles from Paknam.

บาง ๒ baaŋ′ V to be thin, sheer. ความ-- thinness, sheerness. →Ant. หนา.

บอบบาง bɔ̀ɔbbaaŋ′ V to be thin, frail.

บางตา baaŋ′taa′ V to thin out, dwindle, fade (in number). →Ant. หนาตา.

เบาบางลง bawbaaŋ′loŋ′ V to diminish, subside (e.g. of illness, distress, noise).

แบบบาง bɛ̀bbaaŋ′ V 1. to be delicate, frail. 2. to be slim, slender, thin.

ผ้าขาวบาง (ผืน) phâakhǎawbaaŋ′ (phʉ̌yn′) N cheesecloth, gauze.

มีดบาง (เล่ม) mîidbaaŋ′ (lêm′) N paring knife; a small thin-bladed knife.

เยื่อบาง jŷabaaŋ′ N membrane, thin tissue.

หน้าบาง nâabaaŋ′ V to have a proper shame, not be brazen, shameless. →Ant. หน้าหนา, หน้า ด้าน.

เอวบาง ?ewbaaŋ′ V to have a small waist, a slim waistline.

บาง ๓ baaŋ′ Nm some. →Always followed by a clf. →Dist. บ้าง. →Syn. ลาง colloq.

o มีลูกเห็บบ้างบางแห่ง miilûughèb′bâaŋ′-baaŋɔ hɛ̀ŋ′↓ There is some hail in some places.

บางคน baaŋkhon′ someone, some (referring to people), some people. →Syn. บางท่าน eleg.

บางครั้ง baaŋkhráŋ′ sometimes.

o เป็นบางครั้งบางคราว penbaaŋkhráŋ′baaŋkhraaw′ elab. colloq. from time to time, now and then, occasionally, once in a while.

บางคราว baaŋkhraaw′ sometimes.

บางตัว baaŋtua′ some (referring to animals or other things taking ตัว as clf.).

บางท่าน baaŋthân′ eleg. 1. someone, some (referring to people), some people. 2. some of you. →Syn. 1. บางคน com.

บางที baaŋthii′ 1. sometimes, at times. 2. other times. 3. perhaps. →Syn. 1, 2. ลางที.

บาง...บาง... baaŋ′...→ baaŋ′... some..., others... (correlative usage).

บางประการ baaŋprakaan′ of a certain kind, certain, of some sort, some sort, some.

บางราย baaŋraaj′ some case, some one (as a case), some cases.

บางเวลา baaŋweelaa′ sometimes.

บางส่วน baaŋsùan′ 1. some part, some parts. 2. in part, in some parts, partially. 3. partial.

บางสิ่ง baaŋsìŋ′ something; some of the things. →Syn. บางอย่าง.

บางสิ่งบางอย่าง baaŋsìŋ′baaŋjàaŋ′ elab. colloq. idem.

บางหน baaŋhǒn′ sometimes.

บางแห่ง baaŋhɛ̀ŋ′ (in) some places.

บางอย่าง baaŋjàaŋ′ 1. something; of some kind(s), of a certain kind. 2. some, certain (ones). →Syn. บางสิ่ง.

บางโอกาศ baaŋ?ookàad′ (on) some occasions.

บ่าง (ตัว) bàaŋ′ (tua′) N 1. flying lemur, colugo. 2. colloq. flying squirrel.

บ้าง bâaŋ′, bâŋ′ iP 1. some (out of a group). 2. in part, somewhat, to some extent. →Dist.บาง ๓. →Syn. มั่ง ๑ colloq. NOTE. When บ้าง occurs at the end of a question, it suggests that more than one item is expected to be mentioned in the answer; 5th example.

o ขอบ้าง khɔ̌ɔbâaŋ′↓, khɔ̌ɔ′bâŋ↓ Let me have some. Give me some. →Syn. ขอมั่ง colloq.

o มีลูกเห็บบ้างบางแห่ง miilûughèb′bâaŋ′-baaŋhɛ̀ŋ′↓

There is some hail in some places.

o เย็นลงบ้าง jen/loŋbâaŋ/ to cool down a little, somewhat.

o อย่างโน้นบ้างอย่างนี้บ้าง jàaŋnóon/bâŋ/-jàaŋɔ níi/bâŋ 1. a bit of this and a bit of that. 2. unclearly, making little sense. 3. hedgingly, in a roundabout manner.

o คุณจะซื้ออะไรบ้าง khuncasýy/-ʔaraj/bâŋ* What're you going to buy?

บ้างก็. . .บ้างก็. . . bâaŋ/kɔɔ. . .→bâaŋ/kɔɔ. . . some..., and some... (correlative usage).

o บ้างก็มาบ้างก็ไม่มา bâaŋ/kɔmaa/→bâaŋ/kɔmâjɔ maa/ Some do come and some don't come.

บาด ๑ bàad/ 1. to cut (as of a sharp object), wound, scar. 2. to hurt, offend. 3. to get cut, wounded.

ทำ(. . .)บาด tham(. . .)bàad/ V to wound, cut with accidentally.

o ทำมีดบาดมือ thammîid/bàadmyy/ to cut one's hand accidentally with a knife.

บาดเจ็บ bàadcèb/ V 1. to get hurt; to be injured, wounded. N 2. injury, wound.

o ได้รับบาดเจ็บ dâjráb/bàadcèb/ to be injured, get wounded.

o ทหารบาดเจ็บ thahǎan/bàadcèb/ a wounded soldier.

บาดใจ bàad/caj/ V to offend, annoy, hurt the feelings of; to be offending.

บาดตา bàad/taa/ V 1. to offend the eyes, be unpleasant to look at. 2. to hurt one's feelings upon seeing. 3. colloq. to be glaring, dazzling.

o สวยบาดตา sŭaj/bàadtaa/ colloq. to be strikingly beautiful, dazzlingly beautiful.

บาดแผล (แห่ง) bàadphlɛ̌ɛ/ (hɛ̀ŋ/) N wound, cut.

บาดโสตประสาท bàad/-sòod/prasàad/ to offend one's sense of hearing.

บาดหมาง bàadmǎaŋ/ V to be in dissension (with), in dispute (with), to have a rift.

บาดหู bàad/hǔu/ V 1. to offend one's ears, be disagreeable to hear. 2. to hurt one's feelings upon hearing.

มีดบาด mîidbàad/ V to get cut by a knife.

หญ้าบาด jâa/bàad/ V to get cut by a blade of grass.

บาด ๒ in บาดหลวง. See บาทหลวง under บาท ๑.

บาดทะยัก, โรค-- bàad/thajág/, rôogbàad/thajág/ N tetanus.

บาดาล baadaan/ N region under the earth.

น้ำบาดาล náambaadaan/ N underground water.

บาตร,บาตร์ (ใบ) bàad/ (baj/) N alms bowl of a Buddhist priest used as a receptacle for food presented to him by the pious.

คว่ำบาตร khwâmbàad/ V 1. idiom. to turn down; to disapprove of, reject. 2. to excommunicate.

ใส่บาตร sàjbàad/ V to give food to a priest, put food into a priest's bowl.

บาท ๑ (บาท) bàad/ (bàad/) N lit. 1. foot, -ped (as in biped). 2. line (of poetry). →Syn. 1. พระบาท roy., เท้า eleg., ตีน com.

บาทวิถี bàad/wíthǐi/ N eleg. footpath, sidewalk.

บาทหลวง,พระ-- (องค์) bàadlǔaŋ/, phráʔ/bàadɔ lǔaŋ/ (ʔoŋ/) N 1. Roman Catholic priest. 2. any robed Christian clergyman. →Also spelled บาดหลวง.

ฝ่าบาท fàabàad/ P roy. you (inf. sp. to low-ranking royalty).

บาท ๒ bàad/ C 1. tical, baht (monetary unit of Thailand, equivalent to 100 satangs). 2. a unit of weight, equivalent to 15 grams (the weight of a baht coin).

ไม่เต็มบาท mâjtem/bàad/ idiom. colloq. to have a screw loose, to be cracked, touched in head, not all there.

บาน ๑ baan/ C clf. for doors, window sashes, mirrors, picture frames, etc.

บานประตู (บาน) baanpratuu/ (baan/) N door panel; door.

บานพับ (อัน) baanpháb/ (ʔan/) N hinge.

บาน ๒ baan/ V to bloom, blossom, open out.

ชื่นบาน chŷynbaan/ V to be cheerful, happy.

เบ่งบาน bèŋbaan/ V to bloom.

เบิกบาน bə̀əgbaan/ V to be happy, cheerful, merry, joyful.

หน้าบาน nâa/baan/ V colloq. to beam (with pleasure), be delighted.

บาน ๓ baan/ colloq. much, a lot of.

บานตะเกียง baan/takiaŋ/ colloq. a lot.

บานตะไท baan/tathaj/ colloq. a lot, in great

quantity.

ประจันบาน pracanbaan′ V to fight at close quarters, to fight furiously.

บ้าน (หลัง) bâan′ (lǎŋ′) N 1. house, home. 2.
village, community. 3. (as n. mod.) domestic.
→Syn. 1. เรือน. →Ant. 3. ป่า.

กลับบ้านกลับช่อง klàbbâan′klàbchɔ̌ŋ′ elab.
colloq. to go home.

กลางบ้าน klaaŋbâan′ idiom. local, pertaining
to old-fashioned village folklore.

การบ้าน (อย่าง) kaanbâan′ (jàaŋ′) N 1. housework. 2. household affairs, domestic affairs.
3. homework (of students). [3. tr. f. Eng.]

ไก่บ้าน (ตัว) kàjbâan′ (tua′) N domestic fowl.

คนพื้นบ้าน khon′phýynbâan′ N native of a village,
villager.

คู่บ้านคู่เมือง khûubâan′khûumyaŋ′ elab. national;
characteristic of the country as a whole.

งานบ้าน ŋaanbâan′ N housework, household
chores.

เจ้าของบ้าน (คน) câwkhɔ̌ɔŋbâan′ (khon′) N 1.
landlord, landlady. 2. houseowner. 3. host,
hostess. →Also เจ้าบ้าน.

ชานบ้าน chaanbâan′ N the premises (around a
house).

ชาวบ้าน (คน) chaawbâan′ (khon′) N 1. villager,
commoner; the common folk. 2. neighbor.

ชาวบ้านร้านตลาด chaawbâan′-ráan′talàad′ N
elab. colloq. the whole neighborhood.

ตั้งบ้าน ๑ tâŋ′bâan′ to settle down. →See ตั้ง ๓.

ตั้งบ้าน ๒ tâŋbâan′ colloq. much, a lot. →See
ตั้ง ๒.

ตามบ้าน taambâan′ around the house.

ที่บ้าน thîibâan′ at home, those at home; joc.
one's spouse.

บ้านเกิด (แห่ง) bâankə̀əd′ (hɛ̀ŋ′) N birthplace.

o บ้านเกิดเมืองนอน bâankə̀əd′myaŋnɔɔn′ N
elab. colloq. motherland, homeland. →Syn.
ปิตุภูมิ.

บ้านช่อง bâanchɔ̂ŋ′ N colloq. home, house.

o ตึกรามบ้านช่อง tỳgraam′bâanchɔ̂ŋ′ N elab.
colloq. buildings (of all kinds, collectively).

บ้านเดิม (แห่ง) bâandəəm′ (hɛ̀ŋ′) N home town,
native town.

บ้านนอก bâannɔ̂ɔg′ N colloq. 1. the country
(as opposed to the city), countryside, rural area.
2. (as n. mod.) rural, countrified.

o ชาวบ้านนอก (คน) chaawbâannɔ̂ɔg′ (khon′) N
colloq. country people.

บ้านผีสิง (หลัง) bâan′phǐisǐŋ′ (lǎŋ′) N a haunted
house.

บ้านพัก (หลัง) bâanphág′ (lǎŋ′) N home, residence,
quarters, lodging; rest-house.

บ้านเมือง bâanmyaŋ′ N country, the country.

บ้านเรือน (หลัง) bâan′ryan′ (lǎŋ′) N house,
home.

o ละแวกบ้านเรือน lawɛ̂ɛg′bâanryan′ N residential
area; settlement.

บ้านไร่ (หลัง) bâanrâj′ (lǎŋ′) N farm house.

บ้านว่าง (หลัง) bâanwâaŋ′ (lǎŋ′) N vacant house.

ผู้ใหญ่บ้าน (คน,นาย) phûujàjbâan′ (khon′, naaj′)
N elected head of a village.

พวกบ้าน phûagbâan′ N the folks, the family (e.g.
of such and such a person).

พ่อบ้าน (คน) phɔ̂ɔbâan′ (khon′) N head of a
family (male).

เพื่อนบ้าน (คน) phɯ̂anbâan′ (khon′) N neighbor.

o เพื่อนบ้านใกล้เคียง phɯ̂anbâan′klâjkhiaŋ′ N
next door neighbor, immediate neighbors.

แม่บ้าน (คน) mɛ̂ɛbâan′ (khon′) N housewife.

ย้ายบ้าน jáajbâan′ V to move (one's place of residence).

รั้วบ้าน (รั้ว) rúabâan′ (rúa′) N fence.

ละแวกบ้าน lawɛ̂ɛgbâan′ N community, inhabited
or settled area, area where people live.

หน้าบ้าน nâabâan′ N 1. the area in front of a house.
2. facade of a house. 3. in front of the house.

หนูบ้าน (ตัว) nǔubâan′ (tua′) N house rat.

หมอประจำบ้าน (คน) mɔ̌ɔ′pracambâan′ (khon′)
N family doctor.

หมู่บ้าน (หมู่,แห่ง) mùubâan′ (mùu′, hɛ̀ŋ′) N
village, group of houses.

หลังบ้าน lǎŋbâan′ behind the house, in the back
of the house.

อยู่บ้าน jùubâan′ to be at home.

บ้านดอน bâandɔɔn′ pN Bandon, in S Thailand.

บ้านดารา bâandaaraa′ pN Bandara, in N Thailand.

บ้านโป่ง bâanpòoŋ′ pN Banpong, in C Thailand.

บ้านหมี่ bâanmìi′ pN Banmi, name of an amphoe in the chāngwat of Lopburi.

บาป bàab′ N sin; fault.

   บาปกรรม bàabkam′ N 1. sin. V 2. to be sinful.

บ่าย ๑ bàaj′ V to turn (e.g. in such and such direction).

   บ่ายเบี่ยง bàajbìaŋ′ V 1. to evade, avoid. 2. to equivocate, act evasively.

   บ่ายหน้า bàaj′nâa′ V to head for, head toward, face toward.

บ่าย ๒ bàaj′ N 1. afternoon. V 2. to be afternoon.

   เช้า สาย บ่าย เย็น ก็ได้ cháaw′ sǎaj′ bàaj′ jen′ kɔ̂dâaj′ any time during the day; "early morning, late morning, afternoon, evening."

   ตกบ่าย tògbàaj′ 1. to be afternoon. 2. in the afternoon, when the afternoon sets in.

   ตอนบ่าย tɔɔnbàaj′ the afternoon, in the afternoon.

   บ่ายคล้อย bàajkhlɔ́ɔj′ 1. the late afternoon. 2. to be late afternoon.

   บ่ายโมง bàajmooŋ′ 1 P. M., one o'clock in the afternoon.

   บ่ายสองโมง bàaj′sɔ̌ɔŋmooŋ′ 2 P. M., two o'clock in the afternoon.

   เมื่อบ่าย mŷabàaj′ in the afternoon, this afternoon.

   เวลาบ่าย weelaabàaj′ N 1. the afternoon. 2. in the afternoon.

บาล baan′ V to tend, look after.

   กฎมนเทียรบาล kòd′-monthian′baan′ N laws pertaining to royalty.

   โคบาล khoobaan′ N eleg. 1. cowherd. 2. cowboy.

   สันติบาล sǎn′tibaan′ N 1. maintenance of peace. 2. city police.

บาลี baalii′ N Pali (the language of the Buddhist texts).

   ภาษาบาลี phaasǎa′baalii′ N the Pali language.

บ่าว (คน) bàaw′ (khon′) N 1. servant; attendant. P 2. (servant or vendor sp.) I, me.

   คู่บ่าวสาว (คู่) khûu′bàawsǎaw′ (khûu′) N bride and groom.

   เจ้าบ่าว (คน) câwbàaw′ (khon′) N groom.

   บ่าวไพร่ (คน) bàawphrâj′ (khon′) N elab. colloq. servant.

บาศก์ in ลูกบาศก์ (ลูก) lûugbàad′ (lûug′) N cube.

บานาญ bamnaan′ N pension, reward.

   เบี้ยบานาญ bîa′bamnaan′ N pension.

บำบัด bambàd′ V to remedy, cure.

บำเพ็ญ bamphen′ V eleg. to do, perform.

   บำเพ็ญตน bamphen′ton′ V to behave, conduct oneself.

บำรุง bamruŋ′ V to cherish, take care of, care for, support, promote, improve. การ-- improvement (as of a condition), promotion (as of a cause).

   ค่าบำรุง khâa′bamruŋ′ N subscription, membership fee, dues.

   ทะนุบำรุง,ทำนุบำรุง thanú?′bamruŋ′, thamnú?bamɔruŋ′ V 1. to nourish. 2. hort. to tend (plants) with care. 3. to improve.

   น้ำบำรุงผม náam′-bamruŋ′phǒm′ N hair tonic, lotion.

   บำรุงเลี้ยง bamruŋ′líaŋ′ V to feed, nourish, foster, take good care of.

บำเรอ bamrəə′ V 1. to entertain, amuse. 2. to tend, serve. เครื่อง-- entertainment.

   นางบำเรอ (คน) naaŋbamrəə′ (khon′) N 1. "lady of pleasure," e.g. as employed in a night club or dance hall. 2. mistress, unlawful wife.

บำเหน็จ bamnèd′ N 1. reward, bonus, premium, compensation. V 2. to give a reward.

บิ bì?′ V to break off (a small piece) with one's fingers, pinch off.

บิด bìd′ V 1. to twist, wring. 2. colloq. to temporize, to resort to various expedients (e.g. making excuses, inventing diversions) in order to evade obeying a command, to worm out of (a commitment). N 3. short for โรค-- (see below).

   บิดตะกูด bìd′takùud′ idem บิด mng. 2.

   บิดเบือน bìd′byan′ V 1. to twist, distort, misrepresent. 2. to worm out of (a commitment).

   บิดผัน bìd′phǎn′ V to evade.

   บิดพริ้ว bìd′phríw′ V 1. to evade. 2. to refuse (to do something), disobey. การ-- evasion; refusal.

   โรคบิด rôogbìd′ N dysentery.

   ลูกบิดประตู (ลูก,อัน) lûugbìd′pratuu′ (lûug′, ?an′) N doorknob; door handle (i.e. one which can be turned).

เล่นไม้บิด lên'máajbìd' V idiom. to balk, to worm out of (a commitment).

บิดา (คน) bìdaa' (khon') N lit. father. →Syn. พ่อ com., คุณพ่อ eleg.

บิดามารดา (คน) bìdaa'maandaa' (khon') N lit. parents. →Syn. พ่อแม่ com., คุณพ่อคุณแม่ eleg.

ผู้บิดา phûu'bìdaa' N lit. the father: "the one who is the father."

บิน bin' V to fly. การ--, เครื่อง--, นัก-- (see below).

การบิน kaanbin' N 1. flying. 2. aviation.

o สายการบิน sǎaj'kaanbin' 1. an air route. 2. an air line (system or company).

ขวัญบิน khwǎnbin' V idiom. to be startled, terrified, frightened, scared. →Syn. See ตกใจ.

เครื่องบิน (ลำ, เครื่อง) khrŷaŋbin' (lam', khrŷaŋ') N aircraft.

o เครื่องบินขับไล่ (เครื่อง) khrŷaŋbin'khàblâj' (khrŷaŋ') N pursuit plane, fighter plane.

o เครื่องบินทิ้งระเบิด (ลำ) khrŷaŋbin'thíŋraꞓbɔ̀ɔd' (lam') N bomber.

จานบิน (ลำ) caanbin' (lam') N flying saucer.

นักบิน (คน) nágbin' (khon') N aviator, pilot.

บินขึ้น binkhŷn' V to take off (of aircraft).

บินไปบินมา binpaj'binmaa' to fly back and forth, hither and thither.

บินลง binloŋ' V to land (of aircraft).

บินว่อน binwɔ̀n' V to swarm about (in the air) (e.g. of airplanes, of insects).

โบยบิน boojbin' V to fly (of winged creatures).

ป้อมบิน (ลำ) pɔ̂mbin' (lam') N superfortress, flying fortress (aircraft).

ฝูงบิน fǔuŋbin' (fǔuŋ') N milit. a group of airplanes.

เรือบิน (ลำ, เครื่อง) ryabin' (lam', khrŷaŋ') N airplane.

สนามบิน (สนาม, แห่ง) sanǎambin' (sanǎam', hèŋ') N airport, airfield, airstrip.

บิ่น bìn' V to get nicked, notched (of a blade); to get chipped (at the edge).

ทำ(...)บิ่น tham'(...)bìn' to nick, chip (the edge or blade of something).

บ้าบิ่น (1, 2) bâa'bìn'; (3) bâabìn' V 1. to be mad,

reckless, foolhardy, rash. sV 2. madly, recklessly, rashly. N 3. a kind of sweetmeat.

บี. bii' the English letter "B." [f. Eng.]

บี้ bîi' V 1. to crush, press, compress. 2. to be crushed.

บีบ bìib' V to squeeze, press.

บีบคอ bìibkhɔɔ' V to strangle.

บีบคั้น bìibkhán' V 1. to compress, crush, squeeze out. 2. idiom. to oppress.

บีบแตร bìibtrɛɛ' V to blow or honk a horn.

บีบนวด bìibnûad' V to massage by kneading (the flesh).

บีบบังคับ bìib'baŋkháb' V 1. to tyrannize, oppress. 2. to force, compel.

บึกบึน bỳgbyn' V 1. to be tough, strong (implying bodily strength). 2. to be insistent, unyielding.

บึง (บึง) byŋ' (byŋ') N a large swamp.

บึ่ง bỳŋ' V colloq. to go very fast, to speed (as in driving an automobile).

บึ้ง ๑ bŷŋ' V to be sullen, serious, strained, unsmiling (of the face).

บึ้งตึง bŷŋtyŋ' V 1. to be sullen, sulky, cross. 2. to be stern.

หน้าบึ้ง nâabŷŋ' V to scowl, be stern faced, have a sulky face.

บึ้ง ๒ in ก้นบึ้ง kônbŷŋ' N the bottom way down, way down at the bottom.

บึน. See บึกบึน.

บุ bù?' V to line (i.e. to put in a lining).

บุก ๑ bùg' V 1. to invade. 2. to attack, drive forward. 3. to be on the offensive (as in war, sports).

การบุกเข้ายึด kaanbùg'khâwjýd' N invasion.

บุกเข้าไป bùg'khâwpaj' V to invade.

บุกบั่น bùgbàn' V to brave the way, fight one's way (through something courageously).

บุกเบิก bùgbə̀əg' V to clear (land) (as for cultivation).

บุกรุก bùgrúg' V 1. to invade. 2. to trespass.

ฝ่ายบุก fàajbùg' N the offense, the side on the offensive (in sports, war).

บุก ๒ in ดีบุก diibùg' N tin.

แร่ดีบุก rɛ̂ɛ'diibùg' N tin ore.

บุก, บุค búg' V colloq. to book, reserve. [f. Eng.]

บุคคล (คน) bùgkhon' (khon') N person, individual.

บุคคลใด bùgkhon'daj' whoever, any individual.

บุคคลพลัดถิ่น bùgkhon'phládthìn' refugee, displaced person.

ส่วนบุคคล sùan'bùgkhon' private, personal, individual (as opposed to public, collective). →Syn. ส่วนตัว. →Ant. ส่วนรวม.

บุคคลิก in the following entries.

บุคคลิกภาพ bùg'khalíg'kaphâab' N eleg. individuality, personality.

บุคคลิกลักษณะ bùg'khalíg'lág'sanà?' N eleg. psych. personality.

บุ้ง (ตัว,อัน) bûŋ' N 1. hairy caterpillar (tua'). 2. rasp (?an'). →Also 1. ตัวบุ้ง. →Dist. 1. ตัวแก้ว,หนอน.

ผักบุ้ง (ต้น) phàgbûŋ' (tôn') N convolvulus, an aquatic morning glory used as a green vegetable (Convolvulaceae).

บุญ bun' N merit (in the Buddhist sense), virtue.

ใจบุญ cajbun' V 1. to be generous, charitable, 2. to be pious.

ตามบุญตามกรรม taambun'taamkam' letting nature take its course, leaving it to fate.

ทำบุญ thambun' V to perform meritorious deeds, such as the giving of alms: "to make merit."

นักบุญ (คน) nágbun' (khon') N saint.

บอกบุญ bɔ̀ɔgbun' V to solicit contributions (for charity or meritorious deeds).

บุญธรรม buntham'. See entry below.

o บุตรบุญธรรม (คน) bùd'buntham' (khon') N eleg. adopted child. →Syn. See ลูกเลี้ยง. com.

o ลูกบุญธรรม (คน) lûug'buntham' (khon') idem. เป็นบุญ penbun' V to be fortunate.

บุตร (คน) bùd' (khon') N eleg. child (one's direct descendant). →Syn. ลูก com.

บุตรชาย (คน) bùdchaaj' (khon') N eleg. son. →Syn. ลูกชาย com.

บุตรธิดา (คน) bùd'thídaa' (khon') N eleg. sons and daughters.

บุตรสาว (คน) bùdsǎaw' (khon') N eleg. daughter. →Syn. See ลูกสาว com.

บุตรหญิง (คน) bùdjǐŋ' (khon') N eleg. daughter. →Syn. See ลูกสาว com.

บุตรา (คน) bùdtraa' (khon') N lit. son. →Syn. ลูกชาย com.

บุตรี (คน) bùdtrii' (khon') N lit. daughter. →Syn. See ลูกสาว com.

บุบ bùb' V 1. to be indented, deformed, out of shape. 2. to crush lightly, pound lightly (in a pestle).

บุบสลาย bùb'salǎaj' V to be damaged.

บุปผชาติ bùb'phachâad' N lit. flowers.

บุพ bùb'phaɔ "first, former" as in the following entry.

บุพบท bùb'phabòd' N gram. preposition.

บุ๋ม bǔm' V 1. to be depressed (have a depression), be dented. 2. to be concave.

รอยบุ๋ม rɔɔjbǔm' N impression, indentation (in something soft, e.g. the flesh, clay, etc.).

บุ้ย bûj' V 1. to protrude the lips (as when signalling with them). 2. colloq. to signal with the lips. →Comp. ใบ้.

บุ้ยใบ้ bûjbâj' V to signal by means of the lips and gestures.

บุรพ as in บุรพทิศ buraphathíd' N lit.,eleg. east. →Syn. ทิศตะวันออก com. →See บูรพา.

บุรี (แห่ง) burii' (hèŋ') N eleg. city, town. →Chiefly used as final member of compound names of towns.

จันทบุรี can'thaburii' pN Čhanthaburi, a township in C Thailand, SE of Bangkok.

ชลบุรี chon'burii' pN Chonburi (Jolburi), a township on the E coast of the Gulf of Thailand.

บุรีรัมย์ burii'ram' pN Buriram, a township in NE Thailand.

ลพบุรี lób'burii' pN Lopburi, a township in C Thailand, N of Bangkok.

บุรุษ (คน) burùd'*(khon') N eleg. 1. man, male (of people). 2. gram. person. →Syn. 1. ชาย com.

เชษฐบุรุษ (คน) chêed'thaburùd' (khon') N eleg. a great statesman.

บรรพบุรุษ (คน) ban'pháburùd' (khon') N eleg. ancestors, forebears, forefathers.

บุรุษที่หนึ่ง burùd'thîinyŋ' N gram. first person.

บุรุษไปรษณีย์ (คน) burùd'prajsanii' (khon') N mailman, postman.

รัฐบุรุษ (คน) rád'thaburùd' (khon') N statesman.

โรคบุรุษ rôog'burùd' N venereal disease (contracted by a woman). →Cf. โรคผู้หญิง.

วีรบุรุษ (คน) wii'ráburùd' (khon') N hero (especially war hero).

สุภาพบุรุษ (คน) suphâab′burùd′ (khon′) N eleg. gentleman.

บุโรทั่ง buroo′thâŋ′ V colloq. to be old and worn out.

บุหรี่ (มวน) burìi′ (muan′) N cigar; cigarette.

ขี้บุหรี่ khîiburìi′ N cigarette ashes.

คอบุหรี่ (คน) khɔɔ′burìi′ (khon′) N idiom. a heavy smoker.

จุดบุหรี่ cùd′burìi′ V to light a cigarette.

ซองบุหรี่ (อัน,ซอง) sɔɔŋ′burìi′ N cigarette case (ʔan′); flip-top box for cigarettes, cigarette package (of paper)(sɔɔŋ′).

ที่เขี่ยบุหรี่ (ที่,อัน) thîikhìa′burìi′ (thîi′,ʔan′) N ash tray.

นักเลงบุหรี่ (คน) nágleeŋ′burìi′ (khon′) N a heavy smoker.

หีบบุหรี่ (ใบ) hìib′burìi′ (baj′) N cigarette box.

บุ๋ม bǔu′ V to be dented, distorted.

บุ๋บี้ bǔubîi′ V to be dented, out of shape.

บู๊ búu′ V colloq. to fight. [f.Chin.]

บูชา buuchaa′ V 1. to sacrifice, to offer (something as a sacrifice) with veneration (as to a deity). 2. to adore (religiously), to worship.

แท่นบูชา (แท่น) thên′buuchaa′ (thên′) N altar.

บูด bùud′ V 1. to be rancid, spoiled (of food). 2. to be sullen; (one's face) to reflect displeasure or ill-humor.

บูดเบี้ยว,เบี้ยวบูด bùudbîaw′,bîawbùud′ V 1. to be sullen. 2. to be twisted, distorted.

หน้าบูด nâabùud′ V to have a sullen face, a long face.

หน้าเบ้บูดเบี้ยว nâa′bêe′-bùud′bîaw′ to have a puckered up face, a long face, a wry face (as from eating sour things, from having to do something one does not like, from being about to cry).

เหม็นบูด mĕnbùud′ V to smell very bad (of spoiled food).

บูรณะ buuraná?′ V eleg. 1. to reconstruct, rehabilitate. 2. to repair, restore, improve. 3. to maintain, support. การ-- reconstruction, rehabilitation; repair(s), restoration.

บูรพ as in บูรพชน (คน) buu′raphachon′ (khon′)

N lit. ancestor.

บูรพา buuraphaa′ N eleg.,lit. east. →Syn. ตะวัน ออก com. →The literary and the common terms for the eight chief points of the compass are listed under ทิศ.

ชาวบูรพา (คน) chaaw′buuraphaa′ (khon′) N eleg.,lit. Easterner, Oriental.

บูรพาทิศ buuraphaa′thíd′ N eleg.,lit. east.

บุโรทั่ง. See บุโรทั่ง.

เบ้ bêe′ V 1. to be twisted, puckered up, distorted (of facial expression). 2. slang to be broke (have no money). →Comp. 1. เบะ.

ทรัพย์เบ้ sáb′bêe′ V slang to be broke.

หน้าเบ้บูดเบี้ยว nâa′bêe′-bùud′bîaw′ to have a puckered up face, a long face, a wry face (as from eating sour things, from having to do something one does not like, from being about to cry).

เบ่ง bèŋ′* V 1. to swell out, expand, enlarge. 2. to be swollen, enlarged. 3. slang to speed. 4. slang to boast, act big. การ-- slang boasting, showing off one's superiority, acting big.

เบ่งบาน bèŋbaan′ V to bloom.

เบ่งไป bèŋ′pajɔ V slang to go very fast.

เบ่งเสียง bèŋsĭaŋ′ V 1. to shout, talk loud. 2. to increase the volume of the voice (as in singing).

เบ่ง in บ่งเบ่ง bóŋbéŋ′* V slang to make a loud noise; to be loud, noisy.

เบญจ- ben′cazɔ* eleg. combining form meaning "five". →Also ปัญจ-. →Syn. ห้า com.

เบ็ด ๑ (ตัว,อัน,คัน) bèd′ N 1. fishhook (tua′,ʔan′). 2. short for คันเบ็ด (khan′).

คันเบ็ด (คัน) khanbèd′ (khan′) N a fishing rod.

ตกเบ็ด tògbèd′ V to fish with hook and bait.

เบ็ด ๒ in เบ็ดเสร็จ bèdsèd′ total, altogether.

คิดเบ็ดเสร็จ khíd′bèdsèd′ to total, total up.

เบ็ดเตล็ด bèdtalèd′ 1. odds and ends. 2. small and varied, miscellaneous.

การแสดงเบ็ดเตล็ด kaansadɛɛŋ′bèdtalèd′ N skit, short revue.

ของเบ็ดเตล็ด khɔ̌ɔŋ′bèdtalèd′ N miscellaneous little things, trinkets, varieties (such as are sold in a variety store).

งานเบ็ดเตล็ด (อย่าง) ŋaan′bèdtalèd′ (jàaŋ′) N

odd jobs.

เบน **been´** V 1. to turn, turn away, swerve. 2. to change direction, deviate, deflect.

เบนหัว **beenhǔa´** V 1. to turn one's head to one side. 2. (a vehicle) to change direction; to head (a vehicle or mount) in a different direction.

เบี่ยงเบน **bìaŋbeen´** V tech. to deviate.

เบนซิน, เบ็นซิน, น้ำมัน-- **bensin´, námman´bensin´*** N 1. benzine. 2. colloq. gasoline. [f. Eur.]

เบอ **bəə´** V 1. to be severe (of a cut, an open wound). sV 2. seriously, severely, badly (cut, etc.).

เบอร์ **bəə´** N number. [f. Eng.]

หวยเบอร์ (ใบ) **hǔajbəə´ (baj´)** N colloq. lottery ticket. →Syn. ลอตเตอรี่ com., สลาก กินแบ่ง eleg.

เบอร์ลิน **bəəlin´** pN Berlin. [f. Eng.]

เบ้อเร่อ **bə̂ərə̂ə´** V colloq. to be enormously big, huge.

เบะ **bè?´** V 1. to be screwed up (as the face or mouth of one who is about to cry), wry, twisted. sV 2. colloq. plenty, much. →Comp. 1. เบ้.

เบา **baw´** V 1. to be light (in weight). 2. to be low (not loud). 3. colloq. to slow down, stop (as a bus). 4. euphem. to urinate. N 5. euphem. urine. sV 6. softly, lightly, quite lightly. →Ant. 1. หนัก. →Syn. 4, 5. เยี่ยว com.

ข้าวเบา **khâawbaw´** N a rapidly maturing variety of rice. →Ant. ข้าวหนัก.

ความหนักเบา **khwaam´nàgbaw´** N degree of severity.

ใจเบา **cajbaw´** V to be easily influenced, easily swayed, credulous, gullible.

เดินเบา **dəən´baw´** V to walk softly, lightly, quietly.

บรรเทาเบาบาง **banthaw´bawbaaŋ´** V to subside, become less serious (of illness, distress, etc.).

เบาเครื่อง **bawkhrɯ̂aŋ´** V to slow down the engine.

เบาใจ **bawcaj´** V 1. to be light-hearted, to take things easy. 2. to be relieved.

o นำเบาใจ **nâa´bawcaj´** V to be conducive of relief (as from worry).

เบาบางลง **bawbaaŋ´loŋ´** V to diminish, subside (e.g. of illness, distress, noise).

เบา ๆ **bawbaw´** sV softly, lightly, gently, quietly.

เบามือ **baw´myy´** V 1. to be gentle (with), touch lightly. 2. (one's work) to be light, to have little to do.

เบารถ **bawród´** V to slow down a car, stop a car.

เบาแรง **bawrɛɛŋ´** V to be labor-saving, easy to operate.

เบาลง **baw´loŋ** V 1. to become lighter. 2. to slow down.

เบาหวิว **baw´wǐw´** V colloq. to be light as a feather.

เบาโหวง **baw´wǒoŋ´** V colloq. idem.

แบ่งเบา **bɛ̀ŋ´baw´** V to lessen, ease, lighten (as a burden or task).

ผ่อนหนักผ่อนเบา **phɔ̀nnàg´phɔ̀nbaw´** V idiom. to ease tension by compromise or mutual concession.

ย่องเบา **jɔ̂ŋbaw´** V to steal, pilfer by sneaking (into someone's house).

หูเบา **hǔubaw´** V to be credulous.

อย่างเบาที่สุด **jàaŋbaw´thîisùd´** most lightly, in the lightest manner; most gently, softly.

เบ้า (เบ้า, ใบ) **bâw´ (bâw´, baj´)** N 1. crucible. 2. socket.

จมเบ้า **com´bâw´** slang to be glued to one's place, remain in one's place for an inordinately long period.

เบ้าตา (เบ้า) **bâwtaa´ (bâw´)** N eye socket.

เบาะ (ใบ, อัน) **bɔ̀?´ (baj´, ?an´)** N 1. cushion. 2. small, soft, lightly stuffed mattress used for infants.

เบาะ ๆ **bɔ̀?bɔ̀?´** sV lightly, slightly.

เบาะประทับตรา (แผ่น, อัน) **bɔ̀?-pratháb´traa´ (phɛ̀n´, ?an´)** N stamp pad.

เบาะรองเท้า (ตัว, ใบ) **bɔ̀?´-rɔɔŋ´tháaw´ (tua´, baj´)** N footstool, hassock, cushion for the feet.

เบาะแส **bɔ̀?sɛɛ´** N inkling, clue, hint, trace.

o รู้เบาะแส **rúu´bɔ̀?sɛɛ´** to have a vague knowledge about, to have an inkling about.

เบิก **bə̀əg´** V 1. to widen, expand (an opening of any kind). 2. to open widely (e.g. the eyes). 3. to withdraw (money), draw (salary). 4. to order, requisition (as from a storeroom).

ไถเบิก **thǎj´bə̀əg´** V to plow up.

บุกเบิก bùg′bəəg′ V to clear (land) (as for cultivation).

เบิกความ bəəgkhwaam′ V to testify.

เบิกเงิน bəəgŋən′ V 1. to withdraw money (from the bank). 2. to draw (one's salary).

o ใบเบิกเงิน (ใบ) baj′bəəgŋən′ (baj′) N bank. withdrawal slip.

เบิกตัว bəəg′tua′ V to lead in, to announce (the presence of).

เบิกตา bəəg′taa′ V to open the eyes wide (as when frightened).

เบิกทาง bəəg′thaaŋ′ V to make way, clear the way (for traffic); to open a route (to traffic).

เบิกบาน bəəgbaan′ V to be happy, cheerful, merry, joyful.

o เป็นที่เบิกบาน penthîi′bəəgbaan′ enjoyably, joyfully.

เบิกโรง bəəg′rooŋ′ V 1. to perform an introductory play. N 2. an introductory play (before the main performance), curtain raiser.

เบิกสมัย bəəg′samǎj′ V to pioneer, introduce an age, open an era.

เบิ่ง bə̀ŋ′, bə̀əŋ′ V 1. to open the eyes wide, to stare. 2. (a buffalo) to look up or turn the head with a stare.

เบิ่งตา bə̀ŋtaa′, bə̀əŋ′taa′ V to open the eyes wide; to stare.

เบิ้ม bə̂m′* V colloq. to be big, important.

พี่เบิ้ม (คน) phîibə̂m′ (khon′) N colloq. 1. a big shot. 2. a gang leader.

เบี้ย (อัน) bîa′ (ʔan′) N 1. cowrie shell. 2. money.

ดอกเบี้ย dɔ̀ɔgbîa′ N interest (on money loaned or deposited).

เบี้ยน้อยหอยน้อย bîanɔ́ɔj′hɔ̌jnɔ́ɔj′ elab. colloq. poor, having little money.

เบี้ยบำนาญ bîa′bamnaan′ N pension.

เบี้ยประกันภัย bîa′-prakan′phaj′ N insurance fee, premium.

เบี้ยเลี้ยง bîalîaŋ′ N special allowance (as for travel, special expenses, etc.).

เบี้ยหวัด bîawàd′ N annual salary.

เป็นเบี้ยบน pen′bîabon′ idiom. 1. to be superior, on top. 2. to have the advantage, have the upper hand. 3. to outdo.

เป็นเบี้ยล่าง pen′bîalâaŋ′ idiom. to be inferior, lower, underneath. 2. to be at a disadvantage. 3. to be outdone.

แม่เบี้ย mɛ̂ɛbîa′ N hood (of a cobra).

o เป็นแม่เบี้ย pen′mɛ̂ɛbîa′ V colloq. to be overbearing, bossy.

ไล่เบี้ย lâjbîa′ V colloq. 1. to question exhaustively and provocatively. 2. to scold, bawl out (usually unjustly). 3. to bawl (everyone) out right on down the line.

เบี่ยง bìaŋ′ V 1. to sidestep, evade. 2. to swerve.

เบี่ยงตัว bìaŋtua′ V to dodge, swerve.

เบี่ยงบ่าย, บ่ายเบี่ยง bìaŋbàaj′, bàajbìaŋ′ V 1. to evade, avoid. 2. to equivocate, act evasively.

เบี่ยงเบน bìaŋbeen′ V tech. to deviate.

เบียด bìad′ V 1. to press (together). 2. to press or crowd into. 3. to squeeze in. 4. slang to get married.

เบียดกัน bìad′kan′ V to huddle close together, to crowd together.

เบียดบัง bìadbaŋ′ V to embezzle.

เบียดเบียน, เบียดเบียฬ bìadbian′ V 1. to oppress, persecute. 2. to sponge off (of somebody), be an expense (to somebody).

เบียดเสียด bìadsìad′ V to be dense, congested, crowded.

o เบียดเสียดเข้าไป bìadsìad′khâwpaj′ to crowd (one's way) into, edge (one's way) through.

o เบียดเสียดเยียดยัด bìadsìad′jîadjád′ V to be crowded, congested; to be densely profuse.

เบียน bian′ V to oppress, persecute. →Also เบียฬ FS.

เบียดเบียน, เบียดเบียฬ bìadbian′ V 1. to oppress, persecute. 2. to sponge off (of somebody), be an expense (to somebody).

เบียร์ bia′ N beer. [f. Eng.]

เบี้ยว bîaw′ V to be out of shape, distorted, irregular (uneven), misshapen.

บูดเบี้ยว, เบี้ยวบูด bùudbîaw′, bîawbùud′ V 1. to be sullen. 2. to be twisted, distorted.

เบียฬ FS. See เบียน.

เบื่อ bỳa′ V to be tired of (something), bored (with).

น่าเบื่อ nâabỳa′ to be tiresome, boring, tedious.

ความ-- tiresomeness, tediousness.

เบื่อหน่าย bỳanàaj′ V to be tired of (something), bored (with). ความ-- boredom.

o น่าเบื่อหน่าย nâa′bỳanàaj′ to be tiresome, irksome, tedious, wearisome. ความ-- tire-someness, irksomeness.

เหม็นเบื่อ mĕnbỳa′ V colloq. to be fed up, bored, disgusted (with).

เบื้อ (ตัว) bỳa′ (tua′) N wild animal (general term).

เป็นเบื้อ penbỳa′ V colloq. to be mute, silent, dumb, speechless.

เบื้อง bỳaŋ′ C clf. for side, part.

เบื้องขวา bỳaŋkhwǎa′ at the right.

เบื้องต้น bỳaŋtôn′ eleg. 1. the beginning part, elementary part. 2. at the beginning. 3. (as n. mod.) introductory, preliminary. →Ant. เบื้องปลาย.

เบื้องบน bỳaŋbon′ upper part, top; above.

เบื้องปลาย bỳaŋplaaj′ eleg. 1. the final part, end part. 2. at the end. →Ant. เบื้องต้น.

เบื้องแรก bỳaŋrɛ̂ɛg′ at first.

เบื้องล่าง bỳaŋlâaŋ′ below, beneath.

เบื้องว่า bỳaŋ′wâaɔ lit. as for, as to.

เบื้องหน้า bỳaŋnâa′ ahead, in front; in the future.

เบื้องหลัง bỳaŋlǎŋ′ behind, in the rear; in the past.

เบือน byan′ V to turn away.

บิดเบือน bìd′byan′ V 1. to twist, distort, mis-represent. 2. to worm out of (a commitment).

แบ bɛɛ′ V to stretch out, spread out, open.

แบมือ bɛɛmyy′ V 1. to open up the palm of the hand. 2. colloq. to extend the palm, stretch out the hand, i.e. to beg.

แบก bɛ̀ɛg′ V 1. to carry on the shoulder, support with the shoulder; to shoulder.

ค่าจ้างแบก khâacâaŋ′bɛ̀ɛg′ N carrying cost, porterage.

แบกภาระ bɛ̀ɛg′phaará?′ V to shoulder respon-sibility, carry the burden.

แบกหาม bɛ̀ɛghǎam′ V to bear, carry (on the shoulder).

แบ่ง bɛ̀ŋ′* V 1. to divide, to share. 2. to be divided.

แบ่งเบา bɛ̀ŋbaw′ V to lessen, ease, lighten (as a burden, task).

แบ่งปัน bɛ̀ŋ′pan′ to share.

แบ่งเป็น bɛ̀ŋ′penɔ 1. to divide into (e.g. parts). 2. to be divided into.

แบ่งภาระ bɛ̀ŋ′phaará?′ V to distribute the burden or responsibility.

แบ่งรับแบ่งสู้ bɛ̀ŋráb′bɛ̀ŋsûu′ V colloq. to make a noncommittal statement.

แบ่งสันปันส่วน bɛ̀ŋ′sǎn′-pan′sùan′ elab. colloq. 1. to share, divide proportionately. 2. to appor-tion.

แบ่งออกเป็น bɛ̀ŋ′?ɔ̀ɔgpenɔ V to be divided up into (e.g. parts).

สลากกินแบ่ง salàag′kinbɛ̀ŋ′ N eleg. lottery ticket.

ส่วนแบ่ง (ส่วน) sùanbɛ̀ŋ′ (sùan′) N dividend, share, portion, quota.

แบงก์, แบงค์, แบ๊งค์ (แห่ง, ใบ) bɛŋ′, bɛ́ŋ′* N 1. bank (hɛ̀ŋ′). 2. bank note (baj′). [f. Eng.]

แบตเตอรี่ (หม้อ, ท่อน) bɛdtəərîi′, bɛ́dtəərîi′* N battery (mɔ̂ɔ′, large type; thɔ̂ɔn′, flashlight type). →Comp. ถ่านไฟฉาย.

แบน bɛɛn′ V to be flat (as of a pancake, lid, roof).

แบนตะเหลนแป้น bɛɛn′talĕnpɛ̌n′ rM to be very flat.

แบบ ๑ (แบบ) bɛ̀ɛb′ (bɛ̀ɛb′) N 1. model, type, style. 2. pattern, form. C 3. clf. for same. →Syn. 1, 3. ทรง ๑ eleg.

o คนแบบนี้ khon′bɛ̀ɛbníi′ a person of this type.

เครื่องแบบ (ชุด) khrŷaŋbɛ̀ɛb′ (chúd′) N uniform.

ตามแบบ taambɛ̀ɛb′ V to imitate (in style), follow the style or pattern of.

ถอดแบบ thɔ̀ɔdbɛ̀ɛb′ V 1. to reproduce, copy, duplicate. 2. to resemble in every minute detail. 3. to pattern after.

ถ่ายแบบ thàajbɛ̀ɛb′ V to copy, make a copy of.

นางแบบ (คน) naaŋbɛ̀ɛb′ (khon′) N a model (i.e. a woman model for an artist or photographer).

แบบง่าย ๆ bɛ̀ɛb′ŋâajŋâaj′ a simple pattern, com-mon style, ordinary style.

แบบฉบับ (อัน, อย่าง) bɛ̀ɛb′chabàb′ (?an′, jàaŋ′) N pattern, example, model, style (esp. what is traditionally accepted as worthy of imitation).

แบบท่องเที่ยว bɛ̀ɛb′thɔ̂ŋthîaw′ N (in) the style of a tourist.

แบบบังคับ bɛ̀ɛb′baŋkháb′ N rules.

แบบใบสมัคร bɛ̀ɛb′bajsamàg′ N application form,

application blank.

แบบผม (แบบ) bɛ̀ɛbphǒm/ (bɛ̀ɛb/) N hair style.

แบบแผน (อย่าง) bɛ̀ɛbphɛ̌ɛn/ (jàaŋ/) N 1. custom, tradition, established pattern or system, conventional rules. 2. standard reference.

แบบฝึกหัด (ข้อ, บท) bɛ̀ɛb/fʏ́ghàd/ (khɔ̂ɔ/, bòd/) N exercise, drill (in a textbook).

แบบพิมพ์ (แบบ, อัน, ใบ) bɛ̀ɛbphim/ (bɛ̀ɛb/, ʔan/, baj/) N 1. a blank form, printed form with blank spaces to be filled in. 2. a mold.

แบบพื้น ๆ bɛ̀ɛb/phʏ́ynphʏ́yn/ simple or everyday style.

แบบฟอร์ม (ใบ, แผ่น) bɛ̀ɛbfɔɔm/ (baj/, phɛ̀n/) N a form (to be filled in, as an application form).

แบบเรียน (เล่ม) bɛ̀ɛbrian/ (lêm/) N textbook.

แบบสากล bɛ̀ɛb/sǎakon/ modern, occidental style.

แบบอย่าง (แบบ, อัน) bɛ̀ɛbjàaŋ/ (bɛ̀ɛb/, ʔan/) N a set example, pattern.

เป็นแบบ penbɛ̀ɛb/ in the style of, on the pattern of.

แม่แบบ mɛ̂ɛbɛ̀ɛb/ N model, pattern.

เลียนแบบ lianbɛ̀ɛb/ V to imitate.

ออกแบบ ʔɔ̀ɔgbɛ̀ɛb/ V to design.

แบบ ๒, แบ๊บ bɛ̀ɛb/, bɛ́b/ V 1. to be in a state of severe prostration (as from illness, serious injury).

นอนแบบ nɔɔn/bɛ́b/ V to lie helpless, spent (from overexhaustion, serious injury, illness).

บอบแบบ bɔ̀bbɛ́b/ V 1. to be fragile. 2. to be frail (of a person), fragile-looking.

แบบบาง bɛ̀ɛbbaaŋ/ V 1. to be delicate, frail. 2. to be slim, slender, thin.

แบว. See บ้องแบว.

แบะ bɛ̀ʔ/ V 1. to split open, lay open (e.g. fruit). 2. to be spread apart, laid open.

คอแบะ khɔɔbɛ̀ʔ/ having lapels (e.g. a coat) (usually as n. mod.).

หน้าแบะ nâabɛ̀ʔ/ N broad face with wide cheeks.

โบ (อัน) boo/ (ʔan/) N bow. [f. Eng.]

โบแดง boodɛɛŋ/ N blue ribbon (literally a "red ribbon" or "bow" which in Thailand symbolizes an award for the best).

โบก bòog/ V 1. to wave, fan. 2. to apply (mortar) with a waving motion; to cover superficially (with mortar).

โบกธง bòogthoŋ/ V to wave a flag (as in signaling).

โบกมือ bòogmyy/ V to wave the hand (as in saying goodbye).

โบกไม้โบกมือ bòogmáaj/bòogmyy/ V elab. colloq. to wave the hand.

โบนัส boonád/, boonás/ N bonus. [f. Eng.]

โบย booj/ V 1. to whip, beat hard, flog. 2. to fly (of winged creatures).

โบยบิน boojbin/ V to fly (of winged creatures).

โบราณ booraan/, booraan/naʔ V 1. to be ancient, old, antique. 2. to be primitive (i.e. belonging to a former time).

คำโบราณ kham/booraan/ N old saying, adage.

บรมโบราณ bɔrom/booraan/ colloq. extremely ancient, very old.

โบราณกาล booraan/nakaan/ lit. ancient times, former times, antiquity.

โบราณคดี booraan/nakhadii/ N 1. account of antiquities. 2. short for the following entry. นัก- - archeologist.

โบราณคดีวิทยา booraan/nakhadii/wídthajaa/ N archeology.

โบราณวัตถุ booraan/wádthùʔ/ N relics, ancient objects, ruins; archeological finds.

โบร่ำโบราณ boorâm/booraan/ colloq. ancient, historical.

สมัยโบราณ samǎj/booraan/ N 1. ancient times. 2. in ancient times.

สัตว์สี่เท้าโบราณ (ตัว) sàd/sìitháaw/-booraan/ (tua/) eleg., lit. a primitive quadruped.

โบสถ์ (โบสถ์, หลัง) bòod/ (bòod/, lǎŋ/) N 1. temple. 2. a chapel in a temple compound. 3. church.

ใบ baj/ N 1. leaf. 2. blade (as of fan). 3. sail. C 4. clf. for leaves, fruit, eggs, various kinds of containers (e.g. baskets, boxes, cups, bags, basins, etc.); also for slips or sheets of paper (e.g. notes, certificates, tickets). →Mngs. 1-3 chiefly in compounds. →Syn. 4. (when referring to fruit) ลูก com., ผล eleg.; (when referring to eggs) ลูก com., ฟอง eleg.

NOTE (1) ใบ in mng. 1 is a class term, not a general term. The general term for "leaf" is ใบไม้. Specific kinds of leaves are named by using the class term followed by specific terms, e.g. ใบจาก "nipa palm leaf," ใบไผ่ "bamboo leaf," ใบพลู "betel leaf, leaf of the betel vine." (2) All nouns based on ใบ take ใบ as their classifier unless otherwise marked; hence (ใบ) is omitted in the derivatives below.

ใบขับขี่ baj′khàbkhìi′ N operator's license, driver's license.

ใบชา bajchaa′ N tea leaves.

ใบตรวจ (ฉบับ) bajtrùad′ (chabàb′) N certificate (certifying inspection).

ใบตอง bajtɔɔŋ′ N banana leaf, plantain leaf.

ใบเบิกเงิน baj′bòəgŋən′ N bank. withdrawal slip.

ใบปลิว bajpliw′ N hand bill, leaflet.

ใบฝากเงิน baj′fàagŋən′ N bank. deposit slip.

ใบพัด (ใบ, อัน) bajphád′ (baj′, ʔan′) N 1. propeller. 2. fan (for a car radiator), fan blades.

ใบมะพร้าว baj′maphráaw′ N leaflet of the coconut palm.

ใบมีดโกน baj′mîidkoon′ N razor blade.

ใบไม้ bajmáaj′ N leaf, leaves (general term for leaves of a tree or plant).

o ฤดูใบไม้ผลิ (ฤดู) rýduu′bajmáajphlì?′ (rýduu′) N spring (season).

o ฤดูใบไม้ร่วง (ฤดู) rýduu′bajmáajrûaŋ′ (rýduu′) N fall, autumn.

ใบยา bajjaa′ N tobacco leaf.

ใบรับของ baj′rábkhɔɔŋ′ N 1. bill of lading. 2. receipt (acknowledging receipt of merchandise).

ใบรับเงิน baj′rábŋən′ N receipt.

ใบรับรอง baj′rábrɔɔŋ′ N certificate (in regard to qualifications, health, etc.).

ใบเรือ bajrya′ N sail (of a boat).

ใบละพัน bajlaphan′ N 1000-tical bill.

ใบละร้อย bajlarɔ́ɔj′ N 100-tical bill.

ใบลา bajlaa′ N application or request for a leave of absence.

ใบส่งของ baj′sòŋkhɔɔŋ′ N invoice.

ใบสมัคร bajsamàg′ N application, written request.

o แบบใบสมัคร bὲɛb′bajsamàg′ N application blank, application form.

ใบสั่งยา baj′sàŋjaa′ N medical prescription.

ใบสำคัญ (ใบ, ฉบับ) baj′sǎmkhan (baj′, chabàb′)

N certificate, document required to establish one's eligibility for something; identification papers.

o ใบสำคัญต่างด้าว baj′sǎmkhan′-tàaŋdâaw′ N 1. passport. 2. alien identification card.

ใบสุทธิ bajsùdthí?′ N certificate showing level of attainment in school.

ใบเสร็จ bajsèd′ N receipt (showing payment has been made).

ใบหญ้า bajjâa′ N blade of grass.

ใบหน้า bajnâa′ N face, countenance.

ใบเหยียบย่ำ baj′jìabjâm′ N land certificate (issued on the condition of use and improvement, e.g. as to a homesteader).

ใบอนุญาต baj′ʔànújâad′ N permit, license.

ผ้าใบ (ผืน) phâabaj′ (phv̌yn′) N canvas, sailcloth.

o รองเท้าผ้าใบ (คู่, ข้าง) rɔɔŋtháaw′phâabaj′ (khûu′, khâaŋ′) N canvas shoes, tennis shoes, sneakers.

เรือใบ (ลำ) ryabaj′ (lam′) N sailboat.

o แล่นเรือใบ lɛ̂nryabaj′ V to sail.

ลัดใบ lád′baj′ V lit., eleg. to put forth leaves.

แล่นใบ lɛ̂n′baj′ V to sail.

ใบ๊ bâj′ V to gesture, signal silently. →Comp. บุ้ยใบ๊.

คนใบ๊ (คน) khonbâj′ (khon′) N mute person.

ใช้ใบ๊ chájbâj′ V to communicate by signs, gestures; to signal.

บอกใบ๊ bɔ̀ɔgbâj′ V to tell by making signs (when speech is to be avoided); to give a high sign to.

บุ้ยใบ๊ bûjbâj′ V to signal by means of the lips and gestures.

เป็นใบ๊ penbâj′ V to be dumb, mute.

ป

ป pɔɔ′ MIDDLE consonant. Pronounced p initially, b finally. The sound p as an initial consonant is always spelled with ป.

ป.๑. Abbrev. for ปืนใหญ่ artillery, and for ทหารปืนใหญ่ the artillery; artilleryman.

ป.๒. Sometimes used as an abbrev. for ไปรษณีย์. mail, post. →See also ป.ณ.

ปก pòg′ N 1. cover. 2. book-cover. V 3. to cover.

ปกครอง. See next main entry.

ปกคลุม pògkhlum′ V 1. to cover. 2. to be covered.

ปกปิด pògpìd′ V to cover; to conceal, keep secret.

ภาพปก (ภาพ) phâapbòg′ (phâab′) N eleg. cover design, cover photo.

ปกครอง pògkhrɔɔŋ′ V to rule, govern. การ--, ความ--, ผู้-- (see below).

การปกครอง kaanpògkhrɔɔŋ′ N governing; government (as in "form of government"), rule, administration. →Dist. รัฐบาล.

ข้าราชการ(ฝ่าย)ปกครอง (คน, นาย) khâarâadɔ chakaan′(fàaj)pògkhrɔɔŋ′ (khon′, naaj′) N government official (esp. an administrative or law enforcement official).

ความปกครอง khwaam′pògkhrɔɔŋ′ N rule, protection, supervision, custody.

ผู้ปกครอง (คน) phûu′pògkhrɔɔŋ′ (khon′) N 1. ruler. 2. guardian. 3. parents.

ปกติ pògkatì?′, pàkatì?′ V 1. to be normal, routine, usual. 2. to be regular, steady (of the wind). The second pronunciation is literary. →Also ปรกติ. →Ant. อปกติ.

ตามปกติ taam′pògkatì?′ normally, ordinarily, as usual, usually.

เป็นปกติ pen′pògkatì?′ 1. to be normal. 2. as usual.

ผิดปกติ phìd′pògkatì?′ V to be unusual, abnormal, irregular.

ยามปกติ jaam′pògkatì?′ normal times; peacetime.

ปฏิกิริยา patì?′kìrijaa′ N reaction. →Also ปฏิกริยา patì?′kàrijaa′.

ปฏิญาณ pàtijaan′ V to promise (by an oath), to vow. คำ-- (ข้อ, ประการ) promise, vow. →Also ปฏิญญาณ pàtin′jaan′, ปฏิญญา pàtin′jaa′.

ปฏิทิน (ฉบับ) pàtithin′ (chabàb′) N calendar.

ปฏิบัติ pàtibàd′ V 1. to do, act, perform, practise. 2. to apply, put into practice, carry out. 3. to attend, tend, serve. การ-- conduct, behavior, performance, operation (of), treatment (of). คน-- tender, attendant.

ข้อปฏิบัติ khɔ̂ɔ′pàtibàd′ N 1. procedure, practice. 2. obligation (e.g. toward a friend).

นำมาใช้ปฏิบัติ nammaacháj′pàtibàd′ 1. to be put into effect, put into use, put into practice.

ปฏิบัติการ pàtibàd′kaan′ V to conduct matters, do things; to perform, operate, execute, carry out. การ-- operation, action.

o ห้องปฏิบัติการ (ห้อง) hɔ̂ŋ′-pàtibàd′kaan′ (hɔ̂ŋ′) N laboratory.

ปฏิปักษ์ pàtipàg′ N lit. adversary, opponent, enemy.

ปฏิภาค pàtiphâag′ N math. proportion.

ปฏิรูป pàtirûub′ V eleg. to reform.

ปฏิโลม pàtiloom′ sV lit. in the reverse direction; in reverse order. →Ant. อนุโลม.

ปฏิวัติ pàtiwád′ N eleg. 1. revolution, overthrow of a government. V 2. to revolt, stage a revolution. การ-- revolution. นัก-- a revolutionary.

ปฏิสังขรณ์ patìsǎŋkhɔ̌ɔn′ V lit., eleg. 1. to repair, rehabilitate. N 2. repair, rehabilitation; also การ--.

ปฏิสันถาร patìsǎnthǎan′ V lit., eleg. 1. to greet. 2. to chat with. N 3. greeting (to an inferior).

ปฏิเสธ pàtisèeθ′ V eleg. 1. to deny, refuse (e.g. a request). sV 2. negative; in the negative. การ-- refusal, refusing.

ตอบปฏิเสธ tɔ̀ɔb′pàtisèeθ′ to refuse, answer in the negative.

ปฐม pathǒm′, pathǒm′maɔ first; primary, elementary. →See also ประถม.

ปฐมพยาบาล pathǒm′phajaabaan′ N 1. first aid. V 2. to administer first aid.

ปฐมวัย pathǒm′mawaj′ N lit. youth, the early period of life.

ปฐมศึกษา pathǒm′sʉ̀gsǎa′ N primary education.

เป็นปฐม pen′pathǒm′ 1. in the first place. 2. originally, first.

ป.ณ. Abbrev. for ไปรษณีย์ mail, post; post office.

ปณิธาน pàníthaan′ N lit., eleg. resolution, formulation of intent, determination.

ปด pòd′ V eleg. to lie, tell a lie. →Syn. See โกหก com.

ขี้ปดมดเท็จ khîipòd′-mód′théd′ V elab. eleg. to tell a lie, prevaricate.

ป.ต.อ. pɔɔtɔɔ?ɔɔ′. Abbrev. for ปืนต่อสู้อากาศยาน. anti-aircraft gun.

ปทานุกรม (เล่ม) pàthaa′núkrom′ (lêm′) N dictionary.

ปทุมธานี pathum′thaanii′ pN Pathumthani, a township in C Thailand.

ปทุมวัน pathum′wan′ pN Pathumwan, an amphoe in Bangkok.

ปน pon′ V 1. to mix. 2. to be mixed, blended.

ใช้ปนกัน cháj′pon′kan (several people) to use (something) together, share (something, e.g. bathroom).

ดินปนทราย dinponsaaj′ N loam, sandy soil.

ปนเป ponpee′ V 1. to mix together. 2. to mix, be mixed in a disorderly or confused way.

ปะปน pà?pon′ V 1. to mix, mingle, combine, intermingle, mix up. 2. to be intermingled, mixed. 3. to be shared (in use by several people).

ป่น pòn′ V to grind, pulverize.

ป่นปี้ pònpîi′ colloq. to be utterly ruined.

ปม pom′ N 1. knot. 2. a complex.

ปมด้อย (อย่าง, ข้อ) pomdɔ̂j′ (jàaŋ′, khɔ̂ɔ′) N psych. inferiority complex.

ปมเด่น (อย่าง, ข้อ) pomdèn′ (jàaŋ′, khɔ̂ɔ′) N psych. superiority complex.

ปุ่มปม pùm′pom′ N knots, kinks.

o เป็นปุ่มปม penpùm′pom′ to be knotted, kinked.

เป็นปม penpom′ to be knotted, knotty.

ปรก pròg′ V to cover, hang down over, fall (e.g. of hair).

ปรกติ prògkatì?′. See ปกติ.

ปรน ๑ in ผ่อนปรน phɔ̀ɔnpron′ V to reduce, ease, lessen (e.g. terms, restrictions, requirements).

ปรน ๒, ปรนปรือ pron′, pronpryy′ V 1. to bring up, rear. 2. to serve, tend. 3. to feed, nourish. 4. to lavish (e.g. gifts on one's beloved).

ปรนนิบัติ pronnibàd′ V to take care of, tend, serve.

เฝ้าปรนนิบัติ fâw′pronnibàd′ V to be at hand, to serve, wait on regularly.

ปรบ pròb′ V lit., eleg. 1. to flap. 2. to clap.

ปรบมือ pròbmyy′ V lit., eleg. to applaud.

ปรปักษ์ (ฝ่าย, คน) pɔɔrapàg′ (fàaj′, khon′) N eleg. enemy. →Syn. ข้าศึก, ศัตรู com.

ปรมาณู (ปรมาณู) paramaanuu′, pɔɔra′- N 1. atom. 2. (as n. mod.) atom, atomic.

กำลังปรมาณู kamlaŋ′paramaanuu′ N atomic power.

พลังงานปรมาณู phalaŋŋaan′paramaanuu′ N atomic energy.

ระเบิดปรมาณู (ลูก) rabə̀əd′paramaanuu′ (lûug′) N atom bomb, atomic bomb.

ปรวน in แปรปรวน prɛɛpruan′ V to change, vary, fluctuate, be uncertain. →Also ปรวนแปร.

ปรองดอง prɔɔŋdɔɔŋ′ V 1. to reconcile. 2. to compromise. 3. to reach an agreement, be in agreement. 4. to get along well (with somebody).

ปรอท parɔ̀ɔd′ N 1. mercury. 2. thermometer. 3. temperature.

ปรอย prɔɔj′ V to be sparse, light.

ประ prà?′ V 1. to add, affix. 2. to touch lightly, daub. 3. to sprinkle, scatter here and there.

ประปราย prà?praaj′ V 1. to be sprinkling (as of rain). sV 2. sparsely, lightly, sporadically, here and there, in scattered fashion.

o ฝนตกประปราย fŏntòg′prà?praaj′ It is drizzling, raining lightly.

ประพรม prà?phrom′ V to sprinkle.

เปรอะประ prə̀?prà?′ V to be spotted, stained, dirty.

เส้นประ sênprà?′ N broken line, dotted line.

ประกบ(กัน) prakòb′(kan′) V 1. to be placed (together) face to face. 2. to be joined (together), spliced (together)(as of the ends of two pieces of timber overlapped and joined surface to surface).

ประกวด prakùad′ V 1. to contest. 2. to compete. การ-- contest.

ประกวดประขัน prakùad′prakhǎn′ V elab. colloq. to compete; to hold a competition.

ประกวดราคา prakùad′raakhaa′ to offer competing bids (i.e. low bids, as for a government contract).

ประกอบ prakɔ̀ɔb′ V 1. to do, perform. 2. to add, put together, join together, assemble, compose. 3. to consist (of), be composed (of). 4. to be a component, ingredient, constituent (of). 5. to be an accessory, an accompanying feature; to be in addition to. 6. to illustrate. 7. to support (as evidence; as a character, etc.). เครื่อง-- accessories, aids. →Syn. 3. กอปร.

ตัวประกอบ tuaprakɔ̀ɔb′ N 1. math. factor. 2.

theatr. supporting character.

ตัวอย่างประกอบ tuajàaŋ′prakɔ̀ɔb′ an illustrative example.

ประกอบคุณความดี prakɔ̀ɔb′khunkhwaamdii′ lit., eleg. to do good.

ประกอบด้วย prakɔ̀ɔb′dûajɔ to consist of, be composed of

ประกอบอาชีพ prakɔ̀ɔb′ʔaachîib′ eleg. to earn a living.

ภาพประกอบ phâab′prakɔ̀ɔb′ N eleg. illustration (e.g. for a text). →Syn. รูปประกอบ com.

ไม่สมประกอบ mâjsǒm′prakɔ̀ɔb′ V to be imperfect, defective, deformed, abnormal.

รูปประกอบ (รูป) rûub′prakɔ̀ɔb′ (rûub′) N com. illustration (i.e. for a text).

ส่วนประกอบ sùanprakɔ̀ɔb′ N component, constituent.

สารประกอบ sǎan′prakɔ̀ɔb′ N compound.

องค์ประกอบ ʔoŋ′prakɔ̀ɔb′ N component, constituent.

ประกัน prakan′ V 1. to guarantee, insure. 2. to bail (out). N 3. bail, security, guaranty. การ-- guarantee; assurance.

ค้ำประกัน khám′prakan′ V 1. to guarantee, stand surety (for someone for payment of a debt). N 2. guarantee. ผู้-- guarantor.

นายประกัน (คน) naajprakan′ (khon′) N insurer, guarantor, bondsman.

ประกันชีวิต prakan′chiiwíd′ V 1. to insure one's life. N 2. life insurance.

ประกันภัย prakan′phaj′ V 1. to insure (against loss or damage). N 2. insurance. การ-- insurance.

o กรมธรรม์ประกันภัย krommathan′-prakan′phaj′ N lit. insurance policy.

ผัดวันประกันพรุ่ง phàd′wan′-prakan′phrûŋ′ V elab. colloq. to procrastinate, put off.

รับประกัน ráb′prakan′ V to guarantee, insure, assure.

หลักประกัน làg′prakan′ N security, surety, collateral, guaranty.

ประกาย (ประกาย) prakaaj′ (prakaaj′) N spark; sparkle, radiant flashing.

ประกายพรึก,ดาว-- (ดวง,คน) prakaajphrýg′,

daaw′prakaajphrýg′ N 1. the morning star (duaŋ′). 2. slang a young beauty; a young star, starlet (khon′, duaŋ′). →Sometimes also, incorrectly written -พฤกษ์. →Also ดาวรุ่ง. →Opp. 1. ดาวประจำเมือง.

ประกายไฟ prakaajfaj′ N spark.

ประการ prakaan′ C 1. eleg., lit. kind, sort, thing, item, respect, means. 2. point, item. 3. law count (as in an indictment). →Syn. 1. ประเภท, สถาน eleg., ชนิด com. 2, 3. ข้อ com.

ด้วยประการฉะนี้ dûajprakaan′chaníi′ lit. in this manner; for this reason.

ทุกประการ thúg′prakaan′ every, everything; in every respect.

บางประการ baaŋprakaan′ of a certain kind, certain, of some sort, some sort, some.

ประการใด prakaan′daj′ 1. what, whatever; whatsoever; how, however. 2. what? whatever? how? however?

o หล่อนจะทำประการใด lɔ̀ncatham′-prakaan′daj′↓ Whatever will she do?

o ไม่มีมูลความจริงแต่ประการใด mâjmiimuun′-khwaamciŋ′-tɛ̀ɛprakaan′daj′↓ There is no truth whatsoever (in it).

ประการใดประการหนึ่ง prakaan′daj′-prakaan′nỳŋ′ any one (of these things), one thing or the other.

ประการที่สอง prakaan′thîisɔ̌ɔŋ′ secondly, in the second place.

ประการแรก prakaanrɛ̂ɛg′ the first (reason) being; for one thing; in the first place.

เป็นประการสำคัญ penprakaan′sǎmkhan′ as the (most) important thing.

อีกประการหนึ่ง ʔìigprakaan′nyŋ furthermore, also.

ประกาศ (ฉบับ) prakàad′ V 1. to announce, proclaim, declare. N 2. announcement, proclamation, declaration (chabàb′). คำ-- (ข้อ,ฉบับ,อย่าง) announcement.

ที่ประกาศ (ที่) thîiprakàad′ (thîi′) N signboard, billboard.

ประกาศใช้ prakàad′cháj′ V to proclaim, declare (to be law), to promulgate (a decree, a law).

ประกาศว่า prakàad′wâa′ to announce that.

ประกาศสงคราม prakàad′sǒŋkhraam′ V to declare war.

หมายประกาศ mǎajprakàad′ N written announcement, declaration.

ออกประกาศ ʔɔ̀ɔgprakàad′ V to announce, proclaim, declare.

ประกาศนียบัตร (ใบ,ฉบับ)prakàad′sanii′jabàd′* (baj′,chabàb′) N certificate, diploma.

หมอประกาศนียบัตร (คน) mɔ̌ɔprakàad′sanii′ɔ jabàd′ (khon′) N certified doctor, physician.

ประขัน in ประกวดประขัน prakùad′prakhǎn′ V elab. colloq. to compete; to hold a competition.

ประคบ prakhób′ V med. to apply a compress, a pad, a medicinal bag (e.g. on a swelling).

ประคบประหงม prakhób′praŋǒm′ to take very good care of, tend with utmost care.

ประคอง prakhɔɔŋ′ V 1. to grasp gently, support (by holding). 2. to hold, support carefully with both hands. 3. to help (somebody) sit up, stand up, walk, etc.

ประเคน prakheen′ V 1. sacer. to proffer (something to a priest) with both hands. 2. colloq. to hand (something to someone) with both hands; usually used sarcastically. 3. idiom. to strike a blow with (a stick or weapon), using both hands; cf. Eng. "give (someone) the stick."

ประโคม prakhoom′ V 1. to blow, sound (a trumpet). 2. to beat (a percussion instrument). 3. to herald (with drum-beat or fanfare). 4. to play a prelude. 5. colloq. to proclaim.

ประจง pracoŋ′ V lit. to do with great care. →Also บรรจง,ผจง.

ประจบ ๑ pracòb′ V to flatter, fawn, curry favor.

ประจบประแจง pracòb′pracɛɛŋ′ idem.

ประจบ ๒ (กับ,กัน) pracòb′(kaɔ, kan′) V to meet (as of two or more lines, paths meeting). →Cf. บรรจบ.

ประจวบ(กับ) pracùab′(kaɔ) V 1. to be coincident (with); to be concurrent, at the same time (as). sV 2. concurrently. 3. it so happens that.

ประจวบคีรีขันธ์ pracùab′khiiriikhǎn′ pN Prachuap-khirikhan, a township in S Thailand. →Also ประจวบ for short.

ประจักษ์ pracàg′ V 1. to be clear, evident, obvious, perceptible, certain, sure. 2. to realize, comprehend clearly, perceive. sV 3. clearly, surely.

ประจักษ์พยาน pracàg′phajaan′ N 1. eyewitness. 2. (visible) evidence, indication.

เห็นประจักษ์ hěn′pracàg′ V to perceive clearly.

ประจัญ pracan′ V to combat, struggle against, oppose, resist.

ประจัญบาน pracanbaan′ V to fight at close quarters; to fight furiously.

o เรือประจัญบาน (ลำ) rya′pracanbaan′ (lam′) N battleship.

ประจัญหน้า pracan′nâa′ V to confront, encounter, meet face to face.

ประจำ pracam′ V to be fixed, steady, regular, staple, permanent. 2. to be stationed (at), on duty (at), assigned (to). sV 3. constantly, regularly, habitually.

o ตำรวจที่ประจำอยู่ในป้อม tamrùad′-thîipracam′ɔ jùunajpɔ̂m′ police who are stationed in the fortress.

o ไม่ได้มีประจำ mâjdâjmii′pracam′ (they) do not have (it) regularly.

ขาประจำ khǎa′pracam′ N colloq. steady customer, regular customer.

ดาวประจำเมือง (ดวง) daaw′pracammyaŋ′ (duaŋ′) N the evening star. →Opp. ดาวประกายพรึก, ดาวรุ่ง.

ประจำการ pracam′kaan′ V to be on duty.

ประจำชาติ pracam′châad′ national.

o ธงประจำชาติ (ผืน) thoŋ′-pracam′châad′ (phǔyn′) N national flag.

ประจำเดือน pracam′dyan′ 1. monthly. N 2. euphem. menstrual period. →Syn. ระดู com.

ประจำตัว pracam′tua′ individual, private, personal.

o บัตรประจำตัว (ใบ) bàd′-pracam′tua′ (baj′) N identification card.

o หมอประจำตัว (คน) mɔ̌ɔ′-pracam′tua′ (khon′) personal doctor.

ประจำปักษ์ pracam′pàg′ fortnightly.

ประจำปี pracam′pii′ annual, yearly.

ประจำวัน pracam′wan′ daily, everyday.

เป็นประจำ pen′pracam′ constantly, regularly, habitually.

พลประจำเรือ (คน) phon′-pracam′rya′ (khon′) N crew member.

รถยนต์ประจำทาง (คัน) ródjon′-pracam′thaaŋ′ (khan′) N eleg. a regularly scheduled bus, motor coach.

โรงเรียนประจำ rooŋrian′pracam′ N boarding school.

ลมประจำ lom′pracam′ N seasonal wind.

ลักษณะประจำมนุษย์ lágsanà?′-pracam′manúd′ N human nature.

เลขหมายประจำ lêegmǎaj′pracam′ serial number of, identification number of (e.g. a machine, a license).

หมอประจำบ้าน (คน) mɔ̌ɔ′pracambâan′ (khon′) N family doctor.

อาหารประจำ ?aahǎanpracam′ staple food.

ประจิม pracim′ lit., eleg. west. →Syn. ตะวันตก com. →The literary and the common terms for the eight chief points of the compass are listed under ทิศ.

ประจุ (ประจุ) pracù?′ (pracù?′) V 1. to fill; to put in, pack. 2. elect. to charge. N 3. elect. a charge. →Comp. บรรจุ, จุ.

ประจุไฟฟ้า (ประจุ, ตัว) pracù?′fajfáa′ (pracù?′, tua′) N electrical charge.

ประแจ (ดอก, ลูก) pracεε′ (dɔ̀ɔg′, lûug′) N colloq. 1. key. 2. lock, padlock.

ประแจง in ประจบประแจง pracòb′pracεεŋ′ V to flatter, fawn, curry favor.

ประชด prachód′ V to be sarcastic, speak sarcastically, ridicule with sarcasm.

ประชวร prachuan′ V roy. to be sick.

ประชัน prachan′ V to compete.

ประชา- prachaa′, prachaaɔ. Bound form meaning "people, public."

ประชากร prachaa′kɔɔn′ N people, populace.

ประชาชน prachaachon′ N the people, the public, the populace, population.

ประชาชนพลเมือง prachaachon′phonlamyaŋ′ the people (esp. of an area, of a country).

ประชาชาติ prachaachâad′, prachaa′châad′ N a people; a nation.

o ประชาชาติอิหร่าน prachaachâad′?ìràan′ the Iranian people, the Iranian nation.

ประชาธิปไตย prachaa′thíbpataj′, -thípataj′ N democracy.

o พรรคประชาธิปไตย phág′prachaa′thípataj′ N democratic party.

o ระบอบประชาธิปไตย rabɔ̀ɔb′-prachaa′thípataj′ N the democratic form of government, democracy.

ประชาธิปัตย์ prachaathípàd′ N 1. democracy. 2. name of a political party (Democratic Party).

ประชาบาล prachaabaan′ N local government.

o โรงเรียนประชาบาล rooŋrian′prachaabaan′ N public (elementary) school (only in rural areas or areas outside of a municipality).

ประชาศึกษา prachaa′sỳgsǎa′ N public education.

ประชาสงเคราะห์ prachaa′sǒŋkhrɔ́?′ N public welfare.

ประชาสัมพันธ์ prachaa′sǎmphan′ N 1. public relations. V 2. slang to advertise.

ประชิด prachíd′ V 1. to close in, approach. 2. to be adjacent to, very close to.

ประชุม prachum′ V 1. to meet (in a group), assemble; to hold a meeting. N 2. a meeting, conference, session; also การ--.

ที่ประชุม (แห่ง) thîiprachum′ N 1. place of assembly, meeting place (hὲŋ′). 2. assembly, gathering (of people).

ประชุมหารือ prachum′hǎaryy′ V to hold a conference.

เรียกประชุม rîag′prachum′ V to call, convene a meeting.

ห้องประชุม (ห้อง) hɔ̂ŋ′prachum′ (hɔ̂ŋ′) N assembly room, meeting room, (assembly) auditorium.

ประณม, --มือ pranom′, pranom′myy′ V to place one's hands palm to palm in the attitude of adoration or salutation. →Also ประนม, พนม.

ประณาม pranaam′ N a salutation made by placing one's palms together and bowing.

ประณีต pranîid′ V 1. to be fine, delicate, intricate. 2. to be neat, exact, precise. ความ-- fineness; precision and neatness; scrupulousness; elaborateness. →Also ปราณีต.

ประณีตศิลปกรรม pranîid′sǐnlapakam′ N fine work, delicate work (of art or handicraft).

ประดัง pradaŋ′ V 1. to throng; to be multitudinous. 2. to well up, surge in (as of several emotions crowding in at the same time). 3. to pile up (as work).

o ประดังกันเข้ามา pradaŋ'kankhâwmaa' to stream in (of a multitude); to surge in.

ประดับ pradàb' V 1. to decorate, adorn, embellish. 2. to be decorated, inlaid. เครื่อง-- decoration, ornament.

เครื่องประดับกาย khrŷaŋpradàb'kaaj' N ornament (to be worn on the body).

ประดับประดา pradàb'pradaa' V elab. to decorate, embellish.

ประดา ๑ pradaa' colloq. all; entire. →Comp. บรรดา.

เต็มประดา tempradaa' colloq. extremely.

ประดา ๒ pradaa' V to dive and remain submerged (in the water, in the ground) for a long time.

ประดาน้ำ (คน) pradaa'náam' (khon') N a skilled diver.

ประดา ๓ in ประดับประดา pradàb'pradaa' V elab. to decorate, embellish.

ประดิษฐ์ pradìd' V to invent, make, devise.

ประดิษฐาน pradìd'sathǎan' V eleg. 1. to place, put, set. 2. to establish, lay the foundation (of).

ประดุจ pradùd' eleg. like, as, such as, as if.

ประเด็น praden' N point or matter in question, crucial point, issue.

นอกประเด็น nɔ̀ɔg'praden' to be irrelevant, off the subject.

ประเดิม pradəəm' V to start, begin.

ประเดี๋ยว pradǐaw' C 1. a moment. 2. colloq. for a moment, in a moment. 3. just a moment. →Also เดี๋ยว. →Syn. 1. 2. ครู่.

ประเดี๋ยวก่อน pradǐawkɔ̀ɔn' (for) a moment; just a minute.

ประตู (บาน) pratuu' (baan') N 1. door, gate (baan'). C 2. sport goal.

ค่าผ่านประตู khâaphàan'pratuu' N admission charge, gate fee.

บัตรผ่านประตู (ใบ) bàdphàan'pratuu' (baj') N admission ticket.

บานประตู (บาน) baanpratuu' (baan') N door panel; door.

ประตูน้ำ pratuunáam' N 1. lock (as in a canal), water gate. pN 2. Pratunam (Pratoonam), name

of an area in the central part of Bangkok.

ประตูหน้าบ้าน pratuu'nâabâan' the front door.

ประถม prathǒm', prathǒm'macɔ 1. first, primary, elementary. N 2. grade (of an elementary school). →See also ปฐม.

ชั้นประถม chán'prathǒm' N elementary grades, grade school level.

o โรงเรียนชั้นประถม (แห่ง, โรงเรียน) rooŋrian'ɔ chánprathǒm' (hɛ̀ŋ, rooŋrian') N elementary school.

ประถมศึกษา prathǒm'sỳgsǎa' N elementary education. การ-- idem.

o โรงเรียนประถมศึกษา rooŋrian'-prathǒm'sỳgɔ sǎa' N elementary school.

โรงเรียนประถม rooŋrian'prathǒm' N elementary school.

ประท้วง prathúaŋ' V eleg. to protest. คำ-- (ข้อ, ฉบับ, ประการ) protest.

ประทวน. See entry below.

นายทหารชั้นประทวน (นาย, คน) naajthahǎan'chánɔ prathuan' (naaj', khon') N milit. noncommissioned officer.

ประทักษิน prathágsĭn' 1. bearing to the right. 2. clockwise.

ประทัง prathaŋ' V 1. to sustain, maintain, keep up. 2. to sustain against. 3. to resist, keep out, restrain.

o ประทังความหนาว prathaŋ'khwaamnǎaw' 1. to sustain against cold. 2. to keep out the cold.

o ประทังชีวิต prathaŋ'chiiwíd' to sustain life, maintain one's life.

ประทัด (ดอก) prathád' (dɔ̀ɔg') N firecracker.

ประทับ ๑ pratháb' V roy. 1. to stay, remain. 2. to sit, be seated. →Syn. 1. อยู่ com. 2. นั่ง com.

ประทับยืน pratháb'jyyn' V roy. to stand. →Syn. ยืน com.

ประทับแรม pratháb'rɛɛm' V roy. to stay overnight.

ประทับ ๒ pratháb' V 1. to press, press against. 2. to imprint, impress, stamp (as with a seal). sV 3. against, on.

ประทับใจ pratháb'caj' V to impress (one); to be impressive.

ประทับตรา pratháb'traa' V to stamp, seal.
→Syn. ตีตรา,ตอกตรา com.

o เบาะประทับตรา (อัน) bɔ́?-pratháb'traa' (?an')
N stamp pad.

ประทาน prathaan' V roy. to give, offer, bestow.
→Syn. See ให้.

ขอประทาน khɔ̌ɔprathaan' V eleg. def. to beg,
ask, request. →See ขอ com.

o ขอประทานโทษ khɔ̌ɔprathaanthôod' eleg. def.
Kindly pardon me. Kindly excuse me. →Syn.
See ขอโทษ com.

o ขอประทานเสนอ khɔ̌ɔprathaan'sanɔ̌ɔ' eleg.
def. I respectfully submit (this matter for your
consideration). Used especially in official correspondence.

ชลประทาน chonlaprathaan' N irrigation.

ประทานโทษ prathaanthôod' eleg. def. Excuse
me. →Less deferential than ขอ--. →Syn.
See ขอโทษ com.

ประทีป,ดวง-- prathîib', duaŋprathîib' N 1. flame.
2. light, e.g. the light from a flame, a lamp,
or a lantern.

ประทุษร้าย prathúd'saráaj'* V to do harm, inflict
injury. →Also ประทุษฐร้าย prathúd'tharáaj'.

ประเทศ (ประเทศ) prathêed' (prathêed') N 1.
eleg. country, nation. C 2. clf. for same.
→Syn. เมือง com.

> NOTE. A list of the elegant names of some
> countries is given below. In every case the
> common name can be formed by using เมือง
> in place of ประเทศ. Federations are listed
> under สหรัฐ.
> ประเทศกัมพูชา prathêed'kamphuuchaa' N eleg.
> lit. Cambodia.
> ประเทศเขมร prathêedkhaměen' N eleg. Cambodia.
> ประเทศจีน prathêedciin' N eleg. China.
> ประเทศญวน prathêedjuan' N eleg. Annam.
> ประเทศญี่ปุ่น prathêed'jîipʉn' N eleg. Japan.
> ประเทศไทย prathêedthaj' N eleg. Thailand.
> ประเทศฝรั่งเศส prathêed'faràŋsèed' N eleg.
> France.
> ประเทศพม่า prathêedphamáa' N eleg. Burma.
> ประเทศฟิลิปปินส์ prathêed'filibpin' N eleg. the
> Philippines.
> ประเทศมะลายู prathêed'malaajuu' N eleg.
> Malaya.
> ประเทศเยอรมัน prathêed'jəəraman' N eleg.
> Germany.
> ประเทศรัสเซีย prathêed'rádsia' N eleg. Russia.

> ประเทศลังกา prathêed'laŋkaa' N eleg. Ceylon.
> ประเทศลาว prathêedlaaw' N eleg. Laos.
> ประเทศอังกฤษ prathêed'?aŋkrìd' N eleg.
> England.
> ประเทศอาหรับ prathêed'?aaràb' N eleg. Arabia.
> ประเทศอินเดีย prathêed'?india' N eleg. India.

กลุ่มประเทศ (กลุ่ม) klùm'prathêed' (klùm') N
1. group of nations. 2. bloc, coalition.

ต่างประเทศ tàaŋprathêed' 1. a foreign country;
abroad. 2. (as n. mod.) foreign. การ-- foreign
affairs.

ทั่วประเทศ thûaprathêed' all over the country.

ประเทศกลุ่มคอมมิวนิสต์ prathêed'klùm'khɔɔmmiwɔ
níd' the communist bloc of nations.

ประเทศชาติ prathêed'châad' N country.

ประเทศมหาอำนาจ (ประเทศ) prathêed'-mahǎa'ɔ
?amnâad' (prathêed) N 1. the great powers.
2. a great power, a mighty nation.

ประเทศร้อน (ประเทศ) prathêedrɔ́ɔn' (prathêed')
N tropical country.

ประเทศราช prathêed'sarâad' N colony, dependency.

ประเทศสมุน (ประเทศ) prathêed'samǔn' (praɔ
thêed') N satellite country.

ภายในประเทศ phaajnaj'prathêed' 1. inside the
country. 2. (as n. mod.) domestic, internal, inland.

ภูมิประเทศ (แห่ง,อย่าง) phuu'míprathêed' (hɛ̀ŋ',
jàaŋ') N 1. topography; the surface features
of an area. 2. scenery, landscape.

ระหว่างประเทศ rawàaŋ'prathêed' international.

o กฎหมายระหว่างประเทศ kòdmǎaj'-rawàaŋ'ɔ
prathêed' N international law.

ประธาน (คน) prathaan' (khon') N president, chairman, head, chief.

ประธานกรรมการ prathaan'kammakaan' N committee chairman.

เป็นประธาน penprathaan' to be the head; to be
president (of), chairman (of). ผู้-- chairman,
president.

พระประธาน (องค์) phráprathaan' (?oŋ') N the
principal Buddha statue in a Buddhist temple.

รองประธาน (นาย,คน) rɔɔŋ'prathaan' (naaj',
khon') N vice-president, vice-chairman.

ประธานาธิบดี (ท่าน,คน) prathaa'naa'thíbɔdii',
-thíbbɔdii' (thân',khon') N president (of a

country).

o รองประธานาธิบดี rɔɔŋ'prathaa'naa'thíbɔdii' N vice-president (of a country).

ประนม. See ประณม.

ประนาม pranaam' V 1. to brand, stigmatize. 2. to blame, accuse, denounce. →Sometimes confused with ประณาม in spelling.

ประปราย. See under ประ.

ประปา prapaa' N (city) water supply. การ-- idem.

การประปากรุงเทพ ฯ kaanprapaa'kruŋthêeb' Bangkok Water Works.

น้ำประปา náamprapaa' N city water, water (as a municipal utility).

ประเปรียว prà?'priaw' V to be lively, active, agile, sprightly. →See เปรียว.

ประพฤติ praphrýd' V to behave, act. ความ-- behavior, conduct.

ประพฤติตัว praphrýd'tua' to behave oneself.

ประพันธ์ praphan' V eleg. to write, compose. นัก--,ผู้-- poet, writer, author. →Syn. แต่ง com., นิพนธ์ eleg.

คำประพันธ์ (บท) kham'praphan' (bòd') N 1. poetry. 2. writing (esp. poetry, but also prose).

บทประพันธ์ (บท) bòd'praphan' (bòd') N a literary work, composition; a writing.

ประพาส praphâad' V roy. to tour, take a trip, visit.

ประเพณี (อย่าง,แบบ) praphee'nii' (jàaŋ', bɛ̀ɛb') N custom, tradition. →Also ประเวณี ๒.

จารีตประเพณี (อย่าง) caa'rîid'-praphee'nii' (jàaŋ') N custom, tradition.

ประภาคาร (หลัง) praphaa'khaan' (lǎŋ') N lighthouse.

ประเภท praphêed' C eleg. kind, sort, type, category, variety. →Syn. See ชนิด com.

ประมง,ประโมง pramoŋ', pramooŋ' V 1. to fish. N 2. fishing. 3. fisherman. การ-- fishing; fishery.

ชาวประมง (คน) chaawpramoŋ' (khon') N fisherman.

เรือประมง (ลำ) ryapramoŋ' (lam') N fishing boat.

ประมวล pramuan' V to compile, combine, codify.

→Also ประมวญ FS.

ประมวลกฎหมาย pramuan'kòdmǎaj' N code of laws, law code.

ประมวลการสอน (เล่ม) pramuan'kaansɔ̌ɔn' (lêm') syllabus.

ประมาณ pramaan' V 1. to approximate; to estimate. qM 2. about, approximately. →Syn. ราว.

งบประมาณ (งบประมาณ) ŋóbpramaan' (ŋóbpracmaan') N budget.

พอประมาณ phɔɔpramaan' V 1. to be moderate (in quantity). sV 2. moderately, to some degree or extent.

สุด(ที่จะ)ประมาณ sùd'pramaan', sùd'thîicapracmaan' to be inestimable.

เหลือประมาณ lɣapramaan' to be beyond description; to be inestimable.

ประมาท pramàad'* V 1. to be overconfident, careless, negligent. 2. to look down on, bemean, belittle, disparage, make disparaging remarks. ความ-- negligence, carelessness, recklessness.

ลบประมาท sòb'pramàad' to insult, disparage, belittle, speak or act contemptuously to.

หมิ่นประมาท mìn'pramàad' V 1. to be contemptuous of. 2. to insult.

ประมุข (คน) pramúg' (khon') N eleg. head, chief, leader. →Syn. หัวหน้า.

ประมูล pramuun' V to bid (e.g. at an auction).

ประเมิน praməən' V to assess; to estimate.

ประโมง. See ประมง.

ประยุกต์ prajúg' V 1. to make useful; to apply. 2. to be applied.

วิทยาศาสตร์ประยุกต์ wídthajaasàad'prajúg' applied science.

ประโยค (ประโยค) prajòog' (prajòog')* N 1. gram. sentence. C 2. level, grade, degree (as of development, achievement).

ประโยชน์ (อย่าง) prajòod'* (jàaŋ') N advantage, usefulness, benefit, profit, use, interest (in the sense of "benefit").

เกิดประโยชน์ kə̀əd'prajòod' V to be advantageous, beneficial, useful; to be of benefit, do (some)good.

คุณประโยชน์ khun'prajòod' N usefulness, utility, value, beneficialness, advantageousness.

ประโยชน์ของส่วนรวม prajòod'khɔ̌ɔŋsùanruam'

the common interest, common good; the collective advantage.

ประโยชน์ส่วนตัว prajòod'sùantua' personal interest, advantage, gain; individual advantage.

เป็นประโยชน์ penprajòod' to be advantageous, useful.

เปล่าประโยชน์ plàaw'prajòod' to be to no advantage, useless.

ผลประโยชน์ phŏn'prajòod' N 1. benefit, gain, use, advantage, profit; (one's) interest. 2. proceeds.

เพื่อประโยชน์(ของ) phŷaprajòod'(khɔ̌ɔŋ'ɔ) for the benefit (of).

มีประโยชน์ miiprajòod' to be advantageous, useful, of use.

ไร้ประโยชน์ ráj'prajòod' V to be useless, in vain.

หาประโยชน์ hǎa'prajòod' V to seek profit, gain, advantage.

ประลอง pralɔɔŋ' V 1. to test. 2. to practise.

ประลองยุทธ pralɔɔŋ'júd' V eleg. to maneuver, hold maneuvers. →Syn. ซ้อมรบ com.

ประโลม praloom' V to comfort, solace.

หนังสือประโลมโลก (เล่ม) naŋsy̌y'-praloom'ɔ lôog' (lêm') N cheap fiction, esp. love stories.

ประวัติ prawàd', prawàd'tiɔ* N 1. account, story, history. V 2. (see ประวัติถึง below).

ประวัติการ prawàd'kaan' N history, chronicle of events. NOTE. ประวัติการ and ประวัติการณ์ are sometimes interchanged because of spelling confusion.

ประวัติการณ์ prawàd'kaan' N (the) record, events worth recording. →See note above.

o ชนะประวัติการณ์ chaná?'-prawàd'kaan' to break the record.

o เป็นประวัติการณ์ pen'-prawàd'kaan' epoch-making, record-breaking, unprecedented.

ประวัติถึง prawàd'thy̌ŋɔ, prawàd'thy̌ŋ' to think back, recall.

ประวัติศาสตร์ prawàdsàad', prawàd'tisàad' N history.

ประวิง prawiŋ' V to prolong, delay, drag out.

ประเวณี ๑ prawee'nii' N sexual intercourse.

การ-- idem.

ล่วงประเวณี lûaŋprawee'nii' V to commit adultery.

ประเวณี ๒ prawee'nii' N custom, tradition. →Also ประเพณี.

ประสงค์ prasǒŋ' V eleg. to desire, want, wish, need, require. ความ-- wish, desire, purpose, intention.

จุดประสงค์ (ประการ,อย่าง) cùd'prasǒŋ' (prakaan', jàaŋ') N purpose, goal.

ต้องประสงค์ tôŋ'prasǒŋ' V 1. lit.,eleg. to need, require, want. 2. to be needed, desirable.

พึงประสงค์ phyŋ'prasǒŋ' eleg. to be desirable.

วัตถุประสงค์ (อย่าง,ประการ) wádthù?'prasǒŋ' (jàaŋ', prakaan') N aim, purpose, object.

ประสพ prasòb' V eleg. to meet, encounter.

ประสพการณ์ prasòb'kaan' N experience.

ประสพเหตุ prasòb'hèed' eleg. to have an accident.

ประสม prasǒm' V to mix. →Also ผสม.

ประสา prasǎa' N 1. colloq. way, manner, esp. proper ways, accepted ways. 2. in the manner of, like, as. →Also occasionally ผะสา. →See also ภาษา ๒.

o คุยกันประสาเพื่อน khuj'kan'-prasǎa'phŷan' to chat the way friends do.

ตามประสา taam'prasǎa' in the manner of, in the way of, according to the ways of (e.g. a certain station in life, mode of life). →Also ตามภาษา, ตามผะสา.

ประสีประสา prasǐi'prasǎa' N 1. meaning, sense, significance. V 2. to know the ways of, know what is proper.

ไม่ประสา mâjprasǎa' 1. to be ignorant of, have no knowledge of. 2. to be innocent, naive.

ไม่ประสีประสา mâjprasǐi'prasǎa' idem.

รู้ประสา rúu'prasǎa' V colloq. to know what is what, to have horse sense. →Also รู้ภาษา, รู้ผะสา.

ประสาท ๑ prasàad' N anat. nerve.

กวนประสาท kuan'prasàad' V colloq. to get on one's nerves; to drive one crazy.

เส้นประสาท (เส้น) sên'prasàad' (sên') N a nerve.

o โรคเส้นประสาท rôog'sênprasàad' N 1. a nervous disorder; neurosis. 2. nervous breakdown.

โสตประสาท sòod/prasàad/ N eleg. 1. sense
of hearing. 2. anat. auditory nerve.

o บาดโสตประสาท bàad/-sòod/prasàad/ eleg.
to offend one's sense of hearing.

ประสาท ๒ prasàad/ V 1. to confer (upon). 2. to
take pleasure in giving.

ประสาน prasǎan/ V 1. to link, join together. 2.
to meet (join, be joined). 3. to bind (as a
binder). 4. to unite, coordinate.

ตัวประสาน tuaprasǎan/ N binder, binding
medium.

ประสานงาน prasǎan/ŋaan/ V to coordinate the
work (e.g. of different departments). การ--
coordination.

ประสานมือ prasǎan/myy/ V to clasp one's hands,
knitting the fingers together.

ประสิทธิ์,ประสิทธิ- prasìd/, prasìd/thiɔ N success.
→Chiefly in compounds.

ประสิทธิ์ผล prasìd/phǒn/ V to be successful,
give successful results.

ประสิทธิภาพ prasìd/thiphâab/ N eleg. efficiency.

ประสิว in ดินประสิว dinprasǐw/ N saltpeter.

o กรดดินประสิว kròd/dinprasǐw/ N nitric acid.

ประสี in ประสีประสา prasǐi/prasǎa/ N 1. meaning, sense, significance. V 2. to know the ways
of, to know what is proper.

o ไม่ประสีประสา mâjprasǐi/prasǎa/ V 1. to be
ignorant of. 2. to be innocent, naive.

ประสูติ prasùud/ V 1. roy. to be born. 2. to give
birth.

ประเสริฐ prasɤ̀ɤd/ V 1. to be excellent. 2. to be
precious.

ประหงม in ประคบประหงม prakhób/praŋǒm/ to
take very good care of, tend with utmost care.

ประหนึ่ง pranɤ̀ŋ/ lit. as if; like, as.

o ดูประหนึ่งว่า duu/-pranɤ̀ŋ/wâa/ it seems as
though, it looks as if. →Syn. ดูเหมือน.

ประหม่า pramàa/ V to be nervous, get panicky, be
struck with fear.

ประหยัด prajàd/ V to be thrifty; to be frugal; to be
sparing of, economical in the use of (e.g. fuel).

ประหลาด pralàad/ V to be surprising, strange,
unusual.

น่าประหลาด nâa/pralàad/ V to be surprising,

strange, marvelous.

ประหลาดใจ pralàad/caj/ V to wonder, be surprised,
astonished. ความ-- surprise, astonishment.

แปลกประหลาด plɛ̀ɛg/pralàad/ V to be wonderful,
strange, unusual, extraordinary.

ประหวั่น prawàn/ V eleg. to fear, be afraid of.

ประหัต prahàd/ V lit. to kill, destroy.

ประหัตประหาร prahàd/prahǎan/ V elab. eleg.
to kill, destroy.

ประหาร prahǎan/ V to kill, destroy.

ประหัตประหาร prahàd/prahǎan/ V elab. eleg.
to kill, destroy.

ประหารชีวิต prahǎan/chiiwíd/ V eleg. 1. to
execute, put to death. 2. to be executed. →Syn.
1. See ฆ่า com.

o ถูกประหารชีวิต thùugprahǎan/chiiwíd/ to be
executed.

รัฐประหาร (ครั้ง) rád/thaprahǎan/ (khráŋ/) N
coup d'état.

ปรัก in ปรักหักพัง paràg/hàgphaŋ/ V to be ruined,
dilapidated.

ปรักปรำ pràgpram/ V 1. to accuse, blame. 2. to
condemn.

พูดปรักปรำ phûud/pràgpram/ to accuse, blame.

ปรัชญา (ข้อ,เรื่อง) pràdjaa/, pràdchajaa/, pàrád/ɔ
chajaa/, pàrádjaa/ (khɔ̌ɔ/, rɯ̂aŋ/) N philosophy.

ปรัตยุบัน pràd/tajúban/ N present (of time).

ปรับ ๑ pràb/. See entry below.

ปรับทุกข์ pràbthúg/ V to tell one's troubles.

ปรับ ๒ pràb/ V 1. to fine, impose a fine on. 2. to
tune, adjust, correct, clear up.

ทั้งจำทั้งปรับ tháŋcam/tháŋpràb/ both fine and imprisonment: "both to imprison and to fine."

ปรับปรุง pràbpruŋ/ V 1. to improve. 2. to adjust.
3. to smarten up, spruce up. การ-- revision,
reform, improvement.

ปรับไหม pràbmǎj/ V to fine.

o ค่าปรับไหม khâa/pràbmǎj/ N fine, penalty.

ปรัมปรา param/paraa/ ancient, traditional.

ปรากฏ praa/kòd/ V 1. to appear. 2. to become
manifest, clear. 3. to be apparent, ostensible.

ดังปรากฏ daŋpraa/kòd/ as has appeared, as could
be seen, as is manifest, evident.

ปรากฏการณ์ (อย่าง) praakòd/kaan/ (jàaŋ/) N

phenomenon.

ปรากฏว่า praakòd'waa' it appears that, it seems that, it is apparent that.

ปรากฏองค์ขึ้น praakòd''oŋ'-khŷn' (a supernatural being) to make an appearance.

ยังคงปรากฏมี jaŋkhoŋ'-praakòd'mii' there still appears to be.

ปราการ (ปราการ) praakaan' (praakaan') N eleg. wall, enclosure (esp. surrounding a town). →Syn. กำแพง com.

ปราง praaŋ' N lit.,eleg. cheek. →Syn. แก้ม com.

ปร่าง in เปรื่องปร่าง prỳaŋpràaŋ' imit. the crashing sound of broken glass.

ปรางค์,พระ-- (องค์) praaŋ', phrápraaŋ' ('oŋ') N stupa.

ปราจีนบุรี praaciin'burii' pN Prachinburi, a township in SE Thailand. →Also ปราจีน for short.

ปราชญ์ (คน) pràad' (khon') N learned man. นัก-- wise man, learned man, sage, philosopher.

ปราชัย praa'chaj', paraa'chaj' V 1. lit. to fail, be defeated. N 2. lit. failure, defeat; also การ--,ความ--.

ปราณ praan' N breath, life, heart.

ลมปราณ lompraan' N breath.

วายปราณ waajpraan' V lit. to die.

ปราณี. See ปรานี.

ปราณีต. See ประณีต.

ปราด pràad' V 1. to rush, dash. sV 2. swiftly, quickly. C 3. a brief glance, a twinkling, an instant.

ปราดเปรื่อง pràadprỳaŋ' V to be quick (in thinking); to be quick-witted, sharp-witted.

มองปราดเดียว mɔɔŋ'pràaddiaw' in a glance, at a glance.

ปราน in โปรดปราน pròodpraan' V to favor, be favored.

ปรานี praa'nii' V to have mercy on. ความ-- pity, kindness, mercy. →Often written ปราณี.

กรุณาปรานี karunaa'-praa'nii' V to be kind, merciful, kind-hearted.

ปราบ pràab' V 1. to subjugate, conquer, overcome. 2. to suppress, put down, squelch; to subdue, tame, bring under control. 3. to level (a sur-

face).

โครงการปราบยุง khrooŋkaan'-pràab'juŋ' mosquito control program.

ปราบปราม pràabpraam' V 1. to subjugate. 2. to suppress, put down, squelch (opposition); to subdue, tame, bring under control. การ-- suppression; control, controlling.

ปราม praam' V eleg. to prohibit, forbid, stop. →Comp. ปราบ.

ห้ามปราม hâampraam' V to prohibit, forbid.

ปราโมทย์ praamôod' N 1. eleg. joy, delight. V 2. to be delighted, glad.

ปราย praaj' V to scatter, sow, disseminate.

ประปราย prà'praaj' V 1. to be sprinkling (as of rain). sV 2. sparsely, lightly, sporadically, here and there, in scattered fashion.

o ฝนตกประปราย fŏntòg'prà'praaj'↓ It is drizzling, raining lightly.

เปรยปราย prəəjpraaj' V to call out, make a general greeting.

โปรยปราย proojpraaj' V to scatter, sow, disseminate.

ลูกปราย lûugpraaj' N bird shot.

ปรารถนา pràadthanǎa' V eleg. to desire, wish, dream of, want. ความ-- wish, desire.

พึงปรารถนา phyŋ'pràadthanǎa' eleg. to be desirable.

สมปรารถนา sŏm'pràadthanǎa' V eleg. 1. to be in accordance with one's desire. 2. to attain one's desire, have one's wish fulfilled.

ปรารภ(ถึง) praarób'(thŷŋ') V eleg. 1. to mention, speak about. 2. to express one's thoughts out loud. →Syn. 1. กล่าว com.

ปราศจาก pràadsacàag', pràasacàag' to be without, be free from, free of. Sometimes corresponds to -less, -free; see examples.

o ปราศจากชีวิต pràadsacàag'chiiwíd' eleg. without life, lifeless.

o ทำให้ปราศจากเชื้อโรค thamhâj'-pràadsacàag'⊃ chýarôog' to make germfree, hence to sterilize, pasteurize.

ปราศรัย praasǎj' V 1. eleg. to greet, speak to, address cordially. sV 2. cordially, genially. N 3. cordial talk, speech. คำ-- (ฉบับ, เรื่อง,

ครั้ง) cordial speech or address.

ปราสาท (หลัง, แห่ง) praasàad⁄ (lǎŋ⁄, hὲŋ⁄) N castle, palace, mansion.

ปร๋า. See ปรักปร๋า.

ปริ prì?⁄ V to part, come apart, be opened, crack open (by pressure from within).

    ปริปาก prì?pàag⁄ V 1. to open one's mouth (to speak). 2. to utter.

ปริญญา (ปริญญา) parin⁄jaa⁄, prinjaa⁄ (parin⁄jaa⁄, prinjaa⁄) N academic degree, diploma.

    ปริญญากิติมศักดิ์ parin⁄jaa⁄-kìtim⁄masàg⁄ N honorary degree.

    ปริญญาตรี parin⁄jaatrii⁄ N bachelor's degree.

    ปริญญาโท parin⁄jaathoo⁄ N master's degree.

    ปริญญาเอก parin⁄jaa?èeg⁄ N doctor's degree.

ปริบ ๆ. See entry below.

    ทำตาปริบ ๆ thamtaa⁄prìbprìb⁄ V to blink the eyes repeatedly (e.g. when stunned by defeat or sorrow).

ปริ่ม prìm⁄ V to be full to the brim.

ปริมาณ parimaan⁄ N quantity, amount, supply.

ปริมาตร parimâad⁄, pɔɔrimâad⁄ N volume. →Also บริมาตร.

ปริยาย parijaaj⁄ N 1. kind, sort. 2. manner, way.

    โดยปริยาย dooj⁄parijaaj⁄ indirectly.

ปริศนา (ข้อ) prìd⁄sanǎa⁄ (khɔ̌ɔ⁄) N puzzle; riddle.

ปรี่ prìi⁄ V 1. to be full to the brim. 2. to issue forth, rush at, approach menacingly.

ปรีชา priichaa⁄ V eleg. 1. to be smart, clever. N 2. intuition. ความ-- intelligence.

ปรีดา priidaa⁄ V lit. to be glad, happy, delighted.

ปรึกษา prᵞgsǎa⁄ V to consult. →Also ปฤกษา.

    ที่ปรึกษา thîi⁄prᵞgsǎa⁄ N consultant, advisor.

ปรือ ๑ pryy⁄ V 1. to feed. 2. to bring up, rear, train.

    ปรนปรือ pronpryy⁄ V 1. to bring up, rear. 2. to serve, tend. 3. to feed, nourish. 4. to lavish (e.g. gifts on one's beloved).

ปรือ ๒ pryy⁄ V to be drowsy.

    ตาปรือ taa⁄pryy⁄ V to have one's eyes half-closed with drowsiness; to be dozing.

ปรื๋อ prᵞy⁄ sV very rapidly.

    เร็วปรื๋อ rewprᵞy⁄ to be extremely fast, speedy.

    แล่นปรื๋อ lɛ̂nprᵞy⁄ to run fast, to speed (of a car).

ปรุ prù?⁄ V 1. to be perforated, riddled, punched through. 2. to be pitted, pocked.

ปรุง pruŋ⁄ V 1. to combine, put together, compound (ingredients of food, medicine, etc.). 2. to season, flavor (food). เครื่อง-- ingredients; seasonings (for food).

    ปรับปรุง pràbpruŋ⁄ V 1. to improve. 2. to adjust. 3. to smarten up, spruce up. การ-- revision, reform, improvement.

    ปรุงแต่ง pruŋ⁄tὲŋ⁄ V 1. to prepare, combine, compound, concoct. 2. to touch up, dress up, decorate.

  o ส่วนปรุงแต่ง sùan⁄pruŋtὲŋ⁄ N chem. component, constituent.

    ปรุงยา pruŋjaa⁄ V to compound a medicine, concoct a remedy, make up a prescription.

    ปรุงอาหาร pruŋ⁄?aahǎan⁄ V eleg. 1. to cook. 2. to season food. →Syn. 1. ทำกับข้าว com.

ปฤกษา. See ปรึกษา.

ป.ล. Abbrev. for ปัจฉิมลิขิต postscript; equiv. to P. S.

ปลง ploŋ⁄ V 1. to lay down (a burden), put down, relinquish. 2. to decide, reach a conclusion, come to a decision. 3. to realize, come to the realization.

    ปลงใจ ploŋcaj⁄ V to decide, consent, be willing to, agree to.

    ปลงชีพ ploŋ⁄chîib⁄ lit. to kill, assassinate, take (someone's) life. การ-- assassination.

    ปลงชีวิต ploŋ⁄chiiwíd⁄ lit. idem.

    ปลงตก ploŋtòg⁄ V 1. to realize, become aware, come to the realization. 2. to know life (be aware of the vicissitudes of life).

    ปลงพระชนม์ ploŋ⁄phráchon⁄ V roy. to assassinate.

    ปลงศพ ploŋsòb⁄ V eleg. to cremate. →Syn. เผาศพ com.

ปลด plòd⁄ V 1. to take off, remove, detach. 2. to release. 3. to fire, dismiss.

    ปลดทหาร plòd⁄thahǎan⁄ V to demobilize.

    ปลดปล่อย plòdplɔ̀j⁄ V to release, set free, discharge.

    ปลดเปลื้อง plòdplʉaŋ⁄ V 1. to take off, remove. 2. to liberate, release.

    ปลดอาวุธ plòd⁄?aawúd⁄ V to disarm.

ปล้น plôn⁄ V 1. to hold up (with intent to rob). 2.

to commit a robbery.

ปลวก (ตัว) plùag′ (tua′) N termite, white ant
(Isoptera).

จอมปลวก (ลูก) cɔɔmplùag′ (lûug′) N termite
hill.

ปลอก (ปลอก) plɔɔg′ (plɔɔg′) N 1. sheath, casing,
covering, band, i.e. that which covers or binds
all around. C 2. clf. for same.

ปลอกคอ (อัน) plɔɔgkhɔɔ′ (ʔan′) N collar (for
a dog).

ปลอกหมอน (ปลอก) plɔɔgmɔɔn′ (plɔɔg′) N
pillowcase.

ปล่อง (ปล่อง) plɔ̀ŋ′* (plɔ̀ŋ′) N 1. tube. 2. shaft
(as of a mine). 3. opening, vent.

ปล่องควัน plɔ̀ŋkhwan′ N smokestack.

ปล่องไฟ plɔ̀ŋfaj′ N chimney, smokestack.

ปล่องภูเขาไฟ plɔ̀ŋ′phuukhǎwfaj′ N vent, crater
of a volcano.

ปล่องรถไฟ plɔ̀ŋ′ródfaj′ N smokestack of a locomotive.

ยุงก้นปล่อง (ตัว) juŋ′kônplɔ̀ŋ′ (tua′) N anopheles mosquito (carrier of malaria).

ปล้อง (ปล้อง) plɔ́ŋ′ (plɔ́ŋ′) N 1. internode (of a
plant stem). C 2. segment, circular segment,
section.

ปลอด plɔɔd′ V 1. to be free from, lacking in, empty
of. 2. to be solid (in color).

ขาวปลอด khǎaw′plɔɔd′ solid white.

เขตปลอดทหาร (เขต) khèed′plɔɔdthahǎan′
(khèed′) N demilitarized zone.

ปลอดโปร่ง plɔɔdpròoŋ′ V to be clear.

ปลอดภัย plɔɔdphaj′ V to be safe, out of danger.
ความ-- security, safety.

o เขตปลอดภัย (เขต) khèed′plɔɔdphaj′ (khèed′)
N safety zone.

o สัญญาณปลอดภัย sǎnjaan′plɔɔdphaj′ N all-
clear signal.

ปล้อน. See ปลิ้นปล้อน.

ปลอบ plɔ̀ɔb′ V to soothe, console, pacify, comfort.

ปลอบใจ plɔ̀ɔbcaj′ V to soothe, console, comfort.
การ-- comfort, consolation.

ปลอม plɔɔm′ V 1. to falsify, fake, counterfeit,
imitate, forge (e.g. a signature), disguise. 2.
to be false, fake, counterfeit, be an imitation,

a substitute, be adulterated, disguised. →Syn.
2. See เก๊ colloq.

ฟันปลอม (ซี่,ชุด) fanplɔɔm′ N false teeth (sîi′
for individual teeth; chúd′ for a denture).

ปล่อย plɔ̀j′* V 1. to release, let go of, let loose.
2. to abandon.

ปลดปล่อย plòdplɔ̀j′ V to release, set free, discharge.

ปล่อยปละละเลย plɔ̀jplà?′lá?ləəj′ V to neglect,
abandon.

ปล่อยให้ plɔ̀j′hâj⊃ to let, allow.

ละปล่อย lá?′plɔ̀j′ V to let go, abandon.

ปละ plà?′ V 1. to be released. 2. to be abandoned,
neglected. →Chiefly in compounds.

ปล่อยปละละเลย plɔ̀jplà?′lá?ləəj′ V to neglect,
abandon.

ปลัก (ปลัก,แห่ง) plàg′ (plàg′,hὲŋ′) N mud hole,
mud puddle.

ปลั่ง plàŋ′ V to be radiant, shiny. →Chiefly in cpds.
เปล่งปลั่ง plὲŋplàŋ′ V to glow (with health), be
radiant (of looks).

ปลัด palàd′ administrative assistant, deputy.

ปลัดกระทรวง (ท่าน,คน) palàd′krasuaŋ′ (thân′,
khon′) N undersecretary (of a ministry).

o รองปลัดกระทรวง (ท่าน,คน) rɔɔŋ′-palàd′kra⊃
suaŋ′ (thân′, khon′) N deputy undersecretary
(of a ministry).

ปลา (ตัว) plaa′ (tua′) N fish. →Syn. มัจฉา lit.

กัดปลา kàdplaa′ V 1. to have a fishfight. N 2.
fishfight.

ก้างปลา (ชิ้น,อัน) kâaŋplaa′ (chín′,ʔan′) N fish
bone. →Dist. กระดูก.

กินข้าวกินปลา kinkhâaw′kinplaa′ V colloq. to
eat (a meal).

ข้าวปลาอาหาร khâawplaa′ʔaahǎan′ N elab.
food. →Also ข้าวปลา colloq.

งู ๆ ปลา ๆ ŋuuŋuu′plaaplaa′ a little bit, bits
and pieces (of knowledge).

จับปลา càbplaa′ V to fish.

o ฤดูจับปลา rýduu′càbplaa′ N fishing season.

ชิ้นปลามัน chín′plaaman′ idiom. the best part
of things; the juiciest, most desirable portion.

ตาปลา (เม็ด) taaplaa′ (méd′) N corn (callous
growth, as on the toe).

น้ำปลา námplaa′ N fish sauce (a liquid sauce made of fish and used as a salty seasoning in place of salt).

ปลากด plaakòd′ N catfish (Tachysurus).

ปลากระดี่ plaakradìi′ N gourami (esp. Trichogaster), a kind of small fresh-water fish.

ปลากระทิง plaakrathiŋ′ N a kind of fresh-water fish (Mastocembelidae).

ปลากระบอก plaakrabɔ̀ɔg′ N sea mullet (Mugilidae).

ปลากระเบน plaakrabeen′ N ray, skate.

ปลากระป๋อง (ตัว, กระป๋อง) plaakrapɔ̌ŋ′ N canned fish (tua′ for fish that is canned; kraɔpɔ̌ŋ′ for a can of canned fish).

ปลากระสูบ plaakrasùub′ N a kind of fresh-water fish (Hampala macrolepidota).

ปลากระโห้ plaakrahôo′ N a kind of fresh-water fish (Catlocarpio siamensis).

ปลากะพง plaakaphoŋ′ N general name for marine fish of the perch and bass families.

ปลากะรัง plaakaraŋ′ N grouper, a salt-water fish (Epenephelus).

ปลากัด plaakàd′ N Siamese fighting fish (Betta).

ปลาเข็ม plaakhěm′ N needle fish, fish of the Belonidae family.

ปลาเค็ม plaakhem′ N dried salted fish.

ปลาเงินปลาทอง plaaŋən′plaathɔɔŋ′ N small carp with gold and silver coloring. →See ปลาทอง.

ปลาจะละเม็ด plaa′calaméd′ N butterfish, an edible marine fish (Stromateus).

ปลาฉนาก plaachanàag′ N sawfish (Pristis).

ปลาฉลาม plaachalǎam′ N shark.

ปลาช่อน plaachɔ̂ɔn′ N 1. serpent-head, a kind of fresh-water fish. 2. euphem. penis.

ปลาดุก plaadùg′ N fresh-water catfish (Siluridae).

ปลาทอง plaathɔɔŋ′ N goldfish, small carp with gold coloring. →Comp. ปลาเงินปลาทอง.

ปลาทะเล plaa′thalee′ N sea fish, marine fish, salt-water fish (general term).

ปลาทู plaathuu′ N a very common kind of mackerel (Scombridae).

ปลาน้ำจืด plaa′námcɨ̀yd′ N fresh-water fish

(general term).

ปลาปักเป้า plaa′pàgpâw′ N globefish (Tetraodontidae).

ปลาร้า plaaráa′ N fish preserved with salt (often having roasted rice mixed with it).

o ไหปลาร้า (ข้าง) hǎj′plaaráa′ (khâaŋ′) N 1. the clavicle, collarbone. 2. the hollow just above the collarbone.

oo กระดูกไหปลาร้า kradùug′-hǎj′plaaráa′ N the clavicle, collarbone.

ปลาโลมา plaaloomaa′ N dolphin, porpoise.

ปลาวาฬ plaawaan′ N whale.

ปลาสลิด plaasalìd′ N 1. gouramy, a kind of fresh-water fish. 2. euphem. female genitalia.

ปลาหมอ plaamɔ̌ɔ′ N climbing fish (Anabus), a common fresh-water fish.

ปลาหมึก plaamɨ̀g′ N 1. cuttlefish (Sepia). 2. squid.

o ปลาหมึกยักษ์ plaamɨ̀g′jág′ octopus.

ปลาแห้ง plaahɛ̂ɛŋ′ N dried fish.

ปลาไหล plaalǎj′ N fresh-water eel.

หาปลา hǎaplaa′ V to fish. คน-- fisherman.

ปลาบ plàab′ V 1. to flow in with a rush, a surge. sV 2. with a rush, a surge. →Chiefly in combinations.

ปลาบปลื้ม plàabplɨ̂ym′ V to be delighted, glad, overjoyed, to feel a surge of delight, gladness, joy. --ใจ idem.

เสียวปลาบ sǐaw′plàab′ to get a sharp sudden sensation (painful or pleasurable), to have a sudden piercing surge of sensation.

ปลาย plaaj′ N end (of anything); tip. →Ant. ต้น.

เข็มกลัดซ่อนปลาย (ตัว, อัน) khěmklàd′sɔ̂ɔnplaaj′ (tua′, ʔan′) N safety pin.

จุดหมายปลายทาง (อัน, จุด) cùdmǎaj′plaajthaaŋ′ (ʔan′, cùd′) N destination, final goal, aim.

ดาบปลายปืน (เล่ม) dàabplaajpyyn′ (lêm′) N bayonet.

ตอนปลาย (ตอน) tɔɔnplaaj′ (tɔɔn′) 1. the end part, final part. 2. in the end, finally. →Opp. ตอนต้น.

ที่หมายปลายทาง (แห่ง, ที่) thîimǎaj′plaajthaaŋ′ (hɛ̀ŋ′, thîi′) N destination.

เบื้องปลาย bɨ̂aŋplaaj′ eleg. 1. the final part,

end part. 2. at the end. →Ant. เบื้องต้น.

ปลายข้าว plaajkhâaw/ N broken milled rice.

ปลายคน plaajkhon/ old age (with humorous connotation).

ปลายทาง plaajthaaŋ/ N. destination; goal, aim.

ปลายเนิน plaajnəən/ N the foot of a knoll, the
bottom of a slope.

ปลายปี plaajpii/ N year's end, the end of a year.

เสมอต้นเสมอปลาย samɔ̌ə/tôn/-samɔ̌ə/plaaj/ V
idiom. 1. to be consistent. sV 2. consistenly.

หอกปลายปืน (เล่ม) hɔ̀ɔgplaajpyyn/ (lêm/) N
bayonet.

หัวนอนปลายตีน hǔanɔɔn/plaajtiin/ N idiom.
the background of a person (esp. as it bears
upon his social status).

ปล้ำ plâm/ V 1. to wrestle, fight, grapple. 2. to
force by wrestling. 3. idiom. to try hard,
work very hard (on something); to strive with
utmost effort.

ปล้ำปลุก,ปลุกปล้ำ plâmplùg/, plùgplâm/ V 1. to
force (someone) by wrestling; to attack with
force (and with intent to rape, to rob). 2.
idiom. to try hard, exert oneself; to strive
with utmost effort.

มวยปล้ำ muajplâm/ N wrestling.

ปลิง (ตัว) pliŋ/ (tua/) N 1. leech, water leech. 2.
staple, clamp.

ปลิด plìd/ V to pick (off), to pluck.

ปลิ้น plîn/ V 1. to turn inside out. 2. to press out,
force out (e.g. seeds).

ปลิ้นปล้อน plînplɔ̂n/ V to lie, deceive, swindle
with deceptive words.

ปลิว pliw/ V 1. to float (in the air). 2. to be blown,
carried by the wind.

ใบปลิว (ใบ) bajpliw/ (baj/) N handbill, leaflet.

ปลิวว่อน pliw/wɔ̂n/ V to be blown about, be floating in the air in great numbers.

ปลี ๑ (ปลี,หัว) plii/ (plii/,hǔa/) N 1. spathe.
2. spadix or flower cluster (of the banana tree).
3. a prominent muscular mass such as the calf
of the human leg.

แตกปลี tɛ̀ɛg/plii/ V (a plant) to put forth its
spadix or flower cluster, (the panicle) to break
through its spathe.

หัวปลี (หัว) hǔaplii/ (hǔa/) N flower cluster of
the banana tree.

ปลี ๒ in กะหล่ำปลี (หัว,ต้น) kalàm/plii/ N cabbage
(hǔa/, for a head; tôn/, for the plant).

ปลีก plìig/ V to break up, separate; to divide into
small parts, small amounts.

ขายปลีก khǎajplìig/ V to retail, sell at retail.

เงินปลีก ŋənplìig/ N small change, coins of small
denomination.

ซื้อปลีก sýyplìig/ V to buy at retail.

ปลีกตัว plìig/tua/ V to get away (from), separate
oneself (from).

ปลีกย่อย plìig/jɔ̂j/ V 1. to be detailed. 2. to be
trivial, minor.

o เรื่องปลีกย่อย rŷaŋ/-plìig/jɔ̂j/ N small, trivial
matter.

ปลีกเวลา plìig/weelaa/ to squeeze in a bit of time,
make a little time (for some unscheduled or unexpected matter), spare a little time.

ปลื้ม plŷym/ V to be glad, delighted, gratified, pleased.
→Chiefly in combinations.

ปลาบปลื้ม plàabplŷym/ V to be delighted, glad,
overjoyed, to feel a surge of delight, gladness,
joy. --ใจ idem.

ปลื้มใจ plŷymcaj/ V to be delighted, greatly pleased.

ปลุก plùg/ V to arouse, rouse, wake (someone) up.
→Dist. ตื่น "to wake (of oneself)."

นาฬิกาปลุก (เรือน) naalikaa/plùg/ (ryan/) N
alarm clock.

ปลุกใจ plùgcaj/ V 1. to arouse, encourage (e.g.
patriotism, bravery). 2. to be arousing, encouraging.

ปลุกปล้ำ,ปล้ำปลุก plùgplâm/, plâmplùg/ V 1. to
force (someone) by wrestling; to attack with force
(and with intent to rape, rob). 2. idiom. to
try hard, exert oneself; to strive with utmost
effort.

ปลุกปั่น plùgpàn/ V to stir up, incite, arouse (esp.
in connection with crime, wrongdoing).

ปลูก plùug/ V 1. to plant, cultivate (plants, friendship). 2. to construct, build, erect. 3. short
for ปลูกฝี.

ปลูกฝัง plùug/fǎŋ/ V 1. to marry off, establish
(a person). 2. to cultivate, plant, establish

(in the mind).

ปลูกฝี, --ดาษ plùugfǐi′, plùugfǐidàad′ V 1. to
vaccinate (against smallpox). 2. to be vaccinated. การ-- smallpox vaccination.

ปลูกไม่ขึ้น plùug′mâjkhŷn′ can't grow (it); (it)
won't grow, can't be grown.

ปลูกสร้าง plùug′sâaŋ′ V to build, construct.

o สิ่งปลูกสร้าง sìŋ′plùugsâaŋ′ N a construction,
anything constructed.

พืชปลูก phŷydplùug′ N cultivated plant.

เพาะปลูก phɔ́ʔplùug′ V to cultivate (land, plants).
การ-- cultivation.

ปวก in ปวกเปียก pùagpìag′ V 1. to be weak. 2.
to be limp (lacking firmness, stiffness).

ปวง puaŋ′ Nm all, entire.

ทั้งปวง tháŋpuaŋ′ com. all, (of) every kind, (of)
every description. →Cf. also ทั้งนั้น, ทั้งผอง,
ทั้งเพ, ทั้งมวล, ทั้งสิ้น, ทั้งหมด, ทั้งหลาย.

ปวงชน puaŋchon′ writ. every one, all the people.

ปวด pùad′ V 1. to ache. 2. to be in pain. →Syn.
เจ็บ.

เจ็บปวด cèbpùad′ V 1. to be painful, to hurt.
2. to be in pain. ความ-- pain, painfulness.

ปวดท้อง pùadthɔ́ɔŋ′ V to have a stomach ache,
a bellyache.

ปวดฟัน pùadfan′ V to have a toothache.

ปวดมวน pùadmuan′ V to have a colic, a fitful
pain in the abdomen.

ปวดร้าว pùadráaw′ V 1. to have a splitting pain.
2. to ache (as though) splitting.

ปวดศีรษะ pùad′sǐisaʔ′ V eleg. to have a headache. →Syn. ปวดหัว com.

ปวดหลัง pùadlǎŋ′ V to have a backache.

ปวดหัว pùadhǔa′ V com. to have a headache.

ป่วน in ปั่นป่วน pànpùan′ V 1. to be confused,
agitated, in a state of confusion, in turmoil. 2.
to be unstable and fluctuating. ความ-- chaos,
disorder, unrest, agitation, turmoil.

ปั่นป่วนใจ pànpùan′caj′ V (the mind) to be in
turmoil.

ป่วนเปี้ยน pûanpîan′ V colloq. to stay close to,
hang around.

ป่วย pùaj′ V eleg. to be sick, ill. →Dist. เป็นไข้.

เจ็บไข้ได้ป่วย cèbkhâj′dâjpùaj′ V elab. eleg.
to get sick.

ป่วยการ pùajkaan′ V to be no use, in vain, for
nothing.

o ค่าป่วยการ khâa′pùajkaan′ N eleg. fee, service charge, commission.

ป่วยไข้ pùajkhâj′ V eleg. to be sick, ill. การ--
being sick; sickness, illness.

ป่วยเจ็บ, เจ็บป่วย pùajcèb′, cèbpùaj′ V to be sick,
ill. การ-- sickness, illness, being sick.
ความ-- sickness, illness.

ป่วยเป็นไข้ pùaj′penkhâj′ to have a fever, be sick
with fever.

ป่วยเป็นโรค pùaj′penrôog′ to have a disease, be
afflicted with a disease.

ลาป่วย laapùaj′ V to request or take sick leave.

หายป่วย hǎajpùaj′ V to recover, get well.

ปศุสัตว์, ปสุสัตว์ (ตัว) pàsusàd′ (tua′) N eleg.
domestic animals.

ปอ pɔɔ′ N hemp.

แมลงปอ (ตัว) malɛɛŋpɔɔ′ (tua′) N dragonfly.
→Also แมงปอ colloq.

ปอก pɔ̀ɔg′ V to peel, pare, shell.

ปอกลอก pɔ̀ɔglɔɔg′ V to defraud, fleece, skin,
clean (someone) out by pretending love, friendship, interest.

ไข่ปอก (ใบ, ฟอง, ลูก) khàjpɔ̀ɔg′ (baj′, fɔɔŋ′, lûug′)
N boiled eggs with shells removed.

ปอก...ออก pɔ̀ɔgɔ...ʔɔ̀ɔg′ to peel (skin, etc.) off.

ปอง pɔɔŋ′ V 1. to intend. 2. to aim to get.

ปองร้าย pɔɔŋráaj′ V to intend harm; to determine
to do harm.

ป่อง pɔ̀ŋ′* V 1. to bulge, protrude. 2. to be protu-
berant, protruding, bulging out.

แมลงป่อง (ตัว) malɛɛŋpɔ̀ŋ′ (tua′) N scorpion.
→Also แมงป่อง colloq.

ป้อง pɔ̂ŋ′* V to protect, guard, cover up.

ป้องกัน pɔ̂ŋkan′ V 1. to protect, defend. 2. to
take a preventive measure. การ-- defense,
protection; prevention (of disease, crime).

ป้องปัด pɔ̂ŋpàd′ V to ward off (e.g. blows, danger).

ป้องหู pɔ̂ŋhǔu′ V to put one's hand to one's ear
in order to hear better.

ปิดป้อง pìdpɔ̂ŋ′ V to defend, guard; to cover up

 in defense, protect by covering.

ปอด (ข้าง,ปอด) pɔ̀ɔd′ N 1. lung, the lungs (khâaŋ′, pɔ̀ɔd′). V 2. to be flattened. 2. slang to be scared, to flinch.

ปอดบวม pɔ̀ɔdbuam′ N pneumonia. โรค-- idem.

o เป็นปอดบวม penpɔ̀ɔdbuam′ to have pneumonia.

ปอดลอย pɔ̀ɔd′lɔɔj′ V 1. slang to be timorous, faint-hearted. 2. to be scared out of one's wits.

ปอดเสีย pɔ̀ɔd′sǐa′ idem.

ผายปอด phǎajpɔ̀ɔd′ V to administer artificial respiration.

โรคปอด rôogpɔ̀ɔd′ N lung disease.

ปอน in เปียกปอน plàgpɔɔn′ V to be soaked, drenched, completely wet.

ป้อน pɔ̂ɔn′ V 1. to feed (to the mouth). 2. to supply.

ปอนด์ pɔɔn′ C 1. pound. 2. clf. for a loaf of bread (i.e. a pound). [f. Eng.]

ป้อม ๑ (หลัง,แห่ง) pɔ̂m′* (lǎŋ′, hèŋ′) N fortification.

ป้อมตำรวจ pɔ̂m′tamrùad′ N police booth.

ป้อมบิน (ลำ) pɔ̂mbin′ (lam′) N superfortress, flying fortress.

ป้อมปืนกล (ป้อม,แห่ง) pɔ̂m′pyynkon′ (pɔ̂m′, hèŋ′) N pillbox; machine gun nest.

เมืองป้อม myaŋpɔ̂m′ N fortress.

ป้อม ๒ pɔ̂m′* V to be spherical, rounded.

ปอย pɔɔj′ C lock, tuft, bunch (e.g. of hair).

ปะ ๑ pà?′ V to patch, mend (e.g. clothing).

รอยปะ (รอย) rɔɔjpà?′ (rɔɔj′) N patch.

ปะ ๒ pà?′ V to meet, encounter. →Chiefly in compounds. →Syn. พบ.

พบปะ phóbpà?′ V to meet, encounter.

พบปะสนทนา phóbpà?′sǒnthanaa′ to meet and converse.

ปะการัง pakaa′raŋ′ N coral.

ตัวปะการัง (ตัว) tua′-pakaa′raŋ′ (tua′) N coral polyps.

หินปะการัง hǐn′-pakaa′raŋ′ N coral rock.

ปะติดปะต่อ patìd′patɔ̀ɔ′ V elab. colloq. to piece together, put two and two together. →Cf. ติดต่อ.

ปะติ๋ว in ขี้ปะติ๋ว khîipatǐw′ V colloq. to be little, small (in value), trifling, insignificant.

ปะทะ pàthá?′ V 1. to collide; to clash. 2. to encounter and assault; to attack. 3. to strike.

การ-- collision, clash, crash.

การปะทะกัน kaan′-pàthá?′kan N 1. clash. 2. military engagement.

แรงปะทะ rɛɛŋ′pàthá?′ N force of impact.

ปะทะปะทัง pàthá?′pàthaŋ′ V colloq. 1. to sustain, keep from falling. 2. to alleviate temporarily.

o รองท้องพอปะทะปะทังความหิวไปก่อน rɔɔŋthɔ́ɔŋ′ɔ̀ phɔɔpàthá?′pàthaŋ′-khwaamhǐw′pajkɔ̀ɔn′ to have a snack just to alleviate one's hunger temporarily.

ปะทุ pathú?′ V 1. to burst, explode. 2. to break out.

ปะทุขึ้น pathú?′khŷn′ V to pop, explode.

ปะปน pà?pon′ V 1. to mix, mingle, combine, intermingle, mix up. 2. to be mixed, intermingled. 3. to be shared (in use by several people). →See ปน.

ปะปัง in ธุระปะปัง (อย่าง) thúrá?′pà?paŋ′ (jàaŋ′) N colloq. business, work to be done, things that keep one busy.

ปะรำ (หลัง) param′ (lǎŋ′) N pavilion, temporary shelter built for a special occasion.

ปะไร paraj′. Short for เป็นไร q.v.

ปะแล่ม in หวานปะแล่มๆ wǎan′-palêm′palêm′* to be slightly sweet.

ปัก pàg′ V 1. to stick in, insert. 2. to embroider. 3. to be embroidered.

ขวดปักดอกไม้ (ใบ,ลูก) khùad′pàgdɔ̀ɔgmáaj′ (baj′, lûug′) N flower vase.

ปักเขตต์ pàgkhèed′ V to set a boundary.

ปักใจ pàgcaj′ V to set one's mind, fix one's mind.

ปักดำ pàg′dam′ V to transplant (young rice plants).

ปักผม pàgphǒm′ V to stick in the hair.

ปักหลัก pàglàg′ V 1. to drive a post or stake. 2. colloq. to dig in, settle down.

o นกปักหลัก (ตัว) nógpàglàg′ (tua′) N kingfisher.

ปักหัว pàghǔa′ V to dive, plunge head first.

เย็บปักถักร้อย jébpàg′thàgrɔ́ɔj′ V 1. to do needlework. N 2. needlework.

ลงหลักปักราก loŋlàg′pàgrâag′ V elab. to lay the foundation.

ปักกิ่ง pàgkìŋ′ pN Peking. [f. Chin.] →See ปักเพ่ง.

ปักเป้า,ปลา-- (ตัว) pàgpâw′, plaa′pàgpâw′ (tua′) N globefish (Tetraodontidae).

ว่าวปักเป้า (ตัว) wâw′pàgpâw′ (tua′) N a small

diamond-shaped kite with a long tail (called the
female). →Cf. ว่าวจุฬา.

ปักเพ้ง pàgphéŋ/* pN Peiping. [f. Chin.]

ปักษ์ pàg/ N 1. section, part. 2. fortnight. →Only
in special compounds. →Comp. 1. ภาค.

ประจำปักษ์ pracam/'pàg/ fortnightly.

ปักษ์ใต้ pàgtâaj/ N the south, the southern part
(of the country).

ปักษ์เหนือ pàgnʉ̌a/ N the north, the northern part
(of the country).

รายปักษ์ raajpàg/ fortnightly, every two weeks.

ปัง in ขนมปัง (แผ่น,ชิ้น,ปอนด์) khanŏmpaŋ/ N
bread (phèn/ for a slice; chín/ for a piece;
pɔɔn/ for a loaf). [ปัง f. Port.]

ปั้ง pǎŋ/ rM intensifier used with ฟิต "fit," and
แน่น "tight, crowded."

ปัจจัย (อย่าง) pàdcaj/ (jàaŋ/) N eleg. 1. cause,
factor, means. 2. requisite, necessary thing.

จตุปัจจัย catù?/'pàdcaj/ N lit.,eleg. the four
requisites for maintaining the comfort of a
Buddhist priest, viz., food, shelter, clothing and
drugs.

ปัจจุบัน pàdcuban/ N 1. the present. 2. at present,
now, nowadays.

การปัจจุบันพยาบาล kaan/-pàdcuban/phajaabaan/
N first aid.

ในปัจจุบัน najpàdcuban/ at present, now.

ปัจจุบันทันด่วน pàdcuban/thandùan/ suddenly,
urgently, abruptly.

แผนปัจจุบัน phɛ̌ɛn/pàdcuban/ N 1. new plan,
modern plan. 2. (as n. mod.) modern, of the
modern type.

แพทย์ปัจจุบัน (นาย,คน) phɛ̂ɛd/pàdcuban/ (naaj/,
khon/) N modern doctor.

โรคปัจจุบัน (ชนิด) rôog/pàdcuban/ (chaníd/) N
sudden illness (sometimes one which causes
immediate death).

ลมปัจจุบัน lom/pàdcuban/ N a sudden stroke,
attack (of illness).

สมัยปัจจุบัน samǎj/pàdcuban/ N modern times,
the present time.

ปัจฉิม. Bound stem meaning "after, later, last."

ปัจฉิมลิขิต pàdchǐm/líkhìd/ N postscript.
→Abbrev. ป.ล.

ปัจฉิมวัย pàdchǐm/máwaj/ N lit. old age, the
final period of life.

ปัญจ- pan/caꞒ combining form meaning "five."
→Also เบญจ-.

ปัญญา panjaa/ N wisdom; (acquired) knowledge,
intelligence.

จนปัญญา con/panjaa/ V colloq. to be at one's
wit's end; to have run out of ideas (in trying to
figure something out).

หมดปัญญา mòd/panjaa/ V to be at one's wit's end.

ปัญหา (ปัญหา,ข้อ) panhǎa/ (panhǎa/, khɔ̂ɔ/) N 1.
problem, question (matter for discussion or
investigation). 2. riddle, puzzle. 3. point (of
law, of fact).

o ปัญหาเกาหลี panhǎa/kawlǐi/ N the Korean
question; the Korean problem.

แก้ปัญหา kɛ̂ɛ/panhǎa/ V to solve a problem, solve
a riddle.

ตัดปัญหา tàd/panhǎa/ V to eliminate a problem.

ปัญหาเรื้อรัง panhǎa/rýaraŋ/ N chronic problem.

ไม่มีปัญหา mâjmii/panhǎa/ 1. without question;
doubtless, no doubt. 2. there is no question
(about it). อย่าง-- unquestionably, doubtlessly.

หมดปัญหา mòd/panhǎa/ V to be rid of a problem;
to free (oneself) from a vexing problem; a problem to be taken care of, solved.

ปัด ๑ pàd/ V 1. to brush away, brush off (with a brisk
motion), whisk off. 2. to wipe, dust off. 3. to
push away, ward off. →Dist. เช็ด,ปาด.

ที่ปัดน้ำฝน (อัน) thîipàd/námfŏn/ (?an/) N wind-
shield-wiper.

บอกปัด bɔ̀ɔgpàd/ V colloq. to turn down, refuse.

ป้องปัด pɔ̂ŋpàd/ V to ward off (e.g. blows, danger).

ปัดกวาดบ้าน pàdkwàad/bâan/ V to clean house,
i.e. to dust and sweep.

ปัดขึ้น pàd/khŷn/ V math. to raise a fraction to
the next whole number.

ปัดเป่า pàdpàw/ V to ward off, dispel, clear up
(a problem).

ปัดฝุ่น pàdfùn/ V to dust, dust off.

ปัด ๒ pàd/ in ลูกปัด lûugpàd/ N glass beads.

ปัตตานี pàdtaanii/ pN Pattani, in S Thailand.

ปัน pan/ V to share, divide into shares.

ปันผล panphŏn/ V to share the profits.

o เงินปันผล ŋən'panphǒn/ dividend (given to a
shareholder).

ปันส่วน pansùan/ V to ration.

ปั่น pàn/ V 1. to spin (something). 2. to become
confused, be in a tizzy. 3. colloq. to do rapidly, fast. เครื่อง-- instrument for spinning,
turning, churning (something); blender, homo-
genizer.

ปลุกปั่น plùgpàn/ V to stir up, incite, arouse
(esp. in connection with crime, wrongdoing).

ปั่นจักรยาน pàn'càgkrajaan/ colloq. to ride a
bicycle (rapidly).

ปั่นป่วน pànpùan/ V 1. to be confused, agitated,
in a state of confusion, turmoil. 2. to be unstable and fluctuating. ความ-- chaos, disorder, unrest, turmoil, agitation.

o ปั่นป่วนใจ pànpùan'caj/ V (the mind) to be in
turmoil.

ปั่นฝ้าย pànfâaj/ V to spin cotton yarn.

ปั่นหัว pànhǔa/ V to work on someone to change
his views or to incite him to action.

ปั้น ๑ pân/ V to mold (e.g. things of clay, plaster,
etc.).

เครื่องปั้นดินเผา khrŷaŋpân'dinphǎw/ N earthenware.

ช่างปั้น (คน) châaŋpân/ (khon/) N modeller
(one who molds clay, plaster, etc.).

ปั้นน้ำเป็นตัว pânnáam/pentua/ idiom. to make
up a story out of whole cloth, fabricate a lie.

ปั้นปึ่ง pânpỳŋ/ V to be haughtily indifferent to
(someone).

รูปปั้น (รูป) rûubpân/ N molded figure, molded
statue, figurine.

หมายมั่นปั้นมือ mǎajmân/pânmyy/ V elab.
colloq. 1. to resolve, have a strong determination (to do something). 2. to anticipate strongly.

ปั้น ๒ in กำปั้น (อัน) kampân/ (?an/) N fist.

ปั๊ม pám/ N 1. pump. V 2. to pump. [f. Eng.]

ปัสสาวะ pàsǎawá?/, pàdsǎawá?/ N eleg. 1. urine.
V 2. to urinate. →Also 2. ถ่ายปัสสาวะ.
→Syn. เยี่ยว com., vulg.

กระเพาะปัสสาวะ (กระเพาะ) kraphɔ́?'pàdsǎa=
wá?/ (kraphɔ́?/) N eleg. urinary bladder.

ปา paa/ V 1. to throw, toss at. 2. colloq. to

move unexpectedly fast (as of time, money).

ขว้างปา khwâaŋ'paa/ V to throw, hurl (at).

ป่า (แห่ง) pàa/ (hɛ̀ŋ/) N 1. forest, woods. 2. thicket.
3. meadow. 4. (as n. mod.) forest; wild, savage.
คน-- (see below). →Syn. 1. ดง. →Ant. 4.
บ้าน. NOTE. In the meaning "wild" ป่า is
sometimes coupled with เถื่อน. See ป่าเถื่อน
below.

ไก่ป่า (ตัว) kàjpàa/ (tua/) N wild fowl.

เข้าป่าเข้าดง khâwpàa'khâwdoŋ/ V elab. colloq.
to go into the jungle (used esp. in a fig. sense,
i.e. to get away from it all).

ไข้ป่า khâjpàa/ N colloq. malaria. →Syn.
ไข้จับสั่น eleg.

คนป่า (คน) khonpàa/ (khon/) savage, barbarian;
primitive, uncivilized people. →Cf. ชาวบ้านป่า.

เจ้าป่า (องค์) câawpàa/ (?oŋ/) N spirit guardian
of a forest.

ชาวบ้านป่า chaawbâanpàa/ N a person living in
the wilds, e.g. a hunter. →Cf. คนป่า.

ป่าจาก (แห่ง) pàacàag/ (hɛ̀ŋ/) N thicket of nipa
palms.

ป่าชัฏ pàa'chád/ N jungle, deep forest.

ป่าช้า (แห่ง) pàacháa/ (hɛ̀ŋ/) N cemetery.

ป่าดงดิบ (แห่ง) pàa'doŋdìb/ (hɛ̀ŋ/) N tropical
evergreen forest.

ป่าแดง (แห่ง) pàadɛɛŋ/ (hɛ̀ŋ/) N deciduous forest.

ป่าเถื่อน pàa'thỳan/ V to be barbaric, barbarous,
savage, primitive, uncivilized. คน-- savage,
barbarian; primitive, uncivilized people. อย่าง--
primitively, in an uncivilized manner.

ป่าทึบ (แห่ง) pàa'thýb/ (hɛ̀ŋ/) N dense jungle.

ป่าไม้ (ป่า,แห่ง) pàamáaj/ (pàa/,hɛ̀ŋ/) N timber
forest. การ-- forestry.

ป่าสัก in แม่น้ำป่าสัก mɛɛnáampàasàg/ pN the
Pasak River.

ป่าสูง (แห่ง) pàasǔuŋ/ (hɛ̀ŋ/) N tall forest, esp.
of tall trees as found in the highlands.

ผีป่า (ตน) phǐipàa/ (ton/) N forest demon.

แมวป่า (ตัว) mɛɛwpàa/ (tua/) N wildcat, leopard
cat.

ล้มป่า lómpàa/ V to deforest.

สัตว์ป่า (ตัว) sàdpàa/ (tua/) N wild animal,
forest animal.

สุนัขป่า (ตัว) sunág'pàa' (tua') N eleg. wolf.

หมาป่า (ตัว) mǎapàa' (tua') N com. wolf.

หูป่าตาเถื่อน hǔupàa'taathýan' V elab. colloq.
to be ignorant of what is going on, of what is
happening.

ฮาป่า haapàa' (a group of people) to laugh and
hoot, give a roar of laughter (i.e. to give a loud
"ha," indicating either amusement or derision).

ป้า (คน) pâa' (khon') N 1. elder aunt (older sister
of father or mother). P 2. you, Auntie (sp. to
elder aunt or other older woman); she, her,
Auntie (sp. of elder aunt); I, me, Auntie (elder
aunt or older woman sp. to nephew, niece, or
other ygr. person). T 3. Aunt -- (ref. to elder
aunt or other older woman). →Opp. ลุง.
→Dist. อา,น้า.

ป้าสะไภ้ (คน) pâa'sapháj' (khon') N wife of
elder uncle, elder aunt-in-law.

ปาก (ปาก) pàag' (pàag') N 1. mouth, beak, lips.
2. orifice. C 3. clf. for mouths, cast nets.
→Syn. 1. พระโอษฐ์ roy., โอษฐ์ lit.

ขี้ปาก khîipàag' N 1. colloq. gossip, idle talk.
2. the parroting of another's words. 3. a victim of gossip.

คันปาก khanpàag' V colloq. to be itching to
say something.

จุ๊ปาก cú?pàag' V to tut, go "tch, tch!"

ติดปาก tìdpàag' V to be addicted to the use of
a certain word or expression.

เต็มปาก tempàag' idiom. freely, without qualms,
without restraint (of speaking).

ทาปาก thaapàag' V to put on lipstick, apply
lipstick.

บ้วนปาก bûanpàag' V to rinse the mouth.

ปริปาก prì?pàag' V 1. to open one's mouth (to
speak). 2. to utter.

ปากกระบอก pàagkrabɔ̀ɔg' N muzzle (of firearms).

ปากกล้า pàagklâa' V 1. to use bold, strong words.
2. to be fresh (in talking).

ปากกา (ด้าม,ตัว,ปาก) pàagkaa' N 1. pen
(dâam'). 2. pen-point (tua')(short for ตัวปาก
กา). 3. crow's beak (pàag').

o ด้ามปากกา (ด้าม) dâam'pàagkaa' (dâam') N
penholder.

o ตัวปากกา (ตัว) tua'pàagkaa' (tua') N penpoint.

o นามปากกา (นาม) naam'pàagkaa' (naam') N
pen name.

o ปากกาลูกลื่น (ด้าม,อัน) pàagkaa'lûuglŷyn'
(dâam',?an') N ball point pen.

o ปากกาหมึกซึม (ด้าม,อัน) pàagkaa'mŷgsym'
(dâam',?an') N fountain pen.

ปากแข็ง pàag'khěŋ' V 1. to be argumentative.
2. to be unwilling to tell or admit, to be tight-
lipped.

ปากคลอง pàagkhlɔɔŋ' N entrance to a canal.

ปากคัน pàag'khan' V to be loose-tongued.

ปากคำ pàagkham' N 1. spoken word, words.
2. testimony, statement.

o ต่อปากคำ tɔ̀ɔ'pàagkham' 1. to talk back, argue
back and forth. 2. to have words (with someone).

o ให้ปากคำ hâj'pàagkham' to testify, give testimony, make a statement.

ปากคีบ (อัน) pàagkhîib' (?an') N forceps.

ปากจัด pàagcàd' V to have a sharp tongue, be
sharp-tongued, sarcastic, given to giving a
tougue-lashing.

ปากช่อง (แห่ง,ช่อง) pàagchɔ̂ŋ' (hèŋ',chɔ̂ŋ') N
entrance to a passageway.

ปากดี pàag'dii' V to have a loose tongue. Lit.,
"fine-mouthed"; hence used ironically.

ปากถนน (แห่ง) pàag'thanǒn' (hèŋ') N entrance
to a road, street.

ปากทาง pàagthaaŋ' N the beginning of a way,
passage, or route.

o เมืองปากทาง myaŋ'pàagthaaŋ' N town located
at the beginning of a route.

ปากน้ำ (แห่ง) pàagnáam' (hèŋ') N 1. mouth of
a river; estuary. pN 2. Paknam, colloquial name
for สมุทรปราการ Samutprakan, a township at
the mouth of the Čhaophaya R. →Also 1. ปาก
แม่น้ำ pàag'mɛ̂ɛnáam'.

ปากน้ำโพ pàagnáamphoo' pN Paknampho, colloquial
name for นครสวรรค์ Nakhɔn Sawan, a township
in C Thailand.

ปากบอน pàagbɔɔn' V colloq. to be a blabbermouth, tale-bearer, tattler.

ปากเปราะ pàagprɔ̀?' V 1. to be ever ready to
greet. 2. to be ever ready to criticize. 3. (a

dog) to be ever ready to bark (i.e. unnecessarily).

ปากเปล่า pàagplàaw′ sV orally.

ปากเปียกปากแฉะ pàagpìag′pàagchὲ?′ V colloq. to talk oneself blue in the face, i.e. to keep telling, instructing, advising, admonishing.

ปากแม่น้ำ (แห่ง,ปาก) pàag′mɛ̂ɛnáam′ (hὲŋ′, pàag′) N the mouth of a river; estuary. →Also ปากน้ำ.

ปากเสียง pàagsǐaŋ′ N spokesman, mouthpiece.

o เป็นปากเสียง penpàag′sǐaŋ′ V 1. idiom. to be a spokesman, a mouthpiece (for). 2. colloq. to have an argument (with).

ปากหวาน pàagwǎan′ V 1. to speak nicely, throw bouquets (at someone). 2. to be suave, smooth-tongued; to be a sweet talker.

ปากเหยี่ยวปากกา pàagjìaw′pàagkaa′ N idiom. danger, peril, hardship.

ปากแหว่ง pàagwὲŋ′ V to have a harelip.

ผิวปาก phǐwpàag′ V to whistle.

ฝีปาก fǐipàag′ N verbal skill, oratory skill.

o ตีฝีปาก tii′fǐipàag′ V to argue wittily; to wise-crack.

o อวดฝีปาก ?ùad′fǐipàag′ V to show cleverness of verbal expression.

มุมปาก (ข้าง) mumpàag′ (khâaŋ′) N corner of the mouth.

เม้มปาก mémpàag′ V to fold or pull one's lips inward and compress them.

รับปาก rábpàag′ V to agree (to), commit oneself (to) (verbally).

ริมฝีปาก rim′fǐipàag′ N lip.

ลมปาก lompàag′ N 1. colloq. words; speech. 2. idiom. the power of speech, the effect of words.

ลั่นปาก lânpàag′ V 1. to commit oneself, give one's word. 2. to say, speak, declare. →Syn. ลั่นคำ com., ลั่นวาจา eleg.

หญ้าปากคอก jâa′pàagkhɔɔg′ idiom. easy, obvious; so familiar as to remain unnoticed: "the grass (by) the barn door."

ออกปาก ?ɔ̀ɔgpàag′ V colloq. to utter, speak up; to mention, say, speak of.

o ออกปากขอ ?ɔ̀ɔgpàag′khɔ̌ɔ′ V to ask (for something).

อ้าปาก ?âapàag′ V to open one's mouth, to gape.

เอ่ยปาก ?ə̀əjpàag′ V to start to utter, to begin speaking.

ปาง ๑ paaŋ′ C 1. time, period, epoch. 2. the time when, when.

ปาง ๒ paaŋ′ AA almost, close to, nearly. →Syn. เกือบ,จวน,แทบ.

ปาฏิหาริย์ (อย่าง) paa′tìhǎan′ (jàaŋ′) N miracle; magic.

ปาฐก (คน) paa′thòg′ (khon′) N lecturer, speaker.

ปาฐกถา (เรื่อง) paa′thàkathǎa′ (rŷaŋ′) N 1. lecture, speech. V 2. to lecture, make a speech.

แสดงปาฐกถา sadɛɛŋ′paa′thàkathǎa′ V to lecture, give a lecture, make a speech.

ห้องปาฐกถา (ห้อง) hɔ̂ŋ′paa′thàkathǎa′ (hɔ̂ŋ′) N lecture room or auditorium.

ปาด pàad′ V 1. to smooth and level off, make smooth and level (with the edge of a blade, ruler, or other long object). 2. to push together and sweep off with the long edge of something, wipe off (food from a plate, with the length of one's finger). →Dist. เช็ด,ปัด.

ปาน ๑ (แห่ง) paan′ (hὲŋ′) N birthmark.

ปาน ๒ paan′ C 1. extent. 2. (to this or that) extent; like, as. V 3. to be like, comparable to (esp. in ปานกัน below).

ปานกลาง paanklaaŋ′ 1. moderately, in a moderate degree. 2. (as n. mod.) moderate; average.

ปานกัน paan′kan to be comparable, about the same.

ปานฉะนี้ paan′chaníi′ this much, to this extent.

ปานนี้ paan′níi′ to this extent, as (e.g. beautiful) as this, like this.

ปานใด paandaj′ no matter how much, however much; to whatever extent.

ป่าน ๑ pàan′ N 1. ramie. 2. hemp. 3. flax.

กระสอบป่าน (ใบ) krasɔ̀ɔb′pàan′ (baj′) gunny sack, jute bag.

ป่าน ๒ in ป่านนี้ pàanníi′ by this time, by now.

ปาม in สวาปาม sawǎa′paam′ V slang to eat, eat greedily.

ป่าย pàaj′ V 1. to climb. 2. to cast or swing (the legs) onto. →Syn. 1. ปีน.

ปีนป่าย piinpàaj′ V to climb, clamber.

ป้าย ๑ (แผ่น) pâaj/ (phὲn/) N 1. poster, sign, placard, bill. 2. label, tag.

ป้ายหยุดรถ (ป้าย, แผ่น) pâaj/jùdród/ (pâaj/, phὲn/) N 1. bus stop placard. 2. (traffic) stop sign.

ป้าย ๒ pâaj/ V to brush or wipe with a sweeping motion; to paint (in a haphazard way), smear; to daub.

ปาล์ม paam/ N palm (general term). ต้น-- (ต้น) palm tree. [f. Eng.]

ป่าว pàaw/ V to spread widely, broadcast (e.g. news).

ป่าวร้อง pàawróɔŋ/ V 1. to announce, declare, proclaim. 2. colloq. to circulate, spread (e.g. information) around.

ป้ำ in ใจป้ำ cajpâm/ V 1. to be generous, stout-hearted, willing to take a risk. 2. to be reso-lute, determined. →Syn. 2. เด็ดเดี่ยว.

ป้ำเป๋อ pâmpə̌ə/ V colloq. to be forgetful, mixed up.

ปิง in แม่น้ำปิง mɛ̂ɛnáampiŋ/ pN the Mæping (Me Ping), a tributary of the Čhaophraya River in N Thailand. →Also แม่ปิง.

ปิ้ง pîŋ/ V 1. to roast, bake, barbecue. 2. to toast (bread). 3. to be roasted, baked, barbecued. 4. to be toasted.

ขนมปังปิ้ง khanŏmpaŋpîŋ/ N toast.

เข้าปิ้ง khâwpîŋ/ V idiom. to be in hot water, in a tight spot.

ปิงปอง piŋpɔɔŋ/* N pingpong. [f. Eng.]

ปิด pìd/ V 1. to close, cover, cover up. 2. to be closed. →Ant. เปิด.

ปกปิด pògpìd/ V to cover, cover up, conceal, keep secret.

ปิดทอง pìdthɔɔŋ/ V to gild; to cover with gold leaf.

ปิดบัง pìdbaŋ/ V to hide, cover up, conceal, keep secret.

ปิดป้อง pìdpɔ̂ŋ/ V to defend, guard, protect by covering, cover up in defense.

ปิดไฟ pìdfaj/ V to turn out the lights; to turn off the lights, the electricity. →Syn. ดับไฟ. →Ant. เปิดไฟ.

ปิดไม่เข้า pìd/mâjkhâw/ can't close (it), (it) won't

close.

ปิดล้อม pìd/lɔ́ɔm/ V to blockade, block off by surrounding. การ-- blockade (blockading).

ปิดแสตมป์ pìd/satεm/ to put, stick, affix, paste a stamp (on an envelope, in an album).

ปิติ pitì?/ N eleg. 1. delight, gladness, joy. V 2. to be glad, happy, delighted. ความ-- delight, gladness, joy. →Also ปีติ.

ปิตุ in ปิตุภูมิ pìtuphuum/ N eleg.,lit. fatherland, native country. →Syn. บ้านเกิดเมืองนอน elab. colloq.

ปิ่น pìn/ N 1. a straight pin with rounded head, some-times jewelled (used for sticking in the hair). 2. top, head.

ข้าวปิ่นแก้ว khâaw/pìnkɛ̂εw/ N top quality rice.

ปิ่นโต (ใบ, เถา) pìntoo/ (baj/, thǎw/) N a food car-rier, consisting of a set of containers stacked vertically and strapped together; tiffin carrier (Brit.).

ปิ่ม pìm/ AA lit. almost, nearly, on the point of, about to.

ปิ้ม pîm/ AA lit. almost, nearly, on the point of, about to.

ปี pii/ C 1. year. 2. years of age. NOTE. In the spoken language ขวบ is used for years of age of children under 12-13. In the written language normally only ปี is used.

NAMES OF THE TWELVE CYCLICAL YEARS
ปีชวด piichûad/ 1. Year of the Rat.
ปีฉลู piichalǔu/ 2. Year of the Ox.
ปีขาล piikhǎan/ 3. Year of the Tiger.
ปีเถาะ piithɔ̌?/ 4. Year of the Rabbit.
ปีมะโรง piimarooŋ/ 5. Year of the Dragon.
ปีมะเส็ง piimasěŋ/ 6. Year of the Snake.
ปีมะเมีย piimamia/ 7. Year of the Horse.
ปีมะแม piimamεε/ 8. Year of the Goat.
ปีวอก piiwɔ̂ɔg/ 9. Year of the Monkey.
ปีระกา piirakaa/ 10. Year of the Chicken, Cock.
ปีจอ piicɔɔ/ 11. Year of the Dog.
ปีกุน piikun/ 12. Year of the Pig.

กลางปี klaaŋpii/ mid-year, in the middle part of the year.

ต่อปี tɔ̀ɔpii/ per year. →Syn. ปีละ.

ตาปี taapii/ "the year round," in the following expressions.

o ชั่วนาตาปี chûanaa/taapii/ elab. colloq. year

in and year out, forever.

o ตาปีตาชาติ taapii'taachâad' e l a b. c o l l o q.
year in and year out.

ท้ายปี tháajpii' N latter part the year.

ประจำปี pracam'pii' annual, yearly.

ปลายปี plaajpii' N year's end, the end of a year.

ปีกลาย, เมื่อ-- piiklaaj', mɯ̂apiiklaaj' last year
(the preceding year).

ปีก่อน piikɔ̀ɔn' last year.

ปีก่อน ๆ pii'kɔ̀ɔnkɔ̀ɔn' the past years.

ปีเกิด piikə̀əd' N year of birth.

ปีละ piilaɔ yearly, a year, annually. →S y n.
ต่อปี.

o ปีละครั้ง piilakhráŋ' once a year.

o ปีละหนึ่งล้านตัน piilanɯ̀ŋ'láan'-tan' a million
tons annually.

ปีแล้วปีเล่า piiléɛw'piilâw' year after year.

ปีแสง piisɛ̌ɛŋ' C a s t r o n. light year.

ปีหน้า piinâa' N next year.

ปีใหม่ piimàj' N New Year.

o ขึ้นปีใหม่ khɯ̂n'piimàj' to start a new year.

o งานปีใหม่ ŋaan'piimàj' N New Year's festival.

o พรปีใหม่ phɔɔn'piimàj' New Year blessing(s).

รอบปี rɔ̂ɔbpii' N 1. the completion of a year;
anniversary. 2. the twelve-year cycle.

รายปี raajpii' annual, annually.

แรมปี rɛɛmpii' for a year, for a period of years.
เป็น-- i d e m.

หัวปี hǔapii' N 1. the early part of the year. 2.
(as n. mod.) eldest, first-born.

ปี่ (เลา) pìi' (law') N wind instrument (general
term).

ปี่พาทย์ pìiphâad' N Thai orchestra, consisting
of woodwinds and percussion instruments.

เป็นปี่เป็นขลุ่ย penpìi'penkhlùj' i d i o m. harmoniously, in united fashion.

ลิ้นปี่ línpìi' N 1. reed (of woodwind). 2. a n a t.
xiphoid cartilage.

ปี้ in ป่นปี้ pɔ̀npîi' c o l l o q. to be utterly ruined.

ปี๋ pǐi' rM intensifier used with ดำ "black," หลับ
ตา "close the eyes," อิ่ม "full (satiated)."

ปีก (ปีก, ข้าง) pìig' (pìig', khâaŋ') N 1. wing.
2. flank, side.

ปีกกา pìigkaa' N 1. the flank (of a military

force). 2. any shape resembling a " V " (remi-
niscent of a crow in flight). 3. brace, braces,
i.e. the typographical characters {}.

โอบปีก ʔòobplìg' V m i l i t. to flank, envelop or
turn the flank of.

ปีติ piitìʔ' V to be glad. →Also ปิติ.

ปีน piin' V to climb, mount. →S y n. ไต่, ป่าย.

ปีนป่าย piinpàaj' V to climb, clamber.

ปีนัง piinaŋ' Penang, an island off the west coast of
the Malay peninsula.

ปีศาจ (ตน) piisàad' (ton') N devil, demon; ghost.

ปีอาโน (หลัง) pii'ʔaanoo' (lǎŋ') N piano. [f. Eng.]
→Also เปียโน, เปียนโน.

ปึก pɯ̀g' C clf. for a stack (of sheets of paper), a
pack (of cards), a wad (of paper currency).

เป็นปึกแผ่น penpɯ̀g'phɛ̀n' to be firm, solid, stable.

ปึ่ง pɯ̀ŋ' V to behave arrogantly, haughtily, indifferently.

ปั้นปึ่ง pân'pɯ̀ŋ' V to be haughtily indifferent to
(someone).

ปึ้ง pɯ́ŋ' rM intensifier used with แน่น "tight."

ปึ้ด, ปื๊ด pɯ̀d', pɯ́d'* rM intensifier used with ดำ
"dark."

ปืน (กระบอก) pyyn' (krabɔ̀ɔg') N gun.

กระบอกปืน (กระบอก) krabɔ̀ɔgpyyn' (krabɔ̀ɔg')
N gun barrel.

กระสุนปืน (นัด, ลูก) krasǔn'pyyn' (nád', lûug')
N 1. bullet, shell. 2. cartridge. เครื่อง--
firearms and ammunition.

กระสุนปืนใหญ่ (นัด, ลูก) krasǔn'pyynjàj' (nád',
lûug') N artillery shell, projectile.

ไกปืน (ไก) kajpyyn' (kaj') N trigger.

ดาบปลายปืน (เล่ม) dàabplaajpyyn' (lêm') N
bayonet. →S y n. หอกปลายปืน.

ด้ามปืน (ด้าม) dâampyyn' (dâam') N gunstock.

ดินปืน dinpyyn' N gunpowder.

ปืนกล (กระบอก) pyynkon' (krabɔ̀ɔg') N machine
gun.

o ป้อมปืนกล (ป้อม, แห่ง) pɔ̂m'pyynkon' (pɔ̂m',
hɛ̀ŋ') N pillbox; machine gun nest.

ปืนครก (กระบอก) pyynkhróg' (krabɔ̀ɔg') N
m i l i t. mortar.

ปืนต่อสู้อากาศยาน (กระบอก) pyyn'-tɔ̀ɔsûu'ʔaaɔ
kàad'sajaan' (krabɔ̀ɔg') N anti-aircraft gun.

→Abbrev. ป.ต.อ.

ปืนพก (กระบอก) pyynphóg′ (krabɔɔg′) N pistol, revolver.

ปืนยาว (กระบอก) pyynjaaw′ (krabɔɔg′) N 1. shotgun. 2. rifle.

ปืนลูกซอง (กระบอก) pyyn′lûugsɔɔŋ′ (krabɔɔg′) N shotgun.

ปืนสั้น (กระบอก) pyynsân′ (krabɔɔg′) N pistol, revolver.

ปืนใหญ่ (กระบอก) pyynjàj′ (krabɔɔg′) N 1. cannon; artillery piece. 2. artillery. →Abbrev. ป.

o กระสุนปืนใหญ่ (นัด,ลูก) krasǔn′pyynjàj′ (nád′, lûug′) N artillery shell, projectile.

o ทหารปืนใหญ่ (คน) thahǎan′pyynjàj′ (khon′) N 1. artilleryman. 2. the artillery.

เรือปืน (ลำ) ryapyyn′ (lam′) N gunboat.

ลูกปืน (ลูก,นัด) lûugpyyn′ (lûug′, nád′) N 1. bullet, gunshot. 2. ball bearing.

o ลูกปืนใหญ่ (ลูก) lûugpyynjàj′ (lûug′) N cannon ball.

ศูนย์ปืน (ศูนย์,อัน) sǔunpyyn′ (sǔun′, ʔan′) N gun sight.

หอกปลายปืน (เล่ม) hɔɔgplaajpyyn′ (lêm′) N bayonet. →Syn. ดาบปลายปืน.

อาวุธปืน ʔaawúd′pyyn′ N firearms.

ปื้น pŷyn′ C clf. for hand saws.

ปื๋อ pŷy′ rM intensifier used with ดำ "black."

ปุก in ปุกปุย pùgpuj′ V to be downy, fluffy, bushy, shaggy.

ปุถุชน (คน) pùthùchon′ (khon′) N lit. ordinary people; the common man, average man.

ปุ่ม pùm′ N nodule, node, knot, knob, lump.

ปุ่มปม pùm′pom′ N knots, kinks.

ปุ่มรส pùmród′ N taste bud.

เป็นปุ่ม penpùm′ V to be nodulated, knotted, kinky.

ปุย puj′ N fluff; a fluffy fiber or fibrous mass.

ปุกปุย pùgpuj′ V to be downy, fluffy, bushy, shaggy.

ปุยฝ้าย (ปุย) pujfâaj′ (puj′) N cotton fiber, cotton wool.

ปุ๋ย ๑ (อย่าง,ชะนิด) pǔj′ (jàaŋ′, chaníd′) N fertilizer. [f. Chin.]

ปุ๋ย ๒ pǔj′ rM intensifier used with หลับ,นอนหลับ "sleep", having the sense of "soundly."

ปู ๑ (ตัว) puu′ (tua′) N crab.

ปูนา (ตัว) puunaa′ (tua′) N field crab, a small fresh-water crab.

ปูแสม (ตัว) puusamɛ̌ɛ′ (tua′) N small salt-water crab.

ปู ๒ puu′ V 1. to spread out (as a mat). 2. to spread over, to cover (with); to pave (with).

ถนนปูหิน thanǒn′puuhǐn′ N a stone-paved road.

ผ้าปูโต๊ะ (ผืน) phâapuutó?′ (phy̌yn′) N tablecloth, lunch cloth.

ผ้าปูที่นอน (ผืน) phâapuu′thîinɔɔn′ (phy̌yn′) N sheet.

ปู่ (คน) pùu′ (khon′) N 1. paternal grandfather, father's father. P 2. you, he, him, Grandpa (sp. to or about one's paternal grandfather); I, me, Grandpa (paternal grandfather sp. to grandchild).

ปู่ย่า (คน) pùu′jâa′ (khon′) N ancestors: "paternal grandparents."

ปู่ย่าตายาย (คน) pùujâa′taajaaj′ (khon′) N ancestors: "paternal grandparents and maternal grandparents."

หลานปู่ (คน) lǎanpùu′ (khon′) N grandchild in the male line.

ปูน ๑ puun′ N 1. lime. 2. mortar (as for laying bricks).

ถือปูน thy̌ypuun′ V 1. to mortar (e.g. bricks). 2. to plaster.

ปั้นปูน pânpuun′ V to mold lime.

ปูนขาว puunkhǎaw′ N lime.

ปูนซิเมนต์,-ซี- puun′simen, -sii′- N cement. [ซิเมนต์ f. Eng.]

ปูนปั้น puunpân′ N molded lime.

หินปูน hǐnpuun′ N 1. limestone. 2. tartar, calculus (i.e. incrustation on teeth).

ปูน ๒ puun′ V to be equivalent to, comparable to, like.

ปูน ๓ puun′ V to give, destribute (a reward, rewards). →Chiefly in the following expression. [f. Chin.]

ปูนบำเหน็จรางวัล puun′-bamnèd′raaŋwan′ V to reward, distribute rewards.

เป in ปนเป ponpee′ V 1. to mix together. 2. to mix, be mixed in a disorderly or confused way.

เป๋ in ขี้เป๋ khîipěe′ colloq. to be bad, of poor

quality.

เป๋ pěe′ sV to one side, slanted, twisted.

เป๋ง pěŋ′* sV fixed, fixedly; precise, precisely.

   จ้อง (...) เป๋ง cɔ̂ŋ(...)pěŋ′ to stare, stare right

      at.

   ตรงเป๋ง troŋpěŋ′ V 1. to be absolutely correct.

      2. to be absolutely straight.

   เที่ยงเป๋ง thîaŋpěŋ′ at noon sharp.

เป็ด (ตัว) pèd′ (tua′) N duck.

   เป็ดไก่ (ตัว) pèdkàj′ (tua′) N barnyard fowl.

   o หมูเห็ดเป็ดไก่ mǔuhèd′pèdkàj′ N colloq.

      meats of various kinds.

   เป็ดย่าง (ตัว) pèdjâaŋ′ (tua′) N roast duck.

เป็น, เปน pen′ V 1. to be, exist, become (some-

     thing). 2. to be live, alive, living. sV 3. as,

     for, into. 4. able to, knows how to. คำ-- (see

     below). →Ant. 2. ตาย. NOTE. The spelling

     เปน, though not shown in the official dictionary,

     is very common in newpapers.

   o เขาเป็นครู kháwpenkhruu′ He is a teacher.

   o นี่ไม่ใช่ดินสอ เป็นปากกา nîi′mâjchâjdinsɔɔ′→

      penpàagkaa′↓ This is not a pencil, it's a pen.

   o สัตว์เป็น sàd′pen′ live animal.

   o แบ่งออกเป็น ๔ ส่วน bèŋ′ʔɔ̀ɔgpensìi′sùan′ to

      be divided up into four parts.

   o นับเป็น náb′pen′ to know how to count.

   ...กว่า(...) เป็นไหน ๆ ...kwàa′(...)pennǎjnǎj′

      far...-er (than...), far more... (than), more

      ...by far (than...).

   เข้าเป็นสมาชิก khâw′pensamaachíg′ to become

      a member (of).

   ความเป็นความตาย khwaampen′khwaamtaaj′ N

     life and death.

   ค่อยเป็นค่อยไป khɔ̂jpen′khɔ̂jpaj′ to learn or

     acquire ability little by little, in due time.

   คำเป็น (คำ) khampen′ (kham′) N live syllable

     (in the Thai system of writing), i.e. a syllable

     ending in a long vowel or a sonorant. →Opp.

     คำตาย.

   คิดเป็น... khíd′pen⊃ to be figured in such and

     such a kind of money, currency).

   จะเป็นไรไป capen′rajpaj↓ It doesn't matter.

   จะเป็นอย่างไร capen′jàaŋraj′ what will happen;

     what will happen to or become of.

จับเป็น càb′pen′ to catch alive, take alive. →Ant.

   จับตาย.

   o นักโทษคนนี้ต้องจับเป็น nágthôod′khonníi′ tɔ̂ŋ⊃

      càb′pen′↓ (You) have to take this convict alive.

   จับ...เป็น càb⊃...pen′ to know how to catch

     (something).

   o จับนกเป็น càbnóg′pen′ to know how to catch

     birds.

   จำเป็น campen′ V to be necessary.

   ถอดเป็นภาษาไทย thɔ̀ɔd′penphaasǎathaj′ to trans-

     late into Thai.

   ทั้งเป็น tháŋpen′ alive.

   o ฝังทั้งเป็น fǎŋ′tháŋpen′ to bury alive.

   นับเป็น náb′pen′ to know how to count.

   นับเป็น... náb′pen⊃ to be considered, reckoned

     as; to be counted by (e.g. the millions).

   เป็นกบฏ penkabòd′ to rebel, mutiny, commit treason.

   เป็นกระจุก penkracùg′ 1. in bunches, bunched to-

     gether, bunched up. 2. in a mass, in lumps.

   เป็นกระเซิง penkrasəəŋ′ (the hair) to stand out

     form the head, stick out in all directions (as

     when mussed, windblown, too thick, too curly).

   เป็นกระบวน penkrabuan′ 1. in a procession, in

     formation. 2. colloq. in great numbers.

   เป็นกลาง penklaaŋ′ 1. to be neutral (in a contro-

     versy). 2. elect. to be neutral, not charged,

     ความ-- neutrality.

   เป็นกลุ่มเป็นก้อน penklùm′penkɔ̂n′ all in one piece,

     in one lump, all nicely together.

   o รวมเงินเป็นกลุ่มเป็นก้อน ruamŋən′penklùm′

      penkɔ̂n′ to gather the money (from different

     sources) into one lump sum.

   เป็นกอง penkɔɔŋ′ colloq. much, a lot, a heap,

     heaps, abundantly.

   o ดีกว่าเป็นกอง dii′kwàapenkɔɔŋ′ to be much

     better, a lot better.

   o เขามีเงินตั้งเป็นกอง kháwmiiŋən′tâŋpenkɔɔŋ′↓

     He has a heap of money.

   เป็นกองส่องกอง penkɔɔŋ′sɔ̀ɔŋkɔɔŋ′ elab. colloq.

     a lot (of), a whole lot (of), heaps (of).

   o เงินเป็นกองส่องกอง ŋən′-penkɔɔŋ′sɔ̀ɔŋkɔɔŋ′

     lots of money, heaps of money.

   เป็นก้อน penkɔ̂n′ 1. to be lumpy, to form lumps.

     2. in lumps. →See also เป็นกลุ่มเป็นก้อน above.

เป็นกอบเป็นกำ penkɔ̀ɔb/penkam/ elab. colloq.
1. to be solid, substantial, productive, effective,
with tangible results. 2. solidly, substantially,
as a steady thing, as a staple. →Syn. เป็นล่ำ
เป็นสัน.

เป็นกันเอง pen/kanʔeeŋ/ to be intimate, familiar,
informal; to feel at home.

เป็นกามโรค penkaam/marôog/ eleg. to have a
venereal disease.

เป็นก่ายเป็นกอง /penkàaj/penkɔɔŋ/ elab. colloq.
a lot (of), a whole lot (of), heaps (of).

เป็นการ penkaan/ to be successful, effective; to
have succeeded.

o เป็นงานเป็นการ penŋaan/penkaan/ elab.
colloq. to be systematic, business-like.

เป็นการจริงจัง penkaan/ciŋcaŋ/ 1. to be earnest,
to be an earnest matter. 2. earnestly, with all
one's heart.

เป็นการชั่วคราว penkaan/chûakhraaw/ 1. to be
temporary, to be a temporary matter. 2. temporarily, as a temporary thing.

เป็นการด่วน penkaandùan/ 1. to be urgent, to be
an urgent matter. 2. urgently, as an urgent
matter.

เป็นการประจำวัน penkaan/pracamwan/ 1. to be
daily, to be a daily matter. 2. daily, normally,
as a daily routine.

เป็นการยาก penkaanjâag/ 1. to be difficult, to be
a diffcult matter. 2. with difficulty.

เป็นการใหญ่ penkaanjàj/ 1. to be on a grand
scale; to be a great thing; to be overwhelming,
considerable. 2. on a grand scale, to a great
extent, overwhelmingly, considerably.

เป็นกำลัง penkamlaŋ/ colloq. very much, considerably, extremely.

เป็นเกล็ด penklèd/ to be scaly.

เป็นเกลียว penkliaw/ 1. in a coil-like, helical
form. 2. in a twisting, spiraling fashion.

o ตัวเป็นเกลียว tua/penkliaw/ idiom. very
hard, busily (of working).

เป็นเกียรติ, เพื่อ-- penklàd/, phŷa-- as an honor,
in honor (of).

เป็นแก่นสาร penkɛ̀n/sǎan/ 1. to be essential,
substantial, solid. 2. to make sense.

เป็นข้อใหญ่ penkhɔ̀ɔ/jàj/ mainly, chiefly.

เป็นของ in the following examples.

o หล่อนก็ต้องเป็นของเขาแน่ lɔ̀n/-kɔ̀tɔ̂ŋpen/khɔ̌ɔŋ⊃
kháwnɛ̂ɛ/ She must become his for sure.

o โอนเป็นของชาติ ʔoon/penkhɔ̌ɔŋchâad/ to nationalize.

o ที่ตกไปเป็นของรัสเซีย thîitɔ̀gpaj/-penkhɔ̌ɔŋ/⊃
rádsia/ which have gotten into Russian possession.

เป็นขั้น ๆ pen/khânkhân/ step by step, in stages.

เป็นขี้เรื้อน pen/khîirýan/ colloq. to have leprosy,
be a leper.

เป็นขุย penkhǔj/ to be fuzzy, frayed, scaly.

เป็นไข้,ป่วย-- penkhâj/, pùaj/penkhâj/ to have
a fever, be feverish, ill with fever.

เป็นไข้จับสั่น penkhâj/càbsàn/ to have malaria.

เป็นครั้งเป็นคราว penkhráŋ/penkhraaw/ at intervals,
on occasion.

เป็นครั้งแรก penkhráŋrɛ̂ɛg/ for the first time.

เป็นคราว ๆ penkhraawkhraaw/ at intervals, at
times.

เป็นควัน penkhwan/ 1. to be smoky. 2. idiom.
eagerly, energetically; promptly.

เป็นความ penkhwaam/ to be involved in a lawsuit,
have a case in court (either as plaintiff or defendant).

เป็นคุ้งเป็นแคว penkhúŋ/penkhwɛɛ/ idiom.,elab.
colloq. lengthily, at great length (as in telling
a story).

เป็นคุณ penkhun/ 1. to be good, beneficial. 2.
for the benefit (of).

เป็นโคลน penkhloon/ to be muddy.

เป็นงวด ๆ penŋûadŋûad/ in installments, periodically.

เป็นง่อย penŋɔ̂j/ to be lame.

เป็นงานเป็นการ penŋaan/penkaan/ elab. colloq.
to be systematic, business-like.

เป็นง่าม penŋâam/ to be forked.

เป็นเงา penŋaw/ to be glossy.

เป็นเงา ๆ penŋawŋaw/ 1. shadowy. 2. faintly,
dimly.

เป็นเงาตามตัว penŋaw/taamtua/ "as one's shadow
follows one's body," a simile for an inevitable
consequence. Cf. Eng. "as night follows day."

เป็นจริง pencing′ to come true, be realized; to materialize (as a dream, plan). ความ-- the actual facts, (in) actuality.

เป็นจัก ๆ pencàgcàg′ to be toothed, notched, serrated, jagged. →Dist. เป็นแฉก. →Syn. เป็นฟัน, เป็นหยัก.

เป็นจำนวน pencamnuan′ in the amount (of), in amount.

เป็นใจ(กับ) pencaj′(kac) to connive (with), be secretly accessory, be an accomplice (of)(e.g. in wrongdoing). →See also รู้เห็น--.

เป็นแฉก penchɛɛg′ to be fringed, deeply serrated, jagged. →Dist. เป็นจัก ๆ, เป็นฟัน, เป็นหยัก.

เป็นชนวน penchanuan′ to lead to, to cause; to be the prime cause.

เป็นชั้น ๆ penchánchán′ in layers, ranks, grades, classes.

เป็นชิ้นเป็นอัน penchín′pen?an′ elab. colloq. to be a good, solid piece; to be well organized, well constructed. อย่าง-- well, solidly.

เป็นชู้ penchúu′ to be adulterous (usually ref. to a man).

เป็นเชิง penchəəŋ′ as an indication of, suggestive of, suggesting, insinuating; in (such and such) a manner.

เป็นดอก pendɔɔg′ 1. to be flowered, decorated with a floral design. 2. to be in flower.

เป็นต้น pentôn′ as a beginning. →Commonly used in expressions of the type shown below.

o เช่น...เป็นต้น chên′...pentôn′ for example; such as (a list of things), for example. NOTE. This expression serves to encompass a list of whatever is being exemplified; hence เช่น introduces the list and เป็นต้น follows it: "such as apples, oranges, grapes, and bananas, for example."

o ตั้งแต่บัดนี้เป็นต้นไป tâŋtɛɛbàdníi′-pentôn′paj′ from now on.

o ตั้งแต่วันนั้นเป็นต้นมา tâŋtɛɛwannán′-pentôn′maa′ from that day on.

o เป็นต้นว่า pentôn′wâa′ for example.

เป็นต้นเหตุ pentôn′hèed′ to be the cause, the origin.

เป็นตม pentom′ to be muddy.

เป็นต่อ pentɔɔ′ to have an advantage, be leading, be in the lead (in a contest).

เป็นต่อยหอย pentɔj′hɔj′ chatteringly; chattering.

เป็นตับ pentàb′ 1. in rows. 2. in large numbers.

เป็นตัว as in ไม่เป็นตัวเป็นตน mâjpentua′penton′ to be unformed, amorphous, not to have taken shape.

เป็นตัวเมีย pentuamia′ V derog. to be a sissy, be effeminate.

เป็นตาเดียว as in มองเป็นตาเดียว mɔɔŋ′-penc taa′diaw′ (several) to focus their eyes upon, to stare at as with a single eye, simultaneously.

เป็นตำหนิ pentamnì?′ to be a defect, an imperfection, a marring feature.

เป็นตุเป็นตะ pentù?′pentà?′ to make sense, be coherent.

o ฝันเป็นตุเป็นตะ fǎn′-pentù?′pentà?′ to have a life-like dream, a coherent dream.

o พูดเป็นตุเป็นตะ phûud′-pentù?′pentà?′ to speak convincingly (e.g. as though one really has a first-hand knowledge of the matter); to tell coherently.

เป็นแต่ pen′tɛɛc simply, only.

เป็นแถบ ๆ penthɛɛbthɛɛb′ section by section, part by part.

เป็นแถว penthɛ̌w′* 1. in rows. 2. in large numbers.

เป็นทอด ๆ penthɔɔdthɔɔd′ from one to another, in succession, successively.

เป็นท่า penthâa′ proper, comme il faut, in the accepted manner.

o ไม่เป็นท่า mâjpenthâa′ 1. awkward, ungainly. 2. awkwardly; not properly, not in the accepted manner.

เป็นทาง penthaaŋ′ 1. as a way (to). 2. in the form of a line, in a line.

เป็นทางการ penthaaŋ′kaan′ officially.

เป็นที่ penthîi′ in place (generally implying neatness, good order). →Cf. เคลื่อนที่.

o วางของให้เป็นที่ waaŋkhɔɔŋ′hâjpenthîi′ to put things where they belong.

o อยู่เป็นที่ jùu′penthîi′ to live at the same place for a long time (not moving about); (things) to stay in place, be in place.

เป็นที่เข้าใจ penthîi′khâwcaj′ it is understood (that).

เป็นที่ทราบกันว่า penthîi/-sâab/kanwâa/ it is known that, it is commonly known that.

เป็นที่พอใจ penthîi/phɔɔcaj/ to be satisfactory.

เป็นที่เรียบร้อย penthîi/rîabrɔ́ɔj/ 1. to be in good order. 2. well, neatly, carefully, smoothly.

เป็นที่สุด penthîisùd/ colloq. extremely.

เป็นทุกข์ penthúg/ to be dejected, worried.

เป็นทุกข์เป็นร้อน penthúg/penrɔ́ɔn/ elab.colloq. to be dejected, worried, bothered (about something). Cf. Eng. "to be hot and bothered."

เป็นไทย penthaj/ 1. to be Thai. 2. to be free.

เป็นธรรม pentham/ to be fair, just. ความ-- justice.

o มีใจเป็นธรรม miicaj/pentham/ to have a sense of justice.

เป็นธรรมดา penthammadaa/ 1. to be natural, normal, usual. 2. naturally. 3. of course.

เป็นนักเป็นหนา pennág/pennǎa/ elab. colloq. extremely, highly, severely, roundly, unsparingly.

เป็นน้ำ pennáam/ 1. to be liquid (not solid). 2. idiom. fluently, flowingly.

o พูดเป็นน้ำ phûud/pennáam/ idiom. to talk a blue streak.

o พูด...เป็นน้ำ phûud/...pennáam/ to speak (e.g. English) fluently.

เป็นนิตย์ penníd/ constantly, always.

เป็นเนื้อเดียวกัน pennýa/diawkan/ to be homogeneous; to be well-blended, smoothly joined.

เป็นแน่ pennɛ̂ɛ/ for a certainty.

เป็นบ้า penbâa/ 1. colloq. to be crazy, insane. 2. slang very, extremely, terribly.

o ร้อนเป็นบ้า rɔ́ɔn/penbâa/ slang to be terribly hot.

เป็นบุญ penbun/ to be fortunate.

เป็นเบี้ยบน pen/bîabon/ idiom. 1. to be superior, uppermost, on top. 2. to have the advantage, have the upper hand. 3. to outdo.

เป็นเบี้ยล่าง pen/bîalâaŋ/ idiom. to be inferior, lower, underneath. 2. to have a disadvantage. 3. to be outdone.

เป็นเบื้อ penbŷa/ colloq. to be silent, dumb, speechless.

เป็นแบบ penbɛ̀ɛb/ in the style of, on the pattern of.

เป็นใบ้ penbâj/ to be dumb, mute.

เป็นปกติ penpòŋkatì?/ 1. to be normal. 2. as usual.

เป็นปฐม penpathǒm/ in the first place; originally, first.

เป็นปม penpom/ to be knotted, knotty.

เป็นประจำ pen/pracam/ constantly, regularly, habitually.

เป็นประธาน pen/prathaan/ to be the head; to be president (of), chairman (of). ผู้-- chairman, president.

เป็นประโยชน์ penprajòod/ to be advantageous, useful.

เป็นประวัติการณ์ pen/-prawàd/kaan/ to be epoch-making, record-breaking, unprecedented.

เป็นปากเสียง penpàag/sǐaŋ/ 1. idiom. to be a spokesman, a mouthpiece (for). 2. colloq. to have an argument (with).

เป็นปี่เป็นขลุ่ย penpìi/penkhlùj/ idiom. harmoniously, in united fashion.

เป็นปึกแผ่น penpỳg/phɛ̀n/ to be firm, solid, stable.

เป็นปุ่ม penpùm/ to be nodulated, knotted, kinky.

เป็น ๆ penpen/ 1. to be live, alive. 2. live, alive.

o คนเป็น ๆ khon/penpen/ a live person.

o เหมือนกับยังเป็น ๆ mǔan/kajaŋpenpen/ as if still alive.

o จับนกเป็น ๆ càbnóg/penpen/ to catch a bird alive.

เป็นไป penpaj/ to go on, progress; to turn out, develop. การ-- getting along, how one gets along; relationship (between), interaction (between). ความ-- way of life, daily life; the way things go, course of events; story, account.

o เป็นไปได้ penpajdâaj/ to be possible.

o เป็นไปไม่ได้ penpaj/mâjdâaj/ to be impossible.

o เป็นไปสม penpaj/sǒm/ to develop in accordance with.

เป็นไปตาม pen/pajtaam/ 1. to agree with, be according to, be in accordance with. 2. to be (that) way.

เป็นผง penphǒŋ/ to be powdery.

เป็นผล penphǒn/ to be successful, fruitful.

เป็นผลดี penphǒndii/ to be useful, profitable, beneficial; to give good results.

เป็นผลสำเร็จ penphǒn/sǎmrèd/ to be successful, accomplished.

เป็นผลเสียหาย penphǒn′sǐahǎaj′ to be damaging, injurious; to give bad results.

เป็นผื่น penphỳyn′ to have a rash.

เป็นผู้เป็นคน penphûu′penkhon′ e l a b. c o l l o q. to be presentable, like a normal human.

เป็นแผล penphlɛ́ɛ′ to be wounded, have a sore.

เป็นฝรั่ง pen′faràŋ′ to be or act like a European or Occidental.

เป็นฝั่งเป็นฝา penfàŋ′penfǎa′ i d i o m. to be settled down, have a family.

เป็นฝ้า penfâa′ to be fogged (of glass), clouded (of eyes, vision), defective, imperfect (as of diamonds).

เป็นพวง ๆ penphuaŋphuaŋ′ in clusters, bunches, strings.

เป็นพัก ๆ penphágphág′ fitfully, sporadically, at times, in fits and bursts.

เป็นพิเศษ penphíseed′ 1. to be special, particular. 2. especially.

เป็นพิษ penphíd′ to be poisonous, toxic; to have a bad effect.

เป็นพืด penphɣ̂yd′ 1. to be webbed (as a duck's feet). 2. to be ridged (as a mountain chain). 3. (side by side) in a row.

เป็นพื้น penphɣ́yn′ 1. as a foundation, a basis, a background. 2. on the average, generally, basically.

เป็นพุ่ม penphûm′ to be bushy.

เป็นเพื่อน penphɣ̂an′ 1. to be friends. 2. as company, as a friend.

o อยู่เป็นเพื่อน jùu′penphɣ̂an′ to keep (someone) company.

เป็นโพรง penphrooŋ′ 1. to be hollow. 2. to be porous.

เป็นฟัน penfan′ to be toothed, serrated. →D i s t. เป็นแฉก. →S y n. เป็นจัก ๆ, เป็นหยัก.

เป็นฟืน in โกรธเป็นฟืนเป็นไฟ kròod′-penfyyn′ɔ penfaj′ to be furiously angry, to burn with rage.

เป็นภัย penphaj′ to be dangerous, harmful, perilous.

เป็นภูเขา penphuukhǎw′ to be mountainous.

เป็นมัน penman′ 1. to be oily, greasy. 2. to be glossy, shiny.

o เป็นมันวาว penman′waaw′ to be glitteringly glossy or shiny.

เป็นมา pen′maaɔ to happen, occur, arise. ความ-- past events, account of past events (from the beginnings to the present).

เป็นเม็ด penméd′ to be granulated; to be pimply.

เป็นเมือก penmɣ̂ag′ to be slimy, mucilaginous.

เป็นแม่เบี้ย pen′mɛ̂ɛbîa′ c o l l o q. to be overbearing, bossy.

เป็นแม่นมั่น penmɛ̂n′mân′ surely, absolutely.

เป็นโมฆะ penmoo′khá?′ to be void, invalid, useless.

เป็นเยี่ยม penjîam′ to be first-rate, best, top.

เป็นระนาว penranaaw′ 1. in a line, in a row. 2. in large numbers.

เป็นระเบียบ penrabìab′ 1. to be orderly, be in good order. 2. to be well-arranged, well-organized.

เป็นระยะ ๆ penrajá?′-rajá?′ at regular intervals (of time or space); at a constant rate.

เป็นรายตัว penraajtua′ one person at a time, one by one, individually.

เป็นริ้วรอย penríwrɔɔj′ to be scratched, lined with marks or scratches.

เป็นรู penruu′ V to have a hole, be holey, full of holes.

เป็นรูป penrûub′ 1. to be in the form of, be shaped. 2. in shape, into shape.

o เป็นรูปเป็นร่างขึ้น penrûub′penrâaŋ′khɣ̂n to take shape, be getting into shape.

เป็นเรือน penryan′ on the order of (a specified magnitude), by (dozens, hundreds, etc.), by the (dozen, hundred, etc.).

เป็นแรมเดือน penrɛɛm′dyan′ for a month, for a period of months.

เป็นโรค penrôog′ to have a disease, be diseased.

เป็นไร. See entries below.

o จะเป็นไรไป capen′rajpaj↓ It doesn't matter.

o ช่างมันเป็นไร, -ปะไร châŋ′manpenraj′↓, -paraj↓ I don't care about him, about it. I don't care what happens to him, to it. Let it be. Let it go.

o ไม่เป็นไร mâjpenraj′↓ It doesn't matter. That's all right. Not at all. It's nothing. It doesn't make any difference. It's all the same. Never mind. Forget it.

เป็นลม penlom′ to faint.

○ เป็นลมล่วิงส่วาย penlom′-sawĭŋ′sawǎaj′ to feel like fainting.

เป็นลอน penlɔɔn′ to be wavy, undulating.

เป็นลายลักษณ์อักษร pen′-laajlág′ʔàgsɔ̌ɔn′ elab. in writing, in written form.

เป็นลำดับ pen′lamdàb′ 1. in order, serially, successively, in succession, one after another. 2. respectively. 3. progressively, gradually.

เป็นล่ำเป็นสัน penlâm′pensăn′ elab. colloq. 1. to be solid, substantial, coherent, well-founded, well-organized. 2. solidly, substantially, as a staple, as a steady thing. →Syn. เป็นกอบเป็นกำ.

เป็นลิ่ม ๆ penlîmlîm′ in lumps.

เป็นเล่น penlên′ playfully; nonchalantly; triflingly.

เป็นแล้วกัน penlέεw′kan That's settled. That does it. That's all (i.e. we've finished what we had to say).

เป็นวรรคเป็นเวร penwág′penween′ on and on, at great length, continuously, excessively (of speaking, crying).

เป็นเวลา ๑ penweelaa′ 1. to be regular, constant. 2. regularly.

○ ให้กินเป็นเวลา hâjkin′penweelaa′ to feed, provide food regularly (according to a fixed schedule).

เป็นเวลา ๒ penweelaa′, penweelaa⊃ 1. to be (such and such) a length of time. 2. for (such and such) a length of time.

○ เป็นเวลานาน penweelaanaan′ 1. to be a long time. 2. for a long time.

○ เป็นเวลาสองอาทิตย์ penweelaa′sɔ̌ɔŋ′aathíd′ 1. it is two weeks. 2. for two weeks.

○ เป็นเวลา ๖ ปีมาแล้ว penweelaa′-hògpii′maa⊃ lέεw′ 1. it has been six years. 2. for the past six years.

เป็นสนิม pensanǐm′ to be rusty.

เป็นส่วนน้อย pensùan′nɔ́ɔj′ 1. to be the lesser part, a small part. 2. in the minority of cases, in a few instances.

เป็นสองแฉก pensɔ̌ɔŋchὲεg′ to be bifurcated, swallow-tailed.

เป็นสัด pensàd′ to rut, be in heat. Used of both male and female animals; rarely extended collo-

quially to human beings.

เป็นสัตย์ --จริง pensàd′, pensàd′ciŋ′ to be true, to be the truth.

เป็นสาระ pensăa′rá?′ to make sense.

เป็นสาว pensăaw′ 1. to be young, adolescent (of a girl). 2. to be a virgin.

เป็นสาวเป็นแส้ pensăaw′pensὲε′ elab. colloq. to be a young unmarried woman.

เป็นสำคัญ pensămkhan′ 1. to be important. 2. as evidence; as a token.

เป็นสุข pensùg′ to be happy, content.

เป็นสุขใจ pensùg′caj′ to be happy, content, have peace of mind.

เป็นเสน่ห์ pensanèe′ to be charming, attractive.

เป็นเสียงเดียวกัน pensĭaŋ′diawkan′ in one voice, in unison.

เป็นโสด pensòod′ to be single, unmarried.

เป็นหนอง pennɔ̌ɔŋ′ to produce pus, have pus.

เป็นหนอน pennɔ̌ɔn′ to be wormy.

เป็นหนักหนา pennàgnǎa′ very much, extremely, severely, roundly, unsparingly.

เป็นหนี้เป็นสิน pennîi′pensǐn′ elab. eleg. to be in debt, to owe. →Also เป็นหนี้ eleg.

เป็นหมัน penmǎn′ 1. to be sterile, fruitless, barren. 2. to be useless.

เป็นหม้าย penmâaj′ to be widowed.

เป็นหมู่เป็นเหล่า penmùu′penlàw′ elab. in groups.

เป็นหมู่ ๆ penmùumùu′ in groups.

เป็นหยัก penjàg′ 1. to be fluted, undulated with pointed crests. 2. to be toothed, serrated, notched. →Dist. เป็นแฉก. →Syn. 2. เป็นจักๆ, เป็นฟัน.

เป็นหล่มเป็นเลน penlòm′penleen′ elab. to be muddy, sloppy, slushy.

เป็นหลักแหล่ง penlàg′lὲŋ′ 1. permanent, steady, fixed (of a house, dwelling). 2. permanently, steadily.

เป็นหลายครั้ง penlǎaj′khráŋ′ many times, on many occasions.

เป็นห่วง penhùaŋ′ to feel concern for; to be worried, concerned about. ความ-- worry, concern.

เป็นหวัด penwàd′ to catch cold; to have a cold.

เป็นหูเป็นตาแทน penhǔu′pentaa′-thεεn′ elab. colloq., idiom. to keep an eye on things, take charge of things (for someone).

เป็นเหตุให้ penhèed/hâjɔ to cause, be the cause of.

เป็นเหน็บ pennèb/ to feel numb, be numb, (a limb) to go to sleep.

เป็นเหยื่อกระสุน penjʉ̀a/krasʉ̌n/ eleg. to be cannon fodder; to fall prey to a bullet.

เป็นไหนๆ. See ...กว่า(...)เป็นไหนๆ above.

เป็นใหญ่ penjàj/ to have power and authority, be head of, be a big shot. ความ-- being on top, being top man.

เป็นอนุสรณ์ pen/ʔànúsɔɔn/ 1. to be a token, reminder(of). 2. in memory(of), as a memorial (to).

เป็นอย่างๆ penjàaŋjàaŋ/ one by one, separately (ref. to kinds, varieties of things); by kinds, varieties; according to kinds, varieties.

เป็นอย่างดี penjàaŋdii/ 1. quite well. 2. willingly, gladly.

เป็นอย่างมาก penjàaŋmâag/ 1. at most, at the very most. 2. very much.

เป็นอย่างยิ่ง penjàaŋjîŋ/ in the extreme, to the utmost.

เป็นอยู่ penjùu/ V to be, exist, live. ความ-- way of living; existence.

เป็นอริ pen/ʔarì?/ to be enemies.

เป็นอะไร. See entries below.

o เป็นอะไรไป (1) pen/ʔaraj/paj/, pen/ʔarajpaj/; (2) pen/ʔarajpaj↓ 1. to have something happen to one, to be the matter with one; what is the matter with (one)? 2. It doesn't matter.

oo เขาคงเป็นอะไรไป kháwkhoŋpen/ʔarajpaj/↓ Something must have happened to him.

o ไม่เป็นอะไร mâjpen/ʔaraj/ to have nothing wrong with one; there's nothing wrong, nothing is the matter.

เป็นอันขาด pen/ʔankhàad/ definitely, decidedly, positively, absolutely, under any circumstances. →Used in negative or prohibitive constructions.

o อย่าข้ามถนนคนเดียวเป็นอันขาด jàakhâam/thaɔ nɔ̌n/-khondiaw/pen/ʔankhàad/ Don't you ever under any circumstances cross the street alone.

เป็นอันดี pen/ʔandii/ 1. well, very well. 2. willingly, gladly.

เป็นอันตกลง pen/ʔan/tògloŋ/ it's agreed!

เป็นอันมาก pen/ʔanmâag/ lit. very much; in great quantity, in great numbers.

เป็นอันว่า pen/ʔanwâa/ this means that (such and such a course of action follows, is agreed upon).

เป็นอันหนึ่งอันเดียวกัน pen/ʔannʉ̀ŋ/ʔandiaw/kan to be one and the same; to be united, unified; to concur.

เป็นอันตราย pen/ʔantaraaj/ 1. to be harmful, dangerous. 2. to be harmed, endangered.

เป็นอ่าง pen/ʔàaŋ/ to stammer; to be stammering.

เป็นอาจิณ, -อาจิณณ์, -อาจินต์ pen/ʔaa/cin/ habitually, constantly, regularly.

เป็นอาชีพ pen/ʔaachîib/ 1. for a living, as an occupation, as a profession. 2. colloq. habitually, constantly.

เป็นอาทิ pen/ʔaathí?/ for example, as notable examples. →See cross reference.

เป็นอารมณ์ pen/ʔaarom/ seriously.

เป็นอาหาร pen/ʔaahǎan/ as food, for food.

เป็นอื่น pen/ʔʉ̀ʉn/ 1. to be estranged, alienated. unfaithful. 2. to be otherwise, different, something else.

o คิดเป็นอื่น khíd/pen/ʔʉ̀ʉn/ colloq. to think otherwise, have one's own opinion, take (it) to mean something else.

เป็นเอกฉันท์ pen/ʔèeg/kachǎn/ 1. to be unanimous. 2. unanimously.

เป็นเอกราช pen/ʔèeg/karâad/ to be independent.

เป็นเอง pen/ʔeeŋ/ naturally (of itself).

แปลเป็น plɛɛ/penɔ to translate into.

แผลเป็น (แห่ง) phlɛ̌epen/ (hɛ̀ŋ/) N scar.

พูดเป็น phûud/pen/ to be able to speak; to know how to talk.

มียศเป็น miijód/penɔ to have the rank (of).

ไม่เป็น mâjpen/ cannot, unable to (because of not having learned how).

o ว่ายน้ำไม่เป็น wâajnáam/mâjpen/ can't swim.

ไม่เป็นเรื่อง mâjpenrʉ̂aŋ/ to be nonsense.

ไม่เป็นไร mâjpenraj/↓ It doesn't matter. That's all right. Not at all. It's nothing. It doesn't make any difference. It's all the same. Never mind. Forget it.

ไม่เป็นอะไร mâjpen/ʔaraj/ to have nothing wrong with one; there's nothing wrong, nothing is the matter.

สัตว์เป็น (ตัว) sàd/pen/ (tua/) N live animal.

หน้าเป็น nâa/pen/ V to be given to mirth on all occasions, suitable or unsuitable; to be all smiles. →Comp. หน้าทะเล้น.

เห็นผิดเป็นชอบ hěnphìd/penchɔ̂ɔb/ to mistake right for wrong, bad for good.

เป็น in ตะเหลนเป็น talěenpěen/ rM intensifier used with ยาว "long," สูง "high."

เปรต prèed/ N 1. a tall spirit, ghost. 2. an evil-doer (used esp. as a word of abuse).

เปรม preem/ V to be happy, gay, joyful.

เปรย prəəj/ V to say aloud, speak out (to no one in particular).

เปรยปราย prəəjpraaj/ V to call out, make a general greeting.

พูดเปรย ๆ phûud/prəəjprəəj/ to speak without addressing anyone in particular (often with sarcastic intent).

เปรอะ prɔ̀ʔ/ V to be dirty, spattered.

เปรอะประ prɔ̀ʔpràʔ/ V to be spotted, stained, dirty.

เปราะ prɔ̀ʔ/ V to be brittle, fragile.

ปากเปราะ pàagprɔ̀ʔ/ V colloq. 1. to be ever ready to greet. 2. to be ever ready to criticize. 3. (a dog) to be ever ready to bark (i.e. unnecessarily).

เปรี้ยง prîaŋ/ V 1. imit. to crash (of thunder). 2. to be strong, merciless (of the sun). rM 3. intensifier used with ร้อน "hot."

เปรี้ยง ๆ prîaŋprîaŋ/ imit. to go "crash!" (of thunder).

เปรียบ prìab/ V to compare.

ได้เปรียบ dâjprìab/ V to have an advantage (over), have the edge (over). →Dist. ได้ที. →Ant. เสียเปรียบ.

เปรียบเทียบ prìabthîab/ V to compare. คำ-- a comparison (in speech).

เปรียบเหมือน prìabmy̌an/ to be comparable to, analogous to; to be like.

เสียเปรียบ sǐaprìab/ V to be handicapped, have a disadvantage.

หาที่เปรียบมิได้ hǎa/thîiprìab/-mídâaj/ lit. incomparable.

เอาเปรียบ ʔawprìab/ to take advantage of.

เปรียว priaw/ V to be agile, sprightly in movement, active, alert. →Also ประเปรียว.

เปรี้ยว prîaw/ V 1. to be sour. 2. idiom. (a girl) to be bold, daring, flirtatious, saucy.

คนเปรี้ยว khonprîaw/ idiom. 1. a flirt, i.e. a woman who likes to flirt, to be surrounded by men.

เปรี้ยวจี๊ด prîawcíid/ to be extremely sour, sour as vinegar.

เปรี้ยวแจ๊ด prîawcɛ́ɛd/ idem.

เปรี้ยวหวาน prîawwǎan/ N a sweet and sour dish.

o ผัดเปรี้ยวหวาน phàd/prîawwǎan/ N sweet and sour fried food.

เปรื่อง ๑ prỳaŋ/ imit. the clatter of glassware; the crashing sound of broken glass.

เปรื่องปร่าง prỳaŋpràaŋ/ idem.

เปรื่อง ๒ prỳaŋ/ V to be clever, sharp, bright.

เปรื่องปราด prỳaŋpràad/ V to be quick (in thinking); to be quick-witted, sharp-witted.

เปล (หลัง, ปาก) plee/ (lǎŋ/, pàag/) N 1. cradle (lǎŋ/, pàag/). 2. litter (lǎŋ/). 3. hammock (pàag/). →Syn. 1. พระอู่ roy.

เปล่ง plèŋ/* V 1. to radiate. 2. to utter. 3. to be radiant, bright.

เปล่งปลั่ง plèŋ/plàŋ/ V to glow (with health), be radiant (of looks).

เปล่งวาจา plèŋ/waacaa/ V eleg. to say, speak, declare.

เปล่งเสียง plèŋsǐaŋ/ V to utter, announce.

เปล่งอุทาน plèŋ/ʔùthaan/ V to exclaim.

เปลว ๑ pleew/ N flame.

ทองคำเปลว (แผ่น) thɔɔŋkham/pleew/ (phɛ̀n/) N gold leaf.

เปลวเพลิง pleewphləəŋ/ N eleg. flame.

เปลวไฟ pleewfaj/ N flame.

เปลว ๒ pleew/ N fat, lard, adipose tissue.

เปล่า plàaw/* V 1. to be bare, empty, void, blank. sV 2. in vain. 3. No.

เดินเท้าเปล่า dəən/tháawplàaw/ to walk barefooted.

ตัวเปล่า tuaplàaw/ 1. to be shirtless. 2. to be single, unmarried, without family ties.

ตาเปล่า taa/plàaw/ the naked eye.

ตีนเปล่า tiinplàaw/ barefoot, with bare feet.

ปากเปล่า pàagplàaw/ sV orally.

เปล่าประโยชน์ plàaw/prajòod/ to be to no advantage,

useless.

เปล่า ๆ plàawplàaw⁄ 1. in vain, to no avail. 2. free, for nothing. 3. empty, barren, plain.

เปล่าเปลี่ยว plàawplìaw⁄ V to be solitary, lonesome.

เปล่าเลย plàaw⁄ləəj⁄ not a bit, not at all.

มือเปล่า myyplàaw⁄ V 1. to be empty-handed. sV 2. empty-handed; with bare hands; freehand.

ว่างเปล่า wâaŋplàaw⁄ V to be empty, vacant, unoccupied (as a house), uncultivated (as a field).

เสียเปล่า (1) sǐa⁄plàaw⁄; (2) sǐaplàaw⁄ 1. to lose in vain, simply lose, simply waste. 2. uselessly, for nothing.

เปลี้ย plîa⁄ V to be weak, worn out.

ง่อยเปลี้ย ŋɔ̂jplîa⁄ V to be lame.

เปลี่ยน plìan⁄ V to change, vary, alter. การ-- change, alteration.

จุดเปลี่ยน cùdplìan⁄ N turning point.

เปลี่ยนเกียร์ plìankia⁄ to shift gears.

เปลี่ยนใจ plìancaj⁄ V to change one's mind.

เปลี่ยนแปลง plìanplɛɛŋ⁄ V to change, vary, alter, transform. การ-- change, changing, alteration, transformation. ความ-- change, alteration.

เปลี่ยนมือ plìanmyy⁄ V 1. to transfer. 2. to be transferred, to change hands.

เปลี่ยนยางรถ plìan⁄jaaŋród⁄ to change a tire.

เปลี่ยนสี plìansǐi⁄ to turn another color, change color.

เปลี่ยนเสียง plìansǐaŋ⁄ to change one's tone, one's attitude.

ผลัดเปลี่ยน phlàdplìan⁄ V to change.

แลกเปลี่ยน lɛ̂ɛgplìan⁄ V to exchange, barter.

เปลี่ยว plìaw⁄ V 1. (places) to be isolated, lonely, deserted. sV 2. in (its) prime, having attained full strength and vigor, fierce or spirited and difficult to handle (because in its prime) (of cattle).

เปล่าเปลี่ยว plàawplìaw⁄ V to be solitary, lonesome.

เปลี่ยวใจ plìawcaj⁄ V to feel lonely.

เปลี๊ยะ plía?⁄ rM intensifier used with แน่น "tight, crowded."

เปลือก (ชิ้น, อัน) plỳag⁄ (chín⁄, ?an⁄) N integu-

ment, hence husk (of rice), peel, skin, rind (of fruit), shell (of egg, nut), crust (of bread), bark (of tree), etc.

ข้าวเปลือก khâawplỳag⁄ N paddy, unhusked rice.

เปลือกตา plỳagtaa⁄ N eyelid.

เปลือกนอก (ชิ้น, อัน) plỳagnɔ̂ɔg⁄ (chín⁄, ?an⁄) N outermost shell (e.g. epicarp of the coconut).

เปลือง plyaŋ⁄ V 1. to use up, consume (esp. wastefully). 2. to be used up. 3. to waste, be wasteful, extravagant.

หมดเปลือง mòd⁄plyaŋ⁄ V 1. to consume, use up, lose, waste (e.g. money, time, resources). 2. to be consumed, used up, lost, wasted. →See cross reference.

เปลื้อง plyaŋ⁄ V eleg. to take off, strip.

ปลดเปลื้อง plòdplyaŋ⁄ V 1. to take off, remove. 2. to liberate, release.

เปลือย plyaj⁄ V to be bare, naked, unclothed.

เปลือยกาย plyajkaaj⁄ V eleg. to be undressed, naked.

เปอร์เซนต์ pəəsen⁄* percent. [f. Eng.]

เป่า in เต็มเป่า tempaw⁄ colloq. with full strength, with all one's might.

เป่า pàw⁄ V 1. to blow. 2. to play a wind instrument. →Dist. 1. พัด. NOTE. เป่า mng. 1 is not used in describing the action of the wind.

ปัดเป่า pàdpàw⁄ V 1. to ward off, dispel. 2. to clear up (a problem).

เป้า ๑ (อัน, เป้า, แห่ง) pâw⁄ (?an⁄, pâw⁄, hɛ̀ŋ⁄) N target.

ยิงเป้า jiŋpâw⁄ V 1. to shoot at targets. 2. to execute by shooting.

o สนามยิงเป้า (แห่ง) sanǎam⁄jiŋpâw⁄ (hɛ̀ŋ⁄) N target range.

เป้า ๒ in ปักเป้า (ตัว) pàgpâw⁄ (tua⁄) N globefish.

เปาะ pɔ̀?⁄ sV 1. continually, repeatedly. 2. imit. a tapping sound, as of water dripping.

ชม(...)เปาะ chom⁄(...)pɔ̀?⁄ to praise again and again.

เปิด pə̀əd⁄ V 1. to open; to be open, opened. 2. to begin, launch. 3. slang to run at full blast, "open up." →Ant. 1. ปิด.

บอกเปิด bɔ̀ɔgpə̀əd⁄ V colloq., obsolesc. to turn down, turn away, refuse.

เปิดการรุก pə̀ədˈkaanrúgˈ to launch an attack.

เปิดค้างไว้ pə̀ədkháaŋˈwájˈ to be left open.

เปิดฉาก pə̀ədchàagˈ V 1. to raise the curtain (on a scene). 2. idiom. to begin.

เปิดทาง pə̀ədthaaŋˈ V 1. to open the way (to). 2. to yield the right of way.

เปิดบัญชี pə̀ədˈbanchiiˈ V to open an account.

เปิดโปง pə̀ədpooŋˈ V colloq. to reveal a secret.

เปิดผนึก pə̀ədˈphanỳgˈ V 1. to unseal. 2. to be unsealed.

เปิดเผย pə̀ədphə̌əjˈ V 1. to disclose, reveal, uncover, expose; to open up. 2. to be open, frank, outspoken.

เปิดไฟ pə̀ədfajˈ V to turn on the lights. →Ant. ปิดไฟ.

เปิดไม่ออก pə̀ədˈmâjʔɔ̀ɔgˈ can't open (it); (it) won't open.

เปิด(...)ไว้ (1) pə̀ədˈ(...)wájˈ; (2) pə̀ədwájˈ 1. to leave (something) open, open (something) and leave (it) open. 2. to be open, remain open.

เปิดหมวก pə̀ədmùagˈ V to remove one's hat (as a sign of respect).

เปิดหูเปิดตา pə̀ədhǔuˈpə̀ədtaaˈ V idiom., elab. colloq. to keep one's eyes and ears open in order to learn.

เปิดอก pə̀ədʔ ògˈ V idiom. to be open-hearted.

เปิดโอกาศ pə̀ədˈʔookàadˈ V to give an opportunity.

เปีย. See entries below.

ผมเปีย (เปีย, ข้าง) phǒmpiaˈ N queue, pigtail (piaˈ for a single queue; khâaŋˈ for one of a pair).

หางเปีย (หาง) hǎaŋpiaˈ (hǎaŋˈ) N colloq. queue, pigtail.

เปียก pìagˈ V 1. to be wet, soaked. 2. to be soft.

ข้าวเปียก khâawpìagˈ porridge; soggy rice.

ปวกเปียก pùagpìagˈ V 1. to be weak. 2. to be limp (lacking firmness, stiffness). →Ant. แข็ง.

ปากเปียกปากแฉะ pàagpìagˈpàagchɛ̀ʔˈ V elab. colloq. to talk oneself blue in the face, i.e. to keep telling, instructing, advising, admonishing.

เปียกแฉะ pìagchɛ̀ʔˈ V to be wet, watery.

เปียกโชก pìagchôogˈ V to be sopping wet.

เปียกน้ำ pìagnáamˈ V to be wet with water.

เปียกปอน pìagpɔɔnˈ V to be soaked, drenched, completely wet.

แป้งเปียก pɛ̂ɛŋpìagˈ N cornstarch paste, flour paste (homemade), laundry starch (in paste form).

เปี๊ยก píagˈ V to be small, tiny.

เปี้ยน. See ป้วนเปี้ยน.

เปียนโน, เปียโน (หลัง) piannooˈ, pianooˈ (lǎŋˈ) N piano. [f. Eng.] →Also ปิอาโน.

เปี๊ยบ píabˈ sV 1. strictly, exactly. rM 2. intensifier used with แหลม "sharp."

เปี่ยม pìamˈ V to be full, filled.

เปี่ยมไปด้วย pìamˈpajdûaj to be full of, filled with.

เปี้ยว pîawˈ N 1. vertical support for a vine. 2. a kind of small crab. →Usually 2. ปูเปี้ยว puupîawˈ.

วิ่งเปี้ยว wîŋpîawˈ N 1. a relay race in which two vertical poles are used as terminals. V 2. to run such a race.

เปื้อน pŷanˈ V to get dirty (stained), soiled.

ทำ(...)เปื้อน tham(...)pŷanˈ to soil (something).

แปดเปื้อน pɛ̀ɛdpŷanˈ V to be stained, soiled.

ผ้ากันเปื้อน (ผืน) phâaˈkanpŷanˈ (phы̌ynˈ) N apron.

เปื่อย pỳajˈ V 1. to be decomposed, decayed. 2. to be falling apart, breaking up.

แป้ง pɛ̂ɛŋˈ N 1. powder. 2. flour. 3. starch.

โต๊ะเครื่องแป้ง tóʔˈkhrŷaŋpɛ̂ɛŋˈ (tuaˈ) N dressing table, vanity (table), dresser (with mirror).

แป้งกาว pɛ̂ɛŋkaawˈ N library paste (commercial).

แป้งข้าวจ้าว pɛ̂ɛŋˈkhâawcâawˈ N rice flour.

แป้งนม pɛ̂ɛŋnomˈ powdered milk.

แป้งเปียก pɛ̂ɛŋpìagˈ N cornstarch paste, flour paste (homemade), laundry starch (in paste form).

แป้งผัดหน้า pɛ̂ɛŋˈphàdnâaˈ N face powder.

แป้งมัน pɛ̂ɛŋmanˈ potato or cassava flour.

ผัดแป้ง phàdpɛ̂ɛŋˈ V to powder, apply face powder.

แปซิฟิก pɛɛsifîgˈ, pɛɛsifígˈ N the Pacific. [f. Eng.]

แปด ๑ pɛ̀ɛdˈ Nm eight.

แปดสิบ pɛ̀ɛdsìbˈ Nm eighty.

มืดแปดด้าน mŷydˈpɛ̀ɛddâanˈ idiom. to be in the dark, be completely lost (in trying to figure something out).

ร้อยแปด rɔ́ɔjpɛ̀ɛdˈ idiom. various, all sorts of, many different kinds of: "hundred and eight."

สิบแปด sìbpɛ̀ɛd′ Nm eighteen.

แปด ๒. See entries below.

แปดปน pɛ̀ɛdpon′ V to mix.

แปดเปื้อน pɛ̀ɛdpûan′ V to be stained, soiled.

แป๊ด ๆ pɛ́ɛdpɛ́ɛd′* i m i t. "beep beep," the high-
　　pitched sound of a horn.

แป้น (อัน) pɛ̂n′ (ʔan′) N 1. potter's wheel. V 2.
　　to be round and flat.

　　แป้นเกลียว (อัน) pɛ̂nkliaw′ (ʔan′) N nut (for
　　　screw or bolt).

　　ยิ้มแป้น jímpɛ̂n′ to smile broadly.

แปร prɛɛ′ V to change, alter, vary.

　　แปรได้ prɛɛ′dâaj′ to be changeable, variable.

　　แปรปรวน prɛɛpruan′ V to change, vary, fluctuate,
　　　be uncertain.

　　แปรรูป prɛɛrûub′ V to transform, transfigure,
　　　transmute, undergo metamorphosis.

　　ผันแปร phǎnprɛɛ′ V to change, undergo change,
　　　fluctuate, be unstable.

แปร๊ prɛ́ɛ′ rM intensifier used with เรียบ
　　"smooth," อิ่ม "full."

แปร๊ prɛ́ɛ′ rM intensifier used with เขียว "green."

แปรง (อัน) prɛɛŋ′ (ʔan′) N 1. brush. V 2. to
　　brush.

　　แปรงฟัน prɛɛŋfan′ V to brush the teeth.

　　แปรงลบกระดานดำ (อัน) prɛɛŋ′-lób′kradaanɔ
　　　dam′ (ʔan′) N blackboard eraser.

　　แปรงสีฟัน (อัน) prɛɛŋsǐifan′ (ʔan′) N toothbrush.

แปร่ง prɛ̀ŋ′* V (one's speech) to be different, sound
　　wrong; (the voice) to be off pitch.

　　แปร่งหู prɛ̀ŋhǔu′ V to sound odd, different from
　　　usual, not quite right, unlikely, not quite believ-
　　　able.

　　พูดแปร่ง phûudprɛ̀ŋ′ V to have an accent, speak
　　　with an accent.

แปร๊ด prɛ́d′* rM intensifier used with เขียว
　　"green," แดง "red."

แปร๊น prɛ́n′* i m i t. the trumpeting of an elephant.

แประ prɛ̀ʔ′ rM intensifier used with เต็ม "full,"
　　เพียบ "loaded (of a boat)."

แปล plɛɛ′ V to translate, interpret, decode, give
　　the meaning of.　คน-- translator, interpreter.
　　คำ-- (อย่าง) translation, meaning.

　　แปลเป็น (1) plɛɛ′penɔ; (2) plɛɛ′pen′ 1. to trans-

late into. 2. to know how to translate.

แปลว่า plɛɛ′wâaɔ that means.

แปลก plɛ̀ɛg′ V to be strange, unusual, queer.

　　ของแปลก (อย่าง) khɔ̌ɔŋplɛ̀ɛg′ (jàaŋ′) N a
　　　strange thing; something strange, unusual.

　　คนแปลกหน้า (คน) khonplɛ̀ɛgnâa′ (khon′) N
　　　stranger.

　　แปลกใจ plɛ̀ɛgcaj′ V to be surprised, amazed.

　　แปลกตา plɛ̀ɛgtaa′ V to appear different, unusual.

　　แปลกประหลาด plɛ̀ɛg′pralàad′ V to be wonderful,
　　　strange, unusual, extraordinary.

　　ไม่แปลก mâjplɛ̀ɛg′ to be indifferent, not make any
　　　difference.

แปลง ๑ plɛɛŋ′ C plot of land; a paddy field.

แปลง ๒ plɛɛŋ′ V to transform, change. เครื่อง--
　　elect. transformer.

　　ดัดแปลง dàdplɛɛŋ′ V to change, modify, adapt.

　　เปลี่ยนแปลง plìanplɛɛŋ′ V to change, alter.
　　　การ-- change, alteration.

　　แปลงชาติ plɛɛŋchâad′ V to become naturalized,
　　　change one's citizenship.

　　แปลงผัน plɛɛŋphǎn′ V chem. to convert.

แปลน (แปลน) plɛɛn′ (plɛɛn′) plan. [f. Eng.]

　　แปลนบ้าน (แปลน) plɛɛnbâan′ (plɛɛn′) N house-
　　　plan.

แป้ว pɛ̂w′* V to wither, collapse.

แปะ ๑ pɛ̀ʔ′ V to place, set, stick (a flat piece or
　　patch on to a surface, causing it to adhere, or
　　with a view to sticking, affixing, sewing it on).

แปะ ๒ in อีแปะ (อัน) ʔiipɛ̀ʔ′ (ʔan′) N a small
　　Chinese coin of low value. [f. Chin.]

แป๊ะ in แป๊ะเจี๊ยะ pɛ́ʔcía′ʔ′ N gratuity, gratuitous
　　payment, especially in real estate transactions
　　(not considered a bribe). [f. Chin.]

โป poo′ N a kind of gambling game. [f. Chin.]

โป้ in นิ้วโป้ (นิ้ว) níwpôo′ (níw′) N c o l l o q.
　　thumb. →Also นิ้วโป้ง. →S y n. นิ้วหัวแม่มือ c o m.

โป๊ póo′ V c o l l o q. to be barely clothed or covered,
　　to be indecently, scantily clothed.

　　ระบำโป๊ rabam′póo′ N burlesque show, strip
　　　tease.

โป๊กเกอร์, โปเกอร์ (ตา, เกมส์) póogkəə′, pookəə′
　　(taa′, keem′) N poker (card game). [f. Eng.]

โปง pooŋ′ N a covering of cloth.

เปิดโปง pə̀ədpooŋ′ V colloq. to reveal a secret.

โป่ง ๑ (แห่ง) pòoŋ′ (hɛ̀ŋ′) N salt-lick, a place in
which the earth is saline.

โป่ง ๒ pòoŋ′ V 1. to be inflated. 2. to bulge.
ลูกโป่ง (ใบ) lûugpòoŋ′ (lûug′) N com. toy
balloon.

โป้ง in นิ้วโป้ง (นิ้ว) níwpòoŋ′ (níw′) N colloq.
thumb. →Also นิ้วโป้. →Syn. นิ้วหัวแม่มือ
com.

โปน poon′ V 1. to bulge, protrude, be prominent
(protruding). 2. to be swollen, inflated.
ตาโปน taa′poon′ to have protruding eyes; with
protruding eyes.

โปรแกรม prookrɛm′, -krɛɛm′ N program. [f. Eng.]

โปร่ง pròoŋ′ V 1. to be clear (esp. the weather).
2. to be spacious, uncrowded, airy, porous. 3.
to be slender.
ปลอดโปร่ง plɔ̀ɔdpròoŋ′ V to be clear.
โปร่งใจ pròoŋcaj′ V to be unworried, free of
anxiety or care.
โปร่งตา pròoŋtaa′ V 1. to be transparent. 2.
to be uncluttered.
โปร่งแสง pròoŋsɛ̌ɛŋ′ V to be translucent.
โปร่งใส pròoŋ′sǎj′ V to be transparent.
ผ้าโปร่ง phâapròoŋ′ N net fabric, netting.

โปรด prôod′ V 1. to favor. 2. to be favored. AA
3. please, kindly, be pleased to. คน-- favored
person, favorite.
โปรดปราน prôodpraan′ V 1. to favor. 2. to be
favored.

โปรตุเกส prootukèed′ N 1. Portugal. 2. Portuguese.

โปรย prooj′ V to scatter, strew, sow, sprinkle.
โปรยปราย proojpraaj′ V to scatter, sow, disseminate.

โปลิโอไมเอไลติส pooliʔoo′majʔee′lajtís′* N polio-
myelitis. โรค-- idem. [f. Eng.]

โปะ pó?′ V to pile on (thickly)(as paint, plaster;
facial make-up; work; etc.). [prob. f. Chin.]

โป๊ะ (ลูก,ใบ) pó?′ N 1. weir, bamboo stake-trap
for fish (lûug′). 2. lampshade (baj′). [f. Chin.]

ไป paj′ V 1. to go. sV 2. on, off, away, to. 3.
excessively, too. →Comp. มา "to come."
→See also ไป๊ "Go away!" →In mng. 3. short
for เกินไป.

เขาไปแล้ว kháwpajlɛ́ɛw′↓ He has gone.

คะมำตกน้ำไป khamam′-tògnáam′paj′ to fall
head first into the water.

เสร็จสิ้นกันไปที sèd′sîn′-kanpajthii′↓ That's
the end of that! (expression of relief).

อย่าไปเชื่อนักเลย jàapajchŷa′nágləəj′ don't
(you) ever go and believe (in it).

ก็แล้วไป kɔ̂lɛ́ɛw′paj↓ Then let it go, leave it at that.

กลับไป klàbpaj′ V to go back, return (thither).

เกลื่อนไปหมด klŷan′pajmòd′ to be scattered all
over in large numbers.

เกินไป kəənpaj′ excessively, too.

ไกลเกินไป klaj′kəənpaj′ (it) is too far.

ขาไป khǎapaj′ the trip going; (on) the way to,
(on) the way there.

ขึ้นไป khŷnpaj′ V 1. to go up. sV 2. up, upward;
onward.

เข้าไป khâwpaj′ V 1. to go in. 2. to join, enter
(an organization). sV 3. in.

ควบไปด้วย (1) khûab′pajdûajɔ; (2) khûab′pajdûaj′
1. to couple with; to be coupled with. sV 2.
besides, in addition, at the same time.

คิดไป khíd′paj′ to think about it; when one thinks
about it.

จมไปเลย com′pajləəj′ slang very; so very much.

จะเป็นไรไป capen′rajpaj′ That doesn't matter.
It doesn't hurt anything.

จากไป càag′paj′ to go away, leave, depart.

จืดจางไป cỳydcaaŋ′paj′ to fade away.

ตลอดไป talɔ̀ɔd′paj′ throughout, constantly, all
the time.

ต่อไป tɔ̀ɔpaj′, tɔ̀ɔ′pajɔ, tɔ̀ɔpajɔ sV 1. next, following, later on (in time). 2. next, further on (in
space). 3. on (i.e. in continuation). →Dist.
ต่อมา. →For examples see cross reference.
NOTE. This expression implies direction in time
or space from a focal point of reference toward
a point beyond it.

ตั้งแต่นี้ไป tâŋtɛ̀ɛníi′paj′ from this time on, henceforth.

เต็มไปด้วย tem′pajdûajɔ to be full of, filled with.

ถมไป thɔ̌mpaj′, thòm′paj to be abundant, plenty.

ถัดไป thàd′paj′, thàdpaj′ next (in a series).

ถ้าจะว่าไป thâacawâa′paj′ one might say, one

could say, so to speak, as a matter of fact.

ทั่วไป thûapaj′ all over, in general, of the general run; general.

ทิ้ง(...)ไป thíŋ(...)paj′ to throw (something) away, discard (something). →Dist. ทิ้ง(...)ไว้.

โทรศัพท์ไปถึง thoorasàb′pajtȟّŋɔ to telephone, call (someone) up.

นอกไปกว่านั้น nɔ̂ɔg′pajkwàanán′ furthermore, besides, over and above that.

เบ่งไป bèŋ′paj′ V colloq. to go very fast.

เป็นต้นไป pentôn′paj′ (from then) on.

เป็นไป penpaj′ V to go on, progress; to turn out, develop. การ-- getting along, how one gets along; relationship (between), interaction (between). ความ-- the way things go, way of life, daily life; course of events; account, story.

เป็นอะไรไป (1) pen²araj′paj′, pen/²arajpaj′; (2) pen/²arajpaj↓ 1. to have something happen to one, to be the matter with one. What is the matter with (you)? 2. It doesn't matter.

ไปก่อน pajkɔ̀ɔn′ V 1. to walk ahead, go ahead. sV 2. for the time being, temporarily, ahead of time, in advance.

ไปดูหนัง pajduunǎŋ′ to go see a movie, go to the movies.

ไปได้ (1) pajdâaj′↓; (2) pajdâaj′; paj!dâaj′ 1. (He) may go, can go. 2. idiom. how can (you do such and such)! (rhetorical question with element of criticism). See example.

o ใจเสาะไปได้ cajsɔ̀²/pajdâaj′↓, -paj!dâaj′↓ How can you be such a scaredy cat?

ไปถึง pajtȟّŋ′, paj′tȟّŋɔ, pajtȟّŋɔ 1. to arrive; to reach, to arrive at, in. 2. to, at, in. NOTE. Implies motion away from a contextually suggested point of reference; cf. มาถึง.

ไปทุ่ง pajthûŋ′ V colloq. to go to the toilet. →Syn. ไปส่วม com.

ไปเที่ยว pajthîaw′ V to go around (here and there for pleasure), to go out (as for an evening).

ไปนอก pajnɔ̂ɔg′ V to go abroad.

ไปนอน pajnɔɔn′ V to retire, go to bed.

ไปพบ pajphób′ V to meet, go to see.

ไปพลาง pajphlaaŋ′ simultaneously, at the same time.

ไปพลางก่อน pajphlaaŋ′kɔ̀ɔn′ for the time being, in the meantime.

ไปพลาง ๆ pajphlaaŋphlaaŋ′ for the time being, in the meantime.

ไปมา pajmaa′ V 1. to go back and forth, to come and go. sV 2. back and forth, to and fro, this way and that, hither and yon. →As sec. verb often also ...ไป...มา. →Dist. ไปมาแล้ว.

o ไปมาค้าขาย pajmaa′kháakhǎaj′ to engage in trade, travel about on commercial business.

o ไปมาหาสู่ pajmaa′hǎasùu′ elab. colloq. to visit, pay visits.

o วกไปมา wóg′pajmaa′ 1. to turn this way and that; to wend. 2. to be winding (as a road).

o สัญจรไปมา sǎncɔɔn′pajmaa′ to pass back and forth, go back and forth.

o กลับไปกลับมา klàbpaj′klàbmaa′ 1. to change back and forth again and again. 2. to be unreliable. sV 3. back and forth.

o เดินไปเดินมา dəənpaj′dəənmaa′ to walk back and forth, up and down. →Also เดินไปมา.

o เดินวนไปเวียนมา dəən′-wonpaj′wianmaa′ to walk around, walk up and down, walk to and fro (within a certain area).

o ตรงไปตรงมา troŋpaj′troŋmaa′ 1. to be straightforward, honest. 2. faithfully, frankly.

o นึกไปนึกมา nýgpaj′nýgmaa′ to think over and over.

o บินไปบินมา binpaj′binmaa′ to fly back and forth, hither and thither.

o วนไปเวียนมา wonpaj′wianmaa′ 1. to go around, go to and fro (within a certain area); to be winding; to be circuitous. 2. around, to and fro; in a roundabout manner.

o หยักไปหยักมา jàgpaj′jàgmaa′ 1. to zigzag. 2. to be zigzagged, serrated, jagged.

o หักไปหักมา hàgpaj′hàgmaa′ to turn this way and that, be winding (as a road).

ไปมาแล้ว paj′maaléɛw′ to have been (there) already, to have gone (there).

ไปไม่ทันรถ paj′mâjthanród′ to miss the car, train, etc.

ไปร่วม pajrûam′ V to participate, join.

ไปรับ pajráb′ V to go meet (a person), go get (a thing).

ไปหา (1) pajhǎa′; (2) pajhǎaɔ 1. to go to see (a person), to visit. 2. to, toward.

ไปไหน pajnǎj′ Where are you going?

ไปไหนมา pajnǎj′maa′ Where have you been?

ไปไหนมาไหน pajnǎj′maanǎj′ to get around, go hither and thither, travel about.

ไปเอา(. . .)มา paj?aw(. . .)maa′ to get, fetch, go bring (something, someone).

ผ่านไป phàan′paj to pass by, pass on.

ผ่านพ้นไป phàanphón′paj′ to pass by, go by, elapse.

เผลอไป phlɤ̌ɤ′paj′ to forget oneself for a moment.

พลาด(. . .)ไป phlâad′(. . .)paj′ to miss.

มุ่งไปสู่ mûŋ′pajsùu′ to aim at, have the purpose of.

ยาวไป jaaw′paj′ to be too long.

ร่ำไป râmpaj′ constantly, always, repeatedly.

ลงไป loŋpaj′ 1. to go down. 2. downward.

o ลดน้อยลงไป lódnɔ́ɔj′loŋpaj′ to decrease, reduce.

ล่วงไป lûaŋpaj′ to pass (of time).

เลี่ยงหายไป lîaŋhǎaj′paj′ to sneak away.

วิ่งไป wîŋpaj′ to run away, run on, run off.

ส่ง(. . .)ไปขาย sòŋ′(. . .)pajkhǎaj′ to export (something) for sale.

สงบไป saŋòb′paj′ to calm down, quiet down; (an unpleasant matter) to blow over.

สืบไป sɨ̀ybpaj′ 1. further, in continuation. 2. from a given time on, hence: thereafter, hereafter.

หมดไป mòd′paj′ to be used up, consumed, out of stock.

หันไป hǎnpaj′ to turn to, turn toward (away from some point of reference).

ห่างไป hàaŋ′paj′ to be far away.

หายไป hǎaj′paj to disappear, vanish, be missing.

อย่าไปนึกถึง jàapajnýg′thɤ̌ɤɔ do not think of (it).

อยู่ไปเรื่อย ๆ jùu′pajrŷajrŷaj′ to live on, go on as usual.

ออกไป (1) ?ɔ̀ɔg′paj′, ?ɔ̀ɔg′pajɔ; (2) ?ɔ̀ɔgpaj′, ?ɔ̀ɔg′pajɔ V 1. to go out, leave. sV 2. away

from.

เอนไป ?een′pajɔ to tend toward, incline toward.

เอา(. . .)ไป ?aw(. . .)paj′ 1. to take away, take (such and such) away (somewhere). 2. away. See cross reference.

ไป๊ !páj↓ Go away! Go on!

o ออกไป๊ ?ɔ̀ɔg!páj↓ Get out of here!

ไปรษณีย์ prajsanii′* N 1. mail, post. 2. post office.

ดวงตราไปรษณีย์ (ดวง) duaŋtraa′prajsanii′ (duaŋ′) N postage stamp.

ที่ทำการไปรษณีย์ thîithamkaan′prajsanii′ N post office.

บุรุษไปรษณีย์ (คน) burùd′prajsanii′ (khon′) N mailman, postman.

ไปรษณีย์ธนานัติ prajsanii′thanaa′nád′ N postal money order.

ไปรษณียบัตร, -ย- (ใบ) prajsanii′jabàd′, prajɔ sanii′bàd′ (baj′) N postcard.

ไปรษณีย์อากาศ prajsanii′?aakàad′ N air mail.

พัสดุไปรษณีย์ phádsadù?′prajsanii′ N parcel post.

เรียนทางไปรษณีย์ rian′thaaŋprajsanii′ to take a correspondence course.

โรงเรียนทางไปรษณีย์ rooŋrian′thaaŋprajsanii′ N correspondence school.

อากาศไปรษณีย์ ?aakàad′prajsanii′ N air mail.

ไปรษณียากร (ดวง) prajsanii′jaakɔɔn′ (duaŋ′) N postage stamp.

ผ

ผ phɔ̌ɔ′ HIGH consonant. Pronounced ph and used initially only.

ผง phǒŋ′ N dust, powdery substance.

กาแฟผง kaafɛɛ′phǒŋ′ N powdered coffee, instant coffee.

ถังผง (ใบ) thǎŋphǒŋ′ (baj′) N trash can (for litter); wastepaper basket or can.

นมผง nomphǒŋ′ N powdered milk.

เป็นผง penphǒŋ′ to be powdery.

ผงซักฟอก phǒŋ′ságfɔ̂ɔg′ N detergent powder.

ผงก phaŋòg′ V to nod.

ผงกศีรษะ phaŋòg′sǐisà?′ V eleg. to nod one's head (in assent). →Syn. ผงกหัว com.

ผงกหัว phaŋòg′hǔa′ V to nod one's head (in
assent).

ผงะ phaŋà?′ V to stop abruptly, come to a sudden
standstill (as when stunned, shocked).

ผงะหงาย phaŋà?′ŋǎaj′ 1. to fall over backward.
2. to draw back suddenly, pull up short, reel
back.

ผจง phacoŋ′ V lit. to do with great care. →Also
บรรจง,ประจง.

ผจญ phacon′ V to encounter, meet, face, fight.

ผจญภัย phacon′phaj′ V to encounter, face danger.
นัก-- an adventurer.

ผดุง phaduŋ′ V to support, maintain, preserve.

ผดุงครรภ phaduŋ′khan′ V 1. eleg. to render
care and treatment during pregnancy and childbirth. N 2. midwife. →Syn. 2. หมอตำแย
colloq.

  o นางผดุงครรภ (คน) naaŋ′phaduŋkhan′ (khon′)
  N eleg. midwife. →Syn. หมอตำแย colloq.

  o แพทย์ผดุงครรภ (คน) phêɛd′-phaduŋkhan′
  (khon′) N eleg. obstetrician.

ผดุงรักษา phaduŋ′rágsǎa′ V to preserve, take
care of.

ผนวก in ภาคผนวก phâagphanùag′ N appendix,
addendum, supplement.

ผนวช phanùad′ V roy. to enter the priesthood.

ผนัง (ผนัง) phanǎŋ′ (phanǎŋ′) N interior wall (of
brick, plaster, stone, etc., but not one of wood).

ผนังห้อง (ด้าน) phanǎŋ′hɔ̂ŋ′ (dâan′) N wall of
a room, interior wall (of brick, stone, etc.).

ฝาผนัง (ฝา,ด้าน) fǎaphanǎŋ′ (fǎa′,dâan′) N
interior wall (of brick, stone, etc.).

ผนึก phanỳg′ V to seal.

เปิดผนึก pə̀əd′phanỳg′ V to unseal; to be unsealed.

ผม ๑ (เส้น) phǒm′ N hair of the head (sên′ for
a strand of hair). →Dist. ขน ๑.

เกล้าผม klâawphǒm′ V to tie up the hair in a bun.

เซ็ทผม sédphǒm′ V to set the hair, have one's
hair set. [เซ็ท f. Eng.]

ดัดผม dàdphǒm′ V to wave the hair, curl the hair,
have one's hair waved, get a permanent wave.

ทรงผม (ทรง,แบบ) soŋphǒm′ (soŋ′,bɛ̀ɛb′) N
eleg. style of haircut, hair style.

แบบผม (แบบ) bɛ̀ɛbphǒm′ (bɛ̀ɛb′) N hair style.

ผมเปีย (เปีย,ข้าง) phǒmpia′ N queue, pigtail
(pia′ for a single queue; khâaŋ′ for one of
a pair).

ผมมวย phǒmmuaj′ N chignon, bun.

ผมม้า phǒmmáa′ N bangs.

ผมหงอก phǒmŋɔ̀ɔg′ N 1. gray hair. V 2. to be
gray-haired.

ผมหยิก phǒmjìg′ N 1. kinky hair, curly hair,
wavy hair. V 2. to have kinky hair, be curly-
haired, be wavy-haired.

ม้วนผม múanphǒm′ V to curl the hair, put up one's
hair.

มวยผม muajphǒm′ N chignon, bun.

ไรผม rajphǒm′ N 1. the hair line above the forehead. 2. the part or dividing line formed when
the hair is gathered into a topknot. →Dist. 2.
แสก.

เสยผม sə̌əjphǒm′ V to brush back one's hair
with one's fingers.

หวีผม wǐiphǒm′ V to comb the hair.

ผม ๒ phǒm′ P def. m. sp. I, me. →Paired with
คุณ "you." →Comp. ดิฉัน def. w. sp. →Cf.
ผม ๑ to which ผม ๒ is related. →Syn. กระผม
eleg., เกล้ากระผม elab. eleg., กระหม่อม,
หม่อมฉัน roy.

ผมด้วย phǒmdûaj′ me too.

ผมเอง phǒm?eeŋ′ 1. myself, I myself. 2. it's
me. 3. (let) me (try it).

ผยอง phajɔ̌ɔŋ′ V to be arrogant, haughty.

หยิ่งผยอง jìŋ′phajɔ̌ɔŋ′ V to be excessively proud,
be arrogant, haughty.

ผรุสวาจา pharúsawaa′caa′, pharùd′sawaa′caa′ N
eleg. abusive language, harsh words.

ผรุสวาท pharùd′sawâad′ N eleg. abusive words,
vulgar words, curses, obscene language. คำ--
(คำ) idem. →Syn. คำหยาบ com.

ผล phǒn′, phǒnla⊃ N 1. result, outcome. 2. eleg.
fruit. C 3. eleg. clf. for any kind of fruit.
→Syn. 3. ใบ,ลูก com.

ได้ผล dâjphǒn′ V 1. to get results. 2. (something) to be successful, effective.

  o ไม่ได้ผล mâjdâjphǒn′ to be of no avail, useless,
  unsuccessful, ineffective.

บรรลุผล banlú?′phǒn′ V to suceed, be successful,

obtain results.

บังเกิดผล baŋkə̀əd′phŏn′ V eleg. to bear fruit,
    yield results, be successful.

ประสิทธิ์ผล prasìd′phŏn′ V to be successful,
    give successful results.

ปันผล panphŏn′ V to share the profits.

o เงินปันผล ŋən′panphŏn′ dividend (given to a
    shareholder).

เป็นผล penphŏn′ to be successful, fruitful.

เป็นผลดี penphŏn′dii′ to be useful, profitable,
    beneficial; to give good results.

ผลกรรม phŏnlakam′ N retribution (for one's
    evil deeds).

ผลกำไร phŏn′kamraj′ N profit, gain.

ผลคูณ phŏnkhuun′ N math. product.

ผลงาน phŏnŋaan′ N result of work.

ผลเฉลี่ย phŏnchalìa′ N average result.

ผลต่าง phŏntàaŋ′ N math. difference.

ผลบวก phŏnbùag′ N math. sum.

ผลประโยชน์ phŏn′prajòod′ N 1. benefit, gain,
    use, advantage, profit; (one's) interest. 2.
    proceeds.

ผลพลอยได้ (อย่าง) phŏn′phlɔɔjdâaj′ (jàaŋ′) N
    by-product.

ผลไม้ (ใบ,ลูก,ผล) phŏnlamáaj′ (baj′, lûug′,
    phŏn′) N eleg. fruit (general term). →Syn.
    ลูกไม้ com.

o ส่วนผลไม้ (ขนัด) sŭan′phŏnlamáaj′ (khanàd′)
    N orchard.

ผลย้อนหลัง phŏn′jɔ́ɔnlăŋ′ N retroactive effect.

ผลร้าย phŏnráaj′ N unfavorable result, bad
    effect, harmful effect.

ผลลบ phŏnlób′ N math. remainder (after sub-
    traction).

ผลลัพธ์ phŏnláb′ N math. result, final result.

ผลสะท้อน phŏn′sathɔ́ɔn′ N after-effect, resulting
    effect, secondary effect.

ผลสำเร็จ phŏn′sămrèd′ N success, accomplish-
    ment.

ผลสุดท้าย phŏn′sùdtháaj′ N 1. final result. 2.
    at last, finally.

ผลเสียหาย phŏn′sĭahăaj′ N damage, damaging
    result, bad results.

ผลิตผล phalìd′phŏn′, phlìdphŏn′ N eleg. product.

พืชผล (อย่าง,ชนิด) phŷydphŏn′ (jàaŋ′, chaníd′)
    N 1. a plant and its products. 2. agricultural
    products. 3. crops.

มีผล miiphŏn′ 1. to become effective. 2. to result
    (in). 3. to bear fruit.

o มีผลย้อนหลัง miiphŏn′jɔ́ɔnlăŋ′ to be retroactive,
    have a retroactive effect.

o มีผลสืบเนื่อง(มาจาก) miiphŏn′sỳybnŷaŋ′(maaɔ
    càagɔ) to be a consequence (of).

ยังผล(ให้) jaŋphŏn′(hâjɔ) lit. to result (in), have
    the result (of).

ไร้ผล rájphŏn′ to be useless, futile, ineffective.

สัมฤทธิ์ผล sămríd′phŏn′ eleg. to be successful.

เหตุผล (ข้อ,อย่าง,ประการ) hèedphŏn′ (khɔ̂ɔ′,
    jàaŋ′, prakaan′) N reason.

ให้ผล hâjphŏn′ to benefit, give benefits, give results.

ออกผล ʔɔ̀ɔgphŏn′ to produce, bear fruit.

ผละ(จาก) phlà?′(càagɔ) V to turn away (from),
    move away (from), part (with), leave, abandon.

ผละหนี phlà?′nĭi′ to turn away from, part with,
    leave.

ผละออก phlà?′′ɔ̀ɔg′ to part; to leave, abandon.

ผลัก phlàg′ V to push, shove.

ผลักดัน phlàg′dan′ V 1. to push, shove. 2. phys.
    to repel. 3. to put pressure on, to influence.

ผลักไส phlàg′săj′ V to push away.

ผลัด phlàd′ V 1. to change, replace. N 2. relief,
    shift; change. C 3. clf. for same.

ผลัดกัน phlàd′kan′ to take turns, alternate.

ผลัดเปลี่ยน phlàdplìan′ V to change.

ผลัดผ้า phlàdphâa′ V to change clothes.

วิ่งผลัด wîŋphlàd′ N 1. relay race. V 2. to run
    a relay race.

ผลัน. See ผลุนผลัน.

ผลาญ,ล้าง-- phlaan′, láaŋphlaan′ V to destroy,
    ruin, waste.

ผลาม. See ผลีผลาม.

ผลิ phlì?′ V to bud, begin to grow and develop,
    burst forth.

ฤดูใบไม้ผลิ (ฤดู) rýduu′bajmáajphlì?′ (rýduu′)
    N spring (the season).

ผลิต phalìd′, phlìd′ V produce, manufacture.
    การ--production. ผู้-- producer.

ผลิตกรรม phalìd′kam′ N production.

ผลิตผล (อย่าง) phalìd'phǒn' (jàaŋ') N product.

o ผลิตผลพลอยได้ phalìd'phǒn'-phlɔɔjdâaj' N
by-product.

ผลิตภัณฑ์ (สิ่ง, อย่าง) phalìd'phan' (sìŋ', jàaŋ')
N product.

ผลิผลาม phlìiphlǎam' V to hurry, be in great
haste.

ผลึก (ก้อน) phalỳg'*(kɔ̂ɔn') N crystal.

ตกผลึก tòg'phalỳg' V to crystallize (of itself).

ผลุนผลัน phlǔnphlǎn' V to make haste, hasten, take
flight.

ผลุบ phlùb' V to duck (in or out), dart.

ผลุบเข้าผลุบออก phlùbkhâw'phlùbʔɔ̀ɔg' to dash
in and out.

ผลุบโผล่ phlùbphlòo' V 1. to be bobbing up and
down in the water (alternately sinking and rising). 2. to appear and withdraw quickly.

ผวน phǔan' V 1. to turn back, return. 2. to reverse.

ผันผวน phǎnphǔan' V to change back and forth,
fluctuate.

ผวย in ผ้าผวย (ผืน) phâaphǔaj' (phǔyn') N
colloq. blanket.

ผวา phawǎa' V 1. to be startled, frightened. 2.
to rush up to someone with both arms open.

ผสม phasǒm' V 1. to mix, blend. 2. to breed
(animals). 3. biol. to cross, crossbreed.
→Also ประสม.

เก็บเล็กผสมน้อย kèb'lég'-phasǒm'nɔ́ɔj' V elab.
colloq. to save up little by little.

ของผสม (อย่าง) khɔ̌ɔŋphasǒm' (jàaŋ') N
chem., phys. mixture.

ผสมพันธุ์ phasǒm'phan' V to breed.

รัฐบาลผสม (ชุด) rádthabaan'phasǒm' (chúd')
N coalition government.

ส่วนผสม (ส่วน) sùanphasǒm' (sùan') N 1. component, constituent, ingredient. 2. admixture.

ผอง in ทั้งผอง tháŋphɔ̌ɔŋ' lit. all. →Cf. ทั้งปวง.

ผ่อง phɔ̀ŋ'* V to be clean, clear, bright, fair (esp.
of complexion).

ผ่องแผ้ว phɔ̀ŋphɛ̂w' V to be clean, pure (esp. in
the cast of one's mind).

ผ่องใส phɔ̀ŋsǎj' V 1. to be clean, pure, unclouded
(as of the mind, heart). 2. to be happy, gay,

cheerful (as of the face).

ผุดผ่อง phùdphɔ̌ŋ' V to be clear, radiant, sparkling.

ผ่อน phɔ̀ɔn', phɔ̀n' V to lessen, reduce, abate, slacken.

เงินผ่อน ŋanphɔ̀ɔn' N installment.

ผ่อนชำระหนี้ phɔ̀ɔn'-chamrá?'nîi' to pay a debt
by installments.

ผ่อนใช้ phɔ̀ɔncháj' V to pay by installments.

ผ่อนปรน phɔ̀npron' V to reduce, ease, lessen
(e.g. terms, restrictions, requirements).

ผ่อนผัน phɔ̀ɔnphǎn' V 1. idem ผ่อนปรน. 2. to
ease the situation.

ผ่อนสั้นผ่อนยาว phɔ̀nsân'phɔ̀njaaw' V idiom.
to ease tensions by compromise or mutual
concession.

ผ่อนหนักผ่อนเบา phɔ̀nnàg'phɔ̀nbaw' idem.

ผ้าผ่อน (ชิ้น) phâa'phɔ̀ɔn' (chín') N colloq.
clothes.

พักผ่อน phágphɔ̀ɔn' V to rest, take a rest.

ผอม phɔ̌ɔm' V to be thin (not fat), lean.

ซูบผอม sûubphɔ̌ɔm' V to be emaciated, pale and
skinny.

ผอมโซ phɔ̌ɔmsoo' V to be skinny and weak
(because undernourished).

ผอมแห้ง phɔ̌ɔmhɛ̂ɛŋ' V to be gaunt, emaciated
(because diseased).

ผะสา. See ประสา. →Also ภาษา ๒.

ผัก (ชนิด, อย่าง) phàg' (chanìd', jàaŋ') N greens,
vegetable.

ผักกาด (ก้าน, ใบ, ต้น) phàgkàad' N leafy vegetable,
such as leaf lettuce, Chinese cabbage, etc. (ก้าน'
for the stem; ใบ' for the leaf; ต้น' for a severed
head or bunch). ต้น-- (ต้น) lettuce, cabbage plant.

o ผักกาดขาว phàgkàad'khǎaw' N Chinese cabbage.

o ผักกาดหวาน phàgkàad'wǎan' N sugar beet.

o ผักกาดหอม phàgkàad'hɔ̌ɔm' N romaine lettuce.

o หัวผักกาด (หัว) hǔaphàgkàad' (hǔa') N turnip.

ผักชี (ก้าน, ใบ) phàgchii' N coriander (ก้าน'
for the stem; ใบ' for the leaf). ต้น-- (ต้น)
the coriander plant.

o ผักชีไทย phàgchii'thaj' N coriander.

o ผักชีฝรั่ง phàgchii'faràŋ' N parsley.

o ผักชีล้อม phàgchii'lɔ́ɔm' N celery.

ผักดอง phàgdɔɔŋ' N pickled vegetable.

ผักบุ้ง phàgbûŋ' N convolvulus, an aquatic morning

glory used as a green vegetable (Convolvulaceae). ต้น-- (ต้น) the plant.

ร่องผัก rɔ̂ŋphàg/ N vegetable bed.

ส่วนผัก (ไร่) sŭanphàg/ (râj/) N truck garden.

ผัง phăŋ/ N plan, layout.

แผนผัง phɛ̆ɛnphăŋ/ N plan, layout, scheme.

ผัด ๑ phàd/ V 1. to stir fry (i.e. to fry chopped meat
and other things mixed together). N 2. fried
food (a mixture of chopped meat and other
things). →Dist. ทอด.

ข้าวผัด khâawphàd/ N fried rice.

ผัดเปรี้ยวหวาน phàd/prîawwăan/ N sweet and
sour fried food.

ผัด ๒ phàd/ V to powder, apply powder.

ผัดแป้ง phàdpɛ̂ɛŋ/ V to powder, apply face powder.

ผัดหน้า phàdnâa/ V to powder the face.

o แป้งผัดหน้า pɛ̂ɛŋ/phàdnâa/ N face powder.

ผัด ๓ phàd/ V postpone, put off.

ผัดวันประกันพรุ่ง phàd/wan/-prakan/phrûŋ/ V
elab. colloq. to procrastinate, put off.

ผัน phăn/ V 1. to turn, rotate, change. 2. gram.
to recite or produce paradigms, to conjugate,
decline, inflect.

บิดผัน bìd/phăn/ V to evade.

แปลงผัน plɛɛŋphăn/ V chem. to convert.

ผ่อนผัน phɔ̀nphăn/ V 1. to reduce, lessen, ease
(e.g. terms, restrictions, requirements). 2.
to ease the situation.

ผันแปร , แปรผัน phănprɛɛ/, prɛɛphăn/ V to change,
undergo change, fluctuate, be unstable.

ผันผวน phănphŭan/ V to change back and forth,
fluctuate.

ผันอักษร phăn/ʔàgsɔ̆ɔn/ V to recite the tonal
paradigm of a consonant.

ผัว (คน) phŭa/ (khon/) N com. husband. →Syn.
สามี eleg.

น้องผัว (คน) nɔ́ɔŋphŭa/ (khon/) N brother- or
sister-in-law (of a woman in ref. to her husband's yg. brother or sister): "husband's
younger sibling."

ผัวเมีย (คู่) phŭamia/ (khûu/) N husband and
wife, married couple. →Syn. สามีภรรยา eleg.

ผิดผัวผิดเมีย phìdphŭa/phìdmia/ V to commit
adultery.

พ่อผัว (คน) phɔ̂ɔphŭa/ (khon/) N (woman's)
father-in-law. →Comp. พ่อตา (man's) father-
in-law.

พี่ผัว (คน) phîi/phŭa/ (khon/) N brother- or
sister-in-law (of a woman in ref. to her husband's
older brother or sister): "husband's older sibling."

แม่ผัว (คน) mɛ̂ɛphŭa/ (khon/) N (woman's)
mother-in-law. →Comp. แม่ยาย (man's)
mother-in-law.

ผัวะเผียะ phùaʔphìaʔ/ imit. the sound of beating,
slapping, cracking. →Also พัวะเพียะ.

ผา ๑ (ลูก) phăa/ (lûug/) N 1. cliff. 2. rock, stone
(in some compounds).

เงื้อมผา (แห่ง) ŋýamphăa/ (hɛ̀ŋ/) N precipice,
overhanging rock, projecting cliff.

ปะง่อนผา (แห่ง) chaŋɔ̂n/phăa/ (hɛ̀ŋ/) N cliff,
precipice, overhanging rock.

หน้าผา (แห่ง,ลูก) nâaphăa/ (hɛ̀ŋ/,lûug/) N cliff.

หินผา (ลูก) hĭnphăa/ (lûug/) N 1. cliff. 2. rock,
stone.

หุบผา (แห่ง) hùbphăa/ (hɛ̀ŋ/) N valley.

ผา ๒ in เลียงผา (ตัว) lianphăa/ (tua/) N goat
antelope, goral (Naemorhedus goral).

ผ่า phàa/ V to split, cut, hew.

กีบผ่า (กีบ) kìibphàa/ (kìib/) N cloven hoof.

ผ่าตัด phàatàd/ V to operate on (surgically).
การ-- surgery, surgical operation.

o หมอผ่าตัด (คน) mɔ̆ɔ/phàatàd/ (khon/) N com.
surgeon. →Syn. ศัลยแพทย์ eleg.

ผ่าเผย phàaphə̌əj/ V 1. to be dignified, majestic,
proud. sV 2. majestically, proudly.

o สง่าผ่าเผย saŋàa/phàaphə̌əj/ idem.

ผ่าเหล่า phàa/làw/ V idiom. to be a black sheep
of the family. 2. to break with family tradition.

ฟ้าผ่า (ครั้ง) (1) fáa/phàa/; (2) fáaphàa/ 1. lightning to strike. N 2. thunderbolt (khráŋ/).

เสื้อผ่าอก (ตัว) sŷa/phàaʔòg/ (tua/) N an upper
garment which opens down the front.

ผ้า (ชิ้น,ผืน,พับ) phâa/ N cloth (chín/ for a piece
of any size, not regarded in terms of any function; phŷyn/, for a piece having a definite function, as a towel, a blanket, a dust rag; pháb/,
for a roll of cloth).

จักรเย็บผ้า (เครื่อง,คัน) càg/jébphâa/ (khrŷaŋ/,

khan′) N sewing machine.

ซักผ้า ságphâa′ V to wash clothes. คน-- launderer, laundress.

o ร้านซักผ้า (ร้าน) ráan′ságphâa′ (ráan′) N laundry (the establishment).

เนื้อผ้า nýaphâa′ N texture of cloth.

ผ้ากฐิน phâakathǐn′ N yellow robe to be presented to the priest during the กฐิน festival.

ผ้ากันเปื้อน phâakanpŷan′ N apron.

ผ้าขนสัตว์ phâakhǒnsàd′ N 1. wool fabric, woolen cloth. 2. wool blanket.

ผ้าขนหนู phâakhǒnnǔu′ N 1. terry cloth. 2. Turkish towel; washcloth.

ผ้าขาวบาง phâakhǎawbaaŋ′ N cheesecloth, gauze.

ผ้าขาวม้า phâakhawmáa′/* N a long strip of patterned cloth used by men for various purposes (e.g. as a towel, loincloth, sash, or covering for the head).

ผ้าขี้ริ้ว phâakhiiríw′/* N rag.

ผ้าคุลมที่นอน phâakhlum′thîinɔɔn′ N bedspread.

ผ้าเช็ดตัว phâachédtua′ N towel, bath towel.

ผ้าเช็ดมือ phâachédmyy′ N napkin.

ผ้าเช็ดหน้า phâachédnâa′ N handkerchief.

ผ้าชิ้น phâasîn′ N a sarong-like lower garment worn by women.

ผ้าดิบ phâadìb′ N unbleached muslin.

ผ้าถุง phâathǔŋ′ N a sarong-like lower garment worn by women.

ผ้าแถบ phâathὲɛb′ N a strip of cloth used singly by women to wrap around the bosom (in place of all other upper garments).

ผ้านวม phâanuam′ N quilt, comforter.

ผ้าน้ำมัน phâanámman′ N oilcloth.

ผ้านุ่ง phâanûŋ′ N the phanung, a Siamese lower garment comprising a wide strip of cloth with one end twisted and hitched between the legs. Formerly worn by both sexes; now rarely seen.

ผ้าใบ phâabaj′ N canvas, sailcloth.

o รองเท้าผ้าใบ (คู่,ข้าง) rɔɔŋtháaw′phâabaj′ N canvas shoes, tennis shoes, sneakers (khûu′ for a pair; khâaŋ′ for one).

ผ้าปูโต๊ะ phâapuutó?′ N tablecloth, lunchcloth.

ผ้าปูที่นอน phâapuu′thîinɔɔn′ N sheet, bedsheet.

ผ้าโปร่ง phâapròoŋ′ N net fabric, netting.

ผ้าผวย phâaphǔaj′ N colloq. blanket.

ผ้าผ่อน (ชิ้น) phâa′phɔ̀ɔn′ (chín′) N colloq. clothes.

ผ้าผูกคอ (ผืน,อัน,เส้น) phâaphùugkhɔɔ′ N 1. scarf (ph/yn′). 2. tie (?an′, sên′).

ผ้าฝ้าย phâafâaj′ N cotton cloth, cotton fabric.

ผ้าพันคอ phâaphankhɔɔ′ N scarf.

ผ้าพันแผล (ม้วน,ชิ้น) phâaphanphlὲɛ′ N bandage, gauze (múan′ for a roll; chín′ for a piece).

ผ้าม่วง phâamûaŋ′ N a silk loincloth or phanung worn by men.

ผ้ายก phâajóg′ N brocade.

ผ้าสำลี phâasǎmlii′ N flannelet, a cotton fabric napped on one side.

ผ้าห่ม phâahòm′ N 1. blanket. 2. shawl.

o ผ้าห่มนอน phâahòmnɔɔn′ N blanket.

ผ้าไหม phâamǎj′ N silk cloth.

ผ้าอ้อม phâa?ɔ̂ɔm′ N diaper, baby's breechcloth.

เย็บผ้า jébphâa′ to sew.

ร่มผ้า (คัน) rômphâa′ (khan′) N cloth umbrella.

รีดผ้า rîidphâa′ V to iron, press clothes.

เสื้อผ้า (ชิ้น) sŷaphâa′ (chín′) N clothes, clothing.

ห่มผ้า hòmphâa′ V to cover with a blanket or shawl.

ผาก ๑ in หน้าผาก (หน้าผาก) nâaphàag′ (nâaphàag′) N forehead.

ผาก ๒ phàag′ rM intensifier used with แห้ง "dry."

ผาด in the following entries.

งามผาด ŋaamphàad′ V to appear beautiful at first glimpse, to be superficially beautiful (mostly of women). →Dist. งามพิศ.

ผาด ๆ phàadphàad′ 1. briefly, quickly, for a short instant. 2. superficially.

ผาดโผน phàadphǒn′ V to be adventurous, daredevilish.

ผ่าน phàan′ V 1. to pass. sV 2. past, through.

ค่าผ่านประตู khâaphàan′pratuu′ N admission charge, gate fee.

เดินผ่าน dəənphàan′ to walk through, walk past, walk by.

o พา...เดินผ่าน phaa′...dəənphàan′ to take (someone) past, lead (someone) past.

ทหารผ่านศึก (คน,นาย) thahǎan′phàansỳg′ (khon′, naaj′) N war veteran.

ทางผ่าน (ทาง) thaaŋphàan′ (thaaŋ′) N passageway.

บัตรผ่านประตู (ใบ) bàdphàan′pratuu′ (baj′) N admission ticket.

ผ่านเข้าออก phàan′khâw?ɔ̀ɔg′ to pass through, in and out.

ผ่านไป phàan′paj′ to pass by, pass on (going away from the point of reference).

ผ่านไปมา phàan′pajmaa′ to pass by (going back and forth).

ผ่านไปเลย phàan′pajləəj′ to pass and not return.

ผ่านพ้นไป phàanphón′paj′ to pass by, go by, elapse.

ผ่านมา phàan′maa′ to pass by, pass on (going toward the point of reference).

ส่งผ่าน sòŋphàan′ to send (something) through, pass (something) through.

ผาย phǎaj′ V to release, let go, part, separate, diverge.

ผายปอด phǎajpɔ̀ɔd′ V to administer artificial respiration.

ผายลม phǎajlom′ V eleg. to break wind. →Syn. ตด com.

ผายออก phǎaj?ɔ̀ɔg′ V to diverge.

ผึ่งผาย phɣ̀ŋphǎaj′ V to be imposing, strong-looking, manly in bearing.

ผ่าว phàaw′ rM intensifier used with ร้อน "hot."

ผาสุก phǎasùg′ V to be happy. ความ-- happiness, well-being.

ผิง phǐŋ′ V to warm at the fire, bake.

เตาผิง (เตา) tawphǐŋ′ (taw′) N fireplace.

ผิด phìd′ V 1. to be different. 2. to be wrong, incorrect. 3. to miss. ความ-- (see below). →Ant. ถูก ๒.

กระทำผิด kratham′phìd′ V to do wrong, make a mistake. การ-- guilt, wrong-doing.

เข้าใจผิด khâwcajphìd′ V to misunderstand, mistake. การ-- misunderstanding.

ความผิด khwaamphìd′ N guilt, fault, mistake.

o มีความผิด miikhwaamphìd′ to be guilty.

o ทำความผิด tham′khwaamphìd′ V 1. to commit a crime. 2. to do wrong. →Comp. ทำผิด.

ความผิดและถูก khwaamphìd′lɛthùug′ N the rights and wrongs.

ทำผิด thamphìd′ V 1. to make a mistake, make an error. 2. to do wrong. →Comp. ทำความผิด under ความผิด above.

ผิดกฎหมาย phìd′kòdmǎaj′ V to be illegal, unlawful, against the law.

ผิดกัน phìd′kan′ to be of different kinds, to differ, be distinguishable from one another.

ผิดกับ phìd′kaɔ to differ from, be different from, unlike.

ผิดคาด phìdkhâad′ V 1. to be contrary to expectation, disappointing. 2. to be disappointed (in expectations).

ผิดจาก phìd′càagɔ 1. to be different from. 2. to be not (such and such), other than (such and such); to fail (to get something).

o ถ้าผิดจากผู้หญิงคนนี้แล้ว ฉันจะไม่แต่งงานเลยใน ชาตินี้ thâaphìd′càagphûujǐŋ′khonníi′-lɛ́ɛw→ chán′camâjtɛ̀ŋŋaan′-ləəj′ najchâad′níi↓ If I fail to get this woman, then I won't get married at all in this life.

ผิดใจ phìdcaj′ V to have a falling out, to be sore (at).

o ผิดใจกัน(ด้วย) phìdcaj′kan(dûajɔ) to be sore at each other, to have a falling out (about).

ผิดตา phìdtaa′ V to look changed.

ผิดถนัด phìd′thanàd′ to be all wrong, way off, wide of the mark.

ผิดถูก phìd′thùug′ V to be right or wrong.

ผิดธรรมดา phìd′thammadaa′ V to be abnormal, unusual, queer.

ผิดนัด phìdnád′ V to miss an appointment.

ผิดปกติ phìd′pògkatì?′ V to be unusual, abnormal, irregular.

ผิดผัวผิดเมีย phìdphǔa′phìdmia′ V to commit adultery. →Comp. ผิดเมีย.

ผิดแผก(ไปจาก) phìdphɛ̀ɛg′(pajcàag′) colloq. to differ, deviate, be different (from).

o ผิดแผกแตกต่าง phìdphɛ̀ɛg′tɛ̀ɛgtàaŋ′ elab. colloq. to differ, be different.

ผิดพลาด phìdphlâad′ V to be incorrect, wrong, mistaken. ความ-- blunder, mistake, error.

ผิดเพี้ยน phìdphían′ V to differ, deviate, be different.

ผิดเมีย phìdmia′ V to commit adultery with another's wife. →Comp. ผิดผัวผิดเมีย.

ผิดสังเกต phìd′sǎŋkèed′ V to be unusual, queer, abnormal.

○ เห็นผิดสังเกตุ hěnphìd′sǎŋkèed′ V to sense something unusual happening.

ผิดสัญญา phìd′sǎnjaa′ V to break a promise, a contract.

ผิดหวัง phìdwǎŋ′ to be disappointed. ความ-- disappointment.

ผิดหูผิดตา phìdhǔu′phìdtaa′ V elab. colloq. to look changed; to have changed markedly in appearance.

รับผิด rábphìd′ V to admit one's guilt or mistake.

รับผิดชอบ ráb′phìdchɔɔb′ to be responsible (for), accept responsibility (for). ความ-- responsibility.

สำคัญผิด sǎmkhan′phìd′ V to misunderstand, mistake, make a mistaken assumption.

หาผิด(กับ) hǎa′phìd′(kaɔ) V to find fault (with).

เห็นผิดเป็นชอบ hěnphìd′penchɔɔb′ to mistake wrong for right, bad for good.

ผิน phǐn′ V to turn (e.g. one's face).

โผผิน phǒophǐn′ V (a bird) to fly from place to place.

ผิว ๑ phǐw′ N 1. skin, outer surface. 2. complexion.

การถือผิว kaan′thʉ̌yphǐw′ N racial discrimination.

ชาติผิวขาว châad′phǐwkhǎaw′ N the white race.

ชาติผิวดำ châad′phǐwdam′ N the black race.

ชาติผิวเหลือง châad′phǐwlʉ̌aŋ′ N the yellow race.

ผิวคล้ำ phǐwkhlám′ N 1. dark, colored skin. V 2. to be dark-skinned.

ผิวดำ phǐwdam′ N 1. dark skin. V 2. to be dark-skinned.

ผิวน้ำ phǐwnáam′ N water surface.

○ เรือผิวน้ำ (ลำ) rʉa′phǐwnáam′ (lam′) N surface vessel.

ผิวเนื้อ phǐwnʉ́a′ N complexion.

ผิว ๆ phǐwphǐw′ sV lightly, superficially.

ผิวเผิน phǐwphə̌ən′ sV 1. superficial, on the surface, skin-deep. 2. superficially.

ผิวพรรณ phǐwphan′ N complexion.

ผิวหนัง phǐwnǎŋ′ N skin.

○ โรคผิวหนัง (ชนิด) rôog′phǐwnǎŋ′ (chaníd′) N skin disease, dermatitis.

พวกผิวขาว phûagphǐwkhǎaw′ N the white-skinned group, white people.

ผิว ๒. See entry below.

ผิวปาก phǐwpàag′ V to whistle.

ผี (ตน) phǐi′ (ton′) N ghost, spirit.

จานผี (ลำ) caanphǐi′ (lam′) N flying saucer.

ผีเข้าผีออก phǐikhâw′phǐiʔɔ̀ɔg′ V idiom. 1. to be characterized by changing one's mind suddenly without apparent or adequate motive. 2. to be changing, fluctuating, inconsistent.

ผีป่า (ตน) phǐipàa′ (ton′) N forest demon.

ผีพุ่งไต้ (ดวง) phǐiphûŋtâaj′ N shooting star.

ผีสาง (ตน) phǐi′sǎaŋ′ (ton′) N ghost, spirit.

ผีสิง phǐi′sǐŋ′ a spirit which possesses (one), a spirit which haunts (a place).

○ บ้านผีสิง (หลัง) bâan′-phǐi′sǐŋ′ (lǎŋ′) N a haunted house.

ผีเสื้อ (ตัว) phǐisʉ̂a′ (tua′) N butterfly.

ฝากผีฝากไข้(กับ) fàagphǐi′fàagkhâj′(kaɔ) V elab. colloq., idiom. to ask (someone) to take care of one, or of one's body, in the event of sickness or death.

ผึ่ง phʉ̀ŋ′ V to dry (in the open or in the sun), to expose (to the sun, the air).

ผึ่งแดด phʉ̀ŋdɛ̀ɛd′ V to expose to the sun, dry in the sun, sun-dry.

ผึ่งผาย phʉ̀ŋphǎaj′ V to be imposing, strong-looking, manly in bearing.

ผึ่งอากาศ phʉ̀ŋ′ʔaakàad′ V to expose to air, dry in the breeze, air-dry.

ผึ้ง (ตัว) phʉ̂ŋ′ (tua′) N bee. →Also ตัว--.

ขี้ผึ้ง khîiphʉ̂ŋ′ N wax, beeswax.

งวงผึ้ง (งวง) ŋuaŋphʉ̂ŋ′ (ŋuaŋ′) N proboscis or sucking organ of the bee.

น้ำผึ้ง námphʉ̂ŋ′ N honey.

รวงผึ้ง (รวง) ruaŋphʉ̂ŋ′ (ruaŋ′) N bee's nest.

รังผึ้ง (รัง) raŋphʉ̂ŋ′ (raŋ′) N 1. beehive. 2. bee's nest.

ผืน phʉ̌yn′ C strip, sheet, piece; hence clf. for cloth in a form suitable for use and having a definite function, e.g. towels, sheets, curtains, rugs, dust rags, etc; also clf. for a strip or section of land.

ผื่น phʉ̀yn′ N rash.

เป็นผื่น penphʉ̀yn′ to have a rash.

ผุ phù?′ V to be decayed, rotten.

ผุพัง phù?/phaŋ/ V to be dilapidated.

ฟันผุ fanphù?/ N 1. tooth decay, dental caries.
2. decayed tooth. V 3. to have dental caries, decayed teeth.

ผุด phùd/ V to emerge, rise up, appear suddenly, pop into view.

ผุดผ่อง phùdphɔ̀ŋ/ to be bright, clear, radiant, sparkling.

ผุดลุก phùd/lúg/ to sit up, stand up, jump up suddenly.

ผุดลุกผุดนั่ง phùdlúg/phùdnâŋ/ V elab. colloq. to be repeatedly getting up and sitting down again (e.g. because of restlessness, impatience).

ผู้ phûu/ N eleg. person (rarely used alone with this meaning). 2. male (not used with people). 3. element placed in front of verbs to form agent nouns; hence may be translated "-er, one who..." (very productive usage). C 4. clf. for people. →Syn. 3, 4 คน ๑ com. →See 3. คน ๑. NOTE. All nouns based on ผู้ take คน as their classifier unless otherwise marked.

ตัวผู้ tuaphûu/ N male (normally not used with people). →Dist. ชาย ๑, ผู้ชาย "male (of people)." →Opp. ตัวเมีย "female."

o เกษรตัวผู้ (อัน) kees̄ɔɔn/tuaphûu/ (?an/) N bot. stamen.

เป็นผู้เป็นคน penphûu/penkhon/ elab. colloq. to be presentable, like a normal human.

ผู้ก่อการ phûukɔ̀ɔkaan/ N rebel, revolutionist, instigator of disorder.

ผู้กำกับ (คน,นาย) phûukamkàb/ (khon/, naaj/) N 1. director. 2. colloq. chief of police.

o ผู้กำกับการตำรวจ phûukamkàbkaan/tamrùad/ N (district or provincial) chief of police.

o ผู้กำกับการแสดง phûukamkàb/kaansadɛɛŋ/ N stage director, film director.

ผู้กำกับการ (คน,นาย) phûukamkàb/kaan/ (khon/, naaj/) N director, head, the person in charge of things.

ผู้ไกล่เกลี่ย phûu/klàjklìa/ N eleg. mediator, arbitrator.

ผู้ขับ phûukhàb/ N eleg. operator, driver (of a vehicle).

ผู้ขับขี่ phûu/khàbkhìi/ N eleg. operator, driver

(of a vehicle).

ผู้ขาย phûukhǎaj/ N eleg. salesperson, seller, vender.

ผู้คน phûu/khon/ N people.

o ผู้คนผ่านไปมา phûu/khon/ phàan/pajmaa/ passers-by, those passing by.

ผู้คนคว้า phûu/khónkhwáa/ N eleg. researcher, investigator.

ผู้คุ้นเคย phûu/khúnkhəəj/ N eleg. an acquaintance.

ผู้คุม phûukhum/ N warden, prison guard; warder, keeper, one who has custody (of a detained person).

ผู้จรจัด phûu/cɔɔncàd/ N eleg. vagrant, vagabond, homeless wanderer.

ผู้จัดการ phûucàdkaan/ N manager. →Dist. คน จัดการ "person in charge (usually temporarily)."

ผู้ช่วย phûuchûaj/ N 1. assistant, helper, aide. 2. rescuer.

ผู้ชาย phûuchaaj/ N 1. man. 2. male (of people). →Syn. บุรุษ eleg. →Dist. 2. ตัวผู้ "male (of animals)." →Opp. ผู้หญิง.

o เด็กผู้ชาย dèg/phûuchaaj/, -phuu- N boy, lad, little boy. →Sometimes written -พ-. →Also เด็กชาย.

ผู้เชี่ยวชาญ phûuchîawchaan/ N eleg. expert, specialist.

ผู้ซึ่ง phûusŷŋ⊃ lit. who, one who.

o เขาเป็นผู้ซึ่งทุกคนไว้วางใจ kháwpen/phûusŷŋ⊃ thúgkhon/ wájwaaŋ/caj↓ He is one whom everybody trusts.

ผู้เฒ่า phûuthâw/ N eleg. old person, aged person.

ผู้ดี phûudii/ N 1. nobleman, noblewoman. 2. gentleman, gentlewoman. 3. a refined person, person of refinement. →Opp. ไพร่.

ผู้ดู phûuduu/ N eleg. spectator, onlooker, audience.

ผู้ดูแล phûuduulɛɛ/ N eleg. superintendent, overseer, caretaker, keeper.

ผู้ใด phûudaj/ eleg. 1. who, whom, anyone, anybody. 2. who? whom?

o ผู้ใดก็ตาม phûudaj/kɔ̂taam/ whoever.

ผู้ต้องสงสัย phûutɔ̂ŋ/sǒŋsǎj/ N eleg. a suspect, one suspected of a crime, of wrongdoing.

ผู้ต้องหา phûu'tôŋhǎa' N eleg. the accused, a
defendant.

ผู้ตัดสิน phûu'tàdsǐn' N eleg. judge, umpire,
referee.

ผู้ตาม phûutaam' N eleg. follower. →Ant.ผู้นำ.

o เขาเป็นผู้นำ เราเป็นผู้ตาม kháwpen'phûunam'
→ rawpen'phûutaam'↓ He is the leader; we are
his followers.

ผู้ติดตาม phûutìdtaam' N 1. an aide who travels
with his superior. 2. entourage.

ผู้ที่ phûu'thîi⊃ eleg. those who, those whose;
one who, one whose.

ผู้แทน (คน,นาย) phûuthɛɛn' (khon', naaj') N
1. representative (in the legislature). 2. delegate. 3. agent, representative.

o ผู้แทนจำหน่าย (คน) phûuthɛɛn'camnàaj' (khon')
N selling or distributing agent.

o ผู้แทนราษฎร (คน,นาย) phûuthɛɛn'râadsadɔɔn'
(khon', naaj') N people's representative (in
the legislature).

o สภาผู้แทน (สภา) saphaa'phûuthɛɛn' (saphaa')
N House of Representatives, the lower legislative body in a parliamentary government.

ผู้น้อย phûunɔ́ɔj' N 1. an inferior, a junior person,
a younger person. 2. the little fellow. →Ant.
ผู้ใหญ่.

ผู้นำ phûunam' N leader.

o ตำแหน่งผู้นำ tamnèŋ'phûunam' the leadership,
i.e. the position of leader.

ผู้นำทาง phûunamthaaŋ' N guide, one who leads
the way.

ผู้บริหาร phûubɔɔrihǎan' N administrator, executive.

ผู้บังเกิดเกล้า phûubaŋkə̀əd'klâaw' N eleg.
parents. →Syn. พ่อแม่ com.

ผู้บังคับ (คน,นาย) phûubaŋkháb' (khon', naaj')
N commander. →Chiefly in compounds.

o ผู้บังคับการบิน phûubaŋkháb'kaanbin' N air-
commander.

o ผู้บังคับการ (คน,นาย) phûubaŋkháb'kaan'
(khon', naaj') N commander (esp. in the lower
echelons).

ผู้บังคับบัญชา (คน,นาย) phûubaŋkháb'banchaa'
(khon', naaj') N superior, director, head.

ผู้บัญชาการ (คน,นาย) phûubanchaa'kaan' (khon',
naaj') N commander, commanding officer
(esp. in the higher echelons).

ผู้ปกครอง phûupòkhrɔɔŋ' N 1. ruler. 2. guardian.
3. parents.

ผู้เป็นประธาน phûupen'prathaan' N eleg. chairman, president.

ผู้พิทักษ์สันติราษฎร์ (คน,นาย) phûuphíthág'sǎnti⊃
râad' (khon', naaj') N eleg. policeman.

ผู้พิพากษา (คน,นาย) phûuphíphâag'sǎa' (khon',
naaj') N judge.

ผู้พิมพ์จำหน่าย phûuphim'camnàaj' N publisher.
→Also ผู้พิมพ์.

ผู้พูด phûuphûud' N eleg. speaker; one who is
speaking; spokesman.

ผู้ฟัง phûufaŋ' N eleg. listener; those who are
listening; audience.

ผู้มีเกียรติ (ท่าน) phûumiiklàd' (thân') N eleg.
honorable person (i.e. one with rank, distinction).

ผู้อันจะกิน phûu'-miiʔan'cakin' N eleg. a well-
off, well-to-do person.

ผู้มีอาวุโส phûu'miiʔaa'wúsǒo' N eleg. a senior
person (in age, rank or status).

ผู้มีอิทธิพล phûu'miiʔìd'thíphon' N eleg. influential or powerful person.

ผู้เยาว์ phûujaw' N 1. law a minor. 2. lit.
youth, youngster.

ผู้รักษาการแทน phûu'-rágsǎakaan'thɛɛn' N eleg.
acting (chairman, etc.) i.e. an official who serves
on a temporary basis or as a substitute for another.

ผู้ร้าย phûuráaj' N criminal, bandit, wrongdoer,
villain (esp. in a movie or a play).

ผู้ริเริ่ม phûu'ríʔ'rə̂əm' N eleg. originator,
one who originates an idea or invents something.

ผู้รู้ phûurúu' N eleg. one who knows, a well-
informed person.

ผู้เรียบเรียง phûu'rîabriaŋ' N eleg. compiler,
author.

ผู้ลากมากดี phûulâag'-mâag'dii' N elab. colloq.
the nobility, the elite, the people of the upper
classes.

ผู้ว่าราชการ (คน,นาย) phûu'wâarâadchakaan'
(khon', naaj') N governor, commissioner.

o ผู้ว่าราชการจังหวัด (คน,นาย) phûu′wâaraâadↃ chakaan′caŋwàd′ (khon′,naaj′) N provincial governor, governor of a จังหวัด.

o ผู้ว่าราชการภาค (คน,นาย) phûu′wâaraâadchaↃ kaan′phâag′ (khon′,naaj′) N regional governor, governor of a ภาค.

ผู้วิเศษ phûuwísèed′ N one who possesses supernatural powers; magician, sorcerer.

ผู้ส่งข่าว phûu′sòŋkhàaw′ N correspondent (for a newspaper).

ผู้สนับสนุน phûu′-sanàb′sanŭn′ N eleg. supporter.

ผู้สมัคร phûusamàg′ N eleg. 1. candidate (for office, election). 2. applicant.

ผู้สร้าง phûusâaŋ′ N eleg. builder, constructor, creator.

ผู้สังเกตการณ์ phûu′-săŋkèed′kaan′ N an observer, one sent as an observer.

ผู้สำเร็จราชการ (ท่าน) phûusămrèd′raâadchaↃ kaan′ (thân′) N 1. regent, king's regent. 2. viceroy (esp. in former times, the viceroy of India).

ผู้สูงอายุ phûusŭuŋ′/ʔaajú?′/ N lit.,eleg. an elderly person.

ผู้เสนอ phûusanɔ̌ə′ N eleg. a speaker for the affirmative; one who makes a motion or proposal (as in a debate).

ผู้แสดง phûusadɛɛŋ′ N eleg. player, performer; the cast.

o รายนามผู้แสดง raajnaam′phûusadɛɛŋ′ N eleg. the cast (in a performance).

ผู้หญิง phûujǐŋ′ N com. 1. woman. 2. female (of people). →Also หญิง. →Syn. 1. สตรี eleg., อิตถี lit. →Dist. 2. ตัวเมีย female (of animals). →Opp. ผู้ชาย.

o เด็กผู้หญิง dègphûujǐŋ′, -phuu- N girl, lass, little girl. →Sometimes written -พู-. →Also เด็กหญิง.

o ท่านผู้หญิง thânphûujǐŋ′ T 1. Lady --. P 2. Her Ladyship, Madame. →See cross reference.

o ผู้หญิงคนเที่ยว phûujǐŋ′khonthîaw′ N prostitute, streetwalker.

o ผู้หญิงสาว phûujǐŋ′săaw′ N young woman, teen-age girl.

o ผู้หญิงหากิน phûujǐŋ′hǎakin′ N prostitute, streetwalker.

o โรคผู้หญิง rôog′phûujǐŋ′ N veneral disease (contracted by a man). →Cf. โรคบุรุษ.

o เสือผู้หญิง (คน) sʉ̌a′phûujǐŋ′ (khon′) N slang wolf, woman-chaser.

ผู้หลักผู้ใหญ่ phûulàg′phûujàj′ N colloq. adults, grown-ups, elders.

ผู้ใหญ่ phûujàj′ N 1. adult. 2. (one's) superior, (one's) elder. 3. the big fellow. →Ant. 1. เด็ก. 2, 3. ผู้น้อย.

o ชั้นผู้ใหญ่ chán′phûujàj′ senior, high-ranking.

o ผู้ใหญ่บ้าน phûujàjbâan′ N elected head of a village.

ผู้อ่าน phûu?àan′ N eleg. the reader (the one reading).

ผู้อารักขา phûu′?aarágkhăa′ N eleg. protector, guardian.

ผู้อาศัย phûu?aasăj′ N eleg. 1. inhabitant, tenant. 2. dependent (one who lives in someone else's household, receiving part or all his support there).

ผู้อำนวยการ phûu?amnuajkaan′ N director.

o ผู้อำนวยการบริหาร phûu?amnuajkaan′bɔɔrihăan′ N director, administrator, executive.

ผู้อื่น phûu?ʉ̀ʉn′ eleg. (the) other people, others, the others.

ผู้อุปการะ phûu′?ùbpakaa′rá?′ N eleg. patron, supporter.

ผูก phùug′ V tie, bind, fasten.

ผ้าผูกคอ (ผืน,อัน,เส้น) phâaphùugkhɔɔ′ N 1. scarf (phʉ̌ʉn′). 2. tie (?an′, sên′).

ผูกขาด phùugkhàad′ V to monopolize. การ-- monopoly; monopolizing.

ผูกพยาบาท phùug′phajaabàad′ V to be vengeful, vindictive, bear a grudge.

ผูกพัน phùugphan′ V 1. to tie, bind, be tied, bound. 2. (the heart, mind) to be absorbed (with), preoccupied (with), wrapped up (in) (e.g. loved ones, work, obligations). การ-- ties, bonds; being absorbed (in), being wrapped up (in), preoccupation (with).

o ข้อผูกพัน (ข้อ) khɔ̂ɔ′phùugphan′ (khɔ̂ɔ′) N obligation, binding condition; restriction, strings (attached to a deal).

ผูกมัด phùugmád/ V to tie, bind. การ-- tie, bond, obligation.

o ข้อผูกมัด (ข้อ) khɔ̌ɔ/phùugmád/ (khɔ̌ɔ/) N obligation, binding condition; restriction, strings (attached to a deal).

ผูกมิตร phùugmíd/ V to make friends.

ผูกไมตรี phùug/majtrii/ V to make friends.

ผูก(...)ไว้ phùug(...)wáj/ 1. to tie, bind up, keep tied up. 2. to be tied, tied up, kept tied up.

เผชิญ phachəən/ V to confront, to face.

เผชิญหน้า phachəənnâa/ V to face, meet face to face.

เผ็ด phèd/ V to be peppery, hot (in taste, not temperature).

แก้เผ็ด kɛ̂ɛphèd/ V to get back at (someone).

แกงเผ็ด kɛɛŋphèd/ N a variety of hot curry.

เผ็ดจี๋ phèdcǐi/ to be extremely peppery, hot (to the taste).

เผ็ดฉี่ phèdchìi/ to be extremely hot (to the taste).

เผ็ดร้อน phèdrɔ́ɔn/ V 1. to be hot and spicy (of food). 2. to be biting, acrimonious (of things, words, an argument, a song).

เผด็จ phadèd/ V lit. eleg. to cut.

เผด็จการ phadèd/kaan/ V to exercise absolute control, be dictatorial. ผู้-- dictator.

o จอมเผด็จการ cɔɔm/-phadèd/kaan/ N dictator.

o ลัทธิเผด็จการ ládthí?/-phadèd/kaan/ N dictatorship.

เผ่น phèn/* V 1. to jump, leap. 2. to flee.

เผ่นพรวด phènphrûad/ V to jump, leap suddenly.

เผย phəəj/ V to reveal, make known, uncover, expose, open.

เปิดเผย pəədphəəj/ V 1. to disclose, reveal, uncover, expose; to open up. 2. to be open, frank, outspoken.

ผ่าเผย phàaphəəj/ V 1. to be dignified, majestic, proud. sV 2. majestically, proudly.

เผยแผ่ phəəjphɛ̀ɛ/ V to propagate, popularize, spread out.

เผยแพร่ phəəjphrɛ̂ɛ/ idem.

เผยอ phajə̌ə/ V 1. to part (the lips) slightly, open (a door) slightly. 2. to be slightly parted, open. 3. to raise, lift slightly. 4. fig. to be haughty, act big.

เผยอตัว phajə̌ə/tua/ V to raise oneself from a prone position.

เผยอยิ้ม phajə̌ə/jím/ V to smile with slightly parted lips.

เผลอ phlə̌ə/ V 1. to forget oneself, let one's mind wander for a moment. 2. to be unaware, off one's guard.

เผลอไป phlə̌ə/paj/ V to forget oneself for a moment.

เผอิญ pha?əən/ by chance, by accident, accidentally, unexpectedly; it happened that. →Also บังเอิญ.

เผา phǎw/ V 1. to burn, burn up, consume by burning; to cremate. 2. to heat with an open flame, to bake.

การเผาไหม้ kaan/phǎwmâj/ N combustion.

ดินเผา dinphǎw/ N the baked or hardened clay of earthenware. เครื่อง-- earthenware.

เตาเผา (เตา) tawphǎw/ (taw/) N 1. furnace. 2. kiln. 3. incinerator. 4. crematory.

น้ำพริกเผา námphríg/phǎw/ N a condiment of roasted pepper and other ingredients combined to form a paste.

เผาไฟ phǎwfaj/ V to burn.

เผาศพ phǎwsòb/ V com. to cremate. →Syn. ปลงศพ, ฌาปนกิจ eleg.

เผ่า (เผ่า) phàw/ (phàw/) N 1. race, tribe, group (of people). C 2. clf. for same.

เผิน in the following entries.

ผิวเผิน phǐwphə̌ən/ sV 1. superficial, skin-deep. 2. superficially.

เผิน ๆ phə̌ənphə̌ən/ superficially, uncritically.

เผียะ phìa?/ imit. 1. the sound of a slap (as when slapping a child's wrist). C 2. a slap.

เผื่อ phʉ̀a/ Cj 1. provided that; if; in case. Pp 2. for (in the sense of "for the benefit of, as a kindness to"). →Dist. 1. เพื่อ.

เผื่อแผ่ phʉ̀aphɛ̀ɛ/ V 1. to be generous, generous to. 2. to share.

เผื่อว่า phʉ̀a/wâac, phʉ̀a/wâa/ if, supposing, in case.

เผือก ๑ phʉ̀ag/ V to be white (in special senses), albino.

ช้างเผือก (เชือก) cháaŋphʉ̀ag/ (chʉ̂ag/) N white elephant (i.e. an albino elephant).

เผือก ๒ (หัว) phỳag′ N taro (hŭa′ for the rhizome).

เผือด phỳad′ V to be pale, pallid, wan.

ซีดเผือด, เผือดซีด sîid′phỳad′, phỳad′sîid′) V
to be very pale, white as a sheet.

o หน้าซีดเผือด nâa′-sîid′phỳad′ to turn pale
(in the face); the face to turn pale.

เผือดลง phỳad′loŋ to turn pale.

หน้าเผือด nâa′phỳad′ V 1. to become crestfallen,
have one's face fall. 2. to turn pale (in the
face); the face to turn pale.

แผ่ phὲε′ V to spread out, stretch out, expand (lat-
erally), extend.

นอนแผ่ nɔɔnphὲε′ V to lie sprawled out (esp.
on one's back).

เผยแผ่ phɤ̌ɤjphὲε′ V to propagate, popularize,
spread out.

เผื่อแผ่ phỳaphὲε′ V 1. to be generous, generous
to. 2. to share.

แผ่อำนาจ phὲε′/ʔamnâad′ V to extend one's
power.

แผก (ไปจาก) phὲεg′(pajcàag′) V to differ, be different (from), unlike, strange.

ผิดแผก (ไปจาก) phìdphὲεg′(pajcàag′) V to differ,
deviate, be different (from).

แผด in แผดเสียง phὲεdsĭaŋ′ V to roar, scream,
yell, sing at the top of one's voice.

แผน (อย่าง, อัน) phɛ̌ɛn′ (jàaŋ′,ʔan′) N plan,
scheme, representation.

แบบแผน (อย่าง) bὲεbphɛ̌ɛn′ (jàaŋ′) N 1. custom,
tradition, established pattern, conventional rules.
2. standard reference.

แผนการ (อย่าง, อัน) phɛ̌ɛnkaan′ (jàaŋ′,ʔan′) N
plan, project, scheme. →Often incorrectly
spelled -การณ์.

o วางแผนการ waaŋ′phɛ̌ɛnkaan′ V to plan, plot,
to lay out a plan, plot, or scheme.

แผนที่ (แผ่น) phɛ̌ɛnthîi′ (phὲn′) N map.

แผนปัจจุบัน phɛ̌ɛn′pàdcuban′ N 1. new plan, modern plan. 2. (as n. mod.) modern, of the modern
type.

แผนผัง (รูป, อัน, แผ่น) phɛ̌ɛnphǎŋ′ (rûub′,ʔan′,
phὲn′) N plan, layout, scheme.

แผ่น phὲn′* C 1. clf. for thin, flat objects, e.g. sheets

of paper, boards, phonograph records, plates
of glass, etc. 2. class term for such items.

แผ่นดิน (ผืน, แผ่นดิน) phὲndin′ N 1. earth, ground,
land (phỳyn′). 2. nation, kingdom, realm (phὲn⊃
din′). C 3. reign.

o ครองแผ่นดิน khrɔɔŋ′phὲndin′ V to reign.

o งบประมาณแผ่นดิน ŋóbpramaan′phὲndin′ the
national budget.

o แผ่นดินใหญ่ phὲndin′jàj′ N the mainland.

o แผ่นดินไหว (ครั้ง) phὲndin′wǎj′ (khráŋ′) N
earthquake.

o พระเจ้าแผ่นดิน (พระองค์, องค์) phrácâwphὲndin′
(phrá?oŋ′,?oŋ′) N king.

แผ่นเสียง (แผ่น) phὲnsĭaŋ′ (phὲn′) N phonograph
record.

แผนก (แผนก) phanὲεg′ (phanὲεg′) N 1. department,
section, division, subdivision. C 2. clf. for
same.

o แผนกการเงิน phanὲεg′kaanŋɤn′ N finance
department, finance division.

แผล (แผล) phlɛ̌ε′ (phlɛ̌ε′) N 1. wound, cut. 2.
sore (e.g. an infected insect bite).

บาดแผล (แห่ง) bàadphlɛ̌ε′ (hὲŋ′) N wound, cut.

เป็นแผล penphlɛ̌ε′ 1. to be wounded. 2. to have
a sore.

แผลเป็น (แห่ง) phlɛ̌εpen (hὲŋ′) N scar.

แผลเรื้อรัง (แผล) phlɛ̌ε′rýaraŋ′ (phlɛ̌ε′) N
chronic ulcer or sore.

แผลง. See entries below.

คำแผลง (คำ) khamphlɛ̌εŋ (kham′) N a word
whose shape has been altered either by certain
derivational processes, as in the case of ดำเนิน
converted from เดิน, or according to certain
rules of rhyming, as in the case of ฉะฉาด from
ฉาด.

แผลงฤทธิ์ phlɛ̌εŋríd′ V 1. to manifest supernatural
power (usually in order to strike terror). 2. to
act up, show itself. 3. to show (its) effects (as
of poison, drugs). 4. to show one's nature, disposition (e.g. by stubbornness, temper, etc.).

แผลงศร phlɛ̌εŋsɔ̌ɔn′ V to shoot (an arrow).

แผล็บ phlὲb′ sV 1. quickly, swiftly (up and down, in
and out). C 2. an instant.

แผล็บ ๆ phlὲbphlὲb′ sV quickly and repeatedly

(up and down, in and out).

แผ่ว, แผ่ว ๆ phɛ̀w/, phɛ̀wphɛ̀w/* sV softly, lightly, faintly (of sound, voice, touch).

แผ้ว phɛ̂w/* to clear, clean, sweep clear.

ผ่องแผ้ว phɔ̀ŋphɛ̂w/ V to be clean, pure, clear (esp. in the cast of one's mind).

แผ้วถาง phɛ̂w/thǎaŋ/ V to clear the way (by removing weeds, obstacles).

แผ้วพาน phɛ̂wphaan/ V to trouble, disturb, bother.

โผ phǒo/ V 1. to dart, dash. 2. to rush up (to) with arms spread out (to greet or embrace someone).

โผผิน phǒophǐn/ V to fly from place to place (of birds).

โผน. See entries below.

ผาดโผน phàadphǒon/ V to be adventurous, daredevilish.

โลดโผน lôodphǒon/ V 1. to be extraordinary, unusual, unconventional. 2. to be exciting, thrilling. 3. to be adventurous, daredevilish.

โผเผ phǒophěe/ V to be weak, fatigued, tired.

โผล่ phlòo/ V to emerge, come up, show up.

ผลุบโผล่ phlùbphlòo/ V 1. to be bobbing up and down in the water (alternately sinking and rising). 2. to appear and withdraw quickly.

ไผ่ phàj/ N bamboo (the generic term). ต้น-- (ต้น) bamboo stalk, stem.

กอไผ่ (กอ) kɔɔphàj/ (kɔɔ/) N a clump of bamboo.

ใบไผ่ (ใบ) bajphàj/ (baj/) N bamboo leaf.

ไม้ไผ่ (ลำ) májphàj/ (lam/) N bamboo (the wood, the stem).

ฝ

ฝ fɔ̌ɔ/ HIGH consonant. Pronounced f and used initially only.

ฝน ๑ (จ๊ก, ห่า) fǒn/ N 1. rain. 2. shower, rainfall (cág/ com., hàa/ eleg.).

ครึ้มฟ้าครึ้มฝน khrýmfáa/khrýmfǒn/ V elab. colloq. to be very cloudy, look like rain. →Also ครึ้มฝน.

ตรำฝน tramfǒn/ V to be exposed to rain.

น้ำฝน námfǒn/ N rain water.

ฝนขาดเม็ดแล้ว fǒn/-khàadméd/léɛwↆ It has stopped raining.

ฝนชุก fǒnchúg/ it's raining a lot; there's lots of rain.

ฝนซาเม็ดแล้ว fǒn/-saaméd/léɛwↆ The rain is subsiding, letting up.

ฝนตก fǒntòg/ it's raining; it rains.

o ฝนตกชุก fǒntòg/chúg/ it's raining a lot; it rains a lot, there's lot of rain.

o ฝนตกโซก fǒntòg/chôog/ it's pouring, raining in bucketsful.

o ฝนตกหยิม ๆ fǒntòg/-jĭmjĭm/ it's drizzling.

ฝนตั้งเค้า fǒn/tâŋkháw/ it is getting ready to rain, it looks like rain.

ฝนเทียม fǒnthiam/ N artificial rain.

ฝนพรำ fǒn/phram/ it's raining lightly and continuously.

ฝนฟ้าอากาศ fǒnfáa/ʔaakàad/ N elab. weather, climate.

ฝนลงเม็ด fǒn/loŋméd/ↆ It's starting to rain.

ฝนแล้ง fǒnléɛŋ/ there is a drought, there is a shortage of rain.

พลอยฟ้าพลอยฝน phlɔɔjfáa/phlɔɔjfǒn/ idiom. to be included or mixed up with others without actual participation; along with others.

พายุฝน phaajúʔ/fǒn/ N rainstorm.

เม็ดฝน médfǒn/ N rain drop.

ฤดูฝน rýduu/fǒn/ N eleg. rainy season.

ลมฝน lomfǒn/ N rain-bearing wind, rainstorm, rain and wind.

ละอองฝน laʔɔɔŋ/fǒn/ N fine drizzle, rain mist; fine droplets of rain (blown in by the wind).

สายฝน sǎajfǒn/ N the line of fall of a raindrop, the vertical traces of falling raindrops, the pattern of parallel lines seen in a rainfall.

หน้าฝน nâafǒn/ N colloq. rainy season.

หยาดฝน (เม็ด) jàadfǒn (méd/) N eleg. raindrop.

อ้าวฝน ʔâawfǒn/ V (the atmosphere) to be sultry (showing definite signs of rain by high humidity and a sudden increase in temperature).

ฝน ๒ fǒn/ V to whet, sharpen, rub against, abrade.

ฝึกฝน fỳgfǒn/ V to train, practice, drill.

ฝรั่ง ๑ (คน) faràŋ/ (khon/) N Occidental, European, westerner. →Var. หรั่ง.

เป็นฝรั่ง pen/faràŋ/ to be or act like a European

or an Occidental.

ผักชีฝรั่ง phàgchii/faràŋ/ N parsley.

ฝรั่งมังค่า faràŋ/maŋkhâa/ N colloq. Occiden-
tals, westerners.

ฝรั่งอังกฤษ faràŋ/ʔaŋkrìd/ N Englishman.

มันฝรั่ง (หัว) man/faràŋ/ (hŭa/) N Irish potato;
potato. →Dist. มันเทศ "sweet potato."

หมากฝรั่ง (ห่อ,อัน,ก้อน) màag/faràŋ/ (hɔ̀ɔ/, ʔan/,
kɔ̂ɔn/) N chewing gum.

ฝรั่ง ๒ (ใบ,ลูก,ผล) faràŋ/ (baj/, lûug/, phŏn/) N
guava. ต้น-- (ต้น) the guava tree.

ฝรั่งเศส faràŋsèed/ N 1. France. 2. French;
Frenchman. [f. Fr. français]

ชาวฝรั่งเศส (คน) chaawfaràŋsèed/ (khon/) N
the French people.

ประเทศฝรั่งเศส prathêed/faràŋsèed/ N eleg.
France.

ภาษาฝรั่งเศส phaasăa/faràŋsèed/ N French,
the French language.

อินโดจีนฝรั่งเศส ʔindoociin/faràŋsèed/ N French
Indochina (formerly a Fr. colonial federation).

ฝ่อ fɔ̀ɔ/ V to wither, dry out, be abortive (of fruit,
seeds).

ขวัญหนีดีฝ่อ khwănnĭi/diifɔ̀ɔ/ V elab. colloq.
to be startled, frightened, scared out of one's
wits.

ใจฝ่อ cajfɔ̀ɔ/ V to be frightened, have one's
heart shrink with fear.

ฝอย fɔ̆j/* N 1. shreds, fibers. 2. spray, droplets.
3. trivial details. V 4. slang to chat. 5. to
brag.

กุ้งฝอย (ตัว) kûŋfɔ̆j/ (tua/) N small shrimp.

ฝอยความ fɔ̆jkhwaam/ N insignificant point,
trivial details.

ฝอยทอง (อัน,จับ,แผง) fɔ̆jthɔɔŋ/ (ʔan/, càb/,
phɛɛŋ/) N a kind of egg-yolk confection consisting of thin threads of yolk boiled in heavy
syrup.

มูลฝอย (กอง) muunfɔ̆j/ (kɔɔŋ/) N rubbish,
refuse, litter, garbage.

รากฝอย (ราก,เส้น) râagfɔ̆j/ (râag/, sên/) N
fibrous roots of plants.

ฝัก ๑ (ฝัก) fàg/ (fàg/) N 1. hull, pod, case, sheath,
scabbard. C 2. clf. for same.

ถั่วฝักยาว (ฝัก) thùafàgjaaw/ (fàg/) N long-podded
cowpea. ต้น-- (ต้น) long-podded cowpea plant.

ฝักถั่ว (ฝัก) fàgthùa/ (fàg/) N bean pod.

ออกฝัก ʔɔɔgfàg/ V to pod, put forth pods.

ฝัก ๒ in ฝักใฝ่ (ใน,ต่อ) fàgfàj/(naj⊃,tɔ̀ɔ⊃) V to
pay attention (to), be absorbed (in), interested
(in).

ฝัง făŋ/ V 1. to bury, put in the ground. 2. to be
buried.

ปลูกฝัง plùug/făŋ/ V 1. to marry (someone) off.
2. to establish (a person). 3. to cultivate, plant,
establish (in the mind).

ฝังใจ făŋcaj/ V to impress.

ฝังตัว făŋtua/ V to burrow.

ฝังทั้งเป็น făŋ/tháppen/ to bury alive.

ฝังในกระดูก făŋ/najkradùug/ to become a habit,
be deeply ingrained.

ฝังรกราก făŋ/rógrâag/ V to settle down permanently, take up residence.

ฝังราก făŋrâag/ V 1. to be founded, rooted. 2.
to take root.

ฝังศพ făŋsòb/ V to bury a corpse.

○ หลุมฝังศพ (หลุม) lŭm/făŋsòb/ (lŭm/) N grave.

ฝังหัว făŋhŭa/ V to be firmly entrenched in one's
mind, in one's beliefs.

ฝั่ง fàŋ/ N 1. coast, shore. 2. bank (of a river).
→Syn. ตลิ่ง.

ชายฝั่ง (แห่ง) chaajfàŋ/ (hɛ̀ŋ/) N 1. coast, shore.
2. bank, edge of a river.

โดยตลอดรอดฝั่ง doojtalɔ̀ɔd/rɔ̂ɔdfàŋ/ elab. colloq.
idiom. safe and sound.

เป็นฝั่งเป็นฝา penfàŋ/penfăa/ V idiom. to be
settled down, have a family.

ฝั่งทะเล (แห่ง) fàŋthalee/ (hɛ̀ŋ/) N 1. seashore,
seacoast, coast. 2. (as n. mod.) coast, coastal.

ฝั่งน้ำ (ฝั่ง) fàŋnáam/ (fàŋ/) N river bank, bank
of a watercourse.

ฝั่งแม่น้ำ (ฝั่ง) fàŋ/mɛɛnáam/ (fàŋ/) N river bank.

ฝัด fàd/ V to winnow or separate heavier granular
materials from the lighter ones by using a win-
nowing basket (as in separating rice grain from
chaff).

ฝัน făn/ V to dream. ความ-- a dream.

แก้ฝัน kɛ̂ɛfăn/ V to interpret a dream.

เคลิ้มฝัน khlóəmfăn′ V to dream, forget oneself.

นึกฝัน nýgfăn′ V to imagine, dream.

ฝันถึง făn′thўŋɔ to dream about.

ฝันเป็นตุเป็นตะ făn′-pentù?′pentà?′ to have a lifelike dream, a coherent dream.

ฝันร้าย fănráaj′ N 1. a bad dream, a nightmare. V 2. to have a bad dream, a nightmare.

ฝันว่า făn′wâaɔ to dream that.

ใฝ่ฝัน(ถึง) fàjfăn′(thўŋɔ) V to dream (of).

อารมณ์ฝัน ?aarom′făn′ N dreamy mood, day-dreaming mood, reverie.

ฝา ๑ (ฝา,ด้าน) făa′ N 1. lid, cover (făa′). 2. partition, wall (dâan′).

ปิดฝา pìdfăa′ V to put the lid on, cover with a lid.

เป็นฝั่งเป็นฝา penfàŋ′penfăa′ V idiom. to be settled down, have a family.

ฝากระดาน (แผ่น) făakradaan′ (phèn′) N wooden wall, wooden partition of a room.

ฝาครอบ (ใบ) făakhrɔ̀ɔb′ (baj′) N cover, dish cover (used to keep out insects).

ฝาชี (ฝา,อัน) făachii′ (?an′,făa′) N a cover placed over a dish of food as protection against flies and other insects. It is usually made of wire, bamboo or rattan.

ฝาผนัง (ฝา,ด้าน) făaphanăŋ′ (făa′, dâan′) N (interior) wall (of brick, stone, etc.).

ฝาห้อง (ด้าน,ฝา) făahɔ̂ŋ′ (dâan′,făa′) N wall of a room.

ฝา ๒ in ฝาแฝด (คู่,คน) făafɛ̀ɛd′ (khûu′, khon′) N 1. twins, twin. 2. Siamese twins.

เด็กฝาแฝด (คู่,คน) dègfăafɛ̀ɛd′ (khûu′, khon′) N 1. twin children. 2. Siamese twin children.

ลูกฝาแฝด (คู่,คน) lûugfăafɛ̀ɛd′ (khûu′, khon′) N 1. twins, twin children. 2. Siamese twin children.

ฝ่า ๑ fàa′, fâaɔ N palm (of hand), sole (of foot). →Chiefly in compounds.

ฝ่าตีน (ข้าง) fàatiin′ (khâaŋ′) N com. sole of the foot, pad of animal's foot.

ฝ่าเท้า (ข้าง) fàatháaw′ (khâaŋ′) N eleg. sole of the foot, pad of animal's foot.

ฝ่าบาท fàabàad′ P roy. you (inf. sp. to low-ranking royalty).

ฝ่าพระบาท fàa′phrábàad′ P roy. you (royal per-

son of medium rank sp. to another royal person of same or slightly higher rank; inferior sp. to royal person of medium rank).

o ใต้ฝ่าพระบาท tâajfàa′phrábàad′ P roy. you (sp. to high-ranking royalty).

ฝ่ามือ (ข้าง) fàamyy′ (khâaŋ′) N palm of the hand.

ฝ่า ๒ fàa′ V 1. to go through, walk through. 2. to brave (hardship, danger). sV 3. through (e.g. hardship, obstacles, danger).

o เดินฝ่าดง dəən′-fàa′doŋ′ to walk through a forest.

ตีฝ่า tii′fàa′ to attack and break through (e.g. the enemy's line).

ฝ่าฝืน fàafŭyn′ V to violate, disobey. ผู้-- violator.

ฝ่าฟัน,ฟันฝ่า fàafan′, fanfàa′ V to struggle, fight against (obstacles, dangers).

ฝ่าอันตราย fàa′?antaraaj′ V to brave danger, take risks.

ฝ้า fâa′ V to be foggy, cloudy, dim (of glass, of the eyes).

กระจกฝ้า (แผ่น,บาน) kracòg′fâa′ (phèn′, baan′) N frosted glass, opaque glass.

เป็นฝ้า penfâa′ 1. (glass) to be fogged; (the eyes, vision) to be clouded. 2. to be defective, imper-fect (as of diamonds).

ฝาก fàag′ V 1. to deposit, entrust, leave (something) (with someone), put (something) in the care or custody (of). 2. to enroll (e.g. a child in a school).

กาฝาก (ต้น,คน) kaafàag′ N 1. a kind of parasitic climbing plant (tôn′). 2. one who lives at the expense of others (khon′). →Also 1. ต้น-- (ต้น).

ของฝาก (อย่าง,ชิ้น,อัน) khɔ̌ɔŋfàag′ (jàaŋ′,chín′, ?an′) N something entrusted to one person to be delivered to another person; something brought as a gift for someone (e.g. one's hostess or her family).

เงินฝาก ŋənfàag′ N money on deposit.

ฝากครรภ์(กับ) fàag′khan′(kaɔ) V eleg. to have prenatal care (at).

ฝากเงิน fàagŋən′ V to deposit money (in a bank).

o ใบฝากเงิน (ใบ) baj′fàagŋən′ (baj′) N deposit slip.

o สมุดฝากเงิน (เล่ม) samùd′fàagŋən′ (lêm′) N bankbook, passbook.

ฝากชื่อ fàagchŷy′ V idiom. to leave a good name behind for oneself.

ฝากผีฝากไข้(กับ) fàagphǐi′fàagkhâj′(kaɔ) V elab. colloq. to ask (someone) to take care of one, or of one's body, in the event of sickness or death.

ฝากรัก(ไว้กับ) fàagrág′(wájkaɔ) V to propose, to declare one's love, give one's heart (to).

ฝากลวดลาย fàag′lûadlaaj′ V idiom. to leave (with someone) the impression of one's skill, ability, etc.

ฝาก...ไว้ fàagɔ...wáj′ to leave (such and such) (with someone), entrust (such and such)(to the care of someone), deposit, put (such and such) on deposit (with).

รับฝาก rábfàag′ V to accept the care of (something)(for someone), to take (something) into one's care.

ฝาด ๑ fàad′ V to be astringent (in taste).

ต้นฝาด tônfàad′ N a kind of tree whose bark is used in tanning and dying.

ฝาด ๒ in ตาฝาด taafàad′ V to have an illusion, be fooled by one's visual perception.

ฝาด ๓ in the following entries.

เลือดฝาด lɯadfàad′ N colloq. blood.

อมเลือดอมฝาด ʔomlɯ́ad′/ʔomfàad′ V elab. colloq. (the face) to have a good color, a clear, healthy complexion.

ฝาน fǎan′ V to slice, cut thin (using a horizontal or nearly horizontal motion).

ฝ่าย fàaj′ N 1. side, party, group. C 2. clf. for same.

o ทั้งสองฝ่าย tháŋsɔ̌ɔŋfàaj′ both sides.

o อีกฝ่ายหนึ่ง ʔìigfàaj′nɯ̀ŋ the other side, the opposing side, the opponent.

ฝ่ายค้าน fàajkháan′ N 1. the negative side (in a debate). 2. opposition (in politics).

ฝ่ายชาย fàajchaaj′ N 1. the men's side. 2. (as n. mod.) men's, male.

ฝ่ายซ้าย fàajsáaj′ N the Leftists; the Left.

ฝ่ายเดียว fàajdiaw′ 1. one side only, alone. 2. one-sided.

ฝ่ายใดฝ่ายหนึ่ง fàajdaj′fàajnɯ̀ŋ′ one side or the other, either side; any side.

ฝ่ายตามและฝ่ายหนี fàajtaam′lɛfàajnǐi′ the pursuer and the pursued.

ฝ่ายธุระการ fàaj′-thúrá?′/kaan′ 1. (on) the practical side; the practical aspect. 2. (on) the administrative side; the administrative aspect. →Comp. ฝ่ายวิชาการ.

ฝ่ายบุก fàajbùg′ N the offense, the side on the offensive (in sports, war).

ฝ่ายรับ fàajráb′ N 1. the defense, the side on the defensive (in sports, war). 2. the taker, receiver.

ฝ่ายรุกราน fàaj′rúgraan′ N aggressor.

ฝ่ายวิชาการ fàaj′-wíchaa′kaan′ (on) the academic, theoretical, technical side; the academic, theoretical, technical aspect. →Comp. ฝ่ายธุระการ.

ฝ่ายสัมพันธมิตร fàaj′sǎmphan′thamíd′ N the Allied side, the Allies.

ฝ่ายเสนอ fàajsanɔ̌ɔ′ N the affirmative side (in a debate).

ฝ่ายหญิง fàajjǐŋ′ N 1. the women's side. 2. (as n. mod.) women's, female.

ฝ้าย fâaj′ N cotton.

ปั่นฝ้าย pànfâaj′ V to spin cotton yarn.

ปุยฝ้าย (ปุย) pujfâaj′ (puj′) N cotton fiber, cotton wool.

ผ้าฝ้าย phâafâaj′ N cotton cloth, cotton fabric.

ฝ้ายดิบ fâajdìb′ N raw cotton.

สมอฝ้าย (ลูก) samɔ̌ɔfâaj′ (lûug′) N boll of the cotton plant.

ฝิ่น fìn′ N opium. ต้น-- (ต้น) poppy plant.

ดอกฝิ่น (ดอก) dɔ̀ɔgfìn′ (dɔ̀ɔg′) N poppy.

ติดฝิ่น tìdfìn′ V to be addicted to opium.

ฝิ่นเถื่อน fìnthɯ̀an′ N smuggled, illegal opium.

ฝี ๑ (หัว,เม็ด) fǐi′ (hǔa′, méd′) N pustule, boil.

ปลูกฝี plùugfǐi′ V 1. to vaccinate (against smallpox). 2. to be vaccinated. การ-- smallpox vaccination.

ฝีดาษ fǐidàad′ N com. smallpox. Sometimes spelled ฝีดาด, which is considered to be etymologically correct; see ดาด ๑. →Syn. โรคไข้ทรพิษ, ไข้ทรพิษ eleg.

o ปลูกฝีดาษ plùug′/fǐidàad′ V 1. to vaccinate (against smallpox). 2. to be vaccinated.

ฝีในท้อง, โรค-- fǐinajthɔ́ɔŋ′, rôog′-- N colloq. (pulmonary) tuberculosis. →Syn. วัณโรค eleg.

ฝี ๒ in the following entries.

ฝีจักร fǐicàg′ N speed, velocity (of anything propelled by an engine).

ฝีตีน fǐitiin′ N com. speed (of foot), pace.

ฝีเท้า fǐitháaw′ N eleg. speed (of foot), pace.

o เต็มฝีเท้า tem′fǐitháaw′ at full speed.

o เสียงฝีเท้า sǐaŋ′fǐitháaw′ the sound of footsteps.

ฝีปาก fǐipàag′ N verbal skill, oratory skill.

o ตีฝีปาก tii′fǐipàag′ V colloq. to argue wittily, wisecrack.

o ริมฝีปาก rim′fǐipàag′ N lip.

o อวดฝีปาก ʔùad′fǐipàag′ V colloq. to show cleverness of verbal expression.

ฝีมือ fǐimyy′ N manual skill, craftsmanship. การ-- handicraft, handiwork. ช่าง-- skilled craftsman.

o อย่างสุดฝีมือ jàaŋsùd′fǐimyy′ doing one's best, to one's best ability.

ฝีไม้ลายมือ fǐimáaj/laajmyy′ N elab. colloq. craftmanship, workmanship, skill, ability.

ฝึก fỹg′ V to practice, drill, train.

ผู้ฝึกสอน (คน) phûu′fỹgsɔ̌ɔn′ (khon′) N instructor; trainer.

ฝึกฝน fỹgfǒn′ V to practice, drill, train.

ฝึกหัด fỹghàd′ V to practice, drill, train. การ-- practice, drill, training.

o แบบฝึกหัด (ข้อ,บท) bɛ̀ɛb′fỹghàd′ (khɔ̂ɔ′, bòd′) N exercise, drill (in a textbook).

o โรงเรียนฝึกหัดครู rooŋrian′fỹghàdkhruu′ teacher-training school, teacher's college, normal school.

ฝืด fǜyd′ V to be tight, stuck, difficult to move; (machinery) to bind, stick (as when in need of oiling). ความ-- friction.

ฝืดคอ fǜydkhɔɔ′ V 1. to be hard to swallow (as dry bread). 2. to experience difficulty in swallowing (as because of dryness of one's throat).

ฝืดเคือง fǜydkhyaŋ′ V 1. to be poor, hard up. 2. to be scarce, meager. 3. to be difficult and frustrating; to have rough going. อย่าง-- poorly, in poverty, in an impoverished manner.

ฝืน fǚyn′ V to do against, act against, act in opposition, to force.

ฝ่าฝืน fàafǚyn′ V to violate, disobey. ผู้-- violator.

ฝืนใจ fǚyn′caj′ V to force oneself (to do something) against one's will.

ฝืนยิ้ม fǚyn′jím′ V to force a smile.

ฝืนสีหน้า fǚyn′sǐinâa′ V to force oneself to assume a certain facial expression.

ฝุ่น fùn′ N dust, powder.

ปัดฝุ่น pàdfùn′ V to dust, dust off.

ฝูง fǔuŋ′ C flock, herd, pack, swarm, group, crowd, party.

ฝูงชน (กลุ่ม,หมู่) fǔuŋchon′ (klùm′, mùu′) N a crowd, a large group of people.

ฝูงบิน (ฝูง) fǔuŋbin′ (fǔuŋ′) N milit. a group of airplanes.

เพื่อนฝูง (คน) phŷanfǔuŋ′ (khon′) N (one's) friends (collectively).

หลงฝูง lǒŋfǔuŋ′ V 1. stray away from one's own group, herd, flock, etc. 2. to be in the wrong group, herd, flock, etc.

เฝ้า fâw′ V 1. to watch, watch over, keep, take care of. 2. to have an audience with, appear before (royalty). คน-- keeper, watcher.

เข้าเฝ้า khâwfâw′ V to have an audience with (a royal person).

เฝ้าดู fâwduu′ V to keep watching, keep an eye on.

เฝ้าปรนนิบัติ fâw′pronnibàd′ V to be at hand, to serve, wait on regularly.

อยู่กับเหย้าเฝ้ากับเรือน jùu′kajâw′-fâw′karyan′ elab. to stay at home and look after things (considered a good quality for a woman).

เฝือก (ข้าง,อัน) fỹag′ (khâaŋ′, ʔan′) N plaster cast, splint (for setting bones).

เฝื่อน fỹan′ V to have an unpleasant taste, be puckery.

o มีสีหน้าเฝื่อน miisǐinâa′fỹan′ to have the facial expression (usually suppressed) of one who has encountered something unpalatable, unwelcome, humiliating; to be discountenanced, abashed.

แฝก fɛ̀ɛg′ N elephant grass (used for roofing).

แฝง fɛ̌ɛŋ′ V 1. to hide, conceal. 2. to be concealed, kept in secret.

เคลือบแฝง khlŷabfɛ̌ɛŋ′ V to be hidden, concealed, unclear, ambiguous.

นามแฝง (นาม) naamfɛ̌ɛŋ′ (naam′) N pseudonym, assumed name, pen name.

แฝด fɛ̀ɛd′ N (as n. mod.) twin, double, paired.

ฝาแฝด (คู่,คน) fǎafɛ̀ɛd′ (khûu′, khon′) N 1.
twins, twin. 2. Siamese twins.

ลูกแฝด (คน) lûugfɛ̀ɛd′ (khon′) N twins, twin
children.

ใฝ่ fàj′ V to have an interest (in), pay attention (to).
→Sometimes written ไฝ่.

ฝักใฝ่ (ใน,ต่อ) fàgfàj′ (naj⊃, t⊃⊃⊃) V to pay attention (to), be absorbed (in), interested (in).

ใฝ่ใจ (ใน) fàjcaj′ (naj⊃) V to pay close attention
(to), be interested (in), absorbed (in).

ใฝ่ฝัน (ถึง) fàjfǎn′ (thy̌ŋ⊃) V to dream (of).

ใฝ่สูง fàjsǔuŋ′ V to aim high, aspire (e.g. to
social eminence), be ambitious.

o มักใหญ่ใฝ่สูง mágjàj′fàjsǔuŋ′ V elab. colloq.
to be ambitious. ความ-- ambition, ambitiousness. NOTE. This expression is used in an
unfavorable sense in Thai.

o อย่าใฝ่สูงให้เกินศักดิ์ jàafàjsǔuŋ′-hâjkəən′sàg′
Don't set your ambitions beyond your station.

ใฝ่หา fàjhǎa′ V 1. to long for. 2. to seek.

ไฝ (เม็ด) fǎj′ (méd′) N mole (on the skin).

ไฝ่. See ใฝ่.

พ

พ ph⊃⊃′ LOW consonant. Pronounced ph initially,
b finally. The sound ph as an initial low consonant is also less commonly written ภ.

พก phóg′ V 1. to carry on one's person. N 2.
pouch or pocket formed by the tucked or knotted
part at the waist of a sarong or phanung.

โกหกพกลม koohòg′phóglom′ V elab. colloq.
to tell a lie.

แถมพก thɛ̌ɛmphóg′ V 1. to give as lagniappe,
give something free to a customer with the purchase of something else. 2. to give a premium.

ปืนพก (กระบอก) pyynphóg′ (krab⊃⊃g′) N pistol,
revolver.

พกปืน phógpyyn′ V to carry a gun on one's person.

สมุดพก (เล่ม) samùd′phóg′ (lêm′) N student's
report book, report card.

พง phoŋ′ N 1. brush, thicket. 2. a kind of tall grass.

หักร้างถางพง hàgráaŋ′thǎaŋphoŋ′ V elab.
colloq. 1. to clear the land. 2. to clear a path
(e.g. through the jungle).

พงศาวดาร (ฉบับ,เล่ม) phoŋsǎawadaan′ (chabàb′,
lêm′) N historical annals, chronicle.

พจน์ phód′ N eleg. 1. word, speech. 2. gram.
number.

สุนทรพจน์ sǔnthoon′phód′ N eleg. speech.

พจนานุกรม (เล่ม) phódcanaa′núkrom′ (lêm′) N
dictionary.

-พเจ้า. See ข้าพเจ้า under ข้า ๒.

พญา (องค์,คน) phajaa′ (ʔoŋ′, khon′) N 1. king,
chief. T 2. title preceding name of a king, chief.

นางพญา (องค์) naaŋphajaa′ (ʔoŋ′) N queen.

พณ ฯ ท่าน phaná?′/thân′ T eleg.def. 1. Honorable --. P 2. Your Excellency, His Excellency
(sp. to or about high officials). NOTE. Also
written ฯ พณ ฯ and sometimes incorrectly
พณท่าน. The formal reading is พณหัวเจ้า
ท่าน phaná?′/hǔacâaw′-thân′.

พ.ท. ph⊃⊃th⊃⊃′, also read phanthoo′. Abbrev. for
พันโท lieutenant colonel.

พฐู (คน) phathuu′ (khon′) N woman, wife, bride.

ยอดพฐู (คน) j⊃⊃d′phathuu′ (khon′) N best-
beloved (woman), i.e. one's wife or sweetheart.

พ่น phôn′ V 1. to spray, squirt, blow. 2. slang
to boast, brag. 3. to speak. เครื่อง-- sprayer,
spraying apparatus.

ฉีดพ่น chìid′phôn′ V to spray.

พ่นควัน phônkhwan′ V to puff out smoke or fumes
(as a chimney, etc.).

พ้น phón′ V to go beyond, be free from.

ผ่านพ้นไป phàanphón′paj′ to pass by, go by, elapse.

พ้นเคราะห์ phónkhr⊃?′ V to be free from misfortune or bad luck.

พ้นวิสัย phón′wísǎj′ V to be beyond human control,
beyond the power of, beyond the limit of.

พ้นอก phón?òg′ V to be rid of (e.g. one's worry),
freed from; to have (something) off one's chest.

o พ้นอกพ่อแม่ phón?òg′ph⊃⊃mɛ̂ɛ′ to need no paren-
tal care (as a result of being grown-up, of getting married).

มีหนี้สินล้นพ้นตัว mii′-nîisǐn′lónphóntua′ to be
heavily in debt, be head over heels in debt.

รอดพ้น rɔ̂ɔd/phón/ V to escape (from danger),
   be safe, be saved.

หลุดพ้น(จาก) lùd/phón/-(càagɔ) V 1. to be
   released, be free (from). 2. to escape, get
   away (from).

พนม, --มือ phanom/, phanom/myy/ V to place one's
   hands palm to palm in the attitude of adoration
   or salutation. →Also ประณม. →Syn. กระพุ่ม.

พนัก phanág/ N a place for resting one's back or
   for leaning against (e.g. the back of a chair).

พนักเก้าอี้ phanág/kâw?îi/ N the back of a chair.

พนักงาน (คน,นาย) phanágŋaan/ (khon/, naaj/) N
   1. employee, worker, person responsible for a
   task. 2. duty, responsibility.

เจ้าพนักงาน (คน,นาย) câwphanágŋaan/ (khon/,
   naaj/) N official, person in charge.

พนักงานโทรศัพท์ (คน) phanágŋaan/thoorasàb/
   (khon/) N telephone operator.

พนักงานพิมพ์ดีด (คน) phanágŋaan/phimdìid/
   (khon/) N typist.

เสมียนพนักงาน (คน) samĭan/phanágŋaan/ (khon/)
   N employees (in general); clerks and workers.

พนัน phanan/ V to bet, wager, gamble. การ--
   gambling.

นักการพนัน (คน) nágkaan/phanan/ (khon/) N
   gambler.

บ่อนการพนัน (บ่อน) bɔ̀n/kaanphanan/ (bɔ̀n/) N
   gambling house, gambling den.

เล่นการพนัน lênkaan/phanan/ V to gamble, engage
   in gambling.

พเนจร phanee/cɔɔn/ V to wander, roam, travel
   aimlessly.

พบ phób/ V com. 1. to meet, encounter. 2. to
   come upon, find. 3. to meet, join, come together at one point. การ-- meeting, encounter. →Syn. 3. บรรจบ eleg.

ขุดพบ khùdphób/ V to unearth, excavate.

เข้าพบ khâwphób/ V to call on, make a (formal)
   call.

ค้นพบ khónphób/ V to find out, discover. การ--
   discovery.

ไปพบ pajphób/ V to meet, go to see.

พบกัน phób/kan/ to see, meet (each other).

พบ(...)เข้า phób/(...)khâw/ to encounter,

meet up with, run into.

พบปะ phóbpà?/ V to meet, encounter.

o พบปะสนทนา phóbpà?/sŏnthanaa/ to meet and
   converse.

พบพาน phób/phaan/ V to meet, see, encounter.

พบว่า phób/wâaɔ to find out that.

พบหน้า phóbnâa/ V to see, meet (someone).

มาพบ maaphób/ V to come to see, come to meet.

หา(...)พบ hăa(...)phób/ to find (e.g. something
   mislaid).

พม่า phamâa/ N 1. Burma. 2. the Burmese. [f. Bur.]

พ.ย. Abbrev. for พฤศจิกายน November.

พยัก phajág/ V to nod in assent. →Chiefly in the
   following compound.

พยักหน้า phajág/nâa/ V to nod in assent.

o พยักหน้าหงึก ๆ phajág/nâa-ŋy̆gŋy̆g/ to nod the
   head up and down, nod the head several times.

พยัญชนะ (ตัว) phajanchaná?/ (tua/) N consonant.

พยัญชนะต้น phajanchaná?/tôn/ initial consonant.

พยากรณ์ phajaakɔɔn/ V eleg. to forecast, predict,
   prophesy. คำ-- (ข้อ,ประการ,อย่าง) forecast,
   prediction, prophecy.

พยากรณ์อากาศ phajaakɔɔn/?aakàad/ V 1. to give
   a weather forecast. N 2. weather forecast;
   also การ--.

พยางค์ (พยางค์) phajaaŋ/ (phajaaŋ/) N,C syllable.

พยาธิ (ตัว) (1) phajâad/; (2) phajaa/thí?/ N 1.
   parasitic worm (in bodies of people, animals)
   (tua/). 2. sickness, illness.

โรคพยาธิ rookhaa/phajaa/thí?/, rookhaa/phajâad/
   N disease, sickness.

พยาน (คน) phajaan/ (khon/) N witness.

ประจักษ์พยาน (คน) pracàg/phajaan/ N 1. eleg.
   eyewitness (khon/). 2 (visible) evidence, indication.

พยานเอก (คน) phajaan/?èeg/ (khon/) N prime
   witness.

วัตถุพยาน wádthù?/phajaan/ N eleg. tangible
   evidence.

สักขีพยาน sàgkhĭi/phajaan/ N eleg. 1. evidence.
   2. eyewitness.

พยาบาท phajaabàad/ V to be vengeful, vindictive.
   ความ-- vengefulness, vindictiveness, vengeance.
   →Syn. อาฆาต.

ขี้พยาบาท khîiphajaabàad′ V to be given to revenge.

ความอาฆาตพยาบาท khwaam?aakhâad′phajaabàad′ N vengeance, vengefulness.

ผูกพยาบาท phùug′phajaabàad′ V to be vengeful, vindictive, bear a grudge.

พยาบาล phajaabaan′ V to nurse, tend (e.g. the sick). การ-- nursing.

การปัจจุบันพยาบาล kaanpàdcuban′phajaabaan′ N first aid.

นางพยาบาล (คน) naaŋphajaabaan′ (khon′) N nurse (as in a hospital).

ปฐมพยาบาล pathǒm′phajaabaan′ N 1. first aid. V 2. to give first aid.

รถพยาบาล (คัน) ród′phajaabaan′ (khan′) N ambulance.

โรงพยาบาล (โรง, แห่ง) rooŋ′phajaabaan′ (rooŋ′, hèŋ′) N hospital.

พยายาม phajaajaam′ V to try, attempt, endeavor. ความ-- effort, endeavor, try, attempt.

พยุง phajuŋ′ V to help lift, support (e.g. an injured person).

พร (ประการ) phɔɔn′ (prakaan′) N blessing, blessings.

พรปีใหม่ phɔɔn′piimàj′ New Year blessings.

ให้พร hâjphɔɔn′ V to bless, wish (someone) happiness and good fortune. คำ-- blessing.

o อวยชัยให้พร ?uajchaj′hâjphɔɔn′ V elab. to wish (someone) happiness and good fortune.

อวยพร ?uajphɔɔn′ V to bless, bestow a blessing; to wish (someone) well.

พ.ร.บ. (ฉบับ) phɔɔrɔɔbɔɔ′ (chabàb′) Abbrev. for พระราชบัญญัติ act of Parliament.

พรม ๑ phrom′ V to sprinkle.

ประพรม prà?′phrom′ V to sprinkle.

พรมน้ำ phromnáam′ V to sprinkle with water.

พรม ๒ (ผืน) phrom′ (phɣɣn′) N rug, carpet.

พรมเช็ดเท้า (ผืน) phrom′chédtháaw′ (phɣɣn′) N doormat.

พรมน้ำมัน (ผืน, แผ่น) phrom′námman′ (phɣɣn′, phèn′) N linoleum.

พรม ๓ in พรมแดน phromdɛɛn′ N frontier, border.

พรรค (พรรค) phág′ (phág′) N 1. party, group (especially political). C 2. clf. for same.

พรรคการเมือง (พรรค) phág′kaanmyaŋ′ (phág′) N political party.

พรรคชาตินิยม phágchâad′níjom′ N nationalist party.

พรรคพวก (คน) phágphûag′ (khon′) N 1. partisan, fellow member, follower. 2. close friends, members of an intimate circle; clique. →Also สมัคร พรรคพวก elab. colloq.

พรรคสนับสนุน (พรรค) phág′-sanàb′sanǔn′ (phág′) N the party supporting the government.

พรรคเสรีมนังคศิลา phág′-sěerii′manaŋ′khásilaa′ nN Serimanangkasila Party, a political party formerly headed by Phibun (Phibul) Songkhram.

พรรค phan′ C sort, group, class.

o พรรคนั้น phannán′ that sort, that kind; of that sort; such a sort.

พรรณ ๑ phan′ C kind, type, sort.

พรรณไม้ (ชนิด) phanmáaj′ (chaníd′) N kinds, varieties of plants.

พรรณ ๒ phan′ N complexion.

ผิวพรรณ phǐwphan′ N complexion; skin color.

พรรณนา phannanaa′, phanranaa′ V to describe, to explain in detail. การ-- describing, explaining in detail.

พรรษา (พรรษา) phansǎa′ (phansǎa′) N 1. rainy season; the Buddhist Lent. C 2. rainy season; also loosely, year. 3. roy. year (of one's age).

เข้าพรรษา khâwphansǎa′ V to be in the Buddhist Lent (in the rainy season) (July-October).

ออกพรรษา ?ɔɔgphansǎa′ V to be out of the Buddhist Lent (October-July).

พรวด phrûad′ sV 1. abruptly, precipitately, suddenly, hastily. C 2. clf. for a sudden, precipitate action.

เผ่นพรวด phènphrûad′ to jump, leap suddenly.

พรวดเดียว phrûaddiaw′ all at once, in one gulp, in one fell swoop.

พรวด ๆ phrûadphrûad′ sV precipitately, hastily.

พรวดพราด phrûadphrâad′ sV abruptly, precipitately; hastily and tactlessly.

o อย่าพรวดพราดเข้าไป jàaphrûad′phrâad′-khâwɔ paj′ don't just barge in (there).

ลุกพรวด lúg′phrûad′ to stand or sit up abruptly.

พรวน in พรวนดิน phruandin′ V to work the soil, loosen the soil.

พรหม,พระพรหม phrom/, phráphrom/ N Brahma.

พรหมจารี phrommacaa/rii/ N virginity.

  หญิงพรหมจารี (คน) jǐŋ/phrommacaa/rii/ (khon/) N virgin.

พร่อง phrɔ̂ŋ/* V to be decreased, lessened.

  บกพร่อง bògphrɔ̂ŋ/ V 1. to be defective, not up to standard, deficient. 2. to be inefficient, negligent (as of duty). ความ-- deficiency; inefficiency, negligence.

  o ข้อบกพร่อง (ข้อ,ประการ) khɔ̂ɔ/bògphrɔ̂ŋ/ (khɔ̂ɔ/, prakaan/) N weakness, fault, defect, flaw.

  o ขาดตกบกพร่อง khàadtòg/bògphrɔ̂ŋ/ V to be deficient, defective, wanting; to fall short.

พร้อม phrɔ́ɔm/ V to be ready, set, completed.

  เตรียมพร้อม triamphrɔ́ɔm/ V to be prepared, on the alert. การ-- preparedness, readiness.

  ถึงพร้อม thɯ̌ŋphrɔ́ɔm/ V to meet all, have all (requirements), attain (completeness).

  พร้อมกัน phrɔ́ɔm/kan at the same time, simultaneously, all together, unanimously.

  พร้อมกันนี้ phrɔ́ɔm/kanníi/ at the same time (as this), this same time.

  พร้อมกับ phrɔ́ɔm/kaɔ together with, at the same time as.

  พร้อมใจ phrɔ́ɔmcaj/ V to be unanimous, in complete accord, of one mind.

  พร้อมด้วย phrɔ́ɔm/dûajɔ together with, at one and the same time with.

  พร้อมทั้ง phrɔ́ɔm/tháŋɔ together with.

  พร้อมที่จะ phrɔ́ɔm/thîicaɔ to be ready to.

  พร้อม ๆ กัน phrɔ́ɔmphrɔ́ɔm/kan at one and the same time, all together.

  พร้อมเพรียง phrɔ́ɔm/phriaŋ/ V 1. to be complete, ready, fully prepared. 2. to be unanimous, harmonious, in harmony, in unison. sV 3. in unison, all at the same time. ความ-- full cooperation, united or unanimous action, unison.

  พร้อมมูล phrɔ́ɔm/muun/ sV fully, completely, to perfection; in abundance. อย่าง-- perfectly, completely.

  o มี...พร้อมมูล mii/...phrɔ́ɔm/muun/ there are plenty of..., there is everything in the way of..., to have everything in the way of...

พร้อมแล้ว phrɔ́ɔmlɛ́ɛw/ ready, set.

พร้อมสรรพ phrɔ́ɔm/sàb/ V 1. to be ready, all set, fully prepared. sV 2. all ready, all set, fully prepared.

  o มี...พร้อมสรรพ mii/...phrɔ́ɔm/sàb/ to be fully equipped with (such and such); to have (such and such) ready.

พร้อมหน้ากัน phrɔ́ɔmnâa/kan all together.

พรักพร้อม phrág/phrɔ́ɔm/ V to be ready, well prepared.

พรั่งพร้อม phrâŋphrɔ́ɔm/ V to be complete, fully furnished, fully equipped or provided (with).

เพรียบพร้อม phrîabphrɔ́ɔm/ V eleg. to be fully provided (with), fully equipped, furnished, loaded.

เห็นพร้อมกัน hěnphrɔ́ɔm/kan to agree unanimously.

พระ (องค์,รูป) phrá?/ (?oŋ/, rûub/) N 1. lord, god. 2. priest. 3. Buddha image. T 4. conferred title for officials of the third rank; cf. พระยา below, and see list of titles under ขุนนาง. 5. title placed before the name of the Buddha ("Lord Buddha"), before the names of divinities, before places and things associated with Buddhism, sacred places and things, places and things associated with the King, etc.

  คุณพระช่วย khunphrá?/chûaj/↓ Oh, my goodness! (Used esp. by women).

  ดาวพระเกตุ daawphrákèed/ N Neptune (the planet). →The names of the major planets are listed under ดาว.

  ดาวพระเคราะห์ (ดวง) daawphrákhrɔ́?/ (duaŋ/) N planet. →Also ดาวเคราะห์ daawkhrɔ́?/.

  ทรงพระอักษร soŋ/phrá?àgsɔ̌ɔn/ V roy. to write.

  พระคุณ phrákhun/ eleg. N beneficence, benevolence. →Also คุณ com.

  o ขอบพระคุณ khɔ̀ɔbphrákhun/ eleg. def. 1. Thank you! V 2. to thank.

  พระจันทร์ (ดวง) phrácan/ (duaŋ/) N moon.

  พระเจดีย์ (องค์) phráceedii/ (?oŋ/) N pagoda, stupa, a memorial edifice with or without relics preserved inside.

  พระเจ้า (องค์) phrácâaw/, phrácâwɔ (?oŋ/) N 1. God (esp. of a monotheistic religion). 2. ruler, king, lord, god; used in certain compounds only. T 3. King --. 4. element occurring in various royal and religious titles.

o พระเจ้าจักรพรรดิ phrácâwcàgkrapháld′ N 1.
emperor. 2. the emperor of (e.g. Japan).

o พระเจ้าตา (องค์) phrácâwtaa′ (ʔoŋ′) N lit.,
def. term of address for an old ascetic.

o พระเจ้าแผ่นดิน (พระองค์) phrácâwphɛ̀ndin′
(phráʔoŋ′) N king: ruler of the earth.

o พระเจ้าลูกเธอ (พระองค์) phrácâwlûugthəə′
(phráʔoŋ′) N 1. roy. son. T 2. title for a
son of the king, added to other titles, as in
สมเด็จพระเจ้าลูกเธอเจ้าฟ้า, พระเจ้าลูกเธอ
พระองค์เจ้า.

o พระเจ้าวรวงศ์เธอพระองค์เจ้า phrácâwwwɔɔraɔ
woŋthəə′phráʔoŋcâaw′ N 1. prince. T 2.
Prince --, Princess --. →Used for a grandchild
of the king, whose father is a สมเด็จเจ้าฟ้า
and whose mother is at least a หม่อมเจ้า.

o พระเจ้าอยู่หัว (องค์, พระองค์) phrácâwjùuhŭa′
(ʔoŋ′, phráʔoŋ′) N 1. king. T 2. King --.
→See also พระบาทสมเด็จ--.

o พระเจ้าโศก phrácâwʔasòog′ King Asoka.

พระชนม phráchon′ N roy. 1. age. 2. life.

o พระชนมพรรษา phráchon′phansǎa′ N roy.
age. →Syn. อายุ com.

oo เฉลิมพระชนมพรรษา chalə̌əm′-phráchon′phanɔ
sǎa′ to celebrate the king's birthday.

o สิ้นพระชนม sîn′phráchon′ V roy. to die.
→Syn. See ตาย com.

พระทัย phráthaj′ N roy. heart; mind.

พระท่าน phráʔ′thânɔ P colloq. 1. he, him,
the god, the holy being. 2. he, him, the priest.

พระที่นั่ง phráthînâŋ′ N throne.

พระธรรม phrátham′, phrátham′maɔ N the
Dharma, the Buddhist teachings.

o พระธรรมเทศนา phrátham′mathêe′sanǎa′,
-thee′sanǎa′ N Buddhist sermon, preaching.

พระนคร phránákhɔɔn′ pN 1. Phra Nakhɔn, the
township in which Bangkok is located. N 2.
capital city.

o ชาวพระนคร (คน) chaaw′phránákhɔɔn′ (khon′)
N the people of Bangkok, Bangkokians.

พระนอน (องค์) phráʔnɔɔn′ (ʔoŋ′) N a reclining
Buddha (i.e. Buddha image).

พระบรมมหาราชวัง (แห่ง) phrábɔrommahǎa′ɔ

rǎadchawaŋ′ (hɛ̀ŋ′) N eleg. the grand palace.

พระบรมราชินี phrábɔrommaraa′chinii′ N eleg.
1. the supreme queen, highest queen. T 2. Her
Majesty the Queen. →Opp. พระบาทสมเด็จพระ-
เจ้าอยู่หัว the King.

o สมเด็จพระนางเจ้าพระบรมราชินี sŏmdèd′phráɔ
naaŋ′câaw′-phrábɔrommaraa′chinii′ N 1. term
for the highest rank held by a queen. T 2. Her
Majesty the Queen.

พระบรมรูป phrábɔrommarûub′ N eleg. picture
or statue of the king.

พระบรมวงศานุวงศ์ (พระองค์) phrábɔrommawoŋɔ
sǎa′núwoŋ′ (phráʔoŋ′) N eleg. royalty; member of the royal family.

พระบรมศพ phrábɔrommasòb′ N eleg. corpse,
body of a king. การ-- royal funeral.

พระบาดหลวง. See พระบาทหลวง.

พระบาท (พระบาท) phrábàad′ (phrábàad′) N,C
roy. foot. →Syn. See ตีน.

o ฝ่าพระบาท fàa′phrábàad′ P roy. you (royal
person of medium rank sp. to another royal person of same or slightly higher rank; inferior sp.
to royal person of medium rank).

o พระบาทสมเด็จ phrábàad′sŏmdèd′ T His
Majesty -- (not used prior to coronation). For
examples, see the list of names under จักรี.

o พระบาทสมเด็จพระเจ้าอยู่หัว (พระองค์) phráɔ
bàad′-sŏmdèd′phrácâwjùuhŭa′ (pháʔoŋ′) N
1. king. T 2. His Majesty the King. →Opp.
พระบรมราชินี the Queen.

o พระบาทหลวง (องค์) phráʔ′bàadlŭaŋ′ (ʔoŋ′)
N 1. Roman Catholic priest. 2. any robed
Christian clergyman. →Also spelled พระบาด
หลวง.

พระปรมาภิไธย phráparamaa′phíthaj′ N roy.
royal signature, name.

พระประธาน (องค์) phráprathaan′ (ʔoŋ′) N the
principal Buddha statue in a Buddhist temple.

พระปรางค์ (องค์) phrápraaŋ′ (ʔoŋ′) N stupa.

พระพุทธ phráphúd′ N the Lord Buddha.

o พระพุทธเจ้า (พระองค์) phráphúd′thacâaw′
(phráʔoŋ′) N the Lord Buddha.

o พระพุทธรูป (องค์) phráphúd′tharûub′ (ʔoŋ′)
N image of Buddha.

o พระพุทธศาสนา phráphúd'thasàad'sanǎa', -sàasanǎa' N Buddhism.

พระภิกษุ,--สงฆ์ (รูป,องค์) phráphígsù?', phrác phígsù?'sǒŋ' (rûub', ?oŋ') N Buddhist priest, monk.

พระภูมิ phráphuum' N the guardian spirit of one's land.

พระมหากษัตริย์ (องค์,พระองค์) phrámahǎa'kac sàd' (?oŋ', phrá'oŋ') N king: "great king."

พระมหานคร phrámahǎa'nákhɔɔn' N capital city.

พระเมรุ. See entries below.

o งานพระเมรุ ŋaan'phrámeen' N roy. cremation ceremony.

o ทุ่งพระเมรุ thûŋ'phrámeen' pN Phra Men (Phra Meru) ground in Bangkok. Used for special ceremonies, including the cremation of members of the royal family. →Also ท้อง สนามหลวง colloq.

พระยา phrajaa' N 1. term for persons of the second highest rank of conferred nobility. T 2. title placed before the honorific name conferred with the rank. 3. title used in animal stories for the leaders or kings of the animals, as in พระยากบ phrajaa'kòb' the frog leader, the king of the frogs. →See 1, 2. ขุนนาง for a list of conferred titles. →Cf. เจ้าคุณ common term of address for พระยา. →Frequently spelled "Phya" in English transliteration.

o เจ้าพระยา (ท่าน,คน) câwphrájaa' (thân', khon') N 1. term for persons of the highest rank of conferred nobility. T 2. title placed in front of the honorific name conferred with the rank. →See ขุนนาง for a list of conferred titles.

พระเยซู phrájee'suu' N Jesus.

พระรอง (คน) phrárɔɔŋ' (khon') N the male character who plays the role of the hero's companion in a play, motion picture, or story.

พระรัตนไตร phrárád'tanátraj' N the Three Gems (Buddha, his teaching, and his disciples). The element รัตน- means "gem," ไตร means "three."

พระราช- phrárâad'chac. Element placed in front of words denoting actions, decisions, belongings, etc. of the King or other royal personages of the highest rank. NOTE. The element ราช- means "king." It may be often be translated into English as "royal."

o พระราชกฤษฎีกา (ฉบับ) phrárâad'chakrìdsac diikaa' (chabàb') N royal decree.

o พระราชดำรัส phrárâad'chadamràd' N roy. royal speech (speech made by the king).

ooทรงพระราชดำรัส soŋ'phrárâad'chadamràd' V roy. to speak, to order.

o พระราชทาน phrárâadchathaan' V roy. to give, present, grant, confer. →Syn. See ให้.

o ขอพระราชทาน khɔ̌ɔ'phrárâadchathaan' V roy. to beg, request.

o พระราชนิพนธ์ (ฉบับ) phrárâad'chaníphon' (chabàb') N writing or literary work of the king.

o พระราชบัญชา phrárâad'chabanchaa' N roy. royal order.

o พระราชบัญญัติ (ฉบับ) phrárâad'chabanjàd' (chabàb') N law, act.

o ร่างพระราชบัญญัติ râaŋ'-phrárâad'chabanjàd' N 1. bill, proposed legislation. V 2. to draft legislation.

o พระราชไมตรี phrárâad'chamajtrii' N friendship, diplomatic relations.

ooเจริญพระราชไมตรี(กับ) carəən'-phrárâad'c chamajtrii'(kac) V (a kingdom) to maintain diplomatic relations, cultivate friendly relations (with).

o พระราชพิธี phrárâad'chaphíthii' N royal ceremony, rite.

o พระราชวัง (แห่ง) phrárâadchawaŋ' (hèŋ') N royal palace.

o พระราชอาณาจักร phrárâad'cha?aanaacàg' N kingdom, empire.

พระศรีรัตนตรัย in คุณพระศรีรัตนตรัย khun'-phrác sǐi'rád'tanátraj' N the virtues of the Three Gems (Buddha, his teaching, his disciples). →Same as พระรัตนตรัย above, but with the addition of more titles.

พระสงฆ์ (รูป,องค์) phrásǒŋ' (rûub', ?oŋ') N Buddhist priest, monk.

พระสังฆราช phrásǎŋ'kharâad' N chief of all the Buddhist priests in the country, Buddhist supreme patriarch. →Also สมเด็จ--.

พระองค์ phráʔoŋ′ P 1. he, him, she, her (sp. of
high-ranking royalty, of divine beings, of the
Buddha). C 2. clf. for a king, for high-ranking
royalty, divine beings, the Buddha.

o พระองค์เจ้า (องค์) phráʔoŋcâaw′, phráʔoŋɔ
câwɔ(ʔoŋ′) N 1. roy. prince, son of the king
born by a lesser concubine. T 2. Prince --.
→See เจ้าฟ้า. →See also พระเจ้าวรวงค์เธอ
พระองค์เจ้า.

พระอาทิตย์ (ดวง) phráʔaathíd′ (duaŋ′) N com.
the sun. →Syn. ตะวัน eleg.

พระอินทร์ phráʔin′ N Indra.

พระอุโบสถ (หลัง) phráʔùboo′sòd′ (lǎŋ′) N
eleg. temple. →Syn. โบสถ์ com.

พระอู่ phráʔùu′ N roy. cradle. →Syn. เปล
com.

พระเอก phráʔèeg′ N 1. the hero (in a play or
story). 2. husband.

พระโอษฐ์ phráʔòod′ N roy. mouth, lips. →Syn.
ปาก com.

โลกพระอังคาร lôog′phráʔaŋkhaan′ N Mars
(the planet).

วันพระ wanphráʔ′ N Buddhist day of worship.
There are four such days in a lunar month,
corresponding to the four phases of the moon.

พระโขนง phrákhanǒoŋ′ pN Prakhanong, an amphoe
in Bangkok.

พรัก in พรักพร้อม phrágphróom′ V to be ready,
well prepared.

พรั่ง in the following entries.

พรั่งพร้อม phrâŋphróom′ V to be complete, fully
furnished, equipped, or provided (with).

พรั่งพรู phrâŋphruu′ V 1. to gush forth. sV 2.
in a mass, in great quantity.

พรั่น phrân′ V eleg. to be afraid, scared.

พรั่นพรึง phrânphrɯŋ′ V eleg. to fear, be scared.

พร่า phrâa′ V 1. to destroy, ruin. 2. to be blurred.

พร่าพราย phrâaphraaj′ V (one's vision) to be
blurred.

พร่ามัว phrâa′mua′ V to be blurred, indistinct.

เสียงพร่า sĭaŋphrâa′ V to have a faltering voice.

แสงพร่า sɛ̌ɛŋphrâa′ N diffused light.

พร้า (เล่ม) phráa′ (lêm′) N jungle knife, kris.

มีดพร้า (เล่ม) mîid′phráa′ (lêm′) N knives
(of all kinds).

พราก phrâag′ V 1. to part, separate. 2. to be parted,
separated. sV 3. copiously, in large quantity.

พลัดพราก(จาก) phládphrâag′(càagɔ) V to stray,
be separated (from), parted (from).

ไหลพราก lǎjphrâag′ V to stream out (e.g. tears),
flow copiously.

พราง phraaŋ′ V 1. to camouflage. 2. to deceive by
means of camouflage.

พรางตา phraaŋtaa′ V to camouflage.

พรางแสงไฟ phraaŋ′sɛ̌ɛŋfaj′ V to have a blackout.

หลุมพราง (หลุม) lǔmphraaŋ′ (lǔm′) N pitfall.

อำพราง ʔamphraaŋ′ V to conceal, hide, keep
secret.

พราด. See พรวดพราด under พรวด.

พราน (คน) phraan′ (khon′) N hunter.

นายพราน (คน) naajphraan′ (khon′) N hunter,
game hunter.

พรานล่าผู้หญิง (คน) phraan′-lâa′phûujĭŋ′ (khon′)
N lady-killer.

พราย phraaj′ N 1. ghost, spirit, elf. 2. a trace
(of something). V 3. to be brilliant, bright,
glittering.

พร่าพราย phrâaphraaj′ V (one's vision) to be
blurred.

พรายน้ำ phraajnáam′ N 1. a line of air bubbles
in the water. 2. glittering ripples. 3. phos-
phorescence in water. 4. luminous paint on the
dial of a watch or clock.

พรายพราว phraajphraaw′ V to be brilliant,
sparkling, glittering.

พรายแพรว phraajphrɛɛw′ V to be glittering,
dazzling, brilliant.

พรายยิ้ม phraajjím′ N trace of a smile.

แพร่งพราย phrɛ̂ŋphraaj′ V 1. to disclose, spread,
reveal, make known. 2. to leak out, be made
known (to).

ยิ้มพราย jímphraaj′ V to smile radiantly.

พราว phraaw′ V to be sparkling, glittering, brilliant.

พราวพราย phraawphraaj′ V to be brilliant,
sparkling, glittering.

พราวแพรว phraawphrɛɛw′ V to be glittering,
dazzling, brilliant.

พราหมณ์ (คน) phraam′ (khon′) N Brahmin.

พรำ phram′ V to drizzle.

○ พรำ ๆ phramphram′ in a drizzle, lightly and steadily in fine drops (of rain).

พร่ำ phrâm′ V 1. to talk continually (about). 2. to talk copiously, with much repetition of certain words or phrases.

พร่ำเพรื่อ phrâmphrŷa′ sV 1. often, frequently, again and again. 2. excessively, luxuriously, extravagantly.

พร่ำสอน phrâmsɔɔn′ to keep teaching, instructing, advising (someone) repeatedly.

พริก (เม็ด) phríg′ (méd′) N pepper, chili pepper.

ถึงพริกถึงขิง thʉ̆ŋphríg′thʉ̆ŋkhĭŋ′ V 1. to be really hot, peppery, spicy (of food). 2. to be racy, piquant (of conversation). อย่าง-- colloq. hotly, heatedly (of arguing, debating).

น้ำพริก námphríg′ N pepper sauce, hot shrimp-paste sauce. There are many varieties having slightly different ingredients.

พริกขี้หนู phrígkhîinŭu′ N bird pepper, a tiny, very hot variety of chili.

พริกไทย phrígthaj′ N pepper (whole or ground).

พริกแห้ง phríghɛ̂ɛŋ′ N dried red pepper.

พริ้ง phríŋ′ V to be dashingly beautiful.

เพราะพริ้ง phrɔ́ʔphríŋ′ V to be melodious, pleasing to the ear, beautiful (of sound).

พริบ. See entries below.

พริบตา phríbtaa′ V 1. to blink, blink the eyes. C 2. an instant, a wink, a twinkling. →Also 1. กระพริบตา.

○ ในพริบตา,--เดียว naj′phríbtaa′, naj′phríbɔ-taa′diaw′ in the twinkling of an eye, quick as a wink.

ไหวพริบ wăjphríb′ N 1. alertness, astuteness, adroitness, ability to make quick judgements. V 2. to be alert, astute, keen.

พริ้ม phrím′ V to be pretty, gay and beautiful.

พริ้มเพรา phrímphraw′ V to be beautiful, gay and beautiful.

พริ้ว in บิดพริ้ว bìdphríw′ V 1. to evade. 2. to refuse (to do something), disobey. การ-- evasion; refusal.

พรึก. See entry below.

ประกายพริก,ดาว-- (ดวง,คน) prakaajphrýg′, daaw′prakaajphrýg′ N 1. the morning star (duaŋ′). 2. slang a young beauty; a young star, starlet (duaŋ′, khon′). →Sometimes also incorrectly written -พฤกษ์. →Also ดาวรุ่ง. →Opp. 1. ดาวประจำเมือง.

พรึงเพริด in ตะลึงพรึงเพริด talyŋ′phryŋphrɜ̂əd′ V elab. colloq. to be stupefied, stunned (with surprise, fright).

พรืด ๑ phrŷd′* sV 1. in a mass, in great numbers, abundantly. V 2. to be in great numbers.

พรืด ๒ phrŷyd′ imit. 1. the sound of grating, scraping, as when dragging a heavy object; the screeching of tires. C 2. an occurrence of any such sound. sV 3. with a grating, scraping effect. เสียง-- a grating, scraping noise.

○ ขับรถพรืดเดียวก็ถึง khàbród′-phrŷyddiaw′kɔ̂ɔthʉ̆ŋ′↓ One screech of the tires and you're there.

พรุ่ง in the following entries.

ในวันในพรุ่ง najwan′najphrûŋ′ colloq. in a day or two, very soon, in a short time.

ผัดวันประกันพรุ่ง phàd′wan′-prakan′phrûŋ′ V elab. colloq. to procrastinate, put off.

พรุ่งนี้ phrûŋníi′ tomorrow.

พรุน phrun′ V to be porous, full of holes, perforated.

พรู phruu′ sV 1. in a mass, in large amounts. V 2. to gush, fall in great quantity.

พรั่งพรู phrâŋphruu′ V 1. to gush forth. sV 2. in a mass, in great quantity.

พฤกษ,พฤกษ-. See entries below. →See also พรึก.

พฤกษชาติ phrýg′sachâad′ N plant world, vegetable kingdom.

พฤกษศาสตร์ phrýg′sasàad′ N botany.

พฤกษา phrýgsăa′ N eleg. plant, vegetation, tree.

ต้นพฤกษา (ต้น) tôn′phrýgsăa′ (tôn′) N tree, plant.

ร่มพฤกษา rôm′phrýgsăa′ N the shade of a tree.

พฤฒสภา phrýd′thasaphaa′ N House of Elders (the upper house in the Thai Parliament, later replaced by the วุฒิสภา).

พฤติการณ์ phrýdtikaan′ N events, course of events; circumstances; action, behavior.

○ ในพฤติการณ์เช่นนั้น najphrýdtikaan′chênnán′ under such circumstances.

พฤตินัย phrýdtinaj′ N law factual sense. โดย--, ตาม-- in fact, de facto. →Opp. นิตินัย.

พฤศจิกายน phrýdsacìkaa′jon′, phrýsa- N November. เดือน-- idem. →The names of all the months are listed under เดือน.

พฤษภาคม phrýdsaphaa′khom′, phrýsa- N May. เดือน-- idem. →The names of all the months are listed under เดือน.

พฤหัส. See entries below. →Short for วัน-- below, and also for พฤหัสบดี in the next main entry.

ดาวพระพฤหัส, ดาวพฤหัส (ดวง) daaw′phrápháɔrýhàd′, daawphárýhàd′ (duaŋ) N Jupiter (the planet). →The names of the major planets are listed under ดาว.

วันพฤหัส wanphárýhàd′ N Thursday (short name; see entry below). →Also พฤหัส. →The days of the week are listed under วัน.

พฤหัสบดี in วันพฤหัสบดี wan′phárýhàd′sabɔɔdii′ N Thursday. →The days of the week are listed under วัน.

พล ๑ phon′ N 1. troop, troops, forces. 2. soldier; member of military or police force.

กองพล (กอง,กองพล) kɔɔŋphon′ (kɔɔŋ′, kɔɔŋphon′) N milit. division.

o กองพลน้อย (กอง,กองพล) kɔɔŋphonnɔ́ɔj′ (kɔɔŋ′, kɔɔŋphon′) N milit. brigade.

o กองพลใหญ่ (กอง,กองพล) kɔɔŋphonjàj′ (kɔɔŋ′, kɔɔŋphon′) N milit. division.

ขุนพล (คน) khǔnphon′ (khon′) N 1. military commander. 2. war lord.

จอมพล (คน,นาย) cɔɔmphon′ (khon′, naaj′) N 1. field marshal. T 2. Field Marshal --.

จอมพลเรือ (นาย,คน) cɔɔmphonrya′ (naaj′, khon′) N 1. admiral of the fleet. T 2. Admiral --.

ที่ชุมพล thîi′chumphon′ N assembly point for troops.

นายพล (นาย,คน) naajphon′ (naaj′, khon′) N milit. general (of unspecified rank). →See cross reference.

นายพลตำรวจ (นาย,คน) naajphon′tamrùad′ (naaj′, khon′) police general (of unspecified rank).

นายพลตำรวจโท (นาย,คน) naajphon′tamrùadɔ

thoo′ (naaj′, khon′) N 1. police lieutenant general. T 2. Lt. General --.

นายพลเรือ (นาย,คน) naajphonrya′ (naaj′, khon′) N 1. admiral (of unspecified rank). See cross reference.

พลจัตวา (นาย,คน) phon′càdtawaa′ (naaj′, khon′) N 1. brigadier general. T 2. Brigadier General --.

พลตระเวน (นาย,คน) phontraween′ (naaj′, khon′) N patrolman; policeman on his beat.

พลตรี (นาย,คน) phontrii′ (naaj′, khon′) N 1. milit. major general. T 2. Major General --.

พลตำรวจ (นาย,คน) phontamrùad′ (naaj′, khon′) N 1. policeman (lowest police rank). T 2. Officer -- (ref. to a policeman).

พลทหาร (นาย,คน) phonthahǎan′ (naaj′, khon′) N 1. milit. private. T 2. Private --.

พลโท (นาย,คน) phonthoo′ (naaj′, khon′) N 1. milit. lieutenant general. T 2. Lt. General --.

พลร่ม (คน) phonrôm′ (khon′) N 1. milit. paratrooper. 2. slang an illegal voter.

o การทิ้งพลร่ม kaanthíŋ′phonrôm′ N 1. paratroop landing. 2. slang balloting by illegal voters.

พลเรือตรี (นาย,คน) phonryatrii′ (naaj′, khon′) N 1. rear admiral. T 2. Rear Admiral --.

พลเรือโท (นาย,คน) phonryathoo′ (naaj′, khon′) N 1. vice-admiral. T 2. Vice-Admiral --.

พลเรือเอก (นาย,คน) phonrya?èeg′ (naaj′, khon′) N 1. admiral. T 2. Admiral --.

พลอากาศ... phon?aakàadɔ... designation for the highest commissioned ranks of the air force.

พลเอก (นาย,คน) phon?èeg′ (naaj′, khon′) N 1. (full) general (the rank). T 2. General --.

ระดมพล radom′phon′ V to mobilize troops, armed forces.

รี้พล ríi′phon′ N troops, fighting forces.

เรียกพล rîagphon′ V to mobilize troops. การ-- mobilizing, mobilization of troops.

พล ๒ in อิทธิพล ?ìdthíphon′ N power, influence.

พล ๓ pháláɔ N (physical) strength. Used only in compounds, but in final position written พละ, q. v.

พลการ phálákaan′ N force, power (esp. the arbitrary application of power or authority).

พลศึกษา phálásỳgsǎa′ N physical education.

o โรงพลศึกษา (โรง) rooŋ′phálásỳgsǎa′ (rooŋ′)
N gymnasium.

พล ๔ in the following entries.

พลเมือง (คน) phonlamyaŋ′ (khon′) N population.

o การสำรวจพลเมือง kaansǎmrùad′phonlamyaŋ′
N census, i.e. the taking of a census.

o หน้าที่พลเมือง nâathîi′phonlamyaŋ′ N civic
duties.

พลเรือน (คน) phonlaryan′ (khon′) N civilian.

o ข้าราชการ(ฝ่าย)พลเรือน (คน,นาย) khâa‿
râadchakaan′(fàaj)phonlaryan′ (khon′, naaj′)
N civilian government employees (as opposed
to those of the military services).

o คณะกรรมการข้าราชการพลเรือน khanákamma‿
kaan′-khâarâadchakaan′phonlaryan′ N Civil
Service Commission.

พลโลก (คน) phonlalôog′ (khon′) N the peoples
of the world.

พลบ phlób′ N twilight, dusk.

เวลาพลบ weelaaphlób′ N 1. twilight time, dusk.
2. at dusk.

พลวง phluaŋ′ N antimony.

พลอง,ไม้-- (อัน) phlɔɔŋ′, májphlɔɔŋ′ (ʔan′) N
1. wooden staff, club (used as a weapon). 2.
a boy scout staff.

พลอด phlɔ̂ɔd′ V to talk incessantly (esp. with ref.
to lovers).

พลอดรัก phlɔ̂ɔdrág′ V to talk love, make love
(to).

พลอมแพลม phlɔmphlɛm′* V 1. to appear, show
itself, be visible intermittently. sV 2. intermittently, unevenly, sparsely, scantily. 3.
lightly, in a drizzle (of rain).

พลอย ๑ (เม็ด) phlɔɔj′ (méd′) N precious stone,
gem, jewel.

เพชรพลอย phédphlɔɔj′ N jewels, precious
stones (in general).

พลอย ๒ phlɔɔj′ V to join in, follow suit.

ผลพลอยได้ (อย่าง) phǒn′phlɔɔjdâaj′ (jàaŋ′) N
by-product.

พลอยฟ้าพลอยฝน phlɔɔjfáa′phlɔɔjfǒn′ idiom.
to be included or mixed up with others without

actual participation; along with others.

วัตถุพลอยได้ (อย่าง) wádthù?′phlɔɔjdâaj′ (jàaŋ′)
N by-product.

พล่อย,พล่อย ๆ phlɔ̂j′, phlɔ̂jphlɔ̂j′* sV without reflection, thoughtlessly.

พละ phalá?′* N 1. strength, force, power. 2. short
for พลศึกษา physical education. →See พล ๓.

ชั่วโมงพละ chûamooŋ′phalá?′ N physical education period (in a school program).

พลั่ก phlâg′ imit. 1. the sound of a gust of air, the
gushing of liquid. 2. the sound of a punch or
a heavy blow. V 3. to gush forth. sV 4. with
a gushing sound; gushing forth.

พลัง phalaŋ′ N power, strength, force.

พลังงาน phalaŋŋaan′ N tech. energy.

o พลังงานปรมาณู phalaŋŋaan′paramaanuu′ N
atomic energy.

พลังปรมาณู phalaŋ′paramaanuu′ N atomic power.

มีพลังแรง mii′-phalaŋ′rɛɛŋ′ to be powerful, have
much power.

พลั่ง phlâŋ′ sV in streams, gushing forth.

พลั้ง phláŋ′ V to make a slip of the tongue.

พลัด phlád′ V 1. to fall, fall off. 2. to stray from,
get separated from.

พลัดตก phládtòg′ V to fall down, drop down.

พลัดถิ่น phládthìn′ V to be displaced from (one's)
native land, exiled; to be outside of, removed
from (its) natural habitat.

o บุคคลพลัดถิ่น bùgkhon′phládthìn′ refugee,
displaced person.

พลัดพราก(จาก) phládphrâag′(càag‿) V to stray,
be separated (from), parted (from).

พลัดเพริด phládphrɤ̂əd′ V to stray, go astray, be
parted and lost from (the group, the herd, etc.).

พลัดลงมา phlád′loŋmaa′ to fall down, fall off.

พลัน phlan′ sV suddenly, immediately, instantly.
→Chiefly in compounds.

ฉับพลัน chàbphlan′ instantly, promptly, at once,
abruptly. โดย--,ใน--,อย่าง-- idem.

โดยเร็วพลัน doojrewphlan′ quickly.

พลับพลา (หลัง) phlábphlaa′ (lǎŋ′) N pavilion.

พลั่ว (อัน) phlûa′ (ʔan′) N shovel.

พลัสติค phlástìg′ N plastic. [f. Eng.]

พล่า phlâa′ N 1. a Thai salad with raw or partially

cooked meat. V 2. to prepare such a salad.

พลาง phlaaŋ′ sV simultaneously, at the same time, meanwhile.

○ พูดพลางหัวเราะพลาง phûud′phlaaŋ′-hŭarɔ́?′ɔ phlaaŋ′ to talk while laughing, talk and laugh at the same time.

ไปพลาง pajphlaaŋ′ simultaneously, at the same time.

ไปพลางก่อน pajphlaaŋ′kɔ̀ɔn′ for the time being, meanwhile, in the meantime.

ไปพลาง ๆ pajphlaaŋphlaaŋ′ for the time being, meanwhile, in the meantime.

พลาด phlâad′ V 1. to miss, fail. 2. to slip, fall.

ก้าวพลาด kâawphlâad′ V 1. to misstep, miss one's footing. 2. to miscalculate, misjudge.

ผิดพลาด phìdphlâad′ V to be incorrect, wrong, mistaken. ความ-- blunder, mistake, error.

พลาดท่า phlâadthâa′ V 1. to make a false step, a wrong move, a slip. 2. by mischance, if by mischance.

พลาดพลั้ง phlâadphláŋ′ V to make a mistake, a blunder, a slip.

พล่าน phlâan′ V 1. (the brain) to be distracted, in confusion. sV 2. in a confused, disorderly manner (of walking, running). 3. short for เดือด-- below.

เดือดพล่าน dɯ̀adphlâan′ 1. to boil vigorously. 2. colloq. to be furious, boiling mad.

พลุกพล่าน phlúgphlâan′ V to mill around, move about in disorder, with much coming and going (of people, animals, vehicles in large numbers).

วิ่งพล่าน wîŋphlâan′ to run pell-mell, helter-skelter, aimlessly.

พล่าม phlâam′ V to talk endlessly, to prattle.

พลาย in ช้างพลาย (เชือก,ตัว) cháaŋphlaaj′ (chɯ̂ag′, tua′) N bull elephant.

พลาสติก phláadsatìg′, phláastìg′ N plastic. [f. Eng.]

พล้ำ in เผลี่ยงพล้ำ phlîaŋphlám′ V to make a wrong move, a mistake.

พลิก phlíg′ V to turn over (as pages in a book).

พลิกตัว phlígtua′ V to turn (oneself) over (in bed).

พลิกแพลง phlígphlɛɛŋ′ V to change, alter, modify; to make changes, alterations, modifications.

พลี phalii′, phlii′ V to sacrifice. เครื่อง-- sacrificial offerings.

พลีกรรม phalii′kam′, phlii′kam′ N worship, sacrificial worship.

พลุ (ดอก) phlú?′ (dɔɔg′) N 1. flare. 2. a giant firecracker, cannon cracker.

พลุก in พลุกพล่าน phlúgphlâan′ V to mill around, move about in disorder, with much coming and going (of people, animals, vehicles in large numbers).

พลุ่ง phlûŋ′ V to puff, to rush out (esp. of smoke or steam).

พลุ้ย phlúj′ V (the stomach) to be protruding, bulging.

พลู ๑ phluu′ N betel, esp. the leaves. ต้น-- (ต้น) the betel vine. ใบ-- (ใบ) the betel leaf. →Dist. หมาก.

หมากพลู màagphluu′ N betel: "areca and betel."

พลู ๒ in กานพลู kaanphluu′ N clove. ดอก-- (ดอก) flower of the clove tree. ต้น-- (ต้น) the clove tree.

พวก (พวก) phûag′ (phûag′) N 1. group, party. C 2. idem. →Cf. จำพวก. →Syn. 1. กก. 2. หมู่, เหล่า, กก.

พรรคพวก (คน) phágphûag′ (khon′) N 1. partisan, fellow member, follower. 2. close friends, members of an intimate circle; clique.

พวกกบฏ (คน,พวก) phûagkabòd′ (khon′, phûag′) N rebels, the rebel faction.

พวกก่อการร้าย phûagkɔ̀ɔkaan′ráaj′ N trouble-makers, gangsters, saboteurs.

พวกเขา phûagkháw′ N they, them, the others. →Opp. พวกเรา.

พวกเจ้า phûagcâw′ you people, you folks (sup. sp. to a group or crowd).

พวกใต้ดิน phûagtâajdin′ N underground organization.

พวกทุจริต phûag′thúdcarìd′ N crooks.

พวกบ้าน... phûagbâan′... the members of (such and such a) household.

พวกผิวขาว phûagphǐwkhǎaw′ N the white race, white people.

พวกผิวดำ phûagphǐwdam′ N the black race, colored people.

พวกพ้อง phûagphɔ́ɔŋ′ N (one's own) group of

friends, party, gang.

o เห็นแก่พวกพ้อง hĕn′kɛ̀phûagphɔ́ɔŋ′ to think only of the interests of one's own group or party.

พวกเรา phûagraw′ N we, us, our group. →Opp. พวกเขา.

ยกพวก jógphûag′ V to bring or take a whole gang, crowd.

เล่นพวกเล่นพ้อง lênphûag′lênphɔ́ɔŋ′ V e l a b. colloq. to indulge in favoritism. →Also เล่นพวก c o l l o q.

เลือกพวก lŷagphûag′ V to discriminate, be prejudiced (in favor of or against someone depending on his group or party affiliation).

พวง (พวง) phuaŋ′ (phuaŋ′) N 1. garland, cluster, string (as of flowers, fruit, beads). C 2. i d e m. →Mng. 1. chiefly in compounds.

เป็นพวง penphuaŋ′ 1. to be bushy (as a tail). 2. to be bulging (as cheeks). 3. in a cluster, in a bunch, in a string; in clusters, bunches, strings.

เป็นพวง ๆ penphuaŋphuaŋ′ in clusters, bunches, strings.

พวงมาลัย (พวง,อัน) phuaŋmaalaj′ N 1. garland (phuaŋ′). 2. steering wheel (of an automobile) (?an′).

o ถือพวงมาลัย thŷy′phuaŋmaalaj′ to steer, be at the wheel, i.e. have hold of the steering wheel.

พวงหรีด (พวง) phuaŋrìid′ (phuaŋ′) N wreath, garland.

พ่วง ๑ phûaŋ′ V to connect, attach, couple (one vehicle or vessel to another for towing).

พ่วงท้าย phûaŋtháaj′ V 1. to have in tow, pull along behind (e.g. a trailer). 2. c o l l o q. to trail (e.g. a degree after one's name).

รถพ่วง (คัน) ródphûaŋ′ (khan′) N 1. trailer. 2. a vehicle drawn by another vehicle. 3. a train of vehicles coupled to one another.

เรือพ่วง (ลำ) ryaphûaŋ′ (lam′) N 1. tugboat. 2. a boat or train of boats pulled by a tugboat.

พ่วง ๒ in พ่วงพี phûaŋphii′ V to be fat.

พวย (พวย,อัน) phuaj′ (phuaj′,?an′) N spout.

พวยกา (พวย,อัน) phuajkaa′ (phuaj′,?an′) N spout of a teakettle.

พวยพุ่ง phuajphûŋ′ V 1. (liquid) to stream out, pour out, spout forth. 2. (smoke, dust) to puff up, rise up. 3. to throw up beams (of light).

พ.ศ. phɔɔsɔ̌ɔ′ B.E. Abbrev. for พุทธศักราช Buddhist Era.

พสกนิกร phasòg′níkɔɔn′ N e l e g. citizen, people, subjects (of a ruler).

พอ phɔɔ′ V 1. to be enough, sufficient. AA 2. adequately, all right; scarcely, hardly, barely, Cj 3. just as soon as, just as, when.

o พอตกดึกเข้าอีกหน่อย phɔɔtògdỳg′khâw?ìignɔ̀j′ as soon as it got to be a little later in the night.

o พอเขามาเราก็จะกิน phɔɔkháwmaa′→ raw′kɔ̂caɔ kin′↓ As soon as he comes we will eat. →Cf. 4th example under พอจะ below.

ชอบพอ chɔ̂ɔbphɔɔ′ V to be fond of, to love.

พอควร phɔɔkhuan′ fairly, moderately, reasonably.

พอจะ phɔɔcaɔ AA 1. adequately, passably (but barely, i.e. with some reservations); enough to. Cj 2. just as (I, you, he, etc.) was about to; just as (I, you, he, etc.) begin to, (am) about to.

o พอจะเดินไหว phɔɔcadəən′wǎj′ can make it (by walking), can walk it all right.

o พอจะทำได้ phɔɔcatham′dâaj′ can do it; (I) guess (I) can do it, can get by with it.

o โตพอจะทำเองได้ too′phɔɔcatham?eeŋ′-dâaj′ big enough to do (it) oneself.

o พอฉันจะกินข้าวเขาก็มา phɔɔcháncakin′khâaw′→ kháwkɔ̂maa′↓ Just as I was about to eat he came. Cf. 2nd example under พอ above.

o พอจะทำเป็นเข้า ก็เกิดลาออกเสีย phɔɔcatham‍ɔ pen′khâaw′→ kɔ̀kə̀əd′laa?ɔ̀ɔg′sía↓ Just as soon as (they) start to catch on, (they) quit.

พอใจ phɔɔcaj′ V to be satisfied, pleased. ความ-- satisfaction, contentment. →Syn. ชอบพอ, ถูกใจ.

o พึงพอใจ phyŋphɔɔcaj′ V 1. to be satisfied. 2. to satisfy, be satisfactory. ความ-- satisfaction.

o ไม่พอใจ mâjphɔɔcaj′ to be dissatisfied, displeased. ความ-- dissatisfaction, displeasure.

พอใช้ phɔɔcháj′ V to be adequate, passable, fair.

o ดีพอใช้ dii′phɔɔcháj′ fairly good, passably good.

พอดี phɔɔdii′ precisely, exactly, just right (in size, amount, etc.), just the right moment;

just then, at that very moment.

พอดู phɔɔduu/ c o l l o q. quite, noticeably, perceptibly.

o ไกลพอดู klaj/phɔɔduu/ quite far, pretty far.

o นานพอดู naan/phɔɔduu/ quite long (of time).

พอที phɔɔthii/↓ That's enough. Enough! (Hold it!).

พอประมาณ phɔɔpramaan/ V to be moderate (in quantity). sV 2. moderately, to some degree, to some extent.

พอ ๆ กัน phɔɔphɔɔ/kan 1. to be about equal, about the same, alike. 2. about equally.

พอเพียง, เพียงพอ phɔɔphiaŋ/, phiaŋphɔɔ/ V to be sufficient, adequate.

พอฟัดพอเหวี่ยง phɔɔfád/phɔɔwìaŋ/ V e l a b. c o l l o q. to be about the same (in strength). →Also พอฟัด c o l l o q.

พอสบาย phɔɔsabaaj/ V to be just right (for comfort).

พอสมควร phɔɔsŏmkhuan/ V to be reasonable, moderate (in amount, price, etc.).

พอเหมาะพอเจาะ phɔɔmɔ́?/phɔɔcɔ́?/ to be just right, to fit exactly. →Also พอเหมาะ c o l l o q.

พ่อ (คน) phɔ̂ɔ/ (khon/) N 1. c o m. father. P 2. you; he, him; Father (sp. to or of one's father); I, me, Father (father sp. to child). T 3. title used before the first names of boys or, in certain circumstances, of men. 4. element placed before nouns and verbs to form agent nouns having the sense of "male engaged in such and such an occupation," as in พ่อครัว "cook," พ่อค้า "merchant." →S y n. 1. บิดา . e l e g. →See 4. คน ๑.

คุณพ่อ khunphɔ̂ɔ/ P e l e g. 1. you; he, him; Father (sp. to or of one's father). N 2. father (of someone).

พ่อครัว phɔ̂ɔkhrua/ N cook (i.e. male cook).

พ่อค้า phɔ̂ɔkháa/ N merchant, trader, tradesman, shopkeeper.

พ่อเฒ่า phɔ̂ɔthâw/ N an aged man.

พ่อตา phɔ̂ɔtaa/ N (man's) father-in-law.

พ่อทูนหัว (1) phɔ̂ɔ/thuunhŭa/; (2) phɔ̂ɔthuun/hŭa/ N 1. godfather. 2. a beloved boy, an adorable boy.

พ่อบ้าน phɔ̂ɔbâan/ N (male) head of a family.

พ่อผัว phɔ̂ɔphŭa/ N (woman's) father-in-law.

พ่อมด phɔ̂ɔmód/ N wizard, sorcerer.

พ่อแม่ phɔ̂ɔ/mɛ̂ɛ/ N parents: "father and mother." →S y n. บิดามารดา e l e g., ผู้บังเกิดเกล้า e l e g.

พ่อเลี้ยง phɔ̂ɔlíaŋ/ N stepfather.

พ่อสื่อ phɔ̂ɔsỳy/ N male go-between, matchmaker.

พ่อหม้าย phɔ̂ɔmâaj/ N widower.

หลวงพ่อ (องค์) lŭaŋphɔ̂ɔ/ (?oŋ/) N 1. a venerable priest (commanding respect by virtue of high office or great age). 2. a priest who is one's father. 3. the largest Buddha image in a temple. P 4. you; he, him (sp. to or of a priest as defined above.) T 5. title placed before the name of such a priest. nN 6. nickname for a person of high character, with a saintly disposition.

พอก phɔ̂ɔg/ V to put on in layers, pile on thickly.

คอพอก khɔɔphɔ̂ɔg/ V to have a goiter.

พอกพูน phɔ̂ɔgphuun/ V to accumulate, add up, pile up, increase gradually.

พอง phɔɔŋ/ V to swell, be swollen, get a swelling.

ดินสอพอง dinsɔ̆ɔphɔɔŋ/ N a soft, prepared chalk used as an after-bath powder for its cooling effect.

เป็นพุพอง pen/phú?phɔɔŋ/ to be covered with clusters of festering sores (as infected mosquito bites).

พ้อง phɔ́ɔŋ/ V to be allied, alike; to be synonymous; to sound alike; to rhyme (with).

พวกพ้อง phûagphɔ́ɔŋ/ N (one's own) group of friends, party, gang.

พ้องกัน phɔ́ɔŋ/kan to coincide; to be alike; to be synonymous; to rhyme with each other.

เห็นพ้อง (ด้วย) hĕnphɔ́ɔŋ/(dûaj/) V to agree.

พ้อม (ใบ, ลูก) phɔ́ɔm/ (baj/, lûug/) N a large bamboo basket used to hold paddy.

พะ- pha⊃. In recent standard dictionaries prior to the 1950 edition of the official monolingual Thai dictionary, this spelling was used in words like พะนัก, พะนัน, พะม่า, พะยาน, etc. The 1950 edition, however, deletes ะ in such words, writing them พนัก, พนัน, พม่า, พยาน, etc., and this convention is followed here.

พะวง phawoŋ/ V to worry (about).

พะวงถึง (1) phawoŋ/thŷŋ⊃; (2) phawoŋ/thŷŋ/ 1. to worry about. 2. to worry about it.

พะว้าพะวัง phawáa′phawaŋ′ V to hesitate, vacillate, be hesitant, undecided (as because of worry, uneasiness, fear).

พะอืดพะอม phaʔỳyd′phaʔom′ V 1. to feel nauseated, squeamish. 2. to be torn between a desire to speak and the necessity for keeping silence (esp. when someone else's feelings are at stake).

พัก phág′ V 1. to rest, stay over (as at someone's home, at a hotel). C 2. clf. for an interval or period of time.

ที่พัก (ที่,แห่ง) thîiphág′ (thîi′,hὲŋ′) N 1. residence, lodging, quarters. 2. resting place.

น้ำพักน้ำแรง námphág′námrɛɛŋ′ N elab. colloq. 1. (one's own) effort, labor. 2. (one's) personal investment.

บ้านพัก (หลัง) bâanphág′ (lǎŋ′) N 1. home, residence. 2. quarters, lodging.

เป็นพัก ๆ penphágphág′ fitfully, sporadically, at times, in fits and starts, in bursts.

พักผ่อน phágphɔ̀ɔn′ V to rest, take a rest.

พักฟื้น phágfýyn′ V to be in convalescence.

พักรบ phágrób′ V to call a truce, a cease-fire.

พักแรม phágrɛɛm′ V to camp, lodge, stay overnight.

o ที่พักแรม (ที่,แห่ง) thîi′phágrɛɛm′ (thîi′,hὲŋ′) N 1. overnight lodging. 2. campsite.

พัก(...)ไว้ phág(...)wáj′ to leave, set (something) aside temporarily.

พักหนึ่ง phág′nyŋ 1. (for) one moment. 2. (for) a period of time.

พักใหญ่ phágjàj′ for a long time.

ไม่พักต้อง mâjphág′tɔ̂ŋɔ does not wait, without waiting (e.g. to be invited).

โรงพัก (โรง,แห่ง) rooŋphág′ (rooŋ′,hὲŋ′) N colloq. police station.

ลาพัก laaphág′ V to request or take a leave of absence (in order to rest).

สักพัก sàgphág′ for a short time, for a while.

หยุดพัก (ครั้ง,หน) jùdphág′ (khráŋ′,hǒn′) V 1. to take a break, take time out; to rest; to pause, stop to rest. N 2. time out, break, rest, recess.

o หยุดพักกลางวัน jùdphágklaaŋwan′ V 1. to take a midday break, a noon recess. N 2. midday break, noon recess.

หอพัก (หอ,หลัง) hɔ̌ɔphág′ (hɔ̌ɔ′,lǎŋ′) N boarding house, dormitory, hostel.

ห้องพัก (ห้อง) hɔ̂ŋphág′ (hɔ̂ŋ′) N 1. waiting room, lounge (as in a train station). 2. room where one stays temporarily (e.g. a hotel room).

พัง ๑ phaŋ′ V 1. to break, destroy, tear down. 2. to fall in ruins, tumble down, cave in, collapse.

ปรักหักพัง paràg′hàgphaŋ′ V elab. to be ruined, dilapidated.

ผุพัง phùʔ′phaŋ′ V to be dilapidated.

พังทลาย phaŋ′thalaaj′ V to fall in ruins, crumble to pieces, tumble down.

พังระเนระนาด phaŋ′ranee′ranâad′ V to tumble down, collapse, be destroyed, and with the pieces overlapping or lying on top of each other.

พัง ๒ in ช้างพัง (เชือก,ตัว) cháaŋphaŋ′ (chŷag′, tua′) N female elephant.

พังพอน (ตัว) phaŋphɔɔn′ (tua′) N mongoose.

พังพาบ in นอนพังพาบ nɔɔn′phaŋphâab′ to lie face down, lie prone.

พังเพย in คำพังเพย (บท) kham′phaŋphəəj′ (bòd′) N saying.

พัฒนา phádthanaa′ V eleg. 1. to progress, advance. N 2. progress, advancement.

พัฒนาการ phádthanaa′kaan′ N eleg. progress, advancement, development.

พัด (เล่ม,อัน) phád′ (lêm′,ʔan′) V 1. to fan. 2. (the wind) to blow. N 3. fan. →Dist. 2. เป่า.

ใบพัด (ใบ,อัน) bajphád′ (baj′,ʔan′) N 1. propeller. 2. fan (for a car radiator). 3. fan blades.

พัดกระโชก phád′krachôog′ to blow very hard, blow in gusts.

พัดกล้า phádklâa′ to blow strong.

พัดฉิว phádchĭw′ to blow uninterruptedly, continuously.

พัดเฉื่อย phád′chỳaj′ to blow lazily, blow gently and steadily.

พัดโชย phádchooj′ to blow gently.

พัดไฟ phádfaj′ V to fan the fire.

พัดระรวย phád′raruaj′ eleg. to blow softly, gently.

พัดรื่น phádrŷyn′ to blow gently and refreshingly.

พัดลม (อัน,เครื่อง) phádlom′ (ʔan′,khrŷaŋ′) N (electric) fan, air blower.

รำพัด ramphád′ V 1. to dance with fans. 2.

slang to play cards.

ลมพัด lomphád⁄ the wind is blowing.

พัทลุง phádthaluŋ⁄ pN Patthalung, a township in S Thailand.

พัน ๑ phan⁄ V 1. to wind, coil. 2. to wrap around, wind around.

เกี่ยวพัน kìawphan⁄ V to be related (to). การ-- relation, connection.

ติดพัน tìdphan⁄ V 1. to engage, occupy, concern, involve. 2. to be engaged, occupied, involved (in, with). 3. colloq. to be in love (with) (prior to marriage), to court.

ผ้าพันคอ (ผืน) phâaphankhɔɔ⁄ (phɯ̌yn⁄) N scarf. →Syn. ผ้าผูกคอ.

ผ้าพันแผล (ม้วน, ชิ้น) phâaphanphlɛ̌ɛ⁄ N bandage, gauze (múan⁄ for a roll; chín⁄ for a piece).

ผูกพัน phùugphan⁄ V 1. to tie, bind, be tied, bound. 2. (the heart, mind) to be absorbed (with), pre-occupied (with), wrapped up (in) (e.g. loved ones, work, obligations). การ-- ties, bonds; being absorbed (in), wrapped up (in), preoccupation (with).

o ข้อผูกพัน (ข้อ) khɔ̂ɔ⁄phùugphan⁄ (khɔ̂ɔ⁄) N obligation, binding condition; restriction, strings (attached to a deal).

พันพัว, พัวพัน phanphua⁄, phuaphan⁄ V to be in-volved, implicated, mixed up, tangled up.

พัน ๒ phan⁄ Nm 1. thousand. C 2. clf. for thou-sands.

o สองพัน (๒๐๐๐) sɔ̌ɔŋphan⁄ two thousand.

o สองพันสี่ร้อยเก้าสิบเจ็ด (๒๔๙๗) sɔ̌ɔŋphan⁄-sìirɔ́ɔj⁄kâawsìbcèd⁄ two thousand four hundred and ninety seven (BE 2497 = AD 1954).

แองพัน (กอง, กองพัน) kɔɔŋphan⁄ (kɔɔŋ⁄, kɔɔŋɔ phan⁄) N battalion.

นายพันตรี (คน, นาย) naajphantrii⁄ (khon⁄, naaj⁄) N 1. major. T 2. Major --. →Also informally พันตรี.

นายพันโท (คน, นาย) naajphanthoo⁄ (khon⁄, naaj⁄) N 1. lieutenant-colonel. T 2. Lt. Colonel --. →Also informally พันโท. →Abbrev. พ.ท.

นายพันเอก (คน, นาย) naajphanʔèeg⁄ (khon⁄, naaj⁄) N 1. colonel. T 2. Colonel --. →Also informally พันเอก.

ใบละพัน (ใบ) bajlaphan⁄ (baj⁄) N 1000-tical bill.

พันจ่า phancàa⁄ N 1. warrant officer. T 2. title placed before the first name of a warrant officer.

o พันจ่าอากาศ... phancàa⁄ʔaakàadɔ... designa-tion for the warrant officer ranks of the air force.

พันตรี. Shortened form of นาย-- above.

พันโท. Shortened form of นาย-- above.

พันเอก. Shortened form of นาย-- above.

พัน ๓ in เดิมพัน dəəmphan⁄ N the bet, the stake in gambling. →Comp. พัน ๑, ๒.

o วางเดิมพัน waaŋ⁄dəəmphan⁄ V to bet, place a bet.

พันตู phantuu⁄ V lit. to be engaged in fighting or competing.

พันธ์, พันธ- (1) phan⁄, phanthaɔ; (2) phanthá⁄ʔ⁄ V 1. to unite, tie. N 2. colloq. obligation; short for พันธกรณี.

พันธกรณี phanthá⁄ʔ⁄karanii⁄, -kɔranii⁄ N obligation.

พันธบัตร (ใบ, ฉบับ) phanthabàd⁄ (baj⁄, chabàb⁄) N finance bond.

พันธมิตร phanthamíd⁄ N allies, ally.

พันธะ (ข้อ) phanthá⁄ʔ⁄ (khɔ̂ɔ⁄) N obligation, strings (attached to a deal).

พันธุ์ phan⁄ N breed, species, kind, pedigree, lineage.

ผสมพันธุ์ phasǒm⁄phan⁄ V to breed.

พันธุ์ผสม phan⁄phasǒm⁄ N hybrid, half-breed.

พืชพันธุ์ (ชนิด) phɯ̂ydphan⁄ (chaníd⁄) N plant, vegetation.

ศูนย์พันธุ์ sǔun⁄phan⁄ V to be extinct.

สืบพันธุ์ sɯ̀ybphan⁄ V to reproduce (produce offspring). การ-- propagation, reproduction.

สูญพันธุ์ sǔun⁄phan⁄ V to be extinct.

หมดพันธุ์ mòdphan⁄ V to be extinct.

พับ pháb⁄ V 1. to fold. C 2. clf. for a bolt of cloth (a length of cloth which is folded, as in a store).

นั่งพับเพียบ nâŋ⁄phábphîab⁄ to sit (on the floor) with both legs tucked back to one side.

บานพับ (อัน) baanpháb⁄ (ʔan⁄) N hinge.

มีดพับ (เล่ม) mîidpháb⁄ (lêm⁄) N penknife, clasp knife, pocketknife.

ล้มพับ lóm⁄pháb⁄ V to collapse.

พัว in พัวพัน, พันพัว phuaphan⁄, phanphua⁄ V to be involved, implicated, mixed up, tangled up.

พ้วะเพียะ phúaʔphíaʔ⁄ imit. the sound of beating,

slapping, cracking. →Also ผัวะเผียะ.

พัสดุ (สิ่ง,อย่าง) phádsadù?/ (sìŋ/, jàaŋ/) N 1.
goods, articles, things. 2. parcel post.

○ ส่งทางพัสดุ sòŋ/thaaŋphádsadù?/ to send by
parcel post.

คลังพัสดุ (แห่ง) khlaŋ/phádsadù?/ (hèŋ/) N
storehouse.

บัญชีพัสดุ banchii/phádsadù?/ N eleg. inventory,
list of articles.

พัสดุไปรษณีย์ phádsadù?/prajsanii/ N parcel post.

โรงพัสดุ (โรง,แห่ง) rooŋ/phádsadù?/ (rooŋ/,
hèŋ/) N storehouse, warehouse.

พา ๑ phaa/ V to take along, bring along.

คนพาเที่ยว (คน) khon/phaathîaw/ (khon/) N
1. tourist guide. 2. escort.

นำพา namphaa/ V to pay attention to, take an
interest in, care for. →Chiefly in negative or
interrogative constructions.

○ ไม่นำพา mâjnamphaa/ to pay not the slightest
attention to; to ignore (e.g. tradition, a warning).

พากัน phaa/kanɔ AA expression indicating con-
certed action, simultaneous and identical action
by the members of a group.

○ พากันหัวเราะ phaa/kanhŭarɔ́?/ everybody
laughed (together).

พาเงินเชิด phaaŋən/chôəd/ slang to steal
money, lift money, run off with money.

พาซื่อ phaasŷy/ naively, unsuspectingly.

พา...เดินผ่าน phaa/...dəənphàan/ to take (someone) past, lead (someone) past.

พา...ไป phaa/...pajɔ to take (someone) to.

พา...มา phaa/...maa/ to bring (someone).

พึ่งพา phŷŋphaa/ V to depend on (for aid).

พึ่งพาอาศัย phŷŋphaa/?aasăj/ V to depend on for
a living, for aid.

ลักพา lág/phaa/ V (a man) to carry off, elope
with (a woman).

พา ๒ in เกี้ยวพาราสี kîawphaa/raasĭi/ V elab.
colloq. to court, woo; to make love to.

พากภูมิ phâagphuum/ V 1. to be proud. 2. to be
dignified, grand, majestic. →Also spelled
ภาคภูมิ, q.v.

พากเพียร phâagphian/ V to persevere.

พากย์ phâag/ V 1. to narrate. 2. to speak the part

of an actor; this is done with foreign films and
silent films.

พาณิชย์,พาณิชย- phaaníd/, phaaníd/chaɔ N commerce. การ-- commerce, trade.

กระทรวงพาณิชย์ krasuaŋ/phaaníd/ N Ministry
of Commerce.

พาณิชยการ phaaníd/chakaan/ N commerce.

พาด phâad/ V to lean against, lean on, place upon.

ข่าวพาดหัว khàaw/phâadhŭa/ headline news.

พาดพิง(ถึง) phâadphiŋ/(thŷŋɔ) V to concern,
be related to, touch upon, have a bearing on;
to implicate.

พาดหัวข่าว phâad/hŭakhàaw/ to give the headline
news.

พาทย์. See entries below.

ปี่พาทย์ (วง) pìiphâad/ (woŋ/) N Thai orchestra.

พิณพาทย์ (วง) phinphâad/ (woŋ/) N Thai orchestra.

พาน ๑ (ใบ) phaan/ (baj/) N tray with pedestal.

พานหมาก (ใบ) phaanmàag/ (baj/) N betel tray.

พาน ๒. See entries below.

แผ้วพาน phêwphaan/ V to bother, disturb, give
trouble.

พบพาน phóbphaan/ V to meet, see, encounter.

พ่าน in เพ่นพ่าน phênphàan/ V to rove, ramble.

พาบ in นอนพังพาบ nɔɔn/phaŋphâab/ to lie face
down, lie prone.

พาย (อัน,ด้าม) phaaj/ (?an/, dâam/) N 1. paddle,
V 2. to paddle.

พายเรือ phaajrya/ V to paddle (a boat).

ไม่เป็นโล้เป็นพาย mâjpenlóo/penphaaj/ idiom.
to make no sense, be incoherent, not well organized.

ไม้พาย (อัน) májphaaj/ (?an/) N 1. paddle.
2. big wooden spatula.

เรือพาย (ลำ) ryaphaaj/ (lam/) N rowboat.

พ่าย,--แพ้ phâaj/, phâajphée/ V to be defeated, to
lose.

พายัพ phaajáb/ lit.,eleg. northwest. →Syn. ตะวัน
ตกเฉียงเหนือ com. →The literary and the
common terms for the eight chief points of the
compass are listed under ทิศ.

ภาคพายัพ phâag/phaajáb/ N the northwest, the
northwestern part (of Thailand).

พายุ phaajú?/ N storm.

พายุฝน phaajú?/fǒn/ N rainstorm.

พายุฟ้าคะนอง phaajú?-fáa/khanɔɔŋ/ N thunderstorm.

พายุหมุน phaajú?/mǔn/ N cyclone.

พายุหิมะ phaajú?/himá?/ N snowstorm.

ลมพายุ lom/phaajú?/ N windstorm.

พารา in ยางพารา jaaŋ/phaaraa/ N 1. the Para
rubber tree. 2. the rubber obtained from such
a tree.

พาล phaan/ V 1. to be mischievous, bad, ignorant,
troublesome; to stir up trouble. 2. to be bul-
lying, bossy, take one's frustrations out on
someone else. คน-- troublemaker, mischief-
maker; fault-finder.

พาหนะ (คัน,อย่าง,ชนิด) phaahàná?/ (khan/, jàaŋ/,
chaníd/) N vehicle, means of transportation.

ยานพาหนะ (คัน,อย่าง,ชนิด) jaan/phaahàná?/
(khan/, jàaŋ/,chaníd/) N vehicle.

สัตว์พาหนะ (ตัว) sàd/phaahàná?/ (tua/) N
beast of burden.

พ่ำ. See พึมพ่ำ.

พำนัก phamnág/ V lit. eleg. to stay, reside.
[conv. f. พัก]

ที่พำนัก (แห่ง) thîi/phamnág/ (hèŋ/) N 1. residence, dwelling place. 2. place of stay.

พิกล phíkon/* V to be strange, abnormal, peculiar.

พิกลพิการ phíkon/phíkaan/* V elab. colloq.
1. to be abnormal, deformed. 2. to be strange,
odd.

พิกัด phíkàd/ V 1. lit. to limit, fix. N 2. limit.
3. tax, duty.

o ของต้องพิกัด khɔ̌ɔŋ/tɔ̂ŋphíkàd/ lit. taxable
or dutiable articles.

พิการ phíkaan/ V to be disabled, physically handicapped; to have (permanent) physical defects.
คน-- handicapped disabled person, person who
has a physical defect (e.g., is blind, crippled,
etc.)

พิกลพิการ phíkon/phíkaan/* V elab. colloq.
1. to be abnormal, deformed. 2. to be strange,
odd.

พิเคราะห์ phíkhrɔ́?/ V eleg. to deliberate, consider carefully.

พินิจพิเคราะห์ phíníd/phíkhrɔ́?/ V elab. eleg.
to deliberate, consider carefully, examine, look
critically.

พิฆาต phíkhâad/ V lit., eleg. to destroy, ruin, kill.

เรือพิฆาต (ลำ) rya/phíkhâad/ (lam/) N destroyer.

พิง phiŋ/ V to lean against.

พาดพิง(ถึง) phâadphiŋ/(thǔŋ⊂) V to concern,
be related to, touch upon, have a bearing on;
to implicate.

พิจารณา phícaaranaa/ V 1. to consider, deliberate.
2. to take into consideration, examine, look
closely and carefully. การ-- consideration,
deliberation, careful examination.

พิจารณาเสนอ phícaaranaa/sanǝ̌ǝ/ to consider
recommending, consider proposing.

พิจารณาเห็นว่า phícaaranaa/hěnwâa/ to realize
that, think that.

พินิจพิจารณา phíníd/phícaaranaa/ V to study and
examine carefully, consider carefully.

พิชคณิต phíd/chakhaníd/ N algebra. →See คณิต.

พิชิต phíchíd/ V lit. to conquer, subdue, defeat.

พิณ (หลัง) phin/ (lǎŋ/) N harp.

พิณพาทย์ (วง) phinphâad/ (woŋ/) N Thai orchestra.

พิถีพิถัน phíthǐi/phíthǎn/ V to be punctilious, meticulous.

พิทักษ์ phíthág/ V to protect, guard, keep, take care of.

ผู้พิทักษ์สันติราษฎร์ (คน,นาย) phûuphíthág/sǎntirâad/
(khon/,naaj/) N eleg. policeman.

พิทักษ์รักษา phíthág/rágsǎa/ V elab. to protect,
guard, take care of.

พิธี (พิธี) phíthii/ (phíthii/) N ceremony.

งานพิธี ŋaanphíthii/ N ceremony.

ประกอบพิธี prakɔ̀ɔb/phíthii/ V eleg. to conduct
a ceremony, officiate at a ceremony.

พระราชพิธี phrárâad/chaphíthii/ N royal ceremony, state ceremony.

พิธีกรรม phíthii/kam/ N rite, worship, sacrificial
rite.

พิธีการ (อย่าง) phíthii/kaan/ (jàaŋ/) N ceremony;
formal procedure, formality, protocol.

พิธีการเฉลิมฉลอง phíthii/kaan/-chalǝ̌ǝm/chalɔ̌ɔŋ/
N commemoration ceremony.

พิธีฌาปนกิจ phíthii/chaa/panakìd/ N lit.,eleg.
cremation rite.

พิธีรีตอง phíthii′riitɔɔŋ′ N elab. colloq. customary ceremony, traditional ceremony, formality.

พิธีสมรส phíthii′sŏmród′ N eleg. wedding ceremony.

พิโร่ phîthôo′|* E Well! (exclamative expressing surprise and relief). →Comp. พุทโธ่.

พินัยกรรม (ฉบับ) phínajkam′ (chabàb′) N law a will.

พินาศ phínâad′ V eleg. to be destroyed, ruined, demolished. →Syn. See วอดวาย com.

พินิจ phíníd′ to consider attentively, examine closely and carefully.

ดุลพินิจ dun′phíníd′, dunlaphíníd′ N 1. careful, impartial, prudent consideration. 2. equitable judgment.

พินิจพิเคราะห์ phíníd′phíkhrɔ́?′ V elab. eleg. to deliberate, consider carefully, examine, look critically.

พินิจพิจารณา phíníd′phícaaranaa′ V to study and examine carefully, consider carefully.

พินิจพิศดู phíníd′-phíd′duu′, phíníd′phísaduu′ V to consider, look at carefully.

พิบัติ, ภัย-- phíbàd′, phaj′phíbàd′ N eleg. disaster, calamity. →Syn. วิบัติ.

พิพัฒนาการ phíphád′thanaa′kaan′ N eleg. development, progress, advancement, evolution.

พิพากษา phíphâagsǎa′ V to judge. ผู้-- judge. คำ-- (อย่าง) verdict, decision.

พิพาท phíphâad′ V eleg. to quarrel, dispute. กรณีพิพาท (เรื่อง, กรณี) karanii′phíphâad′, kɔ- (rɣaŋ′, karanii′) N dispute, controversy.

พิพิธภัณฑ์ (แห่ง) phíphíd′thaphan′ (hὲŋ′) N museum. พิพิธภัณฑสถาน (แห่ง) phíphíd′thaphan′sathǎan′ (hὲŋ′) N museum. ราชพิพิธภัณฑ์ râad′chaphíphíd′thaphan′ pN The Royal Museum (in Bangkok).

พิภพ phíphób′ N eleg., lit. world, earth. ดาวพระพิภพ, ดาวพิภพ (ดวง) daaw′phráphíphób′, daawphíphób′ (duaŋ′) N Earth. →Also ดาว โลก. →The names of the major planets are listed under ดาว. บรรณพิภพ ban′naphíphób′ N eleg. the literary world, the world of literature.

พิมพ์ phim′ V to print, imprint. การ-- printing; publishing. ผู้-- publisher; printer. ช่าง-- printer.

ตีพิมพ์ tii′phim′ V to print, type, publish.

o ลงตีพิมพ์ loŋtii′phim′ V to publish.

แบบพิมพ์ (แบบ, อัน, ใบ) bὲὲbphim′ (bὲὲb′, ?an′, baj′) N 1. blank form, printed form with blank spaces to be filled in. 2. mold.

พิมพ์(...)จำหน่าย phim′(...)camnàaj′ V to publish (for sale). ผู้-- publisher.

พิมพ์ดีด phimdìid′ V 1. to type, to typewrite. N 2. typing. 3. short for เครื่อง-- typewriter.

o พนักงานพิมพ์ดีด (คน) phanágŋaan′phimdìid′ (khon′) N typist.

o พิมพ์ดีดกระเป๋าหิ้ว phimdìid′krapǎwhîw′ N portable typewriter.

พิมพ์โรเนียว phim′rooniaw′ V to duplicate by means of a Roneo machine (similar to mimeographing).

พิมพ์หนังสือ phim′naŋsɣy′ V 1. to print. 2. to type. เครื่อง-- printing press; any printing device.

เรียงพิมพ์ riaŋphim′ V to set type.

โรงพิมพ์ (โรง) rooŋphim′ (rooŋ′) N printery, press, publishing house.

หนังสือพิมพ์ (ฉบับ) naŋsɣyphim′ (chabàb′) N newspaper. การ-- journalism.

พิมเสน phimsěen′ N chem., bot. borneol. มะม่วงพิมเสน mamûaŋ′phimsěen′ N a variety of mango.

พิราบ in นกพิราบ (ตัว) nógphírâab′ (tua′) N pigeon (Columbidae).

พิรุธ phírúd′ N 1. suspiciuos act; telltale trace (of something wrong). V 2. to act suspiciously, be strange, suspicious. มีพิรุธ miiphírúd′ V to act suspiciously, be suspicious (in action, appearance).

พิโรธ phírôod′ V lit. to be angry, provoked.

พิลึก (1) phílɣ́g′; (2) phílɣ́g′*| V 1. to be odd, strange, queer. E 2. How odd! (expressing reproach, dissatisfaction with another's words or actions).

พิศ phíd′ V eleg. to look at carefully. งามพิศ ŋaamphíd′ V to appear increasingly beautiful upon contemplation, to be profoundly beautiful (used mostly of women). →Dist. งามผาด.

พิศดู phísaduu′, phíd′duu′ V to look at carefully.

o พินิจพิศดู phíníd′-phíd′duu′ V to consider; to regard, look at carefully.

พิศวง phísawǒŋ′ V to be surprised, amazed, puzzled, perplexed; to wonder. ความ-- puzzlement, amazement.

น่าพิศวง nâa′phísawǒŋ′ V to be amazing, astonishing, perplexing. อย่าง-- amazingly, astonishingly, surprisingly.

พิศวงงงงวย phísawǒŋ′ŋoŋŋuaj′ V to be dumfounded, bewildered, perplexed. ความ-- puzzlement, perplexity, bewilderment.

พิศวาส phísawàad′ V 1. to love, to like. N 2. love, affection.

พิเศษ phísèed′ V to be special, extra.

เป็นพิเศษ penphísèed′ 1. to be special, particular. 2. especially.

ลักษณะพิเศษ lág′sanà?′/phísèed′ special feature or character, distinctive feature.

สิทธิพิเศษ sìdthí?′/phísèed′ special privilege.

พิษ phíd′ N 1. poison, venom. 2. bad effect, injury. 3. power, effect.

ทำพิษ thamphíd′ V colloq. 1. to cause trouble. 2. to produce a bad result.

เป็นพิษ penphíd′ V 1. to be poisonous, toxic. 2. to have bad effects.

พิษรัก phídrág′ the poisoning effect of love (as when unrequited or tainted with jealousy).

พิษสง phídsǒŋ′ N power to harm, capacity to do harm, harmful effect.

มีพิษ miiphíd′ V to be poisonous (as a snake).

ยาพิษ (ชนิด) jaaphíd′ (chaníd′) N poison.

o วางยาพิษ waaŋ′jaaphíd′ V to poison.

โรคพิษสุรา rôog′-phíd′suraa′ N alcoholism.

ไอพิษ ʔajphíd′ N poison gas.

พิษณุโลก phísanúlôog′ pN Phitsanulok, a township in N Thailand.

พิสดาร phísadaan′ V 1. to be strange, peculiar, queer, unusual, extraordinary. 2. to be extensive, detailed. ความ-- strangeness, peculiarity.

ข้อความพิสดาร khɔɔkhwaam′/phísadaan′ detailed, extensive, complete account.

โดยพิสดาร dooj′/phísadaan′ extensively, in detail.

วิจิตรพิสดาร wícìd′/phísadaan′ V to be magnificent, gorgeous, elaborately beautiful.

พิสมัย phísamǎj′ V lit. to love, to like.

พิสูจน์ phísùud′ V to prove.

ข้อพิสูจน์ (ข้อ) khɔɔ′phísùud′ (khɔɔ′) N proof.

เครื่องพิสูจน์ khrŷaŋ′phísùud′ N proof, material proof.

พี. phii′ the English letter "P." [f. Eng.]

พี phii′ V to be fat.

พวงพี phuaŋphii′ V to be fat.

พี่ (คน) phîi′ (khon′) N com. 1. older sibling, i.e. older brother or sister. P 2. I, me (older sibling to yg. sibling, husband to wife, older person to slightly younger person); you, he, him, she, her (sp. to or about one's older sibling, one's husband, a slightly older person). T 3. title used with the first name of an older sibling. →Comp. น้อง "younger sibling." →See 2. คุณพี่ below.

คุณพี่ khunphîi′ P eleg. you (younger sibling to older sibling, wife to husband).

พี่แก phîikɛɛ′ colloq. he, that fellow; she, that lady.

พี่เขย phîikhǒəj′ N brother-in-law who is the husband of one's older sister.

พี่ชาย phîichaaj′ N 1. older brother. 2. colloq. (older) buddy.

พี่น้อง phîinɔɔŋ′ N brothers; sisters; brother and sister, brothers and sisters; cousins.

o ญาติพี่น้อง jâad′phîinɔɔŋ′ N relatives.

o พี่น้องร่วมชาติ phîinɔɔŋ′rûamchâad′ (one's) fellow citizens.

พี่ผัว phîi′phǔa′ N brother- or sister-in-law (of a woman in ref. to her husband's older brother or sister): "husband's elder sibling."

พี่เมีย phîi′mia′ N brother- or sister-in-law (of a man in ref. to his wife's older brother or sister): "wife's elder sibling."

พี่เลี้ยง phîilíaŋ′ N 1. nursemaid. 2. sport one who manages, trains or tends an athlete.

พี่สะใภ้ phîisapháj′ N sister-in-law who is the wife of one's older brother.

พี่สาว phîisǎaw′ N older sister.

พี่ใหญ่ phîijàj′ N eldest sibling.

ลูกพี่ (คน) lûugphîi′ (khon′) N cousin who is the child of an elder uncle or aunt; the child of an older sibling.

ลูกพี่ลูกน้อง (คน) lûugphîi′lûugnɔ́ɔŋ′ (khon′) N cousin.

พึง phyŋ′ AA should, ought. →Dist. ควร 2.

  o พึงตีเหล็กเมื่อร้อน phyŋ′-tiilèg′mɯ̂arɔ́ɔn′↓ One should forge while the iron is hot.

พึงประสงค์ phyŋ′prasǒŋ′ eleg. to be desirable.

พึงปรารถนา phyŋpràad′thanǎa′ eleg. to be desirable.

พึงพอใจ phyŋphɔɔcaj′ 1. to be satisfied, pleased, contented. 2. to satisfy, be satisfactory. ความ-- satisfaction.

พึงสังเกต phyŋ′sǎŋkèed′ 1. to be noteworthy. 2. (it) should be noticed (that); note (that).

พึ่ง ๑ phŷŋ′ V to depend on (for help).

พึ่งพา phŷŋphaa′ V to depend on (for help).

  o พึ่งพาอาศัย phŷŋphaa′′aasǎj′ elab. colloq. to depend on for a living, for help.

พึ่ง ๒ phŷŋ′ AA 1. just, just now. 2. (not) yet, (not) just now. →Syn. 1. เพิ่ง. 2. เพิ่ง, เพ่อ.

พึมพำ phympham′ V to murmur, mumble, mutter.

บ่นพึมพำ bòn′phympham′ V to grumble, mutter, murmur.

พืช (อย่าง,ชนิด) phŷyd′ (jàaŋ′, chaníd′) N plants, vegetation.

น้ำมันพืช námman′phŷyd′ N vegetable oil.

พืชปลูก phŷydplùug′ N cultivated plant.

พืชผล (อย่าง,ชนิด) phŷydphǒn′ (jàaŋ′, chaníd′) N 1. a plant and its products. 2. agricultural products. 3. crops.

พืชพันธุ์ phŷydphan′ N plant, vegetation.

พืชเมืองร้อน phŷyd′mɯaŋrɔ́ɔn′ N tropical plants.

พืชยืนต้น phŷyd′jyyntôn′ N perennial plant.

พืชไร่ phŷyd′râj′ N farm crops.

พืชล้มลุก (ต้น,ชนิด) phŷyd′lómlúg′ (tôn′, chaníd′) N any plant whose life cycle is short, as an annual or a biennial.

เมล็ดพืช (เมล็ด) maléd′phŷyd′ (maléd′) N seed.

พืด phŷyd′ N 1. line, row; range (of mountains). C 2. clf. for a range of mountains. →Syn. 1.

ทิว, เทือก.

เป็นพืด penphŷyd′ 1. to be webbed (as a duck's feet). 2. (side by side) in a row.

พืดเขา (พืด) phŷydkhǎw′ (phŷyd′) N mountain range, chain.

พื้น phýyn′ N 1. floor. 2. surface (of earth, water, etc.).

แบบพื้น ๆ bɛ̀ɛb′phýynphýyn′ simple, everyday style.

เป็นพื้น penphýyn′ 1. as a foundation, basis, background. 2. on the average, generally, basically.

พื้นความรู้ phýyn′khwaamrúu′ N background of knowledge, fundamental knowledge (possessed by someone).

พื้นดิน phýyndin′ N the ground, earth, earth-surface.

พื้นที่ phýynthîi′ N terrain, surface of the earth.

พื้นที่ราบ (แห่ง) phýynthîi′râab′ (hὲŋ′) N geog. plain.

พื้นเพ phýynphee′ N background of a person.

พื้นเมือง phýynmɯaŋ′ N (as n. mod.) native, local. See examples below. คน-- a native.

  o ชาวพื้นเมือง (คน) chaawphýynmɯaŋ′ (khon′) N native, native inhabitant.

  o ภาษาพื้นเมือง phaasǎa′phýynmɯaŋ′ N dialect, regional speech.

พื้นรองเท้า phýyn′rɔɔŋtháaw′ N shoe sole.

พื้นราบ (อัน,แห่ง) phýynrâab′ (′an′,hὲŋ′) N 1. geom. plane. 2. geog. plain.

พุ . See entries below.

  น้ำพุ (แห่ง) námphú?′ (hὲŋ′) N fountain, spring, water spout.

เป็นพุพอง penphú?phɔɔŋ′ to be covered with clusters of festering sores (as infected mosquito bites).

พุก in หนูพุก (ตัว) nǔuphúg′ (tua′) N field rat.

พุง phuŋ′ N colloq. belly, stomach. →Syn. ท้อง.

ลงพุง loŋphuŋ′ V colloq. to have a big belly, be paunchy, potbellied.

พุ่ง phûŋ′ V 1. to thrust, throw, hurl. 2. to fly, move at high speed.

ผีพุ่งไต้ (ดวง) phǐiphûŋtâaj′ (duaŋ′) N shooting star.

พวยพุ่ง phuajphûŋ′ V 1. (liquid) to stream out, pour out, spout forth. 2. (smoke, dust) to puff up, rise up. 3. to throw up beams (of light).

พุ่งแหลน phûŋlɛ̌ɛn′ V 1. to throw, hurl a javelin. N 2. javelin throwing.

รบพุ่ง róbphûŋ′ V to fight, wage war, engage in a battle. การ-- fighting, battle, war.

พุทธ phúd′, phúd/thaɔ N Buddha. →Chiefly in cpds.

ถือพุทธ thɯ̌ɯphúd′ V colloq. to profess Buddhism.

พระพุทธ phráphúd′ N the Lord Buddha.

พระพุทธเจ้า (พระองค์) phráphúd/thacâaw′ (phráɔ ʔoŋ′) N the Lord Buddha.

พระพุทธรูป (องค์) phráphúd/tharûub′ (ʔoŋ′) N image of Buddha.

พระพุทธศาสนา phráphúd/thasàadsanǎa′ -sàasaɔ nǎa′ N Buddhism.

พุทธกาล phúd/thakaan′ N 1. the time of the Buddha. 2. the Buddhist era.

พุทธศักราช phúd/thasàgkaràad′ N Buddhist era. →Abbreviated พ.ศ. →Also พุทธศก phúd/ɔ thasòŋ′ lit.

พุทธศาสนา phúd/thasàadsanǎa′ -sàasanǎa′ N Buddhism, Buddhist religion. พระ-- idem.

ศาสนาพุทธ sàadsanǎa/phúd′, sàasanǎa- N Buddhism.

พุทโธ่ phûthôo′↓*, phúdthôo′↓* E Oh my! Gosh! My goodness! (exclamative expressing surprise and discouragement). →Also written พุโธ่, พุ่โท้. →Comp. พิโธ่.

พุทโธ่เอ๋ย phûthôo′!ʔə̌əj′* E What a pity! Too bad! It's a shame. (e.g. on learning about mishap).

พุทรา (ลูก) phúdsaa′ (lûug′) N jujube. ต้น--(ต้น) the jujube tree.

พุ่โท้. Variant spelling of พุทโธ่.

พุธ. See entries below.

ดาวพระพุธ daaw′phráphúd′ N Mercury (the planet). →The names of the major planets are listed under ดาว.

วันพุธ wanphúd′ N Wednesday. →Also พุธ. →The days of the week are listed under วัน.

พุโธ่. Variant spelling of พุทโธ่.

พุ่ม ๑ phûm′ N 1. bush. 2. grove of trees. C 3. clf. for 1. and 2.

เป็นพุ่ม penphûm′ to be bushy.

พุ่มไม้ (พุ่ม) phûmmáaj′ (phûm′) N 1. bush. 2. grove of trees.

พุ่ม ๒ in พุ่มหม้าย, พุ่มม่าย phûmmâaj′ N widowhood.

ตกพุ่มม่าย tòg′phûmmâaj′ V to become widowed.

พุ้ย phúj′ V 1. to paddle. 2. to make a paddling motion with the hands (as when swimming).

พุ้ยข้าวด้วยตะเกียบ phúj′khâaw′-dûajtakìab′ to scoop rice into one's mouth with chopsticks (from a bowl held up to the mouth).

พุ้ยน้ำ phúj′náam′ V to paddle (in water).

พู. Variant spelling of ผู้ in ผู้ชาย, ผู้หญิง, used to render a pronunciation phuuɔ.

พู่ (พู่, พวง) phûu′ (phûu′, phuaŋ′) N tassel, tuft.

พู่กัน (อัน) phûukan′ (ʔan′) N artist's brush.

พูด phûud′ V com. to speak, talk, say. ผู้-- speaker, spokesman. คำ-- (see below). →Dist. บอก "to tell." →Syn. กล่าว eleg.

คำพูด (คำ) khamphûud′ (kham′) N spoken word, utterance.

o เครื่องหมายคำพูด khrɯ̂aŋmǎaj′khamphûud′ quotation marks.

o ภาษาคำพูด phaasǎa′khamphûud′ 1. the spoken language. 2. a colloquialism.

o รักษาคำพูด rágsǎa′khamphûud′ to keep one's word.

ช่างพูด châaŋphûud′ V to be talkative, full of talk.

พูดกรอกหู(ว่า) phûud′-krɔ̀ɔghǔu′(wâaɔ) 1. to talk into a person's ear. 2. to drop a hint or make a complaint which is intended for the ears of a particular person present.

พูดกระทบถึง phûud′-krathób′thɯ̌ŋɔ to speak insinuatingly about, insinuate (something) about (someone).

พูดกันรู้เรื่อง phûud′kanrúuryaŋ′ to be able to communicate or converse together with mutual understanding or comprehension.

พูดคล่อง phûudkhlɔ̂ŋ′ to speak fluently, smoothly, in a facile manner.

พูดคำตอบคำ phûudkham′tɔ̀ɔbkham′ elab. colloq. to say scarcely anything and only when asked, to be taciturn.

พูดง่าย ๆ phûudŋâajŋâaj′ plainly speaking; briefly speaking, in short.

พูดจนน้ำลายแตกฟอง phûud′connámlaaj′tɛ̀ɛgfɔɔŋ′

idiom., colloq. to spout forth, talk volubly.

พูดจ้อ phûudcɔ̂ɔ′ to talk continually, steadily, freely.

พูดจา phûudcaa′ V colloq. to speak, talk.

o พูดจาฉะฉาน phûudcaa′chàʔchǎan′ to speak distinctly.

o พูดจาหยาบโลน phûudcaa′jàabloon′ to use vulgar or obscene language (often with humorous intent).

พูดซุบซิบ phûud′súbsíb′ to whisper, to gossip; to talk in a low, whispering voice.

พูดโดยทั่วไป phûud′doojthûapaj′ generally speaking.

พูดถึง phûud′thɣ̌ŋ⊃ to talk about.

พูดเท็จ phûudthéd′ V eleg. 1. to tell a lie; to lie. 2. to be untrue, false. →Also เท็จพูด. →Syn. 1. See โกหก com.

พูดโทรศัพท์ phûud′thoorasàb′ to talk on the telephone.

พูดน้ำไหลไฟดับ phûud′námlǎj′fajdàb′ V colloq. to chatter away, talk a blue streak, talk rapidly and profusely.

พูดปรักปรำ phûud′pràgpram′ to accuse, blame (verbally).

พูดเป็น phûudpen′ to be able to speak, know how to talk.

พูดเป็นต่อยหอย phûud′-pentɔ̀j′hɔ̌j′ 1. colloq. to chatter, jabber. 2. to be very talkative.

พูดเป็นน้ำ phûud′pennáam′ colloq. to talk a blue streak.

พูด...เป็นน้ำ phûud′...pennáam′ colloq., to speak (e.g. English) fluently.

พูดเป็นวรรคเป็นเวร phûud′-penwág′penween′ colloq. to talk on and on, at great length.

พูดเปรย ๆ phûud′prəəjprəəj′ to speak without addressing anyone in particular (often with sarcastic intent).

พูดแปร่ง phûudprèŋ′ to speak with an accent.

พูดพล่อย ๆ phûud′phlɔ̂jphlɔ̂j′ to speak without reflection, thoughtlessly.

พูดพลางหัวเราะพลาง phûud′phlaaŋ′-hǔarɔ́ʔ/⊃ phlaaŋ′ to talk while laughing, talk and laugh at the same time.

พูดเพ้อ phûudphə́ə′ to talk deliriously, incoher-

ently, to ramble.

พูดไม่จริง phûud′mâjciŋ′ com. to tell an untruth. →Syn. See โกหก com.

พูดไม่ออก phûud′mâjʔɔ̀ɔg′ to be struck dumb, speechless.

พูดล้อ phûudlɔ́ɔ′ to jest, kid, tease.

พูดลอย ๆ phûud′lɔɔjlɔɔj′ to say something without addressing anybody in particular.

พูดเล่น phûudlên′ to speak playfully, to say in fun, to jest.

พูดว่า phûud′wâa⊃ to say that.

พูดเส่ phûudsèe′ to talk evasively, avoid a subject.

พูดเลี้ยดลี้ phûud′sìadsîi′ to speak sarcastically.

พูดหวน ๆ phûud′hǔanhǔan′ to speak curtly.

พูดหวานล้อม phûud′wǎanlɔ́ɔm′ to cajole someone into doing or accepting something.

พูดอย่างคร่าว ๆ phûud′jàaŋkhrâawkhrâaw′ roughly speaking.

พูดอ้อมค้อม phûud′ʔɔ̂ɔmkhɔ́ɔm′ to speak evasively, to beat about the bush.

ภาษาพูด phaasǎaphûud′ N 1. the spoken language. 2. a colloquialism.

หัดพูด hàdphûud′ V to learn to speak.

พูน phuun′ V 1. (the contents) to fill (the container) until heaping full. 2. to pile up, heap up (e.g. dirt). →Sometimes spelled พูล.

พอกพูน phɔ̂ɔgphuun′ V to add up, accumulate, pile up, increase gradually.

เพิ่มพูน phə̂əmphuun′ V to increase, accrue, grow.

พูม in พากพูม phâagphuum′ V 1. to be proud. 2. to be dignified, grand, majestic. →Also spelled ภาคภูมิ, q.v.

พูล. See พูน.

เพ. See entries below.

ทั้งเพ tháŋphee′ colloq. all (of it), the whole thing, in (its) entirety, in toto. →Cf. ทั้งปวง.

พื้นเพ phɣ́ynphee′ N the general background of a person.

เพคะ pheekhá′ Pt eleg. def. w. sp. particle used at the end of statements addressed to royalty. Paired with กระหม่อม m. sp.

เพ่ง phêŋ′* V to stare, gaze, watch closely, direct one's attention to.

เพ่งดู phêŋduu′ V to stare at, gaze at.

เพ่งเล็ง phêŋleŋ′ V 1. to take aim. 2. to focus one's mind or attention on.

เพชฌฆาต (คน) phédchakhâad′ (khon′) N executioner.

เพชร,เพ็ชร,เพ็ชร์ (เม็ด) phéd′ (méd′) N diamond. เครื่อง-- jewelry. →The spelling เพชร is the one given in the 1950 ed. of the official monolingual Thai dictionary. The other spellings are found in older books.

　ช่างเพชร (คน) châaŋphéd′ (khon′) N jeweler.

　เพชรพลอย (เม็ด) phédphlɔɔj′ (méd′) N jewels, precious stones (in general). เครื่อง-- jewelry.

　แหวนเพชร (วง) wɛ̌ɛnphéd′ (woŋ′) N diamond ring.

เพชรบุรี phéd′burii′* pN Phetburi, (Petburi, Pechaburi) a township in S Thailand. Formerly pronounced phéd′chaburii′.

เพชรบูรณ์ phéd′chabuun′* pN Phetchabun, a township N Thailand.

เพ็ญ phen′ N (the) full (moon). →In compounds only.
　จันทร์เพ็ญ can′phen′ N the full moon. →Also เพ็ญจันทร์.
　วันเพ็ญ wanphen′ N day of the full moon.
　o คืนวันเพ็ญ khyyn′wanphen′ N night of the full moon.
　o พระจันทร์วันเพ็ญ phrácan′-wanphen′ N the full moon.

เพดาน pheedaan′ N ceiling.
　เพดานปาก pheedaan′pàag′ N palate, roof of the mouth.

เพนนิซิลิน phennisilin′* N penicillin. [f. Eng.]

เพ่นพ่าน phênphâan′* V to rove, ramble.

เพย in คำพังเพย (บท) kham′phaŋphəəj′ (bòd′) N saying.

เพรา in พริ้มเพรา phrímphraw′ V to be beautiful, gay and beautiful.

เพราะ ๑ phrɔ́ʔ′ V to be melodious, pleasing to the ear, beautiful (of sounds).
　เพราะพริ้ง phrɔ́ʔ′phríŋ′ idem.

เพราะ ๒ phrɔ́ʔ′ Cj 1. because. Pp 2. because of.
　o แต่เขาไม่ทำเช่นนั้น เพราะเขามิได้มาคนเดียว tɛ̀ɛkháwmâjtham′chênnán′→ phrɔ́kháwmídâjᴐ maa′khondiaw′↓ but he didn't do that, because

he didn't come alone.
　o รักเพราะสวย rág′phrɔ́sǔaj′ (he) loves (her) because (she) is beautiful.
　o ไก่งามเพราะขน คนงามเพราะแต่ง kàjŋaam′ᴐ phrɔ́khŏn′→ khonŋaam′phrɔ́tɛ̀ŋ′↓ Fowl are handsome because of their plumage; people are elegant because (of their) raiment. (A rhymed saying.)

เพราะฉะนั้น phrɔ́chanán′ Cj therefore.

เพราะว่า phrɔ́wâa′ Cj because.

เพราะเหตุไร phrɔ́hèed′raj′ why, for what reason.

เพราะเหตุว่า phrɔ́hèed′wâa′ Cj because, for the reason that.

เพริด See entries below.
　ตะลึงพรึงเพริด talyŋ′phryŋphrəəd′ elab. colloq. to be stupefied, stunned (with surprise, fright).
　พลัดเพริด phládphrəəd′ V to stray, go astray, be parted and lost from (the group, the herd, etc.).

เพรียง in พร้อมเพรียง phrɔ́ɔmphriaŋ′ V 1. to be complete, ready, fully prepared. 2. to be unanimous, harmonious, in harmony, in unison. sV 3. in unison, all at the same time.

เพรียบ in เพรียบพร้อม phrîabphrɔ́ɔm′ V eleg. to be fully provided (with), fully equipped, furnished, loaded.

เพรียว phriaw′ V to be slender, slim, streamlined.
　เพรียวลม phriawlom′ V to be streamlined, slender, slim.

เพรื่อ in พร่ำเพรื่อ phrâmphrŷa′ sV 1. often, frequently, again and again. 2. excessively, luxuriously, extravagantly.

เพล pheen′ N sacer. the time between 11.00 A.M. and 12.00 noon.

เพลง (เพลง,บท) phleeŋ′ (phleeŋ′, bòd′) N song.
　ขับเพลง khàbphleeŋ′ V to sing a song.
　แต่งเพลง tèŋphleeŋ′ V to write a song. นัก-- song writer, composer.
　ทำนองเพลง thamnɔɔŋ′phleeŋ′ N melody, tune.
　เนื้อเพลง nýaphleeŋ′ N words, text of a song.
　บทเพลง (บท) bòdphleeŋ′ (bòd′) N song; the text of a song.
　เพลงขับ phleeŋkhàb′ N song (for singing).
　เพลงชาติ phleeŋchâad′ N national anthem.
　เพลงเต้นรำ phleeŋ′tênram′ N dance music.

เพลงมาร์ช phleeŋmáach′, -máad′ N march music. [มาร์ช f. Eng.]

เพลงวอลซ์ phleeŋwɔɔls′ N waltz music. [วอลซ์ f. Eng.]

เพลงสวด phleeŋsùad′ N hymn.

เพลงสวิง phleeŋ′sawiŋ′ N swing music. [สวิง f. Eng.]

เพลงสากล phleeŋ′sǎakon′ N occidental music (popular and classical).

ภาพยนต์เพลง (เรื่อง) phâabphajon′phleeŋ′ (rŷaŋ′) N eleg. musical motion picture.

ร้องเพลง rɔ́ɔŋphleeŋ′ V to sing.

สร้อยเพลง (สร้อย) sɔ̂j′phleeŋ′ (sɔ̂j′) N chorus, refrain.

หนังเพลง (เรื่อง) nǎŋphleeŋ′ (rŷaŋ′) N colloq. musical motion picture.

หีบเพลง (หลัง,เครื่อง,อัน) hìibphleeŋ′ N 1. piano (lǎŋ′). 2. organ (lǎŋ′). 3. accordion (short for หีบเพลงชัก) (khrŷaŋ′). 4. mouth organ, harmonica (short for หีบเพลงปาก) (ʔan′).

o หีบเพลงชัก (เครื่อง) hìibphleeŋ′chág′ (khrŷaŋ′) N accordion.

o หีบเพลงปาก (อัน) hìibphleeŋ′pàag′ (ʔan′) N mouth organ, harmonica.

เพลา ๑ pheelaa′ N lit. 1. time. C 2. time, occasion. →Syn. เวลา com.

เพลา ๒ (อัน) phlaw′ (ʔan′) N axle, shaft.

เพลาะ ๑ phlɔ́ʔ′ V to sew (the straight edges of two pieces of cloth) together.

เพลาะ ๒ in สนามเพลาะ (แห่ง) sanǎamphlɔ́ʔ′ (hɛ̀ŋ′) N trench.

เพลิง phləəŋ′ N eleg. fire, conflagration. →Syn. ไฟ com.

คบเพลิง (ดวง) khóbphləəŋ′ (duaŋ′) N eleg. torch.

เชื้อเพลิง chýaphləəŋ′ N tech. fuel, combustible substance.

o น้ำมันเชื้อเพลิง námman′chýaphləəŋ′ N fuel oil.

ดอกไม้เพลิง (ดอก) dɔ̀ɔgmáajphləəŋ′ (dɔ̀ɔg′) N eleg. fireworks.

ดับเพลิง dàbphləəŋ′ V eleg. to put out a fire. คน-- fireman. →Syn. ดับไฟ com.

o รถดับเพลิง (คัน) ród′dàbphləəŋ′ (khan′) N fire engine.

เปลวเพลิง pleewphləəŋ′ N eleg. flame.

วางเพลิง waaŋphləəŋ′ V eleg. to commit arson.

หมอกเพลิง mɔ̀ɔgphləəŋ′ N nebula.

เพลิดเพลิน phləədphləən′ V to be engrossed, absorbed (in), enraptured (by). ความ-- pleasure, engrossment.

เพลิน phləən′ V 1. to be oblivious. 2. to be engrossed, absorbed (in something). →See also เพลิดเพลิน above.

o อ่านหนังสือเพลิน ʔàan′naŋsɣ̌y′-phləən′ to be engrossed in reading.

เพลีย phlia′ V to be tired out, worn out.

อ่อนเพลีย ʔɔ̀ɔnphlia′ V 1. to be weak, weakened. 2. to be fatigued, exhausted.

เพลี้ย (ตัว) phlía′ (tua′) N plant louse, aphid.

เพลี่ยง in เพลี่ยงพล้ำ phlîaŋphlám′ V to make a wrong move, a mistake.

เพศ (เพศ) phêed′ (phêed′) N,C 1. sex (i.e. distinction in sex). 2. gram. gender.

เพศชาย phêedchaaj′ N male sex; masculine gender.

เพศหญิง phêedjiŋ′ M female sex; feminine gender.

เพื่อนร่วมเพศ (คน) phŷanrûamphêed′ (khon′) N friends of the same sex.

เพอ phəə′ AA (not) yet, (not) as yet, (not) just now. →Syn. พึ่ง ๒,เพิ่ง.

เพ้อ phɔ́ɔ′ V 1. to be delirious, to rave in delirium. 2. to speak incoherently, be raving (as though in delirium).

เพ้อเจ้อ phɔ́ɔcə̂ɔ′ V to ramble, speak incoherently, without making much sense.

เพาะ phɔ́ʔ′ V 1. to plant (seeds). 2. to cultivate. 3. to germinate.

เพาะปลูก phɔ́ʔplùug′ V to cultivate (land; plants). การ-- cultivation.

เพิก ๑ in เพิกถอน phə̀əgthɔ̌ɔn′ V to revoke, annul, retract, withdraw, cancel.

เพิก ๒ in เพิกเฉย(ต่อ,กับ) phə̀əgchə̌əj′(tɔ̀ɔ, kàʔ) V to ignore, neglect, pay no attention (to).

เพิง (หลัง) phəəŋ′ (lǎŋ′) N lean-to.

เพิ่ง phə̂ŋ′* AA 1. just, just now. 2. (not) yet, (not) just now. →Syn. 1. พึ่ง ๒. 2. พึ่ง ๒,เพอ.

เพิ่งจะ phə̂ŋcàɔ AA just, just now.

เพิ่งย่างเข้า phə̂ŋjâaŋ'khâwɔ just about to enter, just entering.

เพิ่ม phə̂əm/ V 1. to increase, add on. sV 2. in addition. การ-- increase, increment.

เงินเพิ่มพิเศษ ŋənphə̂əm'phísèed/ N special auxiliary allowance for employees (in addition to the regular salary).

ได้...เพิ่มอีก dâjɔ...phə̂əm/-ʔìig/ to get (such and such) in addition.

เพิ่มขึ้น phə̂əm'khŷn/ to increase, be increased.

เพิ่มเติม phə̂əmtəəm/ V 1. to add, add to. 2. to be added, added on to. sV 3. in addition, additional.

o แก้ไขเพิ่มเติม kɛ̂ɛkhǎj'phə̂əmtəəm/ V to revise and enlarge.

o ได้...เพิ่มเติม dâjɔ...phə̂əmtəəm/ to gain more (such and such), get (such and such) in addition, get additional (such and such).

o เจาะบ่อน้ำเพิ่มเติมอีก cɔ̀ʔ'bɔ̀ɔnáam/-phə̂əmɔ təəm/-ʔìig/ to drill additional wells.

เพิ่มพูน phə̂əmphuun/ V to increase, accrue, grow.

เพียง phiaŋ/ only, only so much. →Note special combinations given below.

แต่เพียง tɛ̀ɛphiaŋ/ nothing but, only, just.

ถึงเพียงนี้ thŷŋphiaŋ'níi/ to this extent, up to this level.

เพียงแค่ phiaŋkhɛ̂ɛ/ only as far as, only to the point of.

เพียงใด phiaŋdaj/ how, how much, to what extent, to what degree.

เพียงแต่ phiaŋ'tɛ̀ɛɔ only.

o ไม่เพียงแต่ mâjphiaŋ'tɛ̀ɛɔ not only.

เพียงพอ,พอเพียง phiaŋphɔɔ/, phɔɔphiaŋ/ V to be enough, adequate, sufficient. การ-- adequacy, sufficiency.

เพียงไร phiaŋraj/ how, how much, to what extent, to what degree.

เพี้ยน phían/ V to differ slightly, be a little off, be slightly distorted.

ผิดเพี้ยน phìdphían/ V to differ, deviate, be different.

เพียบ ๑ phîab/ V 1. to be in serious or critical condition. 2. (a boat) to be loaded almost to the point of sinking.

เพียบแปร้ะ phîab'prɛ̂ʔ/ (a boat) to be extremely full, heavily loaded.

เพียบหนัก phîabnàg/ V to be in serious, critical condition, in bad shape.

อาการเพียบ ʔaakaan'phîab/ N 1. serious, critical condition. V 2. to be in serious, critical condition.

เพียบ ๒. See นั่งพับเพียบ under พับ.

เพียร phian/ V 1. to persevere, stick to it. 2. to be persevering, diligent, persistent, patient. ความ-- perseverance, persistence, patience.

พากเพียร phâagphian/ V 1. to persevere. 2. to be persevering, persistent, patient.

เพื่อ phŷa/ Cj 1. in order to; for (the purpose of). Pp 2. for (the sake of). →Dist. 1. เผื่อ.

เพื่อจะ phŷacaɔ in order to.

o เพื่อจะได้ (1) phŷacadâj; (2) phŷacadâajɔ, -dâaj/ 1. in order to, in order that, in order to get to (do something). 2. in order to get, obtain.

o เพื่อจะ...ให้ได้ phŷacaɔ...hâjdâaj/ in order to be able to.

เพื่อประโยชน์(ของ) phŷaprajòod/(khɔ̌ɔŋ/) for the benefit (of).

เพื่อเป็นเกียรติ phŷapenkìad/ as an honor, in honor (of).

เพื่อเป็นอนุสรณ์ phŷa/penʔànúsɔ̌ɔn/ 1. as a token (of), a reminder (of). 2. in memory (of), as a memorial (to).

เพื่อว่า phŷa/wâaɔ in order that, so that.

เพื่อเห็นแก่ phŷahěn/kɛ̀ɔ for the sake of.

เพื่อให้ phŷa/hâjɔ in order to, so that, for, (in order) to allow.

เพื่อน (คน) phŷan/ (khon/) N com. friend, companion. →Syn. มิตร eleg., เกลอ colloq.

กว่าเพื่อน kwàaphŷan/ colloq. the most (thus and so), the...-est (of those being compared). →Comp. ที่สุด.

o สวยกว่าเพื่อน sǔaj/kwàaphŷan/ to be the most beautiful one of all, more beautiful than any of the others.

ก่อนเพื่อน kɔ̀ɔnphŷan/ colloq. first, before

other things, before anyone else.

เป็นเพื่อน penphɯ̂an′ 1. to be friends. 2. as company, as a friend.

o อยู่เป็นเพื่อน jùu′penphɯ̂an′ to keep (someone) company.

เพื่อนเกลอ phɯ̂ankləə′ N close friend, pal.

เพื่อนเก่า phɯ̂ankàw′ N old friend, former friend.

เพื่อนคู่ใจ phɯ̂an′khûucaj′ N trusted friend, bosom friend.

เพื่อนคู่หู phɯ̂an′khûuhǔu′ N intimate friend, bosom companion.

เพื่อนชาย phɯ̂anchaaj′ N male friend.

เพื่อนเดินทาง phɯ̂an′dəənthaaŋ′ N travelling companion; fellow traveller.

เพื่อนบ้าน phɯ̂anbâan′ N neighbor.

o ประเทศเพื่อนบ้าน prathêed′phɯ̂anbâan′ neighboring country.

o เพื่อนบ้านใกล้เคียง phɯ̂anbâan′klâjkhiaŋ′ next door neighbor, immediate neighbors.

เพื่อนฝูง phɯ̂anfǔuŋ′ N colloq. friends (collectively).

เพื่อนมนุษย์ phɯ̂anmanúd′ N fellow man.

เพื่อนร่วมชั้น phɯ̂an′rûamchán′ N classmate.

เพื่อนร่วมชาติ phɯ̂an′rûamchâad′ N fellow countryman.

เพื่อนร่วมเพศ phɯ̂an′rûamphêed′ N friend of the same sex.

เพื่อนร่วมโรงเรียน phɯ̂an′rûamrooŋrian′ N schoolmate.

เพื่อนเล่น phɯ̂anlên′ N playmate.

เพื่อนสนิท phɯ̂ansanìd′ N intimate friend.

แพ (แพ,หลัง) phɛɛ′ N 1. raft (phɛɛ′). 2. houseboat (lǎŋ′).

แพยนตร์ (แพ,ลำ) phɛɛ′jon′ (phɛɛ′,lam′) N ferryboat.

เรือแพ rɯa′phɛɛ′ N colloq. watercraft, lit. boats and rafts, house-boats (coll. term).

ล่องแพ lɔ̂ŋphɛɛ′ V to transport, travel on a raft (downstream).

แพ้ phɛ́ɛ′ V 1. to be defeated; to give in, lose. 2. to be defeated by, beaten by.

พ่ายแพ้ phâajphɛ́ɛ′ V to be defeated, to lose.

แพ้ท้อง phɛ́ɛthɔ́ɔŋ′ V to have morning sickness (in pregnancy).

ไม่แพ้ mâjphɛ́ɛ′ no less than, not less than.

o สวยไม่แพ้แม่ sǔaj′-mâjphɛ́ɛ′mɛ̂ɛ′ no less beautiful than (her) mother.

o สูงไม่แพ้พ่อ sǔuŋ′-mâjphɛ́ɛ′phɔ̂ɔ′ no shorter than (his) father.

ยอมแพ้ jɔɔmphɛ́ɛ′ V 1. to surrender, give up, give in. 2. to surrender to, yield to.

แพง phɛɛŋ′ V to be expensive, high in price. →Ant. ถูก ๑.

แพงขึ้น phɛɛŋ′khɯ̂n′ to become more expensive.

แพงดับ phɛɛŋ′dàb′ colloq. to be extremely expensive.

แพ่ง phêŋ′* N "civil," used in legal terms. →Opp. อาญา "criminal."

กฎหมายแพ่ง (ฉบับ) kòdmǎaj′phêŋ′ (chabàb′) N civil law.

แพทย์ (นาย,คน) phêɛd′ (naaj′,khon′) N eleg. doctor, physician. การ-- medicine (as a subject of study, a scientific field); medical matters. →Syn. หมอ com.

จรรยาแพทย์ canjaa′phêɛd′ N medical ethics.

จิตแพทย์ (นาย,คน) cìd′taphêɛd′ (naaj′,khon′) N tech. psychiatrist.

ทันตแพทย์ (นาย,คน) than′taphêɛd′ (naaj′,khon′) N eleg. dentist. →Syn. แพทย์ฟัน eleg., หมอฟัน com.

นายแพทย์ (นาย,คน) naajphêɛd′ (naaj′,khon′) N eleg. (male) physician, doctor. →Syn. หมอผู้ชาย com.

o นายแพทย์หญิง (คน) naajphêɛd′jǐŋ′ (khon′) N eleg. woman physician, doctor. →Syn. หมอผู้หญิง com.

แพทย์ปัจจุบัน (นาย,คน) phêɛd′pàdcuban′ (naaj′, khon′) N eleg. modern doctor.

แพทย์ผดุงครรภ์ (คน) phêɛd′-phaduŋ′khan′ (khon′) N eleg. obstetrician.

แพทยศาสตร์ phêɛdsàad′ N medicine (as a subject of study).

แพทย์สัตว์ (นาย,คน) phêɛdsàd′ (naaj′,khon′) N eleg. veterinarian.

วิชาแพทย์ wíchaa′phêɛd′ N medicine (as a subject of study).

ศัลยแพทย์ (นาย,คน) sǎn′japhêɛd′ (naaj′,khon′) N eleg. surgeon. →Syn. หมอผ่าตัด com.

แพร phrɛɛ′ N silk.

แพร่ phrɛ̂ɛ′ V to spread, disseminate, reveal.

เผยแพร่ phə̌əjphrɛ̂ɛ′ V to propagate, popularize, spread out.

แพร่สะพัด phrɛ̂ɛ′saphád′ V eleg. to spread out, be widespread, widely talked about.

แพร่หลาย phrɛ̂ɛlǎaj′ V to be popular, well-known, widespread.

แพร่ง ๑ phrɛ̂ŋ/* C fork (of a road, path).

แพร่ง ๒ in แพร่งพราย phrɛ̂ŋphraaj/* V 1. to disclose, spread, reveal, make known. 2. to leak out, be made known (to).

แพลง phlɛɛŋ′ to be sprained.

พลิกแพลง phlígphlɛɛŋ′ V 1. to change, alter, modify. 2. to make changes, alterations, modifications.

แพะ (ตัว) phɛ́?′ (tua′) N goat.

ลูกแพะ (ตัว) lûugphɛ́?′ (tua′) N kid.

โพก in โพกหัว phôoghǔa′ V 1. to wear a turban. 2. to wrap a piece of cloth around one's head; to cover the head with a cloth.

โพงพาง phooŋphaaŋ′ N 1. a kind of weir. 2. a children's game.

โพด in ข้าวโพด (ฝัก,เม็ด) khâawphôod′ N corn, i.e. maize (fág′ for ears; méd′ for grains). →Also sometimes incorrectly ข้าวโภชน์.

โพธิ phoo/* N pipal, bo. ต้น-- (ต้น) pipal tree, bo tree (Ficus religiosa).

โพ้น. See entries below.

ไกลโพ้น klaj′phóon′ far away.

โพ้นทะเล phóon′thalee′ N overseas.

โพนทะนา phoon′thanaa′ V to accuse, blame, slander publicly.

โพย. See entries below.

ขอโทษขอโพย khɔ̌ɔthôod′khɔ̌ɔphooj′ V elab. colloq. to apologize.

แฉโพย chɛ̌ɛphooj′ V colloq. to disclose, reveal (a secret).

โพยภัย phooj′phaj′ N danger.

โพยม in โพยมยาน (ลำ,เครื่อง) phajoom′jaan′ (lam′, khrɣaŋ′) N eleg. aircraft.

โพรก phrôog′ V to be loose, not tightly packed.

หลวมโพรก lǔamphrôog′ V to be very loose, too large, very baggy (as of garments).

โพรง (โพรง) phrooŋ′ (phrooŋ′) N hole, cavity.

เป็นโพรง penphrooŋ′ to be hollow.

โพลง phlooŋ′ rM intensifier used with ขาว "white," ลืมตา "open the eyes," ลุก "burn."

โพล้เพล้ phlóophlée′ N twilight, dusk.

เวลาโพล้เพล้ weelaa′phlóophlée′ N twilight time, dusk.

ไพ่ (ใบ,ตัว,สำรับ) phâj′ N playing cards (baj′, tua′ for single cards; sǎmráb′ for decks of cards).

กินไพ่ kinphâj′ V colloq. to win at cards.

ขาไพ่ (ขา,คน) khǎaphâj′ (khǎa′, khon′) N colloq. card player.

ไพ่ตอง (ตา,สำรับ,ใบ) phâjtɔɔŋ′ N 1. a Thai card game (taa′). 2. the cards used in playing the game (sǎmráb′, baj′).

ไพ่ไฟ (ใบ) phâjfaj′ (baj′) N slang fraudulent vote or ballot.

วงไพ่ (วง) woŋphâj′ (woŋ′) N a circle of card players.

เล่นไพ่ lênphâj′ V to play cards.

ไพบูลย์ phajbuun′ V 1. to be abundant, plentiful. 2. to prosper. ความ-- abundance, prosperity.

ไพร (แห่ง) phraj′ (hὲŋ′) N lit. forest, jungle.

สมุนไพร samǔn′phraj′ N medicinal plant, herb.

ไพร่ (คน) phrâj′ (khon′) N commoners, low-class people, vulgar people. →Opp. ผู้ดี.

บ่าวไพร่ (คน) bàawphrâj′ (khon′) N elab. colloq. servants.

ไพร่ฟ้า phrâj′fáa′ N people (of a country).

ไพเราะ phajrɔ́?′ V to be beautiful, sweet, pleasing (of something heard or read). ความ-- sweetness, beauty. อย่าง-- beautifully, in a sweet-sounding manner. →Cf. เพราะ ๑.

ไพล่ phlâj′ V to be contrary to, run counter to (expectations, intentions).

๐ เขมรไม่ออกเสียงตัว "ท" อย่างเรา แต่ไพล่ ไปออกเสียงเป็นตัว "ต" khamě̌en′-mâj?ɔ̀ɔgsǐaŋ′-tuathɔɔ′-jàaŋraw′→ tὲɛphlâjpaj?ɔ̀ɔgsǐaŋ′-pen⊃ tuatɔɔ′↓ The Cambodians do not pronounce the letter "thɔɔ" the way we do, but on the contrary they pronounce it "tɔɔ."

ไพศาล phajsǎan′ V eleg. to be extensive, broad, vast.

ฟ

ฟ fɔɔ/ LOW consonant. Pronounced f initially, b finally (or occ. f in recent loanwords).

ฟก fóg/ V to be bruised.

ฟกช้ำ fógchám/ V to be bruised and swollen.

ฟกช้ำดำเขียว fógchám/damkhǐaw/ V ela b. colloq. to be bruised black and blue.

ฟรังก์ fraŋ/ C franc. [f. Fr.]

ฟรี frii/ V 1. to be free, not charged for. 2. to be free (from work, obligation). sV 3. free, without charge. Also 3. ฟรีๆ [f. Eng.]

ฟลุค flúg/ N 1. a fluke. V 2. to be a fluke, a lucky chance. [f. Eng.]

ฟอก fɔɔg/ V 1. to tan (hides). 2. to purify, cleanse, soap.

ซักฟอก ságfɔɔg/ V to launder, wash (with soap or detergent).

o ผงซักฟอก phǒŋ/ságfɔɔg/ N detergent powder.

ฟอกหนัง fɔɔgnǎŋ/ V to tan hides. การ-- tanning.

o โรงงานฟอกหนัง (โรง) rooŋŋaan/fɔɔgnǎŋ/ (rooŋ/) N tannery.

ฟอง (ลูก,ฟอง,หย่อม) fɔɔŋ/ (lûug/, fɔɔŋ/, jɔ̀ɔm/) N 1. bubbles, foam. C eleg. 2. clf. for eggs. →Syn. 2. ใบ,ลูก com.

ตกฟอง tògfɔɔŋ/ V lit., eleg. to lay eggs. →Syn. See ออกไข่ com.

แตกฟอง tɛ̀ɛgfɔɔŋ/ V to foam, become foamy, break into foam.

o น้ำลายแตกฟอง námlaaj/tɛ̀ɛgfɔɔŋ/ colloq. to spout forth, talk volubly. →Also พูดจน--.

เป็นฟอง penfɔɔŋ/ to be spumed, foamy.

o เป็นฟองฟอด penfɔɔŋ/fɔ̂d/ to be very foamy, frothy (e.g. of waves; of rotting fruit).

ฟองน้ำ (ลูก,ฟอง,หย่อม,อัน) fɔɔŋnáam/ N 1. bubbles (lûug/, fɔɔŋ/); foam (jɔ̀ɔm/). 2. sponge (ʔan/). 3. foam rubber (ʔan/).

ฟองอากาศ (ฟอง,ลูก) fɔɔŋ/ʔaakàad/ (fɔɔŋ/, lûug/) N air bubble.

ฟ่อง in ลอยฟ่อง lɔɔjfɔ̂ŋ/* V to float freely.

ฟ้อง fɔ́ɔŋ/ V 1. to accuse, tell on. 2. to sue, prosecute, take to court. N 3. charge, accusation.

การ-- accusing; accusation. คำ--(ข้อ,ประการ, อย่าง) charge, accusation.

ถอนฟ้อง thɔ̌ɔnfɔ́ɔŋ/ V to withdraw a (legal) charge, withdraw (one's case).

ฟ้องร้อง fɔ́ɔŋrɔ́ɔŋ/ V to sue, bring charges against.

ฟ้องหมิ่นประมาท fɔ́ɔŋ/-mìn/pramàad/ V to sue for libel.

ฟ้องหย่า fɔ́ɔŋjàa/ V to sue for divorce.

ยกฟ้อง jógfɔ́ɔŋ/ V to dismiss a (legal) case.

ยื่นฟ้อง jɥynfɔ́ɔŋ/ V to bring a case to court.

ฟอด ๑ fɔ̂ɔd/, fɔ̂d/ V to be foamy, spongy (esp. of rotten fruit).

เป็นฟองฟอด penfɔɔŋ/fɔ̂d/ to be very foamy, frothy (e.g. of waves; of rotting fruit).

ฟอด ๒ fɔ̂ɔd/ imit. 1. the sound of kissing. C 2. clf. for a kiss.

ฟ่อน fɔ̂n/ C sheaf, bundle (as of grass, hay, rice stalks).

ฟ้อน fɔ́ɔn/ N 1. dance (northern style). V 2. to dance in the northern style.

ฟ้อนรำ fɔ́ɔnram/ V to dance (in any Thai style). →Comp. เต้นรำ.

ฟอโมซา fɔɔmoosaa/ pN Formosa. [f. Eng.]

เกาะฟอโมซา kɔ̀ʔ/fɔɔmoosaa/ pN the Island of Formosa.

ฟอร์ม (ชุด) fɔɔm/ (chúd/) N uniform. [f. Eng.]

แบบฟอร์ม (ใบ,แผ่น) bὲεbfɔɔm/ (baj/, phὲn/) N a form (to be filled in, as an application form).

ฟัก ๑ fág/ V to hatch.

ฟักไข่ fágkhàj/ V to hatch (eggs).

ฟัก ๒ (ลูก,ต้น) fág/ (lûug/, tôn/) N vegetable of the squash or melon family (general term).

ฟักทอง (ลูก,ใบ,ผล) fágthɔɔŋ/ (lûug/, baj/, phǒn/) N pumpkin.

ฟัง faŋ/ V 1. to listen. 2. to listen to. นัก-- good listener. ผู้-- listener; audience.

เครื่องฟังเสียง (เครื่อง) khrɥ̂aŋ/faŋsǐaŋ/ (khrɥ̂aŋ/) N a sound-detecting device.

เงี่ยหูฟัง ŋîahǔu/faŋ/ to cock the ears, i.e. try hard to listen.

เชื่อฟัง chɥ̂afaŋ/ V to heed, pay attention to, obey.

ได้ยินได้ฟัง dâjjin/dâjfaŋ/ ela b. colloq. 1. to hear. 2. to have heard of.

น่าฟัง nâafaŋ/ V to be pleasant to listen to, interesting to listen to, beautiful (to hear).

ฟังขึ้น faŋ'khŷn' V to sound reasonable, plausible.

ฟังดู faŋ'duu' V to sound, seem, appear.

o ฟังดูแปลก faŋ'duuplɛ̀ɛg' to sound strange.

ฟังเทศน์ faŋthêed' V to hear a sermon.

ฟังไม่ขึ้น faŋ'mâjkhŷn' to sound unreasonable, unbelievable, implausible.

ฟังไม่ชัด faŋ'mâjchád' to be unclear, indistinct (of sounds); can't hear clearly.

ฟังไม่ได้ faŋ'mâjdâaj' 1. to sound awful, unpleasant; can't bear to listen (to it). 2. to sound invalid, unreasonable.

ฟังไม่ได้ยิน faŋ'mâjdâjjin' can't hear (because of noise, etc.).

ฟังสับสน faŋ'sàbsŏn' to sound confusing.

ฟังหูไว้หู faŋhŭu'wájhŭu' idiom. to take (things one hears) with a grain of salt.

ฟังให้ขึ้ง faŋ'hâjsýŋ' to listen with deep feeling. →Also ฟังขึ้ง.

ฟัง(...)ออก faŋ'(...)ʔɔ̀ɔg' to make (it) out, be able to understand (something spoken).

o ฟังภาษาออก faŋ'phaasǎa'-ʔɔ̀ɔg' to be able to understand a language (when spoken).

ไม่ตั้งใจฟัง mâjtâŋcaj'faŋ' to be inattentive.

ว่าไม่ฟัง wâa'mâjfaŋ' to be disobedient, naughty, heedless of advice, warnings, commands.

สดับฟัง,สดับตรับฟัง sadàb'faŋ', sadàb'-tràb'faŋ' V elab. eleg. to listen carefully.

ฟัด fád' V 1. to wrestle, wrestle with. 2. colloq. to cuddle and kiss vigorously (as a parent does a small child).

พอฟัดพอเหวี่ยง phɔɔfád'phɔɔwìaŋ' V elab. colloq. to be about the same. →Also พอฟัด. colloq.

ฟัน ๑ (ขี่) fan' (sîi') N 1. tooth, teeth. 2. barb (as of a fish trap).

กัดฟัน kàdfan' V 1. to gnash one's teeth. 2. colloq. to grin and bear (it), be patient.

ขี้ฟัน khîifan' N decaying food particles between the teeth.

เข็ดฟัน khèdfan' V to have one's teeth set on edge (as by the sight or taste of something sour).

จิ้มฟัน cîmfan' V to pick the teeth.

ปวดฟัน pùadfan' V to have a toothache.

เป็นฟัน penfan' to be toothed, serrated. →Dist. เป็นแฉก. →Syn. เป็นจักๆ, เป็นหยัก.

แปรงฟัน prɛɛŋfan' V to brush the teeth.

แปรงสีฟัน (อัน) prɛɛŋ'sǐifan' (ʔan') N toothbrush.

แพทย์ฟัน (คน,นาย) phɛ̂ɛdfan' (khon', naaj') N eleg. dentist. →Syn. ทันตแพทย์ eleg., หมอฟัน com.

ฟันปลอม (ขี่,ชุด) fanplɔɔm' N false teeth. (sîi' for individual teeth; chúd' for a denture).

ฟันผุ fanphù?' N 1. tooth decay, dental caries. 2. decayed tooth. V 3. to have dental caries, decayed teeth.

ฟันฟาง (ขี่) fanfaaŋ' (sîi') N colloq. tooth, teeth.

ฟันหน้า (ขี่) fannâa' (sîi') N front teeth.

ยาสีฟัน jaasǐifan' N toothpaste, dentifrice.

ยิงฟัน jiŋfan' V 1. to show one's teeth (by drawing back the lips). 2. colloq. to grin.

ไรฟัน rajfan' N the teeth (as they are in the mouth).

หมอฟัน (คน) mɔ̌ɔfan' (khon') N com. dentist. →Syn. ทันตแพทย์, แพทย์ฟัน eleg.

ฟัน ๒ fan' V to slash, cut, chop, sever (with a sharp-edged object).

ฆ่าฟัน khâa'fan' V to kill, slay. การ-- killing, slaying, slaughter (of people).

ฟันฝ่า fanfàa' V to struggle, fight against (obstacles, danger). →Also ฝ่าฟัน.

ฟั่น ๑ fân' V to twist (together), roll (into cylindrical form).

ฟั่นเชือก fânchŷag' V to make a rope by twisting several strands of fibers together.

ฟั่นเทียน fânthian' V to make a wax candle, roll wax into a candle.

ฟั่น ๒ in ฟั่นเฟือน fânfyan' V to be out of one's mind.

ฟั้น fán' V to massage (the flesh) vigorously, squeeze (the flesh) hard.

นวดฟั้น nûadfán' V to massage by kneading (the flesh).

ฟัสซิสต์ fássís', fádsís' N Fascist. [f. Eng.]

ฟ้า fáa' N com. sky. →Syn. เวหน lit., นภา lit., eleg.

กลางฟ้า klaaŋfáa' (in) the sky, (in) the middle of the sky.

ขอบฟ้า khɔ̀ɔbfáa' N com. horizon. →Syn.

ขอบจักรวาฬ eleg.

ครึ้มฟ้าครึ้มฝน khrýmfáa′/khrýmfǒn′ V ela b. colloq. to be very cloudy, look like rain.

เจ้าฟ้า (องค์) câawfáa′, câwfáa′ (ʔoŋ′) N 1. prince of the highest rank, i.e. son of the king born by the queen. T 2. Prince --.

เจ้าฟ้าหญิง (องค์) câwfáajǐŋ (ʔoŋ′) N 1. princess of the highest rank, i.e. daughter of the king born by the queen. T 2. Princess --.

ดาดฟ้า (แห่ง) dàadfáa′ (hèŋ′) N deck (of ship or building), (sun-)deck.

ดินฟ้าอากาศ dinfáa′/ʔaakàad′ N weather, climate.

ท้องฟ้า thɔ́ɔŋfáa′ N the sky, the heavens.

นางฟ้า (องค์) naaŋfáa′ (ʔoŋ′) N angel, fairy.

นุ่งลมห่มฟ้า nûŋlom′hòmfáa′ V ela b. colloq. to be naked, in the nude: "clothe oneself with wind and sky."

บนฟ้า bonfáa′ in the sky.

พลอยฟ้าพลอยฝน phlɔɔjfáa′phlɔɔjfǒn′ idio m. to be included or mixed up with others without actual participation; along with others.

ไพร่ฟ้า phrâj′/fáa′ N people (of a country).

ฟ้าคะนอง fáa′khanɔɔŋ′ N eleg. 1. thunder. 2. it thunders.

o พายุฟ้าคะนอง phaajúʔ′-fáa′/khanɔɔŋ′ N thunderstorm.

ฟ้าคำรน fáa′khamron′ lit., eleg. it thunders.

ฟ้าดิน fáa′din′ "heaven and earth," as in the following entries.

o จนฟ้าดินสลาย confáa′dinsalǎaj′ until the end of the world.

o ชั่วฟ้าดินสลาย chûafáa′dinsalǎaj′ forever, till doomsday. →Also ชั่วฟ้าดิน.

ฟ้าผ่า (ครั้ง) (1) fáa′phàa′; (2) fáaphàa′ 1. lightning to strike. N 2. thunderbolt (khráŋ′).

ฟ้าร้อง (ครั้ง) (1) fáa′rɔ́ɔŋ′; (2) fáarɔ́ɔŋ′ 1. to thunder; it thunders. N 2. thunder (khráŋ′).

ฟ้าลั่น (1) fáa′lân′; (2) fáalân′ 1. to thunder; it thunders. N 2. thunder; a thunderclap.

ฟ้าแลบ (1) fáa′lɛ̂ɛb′; (2) fáalɛ̂ɛb′ 1. lightning to flash. N 2. lightning; a flash of lightning.

o ประหนึ่งฟ้าแลบ pranʉ̀ŋ′/fáalɛ̂ɛb′ like a flash of lightning.

ฟ้าสาง (1) fáa′sǎaŋ′, fáasǎaŋ′ to be dawn; day to

dawn, be dawning.

ไฟฟ้า fajfáa′ N electricity. การ-- electricity; electrical works; electrification.

ลมฟ้าอากาศ lomfáa′/ʔaakàad′ N weather, climate.

สวรรค์ชั้นฟ้า sawǎn′chánfáa′ N eleg. colloq. heaven.

สายฟ้า, --แลบ sǎajfáa′, sǎaj′/fáalɛ̂ɛb′ N streak of lightning.

สีฟ้า sǐifáa′ N 1. sky-blue color. V 2. to be sky blue, light blue, pastel blue.

สุดหล้าฟ้าเขียว sùdlâa′fáakhǐaw′ eleg. colloq. very far away, beyond the horizon.

ฟาก ๑ fâag′ N split bamboo flooring.

ตกฟาก tòkfâag′ V colloq. to be born: "drop to the floor."

ฟาก ๒ (ฟาก) fâag′ (fâag′) N side (of street, waterway); shore, bank (of waterway).

o ข้ามฟาก khâamfâag′ to cross a street, a river, a channel.

o สองฟากทาง sɔ̌ɔŋ′/fâagthaaŋ′ (on) both sides of the street or path.

ฟาง ๑ (กอง, ฟ่อน, มัด) faaŋ′ N straw, rice straw (kɔɔŋ′ for a heap; fɔ̂ɔn′ for a sheaf; mád′ for a bundle).

กระดาษฟาง kradàadfaaŋ′ N an absorbent straw paper made by the Chinese, used chiefly as toilet paper.

หมวกฟาง (ใบ) mùagfaaŋ′ (baj′) N straw hat.

ฟาง ๒ in ฟันฟาง (ซี่) fanfaaŋ′ (sîi′) N colloq. tooth, teeth.

ฟาง ๓ in ตาฟาง taa′faaŋ′ V to have blurred vision, see indistinctly (e.g. because of glare, old age).

ฟ่าง in ข้าวฟ่าง khâawfâaŋ′ N millet.

ฟาด fâad′ V 1. to strike, slap, hit hard (with the side of a long object). 2. slang to eat up, stash (all the food) away (by eating).

ฟาดข้อ(กับ) fâadkhɔ̂ɔ′(kaɔ) V slang to argue, fight (with).

ฟ่าม fâam′ V to be dry and mealy (as of oranges or apples that have been kept too long, and have lost their crisp, juicy texture).

ฟาร์ม (แห่ง) faam′ (hèŋ′) N farm. [f. Eng.]

ฟาเรนไฮท์ faarenháj′ N Fahrenheit. [f. Eur.]

ฟิด in ทำจมูกฟิด ๆ thamcamùug/fídfíd/ to go "sniff, sniff," to sniffle (as because of a cold).

ฟิต ๑ fíd/, ffid/ C the English foot (unit of linear measure). [f. Eng.] →Also more commomly ฟุต.

ฟิต ๒ fíd/ V 1. to fix, adjust, fit. 2. to be fit. ความ-- fitness. ช่าง-- mechanic. [f. Eng. fit]

ฟิตปั๋ง fíd/pǎŋ/ V colloq. 1. to be in top shape, tiptop condition. 2. to fit very tight.

ฟิตรถ fídród/ to fix a car, repair a car.

ฟินแลนด์ finlɛɛn/ pN Finland. [f. Eng.]

ฟิล์ม fiim/ N film, esp. photographic film. [f. Eng.]
ฟิล์มถ่ายรูป (ม้วน,แผ่น) fiim/thàajrûub/ N photographic film (múan/ a roll; phɛ̀n/ a sheet).
ล้างฟิล์ม láaŋfiim/ V to develop or process a photographic film.

ฟิลิปปินส์ filibpin/, filíbpin/ pN the Philippines. [f. Eng.]

ฟิวส์ fiw/ N fuse. [f. Eng.]

ฟิสิกส์,ฟิสิคส์ físìg/ N physics. [f. Eng.]
วิชาฟิสิกส์ wíchaa/físìg/ N physics, physics course.

ฟืน (ดุ้น,ท่อน) fyyn/ (dûn/, thɔ̂ɔn/) N firewood.
โกรธเป็นฟืนเป็นไฟ krôod/-penfyyn/penfaj/ idiom. to be furiously angry, burn with rage.
ไม้ฟืน (ดุ้น,ท่อน) májfyyn/ (dûn/, thɔ̂ɔn/) N firewood.

ฟื้น fýyn/ V to recover, revive, bring back, restore.
พักฟื้น phágfýyn/ V to be in convalescence.
ฟื้นไข้ fýynkhâj/ V to recover, recuperate.
ฟื้นความจำ fýyn/khwaamcam/ V to recall; to refresh one's memory.
ฟื้นดิน fýyndin/ V to turn over the soil.
ฟื้นตัว fýyntua/ V to recover, improve, take a turn for the better.
ฟื้นฟู fýynfuu/ V to rehabilitate, revive, restore.
การ-- revival, restoration.
รื้อฟื้น rýyfýyn/ V to revive, bring back.

ฟุ้ง fúŋ/ V to spread in the air, be wafted; to diffuse.
ฟุ้งกระจาย fúŋ/kracaaj/ V to diffuse.
ฟุ้งซ่าน fúŋsâan/ V 1. (one's mind or thoughts) to wander, be jumbled. sV 2. incoherently, in jumbled fashion.
o คิดฟุ้งซ่าน khíd/fúŋsâan/ to think incoherently, (one's) thoughts to be jumbled.
ฟุ้งเฟ้อ fúŋfɔ́ɔ/ V 1. to be extravagant, lavish.

2. to be puffed up with pride, conceited.

ฟุต fúd/ C the English foot (unit of linear measure). [f. Eng.] →Also ฟิต ๑.
นิ้วฟุต níwfúd/ C inch (in the English system). →See นิ้ว.

ฟุตบอลล์ (เกม) fúdbɔn/, fúdbɔɔl (keem/) N 1. soccer, football. 2. short for ลูก-- (see below). นัก-- soccer player. [f. Eng.]
การแข่งขันฟุตบอลล์ kaan/-khɛ̀ŋkhǎn/fúdbɔn/ N soccer game.
ลูกฟุตบอลล์ (ลูก) lûugfúdbɔn/ (lûug/) N soccer ball.

ฟุตปาร์ต,ฟุตปาท fúdpàad/ N footpath, sidewalk. [f. Eng.]

ฟุบ fúb/ V to collapse, fall face down.

ฟุ่มเฟือย fûmfyaj/ V to be extravagant, luxurious.
ความ-- extravagance, luxuriousness, อย่าง-- extravagantly, lavishly.

ฟู fuu/ V to rise (as bread), become fluffy.
ฟื้นฟู fýynfuu/ V to restore, rehabilitate, revive.
เฟื่องฟู fɤ̂aŋfuu/ V to be prosperous, to progress.

ฟูก (ลูก,อัน) fûug/ (lûug/, ʔan/) N colloq. mattress.

เฟ้น ๑ fén/* V to choose, select critically.
เลือกเฟ้น lɯ̂agfén/ V to choose, select critically.

เฟ้น ๒ fén/* V to massage (the flesh) by kneading. →Chiefly in the following compound.
นวดเฟ้น nûadfén/ V to massage (the flesh) by kneading.

เฟ้อ fɔ́ɔ/ V to be in excess. การ-- overabundance, oversupply, excess, inflation (of currency) ความ-- vanity; inflation (of currency).
ท้องเฟ้อ thɔ́ɔŋfɔ́ɔ/ V 1. to suffer from flatulence, excess gas in the stomach. N 2. flatulence.
ฟุ้งเฟ้อ fúŋfɔ́ɔ/ V 1. to be extravagant, lavish.
2. to be puffed up with pride, conceited.

เฟอร์นิเจอร์ (ชิ้น) fɤɤnicɤ̀ɔ/ (chín/) N furniture. [f. Eng.]

เฟิน (ต้น) fɤɤn/ (tôn/) N fern. [f. Eng.]

เฟือ in เหลือเฟือ lɯ̌afya/ V 1. to be more than enough, plentiful. sV 2. more than enough, plentifully. →Also 2. อย่าง--.

เฟื้อ in เอื้อเฟื้อ ʔ̂afýa/ V to be generous (to), to help, support (with kindness).

o มีน้ำใจเอื้อเฟื้อ miinámcaj/ʔɣafɣa/ to be generous.

o เอื้อเฟื้อเผื่อแผ่ ʔɣafɣa/phɣaphὲɛ/ e l a b. to be
generous, liberal; to be generous (to).

เฟือง fyaŋ/ N 1. (screw) thread. 2. cog.

เฟื่อง in เฟื่องฟู fɣaŋfuu/ V to be prosperous, to
progress. →S y n. เจริญ, รุ่งเรือง.

เฟื้อง fɣaŋ/ C bit (a former monetary unit, twelve
and a half satangs).

เฟือน in ฟั่นเฟือน fȃnfyan/ V to be out of one's
mind.

เฟือย in ฟุ่มเฟือย fȗmfyaj/ V to extravagant,
luxurious.

เฟื้อย fɣaj/ rM intens. used with ยาว "long."

แฟง (ลูก) fɛɛŋ/ (lȗug/) N vegetable marrow, a
kind of squash. ต้น-- (ต้น) the plant. →Cf.
ฟัก.

แฟชั่น fɛɛ/chȃn/ N fashion. [f. Eng.]

แฟน fɛɛn/ N 1. c o l l o q. fan, devotee, admirer.
2. s l a n g girl friend, boy friend. [f. Eng.]
→Also, as a hypercorrection, แควน.

แฟ้น in แน่นแฟ้น nȇnfɛ́ɛn/ V to be firm, steady,
secure. sV 2. firmly, securely. อย่าง--
firmly, securely, tightly.

แฟนซี (1) fɛɛnsii/; (2) fɛɛnsȋi/ N 1. costume (as
for a ball), fancy dress. V 2. to be fancy.
[f. Eng.]

แฟบ fȇɛb/ V to be deflated, flat (as a tire).

แฟ้ม (อัน, แฟ้ม) fέɛm/ (ʔan/, fέɛm/) N folder, file,
binder.

แฟร์ fɛɛ/ V c o l l o q. to be fair (i.e. just). [f. Eng.]
ไม่แฟร์ mȃjfɛɛ/↓ It's not fair!

แฟสซิส์ม fέɛssís/ N fascism. [f. Eng.]

ไฟ faj/ N c o m. 1. fire. 2. light. →S y n. 1. เพลิง
e l e g.
กระโจมไฟ (แห่ง, หลัง) kracoom/faj/ (hὲŋ/, lǎŋ/)
N lighthouse. →Also กระโจมไฟ.
ก่อไฟ kɔ̀ɔfaj/ V to start a fire, build a fire.
กองไฟ (กอง) kɔɔŋfaj/ (kɔɔŋ/) N bonfire.
โกรธเป็นฟืนเป็นไฟ kròod/-penfyyn/penfaj/ i d i o m.
to be furiously angry, to burn with rage.
เข้าไต้เข้าไฟ khȃwtȃaj/khȃwfaj/ V e l a b.
c o l l o q. to be getting dark, be twilight.
ควันไฟ khwanfaj/ N smoke.

ค่าน้ำค่าไฟ khȃanáam/khȃafaj/ N cost of utilities
(i.e. water and electricity).

โคมไฟ (ดวง) khoomfaj/ (duaŋ/) N lamp, lantern.

จุดไฟ cùdfaj/ V to kindle, light a fire.

ช่องไฟ (ช่อง) chɔ̀ŋfaj/ (chɔ̀ŋ/) N space between
letters or words.

เชื้อไฟ chɣafaj/ N fuel, kindling.

โซดาไฟ soodaafaj/ N c o l l o q. caustic soda.
[soodaa f. Eng.]

ดวงไฟ (ดวง) duaŋfaj/ (duaŋ/) N 1. ball of fire.
2. a distant light or fire.

ดอกไม้ไฟ (ดอก) dɔ̀ɔgmáajfaj/ (dɔ̀ɔg/) N c o m.
fireworks. →S y n. ดอกไม้เพลิง e l e g.

ดับไฟ dàbfaj/ V c o m. 1. to put out a fire. 2.
to turn off the lights. →Also 1. ดับเพลิง e l e g.
2. ปิดไฟ.

ดินน้ำลมไฟ din/→náam/→lom/→faj/ the four
elements: earth, water, wind, and fire.

ต้นไฟ (แห่ง) tȏnfaj/ (hὲŋ/) N c o m. the source
of a fire.

ติดไฟ tìdfaj/ V 1. to light a fire. 2. to be inflammable.

เตาไฟ (เตา) tawfaj/ (taw/) N stove (for cooking).

ทนไฟ thonfaj/ V 1. to be fireproof, fire resistant,
heat resistant. 2. to withstand fire, endure fire
or heat.

ประกายไฟ prakaajfaj/ N spark.

ปล่องไฟ (ปล่อง) plɔ̀ŋfaj/ (plɔ̀ŋ/) N chimney,
smokestack.

ปิดไฟ pìdfaj/ V to turn out the lights, turn off
the lights, the electricity. →Also ดับไฟ. →Opp.
เปิดไฟ.

เปลวไฟ pleewfaj/ N flame.

เปิดไฟ pə̀ədfaj/ V to turn on the lights, the
electricity. →Opp. ปิดไฟ.

เผาไฟ phǎwfaj/ V to burn.

พูดน้ำไหลไฟดับ phȗud/-námlǎj/fajdàb/ V c o l l o q.
to chatter away, talk a blue streak, talk rapidly
and profusely.

ไพ่ไฟ (ใบ) phȃjfaj/ (baj/) N s l a n g fraudulent
vote or ballot.

ไฟฉาย (ดวง, อัน, กระบอก) fajchǎaj/ (duaŋ/, ʔan/,
krabɔ̀ɔg/) N flashlight, searchlight, spotlight.

ไฟแช็ก fajchég/ N c o l l o q. (cigarette) lighter.

ไฟท้าย (ดวง) fajtháaj′ (duaŋ′) N taillight.

ไฟป่า fajpàa′ N forest fire.

ไฟฟ้า fajfáa′ N electricity. การ-- electricity; electrical works; electrification. เครื่อง-- electrical appliances. ช่าง-- electrician.

o กระแสไฟฟ้า krasɛ̌ɛ′fajfáa′ N electric current.

o กำลังไฟฟ้า. kamlaŋ′fajfáa′ N electric power.

o ขั้วไฟฟ้า (ขั้ว) khûa′fajfáa′ (khûa′) N electrode, terminal.

o เครื่องกำเนิดไฟฟ้า (เครื่อง) khrŷaŋkamnə̀əd′ɔ fajfáa′ (khrŷaŋ′) N electric generator.

o ดวงไฟฟ้า (ดวง) duaŋfajfáa′ (duaŋ′) N electric light.

o เตารีดไฟฟ้า (เตา) tawrîid′fajfáa′ (taw′) N electric iron.

o ประจุไฟฟ้า (ประจุ,ตัว) pracù?′fajfáa′ (pracɔ cù?′,tua′) N electric charge.

o ไฟฟ้าเดินทาง (กระบอก,ดวง) fajfáa′dəənɔ thaaŋ′ (krabɔ̀ɔg′,duaŋ′) N flashlight.

o รถรางไฟฟ้า (คัน) ródraaŋ′fajfáa′ (khan′) N streetcar, tram.

o โรงไฟฟ้า (โรง) rooŋ′fajfáa′ (rooŋ′) N electric power plant.

o ลวดไฟฟ้า (เส้น,ขด) lûad′fajfáa′ (sên′,khɔ̀d′) N electric wire.

สายไฟฟ้า (สาย,เส้น) sǎajfajfáa′ (sǎaj′,sên′) N 1. electric wire. 2. power line.

o เสาไฟฟ้า (เสา) sǎw′fajfáa′ (sǎw′) N lamp post; utility pole, power pole.

o หลอดไฟฟ้า (หลอด) lɔ̀ɔd′fajfáa′ (lɔ̀ɔd′) N electric light bulb.

ไฟรัก fajrág′ N fire, flame of love (i.e. love which burns intensely like a fire).

ไฟลามทุ่ง faj′laamthûŋ′ "the fire spreads over the field," a simile used to describe any chain of events which spreads rapidly.

ไฟสัญญาน (ดวง) faj′sǎnjaan′ (duaŋ′) N signal light.

ไฟสี fajsǐi′ N colored light.

ไฟหน้า (ดวง) fajnâa′ (duaŋ′) N headlight (of a car).

ไฟไหม้ fajmâj′ N 1. a fire, a conflagration. V 2. to be on fire, catch fire.

ไม้ขีดไฟ (กลัก,ก้าน) májkhìidfaj′ N match (klàg′, for a box of matches; kâan′, for individual matches, matchsticks).

รถไฟ (ขบวน) ródfaj′ (khabuan′) N train.

เรือไฟ,เรือกลไฟ (ลำ) ryafaj′, rya′konfaj′ (lam′) N steamboat, steamship, steamer.

โรงสีไฟ (โรง,แห่ง) rooŋsǐifaj′ (rooŋ′,hɛ̀ŋ′) N steam-operated rice mill.

ลนไฟ lonfaj′ V to singe, heat over a flame.

ลูกไฟ (ลูก) lûugfaj′ (lûug′) N sparks, ignited or fiery particles thrown up in the air.

ไวไฟ wajfaj′ V 1. to be inflammable. 2. slang to be quick.

ส่องไฟ sɔ̀ŋfaj′ V to throw a light, throw some light (i.e., cause a light to be thrown in order to illuminate something). →Dist. ส่องแสง "to shine, emit light."

แสงไฟ sɛ̌ɛŋfaj′ N 1. light. 2. firelight.

หม้อไฟ (หม้อ) mɔ̂ɔfaj′ (mɔ̂ɔ′) N 1. a meter for recording the consumption of electricity. 2. a storage battery.

หลอดไฟ (หลอด) lɔ̀ɔdfaj′ (lɔ̀ɔd′) N light bulb.

หินเหล็กไฟ (ก้อน) hǐn′lègfaj′ (kɔ̂ɔn′) N flint rock.

โหมไฟ hǒomfaj′ V to coax a fire (as by fanning, adding fuel).

อยู่ไฟ jùufaj′ V to lie by a fireplace after childbirth (a Thai custom).

ภ

ภ phɔɔ′ LOW consonant. Pronounced ph initially, b finally. The sound ph as an initial low consonant is more commonly written with พ.

ภพ phób′ N lit.,eleg. world, earth, ground.

จักรภพ càgk(r)aphób′ N eleg. empire.

ภยันตราย phajan′taraaj′ N eleg. dangers (of all kinds). →See also ภัยอันตราย,ภัย,อันตราย.

ภรรยา (คน) phanjaa′, phanrajaa′ (khon′) N eleg. wife. →Syn. เมีย com.

ภรรยาน้อย (คน) phanrajaa′nɔ́ɔj′ (khon′) N eleg. minor wife; second, third, or other additional wife. →Syn. เมียน้อย com.

สามีภรรยา,ภรรยาสามี (คู่) sǎamii′phanrajaa′, phanrajaa′sǎamii′ (khûu′) N eleg. married

couple; husband and wife. NOTE. When ภรรยา
is placed first it is for the poetic effect of the
close rhyme between ⊃jaa and sǎa⊃. →Syn.
ผัวเมีย com.

ภราดรภาพ pharaa′dɔraphâab′ N eleg. brother-
hood, fraternity (as in liberty, equality and
fraternity).

ภริยา (คน) phárÍjaa′ (khon′) N eleg.,lit. wife.
→Lit. equiv. of ภรรยา.

ภวังค์ phawaŋ′ N eleg. inattentive, absent, oblivious state of mind.

ภักดี,จงรัก--(ต่อ) phágdii′, coŋrág′phágdii′(tɔɔ⊃)
V to be loyal, faithful (to).

ส่วามิภักดิ์(ต่อ) sawǎa′míphág′(tɔɔ⊃) V eleg.
1. to surrender, yield, submit oneself (to),
submit itself (to)(as a weaker country or king
to a powerful neighbor). 2. to be loyal and
submissive.

-ภัณฑ์ ⊃phan′ N tech. bound stem meaning "equipment, implement(s), paraphernalia." →Comp.
เครื่อง com.

เคมีภัณฑ์ (อย่าง,ชนิด) kheemii′phan′ (jàaŋ′,
chaníd′) N chemicals.

ผลิตภัณฑ์ (สิ่ง,อย่าง) phalìd′phan′, phlìd′phan′
(sìŋ′, jàaŋ′) N product.

ยุทธภัณฑ์ júd′thaphan′ N military equipment,
implements of war.

เวชภัณฑ์ (อย่าง) wêed′chaphan′ (jàaŋ′) N medical supplies.

ภัตต-. Bound form meaning "food, rice."

ภัตตกิจ in กระทำภัตตกิจ kratham′phádtakìd′
eleg. sacer. to eat. →Syn. See กิน com.

ภัตตาคาร (หลัง,ร้าน,แห่ง) phádtaakhaan′ (lǎŋ′,
ráan′,hèŋ′) N eleg. (large) restaurant.
→Comp. ร้านอาหาร com.

ภัตตาหาร phádtaa′hǎan′ N sacer. food. →Syn.
อาหาร com.

ภัย (อย่าง,ประการ) phaj′ (jàaŋ′,prakaan′) N
danger, peril. →Syn. อันตราย. →See also
ภัยอันตราย,ภยันตราย.

ที่หลบภัย (ที่,แห่ง) thîi′lòbphaj′ (thîi′, hèŋ′) N
shelter (from danger).

ประกันภัย prakan′phaj′ N 1. insurance. V 2.
to insure (against loss or damage).

ปลอดภัย plɔɔdphaj′ V to be safe, out of danger.
ความ-- security, safety.

เป็นภัย penphaj′ V to be dangerous, harmful,
perilous.

ผจญภัย phacon′phaj′ V to encounter danger, face
danger. นัก-- adventurer.

โพยภัย phooj′phaj′ N danger.

ภัยทางอากาศ phaj′thaaŋʔaakàad′ N danger from
an air attack.

ภัยธรรมชาติ phaj′thammachâad′ N danger, disaster caused by the elements, by nature.

ภัยพิบัติ phaj′phíbàd′ N eleg. catastrophe, disaster, peril.

ภัยอันตราย phaj′ʔantaraaj′ N elab. danger,
peril. →See also ภยันตราย,อันตราย.

โรคภัยไข้เจ็บ (อย่าง,ชนิด) rôogphaj′khâjcèb′
(jàaŋ′,chaníd′) N elab. disease, sickness.

เสี่ยงภัย sìaŋphaj′ V to risk, take a risk.

หลุมหลบภัย (แห่ง,หลุม) lǔm′lòbphaj′ (hèŋ′,lǔm′)
N air-raid shelter.

ภาค ๑ (ภาค) phâag′ (phâag′) N 1. part, section;
region (i.e. a large geographical area of a country). 2. region (an administrative unit). 3. term,
semester (of school). C 4. clf. for parts, sections, regions, semesters. →Comp. ส่วน,ปักษ์.
NOTE. Thailand is divided into nine administrative regions called ภาค. These are further
subdivided into จังหวัด, อำเภอ, and ตำบล.
For most practical purposes the chief subdivision
of the country is said to be the ǒhangwat. →See
จังหวัด.

ทหารภาคพื้นดิน thahǎan′phâagphýyndin′ N milit.
ground forces.

ผู้ว่าราชการภาค (นาย,คน) phûu′wâarâadchaⴰ
kaan′phâag′ (naaj′, khon′) N regional governor,
governor of a ภาค.

ภาคกลาง phâagklaaŋ′ N 1. the central part (of
a country, a geographical area). 2. (as n. mod.)
central.

o ยุโรปภาคกลาง júrôob′phâagklaaŋ′ Central
Europe.

ภาคใต้ phâagtâaj′ N 1. the south, the southern
part (of the country). 2. (as n. mod.) southern.

ภาคทัณฑ์ phâagthan′ V eleg. to put on probation.

o ถูกภาคทัณฑ์ thùug/phâagthan/ eleg. to be on probation, be put on probation.

ภาคปลาย phâagplaaj/ N 1. final part, section. 2. final semester.

ภาคผนวก phâagphanùag/ N appendix, addendum, supplement.

ภาคพายัพ phâagphaajáb/ N the northwest, the northwestern part (of Thailand).

ภาคเหนือ phâagnɣ̌a/ N the north, the northern part (of the country).

ภาคอีสาน phâag?isǎan/ N the northeast, the northeastern part (of Thailand).

ภูมิภาค phuu/míphâag/ N the provinces, i.e. part of the country lying outside the capital or largest city.

เล่มอภาค samɔ̀ɔ/phâag/ V to be equal (in legal status). ความ-- equality.

ภาค ๒ in ภาคภูมิ phâagphuum/ V 1. to feel proud. 2. to be dignified, grand, majestic. →Also spelled พากพูม.

o ภาคภูมิใจ(ใน) phâagphuum/caj/(najɔ) V 1. to feel proud (of). 2. to have a sense of accomplishment. →Also spelled พากพูมใจ.

ภาคี phaakhii/ N eleg. member, partner.

ชาติภาคี (ชาติ) châad/phaakhii/ (châad/) N eleg. member nations.

ประเทศภาคี (ประเทศ) prathêed/phaakhii/ (praɔ thêed/) N eleg. member countries.

ภาชนะ (อย่าง, ชิ้น, ใบ) phâadchaná?/ (jàaŋ/, chín/, baj/) N eleg. container, vessel, utensil.

ภาพ (ภาพ) phâab/, phâabphaɔ (phâab/) N eleg. 1. picture, image, figure. 2. element used as the final member of certain compounds in the meaning "state, condition"; see example. →Comp. 2. ภาวะ. →Syn. 1. รูป com.

o อิสรภาพ ?ìsaraphâab/ independence: "independent state, condition."

ข่าวภาพ khàawphâab/ N pictorial news.

เจ้าภาพ (คน) câwphâab/ (khon/) N host, hostess.

ช่างภาพ (คน) châaŋphâab/ (khon/) N eleg. photographer, cameraman.

ถ่ายภาพ thàajphâab/ V eleg. to take a picture, to photograph. →Syn. ถ่ายรูป com.

นึกเห็นภาพ nýg/hěnphâab/ V to imagine, visualize, picture (in one's mind).

ภาพข่าว phâabkhàaw/ N eleg. news pictures.

ภาพเขียน phâabkhǐan/ N eleg. a drawing (as opposed to a painting, a photograph).

ภาพถ่าย (ภาพ, ใบ, แผ่น) phâabthàaj/ (phâab/, baj/, phèn/) N eleg. photograph. →Syn. รูปถ่าย com.

ภาพนิ่ง phâabnîŋ/ N 1. slide (for projection), still picture. 2. shadow play figure (made of hide or paper). NOTE. Mng. 2 is used esp. in the south where shadow plays are still seen.

ภาพปก phâabpòg/ N eleg. cover design, cover photo, cover picture. →Also ภาพหน้าปก.

ภาพประกอบ phâabprakɔ̀ɔb/ N eleg. (pictorial) illustration (i.e. for a text).

ภาพเปลือย phâabplyaj/ N eleg. picture of a nude.

ภาพยนตร์ (เรื่อง) phâabphajon/ (rɣ̂aŋ/) N eleg. motion pictures, cinema. →Syn. หนัง com.

o ภาพยนตร์เพลง (เรื่อง) phâabphajon/phleeŋ/ (rɣ̂aŋ/) N eleg. a musical (i.e. musical motion picture).

o โรงภาพยนตร์ (โรง) rooŋ/phâabphajon/ (rooŋ/) N eleg. motion picture theater, cinema. →Syn. โรงหนัง com.

ภาพระบายสี phâab/rabaajsǐi/ N eleg. a painting.

ภาพล้อ phâablɔ́ɔ/ N a caricature.

ภาพวาด phâabwâad/ N eleg. a drawing, a painting (as opposed to a photograph).

ภาพหน้าปก phâab/nâapòg/ N eleg. cover picture (as on a magazine). →Also ภาพปก.

แมกกาซีนภาพ (ฉบับ, เล่ม) mégkaasiin/phâab/ (chabàb/, lêm/) N pictorial magazine. [แมกกา ซีน f. Eng.]

รูปภาพ (รูป, ใบ) rûubphâab/ (rûub/, baj/) N picture.

วาดภาพ wâadphâab/ V to draw a picture.

ห้องภาพ (ห้อง) hɔ̂ŋphâab/ (hɔ̂ŋ/) N photography studio.

ภาย phaaj/ N part, side (as in "inside, outside"). →Used of both space and time. →Comp. ข้าง.

ภายใต้ phaajtâaj/ under, underside, underneath.

ภายนอก phaajnɔ̂ɔg/ outside, exterior, external. การ-- external affairs, outside matter.

ภายใน phaajnaj/ inside, interior; internal; inside

of, within (time or space); การ - - internal
affairs.

o ภายในประเทศ phaaj′najprathêed′ 1. inside
the country. 2. (as n. mod.) domestic, internal,
inland.

o ภายในไม่กี่วัน phaaj′najmâjkìiwan′ within a
few days.

o ภายในระยะ phaaj′najrajá?′ within a distance
of, within a period of.

o ภายในเวลา phaaj′najweelaa′ during, within
the time limit, within the period of.

o ภายในหกเดือน phaaj′najhòɡdyan′ within six
months.

ภายหน้า phaajnâa′ in the future.

o ในภายหน้า najphaajnâa′ in the future.

ภายหลัง phaajlăŋ′ after, afterwards, later on.

o ในภายหลัง najphaajlăŋ′ afterwards, later, in
the future.

o ภายหลังที่ phaajlăŋ′thîi⊃ after (doing thus and
so).

ภาร phaan⊃, phaa′rá⊃. Bound stem meaning "burden,
task, work, duty, responsibility." →Comp.
ภาระ.

ภารกิจ phaa′rákìd′ N work to be done, task,
duty, responsibility.

ภารโรง (คน) phaanrooŋ′ (khon′) N janitor,
custodian.

ภาระ (อย่าง) phaará?′ (jàaŋ′) N burden, task,
work, duty, responsibility. →Comp. ภาร.

แบกภาระ bὲɛg′phaará?′ V to shoulder the
responsibility, carry the burden.

ภาวนา phaawanaa′ V to pray, meditate.

ภาวะ phaawá?′ N state, condition, situation.
→Comp. ภาพ.

นิติภาวะ nítìphaawá?′, nítì?′- N law legal
competency.

o บรรลุนิติภาวะ bunlú?′nítìphaawá?′, -nítì?′-
V law to come of age, reach legal age, attain
one's majority.

ภาวะการเงิน phaawá?′kaanŋɤn′ N financial
condition, financial situation (e.g. of a country).

ภาวะคับขัน phaawá?′khábkhǎn′ a state of crisis
or emergency.

ภาวะเงินเฟ้อ phaawá?′ŋɤnfɤ́ɤ′ N the condition

in which currency is devaluated; the condition
of inflated currency; hence, inflation.

ภาวะฉุกเฉิน phaawá?′chùgchɤ̌ɤn′ N emergency,
state of emergency.

ภาษา ๑ (ภาษา) phaasǎa′ (phaasǎa′) N com.
language, speech.

ต่างภาษา tàaŋphaasǎa′ a different language, a
foreign language.

o ต่างชาติต่างภาษา tàaŋchâad′tàaŋphaasǎa′ ela b.
colloq. (of) different nationality and speech.

ฟังภาษาออก faŋ′phaasǎa′-?ɔ̀ɔg′ to be able to
understand a language when spoken.

ภาษาคน phaasǎakhon′ N human speech.

ภาษาจีน phaasǎaciin′ N Chinese, the Chinese
language.

ภาษาตลาด phaasǎa′talàad′ N the language of
the common people; the unrefined speech of the
market place, of the lower classes.

ภาษาต่างประเทศ phaasǎa′tàaŋprathêed′ N foreign
language.

ภาษาท้องถิ่น phaasǎa′thɔ́ɔŋthìn′ N dialect, regional
speech.

ภาษาไทย phaasǎathaj′ N Thai, the Thai language.

o ภาษาไทยกลาง phaasǎa′thajklaaŋ′ central Thai,
the central Thai language (i.e. the one spoken in
Bangkok).

ภาษาบาลี phaasǎa′baalii′ N Pali language (language of the Buddhist texts).

ภาษาฝรั่งเศส phaasǎa′faràŋsèed′ N French, the
French language.

ภาษาพื้นเมือง phaasǎa′phýynmyaŋ′ N dialect,
regional speech.

ภาษาพูด phaasǎaphûud′ N 1. the spoken language.
2. colloquialism.

ภาษามคธ phaasǎa′makhód′ N Pali, the Pali language.

ภาษาละติน phaasǎa′latin′ N Latin, the Latin
language. [ละติน f. Eng.]

ภาษาหนังสือ phaasǎa′naŋsʉ̌y′ N 1. written language. 2. literary language.

ภาษาอังกฤษ phaasǎa′?aŋkrìd′ N English, the
English language.

ภาษา ๒. See entries below. →Also written ผะสา,
which is considered to be more correct. →See

also ประสา.

ตามภาษา taam/phaasǎa/ in the manner of, according to the ways of.

รู้ภาษา rúu/phaasǎa/ V colloq. to know what is what; to have horse sense.

ภาษิต (บท) phaasìd/(bòd/) N proverb, teaching, motto. →Comp. สุภาษิต.

ภาษี ๑ phaasǐi/ N advantage, upper hand.

มีภาษีกว่า miiphaasǐi/kwàa/ 1. to have an advantage over, have the upper hand. 2. to have more points than (e.g. in a beauty contest).

o มีภาษีเหนือกว่า, มีภาษีดีกว่า miiphaasǐi/-nǎya/ɔ kwàa/, miiphaasǐi/-dii/kwàa/ idem.

ภาษี ๒ phaasǐi/ N tax, tariff, duty. →Comp. อากร.

เก็บภาษี kèb/phaasǐi/ V to collect a tax or duty. การ-- taxation, taxing; the collection of taxes or duty. คน-- tax collector.

ด่านภาษี (ด่าน) dàan/phaasǐi/ (dàan/) N customs station, customs post, customs house.

ภาษีการค้า phaasǐi/kaankháa/ N business tax.

ภาษีเงินได้ phaasǐi/ŋəndâaj/ N income tax.

ภาษีศุลกากร phaasǐi/sǔn/lakaakɔɔn/ N customs duty.

ภาษีอากร phaasǐi/ʔaakɔɔn/ N revenue, i.e. all taxes, duties, fees collected by the government.

โรงภาษี (โรง,แห่ง) rooŋphaasǐi/ (rooŋ/, hɛ̀ŋ/) N customs building.

เสียภาษี sǐa/phaasǐi/ V to pay taxes. ผู้-- taxpayer.

อัตราภาษี ʔàdtraa/phaasǐi/ N tax rate.

ภิกษุ,พระ-- (รูป,องค์) phígsù?/, phráphígsù?/ (rûub/, ʔoŋ/) N eleg. Buddhist priest, monk.

ภู in ภูเขา (ลูก) phuukhǎw/(lûug/) N mountain. →Comp. เขา.

เป็นภูเขา penphuukhǎw/ to be mountainous.

ภูเขาไฟ (ลูก) phuukhǎwfaj/ (lûug/) N volcano.

ภูเขาหิมาลัย phuukhǎw/-hìmaa/laj/ the Himalaya Mountains.

ภู in แมลงภู่ (ตัว) malɛɛŋphûu/ (tua/) N eleg. carpenter bee. See cross reference.

ภูเก็ต phuukèd/ pN Phuket (Puket), a township in S Thailand.

ภูมิ ๑ phuum/, phuu/mí⊃ N 1. earth, place. 2. level,

status, background. Chiefly in compounds.

ปิตุภูมิ pìtùphuum/ N eleg. fatherland, native country. →Comp. มาตุภูมิ.

พระภูมิ phráphuum/ N the guardian spirit of one's land.

ภูมิประเทศ (แห่ง,อย่าง) phuu/míprathêed/ (hɛ̀ŋ/, jàaŋ/) N topography, the surface features of an area; scenery, landscape.

ภูมิพลอดุลเดช phuu/míphon/-ʔàdun/dèed/ nN Phumiphon Adundet (Phumiphol Aduldet), king of Thailand (1946-).

ภูมิภาค phuu/míphâag/ N the provinces, i.e. parts of the country lying outside the capital or largest city.

o ราชการส่วนภูมิภาค râadchakaan/sùanphuu/⊃ míphâag/ N provincial government service.

ภูมิลำเนา phuu/mílamnaw/ N domicile, native habitat, native district.

o ตั้งภูมิลำเนา tâŋ/phuu/mílamnaw/ to take up residence (as in a new district), to settle.

ภูมิศาสตร์ phuumísàad/ N geography.

มาตุภูมิ maa/tùphuum/ N eleg. motherland, native country. →Comp. ปิตุภูมิ.

ยุทธภูมิ (แห่ง) júd/thaphuum/ (hɛ̀ŋ/) N eleg. battlefield, battleground.

ลองภูมิ lɔɔŋphuum/ V colloq. to test the knowledge of, measure the educational level or background of (usually in an attempt to catch someone, expose someone's ignorance).

อุณหภูมิ ʔun/haphuum/ N temperature.

ภูมิ ๒ in the following entries.

ภาคภูมิ phâagphuum/ V 1. to feel proud. 2. to be dignified, grand, majestic. See cross reference.

ภูมิใจ(ใน) phuumcaj/(naj⊃) V 1. to be proud (of). 2. to have a feeling of accomplishment. ความ-- pride.

ภูมิฐาน phuumthǎan/ V to be dignified, grand.

เภสัช (1) pheesàd/; (2) pheesàd/⊃, pheesàd/cha⊃ N 1. eleg.,tech. medicine, drug. 2. initial stem meaning "pharmaceutical, pertaining to drugs." →Syn. 1. ยา com.

เภสัชกร (คน) pheesàd/chakɔɔn/ (khon/) N eleg. pharmacist.

เภสัชกรรม pheesàd/chakam/ N pharmacy.

เภสัชวิทยา pheesàd′wídthajaa′ N pharmacology.

โภค phôog′, phôogkha⊃ N 1. property. V 2. to eat, consume, utilize. →Chiefly in compounds.

    เครื่องอุปโภค khrɯ̂aŋ?ùbpaphôog′ N useful articles.

    บริโภค bɔɔríphôog′ V eleg. to consume, eat.

    โภคทรัพย์ phôogkhasáb′ N eleg. resources (as in "natural resources").

โภชน as in โภชนาหาร phôodchanaa′hǎan′ N eleg. food (in general).

โภชน์. See โพด .

ม

ม mɔɔ′ LOW consonant. Pronounced m both initially and finally.

มกราคม mógkaraa′khom′ N January. เดือน-- idem. →The names of all the months are listed under เดือน .

มคธ makhód′ N 1. an ancient kingdom in India, now called Bihar. 2. Pali, the language of this kingdom.

    ภาษามคธ phaasǎa′makhód′ N the Pali language.

มงกุฎ (อัน,มงกุฎ) moŋkùd′ (?an′, moŋkùd′) N crown.

มงคล moŋkhon′ N 1. eleg. auspicious sign. 2. propitiousness, auspiciousness. 3. a cotton band worn on the head (e.g. by bride and groom) for its auspiciousness.

    อัปมงคล ?àb′pamoŋkhon′ N 1. eleg. bad omen. 2. inauspiciousness. 3. (as n. mod.) inauspicious; defamatory, injurious (to someone's reputation).

    o เป็นอัปมงคล pen′-?àb′pamoŋkhon′ to be inauspicious, ominous.

มณฑป (หลัง) mondòb′ (lǎŋ′) N a structure with a pyramidal spire.

มณฑล (มณฑล) monthon′ (monthon′) N 1. province, monthon (montol). 2. circle. NOTE. Thailand was formerly divided into ten monthon for administrative purposes. This system was discontinued in 1933 (B. E. 2476). The largest administrative subdivision is now the ภาค , of which there are nine. For most practical purposes, however, the chief subdivision of the country is said to be the จังหวัด . →See จังหวัด ,

ภาค .

มณเฑียร. See มนเทียร .

มณี manii′ N lit. precious stones, gems.

มด ๑ (ตัว) mód′ (tua′) N ant.

    มดแดง (ตัว) móddɛɛŋ′ (tua′) N red ant.

มด ๒. See entries below.

    ขี้ปดมดเท็จ khîipòd′-mód′théd′ V elab. eleg. to tell a lie, prevaricate.

    พ่อมด (คน) phɔ̂ɔmód′ (khon′) N wizard, sorcerer.

    มดลูก (มดลูก) módlûug′ (módlûug′) N womb, uterus.

    มดหมอ (คน) mód′mɔ̌ɔ′ (khon′) N colloq. doctor, physician. →Syn. หมอ com., แพทย eleg.

    แม่มด (คน) mɛ̂ɛmód′ (khon′) N witch, sorceress.

มติ mátì?′ N resolution, decision; opinion, idea, view.

    ประชามติ prachaa′mátì?′ N eleg. public resolution, opinion.

    มติมหาชน mátì?′-mahǎa′chon′ N public opinion.

    มีมติให้ mii′mátì?′-hâj⊃ to resolve that, come to a decision that.

    ลงมติ loŋ′mátì?′ to resolve, pass a resolution, come to a decision.

ม.ธ.ก. mɔɔthɔɔkɔɔ′. Abbr. of มหาวิทยาลัยธรรม-ศาสตร์และการเมือง mahǎa′wídthajaalaj′-thammasàad′lɛkaanmɯaŋ′ University of Political and Moral Sciences.

มน ๑ mon′ V to be roundish, somewhat round (not sharply pointed).

มน ๒ in มืดมน mɯ̂ydmon′ V to be dark, obscure.

มนต์,มนตร์ (บท) mon′ (bòd′) N sacred words, prayer, sacrificial formula, incantation, magic spell.

    น้ำมนต์,-มนตร์ námmon′ N holy water.

    เวทมนต์,-มนตร์ (บท) wêedmon′ (bòd′) N magic spell, charm.

    สวดมนต์,-มนตร์ sùadmon′ V 1. to pray. 2. to chant sacred words, utter an incantation.

มนตรี (คน) montrii′ (khon′) N councilor, councilman. →Chiefly in compounds.

    คณะมนตรีความมั่นคง khanámontrii′khwaammânkhoŋ′ N Security Council.

    เทศมนตรี (คน) thêedsamontrii′ (khon′) N city councilman.

    รัฐมนตรี (คน) rádthamontrii′ (khon′) N minister,

i.e. cabinet minister.

o คณะรัฐมนตรี (คณะ) khaná?'/rádthamontrii'/
(khaná?/) N (the) cabinet, council of ministers.

o นายกรัฐมนตรี (คน,ท่าน) naajóg/rádthamon⊃
trii/ (khon/,thân/) N prime minister, premier.

องคมนตรี (ท่าน) ?oŋ/khamontrii/ (thân/) N
privy councilor.

มนเทียร monthian/ N royal household, establishment; palace. Also spelled มณเฑียร.

กฎมนเทียรบาล kòd/monthianbaan/ N laws pertaining to royalty.

มนังคสิลา in พรรคเสรีมนังคสิลา phág/-sěerii/ma⊃
naŋ/khásilaa/ Serimanangkhasila Party, a
political party formerly under the leadership
of Phibun (Phibul) Songkhram.

มนัส manád/ N lit. mind, heart.

มนิลา manilaa/ pN Manila. [f. Eng. or Tag.]

มนุษย,มนุษย- (คน) manúd/,manúd/saja⊃ (khon/)
N eleg. man, human being.

เพื่อนมนุษย (คน) phɣanmanúd/ (khon/) N fellow
man.

มนุษยชาติ manúd/sajachâad/ N mankind.

มนุษยเดินดิน (คน) manúd/-dəən/din/ (khon/) N
an ordinary human being (in the sense of not
possessing supernatural powers).

มนุษยธรรม manúd/sajatham/ N humanity,
humaneness.

มนุษยโลก manúd/sajalôog/ N the world, the
earth, i.e. the world of human beings. →Opp.
เทวโลก "world of the gods."

ลักษณะประจำมนุษย lágsanà?/-pracam/manúd/
N human nature.

โลกมนุษย lôog/manúd/ N the world, the earth.
Same as มนุษยโลก.

สังคมมนุษย (สังคม) sǎŋkhom/manúd/ (sǎŋkhom/)
N human society.

มโน manoo/ N eleg. heart, mind. →Syn. See ใจ.

มโนคติ manoo/khatì?/ N lit. idea, thought.

มโนภาพ manoo/phâab/ N lit. imagination.

มม.,ม.ม. Abbr. for มิลลิเมตร millimeter.

มรกต (เม็ด) mɔɔrakòd/ (méd/) N emerald.

มรณะ mɔɔraná?/ N lit. 1. death. V 2. to die.

มรณภาพ mɔɔ/ranaphâab/ N sacer. death.

o ถึงแก่มรณภาพ thɣŋkɛ̀ɛmɔɔ/ranaphâab/ sacer.

to die. →Syn. See ตาย.

มรดก mɔɔradòg/ N (one's) inheritance. →Also
spelled มฤดก.

รับมรดก ráb/mɔɔradòg/ V to inherit.

มรรยาท manjâad/ N manners, etiquette. →Also
มารยาท.

ตามมรรยาท taam/manjâad/ by courtesy.

ม.ร.ว. Abbrev. for หม่อมราชวงศ์ title for a great-
grandchild of a king.

มรสุม mɔɔrasǔm/ N monsoon.

ลมมรสุม lom/mɔɔrasǔm/ N monsoon wind.

หน้ามรสุม nâa/mɔɔrasǔm/ N monsoon season.

มฤดก márýdòg/, mɔɔradòg/. See มรดก.

มฤตยู marýdtajuu/ N 1. lit. death. 2. Uranus.

ดาวมฤตยู (ดวง) daaw/marýdtajuu/ (duaŋ/) N
Uranus (the planet).

ม.ล. Abbr. for หม่อมหลวง title for a great-great-
grandchild of a king.

มลทิน monthin/ N eleg. stain, blemish, taint,
impurity.

มีมลทิน mii/monthin/ eleg. to be tainted, blemished.

มลายา malaajaa/ pN Malaya. FS. มะลายา. [prob.
f. Eng. f. Mal.] →More often มลายู.

มลายู malaajuu/ pN Malaya. FS. มะลายู. [f. Mal.]
→Also มลายา.

แขกมลายู (คน) khɛ̀ɛg/malaajuu/ (khon/) N
Malayan, Malayan person.

ประเทศมลายู prathêed/malaajuu/ pN Malaya.

สหรัฐมลายู sahàrád/malaajuu/ pN Federated
Malay States.

หมู่เกาะมลายู mùukɔ̀?/malaajuu/ pN the Malay
Archipelago.

แหลมมลายู lɛ̌ɛm/malaajuu/ pN Malay Peninsula.

ม่วง mûaŋ/ V to be purple.

ผ้าม่วง (ผืน) phâamûaŋ/ (phɣ̌yn/) N a silk
loincloth or panung, worn by men.

สีม่วง sǐimûaŋ/ N 1. purple, the color purple.
V 2. to be purple.

ม้วน ๑ muan/ C 1. clf. for cigars, cigarettes.
V 2. to roll (a cigarette).

ม้วน ๒ in ปวดม้วน pùadmuan/ V to have a colic,
a fitful pain in the abdomen.

ม้วน múan/ C 1. roll, reel (e.g. of film). V 2. to
roll, roll up, reel (on a reel), wind, coil, curl.

ม้วนผม múanphŏm′ V to curl one's hair, put up one's hair.

มวย ๑ muaj′ N sport boxing. นัก-- boxer.

ชกมวย chógmuaj′ V to box.

ต่อยมวย tɔ̀jmuaj′ V to box.

มวยปล้ำ muajplâm′ N wrestling.

มวยสากล muajsăakon′ N boxing of European or American style (as opp. to the Thai style).

เวทีมวย (เวที) weethii′muaj′ (weethii′) N boxing ring.

มวย ๒ in ผมมวย phŏmmuaj′ N chignon, bun.

ม้วย (คน) mûaj′ (khon′) N colloq. Chinese girl. [f. Chin.]

ม้วย múaj′ V lit. to die, pass away. →Syn. See ตาย com.

มวล muan′ N 1. tech. mass. C 2. eleg. mass (see below).

ทั้งมวล tháŋmuan′ lit. eleg. all, all (of them): "the whole mass." →Cf. ทั้งปวง.

มหรสพ (อย่าง) mahɔ̌ɔrasòb′ (jàaŋ′) N eleg. entertainment. Also การ--.

โรงมหรสพ (โรง) rooŋ′mahɔ̌ɔrasòb′ (rooŋ′) N eleg. theater, entertainment establishment.

สถานมหรสพ (แห่ง) sathăn′mahɔ̌ɔrasòb′ (hɛ̀ŋ′) N eleg. theater, place of entertainment.

มหันต-. Bound form meaning "great."

มหันตโทษ mahăn′tathôod′ N eleg. 1. heavy punishment or penalty. 2. major offense. →Syn. โทษหนัก com.

มหันตภัย (อย่าง) mahăn′taphaj′ (jàaŋ′) N lit. eleg. great danger. Also มหาภัย. →Comp. ภัย.

มหัศจรรย์ mahàd′sacan′ V eleg. to be miraculous, fantastic, stupendous, amazing. ความ-- miracle; wonder, amazement.

มหา-. Bound form meaning "great."

พระบรมมหาราชวัง (แห่ง) phrábɔrommahăa′ɔ râadchawaŋ′ (hɛ̀ŋ′) N eleg. the grand palace.

พระมหากษัตริย์ (องค์,พระองค์) phrámahăa′ɔ kasàd′(ʔoŋ′,phráʔoŋ′) N king: "great king."

มหาชน mahăa′chon′ N eleg. the public, the majority of people.

o มติมหาชน matì?′-mahăa′chon′ N eleg. public opinion.

o มหาชนรัฐ mahăa′chonnarád′ N republic.

มหาบัณฑิต mahăa′bandìd′ N 1. the holder of a master's degree. 2. a master's degree.

มหาบุรุษ (คน) mahăa′burùd′ (khon′) N eleg. a great man.

มหาประเทศ (ประเทศ) mahăa′prathêed′ (prac thêed′) N eleg. powerful country, great power.

มหาประลัย mahăa′pralaj′ N eleg. great devastation, catastrophe, havoc.

o ระเบิดมหาประลัย rabə̀əd′-mahăa′pralaj′ N devastating bomb.

มหาภัย (อย่าง) mahăa′phaj′ (jàaŋ′) N eleg. great danger. Also มหันตภัย.

มหายาน mahăajaan′ N Mahayana, the northern theistic form of Buddhism (prevailing in Tibet, China and Japan). →Dist. หินยาน.

มหาราช mahăa′râad′ N the Great (as in Alexander the Great).

มหาวิทยาลัย (แห่ง) mahăa′wídthajaalaj′ (hɛ̀ŋ′) N university.

o จุฬาลงกรณมหาวิทยาลัย culaaloŋkɔɔn′-mahăa′ɔ wídthajaalaj′ N Chulalongkorn University.

มหาศาล mahăa′săan′ colloq. great, huge, enormous, tremendous.

มหาเศรษฐี (คน) mahăa′sèedthĭi′ (khon′) N multimillionaire.

มหาสงคราม (ครั้ง,หน) mahăa′sŏŋkhraam′ (khráŋ′, hŏn′) N Great War, World War.

มหาสมุทร (มหาสมุทร) mahăa′samùd′ (mahăa′ɔ samùd′) N ocean.

มหาสารคาม mahăa′săarakhaam′ pN Mahasarakham, a township in NE Thailand.

มหาอำนาจ,ประเทศ-- (ประเทศ) mahăa′ʔamɔ nâad′, prathêed′mahăa′ʔamnâad′ (prathêed′) N eleg. 1. the Great Powers. 2. a great power, a mighty nation.

o มหาอำนาจตะวันตก (ประเทศ) mahăa′ʔamnâad′-tawantòg′ (prathêed′) N eleg. the Western Powers.

มหาดไทย. See entries below.

กรมมหาดไทย krom′mahàadthaj′ N Department of the Interior.

กระทรวงมหาดไทย krasuaŋ′mahàadthaj′ N Ministry of the Interior.

มหาดเล็ก (คน) mahàadlég/ (khon/) N royal page.

มหิมา,มหึมา máhìmaa/, máhɨ̀maa/ V to be enormous, huge, gigantic.

มเหสี (องค์) mahěe/sǐi/ (ʔoŋ/) N roy. queen (wife of a king).

มโหรี (วง) mahǒorii/ (woŋ/) N Thai orchestra with vocal accompaniment (Oriental style).

มโหฬาร mahǒolaan/ V 1. to be splendid, magnificent, grand. 2. to be enormous, spacious. อย่าง-- with great pomp; grandly, in a grand way.

มอง mɔɔŋ/ V to look, look at.

เขม้นมอง khamên/mɔɔŋ/ V 1. to stare at, gaze at. 2. to look at (something) closely, fixedly.

จ้องมอง cɔ̂ŋ/mɔɔŋ/ V to stare at.

จับตามอง càbtaa/mɔɔŋ/ V to keep an eye on, fix one's eyes on.

มองกราด mɔɔŋkràad/ V to look around.

มองการณ์ไกล mɔɔŋ/kaanklaj/ V to be farsighted (have foresight), to foresee an incident or situation.

มองข้าม mɔɔŋkhâam/ V to overlook; to disregard.

มองเขม็ง mɔɔŋ/khaměŋ/ V to stare at, look at fixedly.

มองดู mɔɔŋduu/ V 1. to look. 2. to look at, regard.

มองตาม mɔɔŋtaam/ V to follow (someone) with one's eyes.

มองในแง่ร้าย mɔɔŋ/najŋɛ̀ráaj/ to look at something with a pessimistic view.

มองไม่เห็น mɔɔŋmâjhěn/ can't see (e.g. because of darkness, mental block, etc.).

มองสบตา mɔɔŋ/sòbtaa/ V to meet somebody's eyes, look somebody straight in the eyes.

มองหา mɔɔŋhǎa/ V to look for, search for.

มองเห็น mɔɔŋhěn/ V 1. to see, catch sight of. 2. to conceive (of). 3. to be able to see.

เหลียวมอง lǐawmɔɔŋ/ V to turn (the head) and look.

เหลือบมอง lɨ̀abmɔɔŋ/ V to glance at.

ม่อง mɔ̂ŋ/* V slang to die; to be dead, killed. →Syn. See ตาย.

ม่องทูด mɔ̂ŋthûud/ idem.

ม่องเท่ง mɔ̂ŋthêŋ/ idem.

มองโกเลีย mɔŋkoolia/* pN Mongolia. [f. Eng.]

มอญ mɔɔn/ N Mon (name referring to a people mostly residing in what is now a part of Burma); Pegu.

ชาวมอญ (คน) chaawmɔɔn/ (khon/) N Mon person, Peguan person.

มอด ๑ (ตัว) mɔ́ɔd/ (tua/) N weevil. →Usually ตัว--.

มอด ๒ mɔ́ɔd/ V to die down, die out, be extinguished.

มอบ mɔ̂ɔb/ V 1. to delegate, commit, entrust. 2. to give, present, submit.

มอบหมาย mɔ̂ɔbmǎaj/ V to assign.

o รับมอบหมาย ráb/mɔ̂ɔbmǎaj/ V 1. to accept or receive an assignment, responsibility, transaction. 2. to be in charge, have charge of.

มอบให้ mɔ̂ɔb/hâjɔ 1. to give, present, submit. 2. to assign to.

มอม mɔm/, mɔɔm/ V to be dirty, smeared, covered (e.g. with dirt, grease, paint) (usually of the face).

มอมแมม mɔmmɛm/* V to be dirty, covered with dirt, dusty and dirty, filthy, bedraggled, besmirched.

มอมหน้า mɔɔmnâa/ V to paint the face in order to conceal one's identity.

มอมเหล้า mɔɔmlâw/ V to trick (someone) into getting drunk.

มอย mɔ̂j/* V to doze, doze off.

หน้ามอย nâa/mɔ̂j/ V 1. (one's) face to fall. 2. to be crestfallen, have a long face.

มอร็อคโค mɔɔrɔ́gkhoo/ pN Morocco. [f. Eng.]

มอสเลม mɔ́ɔslem/* N Moslem. [f. Eng.]

มะกรูด (ใบ,ลูก,ผล) makrùud/ (baj/,lûug/,phǒn/) N Kaffir lime, bergamot. ต้น-- (ต้น) Kaffir lime tree, bergamot tree.

มะกอก (ใบ,ลูก,ผล) makɔ̀ɔg/ (baj/,lûug/,phǒn/) N hog plum; olive. ต้น-- (ต้น) olive tree.

น้ำมันมะกอก námman/makɔ̀ɔg/ N olive oil.

มะเกลือ maklya/ N ebony. ต้น-- (ต้น) ebony tree.

มะขาม (ฝัก) makhǎam/ (fàg/) N tamarind. ต้น-- (ต้น) tamarind tree.

มะเขือ (ใบ,ลูก,ผล) makhy̌a/ (baj/,lûug/,phǒn/) N eggplant (the fruit). ต้น-- (ต้น) eggplant (the plant).

มะเขือเทศ (ใบ,ลูก,ผล) makhy̌athêed/ (baj/, lûug/,phǒn/) N tomato. ต้น-- (ต้น) tomato plant.

มะเดื่อ (ใบ,ลูก,ผล) madỳa/ (baj/,lûug/,phǒn/) N

fig. ต้น-- (ต้น) fig tree.

มะนาว (ใบ,ลูก,ผล) manaaw′ (baj′,lûug′,phɔ̌n′)
N lime, lemon. ต้น-- (ต้น) lime tree, lemon
tree.

น้ำมะนาว námmanaaw′ N 1. lemonade, limeade.
2. lemon juice, lime juice.

มะโนลา manoo′laa′ N a type of dance performance
found in S Thailand.

มะปราง (ใบ,ลูก,ผล) mapraaŋ′ (baj′,lûug′,phɔ̌n′)
N marian plum. ต้น-- (ต้น) marian plum
tree.

มะพร้าว (ใบ,ลูก,ผล) maphráaw′ (baj′,lûug′,phɔ̌n′)
N coconut (the fruit). ต้น-- (see below).

กะโหลกมะพร้าว (ลูก,ใบ) kalòog′maphráaw′
(lûug′,baj′) N hard shell of the coconut, i.e.
the endocarp.

กากมะพร้าว kàagmaphráaw′ N coconut meat
residue, i.e. the unusable residue left after the
grated meat has been pressed.

ก้านมะพร้าว (ก้าน) kâan′maphráaw′ (kâan′) N
midrib of a leaflet of a coconut palm pinnate
leaf. →Dist. ทางมะพร้าว.

กาบมะพร้าว (กาบ) kàabmaphráaw′ (kàab′) N
coir; piece of coconut husk (of any size).

งวงมะพร้าว (งวง) ŋuaŋmaphráaw′ (ŋuaŋ′) N
spadix, fruit-bearing stem of the coconut palm.

ต้นมะพร้าว (ต้น) tônmaphráaw′ (tôn′) N the
coconut palm, coco palm (Cocos nucifera).

ทางมะพร้าว (ทาง) thaaŋmaphráaw′ (thaaŋ′) N
1. midrib of the coconut palm pinnate leaf. 2.
coconut palm pinnate leaf. →Dist. ก้านมะพร้าว.

น้ำมะพร้าว náam′maphráaw′ N coconut milk
(i.e. the liquid from a green coconut).

น้ำมันมะพร้าว námman′maphráaw′ N coconut oil.

เนื้อมะพร้าว nýamaphráaw′ N coconut meat.

ใบมะพร้าว (ใบ) bajmaphráaw′ (baj′) N leaf or
leaflet of the coconut palm.

เปลือกมะพร้าว plỳagmaphráaw′ N coconut husk.

มะพร้าวห้าว (ใบ,ลูก,ผล) maphráawhâaw′ (baj′,
lûug′,phɔ̌n′) N ripe coconut.

o เอามะพร้าวห้าวมาขายสวน ʔawmaphráawhâaw′-
maakhǎaj′sǔan′ idiom. to tell someone what
he already knows. Cf. "carry coals to Newcastle."

มะพร้าวแห้ง maphráaw′hɛ̂ŋ′ N dried coconut

meat, copra.

มะพร้าวอ่อน (ใบ,ลูก,ผล) maphráawʔɔ̀ɔn′ (baj′,
lûug′,phɔ̌n′) N young coconut.

ยอดมะพร้าว (ยอด) jɔ̂ɔdmaphráaw′ (jɔ̂ɔd′) N
crown of the coconut palm.

ลูกมะพร้าว (ลูก) lûugmaphráaw′ (lûug′) N
coconut (with or without the outer husk).

มะเฟือง (ใบ,ลูก,ผล) mafyaŋ′ (baj′,lûug′,phɔ̌n′) N
carambola (fruit). ต้น-- (ต้น) carambola tree.

มะม่วง (ใบ,ลูก,ผล) mamûaŋ′ (baj′,lûug′,phɔ̌n′)
N mango (the fruit). ต้น-- (ต้น) mango tree
(Mangifera indica).

มะเมีย mamia′ N eleg. (Year of the) Horse. →The
complete list of the cyclical years is given under
ปี.

มะเมื่อม mamŷam′ rM intensifier used with ดำ
"black."

มะแม mamɛɛ′ N eleg. (Year of the) Goat. →The
complete list of the cyclical years is given under
ปี.

มะระ (ใบ,ลูก,ผล) mará′ (baj′,lûug′,phɔ̌n′) N
bitter melon. ต้น-- (ต้น) bitter melon plant.

มะรืน maryyn′ N the day after tomorrow. →See
มะเรื่อง.

มะรืนนี้ maryynníi′ the day after tomorrow.

มะเร็ง mareŋ′ N cancer.

โรคมะเร็ง rôog′mareŋ′ N cancer (the disease).

มะเรื่อง marŷaŋ′ N the third day from today, three
days from today (i.e. the day after the day after
tomorrow). →See มะรืน.

มะโรง marooŋ′ N (Year of the) Dragon. →The complete list of the cyclical years is given under ปี.

มะละกอ (ใบ,ลูก,ผล) malakɔɔ′ (baj′,lûug′,phɔ̌n′)
N papaya. ต้น-- (ต้น) papaya tree (Carica
papaya).

มะลายา FS. See มลายา.

มะลายู FS. See มลายู.

มะลิ (ดอก) malíʔ′ (dɔ̀ɔg′) N jasmine. ต้น-- (ต้น)
jasmine plant or bush.

ดอกมะลิ (ดอก) dɔ̀ɔgmalíʔ′ (dɔ̀ɔg′) N jasmine
(the flower).

มะเส็ง maseŋ′ N eleg. (Year of the) Snake. →The
complete list of the cyclical years is given under
ปี.

มะเหงก maŋèeg′ N colloq. knuckle (of the hand).

o มะเหงกแน่ะ maŋèeg′nê a threatening expression usually uttered with the knuckle poised as if to strike.

มัก mág′ AA likely to, usually.

มักคุ้น in รู้จักมักคุ้น. See below.

มักง่าย mágŋâaj′ V to be careless, heedless, sloppy, slovenly.

มักจะ mág′caʔ AA likely to, usually.

มักจี่ in รู้จักมักจี่. See below.

มักน้อย mágnɔ́ɔj′ V 1. to be content with little, be satisfied with what little one has. 2. to be unambitious. →Ant. 1. มักมาก. 2. มักใหญ่.

มักมาก mágmâag′ V to be greedy, have an insatiable desire (e.g. for money, sex). →Ant. มักน้อย.

มักใหญ่ mágjàj′ V to be ambitious. →Ant. มักน้อย.

o มักใหญ่ใฝ่สูง mágjàj′fàjsǔuŋ′ V elab. colloq. to be ambitious. ความ-- ambition, ambitiousness. →Used in an unfavorable sense in Thai.

รู้จักมักคุ้น rúucàg′mágkhún′ V elab. colloq. to be acquainted (with), know personally.

รู้จักมักจี่ rúucàg′mágcìi′ V elab. colloq. idem.

เลือกที่รักมักที่ชัง lɨ̂ag′thîirág′-mág′thîichaŋ′ V elab. colloq. to show partiality, show favoritism, play favorites; to be partial in one's likes and dislikes.

มักกัก mâgkàg′. Colloquial var. of มักขัก.

มักขัก mâgkhâg′ rM intens. used with อ้วน "fat."

มัง ๑ maŋ′ colloq. 1. some (out of a number). 2. somewhat, in part, partly, to some extent. →Colloquial var. of บ้าง bâaŋ′.

o ขอมัง khɔ̌ɔ′maŋ↓ colloq. Let me have some! →Syn. ขอบ้าง com.

มัง ๒. See entries below.

มั่งคั่ง mâŋkhâŋ′ V eleg. to be rich, wealthy, prosperous. ความ-- richness, wealthiness. →Syn. มั่งมี eleg., รวย com.

มั่งมี mâŋmii′ V eleg. to be rich, wealthy. ความ-- richness, wealthiness. →Syn. มั่งคั่ง eleg., รวย com.

มังกร (ตัว) maŋkɔɔn′ (tua′) N dragon.

มังค่า in ฝรั่งมังค่า (คน) faràŋ′-maŋ′khâa′ (khon′) N colloq. white people, occidental people.

มังคุด (ใบ,ลูก,ผล) maŋkhúd′ (baj′,lûug′,phǒn′) N mangosteen. ต้น-- (ต้น) mangosteen tree (Garcinia mangostana).

มัจจุราช mádcurâad′ N lit. 1. god of death. 2. death. →Syn. 2. ความตาย com.

มัจฉา mádchǎa′ N lit. fish. →Syn. ปลา com.

มัชฌิม mádchim′, mád′chimmaʔ N 1. lit. mid, middle. 2. tech. medium, mean.

มัชฌิมยาม mád′chimmajaam′ N lit. midnight.

มัชฌิมวัย mád′chimmawaj′ N lit.,eleg. middle age, i.e. the middle period of life.

มัด mád′ V 1. to tie, bind. C 2. clf. for bundles, bunches. →Syn. 1. ผูก.

ผูกมัด phùugmád′ V to tie, bind. การ-- obligation, tie, bond.

o ข้อผูกมัด (ข้อ) khɔ̂ɔ′phùugmád′ (khɔ̂ɔ′) N 1. obligation, binding condition. 2. strings (attached to a deal).

มัดจำ (จำนวน) mádcam′ (camnuan′) N deposit (given as security, as a down payment).

o เงินมัดจำ ŋən′mádcam′ N deposit.

o วางมัดจำ waaŋ′mádcam′ V to give a deposit, make a part payment.

มัธยม mádthajom′ N secondary educational level.

ครูมัธยม (คน) khruu′mádthajom′ N secondary school teacher.

ชั้นมัธยม chán′mádthajom′ N secondary school level.

ชั้นมัธยมบริบูรณ์ chán′-mádthajom′bɔɔribuun′ N the final year of secondary schools.

มัธยมศึกษา mádthajom′sɨ̀gsǎa′ N secondary education.

o โรงเรียนมัธยมศึกษา rooŋrian′-mádthajom′ʔ sɨ̀gsǎa′ N secondary school.

มัธยัสถ์ mádthajád′ V eleg. 1. to be thrifty, economical. 2. to economize. ความ-- thrift, thriftiness, economy.

มัน ๑ man′ N 1. oil, fat, grease. V 2. to be rich, oily; to be fatty, rich in fats, greasy (considered to be a desirable quality with some foods, as nuts, rich cookies, ice cream, etc.). 3. to be glossy.

ของมัน ๆ khɔ̌ɔŋ′manman′ N fatty, oily substance or thing.

ขัดมัน khàdman′ V to be polished, shiny, glossy.

ไขมัน khǎjman′ N fat.

ชิ้นปลามัน chín′plaaman′ idiom. the best part of things, the juiciest, most desirable portion.

ตกมัน tògman′ V (an elephant) to be in must, in rut.

น้ำมัน námman′ N 1. oil. 2. colloq. fuel oil. See cross reference.

เป็นมัน penman′ 1. to be oily, greasy. 2. to be shiny, glossy.

เป็นมันวาว penman′waaw′ to be glitteringly glossy, shiny.

มันขลับ man′khlàb′ to be very shiny, glossy.

มันวับ man′wáb′ to be very glossy.

มันสมอง (ก้อน) mansamɔ̌ɔŋ′ (kɔ̂ɔn′) N anat. brain (the organ, as opposed to สมอง "brains, intellectual power, intelligence").

รสมัน ródman′ N a nutty flavor.

มัน ๒ (หัว) man′ (hǔa′) N 1. potato, yam. V 2. to taste crisp and starchy (used to describe the texture of raw sweet potatoes, water chestnuts, certain green mangoes). NOTE. มัน is a class term for several kinds of plants with starchy tuberous roots.

แป้งมัน pɛ̂ɛŋman′ N cassava or potato starch.

มันเทศ (หัว) manthêed′ (hǔa′) N sweet potato (as opposed to มันฝรั่ง). ต้น-- (ต้น) sweet potato plant.

มันฝรั่ง (หัว) man′faràŋ′ (hǔa′) N potato, Irish potato (as opposed to มันเทศ). ต้น-- (ต้น) potato plant.

มันสำปะหลัง (หัว) man′sǎmpalǎŋ′ (hǔa′) N cassava. ต้น-- (ต้น) cassava plant. →Also incorrectly มันสำปะหรัง.

มัน ๓ man′ P 1. com. it, they, them. 2. derog. or int. he, him, she, her, they, them. →Syn. 2. เขา com. NOTE. มัน is sometimes used in ways corresponding to the English use of "it" as an indefinite subject; 1st and 2nd examples.

o มันยากนาแกนา manjâag′naa′→kɛɛnaa′↓ It is very difficult, you see.

o นั่นมันคนละเรื่อง nân′-mankhonlarŷaŋ′↓ That's a different story, a different matter!

ของมัน khɔ̌ɔŋman′ of it, its.

ช่างมัน,--ปะไร,--เป็นไร châŋ′man↓, châŋ′manɔ paraj↓, châŋ′manpenraj↓ Let it be. Let it go. I don't care about him, about it. I don't care what becomes of him.

ทีใครก็ทีมัน thii′khraj′-kɔ̂thii′man′ When it's a fellow's turn, why then, it's his turn!

มัน ๔ man′ V 1. to feel a strong urge (to do something). 2. to be having great pleasure (in doing something). →Chiefly in compounds.

มันขา man′khǎa′ V 1. to feel a strong urge to do something with one's feet (e.g. to dance). 2. to be greatly enjoying (e.g. dancing).

มันเขี้ยว man′khîaw′ V "to feel like biting (into something)." →Used especially when seeing the temptingly chubby cheeks of a child.

มันเขี้ยวมันมือ mankhîaw′manmyy′ V to be eager to fight; to have a strong urge to do something (with one's hands, or with one's hands and teeth). Cf. Eng. "to feel like tearing into."

มันมือ manmyy′ V 1. to feel a strong urge to do something with one's hands (e.g. to play the piano, to play badminton, etc.). 2. to be having great fun (e.g. playing the piano).

มั่น mân′ V to be firm.

คำมั่นสัญญา (ข้อ,ประการ) khammân′sǎnjaa′ (khɔ̂ɔ′, prakaan′) N promise, pledge. →Also คำมั่น.

เชื่อมั่น chŷa′mân′ to believe firmly.

ตั้งมั่น tâŋ′mân′ 1. to settle down firmly; to establish oneself in a stronghold. 2. to remain firm, steadfast.

ที่มั่น (ที่,แห่ง) thîimân′ (thîi′,hὲŋ′) N fortified place, fortification, stronghold.

เป็นแม่นมั่น penmɛ̂n′mân′ surely, absolutely.

มั่นคง mânkhoŋ′ V to be steadfast, stable, firm (as in purpose), secure. ความ-- firmness, stability, permanence, security.

o คณะมนตรีความมั่นคง khanámontrii′khwaammânɔ khoŋ′ N Security Council.

มั่นใจ mâncaj′ V to be sure, confident, positive, certain. ความ-- confidence, certainty.

ยึดมั่น(ใน) jýd′mân′(najɔ) 1. to hold fast (to). 2. to believe firmly (in).

หมายมั่นปั้นมือ mǎajmân′pânmyy′ eleg. colloq. 1. to resolve, have a strong determination (to do something). 2. to anticipate strongly.

มัว mua′ V 1. to be dim, obscure, cloudy. 2.
    colloq. to be busily engaged in something.

ขุ่นมัว khùnmua′ V 1. to be murky, unclear,
    cloudy. 2. to be dim, blurred. 3. to be sullen,
    ill-humored, gloomy.

พร่ามัว phrâa′mua′ V to be blurred, indistinct.

มัวแต่ muatɛɔ V to be busy with, to spend or
    waste too much time (doing something).

มัวหมอง muamɔɔŋ′ V to be tainted, stained, tar-
    nished. →Often used in respect to one's name.

มัวโอ้เอ้ mua?ôo°êe′ V colloq. to waste time
    unnecessarily.

มืดมัว mŷydmua′ V 1. to be obscure. 2. to be
    overcast, murky.

มั่ว in มั่วสุ่ม mûasùm′ V (people) to assemble,
    congregate, gather together.

มา maa′ V 1. to come. sV 2. coming, hitherward
(in space); 2nd example. 3. coming, i.e. toward
the present, or toward the focal time (as in a
story); 3rd example. 4. sec. vb. corresponding
to English present perfect tense; 4th and 5th
examples.
NOTE. (1) มา is frequently coupled with ไป
"go." See examples under ไปมา below. (2)
It can also be used as a sec. vb. with ไป as
prim. vb.; 4th example.

o มาเร็ว maa!réw′↓ Come quickly!

o กลับมา klàbmaa′ to come back; "return com-
    ing."

o ต่อมาเขาก็ได้แต่งงานกัน tɔɔmaa′→ kháwkɔ̂daâjɔ
    tɛ̀ŋŋaan′kan↓ Later on, they got married.

o ไปมาแล้ว paj′maalɛ́ɛw′ has gone (there), has
    already been (there).

o ที่กล่าวมานี้ thîiklàaw′maanîi′ which (we) have
    mentioned, which has been mentioned.

การมาเรียน kaan′maarian′ N attendance (in
    school).

เกิดมา (1) kɔ̀ad′maa′; (2) kɔ̀ad′maaɔ 1. to be
    born, to have been born. 2. colloq. to happen
    to (e.g. get sick).

ขึ้นมา khŷnmaa′ 1. to come up, rise. 2. to grow,
    increase. sV 3. up, upward; onward. 4. in-
    creasingly.

o วูบขึ้นมา wûub′khŷnmaa′ to flare up.

เข้ามา khâwmaa′ V 1. to come in. sV 2. in.

o เดินเข้ามา(ใน) dəən′khâwmaa′(najɔ) to walk
    in(to), come in(to), enter.

o เดินเข้ามาหา dəən′khâwmaahǎa′ to approach,
    come toward.

o นำ...เข้ามาใช้ nam′...khâwmaacháj′ to
    introduce, bring into use.

ใจมา. See subentries below.

o ใจมาขึ้นเป็นกอง caj′maa′-khŷnpenkɔɔŋ′ 1.
    to take heart, be heartened. 2. to recover
    (as from fright).

o ใจมาตั้งกระบุง caj′maa′-tâŋkrabuŋ′ idem.

ต่อมา tɔ̀ɔ′maa′, tɔ̂ɔmaa′, tɔɔmaaɔ sV 1. next,
following, later on (in time). 2. next, further
on (in space). 3. on (i.e. in continuation). →For
examples see cross reference. NOTE. This
expression implies direction in time or space
from a contextually suggested point toward a
focal point of reference. →Dist. ต่อไป.

ตั้งแต่...เป็นต้นมา tâŋtɛɔ...pentôn′maa′ from
(such and such a time) on (i.e. from the past
toward the present); from (such and such a place)
on (i.e. from a distant point toward a closer one).

ทำมาหากิน thammaa′hǎakin′ V to earn a living.
การ-- making a living, earning a living; occupation, livelihood.

ที่มา (แห่ง) thîimaa′ (hɛ̀ŋ′) N source, origin.

นำ(...)มา nam′(...)maa′ 1. to bring; to lead
(coming this way). 2. to bring about.

o นำมาซึ่ง nam′maa′-sŷŋɔ lit.,eleg. to bring,
    bring in, bring about (e.g. sorrow, misfortune).

o นำมาใช้ nam′maacháj′ to bring into use, intro-
    duce.

เป็นมา pen′maaɔ to happen, occur, arise. ความ--
past events, account of past events (from the
beginnings to the present).

ไปตาม(...)มา pajtaam′(...)maa′ to go fetch
(a person).

ไปมา pajmaa′ V 1. to go back and forth, to come
and go; 1st and 2nd examples. sV 2. back and
forth, to and fro, this way and that, hither and
yon; 3rd and 5th examples. As sec. verb also
...ไป...มา ; 4th and 6th examples.

o ไปมาค้าขาย pajmaa′kháakhǎaj′ colloq. to engage in trade, travel about on commercial business.

o ไปมาหาสู่ pajmaa′hǎasùu′ colloq. to visit, pay visits.

o เดินไปมา dəən′pajmaa′ to walk back and forth.

o เดินโซไปเซมา dəən′-soopaj′seemaa′ to stagger back and forth, this way and that (as a drunk person).

o วกไปมา wók′pajmaa′ 1. to turn this way and that; to wend. 2. to be winding (as a road).

o กลับไปกลับมา klàbpaj′klàbmaa′ 1. to change back and forth again and again. 2. to be unreliable. 3. back and forth.

ไปไหนมา pajnǎjmaa↓ Where have you been?

ไปไหนมาไหน pajnǎj′maanǎj′ to get around, go hither and thither, travel about.

พา(...)มา phaa(...)maa′ to bring. →Cf. เอามา.

มาก่อน maakɔ̀ɔn′ before, in the past.

มาจาก (1) maa′càagɔ; (2) maacàagɔ 1. to come from. 2. from.

มาตาม (1,3) maataam′; (2) maa′taamɔ 1. to come to fetch. 2. to come along, walk along (e.g. a path). 3. along, following.

มาแต่ maatɛ̀ɛɔ from, since.

o มาแต่กำเนิด maatɛ̀ɛkamnə̀əd′ from birth.

o มาแต่เดิม maatɛ̀ɛdəəm′ from the beginning.

มาถึง maathʉ̌ŋ′, maa′thʉ̌ŋɔ, maathʉ̌ŋɔ 1. to arrive; to reach, arrive at or in. 2. to, at, in. NOTE. มาถึง implies motion towards a contextually suggested point of reference; cf. ไปถึง.

มาเที่ยว maathîaw′ 1. to come around (e.g. to someone's house). 2. to come on a pleasure trip (e.g. to a city, a country).

มารับ maaráb′ to come to meet, get, or receive.

มาแล้ว maaléɛw′ 1. ago; 1st and 2nd examples. 2. have, have already (done such and such); 3rd and 4th examples. 3. have come from (doing such and such); 5th example.

o นานมาแล้ว naan′maaléɛw′ long ago, a long time ago.

o เมื่อ ๖ ปีมาแล้ว mʉ̂ahòg′pii′-maaléɛw′ six years ago.

o ท่องมาแล้ว thɔ̂ŋ′maaléɛw′ (I) have studied (my lesson).

o ให้มาแล้ว hâj′maaléɛw′ (he) has already given (it to me).

o กินมาแล้ว kin′maaléɛw′ (I) have already eaten (implying that one has eaten before coming).

มาหา maahǎa′ to come to see, come to visit.

มาเอง maaʔeeŋ′ 1. to come by oneself (unaccompanied). 2. to come of one's own accord. 3. to come oneself (in person).

ยกมากล่าว jók′maaklàaw′ to quote, mention, cite.

ลงมา loŋmaa′ 1. to come down. sV 2. down, downward.

o ยกลงมา jók′loŋmaa′ 1. to move (e.g. troops) down (from the north, or from a hilltop). 2. to take (e.g. a box) down (from the top of a stack).

สืบมา sʉ̀yb′maa′ 1. further, in continuation. 2. from them on (toward the focal time), since then.

เสมอมา samə̌ə′maa′ constantly, regularly (up to the present or to the focal time).

หันมา hǎnmaa′, hǎn′maaɔ to turn toward.

อยู่มาวันหนึ่ง jùumaa′-wan′nyŋ (and) then one day, one day later on.

ออกมา (1) ʔɔ̀ɔg′maa′, ʔɔ̀ɔg′maaɔ; (2) ʔɔ̀ɔgmaa′ V 1. to come out. sV 2. out, forth.

o ยื่นออกมา jʉ̂yn′′ʔɔ̀ɔgmaa′ to stick out, project, protrude.

เอา(...)มา ʔaw(...)maa′ 1. to bring. 2. hither, along, up. →See cross reference. →Cf. พามา.

ม้า (ตัว) máa′ (tua′) N 1. horse. 2. bench.

กำลังม้า kamlaŋ′máa′ C horsepower. [tr. f. Eng.] →Syn. แรงม้า.

เกือกม้า (อัน, ข้าง) kỳagmáa′ (ʔan′, khâaŋ′) N horseshoe.

ขี่ม้า khìimáa′ V 1. to ride a horse. N 2. horseback riding.

แข่งม้า (ครั้ง, นัด, เที่ยว) (1) khὲŋ′máa′; (2) khὲŋɔ máa′ V 1. to race on horseback; to participate in horse racing. N 2. the races, horse races, horse racing (khráŋ′, nád′); a (horse) race (thîaw′). การ-- horse racing.

ควบม้า khûabmáa′ V to gallop (a horse).

คอกม้า (คอก) khɔ̂ɔgmáa′ (khɔ̂ɔg′) N horse stable.

ทรงม้า soŋmáa′ V roy. 1. to be mounted on a

horse. 2. to ride a horse.

ทหารม้า (คน) thahǎan′máa′ (khon′) N cavalryman; the cavalry.

ผ้าขาวม้า (ผืน) phâakhawmáa′* (phɣ̌yn′) N a
long strip of patterned cloth used by men for
various purposes (e.g. as a towel, loincloth,
sash, or covering for the head).

ม้าแข่ง (ตัว) máakhɛ̀ŋ′ (tua′) N race horse.

ม้าต่าง (ตัว) máatàaŋ′ (tua′) N pack horse.

ม้านั่ง (ตัว) máanâŋ′ (tua′) N 1. bench, stool.
2. pew.

ม้ามืด máamɣ̂yd′ N polit. dark horse. [tr.f.
Eng.]

ม้ายาว (ตัว) máajaaw′ (tua′) N 1. bench. 2.
pew.

รถม้า (คัน) ródmáa′ (khan′) N carriage, a
horse-drawn vehicle.

แรงม้า rɛɛŋmáa′ C horsepower. →Syn.
กำลังม้า.

เล่นม้า lênmáa′ V to bet on horses: "to play the
horses." [perh. tr. f. Eng.]

สนามม้า (แห่ง) sanǎammáa′ (hɛ̀ŋ′) N race track.

หน้าม้า (คน) nâamáa′ (khon′) N decoy (only of
a person).

อานม้า (ชุด, อัน) ʔaanmáa′ (chúd′, ʔan′) N
horse saddle.

มาก mâag′ V 1. to be much, many. sV 2. much,
very. Nm 3. many, a lot of. →Ant. น้อย.
→In mng. 3. used chiefly with คน or in the
following expression.

o มากหน้าหลายตา mâagnâa′lǎajtaa′ many people, a lot of people.

ข้างมาก khâaŋmâag′ N the majority (esp. in
voting).

o เสียงข้างมาก sɯ̌aŋ′khâaŋmâag′ the majority
vote.

โดยมาก doojmâag′ by and large, for the most
part, mostly.

น้อยมาก nɔ́ɔjmâag′ very few, very little, very
small in number.

น้ำมาก náam′mâag′ the flood level is above
normal, the flood is high, the tide is high.

เป็นจำนวนมาก pencamnuan′mâag′ 1. in large
quantity, in great numbers. 2. by a great quan-

tity, by a large number.

เป็นอันมาก penʔanmâag′ lit. great, very much;
in great quantity.

ผู้ลากมากดี (คน) phûulâag′-mâag′dii′ (khon′)
N elab. colloq. the nobility, the elite, the
people of the upper class.

มักมาก mágmâag′ V to be greedy, have an insatiable desire (e.g. for money, sex). →Ant. มักน้อย.

มากกว่า mâagkwàa′, mâag′kwàaɔ more, -er;
more than, -er than.

มากเกินควร mâag′kəənkhuan′ 1. more than is
good, proper. 2. much too (e.g. big, small, etc.).

มากเกินไป mâag′kəənpaj′ 1. too much. 2. much
too (e.g. hot).

มากขึ้น mâag′khɣ̂n′ more, more and more.

มากต่อมากนัก mâag′tɔ̀ɔmâag′-nág so much, so
many, a great deal of. →Also มากต่อมาก.

มากที่สุด mâag′thîisùd′ the most, the very most.

o ร้ายมากที่สุด ráajmâag′thîisùd′ the very most
ferocious; the very worst.

มากน้อย. See entries below.

o กี่มากน้อย kìimâagnɔ́ɔj′ colloq. how much,
how many.

o ไม่กี่มากน้อย mâjkìi′mâagnɔ́ɔj′ colloq. not
so much, not so many.

o ไม่มากก็น้อย mâjmâag′kɔ̂nɔ́ɔj′ whether many
or few, whether much or little; if not a (whole)
lot, then (at least) some.

มากมาย mâagmaaj′ V to be much, a lot, many,
a great many; to be numerous, innumerable.

o เป็นจำนวนมากมาย pencamnuan′mâagmaaj′ 1.
in great numbers. 2. by a great quantity, by a
large number.

o มากมายก่ายกอง mâagmaaj′kàajkɔɔŋ′ elab.
colloq. so much, so many, a whole lot, a great
deal.

มากยิ่งขึ้นทุกที mâag′jîŋkhɣ̂n′-thúgthii′ more and
more every minute; progressively more.

ไม่...มากนัก mâjɔ...mâag′nág′ not so very.

ส่วนมาก sùanmâag′ mostly, the greater part.
คน-- the majority (of people); most people.

o เป็นส่วนมาก pensùan′mâag′ for the most part,
mostly.

อย่างมาก jàaŋmâag′ 1. at most, at the maximum.

2. very, much, highly. 3. big, great, maximum.

o เป็นอย่างมาก penjàaŋmâag′ 1. at most, at the very most. 2. very much.

อายุมาก ʔaajúʔ′mâag′ V to be old, aged; to be an older person (as opposed to a young person).

มาด. See entries below.

มาดหมาย mâadmǎaj′ V to expect, anticipate, intend.

มุ่งมาด mûŋmâad′ V to expect, anticipate, aim at, aim for.

มาตร in มาตรว่า mâad′wâaɔ even if, although.

มาตรฐาน mâadtrathǎan′ N standard.

มาตรฐานการครองชีพ mâadtrathǎan′kaankhrɔɔŋɔ chîib′ N standard of living.

มาตรา mâadtraa′* N 1. system of measurement, standard. C 2. section, clause (as of a law).

มาตราชั่ง mâadtraa′châŋ′ N system of weight measurement.

มาตราเมตริก mâadtraa′métrìg′ N metric system.

มาตราส่วน mâadtraa′sùan′ N scale (indicating proportionate size).

อนุมาตรา ʔànúʔ′mâadtraa′ N law subsection, subdivision of a clause or section of a law.

มาตุ in มาตุภูมิ maa′tùphuum′ N eleg. motherland, native country. →Comp. ปิตุภูมิ.

ม่าน (ผืน) mâan′ (phǔyn′) N curtain, drape.

ม่านควัน mâankhwan′ N smoke screen.

ม่านตา mâantaa′ N anat. iris of the eye.

ม่านหน้าต่าง (ผืน) mâannâatàaŋ′ (phǔyn′) N window curtain, window shade, drape.

ม่านเหล็ก mâanlèg′ the Iron Curtain.

o หลังม่านเหล็ก lǎŋ′mâanlèg′ behind the Iron Curtain.

มานะ maanáʔ′ N 1. persistence, perseverance. 2. pride (which prompts to perseverance). V 3. to persevere, be persistent (in a good sense). ความ-- perseverance, persistence.

ม้าม (ลูก) máam′ (lûug′) N spleen.

มาย in มากมาย mâagmaaj′ V to be much, a lot, many; to be numerous, innumerable.

ม้าย ๑ in ม้ายงั้น mâajŋán′ colloq. otherwise, or else, if not. →Short and variant form of ไม่อย่างงั้น. →Also ไม่งั้น.

ม้าย ๒ mâaj′. Bound stem meaning "widowed." →Also spelled หม้าย.

พ่อม้าย (คน) phɔɔmâaj′ (khon′) N widower.

พุ่มม้าย phûmmâaj′ N widowhood.

แม่ม้าย (คน) mɛɛmâaj′ (khon′) N widow.

หญิงม้าย (คน) jǐŋmâaj′ (khon′) N widow.

มายา (อย่าง) maajaa′ (jàaŋ′) N trick, artifice, deception. →Also มารยา.

มาร (ตัว) maan′ (tua′) N 1. Mara, devil, demon, evil spirit. 2. a person who ruins everything, an evildoer, a devil.

ตัวมาร (ตัว) tuamaan′ (tua′) N 1. Mara, devil, demon. 2. a person who ruins everything, an evildoer, a devil.

มาร์ช in เพลงมาร์ช (เพลง) phleeŋmáach′, -máad′ (phleeŋ′) N march music. [มาร์ช f. Eng.]

มารดา (คน) maandaa′ (khon′) N eleg. mother. →Syn. แม่ com.

บิดามารดา (คน) bìdaa′maandaa′ (khon′) N eleg. parents. →Syn. พ่อแม่ com.

มารยา (อย่าง) maanjaa′ (jàaŋ′) N trick, artifice, deception. →Also มายา.

กลมารยา (อย่าง) kon′maanjaa′ (jàaŋ′) N trick, artifice, deception.

มารยาท (อย่าง) maarajâad′ (jàaŋ′) N manners, etiquette. →Also มรรยาท.

มาลัย maalaj′ N garland.

พวงมาลัย (พวง,อัน) phuaŋmaalaj′ N 1. garland (phuaŋ′). 2. steering wheel (of automobile) (ʔan′).

มาลาเรีย,มาเลเรีย maalaaria′, maaleeria′ N malaria. [f. Eng.] →Syn. ไข้จับสั่น.

มิ- míɔ eleg. not. →Used only in special expressions, chiefly in formal contexts. →Comp. ไม่.

จะหลับมิหลับแหล่ calàb′mílàb′lɛ̀ɛ′ to be on the verge of falling asleep. →See แหล่ ๒.

มิฉะนั้น míchanán′ otherwise.

o หรือมิฉะนั้น rʉ̌y′míchanán′ or else, otherwise.

มิชอบ míchɔɔb′ to be wrong, illegal, inappropriate, bad, dishonest.

o คิดมิชอบ khíd′míchɔɔb′ to have evil intentions, have unrighteous thoughts.

o ในทางมิชอบ najthaaŋ′míchɔɔb′ in an unlawful manner, illegally.

มิช้ามินาน mícháa′mínaan′ eleg. not long (of time).

มิใช่ (1) míchâjɔ:; (2) míchâj↓ AA 1. not. 2. no, that's not the case.

มิดีมิร้าย mídii'míráaj' elab. eleg. to be bad, evil, harmful.

o คิดมิดีมิร้าย khíd'mídii'míráaj' elab. eleg. to have evil intentions.

มิได้ (1,3) mídâaj'; (2) mídâjɔ; (4) mídâaj↓ eleg. 1. not get, gain, obtain, procure. 2. didn't; not get to, didn't get to. 3. cannot. 4. No! (general negative). →Syn. ไม่ได้ com.

o โดยมิได้... dooj'mídâjɔ... without...-ing, without being...

o มิได้ขาด mídâjkhàad' incessantly, regularly, constantly, unfailingly.

o มิได้อะไร mídâaj'ʔaraj' 1. is of no use. 2. (one) will not gain anything.

o ยังมิได้ jaŋmídâjɔ eleg. not yet.

o หาค่ามิได้ hǎakhâa'mídâaj' eleg. to be invaluable. May be used by some speakers in the meaning "valueless."

o หาที่เปรียบมิได้ hǎa'thîiprîab'-mídâaj' incomparable, incomparably.

มิน่าเล่า mínâa'lâw↓ No wonder! →Also มิน่าล่ะ. mínâa'lâʔ↓.

มิไย míjaj' regardless of, disregarding (the fact that), even though. →Also incorrectly spelled มิใย.

มิรั้งรอ míráŋ'rɔɔ' not to hesitate; unhesitatingly.

มิรู้วาย mírúu'waaj' unceasingly, ceaselessly, without stopping.

มิว่า míwâa' no matter, disregarding.

มิวาย míwaaj' cannot help, cannot refrain from.

มิหนำซ้ำ mínǎmsám' colloq. in addition, moreover, worse than that.

มิเห็นแก่ míhěn'kɛ̀ɛ without thinking of, without regard to, with disregard for.

มิให้ míhâj' not to let, not to allow, not to permit.

อะไรต่อมิอะไร ʔaraj'tɔ̀ɔmíʔaraj' all sorts of things; what not.

มิจฉา mídchǎa' eleg. wrong, improper, illegal.

มิจฉาชีพ mídchǎa'chîib' N illegal or wrong means of making a living.

มิจฉาทิฐิ míchǎa'thídthìʔ' N wrong view, false idea (esp. a far-reaching distortion of moral

values such as characterizes hardened criminals). →Also มิจฉาทิฏฐิ, มิจฉาทิษฐิ.

มิด míd' entirely, completely.

จมมิด com'míd' V 1. to be entirely submerged. 2. to penetrate completely (as a knife blade into the flesh).

บัง(...)มิด baŋ'(...)míd' to obstruct, hide (something) completely.

มิดชิด mídchíd' completely, entirely, closely, tightly (covered, wrapped, hidden). Also อย่าง--.

มิตร (คน) míd', mídtraɔ (khon') N eleg. friend. →Syn. เพื่อน com., เกลอ colloq.

ญาติมิตร jâadmíd' N 1. relatives and friends. V 2. slang to play cards.

ผูกมิตร phùug'míd' V eleg. to make friends.

มิตรจิตร mídtracìd' N eleg. friendliness.

มิตรภาพ mídtraphâab' N eleg. friendship.

มิตรสหาย (คน) míd'sahǎaj' (khon') N eleg. friend.

มิตรสัมพันธ์ míd'sǎmphan' N eleg. friendly relations.

มิถุนายน míthùnaa'jon' N June. เดือน-- idem. →The names of all the months are listed under เดือน.

มิลลิเมตร minliméed' N millimeter. →Abbr. มม., ม.ม.

มิสเตอร์ místəə' N 1. mister. T 2. Mr.-- →Used in transliterations from English. [f. Eng.]

มี mii' V 1. to have, possess. 2. there is, there are. →Syn. 1. ทรง ๑ eleg., roy.

o มีต้นมะม่วงหลายขนัด miitônmamûaŋ'lǎajkhanàd' There are several rows of mango trees.

ก็มี kɔ̂mii' "is (are) found too." →See cross reference for examples.

เกิดมี kə̀əd'miiɔ 1. to happen (that); there happened to be; to arise, occur, exist. 2. to happen to have.

ตามมีตามเกิด taammii'taamkə̀əd' elab. colloq. according to one's means, as one can afford.

มั่งมี mâŋmii' eleg. to be rich, wealthy. →Syn. มั่งคั่ง eleg., รวย com.

มีกะใจ miikacaj'. Variant spelling of มีแก่ใจ.

มีกำไร miikamraj' to profit, gain a profit.

มีเกียรติ miikìad' eleg. to be honorable (have

honor)(of a person). ผู้-- an honorable person (i.e. one with rank, distinction).

มีแก่ใจ mii'kacaj', mii'kɛɛcaj'* 1. to have the will, the spirit (to do something). 2. to be thoughtful, considerate of others. 3. to be kind enough to, considerate enough to. ความ-- will, spirit; considerateness, thoughtfulness. →Sometimes also spelled มีกะใจ.

มีขนาดเท่า ๆ... miikhanàad'-thâwthâw'- to be of the same size as.

มีครรภ์ miikhan' eleg. to be pregnant. →Syn. See มีท้อง.

มีความผิด miikhwaamphìd' to be guilty.

มีความยินดี miikhwaam'jindii' eleg.to be pleased.

มีค่า miikhâa' to have value (worth); to be valuable, precious.

มีคุณ miikhun' 1. to be beneficial, useful, good. 2. to have value, be of value.

มีเค้า miikháw' to show a trace, a vestige (of).

มีชัย miichaj' eleg. to be victorious, win. ความ-- victory.

มีชีวิต miichiiwíd' 1. to be alive, be living. 2. colloq. to be lively. →Ant. 1. ตาย.

o มีชีวิตชีวา miichiiwíd'chiiwaa' elab. colloq. to be lively.

o สิ่งมีชีวิต sìŋ'miichiiwíd' N living thing.

มีชู้ miichúu' (a married woman) to be adulterous, have a lover.

มีชื่อ miichŷy' to be well known, famous, famed.

o มีชื่อเสียง miichŷysǐaŋ' to be famous, famed.

มีโชค miichôog' to have good luck; to be lucky.

มีใช้ miicháj' 1. to have for use, have available. 2. to be in use, in operation (e.g. machines), in force (e.g. rules).

มีดอก miidɔ̀ɔg' to be in flower. →Dist. เป็นดอก.

มีต่อ miitɔ̀ɔ' (it is) continued (on page...).

o ยังมีต่อ,--ไปอีก jaŋmiitɔ̀ɔ', jaŋmii'tɔ̀ɔpaj?lìg' 1. to be continued. 2. there is still more to come (as of a story).

มีถมไป miithŏm'paj there is plenty, there is a lot.

มีทรัพย์ miisáb' eleg. to be rich, wealthy; to have money. →Syn. มั่งคั่ง, มั่งมี eleg., รวย com.

มีท้อง miithɔ́ɔŋ' V colloq. to be in the family way, be pregnant. →Cf. อุ้มท้อง. →See cross reference.

มีท่าว่า miithâa'wâaɔ there are some indications that, it appears that.

มีทาง miithaaŋ' there is a way, a means; it is possible.

o ไม่มีทาง mâjmiithaaŋ' there is no way, no means; it is impossible.

มีโทษ miithôod' to be harmful, produce ill effects.

มีธุระ miithúrá?' 1. to be busy, occupied. 2. to have an errand (to do).

มีนามโด่งดัง miinaam'dòoŋdaŋ' eleg. to be widely known, renowned. →Syn. มีชื่อโด่งดัง.

มีนามอุโฆษ miinaam'?ùkhôod' eleg. to be widely known, renowned.

มีประโยชน์ miiprajòod' to be advantageous, useful.

มีผล miiphŏn' 1. to become effective. 2. to result (in). 3. to bear fruit.

o มีผลย้อนหลัง miiphŏn'jɔ́ɔnlǎŋ' to be retroactive, be effective retroactively.

o มีผลสืบเนื่อง(มาจาก) miiphŏn'-sỳybnŷaŋ' (maacàagɔ) to be a consequence (of).

มีพิษ miiphíd' to be poisonous (as a snake).

มีมติให้ miimátì?/hâjɔ to resolve, pass a resolution, come to a decision that.

มีมลทิน miimonthin' eleg. to be tainted, blemished.

มีมูล,--ความจริง miimuun', miimuun'khwaamciŋ' to have a factual basis; there is an element or basis of truth.

มีรส miiród' 1. to taste (intr.), have a (particular) flavor. 2. to be tasty.

o มีรสขม miiród'khŏm' to taste bitter.

o มีรสสนุก miiród'sanùg' to be entertaining, amusing; to be great sport.

มีระเบียบ miirabìab' to be neat, well-organized, systematic, in good order. อย่าง-- in good order, in an orderly manner.

มีรากฐาน miirâagthǎan' 1. to have a foundation. 2. (a person) to have a secure position or standing.

มีราคา miiraakhaa' to be valuable, precious.

มีเรือน miiryan' colloq. to be married, have a family (usually of women). →Also มีเหย้ามีเรือน elab. colloq.

มีลาภ miilâab' to get a windfall, have an unexpected piece of good fortune.

มี(...)ไว้ mii(...)wáj′ to have (e.g. food) around, on hand.

มีศีลมีสัตย์ miisǐin′miisàd′ elab. to be trustworthy, honest.

มีสง่า miisaŋàa′ to be dignified, stately, majestic.

มีสตางค์ miisataŋ′ to be rich, have money. คน-- rich person; the rich.

มีสภาพ miisaphâab′ to be in a state or condition.

มีส่วนมีเสียง miisùan′miisǐaŋ′ elab. colloq. to have a share, a part, a voice (in).

มี(...)สำรอง mii′(...)sǎmrɔɔŋ′ to have (such and such) in reserve.

มีสีหน้า miisǐinâa′ to have a (particular) facial expression.

มีเสน่ห์ miisanèe′ to have charm; to be charming, attractive.

มีหน้า (1) mii′nâa′, (2) miinâa′ 1 to dare to, have the nerve to. 2. to have (such and such a) look; to look (thus and so); see example.

o มีหน้าเคร้า miinâa′sâw′ to have a sad look, to look sad.

มีหน้ามีตา miinâa′miitaa′ idiom. to be in a position of respect, esteem, deference.

มีหวัง miiwǎŋ′ to have hopes, be hopeful. →Ant. หมดหวัง.

มีเหย้ามีเรือน miijâw′miiryan′ elab. colloq. to be married, have a family (usually of women). →Also มีเรือน colloq.

มีเหลี่ยมมีคู miilìam′miikhuu′ elab. colloq. to be sly, cunning, crafty.

มีอย่างหรือ miijàaŋ′rý↓ How come? What is that? (expressing indignation, reproach, disappointment).

มี(...)อยู่ mii′(...)jùu⊃ has, have; is, are in possession of; is, are in existence; is, are to be found. →See cross reference.

มีอะไร mii′araj′, mii′′araj′ 1. there is something. 2. to have something. 3. what there is. 4. to have what? 5. there is what? →See cross reference.

มีอันจะกิน mii′an′cakin′ eleg. to be well-off, well-to-do. ผู้-- one who is well off, a well-to-do person.

มีอาชีพ mii′aachîib′ to make a living.

มีอายุ mii′aajú′⊃ colloq. 1. to be (so and so many years) old. 2. to be elderly, up in years. ผู้-- an elderly person.

o มีอายุ ๑๘ ปี mii′aajú′′-sìbpɛ̀ɛd′pii′ (he) is eighteen years old.

มีอาวุโส mii′aa′wúsǒo′ eleg. to be senior (in age, rank, status). ผู้-- a senior person.

มีอิทธิพล mii′ìdthiphon′ eleg. to be influential, powerful (as a person). ผู้-- an influential or powerful person.

ไม่มีปัญหา mâjmii′panhǎa′ 1. without question; no doubt, doubtless. 2. there is no question (about it). อย่าง-- unquestionably, doubtlessly.

ไม่มีวัน mâjmiiwan′ never, there will never be a day (when); not a chance.

o ไม่มีวันอดตาย mâjmiiwan′-′òd′taaj′ will never starve to death.

ยากดีมีจน jâagdii′-mii′con′ elab. colloq. rich or poor.

อย่างไม่มีปี่มีขลุ่ย jàaŋmâjmiipìi′miikhlùj′ idiom. without warning.

มีด (เล่ม) mîid′ (lêm′) N knife.

มีดโกน (เล่ม,อัน) mîidkoon′ (lêm′,′an′) N razor.

o ใบมีดโกน (ใบ) baj′mîidkoon′ (baj′) N razor blade.

มีดดาบ (เล่ม) mîiddàab′ (lêm′) N sword.

มีดตัดเล็บ (อัน) mîid′tàdléb′ (′an′) N nail clipper.

มีดโต้ (เล่ม) mîidtôo′ (lêm′) N hacking knife.

มีดทอง (เล่ม) mîidthɔɔŋ′ (lêm′) N brass fruit knife or paring knife. Brass is used to avoid discoloration of the fruit.

มีดบาง (เล่ม) mîidbaaŋ′ (lêm′) N paring knife; a small, thin-bladed knife.

มีดพร้า (เล่ม) mîid′phráa′ (lêm′) N knives (general term for all sorts and sizes).

มีดพับ (เล่ม) mîidpháb′ (lêm′) N penknife, clasp knife, pocketknife.

หินลับมีด (ก้อน) hǐn′lábmîid′ (kɔ̂ɔn′) N whetstone.

มีนาคม miinaa′khom′ N March. เดือน-- idem. →The names of all the months are listed under เดือน.

มึ่ง myŋ′ P sp. to inf. you. Rude word, paired
   with กู "I, me."

มึน myn′ V to be tipsy, befuddled, groggy.

  มึนชา mynchaa′ to be cold (in disposition).

  มึนซึม mynsym′ to be drowsy, dull.

  มึนตึง myntyŋ′ to be cold (in disposition), to be
    indifferent.

  มึนเมา mynmaw′ V to be drunk, intoxicated.

  มึนหัว mynhŭa′ V to be befuddled, dopey.

มืด mŷyd′ V to be dark. ความ-- darkness.

  เงามืด ŋawmŷyd′ N silhouette, dark shadow.

  เช้ามืด cháawmŷyd′ N the very early morning
    (while still dark).

  เดือนมืด dyanmŷyd′ waning moon. →Opp. เดือน
    หงาย.

  ตลาดมืด (แห่ง) talàad′mŷyd′ (hèŋ′) N black
    market.

  บังมืด baŋmŷyd′ to obstruct light.

  ม้ามืด máamŷyd′ N polit. dark horse. [f. Eng.]

  มืดครึ้ม mŷydkhrým′ to be overcast, cloudy; to
    be overshadowed, darkened.

  มืดตื้อ mŷydtŷy′ 1. colloq. to be pitch dark,
    absolutely dark. 2. fig. (one's mind) to be
    blank (unable to think).

  มืดตื๋อ mŷydtŷy′ colloq. to be completely dark.

  มืดแปดด้าน mŷyd′pɛ̀ɛddâan′ idiom. to be in the
    dark, be completely lost (in trying to figure
    something out).

  มืดมน mŷydmon′ to be dark, obscure.

  มืดมัว mŷydmua′ V 1. to be obscure. 2. to be
    overcast, gloomy.

  มืดสลัว mŷyd′salŭa′ to be dimly lighted.

  หน้ามืด nâamŷyd′ 1. to black out, have a dizzy
    spell. 2. idiom. to lose control of oneself,
    be blind with passion.

มือ (มือ, ข้าง) myy′ (myy′, khâaŋ′) N hand. NOTE.
  มือ is often coupled with ไม้ in elaborate colloquial expressions, e.g. จับไม้จับมือ "to shake
  hands." Here ไม้ is used for the sake of alliteration and does not carry the connotation of
  its literal meaning "wood."

  กวักมือ kwàgmyy′ V to beckon (to), summon
    (a person) by motioning with the hand palm
    downward.

กำมือ kammyy′ V 1. to clench the fist. N 2. grip,
  clutch, clutches. C 3. handful (as of sand).

 o เต็มกำมือ tem′kammyy′ 1. (in the amount of a)
    handful. 2. with one's hand or hands full.

กุญแจมือ (ข้าง, คู่) kuncɛɛ′myy′ (khâaŋ′, khûu′)
  N handcuff.

แก้มือ kɛ̂ɛ′myy′ to ask for a return match, a
  chance to make up for one's loss.

ข้อมือ (ข้อ, ข้อมือ, ข้าง) khɔ̂ɔmyy′ (khɔ̂ɔ′, khɔ̂ɔmyy′,
  khâaŋ′) N wrist.

ขาดมือ khàad′myy′ V to be wanting, in short supply, out of stock; the supply (of something) to
  run out.

คันมือ khan′myy′ colloq. to be itching to do
  something (with the hands).

คามือ khaa′myy′ in the act, red-handed.

 o จับได้คามือ càb′dâaj′-khaa′myy′ to catch in
    the act, catch red-handed.

คู่มือ (เล่ม) khûumyy′ (lêm′) N 1. handbook,
  manual. 2. (as n. mod.) handy, trusty, always at
  hand.

เครื่องมือ (อัน) khrŷaŋmyy′ (ʔan′) N tool, instrument.

 o เครื่องไม้เครื่องมือ (อย่าง, ชิ้น, อัน) khrŷaŋ‿
    máaj′khrŷaŋmyy′ (jàaŋ′, chín′, ʔan′) N elab.
    colloq. implement, tool.

ง่ามมือ ŋâammyy′ N the region between two fingers.

เงื้อมือ ŋýa′myy′ V to raise the hand in a striking
  position.

เงื้อมมือ ŋýammyy′ N idiom. control, power,
  clutches, hands.

 o อยู่ในเงื้อมมือของ jùunajŋýammyy′khɔ̌ɔŋ‿ to
    be in the clutches of.

จับมือ càbmyy′ V 1. to shake hands. 2. to hold
  hands, clasp hands. 3. to grasp (someone's)
  hands.

 o จับไม้จับมือ càbmáaj′càbmyy′ V elab. colloq.
    1. to shake hands. 2. to hold hands.

จูงมือ cuuŋmyy′ V to lead by the hand.

เจ้ามือ (คน) câwmyy′ (khon′) N 1. the dealer
  (in card games); the banker (in gambling games).
  2. colloq. the one who treats.

ช่วยกันคนละไม้คนละมือ chûaj′kan′-khonlamáaj′‿
  khonlamyy′ idiom. (each one) to give a helping

hand.

ชี้มือ chíimyy′ V colloq. to point, point one's
finger.

o ชี้ไม้ชี้มือ chíimáaj′chíimyy′ V elab. colloq.
to point, point one's finger.

ตกถึงมือ tòg′thɣ̌ŋmyy′ to come to the hand of,
come into the possession of.

ตกอยู่ในมือ tòg′jùunajmyy′ to fall into the hands
of.

ต้นมือ tônmyy′ N idiom. the early phase or
stage; the beginning.

เต็มมือ tem′myy′ to fill the hand, fill the hands;
to be covering the hands, all over one's hands.
For examples see cross reference.

ถึงมือ thɣ̌ŋmyy′ 1. to reach, get to. 2. to get
into the hands of.

ถุงมือ (คู่,ข้าง) thǔŋmyy′ (khûu′,khâaŋ′) N
glove, gloves.

ทางขวามือ thaaŋkhwǎa′myy′ to the right.

ทางซ้ายมือ thaaŋsáaj′myy′ to the left.

น้ำมือ námmyy′ N one's own deed, act, action,
hand, hands.

o ตายเพราะน้ำมือลูก taaj′-phrɔ́námmyy′lûug′
to die by the hand of one's own son.

นิ้วมือ (นิ้ว) níwmyy′ (níw′) N finger.

แบมือ bɛɛmyy′ V to open up the palm of the hand.
2. colloq. to extend the palm, stretch out the
hand, i.e. to beg.

โบกมือ bòogmyy′ V to wave one's hand (as in
saying goodbye).

o โบกไม้โบกมือ bòogmáaj′bòogmyy′ elab.
colloq. to wave the hand.

ปรบมือ pròbmyy′ V eleg. to applaud.

ประณมมือ pranom′myy′ V to place one's hands
palm to palm in the attitude of adoration or
salutation. →Also ประนมมือ.

ประสานมือ prasǎan′myy′ V to clasp one's
hands, knitting the fingers together.

ฝ่ามือ (ข้าง) fàamyy′ (khâaŋ′) N palm of the
hand.

ฝีมือ fǐimyy′ N 1. manual skill, craftsmanship.
2. something prepared with one's own hands.
การ-- handicraft, handiwork.

o ช่างฝีมือ (คน) châaŋfǐimyy′ (khon′) N skilled

craftsman.

พนมมือ phanom′myy′ V to place one's hands palm
to palm in the attitude of adoration or salutation.

มันเขี้ยวมันมือ mankhîaw′manmyy′ to be eager
to fight; to have a strong urge to do something
(with one's hands, or with one's hands and teeth).
Cf. Eng. "to feel like tearing into."

มือเก่า (คน,มือ) myykàw′ (khon′,myy′) N an
old hand (at some activity). →Opp. มือใหม่.

มือขวา myykhwǎa′ N 1. right hand. 2. right hand
man. 3. idiom. something one is good at, something one habitually does (either good or bad),
something that is second nature to one.

o การตัดเสื้อเป็นมือขวาของเขา kaantàdsɣ̂a′penɔ
myykhwǎa′khɔ̌ŋkháw′↓* Dressmaking is second
nature to her, comes natural to her. She is good
at dressmaking.

มือดี myy′dii′ V 1. to be a good hand (at some
activity). N 2. a good hand, a good player.
→Opp. มือเลว.

มือเติบ myy′tɤ̀ɤb′ V 1. to have a lavish hand. sV
2. with a lavish hand, lavishly, liberally.

มือเปล่า myy′plàaw′ V 1. to be empty-handed.
sV 2. empty-handed; with bare hands; freehand.

มือเลว myy′leew′ V 1. to be a poor hand (at some
activity). N 2. a poor hand, a poor player.
→Opp. มือดี.

มือไว myy′waj′ V to be thievish, light-fingered.

มือหนึ่ง myynɣ̀ŋ′ V 1. to be first rate. N 2. one
who makes the first play (as in cards, tennis).

มือใหม่ (คน,มือ) myymàj′ (khon′,myy′) N beginner, a new hand (at some activity). →Opp. มือเก่า.

ยื่นมือ jɣ̂ɣnmyy′ V 1. to interfere, intervene. 2.
to offer one's services.

ร่วมมือ rûammyy′ V to cooperate (with). ความ--
cooperation.

รับมือ rábmyy′ V idiom. to encounter, meet,
confront, counteract (usually in a fight or contest
involving the use of the hands).

เร่งมือ rêŋmyy′ V to speed up doing one's work.

ลงมือ loŋmyy′ V idiom. to start, begin, undertake.

ล้นมือ lónmyy′ V. to be too much, too many to
handle.

ลายมือ (ลายมือ,นิ้ว,เส้น) laajmyy′ N 1. handwriting (laajmyy′). 2. fingerprint (níw′). 3. the lines on the palm of the hand (sên′).

ลูกมือ (คน) lûugmyy′ (khon′) N helper, assistant.

ลูกระเบิดมือ (ลูก) lûugrabə̀əd′myy′ (lûug′) N handgrenade.

เล็บมือ (เล็บ) lébmyy′ (léb′) N fingernail.

วางมือ waaŋmyy′ V idiom. to stop or give up doing something.

ว่างมือ wâaŋmyy′ V to be free, unoccupied, have one's hands free (e.g. from work).

หมายมั่นปั้นมือ mǎajmân′pânmyy′ elab. colloq. V 1. to resolve, have a strong determination (to do something). 2. to anticipate strongly.

หยิบมือ jìbmyy′ C a small amount, a pinch (e.g. of salt).

หลุดมือ lùdmyy′ V to slip from the hand.

หัวแม่มือ (ข้าง,นิ้ว) hǔamɛ̂ɛmyy′ (khâaŋ′, níw′) N thumb.

อยู่ในมือ jùunajmyy′ 1. to be in the hands (of), under the control (of). 2. to be at hand, on hand, in stock.

อยู่มือ jùu′myy′ V idiom. to be under control, in hand.

อุ้งมือ ʔûŋmyy′ N the depressed, center part of the palm (of the hand).

เอามือล้วงกระเป๋า ʔawmyy′lúaŋkrapǎw′ V to have or put one's hand(s) in one's pocket(s).

เอื้อมมือ ʔŷammyy′ V to reach out (for), stretch one's hand out (in order to reach something).

มื้อ mýy′ C clf. for meals.

o อาหารสามมื้อ ʔaahǎan′-sǎam′mýy′ three meals.

มื้อกลางวัน (มื้อ) mýyklaaŋwan′ (mýy′) N lunch.

มื้อค่ำ (มื้อ) mýykhâm′ (mýy′) N dinner, evening meal.

มื้อเช้า (มื้อ) mýycháaw′ (mýy′) N breakfast.

อดมื้อกินมื้อ ʔòdmýy′kinmýy′ colloq. to have something to eat at times and be starving at other times (because of poverty).

มุ mú?′ V colloq. to try hard, work hard.

มุก (ตัว) múg′ (tua′) N pearl oyster.

ไข่มุก (เม็ด,สาย) khàjmúg′ N 1. pearl (méd′). 2. (a string of) pearls (sǎaj′). →Sometimes also ไข่มุกด์.

มุกดา,มุกด์ (เม็ด) múgdaa′, múg′ (méd′) N 1. pearl. 2. moonstone.

ไข่มุกด์. See ไข่มุก under มุก.

มุข múg′ N front porch, portico of a building, front balcony.

หน้ามุข nâamúg′ N front balcony, front porch, portico.

มุง muŋ′ V 1. to roof, be roofed with. 2. to crowd around.

มุงจาก muŋcàag′ V to be roofed with nipa palm leaf thatches.

มุงหลังคา muŋ′lǎŋkhaa′ V to roof.

ยืนมุง jyyn′muŋ′ V to stand crowding around.

มุ่ง mûŋ′ V to aim for.

o มุ่งมาด mûŋmâad′ V to expect, anticipate, aim at, aim for.

มุ่งร้าย mûŋráaj′ V to intend to do harm.

มุ่งร้ายหมายขวัญ mûŋráaj′-mǎaj′khwǎn′ V elab. to intend harm, have bad intentions; to bear malice (toward), bear ill-will (toward).

มุ่งหน้า mûŋnâa′ V to head toward determinedly. ความ-- determination.

มุ่งหมาย mûŋmǎaj′ V 1. to have a definite purpose. 2. to aim for. ความ-- purpose, aim, objective.

o จุดมุ่งหมาย (จุด,อย่าง,แห่ง) cùd′mûŋmǎaj′ (cùd′, jàaŋ′, hɛ̀ŋ′) N goal, aim.

มุ่งหวัง mûŋwǎŋ′ V to anticipate, expect, intend.

มุ้ง (หลัง) múŋ′ (lǎŋ′) N mosquito net.

กางมุ้ง kaaŋmúŋ′ V to hang up a mosquito net.

มุ้งลวด múŋlûad′ N 1. screen, wire screen. 2. screened section or cubicle for sleeping in.

มุด múd′ V to crawl under, go underneath, pass through (a low opening), burrow into; to duck under.

มุทะลุ múthalú?′ V to be hot-headed, rash, impetuous.

มุ่น in หมกมุ่น mògmûn′ V to be engrossed (in), preoccupied (with); to devote one's time and energy exclusively (to).

มุบมิบ ๑ múbmíb′ V colloq. to act in a surreptitious manner.

มุบมิบ ๒ as in ทำปากมุบมิบ thampàag′múbmíb′ to work the lips up and down silently. →See also หมุบหมิบ, ขมุบขมิบ.

มุม (มุม) mum′ (mum′) N corner (as of a room);

angle.

จนมุม con/mum/ V idiom. to be cornered, trapped, at bay.

ทุกซอกทุกมุม thúgsɔ̂ɔg/thúgmum/ elab. every nook and cranny.

ทุกซอกเล็กมุมน้อย thúgsɔ̂ɔg/lég/-mum/nɔ́ɔj/ elab. every little nook and corner, every little nook and cranny.

มุมกลับ mumklàb/ N 1. reflex angle. 2. antithesis.

o คิดในมุมกลับ khíd/najmumklàb/ idiom. 1. to take or consider an antithetic point of view. 2. conversely.

มุมเงย mumŋəəj/ N angle of elevation.

มุมฉาก mumchàag/ N right angle.

มุมถนน (แห่ง,มุม) mum/thanɔ̀n/ (hɛ̀ŋ/, mum/) N street corner.

มุมปาก (ข้าง) mumpàag/ (khâaŋ/) N corner of the mouth.

มุมห้อง (มุม) mumhɔ̂ŋ/ (mum/) N corner of a room.

แมงมุม,แมลงมุม (ตัว) mɛŋmum/, malɛɛŋmum/ (tua/) N spider.

เส้นทแยงมุม sên/thajɛɛŋmum/ N diagonal line.

หลบมุม lòbmum/ V to avoid an unpleasant encounter or situation: "to duck into a (safe) corner."

มุสา músǎ/ V lit., eleg. 1. to be false, be a lie. 2. to lie. →Syn. 2. See โกหก.

มูก mûug/ N mucus.

ขี้มูก khîimûug/ N com., vulg. snot. →Syn. น้ำมูก eleg.

น้ำมูก námmûug/ N eleg. nasal mucus. →Syn. ขี้มูก com., vulg.

มูน ๑ muun/ N 1. knoll, mound. V 2. to pile up.

มูนดิน (กอง,แห่ง) muundin/ (kɔɔŋ/, hɛ̀ŋ/) N earth mound. →Also incorrectly written มูลดิน.

มูน ๒ muun/ V to stir coconut cream into (glutinous rice).

มูมมาม muummaam/ sV 1. in a sloppy, messy, uncouth manner (of eating). V 2. to eat in a sloopy, messy, uncouth manner.

มูล ๑ muun/ N excrement, dung. →Syn. ขี้ ๑.

มูลฝอย (กอง) muunfɔ̌j/ (kɔɔŋ/) N rubbish, refuse, litter, garbage.

มูล ๒ muun/ N base, origin, source, root.

เค้ามูล kháwmuun/ N primary source.

มีมูล miimuun/ 1. to have a factual basis. 2. there in an element or basis of truth.

o ไม่มีมูล mâjmiimuun/ to have no grounds, basis.

มูลความจริง muun/khwaamciŋ/ N basis in truth; element of truth.

มูลฐาน muunthǎan/ N 1. foundation, basis. 2. (as n. mod.) fundamental, basic.

มูลนิธิ muun/níthí?/ N foundation, charitable trust.

มูลเหตุ (อย่าง,อัน) muunhèed/ (jàaŋ/, ?an/) N cause, original cause, basic cause.

มูลแห่งความจริง muun/hɛ̀ŋkhwaamciŋ/ N basis of truth.

มูล ๓ in พร้อมมูล phrɔ́ɔm/muun/ sV fully, completely, to perfection; in abundance. อย่าง-- perfectly, completely.

มูล ๔ in มูลค่า muunkhâa/ N value, price.

มูล ๕ in แม่น้ำมูล mɛ̂ɛnáammuun/ pN the Mun River, in E Thailand.

มูล ๖ in มูลดิน. See มูนดิน under มูน ๑.

มูลี่ (ผืน) mûulî/ (phɯ̌ɯn/) N bamboo blind.

เมฆ (ก้อน) mêeg/ (kɔ̂ɔn/) N cloud.

ก้อนเมฆ (ก้อน) kɔ̂ɔnmêeg/ (kɔ̂ɔn/) N patch or mass of clouds.

เม็ด ๑ méd/ N 1. seed, kernel, grain (as of sand). C 2. clf. for seeds, grain, pills, gems, pimples, etc. →See also เมล็ด.

เต็มเม็ดเต็มหน่วย temméd/temnùaj/ elab. 1. full, complete. 2. fully, to the utmost; at full capacity.

เป็นเม็ด penméd/ to be granulated, pimply.

ฝนขาดเม็ดแล้ว fǒn/-khàadméd/lɛ́ɛw↓ It has stopped raining.

ฝนซาเม็ด fǒn/saaméd/ the rain has subsided.

ฝนลงเม็ด fǒn/loŋméd/ it's starting to rain.

เม็ดฝน médfǒn/ N raindrop.

ยาเม็ด (เม็ด) jaaméd/ (méd/) N (medicinal) pill, tablet.

เม็ด ๒ in กลเม็ด (อย่าง) konlaméd/ (jàaŋ/) N trick.

เมตตา mêedtaa/ N 1. kindness, mercifulness. V 2. to be kind to; to take pity on. ความ-- kindness, mercifulness.

เมตตากรุณา mêedtaa/karunaa/ V to be kind,

have mercy. ความ-- mercy, mercifulness, kindness, kindliness.

เมตตาจิต mêedtaa/cìd/ N kindheartedness.

เมตร méd/, méed/ C meter. [f. Fr.]

ไม้เมตร (อัน) máajméd/, máajméed/ (ʔan/) N meter stick.

เมตริก médtrìg/* metric. [f. Eng.]

มาตราเมตริก mâadtraa/médtrìg/ N metric system.

เม่น (ตัว) mên/*(tua/) N porcupine.

เม้ม mém/* V to fold the edge or border in.

เม้มปาก mémpàag/ V to fold or pull one's lips inwards, compressing them.

เมย. See เฉยเมย.

เมล์ mee/ mail. [f. Eng.]

รถเมล์ (คัน) ródmee/ (khan/) N bus.

เรือเมล์ (ลำ) ryamee/ (lam/) N a scheduled passenger motorboat, steam passenger ferry.

เมล็ด (เมล็ด) maléd/ (maléd/) N seed. →See also เม็ด.

เมล็ดพืช (เมล็ด) maléd/phŷyd/ (maléd/) N seed, plant seed.

เมษายน mee/sǎajon/ N April. เดือน-- idem. →The names of all the months are listed under เดือน.

เมา maw/ V 1. to be drunk, intoxicated. 2. to be affected with motion sickness (e.g. seasick, carsick). คน-- one who is drunk (at the given time); contrasts with คนขี้เมา drunkard.

ขี้เมา khîimaw/ V 1. to be given to drunkenness, to be a drunkard; to be habitually drunk. 2. to be given to motion sickness. คน-- drunkard; contrasts with คนเมา one who is drunk. ความ-- drunkenness.

น้ำเมา (อย่าง) námmaw/ (jàaŋ/) N intoxicating beverage (usually undistilled).

มัวเมา muamaw/ V to be addicted (to), possessed (by), crazy (about).

มึนเมา mynmaw/ V to be drunk, intoxicated.

เมาคลื่น mawkhlŷyn/ V to be seasick.

เมายา mawjaa/ V to be drugged, doped, intoxicated with drugs.

เมารถ mawród/ V to be carsick.

เมาเรือ mawrya/ V to be seasick.

เมาเรือบิน maw/ryabin/ V to be airsick.

เมาเหล้า mawlâw/ V to be drunk, intoxicated (by alcohol, alcoholic drinks).

เมาอำนาจ maw/ʔamnâad/ V to be drunk with power.

เมิน məən/ V to turn away.

เมินเลียเถอะ məən/síathəʔ↓ You haven't got a chance. You had better give up the idea.

เมินเลียเถิดที่เราจะเชื่อ məən/síathəʔ/-thîiraw/ɔ cachŷa/↓ Don't ever expect us to believe (it).

เมินหน้า məənnâa/ V to turn the face away, look away.

เมีย (คน) mia/ (khon/) N com. wife. →Syn. ภรรยา eleg.

ตัวเมีย tuamia/ N female. →Usually of nonhumans. →Dist. หญิง, ผู้หญิง female (of people). →Opp. ตัวผู้.

o ม้าตัวเมีย máa/tuamia/ N mare.

น้องเมีย (คน) nɔ́ɔŋmia/ (khon/) N brother- or sister-in-law (of a man in ref. to his wife's yg. brother or sister): "wife's younger sibling."

ผัวเมีย (คู่) phǔamia/ (khûu/) N com. husband and wife, married couple. →Syn. สามีภรรยา eleg.

ผิดผัวผิดเมีย phìdphǔa/phìdmia/ V to commit adultery.

ผิดเมีย phìdmia/ V to commit adultery with another's wife.

พี่เมีย (คน) phîi/mia/ (khon/) N brother- or sister-in-law (of a man in ref. to his wife's older brother or sister). "wife's older sibling."

เมียเก็บ (คน) miakèb/ (khon/) N mistress; illicit wife; secret minor wife or concubine. →Syn. เมียลับ.

เมียน้อย (คน) mianɔ́ɔj/ (khon/) N com. minor wife; second, third, or other additional wife; concubine. →Syn. ภรรยาน้อย eleg.

เมียลับ (คน) mialáb/ (khon/) N mistress; illicit wife; secret minor wife or concubine. →Syn. เมียเก็บ.

เมียหลวง (คน) mialǔaŋ/ (khon/) N principal wife, first wife.

เมียง miaŋ/ V 1. to approach stealthily. 2. to glance stealthily.

เมี่ยง mîaŋ/ N fermented leaves of wild tea plants (used for chewing in place of betel in N Thailand).

เมื่อ mŷa/ C 1. clf. for a time, times. Cj 2. when. Pp 3. at, in (of past time only).

 ○ มาได้ทุกเมื่อ maadâaj/thúgmŷa/ you can come any time.

ขณะเมื่อ khanà?/mŷa/ at the moment when.

ต่อเมื่อ tɔ̀ɔmŷa/ 1. when, only when, at the time that. 2. until, until later when.

ในเมื่อ najmŷa/ when, in the event that.

เมื่อก่อน mŷakɔ̀ɔn/ before, previously.

เมื่อกี้ mŷakîi/ a moment ago, just now.

 ○ เมื่อกี้นี้ mŷakîiníi/ idem.

เมื่อกี๊ mŷakíi/ colloq. a moment ago, just now.

 ○ เมื่อกี๊นี้ mŷakíiníi/ idem.

เมื่อครั้ง mŷakhráŋ/ at the time when.

เมื่อคราว mŷakhraaw/ at the time when.

เมื่อคืนนี้ mŷakhyyn/níi/ last night.

เมื่อคืนวันที่ ๕ mŷakhyyn/wanthîihâa/ on the night of the fifth.

เมื่อคืนวาน mŷakhyyn/waan/ the night before last.

 ○ เมื่อคืนวานนี้ mŷakhyyn/-waan/níi/ idem.

เมื่อเช้า mŷacháaw/ this morning (prior to the present).

 ○ เมื่อเช้านี้ mŷacháaw/níi/ idem.

เมื่อใด mŷadaj/ when; whenever.

เมื่อต้น mŷatônꞎ in the beginning of, in the early part of (e.g. the year, ref. to the past).

เมื่อตะกี้นี้ mŷatakîiníi/ a moment ago, just now.

เมื่อตะกี๊นี้ mŷatakíiníi/ colloq. idem.

เมื่อบ่าย mŷabàaj/ in the afternoon, this afternoon.

เมื่อปีกลาย mŷapiiklaaj/ last year (the preceding year).

เมื่อเย็น mŷajen/ this evening, this late afternoon (prior to present).

เมื่อเร็ว ๆ นี้ mŷarewrew/níi/ just recently.

เมื่อไร mŷaraj/* 1. when? at what time? 2. any time, whenever. →Also เมื่อไหร่.

 ○ เมื่อไรก็ได้ mŷaraj/kɔdâaj/ at any time, any time will do.

เมื่อวันก่อน mŷawankɔ̀ɔn/ the other day.

เมื่อวาน mŷawaan/ yesterday.

 ○ เมื่อวานนี้ mŷawaan/níi/ idem.

เมื่อไหร่ mŷaràj/. Variant form of เมื่อไร.

เมื่ออาทิตย์ก่อน mŷa?aathíd/kɔ̀ɔn/ last week.

ยิ่งเมื่อ jîŋ/mŷaꞎ especially when.

เมือก mŷag/ N slime, mucilaginous substance.

เป็นเมือก penmŷag/ to be slimy, mucilaginous.

เยื่อเมือก jŷamŷag/ N mucous membrane.

เมือง (เมือง) myaŋ/ (myaŋ/) N com. 1. town, city. 2. country. การ-- (see below). →Syn. 1. นคร eleg. 2. ประเทศ eleg.

NOTE. A list of elegant names of countries is shown under ประเทศ. In every case the common names use เมือง in place of ประเทศ.

กลางเมือง klaaŋmyaŋ/ in public, in the open; public, civil.

 ○ สงครามกลางเมือง (ครั้ง) sǒŋkhraam/klaaŋꞎ myaŋ/ (khráŋ/) civil war.

การเมือง kaanmyaŋ/ N politics; political affairs. นัก-- politician.

 ○ ทบวงการเมือง thabuaŋ/kaanmyaŋ/ N political bureau.

 ○ พรรคการเมือง (พรรค) phág/kaanmyaŋ/ (phág/) N political party.

กินเมือง kinmyaŋ/ V to rule, govern (a subject city, state).

เข้าเมือง khâwmyaŋ/ V to enter a country or town; to immigrate. คน-- person entering a country or town; immigrant.

 ○ ด่านเข้าเมือง (ด่าน) dàan/khâwmyaŋ/ (dàan/) N immigration office or post (at the point of entry).

แขกเมือง (คน, ท่าน) khὲɛgmyaŋ/ (khon/, thân/) N an official foreign visitor.

คนต่างเมือง (คน) khon/tàaŋmyaŋ/ (khon/) N foreigner, stranger, esp. a person from another locality.

คู่บ้านคู่เมือง khûubân/khûumyaŋ/ elab. national; characteristic of the country, particularly associated with the country.

เจ้าเมือง (คน, องค์) câwmyaŋ/ (khon/, ?oŋ/) N ruler of a city or country (?oŋ/, if royal).

ชานเมือง (แห่ง) chaanmyaŋ/ (hὲŋ/) N the outskirts of a city or town, environs. →Dist. ชายเมือง.

ชายเมือง (แห่ง) chaajmyaŋ/ (hὲŋ/) N the edge

of town, i.e. the inside edge of a city or town.
→Dist. ชานเมือง.

ชาวเมือง (คน) chaawmyaŋ′ (khon′) N native,
native inhabitant; townspeople.

ดอนเมือง dɔɔnmyaŋ′ pN Don Muang international
airport N of Bangkok.

บ้านเกิดเมืองนอน bâankə̀əd′myaŋnɔɔn′ N e l a b.
c o l l o q. motherland, homeland, native country.
→S y n. ปิตุภูมิ.

บ้านเมือง bâanmyaŋ′ N country, the country.

พลเมือง (คน) phonlamyaŋ′ (khon′) N population.

พื้นเมือง phýynmyaŋ′ native, local. คน-- native.

o ชาวพื้นเมือง (คน) chaawphýynmyaŋ′ (khon′)
N native, native inhabitant.

เมืองกัลกตา, เมืองกัลกัตตา myaŋ′kalkàtaa′, -kalɔ
lákàtaa′, -kankàdtaa′, myaŋ′kanlákàdtaa′, -kanɔ
la′- pN Calcutta.

เมืองกัวลาลัมเปอร์ myaŋ′kualaalampəə′ pN Kuala
Lumpur, capital of the Federation of Malaya.

เมืองขึ้น (เมือง) myaŋkhŷn′ (myaŋ′) N colony,
dependency, subject country.

เมืองจีน (เมือง, แห่ง) myaŋciin′ pN 1. c o m.
China (myaŋ′). 2. Chinatown (hɛ̀ŋ′). →S y n.
1. ประเทศจีน e l e g.

เมืองชล myaŋchon′ pN c o l l o q. Chonburi.

เมืองด่าน (เมือง) myaŋdàan′ (myaŋ′) N border
town.

เมืองท่า (เมือง) myaŋthâa′ (myaŋ′) N seaport
town.

เมืองไทย myaŋthaj′ N c o m. Thailand. →S y n.
ประเทศไทย e l e g.

เมืองนอก myaŋnɔ̀ɔg′ N foreign country, abroad
(esp. of western countries).

o ไปเมืองนอก paj′myaŋnɔ̀ɔg′ to go abroad.

เมืองนอกเมืองนา myaŋnɔ̀ɔg′myaŋnaa′ N e l a b.
c o l l o q. foreign country, abroad (usually the
U. S. A. or in Europe).

เมืองย่างกุ้ง myaŋ′jâaŋkûŋ′ pN Rangoon.

เมืองร้อน (เมือง) myaŋrɔ́ɔn′ (myaŋ′) N tropical
country.

เมืองหลวง (เมือง) myaŋlǔaŋ′ (myaŋ′) N c o m.
capital (of a country or state). →S y n. ราชธานี
e l e g.

เมืองอุตสาหกรรม (เมือง) myaŋ′?ùdsǎa′hàkam′,

-?ùdsǎa′- (myaŋ′) N an industrial city.

เมืองเอก (เมือง) myaŋ?èeg′ (myaŋ′) N principal
province, city, town (esp. from the viewpoint of
strategic importance).

เมืองฮานอย myaŋ′haanɔɔj′ pN Hanoi, a city in
Vietnam.

หัวเมือง (หัวเมือง) hǔamyaŋ′ (hǔamyaŋ′) N
provincial town. →C o m p. บ้านนอก.

เมื่อย mŷaj′ V to be stiff and sore (as from unaccus-
tomed exercise); to be tired, stiff (of muscles).
ความ-- stiffness (of muscles).

เมื่อยขัด mŷajkhàd′ V to feel stiff and sore.

เมื่อยตัว mŷajtua′ V to have a muscular fatigue
all over the body.

เมื่อยล้า mŷajláa′ V to be tired, fatigued, stiff
and sore.

แม่ (คน) mɛ̂ɛ′ (khon′) N 1. c o m. mother. P 2.
you, she, her, Mother (sp. to or of one's mother);
I, me, Mother (mother sp. to child). T 3. title
used in front of the first names of girls or, in
certain circumstances, of women. T 4. e l e g.
title used before the names of pets. →S y n. 1.
มารดา e l e g. →O p p. พ่อ, q.v.

> NOTE. The word แม่ has a number of special
> uses, as listed below.
>
> 1. As the first member of a compound with
> the special sense of "female engaged in such
> and such an occupation," as in แม่ค้า mɛ̂ɛkháa′
> "woman shopkeeper, vendor." →See คน ⊚.
>
> 2. As the first member of a compound with
> the special sense of "master of, head of," as
> in แม่ทัพ mɛ̂ɛtháb′ "general, commander-in-
> chief." →See คน ⊚.
>
> 3. As the first element in แม่น้ำ mɛ̂ɛnáam′
> "river," and in the names of certain rivers,
> as in แม่โขง mɛ̂ɛkhǒoŋ′ "the Mækhong R."
>
> 4. As the first element in certain place
> names, as แม่ฮ่องสอน mɛ̂ɛhɔ̀ŋsɔ̌ɔn′ "Mæ-
> hɔngsɔn" and แม่สะเรียง mɛ̂ɛsarian′ "Mæ-
> sariang."
>
> 5. In compound names for certain contriv-
> ances or devices, as แม่แรง mɛ̂ɛrɛɛŋ′ "jack,
> crane" and แม่เหล็ก mɛ̂ɛlèg′ "magnet."
>
> 6. In the words หัวแม่เท้า hǔamɛ̂ɛtháaw′
> "big toe" and หัวแม่มือ hǔamɛ̂ɛmyy′ "thumb."

คุณแม่ khunmɛ̂ɛ′ P e l e g. 1. you, she, her, Mother
(sp. to or of one's mother). N 2. mother (of
someone).

พ่อแม่ (คน) phɔ̂ɔ′mɛ̂ɛ′ (khon′) N parents: "father

and mother." →Syn. บิดามารดา eleg.,
ผู้บังเกิดเกล้า eleg.

แม่กลอง mɛ̂ɛklɔɔŋ′ pN Mæklong (Me Klong),
colloquial name for สมุทรสงคราม a township
in C Thailand.

o แม่น้ำแม่กลอง mɛ̂ɛnáammɛ̂ɛklɔɔŋ′ pN the
Mæklọng (Me Klong) River in C Thailand.

แม่กุญแจ (ลูก, ดอก) mɛ̂ɛkuncɛɛ′ (lûug′, dɔɔg′)
N lock, padlock.

แม่ไก่ (ตัว) mɛ̂ɛkàj′ (tua′) N hen.

แม่โขง mɛ̂ɛkhǒoŋ′ pN 1. the Mækhong (Mekong)
River, which forms a part of the border between
Thailand and nations to the E. N 2. the brand
name of a liquor made in Bangkok. →Also 1.
แม่น้ำโขง.

แม่คงคา mɛ̂ɛkhoŋkhaa′ N lit. the goddess of
the waters.

แม่ครัว (คน) mɛ̂ɛkhrua′ (khon′) N (female) cook.

แม่ค้า (คน) mɛ̂ɛkháa′ (khon′) N (woman) merchant, shopkeeper, street vendor; market woman.

แม่คุณ mɛ̂ɛkhun′ P you, used in addressing a girl
or a young woman, equiv. to "my dear girl"
or "my dear young lady."

แม่เฒ่า (คน) mɛ̂ɛthâw′ (khon′) N an aged woman.

แม่ทัพ (นาย, คน) mɛ̂ɛtháb′ (naaj′, khon′) N general, commander in chief, leader of an army.

แม่ทูนหัว (1) mɛ̂ɛ′thuunhǔa′, (2) mɛ̂ɛthuun′hǔa′
N 1. godmother. 2. beloved girl, adorable girl.

แม่ธรณี mɛ̂ɛthɔɔ′ranii′ N goddess of the earth.

แม่นม (คน) mɛ̂ɛnom′ (khon′) N com. wet
nurse. →Syn. นางนม eleg.

แม่น้ำ (สาย) mɛ̂ɛnáam′ (sǎaj′) N river.

o ปากแม่น้ำ (แห่ง) pàag′mɛ̂ɛnáam′ (hὲŋ′) N
mouth of a river, estuary.

o ฝั่งแม่น้ำ (ฝั่ง) fàŋ′mɛ̂ɛnáam′ (fàŋ′) N river
bank.

o แม่น้ำโขง mɛ̂ɛnáamkhǒoŋ′ pN the Mækhong
(Mekong) River. →Also แม่โขง.

o แม่น้ำคง mɛ̂ɛnáamkhoŋ′ pN the Salween River.

o แม่น้ำคงคา mɛ̂ɛnáamkhoŋkhaa′ pN the Ganges
River.

o แม่น้ำเจ้าพระยา mɛ̂ɛnáamcâwphrájaa′ pN the
Čhaophraya (Chao Phya)R., at whose mouth
Bangkok is situated. NOTE. Generally called

"Menam" (from the Thai word for "river") in
books in English about Thailand.

o แม่น้ำชี mɛ̂ɛnáamchii′ pN the Chi (Ji) River,
a tributary of the Mun R. in NE Thailand.

o แม่น้ำชุมพร mɛ̂ɛnáamchumphɔɔn′ pN the
Chumphọn River, in S Thailand.

o แม่น้ำน่าน mɛ̂ɛnáamnâan′ pN the Mænan (Me
Nan), a tributary of the Čhaophraya River in N
Thailand. →Also แม่น่าน.

c แม่น้ำบางปะกง mɛ̂ɛnáambaaŋpakoŋ′ pN the
Bangpakong, a river in C Thailand.

o แม่น้ำป่าสัก mɛ̂ɛnáampàasàg′ pN the Pasak River.

o แม่น้ำปิง mɛ̂ɛnáampiŋ′ pN the Mæping (Me Ping),
a tributary of the Čhaophraya River in N Thailand. →Also แม่ปิง.

o แม่น้ำมูล mɛ̂ɛnáammuun′ pN the Mun River in
E Thailand.

o แม่น้ำแม่กลอง mɛ̂ɛnáammɛ̂ɛklɔɔŋ′ pN the
Mæklọng (Me Klong) River in C Thailand.

o แม่น้ำยม mɛ̂ɛnáamjom′ pN the Mæyom (Me
Yom), tributary of the Čhaophraya River in N
Thailand. →Also แม่ยม.

o แม่น้ำลพบุรี mɛ̂ɛnáam′lóbburii′ pN the Lopburi
River in C Thailand.

o แม่น้ำวัง mɛ̂ɛnámwaŋ′ pN the Mæwang (Me
Wang), a tributary of the Čhaophraya River in
N Thailand. →Also แม่วัง.

o ริมแม่น้ำ (ฟาก, ด้าน, ข้าง, แห่ง) rim′mɛ̂ɛnáam′
(fâag′, dâan′, khâaŋ′, hὲŋ′) N river bank, edge
of a river.

o ลำแม่น้ำ (สาย) lam′mɛ̂ɛnáam′ (sǎaj′) N river.

แม่บังเกิดเกล้า (คน) mɛ̂ɛ′-baŋkə̀əd′klâaw′ (khon′)
N one's real mother (as opposed to แม่เลี้ยง
stepmother).

แม่บ้าน (คน) mɛ̂ɛbâan′ (khon′) N housewife.

แม่บุญธรรม (คน) mɛ̂ɛ′buntham′ (khon′) N foster
mother.

แม่เบี้ย mɛ̂ɛbîa′ N hood (of a snake).

แม่แบบ mɛ̂ɛbὲɛb′ model, pattern.

แม่ผัว (คน) mɛ̂ɛphǔa′ (khon′) N (woman's)
mother-in-law.

แม่มด (คน) mɛ̂ɛmód′ (khon′) N witch, sorceress.

แม่ยาย (คน) mɛ̂ɛjaaj′ (khon′) N (man's) mother-
in-law.

แม่เรือน (คน) mɛ̂ɛryan/ (khon/) N female head of a family; housewife.

แม่แรง (อัน) mɛ̂ɛrɛɛŋ/ (ʔan/) N 1. jack, crane. 2. (moral) support, mainstay (used of a woman who stands behind a man in what he does).

แม่ลูกอ่อน (คน, ตัว) mɛ̂ɛlûugʔɔ̀ɔn/ (khon/, tua/) N nursing mother (tua/ for animals).

แม่เลี้ยง (คน) mɛ̂ɛlíaŋ/ (khon/) N stepmother, foster mother.

แม่สะเรียง mɛ̂ɛsariaŋ/, mɛ̂ɛ/sariaŋ/ Mæsariang, a town in NW Thailand.

แม่สื่อ (คน) mɛ̂ɛsỳy/ (khon/) N female go-between (usually one acting as matchmaker).

แม่เสือ (คน) mɛ̂ɛsỹa/ (khon/) N tough woman, esp. one who is given to bawling people out.

แม่หนู mɛ̂ɛnǔn/ P 1. you, she, her (sp. to or of a little girl). T 2. Miss --, little Miss --.

แม่หม้าย (คน) mɛ̂ɛmâaj/ (khon/) N widow.

แม่เหล็ก mɛ̂ɛlèg/ N magnet.

แม่ฮ่องสอน mɛ̂ɛhɔ̀ŋsɔ̌ɔn/ pN Mæhɔŋsɔn, a township in N Thailand.

หัวแม่เท้า (นิ้ว) hǔamɛ̂ɛtháaw/ (níw/) N eleg. big toe. →Syn. หัวแม่ตีน com., vulg.

หัวแม่มือ (นิ้ว) hǔamɛ̂ɛmyy/ (níw/) N thumb.

แม mɛ́ɛ/ Cj even though, even if.

ขอแม (ข้อ) khɔ̌ɔmɛ́ɛ/ (khɔ̂ɔ/) N condition, stipulation.

ถ้าแม thâamɛ́ɛ/ but if, if.

ถึงแม(ว่า) thy̌ŋmɛ́ɛ/(wâaɔ) even if, even though, although.

แมกระทั่ง mɛ́ɛkrathâŋ/ Cj 1. even when. Pp 2. even.

แมกระนั้น mɛ́ɛkranán/ however, yet, nevertheless.

แมจะ mɛ́ɛcaɔ even though.

แม(...)จะ...ก็ตาม mɛ́ɛ(...)caɔ...-kɔ̂taam/ even if, notwithstanding.

แมแต่ mɛ́ɛtɛ̀ɛɔ Pp even.

แมว่า...(ก็ตาม)แต่... mɛ́ɛ/wâaɔ...(kɔ̂taam/) →tɛ̀ɛɔ... even though..., still...; no matter ..., still.... →Also ถึง--.

แมกกาซีน (ฉบับ, เล่ม) mégkaasiin/* (chabàb/, lêm/) N magazine. [f. Eng.]

แมกกาซีนภาพ mégkaasiin/phâap/ N pictorial magazine.

แมง (ตัว) mɛɛŋ/, mɛŋ/ (tua/) N colloq. insect. →Syn. แมลง com.; in cpds. eleg. NOTE. แมง is a colloquial class term for insects and แมลง is the corresponding common or elegant term. In addition แมง is a common class term for some aquatic invertebrates; see 2nd and 3rd subentries.

แมงกะแท้ mɛŋkathée/ N a kind of bug, known for its distinctive odor when crushed (Pentatomidae).

แมงกะพรุน mɛŋkaphrun/ N jellyfish (Medusae).

แมงดา (ตัว, คน) mɛŋdaa/ N 1. king crab or horseshoe crab (tua/). 2. water bug (tua/). 3. vulg. gigolo (khon/).

แมงปอ mɛŋpɔɔ/ N colloq. dragonfly.

แมงป่อง mɛŋpɔ̀ŋ/ N colloq. scorpion.

แมงมุม mɛŋmum/ N colloq. spider.

แมงวัน mɛŋwan/ N colloq. fly, housefly.

แมงหวี่ mɛŋwìi/ N colloq. fruit fly.

แมงลัก mɛŋlág/* N a variety of sweet basil used in cookery.

แม่น mɛ̂n/* V to be accurate, correct, exact, precise.

นักแม่นปืน (คน) nág/mɛ̂npyyn/ (khon/) N sharpshooter.

เป็นแม่นมั่น penmɛ̂n/mân/ surely, absolutely.

แม่นยำ mɛ̂njam/ sV 1. accurately, clearly, vividly, well. V 2. to be accurate, correct. ความ-- N accuracy, precision. NOTE. แม่นยำ is chiefly used to describe the memory, remembering something.

แม้น ๑ mɛ́ɛn/ Cj even though, even if.

แม้น ๒ mɛ́ɛn/ V lit. to resemble, look like, be similar to.

แมนจูเรีย mɛɛncuuria/ pN Manchuria. [f. Eng.]

แมม in มอมแมม mɔmmɛm/* V to be dirty, covered with dirt, dusty and dirty, filthy, bedraggled, besmirched.

แมลง (ตัว) malɛɛŋ/ (tua/) N com. insect. →Also ตัว--. →Syn. แมง colloq. NOTE. In some compounds แมลง is eleg.

o ยาฆ่าตัวแมลง jaa/-khâa/tuamalɛɛŋ/ N insecticide.

แมลงปอ malɛɛŋpɔɔ/ N eleg. dragonfly.

แมลงป่อง malɛɛŋpɔ̀ŋ/ N eleg. scorpion.

แมลงภู่ malɛɛŋphûu/ N eleg. carpenter bee.

○ หอยแมลงภู่ hɔ̌jmalɛɛŋphûu′ N eleg. iridescent sea mussel.

แมลงมุม malɛɛŋ′mum′ N eleg. spider.

○ ใยแมลงมุม (ใย,เส้น) jaj′malɛɛŋmum′ (jaj′,
sên′) N eleg. spider web, cobweb.

แมลงวัน malɛɛŋwan′ N eleg. fly, housefly.

แมลงสาบ malɛɛŋsàab′ N eleg. cockroach.

แมลงหวี่ malɛɛŋwìi′ N eleg. fruit fly.

แมว (ตัว) mɛɛw′ (tua′) N cat. →Comp. เหมียว.

นกเค้าแมว (ตัว) nógkháwmɛɛw′ (tua′) N owl.

แมวน้ำ (ตัว) mɛɛwnáam′ (tua′) N seal, sea lion.

แมวบ้าน (ตัว) mɛɛwbâan′ (tua′) N house cat.

แมวป่า (ตัว) mɛɛwpàa′ (tua′) N wildcat, leopard cat.

แมวสีสวาด (ตัว) mɛɛw′sǐisawàad′ (tua′) N
a bluish gray cat native to Thailand.

แม้ว méw′* N Meo (or Miao), a tribe of hill people
in N Thailand.

โม่ (ลูก,ใบ) môo′ V 1. to grind, mill. N 2. mill
(lûug′, baj′).

โม้ móo′ V colloq. to boast, brag.

โมฆะ,โมฆ mookhá?′ eleg. void, invalid, useless.

เป็นโมฆะ penmookhá?′ to be void, invalid, useless.

โมง mooŋ′ C colloq. o'clock. →Must be used
with a preceding numerative except that "one"
may sometimes be omitted. →Syn. นาฬิกา
eleg.

กี่โมง (1) kìimooŋ′; (2) kìimooŋ′↓ colloq. 1. at
what time? 2. What time is it?

ชั่วโมง chûamooŋ′ C hour.

○ หกชั่วโมง hòg′chûamooŋ′ six hours.

บ่ายโมง bàajmooŋ′ one o'clock in the afternoon,
1 P. M.

บ่ายสองโมง bàajsɔ̌ɔŋmooŋ′ two o'clock in the
afternoon, 2 P. M.

โมงเช้า,หนึ่ง-- mooŋcháaw, nὑŋmooŋcháaw′
seven o'clock in the morning, 7 A. M.

สองโมงเช้า sɔ̌ɔŋmooŋcháaw′ eight o'clock in
the morning, 8 A. M.

หกโมงเช้า hògmooŋcháaw′ six o'clock in the
morning, 6 A. M.

หกโมงเย็น hògmooŋjen′ six o'clock in the evening, 6 P. M.

โมหะ,โมห moohà?′ N lit. passion (in the sense

of a total absence or suspension of reason when
committing a sin, a wrongdoing).

โมโห moohǒo′ V 1. to be angry, angry with. N 2.
anger; usually ความ--. →Syn. กริ้ว roy.,
โกรธ,ฉุน com., โกละ eleg.

โมโหร้าย moohǒoráaj′ V to be very bad-tempered,
susceptible to violent anger.

ไม่ mâj′ AA not.

NOTE 1. This word is often used together with
other adverb-auxiliaries. In such combinations
it usually comes first, e.g. ไม่ค่อย,ไม่อยากจะ,
and many others listed below. In certain instances, however, it regularly follows the other
adverb-auxiliaries, e. g. จะไม่, คงจะไม่,
มักจะไม่, ย่อมจะไม่, ยังไม่, เห็นจะไม่; see
these below.

NOTE 2. Expressions meaning "cannot" are
very numerous. The most general term is
ไม่ได้ mâjdâaj′; 1st example. The expression
ไม่เป็น mâjpen′ means "cannot" in the sense
of not knowing how; 2nd example. The expression ไม่ไหว mâjwǎj′ means "cannot" in the
sense of being physically unable; 3rd example.
Other expressions make use of other verbs
after ไม่. These verbs usually suggest some
result that might have been expected from the
action of the primary verb, but which does not
follow because of some condition which makes
that result impossible; 4th-7th examples. Expressions of this type may indicate either an
actor's inability to perform a given action (4th
example), or the impossibility of the action's
being performed (6th example). Occasionally
the expression functions as a secondary verb;
7th example.

○ ผมไปว่ายน้ำไม่ได้เพราะฝนตก phǒm′pajwâajⴗ
náam′mâjdâaj′→phrɔ́fǒntòg′↓ I can't go swimming because it's raining.

○ ผมว่ายน้ำไม่เป็นเพราะไม่มีใครสอนให้ phǒm′-
wâajnáam′mâjpen′→phrɔ́mâjmiikhraj′sɔ̌ɔnhâj′↓
I can't (don't know how to) swim because I had
no one to teach me how.

○ ผมว่ายน้ำต่อไปไม่ไหวเพราะเหนื่อยมากแล้ว
phǒm′-wâajnáam′-tɔ̀ɔpaj′mâjwǎj′→phrɔ́nὑaj′ⴗ
mâaglέɛw′↓ I can't swim any further because
I'm very tired.

○ ผมมองไม่เห็นเพราะมืด phǒmmɔɔŋ′mâjhěn′→
phrɔ́mɯ̂yd′↓ I can't see because it's dark.

○ ปัญหานั่นเป็นปัญหาที่แก้ไม่ตก panhǎanán′ penpanⴗ
hǎa′-thîikὲɛ′mâjtòg′↓ The problem is an unsolvable one: "one which is unsolvable."

○ ไฟนั่นจุดไม่ติด faj′nán′ cùd′mâjtìd′↓ The fire
won't light: "can't be lit."

○ เด็กคนนั้นชนแก้ไม่หาย dèg′khonnán′ son′-kὲɛ′ⴗ
mâjhǎaj′↓ That child is incorrigibly naughty.

กินไม่เข้า kin/mâjkhâw/ can't eat (it), can't get (it) down; to be inedible.

แก้ไม่ตก kɛɛ/mâjtòg/ can't solve (it), can't figure (it) out; can't be solved, is unsolvable.

แก้ไม่หาย kɛɛ/mâjhǎaj/ to be incorrigible, incurable; incorrigibly.

ขบไม่แตก khòb/mâjtὲɛg/ can't solve (it); can't be solved, unsolvable. Cf. Eng. "it can't be cracked."

ขุดไม่เข้า khùd/mâjkhâw/ can't dig it up.

คง(จะ)ไม่ khoŋ/(ca)mâjɔ surely (will) not, probably (will) not, unlikely to.

ความไม่แน่ใจ khwaam/mâjnɛ̀ɛcaj/ N uncertainty (of mind).

ความไม่ประมาท khwaam/mâjpramàad/ N caution, prudence, carefulness.

ความไม่พอ khwaam/mâjphɔɔ/ N insufficiency.

ความไม่พอใจ khwaam/mâjphɔɔcaj/ N dissatisfaction; displeasure.

ความไม่มั่นคง khwaam/mâjmânkhoŋ/ N instability, unsteadiness, insecurity.

ความไม่ลำเอียง khwaam/mâjlamʔiaŋ/ N impartiality.

ความไม่สงบ khwaam/mâjsaŋòb/ N unrest, disquietude.

คิดไม่ออก khíd/mâjʔɔ̀ɔg/ can't solve (it), can't figure (it) out; can't think (e.g. because of noise, confusion, a headache).

จะไม่ camâjɔ will not, won't.

o จะไม่ไป camâjpaj/ won't go.

ดันไม่เข้า dan/mâjkhâw/ can't push (it) in, can't push it together.

ดึงไม่ออก dyŋ/mâjʔɔ̀ɔg/ can't pull (it) out, can't pull (it) apart.

ดูไม่เห็น duu/mâjhěn/ can't see (e.g. because of darkness).

ดูไม่ออก duu/mâjʔɔ̀ɔg/ can't tell, can't make out (by looking).

โดยไม่... doojmâjɔ without...-ing, without being... .

o โดยไม่ผิด dooj/mâjphìd/ without erring.

o โดยไม่ยาก dooj/mâjjâag/ without difficulty.

o โดยไม่รู้สึกตัว dooj/mâjrúusỳgtua/ without being aware of it, without realizing it.

o ยอมแพ้โดยไม่มีเงื่อนไข jɔɔmphɛ́ɛ/-doojmâjmii/ɔ ŋankhǎj/ to surrender unconditionally.

ตั้งสติไม่อยู่ tâŋ/satìʔ/-mâjjùu/ can't concentrate.

ตัดไม่ขาด tàd/mâjkhàad/ can't sever (it).

ตามไม่ทัน taam/mâjthan/ can't catch up with.

เถียงไม่ขึ้น thǐaŋ/mâjkhŷn/ can't win the dispute, argument; can't argue (e.g. because one's opponent is too clever, or has too high a position).

ทำไม่ลง tham/mâjloŋ/ can't do (it), don't have the heart to do (it).

นอนไม่หลับ nɔɔn/mâjlàb/ can't sleep.

นั่งไม่ลง nâŋ/mâjloŋ/ can't sit down (e.g. because the seat is dirty).

นับไม่ถ้วน náb/mâjthûan/ countless, innumerable; can't count (them).

นึกไม่ออก nýg/mâjʔɔ̀ɔg/ can't recall, can't think of it.

บอกไม่ถูก bɔ̀ɔg/mâjthùug/ can't tell exactly or correctly; (it's) hard to say.

ปลูกไม่ขึ้น plùug/mâjkhŷn/ can't grow (it); (it) won't grow, can't be grown.

ปิดไม่เข้า pìd/mâjkhâw/ can't close (it); (it) won't close.

เปิดไม่ออก pə̀əd/mâjʔɔ̀ɔg/ can't open (it); (it) won't open.

ไปไม่รอด paj/mâjrɔ̂ɔd/ can't go through, can't carry on, can't get anywhere.

พูดไม่จริง phûud/mâjciŋ/ V c o m. to tell an untruth. →Syn. See โกหก c o m.

พูดไม่ออก phûud/mâjʔɔ̀ɔg/ to be struck dumb, speechless.

ฟังไม่ขึ้น faŋ/mâjkhŷn/ to sound unreasonable, unbelievable, implausible.

ฟังไม่ชัด faŋ/mâjchád/ can't hear clearly; to be unclear, indistinct (of sound).

ฟังไม่ได้ยิน faŋ/mâjdâjjin/ can't hear (e.g. because of noise).

ฟังไม่สนิทหู faŋ/-mâjsanìd/hǔu/ to sound odd, different from usual, not quite right; to sound unlikely, not quite believable.

มองไม่เห็น mɔɔŋ/mâjhěn/ can't see (e.g. because of darkness, mental block, etc.).

มักจะไม่ mágcamâjɔ not likely to.

ไม่กี่... mâjkìiɔ not many (followed by a clf.).

o ต่อมาไม่กี่วัน tɔɔmaa'mâjklìwan' not many days later.

ไม่กี่มากน้อย mâjklìmâagnɔ́ɔj' colloq. not so much, not so many.

ไม่เกิน mâjkəən' not to exceed, not more than, no more than, no...-er than.

o สวยไม่เกินแม่ sŭaj'-mâjkəən'mɛ̂ɛ' she is no more beautiful than her mother.

o สูงไม่เกินพ่อ sŭuŋ'-mâjkəən'phɔ̂ɔ' he is no taller than his father.

ไม่เกี่ยว mâjklìaw' not to be concerned, not to concern; to be unrelated.

ไม่ขาด,--สาย mâjkhàad', mâjkhàadsǎaj' without a break, continously. →Comp. ตัดไม่ขาด. "can't sever it."

ไม่ขึ้น. See เถียง--,ปลูก--,ฟัง--,ลุก-- among the subentries of ไม่.

ไม่เข้า. See กิน--,ขุด--,ดัน--,ปิด--,ใส่-- among the subentries of ไม่.

ไม่เข้าใครออกใคร mâjkhâwkhraj'?ɔ̀ɔgkhraj' colloq. be neutral, impartial.

ไม่เข้าเรื่อง mâjkhâwrŷaŋ' 1. to be irrelevant, impertinent, nonsensical. 2. irrelevantly, unnecessarily.

o ยุ่งไม่เข้าเรื่อง jûŋ'mâjkhâwrŷaŋ' colloq. to be unnecessarily meddlesome; to fiddle with things one has no business touching (as of a child).

ไม่คงเส้นคงวา mâjkhoŋsên'khoŋwaa' to be inconsistent.

ไม่ควร mâjkhuan' 1. should not, ought not. 2. to be improper, inappropriate.

ไม่ค่อย mâjkhɔ̂j⊃ colloq. scarcely, hardly, not quite, not very. →Syn. ไม่ใคร่ lit., ไม่สู้ ๒ com. →See cross reference.

ไม่เคย mâjkhəəj' never (e.g. "have never done").

ไม่เคยเลย mâjkhəəj'ləəj' never before.

ไม่ใคร่ mâjkhrâj⊃ lit. scarcely, hardly, not quite, not very. →Syn. ไม่ค่อย colloq., ไม่สู้ ๒ com.

ไม่ชอบ mâjchɔ̂ɔb' 1. to dislike. 2. to be displeased. 3. to be inappropriate, improper, out of keeping (with); to be illegal.

o ไม่ชอบด้วยกฎหมาย mâjchɔ̂ɔb'dûajkòdmǎaj' to

be against the law, unlawful, illegal.

o ไม่ชอบที่จะ mâjchɔ̂ɔb'thîicaɔ ought not, should not.

ไม่ชอบกล mâjchɔ̂ɔbkon' to be inappropriate, funny, strange, peculiar.

ไม่ชั่วแต่ mâjchûa'tɛ̀ɛɔ it is not only; not only.

ไม่ช้า mâjcháa' soon, in a short time, shortly.

o ในไม่ช้า najmâjcháa' idem.

o ไม่ช้าก็เร็ว mâjcháa'kɔrew' sooner or later.

o ไม่ช้าไม่นาน mâjcháa'mâjnaan' soon.

o อยู่มาไม่ช้า jùumaa'mâjcháa' writ. not long afterwards.

ไม่ช่าย mâjchâaj'. A special spelling of ไม่ใช่, used to represent a long-drawn-out pronunciation of the second syllable.

ไม่เชิง mâjchəəŋ' colloq. not exactly, not quite.

o ไม่เชิงอวด mâjchəəŋ'?ùad' (it's) not exactly boasting.

ไม่ใช่ (1) mâjchâj⊃; (2) mâjchâj↓ 1. is not, are not, am not. 2. No, it's not! No!

o ธุระไม่ใช่ thurá?'mâjchâj' colloq. to be none of one's business.

o นี่ไม่ใช่ดินสอ nîi'-mâjchâjdinsɔɔ' this is not a pencil.

o ไม่ใช่เล่น mâjchâjlên' colloq. quite, really.

o ไม่ใช่หรือ mâjchâjrý↓, mâjchâj'rý↓ Isn't it? Aren't you? Don't you?

ไม่ดี mâjdii' to be bad, not good. ความ-- badness, (the) bad.

o ลมไม่ดี lom'mâjdii' colloq. to be in a bad mood.

ไม่เดียงสา mâjdiaŋsǎa' to be innocent, naive, to lack worldly wisdom (as of a child).

ไม่ได้ (1)mâjdâj⊃, mâjdâaj'; (2) mâjdâj⊃, (3) mâjɔ dâaj'; (4) mâjdâaj↓ com. 1. not get, gain, obtain, procure. 2. didn't; not get to, didn't get to. 3. can't, cannot, unable to (as a temporary condition). 4. No! (in ans. to ได้ไหม ; also used prohibitively). →Syn. มิได้ eleg. →Note the various usages of ไม่ได้ listed below.

PRIMARY VERB USAGE (see mng. 1 above). Here ไม่ negates ได้ and the latter functions as a primary verb.

o ไม่ได้ไม่เสีย mâjdâaj'mâjsɪa' to neither lose

nor gain; to break even.

o ไม่ได้ความ (1,2) mâjdâjkhwaam′; (3) mâjdâjco khwaam′↓ 1. to be nonsense, make no sense. 2. nonsensically, senselessly. 3. Nonsense! It doesn't make sense!

o ไม่ได้ผล mâjdâjphŏn′ to get no result; to be of no avail, useless, unsuccessful, ineffective.

o ไม่ได้เรื่อง mâjdâjrŷaŋ colloq. 1. to be no good, useless. 2. to get no result. 3. to make no sense.

ADVERB-AUXILIARY USAGE (see mng. 2 above). Here ไม่ได้, like simple adv. -aux., occurs before the primary verb.

o ยังไม่ได้ถาม jaŋmâjdâjthăam′ haven't yet asked.

o ผมไม่ได้ไปไหน phŏm′-mâjdâjpajnăj↓ I didn't go anywhere.

o ฉันจะไม่ได้ไปเมืองนอกแล้วละ cháncamâjdâjo paj′/myaŋnɔ̂ɔg′-léwla?↓ I won't get to go abroad after all.

SECONDARY VERB USAGE (see mng. 3 above). Here ไม่ได้ follows the primary verb which it modifies. Sometimes it is also followed by another secondary verb which it then negates, and the resulting expression modifies the primary verb, as in the 4th example below.

o ใช้การไม่ได้ chájkaan′mâjdâaj′ cannot be used; is out of order, not in serviceable condition.

o ไปไม่ได้ paj′mâjdâaj′ can't go.

o ไปไกลไม่ได้ pajklaj′mâjdâaj′ unable to go far, can't go far.

o ไปไม่ได้ไกล paj′mâjdâjklaj′ won't go very far, will go (but) not far.

o เป็นไปไม่ได้ penpaj′mâjdâaj′ to be impossible.

o พูดไม่ได้เต็มปาก phûud′mâjdâatempàag′ unable to say conclusively.

o ฟังไม่ได้ faŋ′mâjdâaj′ 1. to sound awful, unpleasant; can't bear to listen (to it). 2. to sound invalid, unreasonable.

o ว่ายน้ำไม่ได้ wâajnáam′mâjdâaj′ can't swim, can't go swimming (for lack of time, etc.).

o สู้(...)ไม่ได้ sûu′(...)mâjdâaj′ can't beat, can't match, can't compete (with), can't compare (with).

o อด(...)ไม่ได้ ?òd′(...)mâjdâaj′ cannot refrain (from).

o อย่างเสียไม่ได้ jàaŋsĭa′mâjdâaj′ against one's will, against one's better judgment (as when giving in to someone's pleading).

ไม่ต้อง mâjtɔ̂ŋo not to have to.

ไม่ต้องการจะ mâjtɔ̂ŋkaan′cao not to want to.

ไม่ต่างอะไรกับ mâjtàaŋ′/?araj′-kao is no different from.

ไม่ต่ำกว่า mâjtàm′kwàao not less than.

ไม่เต็มเต็ง mâjtemteŋ′ idiom. colloq. to have

a screw loose, to be cracked, touched in the head, not all there.

ไม่ถือสา mâjthɣ̌ysăa′ V not to mind, take no offense.

ไม่ทัน mâjthan′ not in time, late.

o ไปไม่ทันรถ paj′-mâjthan′ród′ to miss one's bus, train, etc.

o ไม่ทันไร mâjthan′raj′ colloq. 1. only a short while later. 2. not very long ago.

o ยังไม่ทัน jaŋmâjthan′ not yet, not yet in time to.

o ยังไม่ทัน...ก็... jaŋmâjthan′...→kɔ̂o... no sooner...than.... .

ไม่ทำดี mâjtham′dii′ not to do good.

ไม่เท่าไร mâjthâwràj′* not very; not much, not many.

ไม่(...)เท่าไร, ไม่ค่อย(...)เท่าไร mâj(...)o thâwràj′, mâjkhɔ̂j(...)thâwràj′ not very, not so very, not too; not very much, many; not so very much, many; not too much, many.

ไม่น้อย mâjnɔ́ɔj′ not a little, i.e. quite, considerable.

o รุนแรงไม่น้อย runrɛɛŋ′mâjnɔ́ɔj′ to be quite severe.

ไม่...นัก mâjo...nág not very, not so very (e.g. big), not too (e.g. difficult), not quite (e.g. satisfactory).

ไม่น่า(จะ) mâjnâa′(cao) should not, ought not, unlikely to, not worth ...-ing.

o ไม่น่าจะสงสัย mâjnâa′casŏŋsăj′ indubitable; there is no doubt about it.

o ไม่น่าเชื่อ mâjnâachŷa′ unbelievable, hard to believe.

o ไม่น่าดู mâjnâaduu′ to be not worth seeing, unpleasant to look at, not nice (to see).

o ไม่น่าเลย mâjnâa′!lòɵj↓ It shouldn't have been like that at all! (I, he, she, etc.) shouldn't have (e.g. done that, forgotten that) at all! (implying surprise, disappointment).

ไม่นานเท่าไร mâjnaan′thâwràj′ not very long (of time).

ไม่นำพา mâjnam′phaa′ to pay not the slightest attention to; to ignore (e.g. tradition, a warning).

ไม่แน่ใจ mâjnɛ̂ɛcaj′ V to be uncertain. uncertainty (of mind).

ไม่ประมาท mâjpramàad′ V to be careful. ความ-- caution, prudence, carefulness.

ไม่ประสีประสา mâjprasǐi'prasǎa' to be innocent, naive, not knowing worldly affairs (as of a child). →Also ไม่ประสา.

ไม่เป็น mâjpen' can't, cannot (because of not knowing how).

o ว่ายน้ำไม่เป็น wâajnáam'mâjpen' can't swim, doesn't know how to swim.

ไม่เป็นตัวเป็นตน mâjpentua'penton' to be un-formed, amorphous, not to have taken shape.

ไม่เป็นท่า mâjpenthâa' 1. to be awkward, ungainly. 2. awkwardly, ungracefully, not in the usual manner, not in the accepted manner.

ไม่เป็นประสีประสา mâjpenprasǐi'prasǎa' 1. to be innocent, naive, not knowing worldly affairs. 2. to be ignorant, inexperienced.

ไม่เป็นเรื่อง mâjpenrŷaŋ' to be nonsense, nonsen-sical.

ไม่เป็นไร mâjpenraj'⌉ It doesn't matter. That's all right. Not at all. It's nothing. It doesn't make any difference. It's all the same. Never mind! Forget it!

ไม่พอ mâjphɔɔ' V to be insufficient, inadequate. ความ-- insufficiency.

ไม่พอใจ mâjphɔɔcaj' to be annoyed, dissatisfied, displeased. ความ-- dissatisfaction, displeas-ure.

ไม่พักต้อง mâjphág'tɔ̂ŋɔ does not wait to, without waiting (e.g. to be invited).

ไม่เพียงแต่ mâjphiaŋ'tɛ̀ɛ strong not only.

ไม่มั่นคง mâjmânkhoŋ' V to be unsteady, unstable, insecure. ความ-- instability, unsteadiness, insecurity.

ไม่มากก็น้อย mâjmâag'kɔ̂nɔ́ɔj' whether many or few, whether much or little; if not a (whole) lot, then (at least) some.

ไม่...มากนัก mâj...mâag'nág' not so very...

ไม่มีทาง mâjmiithaaŋ' there is no way, it is not possible.

ไม่มีทางออก mâjmii'thaaŋʔɔ̀ɔg' there is no way out (used both literally and figuratively).

ไม่มีปัญหา mâjmii'panhǎa' 1. unquestionably, without question; doubtless, no doubt. 2. there is no question (about it). อย่าง-- unquestion-ably, doubtlessly.

ไม่มีมูล mâjmiimuun' to have no grounds, basis.

ไม่มีวัน mâjmiiwan' never, there will never be a day (when); there's not a chance.

o ไม่มีวันอดตาย mâjmiiwan'-ʔòd'taaj' will never starve to death.

ไม่มีสาระ mâjmii'sǎa'rá?' 1. to have no sense, be nonsense. 2. to have no substance, be imma-terial.

ไม่ยอม (1) mâjjɔɔmɔ, mâjjɔɔm'; (2) mâjjɔɔm'⌉ 1. to refuse to, decline, be unwilling to. 2. (I) won't have it!

o ไม่ยอมกลับ mâjjɔɔmklàb' to refuse to return.

o ไม่ยอมแพ้ mâjjɔɔmphɛ́ɛ' to refuse to surrender.

o ไม่ยอมออกเสียง mâjjɔɔm'ʔɔ̀ɔgsǐaŋ' to abstain from voting, refuse to vote.

ไม่ยอย mâjjɔ̌j' colloq. quite, significantly (not at all insignificant).

ไม่ยัก mâjjágɔ colloq. strangely enough not; regrettably not; not in the least, not at all; not as expected, not as (one) should; happen not to (contrary to expectation).

o เขาไม่ยักมา kháwmâjjág'maa' He didn't come as expected, strangely enough.

o ไม่ยักชอบ mâjjág'chɔ̂ɔb' to happen not to like (something) (contrary to expectation).

o ไม่ยักรู้ mâjjág'rúu' to happen not to know (contrary to expectation).

ไม่ยี่เจ้ย (1) mâjjîicə̀əj'; (2) mâjjîicə̀əj'⌉ slang 1. not much. 2. It's nothing (expressing either insignificance or contempt).

ไม่ยี่หระ mâjjîirà?' slang not to give a hang, not to care about.

ไม่แยแส mâjjɛɛsɛ̌ɛ' not to pay the slightest atten-tion, to be completely indifferent.

ไม่ไยดี (ต่อ) mâjjajdii'(tɔ̀ɔɔ) to be indifferent (to), not care (for), pay no attention (to).

ไม่รั้งรอ mâjráŋrɔɔ' 1. not to hesitate. 2. unhesi-tatingly.

ไม่รู้จบ mâjrúucòb' 1. unending, endless; recur-ring (decimal). 2. endlessly, without end.

ไม่รู้ไม่ชี้ mâjrúu'mâjchíi' elab. colloq. 1. to pay no attention; to refuse to listen. 2. to refuse to be answerable for the consquences (after a warning has been ignored).

ไม่รู้ไม่เห็น mâjrúu′mâjhěn′ elab. colloq. to know nothing, to have seen nothing (e.g. concerning a crime).

ไม่รู้ลืม mâjrúu′lyym′ 1. to be unforgettable, never to be forgotten. 2. unforgettably. 3. without forgetting.

ไม่รู้วาย mâjrúu′waaj′ unceasingly, ceaselessly.

ไม่เร็วก็ช้า mâjrew′kɔ̂cháa′ sooner or later.

ไม่ลง mâjloŋ′ cannot, unable to, does not have the heart (to). See ทำ--,นั่ง--,วาง-- among the subentries of ไม่.

ไม่ลงรอยกัน mâjloŋrɔɔj′kan′ idiom. to be at odds with each other; to be inharmonious, not on good terms, not to see eye to eye with each other.

ไม่ลำเอียง mâjlam?iaŋ′ to be impartial. ความ-- impartiality.

ไม่เลือกหน้า mâjlŷag′nâa′ without anyone being excepted; without discrimination.

ไม่ว่า (1) mâjwâa′; (2) mâjwâaɔ 1. not to mind, not to complain. 2. no matter, regardless of.

ไม่ว่าง mâjwâaŋ′ 1. to be busy, occupied. 2. to be occupied (as of a bathroom).

ไม่วางตา mâjwaaŋ′taa′ without taking (one's) eyes off (something).

ไม่วาย mâjwaaj′ cannot help, cannot refrain from.

ไม่เว้นแต่ละวัน mâjwén′tɛɛlawan′ colloq. every day, day in and day out.

ไม่ไว้หน้า mâjwájnâa′ without sparing (the feelings of) anyone, without respect for anyone.

ไม่สงบ mâjsaŋòb′ to be unrestful. ความ-- unrest, disquietude.

ไม่สนิทหู. See under ฟัง-- above.

ไม่สบาย mâjsabaaj′ to be sick, ill; to be uncomfortable, ill at ease.

ไม่สมประกอบ mâjsǒm′prakɔ̀ɔb′ to be deformed, abnormal, imperfect, defective.

ไม่สะดวก mâjsaduag′ 1. to be inconvenient. 2. inconveniently, with difficulty.

ไม่(...)สักเท่าไร mâj(...)ságthâwràj′ not so very; not so very much.

ไม่สู้ ๑ mâjsûu′ 1. to give up, withdraw (as from competition). 2. won't fight, won't compete. คน-- weakling, coward.

ไม่สู้ ๒,--จะ mâjsûu′, mâjsûu′caɔ not very, not much, not so. →Syn. ไม่ค่อย colloq. ไม่ใคร่ lit.

o ไม่สู้...นัก mâjsûu′...nág′ not so very, not exceptionally.

ไม่เสียไม่ได้ mâjsǐa′mâjdâaj′ to neither lose nor gain; to break even. →Usually ไม่ได้ไม่เสีย.

ไม่หยอก mâjjɔ̀ɔg′ colloq. quite, really, very.

ไม่เห็นแก่ mâjhěn′kɛ̀ɛ not to think of, not to care about.

ไม่เห็นด้วย mâjhěndûaj′ to disagree.

ไม่เหลียวไม่แล mâjlǐaw′mâjlɛɛ′ elab. colloq. 1. to pay no attention, be indifferent. 2. to neglect, abandon.

ไม่ให้ (1) mâjhâj′; (2,3) mâjhâjɔ 1. not to give. 2. not to let. 3. not to, without, so that not (followed by a verb). →For additional examples see cross reference.

o ไม่ให้นำ(...)เข้ามา mâjhâjnam′(...)khâwɔ maa′ not to bring (something) in, not to allow to bring (something) in.

o ไม่ให้เป็นสมาชิก mâjhâj(...)pen′samaachíg′ not to allow (someone) to become a member.

o ไม่ให้มากเกินไป mâjhâjmâag′kəənpaj not too much.

ไม่ไหว (1) mâjwǎj′; mâjwǎj↓ sV 1. unable to, can't, cannot, is incapable of (because of lack of physical strength or energy). E 2. How impossible!

o ว่ายน้ำต่อไปไม่ไหว wâajnáam′-tɔ̀ɔpaj′mâjwǎj′ can't swim any further.

ไม่อยาก(จะ) mâjjàag(ca)ɔ not to want to, not to wish to.

o ไม่อยากได้ mâjjàagdâaj′ not to wish to have, not to want.

ไม่อย่างงั้น mâjjàŋŋán′ colloq. otherwise, or else, if not.

ไม่ออก. See คิด--, ดู--,ดึง--,นึก--,เปิด--, พูด--,แยก--,อ่าน-- among the subentries of ไม่.

ไม่อะไรก็อะไร mâj?araj′kɔ̂?araj′ colloq. one thing or another, something for sure.

ไม่อั้น mâj?ân′ colloq. 1. not to hold back, stint. 2. without holding back, without stint, without hesitation. →Also 2. อย่าง--.

ไม่...อีกเลย mâj...ʔìigləəj´ never again (do such and such).

ย่อมจะไม่ jɔ̂m´camâjɔ not likely to, not apt to.

ยังไม่ jaŋmâjɔ not yet.

ยังไม่พออีกหรือ jaŋmâjphɔɔ´/ʔìigrýɟ Isn't that enough?

ยิงไม่อยู่ jiŋ´mâjjùu´ cannot drop (e.g. an animal) (by shooting).

แยกไม่ออก jɛ̂ɛg´mâjʔɔ̀ɔg´ 1. cannot be separated, cannot be taken apart. 2. cannot separate (something).

รู้เท่าไม่ถึงการณ์ rúu´thâw´-mâjthʉ̌ŋkaan´ to be blind to a situation, be unable to see what someone is up to.

ลุกไม่ขึ้น lúg´mâjkhŷn´ can't get up.

เลี้ยงไม่เชื่อง líaŋ´mâjchŷaŋ´ to be untameable.

ว่าไม่ฟัง wâa´mâjfaŋ´ to be disobedient, naughty, heedless of advice, warnings, commands.

วางไม่ลง waaŋ´mâjloŋ´ cannot put down (as when fascinated with something).

ใส่ไม่เข้า sàj´mâjkhâw´ can't put it in or on; (it) won't go in, go on.

หยิบไม่ถึง jìb´mâjthʉ̌ŋ´ can't get it, can't take it up (because it's beyond reach).

หรือไม่ rʉ̌ymâj´ or not.

หาไม่ hǎamâj´ lit. otherwise; had it been otherwise. →See cross reference.

หา...ไม่ hǎa...mâj´ lit. not. →For additional examples see cross reference.

o หาควรไม่ hǎakhuan´mâj´ lit. ought not, should not.

o หามีไม่ hǎamii´mâj´ lit. there isn't any.

หาไม่พบ hǎa´mâjphób´ can't find (it).

หายใจไม่ทั่วท้อง hǎajcaj´-mâjthûa/thɔ́ɔŋ´ colloq. fig. to breathe uneasily (as in a tense situation).

เห็นจะไม่ hěn´camâjɔ apparently will not, (it) seems not.

อย่างไม่มีปัญหา jàaŋmâjmii´panhǎa´ without question, no doubt.

อย่างไม่มีปี่มีขลุ่ย jàaŋmâjmiipìi´miikhlùj´ idiom. without warning.

อย่างไม่แยแส jàaŋ´mâjjɛɛsɛ̌ɛ´ uninterestedly,

indifferently.

อย่างไม่ลดละ jàaŋ´-mâjlódlá?´ unrelentingly, without slackening, unceasingly, without letup, without giving in. →Also อย่างไม่ละลด.

อย่างไม่หยุดหย่อน jàaŋ´-mâjjùdjɔ̀n´ incessantly, ceaselessly.

อ่านไม่ออก ʔàan´mâjʔɔ̀ɔg´ 1. can't read (it) (because of illegibility, etc.). 2. fig. can't figure it out.

ไม้ máaj´, májɔ N wood, stick.

NOTE 1. Terms for parts or the whole of plants or trees (e.g. ดอก "flower," ใบ "leaf," ต้น "plant") are normally not used alone, except as classifiers. They are followed by ไม้ if the general meaning is intended, as in ดอกไม้ "flower (of any kind)," ใบไม้ "leaf," ต้นไม้ "tree." Otherwise they are followed by a specific term for the species, as in ดอกกุหลาบ "rose," ใบมะม่วง "mango leaf," ต้นนุ่น "kapok tree."

NOTE 2. The word ไม้ is also used as the first member of compounds referring to certain kinds of secondary written symbols, such as tonal markers, certain vowel symbols, etc. In this usage it corresponds quite closely to the English word "mark" or "marker." See the following entries in the list of derivatives below: ไม้กากบาท, ไม้จัตวา, ไม้ตรี, ไม้ไต่คู้, ไม้โท, ไมมลาย, ไม้ม้วน, ไม้ยมก, ไม้หันอากาศ, ไม้เอก.

NOTE 3. ไม้ is often coupled with มือ "hand," chiefly for the sake of alliteration, in special expressions:
o จับไม้จับมือ càbmáaj´càbmyy´ elab. colloq. to hold hands. จับมือ is the corresponding simple expression.

กล้วยไม้ klûajmáaj´ N orchid. ดอก-- (ดอก) orchid (the flower). ต้น-- (ต้น) orchid (the plant).

กอไม้ (กอ) kɔɔmáaj´ (kɔɔ´) N a clump of trees, shrubs; a bush.

กิ่งไม้ (กิ่ง) kìŋmáaj´ (kìŋ´) N branch, twig (of any kind of plant or tree).

ข้อไม้ข้อมือ (ข้อ,ข้าง) khɔ̂ɔmáaj´khɔ̂ɔmyy´ (khɔ̂ɔ´, khâaŋ´) N elab. colloq. wrist.

เครื่องไม้เครื่องมือ (อย่าง,ชิ้น,อัน) khrŷaŋmáaj´ɔ khrŷaŋmyy´ (jàaŋ´, chín´, ʔan´) N elab. colloq. implements, tools.

จับไม้จับมือ càbmáaj´càbmyy´ V elab. colloq. 1. to hold hands. 2. to shake hands.

ช่วยกันคนละไม้คนละมือ chûaj'kan'-khonlamáaj'ɔ
khonlamyy' elab. colloq. each one gives a
helping hand.

ช่างไม้ (คน) châaŋmáaj' (khon') N carpenter.

ชี้ไม้ชี้มือ chíimáaj'chíimyy' elab. colloq. to
point, point one's finger.

ซีกไม้ (ซีก,ชิ้น) sîigmáaj' (sîig', chín') N a
piece or length of split wood, splinter.

ดอกไม้ (ดอก) dɔ̀ɔgmáaj' (dɔ̀ɔg') N flower,
blossom (general term). →See cross reference.
→See note under ดอก.

ดุ้นไม้ (ดุ้น) dûnmáaj' (dûn') N a piece of wood,
stick.

ต้นไม้ (ต้น) tônmáaj' (tôn') N tree, plant (of
any kind). NOTE. ต้นไม้ is a general term for
trees or plants of any kind. Specific trees and
plants are named by using the class term, ต้น,
followed by specific terms, e.g. ต้นกล้วย
"banana tree," ต้นฝิ่น "poppy plant," ต้นอ้อ
"giant reed." See also ไม้ Note 1.

ถ่านไม้ (ก้อน) thàanmáaj' (kɔ̂ɔn') N charcoal
obtained from wood.

ท่อนไม้ (ท่อน) thɔ̂ɔnmáaj' (thɔ̂ɔn') N a log, a
piece of wood.

ทิวไม้ (ทิว) thiwmáaj' (thiw') N a distant
stretch or line of trees, a long row of trees.

นักเลงหัวไม้ (คน) nágleeŋ'hǔamáaj' (khon') N
colloq. rogue, scamp, gangster, hoodlum,
tough guy.

นางไม้ (องค์) naaŋmáaj' (ʔoŋ') N wood fairy,
female tree spirit.

เนื้อไม้ nýamáaj' N wood texture; wood (exclusive of bark).

บ้านไม้ (หลัง) bâanmáaj' (lǎŋ') N wooden house.

โบกไม้โบกมือ bòogmáaj'bòogmyy' V elab.
colloq. to wave the hand.

ใบไม้ (ใบ) bajmáaj' (baj') N leaf (of any kind).
→See ไม้ Note 1.

ป่าไม้ (แห่ง) pàamáaj' (hɛ̀ŋ') N forest, jungle,
woods. การ-- forestry.

เปลือกไม้ plỳagmáaj' N bark.

ผลไม้ (ผล,ลูก,ใบ) phǒnlamáaj' (phǒn', lûug',
baj') N eleg. fruit (of any kind). →Syn.
ลูกไม้ com. →See ไม้ Note 1.

ฝีไม้ลายมือ fĭimáaj'laajmyy' N elab. colloq.
craftmanship, workmanship, skill, ability.

พรรณไม้ (ชนิด) phanmáaj' (chaníd') N kinds of
plants, varieties of plants.

มาไม้นี้ maa'máajníi' colloq. to come up with
this strategy, to use this approach.

มือไม้ (มือ,ข้าง) myymáaj' (myy', khâaŋ') N
colloq. hand

ไม้กวาด (ด้าม,อัน) májkwàad' (dâam', ʔan') N
broom.

ไม้ก๊อก májkɔ́g' N cork (the material); a cork
(stopper). [ก๊อก f. Eng.]

ไม้กากบาท (อัน) májkaakabàad' (ʔan') N the
fourth tonal marker (⁺). →Syn. ไม้จัตวา.

ไม้กางเขน (อัน) májkaaŋkhěen' (ʔan') N cross.

ไม้แก่น máajkèn' N hardwood tree, hardwood.

ไม้ขอ (อัน) májkhɔ̌ɔ' (ʔan') N hook with a wooden
handle.

ไม้ขีด, --ไฟ (อัน,ก้าน,กลัก) májkhìid', májkhìidɔ
faj' N match, matchstick (ʔan', kâan' for individual matches; klàg' for boxes).

ไม้แขวนเสื้อ (อัน) májkhwɛ̌ɛnsŷa' (ʔan') N coat
hanger.

ไม้คาน (อัน) májkhaan' (ʔan') N a bamboo pole
used for carrying loads on the shoulder.

ไม้จัตวา (อัน) májcàdtawaa' (ʔan') N the fourth
tonal marker (⁺) of the Thai writing system.
→Syn. ไม้กากบาท. →Dist. เสียงจัตวา
"rising tone" (of the spoken language).

ไม้จิ้มฟัน (อัน) májcîmfan' (ʔan') N toothpick.

ไม้ดอก (ต้น,ชนิด) máajdɔ̀ɔg' (tôn', chaníd') N
a flowering plant, i.e. a plant known to bear
flowers.

ไม้เด็ด (ไม้) máajdèd' (máaj') N colloq.
decisive blow, decisive trick, stratagem.

ไม้ตรี (อัน) májtrii' (ʔan') N the third tonal
marker (″) of the writing system. →Dist.
เสียงตรี "high tone" (of the spoken language).

ไม้ตาย (ไม้) máajtaaj' (máaj') N 1. boxing
decisive blow, knock-out blow. 2. decisive trick
or stratagem.

ไม้ไต่คู้ (ตัว,อัน) májtàjkhúu' (tua', ʔan') N the
short vowel marker (˘). →Syn. เลขแปด.

ไม้เถา (ต้น) máajthǎw' (tôn') N creeper, vine,

liana.

ไม้ทัณฑฆาต májthan'thakhâad' N eleg. the cancellation mark (̊) used in the Thai writing system. →Syn. การันต์ com.

ไม้เท้า (อัน) májtháaw' (ʔan') N walking stick.

ไม้โท (อัน) májthoo' (ʔan') N the second tonal marker (̌) of the Thai writing system. →Dist. เสียงโท "falling tone" (of the spoken language); see note under cross reference.

ไม้บรรทัด (อัน) máajbanthád' (ʔan') N ruler, straightedge.

ไม้ไผ่ (ลำ) májphàj' (lam') N bamboo (the wood, the stem).

ไม้พาย (อัน) májphaaj' (ʔan') N 1. paddle. 2. big wooden spatula.

ไม้ฟืน (ดุ้น,ท่อน) májfyyn' (dûn',thɔ̂ɔn') N firewood.

ไม้มลาย májmalaj'* N the vowel symbol ไ, representing the sequence -aj as in ไม้.

ไม้ม้วน májmúan' N the vowel symbol ใ, representing the sequence -aj as in ใบ. NOTE. This symbol is of much rarer usage than is ไ which has the same pronunciation (see entry above).

ไม้มะเกลือ májmaklya' N ebony.

ไม้มืด máajmŷyd' N idiom. surprise blow, surprise attack, assault.

ไม้เมตร (อัน) máajméed' (ʔan') N meter stick.

ไม้ยมก májjamóg' N the repeat symbol ๆ, as in ต่าง ๆ tàaŋtàaŋ'.

ไม้ยัน (อัน) máajjan' (ʔan') N crutch.

ไม้ยืนต้น (ต้น,ชนิด) máajjyyntôn' (tôn',chaníd') N perennial plant.

ไม้รวก (ต้น,ลำ,กอ) májrûag' (tôn',lam',kɔɔ') N a thornless type of bamboo.

ไม้เรียว (อัน) májriaw' (ʔan') N switch, rod (used for whipping, beating).

ไม้แร็กเกต (อัน) máajrégkêd'* (ʔan') N racket (for tennis or badminton). [แร็กเกต f. Eng.]

ไม้เลื้อย (ชนิด) máajlýaj' (chaníd') N climbing plant, vine, liana, creeper.

ไม้สน májsŏn' N 1. pine wood. 2. wood of any coniferous tree.

ไม้สัก májsàg' N teak, teakwood.

ไม้หมอน (อัน,ดุ้น) májmɔɔn' (ʔan',dûn') N railroad tie or sleeper.

ไม้หันอากาศ (อัน) májhăn?aakàad' (ʔan') N the vowel symbol (̌) .

ไม้ออ (ต้น) máj?ɔɔ' (tôn') N reed.

ไม้อัด (แผ่น) máj?àd' (phèn') N plywood.

ไม้เอก (อัน) máj?èeg' (ʔan') N the first tonal marker (̀) of the Thai writing system. →Dist. เสียงเอก "low tone" (of the spoken language); see note under cross reference.

ยอดไม้ (ยอด) jɔɔdmáaj' (jɔ̂ɔd') N tree-top.

ร่มไม้ (แห่ง) rômmáaj' (hèŋ') N shade, umbrage of trees.

เรือนไม้ (หลัง) ryanmáaj' (lăŋ') N wooden house or building.

ลงมือลงไม้,ลงไม้ลงมือ loŋmyy'loŋmáaj', loŋmáaj'ɔ loŋmyy' elab. colloq. to begin to do something.

ลูกไม้ (ใบ,ลูก,ผล) lûugmáaj' (baj',lûug',phŏn') N 1. com. fruit (of any kind). 2. lace. 3. idiom. trick. →Syn. 1. ผลไม้ eleg.

เล่นไม้บิด lên'máajbìd' V idiom. to balk.

เศษไม้ (ชิ้น,ดุ้น) sèedmáaj' (chín',dûn') N piece of wood, splinter.

หน่อไม้ (หน่อ) nɔɔmáaj' (nɔ̀ɔ') N young bamboo shoot.

หน้าไม้ (คัน,อัน) nâamáaj' (khan',ʔan') N crossbow.

หมู่ไม้ mùumáaj' N 1. a group of trees, grove. 2. plants (collectively).

ไมตรี majtrii' friendship.

ความสัมพันธไมตรี khwaam'sămphan'thamajtrii' N friendly relations. Also สัมพันธไมตรี.

ไมตรีจิตต์,-จิต majtrii'cìd' N spirit of friendship.

o ความมีไมตรีจิต khwaammii'-majtrii'cìd' N friendliness.

ไมตรีสาร (ฉบับ) majtrii'săan' (chabàb') N friendship note or message.

สันถวไมตรี sănthawámajtrii' N close, intimate friendship.

o ทูตสันถวไมตรี (นาย) thûud'săn'thawámajtrii' (naaj') N good-will ambassador.

ไมล์ maj' C mile. [f. Eng.]

ย

ย jɔɔ′ LOW consonant. Pronounced j both initially
    and finally. The sound j as an initial low con-
    sonant is also sometimes written ญ.

ยก ๑ jóg′ C 1. round (boxing). 2. folio, signature
    (printing, bookbinding). 3. volumetric unit of
    lumber.

ยก ๒ jóg′ V to lift, raise.
    ผ้ายก (ผืน) phâajóg′ (phɯ̌yn′) N brocade.
    ยกกำลัง jóg′kamlaŋ 1. to mobilize, raise a
      (military) force. 2. m a t h. to raise, be raised
      to the (stated) power.
    o ยกกำลังสอง jóg′kamlaŋsɔ̌ɔŋ to square, be
      squared.
    ยกขึ้น jógkhɯ̂n′ 1. to lift up. 2. to raise, bring
      up (a question).
    ยก(...)ขึ้นบก jóg′(...)khɯ̂nbòg′ to land (e.g.
      troops), put (e.g. troops) ashore.
    ยกตัวอย่าง jóg′tuajàaŋ′ to give an example,
      bring up an example.
    ยกทรง (ตัว) jógsoŋ′ (tua′) N brassière.
    ยกทหาร jóg′thahǎan′ to move troops (to).
    ยกทัพ jógtháb′ 1. to lead (the) troops, lead an
      army. 2. to move the army (to).
    ยกโทษ jógthôod′ to forgive.
    ยกนิ้ว jógníw′ i d i o m. to accept (someone's)
      superiority.
    ยกพวก jógphûag′ to bring or take a whole crowd,
      a gang.
    ยกฟ้อง jógfɔ́ɔŋ′ l a w to dismiss a case.
    ยกมากล่าว jóg′maaklàaw′ e l e g. to quote, men-
      tion, cite.
    ยกยอ ๑ jógjɔɔ′ to fish with a dip-net.
    ยกยอ ๒ jógjɔɔ′ V to flatter.
    ยกย่อง jógjɔ̂ŋ′ V to admire, praise, extol. ความ--
      honor, commendation, praise, laudation.
    ยกลงมา jóg′loŋmaa′ 1. to move (e.g. troops)
      down (from the north, or from a hilltop). 2. to
      take (e.g. a box) down (from the top of a stack).
    ยกเลิก jóglə̂əg′ V to cancel, nullify.
    ยกเว้น jógwén′ V to except, exempt.
    o ยกเว้นแต่ ·jógwén′tὲὲ except, excepting.

ยก(...)ให้ (1,2) jóg′(...)hâj′, jóg′(...)hâjɔ;
    (3,4) jóg′hâj′, jóg′hâjɔ, jóghâj′ 1. to give, offer
    (something)(to). 2. to lift (e.g. something heavy)
    for (someone). 3. to excuse, exempt. 4. to rec-
    ognize (that), accept as true (that).
o ยกโทษให้ jógthôod′hâj′, -hâjɔ to forgive.
o ยกลูกสาวให้ jóg′lûugsǎaw′hâj′, -hâjɔ to give
    one's daughter in marriage.
o ยอมยกให้ว่า jɔɔmjóg′hâjwâa to concede, grant,
    accept as true (that).
หยิบยก, --ขึ้น jìbjóg′, jìbjóg′khɯ̂n V 1. to bring
    up, take up, single out. 2. to be brought up,
    taken up, singled out.

ยง ๑ joŋ′ V to be firm, stable, steady.
    ยืนยง jyynjoŋ′ V 1. to stand firmly, remain
      steadfast. 2. to last, endure. 3. to maintain.

ยง ๒ in ยุยง júʔjoŋ′ V to incite (to something bad).

ยถากรรม, ตาม-- játhǎa′kam′, taam′-játhǎa′kam′
    as circumstances dictate, at the mercy of fate.

ยน jôn′ V 1. to be wrinkled, folded. 2. to be short-
    ened (by pressure, impact, wrinkling), to contract.
    ยนย่อ,ย่อยน jônjɔ̀′, jɔ̀ɔjôn′ V to shrink (back),
      lose one's courage, determination.

ยนต์,ยนตร์ (เครื่อง) jon′ (khrɯ̂aŋ′) N mechanical
    device, motor. →Chiefly in compounds.
    เครื่องยนต์ (เครื่อง) khrɯ̂aŋjon′ (khrɯ̂aŋ′) N mo-
      tor (as of an automobile); machine, mechanism.
    o เครื่องยนต์สูบน้ำ (เครื่อง) khrɯ̂aŋjon′sùubnáam′
      (khrɯ̂aŋ′) N water pump.
    จักรยานยนต์ (คัน) càgkrajaan′jon′, càgkajaan′jon′
      (khan′) N motorcycle.
    ช่างยนต์ (คน) châaŋjon′ (khon′) N mechanical
      engineer.
    แพยนต์ (แพ,ลำ) phɛɛ′jon′ (phɛɛ′, lam′) N
      ferryboat.
    ภาพยนตร์ (เรื่อง) phâabphajon′ (rɯ̂aŋ′) N
      e l e g. motion pictures, cinema. →Syn. หนัง
      c o l l o q.
    ยานยนต์ (อย่าง) jaanjon′ (jàaŋ′) N vehicles
      (motor-driven).
    o กองยานยนต์ (กอง) kɔɔŋ′jaanjon′ (kɔɔŋ′) N
      1. department of motor vehicles. 2. m i l i t.
      motorized unit.
    รถยนต์ (คัน) ródjon′ (khan′) N automobile.

เรือยนต์ (ลำ) ryajon′ (lam′) N motorboat.

หุ่นยนต์ (ตัว) hùnjon′ (tua′) N robot.

ยม in แม่น้ำยม mɛ̂ɛnáamjom′ pN the Mæyom
(Me Yom), a tributary of the Čhaophraya River
in N Thailand.

ยมก in ไม้ยมก májjamóg′ N the repeat symbol
(ๆ) as in ต่าง ๆ.

ยล in แยบยล jɛ̂ɛbjon′ V 1. to be tricky, cunning,
ingenious. N 2. trick.

ยวด ๑ in ยวดยาน (คัน, อย่าง) jûadjaan′ (khan′,
jàaŋ′) N vehicle.

ยวด ๒ in ยวดยิ่ง, ยิ่งยวด jûadjîŋ′, jîŋjûad′ V 1.
to be extreme. sV 2. extremely. →Often rendered in English by "super-," as in "superheated."

ยวน juan′ V colloq. 1. to be annoying, irritating,
provoking. 2. to be provoking, enticing, tempting.

ยั่วยวน jûajuan′ V 1. to entice (sexually), to
flirt. 2. to be enticing.

ยียวน jiijuan′ V 1. to excite sexually (by caressing). 2. to be enticing.

ยวบ jûab′ V 1. to sink deeper (than before). 2. to
cave in, fall in, collapse.

ยศ jód′ N rank, position, authority.

เกียรติยศ kìad′tijód′ N honor.

เครื่องยศ (ชิ้น, อัน) khrŷaŋjód′ (chín′, ʔan′) N
insignia of rank.

ยโส in หยิ่งยโส jìŋ′jasǒo′ V to be arrogant,
impudent.

ยอ ๑ (ปาก) jɔɔ′ (pàag′) N dip-net.

ยกยอ jógjɔɔ′ V to fish with a dip-net.

ยอ ๒ jɔɔ′ V to flatter, wheedle.

ยกยอ jógjɔɔ′ V to flatter.

ยอแสง jɔɔ′sɛ̌ɛŋ′ V to be dim, become dim (of
sunlight, at dusk).

เยินยอ jəənjɔɔ′ V to speak highly of, praise,
laud.

ย่อ jɔ̂ɔ′ V 1. to be brief, abridged. 2. to abbreviate,
abridge, summarize; to reduce. คำ-- (คำ)
abbreviation.

โดยย่อ doojjɔ̂ɔ′ briefly, in brief, in short.

๐ กล่าวโดยย่อ klàaw′doojjɔ̂ɔ′ briefly speaking.

ย่อความ (เรื่อง, บท) jɔ̂ɔkhwaam′ (rŷaŋ′, bòd′)
V 1. to condense, prepare an abstract, a digest.

N 2. digest, abstract.

ย่อตัว jɔ̂ɔtua′ V to lower oneself (by bending the
knees).

ย่อท้อ jɔ̂ɔthɔ́ɔ′ V 1. to lose heart, be discouraged.
2. to feel like giving up, yielding, withdrawing.

ย่อย่น, ย่นย่อ jɔ̂ɔjôn′, jônjɔ̂ɔ′ V to shrink (back),
lose one's courage, determination.

ย่อหน้า jɔ̂ɔnâa′ V to indent (as in writing).

อย่างย่อๆ jàaŋjɔ̂ɔjɔ́ɔ′ in brief.

ยอก ๑ jɔ̂ɔg′ V 1. to prick. 2. to ache (of muscles).

ยอก ๒ in the following entries.

ยอกย้อน jɔ̂ɔgjɔ́ɔn′ V to be complicated, devious.

ยักยอก jágjɔ̂ɔg′ V to embezzle.

ยอง in นั่งยองๆ nâŋ′jɔɔŋjɔɔŋ′ V to sit on one's
heels, to squat.

ย่อง ๑ jɔ̂ŋ/* V to walk quietly, stealthily; to tiptoe.

ย่องเบา jɔ̂ŋbaw′ V to steal, pilfer by sneaking
(into someone's house).

ย่อง ๒ in ยกย่อง jógjɔ̂ŋ/* V to admire, praise,
extol.

ย่อง ๓ in ยิ้มย่อง jímjɔ̂ŋ/* V to smile joyfully.

ยอด (ยอด) jɔ̂ɔd′ (jɔ̂ɔd′) N top, tip, peak.

ยอดเขา (ยอด) jɔ̂ɔdkhǎw′ (jɔ̂ɔd′) N mountain
top, peak, pinnacle.

ยอดจำนวน jɔ̂ɔd′camnuan′ N the total number;
the total.

ยอดมะพร้าว (ยอด) jɔ̂ɔd′maphráaw′ (jɔ̂ɔd′) N
crown of the coconut palm.

ยอดไม้ (ยอด) jɔ̂ɔdmáaj′ (jɔ̂ɔd′) N treetop.

ยอดรัก (คน) jɔ̂ɔdrág′ (khon′) N the dearest
(one), best-beloved (sp. to or about someone
of the opposite sex).

ยอน jɔɔn′ V to insert, gently pulling back and forth,
or turning round and round.

ย้อน jɔ́ɔn′ V 1. to return, come back. 2. to retrace.
3. to proceed in reverse.

นึกย้อน nýgjɔ́ɔn′ V to think back.

มีผลย้อนหลัง miiphǒn′-jɔ́ɔn′lǎŋ′ to be retroactive,
be effective retroactively (as of a law).

ยอกย้อน jɔ̂ɔgjɔ́ɔn′ V to be complicated, devious.

ย้อนรอย jɔ́ɔn′rɔɔj′ V to retrace (one's) steps,
return by the same route.

หวนย้อน hǔanjɔ́ɔn′ V to go back, turn back.

ยอบแยบ jɔ̂bjɛ̂b′/* V colloq. 1. to be too little, in-

sufficient. 2. to be running out, running low.
3. to be poor.

ยอม jɔɔm/ V 1. to let, allow. 2. to agree, consent.
3. to comply (with), submit (to), yield (to).

ไม่ยอม (1) mâjjɔɔm/; (2) mâjjɔɔm/↓ 1. to refuse
to, decline, be unwilling to. 2. (I) won't have it!

o ไม่ยอมออกเสียง mâjjɔɔm/ʔɔɔgsɪaŋ/ to abstain
from voting, refuse to vote.

ยอมจำนน jɔɔm/camnon/ V to surrender, give in,
admit defeat.

ยอมแพ้ jɔɔmphɛɛ́/ V to surrender (to), give up,
give in, yield (to).

o ยอมแพ้โดยไม่มีเงื่อนไข jɔɔmphɛɛ́/-doojmâjmii/
ŋŷankhǎj/ to surrender unconditionally.

ยอมยกให้ว่า jɔɔm/jóg/-hâjwâac to concede,
grant, accept as true (that).

ยอมรับ jɔɔmráb/ V 1. to admit, concede. 2. to
accept, agree to.

ยอมให้ jɔɔm/hâjɔ to allow to (do something).

ยินยอม jinjɔɔm/ V to consent, agree.

o คำยินยอม (ข้อ,ประการ) kham/jinjɔɔm/(khɔɔ́/,
prakaan/) N consent.

ย่อม ๑ jɔ̂m/* V 1. to be smallish, moderate (in size,
price, etc.). 2. to be short of, less (in reckoning only). →Cf. 2. หย่อน.

o แมวขนาดย่อม ๆ mɛɛw/-khanàad/jɔ̂mjɔ̂m/ a
smallish cat.

o ราคาสามบาทย่อมสลึง raakhaa/-sǎambàad/-
jɔ̂m/salʉ̌ŋ/ The price is 3 bahts less a quarter.

ย่อมเยา jɔ̂mjaw/ V to be inexpensive, reasonable,
moderate. →Often also spelled ย่อมเยาว์.

ย่อม ๒ jɔ̂m/* AA liable to, likely to, apt to, tend to
(do something).

ย่อมจะ jɔ̂mcac AA liable to, likely to, apt to.

ย่อมจะไม่ jɔ̂mcamâjc not likely to, not apt to.

ย้อม jɔ́ɔm/ V to dye.

ช่างย้อมผ้า (คน) châaŋjɔ́ɔmphâa/ (khon/) N dyer.

ชุบย้อม chúb/jɔ́ɔm/ V to enliven, give new vigor
to.

ย้อมใจ jɔ́ɔmcaj/ V to stimulate, invigorate.

ย่อย jɔ̀j/* V 1. to break up into small particles, gran-
ulate. 2. to digest, assimilate. 3. to be minor,
subordinate. 4. to be a part, a component.

น้ำย่อย námjɔ̀j/ N gastric juice.

ปลีกย่อย plìigjɔ̀j/ V 1. to be trivial, minor.

o เรื่องปลีกย่อย rŷaŋ/-plìig/jɔ̀j/ N small, trivial
matter.

ไม่ย่อย mâjjɔ̀j/ colloq. quite, significantly:
"not insignificant." →Also ไม่ใช่ย่อย.

ย่อย ๆ jɔ̀jjɔ̀j/ minor, lesser, small.

ย่อยยับ jɔ̀jjáb/ V 1. to collapse, go to pieces, be
ruined, destroyed, go bankrupt. sV 2. ruinously,
severely, heavily; in pieces, till in pieces. →Syn.
1. See วอดวาย.

รายย่อย raajjɔ̀j/ N 1. minor case. 2. minor
party (e.g. to an agreement).

ย้อย jɔ́ɔj/ V 1. to slip down. 2. to hang down, droop.

หยดย้อย jòdjɔ́ɔj/ V to be superb, beautiful.

หินย้อย hǐnjɔ́ɔj/ N stalactite.

ยะ já/ Pt used in questions, corresponding to จ๊ะ,
but impolite.

ยะ jâ/ Pt used in statements, corresponding to จ๊ะ,
but impolite.

ยะลา jálaa/ pN Yala a township in S Thailand.

ยะโล. See ยโล.

ยัก ๑ jág/ V 1. to move, raise. 2. to wriggle, sway.

ยักกระสาย jágkrasǎaj/ slang to change the
topic. 2. to change the method, approach. 3.
to make things hard for someone (e.g. by giving
him the run-around). →Syn. 3. ยักท่า.

ยักคิ้ว jágkhíw/ V to raise or flutter the eyebrows
(indicating assent or acknowledgment, or as when
a man flirts with a woman).

ยักท่า jág/thâa/ colloq. V to make things hard
for someone (e.g. by giving him the run-around).
→Syn. ยักกระสาย.

ยักยอก jágjɔɔg/ V to embezzle.

ยักแย่ยักยัน jágjɛ̀ɛ/jágjan/ V colloq. to hobble;
to move haltingly, with difficulty, clumsily.

ยักไหล่ jáglàj/ V to shrug one's shoulders.

ยัก ๒ in ไม่ยัก mâjjág/ AA strangely enough not;
regrettably not; not in the least, not at all; not
as expected; not as (one) should; happen not to
(contrary to expectation).

o เขาไม่ยักมา kháwmâjjág/maa/ He didn't come
as expected, strangely enough.

o ไม่ยักชอบ mâjjág/chɔ̂ɔb/ to happen not to like
(contrary to expectation).

o ไม่ยักรู้ mâjjág′rúu′ to happen not to know (contrary to expectation).

ยักษ์ (ตน) jág′ (ton′) N giant, ogre.

ยัง ๑ jaŋ′ V to be, have. →Rare. →Syn. มี.

ยังชีวิต jaŋ′chiiwíd′ to have life. Sometimes means "to sustain life."

ยังมี jaŋmii′ (once) there was, were (as at the beginning of a fable).

ยัง ๒ jaŋ′ V to cause, render, bring about; to result in.

ยังผล(ให้) jaŋphǒn′(hâjɔ) lit., eleg. to result (in), have the result (of).

ยัง ๓ jaŋ′ AA 1. still, yet. 2. not yet (in answer to a yes-or-no question).

ค่อยยังชั่ว khɔ̂jjaŋchûa′ to get better, feel better; not so bad.

ยังคง jaŋkhoŋɔ still, yet.

o ยังคงปรากฏมี jaŋkhoŋpraakòd′mii′ there still appears to be, apparently there is still.

ยังดี jaŋdii′ to be good enough, not bad; to be a good thing; to still be good.

ยังเด็ก(อยู่) jaŋdèg′(jùu′) to still be a child.

ยังทำการสอบสวนอยู่ jaŋthamkaan′sɔ̀ɔbsŭan′-jùu′ is still being investigated.

ยังมิ jaŋmíɔ as yet not.

ยังมีต่อ, -- ไปอีก jaŋmiitɔ̀ɔ′, jaŋmiitɔ̀ɔ′paj?lig′ 1. to be continued. 2. there is still more to come (as of a story).

ยังมีตัวอยู่ jaŋmiitua′jùu′ to be still living.

ยังมีหน้า jaŋmiinâa′ to be shameless enough to: "still have the face."

ยังไม่ทัน jaŋmâjthanɔ not yet, not yet in time to.

ยังไม่ทัน...ก็... jaŋmâjthanɔ...kɔ̂ɔ... no sooner...than...

ยังไม่เป็นค่าจ้างพออีกหรือ jaŋmâjpenkhâacâaŋ′ɔ phɔɔ′-?ìigrý′ is that not yet sufficient pay?

ยังเล่าไม่จบ jaŋlâw′mâjcòb′ (I) have not yet finished telling (it).

ยังหรอก jaŋ′rɔgɬ colloq. Not yet.

ยัง(...)อยู่ jaŋ(...)jùu′ to still be in (a place, a state of), still be there, still be around, still be (thus and so), still be (doing such and such).

o ยังเล็กอยู่ jaŋlég′jùu′ to be still small.

o คงจะยังอยู่ที่นี่ khoŋ′cajaŋjùu′-thîinîi′ might

still be here, might still stay here.

อีกทั้งยัง ?ìig′tháŋjaŋɔ furthermore, moreover.

ยัง ๔ jaŋ′ Pp to (a destination, end-point).

คืนยังรุ่ง khyynjaŋrûŋ′ all night long, the whole night through.

ตรงไปยัง troŋ′pajjaŋɔ straight ahead to (some point), directly at, toward (a point).

วันยังค่ำ wanjaŋkhâm′ all day long, the whole day through.

ยัง ๕. Variant of อย่าง, representing the shortened pronunciation in the instances shown below.

ยังกะ, ยังกับ jaŋkaɔ colloq. like, as if.

ยังงั้น jaŋŋán′ colloq. like that. →Variant of อย่างนั้น. →Also written อย่างงั้น. →For examples see อย่างงั้น under อย่าง.

ยังงี้ jaŋŋíi′ colloq. like this. →Variant of อย่างนี้. →Also written อย่างงี้. →For examples see อย่างงี้ under อย่าง.

ยังโง้น jaŋŋóon′ like that. →Variant of อย่างโน้น. →Also written อย่างโง้น. →For examples see อย่างโน้น under อย่าง.

ยังไง jaŋŋaj′ colloq. 1. how, in what way. 2. in any way. →Variant of อย่างไร. →Also written อย่างไง. →For additional examples see อย่างไร under อย่าง.

o ยังไง ๆ jaŋŋaj′jaŋŋaj′ colloq. at any rate; no matter what.

o ดูยังไง ๆ อยู่ duu′-jaŋŋaj′jaŋŋaj′-jùu′ colloq. to look odd, strange, not quite right, unacceptable.

ยังนั้น jaŋnán′ colloq. like that, in that way. →Variant of อย่างนั้น, q.v. under อย่าง.

ยังนี้ jaŋníi′ 1. like this, of this sort. 2. This is it! This is the way! →Variant of อย่างนี้, q.v. under อย่าง.

ยั่ง in ยั่งยืน jâŋjyyn′ V to be enduring, lasting, permanent.

ยั้ง jáŋ′ V to stop, cease, refrain from, restrain; to defer, withhold.

ยั้งคิด jáŋkhíd′ V to ponder, pause to think.

ยับยั้ง jábjáŋ′ V to stop, cease, refrain (from), restrain.

o สิทธิยับยั้ง sìdthí?′/jábjáŋ′ veto power.

ยัด jád′ V 1. to push in, stuff in, cram in. 2. vulg. to eat. →Syn. 2. See กิน com.

ยัดเยียด, เยียดยัด játjîad', jîadjád' V 1. to be stuffed, congested, crowded.

o เบียดเสียดเยียดยัด bìadsìad'jîadjád' V elab. colloq. to be crowded, congested, densely profuse.

o ยัดเยียดให้ játjîad'hâj' to insist upon giving, press upon.

ยัดห่า jád'hàa' V vulg. to eat: "to eat the plague." →See also แดกห่า.

ยัน jan' V 1. to push against, prop, support. 2. to confront. 3. to be intoxicating (of betel).

ไม้ยัน (อัน) máajjan' (ʔan') N crutch.

ยักแย่ยักยัน jágjɛ̀ɛ'jágjan' colloq. to hobble; to move haltingly, with difficulty, clumsily.

ยืนยัน jyynjan' V 1. to confirm. 2. to insist, maintain, stand firm.

ยั่น jân' V to be afraid.

ยับ ๑ jáb' V 1. to be broken, torn, ruined, damaged, bruised, wrinkled. sV 2. till bruised and torn, till battered and broken; severely, heavily (of loss).

ย่อยยับ jɔ̀jjáb' V 1. to collapse, go to pieces, be ruined, destroyed. 2. to go bankrupt. sV 3. ruinously, severely, heavily; in pieces, till in pieces. →Syn. 1. See วอดวาย.

ยับเยิน jábjəən' V 1. to collapse, go to pieces, be ruined, destroyed. 2. to be wrinkled, crumpled (as of cloth, paper), battered (as of a wrecked car), torn, broken, bruised (as of the flesh). sV 3. ruinously, severely, heavily (of loss); in pieces, till in pieces; till ruined, battered and broken, bruised and torn. →Syn. 1. See วอดวาย.

ยุบยับ júbjáb' sV 1. heavily, severely (of loss). V 2. to lose heavily.

ยับ ๒ jáb' V to keep, store.

ยับ ๓ in ยับยั้ง jábjáŋ' V to stop, cease, refrain from, restrain; to defer, withhold.

o สิทธิยับยั้ง sìdthíʔ'jábjáŋ' veto power.

ยั่ว jûa' V 1. to excite, arouse, provoke, irritate. 2. to tease.

ยั่วใจ jûacaj' V 1. to tempt. 2. to be tempting.

ยั่วยวน jûajuan' V 1. to entice (sexually), to flirt. 2. to be enticing.

ยั้วเยี้ย júajía' V to be crawling with, crowded with (e.g. people, creeping things).

ยา ๑ (ชนิด, อย่าง, ขนาน) jaa' (chaníd', jàaŋ', khanăan') 1. medicine, drug. 2. tobacco (ยาสูบ). 3. colloq. cigarette. 4. opium (ยาฝิ่น). NOTE. Where appropriate other clfs. may be used, e.g. ขวด, เข็ม, ช้อน, เม็ด, หยด, หลอด, ห่อ, etc.

ขี้ยา khîjaa' N 1. residuum (of opium). 2. an opium addict. V 3. to be addicted to opium.

เครื่องยา (ชนิด, อย่าง, ขนาน) khrŷaŋjaa' (chaníd', jàaŋ', khanăan') N ingredient (of a drug).

ฉีดยา chìdjaa' V 1. to inject medicine, inoculate. 2. to get an injection, a shot.

น้ำยา námjaa' N 1. com. chemical solution (nontech. term, e.g. as in "permanent wave solution"). 2. a kind of sauce made of fish, coconut cream and other ingredients and served with vermicelli.

ใบยา (ใบ) bajjaa' (baj') N tobacco leaf.

ใบสั่งยา (ใบ) baj'sàŋjaa' (baj') N medical prescription.

ปรุงยา pruŋjaa' V to compound a medicine, concoct a remedy, make up a prescription.

เมายา mawjaa' V to be drugged, doped, intoxicated with drugs.

ยากันเชื้อโรค jaakan'chýarôog' N antiseptic.

ยาแก้บิด jaakɛ̀ɛbìd' N medicine for dysentery.

ยาควินิน jaakhwinin' N quinine. [ควินิน f. Eng.]

ยาฆ่าตัวแมลง jaakhâa'tuamalɛɛŋ' insecticide.

ยาฉีด jaachìd' N medicine for injection.

ยาดม jaadom' N 1. smelling salts. 2. inhalant.

ยาแดง jaadɛɛŋ' N mercurochrome.

ยาถ่าย jaathàaj' N purgative, laxative.

ยานัตถุ์ jaanád' N snuff (tobacco preparation).

ยาพิษ jaaphíd' N poison.

o วางยาพิษ waaŋ'jaaphíd' to poison.

ยาเม็ด (เม็ด) jaaméd' (méd') N (medicinal) pill, tablet.

ยาระบาย jaarabaaj' N laxative.

ยารักษาโรค jaa'-rágsăa'rôog' N medicinal drug.

ยาวิเศษ jaa'wísèed' N miracle drugs.

ยาสมุนไพร jaa'-samŭn'phraj' N medicine prepared with local herbs or medicinal plants.

ยาสลบ jaasalòb' N anesthetic.

ยาสีฟัน jaasǐifan′ N toothpaste, dentifrice.

o ยาสีฟันผง jaasǐifan′phǒŋ N tooth powder.

ยาสูบ jaasùub′ N tobacco.

o กล้องยาสูบ (อัน) klɔ̂ŋ′jaasùub′ (ʔan′) N tobacco pipe.

ยาเส้น jaasên′ N prepared tobacco, pipe tobacco.

ยาเสพติด jaasèebtìd′ N habit-forming drug, narcotic.

เยียวยา jiawjaa′ V eleg. 1. to cure (e.g. a disease). 2. to treat (with medicine).

สูบยา sùubjaa′ V to smoke (tobacco, opium).

หมอยา (คน) mɔ̌ɔjaa′ (khon′) N medical doctor, physician.

ยา ๒ jaa′ V 1. to calk. N 2. dammar, substance used for calking boats. 3. niello, or some type of colored enameling compound inlaid in jewelry and ornamental wares made of metal.

ยาขัดเกือก jaakhàdkỳag′ N com. shoepolish.

ยาขัดรองเท้า jaa′khàdrɔɔŋtháaw′ N eleg. shoepolish.

ลงยา loŋjaa′ V to apply niello or some type of enameling compound; to inlay (something) with niello or an enameling compound.

o เครื่องลงยา khrŷaŋ′loŋjaa′ N 1. nielloware. 2. jewelry or ornamental ware inlaid with colored enameling compound. →Syn. 1. เครื่อง ถม.

ย่า (คน) jâa′ (khon′) N 1. paternal grandmother, father's mother. P 2. you, she, her, Grandma (sp. to or about one's paternal grandmother); I, me, Grandma (paternal grandmother sp. to grandchild).

ปู่ย่า (คน) pùu′jâa′ (khon′) N ancestors ("paternal grandparents").

ปู่ย่าตายาย (คน) pùujâa′taajaaj′ (khon′) N ancestors: "paternal and maternal grandparents."

ยาก jâag′ V 1. to be hard, difficult. 2. to be wanting. คน-- poor people, the poor; poor person.

ข้าวยากหมากแพง khâawjâag′màagpheeŋ′ elab. colloq. famine or hard times to exist, food to be scarce.

ความยากเข็ญ khwaamjâagkhěn′ N 1. hardship. 2. poverty.

โดยไม่ยาก dooj′mâjjâag′ without difficulty.

ตกยาก tògjâag′ V 1. to sink into poverty, become impoverished. 2. to suffer hardship.

เป็นการยาก penkaan′jâag′ 1. to be difficult, to be a difficult matter. 2. with difficulty.

ยากแค้น jâagkhέεn′ V to be impoverished.

ยากจน jâagcon′ V to be poor, poverty-stricken. คน-- poor people; poor person. ความ-- hardship, poverty.

ยากจนข้นแค้น jâagcon′khônkhέεn′ V elab. colloq. to be poor, hard up, needy, impoverished.

ยากดีมีจน jâagdii′-mii′con′ elab. colloq. (whether) rich or poor.

ยากที่จะหวังกัน jâag′thîicawǎŋ′kan 1. hardly to be hoped for. 2. (it is) hard to hope for.

ยากเย็น jâagjen′ V colloq. to be very difficult.

ยุ่งยาก jûŋjâag′ V to be complicated and difficult; to be troublesome. ความ-- difficulty, confusion, trouble, problem.

ว่านอนสอนยาก wâanɔɔn′sɔ̌ɔnjâag′ V elab. colloq. to be untractable, unmanageable, disobedient, unruly.

ว่ายาก wâajâag′ to be disobedient, untractable.

หายาก hǎajâag′ to be scarce, rare, hard to find.

o ของหายาก khɔ̌ɔŋ′hǎajâag′ something rare, something hard to find.

ยาง jaaŋ′ N 1. resin, sap: "yang." 2. rubber. 3. colloq. rubber tire, rubber band.

เครื่องยาง (อย่าง,ชนิด) khrŷaŋjaaŋ′ (jàaŋ′,chaɔníd′) N rubber goods.

ต้นยาง (ต้น) tônjaaŋ′ (tôn′) N rubber tree, i.e. the tree from which latex is derived.

น้ำมันยาง námman′jaaŋ′ N dammar, resin.

ยางแตก jaaŋtὲεg′ to have a flat (tire), a blow-out.

o รถผมยางแตก ródphǒm′jaaŋtὲεg′↓ My car has a flat.

ยางเทียม jaaŋthiam′ N synthetic rubber.

ยางรถ,--ยนต์ (เส้น,ข้าง) jaaŋród′, jaaŋ′ródjon′ (sên′, khâaŋ′) N automobile tire.

ยางรัด (เส้น) jaaŋrád′ (sên′) rubber band.

ยางลบ (อัน,ก้อน,แท่ง) jaaŋlób′ (ʔan′, kɔ̂ɔn′, thɛ̂ŋ′) N (rubber) eraser.

ยางล้อรถ (เส้น) jaaŋ′lɔ́ɔród′ (sên′) N tire (for any kind of wheel or vehicle).

รองเท้ายาง (คู่, ข้าง) rɔɔŋtháawjaaŋ/ (khûu/, khâaŋ/) N eleg. rubber-soled canvas shoes, tennis shoes.

ลาดยาง lâadjaaŋ/ V to be paved with asphalt.

ย่าง ๑ jâaŋ/ V to roast (over an open fire), to barbecue.

เป็ดย่าง (ตัว) pèdjâaŋ/ (tua/) N roast duck.

ย่าง ๒ jâaŋ/ V to step, take a step, set one's foot (in, on, etc.).

o อายุเจ็ดปีย่าง ʔaajú?/-cèdpii/jâaŋ/ eleg. (he's) almost seven years of age, very nearly seven years old.

o อายุย่างเข้าเจ็ดปี ʔaajú?/-jâaŋ/-khâwcèd/pii/ eleg. (he's) going on seven, between six and seven years old.

เพิ่งย่างเข้า phə̂ŋjâaŋ/khâwɔ just about to enter, just entering.

ย่างขึ้น jâaŋ/khŷnɔ V eleg. to begin, enter (the next phase of development, e.g. to begin one's second year of life).

ย่างกุ้ง, เมือง-- jâaŋkûŋ/, myaŋ/jâaŋkûŋ/ pN Rangoon. [f. Bur.]

ยาจก (คน) jaacòg/ N eleg. beggar.

ยาตรา jâadtraa/ V lit., eleg. to move in procession; to march; to walk.

ยาน ๑ jaan/ N eleg. conveyance of any kind (land, sea, or air).

จักรยาน, รถ-- (คัน) càgkajaan/, ród/càgkajaan/ (khan/) N eleg. bicycle.

o จักรยานยนต์ (คัน) càgkajaan/jon/ (khan/) N eleg. motorcycle.

โพยมยาน (ลำ, เครื่อง) phajoom/jaan/ (lam/, khrŷaŋ/) N eleg. aircraft.

ยวดยาน (คัน) jûadjaan/ (khan/) N eleg. vehicle.

ยานพาหนะ (คัน, อย่าง, ชนิด) jaan/phaahàná?/ (khan/, jàaŋ/, chaníd/) N eleg. vehicle.

ยานยนต์ (อย่าง) jaanjon/ (jàaŋ/) N eleg. motor vehicle.

o กองยานยนต์ (กอง) kɔɔŋ/jaanjon/ (kɔɔŋ/) N eleg. 1. department of motor vehicles. 2. milit. motorized unit.

ยาน ๒ jaan/ V to be drooping, sagging.

ย่าน jâan/ N 1. part, section (of a locality), district,

place, area, region. C 2. clf. for same.

ยาม jaam/ N 1. time (as "time of war"), period, era, hour (as "hour of need"). C 2. clf. for same. 3. clf. for three-hour watch periods, the first of which starts at 6 P.M. Normally there are four watch periods in the night, the last ending at 6 A.M. N 4. short for คน-- watchman, guard.

o ยามหนึ่ง jaam/nyŋ 9 P.M.

o สองยาม sɔ̌ɔŋjaam/ midnight.

o สามยาม sǎamjaam/ 3 A.M.

เข้ายาม khâwjaam/ V to be on duty (as a guard, night watchman).

ทหารยาม (คน) thahǎanjaam/ (khon/) N sentry, guard.

มัชฌิมยาม mádchim/majaam/ N lit. midnight.

ยามคับขัน jaam/khábkhǎn/ N time of emergency, troublous times.

ยามค่ำ jaamkhâm/ N 1. evening (from sunset to midnight), evenings. 2. in the evening. ใน-- in the evening.

ยามเข้าตรู่ jaam/cháawtrùu/ N the early morning; early in the morning. ใน-- in the early morning.

ยามดึก jaamdỳg/ late at night.

ยามต้น jaamtôn/ N the first watch period, 6-9 P.M.

ยามปกติ jaam/pògkatì?/ 1. normal times. 2. peacetime.

ยามรักษาการ (คน) jaam/rágsǎakaan/ (khon/) N eleg. guard, sentry.

ยามวิกาล jaam/wíkaan/ N eleg. 1. wrong or inappropriate time, i.e. nighttime. 2. at an inappropriate time; also ใน--. NOTE. Primary reference is to the period from 12:00 noon to 6 A.M. when it is improper for a priest to eat; but ยามวิกาล is commonly used to refer to nighttime as an inappropriate time for some given action or activity.

ยามสงคราม jaam/sǒŋkhraam/ N 1. wartime. 2. in wartime.

ย้ำยาม jâm/jaam/ V to mark the change of a nighttime watch period by beating a gong or drum.

ฤกษ์งามยามดี rə̂əgŋaam/jaamdii/ N ela b. colloq.

auspicious time.

อยู่ยาม jùujaam′ V to be on guard (at a place).

ย่าม ๑ (ย่าม,ใบ) jâam′ (jâam′,baj′) N bag, satchel (with shoulder strap or loop).

ย่าม ๒ in ย่ามใจ jâamcaj′ to become emboldened (as a result of previous success). →Syn. ได้ใจ.

ย่าม ๓ in ยุ่มย่าม jûmjâam′ V 1. to meddle, be meddlesome, be in the way, fool around where one does not belong. 2. to be in disorderly profusion (as of a beard, moustache). 3. to be a wriggling mass (as of worms).

ยาย (คน) jaaj′ (khon′) N 1. maternal grandmother. P 2. you, she, her (sp. to or of one's maternal grandmother, or any elderly woman); I, me (grandmother or elderly person sp. to younger person). T 3. title for girl or woman.

ปู่ย่าตายาย (คน) pùujâa′taajaaj′ (khon′) N ancestors: "paternal and maternal grandparents."

แม่ยาย (คน) mɛ̂ɛjaaj′ (khon′) N (man's) mother-in-law. →Comp. แม่ผัว (woman's) mother-in-law.

ยายชี jaajchii′ N nun. →Syn. See แม่ชี.

ยายหนู jaajnǔu′ P you, she, her (sp. to or of a female child).

ย้าย jáaj′ V 1. to move (i.e. change the location of something); to transfer, relocate (some person or thing). 2. to move (one's location, one's place of residence); to transfer (e.g. change one's place of work).

ย้ายบ้าน jáajbâan′ V to move (one's place of residence).

แยกย้าย jɛ̂ɛgjáaj′ V to separate, go (their) separate ways, spread out, move off separately.

ยาว jaaw′ V to be long (of objects, generally not of time). ความ-- length. →Ant. สั้น.

o เมื่องอกยาวราวหนึ่งแขน mŷaŋɔɔg′jaaw′-raawɔ nỳŋkhɛ̌ɛn′ when the shoot (plant) is about one arm's length long.

เข็มยาว (อัน) khěmjaaw′ (ʔan′) N minute hand (of a clock).

ช่วงยาวคลื่น chûaŋjaawkhlŷyn′ N tech. wave length.

ตามยาว taamjaaw′ lengthwise, longitudinal.

ถั่วผักยาว (ผัก) thùafàgjaaw′ (fàg′) N long-podded cowpea. ต้น-- (ต้น) long-podded cowpea plant.

ปืนยาว (กระบอก) pyynjaaw′ (krabɔɔg′) N shotgun; rifle.

ผ่อนสั้นผ่อนยาว phɔ̀nsân′phɔ̀njaaw′ V idiom. to ease tensions by compromise or mutual concession.

ม้ายาว (ตัว) máajaaw′ (tua′) N 1. bench. 2. pew.

ยาวตะเหลนเป็น jaaw′talěenpěen′ colloq. to be extremely long.

ยาวไป jaaw′paj to be too long.

ยาวเฟื้อย jaawfýaj′ colloq. to be very long, extremely long.

ยาวยืด,ยืดยาว jaawjŷyd′, jŷydjaaw′ V to be lengthy, extensive (of objects; of time).

ยาวเหยียด jaawjìad′ V to be stretched long, long and stretching.

ยืนยาว jyynjaaw′ V 1. to be long-lasting, durable. 2. to be extensive, protracted.

สายตายาว sǎajtaa′jaaw′ to be farsighted (both lit. and fig.).

ย่ำ ๑ jam′ V 1. to mix together, blend. 2. to make (a salad). N 3. a kind of salad.

ย่ำ ๒ in ย่ำเกรง jamkreeŋ′ eleg. to respect, be in awe of.

ย่ำ ๓ in แม่นย่ำ mɛ̂njam′* sV 1. accurately, clearly, vividly, well. V 2. to be accurate, correct. NOTE. แม่นย่ำ is chiefly used to describe the memory, remembering.

ย่ำ jâm′ V 1. to tread down, tramp upon. 2. colloq. to walk.

ใบเหยียบย่ำ (ใบ) baj′jìabjâm′ (baj′) N land certificate (issued on the condition of use and improvement, e.g. as to a homesteader).

ย่ำค่ำ jâmkhâm′ colloq. 6 P.M.

ย่ำต๊อก jâmtɔ́g′ V colloq. to walk, hoof it (e.g. when transportation is not available).

ย่ำเท้า jâmtháaw′ V to mark time (with the feet).

o เดินย่ำเท้า dəən′jâmtháaw′ to march (as soldiers).

ย่ำยาม jâmjaam′ V to mark the change of a watch period at night by beating a gong or drum.

ย่ำยี jâmjii′ V 1. to trample on, crush. 2. to

invade, overrun. 3. to oppress, domineer.

ย่ำรุ่ง jâmrûŋ′ colloq. 6 A.M.

o เวลาย่ำรุ่ง weelaa′jâmrûŋ′ N 1. dawn. 2. at
dawn.

ย้ำ jám′ V to emphasize, confirm, repeat.

ยิกๆ jígjíg′ colloq. repeatedly and in quick
succession.

ยิง jiŋ′ V to shoot, shoot at.

ยิงดับชีพ jiŋ′dàbchîib′ colloq. to shoot to death.

ยิงตก jiŋtòg′ V to shoot down, to drop (by shooting).

ยิงตาย jiŋtaaj′ to shoot to death, shoot dead.

ยิงเป้า jiŋpâw′ 1. to shoot at targets. 2. to execute by shooting.

o สนามยิงเป้า (แห่ง) sanǎam′jiŋpâw′ (hèŋ′)
N target range.

ยิงฟัน jiŋfan′ V 1. to show one's teeth (by drawing back the lips). 2. colloq. to grin.

ยิงไม่อยู่ jiŋ′mâjjùu′ cannot drop (e.g. an animal)
(by shooting).

ระดมยิง radom′jiŋ′ V to fire a volley, concentrate a heavy fire (on).

หยุดยิง jùdjiŋ′ V to cease fire.

ยิ่ง jîŋ′ V 1. to be extreme. sV 2. extremely.
AA 3. especially, increasingly, progressively
(see examples below).

o เมื่อผมตามเขา เขาก็ยิ่งเดินเร็วขึ้น mʉ̂aphǒmɔ
taam′kháw→ kháwkɔ̂jîŋdəən′rewkhŷn′↓ When
I followed him, he walked all the faster.

o ยิ่งนอนก็ยิ่งขี้เกียจ jîŋnɔɔn′kɔ̂jîŋkhîikîad′↓
The more you sleep, the lazier you become.

o ยิ่งเร็วยิ่งดี jîŋrew′jîŋdii′↓ The faster, the
better. The sooner the better.

ยิ่งกว่า jîŋkwàa′ sV more than, to a greater
extent than.

o ยิ่งกว่านั้น jîŋkwàanán′ moreover.

ยิ่งขึ้น jîŋkhŷn′ more, increasing, increasingly.

o ทวียิ่งขึ้น thawii′jîŋkhŷn′ V to accumulate,
increase (of itself).

o มากยิ่งขึ้นทุกที mâag′jîŋkhŷn′thúgthii′ more
and more every minute; progressively more.

ยิ่งนัก jîŋnág′ exceedingly.

ยิ่งยวด, ยวดยิ่ง jîŋjûad′, jûadjîŋ′ V 1. to be
extreme. sV 2. extremely. →Often rendered

in English by "super-," as in "superheated."

ยิ่งๆขึ้นไป jîŋjîŋ′khŷnpaj′ better and better,
more and more, progressively, increasingly.

ยิ่งหนาตา jîŋnǎa′taa′ V to multiply, grow in
number (of itself); to thicken (as of a crowd).

ยิ่งหย่อนกว่า jîŋjɔ̀n′kwàaɔ to differ in superiority
or inferiority (with respect to some quality, as
size, beauty, diligence, etc.). →Often used in
negative constructions.

o สองคนนี้ สวยไม่ยิ่งหย่อนกว่ากันเลย sɔ̌ɔŋkhonɔ
nîi′ sǔaj′-mâjjîŋjɔ̀n′kwàakan′-ləəj′↓ Neither
of these two is inferior to the other in beauty.

o ดูซิว่า สองคนนี้ยิ่งหย่อนกว่ากันแค่ไหน duu′síɔ
wâa′→ sɔ̌ɔŋkhonnîi′ jîŋjɔ̀n′kwàakan′-khɛɛnǎj′↓
See how much these two differ (in superiority
or inferiority)!

ยิ่งใหญ่ jîŋjàj′ V to be great, powerful, important.

ยุ่งยิ่ง jûŋjîŋ′ V to be confused, confusing, entangled, intricate, mixed up, in confusion.

อย่างยิ่ง jàaŋjîŋ′ extremely, exceedingly.

o เฉพาะอย่างยิ่ง, โดย-- chaphɔ́ʔ′jàaŋjîŋ′, dooj⊃
chaphɔ́ʔ′jàaŋjîŋ′ in particular, especially.

o เป็นอย่างยิ่ง penjàaŋjîŋ′ in the extreme, to the
utmost.

ยิน jin′ V to hear. →Chiefly in compounds. The
ordinary word for "to hear" is ได้ยิน, as below.

ได้ยิน dâjjin′ V to hear.

o ได้ยินกับหู dâjjin′kahǔu′ to hear with one's own
ears.

o ได้ยินได้ฟัง dâjjin′dâjfaŋ′ elab. colloq. 1.
to hear. 2. to have heard of.

o ฟังไม่ได้ยิน faŋ′mâjdâjjin′ can't hear (because
of noise, etc.).

ยินดี jindii′ V to be glad, pleased. ความ-- gladness, pleasure (in the sense of "state of being
pleased" only).

o น่ายินดี nâa′jindii′ to be delightful, conducive
to gladness, wonderful.

o ยินดีที่ jindii′thîiɔ is pleased that (such and
such has occurred).

o ยินดีที่จะ jindii′thîicaɔ is glad to (do thus and
so), will be glad to (do thus and so).

o แสดงความยินดี(กับ) sadɛɛŋ′khwaamjindii′(kaɔ)
to congratulate.

ยินยอม jinjɔɔm′ V to consent, agree. คำ-- (ข้อ,ประการ) consent.

ยิบ in the following entries.

ยิบ ๆ jíbjíb′ V to be glittering, flickering.

สู้ยิบตา sûu′jíbtaa′ V idiom. to fight, resist until death.

ยิ้ม jím′ V to smile.

ฝืนยิ้ม fy̌yn′jím′ V to force a smile.

พรายยิ้ม phraajjím′ N trace of a smile.

ยิ้มกริ่ม jímkrìm′ V to be smiling happily, beaming.

ยิ้มกะเรี่ยกะราด jím′-karîa′karâad′ to smile wryly and sheepishly, with embarrassment, confusion.

ยิ้มแฉ่ง jímchɛ̀ŋ′ to smile broadly, happily.

ยิ้มแป้น jímpɛ̂n′ to smile broadly.

ยิ้มพราย jímphraaj′ to smile radiantly.

ยิ้มย่อง jímjɔ̂ŋ′ V to smile joyfully.

ยิ้มแย้ม jímjɛ́ɛm′ V to smile broadly, cheerfully; to beam.

ยิ้มละไม jím′lamaj′ to smile pleasantly.

ยิ้มแห้ง ๆ jím′hɛ́ɛŋhɛ́ɛŋ′ to smile dryly, mirthlessly.

ยิ้มแหย ๆ jím′jɛ̌ɛjɛ̌ɛ′ to smile sheepishly, wryly.

ลักยิ้ม (แห่ง,รอย) lágjím′ (hɛ̀ŋ′,rɔɔj′) N dimple.

อมยิ้ม ʔomjím′ V to smile knowingly, or in a mildly amused and patronizing manner (without parting the lips).

ยี. jii′ the English letter "G." [f. Eng.] →Also จี.

ยี jii′ V to crush with a rubbing motion.

ย่ำยี jâmjii′ V 1. to trample on, crush. 2. to invade, overrun. 3. to oppress, domineer.

ยียวน jiijuan′ V 1. to excite sexually (by caressing). 2. to be enticing.

ยี่ ๑ jîi′ Nm "two," as in the following entries. →Cf. สอง.

เดือนยี่ dyanjîi′ the second lunar month.

ยี่สิบ (๒๐) jîisìb′ Nm twenty.

o ยี่สิบเอ็ด (๒๑) jîisìb′ʔèd′ Nm twenty-one.

ยี่ ๒ in ยู่ยี่ jûujîi′ V to be wrinkled, mussed, crumpled up, distorted.

ยี่เก jîikee′ N colloq. musical folk drama. →Also ลิเก writ.

ยี่เจ้ย in ไม่ยี่เจ้ย (1) mâjjîicə̂əj′; (2) mâjjîicə̂əj′↓

slang 1. not much. 2. It's nothing (expressing either insignificance or contempt). [f. Chin.]

ยี่โถ jîithǒo′ N oleander. ดอก-- (ดอก) oleander flower. ต้น-- (ต้น) oleander plant or shrub.

ยี่ส่ง in ถั่วยี่ส่ง thùajîisŏŋ′ N writ. peanut. →See also ถั่วลิสง, a colloquial variant.

ยี่หระ in ไม่ยี่หระ mâjjîirà? ′ slang not to give a hang, not to care about.

ยี่ห้อ (ยี่ห้อ) jîihɔ̂ɔ′ (jîihɔ̂ɔ′) N 1. brand, brand name, make (of merchandise), trade mark. 2. colloq. type, kind, variety. [f. Chin.]

ยึด jýd′ V 1. to seize, grab, grasp, get hold of. 2. to capture. 3. to confiscate. 4. to hold back; to hold, retain.

o ยึดเป็นอาชีพ jýd′pen?aachîib′ to have or hold as an occupation.

เข้ายึด khâwjýd′ V to capture, seize, occupy.

o การบุกเข้ายึด kaanbùg′khâwjýd′ N invasion.

ยึดครอง jýdkhrɔɔŋ′ V to occupy, take possession of (by force).

ยึดได้ jýd′dâaj′ V to seize, capture.

ยึดมั่น(ใน) jýdmân′(najɔ) 1. to hold fast (to). 2. to believe firmly (in).

ยึดไว้ jýdwáj′ V 1. to confiscate. 2. to hold up, hold together, support, prop (i.e. in order to keep something from falling down, falling apart).

ยึดหลัก jýdlàg′ V 1. to cling to a pole, post. 2. to cling to, hold to a principle.

ยืด jŷyd′ V to stretch, extend, lengthen.

การยืดตัว kaan′jŷydtua′ N 1. stretching. 2. phys. expansion.

ยืดยาว,ยาวยืด jŷydjaaw′, jaawjŷyd′ V to be lengthy, extensive (of objects; of time).

ยืดเยื้อ jŷydjýa′ V to be greatly prolonged, to last a long time.

ยืดเวลา jŷyd′weelaa′ V 1. to get an extension of time, to extend, prolong (the allotted period of) time. 2. to delay.

ยืดหดได้ jŷydhòd′dâaj′ V to be capable of extension and retraction, of stretching and shrinking, elastic.

ยืดหยุ่น jŷydjùn′ V to be elastic. การ-- phys. elasticity. ความ-- elasticity.

ยืน jyyn′ V to stand.

ประทับยืน prath́ab'jyyn' V roy. to stand.

ยั่งยืน jâŋjyyn' V to be enduring, lasting, permanent.

ยืนกราน jyyn'kraan' V 1. to stand firm, remain unyielding. 2. to insist.

ยืนขึ้น jyyn'kĥyn' to stand up.

ยืนต้น jyyntôn' V to remain growing, hence, to be perennial.

o พืชยืนต้น (ต้น,ชนิด) pĥyd'jyyntôn' (tôn', chaɔ níd') N perennial plant.

ยืนที่ jyyntĥi' V 1. to be stable, stabilized. 2. to stay put.

ยืนนาน jyynnaan' V 1. to last, endure. 2. to live long.

ยืนมุง jyyn'muŋ' to stand crowding around.

ยืนยง jyynjoŋ' V 1. to stand firmly, remain steadfast. 2. to last, endure. 3. to maintain.

ยืนยัน jyynjan' V 1. to confirm. 2. to insist, maintain, stand firm.

ยืนยาว jyyn'jaaw' V to be long-lasting, durable, extensive, protracted.

ยืนโรง jyyn'rooŋ' V 1. (someone) to be a mainstay. 2. to have the longest or most prominent role (as in a play); to have the same role every time.

ยืนหยัด jyyn'jàd' V to stand firm, be steadfast, unyielding.

ยืนออ jyyn'?ɔɔ' V to crowd together, be crowded together, stand in a group.

ล้มทั้งยืน lóm'tháŋjyyn' colloq. to fall from a standing position, keel over.

ยื่น ĵyn' V 1. to stretch (out), extend, project. 2. to hand out. 3. to hand in, file, submit.

ยื่นคำขาด ĵyn'khamkhàad' to deliver an ultimatum.

ยื่นใบสมัคร ĵyn'bajsam̀ag' to submit, file an application. ผู้ - - applicant.

ยื่นฟ้อง ĵynf́ɔɔŋ' V to submit a case to court.

ยื่นมือ ĵynmyy' V 1. to interfere, intervene. 2. to offer one's services.

ยื่น(...)ให้ ĵyn'(...)ĥajɔ V to hand over to.

หยิบยื่น jìbĵyn' to give, offer, hand over.

ยืม jyym' V to borrow.

ขอยืม kĥɔɔjyym' V to borrow, ask to borrow.

เช่ายืม cĥaw'jyym' V 1. to rent (from). 2. to take (goods) on a lend-lease basis.

o ให้เช่ายืม ĥajcĥaw'jyym' 1. to rent (to). 2. to lend-lease.

ให้ยืม ĥajjyym' to lend.

ยิ้ม j́ym' colloq. variant of ยืม.

ยื้อ in ยื้อแย่ง j́yĵɛɛŋ' V 1. to seize, take possession of by force. 2. to engage in vigorous rivalry.

ยุ jú?' to urge on, incite, spur, prod.

ยุยง jú-joŋ', jú?joŋ' V to incite (to something bad).

เย้ายุ j́awjú?' V to excite, arouse.

ยุค júg' C age, era, period, time.

ยุคกรุงรัตนโกสินทร์ júg'-kruŋ'ŕadtanákoosĬn' the Ratanakosin (Bangkok) period of Thai history, from 1782 AD (BE 2325) to the present.

ยุคต้น júgtôn' N the first period, the earliest period.

ยุคใหม่ júgmàj' N the new period; the latest period; the modern age.

ยุง (ตัว) juŋ' (tua') N mosquito.

ยุงก้นปล่อง (ตัว) juŋ'kônpl̀ɔŋ' (tua') N anopheles mosquito.

ยุ่ง jûŋ' V 1. to be confused, confusing, entangled, intricate, complicated, involved. 2. colloq. to be a nuisance, a pest, meddlesome. 3. to be involved, associate (with someone). 4. to be involved, occupied, busy. 5. to bother, concern, involve oneself.

ยุ่งเกี่ยวกับ jûŋkìaw'kaɔ V to associate with, get involved with.

ยุ่งยิ่ง jûŋkhĬŋ' V colloq. 1. to be highly involved, complicated, confusing. 2. to have dealings (with), have to do with.

ยุ่งใจ jûŋcaj' V to be worried, perturbed, confused.

ยุ่งไม่เข้าเรื่อง jûŋ'màjkĥawr̂yaŋ' colloq. to be unnecessarily meddlesome; to fiddle with things one has no business touching (as of a child).

ยุ่งยาก jûŋjâag' V 1. to be complicated and difficult. 2. to be troublesome. ความ - - difficulty, confusion, trouble, problem.

ยุ่งยิ่ง jûŋjĬŋ' V to be confused, confusing, entangled, intricate, mixed up, in confusion.

ยุ่งเหยิง jûŋǰəŋ' V to be in great confusion, disorder.

ยุ่งอยู่กับ jûŋ'jùukaɔ colloq. to be involved in, engaged in, busy with.

ยุ้ง (ยุ้ง,หลัง) júŋ' (júŋ',lǎŋ') N 1. barn, store-house, storage bin (for rice). C 2. clf. for same.

ยุตติ. See ยุติ.

ยุติ júdtì?' V to terminate, close, end, cease, con-clude (of itself).

ยุติธรรม júdtitham' V 1. to be just, fair. N 2. jus-tice. การ-- judicial affairs, justice. ความ-- justice. →Also ยุตติธรรม F.S.

กระทรวงยุติธรรม krasuaŋ'júdtitham' N Ministry of Justice.

กระบวนการยุติธรรม krabuankaan'júdtitham' N judicial administration (collectively, viz., the courts, the police, various government depart-ments).

อยุติธรรม ?àjúdtitham' V 1. to be unjust, unfair. N 2. injustice. ความ-- injustice.

ยุทธ-,-ยุทธ júd'thaɔ, ɔjúd', -júd'. Bound form meaning "to fight, to battle," as in the entries below.

กลยุทธ (แบบ,อย่าง) konlajúd' (bɛ̀ɛb',jàaŋ') N 1. eleg. tactics, strategy. 2. strategem. 3. colloq. trick.

การยุทธ kaanjúd' N eleg. fighting, battle.

ประลองยุทธ pralɔɔŋ'júd' V eleg. to maneuver, hold maneuvers. →Syn. ซ้อมรบ com.

ยุทธการ (ครั้ง) júd'thakaan' (khráŋ') N eleg. military operation; battle.

ยุทธบริเวณ (บริเวณ,แห่ง) júd'thabɔɔriween' (bɔɔriween',hɛ̀ŋ') N milit. battle zone, war zone; theater command.

ยุทธภัณฑ์ júd'thaphan' N military equipment, implements of war.

ยุทธภูมิ (แห่ง) júd'thaphuum' (hɛ̀ŋ') N eleg. battlefield, battleground.

ยุทธวิธี júd'thawithii' N milit. strategy; tactics.

ยุทธศาสตร์ júd'thasàad' N military strategy; military science.

ยุทธนา,--การ júd'thanaa', júd'thanaakaan' N eleg. military engagement, battle.

ยุทโธปกรณ júdthoo'pakɔɔn' N eleg. war materiel.

ยุบ júb' V 1. to diminish in size, intensity. 2. to sink, settle (of earth). 3. to cave in, give way, col-lapse. 4. to melt down (e.g. a metal object). 5. to dissolve, abolish.

ยุบยับ júbjáb' sV 1. heavily, severely (of loss). V 2. to lose heavily.

ยุบลงมา júb'loŋmaa' V (a structure) to collapse.

ยุบสภา júb'saphaa' V to dissolve the assembly, the parliament.

ยุพราช (องค์) júbpharâad' (?oŋ') N crown prince.

ยุ่ม in ยุ่มย่าม jûmjâam' V 1. to meddle, be meddle-some, in the way, fool around where one does not belong. 2. to be in disorderly profusion (as of a beard, moustache). 3. to be a wriggling mass (as of worms).

ยุ่ย jûj' V to be ready to fall apart at a touch (as of overcooked food, rotten wood).

แตกยุ่ย tɛ̀ɛg'jûj' V to break up easily into bits, disintegrate (of itself).

ยุ้ย júj' V 1. to protrude, be protruding. 2. (cheeks) to be round, chubby.

ยุโรป júròob', juròob'* N Europe. [f. Eng.]

ชาวยุโรป (คน,พวก) chaaw'juròob' (khon', phûag') N a European (khon'); Europeans (phûag').

ยุว- júwaɔ. Bound form meaning "young, youthful." Same as เยาว์, เยาว- jaw', jawwaɔ.

ยุวชน (คน) júwachon' (khon') N youth, young people. →Used esp. of youth organizations, as formed during World War II.

ยู. juu' the English letter "U." [f. Eng.]

ยู jûu' V to be dented, distorted in shape.

ยู่ยี่ jûujîi' V to be wrinkled, mussed, crumpled up, distorted.

ยูง,นก-- (ตัว) juuŋ', nógjuuŋ' (tua') N the com-mon peafowl (Paro cristatus).

ยูโน juunoo' nN UNO, the United Nations Organiza-tion. [f. Eng.] →Full name under องค์การ.

เย jée' V to be leaning, aslant, not straight.

โยเย jóojée' V to be leaning, aslant, not straight, crooked, out of plumb.

เยก. See โยกเยก under โยก.

เยซู,พระ-- jeesuu', phrájeesuu' nN Jesus.

เย็น jen' V 1. to be cool, cold (of the weather; of inanimate objects; of body parts). N 2. evening. C 3. evening. V 4. to be evening. ความ-- the cold, coldness. →Dist. 1. หนาว. →Ant.

1. ร้อน.

กาแฟเย็น kaafɛɛjen′ N iced coffee.

ข้าวเย็น (มื้อ) khâawjen′ N 1. leftover cooked
    rice, cold rice. 2. s p e c i a l evening meal,
    dinner (mýy′). →S y n. 2. อาหารเย็น.

o กินข้าวเย็น kin′khâawjen′ to eat dinner.

ใจเย็น cajjen′ V to be calm, steady, cool-headed,
    imperturbable. →A n t. ใจร้อน.

ชาเย็น ๑ chaajen′ N iced tea.

ชาเย็น ๒ chaa′jen′ V to be cold, indifferent,
    unfeeling, cool (e.g. toward someone).

เช้า สาย บ่าย เย็น ก็ได้ cháaw′ sǎaj′ bàaj′
    jen′ kɔ̂dâaj′ (it can be) any time during the
    day: "early morning, late morning, afternoon,
    evening."

แช่เย็น chɛ̂ɛ′jen′ V to put (something) on ice.

o งานแช่เย็น ŋaan′-chɛ̂ɛ′jen′ i d i o m. the work
    is shelved, put on ice, remains cold and un-
    touched (sarcastic).

ตอนเย็น tɔɔnjen′ in the evening.

ตู้เย็น (ตู้,ใบ) tûujen′ (tûu′, baj′) N icebox,
    refrigerator.

ที่เย็นๆ thîi′jenjen′ cool places.

น้ำเย็น námjen′ cold water.

เมื่อเย็น mŷajen′ this evening, this late afternoon
    (prior to present).

ยากเย็น jâagjen′ V to be very difficult.

เย็นเจี๊ยบ jencíab′ c o l l o q. to be very cold,
    ice-cold.

เย็นใจ jencaj′ V to be unworried, calm, relaxed,
    composed. →A n t. ร้อนใจ.

เย็นเฉียบ jenchìab′ to be extremely cold, icy
    cold.

เย็นชา jen′chaa′ V 1. to be cold, unresponsive,
    unfeeling, cool (e.g. toward someone). 2. to
    be numb from cold.

เย็นชืด jenchŷyd′ V to be stone-cold, cold and
    tasteless (of food which should be served hot).

เย็นเฉี้ยบ jenchíab′ c o l l o q. to be ice-cold.

เย็นนี้ jenníi′ this evening.

เย็นเยียบ,เยียบเย็น jenjîab′, jîabjen′ V to be
    very cold, bitterly cold.

เย็นลง jen′loŋ′ to get cool, get cooler, cool off.

เย็นวันนี้ jen′wanníi′ this evening.

เย็นหู jenhǔu′ V to be pleasant to listen to.

เยือกเย็น jŷagjen′ V to be very cold, bitterly cold.

ร่มเย็น rômjen′ V 1. to be peaceful, tranquil.
    2. to be shady.

เวลาเย็น weelaajen′ N 1. evening. 2. in the
    evening.

หกโมงเย็น hògmooŋjen′ c o l l o q. 6 P. M. six
    o'clock in the evening.

อยู่เย็นเป็นสุข jùujen′pensùg′ V e l a b. to live in
    happiness, in peace and contentment, to live hap-
    pily.

อาหารเย็น (มื้อ) ʔaahǎanjen′ (mýy′) N e l e g.
    evening meal, dinner.

เย็บ jéb′ V to sew.

ตัดเย็บ tàd′jéb′ V to cut and sew; hence, to tailor,
    make a dress, make a suit, etc.

เย็บปักถักร้อย jébpàg′thàgrɔ́ɔj′ V 1. to do needle-
    work. N 2. needlework.

เย็บผ้า jébphâa′ V to sew.

o เข็มเย็บผ้า (เล่ม) khěm′jébphâa′ (lêm′) N
    sewing needle.

o จักรเย็บผ้า (คัน,เครื่อง) càg′jébphâa′ (khan′,
    khrŷaŋ′) N sewing machine.

เย็บ(...)เสีย jéb′(...)sía′ to sew up.

เย็บ...ใส่ jébɔ...sàj′ to sew or make up (some-
    thing) to wear.

เยย,--หยัน jə́əj′, jə́əjjǎn′ V to mock, ridicule,
    jeer, laugh at.

เย่อ in เย่อหยิ่ง jə̂əjìŋ′ V to be haughty, vain,
    proud.

เย้อ in เย็นเย้อ jənjə́ə′/* V c o l l o q. to be lengthy,
    overlong.

เยอรมนี jəəramanii′ pN Germany. [f. Eng.]

เยอรมัน jəəraman′ N German, Germany. [f. Eng.]

    ประเทศเยอรมัน prathêed′jəəraman′ pN Germany.

เยอะ jə́ʔ′ V c o l l o q. 1. to be a whole lot, a great
    deal, plenty. sV 2. plentifully.

o มีเยอะ miijə́ʔ′ there's a lot, there's plenty.

เยอะแยะ jə́ʔjɛ́ʔ′ c o l l o q. idem เยอะ.

เยา jaw′ V to be little, low (in magnitude).

ย่อมเยา jɔ̂mjaw′ V to be inexpensive, reasonable,
    moderate. →Often also spelled ย่อมเยาว์.

ราคาเยา raakhaajaw′ (a) low or moderate price;
    priced cheaply or moderately. →Often also

spelled ราคาเยาว์.

เย้า jáw/ V to tease.

เย้ายุ jáwjú?/ V to excite, arouse.

เยาว, เยาว- jaw/, jawwaɔ V to be young, youthful. →Also ยุว-.

ผู้เยาว์ (คน) phûujaw/ (khon/) N 1. law a minor. 2. lit. youth, youngster.

ย่อมเยาว์. See ย่อมเยา under เยา.

เยาวชน (คน) jawwachon/ (khon/) N youth, young people, youngsters.

o ศาลเด็กและเยาวชน sǎandèg/lɛjawwachon/ N juvenile court.

เยาว์วัย jawwaj/ V 1. to be young, underage. N 2. childhood.

ราคาเยาว์. See ราคาเยา under เยา.

เยาะ jɔ́?/ V to mock, ridicule, jeer at, laugh at.

หัวเราะเยาะ hǔarɔ́?/jɔ́?/ V to laugh at, ridicule and laugh at.

เยิน in the following entries.

ยับเยิน jábjəən/ V 1. to be collapse, go to pieces, be ruined, destroyed. 2. to be wrinkled, crumpled (as of cloth, paper), crumpled, battered (as of a wrecked car), torn, bruised, broken (as of the flesh). sV 3. severely, ruinously, heavily (of loss); in pieces, till in pieces; till ruined, battered and broken, bruised and torn. →Syn. 1. See วอดวาย.

เยินยอ jəənjɔɔ/ V to speak highly of, praise, laud.

เยิ่น in เยิ่นเย้อ jə̂njə́ə/* V colloq. to be lengthy, overlong.

เยิ้ม jə́əm/ V to ooze, exude.

หยาดเยิ้ม jàadjə́əm/ V 1. to look honey-sweet, rich and sweet, meltingly sweet (as of candied fruit, honeycomb, a woman's eyes). 2. (music) to be rich and sweet, gorgeous, mellifluous.

เยี่ย in ยั้วเยี่ย júajía/ V to be crawling with, crowded with (e.g. people, creeping things); to be moving about in great numbers.

เยี่ยง jîaŋ/ like, in the same manner as, in (such and such a) manner.

เยี่ยงอย่าง jîaŋjàaŋ/ N established example, pattern.

เยียด in the following entries.

เยียดยัด, ยัดเยียด jîadjád/, jádjîad/ V to be stuffed, congested, crowded.

o เบียดเสียดเยียดยัด bìadsìad/jîadjád/ V elab. colloq. to be crowded, congested, densely profuse.

o ยัดเยียดให้ jádjîad/hâj/ to insist upon giving, press upon.

เยียน in เยี่ยมเยียน jîamjian/ V to visit, pay a visit.

เยียบ in เยียบเย็น, เย็นเยียบ jîabjen/, jenjîab/ V to be very cold, bitterly cold.

เยี่ยม ๑ jîam/ V to be first rate, best, top, tops.

ชั้นเยี่ยม chánjîam/ top grade, excellent, best.

โชคดีเยี่ยม chôog/diijîam/ first rate good luck.

เยี่ยม ๒ jîam/ V to visit.

เยี่ยมเยียน jîamjian/ V to visit, pay a visit.

เยี่ยมหน้า jîamnâa/ V to stick one's head out to see; to look out.

เยียว in เยียวยา jiawjaa/ V eleg. 1. to cure (e.g. a disease). 2. to treat (with medicine).

เยี่ยว jîaw/ V 1. com., vulg. to urinate. N 2. com., vulg. urine. →Syn. ปัสสาวะ eleg., เบา euphem.

เยื่อ (แผ่น) jŷa/ (phɛ̀n/) N membrane, fascia, pellicle.

เยื่อบาง jŷabaaŋ/ N membrane, thin tissue.

เยื่อเมือก jŷamŷag/ N mucous membrane.

เยื่อใย jŷajaj/ N attachment, bond, tie (esp. between related objects or persons).

เยื้อ in ยืดเยื้อ jŷydjŷa/ V to be greatly prolonged, to last a long time.

เยือก ๑ jŷag/ V to be cold, very cold.

เย็นเยือก, เยือกเย็น jenjŷag/, jŷagjen/ V to be very cold, bitterly cold. ความ-- chill, coolness, calmness.

เยือกแข็ง jŷagkhɛ̌ŋ/ V to be frozen solid.

เยือก ๒ jŷag/ rM modifier used with ไหว "to quiver, shake."

เยื้อง ๑ jŷaŋ/ V to be diagonally opposite (from).

เยื้อง ๒ in เยื้องกราย jŷaŋkraaj/ V to walk slowly and gracefully, walk with an air (mostly of women).

เยือน jyan/ V eleg. to visit, call on.

แย่ jɛ̂ɛ/ V 1. to be too bad. 2. to be in trouble, in a bad way. 3. to be helpless.

ยักแย่ยักยัน jágjɛ̂ɛ'jágjan' V colloq. to hobble; to move haltingly, with difficulty, clumsily.

แย่หน่อย jɛ̂ɛ'nɔ̀j' too bad; kind of bad.

แย้ (ตัว) jɛ́ɛ' (tua') N a kind of ground lizard.

แยก jɛ̂ɛg' V com. 1. to separate, part, go apart. 2. to divide up (into). 3. to analyze. →Syn. จำแนก eleg.

การแยกตน kaanjɛ̂ɛgton' N phys. fission.

แตกแยก,--กัน tɛ̀ɛgjɛ̂ɛg', tɛ̀ɛgjɛ̂ɛg'kan' V 1. to break up and separate (as a group of friends), to split up. 2. to break off (a friendship). 3. to be split off, separated. การ-- separation, dissociation; (act of) breaking a friendship.

ทางแยก (ทาง) thaaŋjɛ̂ɛg' (thaaŋ') N 1. side road, road or path branching off the main thoroughfare; roads branching from a fork. 2. branch line.

แยกตัวประกอบ jɛ̂ɛg'tuaprakɔ̀ɔb' V math. to factor.

แยกทาง jɛ̂ɛgthaaŋ' V to go separate ways.

แยกธาตุ jɛ̂ɛgthâad' V to analyze chemically.

แยกไม่ออก jɛ̂ɛg'mâj?ɔ̀ɔg' 1. cannot be separated, cannot be taken apart. 2. cannot separate (something).

แยกย้าย jɛ̂ɛgjáaj' V to separate, go (their) separate ways, move off separately.

แยกแยะ jɛ̂ɛg'jé?' V 1. to analyze, split up into components. 2. to branch out, diverge, become differentiated (into multiple components).

สี่แยก (แห่ง) sìijɛ̂ɛg' (hɛ̀ŋ') N intersection where four streets meet (or, in the Thai idiom, where they part).

แยง jɛɛŋ' V to insert, poke into, probe into.

แยงจมูก jɛɛŋ'camùug' to pick one's nose, insert (something) in the nose.

แย่ง jɛ̂ɛŋ' V to struggle to take; to scramble for; to grab, snatch by force.

แก่งแย่ง kɛ̀ŋjɛ̂ɛŋ' V 1. to engage in rivalry, vie (with). 2. to be at odds (with), at loggerheads (with).

ยื้อแย่ง jýyjɛ̂ɛŋ' V 1. to seize, take possession of by force. 2. to engage in vigorous rivalry.

แย่งกัน jɛ̂ɛŋ'kan' V to compete, vie with one another.

แย้ง jɛ́ɛŋ' V 1. to contradict, conflict with. 2. to object. 3. to oppose.

ขัดแย้ง(กัน) khàdjɛ́ɛŋ'(kan) V to be in conflict, disagree (with one another), contradict (one another).

โต้แย้ง tôojɛ́ɛŋ' V 1. to argue, dispute. 2. to contradict.

แย้งขึ้น jɛ́ɛŋ'khŷn' V 1. to interrupt (in talking), break in. 2. to contradict, utter a contrary statement.

แยบ ๑ in the following entries.

แยบคาย jɛ̂ɛbkhaaj' V 1. to be ingenious, skillful, clever. 2. to be right, appropriate, wise.

แยบยล jɛ̂ɛbjon' V 1. to be tricky, cunning, ingenious. N 2. trick.

แยบ ๒ in ยอบแยบ jɔ̂bjɛ̂b'* V colloq. 1. to be too little, insufficient. 2. to be running out, low. 3. to be poor.

แย้ม jɛ́ɛm' V 1. to burst into bloom. 2. to open up, open, part. 3. to reveal (e.g. one's thoughts).

ยิ้มแย้ม jímjɛ́ɛm' V to smile broadly, cheerfully; to beam.

แรกแย้ม rɛ̂ɛgjɛ́ɛm' first-blooming.

o ดอกไม้แรกแย้ม dɔ̀ɔgmáaj'rɛ̂ɛgjɛ́ɛm' a flower which is just beginning to open. →Often used as a simile for a young girl.

แยแส jɛɛsɛ̌ɛ' V to pay attention (to), mind, show interest (in).

ไม่แยแส mâjjɛɛsɛ̌ɛ' not to pay the slightest attention, to be completely indifferent.

แยะ jé?' V colloq. 1. to be a whole lot, a great deal, plenty. sV 2. plentifully.

เยอะแยะ já?jé?' colloq. idem.

แยกแยะ jɛ̂ɛg'jé?' V 1. to analyze, split up into components. 2. to branch out, diverge, become differentiated (into multiple components).

โย jóo' V to be leaning, aslant, not straight.

โยเย jóojee' V to be leaning, aslant, not straight, crooked, out of plumb.

โยกโย jôogjóo' V to be evasive (in speech), drag out (a discussion)(by evasive speech).

โยก jôog' V to sway, oscillate, rock back and forth.

โยกเยก jôogjêeg' V 1. to sway, oscillate. 2. to vacillate. 3. to prevaricate.

โยกโย้ jôogjóo′ V to be evasive (in speech), drag out (a discussion)(by evasive speech).

โยกโยน jôogjoon′ V to rock and sway, pitch and toss.

หัวโยก hŭajôog′ N digging stick (for planting rice).

โยง ๑ joog′ V to link, join, interconnect.

โยง ๒ joog′ N base (in games).

อยู่โยง jùu′joog′ V 1. to remain at base (in games). 2. to hold the fort, i.e. stay on duty (as in an office, a store, etc.) while other employees take time off.

โย่ง jôog′ V colloq. to be tall, high.

โยชน์ jôod′ C a unit of distance, equivalent to about 10 miles.

โยธา in โยธาเทศบาล joothaa′thêesabaan′ N Public Works.

o กรมโยธาเทศบาล krom′-joothaa′thêesabaan′ N Department of Public Works.

โยน ๑ joon′ V to toss, throw, cast.

โยกโยน jôogjoon′ V to rock and sway, pitch and toss.

โยนหลุม joonlŭm′ N a kind of gambling game in which the stakes, consisting of pennies, small cards, or marbles, are thrown or shot toward a hole or holes.

โยนหัวโยนก้อย joonhŭa′joonkɔ̂j′ V colloq. to flip a coin.

โยน ๒ in อ่อนโยน ʔɔ̀ɔnjoon′ V to be gentle, tender.

โยนี (โยนี) joonii′ (joonii′) N lit., anat. vulva; (loosely) female genitalia.

โยม joom′ N 1. one who supports a priest. P 2. I, me (king, parents, older people, or supporters sp. to priest); you (priest sp. to parents, older people, supporters).

ญาติโยม (คน) jâadjoom′ (khon′) N relatives.

โยเย joojee′ V 1. to cry, complain, be given to crying, complaining. 2. to back out (e.g. from a commitment).

ใย ๑ (เส้น) jaj′ (sên′) N fiber, filament; web.

ชักใย chágjaj′ V to form threads, spin a web or cocoon (as spiders, silkworms).

เยื่อใย jŷajaj′ N attachment, bond, tie (esp.

between related objects or persons).

ใยแมลงมุม (ใย, เส้น) jaj′malɛɛŋmum′ (jaj′, sên′) N 1. spider web. 2. cobweb.

เส้นใย (เส้น) sênjaj′ (sên′) N fiber, filament.

ใย ๒ in ห่วงใย hùaŋjaj′ V to be worried, anxious, concerned. ความ-- concern, care.

ไย ๑. See entries below.

มิไย míjaj′ regardless (of), disregarding (the fact that), even though.

ไม่ไยดี (ต่อ) mâjjajdii′ (tɔ̀ɔ=) to be indifferent (to), not care (for), pay no attention (to).

ไย ๒ jaj′ lit. why? wherefore?

ไย่ in หยากไย่ jàagjâj N cobweb. →Also spelled หยักไย่. →Dist. ใยแมลงมุม mng. 1.

ร

ร rɔɔ′ LOW consonant. Pronounced r initially, n finally. →May be confused with ล in pron.

รก ๑ róg′ V 1. to be disorderly, untidy, cluttered, full of clutter, a hodge-podge. 2. to be overgrown, neglected, covered with disorderly plant growth.

รกร้าง rógráaŋ′ V to be deserted, desolate, disorderly and deserted, neglected and uninhabited.

รกรุงรัง róg′ruŋraŋ′ V elab. colloq. to be disorderly, cluttered, untidy, messy, a hodge-podge.

รกหูรกตา róghŭu′rógtaa′ V (a person or thing) to offend the eye (by being out of place in otherwise pleasant or orderly surroundings).

รก ๒ róg′ N placenta.

รกราก rógrâag′ N birthplace, domicile, residence.

o ตั้งรกราก tâŋ′rógrâag′ to settle down permanently, take up residence.

o ฝังรกราก fâŋ′rógrâag′ idem.

รง roŋ′ N gamboge, a kind of gum resin.

รณ ron′ V lit. to fight, battle, wage war.

รณรงค์ ronnaroŋ′ N lit. fighting, battle.

รด ród′ V 1. to water (e.g. plants). 2. to sprinkle (as in certain ceremonies).

รดน้ำ ródnáam′ V 1. to pour water on, to water. 2. to besprinkle with holy water.

หกรด hògród′ V to spill, be spilled (over smthg.).

รถ (คัน) ród′ (khan′) N vehicle. Class term usu-
    ally fol. by a specific term, e.g. รถไฟ. คน--
    colloq. chauffeur; also คนขับรถ com.

ขบวนรถ (ขบวน) khabuanród′ (khabuan′) N 1.
    railroad train. 2. procession of vehicles.

ขับรถ khàbród′ V to drive a car. คน-- driver,
    chauffeur; also คนรถ colloq.

ขึ้นรถ khŷnród′ V to take, board, get on a train
    or bus; to take, get in a car.

ค่ารถ khâaród′ N fare, carfare.

จับรถ càbród′ V to catch a bus or other vehicle.
    [tr. f. Eng.]

เดินรถ dəənród′ V 1. to operate a line, manage
    a fleet of motor vehicles (e.g. a bus line). 2.
    to drive, operate a motor vehicle.

ตกรถ tògród′ V colloq. to miss one's train,
    bus, etc.

ทะเบียนรถ thabianród′ N car registration.

ป้ายหยุดรถ (ป้าย,แผ่น) pâaj′jùdród′ (pâaj′,
    phèn′) N 1. bus stop sign. 2. traffic stop sign.

ยางรถ (เส้น,ข้าง) jaaŋród′ (sên′,khâaŋ′) N
    tire.

รถกระบะ (คัน) ród′krabà?′ (khan′) N hand
    truck, handcart.

รถกุดัง,รถโกดัง (คัน) ród′kudaŋ′, ród′koodaŋ′
    (khan′) N colloq. (motor) truck. →Syn.
    รถบรรทุก eleg.

รถเก๋ง (คัน) ródkěŋ′ (khan′) N sedan (car).

รถเกราะ (คัน) ródkrɔ?′ (khan′) N 1. tank.
    2. armored car.

รถเข็น (คัน) ródkhěn′ (khan′) N pushcart.

รถแข่ง (คัน) ródkhὲŋ′ (khan′) N racing car.

รถจักร (คัน) ródcàg′ (khan′) N locomotive.

รถจักรยาน (คัน) ród′càgkajaan′ (khan′) N
    eleg. bicycle. →Syn. รถถีบ colloq.

o รถจักรยานสามล้อ (คัน) ród′-càgkajaan′ɔ-
    sǎamlɔɔ′ (khan′) N eleg. 1. samlor, pedicab.
    2. tricycle. →Also สามล้อ,รถสามล้อ.

รถเจ๊ก (คัน) ródcég′ (khan′) N colloq. rick-
    shaw. →Syn. รถลาก eleg.

รถเช่า (คัน) ródchâw′ (khan′) N 1. taxi. 2.
    rented car.

รถด่วน (ขบวน,คัน) róddùan′ N express train

(khabuan′); express bus (khan′).

รถดับเพลิง (คัน) ród′dàbphləəŋ′ (khan′) N
    fire engine.

รถโดยสาร (คัน) ród′doojsǎan′ (khan′) N 1.
    passenger car (as opposed to freight car). 2. bus.

รถตอนเดียว (คัน) ród′tɔɔndiaw′ (khan′) N coupé,
    roadster.

รถตีนตะขาบ (คัน) ród′tiintakhàab′ (khan′) N
    caterpillar tractor.

รถถัง (คัน) ródthǎŋ′ (khan′) N milit. tank.

รถถีบ (คัน) ródthìib′ (khan′) N colloq. bicycle.
    →Syn. รถจักรยาน eleg.

รถแท็กซี่ (คัน) ród′thέgsîi′ (khan′) N taxi.
    [แท็กซี่ f. Eng.] →Also รถแท๊กซี่.

รถบดถนน (คัน) ród′bòdthanǒn′ (khan′) N steam
    roller.

รถบรรทุก (คัน) ród′banthúg′ (khan′) N eleg.
    1. truck. 2. freight car. →Syn. 1. รถกุดัง
    colloq.

รถประจำทาง (คัน) ród′-pracam′thaaŋ′ (khan′)
    N eleg. bus, coach. →Syn. รถเมล์ colloq.

รถพยาบาล (คัน) ród′phajabaan′ (khan′) N
    ambulance.

รถพ่วง (คัน) ródphûaŋ′ (khan′) N 1. trailer,
    vehicle drawn by another vehicle. 2. a train
    of vehicles coupled to one another.

รถไฟ (ขบวน) ródfaj′ (khabuan′) N train. การ--
    railway affairs.

o กรมรถไฟ krom′ródfaj′ N State Railways
    Organization.

o ชุมทางรถไฟ (แห่ง) chumthaaŋ′ródfaj′ (hὲŋ′)
    N railroad junction.

o ทางรถไฟ (สาย) thaaŋ′ródfaj′ (sǎaj′) N
    1. railway, railroad. 2. by rail.

o รถไฟด่วน (ขบวน) ródfaj′dùan′ (khabuan′)
    N express train.

o รถไฟหลวง ródfaj′lǔaŋ′ N Royal State Railways.
    Abbrev. as ร.ฟ.ล.

o รางรถไฟ (ราง) raaŋ′ródfaj′ (raaŋ′) N rail-
    road track.

รถม้า (คัน) ródmáa′ (khan′) N horse-drawn
    carriage.

รถเมล์ (คัน) ródmee′ (khan′) N colloq. bus.
    [เมล์ f. Eng. "mail"] →Syn. รถประจำทาง

eleg.

รถยนต์ (คัน) ródjon′ (khan′) N automobile.

o ทางรถยนต์ (ทาง,สาย,เส้น) thaaŋ′ródjon′ N 1. highway (thaaŋ′, sǎaj′, sên′). 2. by automobile.

o รถยนต์เช่า (คัน) ródjon′châw′ (khan′) N eleg. rented automobile.

o รถยนต์โดยสาร (คัน) ródjon′doojsǎan′ (khan′) N eleg. bus.

o รถยนต์ประจำทาง (คัน) ródjon′-pracam′ɔthaaŋ′ (khan′) N eleg. a regularly scheduled bus, motor coach.

o รถยนต์พระที่นั่ง (คัน) ródjon′phráthîinâŋ′ (khan′) N roy. royal limousine.

รถรบ (คัน) ródrób′ (khan′) N 1. (military) tank. 2. military vehicle.

o กองรถรบ (กอง) kɔɔŋ′ródrób′ (kɔɔŋ′) N armored unit.

รถรา (คัน) ród′raa′ (khan′) N colloq. vehicles (collectively).

รถราง (คัน) ródraaŋ′ (khan′) N streetcar, trolley car, tram.

o รถรางไฟฟ้า (คัน) ródraaŋ′fajfáa′ (khan′) N streetcar, tram.

รถลาก (คัน) ródlâag′ (khan′) N eleg. rickshaw. →Syn. รถเจ๊ก colloq.

รถละเบียง,รถเสบียง (คัน) ród′sabiaŋ′ (khan′) N dining car, restaurant car, diner.

รถสามล้อ (คัน) ród′sǎamlɔ́ɔ′ (khan′) N colloq. samlor, pedicab. →Also สามล้อ,รถจักรยานสามล้อ.

รถหวอ (คัน) ródwɔ̌ɔ′ (khan′) N colloq. ambulance, fire engine, police car (i.e. any vehicle with a siren).

รถหุ้มเกราะ (คัน) ród′hûmkrɔ̀ʔ′ (khan′) N armored car.

รางรถ (ราง) raaŋród′ (raaŋ′) N railroad tracks, streetcar tracks.

โรงเก็บรถ (โรง) rooŋkèbród′ (rooŋ′) N garage. →Also โรงรถ. →Dist. อู่รถ.

อู่รถ (อู่) ʔùuród′ (ʔùu′) N garage (for sheltering or repairing cars). →Dist. โรงเก็บรถ.

ร.น. rɔɔnɔɔ′. Abbrev. for ราชนาวี the Royal Navy.

รน ron′ V to be restless, unable to stay still.

ดิ้นรน dînron′ V to struggle, struggle to free oneself.

รนหา ronhǎa′ to look for, go out of one's way to look for, place oneself in the way of (e.g. danger, trouble).

ร้อนรน rɔ́ɔnron′ V to be anxious (e.g. for news, for help).

รน rôn′ V to shorten, move closer (in time or space).

รน in กระตือรือร้น kratyy′ryyrón′ to be anxious, enthusiastic, eager, in a rush (e.g. to do something).

รบ rób′ V to fight, battle. การ-- (the) fighting, (a) battle. นัก-- warrior, fighter.

ซ้อมรบ sɔ́ɔmrób′ V to hold maneuvers. →Syn. ประลองยุทธ eleg.

แนวรบ (แนว,ด้าน) nɛɛwrób′ (nɛɛw′, dâan′) N battle line, fighting front. →Also แนวหน้า.

พักรบ phágrób′ V to call a truce, a cease-fire.

รถรบ (คัน) ródrób′ (khan′) N 1. (military) tank. 2. military vehicle.

o กองรถรบ (กอง) kɔɔŋ′ródrób′ (kɔɔŋ′) N armored unit.

รบกวน róbkuan′ V to bother, trouble, annoy, vex. ความ-- bothersomeness, annoyance; disturbance, distraction.

รบพุ่ง róbphûŋ′ V to fight, wage war, engage in a battle.

รบเร้า róbráw′ V to beg, beseech repeatedly.

เรือรบ (ลำ) ryarób′ (lam′) N warship.

o กองเรือรบ (กอง) kɔɔŋ′ryarób′ (kɔɔŋ′) N fleet (of warships).

สนามรบ (แห่ง) sanǎamrób′ (hɛ̀ŋ′) N battlefield.

สู้รบ sûurób′ V to fight, battle.

ร.ฟ.ล. Abbrev. for รถไฟหลวง Royal State Railways.

รม ๑ rom′ V to subject to, expose to (smoke, fume, flame, etc.).

รมควัน romkhwan′ V to smoke, be smoked (as a piece of glass).

รม ๒ in หอยนางรม (ตัว) hɔ̌jnaaŋrom′ (tua′) N oyster. →Also หอยอีรม.

ร่ม (คัน) rôm′ N 1. shade. 2. umbrella (khan′). 3. to be shaded.

โดดร่ม dòodrôm′ V 1. to make a parachute jump;

to bail out (of a plane). 2. **slang** to play
truant.

ในร่ม najrôm´ 1. in the shade, indoors. 2.
(as n. mod.) indoor.

ในร่มผ้า naj´rômphâa´ under one's garment (ref.
to any part of the body covered by clothes).

พลร่ม (คน) phonrôm´ (khon´) N 1. paratrooper.
2. **slang** illegal voter.

ร่มครึ้ม rôm´khrým´ V to be nice and shady,
cool and shady.

ร่มชูชีพ (ผืน) rôm´chuuchîib´ (phv̆yn´) N parachute.

ร่มผ้า (คัน) rômphâa´ (khan´) N cloth umbrella.

ร่มไม้ (แห่ง) rômmáaj´ (hὲŋ´) N shade, umbrage
of trees.

ร่มเย็น rômjen´ V 1. to be peaceful, tranquil.
2. to be shady.

ร.ม.ต. rɔɔmɔɔtɔɔ´. Abbrev. for รัฐมนตรี minister,
minister of state.

รมย์ in รื่นรมย์ rŷynrom´ V 1. to be pleased, find
pleasure, enjoyment. →Often รู้สึก--.

ร.ร. Abbrev. for โรงเรียน school.

รวง (รวง) ruaŋ´ (ruaŋ´) N ear of paddy, ear of
corn.

ตกรวง tògruaŋ´ V (ears of paddy) to set.

รวงผึ้ง (รวง) ruaŋphŷŋ´ (ruaŋ´) N bee's nest.

ร่วง rûaŋ´ V to fall, drop, drop off (as leaves from
a tree).

ท้องร่วง thɔ́ɔŋrûaŋ´ V eleg. 1. to have diarrhea,
N 2. diarrhea.

o โรคท้องร่วง rôog´thɔ́ɔŋrûaŋ´ N eleg. diarrhea.

ทำ(...)ร่วง tham´(...)rûaŋ´ to make (something) fall off.

ร่วงโรย rûaŋrooj´ V 1. to deteriorate, degenerate. 2. to be withered, wilted. 3. to have lost
(its) vitality, vigor.

ฤดูใบไม้ร่วง (ฤดู) rýduu´bajmáajrûaŋ´ (rýduu´)
N fall, autumn.

รวด ๑ rûad´ C round, time.

รวดเดียว rûaddiaw´ all at once, all at one time.

รวด ๒ in รวดเร็ว rûadrew´ V 1. to be fast, quick.
sV 2. quickly.

o ในเวลาอันรวดเร็ว najweelaa´ʔanrûadrew´

in a very short time, very quickly (of time).

รวน ruan´ V 1. to provoke, irritate, pick a fight,
a quarrel with (someone)(by means of provoking
or irritating speech). 2. to pan-fry (as meat).
3. to be shaky, loose (of teeth, posts, etc.). 4.
to be crooked, out of line (e.g. of teeth, rows of
things).

รวนเร ruanree´ V to be uncertain, wavering.

ร่วน rûan´ V to be friable, loose, crumbly (as soil).

หัวเราะร่วน hŭaró?´rûan´ to laugh heartily.

รวบ rûab´ V 1. to grasp, grab; to gather together.
2. **slang** to seize, arrest.

รวบรวม rûabruam´ V to collect, gather together.

รวบรัด rûabrád´ V to cut short, make brief.

รวม ruam´ V to combine, add, add up, sum up,
include.

จุดรวม cùdruam´ N center, hub (fig. sense):
"combined points".

รวบรวม rûabruam´ V to collect, gather together.

รวมกลุ่ม ruamklùm´ V to form a group, gather
into a group, assemble.

รวมกัน ruamkan´ to put together, combine; to
be put together, combined.

รวมความ ruamkhwaam´ V to sum up, summarize.

o รวมความว่า ruamkhwaam´wâa´ in short, briefly.

รวมทั้ง ruam´tháŋᵓ 1. to include. 2. including.

รวมทั้งหมด ruam´tháŋmòd´ altogether.

ส่วนรวม sùanruam´ 1. the group as a whole. 2.
common, collective. 3. broadly, on the whole,
in general. →Ant. ส่วนตัว, ส่วนบุคคล.

o ประโยชน์ของส่วนรวม prajòod´khɔ̌ɔŋsùanruam´
the common interest, common good; the collective advantage.

รวม ๑ rûam´ V 1. to share, join in, participate.
sV 2. in participation, jointly, together.

เข้าร่วม khâwrûam´ V to join; to participate (in).

แถลงการณ์ร่วม thalɛ̌ɛŋkaan´rûam´ N joint communique.

ทางร่วม (ทาง,สาย) thaaŋrûam´ (thaaŋ´, sǎaj´)
N junction, merging street or highway.

พี่น้องร่วมชาติ phîinɔ́ɔŋ´rûamchâad´ (one's) fellow
citizens.

เพื่อนร่วมชั้น (คน) phŷan´rûamchán´ (khon´) N
classmate.

เพื่อนร่วมชาติ (คน) phɯ̂an'rɯ̂amchâad' (khon')
N (one's) countryman.

เพื่อนร่วมเพศ (คน) phɯ̂an'rɯ̂amphêed' (khon')
N friend of the same sex.

เพื่อนร่วมโรงเรียน (คน) phɯ̂an'rɯ̂amrooŋrian'
(khon') N schoolmate.

มีส่วนร่วม miisùan'rɯ̂am' to have a part, a share
(in).

ร่วมกัน rɯ̂amkan' 1. to join together (as in an
activity). 2. mutual, common. 2. together.

o นอนร่วมกัน nɔɔn'rɯ̂amkan' to sleep together.

o ผลประโยชน์ร่วมกัน phŏnprajòod'rɯ̂amkan' N
mutual benefit.

ร่วมกับ rɯ̂am'kaɔ together with, in conjunction
with, with.

ร่วมใจกัน rɯ̂amcaj'kan' to be united in mind and
spirit.

ร่วมโต๊ะ rɯ̂amtó?' V to join someone at the table;
to eat together.

ร่วมมือ rɯ̂ammyy' V to cooperate (with). การ--
cooperating, cooperation. ความ-- cooperation.

ร่วมไม้ร่วมมือ rɯ̂ammáaj'rɯ̂ammyy' V elab.
colloq. to cooperate.

ร่วมแรงร่วมใจ rɯ̂amrɛɛŋ'rɯ̂amcaj' V elab.
colloq. to be united in action and spirit.

ร่วมวง rɯ̂amwoŋ' V to join a group or party.

ร่วมสายโลหิต rɯ̂amsăaj'loohìd' eleg. of the
same blood, of the same parents.

ร่วม ๒ rɯ̂am' qM almost, about, nearly. →Syn.
See เกือบ.

o ร่วมปี rɯ̂ampii' almost a year.

o ร่วมพันปี rɯ̂am'phanpii' almost a thousand
years.

รวย ruaj' V colloq. to be rich, wealthy. →Syn.
มั่งคั่ง, มั่งมี eleg. →Ant. จน.

ร่ำรวย râmruaj' V to be rich, wealthy.

รส ród' N taste.

ปรุงรส chɯɯród' V to bring out, enhance the flavor.

มีรสสนุก miiród'sanùg' to be entertaining, amusing; to be great sport.

รสชาติ ródchâad' N taste, flavor.

รสนิยม ród'níjom' N taste (perceptive judgment), liking, preference.

ลิ้มรส límród' V to taste.

ออกรส ?ɔ̀ɔgród' V 1. to be tasty. 2. to be enjoyable, zestful (as of a conversation).

โอชารส ?oochaaród' V eleg. to be delicious.
→Syn. อร่อย com.

ร.ส.พ. rɔɔsɔɔphɔɔ'. Abbrev. for องค์การรับส่งสินค้า
และพัสดุภัณฑ์ Express Transportation Bureau
(E.T.B).

รอ rɔɔ' V to wait, wait for, await. →Syn. คอย,
ท่า ๔.

รอคอย rɔɔkhɔɔj' V to wait, wait for.

รอช้า rɔɔcháa' V to hesitate, delay.

รอท่า rɔɔthâa' V to wait.

o โดยไม่รอท่า dooj'mâjrɔɔthâa' without waiting,
without hesitation.

รั้งรอ ráŋrɔɔ' V to hesitate, delay, prolong.
→Also รอรั้ง rɔɔráŋ'.

รีรอ riirɔɔ' V to hesitate, hold back, pause from
uncertainty of mind.

รอก (ลูก) rɔ̂og' (lûug') N pulley.

ลูกรอก (ลูก) lûugrɔ̂og' (lûug') N pulley.

รอง rɔɔŋ' V 1. to underlay, place beneath, be placed
beneath. 2. to collect (a liquid). sV 3. next on
down (as in size, age, position) (1st and 2nd examples). N 4. initial element in noun cpds.; trans-
latable as "vice- (as in vice-president), deputy,
second, runner-up" (3rd example).

o คนหัวปีเป็นหมอ คนรองเป็นครู khonhŭapii'penɔ
mɔ̌ɔ'→ khonrɔɔŋ'penkhruu'↓ The oldest (son,
daughter) is a doctor; the next (oldest) is a teacher.

o คนที่ยืนรองลงมาเป็นนางสาวไทย khonthîijyyn'-
rɔɔŋ'loŋmaa'→ pennaaŋsăaw'thaj'↓ The one
standing next below is Miss Thailand.

o รองประธานาธิบดี (นาย,คน) rɔɔŋ'-prathaa'ɔ
naa'thíbɔdii' (naaj',khon') N vice-president
(of a country).

จานรอง (ใบ) caanrɔɔŋ' (baj') N saucer.

ชั้นรอง chánrɔɔŋ' N the next step (shelf, level,
etc.) down.

ต่อรอง tɔ̀ɔrɔɔŋ' V to bargain for a reduction,
to haggle.

ทดรอง thódrɔɔŋ' V to lay out money in advance,
to pay (for something) pending reimbursement.

พระรอง (คน) phárɔɔŋ' (khon') N the male
character who plays the role of the hero's com-

panion in a play, motion picture, or story.

รองท้อง rɔɔŋthɔ́ɔŋ′ V to eat just enough to prevent hunger.

รองเท้า (ข้าง,คู่) rɔɔŋtháaw′ N eleg. shoe,
shoes (khâaŋ′ for one of a pair; khûu′ for
pairs).

o รองเท้าแตะ rɔɔŋtháawtɛ̀ʔ′ N slippers.

o รองเท้าผ้าใบ rɔɔŋtháaw′phâabaj′ N canvas
shoes, tennis shoes, sneakers.

o รองเท้ายาง rɔɔŋtháawjaaŋ′ N rubber-soled
canvas shoes, tennis shoes, sneakers.

o รองเท้าส้นสูง rɔɔŋtháaw′sônsǔuŋ′ N high-
heeled shoes.

รองนางสาวไทย (คน) rɔɔŋ′naaŋsǎawthaj′
(khon′) N runners-up for Miss Thailand.

รองประธาน (คน,นาย) rɔɔŋ′prathaan′ (khon′,
naaj′) N vice-president, vice-chairman.

รองประธานาธิบดี (นาย,คน) rɔɔŋ′-prathaa′ɔ
naa′thíbɔdii′ (naaj′,khon′) N vice-president
(of a country).

รองปลัดกระทรวง (นาย,คน) rɔɔŋ′-palàd′kraɔ
suaŋ′ (naaj′,khon′) N deputy undersecretary
(of a ministry).

รองรับ rɔɔŋráb′ V to catch (smthg.) in a container placed underneath for the purpose.

รับรอง rábrɔɔŋ′ V 1. to entertain (guests). 2.
to certify, guarantee, vouch; to confirm, sanction, recognize, approve; to sponsor; to second
(a motion). การ-- reception; confirmation,
recognition; guarantee; sponsorship.

o ใบรับรอง (ใบ) bajrábrɔɔŋ′ (baj′) N certificate (in regard to qualifications, health, etc.).

รอง (ร่อง) rɔ̂ŋ′*(rɔ̂ŋ′) N 1. groove, channel,
ditch, furrow. 2. crack, space (e.g. between
boards in the floor). 3. (vegetable) bed.

ท้องร่อง (ท้องร่อง) thɔ́ɔŋrɔ̂ŋ′ (thɔ́ɔŋrɔ̂ŋ′) N
irrigation ditch.

นำร่อง namrɔ̂ŋ′ V to pilot, navigate (a ship).
คน-- pilot. ผู้-- pilot.

ร่องน้ำ (ร่อง) rɔ̂ŋnáam′ (rɔ̂ŋ′) N 1. channel.
2. the deeper part of a stream or waterway.

ร่องผัก (ร่อง) rɔ̂ŋphàg′ (rɔ̂ŋ′) N vegetable bed.

ร่องรอย rɔ̂ŋrɔɔj′ N trace, mark, sign, evidence.

ร้อง rɔ́ɔŋ′ V 1. to cry, utter characteristic cries

(of birds and animals); to cry out (of people).
2. to sing. นัก-- singer. →Also 2. ร้องเพลง.

ขอร้อง khɔ̌ɔrɔ́ɔŋ′ V to request, beseech, entreat.

o คำขอร้อง (ฉบับ,ข้อ,อย่าง) kham′khɔ̌ɔrɔ́ɔŋ′
N 1. (written) petition (chabàb′). 2. request
(for help)(khɔ̂ɔ′, jàaŋ′).

ขับร้อง khàbrɔ́ɔŋ′ V eleg. to sing.

คำร้อง (ข้อ,ฉบับ) khamrɔ́ɔŋ′ (khɔ̂ɔ′, chabàb′)
N petition.

เนื้อร้อง nýarɔ́ɔŋ′ N words, text of a song.

ป่าวร้อง pàawrɔ́ɔŋ′ V 1. to announce, declare,
proclaim. 2. colloq. to circulate, spread
(e.g. information) around.

ฟ้องร้อง fɔ́ɔŋrɔ́ɔŋ′ V to sue, bring charges against.

ฟ้าร้อง (ครั้ง) (1) fáa′rɔ́ɔŋ′; (2) fáarɔ́ɔŋ′ 1. to
thunder; it thunders. N 2. thunder (khráŋ′).

ร้องขอ rɔ́ɔŋkhɔ̌ɔ′ V 1. to cry for (e.g. help). 2.
to beg for, request.

ร้องจ๋า rɔ́ɔŋcǎa′ V colloq. to cry loudly (as
of an infant).

ร้องทัก rɔ́ɔŋthág′ V to greet, hail, speak to
(loudly).

ร้องทุกข์ rɔ́ɔŋthúg′ V to complain, make a complaint.

ร้องเพลง rɔ́ɔŋphleeŋ′ V to sing, sing a song.

ร้องเรียก rɔ́ɔŋrîag′ V to call, call out to.

ร้องเรียน rɔ́ɔŋ′rian′ V eleg. to request, complain, petition.

ร้องลั่น rɔ́ɔŋ′lân′ V colloq. to shout, scream,
cry out loudly.

ร้องโวยวาย rɔ́ɔŋ′woojwaaj′ V colloq. to shout,
cry, scream (as for help).

ร้องไห้ rɔ́ɔŋhâj′* V to cry, weep. →Dist. ร่อง.

ร่ำร้อง râmrɔ́ɔŋ′ V to beg, ask, request, beseech
repeatedly.

เรียกร้อง rîagrɔ́ɔŋ′ V 1. to demand, claim, make
a demand for.

โห่ร้อง hòorɔ́ɔŋ′ V to cheer, hail, acclaim.

ร้องเมือง rɔɔŋmyaŋ′ pN name of a street in Bangkok.

ร่องแร่ง rɔ̂ŋrɛ̂ŋ′* to be hanging and swaying precar-
iously (as a partly broken branch of a tree).

รอด rɔ̂ɔd′ V to escape (from danger); to be safe,
saved.

จนแล้วจนรอด conlɛ́ɛw′conrɔ̂ɔd′ colloq. on and

on, over and over.

โดยตลอดรอดฝั่ง doojtalɔ̀ɔd/rɔ̂ɔdfàŋ/ elab. colloq., idiom. safe and sound.

รอดตาย rɔ̂ɔdtaaj/ V to survive, escape death.

รอดพ้น rɔ̂ɔd/phón/ V to escape (from danger), be safe, be saved.

รู้แล้วรู้รอด rúulɛ́ɛw/rúurɔ̂ɔd/ elab. colloq. once and for all.

เอาชีวิตรอด ʔaw/-chiiwíd/rɔ̂ɔd/ to save one's own life.

เอาตัวรอด ʔawtua/rɔ̂ɔd/ 1. to save oneself, get oneself to safety, to save one's own skin. 2. to manage to live; to make something of one's life.

o หนีเอาตัวรอด nǐi/-ʔawtua/rɔ̂ɔd/ to flee to safety, flee saving one's own skin.

รอน rɔɔn/ V eleg. to cut, sever (something).

ตัดรอน tàd/rɔɔn/ V eleg. to cut, sever.

รอน ๆ rɔɔnrɔɔn/ V eleg. 1. to be fading, setting (of the sun). AA 2. almost, nearly.

รอนแรม rɔɔnrɛɛm/ V lit. to go on a trip (overnight or longer), to journey spending the night out.

ร่อน rɔ̂n/* V 1. to sift, winnow, separate. V 2. to hover (in flight); to glide.

เร่ร่อน, ร่อนเร่ rêerɔ̂n/, rɔ̂nrêe/ V to wander, roam about.

ร้อน rɔ́ɔn/ V 1. to be hot. 2. to be urgent. ความ-- heat. →Ant. 1. เย็น, หนาว.

ขี้ร้อน khîirɔ́ɔn/ V to be sensitive to hot weather.

ใจร้อน cajrɔ́ɔn/ V 1. to be hasty, impetuous. 2. to be burning with impatience, anxious (e.g. to get something done). →Ant. ใจเย็น.

เดือดร้อน d̀yadrɔ́ɔn/ V 1. to be in trouble. 2. to worry, feel anxious, unhappy, upset. ความ-- trouble; worry.

o เป็นที่เดือดร้อน penthîi/d̀yadrɔ́ɔn/ to be troublesome.

ตัวร้อน tuarɔ́ɔn/ V to have a high (body) temperature.

แถบร้อน (แถบ) thɛ̀ɛbrɔ́ɔn/ (thɛ̀ɛb/) N hot region, tropical zone.

ทุกข์ร้อน thúgrɔ́ɔn/ V to suffer, be unhappy, be in trouble. ความ-- trouble, suffering, un-

happiness, woe.

ธุระร้อน (อย่าง) thúrá?/rɔ́ɔn/ (jàaŋ/) N urgent business.

บ่อน้ำร้อน (บ่อ) bɔ̀ɔ/námrɔ́ɔn/ (bɔ̀ɔ/) N hot spring.

ประเทศร้อน (ประเทศ) prathêed/rɔ́ɔn/ (prathêed/) N eleg. tropical country.

เป็นทุกข์เป็นร้อน penthúg/penrɔ́ɔn/ V elab. colloq. to be dejected, worried, bothered (about something). Cf. Eng. "to be hot and bothered."

เผ็ดร้อน phèdrɔ́ɔn/ V 1. to be hot and spicy (of food). 2. to be heated, acrimonious (of speech).

เมืองร้อน (เมือง) myaŋrɔ́ɔn/ (myaŋ/) N colloq. tropical country.

ร้อนขึ้น rɔ́ɔn/khŷn/ 1. to heat up, get hotter. 2. to be warmer.

ร้อนเงิน rɔ́ɔnŋən/ V to be in desperate need of money.

ร้อนจัด rɔ́ɔncàd/ to be extremely hot.

ร้อนจี๋ rɔ́ɔncǐi/ colloq. to be burning hot, extremely hot. 2. to be extremely urgent.

ร้อนใจ rɔ́ɔncaj/ V to be worried, anxious, perturbed. ความ-- worry, anxiety. →Ant. เย็นใจ.

o เดือดเนื้อร้อนใจ d̀yadnýa/rɔ́ɔncaj/ V elab. colloq. to worry, be upset. →See เดือดร้อน.

ร้อนฉี่ rɔ́ɔnchìi/ colloq. to be sizzling hot.

ร้อนถึง rɔ́ɔn/thŷŋⵀ idiom. to involve (someone) in trouble.

ร้อนเป็นไฟ rɔ́ɔn/penfaj/ to be hot like fire.

ร้อนเปรี้ยง rɔ́ɔnprîaŋ/ to be very hot (of the sun).

ร้อนผ่าว rɔ́ɔnphàaw/ to be scorchingly hot, intensely hot.

ร้อนเย็น rɔ́ɔn/jen/ V to be hot and/or cold. ความ-- temperature (esp. to the touch).

ร้อนรน rɔ́ɔnron/ V to be anxious (e.g. for news, for help).

ร้อนแรง rɔ́ɔn/rɛɛŋ/ V to be burning, flaming, rousing.

ร้อนหนาว rɔ́ɔn/nǎaw/ V to be hot and/or cold. ความ-- temperature (of weather, sensation).

ร้อนอกร้อนใจ rɔ́ɔn?òg/rɔ́ɔncaj/ V elab. colloq. to be worried and unhappy, be anxious. ความ-- elab. colloq. worry, anxiety.

ร้อนอบอ้าว rɔ́ɔn/?òb/?âaw/ V to be hot and sultry.

รีบร้อน rîibrɔ́ɔn/ V to hurry, be in a big hurry.

เร่งร้อน rêŋrɔ́ɔn′ V 1. to hurry, be in a hurry.
2. to hurry, rush (someone). 3. to be urgent,
pressing.

เร้าร้อน ráwrɔ́ɔn′ V to be aroused, inflamed,
burn (e.g. with passion, desire, impatience).

ฤดูร้อน rýduurɔ́ɔn′ N lit., eleg. summer, the
hot season.

เลือดร้อน lŷadrɔ́ɔn′ V 1. to be warm-blooded
(as of animals, birds). 2. to be hot-tempered,
quick-tempered, hot-headed, hot-blooded, impetuous.

สด ๆ ร้อน ๆ sòdsòd′rɔ́ɔnrɔ́ɔn′ V 1. idiom.
to be red-hot, fresh, new, most recent, the
latest. sV 2. just now, freshly.

หน้าร้อน nâarɔ́ɔn′ N colloq. summer, the hot
season.

ร้อบ rɔ̂ɔb′ 1. around. C 2. round, cycle.

โดยรอบ doojrɔ̂ɔb′ around, all around.

ในรอบ najrɔ̂ɔb′ in the course of, in the period of.

รอบข้าง rɔ̂ɔbkhâaŋ′ on all sides, all around.

รอบคอบ rɔ̂ɔbkhɔ̂ɔb′ to be careful, circumspect,
cautious. ความ-- carefulness, circumspec-
tion, caution.

รอบนอก rɔ̂ɔbnɔ̂ɔg′ 1. outside, outer area, periphery; outer part, outer layer. 2. outside (of),
around the periphery (of).

o รอบนอกของ rɔ̂ɔbnɔ̂ɔg′khɔ̌ɔŋɔ beyond, outside
of (e.g. the city limits).

รอบปี rɔ̂ɔbpii′ N 1. the completion of a year;
anniversary. 2. the twelve-year cycle.

รอบ ๆ rɔ̂ɔbrɔ̂ɔb′ around, around and around,
all around.

รอบรู้ rɔ̂ɔbrúu′ V to know extensively, be well-
informed.

รอบโลก rɔ̂ɔblôog′ around the world.

ล้อมรอบ lɔ́ɔmrɔ̂ɔb′ V to surround; to circle
around.

หมุนรอบ mǔnrɔ̂ɔb′ V to rotate, revolve, turn
around.

รอม in เก็บหอมรอมริบ, q.v. under เก็บ. (รอม
is used to provide a rhyme for หอม).

รอมร่อ rɔmmarɔ̂ɔ′* colloq. almost, about, on the
point of.

ร้อย (รอย) rɔɔj′ (rɔɔj′) N 1. trace, mark, line,

track, vestige.

เข้าชุดเข้ารอย khâwchúd′khâwrɔɔj′ V elab.
colloq. to fit (in with a set, a series), to match.

เจริญรอย carəən′rɔɔj′ V eleg. to follow (fig.).

o เจริญรอยพระยุคลบาท carəən′-rɔɔj′phrájúkhon′ɔ
bàad′ V roy. to follow in the king's footsteps.

ตามรอย taamrɔɔj′ V 1. to follow the track, mark,
or footprint, to track. 2. to follow in the steps
(of someone).

เป็นริ้วรอย penríw′rɔɔj′ V to be scratched.

ย้อนรอย jɔ́ɔn′rɔɔj′ V to retrace (one's) steps,
return by the same route.

ร่องรอย rɔ̂ŋrɔɔj′ N trace, mark, sign, evidence.

รอยขีด (รอย) rɔɔjkhìid′ (rɔɔj′) N scratch.

รอยเท้า rɔɔjtháaw′ N eleg. footprint.

รอยร้าว (รอย) rɔɔjráaw′ (rɔɔj′) N crack,
fissure.

ลงรอย loŋrɔɔj′ V idiom. to be in good harmony,
in agreement, to get along well (with someone).

สะกดรอยตาม sakòd′rɔɔj′-taam′ to follow after,
to trail, track.

ร้อย in the following entries.

กระจ้อยร่อย kracɔ̂jrɔ̂j′* V colloq. to be tiny.

ร้อยหรอ rɔ̂jrɔ̌ɔ′* V to decrease, become less and
less.

ร้อย ๑ rɔ́ɔj′ Nm 1. hundred. C 2. clf. for hundreds.

กองร้อย (กอง, กองร้อย) kɔɔŋrɔ́ɔj′ (kɔɔŋ′, kɔɔŋɔ
rɔ́ɔj′) N milit. company.

นายร้อยตรี (นาย, คน) naajrɔ́ɔjtrii′ (naaj′, khon′)
N 1. second lieutenant. T 2. Lieutenant--.

นายร้อยโท (นาย, คน) naajrɔ́ɔjthoo′ (naaj′, khon′)
N 1. first lieutenant. T 2. Lieutenant--.

นายร้อยเอก (นาย, คน) naajrɔ́ɔjʔèeg′ (naaj′,
khon′) N 1. (army) captain. T 2. Captain--.

ในร้อย najrɔ́ɔj′ (so and so much) in a hundred,
out of a hundred.

o สิบในร้อย sìb′najrɔ́ɔj′ ten in a hundred, ten
out of a hundred.

ใบละร้อย (ใบ) baj′larɔ́ɔj′ (baj′) N a hundred-
tical bill.

ร้อยตรี (นาย, คน) rɔ́ɔjtrii′ (naaj′, khon′) N 1.
second lieutenant. T 2. Lieutenant--. →Short-
ened form of นายร้อยตรี.

ร้อยโท (นาย, คน) rɔ́ɔjthoo′ (naaj′, khon′) N

1. first lieutenant. T 2. Lieutenant --. →Short-
ened form of นายร้อยโท.

ร้อยแปด rɔ́ɔjpὲɛd/ idiom. various, all sorts of,
many different kinds of: "a hundred and eight."
→Dist. ร้อยเอ็ดเจ็ด-.

ร้อยละ (...) (1) rɔ́ɔj/lá?/; (2) rɔ́ɔj/laʔ... N
1. percentage. 2. (so and so much) percent.

o คิดเป็นร้อยละ khíd/-penrɔ́ɔj/la?/ figure (it)
by percentage, think in terms of percentages,
think of it percentagewise.

o จำนวนร้อยละ (...) (1) camnuan/-rɔ́ɔj/lá?/;
(2) camnuan/-rɔ́ɔj/laʔ... N 1. percentage.
2. (so and so much) percent.

ร้อยห้า rɔ́ɔjhâa/ one hundred and five.

ร้อยเอก (นาย,คน) rɔ́ɔj?èeg/ (naaj/,khon/) N
1. (army) captain. T 2. Captain --. →Shortened
form of นายร้อยเอก.

ร้อยเอ็ด rɔ́ɔj?èd/ Nm 1. one hundred and one.
pN 2. Rɔi-et, a township in NE Thailand.

ร้อยเอ็ดเจ็ดหัวเมือง rɔ́ɔj?èd/cèd/hŭamyaŋ/
idiom. countless provinces, all over the country. →Dist. ร้อยแปด which is not used with
places.

โรงเรียนนายร้อย rooŋrian/naajrɔ́ɔj/ N cadet
academy.

เหยียบร้อย jìabrɔ́ɔj/ as many as a hundred, close
to a hundred.

ร้อย ๒ rɔ́ɔj/ V to string, thread.

o ร้อยเข็ม rɔ́ɔjkhĕm/ to thread a needle.

o ร้อยเชือกเข้าหลอด rɔ́ɔjchŷag/khâwlɔ̀ɔd/ to
thread a string through a tube, insert a string
into a tube.

เย็บปักถักร้อย jébpàg/thàgrɔ́ɔj/ V 1. to do needlework. N 2. needlework.

ร้อยกรอง rɔ́ɔjkrɔɔŋ/ V 1. to string (e.g. flowers
into a garland, beads into a necklace, thus
making a thing of beauty). 2. to compose verse.
N 3. verse.

ร้อยแก้ว rɔ́ɔjkɛ̂ɛw/ N prose.

เรียบร้อย rîabrɔ́ɔj/ V 1. to be neat, tidy, in good
order, in good shape. 2. to be ready, all set.
3. to be polite, well-mannered.

ร้อยเอ็ด rɔ́ɔj?èd/ pN Rɔi-et, a township in NE
Thailand.

ร้อแร้ rɔ̂ɔrɛ́ɛ/ V to be near death, about to die,
dying.

ระ rá?/ V to strike, hit, touch one after the other
(often superficially).

ตึกระฟ้า (หลัง) tỳg/-rá?/fáa/ (lăŋ/) N skyscraper.

ระกา rakaa/ N (Year of the) Chicken, Cock. →The
complete list of the cyclical years is given
under ปี.

ระกำ ๑ (ลูก,ผล) rakam/ (lûug/,phŏn/) N a kind
of red, edible fruit. ต้น-- (ต้น) a type of
palm (which bears the above fruit).

น้ำมันระกำ námman/rakam/ N oil of wintergreen.

ระกำ ๒ rakam/ N sorrow, grief, suffering, trouble.

ระกำใจ rakam/caj/ V to be grieved and hurt.

ระเกะระกะ rakè?/rakà?/ V eleg. to be scattered
about, lying around in a disorderly manner.

ระคน rakhon/ V eleg. to be mixed, combined,
blended.

ระคาย rakhaaj/ V eleg. to be irritating, rough,
unpleasant.

ระแคะระคาย rakhé?/rakhaaj/ N hint, inkling,
intimation.

ระฆัง (ใบ,ลูก) rakhaŋ/ (baj/,lûug/) N bell (esp.
a big one). →Dist. กระดิ่ง.

หอระฆัง (หอ) hɔ̌ɔ/rakhaŋ/ (hɔ̌ɔ/) N bell tower.

ระงม raŋom/ V to be loud, noisy.

ระงับ raŋáb/ V 1. to stop, halt, hold up (e.g. an
activity, action). 2. to curb, hold back, suppress, repress.

ระงับใจ raŋáb/caj/ V 1. to restrain oneself, keep
oneself from doing something. 2. to suppress
one's feelings or desires.

ระดม radom/ V to mobilize, gather, assemble.

ระดมพล radom/phon/ V to mobilize troops.

ระดมยิง radom/jiŋ/ V to fire a volley, concentrate a heavy fire (on).

ระดับ radàb/ N level.

ระดับตา radàb/taa/ N eye level.

ระดับน้ำ radàb/náam/ N water level.

ระดับน้ำทะเล radàb/náamthalee/ N sea level.

ระดับสูง radàb/sǔuŋ/ N high altitude; high level.

ระดู raduu/ N com. menstruation, menses. →Syn.
ประจำเดือน euphem. →Comp. ฤดู.

ผ้าซับระดู (ผืน,อัน) phâa/-sáb/raduu/ (phŷyn/,

ʔan′) N sanitary napkin (e.g. Kotex).

ระทม rathom′ V to be broken-hearted, grief-stricken.

ระนอง ranɔɔŋ pN Ranong, a township in S Thailand.

ระนาด ๑ (เครื่อง) ranâad′ (khrɨ̂aŋ′) N xylophone.

ระนาด ๒, ระเน-- ranâad′, ranee′ranâad′ lying on top of one another, left in a mess, turned into a shambles.

ระนาว ranaaw′ N line, row. →Syn. ตับ, แถว, แนว.

เป็นระนาว penranaaw′ 1. in a line, in a row. 2. in large numbers.

ระเนระนาด. See ระนาด ๒.

ระบบ ·rabòb′ N eleg. system, form, custom, manner.

ระบม rabom′ V to be stiff and sore, painful (all over).

ระบอบ (ระบอบ) rabɔ̀ɔb′ (rabɔ̀ɔb′) N eleg. system, order.

ระบอบการปกครอง rabɔ̀ɔb′kaanpògkhrɔɔŋ′ N eleg. form of goverment, system of government.

ระบอบประชาธิปไตย rabɔɔb′-prachaa′thípataj′ eleg. the democratic form of government, the democratic system, democracy.

ระบอบเศรษฐกิจ rabɔ̀ɔb′-sèed′thakìd′ eleg. economic system.

ระบาด rabàad′ V to spread, extend far and wide in all directions, be dispersed.

โรคระบาด (โรค, ชนิด) rôog′rabàad′ (rôog′, chaníd′) N epidemic.

ระบาย rabaaj′ V 1. to drain, let out, release. 2. to paint.

ยาระบาย jaarabaaj′ N laxative.

ระบายสี rabaajsǐi′ V to color, paint (a picture).

ระบำ rabam′ N dance (i.e. one which is a performance).

จับระบำ càb′rabam′ V to dance (ref. to a group performance on stage).

เต้นระบำ tên′rabam′ V to dance (as a solo or group performance).

นางระบำ (คน) naaŋrabam′ (khon′) N dancing girl, (woman) dancer.

ระบำโป๊ rabam′póo′ N colloq. burlesque show, strip tease.

ระบือ rabyy′ V eleg. 1. to spread, diffuse. 2. to be renowned, well-known.

ระบุ rabù′ V to specify, mention specifically.

ระเบิด rabə̀əd′ N 1. bomb. V 2. to explode, burst, blast. การ-- explosion.

ทิ้งระเบิด thíŋ′rabə̀əd′ V to bomb.

ทุ่นระเบิด thûnrabə̀əd′ N explosive underwater mine.

ระเบิดปรมาณู (ลูก) rabə̀əd′paramaanuu′ N atomic bomb.

ระเบิดเวลา (ลูก) rabə̀əd′weelaa′ (lûug′) N time bomb.

ระเบิดไฮโดรเยน (ลูก) rabə̀əd′hajdroojên′* (lûug′) N hydrogen bomb. [ไฮโดรเยน f. Eng.]

ลูกระเบิด (ลูก) lûugrabə̀əd′ (lûug′) N bomb.

ระเบียง (ระเบียง) rabiaŋ′ (rabiaŋ′) N porch, veranda.

ระเบียงบ้าน rabiaŋbâan′ N porch, veranda.

ระเบียบ (ระเบียบ, ข้อ) rablab′ (rablab′, khɔ̂ɔ′) N 1. order (as of things arranged in a sequence). 2. system, form (as of government). 3. rules, regulations.

เป็นระเบียบ penrablab′ 1. to be orderly, in good order. 2. to be well-arranged, well-organized.

เป็นระเบียบเรียบร้อย penrablab′rîabrɔ́ɔj′ V 1. to be ship-shape, in good order, fine. 2. to be well arranged, well organized.

มีระเบียบ miirablab′ to be neat, well-organized, systematic, in good order. อย่าง-- in good order, in an orderly manner.

ระเบียบการ (ฉบับ, เล่ม) rablabkaan′ (chabàb′, lêm′) N 1. (printed) information (e.g. about the policies and general nature of a club, school, society, institution). 2. schedule, prospectus.

ระเบียบการประชุม rablab′kaanprachum′ N com. agenda. →Syn. ระเบียบวาระ eleg.

ระเบียบวาระ rablab′waa′rá′ N eleg. agenda. →Syn. ระเบียบการประชุม com.

ระเบียบวินัย rablab′wínaj′ N order and discipline.

ระมัด in ระมัดระวัง ramád′rawaŋ′ V elab. to be cautious, heedful, careful. ความ-- caution, care, carefulness.

ระยอง rajɔɔŋ′ pN Rayọng, a township in SE Thailand.

ระยะ rajá?′ N 1. distance. 2. period, stage (as of development), interval (of space or time). C 3. clf. for periods, stages, intervals.

ช้วระยะ chûarajá?′ interval of space or time.

ในระยะ najrajá?′ within (a period of time, a range of distance).

เป็นระยะ ๆ penrajá?′rajá?′ at regular intervals (of space or time), at a constant rate.

ระยะใกล้ rajá?′klâj′ N short distance, short range.

ระยะไกล rajá?′klaj′ N long distance, long range.

ระยะเดิน rajá?′dəən′ walking distance.

ระยะทาง rajá?′thaaŋ′ N distance.

ระยะเวลา rajá?′weelaa′ N interval, period of time.

o ช้วระยะเวลา chûarajá?′weelaa′ (for) a period of, (for) a time interval of.

o ในระยะเวลา najrajá?′weelaa′ within (a length of time).

ระยับ rajáb′ sV glitteringly, glisteningly.

ระย้า rajáa′ V 1. to be pendent, hanging (as ornaments, decorations). N 2. pendant, tassel; hanging ornament or decoration.

ระยำ rajam′ V derog. to be evil, base, vile.

ระโยง (สาย) rajooŋ′ (sǎaj′) N stay, guy.

ระโยงระยาง (สาย) rajooŋ′rajaaŋ′ (sǎaj′) N elab. 1. rigging, stay, guy. 2. a large number of strings, ropes, wires, cables, connected or suspended in a disorderly fashion.

ระรวย raruaj′ eleg. rM 1. modifier meaning "lightly, softly," used with หอม "fragrant," พัด "to blow." V 2. to be faint, light (of a pleasant odor).

ระราน rá?′raan′ V 1. to oppress, browbeat, bully. 2. to be aggressive.

ระรื่น rarŷyn′ V lit. 1. to be pleasant, sweet (of sounds, odors). 2. to be happy. sV 3. sweetly. 4. happily.

ระเริง (อยู่ใน, อยู่กับ) rarəəŋ′(jùunajɔ, jùukaɔ) V lit. eleg. to be captivated (by), fascinated (by), abandoned (to), excessively given to the enjoy-

ment (of)(e.g. a moth fluttering around a light, a man given to sinful pleasures).

หลงระเริง(อยู่ใน, อยู่กับ) lǒŋ′rarəəŋ′(jùunajɔ, jùukaɔ) idem (with the added element of going astray, falling into this condition).

ระลอก (ลูก) ralɔɔg′ (lûug′) N ripple, wave. →Also ละลอก.

ระลึก(ถึง) ralýg′(thŷŋɔ) V to recall, remember, recollect, think (of). →Also รำลึก.

ของที่ระลึก khɔɔŋ′thîiralýg′ N souvenir.

วันที่ระลึก wan′thîiralýg′ N memorial day.

สมุดที่ระลึก (เล่ม) samùd′thîiralýg′ (lêm′) N memorial volume, book, or notebook given as a souvenir on a special occasion.

ระวัง rawaŋ′ V to take care, be careful; to beware of, watch out for, be careful of.

คอยระวัง khɔɔjrawaŋ′ to keep watching out, keep on the alert.

ระมัดระวัง ramád′rawaŋ′ V elab. to be cautious, heedful, careful. ความ-- caution, care, carefulness.

ระวังตัว rawaŋ′tua′ 1. to be on the alert, on guard. 2. to take care of oneself.

ระแวดระวัง rawɛɛd′rawaŋ′ V elab. to keep a careful watch for; to be extremely cautious.

ระวาง rawaaŋ′ N tonnage.

ค่าระวาง khâarawaaŋ′ N freight charges.

o ค่าระวางบรรทุก khâarawaaŋ′banthúg′ N eleg. shipping charge, freightage.

ระวางขับน้ำ rawaaŋ′khàbnáam′ N displacement (of a ship).

ระแวง rawɛɛŋ′ V to mistrust, suspect, doubt. ความ-- mistrust, suspicion.

ระแวด in ระแวดระวัง rawɛɛd′rawaŋ′ V elab. to keep a careful watch for; to be extremely cautious.

ระส่ำระสาย rasàm′rasǎaj′ V to be scattered in disorder, dispersed, in confusion, in a state of unrest. ความ-- unrest, disorder, confusion, disunity, dispersion.

ระหง rahǒŋ′ V eleg. to be tall and slender.

ระหว่าง rawàaŋ′ N 1. interval (of space or time). C 2. period, interval (of time). Pp 3. between, among, during. →In mng. 2 occurs with demonstratives, but not with numerals.

ในระหว่าง najrawàaŋ/ 1. between, among. 2. in the midst of, during.

ระหว่าง...กับ... rawàaŋɔ...kaɔ... between (such and such a place or time) and (another place or time).

ระหว่างชาติ rawàaŋchâad/ international.

ระหว่างประเทศ rawàaŋprathêed/ international.

o กฎหมายระหว่างประเทศ kòdmǎaj/rawàaŋpraɔthêed/ N international law.

ระหัด (เครื่อง) rahàd/ (khrɯ̂aŋ/) N 1. noria, irrigation treadmill; irrigating pump. 2. cotton gin.

ระเหย rahə̌əj/ V to evaporate, vaporize, volatilize. →Occasionally also ละเหย.

ระแหง ๑ rahɛ̌ɛŋ/ earth that is dried and cracked.
ทั่วทุกหัวระแหง thûa/-thúghǔa/rahɛ̌ɛŋ/ everywhere.

ระแหง ๒ rahɛ̌ɛŋ/ pN Rahæng, an amphoe in čhangwat Tak.

ระโหย rahǒoj/ V to feel tired, weary.

ระอา raʔaa/ V to be tired, bored, fed up.
เอือมระอา ʔyam/raʔaa/ V elab. to be tired, fed up.

ระอิดระอา raʔìd/raʔaa/ V elab. to be tired, bored, fed up.

ระอุ raʔù?/ V 1. to be very hot. 2. to be thoroughly done, cooked through (as of rice).

รัก ๑ rág/ V to love. ความ-- love. คน-- lover.

คู่รัก (คน) khûurág/ (khon/) N lovers, sweethearts; (one's) sweetheart.

จงรัก coŋrág/ V to be loyal, faithful (to).

ที่รัก thîirág/ dear, beloved.

น่ารัก nâarág/ V to be lovable, lovely, attractive, charming, cute. ความ-- loveliness, lovableness, attractiveness.

ฝากรัก(ไว้กับ) fàag/rág/(wájkaɔ) V to propose, declare one's love, give one's heart (to).

พิษรัก phídrág/ N the poisoning effect of love (as when unrequited or tainted with jealousy).

ไฟรัก fajrág/ N fire, flame of love (i.e. love which burns intensely like a fire).

ยอดรัก (คน) jɔ̂ɔdrág/ (khon/) N the dearest (one), best-beloved (sp. to or about someone

of the opposite sex).

รักใคร่กัน rágkhrâj/kan to love one another, love each other.

รักชาติ rágchâad/ V to be patriotic. ความ-- patriotism.

รักแรก rágrɛ̂ɛg/ N first love.

เลือกที่รักมักที่ชัง lŷag/thîirág/-mág/thîichaŋ/ V elab. colloq. to show partiality, show favoritism, play favorites; to be partial in one's likes and dislikes.

สาวคนรัก (คน) sǎaw/khonrág/ (khon) N a man's sweetheart.

หลงรัก lǒŋrág/ V to be madly in love with, infatuated with, crazy over (someone).

รัก ๒, ต้นรัก (ต้น) rág/, tônrág/ (tôn/) N 1. a flowering shrub. 2. a tree yielding black lacquer.

รักบี้ rágbîi/ N rugby. [f. Eng.]

รักเร่ rágrêe/ N dahlia. ดอก-- (ดอก) dahlia (the flower). ต้น-- (ต้น) dahlia (the plant).

รักแร้ (ข้าง, รักแร้) rágrɛ́ɛ/ (khâaŋ/, rágrɛ́ɛ/) N armpit.

รักษา rágsǎa/ V 1. to watch over, take care of, care for, keep, rear. 2. to treat (e.g. an illness). การ-- care, maintenance, preservation; cure, remedy.

ยารักษาโรค (ขนาน) jaarágsǎa/rôog/ (khanǎan/) N medicine, medicinal drug.

รักษาการ rágsǎakaan/ V to be on guard, on duty, in charge.

o ยามรักษาการ (คน) jaam/rágsǎakaan/ (khon/) N guard, sentry.

o รักษาการแทน rágsǎakaan/thɛɛn/ to act temporarily in place of. ผู้-- acting--; an official who serves temporarily, or as a substitute for another (in an administrative capacity).

รักษาคำพูด rágsǎa/khamphûud/ to keep (one's) word.

รัง ๑, ต้นรัง (ต้น) raŋ/, tônraŋ/ (tôn/) N a kind of timber tree. ไม้-- (ต้น, แผ่น) timber or wood of same.

รัง ๒ (รัง) raŋ/ (raŋ/) N nest.

รังไข่ (รัง) raŋkhàj/ (raŋ/) N ovary.

รังดุม (รัง) raŋdum/ (raŋ/) N buttonhole. →Also รังกระดุม.

รังผึ้ง (รัง) raŋphŷŋ′ (raŋ′) N 1. beehive. 2. bee's nest.

รัง ๓ raŋ′ Pp only, for, only for, only to.

o รังคนนินทา raŋ′khonninthaa′ only for others to slander.

รังแต่ raŋ′tɛ̀ɛⲟ Pp only to, only for.

รัง ๔ in the following entries.

รุงรัง ruŋraŋ′ V to be untidy, messy, unkempt, disorderly, disheveled.

เรื้อรัง rýaraŋ′ V to be chronic.

รั้ง ráŋ′ V 1. to pull. 2. to delay, hold back. 3. to hold (a position). 4. to control, govern.

รั้งท้าย ráŋtháaj′ V to be the last (e.g. in line or in rank).

รั้งเมือง ráŋmyaŋ′ to govern a city or state.

รั้งรอ, รอรั้ง ráŋrɔɔ′, rɔɔráŋ′ V to hesitate, delay, prolong.

หยักรั้ง jàgráŋ′ V (clothing) to be pulled high, hiked up, gathered up (as of a skirt, trouser legs). NOTE. According to some speakers this expression implies that the lower edge of the garment is uneven, or has one portion pulled up higher than another.

รังเกียจ raŋkìad′ V to mind, dislike, be prejudiced against, have an aversion to. ความ-- objection, aversion, dislike.

o น่ารังเกียจ nâa′raŋkìad′ V 1. to be objecttionable, repugnant, offensive. 2. to arouse aversion.

รังแก raŋkɛɛ′ V to pick on, molest, bully, persecute.

รังควาน raŋkhwaan′ V 1. to disturb, annoy. 2. to raid, attack, harass by violent means.

รังแค in ขี้-- khîiraŋkhɛɛ′ N com. dandruff. →Syn. ขี้หัว colloq.

รังสี raŋsǐi′ N ray, light, radiation.

กัมมันตภาพรังสี kamman′taphâab′-raŋsǐi′ N phys. radioactivity.

กัมมันตรังสี kamman′taraŋsǐi′ phys. radioactive.

รัชกาล rádchakaan′ N 1. reign. 2. the reign of.

รัชกาลที่ ๕ rádchakaan′thîihâa′ the reign of King Rama V.

รัชทายาท (องค์) rádchathaa′jâad′ (ʔoŋ′) N roy. royal heir to the throne.

รัฐ (รัฐ) rád′ (rád′) N state, nation. NOTE. When used as the first member of certain cpds., this word has the pronunciation rád′thaⲟ. Such cpds. are treated below as independent dictionary entries.

เจ้าหน้าที่ของรัฐ câwnâathîi′khɔ̌ɔŋrád′ (a) government official, (an) official of the government.

สยามรัฐ sajǎamrád′ N "The Siamese Nation," name of a newspaper published in Bangkok. Transliterated by the publisher as "Siam Rath."

สหปาลีรัฐ sahà?′paalirád′ N united states.

สหรัฐ sahàrád′ N federated states.

รัฐธรรมนูญ rád′thathammanuun′ N constitution (of a nation).

รัฐนิยม (ฉบับ) rád′thanijom′ (chabàb′) N state convention or code of conduct (issued for the public during World War II).

รัฐบาล (ชุด) rádthabaan′ (chúd′) N the government. →Dist. การปกครอง under ปกครอง.

ทำเนียบรัฐบาล (แห่ง , ทำเนียบ) thamnîab′rádⲟthabaan′ (hɛ̀ŋ′, thamnîab′) N the prime minister's office; the government office.

รัฐบาลกลาง rádthabaan′klaaŋ′ N central government.

รัฐบาลท้องถิ่น rádthabaan′thɔ́ɔŋthìn′ N local government.

รัฐบาลผสม rádthabaan′phasǒm′ N coalition government.

โรงเรียนรัฐบาล (โรงเรียน , แห่ง) rooŋrian′rádⲟthabaan′ (rooŋrian′, hɛ̀ŋ′) N government school, public school.

องค์การรัฐบาล (องค์การ , แห่ง) ʔoŋkaan′rádthaⲟbaan′ (ʔoŋkaan′, hɛ̀ŋ′) N (a) government organization.

รัฐบุรุษ (นาย , ท่าน) rád′thaburùd′ (naaj′, thân′) N eleg. statesman.

รัฐประศาสน์ rád′thaprasàad′ N eleg. government administration (as an activity).

รัฐประศาสโนบาย (อัน , อย่าง) rád′thaprasǎa′ⲟsanoo′baaj′ (ʔan′, jàaŋ′) N eleg. administative policy of the government.

รัฐประหาร (ครั้ง) rád′thaprahǎan′ (khráŋ′) N eleg. coup d'état.

รัฐมนตรี (คน , ท่าน) rádthamontrii′ (khon′, thân′)

N (a) minister (of the government). →Abbrev. ร.ม.ต.

คณะรัฐมนตรี (คณะ) kháná?/rádthamontrii/ (kháɔ ná?/) N (the) cabinet, council of ministers.

นายกรัฐมนตรี (นาย,คน) naajóg/rádthamontrii/ (naaj/, khon/) N prime minister; premier.

o สำนักนายกรัฐมนตรี sămnág/-naajóg/rádthaɔ montrii/ N Office of the President of the Council of Ministers.

รัฐมนตรีช่วยว่าการ (คน,นาย) rádthamontrii/ɔ chûajwâakaan/ (khon/, naaj/) N deputy minister (of the government).

รัฐมนตรีลอย (คน,นาย) rádthamontrii/lɔɔj/ (khon/, naaj/) N minister without portfolio.

รัฐมนตรีว่าการ (คน,นาย) rádthamontrii/wâaɔ kaan/ (khon/, naaj/) N minister (of the government).

รัฐมนตรีสั่งราชการ (คน,นาย) rádthamontrii/ɔ sàŋrâadchakaan/ (khon/, naaj/) N acting minister (of the government).

รัฐศาสตร์ rádthasàad/ N political science.

รัฐสภา rádthasaphaa/ N parliament, congress.

รัด rád/ V 1. to bind, tie, fasten (something) tightly. 2. to be tight (as of garments).

กระทัดรัด krathádrád/ V to be well-proportioned and somewhat small in size; to be compact; to be short and to the point; to be well-fitting.

กอดรัด kɔ̀ɔd/rád/ V to embrace, hug.

ยางรัด (เส้น) jaaŋrád/ (sên/) N rubber band.

รวบรัด rûabrád/ V to cut short, make brief.

รัดกุม rádkum/ V 1. to fit well (of clothes). 2. to be airtight, i.e. without any loopholes (as of rules).

เร่งรัด rêŋrád/ V 1. to expedite, hasten, speed up, urge (someone) on, hurry. 2. to be urgent, pressing.

รัตน์,รัตน- (เม็ด) rád/, rádtanáɔ-, rádtaná?/ (méd/) N eleg. jewel, gem.

รัตนตรัย rád/tanátraj/ N the Three Gems (of Buddhism, viz. Buddha, his teaching, his disciples). →Also พระ--.

o คุณพระศรีรัตนตรัย khun/-phrásĭi/rád/tanátraj/ the Virtues of the Three Gems.

รัตนโกสินทร์ rád/tanákoosĭn/ pN Bangkok (official

name). กรุง-- idem. →See พระนคร.

รั้น rán/ V to be stubborn.

รับ ráb/ V 1. to receive, accept, take on. 2. to eat (something); shortened form of รับประทาน. เครื่อง-- (radio) receiver.

ขอรับ khɔ̌ɔráb/ Pt eleg. def. m. sp. 1. particle used as the final element of statements and questions. 2. Yes! (in answer to a question). 3. particle placed after name or kin term to address or call the attention of someone. 4. Yes? (used as a reply when called or spoken to). For examples, see ครับ. →Syn. ครับ def. m. sp.

ขอรับอนุญาต khɔ̌ɔráb/?ànújâad/, khɔ̌ɔ/-ráb/?ànúɔ jâad/ to apply for permission.

ขานรับ khăan/ráb/ V to answer (a call), to call in reply.

เข้ารับตำแหน่ง khâwráb/tamnɛ̀ŋ/ to assume an official position.

เครื่องรับวิทยุ khrŷaŋráb/wídthajú?/ N (radio) receiver. →Also เครื่องรับ.

ได้รับ dâjráb/ V 1. to receive, get, obtain. 2. to have received. →See cross reference.

ต้อนรับ tɔ̂ɔnráb/ V to welcome, receive (e.g. guests).

ตอบรับ tɔ̀ɔbráb/ V to say yes, answer in the affirmative; to accept.

ใบรับเงิน (ใบ) bajráb ŋən/ (baj/) N receipt.

ไปรับ pajráb/ V to go meet (a person), to go get (a thing).

ฝ่ายรับ fàajráb/ N the defense, the side on the defensive (in sports, war); taker, receiver.

ยอมรับ jɔɔmráb/ V 1. to admit, concede. 2. to accept, agree to.

รองรับ rɔɔŋráb/ V to catch (smthg.) in a container placed underneath for the purpose.

รับกับ ráb/kaɔ 1. to match. 2. be in line with. 3. to become, be becoming to (someone).

รับขวัญ rábkhwăn/ V lit. to caress, kiss.

รับแขก rábkhɛ̀ɛg/ V to receive, welcome, entertain a guest or visitor.

o ห้องรับแขก (ห้อง) hɔ̂ŋ/rábkhɛ̀ɛg/ (hɔ̂ŋ/) N living room.

รับจ้าง rábcâaŋ/ V to take employment, to hire (oneself) out. คน-- employee.

รับช่วง rábchûaŋ′ V to inherit, take over, receive something which has been passed on and is to be harbored or used and often passed on again, (as a tradition, a business, used clothing, a subcontract).

รับใช้ rábcháj′ V to serve, to be a servant, to give service to. คน-- servant, a person who attends to the wants of another person.

รับซื้อ rábsýy′ V to purchase.

รับทราบ rábsâab′ V eleg. 1. to acknowledge. 2. to bear (something) in mind.

รับประกัน ráb′prakan′ V to guarantee, insure, assure.

รับประทาน rábprathaan′ V eleg. to eat (something). →Syn. See กิน com.

o รับประทานอาหาร rábprathaan′/ʔaahǎan′ eleg. to eat. การ-- eating.

o ห้องรับประทานอาหาร (ห้อง) hɔ̂ŋ′-rábprathaan′/ʔaahǎan′ (hɔ̂ŋ′) N eleg. dining room.

รับปาก rábpàag′ V to agree (to), commit oneself (to) (verbally).

รับผิด rábphìd′ V to admit one's guilt or mistake.

รับผิดชอบ rábphìdchɔ̂ɔb′ V to be responsible (for), accept responsibility (for). ความ-- responsibility.

รับฝาก rábfàag′ V to accept taking care of (something for someone). →See ฝาก.

รับมรดก ráb′mɔɔradòg′ V to inherit.

รับมอบหมาย ráb′mɔ̂ɔbmǎaj′ V 1. to accept or receive an assignment, responsibility, transaction. 2. to be in charge, have charge of.

รับมือ rábmyy′ V idiom. to encounter, meet, confront, counteract (usually in a fight or contest involving the hands).

รับรอง rábrɔɔŋ′ V 1. to entertain (guests). 2. to certify, guarantee, vouch; to confirm, sanction, recognize, approve; to sponsor; to second (a motion). การ-- reception; confirmation, recognition; guarantee; sponsorship.

o ใบรับรอง (ใบ) bajrábrɔɔŋ′ (baj′) N certificate.

รับราชการ ráb′râadchakaan′ V to work for the government, serve as a government official.

รับรู้ rábrúu′ V 1. to acknowledge. 2. to take responsibility.

รับเลือก,--ตั้ง ráblŷag′, ráb′lŷagtâŋ′ V to be elected, chosen.

รับไว้ ráb′wáj′ 1. to accept (and keep) (something). 2. to admit (e.g. patients to hospital).

รับสั่ง rábsàŋ′ V roy. 1. to order. 2. to speak, say. N roy. 3. order, command.

รับสารภาพ ráb′sǎaraphâab′ V to confess, plead guilty.

รับหลักการ ráb′làgkaan′ V to accept in principle.

รับเหมา rábmǎw′ V to contract (for work); to accept a contract.

รับอาสา ráb′ʔaasǎa′ V to volunteer.

รายรับ raajráb′ N 1. income. 2. debit.

ริ้ว rua′ V 1. to beat in quick, short strokes (as a drum). 2. to roll (as one's tongue).

รั่ว rûa′ V to leak.

รั่วไหล rûalǎj′ V to leak, leak out (e.g. water; news).

รั้ว (รั้ว) rúa′ (rúa′) N fence.

กั้นรั้ว kânrúa′ V to put up a fence.

ตะเกียงรั้ว (ดวง) takiaŋrúa′ (duaŋ′) N lantern.

รั้วบ้าน (รั้ว) rúabâan′ (rúa′) N fence around a house.

ล้อมรั้ว lɔ́ɔmrúa′ V to fence, put up a fence (around).

รัศมี rásamǐi′ N 1. rays (of light). 2. radius, range.

รัศมีทำการ rásamǐi′thamkaan′ N effective radius, range of operation.

รัษฎากร rásadaa′kɔɔn′ N eleg. national revenue.

รัสเซีย rádsia′ N Russia. [f. Eng.]

โซเวียตรัสเซีย soowîad′rádsia′ N Soviet Russia.

รา ๑ raa′ N 1. mold, fungus. V 2. to break up, disband gradually. 3. to lessen, reduce, abate, subside.

ขึ้นรา khŷnraa′ V to get mildewed, moldy.

รา ๒ in รถรา (คัน) ród′raa′ (khan′) N colloq. vehicles (collectively).

ร่า râa′ 1. cheerfully. 2. openly.

ร่าเริง râareəŋ′ V to be jovial, cheerful, in high spirits.

เร่อร่า rə̂ərâa′ sV intrusively, awkwardly, clumsily.

ร้า in ปลาร้า plaaráa′ N fish preserved with salt

(often having roasted rice mixed with it).

ราก ๑ (ราก) râag´ N 1. root (of a plant). 2.
foundation (of a building).

ฝังราก fǎŋrâag´ V 1. to be founded, rooted. 2.
to take root.

รกราก rógrâag´ N birthplace, domicile, residence.

o ตั้งรกราก tâŋ´rógrâag´ to settle down permanently, take up residence. →Also ฝังรกราก
fǎŋ´rógrâag´.

รากแก้ว (ราก) râagkɛ̂ɛw´ (râag´) N taproot.

รากเง่า râagŋâw´ N 1. root. 2. origin, source.

รากฐาน râagthǎan´ N 1. foundation. 2. basis.
3. secure position or standing (of a person).

รากตึก (ราก) râagtỳg´ (râag´) N foundation of
a building.

o ลงรากตึก loŋ´râagtỳg´ to lay the foundation
of a building.

รากฝอย (ราก, เส้น) râagfɔ̌j´ (râag´, sên´) N
fibrous roots of plants.

ลงหลักปักราก loŋlàg´pàgrâag´ e l a b. to lay the
foundation.

ราก ๒ râag´ V v u l g. to puke, vomit, throw up.
→S y n. See อ้วก c o m.

ไข้รากสาดน้อย khâjrâagsàad´nɔ́ɔj´ N typhoid
fever.

ไข้รากสาดใหญ่ khâjrâagsàad´jàj´ N typhus.

ราค, ราคะ raa´khá?´ N e l e g. lust, sexual desire.

ราคา (ราคา) raakhaa´ (raakhaa´) N price.

กดราคา kòd´raakhaa´ N to underprice.

เกี่ยงราคา kìaŋ´raakhaa´ V to argue over the
price.

ขึ้นราคา khŷn´raakhaa´ V to raise the price.

ตั้งราคา tâŋ´raakhaa´ V to set a price.

ตีราคา tii´raakhaa´ V to name the price, put a
value (on), make a price estimate, appraise.

มีราคา mii´raakhaa´ V to be valuable, precious.

ราคาขายส่ง raakhaa´khǎajsòŋ´ wholesale price.

ราคาตก raakhaa´tòg´ price to fall, drop off.

ราคาถูก raakhaa´thùug´ 1. low price. 2. to be
cheap, inexpensive, low-priced.

ราคาแพง raakhaa´phɛɛŋ´ 1. a high price. 2.
to be expensive, high-priced.

ราคาย่อมเยา raakhaa´jɔ̂mjaw´ 1. a low or mod-

erate price. 2. priced cheaply or moderately.
→Often also spelled ราคาย่อมเยาว์.

ลดราคา lód´raakhaa´ V to reduce the price;
to give a discount; to put on sale; to have a sale.

เสียราคา sǐa´raakhaa´ V to go down in price,
decrease in value.

หมดราคา mòd´raakhaa´ V to become worthless,
valueless.

ราคี raakhii´ N l i t. defect, flaw, blemish, stain,
impurity.

ราง ๑ (ราง) raaŋ´ (raaŋ´) N 1. rail, track. 2.
groove, trough.

เครื่องราง (ชิ้น) khrŷaŋraaŋ´ (chín´) N amulet.

ตกราง tògraaŋ´ V to be derailed.

รถราง (คัน) ródraaŋ´ (khan´) N streetcar,
trolley car, tram.

รางรถ (ราง) raaŋród´ (raaŋ´) N track of a
railroad or streetcar.

ราง ๒ raaŋ´ V to be vague, indistinct, blurred
(esp. of a mental image). →Sometimes spelled
ลาง.

ราง ๆ raaŋraaŋ´ V 1. to be vague, indistinct.
sV 2. indistinctly.

ร่าง (ร่าง) râaŋ´ (râaŋ´) N 1. shape, structure.
2. e l e g. body. V 3. to make a draft, sketch,
outline. →S y n. 2. ตัว c o m.

ต้นร่าง (ฉบับ) tônrâaŋ´ (chabàb´) N original
writing, manuscript.

ร่างกาย (ร่าง) râaŋkaaj´ (râaŋ´) N e l e g.
the body.

o ทำร้ายร่างกาย thamráaj´râaŋkaaj´ V to assault,
do bodily harm.

ร่างพระราชบัญญัติ râaŋ´phrárâad´chabanjàd´ N
1. bill, proposed legislation. V 2. to draft a bill.

รูปร่าง rûubrâaŋ´ N appearance, form, figure,
shape.

เรือนร่าง ryanrâaŋ´ N e l e g. (human) body,
figure, form.

ร้าง ráaŋ´ V to be deserted, abandoned, uninhabited,
unoccupied.

รกร้าง rógráaŋ´ V to be deserted, desolate,
disorderly and deserted, neglected and uninhabited.

เริดร้าง rə̂əd´ráaŋ´ V 1. to be neglected, forsaken,

abandoned. 2. to be separated (e.g. of husband and wife).

เลิกร้าง lɤ̂ɤg'ráaŋ' V to divorce, abandon.

หย่าร้าง jàa'ráaŋ' V to divorce.

หักร้างถางพง hàgráaŋ'thǎaŋphoŋ' V elab. colloq. 1. to clear land. 2. to clear a path (e.g. through the jungle).

รางวัล (รางวัล,อย่าง) raaŋwan' (raaŋwan', jàaŋ') N prize, reward, award.

รางวัลชมเชย raaŋwan'chomchǝǝj' N honorable mention.

ราช-, -ราช râad'chaɔ, râadchaɔ, ɔrâad'. Bound form meaning "king, royal" as in the derivatives below. NOTE. Place names beginning in ราช- are listed as independent entries.

จอมราช cɔɔm'râad' N lit. king.

ประเทศราช prathêed'sarâad' N eleg. colony, dependency. →Syn. เมืองขึ้น com.

พระราช- phrárâad'chaɔ. Bound form placed in front of words denoting actions, decisions, belongings, etc. of the king or other royal personages of the highest rank. May best be translated "royal" in English.

พระราชกฤษฎีกา (ฉบับ) phrárâad'chakrìdsadiiɔ kaa' (chabàb') N roy. royal decree.

พระราชดำรัส phrárâad'chadamràd' N roy. royal speech (speech made by the king).

พระราชทาน phrárâad'chathaan' V roy. to give, present, grant, confer. →Syn. See ให้.

พระราชบัญญัติ (ฉบับ) phrárâad'chabanjàd' (chaɔ bàb') N law, act.

พระสังฆราช phrásǎŋ'kharâad' N chief of all the Buddhist priests in the country, Buddhist supreme patriarch.

ราชการ râadchakaan' N 1. government service. 2. government job.

o กึ่งราชการ kɯ̀ŋ'râadchakaan' semiofficial.

o ข้าราชการ (นาย,คน) khâarâadchakaan' (naaj', khon') N government official.

o ข้าราชการปกครอง (นาย,คน) khâarâadchaɔ kaan'pògkhrɔɔŋ' (naaj', khon') N government official (esp. an administrative or law enforcement official).

o ข้าราชการพลเรือน (นาย,คน) khâarâadchaɔ

kaan'phonlaryan' (naaj', khon') N civil employee.

o ทางราชการ thaaŋrâadchakaan' 1. official(ly). 2. colloq. the government, the authorities. →Cf. ทางบ้าน.

o ผู้ว่าราชการ (คน,ท่าน) phûu'wâarâadchakaan' (khon', thân') N governor, commissioner.

o ผู้สำเร็จราชการ (ท่าน) phûusǎmrèd'râadchaɔ kaan' (thân') N 1. king's regent. 2. viceroy (esp. in former times the viceroy of India).

o ราชการทหาร râadchakaan'thahǎan' N military service.

o ราชการส่วนกลาง râadchakaan'sùanklaaŋ' N central government service.

o ราชการส่วนท้องถิ่น râadchakaan'sùanthɔ́ɔŋthìn' N municipal government service, local government service.

o ราชการส่วนภูมิภาค râadchakaan'sùanphuumiɔ phâag' N provincial government service.

o วันหยุดราชการ (วัน) wanjùd'râadchakaan' (wan') N official holiday.

o ว่าราชการ wâa'râadchakaan' V to administer the affairs of the state. ผู้-- governor, commissioner.

ราชทัณฑ์ râad'chathan' N eleg. official punishment.

o กรมราชทัณฑ์ krom'râadchathan' N Penitentiary Department.

ราชทูต (คน,นาย) râadchathûud' (khon', naaj') N royal envoy.

o อัครราชทูต (คน,นาย) ʔàg'kharâadchathûud' (khon', naaj') N minister (esp. one who is the head of a delegation).

o เอกอัครราชทูต (คน,นาย,ท่าน) ʔèeg'ʔàg'khaɔ râadchathûud' (khon', naaj', thân') N ambassador.

ราชธานี (แห่ง) râadchathaa'nii' (hɛ̀ŋ') N eleg. the capital (city). →Syn. เมืองหลวง com.

ราชนาวี râadchanaa'wii' N royal navy.

ราชบัณฑิต (นาย) râad'chabandìd' (naaj') N member of the Royal Academy.

o ราชบัณฑิตสถาน râad'chabandìd'sathǎan' N Royal Academy.

ราชบัลลังก์ râad'chabanlaŋ' N eleg. throne.

ราชพิพิธภัณฑ์ (แห่ง) râad/chaphiphíd/thaphan/ (hὲŋ/) N Royal Museum (in Bangkok).

ราชวงค์ (ราชวงค์) râadchawoŋ/ (râadchawoŋ/) N dynasty.

o หม่อมราชวงค์ mɔ̀mrâadchawoŋ/ N 1. royal great-grandchild. T 2. title used before the first name of same. →Abbrev. ม.ร.ว.

ราชวงค์านุวงค์ (องค์,พระองค์) râad/chawoŋɔ sɑ̌a/núwoŋ/ (ʔoŋ/,phráʔoŋ/) N royalty; member of the royal family.

ราชวัง (แห่ง) râadchawaŋ/ (hὲŋ/) N royal palace.

o พระบรมมหาราชวัง (แห่ง) phrábɔrommahɑ̌aɔ râadchawaŋ/ (hὲŋ/) N eleg. the grand palace.

ราชสมบัติ râad/chasɔ̌mbàd/ N throne, kingdom.

o ครองราชสมบัติ khrɔɔŋrâad/chasɔ̌mbàd/ V to reign.

o สละราชสมบัติ salàʔ/-râad/chasɔ̌mbàd/ V to abdicate.

o เสวยราชสมบัติ sawɔ̌əj/râad/chasɔ̌mbàd/ V to reign.

ราชสำนัก râad/chasɑ̌mnág/ N royal court, household.

ราชสีห์ (ตัว) râadchasǐi/ (tua/) N lion, king lion (in fables).

ราชอาณาจักร râad/chaʔaanaacàg/ N kingdom, empire. →Also พระ--.

สมบูรณาญาสิทธิราช sɔ̌mbuuranaa/jaa/sìdthírâad/ absolute monarchy.

อุปราช (องค์) ʔùbparâad/ (ʔoŋ/) N viceroy.

เอกราช ʔèeg/karâad/ N independence, freedom, liberty.

ราชดำเนิน râad/damnəən/, râad/chadamnəən/ pN Ratdamnoen or Ratchadamnoen (Ave. in Bangkok).

ราชบุรี râad/burii/, râad/chaburii/ pN Ratburi or Ratchaburi, a township in S Thailand.

ราชา (องค์) raachaa/ (ʔoŋ/) N king.

ราชินี raa/chinii/ N queen. →Chiefly in combination with titles, as below.

พระบรมราชินี phrábɔrommaraa/chinii/ N eleg. 1. the supreme queen, highest queen. T 2. Her Majesty the Queen. →Opp. พระบาทสมเด็จ พระเจ้าอยู่หัว the king.

ราด râad/ V to pour over, onto; to top.

เรี่ยราด rîarâad/ V to be scattered all over.

ราตรี raatrii/ N eleg. night. →Syn. คืน com.

ชุดราตรี (ชุด) chúd/raatrii/ (chúd/) N evening dress, evening wear (for both men and women).

ราตรีสวัสดิ์ raatrii/sawàd/ eleg.,obs. Good night.

ราน raan/ V to cut, sever, trim.

รุกราน rúgraan/ V to invade, attack.

o ฝ่ายรุกราน fàaj/rúgraan/ N aggressor.

ร้าน (ร้าน,แห่ง) ráan/ (ráan/,hὲŋ/) N store, shop.

เจ้าของร้าน (คน) câwkhɔ̌oŋráan/ (khon/) N storekeeper, proprietor of a store.

ชาวบ้านร้านตลาด (คน) chaawbâan/-ráan/talàad/ (khon/) elab. colloq. the whole neighborhood.

ร้านกาแฟ ráan/kaafεε/ N coffee-shop.

ร้านขายของ ráan/khǎajkhɔ̌oŋ/ N store, shop.

ร้านขายเครื่องเขียน ráan/khǎajkhrɤ̂aŋkhǐan/ N stationery store.

ร้านขายเครื่องกระป๋อง ráan/khǎajkhrɤ̂aŋkrapɔ̌ŋ/ N grocery store, esp. one selling mostly canned goods.

ร้านขายยา ráan/khǎajjaa/ N drug store, pharmacy.

ร้านขายเสื้อผ้า ráan/khǎajsŷaphâa/ N clothing store.

ร้านขายหนังสือ ráan/khǎajnaŋsɤ̌ɤ/ N book store.

ร้านขายอาหาร ráan/khǎajʔaahǎan/ N restaurant, food stall (selling ready-to-eat food).

ร้านค้า ráankháa/ N store.

ร้านซักผ้า ráan/ságphâa/ N laundry (establishment).

ร้านตัดผม ráan/tàdphǒm/ N barber shop.

ร้านตัดเสื้อ ráan/tàdsŷa/ N tailor shop, dressmaker's.

ร้านอาหาร ráan/ʔaahǎan/ N restaurant, food stall (selling ready-to-eat food). →Comp. ภัตตาคาร eleg.

ห้างร้าน (แห่ง) hâaŋ/ráan/ (hὲŋ/) N stores and shops, commercial establishments.

ออกร้าน ʔɔ̀ɔgráan/ V to set up a temporary stall or shop (esp. in a fair).

ราบ râab/ V to be flat, smooth, level, plain. →Chiefly in compounds.

ทหารราบ (คน) thahǎanrâab/ (khon/) N infantryman.

ที่ราบ thîirâab/ N geog. plain.

o ที่ราบสูง (แห่ง) thîirâabsǔuŋ/ (hὲŋ/) N plateau.

ทุ่งราบ (แห่ง) thûŋrâab/ (hὲŋ/) N open plain
(not used of desert country).

พื้นราบ (อัน, แห่ง) phýynrâab/ (ʔan/, hὲŋ/) N
1. geom. plane. 2. geog. plain.

ราบคาบ râabkhâab/ V 1. to be peaceful, tranquil.
2. to be subdued.

ราบรื่น râabrŷyn/ V 1. to be smooth. 2. to progress smoothly.

ราบเรียบ râabrîab/ V to be smooth, level.

หมอบราบคาบแก้ว mɔ̀ɔbrâab/khâabkɛ̂ɛw/ elab.
colloq. to give in, surrender, yield completely.

ราม in ตึกรามบ้านช่อง tỳgraam/bâanchɔ̂ŋ/ N elab.
colloq. buildings (of all kinds, collectively).

รามเกียรติ์ raammakian/ N Ramakian, a Thai epic
derived from the famous Ramayana epic of India.

ราย (ราย) raaj/ (raaj/) N 1. instance, case (as
"accident case"). 2. issue (as of a newspaper).
3. list, table (usually in compounds). 4. person, party. C 5. clf. for instances, cases;
issues; persons, parties.

o ราย ๒ เดือน raaj/sɔ̌ɔŋdyan/ bimonthly.

o ราย ๓ เดือน raaj/sǎamdyan/ quarterly.

เป็นรายตัว penraaj/tua/ one person at a time,
one by one, individually.

รายการ (รายการ) raajkaan/ (raajkaan/) N
1. list, list of items. 2. item (in a list of
items).

รายงาน raajŋaan/ N 1. report. V 2. to report.

o รายงานข่าว (กระแส,สาย,ฉบับ) (1) raajŋaanↄ
khàaw/; (2) raajŋaan/khàaw/ N 1. news, report
(krasɛ̌ɛ/, sǎaj/, chabàb/). V 2. to report news.

รายจ่าย raajcàaj/ N expenditures, expenses.

รายชื่อ raajchŷy/ N colloq. list of names, roll,
register. →Syn. รายนาม eleg.

o รายชื่ออาหาร raajchŷy/ʔaahǎan/ N menu.

รายเดือน raajdyan/ monthly.

รายได้ raajdâaj/ N income, earnings.

รายนาม raajnaam/ N eleg. list of names, roll,
register. →Syn. รายชื่อ com.

o รายนามผู้แสดง raajnaam/phûusadɛɛŋ/ N
eleg. the cast (in a performance).

รายปักษ์ raajpàg/ fortnightly.

รายปี raajpii/ annual, annually.

รายย่อย raajjɔ̂j/ N 1. minor case. 2. minor

party (e.g. to an agreement).

รายรับ raajráb/ N income; debit.

รายละเอียด raajlaʔìad/ N the details, particulars.

รายวัน raajwan/ N a daily; daily issue (as of a
newspaper).

รายสัปดาห์ raaj/sàbdaa/ a weekly; weekly issue
(as of a newspaper, magazine).

เรียงราย riaŋraaj/ V 1. to be scattered all around.
2. to be lined up; to be arranged in lines.

ร่าย ๑ râaj/ N a kind of Thai poetry.

ร่าย ๒ in ร่ายมนต์ râaj/mon/ V to utter a magic
incantation, formula.

ร่าย ๓ in ร่ายรำ, รำร่าย râajram/, ramrâaj/ V
to dance.

ร้าย ráaj/ V to be fierce, cruel, wicked, bad. →Syn.
ชั่ว, เลว. คน--, ผู้-- criminal, wrongdoer; villain (esp. in a play, movie). →Ant. ดี.

ก่อการร้าย kɔ̀ɔ/kaanráaj/ to make trouble, cause
violence.

o พวกก่อการร้าย phûagkɔ̀ɔ/kaanráaj/ N trouble-
makers, gangsters, saboteurs.

คิดร้าย khídráaj/ V to intend to do harm, to plot
against.

คุ้มดีคุ้มร้าย khúmdii/khúmráaj/ V elab. colloq.
1. to be alternately sane and insane. 2. to be
half crazy, mentally unhinged. 3. to be erratic,
changeable in temper.

เคราะห์ร้าย khrɔ́ʔráaj/ V 1. to be unfortunate,
unlucky. 2. unfortunately, unluckily; it's unfortunate (that). →Ant. เคราะห์ดี.

ดุร้าย dùʔráaj/ V to be ferocious.

ทำร้าย thamráaj/ V eleg. to do harm; to harm.

o ลอบทำร้าย lɔ̂ɔb/thamráaj/ V eleg. to ambush,
attack or assault by surprise.

ประทุษร้าย prathúd/saráaj/ V lit. to harm.

ปองร้าย pɔɔŋráaj/ V lit. to intend to do harm.

ผลร้าย phǒnráaj/ N unfavorable, bad, harmful,
deleterious effect or result.

ฝันร้าย fǎnráaj/ N 1. a bad dream, a nightmare.
V 2. to have a bad dream, a nightmare.

มิดีมิร้าย mídii/míráaj/ V elab. eleg. to be
bad, evil, harmful.

o คิดมิดีมิร้าย khíd/-mídii/míráaj/ elab. eleg.
to have evil intentions.

มุ่งร้ายหมายขวัญ mûŋráaj'-mǎaj'khwǎn' V lit.
elab. eleg. to intend harm, have bad intentions, bear ill will (toward).

โมโหร้าย moohǒo'ráaj' V to be very bad-tempered, susceptible to violent anger.

ร้ายกาจ ráajkàad' V 1. to be fierce, cruel, harsh,
severe. 2. to be wicked.

ร้ายแรง ráajrɛɛŋ' V to be severe, serious, bad
(as of a fire, illness, etc.).

ลางร้าย laaŋráaj' N bad omen.

วายร้าย waajráaj' colloq. devilish. อย่าง--
slang extremely.

ใส่ร้าย sàjráaj' V to smear, slander.

เหล่าร้าย làwráaj' N gangsters, hoodlums.

โหดร้าย hòodráaj' V to be cruel, atrocious.
→Syn. ทารุณ eleg.

ราว ๑ (ราว) raaw' (raaw') N 1. line (e.g. clothes-
line). 2. railing.

ราวบันได raaw'bandaj' N eleg. railing (of a
staircase), banister.

เรื่องราว rɣaŋraaw' N story, account; matter;
happening; case.

วิ่งราว wîŋraaw' V to snatch and run away.

ราว ๒ raaw' V 1. to be about the same, to approximate. qM 2. about, around. →Syn. ประมาณ.

o อายุอานามก็คงราวๆผม ?aajú?'?aanaam kɔŋ
khoŋraawraaw'phǒm'↓ He must be about my
age.

o ราวหกโมง raaw'hògmooŋ' about 6 o'clock,
around 6 o'clock.

ในราว najraaw' about, around.

ราวกับ(ว่า) raaw'ka(wâa')ᴐ eleg. like, as;
as if, as though. →Syn. อย่างกับ com.

ราวจะ raaw'caᴐ AA eleg. as if to, as though.
→Syn. อย่างจะ com.

ร้าว ráaw' V to be cracked, to crack (of itself).

ก้าวร้าว kâawráaw' V 1. to show disrespect.
sV 2. disrespectfully, abusively.

แตกร้าว tɛɛgráaw' V 1. to be cracked. 2. to be
divided, disunited.

ปวดร้าว pùadráaw' V to have a splitting pain,
to ache (as though) splitting.

รอยร้าว (รอย) rɔɔjráaw' (rɔɔj') N crack,
fissure.

ราวี raawii' V lit. 1. to fight, attack, invade. 2.
to molest, disturb.

ราศี raasǐi' N 1. zodiac. 2. grandeur, splendor,
dignity, good quality. →Also ราสี.

ราษฎร,ราษฎร์ râadsadɔɔn', râad' N populace,
citizenry, subjects (of a king).

ทวยราษฎร์ thuajrâad' N lit. people, citizenry.

ผู้แทนราษฎร (นาย) phûuthɛɛn'râadsadɔɔn' (naaj')
N people's representative (in the legislature).

o สภาผู้แทนราษฎร (สภา) saphaa'-phûuthɛɛn'ᴐ
râadsadɔɔn' (saphaa') N House of Representatives, the lower legislative body in a parliamentary government.

โรงเรียนราษฎร์ (โรงเรียน) rooŋrian'râad'
(rooŋrian') N private school. →Opp. โรงเรียน
หลวง,โรงเรียนรัฐบาล.

ราสี ๑. See ราศี.

ราสี ๒ in เกี้ยวพาราสี kîawphaa'raasǐi' V elab.
colloq. to court, woo; to make love to.

รำ ๑ ram' V to dance (in Thai fashion).

เต้นรำ tênram' V to dance (ballroom dancing).

ฟ้อนรำ fɔɔn'ram' V to dance (in Thai fashion).

ร่ายรำ,รำร่าย râajram', ramrâaj' V to dance.

รำพัด ramphád' V 1. to fan-dance. 2. slang
to play cards.

รำวง ramwoŋ' N 1. a Thai folk dance in which
the couples move around in circles. V 2. to
dance the รำวง.

รำ ๒ ram' N bran.

ร่ำ ๑ râm' V to scent, perfume.

ร่ำ ๒ râm' 1. initial element in verbs describing
repetitive actions. sV 2. repeatedly. V 3.
Short for ร่ำร้อง below.

o พูดร่ำรำพัน phûud'-râm'ramphan' to talk
repeatedly and at length (about something).

ร่ำไป râmpaj' constantly, always, repeatedly.

ร่ำร้อง râmrɔ́ɔŋ' V to beg, ask, request, beseech
repeatedly.

ร่ำลา râmlaa' V to bid farewell, say goodbye
(usually implying repeated farewells).

ร่ำลือ râmlyy' V to rumor, talk about repeatedly
and widely.

ร่ำไห้ râmhâj' V to weep and wail incessantly,
lament repeatedly.

ร่ำ ๓ in ร่ำรวย râmruaj/ V to be rich, wealthy. ความ-- wealthiness.

ร่ำ ๔ in ร่ำไร râmraj/ V to dally, waste time (by doing the same thing over and over); to be slow (in getting something done). →Syn. ชักช้า.

ร่ำคาญ ramkhaan/ V 1. to be annoyed, vexed. 2. to be bored. ความ-- annoyance; ennui, boredom.

น่าร่ำคาญ nâa/ramkhaan/ V to be annoying, disturbing.

ร่ำคาญใจ ramkhaan/caj/ V to feel annoyed.

ร่ำพัน (ถึง) ramphan/(thy̆ŋɔ) V to talk at length (about), complain at length (about), lament.

ร่ำพึง ramphyŋ/ V to ponder.

   o ร่ำพึงตัวว่า ramphyŋ/tua/-wâa/ to think to oneself saying.

ร่ำร่ำ ramram/ AA colloq. be on the point of, about to; almost, about, nearly.

ร่ำไร ramraj/ sV indistinctly in the distance.

ร่ำลึก (ถึง) ramlýg/(thy̆ŋɔ) V eleg. to recall, recollect, think back (on), bring back to mind. →Also more commonly ระลึก.

ริ rí?/ V to begin, start, originate. ผู้-- originator.

ริเริ่ม rí?/rə̂əm/ V to originate, initiate. ผู้-- originator.

ริอ่าน rí?/?àan/ V 1. to plan. 2. to try, attempt.

ริกๆ rígríg/ sV tremblingly, shiveringly.

ริดสีดวง rídsíiduaŋ/* N a class term for several maladies, as in the following examples.

ริดสีดวงตา rídsíiduaŋ/taa/ N trachoma.

ริดสีดวงทวาร rídsíiduaŋ/thawaan/ N eleg. hemorrhoids, piles.

ริน rin/ V 1. to decant, pour out. sV 2. slowly, little by little.

ไหลริน lǎj/rin/ to flow slowly, trickle.

ริ้น (ตัว) rín/ (tua/) N gnat, sandfly.

ริบ ríb/ V to confiscate (something).

เก็บหอมรอมริบ kèbhɔ̌ɔm/rɔɔmríb/ V elab. colloq. to save up.

ริบหรี่ ríbrìi/ V to be dim, faint (of light).

ริม ๑ (ริ่ม) rim/ (rim/) N edge, edging, rim, brim.

ริมถนน rim/thanǒn/ N roadside, edge of a road.

ริมทาง rimthaaŋ/ N wayside.

ริมน้ำ rimnáam/ N the water's edge, bank.

ริมฝีปาก rim/fǐipàag/ N lip, lips.

ริมแม่น้ำ (ด้าน, ข้าง, แห่ง) rim/mɛ̂ɛnáam/ (dâan/, khâaŋ/, hɛ̀ŋ/) N river bank, edge of a river.

ริม ๒ rim/ C ream (of paper). [f. Eng.] →Also ริ่ม.

ริ้ว ríw/ N stripe, line, streak.

ขี้ริ้ว khîiríw/ V to have no looks at all, be plain and homely, unattractive (used of people).

ริ้วรอย ríw/rɔɔj/ N 1. scratch mark. 2. lines, wrinkles (e.g. on the face).

   o เป็นริ้วรอย penríw/rɔɔj/ V to be scratched, lined with marks or scratches.

ริษยา rídsajǎa/ V to be jealous, envious. ความ-- jealousy, envy.

รี ๑ rii/ V to be tapering, oblong, oval.

รี ๒ in รีรอ riirɔɔ/ V to hesitate, hold back, pause from uncertainty of mind.

รี่ rîi/ V to rush, dash straight (toward).

เดินรี่ dəənrîi/ V to walk straight (to).

ตรงรี่ troŋ/rîi/ V to advance, move quickly straight (toward).

รี้ in รี้พล ríi/phon/ N troops, fighting forces.

รีด rîid/ V 1. to squeeze (smthg.). 2. to press, iron.

ซักรีด ság/rîid/ V 1. to wash and iron, launder. 2. to clean and press.

เตารีด (เตา, อัน) tawrîid/ (taw/, ?an/) N iron (for pressing clothing).

รีดนม rîidnom/ V to milk.

รีดผ้า rîidphâa/ V to iron clothing.

รีดลูก rîidlûug/ V to abort, have an abortion. →Dist. แท้งลูก.

รีบ rîib/ V to hurry, hasten.

รีบกระวีกระวาด rîib/krawii/krawâad/ to hurry.

รีบร้อน rîibrɔ́ɔn/ V to hurry, be in a big hurry.

รีบรุด rîibrúd/ V to advance or move ahead hurriedly, go (somewhere) in a hurry.

รีบเร่ง, เร่งรีบ rîibrêŋ/, rêŋrîib/ V to expedite, speed up, hasten, hurry.

ริ่ม. See ริม ๒.

รีวิว riiwiw/ N revue. [f. Eng.]

รี rý/ Cj 1. or. Pt 2. particle used to convert a statement into a yes-or-no question. →Variant of หรือ.

รื่น rŷyn/ V to be refreshing, pleasant, merry.

ราบรื่น râabrŷyn/ V to be smooth, progress

smoothly.

รื่นรมย์ rŷynrom′ V to be pleased, find pleasure, enjoyment. →Often รู้สึก--.

รื่นเริง rŷynrəəŋ′ V to be cheerful, jovial, gay, hilarious, merry. การ-- amusement, entertainment.

o งานรื่นเริง ŋaan′rŷynrəəŋ′ N a party, gathering for entertainment, festivity.

รือ ๑ in หารือ hǎaryy′ V to consult, confer.

รือ ๒ in กระตือรือร้น kratyy′ryyrón′ to be enthusiastic, eager, anxious, in a rush (e.g. to do something).

รื้อ rýy′ V to tear up, tear apart, demolish, dismantle.

รื้อจัด rýy′càd′ V to rearrange.

รื้อถอน rýythɔɔn′ V to tear out (an installation), tear down (a house, building).

รื้อฟื้น rýyfýyn′ V to revive, bring back.

รุ rú?′ V to clear off, clean out, get rid of.

รุก rúg′ V 1. to advance, advance into, invade. 2. to pursue or press an advantage. การ-- attack, invasion.

บุกรุก bùgrúg′ V 1. to invade. 2. to trespass. การ-- invasion; trespassing.

ฝ่ายรุก fàajrúg′ N the offense, the side on the offensive (in sports, war).

รุกราน rúgraan′ V to invade, attack. ผู้-- aggressor, invader.

o ฝ่ายรุกราน fàaj′rúgraan′ N aggressor.

รุกล้ำ rúglám′ V 1. to intrude, trespass. 2. to penetrate, advance into (by force).

หมากรุก (สำรับ, กระดาน) màagrúg′ N chess (sǎmráb′ for sets; kradaan′ for games).

รุ่ง. See รุ่งริ่ง.

รุ่ง rûŋ′ N 1. dawn, daybreak. V 2. to get light (in the morning), day to break. →Syn. 1. อรุณ eleg.

คืนยังรุ่ง khyynjaŋrûŋ′ all night long.

ดาวรุ่ง (ดวง, คน) daawrûŋ′ N 1. the morning star (duaŋ′). 2. a renowned beauty (khon′, duaŋ′). →Also ดาวประกายพรึก. →Opp. ดาวประจำเมือง.

ย่ำรุ่ง jâmrûŋ′ 6 A.M.; dawn, early in the morning.

รุ่งขึ้น, วัน-- rûŋkhŷn′, wan′rûŋkhŷn′ the next day.

o ในวันรุ่งขึ้น najwan′rûŋkhŷn′ on the following day.

รุ่งเช้า rûŋcháaw′ at daybreak.

รุ่งเรือง rûŋryaŋ′ V 1. to be prosperous, flourishing, thriving, civilized. 2. to be luminous, brilliant. ความ-- prosperity, civilization. →Syn. 1. เจริญ, เฟื่อง. 2. สว่าง.

o เจริญรุ่งเรือง carəən′rûŋryaŋ′ V to prosper, be civilized. ความ-- prosperity, civilization.

รุ่งโรจน์ rûŋrôod′ V 1. to be glorious, flourishing. 2. to be bright, brilliant.

รุ่งสว่าง rûŋ′sawàaŋ′ at dawn, at daybreak.

รุ่งสาง rûŋsǎaŋ′ 1. day to break. 2. at dawn, at daybreak.

รุ่งอรุณ rûŋ′ʔarun′ dawn; at dawn.

หามรุ่งหามค่ำ hǎamrûŋ′hǎamkhâm′ colloq. all day and all night; day and night.

รุ้ง (สาย) rún′ (sǎaj′) N rainbow.

สายรุ้ง (สาย) sǎajrún′ (sǎaj′) N 1. writ. rainbow. 2. com. streamers, long and narrow strips of colored paper or cloth, used as decoration, for throwing at carnivals, etc.

เส้นรุ้ง (เส้น) sênrún′ (sên′) N geog. latitude.

รุ่งริ่ง rûŋraŋ′ V to be untidy, messy, unkempt, disorderly, disheveled.

รกรุ่งริ่ง róg′rûŋraŋ′ V to be disorderly, cluttered, untidy, messy, a hodgepodge.

รุด rúd′ V to move forward in a hurry, proceed with dispatch.

รีบรุด rîibrúd′ V to advance or move ahead hurriedly, go (somewhere) in a hurry.

รุน in รุนแรง runrɛɛŋ′ V to be severe, violent, fierce, strong.

รุ่น rûn′ C 1. period, age, time. 2. group, class, batch. V 3. to be young, adolescent, in one's teens.

รุ่นจิ๋ว rûncǐw′ in the class of small things, of the tiny variety, midget.

แรกรุ่น rɛ̂ɛgrûn′ adolescent, young.

อนุชนรุ่นหลัง ʔànúchon′rûnlǎŋ′ N people of the younger generation.

รุม rum′ V to crowd around; to mob.

รุมล้อม rumlɔ́ɔm′ V to crowd around, surround, encircle.

รุ่มร่าม rûmrâam′ V to be ill-fitting, oversized.

รู (รุ) ruu′ (ruu′) N hole; perforation.

  เจาะรู cɔ̀ʔruu′ V to make a hole.

  เป็นรู penruu′ V 1. to have a hole. 2. to be full of holes.

รูจมูก (รู) ruucamùug′ (ruu′) N nostril.

รู้ rúu′ V to know (e.g. a subject, not a person). ความ-- (see below). ผู้-- one who knows, a well-informed person. →Comp. ทราบ eleg.

ความรู้ khwaamrúu′ N knowledge.

  o พื้นความรู้ phýyn′khwaamrúu′ N background of knowledge, fundamental knowledge (possessed by someone).

  o วิชาความรู้ wíchaa′khwaamrúu′ N knowledge.

น่ารู้ nâa′rúu′ V to be of interest, interesting, i.e. interesting to know, worth knowing.

ไม่ยักรู้ mâjjág′rúu′ to happen not to know (contrary to expectation).

ไม่รู้จบ mâjrúucòb′ 1. unending, endless; recurring (decimal). 2. endlessly, without end.

ไม่รู้ไม่ชี้ mâjrúu′mâjchíi′ elab. colloq. 1. to pay no attention; to refuse to listen. 2. to refuse to be answerable for the consequences (e.g. after a warning has been ignored).

ไม่รู้ไม่เห็น mâjrúu′mâjhěn′ elab. colloq. to know nothing, to have seen nothing (e.g. concerning a crime).

ไม่รู้ลืม mâjrúulyym′ 1. to be unforgettable, never to be forgotten. 2. unforgettably. 3. without forgetting.

ไม่รู้วาย mâjrúuwaaj′ lit. unceasingly, ceaselessly.

รอบรู้ rɔ̂ɔbrúu′ V to know extensively, to be well-informed.

รับรู้ rábrúu′ V 1. to acknowledge. 2. to take responsibility.

รู้แก่ใจ rúu′kɛ̀ɛcaj′ to know full well, to be fully aware.

รู้แกว (ว่า) rúukɛɛw′(wâaɔ) to get an inkling, a notion (that); to get wind (that).

รู้จัก rúucàg′ V to be acquainted with, to know (a person); to know how (to do something).

  o รู้จักมักคุ้น rúucàg′mágkhún′ V elab. colloq. to be acquainted (with), know personally.

  o รู้จักมักจี่ rúucàg′mágcìi′ V elab. colloq.

idem.

รู้แจ้งเห็นจริง rúucɛ̂ɛŋ′hěnciŋ′ V elab. colloq. to perceive and understand clearly.

รู้ใจ rúucaj′ V to know what is in the mind of (someone).

รู้ดี rúu′dii′ 1. to know well. 2. to presume to know; to know better; to know it all. →In mng. 2 used sarcastically, reproachfully, as in the following examples.

  o รู้ดี ฉันสั่งอย่างนี้ ทำไมไปทำอย่างนั้น rúu′dii′→ chánsàŋ′jàaŋníi′→thammaj′-pajtham′jàaŋnán′ You know so much, huh? I told you to do it this way; why did you go and do it that way?

  o รู้ดี ทำไมไม่ถามเสียก่อน rúu′dii′→thammaj′ɔ mâjthǎam′-síakɔ̀ɔn′ You know it all, huh? Why didn't you ask (me) first?

รู้ตัว rúutua′ V to be aware, conscious. ความ-- awareness, consciousness.

รู้ทัน rúu′than′ V to know at once what another is driving at. →Dist. รู้เท่า.

รู้ที่ rúuthii′ V to know what is on someone's mind, sense someone else's wishes.

รู้เท่า rúu′thâw′ V to know what someone is up to, know what is behind (someone's behavior); to be on to (someone's intentions). →Dist. รู้ทัน.

  o รู้เท่าไม่ถึงการณ์ rúu′thâw′-mâjth̭ýŋkaan′ to be blind to a situation, be unable to see what someone is up to.

รู้เบาะแส rúu′bɔ̀ʔsɛ̌ɛ′ to have a vague knowledge about, have an inkling about.

รู้ภาษา rúuphaasǎa′ V colloq. to know what is what, have horse sense. →Also รู้ประสา.

รู้มาก rúu′mâag′ V idiom. to take advantage of. →Contrast the expression มีความรู้มาก miiɔ khwaamrúu′mâag′ to have a lot of knowledge, to know a lot (about things).

รู้เรื่อง rúurŷaŋ′ V 1. to understand. 2. to know or understand the matter. 3. to be understandable.

รู้แล้วรู้รอด rúulɛ́ɛw′rúurɔ̂ɔd′ elab. colloq. once and for all.

รู้สึก rúusȳg′ V to feel. ความ-- feeling.

  o รู้สึกตัว rúusȳgtua′ 1. to come to feel, realize, come to awareness. 2. to recover consciousness.

○ รู้สึกตัวว่า rúusỳgtua/wâa/ to have come to feel that, realize that.

รู้หนังสือ rúunaŋsỹy/ V to be literate, able to read.

รู้เห็น rúu/hĕn/ V 1. to know, have experience. 2. to see, witness. 3. to witness (e.g. wrong-doing) with acquiescence.

○ รู้เห็นเป็นใจ rúuhĕn/pencaj/ elab. to witness (i.e. have full knowledge of the facts) and to connive, be secretly accessory, be an accomplice (e.g. in wrongdoing). →See also เป็นใจ.

เรียนรู้ rianrúu/ V to learn.

ล่วงรู้ lûaŋrúu/ V to know in advance, be known in advance.

สอดรู้สอดเห็น sɔ̀ɔdrúu/sɔ̀ɔdhĕn/ V elab. colloq. to be inquisitive, curious, meddling, nosy. →Also สอดรู้.

 สู่รู้ sùu/rúu/ V 1. to think one knows it all, knows better. 2. to know more than is good for one. →Syn. 1. อวดรู้. NOTE. This expression is often used chidingly.

เสียรู้ sĭa/rúu/ V to be outwitted.

อยากรู้ jàagrúu/ to be curious, anxious to know.

รูด rûud/ V to slide, draw, pull.

รูป (รูป,ใบ) rûub/ N 1. picture (rûub/,baj/). 2. form, shape (rûub/). C 3. clf. for pictures, idols. 4. clf. for priests. →Syn. 1,3. ภาพ eleg. 2. ทรง eleg.

เข้ารูป khâwrûub/ V 1. to fit in (with), conform (to). 2. to be fitted, form-fitting (as a dress). 3. to form, take shape.

ชักรูป chágrûub/ slang to take a picture, to photograph.

ถ่ายรูป thàajrûub/ com. to take a picture, to photograph. →Syn. ถ่ายภาพ eleg., ชักรูป slang.

○ กล้องถ่ายรูป (กล้อง) klɔ̂ŋ/thàajrûub/ (klɔ̂ŋ/) N camera.

○ ฟิล์มถ่ายรูป (ม้วน,แผ่น) fiim/thàajrûub/ N photographic film (múan/ a roll; phèn/ a sheet). [ฟิล์ม f. Eng.]

เป็นรูป penrûub/ 1. to be in the form of, be shaped. 2. in shape, into shape.

○ เป็นรูปเป็นร่างขึ้น penrûub/penrâaŋ/-khŷn/ to take shape, to be getting into shape.

แปรรูป prɛɛ/rûub/ V eleg. to transform, transfigure, transmute, undergo metamorphosis.

พระบรมรูป phráborom/marûub/ N eleg. picture, statue of the king.

พระพุทธรูป (องค์) phráphúd/tharûub/ (ʔoŋ/) N image of Buddha.

รูปจำลอง rûubcamlɔɔŋ/ N miniature, scale model.

รูปฉาย (แผ่น,ใบ) rûubchǎaj/ (phèn/, baj/) N photograph.

รูปโฉม rûubchŏom/ N figure, shape, appearance, build.

รูปถ่าย (รูป,ใบ) rûubthàaj/ (rûub/, baj/) N com. photograph. →Syn. ภาพถ่าย eleg.

รูปทรง rûubsoŋ/ N eleg. figure, form, build.

รูปประกอบ (รูป) rûubprakɔ̀ɔb/ (rûub/) N illustration, accompanying figure (in a text).

รูปปั้น (รูป) rûubpân/ (rûub/) N molded figures, figurines.

รูปภาพ (รูป,ใบ) rûubphâab/ (rûub/, baj/) N picture.

รูปร่าง rûubrâaŋ/ N appearance, form, figure, shape.

รูปลักษณะ rûub/lágsanà?/ N appearance, feature, form.

รูปสลัก (รูป,ชิ้น) rûubsalàg/ (rûub/, chín/) N sculpture.

รูปสามเหลี่ยม (รูป) rûubsǎamlìam/ (rûub/) N triangle.

รูปสี่เหลี่ยม (รูป) rûubsìilìam/ (rûub/) N quadrangle, rectangle.

รูปหล่อ rûublɔ̀ɔ/ V 1. colloq. to be handsome, good-looking (of men only). N 2. molded figure.

รูปหุ่น rûubhùn/ N model, mannequin, dressmaker's dummy.

ล้างรูป láaŋrûub/ V to develop a photographic film or print.

สำเร็จรูป sǎmrèd/rûub/ ready-made, prepared, prefabricated.

อัดรูป ʔàdrûub/ V to print a picture.

รูปพรรณ rûubpàphan/ N 1. characteristic, appearance, description. 2. gold or silver ornamental article.

ทองรูปพรรณ (ชิ้น) thɔɔŋ/rûubpàphan/ (chín/) N gold made into ornaments and other articles, ornamental gold (as opposed to gold bars).

รูเมเนีย ruumeenia′ pN Rumania. [f. Eng.]

เร in เรรวน reeruan′ V to be uncertain, wavering.

เร่ rêe′ V to wander, rove.

  เร่ขาย rêekhǎaj′ V to peddle.

  เร่ร่อน, ร่อนเร่ rêerɔ̂n′, rɔ̂nrêe′ V to wander,
roam about.

  o ใช้ชีวิตอย่างเร่ร่อน cháj′chiiwíd′-jàaŋrêerɔ̂n′
to lead the life of a vagrant.

เรขาคณิต reekhǎa′khaníd′ N geometry.

เร่ง rêŋ′* V 1. to hurry, speed up, accelerate, urge,
urge on. 2. to be urgent, pressing.

  รีบเร่ง, เร่งรีบ rîibrêŋ′, rêŋrîib′ V to expedite,
speed up, hasten, hurry.

  เร่งมือ rêŋmyy′ V to speed up one's work.

  เร่งร้อน rêŋrɔ́ɔn′ V 1. to hurry, be in a hurry.
2. to hurry, rush (someone). 3. to be urgent,
pressing.

  เร่งรัด rêŋrád′ V 1. to expedite, hasten, speed
up, urge (someone) on, hurry. 2. to be urgent,
pressing.

  เร่งเร้า rêŋráw′ V to urge, urge on.

เรณู reenuu′ N 1. eleg. pollen. nN 2. first name
for a woman.

เรดาณ์ (เครื่อง) reedâa′, reedaa′ (khrŷaŋ′) N
radar. [f. Eng.]

เรยอง, เรยอน reejɔŋ′, reejɔn′* N rayon. [f. Eng.]

เร็ว rew′ V 1. to be fast, quick, rapid. 2. to be
early (ahead of time). sV 3. fast, quickly,
rapidly. ความ-- speed. →Ant. ช้า. →Syn.
2. เนิ่น, 3. ทันใจ.

  ใจเร็ว cajrew′ V to be hasty, impetuous, impulsive. ความ-- hastiness, rashness.

  โดยเร็ว, --พลัน doojrew′, dooj′rewphlan′ quickly.

  ในเร็วๆวัน najrewrew′wan′ soon, in the near
future.

  ไม่ช้าก็เร็ว mâjcháa′kɔ̀rew′ sooner or later.
→Also ไม่เร็วก็ช้า mâjrew′kɔ̀cháa′.

  รวดเร็ว rûadrew′ V to be fast, quick.

  o ในเวลาอันรวดเร็ว najweelaa′ʔanrûadrew′ in
a very short time, very quickly.

  เร็วจี๋ rewcǐi′ colloq. to be extremely fast.

  เร็วๆนี้ rewrew′níi′ soon, in the near future.

  o ในเร็วๆนี้ najrewrew′níi′ soon, in the near
future.

  o เมื่อเร็วๆนี้ mŷarewrew′níi′ just recently.

วิ่งเร็ว wîŋrew′ 1. to race; to run fast. N 2.
sports a dash.

อัตราเร็ว ʔàdtraa′rew′ N velocity, speed.

เรอ rəə′ V to belch, eructate.

เร่อ in เร่อร่า rə̂ərâa′ sV intrusively, awkwardly,
clumsily.

เรอะ rə́′. Colloq. variant of หรือ. →See also เหรอ.

เรา raw′ P 1. we, us. 2. I, me (when speaking to
oneself, to an inferior, or to an intimate).

  ของเรา khɔ̌ɔŋraw′ 1. our, ours. 2. my, mine.

  คนเรา khon′raw′ N we people, we humans.

  พวกเรา phûagraw′ N we, us, our group.

เร้า in the following entries.

  เร่าร้อน râwrɔ́ɔn′ V to be inflamed, aroused,
burn (e.g. with passion, desire, impatience).

  เร่าๆ râwrâw′ sV 1. agitatedly, anxiously. 2.
expressively and incessantly.

เร้า ráw′ V to stimulate, arouse, stir, incite.

  รบเร้า róbráw′ V to beg, beseech repeatedly.

  เร่งเร้า rêŋráw′ V to urge, urge on.

  เร้าใจ ráw′caj′ V to arouse, incite, encourage.

เราะ rɔ́ʔ′ V 1. to walk along (e.g. a fence) (in order
to find a way in or out). 2. to chip off, break
off little by little.

เริง in the following entries.

  ร่าเริง râarəəŋ′ V to be jovial, cheerful, in high
spirits.

  รื่นเริง rŷnrəəŋ′ V to be jovial, gay, hilarious,
merry. การ-- amusement, entertainment.

  o งานรื่นเริง ŋaan′rŷnrəəŋ′ N a party, gathering
for entertainment, festivity.

เริด in เริดร้าง rəəd′ráaŋ′ V 1. to be neglected,
forsaken, abandoned. 2. to be separated (e.g.
of husband and wife).

เริ่ม rə̂əm′ V to begin, start. →Syn. ตั้งต้น.

  ริเริ่ม rí′rə̂əm′ V to originate, initiate. ผู้--
originator.

  เริ่มด้วย rə̂əm′dûajɔ to begin with, to begin by
(doing such and such).

  เริ่มต้น rə̂əmtôn′ V to begin, start, commence.

  o จุดเริ่มต้น cùd′rə̂əmtôn′ N starting point.

เริ่มแรก, แรกเริ่ม rə̂əmrɛ̂ɛg′, rɛ̂ɛgrə̂əm′ N 1. beginning. 2. originally, in the beginning, from the start.

แรกเริ่มเดิมที rɛ̂ɛgrə̂əm′dəəmthii′ elab. originally, in the beginning.

เรี่ย ๑ rîa′ V to be almost touching, to touch slightly, to hang down nearly touching (as drapery reaching almost to the floor).

เรี่ยราด rîaraad′ V to be scattered all over.

เรี่ยๆ rîarîa′ slightly above, slightly touching.

ไร่เรี่ย râjrîa′ V to be about equal, about the same. →Usually ไล่เลี่ย.

เรี่ย ๒ in เรี่ยไร rîaraaj′* V to solicit contributions, take up a collection.

เรียก rîag′ V 1. to call. 2. to be called.

กวักมือเรียก kwàgmyy′rîag′ V to summon, call (someone) over (by beckoning with one's hand).

ที่เรียกกันว่า thîirîag′kanwâa′ which is called, which they call.

ร้องเรียก rɔ́ɔŋrîag′ V to call, call out to.

เรียกขวัญ rîagkhwǎn′ V to call (back) the protecting spirit.

เรียก(...)คืน rîag(...)khyyn′ V to recall, revoke.

เรียกชื่อ rîagchŷy′ V 1. to call the name (of). 2. to call the roll.

เรียกได้ว่า rîag′dâjwâa′ can be regarded as.

เรียกประชุม rîag′prachum′ V to call, convene a meeting.

เรียกพล rîagphon′ V to mobilize troops. การ-- mobilization (of troops).

เรียกร้อง rîagrɔ́ɔŋ′ V to demand, claim, make a demand for.

o ข้อเรียกร้อง (ข้อ) khɔ̂ɔ′rîagrɔ́ɔŋ′ (khɔ̂ɔ′) N demand, request.

เรียก(...)ว่า (1) rîag′(...)wâa′; (2) rîag′wâa′ 1. to call (such and such)(by the name of). 2. to be called (such and such).

เรียก(...)ให้มา rîag′(...)hâjmaa′ to call (to someone) to come, call (someone) over.

หมายเรียก (ฉบับ) mǎajrîag′ (chabàb′) N subpoena, summons. →Also หมายเรียกตัว.

เรียง riaŋ′ V to put in order, arrange in order. ความ-- essay.

เรียงความ (เรื่อง, บท) riaŋkhwaam′ (rŷaŋ′, bòd′) N 1. essay. V 2. to write an essay, composition.

เรียงพิมพ์ riaŋphim′ V to set type.

เรียงราย riaŋraaj′ V 1. to be scattered all around. 2. to be lined up; to be arranged in lines.

เรียงลำดับ riaŋ′lamdàb′ to be arranged in order (of)(e.g. in order of height).

เรียบเรียง rîabriaŋ′ V to compose, compile, arrange. ผู้-- compiler, author.

เรียน rian′ V 1. com. to study, learn. 2. eleg. to inform, tell (particularly when sp. to a superior). 3. a term of respect used in the salutation of a letter (followed by the name of the addressee). การ-- learning, study. นัก-- student, pupil. →Syn. 2. บอก com.

กราบเรียน kràabrian′ V 1. elab. eleg. sp. to sup. to inform, tell. 2. term of respect used in the salutation of a letter (followed by the name of the addressee). →Cf. กราบเท้า.

การมาเรียน kaan′maarian′ N attendance (in school)

ขาดเรียน khàadrian′ V to be absent from school, miss school, cut classes.

คงแก่เรียน khoŋkarian′* V to be learned, erudite.

บทเรียน (บท) bòdrian′ (bòd′) N lesson.

แบบเรียน (เล่ม) bɛ̀ɛbrian′ (lêm′) N textbook.

ร้องเรียน rɔ́ɔŋ′rian′ V to request, petition, complain.

เรียนถาม rianthǎam′ V eleg. def. to ask, inquire.

เรียนทางไปรษณีย์ rian′thaaŋprajsanii′ to take a correspondence course.

เรียนรู้ rianrúu′ V to learn.

เรียนหนังสือ rian′naŋsǔy′ V to study.

โรงเรียน (โรงเรียน, แห่ง) rooŋrian′ (rooŋrian′, hɛ̀ŋ′) N school, schoolhouse.

เล่าเรียน lâwrian′ eleg. to learn, study.

หนังสือเรียน (เล่ม) naŋsǔyrian′ (lêm′) N schoolbook.

ห้องเรียน (ห้อง) hɔ̂ŋrian′ (hɔ̂ŋ′) N classroom.

เรียบ rîab′ V 1. to be smooth, plain, even. 2. to be neat, orderly.

ราบเรียบ râabrîab′ V to be smooth, level.

เรียบแปร้ rîabprɛ́ɛ′ very neat and smooth, slicked

down (of the hair).

เรียบร้อย rîabrɔ́ɔj′ V 1. to be neat, tidy, in good order, in good shape. 2. to be ready, all set. 3. to be polite, well-mannered.

o โดยเรียบร้อย dooj′rîabrɔ́ɔj′ 1. in good condition, in fine shape. 2. smoothly, in an orderly manner.

o เป็นที่เรียบร้อย penthîi′rîabrɔ́ɔj′ 1. to be in good order. 2. well, neatly, carefully, smoothly.

o เป็นระเบียบเรียบร้อย penrabìab′rîabrɔ́ɔj′ V 1. to be ship-shape, in good order, fine. 2. to be well-arranged, well-organized.

เรียบเรียง rîabriaŋ′ V to compose, compile, arrange. ผู้-- compiler, author.

เรียบๆ rîabrîab′ V to be plain, simple, ordinary, natural. →Ant. ฉูดฉาด.

o สีเรียบๆ sǐi′rîabrîab′ plain color, subdued color.

เรียม riam′ P lit. m. sp. I, me. →Syn. ผม ๒.

เรี่ยม rîam′ V 1. to be clean, clear, spotless. 2. colloq. to be perfect, excellent, very good.

เรียว riaw′ to be tapering.

ไม้เรียว májriaw′ (ʔan′) N switch, rod (used for whipping, beating).

เรี่ยว rîaw′ N strength, power. →Syn. กำลัง.

เรี่ยวแรง rîawrɛɛŋ′ N strength.

หัวเรี่ยวหัวแรง hǔarîaw′hǔarɛɛŋ′ N elab. colloq. mainstay, principal force.

เรือ (ลำ) rya′ (lam′) N com. boat, ship. →Syn. นาวา lit., eleg.

กองทัพเรือ (กองทัพ) kɔɔŋtháb′rya′ (kɔɔŋtháb′) N navy, naval forces.

จอมพลเรือ (นาย,คน) cɔɔmphonrya′ (naaj′, khon′) N 1. admiral of the fleet. T 2. Admiral --.

ชาวเรือ (คน) chaawrya′ (khon′) N seafarer.

เดินเรือ dəənrya′ V 1. to navigate, direct a ship on its course. 2. to operate a shipping line, ships. การ-- navigation.

ทหารเรือ (คน) thahǎanrya′ (khon′) N sailor, member of the navy. →Dist. กะลาสี.

o นายทหารเรือ (นาย,คน) naajthahǎanrya′ (naaj′, khon′) N naval officer.

ทัพเรือ (กอง) thábrya′ (kɔɔŋ′) N navy.

ท่าเรือ (แห่ง,ท่า) thâarya′ (hὲŋ′, thâa′) N 1. harbor, port, seaport. 2. pier.

นายพลเรือ (นาย,คน) naajphonrya′ (naaj′, khon′) N 1. admiral (of unspecified rank). T 2. Admiral --.

นายพลเรือตรี (นาย,คน) naajphon′ryatrii′ (naaj′, khon′) N 1. rear admiral. T 2. Rear Admiral --. →Also พลเรือตรี.

นายพลเรือโท (นาย,คน) naajphon′ryathoo′ (naaj′, khon′) N 1. vice-admiral. T 2. Vice-Admiral --. →Also พลเรือโท.

นายพลเรือเอก (นาย,คน) naajphon′rya?èeg′ (naaj′, khon′) N 1. admiral. T 2. Admiral -- →Also พลเรือเอก.

นายเรือ (นาย,คน) naajrya′ (naaj′, khon′) N captain (of a ship).

นายเรือตรี (นาย,คน) naajryatrii′ (naaj′, khon′) N 1. ensign (naval rank). T 2. Ensign --. →Also เรือตรี.

นายเรือโท (นาย,คน) naajryathoo′ (naaj′, khon′) N nav. 1. lieutenant junior grade. T 2. Lieutenant --. →Also เรือโท.

นายเรือเอก (นาย,คน) naajrya?èeg′ (naaj′, khon′) N nav. 1. lieutenant senior grade. T 2. Lieutenant --. →Also เรือเอก.

ใบเรือ (ใบ) bajrya′ (baj′) N sail (of a boat). →Also ใบ.

พายเรือ phaajrya′ V to paddle (a boat).

เรือกลไฟ (ลำ) ryakonfaj′ (lam′) N steamship, steamer.

เรือกวาดทุ่นระเบิด (ลำ) ryakwàad′thûnrabə̀əd′ (lam′) N mine sweeper.

เรือกำปั่น (ลำ) ryakampàn′ (lam′) N ship, merchant ship.

เรือคุ้มกัน (ลำ) rya′khúmkan′ (lam′) N convoy, armed ship used as an escort.

เรือจ้าง (ลำ) ryacâaŋ′ (lam′) N sampan (taxi boat propelled by oar).

เรือดำน้ำ (ลำ) ryadamnáam′ (lam′) N submarine.

เรือเดินทะเล (ลำ) ryadəən′thalee′ (lam′) N sea-going steamer.

เรือเดินสมุทร (ลำ) ryadəən′samùd′ (lam′) N ocean-going steamer.

เรือตรี. See นาย-- under เรือ above.

เรือทิ้งทุ่นระเบิด (ลำ) rya'thíŋthûnrabə̀əd' (lam')
N mine layer.

เรือโท. See นาย-- under เรือ above.

เรือธง (ลำ) ryathoŋ' (lam') N flagship.

เรือบด (ลำ) ryabòd' (lam') N small boat
(propelled by oar), canoe.

เรือบรรทุกเครื่องบิน (ลำ) rya'-banthúg'khrŷaŋ=
bin' (lam') N aircraft carrier.

เรือบิน (ลำ, เครื่อง) ryabin' (lam', khrŷaŋ') N
airplane.

เรือใบ (ลำ) ryabaj' (lam') N sailboat.

เรือประจัญบาน (ลำ) rya'pracanbaan' (lam')
N battleship.

เรือประมง (ลำ) ryapramoŋ' (lam') N fishing
boat.

เรือปืน (ลำ) ryapyyn' (lam') N gunboat.

เรือผิวน้ำ (ลำ) rya'phĭwnáam' (lam') N surface vessel.

เรือพ่วง (ลำ) ryaphûaŋ' (lam') N 1. tugboat.
2. a boat or train of boats pulled by a tugboat.

เรือพาย (ลำ) ryaphaaj' (lam') N a boat propelled by paddling.

เรือพิฆาต (ลำ) rya'phíkhâad' (lam') N destroyer.

เรือไฟ (ลำ) ryafaj' (lam') N steamboat.

เรือเมล์ (ลำ) ryamee' (lam') N a scheduled
passenger motorboat, steam passenger ferry.

เรือยนต์ (ลำ) ryajon' (lam') N motorboat.

เรือรบ (ลำ) ryaró b' (lam') N warship.

o กองเรือรบ (กอง) kɔɔŋ'ryaró b' (kɔɔŋ') N
fleet (of warships).

o กำลังเรือรบ kamlaŋ'ryaró b' N naval power,
strength.

เรือลาดตระเวน (ลำ) rya'lâadtraween' (lam')
N cruiser.

เรือสำปั้น (ลำ) ryasămpân' (lam') N sampan.

เรือสำเภา (ลำ) ryasămphaw' (lam') N Chinese
junk.

เรือสินค้า (ลำ) ryasĭnkháa' (lam') N cargo
boat, freighter.

เรือเหาะ (ลำ) ryahɔ̀ʔ' (lam') N aircraft.

เรืออากาศ... rya'ʔaakàadɔ... designation for
the lowest commissioned ranks of the air force.

เรือเอก. See นาย-- under เรือ above.

ลงเรือ loŋrya' V to board a boat.

ลูกเรือ (คน) lûugrya' (khon') N crew.

หัวเรือ hŭarya' N bow, prow.

อู่ต่อเรือ (อู่) ʔùu'tɔ̀ɔrya' N shipyard.

อู่เรือ (อู่) ʔùurya' (ʔùu') N dock.

เรื่อ, เรื่อๆ rŷa', rŷarya' sV light, faint (mostly
used with แดง "red," ชมพู "pink.").

แดงเรื่อ dɛɛŋrŷa' to be light red, a faint red.

เรื้อ in เรื้อรัง rýaraŋ' V to be chronic.

o ปัญหาเรื้อรัง panhăa'rýaraŋ' N chronic problem.

o แผลเรื้อรัง (แผล) phlɛ̆ɛ'rýaraŋ' (phlɛ̆ɛ') N
chronic ulcer or sore.

เรือก in เรือกสวน (ขนัด) rŷagsŭan' (khanàd')
N orchard, garden.

เรือง ryaŋ' V to be bright, glowing, fluorescent.

ดาวเรือง daawryaŋ' N marigold. ดอก-- (ดอก)
marigold (the flower). ต้น-- (ต้น) marigold
(the plant).

รุ่งเรือง rûŋryaŋ' V 1. to be prosperous, civilized.
2. to be luminous, brilliant. →Syn. 1. เจริญ,
เฟื่อง. 2. สว่าง.

เรืองนาม ryaŋnaam' V eleg. to be famous,
renowned.

เรื่อง (เรื่อง) rŷaŋ' (rŷaŋ') N 1. story, subject,
subject matter. C 2. clf. for stories, plays,
anecdotes, etc. Pp 3. about, concerning.

ก่อเรื่อง kɔ̀ɔrŷaŋ' V to start or cause trouble.

เกิดเรื่อง kə̀ədrŷaŋ' trouble arises.

คุยกันถึงเรื่อง khuj'kanthy̆ŋrŷaŋ' to chat about.

เค้าเรื่อง kháwrŷaŋ' N outline, scheme, plot of
a story.

โครงเรื่อง khrooŋrŷaŋ' N plot, outline, structure
(of a story).

ด้วยเรื่อง dûajrŷaŋ' about, concerning, over, with
regard to, in the matter of, in the case of.

o ด้วยเรื่องอะไร dûajrŷaŋ'/ʔaraj' about what?

ตามเรื่อง taamrŷaŋ' sV colloq. 1. accordingly,
as the circumstances allow (or require). 2.
for the heck of it.

ท้องเรื่อง thɔ́ɔŋ'rŷaŋ' N the subject matter,
the essence of a story, the story itself.

เนื้อเรื่อง nýarŷaŋ' idem.

ในเรื่อง najrŷaŋ' 1. in (such and such a) case,

event, matter. 2. in regard to, in the matter
of, in the case of.

ไม่ได้เรื่อง mâjdâjrŷaŋ′ colloq. 1. to be no
good, useless. 2. to get no result. 3. to make
no sense.

ไม่เป็นเรื่อง mâjpenrŷaŋ′ to be nonsense, nonsensical.

รู้เรื่อง rúurŷaŋ′ V 1. to understand. 2. to know,
understand the matter. 3. to be understandable.

เรื่องควรรู้ rŷaŋ′khuanrúu′ things (or stories)
worth knowing.

เรื่องเงินๆทองๆ rŷaŋ′-ŋənŋən′thɔɔŋthɔɔŋ′ N
financial matter.

เรื่องจุกจิก rŷaŋ′cùgcìg′ N trivial matter, petty
matter, trifle.

เรื่องปลีกย่อย rŷaŋ′-plìig′jɔ̀j′ N trivial matter.

เรื่องราว rŷaŋraaw′ N story, account; matter;
happening; case.

เรื่องลึกลับ rŷaŋ′lýgláb′ N 1. mysterious subject.
2. mystery story.

เรื่องส่วนตัว rŷaŋ′sùantua′ N personal matter,
private affair.

เรื่องสั้น (เรื่อง) rŷaŋsân′ (rŷaŋ′) N short story.

o ชุมนุมเรื่องสั้น chumnum′rŷaŋsân′ N anthology
of short stories.

เรื่องอะไรกัน rŷaŋ′ʔaraj′-kan′↓ What's the matter? What's up? What for?

เรื่องอ่านเล่น (เรื่อง) rŷaŋ′ʔàanlên′ (rŷaŋ′)
N something which is read for pleasure, light
reading. →Often used instead of the more specific terms นวนิยาย "novel," เรื่องสั้น "short
story," etc.

หัวเรื่อง (เรื่อง, ข้อ) hŭarŷaŋ′ (rŷaŋ′, khɔ̂ɔ′) N
title, heading.

หาเรื่อง hǎarŷaŋ′ V 1. to look for trouble, invite
trouble. 2. to start trouble, dissension.

เอาเรื่อง ʔawrŷaŋ′ V 1. to be strict, severe,
stern. 2. to cause trouble; to make an issue
(of something). sV 3. colloq. quite, quite a
bit, considerably.

เรือด (ตัว) rŷad′ (tua′) N bedbug. →Also ตัว--.

เรือน ๑ (หลัง) ryan′ (lǎŋ′) N 1. house, household;
housing. C 2. clf. for clocks, watches. →Syn.
1. บ้าน.

การเรือน (อย่าง) kaanryan′ (jàaŋ′) N 1. housework. 2. household affairs. 3. home economics.

ครัวเรือน (ครัวเรือน) khruaryan′ (khruaryan′)
N family, household.

เครื่องเรือน (ชิ้น, ชุด) khrŷaŋryan′ N furniture
(chín′ for a piece; chúd′ for a set or suite).

ชานเรือน chaanryan′ N (uncovered) porch.

บ้านเรือน bâan′ryan′ N house, home.

มีเรือน miiryan′ V colloq. to be married, have
a family (usually of a woman).

มีเหย้ามีเรือน miijâw′miiryan′ V elab. colloq.
to be married, have a family (usually of a woman).

แม่เรือน (คน) mɛ̂ɛryan′ (khon′) N female head
of a family; housewife.

เรือนกาย ryankaaj′ N eleg. (human) body, form.

เรือนจำ (แห่ง) ryancam′ (hɛ̀ŋ′) N eleg. jail,
prison. →Syn. คุก com.

เรือนไม้ (หลัง) ryanmáaj′ (lǎŋ′) N wooden house,
building.

เรือนร่าง ryanrâaŋ′ N eleg. (human) body, figure,
form. →Syn. เรือนกาย.

เรือนหอ (หลัง) ryanhɔ̌ɔ′ (lǎŋ′) N bridal house,
a house built for a newly wedded couple.

อยู่กับเหย้าเฝ้ากับเรือน jùu′kajâw′-fâw′karyan′
elab. colloq. to stay at home and look after
things (considered a good quality for a woman).

เรือน ๒ ryan′ C amount, quantity.

เป็นเรือน penryan′ on the order of (a specified
magnitude), by (dozens, hundreds, etc.), by the
(dozen, hundred, etc.).

เรือน ๓ in พลเรือน (คน) phonlaryan′ (khon′) N
civilian.

เรือน in the following entries.

ขี้เรือน khîiryan′ N colloq. leprosy.

o เป็นขี้เรือน pen′khîiryan′ to have leprosy, be
a leper.

โรคเรือน rôogryan′ N leprosy.

เรื่อย sV continuously.

เรื่อยเจื้อย rŷajcŷaj′ on and on, continuously.

เรื่อยๆ rŷajrŷaj′ V 1. to be so-so, as usual. sV
2. continuously, regularly. 3. leisurely, in a
leisurely manner.

แร่ rɛ̂ɛ′ N ore, mineral.

น้ำมันแร่ námman′rɛ̂ɛ′ N mineral oil.

น้ำแร่ námrɛɛ′ N mineral water.

แร่ดีบุก rɛɛ′diibùg′ N tin ore.

แร่วูลแฟรม rɛɛ′wuunfrɛɛm′, -wuul- N tungsten
  ore, wolframite. [วูลแฟรม f. Eng.]

สินแร่ sǐnrɛɛ′ N ore.

เหมืองแร่ (เหมือง) mǎŋrɛɛ′ (mǎŋ′) N ore
  mine.

แรก rɛɛg′ V to be first.

  ข้อแรก khɔ̂ɔrɛɛg′ the first item, first point.

  ขั้นแรก khânrɛɛg′ 1. the initial step. 2. initial,
    primary.

  ครั้งแรก khráŋrɛɛg′ the first time.

  o ในครั้งแรก najkhráŋrɛɛg′ 1. in the first place.
    2. the first time.

  o เป็นครั้งแรก penkhráŋrɛɛg′ for the first time.

  ชั้นแรก chánrɛɛg′ 1. first step, first shelf, first
    class. 2. at first.

  o ในชั้นแรก najchánrɛɛg′ at first.

  ตอนแรก tɔɔnrɛɛg′ 1. the first part, the beginning
    part. 2. at first.

  แต่แรก tɛ̀ɛrɛɛg′ at first, from the beginning.

  ทีแรก thiirɛɛg′ 1. at first, the first time. 2. in
    the first place.

  เบื้องแรก bŷaŋrɛɛg′ eleg. at first.

  ประการแรก prakaan′rɛɛg′ eleg. for one thing,
    the first (reason being), in the first place.

  รักแรก rágrɛɛg′ N first love.

  เริ่มแรก, แรกเริ่ม rə̂əmrɛɛg′, rɛɛgrə̂əm′ N 1.
    beginning. 2. originally, in the beginning, from
    the start.

  แรกเกิด rɛɛgkə̀əd′ newborn.

  แรกแย้ม rɛɛgjɛ́ɛm′ first-blooming.

  o ดอกไม้แรกแย้ม dɔ̀ɔgmáaj′rɛɛgjɛ́ɛm′ a flower
    which is just beginning to open. →Often used
    as a simile for a young girl.

  แรกรุ่น rɛɛgrûn′ adolescent, young.

  แรกเริ่มเดิมที rɛɛgrə̂əm′dəəmthii′ elab. origi-
    nally, in the beginning.

แรกเกต, ไม้-- (อัน) régkêd′, máajrégkêd′*(ʔan′)
  N racket (as for tennis). [แร็กเกต f. Eng.]

แรง rɛɛŋ′ N 1. power, force, strength, energy.
    V 2. to be powerful, strong, energetic. sV 3.
    forcefully, hard, powerfully, strongly.

  กำลังแรง kamlaŋrɛɛŋ′ N power.

ขอแรง khɔ̌ɔrɛɛŋ′ V to ask (someone) to lend a
  hand, ask for assistance (in doing work).

แข็งแรง khěŋrɛɛŋ′ V to be strong, powerful.

เต็มแรง temrɛɛŋ′ with full force, with all one's
  might.

ทุนแรง thûnrɛɛŋ′ V to save on energy, effect an
  economy on energy, power, labor.

น้ำพักน้ำแรง námphág′námrɛɛŋ′ N elab. colloq.
  1. (one's own) effort, labor. 2. (one's) personal
  investment.

เบาแรง bawrɛɛŋ′ V to be labor-saving, easy to
  operate.

แม่แรง (อัน) mɛ̂ɛrɛɛŋ′ (ʔan′) N 1. jack; crane.
  2. (moral) support, mainstay (used of a woman
  who stands behind a man in what he does).

ร่วมแรงร่วมใจ rûamrɛɛŋ′rûamcaj′ V elab. to
  be united in action and spirit.

ร้อนแรง rɔ́ɔn′rɛɛŋ′ V to be burning, flaming,
  rousing.

ร้ายแรง ráaj′rɛɛŋ′ V to be severe, serious, bad
  (as of a fire, an illness, etc.).

เรี่ยวแรง rîawrɛɛŋ′ N strength.

แรงคน rɛɛŋkhon′ N manpower.

แรงงาน rɛɛŋŋaan′ N labor.

  o ค่าแรงงาน khâa′rɛɛŋŋaan′ N wages, pay
    (for labor).

แรงดัน rɛɛŋdan′ N pressure.

แรงเทียน rɛɛŋthian′ C candle power; watt.

แรงม้า rɛɛŋmáa′ C horsepower. →Syn. กำลังม้า.

ลงแรง loŋrɛɛŋ′ V to expend energy.

  o ลงทุนลงแรง loŋthun′loŋrɛɛŋ′ V to put money
    and effort into (a project).

ลมแรง lomrɛɛŋ′ V to be windy.

สิ้นแรง sînrɛɛŋ′ V to be exhausted.

หมดแรง mòdrɛɛŋ′ V to be exhausted, lose all
  one's strength or energy.

หัวเรี่ยวหัวแรง hǔarîaw′hǔarɛɛŋ′ N elab.
  colloq. mainstay, principal force.

หัวแรง hǔarɛɛŋ′ N mainstay, principal force.

เหลือบ่ากว่าแรง lɥ̌abàa′kwàarɛɛŋ′ elab. colloq.
  to be more than one can do, take on, shoulder.

อ่อนแรง ʔɔ̀ɔnrɛɛŋ′ V to be tired, weary, weakened.

เอาแรง ʔawrɛɛŋ′ V to build up a reserve of
  strength, energy.

แร่ง ๑ (อัน) rêŋ/*(ʔan/) N sieve, strainer.

แร่ง ๒. See ร่องแร่ง.

แร้ง (ตัว) réeŋ/ (tua/) N w r i t. c o m. vulture.
→Also อีแร้ง c o m.

แรด (ตัว) rêed/ (tua/) N rhinoceros.

นอแรด (อัน) nɔɔrɛ̂ed/ (ʔan/) N rhinoceros horn.

แร้น in แร้นแค้น rέεnkhέεn/ V to be poverty-
stricken, needy.

แรม ๑ reem/ V to wane (of the moon).

ข้างแรม khâaŋreem/ (period of) the waning moon.

วันแรม ๑ ค่ำ wanreem/nɣ̀ŋkhâm/ the first day
of the waning moon.

แรม ๒ rεεm/ V to spend (the night).

ค้างแรม kháaŋreem/ V c o m. to stay overnight,
spend the night. →Syn. แรมคืน e l e g.

ประทับแรม pratháb/reem/ V r o y. to stay overnight.

พักแรม phágreem/ V to camp, lodge, stay overnight.

o ที่พักแรม (ที่,แห่ง) thîi/phágreem/ (thîi/, hὲŋ/)
N 1. overnight lodging. 2. campsite.

รอนแรม rɔɔnreem/ V l i t. to go on a trip (overnight or longer), to journey spending the night
out.

แรมคืน reemkhyyn/ V e l e g. to spend the night.
→Syn. ค้างคืน c o m.

แรมเดือน, เป็น-- reemdyan/, penreemdyan/ for
a month, for a period of months.

แรมปี, เป็น-- reempii/, penreempii/ for a year,
for a period of years.

โรงแรม (โรง,แห่ง) rooŋreem/ (rooŋ/, hὲŋ/)
N hotel. →Syn. โฮเต็ล.

แร้ว (อัน) réεw/ (ʔan/) N snare, trap (that en-
snares).

ติดแร้ว tìdréεw/ V to get trapped, stuck in a trap.

โร roo/ V (the abdomen) to be distended, swollen.

โร้ rôo/ sV 1. distinctly (such that it attracts attention); obviously, clearly. 2. quickly.

o แดงโร้ dεεŋ/rôo/ to be distinctly red, bright
red.

โรค (อย่าง,ชนิด) rôog/ (jàaŋ/, chaníd/) N disease,
sickness.

กามโรค kaam/marôog/ N e l e g.,t e c h. venereal
disease. →Syn. โรคบุรุษ,โรคผู้หญิง.

กาฬโรค kaa/larôog/ N plague.

ขี้โรค khîirôog/ V to be sickly, unhealthy.

เชื้อโรค chýarôog/ N disease germs.

ตัวโรค (ตัว) tuarôog/ (tua/) N microbe.

ติดโรค tìd/rôog/ V to contract a disease, catch
a (contagious) disease.

เป็นโรค penrôog/ to have a disease, be diseased.

ยารักษาโรค jaa/-rágsǎa/rôog/ N medicine, medicinal drug.

โรคกระดูกอ่อน rôog/kradùug?ɔ̀ɔn/ N rickets.

โรคกุฏฐรัง rôog/kùdthǎŋ/ N leprosy.

โรคเกลื้อน rôogklýan/ N chloasma, a skin disease.

โรคขาดอาหาร rôog/khàad?aahǎan/ N malnutrition,
undernourishment.

โรคไข้ทรพิษ rôog/khâjthɔɔraphíd/ N e l e g. smallpox. →Also ไข้ทรพิษ. →Syn. ฝีดาษ c o m.

โรคไข้รากสาดน้อย rôog/-khâjrâagsàad/nɔ́ɔj/ N
typhoid.

โรคไข้รากสาดใหญ่ rôog/-khâjrâagsàad/jàj/ N
typhus.

โรคคอตีบ rôog/khɔɔtìib/ N diphtheria.

โรคคุดทะราด rôog/khúdtharâad/ N yaws.

โรคจิต (ชนิด) rôogcìd/ (chaníd/) N mental
disease.

โรคชัก rôogchág/ N c o l l o q. disease characterized by convulsions.

โรคดีซ่าน rôog/diisâan/ N jaundice.

โรคตาแดง rôog/taadεεŋ/ N conjunctivitis.

โรคติดต่อ (ชนิด) rôog/tìdtɔ̀ɔ/ (chaníd/) N
contagious disease.

โรคท้องผูก rôog/thɔ́ɔŋphùug/ N constipation.

โรคท้องร่วง rôog/thɔ́ɔŋrûaŋ/ N e l e g. diarrhea.

โรคท้องเสีย rôog/thɔ́ɔŋsǐa/ N c o l l o q. diarrhea.

โรคบาดทะยัก rôog/bàadthajág/ N tetanus.

โรคบิด rôogbìd/ N dysentery.

โรคบุรุษ rôog/burùd/ N venereal disease (contracted by a woman). →Cf. โรคผู้หญิง.

โรคปอดบวม rôog/pɔ̀ɔdbuam/ N pneumonia.

โรคปัจจุบัน rôog/pàdcuban/ N sudden illness
(sometimes one which causes immediate death).

โรคผิวหนัง (ชนิด) rôog/phǐwnǎŋ/ (chaníd/) N
dermatitis.

โรคผู้หญิง rôog/phûujǐŋ/ N venereal disease
(contracted by a man). →Cf. โรคบุรุษ.

โรคฝีเนื้อร้าย rôog'fǐinýaráaj' N eleg. cancer. →Syn. โรคมะเร็ง com.

โรคฝีในท้อง rôog'fǐinajthɔ́ɔŋ' N colloq. (pulmonary) tuberculosis. →Syn. วัณโรค eleg.

โรคพิษสุรา rôog'phídsuraa' N alcoholism.

โรคภัยไข้เจ็บ (อย่าง,ชนิด) rôogphaj'khâjcèb' (jàaŋ',chaníd') N elab. disease, sickness.

โรคมะเร็ง rôog'mareŋ' N com. cancer. →Syn. โรคฝีเนื้อร้าย eleg.

โรคระบาด (โรค,ชนิด) rôog'rabàad' (rôog', chaníd') N eleg. epidemic.

โรคเรื้อน rôogrýan' N leprosy.

โรคลงราก rôog'loŋrâag' N vulg. cholera. →Syn. โรคห่า vulg., โรคอหิวา eleg.

โรคลมบ้าหมู rôog'-lom'bâamǔu' N epilepsy.

โรคลักปิดลักเปิด rôog'-lágkapìd'lágkapə̀əd' N scurvy.

โรคโลหิตจาง rôog'-loohìd'caaŋ' N anemia.

โรคศิลปะ rôog'sǐnlapà?' N medicine (as an art or science); therapeutics.

โรคเส้นประสาท rôog'sênprasàad' N 1. a nervous disorder; neurosis. 2. nervous breakdown.

โรคไส้ตัน rôog'sâjtan' N appendicitis.

โรคหนองใน rôog'nɔ̌ɔŋnaj' N gonorrhea.

โรคหลอดลมอักเสบ rôog'-lɔ̀ɔdlom''àgsèeb' N bronchitis.

โรคหวัด rôogwàd' N common cold.

โรคหัด rôoghàd' N measles.

โรคหัวใจ rôog'hǔacaj' N heart disease.

โรคห่า rôoghàa' N vulg. 1. cholera. 2. any virulent disease which destroys large numbers of men or animals; hence also, plague, rinderpest, anthrax.

โรคหิด rôoghìd' N scabies (in man only).

โรคหืด rôoghỳyd' N asthma.

โรคเหน็บชา rôog'nèbchaa' N beriberi.

โรคอหิวา rôog''àhiwaa' N eleg. cholera. →Syn. โรคห่า,โรคลงราก vulg.

โรคอัมพาต rôog''ammaphâad' N paralysis.

วัณโรค wannarôog' N eleg. tuberculosis, consumption. →Syn. โรคฝีในท้อง colloq.

อมโรค ?om'rôog' V to be sickly, unhealthy.

อหิวาตกโรค ?àhiwaa'tàkarôog' N eleg. cholera.

โรคา rookhaa' N lit. disease, sickness. Cf. โรค.

โรคาพยาธิ rookhaa'phajâad', rookhaa'phajaa'= thí?' N lit. disease, sickness.

โรง (โรง) rooŋ' (rooŋ') N 1. building, structure; normally not used alone except as clf. C 2. clf. for buildings whose names have โรง as their first element, except where otherwise noted in the list of derivatives below.

ภารโรง (คน) phaanrooŋ' (khon') N janitor, custodian.

ยืนโรง jyyn'rooŋ' V 1. (someone) to be a mainstay. 2. to have the longest or most prominent role (as in a play); to have the same role every time.

โรงกระษาปณ์ rooŋkrasàab' N mint (i.e. where money is coined).

โรงเก็บ rooŋkèb' N storehouse.

โรงเก็บรถ rooŋ'kèbród' N garage.

โรงฆ่าสัตว์ rooŋ'khâasàd' N slaughterhouse.

โรงงาน (โรง,แห่ง) rooŋŋaan' (rooŋ',hɛ̀ŋ') N factory, workshop, plant.

o โรงงานฟอกหนัง rooŋŋaan'fɔ́ɔgnǎŋ' N tannery.

o โรงงานอุตสาหกรรม rooŋŋaan''ùsǎa'hakam', -?ùdsǎa'- N factory, industrial plant.

โรงจำนำ rooŋ'camnam' N pawnshop.

โรงช่างแสง rooŋ'châaŋsɛ̌ɛŋ' N arsenal.

โรงซ่อม rooŋsɔ̂m' N repair shop.

โรงซักผ้า rooŋ'ságphâa' N laundry (establishment).

โรงตำรวจ (แห่ง) rooŋ'tamrùad' (hɛ̀ŋ') N colloq. police station. →Syn. โรงพัก.

โรงเต้นรำ (แห่ง) rooŋ'tênram' (hɛ̀ŋ') N dance pavilion, dance hall, ballroom.

โรงทหาร (โรง,แห่ง,หลัง) rooŋ'thahǎan' (rooŋ', hɛ̀ŋ',lǎŋ') N military barracks.

โรงนา rooŋnaa' N farm shack, farm shed.

โรงไปรษณีย์ (แห่ง) rooŋ'prajsanii' (hɛ̀ŋ') N colloq. post office.

โรงพยาบาล (โรง,แห่ง) rooŋ'phajaabaan' (rooŋ', hɛ̀ŋ') N hospital.

o โรงพยาบาลศิริราช rooŋ'phajaabaan'-sirìrâad' pN the Sirirat (Siriraj) Hospital, in Thonburi.

โรงพละศึกษา rooŋ'phálásỳgsǎa' N gymnasium.

โรงพัก (โรง,แห่ง) rooŋphág' (rooŋ',hɛ̀ŋ') N colloq. police station. →Syn. โรงตำรวจ.

โรงพัสดุ (โรง,แห่ง) rooŋ'phádsadù?' (rooŋ', hὲŋ') N storehouse, warehouse.

โรงพิมพ์ (โรง,แห่ง) rooŋphim' (rooŋ,hὲŋ') N printing establishment, press, printery, publishing house.

โรงไฟฟ้า rooŋ'fajfáa' N electric power plant.

โรงภาพยนตร์ (โรง,แห่ง) rooŋ'phâabphajon' (rooŋ',hὲŋ') N eleg. moving-picture theater.

โรงภาษี (โรง,แห่ง) rooŋ'phaasĭi' (rooŋ',hὲŋ) N customs building.

โรงมหาสพ rooŋ'mahɔ̌ɔrasòb' N eleg. theater, entertainment establishment.

โรงรถ rooŋród' N garage.

โรงรับจำนำ rooŋráb'camnam' N pawnshop.

โรงเรียน (โรงเรียน,โรง,แห่ง) rooŋrian' (rooŋrian',rooŋ',hὲŋ') N school, schoolhouse.

o โรงเรียนกินนอน rooŋrian'kinnɔɔn' N com. boarding school. →Syn. โรงเรียนประจำ eleg.

o โรงเรียนเกษตรกรรม rooŋrian'kasèedtakam' N school of agriculture.

o โรงเรียนชั้นประถม rooŋrian'chánprathŏm' N elementary school, grade school.

o โรงเรียนดัดสันดาน rooŋrian'-dàd'sǎndaan' N reform school.

o โรงเรียนทางไปรษณีย์ rooŋrian'thaaŋprajsanii' N correspondence school.

o โรงเรียนเทศบาล rooŋrian'thêesabaan' N municipal school.

o โรงเรียนนายร้อย rooŋrian'naajrɔ́ɔj' N cadet academy.

o โรงเรียนประจำ rooŋrian'pracam' N eleg. boarding school. →Syn. โรงเรียนกินนอน com.

o โรงเรียนประชาบาล rooŋrian'prachaabaan' N public (elementary) school (only in rural areas or areas outside of a municipality).

o โรงเรียนประถมศึกษา rooŋrian'-prathŏm'sy̆gɔ sǎa' N elementary school.

o โรงเรียนฝึกหัดครู rooŋrian'fy̆ghàdkhruu' N teacher-training school, teachers college, normal school.

o โรงเรียนพาณิชยการ rooŋrian'phaních'chakaan' pN School of Commerce (a Government school in Bangkok).

o โรงเรียนมัธยมศึกษา rooŋrian'-mádthajom'sy̆gɔ sǎa' N secondary school.

o โรงเรียนรัฐบาล rooŋrian'rádthabaan' N public school. →Opp. โรงเรียนราษฎร์. →Syn. โรงเรียนหลวง.

o โรงเรียนราษฎร์ rooŋrian'râad' N private school. →Opp. โรงเรียนรัฐบาล,โรงเรียนหลวง.

o โรงเรียนหยุด rooŋrian'jùd' school is closed, is over, is out. →Comp. หยุดโรงเรียน.

o โรงเรียนอนุบาล rooŋrian'?ànúbaan' N kindergarten.

o โรงเรียนอาชีพ rooŋrian'?aachîib' N vocational school, trade school.

o หยุดโรงเรียน jùd'rooŋrian' to skip school, stay out of school. →Comp. โรงเรียนหยุด.

โรงแรม (โรง,แห่ง) rooŋrɛɛm' (rooŋ',hὲŋ') N hotel. →Syn. โฮเต็ล.

โรงละคร rooŋlakhɔɔn' N theater, playhouse.

โรงเลื่อย (โรง,แห่ง) rooŋlŷaj' (rooŋ,hὲŋ') N sawmill.

โรงศาล rooŋsǎan' N colloq. court of justice.

o ขึ้นโรงขึ้นศาล khŷnrooŋ'khŷnsǎan' V elab. colloq. to appear in court, go to court.

โรงสวด rooŋsùad' N colloq. church, church building.

โรงสินค้า (โรง,หลัง) rooŋsĭnkháa' (rooŋ',lǎŋ') N warehouse.

โรงสี,--ข้าว (โรง,แห่ง) rooŋsĭi', rooŋsĭikhâaw' (rooŋ',hὲŋ') N rice mill.

o โรงสีไฟ rooŋsĭifaj' N steam rice mill.

โรงหนัง (โรง,แห่ง) rooŋnǎŋ' (rooŋ,hὲŋ') N movie (theater). →Syn. โรงภาพยนตร์.

โรงหมอ (โรง,แห่ง) rooŋmɔ̌ɔ' (rooŋ',hὲŋ') N hospital, clinic (usually private).

โรงอุตสาหกรรม (โรง,แห่ง) rooŋ'?ùsǎha'hakam', -?udsǎ'- (rooŋ',hὲŋ') N industrial plant.

เหล้าโรง (ขวด) lâwrooŋ' (khùad') N an alcoholic beverage distilled from fermented rice.

โรจน์ in รุ่งโรจน์ rûŋrôod' V 1. to be glorious, flourishing. 2. to be bright, brilliant.

โรเนียว in พิมพ์โรเนียว,อัดโรเนียว phim'rooniaw', ?àd'rooniaw' V to duplicate by means of a Roneo machine (a process similar to mimeographing). [f. Eng.]

โรม ๑,--รัน room′, roomran′ V lit. to attack, fight.

โรม ๒ room′ pN Rome. [f. Eng.]

โรย rooj′ V 1. to sprinkle, scatter about on top of something. 2. to wither and drop off (of flower parts). 3. to be weary, exhausted.

  ถนนโรยกรวด (ลาย, ถนน) thanŏn′roojkrùad′ (sǎaj′, thanŏn′) N gravel road, driveway.

  ร่วงโรย rûaŋrooj′ V 1. to deteriorate, degenerate. 2. to be withered, wilted. 3. to have lost (its) vitality, vigor.

  อิดโรย ʔìdrooj′ V eleg. to be fatigued. →Syn. เหนื่อย com.

ไร ๑ raj′ 1. something, anything. 2. what? →Cf. อะไร. →Usually in special combinations only, as in the examples below.

  ช่าง(มัน)เป็นไร, -ปะไร châŋ′(man)penraj′↓, châŋ′(man)paraj′↓ Let it be. Let it go. I don't care. I don't care what happens to him.

  ทีไร thiiraj′ whenever, any time, whatever time.

  เท่าไร thâwràj′* 1. how much? how many? to what extent? 2. how much, how many. →See cross reference.

  เพียงไร phiaŋraj′ how much, to what level.

  เมื่อไร mŷaraj′ 1. when? 2. any time, whenever.

  ไม่เป็นไร mâjpenraj′↓ It doesn't matter. Never mind.

  เหตุไร hèed′raj′ 1. why? for what reason? 2. whatever reason.

  อย่างไร jàaŋraj′ 1. how? what? in what way? 2. how, what, in what way, in any way. 3. odd, strange, not quite right, unacceptable. →Also ยังไร, ยังไง. →For examples see cross reference.

ไร ๒ (ตัว) raj′ (tua′) N fowl louse.

ไร ๓. See entries below.

  ไรผม rajphŏm′ N 1. the hair line above the forehead. 2. the part or dividing line formed when the hair is gathered into a topknot. →Dist. 2. แสก.

  ไรฟัน rajfan′ N the teeth (as they are in the mouth).

ไร ๔ in เรี่ยไร rîaraaj′* V to solicit contributions, take up a collection.

ไร ๕ in ไรๆ rajraj′ sV indistinctly in the distance. →Usually in the following expression.

  o เห็นไรๆ hěn′rajraj′ to see vaguely, indistinctly in the distance.

ไร่ ๑ râj′ N 1. farm, plantation. C 2. a square surface measure equal to 1600 square meters (2.53 ไร่ equals one acre).

  ชาวไร่ชาวนา (คน) chaawrâj′chaawnaa′ (khon′) N elab. colloq. farmers.

  ทำไร่ thamrâj′ V to do farming, do crop-farming. →Syn. ทำนา.

  ที่ไร่ที่นา (แปลง) thîirâj′thîinaa′ (plɛɛŋ′) N elab. colloq. field, farm.

  พืชไร่ phŷyd′râj′ N farm crops.

  ไร่นา, --สาโท (แปลง) râjnaa′, râjnaa′sǎathoo′ (plɛɛŋ′) N elab. colloq. field, farm.

ไร่ ๒ in ไร่เรี่ย râjrîa′ to be about equal, about the same. →Usually ไล่เลี่ย.

ไร้ ráj′ V to be without; to lack.

  ไร้ความคิด ráj′khwaamkhíd′ V to be unthinking, not using one's head.

  ไร้ค่า ráj′khâa′ V to be valueless, worthless.

  ไร้งาน ráj′ŋaan′ V to be unemployed, out of a job.

  ไร้เดียงสา ráj′diaŋsǎa′ V to be innocent, naive, to lack worldly wisdom (as of a child).

  ไร้ประโยชน์ ráj′prajòod′ V to be useless, in vain.

  ไร้ผล ráj′phŏn′ V to be useless, futile, ineffective.

  ไร้สติ ráj′satì?′ V 1. to be unconscious. 2. to be crazy, insane.

  ไร้สาระ ráj′sǎará?′ V to make no sense, be nonsensical.

ไรเฟิล (กระบอก) rajfə̂n′, rajfə̂l′* (krabɔɔg′) N rifle. [f. Eng.]

ฤ

ฤ rý?′ A symbol used in the Thai writing system which functions as a consonant plus vowel combination pronounced rý-, rí-, or rəə. It is not considered one of the 44 letters of the alphabet since it is not a simple consonant. In dictionary arrangements, however, it is placed after ร.

ฤกษ์ rə̂əg′ N auspicious time.

ดาวฤกษ์ (ดวง) daawrɔ̂əg′ (duaŋ′) N fixed star.

ได้ฤกษ์ dâjrɔ̂əg′ to reach the auspicious moment.

ฤกษ์งามยามดี rɔ̂əgŋaam′jaamdii′ N elab.
colloq. auspicious time.

ฤกษ์ดี rɔ̂əgdii′ N propitious, auspicious time.

ฤดู (ฤดู) rýduu′ (rýduu′) N eleg. season.
→Comp. ระดู. →Syn. หน้า ๒.

ฤดูกาล rýduu′kaan′ N season, time.

ฤดูเก็บเกี่ยว rýduu′kèbkìaw′ N harvest, harvesttime, harvesting season.

ฤดูใบไม้ผลิ (ฤดู) rýduu′bajmáajphlì?′ (rýduu′)
N spring (the season).

ฤดูใบไม้ร่วง (ฤดู) rýduu′bajmáajrûaŋ′ (rýduu′)
N fall, autumn.

ฤดูฝน rýduu′fǒn′ N rainy season.

ฤดูร้อน rýduu′rɔ́ɔn′ N summer, the hot season.

ฤดูแล้ง rýduu′lɛ́ɛŋ′ N the dry season.

ฤดูหนาว rýduu′nǎaw′ N winter, the cold season.

วสันตฤดู wásǎn′tàrýduu′ N eleg. spring (the
season).

ฤทธิ์ ríd′ N 1. supernatural power. 2. effect.

แผลงฤทธิ์ phlɛ̌ɛŋríd′ V 1. to manifest supernatural power (usually in order to strike terror).
2. to act up, show itself. 3. to show (its) effects
(as of poison, drugs). 4. to show one's nature,
disposition (e.g. by stubbornness, temper, etc.).

ออกฤทธิ์ ?ɔ̀ɔgríd′ V 1. to show (its) effects (as
of poison, drugs). 2. to show one's nature, disposition (e.g. by stubbornness, temper, etc.).

อิทธิฤทธิ์ ?ìdthiríd′ N supernatural power, force
(esp. of a violent, destructive nature).

ฤทัย rythaj′ N lit. mind, heart. →Syn. See ใจ.

ฤษี (องค์) rysǐi′ (?oŋ′) N hermit, anchorite.
→More commonly ฤๅษี ryysǐi′.

ฤๅ

ฤๅ ryy′. A symbol used in the Thai writing system
which functions as a consonant plus vowel combination pronounced ryy′, ryyɔ.

ฤๅษี (ตน, องค์) ryysǐi′ (ton′, ?oŋ′) N hermit,
anchorite.

ล

ล lɔɔ′ LOW consonant. Pronounced l initially, n
finally (or occ. l in recent loanwords). The sound
l as an initial low consonant is also rarely written ฬ. →May be confused with ร in pron.

ลง loŋ′ V 1. to descend. 2. to get out of, get off
(a car, train, etc.). 3. to put (something) down.
4. to release, drop. sV 5. down. →A special use
of this word is given in the three examples below. →Ant. ขึ้น.

o ลงได้กินเหล้าละก็ เป็นเมาทุกที loŋ′dâjkinlâw′-
lakɔɔ→penmaw′thúgthii↓ Whenever he drinks,
he gets drunk.

o ลงบทชอบขึ้นมาละก็ loŋ′-bòdchɔ̂ɔb′khŷnmaa′-
lakɔɔ→ whenever one happens to like (someone
or something); whenever a liking arises; whenever love arises.

o ลงบทฉันชอบขึ้นมาละก็ loŋbòd′chánchɔ̂ɔb′-khŷnɔ
maa′-lakɔɔ→ whenever I happen to like (something).

ก้าวลง kâaw′loŋɔ to step down (from).

แก่ลง kɛ̀ɛ′loŋ to grow older.

ขาลง khǎaloŋ′ the downward trip; on the way down.

ขึ้นลง khŷnloŋ′ V 1. to fluctuate, rise and fall;
to be fluctuating, inconstant. 2. to go up and
down, take off and land. sV 3. up and down.

ค่ำลง khâm′loŋ 1. to become dark. 2. at dusk.

เงียบลง ŋîab′loŋ to quiet down.

จบลง còb′loŋ to end, be concluded.

ช้าลง cháa′loŋ to get slower, slow down, slow up.

ซาลง saa′loŋ to subside, abate.

o ฝนซาลง fǒn′saa′loŋ the rain is subsiding.

ได้ลงคอ dâjloŋkhɔɔ′ to be unfeeling enough to.

o ลูกฆ่าพ่อได้ลงคอ lûug′-khâa′phɔ̂ɔ′-dâjloŋkhɔɔ′↓
The son killed his father in cold blood.

o คุณนี่ช่างทำได้ลงคอนะ khun′nîi→châŋtham′dâjɔ
loŋkhɔɔ′-ná↓ How could you have the heart to
do this?

ตกลง tògloŋ′ V to agree (to something).

o ข้อตกลง (ข้อ) khɔ̂ɔ′tògloŋ (khɔ̂ɔ′) N 1.
agreement, settlement. 2. points of agreement.

o ตกลงใจ tògloŋcaj′ V to decide, to make up

one's mind.

o เป็นอันตกลง pen'an'tògloŋ'⌡ It's agreed.

ตลอดลงมา talòod'loŋmaa' all the way down to.

ทรุดลง súd'loŋ to get worse, take a turn for the worse (of a patient).

น้อยลง nɔ́ɔj'loŋ to decrease, diminish, dwindle.

นั่งลง nâŋ'loŋ to sit down.

น้ำลง námloŋ' N ebb tide. →Opp. น้ำขึ้น.

บรรเทาลง banthaw'loŋ to alleviate, reduce (e.g. pressure).

บินลง binloŋ' to land (of aircraft).

เบาบางลง bawbaaŋ'loŋ' to diminish, subside (e.g. illness, distress, noise).

ฝนลงเม็ด fǒn'loŋméd'⌡ It's starting to rain.

เย็นลง jen'loŋ to get cool, get cooler, cool down.

ลงกลอน loŋklɔɔn' V to bolt, latch (a door, window).

ลงข่าว loŋkhàaw' V to print, publish the news.

ลงแขก loŋkhὲɛg' V idiom. to hold a bee, get the help of one's neighbors on a given day (esp. for transplanting or harvesting rice).

ลงความเห็น loŋ'khwaamhěn' V to conclude, come to a general conclusion, come to an agreement.

ลงคอ ๑. See entry below.

o หวัดลงคอ wàd'loŋkhɔɔ' to have a sore throat, a cold with phlegm.

ลงคอ ๒. See ได้ลงคอ above.

ลงคะแนน loŋ'khanɛɛn' V 1. to cast a vote, cast a ballot. 2. to write down, record the score.

ลงชื่อ loŋchŷy' V colloq. to sign, sign one's name. →Syn. See เซ็นชื่อ com.

ลงท้อง loŋthɔɔŋ' V colloq. to suffer from diarrhea.

ลงทะเบียน loŋ'thabian' V to register, to be registered.

o จดหมายลงทะเบียน còdmǎaj'loŋthabian' N registered mail.

ลงทัณฑ์ loŋthan' V eleg. to punish. →Syn. See ทำโทษ.

ลงท้าย loŋtháaj' V 1. to be at the end. 2. to end, bring to an end, close. sV 3. finally, at last.

ลงทุน loŋthun' V to invest, make an investment.

o ลงทุนลงแรง loŋthun'loŋrɛɛŋ' V to put money and effort into (a project).

ลงโทษ loŋthôod' V 1. to punish. 2. to take disciplinary action. →Syn. See ทำโทษ.

o บทลงโทษ (ฉบับ,บท,ข้อ) bòd'loŋthôod' (chabàb', bòd', khɔɔ') N penal code.

ลงนาม loŋnaam' V eleg. to sign, sign one's name. การ-- signing, act of signing. →Syn. See เซ็นชื่อ com.

ลงบัตร loŋbàd' to cast a ballot.

ลงไป loŋpaj' 1. to go down. 2. down, downward.

ลงพุง loŋphuŋ' V colloq. to have a big belly, be paunchy, potbellied.

ลงมติ loŋ'mátì?' V to resolve, pass a resolution, come to a decision.

ลงมา loŋmaa' 1. to come down. 2. down, downward.

o ทุกคนตั้งแต่พระเจ้าแผ่นดินลงมา thúgkhon'-tâŋɔ tὲɛphrácâwphὲndin'loŋmaa' everyone from the king down.

o ลดต่ำลงมา lódtàm'loŋmaa' to get lower down.

ลงมือ loŋmyy' V idiom. to start, begin, undertake, set one's hand to. →Syn. ตั้งต้น.

ลงรถ loŋród' V to get out of a car, get off a vehicle (e.g. a bus, streetcar).

ลงรถไฟ loŋ'ródfaj' V to get off a train.

ลงรอย loŋrɔɔj' V idiom. to be in good harmony, in agreement, to get along well (with someone).

ลงรากตึก loŋ'râagtỳg' to lay the foundation of a building.

ลงเรือ loŋrya' V to board a boat.

ลงแรง loŋrɛɛŋ' V to expend energy.

o ลงทุนลงแรง loŋthun'loŋrɛɛŋ' V to put money and effort into (a project).

ลงวันที่ ๖ loŋ'wanthîihòg' dated the sixth.

ลงหลักปักราก loŋlàg'pàgrâag' V elab. to lay the foundation.

ลงเอย loŋ?əəj' V colloq. to end up, conclude, be settled.

ลดลง lód'loŋ to subside, become lower.

ลด(...)ลง lód'(...)loŋ to decrease, lower, reduce.

ล้มลง lóm'loŋ' to fall down, to collapse.

ล้มลงนอน lóm'loŋnɔɔn' to lie down.

เลวลง leew'loŋ to become worse.

สงบลง saŋòb'loŋ to die down, subside.

หย่อนลง jɔ̀ɔn'loŋ, jɔ̀n'loŋ 1. to put down, lower.
   2. to slow down. 3. to slacken (e.g. a rope).
   4. to decrease, diminish.
หารลงตัว hǎan'loŋtua' to be divisible (mathemat-
   ically).
อ่อนกำลังลง ʔɔ̀ɔn'kamlaŋ'loŋ to be weakened.
อ่อนเพลียลง ʔɔ̀ɔnphlia'loŋ to get weak, get weaker.
อ่อนลง ʔɔ̀ɔn'loŋ to get weaker, become milder,
   softer, less rigid.
ลงเล้ง in เสียงลงเล้ง (เสียง) sǐaŋ'lóŋléŋ'*
   (sǐaŋ') N slang loud noise (e.g. of quarreling, debating).
ลด lód' V to lower, reduce, decrease, discount.
   ลดราคา lód'raakhaa' to reduce the price; to give
      a discount; to put on sale; to have a sale.
   ลดลง lód'loŋ to subside, become lower.
   ลด(...)ลง lód'(...)loŋ to decrease, lower,
      reduce.
   ลดละ,ละลด lódlá?', lá?lód' V to give in, yield,
      let up.
   o อย่างไม่ลดละ jàaŋ'-mâjlódlá?' unrelentingly,
      without slackening, unceasingly, without letup,
      without giving in.
   ลดเลี้ยว lódlíaw' V to be winding.
   ลดหย่อน lódjɔ̀ɔn' to decrease, reduce, lower.
   ลดหลั่น lódlàn' to be descending in regular order,
      to cascade.
ล.ท. lɔɔ thɔɔ'. Abbrev. for หลังเที่ยง "after
   noon"; hence, P.M.
ลน ๑ lon' V to singe, hold over a flame.
   ลนไฟ lonfaj' V to singe, hold over a flame.
ลน ๒ lon' V to be excited, flustered, panicky.
   →Chiefly in compounds.
   ลนลาน lonlaan' V to show signs of agitation or
      perturbation, act flustered, flurried, agitated,
      panicky.
   ลุกลน,ลุกลี้-- lúglon', lúglíi'lúglon' V elab.
      colloq. to be in a flurry, to act in a nervous
      hurry.
ล้น lón' V 1. to be filled to overflowing. 2. to
   overflow, spill over.
   ล้นค่า lónkhâa' V eleg. to be invaluable, price-
      less.
   ล้นมือ lónmyy' V idiom. to be too much or too

many to handle.
   ล้นหลาม lónlǎam' V to be overloaded, overflowing,
      overcrowded.
ลบ lób' V 1. to erase. 2. to subtract; minus.
   ขั้วลบ (ขั้ว) khûalób' (khûa') N cathode; negative
      pole.
   แปรงลบกระดานดำ (อัน) prɛɛŋ'-lób'kradaandam'
      (ʔan') N blackboard eraser.
   ยางลบ (แท่ง) jaaŋlób' (thɛ̂ŋ') N eraser (made
      of rubber).
   ลบล้าง lóbláaŋ' V to wipe out, eradicate, wash
      away.
   ลบเลือน lóblyan' V to fade away.
   ลบหลู่ lóblùu' V 1. to show disrespect, contempt,
      disdain, ungratefulness (toward parents, guardian,
      teacher, or other benefactor particularly deserv-
      ing of respect).
ลพบุรี lób'burii' pN Lopburi, a township in C Thailand. →See also ละโว้.
ลม lom' N 1. wind, breeze, air. 2. air, mood, humor. 3. faint, swoon. →Syn. 2. อารมณ์.
   โกหกพกลม koohòg'phóglom' elab. colloq. to
      tell a lie.
   ดินน้ำลมไฟ din'→náam'→lom'→faj' the four
      elements: earth, water, wind, and fire.
   ได้ลม dâjlom' V 1. to get some air, get a breeze.
      2. to catch the wind.
   ต้องลม tɔ̂ŋ'lom' V to be blown by the wind, catch
      the wind (as a weathervane, a windmill, grass).
   ตามลม taamlom' V 1. to move leeward, go with
      the wind. sV 2. leeward, with the wind.
   ติดลม tìdlom' V to catch the wind.
   ใต้ลม tâajlom' downwind, leeward, on the leeward
      side. →Cf. เหนือลม.
   ทวนลม thuanlom' V 1. to move windward, go
      against the wind. sV 2. windward, against the
      wind.
   o ทำหูทวนลม thamhǔu'thuanlom' idiom. to
      pretend not to hear, turn a deaf ear.
   นุ่งลมห่มฟ้า nûŋlom'hòmfáa' elab. colloq. to
      be naked, in the nude: "clothe oneself with wind
      and sky."
   เป็นลม penlom' to faint.
   เป็นลมสวิงสวาย penlom'-sawǐŋ'sawǎaj' elab.

colloq. to feel like fainting.

พัดลม (อัน, เครื่อง) phádlom/ (ʔan/, khrŷaŋ/) N (electric) fan, air blower.

เพรียวลม phriawlom/ V to be streamlined, slender, slim.

ลมจัด lom/càd/ to be windy.

ลมจับ lom/càb/ V colloq. to faint, collapse.

ลมทะเล lom/thalee/ N sea breeze.

ลมบ้าหมู lom/bâamǔu/ N 1. whirlwind. 2. epilepsy; short for โรค--.

o โรคลมบ้าหมู rôog/-lom/bâamǔu/ N epilepsy.

ลมประจำ lom/pracam/ N seasonal wind.

ลมปราณ lompraan/ N breath.

ลมปัจจุบัน lom/pàdcuban/ N a sudden stroke, attack (of illness), fainting fit.

ลมปาก lompàag/ N 1. colloq. words, speech. 2. idiom. the power of speech, the effect of words.

ลมฝน lomfǒn/ N rain-bearing wind, rainstorm, rain and wind.

ลมพัด lomphád/ the wind is blowing.

ลมพัดจัด lom/phádcàd/ the wind is blowing hard.

ลมพายุ lom/phaajúʔ/ N windstorm.

ลมฟ้าอากาศ lomfáa/ʔaakàad/ N weather, climate.

ลมมรสุม lom/mɔɔrasǔm/ N monsoon wind.

ลมไม่ดี lom/mâjdii/ colloq. to be in a bad mood.

ลมสินค้า lom/sǐnkháa/ N trade winds.

ลมเสีย lom/sǐa/ V to be in a bad mood.

ลมหายใจ lom/hǎajcaj/ N breath.

ล่องลม lɔ̂ŋ/lom/ V to be carried by the wind, float with the wind.

ส่ายลม sǎajlom/ N breeze, drift of air, air current.

เหนือลม nŷalom/ upwind, windward, on the windward side. →Cf. ใต้ลม.

ล่ม lôm/ V 1. to sink, capsize, overturn. 2. to be ruined, destroyed (e.g. a crop).

ล่มจม lômcom/ V 1. to go bankrupt. 2. to collapse, fall (as a government).

ล้ม lóm/ V 1. to fall (from an upright position), keel (over), topple. 2. eleg. to die (esp. of an elephant). 3. to fell. 4. to kill. 5. to cancel, abandon (plans, intentions). →Dist. 1. ตก.

ล้มคว่ำ lómkhwâm/ V to fall face down.

ล้มเจ็บ lómcèb/ V to fall sick.

ล้มตัวลงนอน lómtua/loŋnɔɔn/ V 1. to lie down, lay oneself down. 2. to flop down (as on a bed).

ล้มตาย lóm/taaj/ V to die, be killed.

ล้มทั้งยืน lóm/tháŋjyyn/ colloq. to fall from a standing position, keel over.

ล้มพับ lóm/pháb/ V to collapse.

ล้มลง lóm/loŋ to fall down, collapse.

ล้มลงนอน lóm/loŋnɔɔn/ to lie down.

ล้มละลาย lóm/lalaaj/ V to go bankrupt.

ล้มล้าง lómláaŋ/ V to overthrow, abolish.

ล้มลุก lómlúg/ V to fall and rise again and again.

o พืชล้มลุก (ต้น, ชนิด) phŷyd/lómlúg/ (tôn/, chaɔ níd/) N any plant whose life cycle is short, as an annual or biennial.

o ล้มลุกคลุกคลาน lómlúg/khlúgkhlaan/ V elab. colloq. to fall down and scramble up again and again.

ล้มเลิก, เลิกล้ม lómlêɔg/, lêɔglóm/ V to abandon, quit, give up, abolish.

ล้มหงาย lómŋǎaj/ V to fall on one's back.

ล้มหมอนนอนเสื่อ lómmɔɔn/nɔɔnsỳa/ V elab. colloq. to fall sick, be brought to bed because of illness.

ล้มเหลว lómlěew/ V to fail. ความ-- failure, flop.

หกล้ม hòglóm/ V to tumble, fall over.

ลวก lûag/ V 1. to scald, burn, or scorch superficially. 2. to cook briefly, parboil; to soft boil (an egg). sV 3. carelessly, in a slovenly manner.

ไข่ลวก (ฟอง, ลูก, ใบ) khàjlûag/ (fɔɔŋ/, lûug/, baj/) N soft-boiled egg.

ลวกๆ lûaglûag/ sV roughly, carelessly, in a slovenly manner.

ลวง luaŋ/ V to deceive.

ลวงตา luaŋtaa/ V to deceive the eyes.

ล่อลวง lɔ̂ɔluaŋ/ V to deceive, delude, lure.

หลอกลวง lɔ̂ɔgluaŋ/ V to dupe, deceive.

ล่วง lûaŋ/ V 1. to pass (of time). 2. to go beyond (a certain limit). sV 3. beyond (a certain limit).

ล่วงเกิน lûaŋkəən/ to trespass against, offend, show disrespect to (someone).

ล่วงประเวณี lûaŋprawee/nii/ V to commit adultery.

ล่วงไป lûaŋpaj/ to pass by (of time).

ล่วงรู้ lûaŋrúu′ V to know in advance, be known in advance.

ล่วงลับ lûaŋláb′ V eleg. to be deceased, pass away.

ล่วงล้ำ lûaŋlám′ V to intrude, trespass.

ล่วงเลย lûaŋləəj′ 1. to pass by, elapse. 2. to go beyond, pass beyond.

ล่วงหน้า lûaŋnâa′ V 1. to go before. sV 2. in advance, previously, beforehand.

o ล่วงหน้าไปก่อน lûaŋnâa′pajkɔ̀ɔn′ to advance, go ahead.

ลุล่วง lú?lûaŋ′ V to be finished, completed, accomplished.

ล้วง lúaŋ′ V 1. to reach into (e.g. a pocket, deep drawer, hole). 2. to reach in for (something) (out of a pocket, deep drawer, etc.).

ล้วงกระเป๋า lúaŋ′krapǎw′ V 1. to pickpocket. 2. to put one's hand(s) in one's pocket(s). 3. to reach into one's pocket(s) (as when reaching for something, taking something out). นัก-- pickpocket.

เอามือล้วงกระเป๋า ?awmyy′-lúaŋ′krapǎw′ 1. to put one's hand(s) in one's pocket(s). 2. with one's hand(s) in one's pocket(s).

ลวด (เส้น,ขด) lûad′ N wire (sên′ for a piece, a strand; khɔ̀d′ for a roll).

ขดลวด (ขด) khɔ̀dlûad′ (khɔ̀d′) N 1. a coil of wire. 2. elect. coil.

มุ้งลวด múŋlûad′ N 1. screen, wire screen. 2. screened section or cubicle for sleeping in.

ลวดไฟฟ้า lûad′fajfáa′ N electric wire.

ลวดลาย (แบบ) lûadlaaj′ (bɛ̀ɛb′) N 1. pattern, decorative design. 2. colloq. some special talents, skills or abilities of a person.

o ฝากลวดลาย fàag′lûadlaaj′ V colloq. to leave (with someone) an impression of one's skills.

o ออกลวดลาย ?ɔ̀ɔg′lûadlaaj′ V colloq. to demonstrate, show off one's special skills.

ลวดหนาม lûadnǎam′ N barbed wire.

วงลวด (วง) woŋlûad′ (woŋ′) N a loop of wire.

ลวน in ลวนลาม luanlaam′ V to overstep the rules of propriety; to be impertinent, act impertinently, make impertinent advances.

ล้วน lúan′ sV entire, pure; entirely, purely, completely.

ล้วนแต่ lúan′tɛ̀ɛɔ nothing but, all, entirely, completely.

ล้วนๆ lúanlúan′ entirely, completely.

ลหุ lahù?′, lahùɔ minor, of lesser importance. →Chiefly in compounds.

o อาปัญญากรรมขั้นลหุ ?àadchajaakam′-khân′lahù?′ a petty crime.

ลหุโทษ lahùthôod′ N 1. light punishment or penalty. 2. minor offense, misdemeanor. →Syn. โทษเบา com.

ล่อ ๑ (ตัว) lɔ̀ɔ′ (tua′) N mule. →Also ฬ่อ FS.

ล่อ ๒ lɔ̀ɔ′ V 1. to lure, tempt, allure, seduce. 2. slang to take food or drink. 3. slang to hit, strike.

เครื่องล่อ (อย่าง) khrŷaŋlɔ̀ɔ′ (jàaŋ′) N decoy, something used as an inducement or lure.

ล่อใจ lɔ̀ɔcaj′ V to entice, tempt.

o เครื่องล่อใจ khrŷaŋlɔ̀ɔcaj′ N an enticement.

ล่อลวง lɔ̀ɔluaŋ′ V to deceive.

ล่อ ๓ in ล่อแหลม lɔ̀ɔlɛ̌ɛm′ V to be risky, dangerous, critical.

ล้อ ๑ (ล้อ,เล่ม) lɔ́ɔ′ N 1. wheel (lɔ́ɔ′). 2. a crudely made cart drawn by two oxen, used for hauling rice sheaves (lêm′). V 3. to roll (a wheel or wheel-shaped object). →Syn. 2. เกวียน.

รถจักรยานสามล้อ (คัน) ródcàgkrajaan′sǎamlɔ́ɔ′ (khan′) N eleg. 1. pedicab, samlor. 2. tricycle.

ล้อรถ (ล้อ) lɔ́ɔród′ (lɔ́ɔ′) N wheel of a vehicle.

o ยางล้อรถ (เส้น) jaaŋ′lɔ́ɔród′ (sên′) N (rubber) tire.

ล้อเลื่อน (คัน) lɔ́ɔlŷan′ (khan′) N lit. vehicles (collective term).

ลูกล้อ (อัน,ลูก) lûuglɔ́ɔ′ (?an′,lûug′) N wheel (of any kind).

สามล้อ (คัน) sǎamlɔ́ɔ′ (khan′) N colloq. samlor, pedicab.

ห้ามล้อ hâamlɔ́ɔ′ V 1. to brake, put on the brake(s). N 2. brake.

o เครื่องห้ามล้อ (เครื่อง) khrŷaŋhâamlɔ́ɔ′ (khrŷaŋ′) N brake.

ลอ ๒ lɔɔ′ V to tease, mock.

ต่อล้อต่อเถียง tɔɔlɔɔ′tɔɔthǐaŋ′ V elab.colloq.
to keep arguing, talk back. 2. to refute, contradict, argue back and forth.

ภาพล้อ (ภาพ) phâablɔɔ′ (phâab′) N caricature.

ล้อเล่น lɔɔlên′ V to tease, kid, joke.

ล้อเลียน lɔɔlian′ V to mock, ridicule by mimicry.

หยอกล้อ jɔɔglɔɔ′ V to tease, kid, play with.

ลอก lɔɔg′ V 1. to copy, make a copy. 2. to skin,
peel. 3. to dredge, take out (mud).

คัดลอก, ลอกคัด khád′lɔɔg′, lɔɔg′khád′ V to copy,
imitate.

ปอกลอก pɔɔglɔɔg′ V to defraud, fleece, skin,
clean (someone) out by pretending love, friendship, interest.

ลอกคราบ lɔɔgkhrâab′ V 1. to molt, slough. 2.
slang to strip (someone) of clothing.

ลอกแลก lɔɔglɛ̂ɛg′* V to have a restless, shifting manner (now attentive, now inattentive; now looking
here, now there; not paying consistent and considered respect).

ตาลอกแลก taa′lɔɔglɛ̂ɛg′ V 1. to have restless
eyes. 2. (a man) to have eyes which are always
looking at the women. N 3. restless eyes; a
roving eye.

ลอง lɔɔŋ′ V to try, try out, try on.

ทดลอง thódlɔɔŋ′ V to experiment, test, try out.
การ-- experiment, test, trial.

ลองคิดดู lɔɔŋkhíd′duuᵓ, lɔɔŋ′khídduu′ V to think
(it) over.

ลองใจ lɔɔŋ′caj′ V to test another's feelings,
attitude, willingness, reaction.

ลองดี lɔɔŋ′dii′ V colloq. to put to the test
(as a law, by defying it, or a person, to determine his capabilities).

ลองดู lɔɔŋ′duu′ V to try, try out, try and see
(what something is like).

ลองตัว lɔɔŋ′tua′ V to try on (for size).

ลองภูมิ lɔɔŋ′phuum′ V to test the knowledge of,
measure the educational level or background of
(usually in an attempt to catch someone, expose
someone's ignorance).

ล่อง lɔ̂ŋ′* V 1. to float, cause to float along. 2. to
follow along (a stream, railroad).

o ล่องซุง lɔ̂ŋsuŋ′ to float logs downstream.

ขาล่อง (เที่ยว) khǎalɔ̂ŋ′ (thîaw′) N 1. the downstream trip, the south-bound trip. 2. on the way
downstream, on the way south.

เที่ยวล่อง (เที่ยว) thîawlɔ̂ŋ′ (thîaw′) N 1. the
downstream trip, south-bound trip, return trip.
2. on the way downstream, on the way south.

ล่องลม lɔ̂ŋlom′ V to be carried by the wind, float
with the wind.

ล่องลอย lɔ̂ŋlɔɔj′ V to wander, drift, float aimlessly.

ล่องหน lɔ̂ŋhǒn′ V to move about invisibly (by
magic).

ลอด lɔɔd′ V 1. to pass through or under (e.g. an
obstacle, barrier, fence, etc.). 2. short for
เล็ดลอด below.

เล็ดลอด, ลอดเล็ด lédlɔɔd′, lɔɔdléd′ V to slip or
sneak (in, out, through, etc.), move secretly and
quietly.

ลอตเตอรี่ (ฉบับ, ใบ) lɔ́dtəərîi′*(chabàb′, baj′) N
com. lottery ticket. [f. Eng.] →Also ตั๋ว--.
→Syn. หวยเบอร์ colloq., สลากกินแบ่ง eleg.

ลอน (ลอน) lɔɔn′ (lɔɔn′) N wave, undulation.
→Syn. คลื่น. →Dist. งอ, หยิก.

เป็นลอน penlɔɔn′ V to be wavy, undulating.

ล่อนจ้อน lɔ̂ncɔ̂n′* V to be nude, naked, bare.

ลอนดอน, กรุง-- lɔɔndɔɔn′, kruŋ′lɔɔndɔɔn′ pN
London.

ลอบ ๑ (ลูก, ใบ) lɔɔb′ (lûug′, baj′) N a kind of
bamboo fishtrap.

ลอบ ๒ lɔɔb′ V eleg. 1. to move stealthily, sneak.
2. to do (something) secretly. →Syn. แอบ.

ลอบเข้าไปใน lɔɔb′khâwpajnajᵓ eleg. to steal
into.

ลอบทำร้าย lɔɔb′thamráaj′ V eleg. to ambush,
attack or assault by surprise.

ลอบหนี lɔɔbnǐi′ V eleg. to sneak away.

ลักลอบ láglɔɔb′ V to act under cover, in secret.

o ลักลอบเอาฝิ่นเข้ามาในประเทศ láglɔɔb′ʔawfìn′-
khâwmaanajprathêed′ to smuggle opium into the
country.

ล้อม lɔ́ɔm′ V 1. to surround, encircle. 2. to besiege.

ปิดล้อม pìd′lɔ́ɔm′ V to blockade, block off by
surrounding.

พูดหว่านล้อม phûud'wàanlɔ́ɔm' V to cajole someone into doing or accepting something.

ล้อมรอบ lɔ́ɔmrɔ̂ɔb' V 1. to surround. 2. to circle around.

ล้อมรั้ว lɔ́ɔmrúa' V to fence, put a fence around,
surround with a fence.

ล้อมหน้าล้อมหลัง lɔ́ɔmnâa'lɔ́ɔmlǎŋ' V to surround,
crowd around.

วงล้อม woŋlɔ́ɔm' N an encirclement.

แวดล้อม wɛ̂ɛdlɔ́ɔm' V 1. to surround. 2. to be
surrounded.

o สถานการณ์แวดล้อม sathǎa'nákaan'wɛ̂ɛdlɔ́ɔm'
N circumstance.

o สิ่งแวดล้อม (สิ่ง, อย่าง) sìŋ'wɛ̂ɛdlɔ́ɔm' (sìŋ',
jàaŋ') N environment, surroundings.

ห้อมล้อม hɔ̂mlɔ́ɔm' V to surround, gather around.

ลอย lɔɔj' V to float, drift.

ข่าวโคมลอย khàaw'khoomlɔɔj' N unfounded
rumor, unsubstantiated news.

ใจลอย cajlɔɔj' V to be absent-minded, have
one's mind wander.

ตาลอย taalɔɔj' V 1. to have vacant eyes. sV 2.
with vacant eyes.

ปอดลอย pɔ̀ɔdlɔɔj' V slang to be timorous,
faint-hearted. 2. to be scared out of one's wits.

พูดลอยๆ phûud'lɔɔjlɔɔj' to say something without
addressing anybody in particular.

ลอยคอ lɔɔjkhɔɔ' V to float with the head above
water.

ลอยชาย lɔɔjchaaj' V 1. to saunter along (e.g.
when speed is needed). sV 2. saunteringly.

ลอยน้ำ lɔɔjnáam' V to float in water.

ลอยฟ่อง lɔɔjfɔ̂ŋ' V to float freely.

เลิศลอย lə̂ədlɔɔj' V 1. to be excellent, superlative. sV 2. highly, to the highest degree.

เลื่อนลอย lʉ̂anlɔɔj' V to drift, wander aimlessly
(as of thoughts).

ละ ๑ lá?' V to leave, desert. →Chiefly in compounds. →Often coupled with ทิ้ง.

ลดละ, ละลด lódlá?', lá?lód' V to give in, yield,
let up.

o อย่างไม่ลดละ jàaŋ'-mâjlódlá?' unrelentingly,
without slackening, unceasingly, without letup,
without giving in.

ละทิ้ง lá?'thíŋ' V to abandon, desert, neglect.

ละเลย lá?'ləəj' V to neglect.

o ปล่อยปละละเลย plɔ̀jplà?'-lá?'ləəj' V to neglect,
abandon.

ละเว้น lá?'wén' V to abstain from, keep away
from, shun.

ละ ๒ lá?', la‿ per (as in per day, per year, etc.).
→Dist. ทุก. →Cf. ต่อ (see note under ปีละ
below).

ข้างละ khâŋla‿ per side, (on) each side.

o ข้างละห้าคน khâŋlahâa'khon' five persons on
each side.

คนละทิศละทาง khonlathíd'lathaaŋ' each one in
a different direction.

คนละไม้คนละมือ khonlamáaj'khonlamyy' e l a b.
c o l l o q. each a hand, as in ช่วยกัน-- chûaj'‿
kan-khonlamáaj'khonlamyy' each one gives a
helping hand.

คราวละ khraawla‿ each time.

แต่ละ tɛ̀ɛla‿* each and every (one of), every single
(followed by a clf.). →See cross reference.

o แต่ละปี tɛ̀ɛlapii' (in) each year.

o ไม่เว้นแต่ละวัน mâjwén'tɛ̀ɛlawan' every single
day, without missing a single day, day in day out.

ทีละ thiila‿ "at a time," as in the following entries.

o ทีละขั้น ๒ ขั้น thiilakhân's̀ɔɔŋkhân' one or two
steps at a time.

o ทีละคน thiilakhon' one (person) at a time.

o ทีละน้อย thiilanɔ́ɔj' little by little, a little at
a time.

o ทีละเล็กละน้อย thiilalég'lanɔ́ɔj' e l a b. little
by little, a little at a time.

ใบละพัน (ใบ) bajlaphan' (baj') N 1000-tical bill.

ใบละร้อย (ใบ) bajlá?rɔ́ɔj' (baj') N 100-tical bill.

ปีละ piila‿ per year, a year, yearly. →Cf. ต่อปี.
NOTE. Distinguish the positions of ต่อปี and
ปีละ in the examples below.

o ได้เงินพันบาทต่อปี dâjŋən'phanbàad'-t̀ɔɔpii'
gets a thousand bahts per year.

o ได้เงินปีละพันบาท dâjŋən'-piilaphan'bàad' gets
a thousand bahts annually.

ร้อยละ (...) (1) rɔ́ɔj'lá?'; (2) rɔ́ɔj'la‿... N 1.
percentage. 2. (so and so much) percent.

วันละ wanla‿ per day, a day, daily.

o วันละครั้ง wanlakhráŋ′ once a day, once daily.

ละ ๓ lá?, la?, laⸯ Pt particle used often with mildly entreative and/or mildly corroborative force.

o แต่พึ่งเชื่อได้ละหรือว่า tɛ̀ɛ′-phyŋchŷa′dâjlaⸯ
rýywâa′ but should it be believable that.

ดีละ dii′la?↓ Very well! O. K. ! All right then!
(as when indignant).

ถูกละ thùug′la? true enough; of course.

o ถูกละอย่างที่เราเรียกกันว่า... thùug′la?→
jàaŋthîirawrîag′kanwâa′... Of course, the
kind that we call... .

ละ ๔ in ละก็,ละก้อ lakɔ̂ɔ′ Pt 1. particle sometimes used at the end of a conditional clause,
often with the force of a mild entreaty. 2. particle used at the end of the subject of a predication, in a corroborative sense: "you know,"
"after all," "why then," etc.

o (ถ้า)ยังไงๆละก็ แวะที่ร้านของฉันบ้างนะ (thâaⸯ)
jaŋŋaj′jaŋŋaj′-lakɔ̂ɔ′→ wɛ́?′-thîiráan′khɔ̌ɔŋⸯ
chán′bâŋná↓ If (you can manage it) one way
or another, why then drop in to my store for a
bit.

o หากคุณชอบละก็... hàag′khunchɔ̂ɔb′-lakɔ̂ɔ′→
if you like it, why then... .

o เด็กละก็เป็นอย่างนี้ dèg′lakɔ̂ɔ′→ pen′jàaŋníi↓
Well, children are like that, you know.

o เดี๋ยวก็คงจะมา ผู้หญิงละก็แต่งตัวช้าเสมอ dǐaw′ⸯ
kɔ̌khoŋcamaa′↓ phûujǐŋ′lakɔ̂ɔ′→tɛ̀ɛŋtuacháa′ⸯ
samɔ̌ə′↓ She'll be along in a minute; women,
you know, always take their time dressing.

เอาละ ?aw′la?↓, ?awla?′↓ All right. Ready.
O. K.

ละ lâ′ Pt particle with mildly entreative force,
similar to but not interchangeable with ละ ๓,
in the following examples.

o นอนหลับสบายดีทีเดียว คุณละครับ nɔɔnlàb′-saⸯ
baajdii′thiidiaw′→ khun′lâkhráb′↓ I slept quite
well. And you?

บอกแล้วไหมล่ะ bɔɔgléɛw′májlâ↓ I told you so.
Didn't I tell you? See, I told you, didn't I?

อะไรอีกล่ะ ?araj′?ìiglâ′ What now? What else?
(as when irritated).

ละคร (เรื่อง,โรง) lakhɔɔn′ N 1. drama, play,
theatrical performance (rŷaŋ′). 2. theatrical

group, theater (rooŋ′). การ-- drama, play.
นัก-- devotee of the theater; authority on drama
and dramatics.

ตัวละคร tualakhɔɔn′ N character (in a play).

โรงละคร (โรง) rooŋlakhɔɔn′ (rooŋ′) N theater.

ละครตลก (เรื่อง) lakhɔɔn′talòg′ (rŷaŋ′) N
farce, comedy.

ละครลิง lakhɔɔnliŋ′ (a) monkey circus.

ละครสัตว์ (โรง,คณะ) lakhɔɔnsàd′ (rooŋ′, khaná?′)
N circus.

เล่นละคร lên′lakhɔɔn′ V com. to act, play, put
on an act, a play.

แสดงละคร sadɛɛŋ′lakhɔɔn′ V eleg. idem.

ละม่อม. See entries below.

โดยละม่อม doojlamɔ̂m′* gently, without force or
violence.

ละมุนละม่อม lamun′lamɔ̂m′* V 1. to be gentle,
tender. 2. to be polite, well-mannered.

ละมั่ง (ตัว) lamâŋ′ (tua′) N a deer sp. (Cervus eldi).

ละม้าย lamáaj′ V eleg. to resemble, look like.
→Syn. See คล้าย.

ละม้ายคล้ายคลึง lamáaj′khláajkhlyŋ′ V elab.
eleg. to resemble, look like.

ละมุด (ลูก,ผล,ใบ) lamúd′ (lûug′, phǒn′, baj′) N
fruit of the fol. tree. ต้น-- (ต้น) a kind of
fruit tree (Mimusops kauki).

ละมุน. See entries below.

ละมุนละม่อม lamun′lamɔ̂m′ V 1. to be gentle,
tender. 2. to be polite, well-mannered.

ละมุนละไม lamun′lamaj′ V to be gentle, tender,
sweet, pleasant.

อ่อนละมุน ?ɔ̀ɔn′lamun′ V to be gentle, soft,
smooth, graceful.

ละเมอ laməə′ V to talk in one's sleep.

ละเมาะ,ป่า-- (แห่ง) lamɔ́?′, pàa′lamɔ́?′ (hɛ̀ŋ′)
N grove.

ละเมิด lamə̂əd′ V to violate, infringe, break.

ละโมบ lamôob′ V to be greedy, covetous, grasping.

ละโมบโลภลาภ lamôob′lôoblâab′ V elab. eleg.
to be greedy.

ละไม lamaj′ V to be attractive, sweet.

ยิ้มละไม jím′lamaj′ V to smile pleasantly.

ละมุนละไม lamun′lamaj′ V to be gentle, tender,
sweet, pleasant.

ละลอก (ลูก) lalɔ́ɔg/ (lûug/) N ripple, wave.
→Also ระลอก.

ละลาบละล้วง lalâab/lalúaŋ/ V to intrude, act intrusively or presumptuously, trespass.

ละลาย lalaaj/ V to dissolve, melt.
ล้มละลาย lóm/lalaaj/ V to go bankrupt.

ละล้าละลัง lalâa/lalaŋ/ V to be worried, distressed, agitated (because in a dilemma).

ละล่ำละลัก lalâm/lalág/ sV with gasps, between gasps (as when speaking while breathless from exertion or excitement).

ละเลง laleeŋ/ V to smear, spread (usually with a circular motion).

ละวา in ตายละวา taaj/lawaa/ E excl. expressing dismay.

ละแวก lawɛ̂ɛg/ N district, vicinity, area.
ละแวกบ้าน lawɛ̂ɛg/bâan/ N community, inhabited or settled area, area where people live.

ละโว้ lawóo/ pN Lavo, the ancient name for Lopburi (ลพบุรี).

ละห้อย lahɔ̌j/* V to be mournful, sad.
หน้าละห้อย nâa/lahɔ̌j/ V to look sad, depressed.

ละหุ่ง,ต้น-- (ต้น) lahùŋ/, tônlahùŋ/ (tôn/) N the caster-oil plant.
น้ำมันละหุ่ง námman/lahùŋ/ N castor oil.

ละเหย lahə̌əj/ V to evaporate, vaporize, volatilize.
→Usually ระเหย.

ละเหี่ย lahìa/ V to feel tired, weary, exhausted.
ละเหี่ยใจ lahìa/caj/ V to feel disheartened, physically and mentally tired.

ละออง la?ɔɔŋ/ N fine particles, dust, powder.
ละอองเกสร (เม็ด) la?ɔɔŋ/keesɔ̌ɔn/ (méd/) N pollen, pollen grain.
ละอองน้ำ la?ɔɔŋ/náam/ N fine spray, mist; condensed water (e.g. on a glass of cold water).
ละอองฝน la?ɔɔŋ/fǒn/ N drizzle, rain mist, fine droplets of rain.

ละอาย la?aaj/ V to be ashamed, shy, bashful.
ความ-- shame, bashfulness.
ละอายใจ la?aaj/caj/ V to be ashamed.

ละเอียด la?ìad/ V 1. to be fine, delicate, detailed, in detail. 2. to be meticulous, careful, thorough, thoroughgoing.
โดยละเอียด doojla?ìad/ minutely, in detail.

รายละเอียด raajla?ìad/ N the details, the particulars.
ให้ละเอียด hâjla?ìad/ in detail, thoroughly.

ลัก lág/ V to steal. →Syn. ขโมย.
ลักพา lág/phaa/ V (a man) to carry off, elope with (a woman).
ลักยิ้ม (แห่ง,ข้าง,รอย) lágjím/ (hɛ̀ŋ/, khâaŋ/, rɔɔj/) N dimple.
ลักลอบ láglɔ̂ɔb/ V to act under cover, in secret.
o ลักลอบเอาฝิ่นเข้ามาในประเทศ láglɔ̂ɔb/?awfìn/-khâwmaanajprathêed/ to smuggle opium into the country.
ลักเล็กขโมยน้อย lág/lég/-khamooj/nɔ́ɔj/ V elab. to pilfer.
ลักปิดลักเปิด lágkapìd/lágkapə̀əd/ N scurvy. →Also โรค--.
ลักลั่น láglân/ V to be out of order, mixed up (esp. in regard to consecutiveness of size or height).
ลักษณ. See entries below. →Cf. ลักษณะ.
ลายลักษณ์อักษร laajlág/?àgsɔ̌ɔn/ N elab. eleg. writing, script.
o เป็นลายลักษณ์อักษร penlaajlág/?àgsɔ̌ɔn/ elab. eleg. in writing, in written form.
ลัญฉลักษณ์ (ตัว) sǎn/jalág/ (tua/) N eleg. symbol. →Syn. เครื่องหมาย.
ลักษณะ (อย่าง) lágsanà?/ (jàaŋ/) N physical characteristics, appearance; characteristic; manner.
คุณลักษณะ khun/nalág/sanà?/ N quality, qualities, attributes (of a desirable nature).
บุคคลิกลักษณะ bùg/khalíg/lág/sanà?/ N eleg. personality.
รูปลักษณะ rûub/-lág/sanà?/ N appearance, feature, form.

ลัง (ใบ,ลูก) laŋ/ (baj/, lûug/) N crate, wooden box.
ลังกา laŋkaa/ pN colloq. Ceylon.
ลังเล laŋlee/ V to hesitate, waver, be uncertain.
ความ-- hesitation.
ลังเลใจ laŋlee/caj/ V to hesitate, waver.
อาการลังเล ?aakaan/laŋlee/ N hesitation, hesitating manner.

ลัด ๑ lád/ V to take a short cut, cut across.
ทางลัด (ทาง) thaaŋlád/ (thaaŋ/) N short cut.
ลัดเลาะ ládlɔ́?/ V to take short cuts and to skirt.
ลัด ๒ as in ลัดใบ ládbaj/ V lit., eleg. to put

forth leaves.

ลัทธิ (ลัทธิ) ládthí?⁄ (ládthí?⁄) N doctrine, belief, creed, practice, "ism."

ลัทธิคอมมิวนิสต์ ládthí?⁄khɔmmiwnis⁄, -níd⁄ N communism.

ลัทธิจักรวรรดินิยม ládthí?⁄-càgkrawàd⁄níjom⁄, -kawàd⁄- N imperialism.

ลัทธิชาตินิยม ládthí?⁄-châad⁄níjom⁄ N nationalism.

ลัทธิประชาธิปไตย ládthí?⁄-prachaa⁄thíbpataj⁄ N democracy.

ลัทธิเผด็จการ ládthí?⁄-phadèd⁄kaan⁄ N dictatorship.

ลัทธิไสยศาสตร์ ládthí?⁄sǎjjasàad⁄ N the doctrine or practice of magic (as derived from Brahmanism, and dealing esp. with spells and incantations).

ลัทธิหาเมืองขึ้น ládthí?⁄-hǎa⁄myaŋkhŷn⁄ N colloq. colonialism. →Syn. ลัทธิอาณานิคม eleg.

ลัทธิอาณานิคม ládthí?⁄-?aanaa⁄níkhom⁄ N eleg. colonialism. →Syn. ลัทธิหาเมืองขึ้น.

ลั่น ๑ lân⁄ V 1. to fire, shoot, release, set off. 2. to go off, fire (as of a gun), make a loud noise. sV 3. loud, loudly.

ฟ้าลั่น fáa⁄lân⁄ 1. to thunder; it thunders. N 2. thunder; a thunderclap.

ร้องลั่น rɔ́ɔŋ⁄lân⁄ V to shout, scream, cry out loudly.

ลั่นกลอน lânklɔɔn⁄ V to bolt, latch (a door, window).

ลั่นกุญแจ lânkuncɛɛ⁄ V to lock.

ลั่นไก lân⁄kaj⁄ V 1. to pull the trigger. 2. to go off.

ลั่นคำ lân⁄kham⁄ V 1. to say, speak, declare. 2. to commit oneself, give one's word.

ลั่นปาก lân⁄pàag⁄ idem.

ลั่นวาจา lân⁄waacaa⁄ V eleg. idem.

หัวเราะลั่น hǔarɔ́?⁄lân⁄ V to roar with laughter.

ลั่น ๒ in ลักลั่น láglân⁄ V to be out of order, mixed up (in reg. to consecutiveness of height, etc.).

ลับ ๑ láb⁄ V 1. to be secret, hidden. 2. to disappear. ความ-- secret.

ของลับ (อัน) khɔ̌ɔŋláb⁄ (?an⁄) N genitalia, private parts.

เคล็ดลับ khlédláb⁄ N secret means, secret technique.

เมียลับ (คน) mialáb⁄ (khon⁄) N 1. mistress. 2. illicit wife. 3. secret minor wife or concubine. →Syn. เมียเก็บ.

ล่วงลับ lûaŋláb⁄ V to pass away (die).

ลับตา lábtaa⁄ V to be out of sight, to disappear.

ลับหลัง láblǎŋ⁄ V 1. to have the back turned. sV 2. behind (someone's back), (while his) back is turned.

ลี้ลับ líiláb⁄ V to be secret.

ลึกลับ lýgláb⁄ V to be mysterious. ความ-- mystery.

o เรื่องลึกลับ rŷaŋ⁄lýgláb⁄ N mystery story.

สายลับ (คน,สาย) sǎajláb⁄ N 1. spy, secret informer (khon⁄). 2. intelligence channel (sǎaj⁄).

ลับ ๒ láb⁄ V to whet, sharpen.

หินลับมีด (ก้อน) hǐn⁄lábmîid⁄ (kɔ̂ɔn⁄) N whetstone.

ลับ ๓ in ลิบลับ líbláb⁄ rM intensifier used with expressions implying distance or comparison. →See under ลิบ.

ลัพธ์ in ผลลัพธ์ phǒnláb⁄ N result, final result.

ลา ๑ (ตัว) laa⁄ (tua⁄) N donkey. →Also ฬา FS.

ลา ๒ laa⁄ C eleg. time. →Of limited use.

ลา ๓ laa⁄ V 1. to take one's leave, say good-by (upon one's departure). 2. to request or take leave, leave of absence, time off. การ-- taking one's leave; requesting leave of absence, time off.

กราบลา kràablaa⁄ V to take leave of (one's elders or superiors). This is often done by prostrating oneself.

ใบลา (ใบ) bajlaa⁄ (baj⁄) N application for a leave of absence.

ร่ำลา râmlaa⁄ V to bid farewell, say goodbye (usually implying repeated farewells).

ลากลับ laaklàb⁄ V to take one's leave, say good-by (when departing to return home, return to work, etc.).

ลาก่อน laakɔ̀ɔn⁄ good-bye. →Used only by one who is leaving, departing.

ลาป่วย laapùaj⁄ V to request or take sick leave.

ลาพัก laaphág⁄ V to request or take a leave of absence (in order to rest).

ลาหยุด laajùd′ V to request or take a leave of absence, ask for, take time off.

ลาออก laa?ɔ̀ɔg′ V to resign.

ล่า ๑ lâa′ V to hunt.

ล่าสัตว์ lâasàd′ V to hunt, hunt game.

ล่า ๒ lâa′ to withdraw, retreat.

○ ต้องล่าทัพกลับไป tɔ̂ŋlâa′tháb′klàbpaj′ he had to withdraw his armies.

ล่าถอย lâathɔ̌ɔj′ V to withdraw, draw back.

ล่า ๓ lâa′ V to be late.

ข่าวล่า khàawlâa′ late news.

ข่าวล่าที่สุด khàawlâa′thîisùd′ the latest news.

ล่าช้า lâacháa′ V 1. to be tardy, late. 2. to be slow.

ล้า láa′ V 1. to lag. 2. to be tired. →Usually in special phrases, as in the entries below.

เมื่อยล้า mŷajláa′ V to be tired, fatigued, stiff and sore.

ล้าสมัย láa′samǎj′ V to be out-of-date, behind the times. →Syn. หมดสมัย.

ล้าหลัง láalǎŋ′ V to lag behind, be behind (in time or space), be backward. ความ-- backwardness.

ลาก lâag′ V to pull, draw, drag, haul, tow.

ผู้ลากมากดี (คน) phûulâag′-mâag′dii′ (khon′) N elab. colloq. the nobility, the elite, the people of the upper classes. →Cf. ผู้ดี.

รถลาก (คัน) ródlâag′ (khan′) N eleg. rickshaw. →Syn. รถเจ๊ก colloq.

ลากเกวียน lâagkwian′ to pull a cart.

ลากพื้น lâagphýyn′ V to be dragged along the floor.

ลาง ๑ laaŋ′ N omen, prophetic sign.

ถือโชคถือลาง thɣ̌ychôog′thɣ̌ylaaŋ′ V elab. colloq. to be superstitious. →Also ถือลาง.

ลางดี laaŋdii′ N good omen.

ลางร้าย laaŋráaj′ N bad omen.

ลาง ๒. See ราง.

ลาง ๓ laaŋ′ Nm some. →More commonly บาง ๓.

ลางที laaŋthii′ sometimes, at times; other times. →More commonly บางที.

ล่าง lâaŋ′ below. →Ant. บน ๑.

ข้างล่าง khâŋlâaŋ′ 1. lower part. 2. below, down below. 3. downstairs. →Opp. ข้างบน.

ชั้นล่าง chánlâaŋ′ downstairs, lower story, lower layer, lower shelf. →Opp. ชั้นบน.

ล้าง láaŋ′ V 1. to wash, wash off (of things other than hair or clothes). 2. fig. to wipe out (esp. in certain expressions). →Dist. 1. ซัก "wash (clothes)," สระ "wash (the hair)."

กวาดล้าง kwàadláaŋ′ V 1. to clean out, wipe out. 2. fig. to purge, eliminate, kill off.

ทำลายล้าง thamlaaj′láaŋ′ V to destroy, wipe out.

ชะล้าง chá?láaŋ′ V to rinse, wash away, cleanse.

ลบล้าง lóbláaŋ′ V to wipe out, eradicate, wash away.

ล้มล้าง lómláaŋ′ V to overthrow, abolish.

ล้างแค้น láaŋkhɛ́ɛn′ V to get rid of one's resentment (usually by taking revenge).

ล้างชีวิต láaŋ′chiiwíd′ V lit. to kill, destroy.

ล้างผลาญ láaŋphlǎan′ V eleg. to destroy, ruin, waste.

ล้างฟิล์ม láaŋfiim′ V to develop or process a photographic film.

ล้างรูป láaŋrûub′ V to develop a photographic film or print.

ล้างหน้า láaŋnâa′ V to wash the face.

○ ที่ล้างหน้า (ที่) thîiláaŋnâa′ (thîi′) N 1. washbasin, lavatory.

○ อ่างล้างหน้า (ใบ) ?àaŋ′láaŋnâa′ (baj′) N washbasin.

ล้างออก láaŋ?ɔ̀ɔg′ to wash off; to be washed off.

ลางสาด (ใบ,ลูก,ผล,พวง) laaŋsàad′ N lansa, a kind of fruit (baj′, lûug′, phǒn′ for individual fruits; phuaŋ′ for bunches). ต้น-- (ต้น) lansa (the tree) (Lansium domesticum).

ลาด ๑ lâad′ V 1. to cover, spread over, pave (with); to be covered, paved (with). N 2. cover, spread (in certain compounds).

ลาดตระเวน lâadtraween′ V to patrol, make the rounds to inspect (a place, an installation).

○ เรือลาดตระเวน (ลำ) rya′lâadtraween′ (lam′) N cruiser (a class of warship).

ลาดพระบาท lâad′phrábàad′ N a covering, carpet placed on the ground for the king to walk on.

ลาดยาง lâadjaaŋ′ V to be paved with asphalt.

ลาด ๒ lâad′ V 1. to slant, incline, slope. N 2. slope, incline. →Dist. 1. ชัน ๒.

o ลาดลงทางแม่น้ำ lâad'loŋthaaŋmɛ̂ɛnáam' (the terrain) slopes downward to the river.

o ลาดเขา lâadkhǎw' the slope of a hill.

ลาด ๓ in ลาดเลา lâadlaw' N 1. situation, layout (as it bears upon some future move, course of action). 2. clue, sign, trace.

ลาน ๑ (อัน) laan' (ʔan') N spring (as of a watch).

ลาน ๒ (แห่ง) laan' (hɛ̀ŋ') N an open, wide, level area such as a courtyard, lawn, terrace, field.

ลาน ๓ (ต้น) laan' (tôn') N a kind of palm tree.

ลาน ๔ laan' V to be excited, flustered, panicky.

    ลนลาน lonlaan' V to show signs of agitation or perturbation, act flustered, flurried, agitated, panicky.

    ลานตา laantaa' V colloq. to make one's eyes spin (because of fantastically large numbers).

ล้าน ๑ láan' V to be bald.

    หัวล้าน hǔaláan' V to be baldheaded.

ล้าน ๒ láan' Nm 1. million. C 2. idem.

    สิบล้าน sìbláan' Nm ten million. →Also โกฏิ.

ลาภ lâab' N a windfall, an unexpected piece of good fortune.

    ละโมบโลภลาภ lamôob'lôoblâab' V elab. eleg. to be greedy.

ลาม laam' V 1. to spread all over. 2. to be presumptuous.

    ไฟลามทุ่ง faj'laamthûŋ' "the fire spreads over the field," a simile used to describe any chain of events which spreads rapidly.

    ลวนลาม luanlaam' V to overstep the rules of propriety; to be impertinent, act impertinently, make impertinent advances.

    ลุกลาม lúglaam' V to spread (as of a fire).

ล่าม ๑ lâam' V 1. to chain, put a rope around (the neck of). 2. to tether, tie up.

ล่าม ๒ (คน) lâam' (khon') N interpreter.

ลามก laamóg' V to be obscene, lewd, indecent.

    ความ-- lewdness, obscenity.

ลาย (ลาย) laaj' (laaj') N 1. design, pattern. V 2. to be striped.

    ตาลาย taalaaj' V 1. to have blurred vision, have double or multiple vision. 2. to have a whirling sensation.

    ลวดลาย (แบบ) lûadlaaj' (bɛ̀ɛb') N 1. pattern,

decorative design. 2. colloq. some special talents, skills or abilities of a person.

ลายกนก,ลายกระหนก (ลาย) laajkanòg', laajɔkranòg' (laaj') N generic term for a kind of decorative pattern characteristic of Thai art.

ลายคราม (ชิ้น) laajkhraam' (chín') N china having a design in indigo. →Usually refers to antique Thai (Siamese) ware. →Also เครื่อง--.

ลายเซ็น (ลายเซ็น) laajsen' (laajsen') N signature, autograph.

ลายดุน (ลาย) laajdun' (laaj') N embossed design in high relief.

ลายมือ (ลายมือ,อัน,เส้น) laajmyy' N 1. handwriting (laajmyy'). 2. finger print (ʔan'). 3. the lines on the palm of the hand (sên').

o ฝีไม้ลายมือ fǐimáaj'laajmyy' N elab. colloq. craftsmanship, workmanship, skill, ability.

ลายลักษณ์อักษร laajlág'ʔàgsɔ̌ɔn' N elab. eleg. writing, script.

o เป็นลายลักษณ์อักษร penlaajlág'ʔàgsɔ̌ɔn' elab. eleg. in writing, in written form.

ลาว laaw' N Lao, Laos, Laotian.

    ประเทศลาว (ประเทศ) prathêedlaaw' (prathêed') N eleg. Laos. →Syn. เมืองลาว com.

ลำ lam' C 1. clf. for boats, ships, airplanes; for long objects, approximately cylindrical in form, as a plant stem, a beam of light. N 2. courseway, passageway.

    แก้ลำ kɛ̂ɛ'lam' V to retaliate; to have a return match, a return engagement.

ลำกล้อง (อัน) lamklɔ̂ŋ' (ʔan') N gun barrel.

ลำแข็ง lamkhɛ̌ŋ' N 1. idiom. personal effort, endeavor. 2. shin (rarely used in this meaning; more commonly หน้าแข้ง).

ลำคลอง (สาย) lamkhlɔɔŋ' (sǎaj') N canal.

ลำคอ (ลำคอ) lamkhɔɔ' (lamkhɔɔ') N throat.

ลำต้น (ลำต้น) lamtôn' (lamtôn') N trunk (of a tree).

ลำตัว (ลำตัว) lamtua' (lamtua') N trunk (of the body), torso.

ลำธาร (แห่ง,สาย) lamthaan' (hɛ̀ŋ', sǎaj') N stream.

ลำน้ำ (สาย) lamnáam' (sǎaj') N water passage.

ลำแสง (ลำ) lamsɛ̌ɛŋ' (lam') N beam of light.

ลำไส้ (ขด) lamsâj⁄ (khòd⁄) N bowel, intestine.

ล่ำ lâm⁄ V to be stout, sturdy, husky.

เป็นล่ำเป็นสัน penlâm⁄pensǎn⁄ V elab. colloq.
1. to be solid, substantial, coherent, well-
founded, well-organized. 2. solidly, substantially, coherently, as a staple, as a steady thing.
→Syn. เป็นกอบเป็นกำ.

ล่ำสัน lâmsǎn⁄ V to be strong, robust, muscular.

ล้ำ lám⁄ V 1. to go beyond, exceed, pass. sV 2.
exceedingly, extremely.

ความเหลื่อมล้ำ khwaam⁄lỳamlám⁄ N inequality,
disparity, difference.

รุกล้ำ rúg⁄lám⁄ V 1. to intrude, trespass. 2.
to penetrate, advance into (by force).

ล่วงล้ำ lûaŋlám⁄ V to intrude, trespass.

ล้ำเลิศ lámlə̂əd⁄ V to be excellent, superb.

สูงล้ำ sǔuŋ⁄lám⁄ V to be exceedingly high.

ลำเค็ญ lamkhen⁄ V eleg. to be poor, hard-pressed,
hard up. ความ-- hardship, adversity.

ลำดับ lamdàb⁄ N 1. order, orderly arrangement.
V 2. to arrange in proper order. →Syn. 1.
อันดับ.

โดยลำดับ doojlamdàb⁄ progressively, gradually.

ตามลำดับ taamlamdàb⁄ 1. in order, in series,
consecutively. 2. respectively. 3. progressively, gradually. 4. in order (of)(e.g. height).

เป็นลำดับ penlamdàb⁄ 1. in order, serially, successively, in succession, one after another. 2.
respectively. 3. progressively, gradually.

เรียงลำดับ riaŋ⁄lamdàb⁄ to be arranged in order
(of)(e.g. height).

เลขลำดับ (ตัว) lêeg⁄lamdàb⁄ (tua⁄) N ordinal
number.

ลำตัด lamtàd⁄ N antiphony, improvised antiphonal
singing.

ลำเนา in ภูมิลำเนา phuu⁄mílamnaw⁄ N native
habitat, native district.

o ตั้งภูมิลำเนา tâŋ⁄phuu⁄mílamnaw⁄ to take up
residence (as in a new place), to settle.

ลำบาก lambàag⁄ V 1. to be hard, difficult, troublesome, bothersome, a bother, a hardship; to
cause trouble, hardship. 2. to be in difficulty,
trouble; to be subjected to hardship, trouble,
bother. 3. to trouble oneself. ความ-- diffi-

culty, trouble.

o จะไปไหนก็ลำบาก capajnǎj⁄kɔlambàag⁄ (it's)
hard to go anywhere (e.g. without a car).

ฐานะลำบาก thǎaná?⁄lambàag⁄ N difficult position.

ลำปาง lampaaŋ⁄ pN Lampang, a township in N
Thailand.

ลำพอง lamphɔɔŋ⁄ V to feel strong and brave. 2.
to be high-spirited. 3. to become puffed up,
self-important.

ลำพัง lamphaŋ⁄ by oneself, alone, singly, single-
handed.

โดยลำพัง dooj⁄lamphaŋ⁄ by oneself, singlehandedly.

ตามลำพัง taamlamphaŋ⁄ alone, by oneself.

แต่ลำพัง tὲɛlamphaŋ⁄ alone, by oneself.

ลำพังแต่ lamphaŋ⁄tὲɛ alone (as in "he alone").

ลำพูน lamphuun⁄ pN Lamphun, a township in N
Thailand.

ลำแพน (ผืน) lamphɛɛn⁄ (phỹyn⁄) N bamboo mat.

ลำโพง (อัน) lamphooŋ⁄ (?an⁄) N loudspeaker,
megaphone.

ลำไพ่ lamphâj⁄ N supplementary income (from
outside work).

ลำไย (ลูก,ผล) lamjaj⁄ (lûug⁄, phǒn⁄) N longan(fruit).
ต้น-- (ต้น)longan tree (Euphoria longana).

ลำลอง lamlɔɔŋ⁄ V to be casual, informal (of dress).

o เครื่องลำลอง (ชุด) khrŷaŋ⁄lamlɔɔŋ⁄ (chúd⁄)
N casual wear, informal wear.

o แต่งกายลำลอง tὲŋkaaj⁄lamlɔɔŋ⁄ to dress casually or informally, wear one's sports clothes.

ลำลึก lamlýg⁄ V to recall, remember, bring to mind,
think of. →Also more commonly รำลึก.

ลำเลิก lamlə̂əg⁄ V to recount, extol one's meritorious deeds done to others in the past.

ลำเลียง lamliaŋ⁄ V to transport (in small quantities),
to lighter. การ-- transporting (in small quantities, as by lighter).

เรือลำเลียง (ลำ) rya⁄lamliaŋ⁄ (lam⁄) N lighter.

สายลำเลียง (สาย) sǎaj⁄lamliaŋ⁄ (sǎaj⁄) N
supply line.

ลำเอียง lam?iaŋ⁄ V to be inclined (toward), to be
partial. ความ-- partiality, inclination.

ลิเก likee⁄ N com. musical folk drama. →Also
ยี่เก colloq.

ลิขสิทธิ์ lígkhasìd⁄ N eleg. copyright.

ลิขิต líkhìd′ V lit. 1. to write. N 2. writings; a writing; a letter.

ปัจฉิมลิขิต pàdchǐm′líkhìd′ N postscript, P.S. →Abbrev. ป.ล.

ลิง ๑ (ตัว) liŋ′ (tua′) N monkey.

ลิงคน (ตัว) liŋkhon′ (tua′) N orang-utan.

ลิงทโมน (ตัว) liŋ′thamoon′ (tua′) N (a) big monkey. →Often used as a simile to describe mischievous children.

ลิงป่า (ตัว) liŋpàa′ (tua′) N orang-utan.

ลิงเสน (ตัว) liŋsěen′ (tua′) N rufous monkey, stump-tailed monkey.

ลิงแสม (ตัว) liŋsamɛ̌ɛ′ (tua′) N crab-eating monkey.

ลิงหอย (ตัว) liŋhɔ̌j′ (tua′) N a small species of monkey.

ลิง ๒ in ลิงโลด liŋlôod′ V to be jubilant, joyful; to jump up and down with joy.

ลิตร líd′ V liter. [f. Eur.]

ลิ้น (ลิ้น) lín′ (lín′) N 1. tongue. 2. reed, valve.

ลิ้นไก่ línkàj′ N uvula.

o พูดลิ้นไก่สั้น phûud′-línkàj′sân′ V to be drunken in speech: "to talk (like someone) with a short uvula."

ลิ้นชัก (ลิ้นชัก) línchág′ (línchág′) N drawer.

ลิ้นทะเล (อัน) lín′thalee′ (ʔan′) N cuttlebone, used to make a powder for polishing and as medicine.

ลิ้นปี่ línpìi′ N 1. reed (of a woodwind). 2. anat. xiphoid cartilage.

เล่นลิ้น lênlín′ V idiom. to deflect the point of a remark or criticism by a clever or witty reply.

แลบลิ้น lɛ̂ɛblín′ V to stick out the tongue.

ลิ้นจี่ (ลูก,ผล) líncìi′ (lûug′, phǒn′) N litchi (or lichee)(the fruit). ต้น-- (ต้น) litchi (the tree).

ลินิน linin′ N linen. [f. Eng.]

ลิบ líb′ rM intensifier used with expressions implying distance (e.g. ไกล "far," สูง "high," ห่างกัน "far apart from each other"), or comparison (e.g. ผิดกัน "different from each other," แพงกว่ากัน "one more expensive than the other").

ลิบลับ líbláb′ idem.

ลิบๆ líblíb′ sV (visible) in the distance, (visible) way (up), way (far away).

ลิบลิ่ว líblîw′ idem ลิบ.

ลิปสติก (อัน,แท่ง) líbsatìg′, líbsatíg′ (ʔan′, thɛ̂ŋ′) N lipstick. [f. Eng.]

ลิ่ม (อัน) lîm′ (ʔan′) N wedge.

เป็นลิ่มๆ pen′lîmlîm′ in clots (as of blood).

ลิ้ม lím′ V eleg. to taste. →Syn. ชิม.

ลิ้มรส límród′ V eleg. to taste.

ลิลิต (เรื่อง) lílíd′ (rɯ̂aŋ′) N a mixed form of Thai versification.

ลิ่ว lîw′ rM intensifier used with expressions implying distance or comparison. →See also ลิบ.

ลิสง in ถั่วลิสง thùalisǒŋ′ N colloq. peanut. →Var. of ถั่วยี่สง eleg., lit.

ลี้ líi′ V 1. to escape. 2. to hide.

ลี้ลับ líiláb′ V to be secret.

ลีบ lîib′ V to be abortive, undeveloped.

ลีลา liilaa′ N eleg. 1. graceful poise or movement. 2. rhythm.

ลีลาศ liilâad′ N eleg. 1. dance. V 2. to dance.

งานลีลาศ ŋaan′liilâad′ N eleg. dancing party, dance. →Refers to ballroom dancing.

ลึก lýg′ V to be deep. ความ-- depth.

ลึกซึ้ง lýgsýŋ′ V to be profound, deeply-felt.

ลึกลับ lýgláb′ V to be mysterious. ความ-- mystery.

o เรื่องลึกลับ rɯ̂aŋ′lýgláb′ N mystery story.

ลึงค์ lyŋ′ N 1. gram. gender. 2. eleg. sex. 3. eleg. penis.

ลื่น lɯ̂yn′ V to be slippery, smooth.

ปากกาลูกลื่น (ด้าม,อัน) pàagkaa′lûuglɯ̂yn′ (dâam′, ʔan′) N ball point pen.

ลืม ๑ lyym′ V to forget.

ขี้ลืม khîilyym′ V to be forgetful, absent-minded.

ขี้หลงขี้ลืม khîilǒŋ′khîilyym′ V eleg. colloq. to be forgetful, absent-minded.

ไม่รู้ลืม mâjrúu′lyym′ to be unforgettable, never to be forgotten. 2. unforgettably. 3. without forgetting.

ลืมตัวลืมตน lyymtua′lyymton′ V elab. colloq. to forget oneself.

ลืมเลือน lyym′lɯan′ V to fade away (of memory).

ลืมเสียเถิด lyym′síathə?′↓ Forget it. Let's forget it.

ลืม(เสีย)สนิท lyym/(sía)sanìd/ V to forget completely.

ลืม ๒ lyym/ V to open (the eyes).

ลืมตา lyymtaa/ V 1. to open the eyes. 2. to have one's eyes open. →Opp. หลับตา.

o ลืมตาโพลง lyymtaa/phloon/ to have one's eyes wide open (e.g. instead of being asleep).

ลืมหูลืมตา lyymhǔu/lyymtaa/ V elab. colloq. to open one's eyes to, or become aware of what is going on around one.

ลือ lyy/ V to rumor, be rumored. →Also ฦๅ FS.

ข่าวลือ (เรื่อง) khàawlyy/(rŷaŋ/) N rumor.

ข่าวเล่าลือ (เรื่อง) khàaw/lâwlyy/(rŷaŋ/) N rumor.

คำเล่าลือ (เรื่อง,อย่าง,ประการ) kham/lâwlyy/ (rŷaŋ/, jàaŋ/, prakaan/) N rumor.

ลือฉา lyychaa/ V to be well-known, widely spoken of.

ลือชื่อ lyychŷy/ V 1. (people, everyone) to talk about (it), spread (it) around: "spread the name." 2. to be well-known, famous, widely spoken of. →Also เลื่องชื่อลือนาม.

ลือนาม lyynaam/ V eleg. to be famous, renowned, well-known.

ลื้อ ๑ lýy/ P you. →Paired with อั๊ว "I, me." →Often used among men who are intimates. [f. Chin.]

ลื้อ ๒ lýy/ N a tribe of hill people in N Thailand.

ลุ lú?/ V to reach, get to. →Chiefly in the following expressions.

ลุแก่โทษ lúkὲεthôod/ V eleg. to confess and ask forgiveness.

ลุแก่อำนาจ lú?/kὲε?amnâad/ V to overstep one's authority.

ลุล่วง lú?lûaŋ/ V to be done, finished, completed, accomplished.

ลุก lúg/ V to get up, rise, arise.

ขนลุก khǒnlúg/ V to have the hair stand on end (as when frightened).

ผุดลุกผุดนั่ง phùdlúg/phùdnâŋ/ V elab. colloq. to be repeatedly getting up and sitting down again (e.g. because of restlessness, impatience).

ลมลุก lómlúg/ V to fall and rise again and again.

ลมลุกคลุกคลาน lómlúg/khlúgkhlaan/ V elab.

colloq. to fall down and scramble up again and again.

ลุกขึ้น lúgkhŷn/ to get up, arise (as from bed).

ลุกช่วง lúg/chûaŋ/ V eleg. to blaze up brightly.

ลุกโพลง lúg/phlooŋ/ V colloq. to blaze up brightly.

ลุกไม่ขึ้น lúg/mâjkhŷn/ can't get up (e.g. because of illness, disability, etc.).

ลุกลน,ลุกลี้-- lúglon/, lúglíi/lúglon/ V elab. colloq. to be in a flurry, act in a nervous hurry.

ลุกลาม lúglaam/ to spread (as of a fire).

ลุกไหม้ lúg/mâj/ V to burn. การ-- combustion.

ลุกฮือ lúg/hyy/ V 1. to flare up all at once (of a fire). 2. to rise up all at once, suddenly and all together (as of a mob).

ลุง (คน) luŋ/ (khon/) N 1. elder uncle (older brother of father or mother). P 2. you, Uncle (sp. to elder uncle or other older man); he, him, Uncle (sp. of elder uncle); I, me, Uncle (elder uncle or older man sp. to nephew, niece, or other ygr. person). T 3. Uncle-- (ref. to one's elder uncle or other older man). →Opp. ป้า. →Cf. อา,น้า.

คุณลุง khunluŋ/ N 1. elder uncle. P 2. eleg. you, he, him (sp. to or of one's elder uncle, or other highly respected older man).

ลุงแชม luŋsεεm/ N "Uncle Sam," i.e. the U.S.

ลุ่ม ๑ lûm/ V 1. to be low, low-lying (esp. of land). N 2. lowland, basin.

ที่ลุ่ม (แห่ง,ที่) thîilûm/ (hὲŋ/, thîi/) N lowland, basin.

ลุ่มน้ำ (แห่ง) lûmnáam/ (hὲŋ/) N river basin.

ลุ่มๆดอนๆ lûmlûm/dɔɔndɔɔn/ V to be uneven (on the surface). ความ-- unevenness, ups and downs.

ลุ่ม ๒ in ลุ่มหลง lûmlǒŋ/ V to be crazy (about), infatuated (with), madly in love (with).

ลุย luj/ V to wade; to go through, wade through.

ลุยโคลน lujkhloon/ V to wade through mud, wade in mud.

ลุย in ทิ้งกันลุย thíŋ/kanlûj/ colloq. to leave (one's opponent) far behind; to outscore by a wide margin.

ลู่ (ลู่) lûu/ (lûu/) N 1. track, path, way. 2. to bend,

incline. →Syn. See ทาง ๑.

ลู่ทาง (ลู่ทาง) lûuthaaŋ′ (lûuthaaŋ′) N means, way.

ออกนอกลู่นอกทาง ?ɔ̀ɔg′-nɔ̀ɔglûu′nɔ̀ɔgthaaŋ′ 1. to get off course. 2. to do something wrong.

เอนลู่ ?een′lûu′ V to bend, incline (as with the wind).

ลูก (คน,ตัว,ลูก) lûug′ N 1. com. child (khon′) (used only as a relationship term). 2. offspring (tua′)(of animals, usually in cpds.). 3. fruit (lûug′)(of trees, usually in cpds.). P 4. I, me (child sp. to parents); you (parent sp. to child); he, him, she, her (sp. of one's child, of some-one's child). C 5. clf. for fruit of any kind; for mountains; for certain round or small ob-jects. →Dist. 1. เด็ก. →Syn. 1. บุตร eleg., 3. ผล eleg., 5. (when referring to fruit) ใบ com., ผล eleg.

> NOTE. As the first member of a compound, ลูก often refers to one of the following. (1) persons of a group, or those standing in a subor-dinate or dependent relationship to others: ลูก จ้าง "employee, hireling"; ลูกค้า "customer." (2) the young of animals and birds, and also larvae: ลูกแกะ "lamb"; ลูกเป็ด "duckling"; ลูกน้ำ "mosquito larva." (3) certain types of fruit: ลูกมะพร้าว "coconut" (but most kinds of fruit are not preceded by ลูก). (4) certain subsidiary devices: ลูกกุญแจ "key." (5) certain ball- or cube-like objects of various kinds: ลูกตา "eyeball."

ชั่วลูกชั่วหลาน chûalûug′chûalǎan′ elab. genera-tion after generation. →Compare ลูกหลาน.

ตกลูก tòglûug′ V to give birth, drop young (of animals).

แท้งลูก théɛŋlûug′ V to miscarry, have a mis-carriage, have an (accidental) abortion. →Dist. รีดลูก.

มดลูก (มดลูก) módlûug′ (módlûug′) N womb, uterus.

ลูกกบ (ตัว) lûugkòb′ (tua′) N tadpole.

ลูกกรง (ด้าน,อัน,ซี่) lûugkroŋ′ N 1. balustrade, railing (dâan′,?an′). 2. the sides of a cage or pen (i.e. one having upright bars)(dâan′). 3. bar of a balustrade, cage, pen (sîi′); in this sense usually ซี่ลูกกรง.

ลูกกระดุม (เม็ด) lûugkradum′ (méd′) N button.

ลูกกระเดือก (ลูก) lûugkradÿag′ (lûug′) N Adam's apple.

ลูกกระโปก (ลูก) lûugkrapòog′ (lûug′) N com., vulg. testicles. →Syn. ลูกอัณฑะ eleg., ไข่ colloq.,euphem.

ลูกกระสุน (นัด,ลูก) lûugkrasǔn′ (nád′,lûug′) N 1. bullet, shot, pellet, projectile. 2. cartridge.

ลูกกลอน (ลูก) lûugklɔɔn′ (lûug′) N bolus, a wet lump or tablet of freshly prepared medicine.

ลูกกลิ้ง (ลูก,อัน) lûugklîŋ′ (lûug′,?an′) N roller (for compacting, pulverizing, printing, etc.).

ลูกกวาด (เม็ด,ก้อน,ลูก) lûugkwàad′ (méd′,kɔ̂ɔn′, lûug′) N candy, esp. bonbons, hard candies.

ลูกกุญแจ (ดอก) lûugkuncɛɛ′ (dɔ̀ɔg′) N key.

ลูกเกด (เม็ด) lûugkèed′ (méd′) N colloq. raisin.

ลูกแก้ว (ลูก) lûugkɛ̂ɛw′ (lûug′) N (glass)marble(s).

ลูกแกะ (ตัว) lûugkɛ̀?′ (tua′) N lamb.

ลูกไก่ (ตัว) lûugkàj′ (tua′) N chick, baby chicken.

ลูกข่าง (ลูก) lûugkhàaŋ′ (lûug′) N top (the toy).

ลูกขุน (คน) lûugkhǔn′ (khon′) N juror.

o คณะลูกขุน (คณะ) khaná?′lûugkhǔn′ (khaná?′) N jury.

ลูกเขย (คน) lûugkhɤ̌əj′ (khon′) N com. son-in-law.

ลูกความ (คน) lûugkhwaam′ (khon′) N litigant.

ลูกค้า (คน) lûugkháa′ (khon′) N customer.

ลูกคิด (อัน) lûugkhíd′ (?an′) N abacus.

o ดีดลูกคิด dìid′lûugkhíd′ V 1. to figure or cal-culate with an abacus. 2. colloq. to scheme, figure the angles.

ลูกเงาะ (ลูก) lûugŋɔ́?′ (lûug′) N rambutan, a kind of fruit.

ลูกจ๊อก (คน) lûugcɔ́ɔg′ (khon′) N slang sub-ordinate; low ranking employee, person of the lower ranks.

ลูกจ้าง (คน) lûugcâaŋ′ (khon′) N colloq. hireling, employee.

ลูกเจี๊ยบ (ตัว) lûugcíab′ (tua′) N colloq. chick.

ลูกชาย (คน) lûugchaaj′ (khon′) N com. son. →Syn. บุตรชาย eleg.

ลูกโซ่ (อัน) lûugsôo′ (?an′) N link (of a chain).

ลูกดุม (เม็ด) lûugdum′ (méd′) N button.

ลูกเด็กเล็กแดง (คน) lûugdèg′légdɛɛŋ′ (khon′)

N elab. colloq. infants and young children (collectively). →Also ลูกเล็กเด็กแดง.

ลูกโดด (ลูก) lûugdòod/ (lûug/) N ball, bullet, slug (whatever is discharged singly).

ลูกตะกั่ว (ลูก) lûugtakùa/ (lûug/) N slang bullet, slug of lead.

ลูกตัว (คน) lûugtua/ (khon/) N com. one's real child (related by blood). →Dist. ลูกเลี้ยง.

ลูกตา (ลูก) lûugtaa/ (lûug/) N anat. eyeball.

ลูกตาดำๆ lûugtaa/damdam/ N idiom. a baby, a child.

ลูกตุ้ม (ลูก) lûugtûm/ (lûug/) N 1. pendulum. 2. heavy pendant. 3. plummet.

ลูกเต็นนิส (ลูก) lûugtenníd/, -nís/ (lûug/) N tennis ball. [เต็นนิส f. Eng.]

ลูกเต้า (คน) lûugtâw/ (khon/) N (one's own) children (i.e. related by blood).

ลูกเต้าเล่าอ่อน (คน) lûugtâw/láw?ɔɔn/ (khon/) N elab. colloq. (one's own) children (esp. very young children).

ลูกเต๋า (ลูก) lûugtǎw/ (lûug/) N die, dice.

ลูกแถว (คน) lûugthɛ̌w/ (khon/) N 1. colloq. person standing in line (other than at the head). 2. men in the lower ranks, the rank and file (in the police force, army). →Dist. หัวแถว.

ลูกทรงกลม (ลูก) lûug/soŋklom/ (lûug/) N sphere, spherical body.

ลูกธนู (ลูก,ดอก) lûugthanuu/ (lûug/,dɔ̀ɔg/) N arrow.

ลูกน้อง (คน) lûugnɔ́ɔŋ/ (khon/) N colloq. underling, subordinate.

ลูกน้ำ (ตัว) lûugnáam/ (tua/) N mosquito larva.

o จุดลูกน้ำ cùd/lûugnáam/ N colloq. the comma.

ลูกบอลล lûugbɔn/, lûugbɔɔl/ N ball. [บอลล f. Eng.]

ลูกบ้าน (คน) lûugbâan/ (khon/) N colloq. 1. villagers. 2. members of a household.

ลูกบาศก์ (ลูก) lûugbàad/ (lûug/) N cube.

o ลูกบาศก์เมตร lûugbàad/méed/ N cubic meter.

ลูกบิด (ลูก,อัน) lûugbìd/ (lûug/,?an/) N door-knob, door handle (i.e. one which can be turned).

ลูกบุญธรรม (คน) lûugbuntham/ (khon/) N eleg. adopted child. →Syn. See ลูกเลี้ยง com.

ลูกปัด lûugpàd/ N glass beads.

ลูกปา lûugpaa/ N confetti (for throwing).

ลูกปืน (ลูก,นัด) lûugpyyn/ (lûug/,nád/) N 1. bullet, gunshot. 2. ball bearing.

ลูกโป่ง (ลูก,ใบ) lûugpòoŋ/ (lûug/,baj/) N com. toy balloon.

ลูกผู้ชาย (คน) lûugphûuchaaj/ (khon/) N 1. son. 2. colloq. a (real) man (i.e. one with manly qualities). 3. (as n. mod.) manly.

ลูกผู้หญิง (คน) lûugphûujiŋ/ (khon/) N 1. daughter. 2. colloq. a (real) woman (i.e. one with womanly qualities). 3. (as n. mod.) womanly.

ลูกฝาแฝด,ลูกแฝด (คน) lûugfǎafɛ̀ɛd/, lûugfɛ̀ɛd/ (khon/) N 1. twin, twins. 2. Siamese twins.

ลูกพี่ลูกน้อง (คน) lûugphîi/lûugnɔ́ɔŋ/ (khon/) N cousin, cousins in general.

ลูกแพะ (ตัว) lûugphέ?/ (tua/) N kid.

ลูกไฟ (ลูก) lûugfaj/ (lûug/) N sparks, ignited or fiery particles thrown up in the air.

ลูกมะพร้าว (ลูก) lûugmaphráaw/ (lûug/) N coco-nut (with or without the outer husk).

ลูกมือ (คน) lûugmyy/ (khon/) N colloq. assistant.

ลูกไม้ (ลูก,ผล,ใบ,อย่าง) lûugmáaj/ N 1. com. fruit (of any kind) (lûug/,phǒn/,baj/). 2. lace (for trimming). 3. slang trick (jàaŋ/). →Syn. 1. ผลไม้ eleg.

ลูกยอ (ลูก) lûugjɔɔ/ (lûug/) N colloq. flattering words.

ลูกรอก (ลูก,อัน) lûugrɔ̂ɔg/ (lûug/,?an/) N pulley.

ลูกระเบิด (ลูก) lûugrabə̀əd/ (lûug/) N bomb.

ลูกเรือ (คน) lûugrya/ (khon/) N crew (of a boat).

ลูกล้อ (อัน) lûuglɔ́ɔ/ (?an/) N wheel.

ลูกเล็กเด็กแดง lûuglég/dègdɛɛŋ/ N elab. colloq. young children (collectively). →Also ลูกเด็กเล็กแดง.

ลูกเลี้ยง (คน) lûuglíaŋ/ (khon/) N com. 1. step-child. 2. adopted child. →Dist. ลูกตัว. →Syn. ลูกบุญธรรม,บุตรเลี้ยง,บุตรบุญธรรม eleg.

ลูกโลก (ลูก) lûuglôog/ (lûug/) N globe (depicting the earth).

ลูกไล่ (คน) lûuglâj/ (khon/) N colloq. one who is always picked on by others.

ลูกศร (ลูก,ดอก) lûugsɔ̌ɔn/ (lûug/,dɔ̀ɔg/) N arrow.

ลูกศิษย์ (คน) lûugsìd/ (khon/) N student, pupil, follower, disciple.

o ลูกศิษย์วัด (คน) lûugsìd'wád' (khon') N an attendant at a monastery, a boy who serves the priest.

ลูกสมุน (คน) lûugsamŭn' (khon') N colloq. subordinate, underling.

ลูกสวรรค์ (ลูก) lûugsawăn' (lûug') N eleg. toy balloon (esp. gas-inflated, such as are seen at festivals).

ลูกสะไภ้ (คน) lûugsapháj' (khon') N com. daughter-in-law.

ลูกสาว (คน) lûugsăaw' (khon') N com. daughter. →Syn. บุตรี lit., บุตรสาว,บุตรหญิง, ธิดา eleg.

ลูกสุดท้อง (คน) lûugsùdthɔ́ɔŋ' (khon') N com. the last-born child, youngest child.

ลูกสูบ (ลูก,อัน) lûugsùub' (lûug', ʔan') N piston.

ลูกเสือ (คน,ตัว) lûugsɰ̌a' N 1. boy scout (khon'). 2. tiger cub (tua').

ลูกหญิง (คน) lûugjĭŋ' (khon') N com. daughter.

ลูกหนัง (ลูก) lûugnăŋ' (lûug') N ball. →Now more commonly ลูกบอลล.

ลูกหนี้ (คน) lûugnîi' (khon') N debtor.

ลูกหมา (ตัว) lûugmăa' (tua') N com. puppy.

ลูกหมากรากไม้ (ลูก,ใบ,ผล) lûugmàag'-râag'ɔ máaj' (lûug', baj', phŏn') N elab. colloq. fruit.

ลูกหยี (พวง,ลูก,เม็ด) lûugjĭi' N a kind of sour fruit (phuaŋ' for clusters; lûug' for individual fresh fruits; méd' for the prepared fruit).
ต้น-- (ต้น) the tree bearing such fruit.

ลูกหลาน (คน) lûuglăan' (khon') N descendants.

o เกิดลูกหลาน kɤ̀ɤd'lûuglăan' to have descendants.

ลูกหัวปี (คน) lûughŭapii' (khon') com. the first-born child, eldest child.

ลูกหิน (ลูก) lûughĭn' (lûug') N agate marble(s).

ลูกเห็บ (ลูก) lûughèb' (lûug') N hail (the hail-stones).

ลูกเหม็น (ลูก) lûugmĕn' (lûug') N moth ball.

ลูกแหง (ตัว) lûugŋɛ̀ɛ' (tua') N a calf of the water buffalo.

ลูกอ่อน (คน,ตัว) lûugʔɔ̀ɔn' (khon', tua') N 1. baby, infant, very young child (khon'). 2. very young animal (tua').

o แม่ลูกอ่อน (คน,ตัว) mɛ̂ɛlûugʔɔ̀ɔn' (khon', tua')

N nursing mother (tua' for animals).

ลูกอัณฑะ (ลูก) lûugʔanthá?' (lûug') N eleg. testicles. →Syn. ลูกกระโปก com.,vulg.

ลูกอุกกาบาต (ลูก) lûug'ʔùgkaa'bàad' (lûug') N meteor.

ออกลูก ʔɔ̀ɔglûug' V colloq. to bear a child, give birth. →Syn. คลอดลูก,คลอดบุตร eleg.

ลูบ lûub' V to stroke, pat, pet.

ลูบคม lûub'khom' idiom. V to insult someone by outdoing him.

ลูบคลำ lûub'khlam' V to caress, fondle, stroke gently, pet.

o กอดจูบลูบคลำ kɔ̀ɔd'cùub'-lûub'khlam' V colloq. to pet, to neck.

ลูบไล้ lûubláj' V to stroke, rub lightly back and forth, apply (powder or perfume) with gentle strokes.

ลูบหน้าปะจมูก lûub'nâa'-pà?'camùug' V idiom. to come upon something one wasn't looking for (as in an investigation where evidence implicating the investigator turns up).

เล็ก lég' V to be small, little (in size). →Dist. น้อย.

เก็บเล็กผสมน้อย kèb'lég'-phasŏm'nɔ́ɔj' V elab. colloq. to save up little by little.

มหาดเล็ก (คน) mahàadlég' (khon') N royal page.

ลักเล็กขะโมยน้อย lág'lég'-khamooj'nɔ́ɔj' V elab. colloq. to pilfer.

ลูกเล็กเด็กแดง lûuglég'dègdɛɛŋ' N elab. colloq. infants and young children (collectively). →Also ลูกเด็กเล็กแดง.

เล็กกระจ้อยร่อย lég'-kracɔ̂ɔj'rɔ̂j' V to be tiny, very small.

เล็กน้อย légnɔ́ɔj' sV 1. a little bit. 2. little by little. NOTE. In mng. 2. เล็ก follows one verb, น้อย follows a second, often nearly synonymous verb, as in เก็บเล็กผสมน้อย and ลักเล็กขะโมย น้อย in the first and third entries above.

o โตกว่า...เล็กน้อย too'kwàaɔ...légnɔ́ɔj' a little bit bigger than.

เล็กมาก légmâag' V to be very small, minute.

เล็กๆ léglég' small, little.

เล็กๆน้อยๆ léglég'nɔ́ɔjnɔ́ɔj' elab. trifling, slight.

เล็กเชอร์ légchəə' V 1. to lecture. N 2. lecture,

esp. in the classroom. [f. Eng.]

เลข (ตัว, จำนวน, วิชา, ข้อ) lêeg/ N 1. numeral, number, figure (tua/, camnuan/). 2. arithmetic (wíchaa/). 3. arithmetic problem (khɔ̌ɔ/).

  คิดเลข khídlêeg/ V to calculate, compute, figure. เครื่อง-- adding machine, calculating machine, computer.

  โจทย์เลข (ข้อ) còodlêeg/ (khɔ̌ɔ/) N arithmetic problem.

  ตัวเลข (ตัว, จำนวน) tualêeg/ (tua/, camnuan/) N numeral, figure.

  ทดเลข thódlêeg/ V 1. arith. to carry a number (in addition). 2. to figure (on scratch paper).

  โทรเลข (ฉบับ) thooralêeg/ (chabàb/) N telegram, cablegram.

  เลขคณิต (วิชา) lêegkhaníd/ (wíchaa/) N arithmetic.

  เลขคี่ lêegkhîi/ N odd number.

  เลขคู่ lêegkhûu/ N even number.

  เลขที่ ๕๖ lêegthîi/hâasìbhòg/ number 56.

  เลขแปลก (ตัว, อัน) lêegpὲɛd/ (tua/, ʔan/) N the short vowel marker (˘). →Syn. ไม้ไต่คู้.

  เลขลำดับ lêeg/lamdàb/ N ordinal number.

  เลขหน่วย lêegnùaj/ N cardinal number.

  เลขหมาย, หมายเลข lêegmǎaj/, mǎajlêeg/ N numeral, number.

  วิชาเลข (วิชา) wíchaalêeg/ (wíchaa/) N arithmetic.

เลขา (คน) leekhǎa/ (khon/) N 1. colloq. secretary; short for เลขานุการ. 2. lit. writing; chiefly in the following derivative.

  พระราชหัตถเลขา (ฉบับ) phrárâad/chahàdthaɔ leekhǎa/ (chabàb/) N roy. the king's writings.

เลขาธิการ (คน) leekhǎa/thíkaan/ (khon/) N secretary of a large organization (i.e. one holding a position of authority), secretary-general.

  เลขาธิการ ก.พ. leekhǎa/thíkaan/-kɔɔphɔɔ/ N Secretary-General of the Civil Service Commission.

  เลขาธิการมหาวิทยาลัย (คน) leekhǎa/thíkaan/-mahǎa/wídthajaalaj/ (khon/) N registrar.

เลขานุการ (คน) leekhǎa/núkaan/ (khon/) N secretary (in an office).

เลขานุการินี (คน) leekhǎa/núkaa/rinii/ (khon/) N

female secretary.

เลง in นักเลง (คน) nágleeŋ/ (khon/) N 1. rogue, rascal, gambler. 2. bold person, sporting person. 3. big-hearted person. 4. person who is an authority on something.

เล็ง leŋ/ V to take aim.

  เพ่งเล็ง phêŋleŋ/ V 1. to take aim. 2. to focus one's mind or attention on.

  เล็งเห็น leŋ/hěn/ V to see, foresee.

เล้ง léŋ/* slang to reprove, scold, chide with a loud voice.

  เสียงล้งเล้ง (เสียง) sǐaŋ/lóŋléŋ/ (sǐaŋ/) N slang loud noise (e.g. of quarreling, debating).

เล็ด in เล็ดลอด lédlɔ̂ɔd/ V to slip or sneak (in, out, through, etc.), move secretly and quietly.

เลน leen/ N very wet mud, mud and water (as in a swampy place).

เล่น lên/* V 1. to play. 2. idiom. to play around with, busy oneself with (see example below). sV 3. for fun, for amusement. การ-- game; play, playing. เครื่อง-- toy, toys, playthings.

  ○ เขาชอบเล่นกุหลาบ kháwchɔ̂ɔb/lênkulàab/↓ He likes to grow roses.

  กระดานเล่นคลื่น (แผ่น) kradaan/lênkhlɔ̂ɔn/ (phὲn/) N surfboard.

  ของเล่น (อย่าง, ชิ้น) khɔ̌ɔŋlên/ (jàaŋ/, chín/) N toy, plaything. →See Note 2 under เครื่อง.

  ขี่เล่น khìi/lên/ to ride for pleasure.

  ขี้เล่น khîilên/ V to be given to playing, to be playful.

  ชื่อเล่น (ชื่อ) chŷylên/ (chŷy/) N nickname.

  เดินเล่น dəənlên/ to go for a stroll, walk for pleasure.

  นั่งเล่น nâŋlên/ to be just sitting, sitting relaxing, sitting enjoying oneself.

  ○ ห้องนั่งเล่น (ห้อง) hɔ̂ŋ/nâŋlên/ (hɔ̂ŋ/) N lounge (as in a hotel or school).

  เป็นเล่น penlên/ playfully; nonchalantly; triflingly.

  พูดเล่น phûudlên/ to speak playfully, say (something) in fun, to jest.

  เพื่อนเล่น (คน) phŷanlên/ (khon/) N playmate.

  ไม่ใช่เล่น mâjchâjlên/ colloq. quite.

  เล่นการพนัน lên/kaanphanan/ V to gamble, engage in gambling.

เล่นการเมือง lên′kaanmyaŋ′ V to play politics.

เล่นงาน lênŋaan′ V colloq. 1. to hit, strike, attack, hurt. 2. to scold. 3. to take serious measures against.

เล่นชู้ lênchúu′ V (a woman) to commit adultery.

เล่นซ่อนหา lên′sɔ̂ɔnhǎa′ V to play hide-and-seek.

เล่นดนตรี lên′dontrii′ V to play (music). นัก-- musician.

เล่นตัว lêntua′ V idiom. to play hard to get, act as though reluctant.

เล่นตา lêntaa′ V to flirt with the eyes.

เล่นน้ำ lênnáam′ V to play in the water.

เล่นพวกเล่นพ้อง lênphûag′lênphɔ́ɔŋ′ V elab. colloq. to indulge in favoritism. →Also เล่นพวก colloq.

เล่นไพ่ lênphâj′ V to play cards.

เล่นไม้บิด lên′máajbìd′ V idiom. to balk; to worm out of (a commitment).

เล่นละคร lên′lakhɔɔn′ V 1. to act, play, put on an act, a play. นัก-- actor, actress.

เล่นลิ้น lênlín′ V idiom. to deflect the point of a remark or criticism by a clever or witty reply.

เล่นว่าว lênwâw′ V to fly kites.

เล่นหัว lênhǔa′ V to laugh and play.

เล่นเอา lên′ʔawɔ V colloq. to make, cause to.

o ยานี้เล่นเอาฉันง่วงนอน jaa′níi′ lên′-ʔawɔ chán′ŋûaŋnɔɔn′↓ This medicine makes me sleepy.

เล่นเอาเถิด lên′ʔawthə̀əd′ V to play tag, play catch.

วิ่งเล่น wîŋlên′ V to run and play (as children).

สมัครเล่น samàg′lên′ V to be amateur.

อ่านเล่น ʔàanlên′ V to read for pleasure.

o หนังสืออ่านเล่น (เล่ม) naŋsʏ̌y′ʔàanlên′ (lêm′) N a book for light reading (as a novel, fiction).

เลนซ์,เลนส์ (อัน) len′, lens′ (ʔan′) N lens. [f. Eng.]

เลนินกราด leeninkràad′ pN Leningrad. [f. Eur.]

เล็บ (เล็บ) léb′ (léb′) N 1. nail (of the finger or toe). 2. claw.

กรงเล็บ kroŋléb′ N claws (when spread out).

เขี้ยวเล็บ khîaw′léb′ N 1. fangs and claws. 2. colloq. power to destroy.

เครื่องแต่งเล็บ (ชุด) khrŷaŋtɛ̀ŋléb′ (chúd′) N manicure set.

เล็บเท้า (เล็บ) lébtháaw′ (léb′) N toenail.

เล็บมือ (เล็บ) lébmyy′ (léb′) N fingernail.

วงเล็บ (อัน,วงเล็บ) woŋléb′ (ʔan′,woŋléb′) N 1. parenthesis. V 2. to parenthesize, put in parentheses.

เล็ม lem′ V 1. to graze (of cattle), to nibble, browse. 2. to cut a little (e.g. hair).

และเล็ม lɛ́ʔlem′ V 1. to nibble. 2. to do little by little, do gradually.

เล่ม lêm′* C clf. for sharp-pointed objects (e.g. knives, axes, pins, needles, swords, etc.); for candles, books, carts, et al.

เลย ๑ ləəj′ V 1. to be beyond. sV 2. (utterly) and then some, exceedingly. 3. at all (after a negative). sV 4. on, onward, further. AA 5. so, then, consequently.

o เลยบ้านนี้ไปเป็นที่ของเราทั้งหมด ləəj′bâanníiɔ paj′→penthîi′khɔ̌ɔŋrawtháŋmòd′↓ All the property beyond this house is ours.

o เคราะห์ดีจังเลย khrɔ́ʔdii′caŋləəj′↓ How awfully lucky!

o ไม่ดีเลย mâjdii′ləəj′ not at all good, not good at all.

o คุณจะต้องเดินเลยไปอีกถนนหนึ่ง khuncatɔ̂ŋdəənɔ ləəj′-paj′ʔìigthanǒn′nyŋ↓ You'll have to walk one block further.

o ผมจะเลยไปบ้านเพื่อนของผม phǒmcaləəj′-pajɔ bâan′phŷankhɔ̌ɔŋphǒm′↓ I will then go on to my friend's house.

o วานนี้ไม่สบาย เลยนอนทั้งวัน waan′níi′ mâjsaɔ baaj′→ ləəjnɔɔn′tháŋwan′ Yesterday I was sick, so I was in bed all day.

ขั้งกระไรเลย châŋkrarajləəj′ How could he! How come? (expressing reproach, indignation).

ปล่อยให้เลยตามเลย plɔ̀j′-hâjləəj′taamləəj′ colloq. to let the thing go even though it is wrong.

ล่วงเลย lûaŋləəj′ 1. to pass by, elapse. 2. to go beyond, pass beyond.

ละเลย láʔ′ləəj′ to neglect.

เลยธง ləəj′thoŋ′ V idiom. to go too far, to exceed moderation.

เลย ๒ ləəj/ pN Loei, a township in NE Thailand.

เลว leew/ V to be bad, poor (in quality), low (in quality, character, etc.). →Syn. ชั่ว com., ทราม eleg. →Ant. ดี.

   ทหารเลว (คน) thahǎanleew/ (khon/) N ordinary soldier (i.e. without rank).

   มือเลว myy/leew/ V 1. to be a poor hand (at some activity). N 2. a poor hand, a poor player. →Opp. มือดี.

   เลวทราม leewsaam/ V to be bad, vile, low, base.

   เลวลง leew/loŋ to become worse, get worse.

เล่ห์ (เล่ห์) lêe/ (lêe/) N trick, deception.

   เจ้าเล่ห์ câwlêe/ V colloq. to be crooked, dishonest, tricky (of people).

   เล่ห์กระเท่ห์ (อย่าง) lêe/krathêe/ (jàaŋ/) N trick, cunning, deceit.

   o ทำเล่ห์กระเท่ห์ thamlêe/krathêe/ to act cunningly, practise deception or intrigue.

   เล่ห์กล (อย่าง) lêekon/ (jàaŋ/) N trick.

   เล่ห์เหลี่ยม (อย่าง) lêelìam/ (jàaŋ/) N trick, cunning angle or pitch (as in advertising, trading).

เลหลัง leelǎŋ/ V to auction.

เลอ in the following entries.

   เลอโฉม ləə/chǒom/ V lit. to be very beautiful, of great beauty, of incomparable beauty.

   เลอเลิศ ləə/lə̂əd/ V 1. to be great, incomparable, unsurpassable. sV 2. excellently, exquisitely, extremely.

   เลอศักดิ์ ləə/sàg/ V to be of the highest rank.

เล่อล่า lə̂əlâa/ V 1. to have a confused or excited expression or manner (as when bewildered, out of place, overwrought, frightened, excited). sV 2. excitedly. 3. intruding unwittingly.

เลอะ lé?/ V to be dirty, splattered (as with ink), messy, soiled.

   ทำเลอะ thamlé?/ V to soil, dirty, mess, muddle.

   เลอะเทอะ lé?thé?/ V 1. to be dirty, soiled, messy, disorderly. 2. colloq. (someone) to be mixed up, confused.

   เลอะเลือน lé?lyan/ V to be unclear, blurred, faded, vague.

เละ lé?/ V 1. to be mushy. 2. to be reduced to a paste, become paste-like.

เละเทะ lé?/thé?/ V to be messed up, disorderly.

เลา ๑ (ต้น) law/ (tôn/) N a kind of grass.

เลา ๒ law/ C clf. for reed instruments.

เลา ๓ in ลาดเลา lâadlaw/ N 1. situation, layout (as it bears upon some future move, course of action). 2. clue, sign, trace.

เล่า ๑ lâw/ V to tell (a story, happening), narrate.

   บอกเล่า bɔ̀ɔglâw/ V to tell, relate (by word of mouth).

   เล่า...จ้อ lâwɔ...cɔ́ɔ/ 1. to talk, tell (about) endlessly. 2. to relate eloquently.

   เล่านิทาน lâwníthaan/ V to tell a story, a legend.

   เล่าเรียน lâwrian/ V to study.

   เล่าลือ as in ข่าวเล่าลือ (เรื่อง) khàaw/lâwlyy/ (rŷaŋ/) N rumor. คำ-- rumor(s).

เล่า ๒ lâw/ Pt particle with mildly entreative or corroborative force, similar to ละ.

   มิน่าเล่า mínâa/lâw No wonder! →Also มิน่าละ.

   ...แล้ว...เล่า ...lέɛw/...lâw/ 1. (with verbs) again and again, time and again, on and on. 2. (with classifiers) from one...to another; one... after another.

   o เตือนแล้วเตือนเล่า tyanlέɛw/tyanlâw/ V elab. colloq. to warn time and again.

   o ครั้งแล้วครั้งเล่า khráŋlέɛw/khráŋlâw/ elab. colloq. again and again, time and again, time after time.

   o สถานีแล้วสถานีเล่า sathǎanii/lέɛw/-sathǎanii/ɔ law/ elab. colloq. (from) station to station, (from) one station to another, station after station.

   อนึ่งเล่า ?anŷŋ/lâw/ and, also, besides.

เล้า (เล้า) láw/ (láw/) N pen, coop, enclosure (for animals).

   ลูกเต้าเล้าอ่อน (คน) lûugtâw/láw?ɔ̀ɔn/ (khon/) N elab. colloq. children (esp. young children).

   เล้าไก่ (เล้า) láwkàj/ (láw/) N chicken coop.

เล้าโลม láwloom/ V to console, soothe, appease.

เลาะ lɔ́?/ V 1. to skirt, go along the edge of. 2. to remove stitches, take the hem out.

   ลัดเลาะ ládlɔ́?/ V to skirt and take shortcuts.

เลิก ๑ lə̂əg/ V to quit, finish, be through, be over; to end, discontinue; to give up; to break up.

   บอกเลิก bɔ̀ɔg/lə̂əg/ V 1. to revoke. 2. to give

notice of termination (of an agreement). 3. to cancel (a subscription, membership, reservation).

ยกเลิก jóglə̂əg′ V to cancel, nullify.

เลิกกัน lə̂əg/kan V 1. colloq. (married people) to be separated, divorced. 2. to break off friendship, dealings with each other. 3. that's all; we've finished (commonly used in ending a telephone conversation).

เลิกกิจการ lə̂əg/kìdcakaan′ to quit the business, give up a business.

เลิกคิด lə̂əgkhíd′ V to give up the idea, stop thinking about something.

เลิกทัพ lə̂əgtháb′ V to withdraw (troops from the fighting zone).

เลิกทาส lə̂əgthâad′ V to abolish slavery.

เลิกพูดกัน lə̂əgphûud/kan 1. to be through (with one's conversation). 2. to be not on speaking terms. 3. to be out of the question (i.e. dismissed from discussion).

เลิกร้าง lə̂əgráaŋ′ V to be divorced, separated.

เลิกล้ม lə̂əglóm′ V to give up, abandon, abolish, cancel.

หนังเลิก nǎŋ′lə̂əg′ the show (movie) is over.

เลิก ๒ lə̂əg′ V to lift, lift up, raise (thereby revealing what was covered; used esp. of cloth, clothing).

เลิกคิ้ว lə̂əgkhíw′ V to raise the eyebrows.

เลิ่กลั่ก lə̂glâg/* V to have a bewildered, anxious, or shocked expression or manner.

เลินเล่อ lə̂ənlə̂ə′ V to be careless, negligent.

เลิศ lə̂əd′ V to be excellent, best, top.

ชนะเลิศ chaná?/lə̂əd′ V 1. to win the championship. N 2. championship.

ประนิดเลิศ chaníd/lə̂əd′ of the best quality.

ผลเลิศ phǒnlə̂əd′ the best result.

เลิศลอย lə̂ədlɔɔj′ V 1. to be excellent, superlative. sV 2. highly, to the highest degree.

เลีย lia′ V 1. to lick. 2. slang to seek favors by flattering or fawning.

เลี่ย. See ไล่เลี่ย.

เลียง ๑ in เลียงผา (ตัว) liaŋphǎa′ (tua′) N goat antelope, goral (Naemorhedus goral).

เลียง ๒ in ไล่เลียง lâjliaŋ′ V 1. to make detailed

inquiries. 2. to cross-examine.

เลี่ยง lîaŋ′ V to sneak away; to evade, avoid.

เลี้ยง líaŋ′ V 1. to feed, nourish. 2. to take care of, look after, keep. 3. to treat (i.e. provide a treat for). 4. to tame, domesticate. การ-- feast, banquet; feeding, taking care of. คน-- person who takes care of, looks after (a pet, a child); person who provides a treat.

o ผมจะเลี้ยงคุณคราวนี้ phǒmcalíaŋ/khun′-khraaw‍ɔ níi↓ I'll treat you this time.

การเลี้ยงน้ำชา (ครั้ง) kaanlíaŋ/námchaa′ (khráŋ′) N tea party.

อุปเลี้ยง chúblíaŋ′ V to foster, raise, rear (esp. children who are not one's own).

เด็กเลี้ยงแกะ (คน) dèg/líaŋkὲ?/ (khon′) N 1. shepherd boy. 2. one who cries wolf.

น้องเลี้ยง (คน) nɔ́ɔŋlíaŋ/ (khon′) N younger sibling related through one parent, through a stepparent, or by adoption; hence a younger half brother, stepbrother, foster brother, half sister, etc.

น้ำเลี้ยง námlíaŋ/ N 1. sap. 2. biol. culture solution.

บำรุงเลี้ยง bamruŋ/líaŋ′ V to feed, nourish, foster, take good care of.

บุตรเลี้ยง (คน) bùdlíaŋ/ (khon′) N eleg. stepchild; adopted child. →Syn. See ลูกเลี้ยง com.

เบี้ยเลี้ยง bîalíaŋ/ N allowance (for food).

พ่อเลี้ยง (คน) phɔ̂ɔlíaŋ/ (khon′) N stepfather; foster father.

พี่เลี้ยง (คน) phîilíaŋ/ (khon′) N 1. nursemaid, nurse. 2. sports one who manages, trains, or tends an athlete. 3. older sibling related through one parent, through a stepparent, or by adoption; hence an older half brother, stepbrother, foster brother, half sister, etc.

แม่เลี้ยง (คน) mɛ̂ɛlíaŋ/ (khon′) N stepmother; foster mother.

ลูกเลี้ยง (คน) lûuglíaŋ/ (khon′) N 1. stepchild. 2. adopted child. →Dist. ลูกตัว. →Syn. ลูกบุญธรรม,บุตรเลี้ยง,บุตรบุญธรรม eleg.

เลี้ยงแขก líaŋkhὲɛg′ V to give a banquet; to feast.

เลี้ยงชีพ,หา-- líaŋchîib′, hǎa′líaŋchîib′ V to make a living.

เลี้ยงดู líaŋduu′ V 1. to raise, bring up. 2. to take care of, look after. 3. colloq. to feast. →Also in mng. 3 เลี้ยงดูปูเสื่อ elab. colloq.

เลี้ยงตัว líaŋ′tua′ V 1. colloq. to balance one-self. 2. to support oneself, earn a living. →Syn. ทรงตัว.

เลี้ยงไม่เชื่อง líaŋ′mâjchʸaŋ′ to be untameable.

เลี้ยงไว้ดูเล่น líaŋ′wájduulên′ to keep, raise (e.g. a pet) for one's pleasure in watching (it).

เลี้ยงส่ง líaŋsòŋ′ V to give a farewell party.

เลี้ยงสัตว์ líaŋsàd′ V to raise, breed animals. การ-- animal husbandry.

สัตว์เลี้ยง (ตัว) sàdlíaŋ′ (tua′) N domesticated animal; pet.

เลียน lian′ V to imitate, copy.

ล้อเลียน lɔ́ɔlian′ V to mock, ridicule by mimicry.

เลียนแบบ lianbɛ̀ɛb′ V to copy, imitate.

เลียน ๑ lían′ V to be cleared away until nothing is left.

ผ้าเลียน (ชิ้น) phâalían′ (chín′) N plain cotton fabric (without any design). →Opp. ผ้าดอก.

เลียน ๒ lían′ V to be greasy (to the taste).

อาหารเลียน ?aahǎan′lían′ N greasy food.

เลียบ líab′ V to go along the edge of, to skirt.

เลียบเคียง líabkhiaŋ′ V to speak in a roundabout manner in order to draw a person out.

เลี่ยม líam′ V 1. to plate, cover, be plated, covered with a thin sheet of metal. 2. to enframe, be enframed with a thin strip of metal.

เลี่ยมเงิน líamŋɔn′ V 1. to plate, cover, be plated, covered with a thin sheet of silver. 2. to enframe, be enframed with a thin strip of silver.

เลี้ยว líaw′ V to turn (and proceed in another direc-tion); to veer.

ลดเลี้ยว lódlíaw′ V 1. (a path) to wind, be wind-ing. 2. to follow a winding path.

เลี้ยวขวา líawkhwǎa′ V to turn right.

หัวเลี้ยว (แห่ง) hǔalíaw′ (hèŋ′) N corner (of a street).

หัวเลี้ยวหัวต่อ (ตอน) hǔalíaw′hǔatɔ̀ɔ′ (tɔɔn′) N elab. transition, turning point.

เลือก lʸag′ V to choose, pick out, select, elect. การ-- selection, choice.

คัดเลือก khádlʸag′ V to choose, select, sort out, pick out.

โดยไม่เลือกสัญชาติภาษา dooj′-mâjlʸag′-sǎnᴐchâad′ phaasǎa′ regardless of language or nationality.

โดยไม่เลือกหน้า dooj′-mâjlʸag′nâa′ without dis-crimination; without excepting anyone.

ได้รับเลือกเป็น dâjráb′lʸag′-penᴐ V to be elected, chosen (something, e.g. chairman).

เลือกคู่ lʸagkhûu′ V to find a mate.

เลือกตั้ง lʸagtâŋ′ V to choose, elect. การ-- election.

o ได้รับเลือกตั้งเป็น dâjráb′lʸagtâŋ′-penᴐ V to be elected (something, e.g. president).

o วันเลือกตั้ง (วัน) wan′lʸagtâŋ′ (wan′) N election day.

o สิทธิ์เลือกตั้ง sìd′lʸagtâŋ′ N right to vote; eligibility to vote.

เลือกที่รักมักที่ชัง lʸag′thîirág′-mág′thîichaŋ′ V elab. colloq. to show partiality, show favor-itism, play favorites; to be partial in one's likes and dislikes.

เลือกเฟ้น lʸagfén′ V to choose, select carefully.

เลือกเอา lʸag′?awᴐ to choose, select.

เลือกเอาเอง lʸag′?aw?eeŋ′↓ Make your own selection! Take your pick!

เลื่อง lʸaŋ′ V to spread widely, be spread widely. →Chiefly in the following entries.

เลื่องชื่อลือนาม lʸaŋchʸy′lʸynaam′ V 1. (people, every one) to talk about (it), spread (it) around: "spread the name." 2. to be well-known, famous, widely spoken of. →Also ลือชื่อ.

เลื่องลือ lʸaŋlyy′ V 1. (people, everyone) to speak (of), spread far and wide. 2. to be spread far and wide, widely known.

o เลื่องลือระบือ lʸaŋlyy′rabyy′ idem.

o เสียงเลื่องลือ (เสียง) sĭaŋ′lʸaŋlyy′ (sĭaŋ′) N rumor.

เลือด lʸad′ N com. blood. →Syn. โลหิต eleg.

ก้อนเลือด (ก้อน) kɔ̂ɔnlʸad′ (kɔ̂ɔn′) N blood clot.

กินเลือดกินเนื้อ kinlʸad′kinnʸa′ V colloq. fig. to eat someone up alive (as with anger).

นองเลือด nɔɔŋ′lʸad′ V to be bloody, covered with blood, sanguinary.

บ้าเลือด bâa'lŷad' V to be blood-crazed.

เลือดกำเดา lŷadkamdaw' N writ blood from a nosebleed. →Syn. เลือดน้ำเดา colloq.

เลือดขึ้นหน้า lŷad'khŷnnâa' (the) blood rushes to one's face (with anger).

เลือดตาแทบกระเด็น lŷadtaa'thἓɛbkraden' idiom. with so much effort, with the greatest trouble (such that the blood almost comes out one's eyes).

เลือดน้ำเดา lŷadnámdaw' N colloq. blood from a nosebleed. →Syn. เลือดกำเดา writ.

เลือดเนื้อเชื้อไข lŷadnýa'chýakhăj' elab. (one's) flesh and blood (usually ref. to one's children or grandchildren).

เลือดเนื้อเชื้อสาย lŷadnýa'chýasăaj' elab.(one's) flesh and blood, i.e. descendants.

เลือดเย็น lŷadjen' V to be cold-blooded (as of fish, reptiles). อย่าง-- cold-bloodedly.

เลือดร้อน lŷadrɔ́ɔn' V 1. to be warm-blooded (as of animals, birds). 2. to be hot-tempered, quick-tempered, hot-blooded, impetuous.

เลือดไหล lŷadlăj' V to bleed.

เลือดออก lŷad'ɔ́ɔg' V to bleed.

สายเลือด săajlŷad' N color (referring to rosiness of complexion).

สีแดงเลือดนก sǐidɛɛŋ'lŷadnóg' N 1. bright red. V 2. to be bright red.

สีเลือดหมู sǐilŷadmǔu' N 1. dark red, maroon. V 2. to be dark red, maroon-colored.

เส้นเลือด (เส้น) sênlŷad' (sên') N blood vessel.

หน้าเลือด nâa'lŷad' V idiom. to be selfish and hard-hearted (as a merchant who overcharges); to be a bloodsucker.

ห้อเลือด hɔ́ɔlŷad' V 1. to be bruised; to have a hematoma. N 2. hematoma.

อมเลือดอมฝาด ʔomlŷad'/ʔomfàad' V elab. colloq. (the face) to have good color, a clear, healthy complexion.

เลือน lyan' V to fade away, blur; to be blurred, vague.

ลบเลือน lóblyan' V to fade away; to become blurred and indistinct (as with the wear of time).

ลืมเลือน lyymlyan' V 1. to be forgotten, to be faded (from memory). 2. (the memory) to fade away.

เลอะเลือน lɤʔlyan' V to be unclear, blurred,

faded, vague.

เลือนลาง lyanlaaŋ' V to be vague, indistinct.

เลือนหาย lyanhăaj' V to fade away.

เลื่อน (เล่ม,คัน) lŷan' (lêm', khan') V 1. to move, move along, slide, shift, change position. 2. to be promoted. 3. to postpone. N 4. sled.

ล้อเลื่อน (คัน) lɔ́ɔlŷan' (khan') N vehicles (collective term).

เลื่อนขึ้น lŷan'khŷn' V to move up, rise (in rank), be promoted.

เลื่อนชั้น lŷanchán' V to be promoted to a higher step, grade, level.

เลื่อนตำแหน่ง (ให้) lŷan'tamnὲŋ'-(hâjɔ) V to promote to a higher position.

o ได้เลื่อนตำแหน่ง dâjlŷan'tamnὲŋ' V to be promoted.

เลื่อนยศ lŷanjód' V to promote, be promoted to a higher rank.

เลื่อนลอย lŷanlɔɔj' V to drift (as one's thoughts).

เลื่อม (อัน) lŷam' (ʔan') N 1. sequin. V 2. to be glossy, lustrous.

เป็นมันเลื่อม penman'lŷam' to be glossy, lustrous.

เลื่อมใส lŷamsăj' V 1. to be thoroughly convinced, be impressed, believe whole-heartedly. 2. to have faith in. ความ-- faith, confidence, an inclination to believe. อย่าง-- devotedly, devoutly. →Syn. ศรัทธา,เชื่อถือ.

เลื่อย (ปื้น,อัน) lŷaj' N 1. saw (pŷyn',ʔan'). V 2. to saw.

ขี้เลื่อย khîilŷaj' N sawdust.

o หัวขี้เลื่อย hŭakhîilŷaj' V colloq. to have the head filled with sawdust, i.e. to be stupid, unintelligent.

โรงเลื่อย (โรง,แห่ง) rooŋlŷaj' (rooŋ',hὲŋ') N sawmill.

เลื่อยจักร (เครื่อง) lŷajcàg' (khrŷaŋ') N motor-driven saw.

เลื้อย lýaj' V 1. to crawl (of snakes). 2. to creep, climb (of plants). →Dist. คลาน,ไต่.

ไม้เลื้อย (ต้น,เถา) máajlýaj' (tôn',thăw') N vine, liana, creeper.

สัตว์เลื้อยคลาน (ตัว) sàd'lýajkhlaan' (tua') N reptile.

แล ๑ lɛɛ' V to see, watch, look.

ดูแล duulɛɛ′ V to look after, take care of, tend, supervise. ผู้-- superintendent, overseer, caretaker, keeper.

ลับแล (อัน) láblɛɛ′ (ʔan′) N portable screen.

แลดู lɛɛduu′ V to look.

แลเห็น lɛɛhĕn′ V to see.

เหลียวแล lĭawlɛɛ′ V to care; to pay attention.

แล ๒ lɛɛ′ Pt particle having emphatic or corroborative force. →Also แหล่.

ดีนักแล dii′náglɛɛ′ very very good, excellent, magnificent.

แล ๓ lɛɛ′ Cj and. →More commonly และ.

กันแลกัน kan′lɛɛkan′ one another, each other.

แล่ lɛɛ′ V to slice (with horizontal motion).

แลก lɛɛg′ V to exchange, swap.

แลกเปลี่ยน lɛɛgplìan′ V to trade, swap, barter, exchange.

อัตราแลกเปลี่ยน ʔàdtraa′lɛɛgplìan′ N rate of exchange.

แลก. See ล้อกแลก.

แลง in ดินแลง, ศิลาแลง dinlɛɛŋ′, silaa′lɛɛŋ′ N laterite (reddish soil, soft when wet, but hard as rock and porous when dry).

แล่ง lɛŋ′* V to split, break.

แล้ง lɛɛŋ′ V to be dry (as of the season), lacking rain, arid.

ฝนแล้ง fŏnlɛɛŋ′ there is a drought, there is a shortage of rain.

ฤดูแล้ง (ฤดู) rýduulɛɛŋ′ (rýduu′) N eleg. dry season.

หน้าแล้ง (หน้า) nâalɛɛŋ′ (nâa′) N colloq. dry season.

แห้งแล้ง hɛ̂ŋlɛɛŋ′ V 1. to be dry, arid. 2. to be dreary, empty of life and freshness.

แลติจูต (เล่น) lédticúud′*(sên′) N latitude. [f. Eng.]

แล่น lɛ̂n′* V 1. to run, move (usually of powered vehicles). 2. to sail (of a boat).

ชั่วแล่น chûalɛ̂n′ colloq. (for) a brief moment, momentarily; momentary.

o ความคิดชั่วแล่น khwaamkhíd′chûalɛ̂n′ N passing fancy.

แล่นฉิว lɛ̂nchĭw′ to run or sail swiftly and smoothly, swiftly and uninterruptedly.

แล่นใบ lɛ̂nbaj′ V to sail.

แล่นเรือ lɛ̂nrya′ V to sail, run a boat.

แลบ lɛɛb′ V 1. to flash (as lightning). 2. to project, be showing.

ฟ้าแลบ (1) fáa′lɛɛb′; (2) fáalɛɛb′ 1. (lightning) to flash. N 2. lightning; a flash of lightning.

แลบลิ้น lɛɛblín′ V to put out the tongue.

แลบออกมา lɛɛb′ʔɔ̀ɔgmaa′ to project, stick out, show.

แล้ว lɛ́ɛw′ V 1. to be finished. sV 2. already. Cj 3. then, afterwards, later.

o จะ แล้วฉันจะทำให้ câ′→lɛ́ɛwchán′-catham′ɔ hâj′↓ Yes, I'll do it for (you) later.

ก็แล้วไป kɔ̂lɛ́ɛw′paj′↓ colloq. Then let it go, leave it at that.

ครั้งแล้วครั้งเล่า khráŋlɛ́ɛw′khráŋlâw′ elab. colloq. again and again; time and again.

ครั้นแล้ว khránlɛ́ɛw′ then; and then.

จนแล้วจนรอด conlɛ́ɛw′conrɔ̂ɔd′ colloq. on and on; over and over.

จบแล้ว còblɛ́ɛw′ V to have ended, finished.

ดีแล้ว diilɛ́ɛw′↓, dii′lɛ́w↓ That's good.

ที่แล้ว as in เดือนที่แล้ว dyan′thîilɛ́ɛw′ (in the) last month, the previous month.

นอกจาก...แล้ว ยัง...ด้วย nɔ̂ɔgcàag′...lɛ́ɛw′→jaŋɔ...dûaj′ not only...but also.

เป็นที่สุดที่แล้ว pen′thîisùd′thîilɛ́ɛw′ elab. colloq. extremely.

พร้อมแล้ว phrɔ́ɔmlɛ́ɛw′ V to be ready, prepared.

พอแล้ว phɔɔlɛ́ɛw′↓ That's enough.

รู้แล้วรู้รอดไป rúulɛ́ɛw′rúurɔ̂ɔd′-paj elab. colloq. once and for all.

ล้วนแล้วไปด้วย lúanlɛ́ɛw′pajdûaj′ to be full of.

แล้ว(...)ก็... lɛ́ɛw(...)kɔ̂ɔ... and then.

o แล้วก็หยุด lɛ́ɛwkɔ̂jùd′ and then (he) stopped.

o แล้วเขาก็มา lɛ́ɛwkháw′kɔ̂maa′ and then he came.

แล้วก็แล้วไป lɛ́ɛw′kɔ̂lɛ́ɛw′-paj↓ Let bygones be bygones.

แล้วกัน ๑. See entries below.

o ก็แล้วกัน kɔ̂lɛ́ɛw′kan 1. mildly hortatory expression: let's: you might (do such and such). Often indicates indifference: go ahead and (do such and such; it would be all the same to me). 2. that's it, that all there is to it.

○ เป็นแล้วกัน penlɛɛw′kan↓ That's settled. That does it. That's all (i.e. we've finished what we had to say).

แล้วกัน ๒ lɛɛw′kan↓ E excl. indicating surprise and disappointment.

แล้วแต่ lɛɛw′tɛ̀ɛ⊃ (the choice) depends on, is up to, depends on whether.

○ แล้วแต่คุณ lɛɛw′tɛ̀ɛkhun↓ It's up to you!

○ แล้วแต่ซี่ lɛɛwtɛ̀ɛ′si↓ It's up to (him)(I don't care).

แล้วเสร็จ lɛɛw′sèd′ V to be finished, completed.

หาไม่แล้ว hǎa′mâjlɛɛw′ lit. otherwise.

และ lɛ́ʔ′, lɛ́ʔ′, lɛ⊃ Cj and.

กันและกัน kan′lekan′ each other, one another (often preceded by ต่อ,ซึ่ง,แห่ง).

ทั้ง...และ... tháŋ⊃...lɛ⊃... both...and...

○ ทั้งหญิงและชาย tháŋjĭŋ′lechaaj′ both men and women.

และอื่นๆ lɛʔ′ỳynʔỳyn′ and so on, and so forth: "and others."

และเล็ม lɛ́ʔlem′ V to nibble.

โล. Shortened form of กิโล kiloo′ C kilo (kilogram, kilometer).

โล่ (โล่,อัน) lôo′ (lôo′, ʔan′) N shield. →Also โล่ห์.

โล้ lóo′ V 1. to rock, swing. V 2. to row. N 3. a kind of row boat.

ไม่เป็นโล้เป็นพาย mâjpenlóo′penphaaj′ idiom. to make no sense, be incoherent, not well organized.

โล้ชิงช้า lóo′chiŋcháa′ V to swing (on a swing).

โล้เรือ lóorya′ V to row a boat, sail a boat.

โลก (โลก) lôog′ (lôog′) N the world, the earth.

ขวางโลก khwǎaŋlôog′ V to do things in opposition to what other people usually do. Cf. Eng. "crosswise with the world."

ชาวโลก (คน) chaawlôog′ (khon′) N inhabitants of the earth.

แชมเปี้ยนโลก (คน) chɛɛmpîanlôog′ (khon′) N sports world champion. [แชมเปี้ยน f. Eng.]

ซีกโลก (ซีก) sîiglôog′ (sîig′) N hemisphere.

ดาวโลก (ดวง) daawlôog′ (duaŋ′) N the earth.

ตลาดโลก talàad′lôog′ N the world market.

แถบขั้วโลก (แถบ) thɛ̀ɛb′khûalôog′ (thɛ̀ɛb′) N the polar regions.

ปัญหาโลกแตก (ปัญหา,ข้อ) panhǎa′lôogtɛ̀ɛg′ (panɔ hǎa′, khɔ̌ɔ′) N problem which cannot be solved.

ลูกโลก (ลูก) lûuglôog′ (lûug′) N globe (depicting the earth).

โลกพระอังคาร lôog′phráʔaŋkhaan′ N Mars (the planet).

โลกมนุษย์ (โลก) lôog′manúd′ (lôog′) N the world, the earth.

ศาลโลก (ศาล) sǎan′lôog′ (sǎan′) N International Court, World Court.

สากลโลก sǎa′konlalôog′ N the universe.

เห็นโลก hěn′lôog′ V colloq. to be experienced in worldly affairs.

องค์การอนามัยแห่งโลก ʔoŋkaan′-anaamaj′hèŋlôog′ nN World Health Organization.

โลกียชน (คน) loo′kiijachon′ (khon′) N ordinary people, the common man.

โลง (โลง,ใบ) looŋ′ (looŋ′, baj′) N coffin.

โล่ง lôoŋ′ V to be open, empty, clear.

โล่งใจ lôoŋcaj′ V to feel relieved, free, at ease.

โล่งอก lôoŋʔòg′ idem.

โล้งเล้ง. See ล้งเล้ง.

โลด lôod′ V to jump.

กระโดดโลดเต้น kradòod′lôodtên′ V to hop and skip about (merrily, as children do).

ลิงโลด liŋlôod′ V to be excited, wild (as with joy), to jump with joy.

โลดโผน lôodphǒon′ V 1. to be exciting, thrilling. 2. to be extraordinary, unusual, unconventional. 3. to be adventurous, daredevilish.

โลน (ตัว) loon′ V 1. to be rude, obscene, indecent, vulgar (often ref. to language meant to be humorous). N 2. crab louse (pubic louse)(tua′).

หยาบโลน jàabloon′ V to be rude, vulgar (often ref. to language meant to be humorous).

โลภ lôob′ V to be greedy, covetous. ความ-- greed, covetousness. →Syn. เห็นแก่ได้.

ละโมภโลภลาภ lamôob′lôoblâab′ V elab. eleg. to be greedy.

โลม in เล้าโลม láwloom′ V to console, soothe, appease.

โลมา in ปลาโลมา (ตัว) plaaloomaa′ (tua′) N dolphin, porpoise.

โลเล loolee′ V to be ever-changing, unreliable,

uncertain, unpredictable.

โล่ห์. Variant spelling of โล่.

โลหกรรม loohàkam/ N metallurgy.

โลหกิจ as in กรมโลหกิจ (กรม) krom/loohàkìd/ (krom/) N Department of Mines.

โลหะ (อย่าง,ชนิด) loohà?/ (jàaŋ/,chaníd/) N metal. ช่าง-- metalworker.

โลหะเจือ loohà?/cya/ N alloy.

โลหิต loohìd/ N eleg. blood. →Syn. เลือด com.

ความดันโลหิต khwaamdan/loohìd/ N blood pressure.

เม็ดโลหิตแดง (เม็ด) méd/-loohìd/dɛɛŋ/ (méd/) N red blood corpuscle.

โรคโลหิตจาง rôog/-loohìd/caaŋ/ N anemia.

สายโลหิต sǎaj/loohìd/ N 1. blood line, lineage. 2. artery (in the fig. sense only, e.g. referring to a river).

เส้นโลหิต (เส้น) sên/loohìd/ (sên/) N blood vessels.

o เส้นโลหิตดำ (เส้น) sên/-loohìd/dam/ (sên/) N vein.

o เส้นโลหิตแดง (เส้น) sên/-loohìd/dɛɛŋ/ (sên/) N artery.

โละ ló?/ V slang to discard. [f. Chin.]

ไล่ lâj/ V 1. to chase. 2. to recite, tell, play, sing (a sequence of learned items in a fixed order, as the alphabet, multiplication tables, musical scale, solfa, etc.).

ขับไล่ khàblâj/ V to drive away, chase away, repel.

ต้นไม้ต้นไล่ (ต้น) tônmáaj/tônlâj/ (tôn/) N elab. colloq. tree.

ลูกไล่ (คน) lûuglâj/ (khon/) N one who is always picked on by others.

ไล่กวด lâjkùad/ V to chase, run after.

ไล่ทัน lâjthan/ V to catch up with, overtake.

ไล่เบี้ย lâjbîa/ V colloq. 1. to question exhaustively and provocatively. 2. to scold, bawl out (usually unjustly). 3. to bawl (everyone) out right on down the line.

ไล่เลี่ย lâjlîa/ V to be about equal, about the same.

ไล่เลียง lâjliaŋ/ V 1. to make detailed inquiries. 2. to cross-examine.

ไล่หลัง lâjlǎŋ/ V to follow behind.

ไล่(...)ออก lâj(...)?ɔɔg/ 1. to dismiss (someone)(from a position), fire (someone). 2. to turn (someone) out, chase (a person or animal) out.

สอบไล่ sɔɔblâj/ V 1. to take a final examination. N 2. final examination.

ไล้ in ลูบไล้ lûublâj/ V to stroke, rub lightly back and forth, apply (something on the body) with gentle strokes.

ฦ lý?/ A symbol used in the Thai writing system which functions as a consonant plus vowel combination pronounced lýc. It is very rarely used. No examples occur in this book.

ฦๅ

ฦๅ ๑ lyy/ A symbol used in the Thai writing system which functions as a consonant plus vowel combination pronounced lyy/. It is very rarely used.

ฦๅ ๒ FS. See ลือ.

ว

ว wɔɔ/ LOW consonant. Pronounced w both initially and finally.

วก wóg/ V to turn back, switch back.

วกไปมา wóg/pajmaa/ 1. to turn this way and that; to wend. 2. to be winding (as a road).

วกไปเวียนมา wógpaj/wianmaa/ 1. to go back and forth or round and round (between two or more places or subjects). 2. to be winding (as of a road).

วกมา wóg/maa/ to come back to, return to.

วกเวียน wógwian/ V 1. to go back and forth or round and round (between two or more places or subjects). 2. to be winding (as of a road).

วง (วง) woŋ′ (woŋ′) N 1. circle, ring, group. C 2. clf. for rings (e.g. fingerring), circles (e.g. card-playing circle), groups (as an orchestra). V 3. to circle around.

แตรวง (วง) trɛɛwoŋ′ (woŋ′) N brass band.

ร่วมวง rûamwoŋ′ V to join a group or party.

รำวง (วง) ramwoŋ′ (woŋ′)· N 1. a Thai folk dance in which the couples move around in circles. V 2. to dance the รำวง.

วงกลม woŋklom′ N circle.

วงการ woŋkaan′ N 1. circle. 2. field, realm.

o วงการที่เชื่อถือได้ woŋkaan′thîichŷathŷy′dâaj′ reliable sources (as of news).

o วงการแพทย์ woŋ′kaanphɛ̂ɛd′ N medical circles.

o วงการเมือง woŋ′kaanmyaŋ′ N political circles.

วงแขน woŋkhɛ̌ɛn′ N 1. embrace, encircling arms. 2. sew. armhole.

วงโคจร woŋ′khoocɔɔn′ N orbit.

วงงาน woŋŋaan′ N sphere of activity, field of work.

วงจร woŋcɔɔn′ N (electrical) circuit.

วงดุริยางค์ woŋ′durijaaŋ′ N orchestra.

วงไพ่ woŋphâj′ N a circle of card players.

วงลวด woŋlûad′ N a loop of wire.

วงล้อม woŋlɔ́ɔm′ N an encirclement.

วงเล็บ (อัน) woŋléb′ (ʔan′) N parenthesis.

วงเวียน (อัน, วง) woŋwian′ N 1. compass (ʔan′). 2. traffic circle (woŋ′).

วงแหวน woŋwɛ̌ɛn′ N ring, gasket, washer.

วงศ์ woŋ′ N race, family, stock. →Also occurs as a bound form, as in the entry below.

ราชวงศ์ (ราชวงศ์) râadchawoŋ′ (râadchawoŋ′) N dynasty.

วงศ์วาน (คน) woŋwaan′ (khon′) N kin, family, relatives.

วงศ์สกุล woŋ′sakun′ N family, lineage.

วงศ์คณาญาติ (คน) woŋsǎ′khanaajâad′ (khon′) N elab. relatives, kin.

วน ๑ won′ V to circulate, revolve, whirl.

น้ำวน námwon′ N whirlpool.

วนไปเวียนมา wonpaj′wianmaa′ 1. to go around, go to and fro (within a certain area); to be wind-

ing (as of a road); to be circuitous. 2. around, to and fro; in a roundabout manner.

o เดินวนไปเวียนมา dəən′-wonpaj′wianmaa′ to walk around, walk to and fro, pace back and forth.

วนเวียน wonwian′ V 1. to go around (within an area); to be circuitous; to be winding (as of a road); to go through a cycle. 2. colloq. to hang around (in an area). sV 3. around, in a roundabout manner.

วน ๒ as in วนศาสตร์ wanasàad′ N forestry.

วรรค (วรรค) wág′ (wág′) N 1. section, phrase; line (of poetry), metric group. 2. pause or space in writing. C 3. clf. for sections, phrases, lines, metric groups.

เป็นวรรคเป็นเวร penwág′penween′ elab. colloq. on and on, at great length, continuously, excessively (of speaking, crying).

เว้นวรรค wénwág′ V to leave spaces (between phrases, clauses, sentences).

วรรณ, วรรณะ wan′, wanná?′ N 1. color, complexion. 2. caste.

วรรณ- wannaɔ. Bound form meaning "writing, composition," as in the entries immediately below.

วรรณกรรม (ชิ้น) wan′nakam′ (chín′) N literary work.

วรรณคดี (เรื่อง, เล่ม) wan′nakhadii′ (rŷaŋ′, lêm′) N literature.

วรรณยุกต์ (อัน) wan′najúg′ (ʔan′) N the tone marks in the Thai system of writing.

วรวงศ์เธอ. See พระเจ้าวรวงศ์เธอพระองค์เจ้า.

วสันตฤดู wásǎn′tàrýduu′ N eleg. spring (the season).

วอ (หลัง) wɔɔ′ (lǎŋ′) N palanquin.

วอก wɔɔg′ N (Year of the) Monkey. →The complete list of the cyclical years is given under ปี.

วอกแวก wɔ̂gwɛ̂g′* V to be distracted, unsettled.

ว่อง in ว่องไว wôŋwaj′* V to be agile.

วอด wɔɔd′ V to be consumed, exhausted.

วอดวาย wɔɔdwaaj′ V to be ruined, destroyed. →Syn. ฉิบหาย colloq. vulg. ย่อยยับ, ยับเยิน com., พินาศ, วินาศ eleg.

วอน wɔɔn′ V 1. to implore; usually in compounds, as below. 2. colloq. to ask for (e.g. trouble, punishment) (as when a child misbehaves).

วอนขอ wɔɔnkhɔ̌ɔ′ V to plead, beg for.

วิงวอน wiŋwɔɔn′ V eleg. to implore, beseech.

อ้อนวอน ʔɔ̂ɔnwɔɔn′ V com. to implore, beseech.

วอน in the following entries.

บินว่อน bin′wɔ̀n′* to swarm about (in the air)(e.g.
of airplanes, insects).

ปลิวว่อน pliw′wɔ̀n′* to be blown about, be floating
in the air in great numbers.

วอบ in วอบแวบ wɔ̂bwɛ̂b′* V colloq. to be flashing, shining, glittering.

วอลซ์ wɔɔl′, wɔɔls′ N waltz. [f. Eng.]

เพลงวอลซ์ (เพลง) phleeŋwɔɔls (phleeŋ′) N
waltz music.

วะ wá′ Pt rustic or vulgar final particle used in
place of the polite form ครับ.

o อะไรวะ? ʔaraj′wá↓ vulg. Well, what is it?

วัง ๑ (วัง) waŋ′ (waŋ′) N palace.

ราชวัง (แห่ง) râadchawaŋ′ (hɛ̀ŋ′) N royal
palace.

วัง ๒ (แห่ง) waŋ′ (hɛ̀ŋ′) N a deep pool (in a
larger body of water); an underwater abyss.

วังน้ำวน waŋ′námwon′ N whirlpool.

วัง ๓ in แม่น้ำวัง mɛ̂ɛnáamwaŋ′ pN the Mæwang
(Me Wang), a tributary of the Čhaophaya River
in N Thailand. →Also แม่วัง.

วังชา in กำลังวังชา kamlaŋ′waŋchaa′ N elab.
colloq. bodily strength.

วังเวง waŋweeŋ′ V 1. to feel lonely and nostalgic,
awed and nostalgic. 2. to evoke feelings of
loneliness and nostalgia, awe and nostalgia.

วัฒนธรรม wád′thanátham′ N culture.

กระทรวงวัฒนธรรม krasuaŋ′wád′thanátham′ N
Ministry of Culture.

องค์การศึกษาวิทยาศาสตร์และวัฒนธรรมแห่งสห-
ประชาชาติ ʔoŋkaan′sy̆gsǎa′ wídthajaaɔ
sàad′ lɛwád′thanatham′-hɛ̀ŋ′sahàprachaaɔ
châad′ nN The United Nations Educational,
Scientific and Cultural Organization (UNESCO).

วัฒนา wádthanaa′ V eleg. to progress, grow.
ความ-- progress. →Syn. เจริญ com.

เจริญวัฒนา carəən′wádthanaa′ V elab. eleg.
to progress and advance.

วัฒนาถาวร wádthanaa′thǎawɔɔn′ eleg. to progress, advance everlastingly; to progress and
be enduring; to be everlasting. ความ-- endur-

ing progress.

วัณ- in วัณโรค wannarôog′ N eleg. tuberculosis.
→Syn. ฝีในท้อง colloq.

วัด ๑ wád′ V to measure.

เครื่องวัด (อัน,อย่าง,ชนิด) khrŷaŋwád′ (ʔan′,
jàaŋ′,chaníd′) N 1. measuring implement;
yardstick. 2. meter, gauge.

o เครื่องวัดความดันอากาศ (อัน) khrŷaŋwád′-
khwaamdan′ʔaakàad′ (ʔan′) N barometer.

วัด ๒ (วัด) wád′ (wád′) N wat, temple, temple
compound.

งานวัด ŋaanwád′ N a fair held within the grounds
of a Buddhist temple.

นครวัด nakhɔɔn′wád′ pN Angkor Wat, ancient
temple of the Khmer (in Cambodia).

วัดพระแก้ว wádphrákɛ̂ɛw′ pN Wat Phra Kæo,
common name for วัดพระศรีรัตนศาลดาราม,
q.v. below.

วัดพระเชตุพน wádphráchêed′tuphon′ pN Wat
Phrachettuphon, official name for the Temple
of the Reclining Buddha in Bangkok. →Also commonly called วัดโพธิ์.

วัดพระศรีมหาธาตุ wádphrásǐi′-mahǎa′thâad′
pN Wat Phrasimahathat, name of the oldest wat
in Nakhɔn Sithammarat in S Thailand.

วัดพระศรีรัตนศาลดาราม wádphrásǐi′rádtanásàaɔ
sadaa′raam′ pN Wat Phrasiratanasasadaram,
official name for the Temple of the Emerald
Buddha in Bangkok. Also commonly called
วัดพระแก้ว.

วัดโพธิ์ wádphoo′ pN Wat Pho, common name for
วัดพระเชตุพน, q.v. above.

วัดวาอาราม (วัด,แห่ง) wádwaa′ʔaaraam′ (wád′,
hɛ̀ŋ′) N elab. colloq. wats and temples.

วัตถุ wádthù′ N eleg. object, article. 2. material(s)
(as "raw materials").

ถาวรวัตถุ (อย่าง,สิ่ง) thǎawɔɔn′wádthù′ (jàaŋ′,
sìŋ′) N eleg. permanent, enduring object
(as a building, monument).

โบราณวัตถุ booraan′wádthù′ N eleg. relics,
ancient objects, ruins; archeological finds.

วัตถุดิบ wádthù′dìb′ N eleg. raw materials.

วัตถุประสงค์ (อย่าง,ประการ) wádthù′prasǒŋ′
(jàaŋ′,prakaan′) N eleg. aim, purpose, object.

วัตถุพยาน wádthù?/phajaan/ N eleg. tangible evidence.

วัตถุพลอยได้ (อย่าง) wádthù?/phlɔɔjdâaj/ (jàaŋ/) N eleg. by-product.

วัตร in กิจวัตร (อย่าง) kìdcawád/ (jàaŋ/) N eleg. routine; routine matter.

วัน wan/ N 1. day. C 2. day.

THE DAYS OF THE WEEK

วันอาทิตย์ wan?aathíd/ Sunday.
วันจันทร์ wancan/ Monday.
วันอังคาร wan?aŋkhaan/ Tuesday.
วันพุธ wanphúd/ Wednesday.
วันพฤหัส wanpháryhàd/ Thursday (short name).
วันพฤหัสบดี wanpháryhàd/sabɔɔdii/ Thursday.
วันศุกร์ wansùg/ Friday.
วันเสาร์ wansǎw/ Saturday.

กลางวัน klaaŋwan/ (in the) daytime, (by) day.
o อาหารกลางวัน (มื้อ) ?aahǎan/klaaŋwan/ (mýy/) N eleg. luncheon, midday meal.

แต่วัน tɛwan/ early, before the usual time, before the appointed time.

แต่วันๆ. See วันๆ below.

ทุกวัน thúgwan/ every day.

ทุกวันนี้ thúgwanníi/ nowadays, today.

เที่ยงวัน thîaŋwan/ N midday, noon.

นับวันแต่ nábwan/tɛ̀ɛ⊃ day by day, as days go by.

ในเร็วๆวัน najrewrew/wan/ soon, in the very near future.

ในวันในพรุ่ง najwan/najphrûŋ/ colloq. in a day or two, very soon, in a short time.

ในวันหน้า najwan/nâa/ some other day (in the future), some future day.

ประจำวัน pracam/wan/ daily; everyday, routine.

ไปวันๆ paj/wanwan/ to go early, ahead of time.

ผัดวันประกันพรุ่ง phàdwan/-prakan/phrûŋ/ V elab. colloq. to procrastinate, put off.

แมลงวัน (ตัว) malɛɛŋwan/ (tua/) N com. fly, housefly. →Also แมงวัน colloq.

ไม่มีวัน mâjmiiwan/ never, there will never be a day (when); not a chance.

o ไม่มีวันอดตาย mâjmiiwan/-?òd/taaj/ will never starve to death.

รายวัน raajwan/ a daily, daily issue (as of a newspaper).

วันก่อน wankɔ̀ɔn/ the other day.

วันก่อนๆ wan/kɔ̀ɔnkɔ̀ɔn/ the previous days.

วันเกิด wankə̀əd/ N birthday.

วันขึ้นปีใหม่ wankhŷn/piimàj/ N New Year's Day.

วันขึ้น ๑ ค่ำ wankhŷn/nỳŋkhâm/ the first day of the waxing moon.

วันคล้ายวันเกิด wankhláajwankə̀əd/ N lit. birthday.

วันเฉลิม wanchalə̌əm/ N 1. day of celebration. 2. colloq. the king's birthday; abbrev. for the following entry.

วันเฉลิมพระชนมพรรษา wanchalə̌əm/-phráchon/⊃ phansǎa/ N roy. anniversary of the king's birthday.

วันชาติ wanchâad/ N National Day.

วันดีคืนดี wandii/khyyndii/ elab. colloq. one fine day, on a certain day.

วันที่... wanthîi⊃ the (such and such numbered) day, the ...-th (e.g. the fifth).

o เมื่อคืนวันที่ ๕ mŷakhyyn/wanthîihâa/ on the night of the fifth.

o ลงวันที่ ๕ loŋ/wanthîihâa/ dated the fifth.

o วันที่ ๑๐ เดือนตุลาคม wanthîisìb/dyantulaa/⊃ khom/ the tenth of October.

วันที่ระลึก wan/thîiralýg/ N memorial day.

วันนี้ wanníi/ today.

o เย็นวันนี้ jen/wanníi/ this evening.

วันพระ wanphrá?/ N Buddhist day of worship. There are four such days in a lunar month, corresponding to the four phases of the moon.

วันเพ็ญ wanphen/ N full moon day.

o คืนวันเพ็ญ khyyn/wanphen/ N full moon night.

วันมะรืน wan/maryyn/ the day after tomorrow.

วันยังค่ำ wanjaŋkhâm/ from morn till night, all day long.

o วันยังค่ำคืนยังรุ่ง wanjaŋkhâm/khyynjaŋrûŋ/ colloq. all day and all night.

วันรุ่งขึ้น, ใน-- wan/rûŋkhŷn/, najwan/rûŋkhŷn/ (on) the next day, the following day, on the morrow.

วันแรม ๑ ค่ำ wanrɛɛm/nỳŋkhâm/ the first day of the waning moon.

วันละ wan/la⊃ per day, a day, daily.

วันๆ wanwan/ ahead of time, before the appointed time.

o แต่วันๆ tɛwan/wan/ idem. →See also แต่วัน.

o มาวันๆ maa′wanwan′ to come early, before the appointed time. →Also มาแต่วันๆ.

วันสงกรานต์ wan′sǒŋkraan′ N Songkran Day, the old Thai New Year's day which falls between April 13 and April 15.

วันหน้า wannâa′ one day, some day, some other day. →Used of future time only. →Also ใน--.

วันหนึ่ง wan′nyŋ one day.

o วันหนึ่งๆ wan′nyŋ-wan′nyŋ 1. from day to day, from one day to the next. 2. in any one day.

o อยู่มาวันหนึ่ง jùumaa′-wan′nyŋ (and) then one day, one day later on.

วันหยุด (วัน) wanjùd′ (wan′) N holiday, day off.

o วันหยุดราชการ (วัน) wanjùd′râadchakaan′ (wan′) official holiday.

วันหยุดงาน wan′jùdŋaan′ day of rest, day off, holiday.

หายวันหายคืน hǎajwan′hǎajkhyyn′ elab. colloq. to recover quickly (from sickness); to improve (in health) from day to day.

วับ wáb′ sV 1. in a flash. rM 2. intensifier used with เช่ง "beautiful," มัน "glossy."

o หายวับไปกับตา hǎaj′wáb′pajkataa′ to vanish in a flash before one's eyes.

วับๆ wábwáb′ V to be twinkling.

วับวาบ wábwâab′ V to be flashing, dazzling, glaring.

วัย waj′ N age, stage, period (of human life).

เจริญวัย caraən′waj′ V eleg. to grow up.

เยาว์วัย jaw′waj′ V eleg. 1. to be young, under-age. N 2. childhood.

วัยกลางคน waj′klaaŋkhon′ N 1. middle age (of people). Among the Thai approx. 35-50 years of age. 2. (as n. mod.) middle-aged. →Also อายุกลางคน. →Comp. ปรา.

วัยฉกรรจ์ waj′chakan′ N youth, young adulthood.

วัยชรา waj′charaa′ N eleg. old age, period of old age.

วลัย in เถาวัลย์ (ต้น,เถา) thǎwwan′ (tôn′,thǎw′) N vines, climbers (in general).

วัว (ตัว) wua′ (tua′) N bovine (animal), ox, cow, cattle. →Also sometimes งัว.

เนื้อวัว ný awua′ N beef.

วัวกระทิง (ตัว) wuakrathiŋ′ (tua′) N gaur (Bos

gaurus), a kind of wild ox.

วัวควาย wuakhwaaj′ N cattle, livestock (in general).

วัวตัวผู้ (ตัว) wua′tuaphûu′ (tua′) N bull.

วัวตัวเมีย (ตัว) wua′tuamia′ (tua′) N cow.

วัวต่าง (ตัว) wuatàaŋ′ (tua′) N pack ox.

วัวนม (ตัว) wuanom′ (tua′) N milch cow.

วิ่งวัว (เที่ยว) wiŋwua′ (thîaw′) V 1. to run a race, to race. N 2. race.

หน้าวัว (ต้น,ดอก) nâawua′ (tôn′,dɔɔg′) N bot. anthurium (Anthurium), a handsome plant.

ว่า ๑ waa′ C wa, a Thai linear meas. eq. to a fathom or two yards (meas. by extending both arms). →Equal to four ศอก, q.v.

ตารางว่า taaraaŋwaa′ square wa, i.e. about four square yards (under 4 sq. meters).

ว่า ๒ in ตายละว่า taaj′lawaa′ E excl. of dismay.

ว่า wâa′, wâaɔ V 1. to say. 2. to scold, criticize, speak disparagingly (to or about someone). sV 3. saying; thus, that. NOTE. Verbs of saying asking, knowing, etc., are fol. by ว่า which is usually trans. as "that" (occ. "whether") or not translated.

o คุณพูดว่าอะไร khunphûud′wâaʔaraj↓ What did you say?

o เขาถามว่ามีห้องว่างไหม kháwthǎam′wâamiihɔŋɔ wâaŋ′máj↓ He asked whether there were any rooms.

o ผมคิดว่าเขาเก่ง phǒmkhíd′wâakháwkèŋ↓ I think (that) he is clever.

เกรงว่า kreeŋ′wâaɔ to fear that, to be afraid that.

เข้าใจว่า khâwcaj′wâaɔ to understand that.

คล้ายกับว่า khláaj′kawâaɔ as if, as though.

คำว่า kham′wâaɔ the word "..."

คือว่า khyywâa′ that is, that is to say.

จะว่าอย่างไร cawâa′jàaŋraj′↓ What (do you) wish to say?

ฉวยว่า chǔaj′wâaɔ if, in case.

เช่นว่า chênwâa′ as mentioned.

ด่าว่า dàa′wâa′ to speak disparagingly or abusively to, of; to scold; to swear at.

ดุว่า dùʔ′wâa′ V to bawl out, reprimand, scold.

ดูว่า duu′wâaɔ to see that.

ต่อว่า tɔɔ′wâa′ V to come (to someone) with a grievance, complain (to), remonstrate (with).

ต่อว่าต่อขาน tɔɔwâa′tɔɔkhǎan′ V colloq.

(parties) to argue over grievances or complaints (which stand between them).

ตอบว่า tɔ̀ɔb/wâaɔ to reply that.

แต่ว่า tɛ̀ɛwâa/ but.

ถ้าจะว่าไป thâacawâa/paj one might say, one
could say, so to speak, as a matter of fact.

ถึงแม้ว่า thʉ̆ŋmɛ́ɛ/wâa/ although, even though.

ถือว่า thʉ̌ywâaɔ to hold (the belief) that, believe
that, consider that, take (it to mean) that, claim
that.

ทราบว่า sâab/wâaɔ eleg. to know that; it was
learned that.

นับว่า náb/wâaɔ to be regarded, counted as, taken
as, considered to be.

ปรากฏว่า praakòd/wâa/ it appears that.

เป็นอันว่า penʔan/wâa/ this means that (such and
such a result ensues, such and such a course of
action is settled on).

ฝันว่า fǎn/wâa/ to dream that.

พูดว่า phûud/wâaɔ to say that.

เพราะว่า phrɔ́wâa/ because.

เพื่อว่า phŷa/wâaɔ in order that.

ไม่ว่า (1) mâjwâa/; (2) mâjwâaɔ 1. not to mind,
not to complain. 2. no matter, regardless of.

รวมความว่า ruamkhwaam/wâa/ in short, briefly.

ราวกับว่า raaw/kawâaɔ as if, as though.

รู้ว่า rúu/wâaɔ to know that.

เรียก(...)ว่า (1) rîag/(...)wâa/; (2) rîag/wâa/
1. to call (such and such) (by the name of). 2.
to be called (such and such).

ว่ากล่าว wâa/klàaw/ V to advise, admonish,
reprove.

ว่าการ wâakaan/ V to direct things, administer;
to be in charge.

o ที่ว่าการ thîiwâakaan/ N administrative office
(usually of the government).

o รัฐมนตรีช่วยว่าการ (นาย,คน) rádthamontrii/ɔ
chûajwâakaan/ (naaj/,khon/) N deputy minister
(of the government).

o รัฐมนตรีว่าการ (นาย,คน) rádthamontrii/wâaɔ
kaan/ (naaj/,khon/) N minister (of the government).

ว่าความ wâakhwaam/ V 1. to litigate; to plead a
case in court. 2. to act as arbiter (in a dispute).

ว่าง่าย wâaŋâaj/ V to be obedient, tractable.

o เด็กว่าง่าย dèg/wâaŋâaj/ an obedient child.

ว่าจ้าง wâacâaŋ/ V to hire, employ, engage.

ว่าด้วย wâadûajɔ to be concerned with, to deal with.

ว่าต่าง wâatàaŋ/ to act for (in a law suit).

ว่าตาม wâataam/ to say after.

ว่าแต่ wâa/tɛ̀ɛ V 1. to criticize (1st example).
2. speaking specifically of (2nd example).

o ว่าแต่คนอื่น แต่คุณก็ทำเอง wâa/tɛ̀ɛkhonʔỳyn/→
tɛ̀ɛkhun/kɔ̀thamʔeeŋ/↓ (You) criticize others,
but you do (the same thing) yourself.

o ว่าแต่คุณเถอะ คุณจะไปไหม wâa/tɛ̀ɛkhun/thə?/→
khuncapaj/máj↓ Speaking about you, now, are
you going to go? Coming to you, now, are you
going to go?

ว่านอนสอนง่าย wâanɔɔn/sɔ̌ɔŋŋâaj/ V elab.
colloq. to be tractable, easily led, compliant,
obedient.

ว่านอนสอนยาก wâanɔɔn/sɔ̌ɔnjâag/ V elab.
colloq. to be untractable, unmanageable, disobedient, unruly.

ว่าไม่ฟัง wâa/mâjfaŋ/ V to be disobedient, naughty,
heedless of advice, warnings, commands.

ว่ายาก wâajâag/ V to be disobedient, untractable.

ว่าราชการ wâa/râadchakaan/ V to administer
the affairs of the state. ผู้-- governor, commissioner.

สัญญาว่า sǎnjaa/wâaɔ to promise that; to contract
to (do something).

หาว่า hǎa/wâaɔ to accuse of, charge that, claim
that.

หากว่า hàag/wâaɔ if, in the event that.

อย่างว่า jàaŋwâa/ colloq. as stated, as said,
as it is said (e.g. in a proverb).

ว่า ๑ !wáa/ E excl. expressing unpleasant surprise,
displeasure.

ว่า ๒. See entries below.

ว่าวุ่น wáawûn/ V to be in a state of confusion,
indecision.

ว่าเหว่ wáawèe/ V to be lonesome, lonely and
lost. ความ-- loneliness.

ว่าเหว่ใจ wáawèe/caj/ V to be lonesome.

วาง waaŋ/ V to place, lay.

ไม่วางตา mâjwaaŋ/taa/ without taking (one's)

eyes off (something).

วางก้าม waaŋkâam/ V idiom. to act big.

วางข้อบังคับ waaŋ/khɔ̂ɔbaŋkháb/ to establish regulations.

วางไข่ waaŋkhàj/ V eleg. to lay eggs. →Syn. ออกไข่ com.

วางโครงการ waaŋ/khrooŋkaan/ to lay plans.

วางใจ waaŋcaj/ V to trust, have confidence in. ความ-- trust.

วางเดิมพัน waaŋ/dəəmphan/ colloq. to bet, place a bet.

วางตน waaŋton/ V eleg. 1. to behave, conduct oneself. 2. to place oneself.

วางตัว waaŋtua/ V com. 1. to behave, conduct oneself. 2. to place oneself.

วางท่า waaŋthâa/ V to put on airs, to pose.

วางนโยบาย waaŋ/nájoobaaj/ to lay down, establish a policy.

วางแผนการ waaŋ/phɛ̌ɛnkaan/ to plan, plot, lay plans.

วางเพลิง waaŋphləəŋ/ V eleg. to commit arson.

วางมัดจำ waaŋ/mádcam/ to give a deposit, make a part payment.

วางมือ waaŋmyy/ V to stop or give up doing something.

วางยาพิษ waaŋ/jaaphíd/ V to poison.

วางระเบียบ waaŋ/rabìab/ 1. to establish regulations. 2. to set up a system.

วางรากฐาน waaŋ/râagthǎan/ to lay, establish a foundation.

วาง(...)ไว้ (1) waaŋ/(...)wáj/; (2) waaŋ/wáj/ 1. to place, lay, set up, fix, establish stipulate (something). 2. to be laid, set up, established.

วางหลัก waaŋlàg/ to set up a principle.

วางหูโทรศัพท์ waaŋhǔu/thoorasàb/ to hang up the telephone receiver.

วางอาวุธ waaŋ/ʔaawúd/ to lay down arms.

วางอุบาย waaŋ/ʔubaaj/ to set up a trap or stratagem.

ไว้วางใจ wájwaaŋcaj/ V to trust, have faith in.

ว่าง wâaŋ/ V 1. to be free, at leisure. 2. to be vacant, unoccupied.

ของว่าง khɔ̌ɔŋwâaŋ/ N snack.

ช่องว่าง (ช่อง,แห่ง) chɔ̂ŋwâaŋ/ (chɔ̂ŋ/, hɛ̀ŋ/) N

vacant or unoccupied space or room, gap, blank space (as on an application).

ที่ว่าง (ที่,แห่ง) thîiwâaŋ/ (thîi/, hɛ̀ŋ/) N vacancy, unoccupied space, unoccupied land.

ไม่ว่าง mâjwâaŋ/ 1. to be busy, occupied. 2. to be occupied (as of a bathroom).

ว่างงาน wâaŋŋaan/ V 1. to be unoccupied, have leisure; to have run out of work, have finished the work at hand. 2. to be unemployed. คน-- unemployed person; unoccupied person.

ว่างเปล่า wâaŋplàaw/ V to be empty, vacant, unoccupied (as a house), uncultivated (as a field).

ว่างมือ wâaŋmyy/ to be free, unoccupied, have one's hands free (e.g. from work).

ว่างๆ wâaŋwâaŋ/ in (one's) spare time, in (one's) free time.

เวลาว่าง weelaa/wâaŋ/ N free time, spare time, leisure time.

อาหารว่าง ʔaahǎan/wâaŋ/ N snack, food taken between meals.

ว้าง. See entries below.

เวิ้งว้าง wə́əŋwáaŋ/ to be wide, vast, vast and empty. 2. to be affected by a sense of the vastness and emptiness of one's surroundings.

อ้างว้าง ʔâaŋwáaŋ/ to be lonely, lonesome.

วาจา waacaa/ N eleg. (spoken) word; utterance.

เปล่งวาจา plèŋ/waacaa/ V eleg. to say, speak, declare.

ผรุสวาจา pharùd/sawaacaa/ N eleg. abusive language, harsh word.

ลั่นวาจา lân/waacaa/ V eleg. 1. to speak, say, declare. 2. to commit oneself, give one's word. →Syn. ลั่นคำ,ลั่นปาก com.

วาด wâad/ V to draw, make a drawing.

ภาพวาด (ภาพ) phâabwâad/ (phâab/) N eleg. a drawing, a painting.

วาดเขียน wâadkhǐan/ V to draw.

วาดภาพ wâadphâab/ V eleg. to draw a picture.

วาตภัย waa/taphaj/ N eleg. disaster from a windstorm.

วาทศิลป์ waa/thásǐn/, waa/tháʔsǐn/ N oratory, rhetoric, art of speaking effectively.

วาที in โต้วาที tôo/waathii/ V 1. to debate. N 2. short for การ-- debate.

วาน ๑ waan′ V to ask (someone) to do something for one.

วาน ๒ waan′. See the entries below.

    คืนวาน khyynwaan′ last night. →Syn. เมื่อคืน.

    เมื่อวาน mɯ̂awaan′ yesterday.

    วานซืน,--นี้ waansyyn′, waansyyn′níi′ the day before yesterday.

    วานนี้ waan′níi′ yesterday.

    o เมื่อวานนี้ mɯ̂awaan′níi′ yesterday.

ว่าน in ว่านเครือ wâankhrya′ N relatives; lineage, family.

วานร (ตัว) waanɔɔn′ (tua′) N lit. monkey.

วาบ wâab′ V to flash up, flare up suddenly.

    ใจหายวาบ cajhǎaj′wâab′ V to be shocked, stunned with fear.

    วับวาบ wábwâab′ V to be flashing, dazzling, glaring.

    วูบวาบ wûubwâab′ V to be flashing, flaring, glaring, glittering.

    แวบวาบ wɛ̂bwâab′ V to be flashing, dazzling, glittering.

วาย. waaj′ the English letter "Y." [f. Eng.] →Also ไว๊.

วาย waaj′ V to end, decrease, finish.

    ไม่วาย mâjwaaj′ cannot help, cannot refrain from.

    วายชนม์ waajchon′ V lit. to die.

    วายปราณ waajpraan′ V lit. to die.

    วายร้าย waajráaj′ colloq. devilish. อย่าง-- slang extremely.

    วายวอด in ฉิบหายวายวอด chìbhǎaj′waajwɔ̂ɔd′, chíb -- V to perish, be utterly ruined, destroyed. NOTE. Used by men sp. to men who are intimates; otherwise insulting. Cf. ฉิบ.

    วุ่นวาย wûnwaaj′ V 1. to be in confusion, in a turmoil. 2. to concern oneself, bother oneself, make a fuss, fuss over. การ-- disturbance, tumult.

    o วุ่นวายใจ wûnwaaj′caj′ V to be confused, perturbed.

ว่าย wâaj′ V to swim. →Chiefly in compounds.

    ว่ายน้ำ wâajnáam′ V to swim.

    แหวกว่าย wɛ̀ɛgwâaj′ V to swim about.

วาร,วาระ waan′, waaráʔ, waará?′ N eleg. 1. time, occasion, period. 2. lit. day. C 3. time,

occasion, period.

    ในวาระ najwaará?′ eleg. on the occasion.

    ระเบียบวาระ rabìab′waará?′ N eleg. agenda.

    วารสาร (ฉบับ,เล่ม) waarasǎan′ (chabàb′,lêm′) periodical, magazine, journal.

    วาระดิถี waarádìthǐi′ elab. eleg. day.

    อีกวาระหนึ่ง ?ìig′-waará?′nỳŋ′ eleg. once more, again.

วาว waaw′ V to be bright, shiny, flashing.

    เป็นมันวาว penman′waaw′ to be glossy, shiny.

    แวววาว wɛɛwwaaw′ V to be glittering, glaring.

ว่าว (ตัว) wâw′* (tua′) N kite (for flying).

    ชักว่าว chágwâw′ V to fly a kite.

    ว่าวจุฬา (ตัว) wâwculaa′ (tua′) N star-shaped kite (called the male).

    ว่าวปักเป้า (ตัว) wâwpágpâw′ (tua′) N a diamond-shaped kite with a long tail (called the female).

วาสนา wâasanǎa′ N fortune, fate, luck (as a consequence of deeds in a previous existence).

วาฬ in ปลาวาฬ (ตัว) plaawaan′ (tua′) N whale.

วิกฤต,วิกฤติ wíkrìd′ N lit. eleg. crisis.

    วิกฤตกาล,วิกฤติกาล wíkrìdtakaan′ N crisis, time of crisis.

วิกล in วิกลจริต wíkon′carìd′ V eleg. to be insane.

วิกาล wíkaan′ sV eleg. wrong, inappropriate, odd (of time). →See note under subentry.

    ยามวิกาล jaam′wíkaan′ N eleg. 1. wrong or inappropriate time, i.e. nighttime. 2. at an inappropriate time. →Also 2. ใน--. NOTE. Primary reference is to the period from 12.00 noon to 6 A.M. when it is improper for priests to eat; but ยามวิกาล is commonly used to refer to nighttime as an inappropriate time for some given action or activity.

วิเคราะห์ wíkhrɔ́?′ V eleg. to analyze. การ-- analysis.

วิง ๑ in วิงวอน wiŋwɔɔn′ V eleg. to implore, beg, beseech. ความ-- pleading, supplication, imploring, begging for mercy. คำ-- (ข้อ,ฉบับ, อย่าง,ประการ) supplication, plea.

วิง ๒ in วิงเวียน wiŋwian′ V to be giddy, dizzy.

วิ่ง wîŋ′ V 1. to run. 2. colloq. to get busy (contacting e.g. an official for a permit, a donor for a contribution).

วิ่งแข่ง wîŋkhὲŋ′ V to race.

วิ่งควบ wîŋkhûab′ V to gallop.

วิ่งจี๋ wîŋ′cǐi′ to run swiftly; to dart.

วิ่งฉิว wîŋ′chĭw′ to run swiftly and smoothly, swiftly and uninterruptedly (of vehicles, ships).

วิ่งตื๋อ wîŋ′tǐyy′ to run very fast (of people, animals).

วิ่งเต้น wîŋtên′ V 1. to run and hop about (as children). 2. colloq. to scurry around, busy oneself, bend every effort (as when trying to obtain support for one's purpose, or when organizing things).

วิ่งเปี้ยว wîŋpîaw′ N 1. a relay race in which two vertical poles are used as terminals. V 2. to run such a race.

วิ่งผลัด wîŋphlàd′ N 1. a relay race. V 2. to run a relay race.

วิ่งราว wîŋraaw′ V to snatch and run away.

วิ่งเร็ว wîŋrew′ 1. to run fast, race (on foot). N 2. sports a dash.

วิ่งวัว wîŋwua′ N 1. race. V 2. to run a race, to race.

วิ่งวุ่น wîŋwûn′ V to run around busily (as when organizing something).

วิ่งหนี wîŋnǐi′ V to run away.

วิ่งเหย่าๆ wîŋ′jàwjàw′ to run slowly, trot along.

วิ่งเหยาะๆ wîŋ′jɔ́ʔjɔ́ʔ′ idem.

วิจัย wícaj′ V to do research, investigate. การ--　research, investigation.

งานวิจัย ŋaanwícaj′ N research work.

วิจารณ์ wícaan′ V 1. to criticize, comment. 2. to ponder, reflect.

คำวิจารณ์ (ข้อ,อย่าง,ประการ) kham′wícaan′ (khɔ̂ɔ′, jàaŋ′, prakaan′) N commentary, criticism.

นักวิจารณ์ (คน) nágwícaan′ (khon′) N critic, commentator.

นักวิจารณ์ข่าว (คน) nágwícaan′khàaw′ (khon′) N news commentator.

วิพากษ์วิจารณ์ wíphâag′wícaan′ V elab. to criticize, comment (critically), pass judgment.

วิจิตร wícìd′ V eleg. to be beautiful, splendid.

วิจิตรพิสดาร wícìd′phídsadaan′ V elab. to be magnificent, gorgeous, fantastically beautiful,

elaborately beautiful.

วิชา (วิชา) wíchaa′ (wíchaa′) N 1. subject (of study). 2. knowledge.

กวดวิชา kùadwíchaa′ V 1. to be tutored, coached, taught (in order to make up a deficiency in one's studies). 2. to tutor, coach, teach (in order to help someone make up a deficiency). →In mng. 2. usually followed by ให้.

วิชาการ wíchaakaan′ N 1. knowledge. 2. technology. 3. (as n. mod.) academic, theoretical, technical. นัก-- scholar.

o ฝ่ายวิชาการ fàaj′wíchaakaan′ (on) the academic, theoretical, technical side; the academic, theoretical, technical aspect. →Comp. ฝ่ายธุระการ.

วิชาครู wíchaakhruu′ N education (as a subject of study).

วิชาความรู้ wíchaa′khwaamrúu′ N knowledge.

วิชาคำนวน wíchaa′khamnuan′ N mathematics.

วิชาชีพ wíchaa′chîib′ N vocational education, vocational study.

วิชาแพทย์ wíchaa′phɛ̂ɛd′ N medicine (as a subject of study).

วิชาเลข wíchaa′lêeg′ N arithmetic.

วิญญาณ (ดวง) winjaan′ (duaŋ′) N spirit, soul.

วิด wíd′ V to dip up, scoop up, bail.

วิตก wítòg′ V to worry, be anxious.

น่าวิตก nâa′wítòg′ V to be worrisome, alarming.

หวั่นวิตก wàn′wítòg′ V to be worried, apprehensive.

วิตถาร wíd(ta)thǎan′ V eleg. to be unconventional, abnormal, peculiar.

วิตมิน, วิตามิน wítamin′ N vitamin. [f. Eur.]

วิถี wíthǐi′ N eleg. way, path, course. →Syn. See ทาง ๑.

บาทวิถี bàad′wíthǐi′ N eleg. footpath, sidewalk.

วิถีทาง wíthǐi′thaaŋ′ N elab. way, path.

วิทย in วิทยฐานะ wídthajáʔ′thǎaná?′ N academic, educational standing.

รับรองวิทยฐานะ rábrɔɔŋ′-wídthajá?′thǎaná?′ to accredit, be accredited.

วิทยา wídthajaa′ N knowledge. →Chiefly in compounds and often equiv. to -ology.

จิตวิทยา cìdtawídthajaa′ N psychology.

ชีววิทยา chii′wawídthajaa′ N biology.

เภสัชวิทยา pheesàd′wídthajaa′ N pharmacology.

วิทยาการ wídthajaakaan′ N science, knowledge.

วิทยานิพนธ์ (เล่ม, ฉบับ) wídthajaa′níphon′ (lêm′, chabàb′) N eleg. thesis, dissertation.

วิทยาลัย (แห่ง) wídthajaalaj′ (hὲŋ′) N college, school.

o มหาวิทยาลัย (แห่ง) mahăa′wídthajaalaj′ (hὲŋ′) N university.

วิทยาศาสตร์ wídthajaasàad′ N science, i.e., the field of knowledge known as "the sciences." การ-- scientific matters, affairs. นัก-- scientist.

o วิทยาศาสตร์บริสุทธิ์ wídthajaasàad′bɔɔrisùd′ N pure science.

o วิทยาศาสตร์บัณฑิต (คน) wídthajaasàad′banɔ dìd′ N 1. a Bachelor of Science (khon′). 2. the Bachelor of Science degree.

o วิทยาศาสตร์ประยุกต์ wídthajaasàad′prajúg′ N applied science.

ศิลปวิทยา sĭnlapà?′wídthajaa′ N arts and sciences.

สุขวิทยา sùg′khawídthajaa′ N hygiene.

วิทยุ (เครื่อง) wídthajú?′ (khrɯ̂aŋ′) N radio, wireless. →Also เครื่อง--.

การส่งวิทยุ kaansòŋ′wídthajú?′ N radio broadcast; radio broadcasting.

เครื่องรับวิทยุ khrɯ̂aŋráb′wídthajú?′ N radio receiver. →Also เครื่องรับ.

เครื่องส่งวิทยุ khrɯ̂aŋsòŋ′wídthajú?′ N radio transmitter. →Also เครื่องส่ง.

วิทยุกระจายเสียง wídthajú?′kracaajsĭaŋ′ N radio broadcast.

วิทยุโทรภาพ (เครื่อง) wídthajú?′thooraphâab′ (khrɯ̂aŋ′) N television; television set.

สถานีวิทยุ (สถานี, แห่ง) sathăanii′wídthajú?′ (sathăanii′, hὲŋ′) N radio station.

วิเทโศบาย withee′sŏobaaj′ N foreign policy.

วิธี (วิธี) wíthii′ (wíthii′) N method, way, means. →Syn. ทาง ๑.

ด้วยวิธี dûajwíthii′ by means of.

โดยสันติวิธี dooj′săn′tìwíthii′ by peaceful means.

ยุทธวิธี júd′thawíthii′ N strategy; tactics.

วิธีการ (อย่าง, วิธี) wíthii′kaan′ (jàaŋ′, wíthii′) N method, procedure.

วิธีทำ (วิธี) wíthii′tham′ (wíthii′) N the way

to do, the method of doing (something), procedure.

วิ่น wîn′ V to be torn, chipped.

ขาดวิ่น khàadwîn′ V to be torn raggedly.

วินัย (ข้อ) wínaj′ (khɔ̂ɔ′) N eleg. 1. discipline. 2. rules of conduct.

ระเบียบวินัย rabìab′wínaj′ N order and discipline.

วินาที wínaathii′ C second (unit of time).

วินาศ wínâad′ V eleg. to be ruined, destroyed, annihilated. →Syn. See วอดวาย com.

วินาศกรรม wínâad′sakam′ N eleg. sabotage, (man-made) destruction. →Also การ--.

o ก่อการวินาศกรรม kɔ̀ɔkaan′-wínâad′sakam′ V eleg. to engage in sabotage, cause destruction. ผู้-- saboteur.

วินิจฉัย wínídchăj′ V eleg. to decide, judge, contemplate, consider.

วิบัติ wíbàd′ N eleg. calamity, destruction, catastrophe. →Syn. พิบัติ eleg.

วิบาก wíbàag′ N eleg. adversity, calamity (as a consequence of evil deeds in a previous life); retribution.

วิ่งวิบาก wîŋ′wíbàag′ N 1. obstacle race. V 2. to run an obstacle race.

วิปริต wíparìd′* V eleg. 1. to be abnormal, unusual. 2. to be adverse.

อากาศวิปริต ?aakàad′wíparìd′ eleg. adverse weather.

วิพากษ์ wíphâag′ V eleg. to criticize, judge.

วิพากษ์วิจารณ์ wíphâag′wícaan′ V elab. to criticize, comment (critically), pass judgment.

วิมาน (หลัง) wímaan′ (lăŋ′) N 1. celestial mansion, celestial castle. 2. paradise.

วิลาส wílâad′ V eleg. to be charming, attractive.

วิไล wílaj′ V eleg. to be beautiful.

วิว wiw′ N view. [f. Eng.]

วิวัฒน์ wíwád′ N eleg. prosperity, advancement.

วิวัฒนาการ wíwád′thanaa′kaan′ N eleg. 1. evolution, progress, advancement, development. V 2. to evolve, progress, advance, develop. ความ-- evolution.

วิวาท wíwâad′ V eleg. to quarrel. →Syn. ทะเลาะ. ทะเลาะวิวาท thalɔ́?′wíwâad′ V elab. eleg. to quarrel.

วิวาห์, วิวาห- wíwaa′, wíwaa′hàɔ N eleg. marriage.

ชีวิตวิวาห์ chiiwíd/wíwaa/ N eleg. married life.

วิวาหมงคล wíwaa/hàmoŋkhon/ N eleg. wedding, wedding ceremony.

วิเวก wíwêeg/ N 1. solitude, quietude, loneliness. V 2. to be lonely, tranquil, serene. ความ-- solitude, quietness.

วิศวกร (คน) wísawakɔɔn/ (khon/) N eleg. engineer.

วิศวกรรม wísawákam/ N eleg. engineering. →Also การ--.

วิศวกรรมไฟฟ้า wísawákam/fajfáa/ N electrical engineering.

วิศวกรรมศาสตร์ wísawákam/masàad/ N engineering.

วิเศษ wísèed/ V 1. to be excellent, superb, supreme, splendid. 2. to be miraculous, supernatural, magic. ผู้-- one who possesses supernatural powers, magician, sorcerer.

ยาวิเศษ jaa/wísèed/ N miracle drugs.

วิเศษณ์ wísèed/ N gram. modifier (as an adjective, an adverb).

กริยาวิเศษณ์ kàrijaa/wísèed/, -wísèed/ N adverb.

คำวิเศษณ์ (คำ) kham/wísèed/, -wísèed/ (kham/) N gram. modifier.

วิสกี้ wídsakîi/ N wiskey. [f. Eng.]

วิสัย wísǎj/ eleg. 1. (one's) habit, nature, mental nature, disposition. 2. boundary, limit.

พ้นวิสัย phón/wísǎj/ V to be beyond human control, beyond the power of, beyond the limit of.

สุดวิสัย sùd/wísǎj/ V to be impossible to do, be beyond human power. การ-- impossibility.

o เหตุสุดวิสัย hèed/-sùd/wísǎj/ N unavoidable circumstances, circumstances beyond one's control.

วิสามัญ wísǎa/man/ eleg. extraordinary, special, irregular. →Ant. สามัญ.

วิสามัญศึกษา wísǎa/man/-sʉ̀gsǎa/ N eleg. 1. secondary education. 2. (formerly) technical education. →Opp. สามัญศึกษา.

วิสาสะ (กับ) wísǎa/sà?/(kaɔ) V eleg. 1. to converse, associate (with) in a friendly manner. N 2. acquaintance, intimacy.

วิหาร (หลัง) wíhǎan/ (lǎŋ/) N temple.

วี. wii/ the English letter "V." [f. Eng.]

วีต in ข้าววีต khâawwíid/ N wheat. [f. Eng.]

วีร. See entries below.

วีรกรรม wii/rakam/ N eleg. heroic performance.

วีรชน (คน) wii/rachon/ (khon/) N eleg. hero, heroic person.

วีรบุรุษ wii/ráburùd/ N eleg. hero.

วีรสตรี wii/rásàtrii/ N eleg. heroine.

วิวัน wîi/wan/ N day.

วิแวว wîi/wɛɛw/ N inkling, indication, vague hint or notion.

วุฒิ. See entries below.

คุณวุฒิ khun/nawúd/thí?/ N qualification, competence.

o ทรงคุณวุฒิ soŋ/-khun/nawúd/thí?/ V to be qualified, competent.

วุฒิสภา wúd/thísaphaa/ N Senate (the upper house of the Thai legislature, replacing the earlier พฤฒสภา).

วุฒิสมาชิก (คน, นาย, ท่าน) wúdthí?/samaachíg/ (khon/, naaj/, thân/) N member of the Senate.

วุ่น wûn/ V 1. to be busy (with). 2. to fuss over. 3. to be confused.

ว้าวุ่น wáawûn/ V to be in a state of confusion, indecision.

วิ่งวุ่น wîŋwûn/ V to run around busily (as when organizing something).

วุ่นวาย wûnwaaj/ V 1. to be in confusion, in a turmoil. 2. to concern oneself, bother oneself, make a fuss, fuss over. การ-- disturbance, tumult. ความ-- confusion, turbulence.

วุ่นวายใจ wûnwaaj/caj/ V to be confused, perturbed.

วุ้น wún/ N gelatin, jelly, agar-agar.

วุ้นเส้น wúnsên/ N bean thread, bean vermicelli.

วูบ wûub/ V 1. (a flame) to flare (up); (a candle, a light) to flare up and go out, be suddenly extinguished. C 2. gust (of wind). sV 3. (extinguished) suddenly. 4. in a gust, in gusts.

ดับวูบ dàbwûub/ 1. to go out, be extinguished, snuffed out suddenly (of a flame, light). 2. to blank out, pass out suddenly (of a person).

วูบขึ้นมา wûub/khŷnmaa/ (fire, anger, sexual desire etc.) to flare up, rise up suddenly.

วูบวาบ wûubwâab/ V to be flashing, flaring,

glaring, glittering.

วูลแฟรม wuulfrɛɛm/* tungsten, wolfram, wolframite.
[f. Eng.]

วู่วาม wûuwaam/ V 1. to spread, flare (up) (as of
fire, anger, love). 2. to act hastily, without
due judgment.

เวง. See วังเวง.

เวจ (ห้อง,แห่ง,ที่) wéd/* (hɔŋ/, hɛ̀ŋ/, thîi/) N
vulg. toilet. →Syn. ส้วม com., บริษัท
euphem.

เวช-. See entries below.

o เวชกรรม wêed/chakam/ N lit. treatment of
diseases.

o เวชภัณฑ์ (อย่าง) wêed/chaphan/ (jàaŋ/) N
lit. medical supplies.

o เวชศาสตร์ wêedchasàad/ N lit. medical
science.

เวทนา wêed/thanaa/ V eleg. to pity. ความ--
pity.

น่าเวทนา nâawêed/thanaa/ to be pitiful, pathetic.

เวทมนตร์,-มนต์ (บท) wêedmon/ (bòd/) N magic
spell, charm.

เวที (เวที) weethii/ (weethii/) N 1. stage (of
theater); platform.

เวทีมวย (เวที) weethii/muaj/ (weethii/) N
boxing ring.

เวน in เวนคืน ween/khyyn/ V to surrender back
(e.g. land, rank, to king or government).

เว้น wén/* V to omit, skip, skip over.

งดเว้น ŋódwén/ V to refrain (from), abstain
(from).

ไม่เว้นแต่ละวัน mâjwén/tɛɛlawan/ every single
day, without missing a single day, day in and
day out.

ยกเว้น jógwén/ V to except, exempt.

ละเว้น lá?/wén/ V to abstain from, keep away
from, shun.

เว้นแต่ wéntɛɛ/, wéntɛɛɔ except, unless, excepting.

เว้นวรรค wénwág/ V to leave spaces (between
phrases, clauses, sentences).

เวร ๑ ween/ N 1. turn; shift (as of work, duty).
C 2. clf. for same.

ถึงเวร thy̌ŋween/ 1. to reach (someone's) turn

(to do something). 2. to be time for (a given)
shift (of duty, work).

เป็นวรรคเป็นเวร penwág/penween/ elab. colloq.
on and on, at great length, continuously, excessively (of speaking, crying).

อยู่เวร jùuween/ to be on duty.

เวร ๒ ween/ N 1. bad deeds, sins, misfortune.
2. grudge, ill-will.

จองเวร,--จองกรรม(ต่อ) cɔɔŋ/ween/, cɔɔŋ/ɔ
ween/-cɔɔŋ/kam/-(tɔ̀ɔɔ) V elab. 1. to hold
a grudge (against). 2. to seek revenge.

เวรกรรม ween/kam/ N 1. fate, misfortune (as
a result of karma). E 2. excl. expressing one's
feelings toward some misfortune, ill fate, bad
luck.

เวลา weelaa/ N com. 1. time. C 2. time, occasion.
Often rendered in English by a conjunction or
preposition: while; at (the time when); at (a
specific hour). →Syn. เพลา ๑ lit.

o เวลาสองโมง weelaa/sɔ̌ɔŋmoon/ 1. it's two
o'clock. 2. at two o'clock.

o เวลาประชุมซีอาโต weelaa/-prachum/siiʔaa/tôo/
at the SEATO Conference.

ก่อนเวลา kɔ̀ɔn/weelaa/ early, ahead of time.

กินเวลา kin/weelaa/ to take time; to take, last
(so and so many hours, days, etc.).

ฆ่าเวลา khâa/weelaa/ to kill time. [tr. f. Eng.]

เจียดเวลา cìad/weelaa/ to take a bit of time off,
spare a little time (for some purpose).

ชั่วเวลา chûaweelaa/ for, in (the time of); (for,
in) a period (of).

o ชั่วเวลาสองชั่วโมง chûaweelaa/sɔ̌ɔŋchûamoon/
for two hours; in two hours.

o ชั่วเวลาอีกไม่ช้า chûaweelaa/ʔìigmâjcháa/ it
won't be long now (until something takes place).

ช่วงเวลา chûaŋweelaa/ N spell, period of time.

ได้เวลา dâjweelaa/ V 1. to reach the time (of).
2. it's the time (to do such and such).

ตรงเวลา troŋ/weelaa/ V to be on time, punctual.

ตลอดเวลา talɔ̀ɔd/weelaa/ all the time.

ตารางเวลา taaraaŋ/weelaa/ N timetable.

ทันเวลา than/weelaa/ in time.

ในเวลา najweelaa/ at (such and such a) time, at
the time of, in, during.

o ในเวลากลางดึก najweelaa'klaaŋdỳg' in the deep of the night.

o ในเวลานี้ najweelaaníi' at this time, at the present time, nowadays.

o ในเวลาไม่ช้า najweelaa'mâjcháa' soon, shortly, in a short time.

o ในเวลาอันรวดเร็ว najweelaa''?anrûadrew' in a very short time, very quickly (of time).

บางเวลา baaŋweelaa' sometimes.

ปลีกเวลา plìig'weelaa' to squeeze in a bit of time, make a little time (for some unscheduled, or unexpected matter), spare a little time.

เป็นเวลา ๑ penweelaa' 1. to be regular, constant. 2. regularly.

เป็นเวลา ๒ penweelaa', penweelaaɔ 1. to be (such and such) a length of time. 2. for (such and such) a length of time.

o เป็นเวลานาน penweelaanaan' 1. to be a long time. 2. for a long time.

o เป็นเวลา ๖ ปีมาแล้ว penweelaa'-hògpii'maaɔ lέεw' 1. it has been six years. 2. for the past six years.

ระเบิดเวลา (ลูก) rabə̀əd'weelaa' (lûug') N time bomb.

ระยะเวลา rajá?'weelaa' N interval, period of time.

o ชั่วระยะเวลา chûarajá?'weelaa' (for) a period of, (for) a time interval of.

o ในระยะเวลา najrajá?'weelaa' within (a length of time).

เวลากลางคืน weelaa'klaaŋkhyyn' N 1. nighttime. 2. at night. ใน-- at night, in the nighttime.

เวลาค่ำ weelaakhâm' N (in the) evening, (at) night. →Syn. ตอนค่ำ.

เวลาเช้า weelaacháaw' N 1. morning, morning time. 2. in the morning. →Syn. ตอนเช้า.

เวลาตะวันตกดิน weelaa'-tawan'tògdin' eleg. at sunset.

เวลาเท่าไรครับ weelaa'thâwràj'-khráb' What time is it? →Also กี่โมงครับ.

เวลาเที่ยง weelaathîaŋ' N 1. noon. 2. at noon. →Syn. ตอนเที่ยง.

เวลานอน weelaanɔɔn' N 1. bed time. 2. when (one) goes to bed, while lying down, while sleeping.

เวลานี้ weelaaníi' at this time, nowadays.

เวลาบ่าย weelaabàaj' N 1. the afternoon. 2. in the afternoon. →Syn. ตอนบ่าย.

เวลาพลบ weelaaphlób' N 1. twilight time, dusk. 2. at dusk.

เวลาโพล้เพล้ weelaa'phlóophlée' idem.

เวลาย่ำรุ่ง weelaa'jâmrûŋ' N 1. dawn. 2. at dawn.

เวลาเย็น weelaajen' N 1. evening. 2. in the evening. →Syn. 1. เวลาสายัณห์ lit., 1.2. ตอนเย็น.

เวลาว่าง weelaawâaŋ' N free time, spare time, leisure time.

เวลาสันติ weelaa'sǎntì?' N 1. peace time. 2. in time of peace.

เวลาสาง weelaasǎaŋ' N 1. the dawn. 2. at dawn.

หมดเวลา mòd'weelaa' the time is up.

เวหา weehǎa' N lit. sky. →Syn. ฟ้า com., นภา lit., eleg.

เว้า ๑ wáw' V 1. to talk to, speak to. 2. colloq. to court, woo.

เว้า ๒ wáw' V to be concave.

กระจกเว้า (แผ่น,บาน) kracòg'wáw' (phèn', baan') N cancave mirror.

เว้าแหว่ง wáwwèŋ' V to be jagged, irregular, curving in and out (as of a coastline, a jaggedly torn hemline, a nibbled piece of bread).

เวิ้ง in เวิ้งว้าง wə́əŋwáaŋ' V 1. to be wide, vast, vast and empty. 2. to be affected by a sense of the vastness, emptiness of one's surroundings.

เวียง wiaŋ' N archaic, dial. city, town.

เวียงจันทร์ wiaŋcan' N Vientiane, a city in Laos.

เวียตนาม wîadnaam' N Vietnam. [f. Viet.]

เวียตมินห์ wîadmin' N Vietminh. [f. Viet.]

เวียน wian' V to circle; to turn (round and round).

บันไดเวียน (อัน,บันได) bandaj'wian' (?an', banɔ daj') N eleg. spiral staircase.

วกไปเวียนมา wógpaj'wianmaa' 1. to go back and forth, or round and round (between two or more places or subjects). 2. to be winding (as of road).

วกเวียน wógwian' idem.

วงเวียน (อัน,วง) woŋwian' N 1. compass (?an'). 2. traffic circle (woŋ').

วนไปเวียนมา wonpaj′wianmaa′ elab. to go
around, go to and fro (within a certain area);
to be winding (as of a road); to be circuitous.
2. around; to and fro; in a roundabout manner.

o เดินวนไปเวียนมา dəən′-wonpaj′wianmaa′
elab. to walk around, walk to and fro, pace back
and forth.

วนเวียน wonwian′ V 1. to go around (within an
area); to be winding (as of a road); to be circuitous; to go through a cycle. 2. colloq. to hang
around (in an area). sV 3. around, in a roundabout manner.

วิงเวียน wiŋwian′ V to be giddy, dizzy.

เวียนหัว wianhŭa′ V to feel giddy, dizzy.

หนังสือเวียน (ฉบับ) naŋsɣy′wian′ (chabàb′) N
circular.

หมุนเวียน mŭnwian′ V to rotate, turn.

แวก. See วอกแวก.

แวง in เส้นแวง (เส้น) sênwɛɛŋ′ (sên′) N geog.
longitude. →Opp. เส้นรุ้ง.

แว้ง wέɛŋ′ V 1. to turn back or sideways (in order
to strike or bite). 2. to betray friendship or
kindness (by backbiting, double-crossing, etc.).

แวด in แวดล้อม wɛɛdlɔ́ɔm′ V 1. to surround. 2.
to be surrounded.

สถานการณ์แวดล้อม sathǎa′nákaan′wɛɛdlɔ́ɔm′
N circumstance.

สิ่งแวดล้อม (สิ่ง, อย่าง) sìŋ′wɛɛdlɔ́ɔm′ (sìŋ′,
jàaŋ′) N environment, surroundings.

แว่น ๑ (อัน) wên′* (ʔan′) N 1. lens. 2. glasses,
spectacles. C 3. clf. for thin round slices (as
of sausage, cucumber). →Comp. 1. กระจก.

แจกแว่น cὲɛgwên′ V slang to give (someone)
a black eye.

แว่นขยาย (อัน) wênkhajǎaj′ (ʔan′) N magnifying
lens, magnifying glass.

แว่นตา (อัน) wêntaa′ (ʔan′) N glasses, spectacles.

o ซองแว่นตา (ซอง) sɔɔŋ′wêntaa′ (sɔɔŋ′) N
eyeglass case.

แว่น ๒ in แว่นแคว้น (แว่นแคว้น) wênkhwέɛn′*
(wênkhwέɛn′) N territory, province, state.

แวบ wêb′* V 1. to flash. 2. slang to shirk, sneak
away from, evade one's work or duty. C 3.

colloq. a flash, a short instant of time, a split
second.

ชั่วแวบเดียว chûawêb′diaw′ for a split second.

วอบแวบ wɔbwêb′ V colloq. to be flashing,
shining, glittering.

แวบวาบ wêbwâab′ V to be flashing, dazzling,
glittering.

แวว wεεw′ N 1. look, expression. 2. keen observation. 3. sign, inkling.

วี่แวว wîiwεεw′ N inkling, indication, vague hint
or notion.

แววตา wεεwtaa′ N expression of the eye, gleam
in the eye.

แวววาว wεεwwaaw′ V to be glittering, glaring.

แว่ว wêw′* V 1. to hear indistinctly. 2. to be heard
indistinctly.

แว่วเสียง wêwsǐaŋ′ V to hear indistinctly.

แวะ wέʔ′ V to stop in, drop in (to see someone).

โวย wooj′ N imit. the sound of a call, of an answer
to a call.

ร้องโวยวาย rɔ́ɔŋ′woojwaaj′ to shout, cry, scream
(as for help).

โว้ย ๑ wóoj′ idem. โวย.

โว้ย ๒ Pt rustic or vulgar final particle. →Cf. วะ.

โวหาร woohǎan′ N 1. eloquence, oratory. 2. idiomatic use of the language.

ไว waj′ V to be quick (either physically or mentally).

ฉับไว chàbwaj′ quickly, instantly, promptly.

มือไว myywaj′ V idiom. to be thievish, light-
fingered.

ว่องไว wɔ̂ŋwaj′ V to be agile.

ไวไฟ wajfaj′ V 1. to be inflammable. 2. slang
to be quick.

ไว้ wáj′ V 1. to keep, leave, place, put (something
somewhere). sV 2. up, away (completive sense;
often in the sense of keeping for use, or to have
on hand; also in the sense of being left in a certain position).

กอง(...)ไว้ kɔɔŋ′(...)wáj′ to heap, pile (something) up.

กำหนด(...)ไว้ (1) kamnòd′(...)wáj′; (2) kamnòd′ɔ
wáj′ 1. to fix, stipulate (something). 2. to be
fixed, stipulated.

เก็บ(...)ไว้ kèb′(...)wáj′ to store up, put up,

keep (something).

ขัง (. . .) ไว้ khǎŋ′(. . .)wáj′ to cage, pen (something) up.

ไข่ไว้ khàj′wáj′ to lay eggs (and leave them).

ค้างไว้ kháaŋ′wáj′ 1. to remain, be left. 2. to be left unfinished, partly done. 3. to be in debt, be owing.

งด (. . .) ไว้ ŋód′(. . .)wáj′ to postpone (something), put (something) aside for the time being.

จำ (. . .) ไว้ (1,2) cam′(. . .)wáj′; (3) cam′wáj′↓ V 1. to confine, lock up, put away. 2. to fix in one's mind. 3. Remember that!

ดักกับไว้ dàgkàb′wáj′ to set out a trap.

ทรงไว้(ซึ่ง) soŋwáj′(sŷŋɔ) V lit., eleg. to possess (e.g. quality, dignity).

ทำ (. . .) ไว้ tham′(. . .)wáj′ to make up, prepare (something); to have made, have done (something).

ทิ้ง (. . .) ไว้ thíŋ′(. . .)wáj′ to leave (something) (in a certain place). →Dist. ทิ้ง (. . .) ไป, ทิ้ง (. . .) เสีย.

เปิด (. . .) ไว้ (1) pə̀əd′(. . .)wáj′; (2) pə̀əd′wáj′ 1. to leave (something) open, open (something) and leave (it) open. 2. to be open, be kept open.

ผูก (. . .) ไว้ (1) phùug′(. . .)wáj′; (2) phùug′wáj′ 1. to tie (something) up, keep (something) tied up. 2. to be tied, tied up, kept tied up.

ฝาก (. . .) ไว้ fàag′(. . .)wáj′ to leave (something) (with someone), entrust (something) (to someone's care), deposit, put (something) on deposit (with).

ฟังหูไว้หู faŋhǔu′wájhǔu′ idiom. to take (things one hears) with a grain of salt.

มี (. . .) ไว้ mii′(. . .)wáj′ to have (something) on hand.

ไม่ไว้หน้า mâjwáj′nâa′ without sparing (the feelings of) anyone, without respect for anyone.

ยึด (. . .) ไว้ jýd′(. . .)wáj′ 1. to confiscate. 2. to hold up, hold together, support, prop (something) (i.e. in order to keep it from falling down, falling apart).

รับ (. . .) ไว้ ráb′(. . .)wáj′ 1. to accept (and keep) (something). 2. to admit (e.g. patients to hospital).

เลี้ยง (. . .) ไว้ líaŋ′(. . .)wáj′ to raise, breed (animals), keep (pets).

วาง (. . .) ไว้ (1) waaŋ′(. . .)wáj′; (2) waaŋ′wáj′ 1. to place, lay, set up, establish, fix, stipulate (something). 2. to be laid, set up, established.

เว้นไว้แต่ wén′wájtɛ̀ɛɔ except, excepting.

ไว้ใจ wájcaj′ V to trust, have faith in. ความ-- trust.

o น่าไว้ใจ nâa′wájcaj′ to be trustworthy.

ไว้ชีวิต wáj′chiiwíd′ V to spare the life (of).

ไว้ทุกข์ wájthúg′ V to be in mourning.

ไว้วางใจ wájwaaŋcaj′ V to trust, have faith in.

ไว้อาลัย wáj′ʔaalaj′ (a ceremony, act, speech) to be in memory (of).

สกัด (. . .) ไว้ sakàd′(. . .)wáj′ to cut off, intercept, block, halt (something which is in motion).

เอา (. . .) ไว้ (1) ʔaw′(. . .)wáj′, -wájɔ; (2,3) ʔawɔ wáj′, -wájɔ 1. to take (and keep), keep, put, put down, put away. 2. to put off, postpone. 3. up, away, off (as in store up, put away, etc.; in this sense similar to ไว้ as a secondary verb). →For additional examples see cross reference.

o กาเอาไว้ kaa′ʔawwáj′ V to mark, mark off (as with an x, check mark, etc.).

o เก็บเอาไว้ kèb′ʔawwáj′ to store up, put up, keep.

ไวย. waaj′* the English letter "Y." [f. Eng.] →Also วาย.

ไวยากรณ์ wajjaakɔɔn′ N grammar.

ไวโอลิน (คัน) waj°oolin′ (khan′) N violin. [f. Eng.]

ไวโอเล็ต (ดอก) waj°ooléd′ (dɔɔg′) N violet (the flower). [f. Eng.]

ศ

ศ sɔɔ′ HIGH consonant. Pronounced s initially, d finally. The sound s as an initial high consonant is most frequently written with ส, but it is also in rare instances written with ษ.

ศก ๑ sòg′ C eleg. era, year.

o เถลิงศกใหม่ thalə̌əŋ′sògmàj′ to begin a new era, a new year.

o ศกนี้ sògníi′ this era; this year.

คริสตศก khríd'tasòg' N the Christian Era.
　[คริสต f. Eng.] →Also คริสตศักราช.

พุทธศก phúd'thasòg' N The Buddhist Era. →Also
　พุทธศักราช.

ศก ๒ in หยักศก jàgsòg' V (hair) to be wavy.
　→Also หยักโศก.

ศตวรรษ sàdtawád' C century.

ศพ (ศพ) sòb' (sòb') N corpse.

　กระบวนศพ krabuan'sòb' N funeral procession.

　งานศพ ŋaansòb' N funeral.

　ซากศพ (ซาก) sâagsòb' (sâag') N corpse,
　　remains (of a person).

　ปลงศพ ploŋsòb' V eleg. to cremate.

　เผาศพ phǎwsòb' V com. to cremate.

　ฝังศพ fǎŋsòb' V to bury a corpse.

　o หลุมฝังศพ (หลุม) lǔm'fǎŋsòb' (lǔm') N grave.

　พระบรมศพ phrábɔrommasòb' N roy. corpse
　　of a king. การ-- roy. royal funeral.

ศร (ลูก,ดอก,คัน) sɔ̌ɔn' N 1. arrow (lûug', dɔ̀ɔg').
　　2. bow (khan'). →Chiefly in compounds.

　โก่งศร kòoŋsɔ̌ɔn' V to draw a bow.

　คันศร (คัน) khansɔ̌ɔn' (khan') N bow (the
　　weapon).

　ลูกศร (ลูก,ดอก) lûugsɔ̌ɔn' (lûug', dɔ̀ɔg') N
　　arrow.

ศรัทธา sàdthaa' N 1. confidence, faith. V 2. to
　　have faith. →Syn. 2. เลื่อมใส,เชื่อถือ.

ศรี sǐi' N 1. splendor, beauty, excellence, dignity,
　　virtue, glory, good fortune, wealth, (i.e. the
　　summation of all these things). 2. element
　　occurring in place names, as in second entry
　　below.

　คุณพระศรีรัตนตรัย khun'-phrásǐi'rád'tanátraj'
　　N the Virtues of the Three Gems.

　นครศรีธรรมราช nakhɔɔn'-sǐi'thammarâad' N
　　Nakhɔn Sithammarat (Nakorn Sritamarat or
　　Sridhamaraj), a township in S Thailand.

ศอก sɔ̀ɔg' C 1. cubit, i.e. a linear measure based
　　on the distance from elbow to fingertips, equiva-
　　lent to about half a yard. Four ศอก equal
　　one วา, q.v. N 2. elbow (chiefly in com-
　　pounds).

　ข้อศอก (ข้อศอก,ข้าง) khɔ̂ɔsɔ̀ɔg' (khɔ̂ɔsɔ̀ɔg',
　　khâaŋ') N elbow.

ตีศอก tiisɔ̀ɔg' V boxing　to hit with the elbow.

อกสามศอก ʔòg'sǎamsɔ̀ɔg' V 1. (a man) to be
　　broad-chested. 2. to be a masculine type, a
　　he-man.

ศักดิ์ sàg' N rank, authority, status.

　เกียรติศักดิ์ kìadtisàg' N prestige.

　ทรงศักดิ์ soŋsàg' V eleg. to possess rank (posi-
　　tion).

　บรรดาศักดิ์ bandaasàg' N the conferred title of
　　rank of the nobility. →See note under ขุนนาง.

　ศักดิ์สิทธิ์ sàgsìd' V to be holy, sacred. ความ--
　　sacredness.

ศักราช sàgkarâad'* N era (of time reckoning).

　คริสตศักราช khríd'sàgkarâad' N the Christian
　　era, A.D. [คริสต f. Eng.] →Abbrev. ค.ศ.
　　→Also คริสตศก.

　จุลศักราช cun'lasàgkarâad' N the Thai minor era,
　　beginning March 21, 638 A.D. →Abbrev. จ.ศ.

　พุทธศักราช phúd'thasàgkarâad' N the Buddhist
　　era, B.E. →Abbrev. พ.ศ.　→Also พุทธศก.

ศัตรู (คน,ตัว) sàdtruu' N com. enemy, foe (khon'
　　for persons; tua' for animals). →Syn. ข้าศึก
　　com., ปรปักษ์ eleg.

ศัพท์ (คำ,ตัว) sàb' (kham', tua') N vocabulary,
　　words, word.

　คุณศัพท์,คำ-- (ตัว) khunnasàb', kham'khunnasàb'
　　(kham') N adjective.

　ทับศัพท์ thábsàb' V 1. to borrow a word (from
　　another language), to transliterate. 2. to be
　　borrowed, transliterated.

　โทรศัพท์ (เครื่อง) thoorasàb' (khrɣ̂aŋ') N 1.
　　telephone. V 2. to telephone.

ศัลย,ศัลย์. See entries below.

　ศัลยแพทย์ (นาย,คน) sǎn'japhɛ̂ɛd' (naaj', khon')
　　N eleg. surgeon. →Syn. หมอผ่าตัด com.

　โศกศัลย์ sòogsǎn' V to be very sad, grieved.

ศัสตราวุธ. See ศาสตราวุธ.

ศานติภาพ sǎantiphâab' N peacefulness, peace.

ศาล ๑ (ศาล,แห่ง) sǎan' (sǎan',hèŋ') N court of
　　law. →Syn. โรงศาล colloq.

　ขึ้นศาล khɣ̂nsǎan' V to appear in court, go to court.

　จ่าศาล (คน) càasǎan' (khon') N court clerk.

　โรงศาล (โรง) rooŋsǎan' (rooŋ') N colloq.
　　court of law.

ศาลแขวง sǎankhwɛ̌ɛŋ/ N district court.

ศาลฎีกา sǎandiikaa/ N supreme court.

ศาลเด็กและเยาวชน sǎandèg/lɛjawwachon/ N juvenile court.

ศาลแพ่ง sǎanphɛ̂ŋ/ N civil court.

ศาลอาญา sǎan?aajaa/ N criminal court.

ศาลอุทธรณ์ sǎan?ùthɔɔn/ N appellate court.

ศาล ๒ in มหาศาล mahǎa/sǎan/ colloq. great, huge, enormous, tremendous.

ศาล ๓ (แห่ง) sǎan/ (hɛ̀ŋ/) N small shrine in the form of a house, intended as a residence for a spirit.

ศาลา (หลัง) sǎalaa/ (lǎŋ/) N 1. a pavilion, used as a shelter and a place for rest and relaxation. 2. a hall, a public building (in compounds, and as an element in proper nouns, e.g. in names of theaters).

ศาลากลาง sǎalaaklaaŋ/ N city hall, town hall.

สุขศาลา sùg/sǎalaa/ N medical station.

ศาสตร์ sàad/ N (branch or field of) knowledge.
→Chiefly in compounds, usually as the second member. Sometimes to be translated "-ology."
→See also ศาสตราจารย์.

กลศาสตร์ konlasàad/ N mechanics (the science).

เกษตรศาสตร์ kasěedsàad/ N agriculture (as a science), agricultural science.

ดาราศาสตร์ daaraasàad/ N astronomy.

ประวัติศาสตร์ prawàd/tisàad/ N history.

พฤกษศาสตร์ phrýg/sasàad/ N botany.

แพทยศาสตร์ phɛ̂ɛdsàad/ N medicine (as a science).

ภูมิศาสตร์ phuumísàad/ N geography.

ยุทธศาสตร์ júd/thasàad/ N military strategy; military science.

รัฐศาสตร์ rádthasàad/ N political science.

วนศาสตร์ wanasàad/ N forestry.

วิทยาศาสตร์ wídthajaasàad/ N science, i.e., the fields of knowledge known as "the sciences."

วิศวกรรมศาสตร์ wí/sawákam/masàad/ N engineering.

เศรษฐศาสตร์ sèed/thasàad/ N economics.

สัตวศาสตร์ sàd/tawasàad/ N zoology.

อักษรศาสตร์ ?àgsɔ̌ɔnsàad/, ?àgsɔ̌ɔrasàad/ N liberal arts.

ศาสตราจารย์ (คน) sàadsatraa/caan/, sàasa- (khon/) N professor. →Cf. อาจารย์.

ศาสตราวุธ saadtraa/wúd/ N eleg. weapons.

ศาสนา (ศาสนา) sàasanǎ/ (sàasanǎa/) N religion.

พุทธศาสนา phúd/thasàasanǎa/ N Buddhism, Buddhist religion. →Also พระ--.

ศาสนาคริสต์ sàasanǎa/khríd/ N Christianity.

ศาสนาพราหมณ์ sàasanǎa/phraam/ N Brahmanism.

ศาสนาพุทธ sàasanǎa/phúd/ N Buddhism.

ศาสนาอิสลาม sàasanǎa/?ìsalaǎm/ N Islam, Mohammedanism.

หมอสอนศาสนา (คน) mɔ̌ɔ/-sɔ̌ɔn/sàasanǎa/ (khon/) N missionary.

ศิริราช in โรงพยาบาลศิริราช rooŋphajaabaan/ɔ sirìrâad/* pN the Sirirat (Siraraj) Hospital in Thonburi.

ศิลป, ศิลป์ sǐnlapà?/, sǐnlápaɔ, sǐn/ N 1. art. 2. arts, crafts.

วาทศิลป, -ศิลป์ waa/thásǐn/ N rhetoric, oratory, art of speaking effectively.

ศิลปกรรม sǐnlápakam/ N art object, work of art, artistic work.

o ประณีตศิลปกรรม pranîid/sǐnlápakam/ N fine work, delicate work (of art or handicraft).

ศิลปวิทยา sǐnlapà?/wídthajaa/ N arts and sciences.

ห้องศิลป (ห้อง, แห่ง) hɔ̌ŋsǐn/ (hɔ̂ŋ/, hɛ̀ŋ/) N art studio.

ศิลปะ in โรคศิลปะ rôog/sǐnlapà?/ N medicine (as an art or science); therapeutics.

ศิลปากร sǐnlápaakɔɔn/ N fine arts.

ศิลปิน (คน) sǐnlápin/ (khon/) N artist.

ศิลา (ก้อน, แผ่น) sǐlaa/ (kɔ̂ɔn/, phɛ̀n/) N stone, rock. The clf. phɛ̀n/ is used for a flat stone.

ศิษย์ (คน) sìd/ (khon/) N disciple, pupil, student.

ลูกศิษย์ (คน) lûugsìd/ (khon/) idem.

ศีรษะ (ศีรษะ) sǐisà?/ (sǐisà?/) N eleg. head.
→Syn. หัว com.

กะโหลกศีรษะ (กะโหลก, ใบ) kalòog/sǐisà?/ (kaɔ lòog/, baj/) N anat. skull.

ผงกศีรษะ phaŋòg/sǐisà?/ V to nod one's head.

ศีล (ข้อ) sǐin/ (khɔ̂ɔ/) N religious rule, precept, commandment.

ถือศีล thɯ̌ɯsǐin/ V to observe religious precepts.

มีศีลมีสัตย์ miisǐin/miisàd/ V elab. colloq. to

be trustworthy, honest.

ศีลธรรม sǐin'tham', sǐinlatham' N code of precepts, moral code.

ศึก ๑ sỳg' N battle, war. การ-- war; martial
affairs. →Syn. สงคราม.

ข้าศึก (คน) khâasỳg' (khon') N enemy.

ขุนศึก (คน,ประเทศ) khǔnsỳg' N 1. a powerful
military leader, war lord (khon'). 2. a nation
with great military power (prathêed').

เชลยศึก (คน) chaləəj'sỳg' (khon') N captive,
prisoner of war.

ทหารผ่านศึก (นาย,คน) thahǎan'phàansỳg' (naaj',
khon') N war veteran.

ไส้ศึก (คน) sâjsỳg' (khon') N traitor; spy (in
wartime).

หย่าศึก jàa'sỳg' V to cease fire, cease hostilities.

ศึกษา sỳgsǎa' V to study, be educated. การ--
education. นัก-- student (in higher institu-
tions). นักการ-- educator.

ประถมศึกษา prathǒm'sỳgsǎa' N elementary
education. →Also การ--.

o โรงเรียนประถมศึกษา rooŋrian'-prathǒm'sỳgɔ
sǎa' N elementary school.

พลศึกษา phálá'sỳgsǎa' N physical education.

มัธยมศึกษา mádthajom'sỳgsǎa' N secondary
education.

วิสามัญศึกษา wísǎa'man'-sỳgsǎa' N 1. secondary
education. 2. (formerly) technical education.
→Opp. สามัญศึกษา.

สามัญศึกษา sǎaman'sỳgsǎa' N 1. elementary
education. 2. (formerly) general education.
→Opp. วิสามัญศึกษา.

องค์การศึกษาวิทยาศาสตร์และวัฒนธรรมแห่งสห-
ประชาชาติ ʔoŋkaan'sỳgsǎa'wídthajaasàad'
lɛwád'thanatham'-hɛ̀ŋ'sahàprachaachâad' nN
the United Nations Educational, Scientific and
Cultural Organization (UNESCO).

อุดมศึกษา ʔùdom'sỳgsǎa' N college education;
higher education.

ศึกษาธิการ (คน) sỳgsǎa'thíkaan' (khon') education
officer, superintendent.

กระทรวงศึกษาธิการ krasuaŋ'sỳgsǎa'thíkaan'
N Ministry of Education.

ศุกร์ sùg'. See entries below.

ดาวพระศุกร์ (ดวง) daawphrásùg' (duaŋ') N
(the planet) Venus. →The names of the major
planets are listed under ดาว.

วันศุกร์ wansùg' N Friday. →The days of the
week are listed under วัน.

ศุลกากร,ภาษี-- sǔnlakaakɔɔn', phaasǐi'sǔnlakaakɔɔn'
N customs duty.

ศูนย์ sǔun' N 1. zero, nought. V 2. to disappear.
→Also spelled สูญ.

ขีดศูนย์ (ขีด) khìidsǔun' (khìid') N zero line,
zero point; rest point (of a balance).

ดับศูนย์ dàbsǔun' V lit. to die out, to be extinct.

ตัวศูนย์ tuasǔun' N cipher, the arithmetical figure
zero.

ศูนย์กลาง sǔunklaaŋ' N center (as "center of
trade").

o จุดศูนย์กลาง cùd'sǔunklaaŋ' N center, center
point.

ศูนย์พันธุ์ sǔunphan' V to be extinct.

ศูนย์เสีย sǔunsǐa' V 1. to disappear, be lost.
2. to lose (something).

ศูนย์หาย sǔunhǎaj' V to disappear, be lost.

สาบศูนย์ sàabsǔun' V to disappear, be lost; to
become extinct.

เส้นศูนย์สูตร (เส้น) sên'sǔunsùud' (sên') N
equator.

ศูนยากาศ sǔun'jaakàad' N vacuum. →Often spelled
สูญญากาศ.

เศรษฐ--. See entries below.

เศรษฐกรรม sèed'thakam' N economics.

เศรษฐการ in กระทรวงเศรษฐการ krasuaŋ'ɔ
sèed'thakaan' Ministry of Economics.

เศรษฐกิจ sèed'thakìd' N economy, economic
affairs. →Also การ--.

o ในทางเศรษฐกิจ najthaaŋ'-sèed'thakìd' in
an economical way; economically.

o ระบอบเศรษฐกิจ rabɔ̀ɔb'sèed'thakìd' N economic system.

เศรษฐศาสตร์ sèed'thasàad' N economics (as
a science).

เศรษฐี (คน) sèedthǐi' (khon') N rich person,
person of wealth, millionaire. →Cf. เศรษฐ--.

มหาเศรษฐี (คน) mahǎa'sèedthǐi' (khon') N
multimillionaire.

เศร้า sâw/ V to be sad, sorrowful, melancholy.
→Syn. สลด.

 เศร้าใจ sâwcaj/ V to grieve, be sad.

 เศร้าโศก sâwsòog/ V to be sad, sorrowful.
 →Also โศกเศร้า.

 เศร้าหมอง sâwmɔ̌ɔŋ/ V to be sad.

 หน้าเศร้า nâa/sâw/ V 1. to look sad, have a sad face. N 2. a sad face.

เศษ sèed/ N 1. remainder; remnant; fraction. 2. math. numerator. 3. eleg. (and a) fraction. →In meaning 3, เศษ usually follows a classifier, and may be translated "over, more than, a little more than; after (a specified time)." →Opp. 2. ส่วน. →Syn. 3. กว่า colloq. →Comp. 3. ครึ่ง.

o เศษหนึ่งส่วนสี่ sèednỳŋ/sùansìi/ one fourth: "numerator one, denominator four."

o ร้อยปีเศษ rɔ́ɔjpiisèed/ over a hundred years (but less than two hundred).

o ๔ โมงเศษ sìimooŋsèed/ after four o'clock (but not yet half past).

o ๕ หน้าเศษ hâanâasèed/ over five pages (but less than six), five pages and a fraction.

o เงินเขาหายไปร้อยเศษ ŋənkháwhǎaj/pajrɔ́ɔj/= sèed/↓ He lost his money, a hundred and some odd (bahts, dollars).

o อีกประมาณ ๕ ไมล์เศษ ก็ถึงบ้าน ʔìigpramaan/ hâamaj/sèed/→kɔ̀thỳŋbâan/↓ Another five miles or so, and we'll be home: "about five more miles and a fraction."

 เศษกระดาษ sèedkradàad/ N waste paper, piece of paper, scrap of paper.

 เศษไม้ (ชิ้น, ดุ้น) sèedmáaj/ (chín/, dûn/) N a piece of wood, a splinter.

 เศษ ๆ sèedsèed/ (and a) small fraction; hence, just a little more than, just over, just after. →Syn. กว่า ๆ.

o ๕ ไมล์เศษ ๆ hâamaj/sèedsèed/ just over five miles.

 เศษสตางค์ (สตางค์) sèed/sataŋ/ (sataŋ/) N small change (money).

 เศษส่วน sèedsùan/ N math. fraction.

 เศษอาหาร sèed/ʔaahǎan/ N 1. food particles. 2. food scraps.

เศียร sǐan/ N lit., eleg., roy. head. →Syn. See หัว com.

โศก ๑ sòog/ N 1. sorrow, grief. V 2. to be sad.

 โศกศัลย์ sòogsǎn/ V to be very sad, grieved.

 โศกเศร้า sòogsâw/ V to be sad, sorrowful.

 ความ-- sorrow, sadness, grief. →Also เศร้าโศก.

 สีโศก sǐisòog/ N 1. chartreuse. V 2. to be chartreuse-colored.

โศก ๒ in หยักโศก jàgsòog/ V (hair) to be wavy. →Also หยักศก.

โศกา sǒokaa/ V lit. to cry, weep. →Syn. ร้องไห้.

ษ

ษ sɔ̌ɔ/ HIGH consonant. Pronounced s initially, d finally. A rare letter in word initial. The sound s as an initial high consonant is usually written with ส, occasionally with ศ. Words of frequent occurrence having ษ in non-initial position include the following.

o ไปรษณีย์ prajsanii/ N mail, post.

o เมษายน mee/sǎajon/ N April.

o รักษา rágsǎa/ V to take care of.

o บุรุษ burùd/ N eleg. man.

ษมา in ขอษมา khɔ̌ɔsamaa/* V to ask forgiveness, apologize. →Also ขอสมา.

ส

ส sɔ̌ɔ/ HIGH consonant. Pronounced s initially, d finally, or occasionally s finally in recent loanwords. The sound s as an initial high consonant is also sometimes written with ศ, more rarely with ษ.

สกปรก sògkapròg/ V to be dirty.

 พูดสกปรก phûud/sògkaprog/ V colloq. to speak obscenely.

สกลนคร sakon/nakhɔɔn/ pN Sakonnakhɔn, a township in NE Thailand.

สกัด sakàd/ V 1. to chisel out. 2. to extract. 3. to intercept, obstruct, block, hinder. →Also สะกัด.

ตีสกัด tii′sakàd′ V to block, intercept (esp. in battle).

สกัดกั้น sakàd′kân′ V to block the way, obstruct the advance. การ-- blockade, blocking or obstructing action.

สกัด(...)ไว้ sakàd′(...)wáj′ to cut off, intercept, block, halt (something which is in motion).

สกุล sakun′ N family, lineage.

นามสกุล (นามสกุล) naamsakun′ (naamsakun′) N surname, family name, last name.

มีสกุล mii′sakun′ V to be of noble birth, of a respectable family.

วงศ์สกุล woŋ′sakun′ N family, lineage.

ส่ง ๑ sòŋ′ V to lift loosely (e.g. heaped grain stalks, straw, rice)(esp. in order to allow grain, particles, water, etc. to sift or drop through).

ส่ง ๒ in พิษส่ง phídsòŋ′ N power to harm, capacity to do harm, harmful effect.

ส่ง sòŋ′ V 1. to send, ship. 2. to see (someone) off, take (a person to some destination). การ-- sending, shipping, dispatch; transmission; delivery. เครื่อง-- (radio) transmitter.

การส่งวิทยุ kaansòŋ′wídthajú?′ N radio broadcast; radio broadcasting.

ขนส่ง khǒnsòŋ′ V to transport. การ-- transportation.

ขายส่ง khǎajsòŋ′ V to wholesale (i.e. sell in quantity to a distributor).

เครื่องส่งวิทยุ khrɣaŋsòŋ′wídthajú?′ N (radio) transmitter. →Also เครื่องส่ง.

ผู้ส่งข่าว (คน) phûu′sòŋkhàaw′ (khon′) N correspondent (for a newspaper).

เลี้ยงส่ง líaŋsòŋ′ V to give a farewell party.

ส่งกลิ่น sòŋklìn′ V to smell, give out an odor.

ส่งจดหมาย sòŋ′còdmǎaj′ V to send a letter.

ส่งท้าย sòŋtháaj′ V to bid farewell (at the end of a season, of the old year, etc.).

ส่ง(...)ไปขาย sòŋ(...)pajkhǎaj′ to send (something) to be sold.

ส่งผ่าน sòŋphàan′ to send (something) through, pass (something) through.

ส่งภาษาอังกฤษ sòŋ′-phaasǎa′?aŋkrìd′ colloq. to be talking in English.

ส่งเสริม sòŋsɤ̌ɤm′ V to encourage, promote,

enhance.

ส่งเสียง sòŋsǐaŋ′ V to utter, produce a sound (with the voice).

ส่ง(...)ออก sòŋ(...)?ɔ̀ɔg′ 1. to send (something) out. 2. to export (something).

ส่งกรานต์ sǒŋkraan′ N the old Thai New Year celebration, which falls between April 13 and April 15.

วันส่งกรานต์ wan′sǒŋkraan′ N Songkhran Day.

ส่งขลา sǒŋkhlǎa′ pN Songkhla, a township in S Thailand.

สงคราม (ครั้ง,หน) sǒŋkhraam′ (khráŋ′,hǒn′) N war. การ-- war; martial affairs. →Syn. ศึก ๑.

มหาสงคราม (ครั้ง,หน) mahǎa′sǒŋkhraam′ (khráŋ′, hǒn′) N a great war, a world war.

ยามสงคราม jaam′sǒŋkhraam′ N 1. wartime. 2. in wartime.

สงครามกลางเมือง sǒŋkhraam′klaaŋmyaŋ′ N civil war.

สงครามโลก sǒŋkhraam′loog′ N world war.

o สงครามโลกครั้งที่สอง sǒŋkhraam′loog′-khráŋꞈthîisɔ̌ɔŋ′ World War II.

สงเคราะห์ sǒŋkhrɔ́?′ V 1. eleg. to help, assist. N 2. assistance.

สงฆ์ (รูป,องค์) sǒŋ′ (rûub′,?oŋ′) N Buddhist priest, monk.

พระภิกษุสงฆ์ (รูป,องค์) phráphígsù?′sǒŋ′ (rûub′, ?oŋ′) N Buddhist priest, monk.

พระสงฆ์ (รูป,องค์) phrásǒŋ′ (rûub′,?oŋ′) N Buddhist priest, monk.

สงบ saŋòb′ V to become calm, quiet; to subside. ความ-- calm, tranquility, peacefulness, quietude.

ความไม่สงบ khwaam′mâjsaŋòb′ N unrest, disquietude.

สงบไป saŋòb′paj′ to calm down, quiet down; (an unpleasant matter) to blow over.

สงบลง saŋòb′loŋ′ to die down, subside.

สงบศึก saŋòb′sɤ̀g′ V 1. to cease fighting. N 2. truce.

สงบสงัด saŋòb′saŋàd′ V to be tranquil, quiet.

สงบสุข saŋòb′sùg′ V to be peaceful, tranquil. ความ-- peacefulness, peace.

สงบเสงี่ยม saŋòb′saŋìam′ V to be quiet, modest, polite, well-behaved.

สงบอารมณ์ saŋòb/'ʔaarom/ V to calm down, calm oneself.

สงวน saŋŭan/ to keep, save, reserve, preserve, conserve. การ-- preservation; conservation.

ของสงวน khɔ̌ɔŋsaŋŭan/ N euphem. bust, breasts. →Syn. นม com.

สงสัย sǒŋsǎj/ V 1. to doubt, be doubtful. 2. to suspect, have a notion (that). ความ-- doubt; suspicion. นัก-- skeptic.

ข้อสงสัย (ข้อ) khɔ̂ɔ/sǒŋsǎj/ (khɔ̂ɔ/) N points of doubt.

ขี้สงสัย khîisǒŋsǎj/ V to be skeptical, given to skepticism.

ต้องสงสัย in the following entries.

o โดยมิต้องสงสัย dooj/-mítɔ̂ŋ/sǒŋsǎj/ lit., eleg. without doubt.

o ผู้ต้องสงสัย (คน) phûutɔ̂ŋ/sǒŋsǎj/ (khon/) eleg. a suspect.

o อย่างไม่ต้องสงสัย jàaŋ/-mâjtɔ̂ŋ/sǒŋsǎj/ com. without doubt.

น่าสงสัย nâa/sǒŋsǎj/ V 1. to be doubtful, suspicious, questionable. 2. to lead (one) to suspect.

สงสาร sǒŋsǎan/ V to pity, take pity on, feel compassion for, sympathize with ความ-- pity.

ขี้สงสาร khîisǒŋsǎan/ V to be overly sympathetic, readily sympathetic, compassionate.

น่าสงสาร (1) nâasǒŋsǎan/; (2) nâa/sǒŋsǎan/↓ V 1. to be pitiful, pitiable, pathetic. 2. What a pity!

สงัด saŋàd/ V to be tranquil, peaceful, quiet.

สงบสงัด saŋòb/saŋàd/ V to be quiet.

สง่า saŋàa/ V to be dignified, stately, majestic.

มีสง่า miisaŋàa/ V to be dignified, stately, majestic.

สง่างาม saŋàa/ŋaam/ V to be stately, handsome and dignified, grand, majestic. ความ-- grandeur, splendor, stateliness.

สด sòd/ V 1. to be fresh, raw, uncooked. 2. to be bright (of colors).

ของสด khɔ̌ɔŋsòd/ N fresh, raw foods (of any kind). →Opp. ของแห้ง, ของข่า.

ของสดของคาว khɔ̌ɔŋsòd/khɔ̌ɔŋkhaaw/ N fresh, raw foods (often esp. raw meats).

เขียวสด khǐawsòd/ V to be bright green.

เงินสด ŋənsòd/ N cash.

ตลาดสด (แห่ง) talàad/sòd/ (hɛ̀ŋ/) N food market where raw, perishable foods are sold.

นมสด nomsòd/ N fresh milk.

สดชื่น sòdchŷyn/ V to be fresh, lively, cheerful.

สดๆร้อนๆ sòdsòd/rɔ́ɔnrɔ́ɔn/ V idiom. 1. to be red-hot, fresh, new, most recent, the latest. sV 2. just now, freshly.

สดละอาด sòd/sa'ʔàad/ V to be clean and fresh.

สดใส sòdsǎj/ V to be clear (as of the weather), fresh, cheerful.

สีสด sǐisòd/ N bright color.

สดับ sadàb/ V lit.,eleg. to listen.

สดับตรับฟัง sadàb/-tràb/faŋ/ V elab. eleg. to listen, listen carefully.

สดุดี sadùʔdii/ V lit.,eleg. to praise, laud.

สต. Abbrev. for สตางค์ "satang."

สตรี (คน) sàtrii/, sàdtrii/ (khon/) N eleg. woman, lady. →Also สัตรี F.S. →Syn. ผู้หญิง com. NOTE. The pronunciation sàdtrii is now generally avoided.

โรงเรียนสตรี (โรงเรียน) rooŋrian/sàtrii/ (rooŋɔ rian/) N girls' school.

สตรีเพศ sàtrii/phêed/ N the female sex.

สุภาพสตรี (คน) sùphâab/sàtrii/ (khon/) N eleg. lady.

สตางค์ sataŋ/* C 1. satang, a coin equivalent to a cent, i.e. a hundredth part of a baht or tical. N 2. money. →Also shortened to ตัง. →Abbrev. สต.

มีสตางค์ miisataŋ/ V to have money, be rich. คน-- rich person; the rich.

เศษสตางค์ (สตางค์) sèed/sataŋ/ (sataŋ/) N small change.

สตางค์แดง (อัน) sataŋdɛɛŋ/ (ʔan/) N penny.

สตางค์สิบ (อัน) sataŋsìb/ (ʔan/) N ten-satang coin, dime.

สตางค์ห้า (อัน) sataŋhâa/ (ʔan/) N five-satang coin, nickel.

สติ satìʔ/ N mind, consciousness, sense, sensibility.

คืนสติ khyyn/satìʔ/ V to regain consciousness.

ได้สติ dâjsatìʔ/ V 1. to come to (oneself), regain consciousness. 2. to come to one's senses, regain one's common sense.

o ไม่ได้สติ mâjdâjsatì?⌐ colloq. Nonsense!
Awful! (expressing derision, disapproval).

ตั้งสติ tâŋ'satì?/ V to concentrate.

ไร้สติ ráj'satì?/ V 1. to be unconscious. 2. to
be crazy, insane.

สติปัญญา satì?/panjaa/ N intelligence, keenness
of mind, wisdom.

สิ้นสติ sîn'satì?/ V to lose consciousness.

เสียสติ sĭa'satì?/ V to be insane, crazy.

หมดสติ mòd'satì?/ V to lose consciousness.

สถาน (แห่ง) sathăn' (hèŋ') N 1. place, locality,
location. C 2. eleg. kind, sort, thing, item,
point, respect, means. →Syn. 1. ที่,แหล่ง
com. 2. ประการ eleg., ชนิด com.

o ในสถานแรก najsathăn'rɛ̂ɛg' in the first
place; for one thing.

o มีความผิดหลายสถาน miikhwaamphìd'lăajsa⊃
thăn' to have several offenses.

กรีฑาสถาน (แห่ง) kriithaa'sathăn' (hèŋ') N
sports arena, stadium.

พิพิธภัณฑ์สถาน (แห่ง) phíphídthaphan'sathăan'
(hèŋ') N museum.

ราชบัณฑิตสถาน râadchabandìd'sathăan' N Royal
Academy.

สถานกงสุล (แห่ง) sathăan'koŋsŭn' (hèŋ') N
consulate.

สถานที่ (แห่ง) sathăanthîi' (hèŋ') N 1. place,
site. 2. building, plant, station, i.e. place
equipped for a particular kind of work, activity,
etc.

o สถานที่ก่อสร้าง sathăanthîi'kɔ̀ɔsâaŋ' N construction site.

สถานทูต (แห่ง) sathăanthûud' (hèŋ') N 1. legation; short for สถานอัครราชทูต. 2. embassy;
short for สถานเอกอัครราชทูต.

สถานมหรสพ (แห่ง) sathăan'mahɔ̌orasòb' (hèŋ')
N eleg. theater, place of entertainment.

สถานอัครราชทูต (แห่ง) sathăan'?àgkharâadcha⊃
thûud' (hèŋ') N legation. →Also สถานทูต.

สถานเอกอัครราชทูต (แห่ง) sathăan'?èeg'?àg⊃
kharâadchathûud' (hèŋ') N embassy. →Also
สถานทูต.

สถานการณ์ sathăanákaan' N condition; situation.

สถานการณ์แวดล้อม sathăanákaan'wɛ̂ɛdlɔ́ɔm' N

circumstance.

สถานี (สถานี,แห่ง) sathăanii' (sathăanii',hèŋ') N
station.

นายสถานี (คน) naaj'sathăanii' (khon') N station-
master.

สถานีตำรวจ (สถานี,แห่ง) sathăanii'tamrùad'
(sathăanii',hèŋ') N police station.

สถานีรถไฟ (สถานี,แห่ง) sathăanii'ródfaj' (sa⊃
thăanii',hèŋ') N railroad station.

สถานีวิทยุ (สถานี,แห่ง) sathăanii'wídthajú?/
(sathăanii',hèŋ') N radio station.

สถาบัน (แห่ง) sathăa'ban' (hèŋ') N institute.

สถาปนา sathăa'panaa' V to construct, establish,
install.

สถาปนิก (คน) sathăa'paníg' (khon') N architect.

สถาปัตยกรรม sathăa'pàdtajakam' N architecture.

สถิต sathìd' V 1. lit.,eleg. to remain, dwell, reside.
2. phys. static. →Sometimes also สถิตย์.

สถิติ sathìtì?/ N statistics; record (as of births and
deaths.

o สถิติคนตาย sathìtì?/khontaaj' record of deaths.

สน ๑ sŏn' N pine. ต้น-- (ต้น) 1. pine tree
(Pinus). 2. any closely related coniferous tree.

น้ำมันสน námman'sŏn' N turpentine.

ไม้สน májsŏn' N pine wood, wood of a coniferous
tree.

สน ๒ in the following entries.

สนเข็ม sŏnkhĕm' V to thread a needle.

สนใจ sŏncaj' V to be interested (in). ความ--
interest (in something). →Syn. ที่ง.

o น่าสนใจ nâa'sŏncaj' V to be interesting.

สน ๓ in the following entries.

ขัดสน khàdsŏn' V to lack, be short of, be in need
of; to be poor, in want, needy.

สับสน sàbsŏn' V to be confused, mixed up.

ส้น (ส้น) sôn' (sôn') N heel (of the foot). →Also
spelled ซ้น.

ส้นตีน (ส้น) sôntiin' (sôn') N com.,vulg. heel.

ส้นเท้า (ส้น) sôntháaw' (sôn') N eleg. heel.

ส้นสูง sônsŭuŋ' N 1. high heels, i.e. high-heeled
shoes. 2. (shoes) to have high heels.

สนทนา sŏnthanaa' V eleg. to converse. การ--
a conversation. →Syn. คุย com.

พบปะสนทนา phóbpà?/sŏnthanaa' to meet and

converse.

สนเท่ห์ sǒnthêe/ V 1. to wonder. 2. to be in doubt, be puzzled, amazed.

สนธิสัญญา (ฉบับ) sǒnthí?/sǎnjaa/ (chabàb/) N treaty.

สนม (คน) sanǒm/ (khon/) N concubines of the king (general term). →See เจ้าจอม.

  สนิทสนม sanìd/sanǒm/ V to be intimate, very close.

สนอง sanɔ̌ɔŋ/ V eleg. to answer, respond.

  สนองคุณ sanɔ̌ɔŋ/khun/ V eleg. to repay the kindness of, pay back benefits received (e.g. from one's parents, native land, etc.).

  สนองตอบ sanɔ̌ɔŋ/tɔ̀ɔb/ V lit., eleg. to answer, respond.

สนั่น sanàn/ V to be very loud, to thunder, rumble.

  สนั่นหวั่นไหว sanàn/wànwǎj/ to be very loud, jarring, rumbling, thundering.

สนับ as in สนับสนุน sanàb/sanǔn/ V to support, back, encourage. ผู้-- supporter.

  พรรคสนับสนุน phág/-sanàb/sanǔn/ N the party supporting the government.

สนาน in สนุกสนาน sanùg/sanǎan/ V to have fun, enjoy oneself, have a good time.

สนาม (แห่ง, สนาม) sanǎam/ (hɛ̀ŋ/, sanǎam/) N 1. lawn; yard. 2. field (as for sports, airplanes).

  ท้องสนามหลวง thɔ́ɔŋsanǎamlǔaŋ/ pN colloq. Phra Men (Phra Meru) Ground, the place in Bangkok where all official ceremonies are held. →Also ทุ่งพระเมรุ.

  สนามกีฬา sanǎamkiilaa/ N stadium; field (for sports).

  สนามบิน sanǎambin/ airport, airfield, airstrip.

  สนามเพลาะ sanǎamphlɔ́?/ N trench.

  สนามม้า sanǎammáa/ N race track, horse-race field.

  สนามแม่เหล็ก sanǎam/mɛ̂ɛlèg/ N magnetic field.

  สนามยิงเป้า sanǎam/jiŋpâw/ N target range.

  สนามรบ sanǎamrób/ N battlefield.

  สนามเล่น sanǎamlên/ N playground.

  สนามหญ้า sanǎamjâa/ N lawn; yard (of house).

  สวนสนาม sǔansanǎam/ V 1. to parade. N 2. (military) parade.

สนิท sanìd/ V 1. to be tight, close, snug, intimate.

sV 2. completely.

  เชื่อสนิท chɣ̂a/sanìd/ V to believe completely.

  ตีสนิท tii/sanìd/ V colloq. to pretend to be acquainted, to behave like a close friend in order to obtain a favor.

  เพื่อนสนิท (คน) phɣ̂ansanìd/ (khon/) N intimate friend.

  ฟังไม่สนิทหู faŋ/-mâjsanìd/hǔu/ to sound odd, different from usual, not quite right; to sound unlikely, not quite believable.

  ลืม(เสีย)สนิท lyym/(sǐa)sanìd/ to have forgotten completely.

  สนิทสนม sanìd/sanǒm/ V to be intimate, very close. ความ-- closeness, intimacy.

  หลับสนิท làb/sanìd/ to be sound asleep.

  หายสนิท hǎaj/sanìd/ to be completely cured, healed; to recover completely.

สนิม sanǐm/ N rust.

  ขี้สนิม khîisanǐm/ N colloq. rust.

  ขึ้นสนิม khɣ̂nsanǐm/ V to rust, get rusty.

  เป็นสนิม pensanǐm/ V to be rusty.

สนุก sanùg/ V 1. to have fun, enjoy oneself, have a good time. 2. to be fun, amusing, entertaining. ความ-- amusement, fun, a good time.

  น่าสนุก nâa/sanùg/ V to be fun.

  สนุกดี sanùg/dii/ V 1. to be fun, amusing, entertaining. 2. to have fun, have a good time.

  สนุกสนาน sanùg/sanǎan/ V elab. to have fun, enjoy oneself, have a good time.

  สนุกๆ sanùg/sanùg/ V 1. to be fun, amusing, entertaining. sV 2. for fun, just for fun.

สนุน in สนับสนุน sanàb/sanǔn/ V to support, back, encourage.

สบ ๑ sòb/ V to meet, find, come upon.

  สบใจ sòbcaj/ V 1. to please, satisfy. 2. to be pleased (with).

  สบโชคดี sòb/chôogdii/ to have good luck.

  สบตา sòbtaa/ V to meet someone's eyes, look someone straight in the eye.

  สบเหมาะ sòbmɔ̀?/ V to be opportune.

สบ ๒ in สบประมาท sòb/pramàad/ to insult, disparage, belittle, speak or act contemptuously to.

สบถ sabòd/ V to swear. คำ-- (คำ) swearword.

  ขี้สบถสาบาน khîisabòd/sǎabaan/ V to be in the

habit of swearing.

สบัด. See สะบัด.

สบาย sabaaj/ V 1. to be well (in health), happy,
comfortable. 2. (a place) to be comfortable.
ความ-- well-being, comfort, ease, happiness.

ความสุขสบาย khwaamsùg/sabaaj/ N happiness,
well-being.

ตามสบาย taamsabaaj/ V 1. to be at ease, feel
at home. sV 2. leisurely; comfortably.

พอสบาย phɔɔsabaaj/ V to be just right (for comfort).

สบายใจ sabaajcaj/ V to be content, contented,
free of care.

สบายดี sabaajdii/ V 1. to be well. 2. (a place)
to be comfortable. sV 3. well, comfortably.

o สบายดีหรือ? sabaaj/diirɣy/↓ How are you?
(common greeting).

สบู่ (ก้อน) sabùu/ (kɔ̂ɔn/) N soap. [f. Port.] →Also
spelled สะบู่.

สปริง (อัน) sapring/ (ʔan/) N spring. [f. Eng.]

สภา (สภา) saphaa/ (saphaa/) N council, organization, (legislative) body, assembly, house (of
a legislature), institution, association.

เนติบัณฑิตสภา nee/tìbandìd/saphaa/ N bar
association.

พฤฒสภา phrýd/thasaphaa/ N House of Elders
(the upper house of the Thai Parliament, later
replaced by the วุฒิสภา).

ยุบสภา júb/saphaa/ V to dissolve a legislative
body.

รัฐสภา rád/thasaphaa/ N parliament, congress.

วุฒิสภา wúd/thísaphaa/ N Senate (the upper house
of the Thai Parliament, replacing the earlier
พฤฒสภา).

สภากาชาด saphaakaachâad/ N the Red Cross.

o สภากาชาดสากล saphaakaachâad/sǎakon/ N
the International Red Cross.

สภานิติบัญญัติ saphaa/nítìbanjàd/, nítì?/- N
legislative body.

สภาผู้แทนราษฎร saphaa/-phûuthɛɛn/râadsadɔɔn/
N House of People's Representatives (the lower
house of the Thai Parliament; also, the House
of Representatives of the U.S. Congress).
→Also สภาผู้แทน.

สภาสามัญ saphaa/sǎaman/ N the House of Commons.

สภาสูง saphaa/sǔuŋ/ N the upper house (of a
legislative body).

สภาพ saphâab/ N condition, state.

มีสภาพ miisaphâab/ V to be in a state or condition
(of).

สภาวะ saphaa/wá?/ N condition, state.

สม ๑ sǒm/ V 1. to fit, be fitting, appropriate. sV
2. as befits; appropriately.

สมควร sǒmkhuan/ V to be fitting, proper, suitable, appropriate.

o พอสมควร phɔɔsǒmkhuan/ V 1. to be reasonable,
moderate. sV 2. reasonably, moderately.

o สมควรจะ sǒmkhuan/ca⊃ ought to.

o เห็นสมควร hěn/sǒmkhuan/ to see fit to; to think
it appropriate.

สมใจ sǒmcaj/ V 1. to be pleasing, satisfying.
sV 2. to one's heart's content, to one's satisfaction, enough. →Syn. จุใจ.

สมน้ำหน้า (1) sǒm/námnâa/; (2) sǒm/námnâa/↓
1. to get one's just deserts; to serve (somebody)
right. 2. It serves (you, him) right!

สมประกอบ sǒmprakɔ̀ɔb/ V to be whole, complete,
without defect (esp. of the body).

o ไม่สมประกอบ mâjsǒm/prakɔ̀ɔb/ V to be deformed, abnormal, imperfect, defective.

สมปรารถนา sǒmpràad/thanǎa/ V eleg. to be in
accordance with one's desire; to attain one's
desire, have one's wish fulfilled.

สมหวัง sǒmwǎŋ/ V 1. to fulfil one's hopes. sV
2. as desired.

สมอยาก sǒmjàag/ V to fulfil one's craving.

เหมาะสม mɔ̀?/sǒm/ V to be suitable, appropriate,
proper.

ให้สมกับ hâjsǒm/ka⊃ 1. so as to suit, satisfy.
2. as befits.

สม ๒ sǒm/ V to join, combine. →Chiefly in compounds.

สมคบ sǒmkhób/ V to conspire, join together (in
a conspiracy, plot, practical joke).

สมทบ sǒmthób/ V to join, combine.

สมรส sǒmród/ V 1. eleg. to marry. N 2. marriage, wedding; also การ--. →Syn. 1. แต่งงาน.

○ พิธีสมรส phíthii′sŏmród′ N wedding ceremony.

ส้ม (ใบ,ลูก,ผล) sôm′ (baj′,lûug′,phŏn′) N orange.

แกงส้ม kɛɛŋsôm′ N a sour soup made with tamarind paste.

ดอกส้ม (ดอก) dɔ̀ɔgsôm′ (dɔ̀ɔg′) N orange blossom.

น้ำส้ม námsôm′ N 1. vinegar. 2. orange juice. 3. orange drink, orange squash, beverage flavored with orange.

ส้มโอ (ใบ,ลูก,ผล) sôm?oo′ (baj′,lûug′,phŏn′) N pomelo.

สีส้ม sĭisôm′ N orange (the color).

สมการ (สมการ) samakaan′ (samakaan′) N math. equation.

สมณะ (รูป) samaná?′, sŏmmaná?′ (rûub′) N Buddhist priest.

สมเด็จ sŏmdèd′. An element used in certain royal titles and designations. See entries below.

พระบาทสมเด็จ phrábàad′sŏmdèd′ T His Majesty (not used prior to coronation).

พระบาทสมเด็จพระเจ้าอยู่หัว (พระองค์) phrác̣bàad′-sŏmdèd′phrácâwjùuhŭa′ (phrá?oŋ′) N 1. king. T 2. His Majesty the King. →Opp. พระบรมราชินี the queen.

สมเด็จเจ้าฟ้า (องค์) sŏmdèd′câwfáa′ (?oŋ′) N prince of the highest rank, i.e. the son of the king born by the queen. →See พระองค์เจ้า.

สมเด็จพระนางเจ้าพระบรมราชินี sŏmdèd′phrác̣naaŋ′câaw′ phráborom′maraachinii′ N 1. term for the highest rank held by a queen. T 2. Her Majesty the Queen.

สมนาคุณ sŏmmanaa′khun′ V eleg. to return a favor, give a token or gift in return for benefits received.

สมบัติ sŏmbàd′ N wealth, property, treasure. →Syn. ทรัพย์ eleg., สิน, เงิน com.

คุณสมบัติ khun′sŏmbàd′, khun′nasŏmbàd′ N quality, property.

ทรัพย์สมบัติ sáb′sŏmbàd′ N property, possessions, wealth.

ราชสมบัติ râad′chasŏmbàd′ N 1. throne. 2. kingdom.

○ ครองราชสมบัติ khrɔɔŋrâad′chasŏmbàd′ V to reign.

○ สละราชสมบัติ salà?′-râad′chasŏmbàd′ V roy. to abdicate.

สมบัติผู้ดี (ข้อ) sŏmbàd′phûudii′ (khɔ̂ɔ′) N principles of good conduct for persons of refinement.

สมบุกสมบัน sŏmbùg′sŏmban′ V 1. to experience hardship, have a hard life, have rough going, do hard work, go through a lot of trouble. sV 2. unsparingly. อย่าง-- unsparingly.

สมบูรณ์ sŏmbuun′ V 1. to be abundant, plentiful; to abound. 2. to be rich, fertile. 3. to be whole, complete, perfect. 4. to be healthy. →Syn. 1, 2. อุดม ๑.

สมบูรณาญาสิทธิราช sŏmbuuranaa′jaa′sìdthirâad′ N absolute monarchy.

สมเพช sŏmphêed′ V to pity, take pity on.

สมภพ sŏmphób′ V roy. to be born.

เสด็จสมภพ sadèd′sŏmphób′ V roy. to be born.

สมภาร sŏmphaan′ N Buddhist abbot.

สมมุติ(ว่า) sŏmmúd′(wâac) V to suppose, assume (that).

สมรภูมิ samɔɔraphuum′ N battlefield.

สมรรถภาพ samàd′thaphâad′ N 1. ability; capability. 2. efficiency.

สมเสร็จ (ตัว) sŏmsèd′ (tua′) N tapir.

สมอ ๑ (สมอ,อัน) samɔɔ′ (samɔɔ′,?an′) N anchor.

ถอนสมอ thɔ̌ɔnsamɔɔ′ V to lift anchor.

ทอดสมอ thɔ̂ɔdsamɔɔ′ V to cast anchor, drop anchor.

สมอเรือ samɔɔrya′ N anchor.

สมอ ๒, สมอฝ้าย (ลูก) samɔɔ′, samɔɔfâaj′ (lûug′) N boll of the cotton plant. →See also ฝ้าย.

สมอ ๓ (ลูก) samɔɔ′ (lûug′) N olive-like fruit of a certain tree. ต้น-- (ต้น) the tree bearing such fruit.

สมอง samɔɔŋ′ N 1. brain. 2. intellect, intelligence. →See also ขมอง.

มันสมอง (ก้อน) mansamɔɔŋ′ (kɔ̂ɔn′) N the brain (body part).

สมัคร samàg′ V to volunteer, apply, make application. ผู้-- candidate, applicant.

ใบสมัคร (ใบ) bajsamàg′ (baj′) N application, written request.

สมัครใจ samàg′caj′ V to be willing. ความ-- willingness.

สมัครพรรคพวก (คน) samàg′phágphûag′ (khon′) N elab. colloq. 1. partisans, fellow members,

followers. 2. close friends, members of an
intimate circle; clique.

สมัชฌา samádchaa′ N assembly, meeting.

   สมัชฌาทั่วไป samádchaa′thûapaj′ N General
Assembly (of the United Nations).

สมัย (สมัย) samǎj′ (samǎj′) C time, period, era,
age, reign.

   กำลังอยู่ในสมัย kamlaŋjùu′najsamǎj′ to be currently in fashion, in style.

   ทันสมัย than′samǎj′ V to be up-to-date, modern.

   ล้าสมัย láa′samǎj′ V to be out-of-date, behind
the times.

   สมัยกรุงศรีอยุธยา samǎj′-kruŋsǐi′ʔajúdthajaa′
N the Ayuthaya period (of Thai history).

   สมัยก่อน samǎj′kɔɔn′ N 1. former times, the old
days. 2. formerly, in the old days.

   สมัยก่อนประวัติศาสตร์ samǎj′-kɔɔn′prawàd′tiɔ
sàad′ the prehistoric era.

   สมัยเก่า samǎj′kàw′ N 1. former times, the old
days. 2. old-fashioned.

   สมัยเจี๊ยบ samǎj′cíab′ very fashionable, chic.

   สมัยเดียวกัน samǎj′diawkan′ contemporary;
contemporaneous.

   สมัยนี้ samǎj′níi′ at the present time, nowadays.

   สมัยโบราณ samǎj′booraan′ N ancient times;
in ancient times.

   สมัยปัจจุบัน samǎj′pàdcuban′ N modern times,
the present time.

   สมัยหลังสงคราม samǎj′-lǎŋ′sǒŋkhraam′ the
postwar period.

   สมัยหิน samǎj′hǐn′ N the Stone Age.

   สมัยใหม่ samǎjmàj′ N 1. modern times, the present time. 2. (as n. mod) modern, up-to date.

   ○ สมัยใหม่จ๋า samǎj′màjcǎa c o l l o q. to be real
modern, ultramodern.

   ○ หัวสมัยใหม่ hǔa′samǎjmàj′ to be modernminded.

   หมดสมัย mòd′samǎj′ V to be out-of-date, out of
fashion.

สมา in ขอสมา ·khɔɔsamaa′* V to ask forgiveness,
apologize. →Also ษมา.

สมาคม (สมาคม) samaakhom′ (samaakhom′) N
1. club, society, association, organization. V
2. to associate.

   สมาคมกรรมกร (สมาคม) samaakhom′kammakɔɔn′

(samaakhom′) N labor organization.

สมาชิก (คน,นาย) samaachíg′*(khon′,naaj′) N
member.

   เข้าเป็นสมาชิก khâwpen′samaachíg′ to become
a member (of), to join (an organization).

   วุฒิสมาชิก (คน,นาย,ท่าน) wúdthí?′samaachíg′
(khon′, naaj′, thân′) N member of the Senate
(the upper house of the Thai Parliament).

   สมาชิกภาพ samaa′chígkaphâab′, samaachíg′phâab′
N membership.

   สมาชิกสภาผู้แทนราษฎร samaachíg′-saphaa′phûuɔ
theɛn′-râadsadɔɔn′ N Member of the House of
Representatives. →Abbrev. ส.ส.

สมาธิ ๑ samaathí?′* N concentration (as in study,
meditation).

สมาธิ ๒,-ธิ์ in ขัดสมาธิ khàdsamàad′ V to sit with
knees apart and legs crossed under (usually on
the floor).

สมาน samǎan′ V to join together, unite.

สม่ำ in สม่ำเสมอ samàm′samǒə′ V to be constant,
uniform, regular.

สมุด (เล่ม) samùd′ (lêm′) N notebook, folio.

   สมุดฉีก samùd′chìg′ N scratch pad, writing
tablet (with leaves which can be torn out).

   สมุดที่ระลึก samùd′thîiralýg′ N memorial volume,
book, or notebook given as a souvenir on a special
occasion.

   สมุดฝากเงิน samùd′fàagŋən′ N bankbook, passbook.

   สมุดพก samùd′phóg′ N student's report book (in
which the teacher and guardian record his grade,
health and conduct).

   หอสมุด (แห่ง) hɔɔsamùd′ (hèŋ′) N library.

   ห้องสมุด (ห้อง,แห่ง) hɔ̂ŋ′samùd′ (hɔ̂ŋ′, hèŋ′) N
1. study (room in a house). 2. library.

สมุทร (สมุทร) samùd′ (samùd′) N sea, ocean.
→Chiefly in compounds.

   คาบสมุทร khâab′samùd′ N peninsula.

   มหาสมุทร (มหาสมุทร) mahǎa′samùd′ (mahǎa′ɔ
samùd′) N ocean.

   เรือเดินสมุทร (ลำ) ryadəən′samùd′ (lam′) N
ocean-going steamer.

   สมุทรปราการ samùd′praakaan′ pN Samutprakan,
a township in C Thailand, at the mouth of the
Čhaophraya R. →Colloquial name is ปากน้ำ.

สมุทรสงคราม samùd'sǒŋkhraam' pN Samutsong-
khram, a township in C Thailand. →Colloquial
name is แม่กลอง.

สมุทรสาคร samùd'sǎakhɔɔn' pN Samutsakhɔn,
a township in C Thailand. →Colloquial name is
ท่าจีน.

สมุน (คน) samǔn' (khon') N underling, subordinate. ลูก-- underling.

ประเทศสมุน (ประเทศ) prathêed'samǔn' (pracɔ
thêed') N satellite country.

สมุนไพร samǔn'phraj' N medicinal plant, herb.

สมุหบัญชี (คน) samù?'banchii', samùhà?'banchii'
(khon') N accountant.

สโมสร (สโมสร,แห่ง) samoosɔ̌ɔn'/*(samoosɔ̌ɔn',
hèŋ') N 1. club, association. 2. clubhouse.
V 3. eleg. to gather together, meet.

งานสโมสร ŋaan'samoosɔ̌ɔn' N party (social
gathering).

สยดสยอง in น่าสยดสยอง nâa'-sajòd'sajɔ̌ɔŋ' V
to be horrible, dreadful.

สยาม sajǎam' N Siam, former name for Thailand.
สยามรัฐ sajǎamrád' nN a Bangkok daily newspaper, "The Siamese Nation." Transliterated
by the publisher as "Siam Rath."

สรง sǒŋ' V roy., s a c e r. to bathe.

สรร sǎn' V to choose, select.

สรรค์ in สร้างสรรค์ sâaŋsǎn' V to establish,
construct, create.

สรรพ (1) sàbphacɔ, sǎnphacɔ; (2) sàb' 1. e l e g. bound
initial element meaning "all, all kinds of." sV
2. completely. →Mng. 2. of restricted occurrence. NOTE. Usually each compound has its
own preferred alternant of the pronunciations
listed for mng. 1.

o จนสุดสรรพกำลัง consùd'sǎn'phakamlaŋ' with
all one's strength, to the utmost of one's
strength.

พร้อมสรรพ phrɔ́ɔmsàb' V 1. to be ready, all set,
fully prepared. sV 2. all ready, all set, fully
prepared.

สรรพคุณ sàbphakhun' N properties, qualities.

สรรพนาม sàbphanaam' N g r a m. pronoun.
คำ-- i d e m.

สรรพสัตว์ sàbphasàd', sǎnphasàd' N animals

(as a whole), all animals, animals of all kinds.

เสร็จสรรพ sèdsàb' V to finish up.

สรรพสามิต sǎnphasǎamíd' N excise. →Chiefly in cpds.

สรรพากร sǎnphaakɔɔn' N revenue. →Chiefly in cpds.

สรรเสริญ sǎnrasɔ̌ən', sǎnsɔ̌ən' V to praise, laud.

สรวง sǔaŋ' N heaven. →Usually in the cpd. below.
สรวงสวรรค์ sǔaŋsawǎn' N heaven.

สร้อย (สาย,เส้น) sɔ̂j'* (sǎaj', sên') N 1. ornamental
chain; string of jewels, pearls, etc. 2. short for
สร้อยเพลง below.

สร้อยข้อมือ sɔ̂j'khɔ̂ɔmyy' N bracelet.

สร้อยคอ sɔ̂jkhɔɔ' N necklace.

สร้อยเพลง sɔ̂j'phleeŋ' N refrain, chorus.

สายสร้อย (สาย,เส้น) sǎajsɔ̂j' (sǎaj',sên') N
ornamental chain; string of jewels, pearls, etc.

สระ ๑ (ตัว) sarà?' (tua') N vowel.

o สระ -า sarà?aa' the vowel -aa, the -aa vowel.

สระ ๒ (สระ,แห่ง) sà?'*(sà?',hèŋ') N pool, pond.
→S y n. บ่อ. →Also สระน้ำ.

สระอาบน้ำ sà?'?àabnáam' N swimming pool.

สระ ๓ sà?'* V to shampoo, wash (the hair). →D i s t.
ล้าง,ซัก.

สร่าง sàaŋ' V (an abnormal physical or emotional
state) to subside, get better.

o ไข้สร่างแล้ว khâj'-sàaŋ'lɛ́ɛw' the fever has
subsided.

สร่างไข้ sàaŋ'khâj' V to recover from a fever.

สร่างเมา sàaŋ'maw' V to become sober (after
being drunk).

สร้าง sâaŋ' V 1. to build, construct. 2. to be built.
การ-- construction, building. ผู้-- builder;
creator.

ก่อสร้าง kɔ̀ɔsâaŋ' V to build, construct. ช่าง--
builder.

o สถานที่ก่อสร้าง sathǎanthîi'kɔ̀ɔsâaŋ' N construction site.

โครงสร้าง khrooŋsâaŋ' N structure, arrangement of constituents.

จัดสร้าง càdsâaŋ' V to build, construct, have
(something) built, constructed.

สร้างขึ้น sâaŋ'khŷn' 1. to build up, establish. 2.
to be built, constructed, to be founded, established.

สร้างสรรค์ sâaŋsǎn' V to establish, construct,
create.

สรุป sarùb/ V 1. to summarize. 2. to conclude.

  สรุปข่าว sarùb/khàaw/ V 1. to give a news summary. N 2. news summary.

  สรุปความ sarùb/khwaam/ V 1. to sum up, summarize, conclude. N 2. conclusion.

สลด salòd/ V to be sad, sorrowful, melancholy. →Syn. เศร้า.

สลบ salòb/ V 1. to faint, lose consciousness. 2. to be unconscious.

  ยาสลบ jaasalòb/ N anesthetic.

  สลบเหมือด salòb/mỳad/ V slang to be unconscious.

สลอน salɔ̌n/* V to be conspicuous or prominent in large numbers.

สละ salà?/ V to renounce, sacrifice.

  สละเงินช่วย salà?/ŋən/-chûajɔ to donate money to.

  สละราชสมบัติ salà?/râad/chasǒmbàd/ V roy. to abdicate.

  เสียสละ sǐasalà?/ V to make a sacrifice.

สลัก ๑ (อัน) salàg/ (?an/) N bolt (movable bar).

สลัก ๒ salàg/ V to carve, chisel. ช่าง-- sculptor. →Comp. จำหลัก, ฉลัก.

  แกะสลัก kɛ̀?/salàg/ V to carve.

  รูปสลัก (รูป, ชิ้น) rûubsalàg/ (rûub/, chín/) N sculpture.

  สลักสำคัญ salàg/sǎmkhan/ N colloq. to be important.

สลัด ๑, โจร-- (คน) salàd/, coon/salàd/ (khon/) N pirate.

สลัด ๒ salàd/ N salad. [f. Eng.]

สลัด ๓ salàd/ V to shake off, throw away, reject.

สลับ salàb/ V to alternate.

สลัว salǔa/ V to be dim.

  มืดสลัว mỳyd/salǔa/ V to be dim, dimly lighted.

สลาก (ฉบับ, ใบ) salàag/ (chabàb/, baj/) N eleg. ticket; label. →Comp. ฉลาก.

  จับสลาก càb/salàag/ V to draw lots.

  สลากกินแบ่ง (ฉะบับ, ใบ) salàag/kinbɛ̀ŋ/ (chabàb/, baj/) N eleg. lottery ticket. →Syn. ลอตเตอรี่, ตั๋วลอตเตอรี่ com., หวยเบอร์ colloq.

สลาง salǎaŋ/ V to be prominent, projecting conspicuously.

สลาย salǎaj/ V to disintegrate, decompose, crum-

ble.

จนฟ้าดินสลาย confáa/dinsalǎaj/ till the end of the world, forever, for all eternity.

แตกสลาย tɛ̀ɛg/salǎaj/ V to be ruined, go to pieces.

สลิด in ปลาสลิด (ตัว) plaasalìd/ (tua/) N 1. gouramy, a kind of fresh water fish. 2. euphem. female genitalia.

สลึง salǔŋ/ C the Thai quarter, i.e. a 25 satang piece; 25 satangs.

สวด sùad/ V to chant, read aloud, recite prayers.

  เพลงสวด (เพลง) phleeŋsùad/ (phleeŋ/) N hymn.

  โรงสวด (โรง) rooŋsùad/ (rooŋ/) N colloq. church, church building.

  สวดมนต์, -มนตร์ sùadmon/ V 1. to pray by reciting prayers. 2. to chant sacred words, utter an incantation. →Dist. อธิษฐาน.

สวน ๑ (ขนัด, แห่ง) sǔan/ (khanàd/, hɛ̀ŋ/) N 1. garden. 2. plantation.

  ชาวสวน (คน) chaawsǔan/ (khon/) N gardener, planter.

  ทำสวน thamsǔan/ V to do gardening, orchard work, plantation work.

  เรือกสวน (ขนัด) rɣagsǔan/ (khanàd/) N orchard, garden.

  สวนครัว (แห่ง, สวน) sǔankhrua/ (hɛ̀ŋ/, sǔan/) N kitchen garden, vegetable garden.

  สวนดอกไม้ (ขนัด) sǔan/dɔ̀ɔgmáaj/ (khanàd/) N flower garden.

  สวนผลไม้ (ขนัด) sǔan/phǒnlamáaj/ (khanàd/) N orchard.

  สวนผัก (ขนัด) sǔanphàg/ (khanàd/) N truck garden.

  สวนสัตว์ (แห่ง) sǔansàd/ (hɛ̀ŋ/) N zoo, zoological garden.

สวน ๒ sǔan/ V 1. to pass (moving in the opposite direction, as cars in two-way traffic). 2. to take an enema.

  ไต่สวน tàjsǔan/ V to inquire into, investigate.

  สวนสนาม sǔansanǎam/ V 1. to parade. N 2. military parade.

  สอบสวน sɔ̀ɔbsǔan/ V to investigate. การ-- investigation.

  สืบสวน sɣybsǔan/ V to investigate.

ส่วน sùan/ N, C 1. part, portion. 2. math. denom-

inator. Pp 3. on the part of, as for. →Comp. 1.
ภาค ๑, ท่อน, ตอน, ปั้น. →Opp. 2. เศษ.

ขยายส่วน khajǎaj'sùan' V to enlarge proportionately (as in drawing a map).

ตามส่วน taamsùan' in proportion.

บางส่วน baaŋsùan' 1. some part, some parts. 2.
in part, in some parts, partially. 2. partial.

ปันส่วน pansùan' V to ration.

มาตราส่วน mâadtraa'sùan' N scale (indicating
proportionate size).

มีส่วน miisùan' V to have a share, a part (in).

มีส่วนมีเสียง miisùan'miisǐaŋ' V elab. colloq.
to have a share, a part, a voice (in).

มีส่วนร่วม miisùan'rûam' V to have a share, a
part (in).

ราชการส่วนท้องถิ่น râadchakaan'sùanthɔ́ɔŋthìn'
N municipal government service, local government service.

ราชการส่วนภูมิภาค râadchakaan'sùanphuu'miɔ
phâag' N provincial government service.

เศษส่วน sèedsùan' N math. fraction.

เศษหนึ่งส่วนสี่ sèednỳŋ'sùansìi' one fourth:
"numerator one, denominator four."

ส่วนกลาง sùanklaaŋ' N 1. the central part. 2.
central.

o ราชการส่วนกลาง râadchakaan'sùanklaaŋ'
Central Government Service.

ส่วนควบ sùankhûab' N component part.

ส่วนเฉลี่ย sùanchalìa' N eleg. 1. the average.
2. share, portion.

ส่วนได้เสีย sùandâaj'sǐa' N an interest (i.e. an
involvement in gain or loss). →Also ส่วนได้
ส่วนเสีย.

o ฝ่ายที่มีส่วนได้เสีย fàaj'-thîimii'sùandâaj'sǐa'
the interested party, parties.

ส่วนตัว sùantua' private, personal, individual
(as opposed to public, collective). →Syn. ส่วน
บุคคล. →Ant. ส่วนรวม.

o ประโยชน์ส่วนตัว prajòod'sùantua' personal
interest, advantage, gain; individual advantage.

o เรื่องส่วนตัว rŷaŋ'sùantua' personal matter,
private affair.

ส่วนตัวฉัน sùantua'chán' as for me; I, for my
part.

ส่วนนอก sùannɔ̂ɔg' the outer part.

ส่วนน้อย sùannɔ́ɔj' the minority, the lesser part.

o คนส่วนน้อย khon'sùannɔ́ɔj' N the minority.

o เป็นส่วนน้อย pensùan'nɔ́ɔj' 1. to be the lesser
part, a small part. 2. in the minority of cases,
in a few instances.

ส่วน...ใน... as in ส่วนหนึ่งในสี่ของนิ้ว sùanɔ
nỳŋ'-najsìi'khɔ̌ɔŋníw' a quarter of an inch.

ส่วนบุคคล sùanbùgkhon' personal, private, individual (as opposed to public, collective). →Syn.
ส่วนตัว. →Ant. ส่วนรวม.

ส่วนแบ่ง sùanbɛ̀ŋ' N share.

ส่วนประกอบ sùanprakɔ̀ɔb' N component, constituent.

ส่วนปรุงแต่ง sùan'pruŋtɛ̀ŋ' N chem. component,
constituent.

ส่วนผสม sùanphasǒm' N 1. component, constituent,
ingredient. 2. admixture.

ส่วนภูมิภาค sùanphuu'miphâag' N 1. province.
2. (as n. mod.) provincial.

ส่วนมาก sùanmâag' the greater part; the majority.

o คนส่วนมาก khon'sùanmâag' the majority of
people, most people.

o เป็นส่วนมาก pensùan'mâag' 1. to be the greater
part. 2. for the most part.

ส่วนรวม sùanruam' 1. the group as a whole. 2.
common, collective. 3. broadly, on the whole,
in general. →Ant. ส่วนตัว,ส่วนบุคคล.

o ประโยชน์ของส่วนรวม prajòod'khɔ̌ɔŋsùanruam'
the common interest, common good; the collective advantage.

o เป็นส่วนรวม pensùan'ruam' 1. to be common,
mutual. 2. on the whole, as a whole.

ส่วนลด sùanlód' N discount, deduction.

ส่วนใหญ่ sùanjàj' the larger part, the major part,
the majority.

o เป็นส่วนใหญ่ pensùan'jàj' 1. to be the larger
part, a large part. 2. for the most part, mostly.

สัดส่วน sàdsùan' N proportion. →Also ส่วนสัด.

หุ้นส่วน hûnsùan' N partnership (as in a business).

ส่วม sǔam' V eleg. to put on, wear. →Syn. ใส่ 2.

น่าส่วม nâasǔam' V eleg. (clothing, jewelry)
to be pretty, nice-looking, comfortable to wear.

ส่วมกอด sǔamkɔ̀ɔd' V to embrace.

สวมนิ้ว sǔamníw′ V to wear on the finger.

สวมรองเท้า sǔamrɔɔŋtháaw′ V to wear shoes.

ล้วม (ส้วม) sûam′ (sûam′) N toilet. →Syn. บริษัท euphem., เว็จ vulg.

ล้วมสาธารณ (แห่ง) sûam′-sǎa′thaaraná? (hɛ̀ŋ′) N public toilet, rest room.

สวย sǔaj′ V to be pretty (of things that are seen). คน-- a pretty girl. →Cf. สะสวย.

ข้าวสวย khâawsǔaj′ boiled or steamed rice (in which each grain is nicely separate).

สวยขึ้น sǔaj′khŷn′ V to get pretty, prettier; to become more attractive.

สวยงาม sǔajŋaam′ V to be beautiful. ความ-- beauty.

สวยเฉี่ยว sǔajchìaw′ to be strikingly beautiful.

สวยบาดตา sǔaj′bàadtaa′ to be strikingly beautiful, dazzlingly beautiful.

หายสวย hǎajsǔaj′ V to lose (one's) beauty.

สวรรค์ (สวรรค์,แห่ง,ชั้น) sawǎn′ (sawǎn′, hɛ̀ŋ′, chán′) N heaven, paradise.

นครสวรรค์ nakhɔɔn′sawǎn′ pN Nakhon Sawan (Nakorn Sawan), a township in C Thailand.

ลูกสวรรค์ (ลูก) lûugsawǎn′ (lûug′) N eleg. toy balloon (esp. gas-inflated, such as are seen at festivals).

สรวงสวรรค์ sǔaŋsawǎn′ N elab. heaven.

สวรรค์ชั้นฟ้า sawǎn′chánfáa′ N elab. heaven.

สวรรคต sawǎnkhód′, sawǎnnakhód′ V roy. to die.

เสด็จสวรรคต sadèd′sawǎnkhód′ V roy. to die.

สวะ (ต้น,แพ) sawà?′ N 1. floating weeds (tôn′ for a single plant; phɛɛ′ for a mass floating together like a raft). V 2. slang to be low-class, of bad quality, no good.

สวัสดิ-,สวัสดิ์. See entries below.

ราตรีสวัสดิ์ raatrii′sawàd′ eleg. Good night. (obsolete).

สวัสดิภาพ sawàd′diphâab′ N safety, welfare.

อรุณสวัสดิ์ ?arun′sawàd′ eleg. Good morning. (obsolete).

สวัสดี sawàd′dii′. This expression is used in greeting or leave-taking at any time of the day or night; hence it may be translated "hello," "good morning," "good day," etc.

ความสุขสวัสดี khwaamsùg′sawàddii′ N well-being.

ส่าง sawàaŋ′ V 1. to be bright, light, lighted. 2. to dawn. ความ-- brightness, brilliance, luminosity; light.

รุ่งสว่าง rûŋ′sawàaŋ′ at dawn, at daybreak.

สว่างจ้า sawàaŋ′câa′ to be extremely bright, dazzlingly bright.

สว่างดี sawàaŋ′dii′ to be nice and bright.

สว่างไสว sawàaŋ′sawǎj′ V to shine brightly all over, be bright with light.

แสงสว่าง sɛ̌ɛŋ′sawàaŋ′ N light.

หูตาสว่าง hǔutaa′sawàaŋ′ V 1. to be wide awake. 2. to be well-informed, wide awake about what is going on.

สวาด in สีสวาด sǐisawàad′ N 1. bluish gray. V 2. to be bluish gray.

แมวสีสวาด (ตัว) mɛɛw′sǐisawàad′ (tua′) N a bluish gray cat native to Thailand.

สวาท sawàad′ V 1. to be lovely, delightful. 2. colloq. to love.

สวาปาม sawǎapaam′ V slang to eat, eat greedily.

สวามิ in สวามิภักดิ์(ต่อ) sawǎa′míphág′(tɔ̀ɔ=) V eleg. 1. to surrender, yield, submit oneself (to), submit itself (to)(as a weaker country or king to a powerful neighbor). 2. to be loyal and submissive.

สวิง ๑ (ปาก) sawǐŋ′ (pàag′) N a kind of small fishing-net, a dip-net.

สวิง ๒ sawiŋ′* "swing," as in the entries below. [f. Eng.]

เพลงสวิง (เพลง) phleeŋ′sawiŋ′ (phleeŋ′) N swing music.

หมัดสวิง màd′sawiŋ′ N boxing a swing.

สวิงสวาย sawǐŋ′sawǎaj′ V 1. to have a feeling of faintness, dizziness. sV 2. slang recklessly, wildly.

o เป็นลมสวิงสวาย penlom′-sawǐŋ′sawǎaj′ V to feel like fainting.

o ขับรถสวิงสวาย khàbród′-sawǐŋsawǎaj′ to drive recklessly, wildly.

สวิตเซอร์แลนด์ sawídsəəlɛɛn′ pN Switzerland. [f. Eng.]

ส.ส. (คน,นาย) sɔ̌ɔsɔ̌ɔ′ (khon′, naaj′). Abbrev. for สมาชิกสภาผู้แทนราษฎร Member of the House of Representatives.

สสาร (ชนิด) sà?sǎan′ (chaníd′) N phys. matter.

สห- sahàɔ, sahàʔɔ. Bound element meaning "united"; sometimes corresponding to Eng. co-, con-, etc. →See following entries.

สหกรณ์ sahàkɔɔn′ N cooperative.

สหประชาชาติ sahàprachaachâad′ N the United Nations.

สหปาลีรัฐอเมริกา sahàʔ/paaliirád′/-ʔameerikaa′ N the United States of America.

สหพันธ์ sahàphan′ N federation.

สหภาพ (สหภาพ) sahàphâab′ (sahàphâab′) N union.

สหภาพโซเวียต sahàphâab′soowîad′ N the Soviet Union.

สหรัฐ (สหรัฐ) sahàrád′ (sahàrád′) N federated states.

สหรัฐมะลายู sahàrád′malaajuu′ N the Federated Malay States.

สหรัฐอเมริกา sahàrád′ʔameerikaa′ N the United States of America.

สหราชอาณาจักร sahàrâad′chaʔaanaacàg′ N the United Kingdom.

สหาย (คน) sahǎaj′ (khon′) N eleg. friend. →Syn. เพื่อน com.

มิตรสหาย (คน) míd′sahǎaj′ (khon′) N friend.

ส่อ. See entries below.

ดินสอ (แท่ง) dinsɔ̌ɔ′ (thɛ̂ŋ′) N pencil.

ดินสอพอง dinsɔ̌ɔphɔɔŋ′ N a soft, prepared chalk used as an after-bath powder for its cooling effect.

ส่อ sɔ̀ɔ′ V to indicate, point out, show.

สอง sɔ̌ɔŋ′ Nm com. two. →Cf. ยี่,ทวิ-,ทวี,โท.

กำลังสอง kamlaŋsɔ̌ɔŋ′ N math. square, the second power. →Often best translated "squared," "to the second power."

จักรยานสองล้อ (คัน) càgkajaan′sɔ̌ɔŋlɔ́ɔ′ (khan′) N bicycle.

ชั้นสอง chánsɔ̌ɔŋ′ second class (accomodations); the second story, second level.

ตีสอง tiisɔ̌ɔŋ′ colloq. 2 A.M. →Syn. ๒ นาฬิกา writ.

สองครั้ง sɔ̌ɔŋkhráŋ′ two times, twice.

สองคืน sɔ̌ɔŋkhyyn′ two nights, for two nights.

สองจิตสองใจ sɔ̌ɔŋcìd′sɔ̌ɔŋcaj′ V elab. colloq. to hesitate, be hesitant, undecided, be of two minds (about something).

สองใจ sɔ̌ɔŋcaj′ V idiom. to be unfaithful, to have two loves.

สองตารางไมล์ sɔ̌ɔŋ′taraaŋmaj′ two square miles.

สองต่อสอง sɔ̌ɔŋtɔ̀ɔsɔ̌ɔŋ′ just the two (persons), tête-à-tête, in privacy.

สองที sɔ̌ɔŋthii′ two times, twice.

สองเท่า sɔ̌ɔŋthâw′ twofold, two times, twice (as much, as big, etc.).

สองพัน sɔ̌ɔŋphan′ Nm two thousand.

สองสามวัน sɔ̌ɔŋsǎamwan′ two or three days.

สองแสน sɔ̌ɔŋsɛ̌ɛn′ Nm two hundred thousand.

สองหน sɔ̌ɔŋhǒn′ two times, twice.

ส่อง sɔ̀ŋ′* V 1. to shine. 2. to illuminate, shine light on or through. 3. to look through (telescope, binoculars). 4. to look into (a mirror).

กล้องส่องทางไกล (อัน) klɔ̂ŋ′sɔ̀ŋthaaŋklaj′ (ʔan′) N 1. binoculars. 2. spyglass.

ส่องกระจก sɔ̀ŋkracòg′ V 1. to look into a mirror. 2. to look through a lens.

ส่องจ้า sɔ̀ŋcâa′ to shine brightly.

ส่องดู sɔ̀ŋduu′ V 1. to look at (through an optical instrument or by means of a mirror). 2. to look through (an optical instrument). 3. to throw a light on and see.

ส่องไฟ sɔ̀ŋfaj′ V to throw a light, throw some light (i.e., cause a light to be thrown in order to illuminate something). →Dist. ส่องแสง.

ส่องแสง sɔ̀ŋsɛ̌ɛŋ′ V (a source of light) to shine, emit light. →Dist. ส่องไฟ.

สอดส่อง sɔ̀ɔdsɔ̀ŋ′ V 1. to scrutinize. 2. to watch carefully.

สอด sɔ̀ɔd′ V to insert, thrust in (between or among). →Used especially in various figurative senses.

แซกสอด,แทรกสอด sɛ̂ɛgsɔ̀ɔd′ V 1. to interfere, intervene. 2. to have (something) interwoven, be threaded (with). sV 3. by inserting; interweavingly.

สอดคล้อง sɔ̀ɔd′khlɔ́ɔŋ′ V to be in line (with), in agreement (with).

สอดพูด sɔ̀ɔd′phûud′ V to interrupt, break in (by) speaking.

สอดรู้ sɔ̀ɔd′rúu′ V to be inquisitive, curious, meddling.

สอดส่อง sɔ̀ɔdsɔ̀ŋ′ V 1. to scrutinize. 2. watch

carefully.

สอน sɔ̌ɔn′ V to teach. การ-- teaching. คำ--
(ข้อ,ประการ) doctrine, teaching.

ประมวลการสอน (เล่ม) pramuan′kaansɔ̌ɔn′
(lêm′) N syllabus.

ผู้ฝึกสอน (คน) phûu′fỳgsɔ̌ɔn′ (khon′) N instructor; trainer.

ว่านอนสอนง่าย wâanɔɔn′sɔ̌ɔnŋâaj′ V elab.
colloq. to be tractable, easily led, compliant,
obedient.

ว่านอนสอนยาก wâanɔɔn′sɔ̌ɔnjâag′ V elab.
colloq. to be untractable, unmanageable,
disobedient, unruly.

สั่งสอน sàŋsɔ̌ɔn′ V to teach, counsel, instruct,
sermonize. คำ-- teaching, counsel, precept.

หมอสอนศาสนา (คน) mɔ̌ɔ′sɔ̌ɔnsàasanǎa′ (khon′)
N missionary.

สอน ๑ sɔ̌n′* V (the eyes) to be slightly crossed.
ตาสอน taa′sɔ̌n′ V to be slightly cross-eyed.

สอน ๒ in สำส่อน sǎmsɔ̌n* sV 1. promiscuous,
undiscriminating, indiscriminate (in one's as-
sociations, behavior). 2. mixed, jumbled, indiscriminately mingled. 3. promiscuously, undis-
criminatingly, indiscriminately.

สอบ sɔ̀ɔb′ V 1. to examine, test, check. 2. to take
an examination. การ-- examination, test (as
in school).

การสอบแข่งขัน kaansɔ̀ɔb′khɛ̀ŋkhǎn′ N competitive examination.

ข้อสอบ (ข้อ) khɔ̂ɔsɔ̀ɔb′ (khɔ̂ɔ′) N 1. examination
questions. 2. examination.

ตรวจสอบ trùadsɔ̀ɔb′ V to check, verify.

สอบซ้อม sɔ̀ɔbsɔ́ɔm′ V to take or give a test, a
quiz (other than a final examination).

สอบได้ sɔ̀ɔbdâaj′ V to pass (an examination or
course, in school).

สอบถาม sɔ̀ɔbthǎam′ V 1. to inquire into. 2. to
question (somebody) (as in an investigation).

สอบไล่ sɔ̀ɔblâj′ V 1. to take a final examination.
N 2. final examination.

o สอบไล่ได้ sɔ̀ɔb′lâjdâaj′ V to pass an examination.

o สอบไล่ตก sɔ̀ɔb′lâjtòg′ V to fail in an examination.

สอบสวน sɔ̀ɔbsŭan′ V to investigate. การ--
investigation.

สอพลอ sɔ̌ɔphlɔɔ′ V to fawn (on), curry favor (esp.
by pretending willingness, agreement).

ส้อม (คัน) sɔ̂m′* (khan′) N fork. →Usually ช้อม.

สอย ๑ sɔ̌j′* V 1. to gather, pick (fruit, flowers) by
means of a long pole with a basket or prong on
the end. 2. to stitch lightly.

สอย ๒ in ใช้สอย chájsɔ̌j′* V to expend, use, make
use of. →See cross reference.

สอย ๓ in ติดสอยห้อยตาม tìdsɔ̌j′hɔ̂jtaam′* V elab.
colloq. to follow, accompany.

สะกด ๑ sakòd′ V 1. to follow after, trail. 2. to
spell (a word).

สะกดรอยตาม sakòd′rɔɔj′-taam′ V to follow
after, trail, track.

สะกด ๒ sakòd′ V 1. to control, check, suppress.
2. to put to sleep (by magic or hypnotism).

สะกดจิต sakòd′cìd′ V to hypnotize.

สะกดใจ sakòd′caj′ V to control oneself, restrain
oneself.

สะกดอกสะกดใจ sakòd′ʔòg′-sakòd′caj′ V elab.
colloq. to control oneself, restrain oneself,
suppress one's emotions.

สะกัด. See สกัด.

สะกิด sakìd′ V 1. to tap, nudge gently (in order to
get someone's attention). 2. to scratch, pick
gently (as with one's fingernail).

สะกิดใจ sakìd′caj′ V 1. to remind one. 2. to
make one become suddenly aware (of).

สะเก็ด (ชิ้น, อัน, แผ่น) sakèd′ (chín′, ʔan′, phɛ̀n′)
N 1. fragment, piece, flake, chip. 2. scab.

สะดวก sadùag′ V to be convenient. ความ-- con-
veniences, facilities, accommodations; convenience.

o ให้ความสะดวก (แก่) hâjkhwaam′sadùag′(kaɔ)
to be accommodating (toward).

โดยสะดวก doojsadùag′ conveniently.

สะดือ (สะดือ) sadyy′ (sadyy′) N navel.

สะดุ้ง sadûŋ′ V to startle; to be startled.

สะดุ้งเฮือก sadûŋ′hŷag′ V to start suddenly,
start with a gasp, be startled.

สะดุด sadùd′ V 1. to stumble. 2. to stumble over,
trip over (something).

สะดุดใจ sadùd'caj' V to be struck (by), have one's attention arrested, get suspicious.

สะดุดตา sadùd'taa' V to strike the eyes, be eye-catching, noticeable.

สะตึ satẙ?' V 1. (a person) to be good-for-nothing. 2. to be of poor quality, worthless.

สะทก in สะทกสะท้าน sathóg'satháan' V to be afraid, frightened; to shake with fear.

สะท้อน sathɔ́ɔn' V 1. to reflect. 2. to recoil, rebound, bounce. 3. eleg. a kind of fruit (Sandoricum indicum). →Syn. กระท้อน com.

ผลสะท้อน phǒn'sathɔ́ɔn' N after-effect, resulting effect, secondary effect.

สะท้าน satháan' V to shake, tremble, shiver, quiver.

สะทกสะท้าน sathóg'satháan' V to be afraid, frightened; to shake with fear.

สะเทิน sathəən' V 1. to be half-(this, half-that). 2. elect., chem. to be neutral.

สะเทินน้ำสะเทินบก sathəən'náam'-sathəən'bòg' V eleg. to be amphibious.

สะเทือน sathyan' V eleg. to shake, tremble, vibrate. ความ-- vibration, tremor.

สะเทือนใจ sathyan'caj' V 1. (one's feelings) to be touched. 2. to be deeply moved, touched, hurt, wounded.

สะบัด sabàd' V 1. to flutter (in the wind). 2. to shake oneself, shake (oneself) free. 3. to shake (something).

สะบัดร้อนสะบัดหนาว sabàd'rɔ́ɔn'-sabàd'nǎaw' V 1. to feel alternately hot and cold, esp. when in fever. 2. (the weather) to alternate between hot and cold. 3. colloq. to be nervous (because of anxiety).

สะบัดหน้า sabàd'nâa' V to turn the face away quickly (as when angry).

สะบั้น sabân' V 1. to be severed, broken or cut apart. sV 2. apart. 3. slang very much; very.

อย่างสะบั้นหั่นแหลก jàaŋsabân'-hàn'lὲɛg' slang a great deal, extremely, unsparingly.

สะบู่. See สบู่.

สะเบียง. See เสบียง.

สะพรั่ง saphrâŋ' sV profusely, in great quantity, all over.

สะพัด in แพร่สะพัด phrɛ̂ɛ'saphád' V to spread out, be widespread, widely talked about.

สะพาน (สะพาน) saphaan' (saphaan') N bridge.

ราวสะพาน raaw'saphaan' N railing or balustrade of a bridge.

สะพาย saphaaj' V to wear over the shoulder, carry on the shoulder.

สะเพร่า saphrâw' V to be careless.

สะใภ้ sapháj' N female relative by marriage, i.e. the wife of a blood relative within a given family. The term designates a woman as an in-law of her husband's blood relatives. Generally combined with kinship terms. →Opp. เขย.

น้องสะใภ้ (คน) nɔ́ɔŋsapháj' (khon') N sister-in-law who is the wife of one's younger brother.

บุตรสะใภ้ (คน) bùd'sapháj' (khon') N eleg. daughter-in-law. →Syn. ลูกสะใภ้ com.

ป้าสะใภ้ (คน) pâa'sapháj' (khon') N wife of elder uncle, i.e. elder aunt-in-law.

พี่สะใภ้ (คน) phîisapháj' (khon') N sister-in-law who is the wife of one's older brother.

ลูกสะใภ้ (คน) lûugsapháj' (khon') N daughter-in-law. →Syn. บุตรสะใภ้ eleg.

สะวิง. See สวิง.

สะสม sà?sǒm' V to store, accumulate.

สะสวย sà?sǔaj' V to be beautiful, pretty. →Cf. สวย.

สะสาง sà?sǎaŋ' V 1. to solve, clear up (a problem). 2. to clear up (accumulated work). →Cf. สาง.

สะอาด sa?àad' V to be clean. ความ-- cleanliness; cleanness.

สดสะอาด sòd'sa?àad' V to be fresh and clean.

สะอาดสะอ้าน sa?àad'sa?âan' V elab. colloq. to be spick-and-span, clean.

สะอึก sa?ẙg' V to hiccup.

สะอึกสะอื้น sa?ẙg'sa?ɯ̂n' V elab. colloq. to sob.

สะอื้น sa?ɯ̂n' V to sob.

สะอื้นไห้ sa?ɯ̂n'hâj' V to sob.

สะเอว (สะเอว) sa?ew'* (sa?ew') N eleg. waist (body-part). →Syn. เอว com.

สัก ๑ sàg' N teak. ต้น-- (ต้น) the teak tree (Tectona grandis).

ไม้สัก májsàg' N teak, teakwood.

สัก ๒ sàg' V to tattoo. →Comp. สลัก ๒.

ลัก ๓ sàg′, ság′ qM as little as, merely, just (minimizing the quantity or amount). →Ant. ตั้ง ๒. NOTE. Often pronounced ság′ in the spoken language and hence sometimes spelled ขัก.

ลักครั้ง sàgkhráŋ′, ságkhráŋ′ once, just once, just this once.

ลักตั้ง sàgtâŋ′, ságtâŋ′ colloq. just for (the needed) period of time. →See ตั้ง ๑.

ลักเท่าไร ságthâwràj′ 1. (just) how much? (just) how many? 2. how much, how many; however much, however many. →For additional examples see cross reference.

o เขาจะวิ่งเร็วลักเท่าไร ก็ไม่ทัน kháwcawîŋrew′- ságthâwràj′→kɔ̂mâjthan′↓ No matter how fast he runs, he still won't make it.

o ไม่ห่างจากที่นั่นลักเท่าไร mâjhàaŋ′càagthînân′- ságthâwràj′ not so very far from there.

ลักนิดเดียว ságníd′diaw′ a little bit, the slightest.

ลักพัก ságphág′ for a short time, for a while.

ลักสองวัน ságsɔ̌ɔŋwan′ just a couple of days.

ลักหน่อย ságnɔ̀ɔj′ a little, a little bit.

ลักขี in ลักขิพยาน sàgkhǐi′phajaan′ N eleg. 1. witness, eyewitness. 2. evidence.

ลั่ง sàŋ′ V to order, give orders to, command. คำ-- (ข้อ,อย่าง,ประการ) order, command, instruction.

รับลั่ง rábsàŋ′ V roy. 1. to order. 2. to speak, say. N 3. order, command.

ลั่งการ sàŋkaan′ V to give orders, instructions.

ลั่งน้ำมูก sàŋ′námmûug′ V eleg. to blow the nose.

ลั่งสอน sàŋsɔ̌ɔn′ V to teach, counsel, instruct, sermonize. คำ-- (ข้อ,ประการ) teaching, counsel, precept.

ลั่งเสีย sàŋ′sǐa′ V to give parting instructions (before one leaves the country, before one dies).

หมายลั่ง (ใบ,ฉบับ) mǎajsàŋ′ (baj′,chabàb′) N law writ, formal written warrant.

ลังกะสี sǎŋkasǐi′ N 1. zinc. 2. galvanized iron.

ลังกัด sǎŋkàd′ V 1. to be under (the jurisdiction of). 2. to be affiliated with, belong to (e.g. a political party).

ลังเกต sǎŋkèed′ V to observe, notice. ความ-- observation. →Often incorrectly spelled ลังเกตุ.

ข้อลังเกต (ข้อ) khɔ̂ɔ′sǎŋkèed′ (khɔ̂ɔ′) N observation, item or comment based on observation.

ช่างลังเกต châŋsǎŋkèed′ V to be observant.

น่าลังเกตลังกา nâa′-sǎŋkèed′sǎŋkaa′ V elab. colloq. 1. to be worthy of notice. 2. to be noticeable.

ผิดลังเกต phìd′sǎŋkèed′ V to be unusual, queer, abnormal.

o เห็นผิดลังเกต hěnphìd′sǎŋkèed′ to sense something unusual happening.

พึงลังเกต phyŋ′sǎŋkèed′ 1. to be noteworthy. 2. (it) should be noticed (that); note (that).

o ข้อพึงลังเกต khɔ̂ɔphyŋ′sǎŋkèed′ N a noteworthy point.

ลังเกตการณ์ sǎŋkèed′kaan′ V to observe. ผู้-- an observer.

ลังเกตง่าย sǎŋkèed′ŋâaj′ V to be easily observable, noticeable.

ลังเกตเห็น sǎŋkèed′hěn′ V to notice, observe.

ลังข์ in หอยลังข์ (ตัว) hɔ̌jsǎŋ′ (tua′) N conch.

ลังขยา sǎŋkhajǎa′ N custard.

ลังขาร sǎŋkhǎan′ N eleg. the body; the physical and mental constitution of the body.

ลังเขป. See entries below.

โดยลังเขป dooj′sǎŋkhèeb′ briefly; in brief.

พอเป็นลังเขป phɔɔ′pensǎŋkhèeb′ idem.

ลังคม (ลังคม) sǎŋkhom′ (sǎŋkhom′) N 1. society. 2. (as n. mod.) social.

ทางลังคม thaaŋ′sǎŋkhom′ social.

ลังคมมนุษย์ (ลังคม) sǎŋkhom′manúd′ (sǎŋkhom′) N human society.

ลังคมวิทยา sǎŋkhom′wídthajaa′ N social science.

ลังคมสงเคราะห์ sǎŋkhom′sǒŋkhrɔ́?′ N social welfare.

ลาวลังคม (คน) sǎaw′sǎŋkhom′ (khon′) N 1. a much-photographed beauty, a pin-up girl. 2. a well-known beauty of loose morals.

ลังเคราะห์ sǎŋkhrɔ́?′ V chem. 1. to synthesize. 2. to be synthetic. การ-- chem. synthesis.

ลังฆราช in พระลังฆราช phrásǎŋ′kharâad′ N chief of all the Buddhist priests in the country, Buddhist supreme patriarch.

ลังวร sǎŋwɔɔn′ V to be aware (of), pay attention (to), be mindful (of).

สังวรไว้ sǎŋwɔɔn/wáj/ to bear in mind.

สังวาส sǎŋwâad/ V eleg.,tech. 1. to copulate.
2. to sleep together, cohabit.

สังเวช sǎŋwêed/ V to feel pity, feel pity and sorrow.

น่าสังเวช nâa/sǎŋwêed/ V to be pitiable, pitiful,
such as to evoke pity.

สังหรณ์ as in สังหรณ์ใจ sǎŋhɔ̌ɔn/caj/ V to have
a premonition, a presentiment.

สังหาร .sǎŋhǎan/ V eleg. to kill, destroy.

สัญจร sǎncɔɔn/ V eleg. 1. to pass, go along (e.g.
a street). 2. to wander. N 3. passage, passageway, road, thoroughfare.

ทางสัญจร (สาย,ทาง) thaaŋ/sǎncɔɔn/ (sǎaj/,
thaaŋ/) N eleg. 1. thoroughfare, passageway.
2. any area traversed by pedestrian or vehicular traffic.

สัญจรไปมา sǎncɔɔn/pajmaa/ V to pass back and
forth, go back and forth. คน-- passer-by.

สัญชาตญาณ sǎnchâad/tajaan/ N instinct.

สัญชาติ sǎnchâad/ N law citizenship. →Dist.
เชื้อชาติ.

o สัญชาติอเมริกัน เชื้อชาติไทย sǎnchâad/ʔameeᵓ
rikan/-chýachâad/thaj/ (of) American citizenship, Thai nationality.

สัญชาติญาณ sǎnchâad/tijaan/. →Var. of สัญชาตญาณ.

สัญญลักษณ์ (ตัว) sǎn/jalág/ (tua/) N symbol.

สัญญา (ฉบับ) sǎnjaa/ V 1. to promise, agree, contract. N 2. promise, agreement, contract,
treaty (chabàb/). คำ-- (ข้อ,ประการ) a promise.

กติกาสัญญา (ฉบับ) kàtikaa/sǎnjaa/ (chabàb/)
N agreement, pact.

เซ็นสัญญา sen/sǎnjaa/ V to sign a contract.

ผิดสัญญา phìd/sǎnjaa/ V to break a promise,
break a contract.

สนธิสัญญา (ฉบับ) sǒnthíʔ/sǎnjaa/ (chabàb/) N
treaty.

สัญญากับ sǎnjaa/kaᵓ to make an agreement with,
promise (a person).

สัญญาว่า sǎnjaa/wâa/ to promise that.

สัญญาสันติภาพ sǎnjaa/sǎntiphâab/ N peace treaty.

เสียสัญญา sǐa/sǎnjaa/ V to break a promise.

ให้สัญญา hâj/sǎnjaa/ V to promise.

สัญญาณ sǎnjaan/ N signal.

กองสัญญาณ (กอง) kɔɔŋ/sǎnjaan/ (kɔɔŋ/) N
milit. signal corps.

สัญญาณปลอดภัย sǎnjaan/plɔ̀ɔdphaj/ N all-clear
signal.

สัญญาณภัยทางอากาศ sǎnjaan/-phaj/thaaŋ?aakàad/
N air-raid warning.

สัณฐาน (แบบ,ชนิด) sǎnthǎan/ (bὲὲb/,chaníd/) N
1. shape, appearance. C 2. shape.

สัด ๑ in สัดส่วน sàdsùan/ N proportion.

สัด ๒ sàd/ V to mate, copulate (of animals).

เป็นสัด pensàd/ V to rut, be in heat. Used of both
male and female animals; rarely extended col-
loquially to human beings.

สัตย์ sàd/ N 1. truth, veracity. 2. promise, pledge,
word of honor. ความ-- truth; honesty.

ซื่อสัตย์ sŷysàd/ V 1. to be honest. 2. to be faithful, loyal. ความ-- honesty; faithfulness, loyalty.
→Also สัตย์ซื่อ.

มีศีลมีสัตย์ miisǐin/miisàd/ V elab. colloq. to
be trustworthy, honest, upright.

เสียสัตย์ sǐasàd/ V to be untrue (to).

ให้สัตย์ hâjsàd/ V to promise.

สัตยาบัน sàdtajaa/ban/ N ratification.

สัตรี FS. →See สตรี.

สัตว์,สัตว- (ตัว) sàd/, sàd/tawaᵓ (tua/) N animal,
beast.

ขนสัตว์ (เส้น) khǒnsàd/ (sên/) N fur, wool,
animal hair.

เนื้อสัตว์ nýasàd/ N meat, flesh.

ปศุสัตว์,ปสุสัตว์ (ตัว) pàsusàd/ (tua/) N eleg.
domestic animals.

แพทย์สัตว์ (นาย,คน) phὲὲdsàd/ (naaj/, khon/) N
eleg. veterinarian. →Syn. หมอสัตว์ com.

ล่าสัตว์ lâasàd/ V to hunt (game).

เลี้ยงสัตว์ líaŋsàd/ V to raise, breed animals.
การ-- animal husbandry.

สวนสัตว์ (แห่ง) sǔansàd/ (hὲ̀ŋ/) N zoo, zoological
garden.

สัตว์กินนม sàd/kinnom/ N com. mammal.

สัตว์กินเนื้อ sàd/kinnýa/ N carnivorous animal.

สัตว์จตุบาท sàd/càtubàad/ N lit.,eleg. quadruped.

สัตว์ต่าง sàdtàaŋ/ N pack animal.

สัตว์น้ำ sàdnáam/ N aquatic animal.

ลัตว์บก sàdbòg′ N land animal.

ลัตว์ป่า sàdpàa′ N wild animal, forest animal; wildlife.

○ การสงวนพันธุ์ลัตว์ป่า kaan′-saŋŭanphan′sàdpàa′ wildlife conservation.

ลัตว์พาหนะ sàd′phaahàná?′ N beast of burden.

ลัตว์เลี้ยง sàdlíaŋ′ N domesticated animal, pet.

ลัตว์เลี้ยงลูกด้วยนม sàd′-líaŋlûug′dûajnom′ eleg., zool. mammal.

ลัตว์เลื้อยคลาน sàd′lýajkhlaan′ N reptile.

ลัตว์วิทยา sàd′tawáwídthajaa′ N zoology.

ลัตว์สองเท้า sàd′sɔ̌ɔŋtháaw′ N biped, two-legged creature (as a fowl).

ลัตว์สี่เท้า sàd′sìitháaw′ N eleg. quadruped.

หมอลัตว์ (คน) mɔ̌ɔsàd′ (khon′) N veterinarian.

ลั่น ๑ (ลั่น) săn′ (săn′) N 1. ridge. 2. the back of a blade, the non-cutting edge of a knife.

คมลั่น khomsăn′ V to have clean-cut (features), be handsome (referring to men).

ล่ำลั่น lâmsăn′ V to be strong, robust, muscular.

ลั่นดอน (แห่ง) săndɔɔn′ (hὲŋ′) N sand bar (at the mouth of a river).

ลั่นหลัง (ลั่นหลัง) sănlăŋ′ (sănlăŋ′) N 1. dorsal ridge; spine. 2. back (body part).

○ กระดูกลั่นหลัง (ชิ้น) kradùugsănlăŋ′ (chín′) N 1. vertebra. 2. backbone, spine.

○ ไขลั่นหลัง khǎj′sănlaŋ′ N spinal cord.

○○ไข้ไขลั่นหลัง khâj′-khǎj′sănlăŋ′ N polio.

○ ลั่นหลังยาว sănlăŋ′jaaw′ V idiom. to be lazy.

ลั่น ๒ in สีลั่น sǐi′săn′ N color.

ลั่น sàn′ V 1. to tremble, vibrate. 2. to ring (of bells).

ไข้จับลั่น khâj′càbsàn′ N eleg. malaria. →Syn. ไข้ป่า colloq.

ใจลั่น cajsàn′ V to be frightened, have one's heart quiver with fear.

ตัวลั่น tuasàn′ V to tremble all over.

ลั่นแด็กๆ sàn′dὲgdὲg′ to tremble violently without stopping.

ลั้น sân′ V to be short (in length). →Dist. เตี้ย. →Ant. ยาว.

เข็มลั้น (อัน) khěmsân′ (?an′) N hour hand (of a clock).

คลื่นลั้น khlŷynsân′ N tech. short wave.

ปืนลั่น pyynsân′ N pistol, revolver.

ผ่อนลั่นผ่อนยาว phɔ̀nsân′phɔ̀njaaw′ V elab. colloq. to ease tensions by compromise or mutual concession.

พูดลิ้นไก่ลั่น phûud′-línkàj′sân′ V to be talking drunk: "talk (like someone) with a short uvula."

เรื่องลั้น (เรื่อง) rŷaŋsân′ (rŷaŋ′) N short story.

○ ชุมนุมเรื่องลั้น chumnum′rŷaŋsân′ N anthology of short stories.

วงจรลั้น woŋcɔɔn′sân′ N elect. short circuit.

สายตาลั้น săajtaa′sân′ V 1. to be nearsighted. 2. to be short-sighted.

ลั่นดาน săndaan′ N disposition, character.

ดัดลั่นดาน dàd′săndaan′ V to reform (a person).

○ โรงเรียนดัดลั่นดาน rooŋrian′-dàd′săndaan′ N reform school.

ลั่นโดษ săndòod′ V 1. to be contented (with what one has or is). 2. to be solitary. ความ-- contentment; solitude.

ลั่นติ săntì?′, sănti⊃ N peace, calm. →Chiefly in compounds.

โดยลั่นติวิธี dooj′săntìwíthii′ by peaceful means.

ในยามลั่นติ najjaam′săntì?′ in times of peace, in peacetime.

ผู้พิทักษ์ลั่นติราษฎร์ (คน, นาย) phûuphíthág′săn⊃ tirâad′ (khon′, naaj′) N eleg. policeman.

ลั่นติบาล săntibaan′ N 1. eleg. maintenance of the peace. 2. the city police.

ลั่นติภาพ săntiphâab′ N peace, peacetime; peacefulness.

○ ลัญญาลั่นติภาพ sănjaa′săntiphâab′ N peace treaty.

ลั่นติสุข săntisùg′ N peace, peace and happiness.

ลั่นถว in ลั่นถวไมตรี săn′thawámajtrii′ N close friendship, intimate friendship.

ทูตลั่นถวไมตรี (นาย) thûud′săn′thawámajtrii′ N good-will ambassador.

ลั่นทัด sănthád′ V 1. to be proficient, skilled, adept, experienced. sV 2. medium, average, good, just right.

รูปร่างลั่นทัด rûubrâaŋ′sănthád′ V to be of medium build, of a good size, well-proportioned.

วงการลั่นทัดกรณี woŋkaan′-sănthád′kɔɔranii′ N well-informed circles or sources.

ส้นนิบาต sănníbàad′ N 1. assembly, gathering, congress. 2. league.

    ส้นนิบาตชาติ sănníbàad′châad′ N the League of Nations.

    ส้นนิบาตอาหรับ sănníbàad′ʔaaràb′ N the Arab League.

ส้นนิษฐาน sănníthăan′* V to presume.

ส้บ ๑ sàb′ V to hack, chop, slash.

    ส้บไก sàb′kaj′ V to pull the trigger (of a gun).

    ส้บ(...)รอบๆ sàb′(...)rɔɔbrɔɔb′ to hack (it) all the way around, make a series of slashes all around (it).

ส้บ ๒ sàb′ V to change, alter, switch.

    ส้บเปลี่ยน sàbplìan′ V to change, alter, switch.

ส้บปะรด (หัว,ใบ,ลูก,ผล) sàbparód′ (hŭa′, baj′ lûug′, phŏn′) N pineapple.

ส้บปล้บ sàbplàb′ V to be deceitful in speech (in the sense of saying one thing to one person, and another to another).

ส้บสน sàbsŏn′ V to be confused.

    ฟังส้บสน faŋ′sàbsŏn′ V to sound confusing.

ส้บปดน sàbpadon′ V to be obscene, indecent.

ส้บดาห์ sàbdaa′ C eleg. week.

ส้บโดกส้บปดน sàbpadòog′sàbpadon′ V elab. colloq. to be obscene, indecent.

ส้บรังเค sàbparaŋ′khee′ V colloq. to be in poor condition, dilapidated, worn out.

ส้บปหงก sàbpaŋòg′ V to nod (as when sleepy).

ส้บเพเหระ sàbphee′hěerá?′ N colloq. stuff, junk.

ส้บพยอก sàbphajɔɔg′ V to tease (in a friendly way).

ส้มปทาน sămpathaan′ N 1. concession, the exclusive right (to operate a mine, to cut timber, etc.). 2. the granting of such rights.

ส้มประสิทธิ์ sămprasìd′ N tech. coefficient.

ส้มผัส,ส้มผัสส์ sămphàd′ V 1. eleg. to feel, touch. 2. to rhyme. N 3. the senses. 4. rhyme. การ-- contact.

    o ส้มผัสทั้งห้า sămphàd′tháŋhâa′ the five senses.

    ส้มผัสรส sămphàd′ród′ V to taste.

ส้มพันธ์,ส้มพันธ- sămphan′, sămphan′thaɔ N relationship, association, alliance. →Also ความ--.

    เกลียวส้มพันธ์ kliaw′sămphan′ N the bonds of a relationship.

    มิตรส้มพันธ์ míd′sămphan′ N friendly relations.

ส้มพันธ์ทางการทูต sămphan′thaaŋkaanthûud′ N diplomatic relations.

ส้มพันธภาพ sămphan′thaphâab′ N relation, relationship, state of being allied, bonds of friendship.

ส้มพันธมิตร sămphan′thamíd′ N 1. alliance. 2. allies.

    o ฝ่ายส้มพันธมิตร fàaj′sămphan′thamíd′ N the Allied side, the Allies.

ส้มพันธไมตรี sămphan′thamajtrii′ N friendly relations, friendship. →Also ความ--.

ส้มภาร,ส้มภาระ (อย่าง) sămphaa′rá?′ (jàaŋ′) N eleg. equipment, provisions, material, supplies, belongings.

ส้มภาษณ์ sămphâad′ V 1. to interview. N 2. interview.

ส้มฤทธิ์ ๑ in ทองส้มฤทธิ์ thɔɔŋ′sămríd′ N bronze. →Also called ทองบรอนซ์.

ส้มฤทธิ์ ๒ in ส้มฤทธิ์ผล sămríd′phŏn′ N to be successful.

สา ๑. See entries below.

    เดียงสา diaŋsăa′. Bound form meaning "worldly wisdom," used in the following negative expressions; not used in the positive.

    o ไม่เดียงสา,ไร้เดียงสา mâjdiaŋsăa′, ráj′diaŋɔ săa′ to be innocent, naive, to lack worldly wisdom (as of a child).

    ถือสา thɯ̆ysăa′ V to mind (something said or done), take offense.

สา ๒ in สาใจ,สาแก่ใจ săa′caj′, săa′kacaj′, -kɛ̀ɛ- to feel satisfied, do something to one's heart's content (esp. when getting the better of somebody, when giving him what he deserves).

สา ๓. See สาเหตุ.

สาก ๑ (อัน) sàag′ (ʔan′) N pestle.

สาก ๒ sàag′ V to be coarse, rough.

สากล săakon′ N 1. universe. 2. (as n. mod.) universal (commonly used to refer to Occidental customs and ways).

    แบบสากล bɛ̀ɛb′săakon′ modern, European, Occidental.

    เพลงสากล (เพลง) phleeŋ′săakon′ (phleeŋ′) N occidental music (popular and classical).

    มวยสากล muaj′săakon′ N boxing of European or American style (as opp. to the Thai style).

สภากาชาดสากล saphaakaachâad/săakon/ N International Red Cross.

สาเก (ลูก,ผล) săakee/ (lûug/, phŏn/) N bread-fruit.

สาขา (ส่ายขา,แห่ง) săakhăa/ (săakhăa/, hɛ̀ŋ/) N branch; offshoot; subdivision; tributary.

สาคู săakhuu/ N 1. sago. 2. tapioca. ต้น-- (ต้น) the sago palm. [f. Mal.]

สาง ๑ săaŋ N ghost, spirit. →Chiefly in the following compound.

ผีสาง (ตน) phǐi/săaŋ/ (ton/) N ghost, spirit.

สาง ๒ săaŋ/ V to unravel, comb. →Cf. สะสาง.

สาง ๓ săaŋ/ V to dawn, be dawn, be dawning.

ฟ้าสาง fáa/săaŋ/ day to dawn, be dawning.

รุ่งสาง rûŋsăaŋ/ 1. day to break. 2. at dawn, at daybreak.

เวลาสาง weelaasăaŋ/ N dawn.

สาด săad/ V to toss out, throw, splash, douse (e.g. as when throwing water from a cup or bucket). →Sometimes coupled with เท "to pour."

ฝนสาด fŏnsàad/ the rain to splash in.

สาดทิ้งเททิ้ง sàadthíŋ/theethíŋ/ V elab. colloq. to throw out.

สาธยาย săa/thajaaj/ V eleg. to recite, explain, relate.

สาธารณ săa/thaaraná?/, săa/thaaranác public, common. →Chiefly in compounds. →Also สาธารณะ FS.

สวนสาธารณ (แห่ง) sŭan/-săa/thaaraná?/ (hɛ̀ŋ/) N public park.

ส้วมสาธารณ (แห่ง) sûam/-săa/thaaraná?/ (hɛ̀ŋ/) N public toilet, rest room.

สาธารณชน săa/thaaranáchon/ N the public.

สาธารณสุข săa/thaaranásùg/ N public health. การ-- affairs of public health.

สาน săan/ V to weave, plait (bamboo).

การจักสาน kaan/càgsăan/ N making of wickerwork, making of woven or plaited articles, such as mats, screens, baskets, etc.

ช่างจักสาน (คน) châŋcàgsăan/ (khon/) N wickerworker.

หมวกสาน (ใบ,ลูก) mùagsăan/ (baj/, lûug/) N plaited hat, woven hat.

สาบ ๑ sàab/ N an unpleasant, rank smell (as of body odors).

แมลงสาบ (ตัว) malɛɛŋsàab/ (tua/) N cockroach.

สาบควาย sàabkhwaaj/ N the odor of the water buffalo.

เหม็นสาบ mĕnsàab/ V to smell, to stink (as of someone who needs a bath).

สาบ ๒ in สาบศูนย์, -สูญ sàabsŭun/ V to disappear, be lost; to become extinct.

สาบ ๓ in ทะเลสาบ (แห่ง) thaleesàab/ (hɛ̀ŋ/) N lake. →Also written -สาป.

สาบาน săabaan/ V to take an oath, swear.

สาป ๑ sàab/ V 1. to curse, put a curse on. N 2. curse. คำ-- spell, curse.

สาปแช่ง sàabchɛ̀ŋ/ V to curse.

สาป ๒. See สาบ ๓.

สาม ๑ săam/ Nm com. three. →Comp. ตรัย,ตรี.

ชั้นสาม chánsăam/ third class (accomodations); the third story, third level.

รูปสามเหลี่ยม (รูป) rûubsăamlìam/ (rûub/) N triangle.

สองสามวัน sɔ̌ɔŋsăamwan/ two or three days, a few days.

สามขา (อัน) săamkhăa/ (ʔan/) N tripod.

สามทุ่ม săamthûm/ colloq. 9 P.M.

สามพัน săamphan/ three thousand.

สามล้อ (คัน) săamlɔ́ɔ/ (khan/) N colloq. samlor, pedicab.

สามวินาที săam/wínaathii/ three seconds.

สามสิบ săamsìb/ Nm thirty.

สามเส้า săam/sâw/ 1. three pillars, supports. 2. having three members, tripartite.

สิบสาม sìbsăam/ thirteen.

สาม ๒ in สามเณร (รูป,องค์) săammaneen/ (rûub/, ʔoŋ/) N one who enters priesthood while under the age of twenty. →Also เณร.

สามัคคี săamágkhii/ V to unify, unite. ความ-- cooperation; harmony, unison, unity, union.

สามัญ săaman/ common, ordinary. →Ant. วิสามัญ.

สภาสามัญ saphaa/săaman/ N the House of Commons.

สามัญชน (คน) săaman/chon/ (khon/) N common people, ordinary people.

สามัญศึกษา săaman/sy̆gsăa/ N 1. elementary education. 2. (formerly) general education. →Opp. วิสามัญศึกษา.

เสียงสามัญ sĭaŋsăaman′ N g r a m. the mid tone.

สามารถ săamâad′ V 1. to be able, capable. AA 2. able to, capable of. ความ-- ability. →Also 2. สามารถจะ. NOTE. As an adv. -aux. frequently used in connection with postposed ได้, as in the following example.

o เท่าที่สามารถกระทำได้ thâw′-thîisăamâad′-kratham′dâaj′ as much as one can do.

สามี (คน) săamii′ (khon′) N e l e g. husband. →S y n. ผัว c o m.

สามีภรรยา (คู่) săamii′phanrajaa′ (khûu′) N e l e g. married couple, husband and wife.

สาย ๑ săaj′ N 1. line (esp. in the fig. sense of a channel, route, as in "telephone line"). C 2. clf. for rivers, canals, roads; for ornamental chains, necklaces; for wires, cables, and for other line-like objects. เครื่อง-- stringed instrument. →D i s t. 1. เส้น.

เชื้อสาย chýasăaj′ N lineage, family, descendants.

ทางสายสำคัญ thaaŋ′-săaj′sămkhan′ a major route, an important road.

รถไฟสายเหนือ ródfaj′săajnўa′ the northern railways, the northern line.

รับสาย rábsăaj′ V to answer the telephone.

สายการบิน (สาย) săaj′kaanbin′ (săaj′) N 1. air route. 2. air line (system or company).

สายดิ่ง (สาย) săajdìŋ′ (săaj′) N sounding line.

สายตา săajtaa′ N 1. sight, eye-sight. 2. line of vision.

o กวาดสายตา kwàad′săajtaa′ V to sweep (with one's gaze).

o มีสายตาไม่กินกัน miisăajtaa′-mâjkin′kan i d i o m. (they) don't like each other's looks, don't get along.

o สายตายาว săajtaa′jaaw′ V to be farsighted (both lit. and fig.).

o สายตาสั้น săajtaa′sân′ V 1. to be nearsighted (in vision). 2. to be short-sighted.

สายโทรศัพท์ (สาย) săaj′thoorasàb′ (săaj′) N telephone line.

สายน้ำ (สาย) săajnáam′ (săaj′) N 1. stream. 2. current.

สายบังเหียน (สาย) săaj′baŋhĭan′ (săaj′) N bridle.

สายบัว (สาย, ก๋า) săajbua′ N stem of a variety of lotus (săaj′ for individual stems; kam′ for bunches).

o ถอนสายบัว thɔ̌ɔn′săajbua′ V i d i o m. to curtsy.

สายฝน săajfŏn′ N the line of fall of a raindrop, the vertical traces of falling raindrops, the pattern of parallel lines seen in a rainfall.

สายฟ้าแลบ (สาย) săajfáalɛ̂ɛb′ (săaj′) N lightning streak.

สายไฟฟ้า (สาย) săajfajfáa′ (săaj′) N 1. electric wire. 2. power line.

สายไม่ว่าง săaj′mâjwâaŋ′↓ The line is busy.

สายรุ้ง (สาย) săajrúŋ′ (săaj′) N 1. w r i t. rainbow. 2. c o m. streamers, long strips of colored paper or cloth used for decoration, for throwing at carnivals, etc. →Also 1. รุ้ง c o m.

สายลม săajlom′ N breeze, drift of air, air current.

สายลับ (คน, สาย) săajláb′ N 1. spy, secret informer (khon′). 2. intelligence channel (săaj′).

สายโลหิต (สาย) săaj′loohìd′ (săaj′) N 1. blood line, lineage. 2. artery (fig. sense only, e.g. referring to a river). →D i s t. เส้นโลหิต.

o ร่วมสายโลหิต rûamsăaj′loohìd′ of the same blood, of the same parents.

สายสมอ (สาย) săajsamɔɔ′ (săaj′) N cable of an anchor.

สายสร้อย (สาย, เส้น) săajsɔ̂j′ (săaj′, sên′) N ornamental chain.

สายเสียง săajsĭaŋ′ N vocal cords. →Also เส้นเสียง.

สายอากาศ (สาย) săaj ʔaakàad′ (săaj′) N antenna, aerial.

สาย ๒ săaj′ N 1. the late morning. V 2. to be late (in the morning), be late morning; to be late (with respect to some expected or appointed time in the morning); to be too late (with respect to accomplishing some purpose). sV 4. late (in the morning). →D i s t. 3, 4. ช้า. →O p p. เช้า. NOTE. In the expressions สายเกินไป, สายเสีย แล้ว listed below, no particular time of day is implied.

เช้า สาย บ่าย เย็น ก็ได้ cháw′ săaj′ bàaj′ jen′ kɔ̂dâaj′ (it can be) any time during the day:

"early morning, late morning, afternoon, evening."

ตอนสาย tɔɔnsǎj′ N 1. the late morning. 2. in the late morning.

สายเกินไป sǎj′kəənpaj′ it is too late.

สายๆ sǎjsǎj′ V 1. to be late morning. sV 2. in the late morning, late in the morning.

สายเสียแล้ว sǎj′sǐaléɛw′ it is too late.

ส่าย sàaj′ V 1. to sway. 2. to move in a zigzag course.

ส่ายไปส่ายมา sàajpaj′sàajmaa′ V to sway from side to side.

ส่ายหน้า sàajnâa′ V to shake the head from side to side, indicating a negative reply.

สายชู in น้ำส้มสายชู námsôm′sǎajchuu′ N vinegar. →Also น้ำส้ม.

สายัณห์ sǎajan′ N lit. evening. →Syn. เย็น com.

สาร ๑ sǎn′, sǎaraɔ N 1. substance, essence. 2. official letter, message. →Comp. สาระ.

แก่นสาร kènsǎn′ N essence, essentials, substance.

ข่าวสาร (ชิ้น, เรื่อง) khàawsǎn′ (chín′, rŷaŋ′) N news.

o สำนักข่าวสารอเมริกัน sǎmnág′-khàawsǎn′ɔ ʔameerikan′ the U.S. Information Service.

ข้าวสาร khâawsǎn′ N raw, husked rice. →Opp. ข้าวสุก.

ไมตรีสาร (ฉบับ) majtrii′sǎn′ (chabàb′) N friendship note, message.

สารคดี (เรื่อง, บท) sǎarakhadii′ (rŷaŋ′, bòd′) N (written) article, account (non-fiction).

สารเคมี sǎn′kheemii′ N chemicals.

สารประกอบ sǎn′prakɔɔb′ N compound.

สารหนู sǎnnǔu′ N arsenic.

สื่อสาร sỳysǎn′ V to communicate.

สาร ๒ in โดยสาร doojsǎn′ V to travel (by means of a conveyance), to take passage.

สาร ๓ in ช้างสาร cháaŋsǎn′ N elephant, esp. a large, powerful one.

สารบัญ, สารบาญ sǎaraban′, sǎarabaan′ N table of contents.

สารพัด sǎaraphád′ N 1. everything, all things. 2. all, every, all kinds of, (of) all kinds.

o ยาแก้สารพัดโรค jaakɛ̂ɛ′-sǎaraphád′rôog′

1. cure-all drug. 2. panacea.

สารภาพ sǎaraphâab′ V to admit, confess.

รับสารภาพ ráb′sǎaraphâab′ V to confess, plead guilty.

สารวัตร sǎarawád′ N (police) inspector.

สาระ sǎará?′ N substance, essence. →Comp. สาร.

ไม่มีสาระ mâjmii′sǎará?′ 1. to have no sense, be nonsense. 2. to have no substance, be immaterial.

ไร้สาระ ráj′sǎará?′ to make no sense, be nonsensical.

สาระแน sǎaránɛɛ′ V colloq. to be meddlesome, get involved (in something which is none of one's business); to look for trouble.

สาราณียกร sǎaraa′niijakɔɔn′ N editor (usually of publications produced by students). →Cf. บรรณา ธิการ.

สารานุกรม (เล่ม) sǎaraa′núkrom′ (lêm′) N encyclopedia.

สาละวน sǎalawon′ V to be busy.

สาลิกา in นกสาลิกา (ตัว) nógsǎalikaa′ (tua′) N the common myna.

สาลี sǎalii′, sáalii′ N wheat. →Chiefly in compounds.

ข้าวสาลี khâaw′sáalii′ N wheat.

แป้งสาลี pɛ̂ɛŋ′sáalii′ N wheat flour.

สาว sǎaw′ N,C 1. young woman; adolescent girl. 2. unmarried woman or girl. V 2. (a woman) to be young, adolescent. คน-- young woman. →Opp. หนุ่ม, used of men.

ไก่สาว (ตัว) kàjsǎaw′ (tua′) N pullet.

คู่บ่าวสาว (คู่) khûu′bàawsǎaw′ (khûu′) N bride and groom.

เจ้าสาว (คน) câwsǎaw′ (khon′) N bride.

น้องสาว (คน) nɔ́ɔŋsǎaw′ (khon′) N younger sister.

นางสาว (คน) naaŋsǎaw′ (khon′) N 1. young woman, miss. T 2. title placed before the first name of an unmarried woman, hence "Miss --." →Abbrev. น.ส.

เป็นสาว pensǎaw′ 1. to be young, adolescent (of a girl). 2. to be a virgin.

เป็นสาวเป็นแล้ pensǎaw′pensɛ̂ɛ′ colloq. to be a young unmarried woman.

ผู้หญิงสาว (คน) phûujiŋ′sǎaw′ (khon′) N young

woman.

พี่สาว (คน) phîisǎaw′ (khon′) N older sister.

ลูกสาว (คน) lûugsǎaw′ (khon′) N daughter.
→Syn. See cross reference.

สาวคนรัก (คน) sǎaw′khonrág′ (khon′) N a
man's sweetheart.

สาวใช้ (คน) sǎawcháj′ (khon′) N maid, maidservant.

สาวทึมทึก (คน) sǎaw′thymthýg′ (khon′) N spinster.

สาวสังคม (คน) sǎaw′sǎŋkhom′ (khon′) N 1.
a much-photographed beauty, a pin-up girl.
2. a well-known beauty of loose morals.

หญิงสาว jǐŋsǎaw′ N young girl, young woman.

หนุ่มสาว (คน,คู่) nùm′sǎaw′ N 1. young people,
teenagers (of both sexes)(khon′). 2. young
couple (khûu′).

หนุ่มๆสาวๆ nùmnùm′sǎawsǎaw′ N colloq.
young men and women, young people, teenagers.
→Also คน--.

หลานสาว (คน) lǎansǎaw′ (khon′) N 1. granddaughter. 2. niece.

สาวก (คน) sǎa′wóg′ (khon′) N disciple, follower.

สาสน์,สาส์น (ฉบับ) sàad′, sǎan′ (chabàb′) N official letter.

สาส์นตราตั้ง sǎan′traatâŋ′ N credentials.

สาสนา. See ศาสนา.

สาหร่าย (ต้น) sǎaràaj′ (tôn′) N aquatic weed,
algae.

สาหัส sǎahàd′ V 1. to be serious, critical. 2. seriously, critically; very, exceedingly, severely.

มีบาดแผลสาหัส mii′-bàadphlἔἔ′sǎahàd′ V to be
seriously wounded.

สาเหตุ (อย่าง,ประการ) sǎahèed′ (jàaŋ′, prakaan′)
N,C origin, cause.

สำ in สำส่อน sǎmsɔ̀n/*sV 1. promiscuous, undiscriminating, indiscriminate (in one's associa-
tions, behavior). 2. mixed, jumbled, indiscriminately mingled. 3. promiscuously, undis-
criminatingly, indiscriminately. การ-- being
promiscuous; promiscuity. ความ-- promis-
cuousness; promiscuity. คน-- low class person; rabble.

สำคัญ ๑ sǎmkhan′ V to be important, significant,

meaningful. ความ-- importance, significance.

ใบสำคัญ (ใบ,ฉบับ) baj′sǎmkhan′ (baj′,chabàb′)
N certificate, document required to establish
one's eligibility for something; identification
papers.

o ใบสำคัญต่างด้าว baj′sǎmkhan′-tàaŋdâaw′ N
1. passport. 2. alien identification card.

เป็นสำคัญ pen′sǎmkhan′ 1. to be the main thing.
the significant thing. 2. as evidence; as a token.

สำหลักสำคัญ sǎmlàg′sǎmkhan′ V colloq. to be
important.

สำคัญ(ว่า) ๒ sǎmkhan′(wâaɔ) V to assume, think,
understand, believe (that)(usually mistakenly).

สำคัญผิด sǎmkhan′phìd′ V to misunderstand,
mistake, make a mistaken assumption.

สำแดง sǎmdɛɛŋ′ V lit. to show, reveal. [conv.f.
แสดง]

สำนวน ๑ (สำนวน) sǎmnuan′ (sǎmnuan′) N idiom,
wording, phrasing, turn of phrase, special phrase,
style (of writing).

สำนวน ๒ sǎmnuan′ C law case.

สำนัก (สำนัก,แห่ง) sǎmnág′ (sǎmnág′,hὲŋ′) N 1.
lodging place; residence. 2. institution (as in
"educational institution"). 3. office.

ราชสำนัก râad′chasǎmnág′ N royal court, household.

สำนักข่าวสารอเมริกัน sǎmnág′-khàawsǎan′ʔameeɔ
rikan′ U.S. Information Service.

สำนักงาน (แห่ง) sǎmnágŋaan′ (hὲŋ′) N office.

สำนักนายกรัฐมนตรี sǎmnág′-naajóg′rádthamontrii′
N Office of the President of the Council of Ministers.

สำนึก sǎmnýg′ V to be conscious of, aware of (esp.
one's shortcomings, guilt). →Comp. นึก.

สำเนา (ฉบับ) sǎmnaw′ (chabàb′) N duplicate copy.

เครื่องอัดสำเนา (เครื่อง) khrŷaŋʔàd′sǎmnaw′
N duplicator, mimeograph.

สำเนียง sǎmniaŋ′ N 1. the sound (of speech). pronunciation, accent. 2. lit.,eleg. sound (of the
voice), tone, voice. [conv.f. เสียง]

สำปะหลัง in มันสำปะหลัง (หัว) man′sǎmpalǎŋ′
(hǔa′) N cassava. →Also incorrectly มัน
สำปะหรัง.

สำปั้น in เรือสำปั้น (ลำ) ryasǎmpân′ (lam′) N

sampan.

ลำเภา in เรือลำเภา (ลำ) ryasămphaw/ (lam/)
N Chinese junk.

สำมะโนครัว sămmanoo/khrua/ N census.
ทะเบียนสำมะโนครัว thabian/sămmanoo/khrua/
N census, i.e. census report or record.

สำรวจ sămrùad/* V to explore, survey. การ--
exploration, survey. นัก-- explorer.
การสำรวจพลเมือง kaan/-sămrùad/phonlamyaŋ/
N census, i.e. the taking of a census.

สำรวม sămruam/ V 1. to control oneself, keep
oneself quiet, be proper (in one's bearing), be
composed, behave sedately and with propriety.
sV 2. quietly, sedately, decorously, with propriety, with composure.

สำรวย sămruaj/ V 1. to be pretty, beautiful, elegant, well-dressed (esp. of women). 2. to consider oneself too fine to work (used of both m.
and w.). [conv. f. สวย]

สำรวล sămruan/ V to laugh happily, be cheerful.

สำรอก sămrɔ̀ɔg/ V eleg. to vomit. →Syn. See
อ้วก com.

สำรอง sămrɔɔŋ/ V 1. to keep in reserve. 2. to be
in reserve.
มี(...)สำรอง mii/(...)sămrɔɔŋ/ to have (such
and such) in reserve.

สำรับ sămráb/ C set (of things occuring in sets);
deck (of cards); suit (of clothes); tray (of food).
เก็บสำรับ kèb/sămráb/ V to clear (the table);
to put up the (food-)tray.

สำราญ sămraan/ V to feel happy, content.

สำเร็จ sămrèd/* V 1. to finish, complete, accomplish. 2. to be successful. 3. to be finished,
completed. sV 4. prepared, ready-made (e.g.
prepared food). 5. to completion. 6. successfully. ความ-- success. [conv. f. เสร็จ]
ผลสำเร็จ phŏn/sămrèd/ N success, accomplishment.
o เป็นผลสำเร็จ penphŏn/sămrèd/ to be successful, accomplished.
ผู้สำเร็จราชการ (คน) phûusămrèd/râadchakaan/
(khon/) N 1. regent, king's regent. 2. viceroy
(esp. in former times the viceroy of India).
เรียนสำเร็จ rian/sămrèd/ V eleg. to graduate,

complete one's studies.

สำเร็จโทษ sămrèd/thôod/ V eleg. to execute,
put to death. →Syn. See ฆ่า com.

สำเร็จรูป sămrèd/rûub/ ready-made, prepared,
prefabricated.

สำลัก sămlág/ V to choke (intr.), choke on, be suf-
focated.
สำลักน้ำ sămlág/náam/ to choke on water.

สำลี sămlii/ N absorbent cotton, cotton wool.
ผ้าสำลี (ชิ้น,ผืน,พับ) phâasămlii/ (chín/, phŷyn/,
pháb/) N flannelet, cotton fabric napped on one
side.

สำหรับ sămràb/ Pp 1. for. Cj 2. for (doing such
and such).
o สำหรับประเทศของตน sămràb/-prathêed/khɔɔŋɔ
ton/ for one's own country.
o ไม่ดีสำหรับดื่ม mâjdii/sămràbdỳym/ not good
to drink, not good for drinking.

สำหลัก in สำหลักสำคัญ sămlàg/sămkhan/ V colloq.
to be important.

สำเหนียก sămnìag/ V to be conscious of, mindful
of; to pay attention to, listen attentively to.

สำอาง sămʔaaŋ/ V to be nice-looking, look nice.
เครื่อง-- cosmetics.

สิ sî/, sìɔ Pt particle indicating definiteness or
emphasis. →Var. of ซี.

สิง sĭŋ/ V (a ghost) to haunt, possess, stay.
ผีสิง (ตน) phĭi/sĭŋ/ (ton/) a spirit which possesses (one), a spirit which haunts (a place).
o บ้านผีสิง bâan/-phĭi/sĭŋ/ a haunted house.

สิ่ง sìŋ/ C eleg. thing. →Comp. อย่าง.
ทุกสิ่งทุกอย่าง thúgsìŋ/thúgjàaŋ/ everything.
บางสิ่ง baaŋsìŋ/ something; some of the things.
→Also บางอย่าง.
สิ่งกรอง sìŋkrɔɔŋ/ N chem. filtrate.
สิ่งของ (อย่าง,สิ่ง) sìŋkhɔ̌ɔŋ/ (jàaŋ/, sìŋ/) N
things.
สิ่งมีชีวิต sìŋ/miichiiwíd/ N living things.
สิ่งแวดล้อม sìŋ/wɛɛdlɔ́ɔm/ N environment, surroundings.

สิงคโปร์ sĭŋkhapoo/ pN Singapore. [f. Mal.]

สิงโต (ตัว) sĭŋtoo/ (tua/) N 1. a legendary Chinese
beast resembling a lion. 2. statuary representing 1. 3. lion. →Also สิงห์โต. →Cf. สิงห์.

สิงห์ sĭŋ′ N lion. →Chiefly in cpds. →Cf. สีห์,สิงโต.

สิงหบุรี sĭŋ′burii′ pN Singburi, a township in C
Thailand. →Cf. สิงห์.

สิงหาคม sĭŋhăa′khom′ N August. เดือน-- idem.
→The names of all the months are listed under
เดือน. →Cf. สิงห์.

สิทธิ์,สิทธิ (อย่าง) sìd′, sìdthí?′, sìdthí⊃ (jàaŋ′)
N right(s), privilege(s).

กรรมสิทธิ์ kammasìd′ N 1. ownership. 2. rights.

มีสิทธิ์ miisìd′ to have the right to, to be authorized.

ลิขสิทธิ lígkhasìd′ N copyright.

ศักดิ์สิทธิ์ sàgsìd′ V to be holy, sacred.

สมบูรณาญาสิทธิราช sŏmbuuranaa′jaa′sìdthíráad′
N absolute monarchy.

สิทธิพิเศษ sìdthí?′phisèed′ N special privileges.

สิทธิยับยั้ง sìdthí?′jábjáŋ′ N veto power.

สิน ๑ sĭn′ N com. wealth, goods. →Chiefly in
cpds. →Syn. ทรัพย์,สมบัติ eleg., เงิน com.

คลังออมสิน (แห่ง) khlaŋ′?ɔɔmsĭn′ (hèŋ′) N
(Thai) government savings bank.

ทรัพย์ในดินสินในน้ำ sáb′najdin′-sĭn′najnáam′
elab. eleg. the natural resources of earth
and water: "treasure-in-the earth, wealth-in-
the water."

ทรัพย์สิน sábsĭn′ N com. property, holdings,
assets, wealth.

เป็นหนี้เป็นสิน pennîi′pensĭn′ V elab. colloq.
to be in debt. →Syn. เป็นหนี้ com.

สินค้า (อย่าง,ชนิด) sĭnkháa′ (jàaŋ′, chaníd′) N
products, produce, commodities, merchandise,
goods, cargo, freight.

o เรือสินค้า (ลำ) ryasĭnkháa′ (lam′) N cargo
boat, freighter.

o โรงสินค้า (โรง,หลัง) rooŋ′sĭnkháa′ (rooŋ′,
lăŋ′) N warehouse.

o ลมสินค้า lom′sĭnkháa′ N trade wind.

o สินค้าขาเข้า sĭnkháa′khăakhâw′ N import,
i.e. import commodity.

o สินค้าขาออก sĭnkháa′khăa?ɔɔg′ N export,
i.e. export commodity.

o สินค้าเข้า sĭnkháa′khâw′ N import.

o สินค้าออก sĭnkháa′?ɔɔg′ N export.

สินจ้าง sĭncâaŋ′ N remuneration.

สินบน sĭnbon′ N bribe.

o กินสินบน kin′sĭnbon′ V to accept bribes.

o ติดสินบน tìd′sĭnbon′ V 1. to bribe. 2. to give
a reward for information (as the police to someone who aids in discovering a wrongdoer).

สินแร่ sĭnrɛɛ′ N ore.

หนี้สิน nîi′sĭn′ N debts, liabilities.

สิน ๒ in ตัดสิน tàdsĭn′ V to decide, judge.

สิ้น sîn′ V 1. to end, come to an end, terminate.
2. to be used up, exhausted. sV 3. up, all up,
completely, entirely. →Dist. เสร็จ. →Comp.
หมด,จบ.

ทั้งสิ้น tháŋsîn′ all, all of (it); entire(ly), total(ly).
→Cf. ทั้งปวง.

สิ้นใจ sîncaj′ V to die. →Syn. See ตาย com.

สิ้นชีพ sînchîib′ V eleg. to die. →Syn. ตาย.

สิ้นชีวิต sîn′chiiwíd′ V eleg. to die.

สิ้นเชิง sînchəəŋ′ lit., eleg. completely, totally.
โดย-- idem.

สิ้นดี sîndii′ colloq. much, very, extremely.

สิ้นพระชนม์ sîn′phráchon′ V roy. to die. →Syn.
See ตาย com.

สิ้นแรง sînrɛɛŋ′ V to be exhausted.

สิ้นสติ sîn′satì?′ V to lose consciousness.

สิ้นสุด sînsùd′ V to end, expire, terminate.

สิ้นหวัง sînwăŋ′ V to despair, give up hope.

สิ้นอยาก sînjàag′ V to lose one's desire (to do
something).

สิ้นอาลัยตายอยาก sîn′-?aalaj′taajjàag′ V elab.
colloq. to lose all hope, be in despair, be
utterly discouraged.

เสร็จสิ้นกันไปที sèd′sîn′-kanpajthii↓ "That's the
end of that!" (expression of relief).

หมดสิ้น mòd′sîn′ V to be exhausted, used up, spent.

สืบ sìb′ Nm, C com. ten. →Cf. ทศ eleg.

นายสืบ. See entries below.

o จ่านายสิบ câa′naajsìb′ N 1. sergeant major.
T 2. Sergeant Major --.

o นายสิบตรี (นาย,คน) naajsìb′trii′ (naaj′, khon′)
N 1. private first class. T 2. Private --.

o นายสิบโท (นาย,คน) naajsìb′thoo′ (naaj′, khon′)
N 1. corporal. T 2. Corporal --.

o นายสิบเอก (นาย,คน) naajsìb′?èeg′ (naaj′,
khon′) N 1. sergeant. T 2. Sergeant --.

ยี่สิบ jîisìb′ Nm twenty.

o ยี่สิบเอ็ด jîisìbʔèd′ Nm twenty one.

สามสิบ sǎamsìb′ Nm thirty.

สิบปีที่แล้ว sìbpii′thîiléɛw′ the preceding decade.

สิบสอง sìbsɔ̌ɔŋ′ Nm twelve.

สิบสาม sìbsǎam′ Nm thirteen.

สิบเอ็ด sìbʔèd′ Nm eleven.

สิว (เม็ด) sǐw′ (méd′) N pimple, acne.

สิ่ว (เล่ม,อัน) sìw′ (lêm′,ʔan′) N chisel.

สิวิไลซ์ siwilaj′ V to be civilized. ความ-- civilization. [f. Eng.] →Cf. อารย-,อารยะ.

สี ๑ (สี) sǐi′ (sǐi′) N 1. color. 2. dye.

ทาสี thaasǐi′ V 1. to paint, cover with paint.
2. to be painted, covered with paint.

ไฟสี fajsǐi′ N colored lights.

ระบายสี rabaaj′sǐi′ V to color, paint (a picture
or drawing).

สีขาว sǐikhǎaw′ N 1. white. V 2. to be white.
→Also 2. ขาว.

สีเขียว sǐikhǐaw′ N 1. green. V 2. to be green.
→Also 2. เขียว.

สีไข่ไก่ sǐikhàjkàj′ N 1. eggshell color, cream
color. V 2. to be cream-colored.

สีคราม sǐikhraam′ N 1. the color indigo. V 2.
to be indigo-colored.

สีคล้ำ sǐikhlám′ N 1. a dark color. V 2. to be
dark (in color). →Also 2. คล้ำ.

o ผิวสีคล้ำ phǐw′sǐikhlám′ V to be swarthy,
dark-complexioned.

สีชมพู sǐichomphuu′ N 1. pink. V 2. to be pink.

สีดำ sǐidam′ N 1. black. V 2. to be black.
→Also 2. ดำ.

สีดำแดง sǐidamdɛɛŋ′ N 1. red-tinged black, reddish black. V 2. to be reddish black. →Also
2. ดำแดง.

สีแดง sǐidɛɛŋ′ N 1. red. V 2. to be red. →Also
2. แดง.

o สีแดงเข้ม sǐidɛɛŋ′khêm′ deep red.

o สีแดงแจ็ด sǐidɛɛŋ′chéd′ bright red.

สีตก sǐitòg′ 1. the colors fade. V 2. to have
colors that fade.

o สีไม่ตก sǐi′mâjtòg′ 1. the colors are fast.
V 2. to be colorfast. →Compare the following.

o สีชะนิดไม่ตก sǐi′-chaníd′mâjtòg′ fast colors.

สีเทา sǐithaw′ N 1. gray. V 2. to be gray.
→Also 2. เทา.

สีน้ำเงิน sǐinámŋən′ N 1. blue. V 2. to be blue.

สีน้ำตาล sǐinámtaan′ N 1. brown. V 2. to be
brown.

สีฟ้า sǐifáa′ N 1. sky-blue. V 2. to be sky-blue,
light blue, pastel blue.

สีม่วง sǐimûaŋ′ N 1. purple. V 2. to be purple.
→Also 2. ม่วง in some contexts.

สีย้อมผ้า sǐi′jɔ́ɔmphâa′ N dye (for fabric).

สีเลือดหมู sǐilɯ̂admǔu′ N 1. dark red, maroon.
V 2. to be dark red, maroon-colored.

สีโศก sǐisòog′ N 1. chartreuse. V 2. to be
chartreuse-colored.

สีสด sǐisòd′ bright colors.

สีส้ม sǐisôm′ N 1. orange. V 2. to be orange.

สีสวาด sǐisawàad′ N 1. bluish gray. V 2. to
be bluish gray.

o แมวสีสวาด (ตัว) mɛɛw′sǐisawàad′ (tua′) a
bluish gray cat native to Thailand.

สีสัน sǐi′sǎn′ N color.

สีแสด sǐisɛ̀ɛd′ N 1. red-orange. V 2. to be
red-orange.

สีหน้า sǐinâa′ N facial expression.

o ฝืนสีหน้า fɯ̌ɯn′sǐinâa′ to force oneself to assume
a certain facial expression.

o มีสีหน้าสลด miisǐinâa′salòd′ to have a sad facial
expression, to look sad.

สีหม่น sǐimòn′ N 1. dull color, gray. V 2. to be
dull-colored, gray.

สีเหลือง sǐilɯ̌aŋ′ N 1. yellow. V 2. to be yellow.
→Also 2. เหลือง.

สี ๒ sǐi′ V 1. to rub across, rub against. 2. to
scrub; to brush (the teeth). 3. to mill (grain).

ขัดสี khàd′sǐi′ V 1. to scrub, scour. 2. to polish.
การ-- friction; abrasion.

โรงสี (โรง) rooŋsǐi′ (rooŋ′) N rice mill.

สีซอ sǐisɔɔ′ V to play a stringed instrument
(with a bow).

สีฟัน sǐifan′ V to brush the teeth.

o แปรงสีฟัน (อัน) prɛɛŋsǐifan′ (ʔan′) N toothbrush.

o ยาสีฟัน jaasǐifan′ N tooth paste, dentifrice.

เสียดสี sìadsǐi′ V 1. to rub (against). 2. to sneer,

be sarcastic. 3. to satirize.

สี่ ๓ in บัดสี bàdsǐi′ V 1. to feel ashamed, be ashamed. 2. to be shameful, disgraceful.

สี่ ๔ in สี่ข้าง (ข้าง) sǐikhâaŋ′ (khâaŋ′) N side (of the body).

สี่ ๕ in สี่ผึ้ง sǐiphɣ̂ŋ′ N resinous substance (as used in lip balm). →Dist. ขี้ผึ้ง.

สี่ ๖ in สี่เสียด sǐisìad′ N cutch, catechu. ต้น-- acacia catechu and similar trees.

สี่ sìi′ Nm c o m. four. →Cf. จัตวา.

ลี่กั๊ก (แห่ง) sìikág′ (hὲŋ′) N crossroads.

สี่เท้า sìitháaw′ c o m. four-legged, quadruped. →Syn. จตุบาท lit.,eleg.

สี่แยก (แห่ง) sìijὲɛg′ (hὲŋ′) N intersection where four streets meet (or, in the Thai idiom, where they part).

สี่สิบ sìisìb′ Nm forty.

สี่เหลี่ยม sìilìam′ quadrilateral.

o รูปสี่เหลี่ยม (รูป) rûubsìilìam′ (rûub′) N quadrilateral.

o สี่เหลี่ยมคางหมู (รูป) sìilìam′khaaŋmǔu′ (rûub′) N trapezoid.

o สี่เหลี่ยมด้านขนาน (รูป) sìilìam′dâankhanǎan′ (rûub′) N parallelogram.

สุ่มสี่สุ่มห้า sùmsìi′sùmhâa′ sV elab. colloq. at random, haphazardly, by guesswork.

สี่ดอ in ข้างสี่ดอ (เชือก,ตัว) cháaŋ′sǐidɔɔ′ (chɣ̂ag′, tua′) N a tuskless bull elephant.

สีห-, -สีห์. Bound form meaning "lion." →Cf. สิงห์.

ราชสีห์ (ตัว) râadchasǐi′ (tua′) N lion, king lion (as in fables).

สึก ๑ sɣg′ V to wear down, be worn down.

สึกหรอ sɣgrɔɔ′ V to wear out, be worn down, worn out. ความ-- wear, depreciation.

สึก ๒ sɣg′ V sacer. to retire from priesthood.

สึก ๓ in รู้สึก rúusɣg′ V to feel.

สืบ ๑ sɣ̀yb′ V to search for the facts, seek clues. นัก-- detective.

สืบถาม sɣ̀ybthǎam′ V to inquire into, make inquiries.

สืบพยาน sɣ̀yb′phajaan′ V to examine a witness.

สืบสวน sɣ̀ybsǔan′ V to investigate.

สืบ ๒ sɣ̀yb′ V to pass on, continue, be passed on.

สืบเชื้อสาย sɣ̀yb′chýasǎaj′ V to continue the line

(as a male descendant).

สืบต่อ sɣ̀yb′tɔɔ′ V to succeed, come after.

สืบเนื่อง sɣ̀ybnɣ̂aŋ′ V 1. to pass on, continue, be passed on. 2. to derive (from), be a consequence (of).

o มีผลสืบเนื่อง(มาจาก) miiphǒn′-sɣ̀ybnɣ̂aŋ′ɔ (maacàagɔ) to be a consequence (of).

o สืบเนื่องลงมา sɣ̀ybnɣ̂aŋ′loŋmaa′ to continue, be handed down (from generation to generation).

สืบไป sɣ̀yb′paj′ 1. further, in continuation. 2. from a given time on, hence: thereafter, hereafter.

สืบพันธุ์ sɣ̀ybphan′ V to reproduce (produce offspring). การ-- propagation, reproduction.

สืบมา sɣ̀yb′maa′ 1. further, in continuation. 2. from then on (toward the focal time), since then.

สือ in หนังสือ (เล่ม) naŋsɣ̌y′* (lêm′) N book.

สื่อ sɣ̀y′ V 1. to take or bring messages (between parties, factions); to transmit. N 2. message carrier; go-between (usually one who acts as a matchmaker); medium of communication or transmission. 3. phys.,elect. conductor.

เป็นสื่อ pensɣ̀y′ to be or act as a conductor, message carrier, go-between (in arranging a match, marriage).

ผู้สื่อข่าว (คน) phûusɣ̀ykhàaw′ (khon′) N newspaper reporter.

พ่อสื่อ (คน) phɔ̂ɔsɣ̀y′ (khon′) N male go-between (usually one who acts as a matchmaker).

แม่สื่อ (คน) mὲɛsɣ̀y′ (khon′) N female go-between (usually one who acts as a matchmaker).

สื่อสาร sɣ̀ysǎan′ V to communicate.

สุก ๑ sùg′ V 1. to be ripe. 2. to be cooked, done (of food). →Ant. ดิบ. →Cf. งอม.

ข้าวสุก khâawsùg′ N cooked rice, boiled rice. →Opp: ข้าวสาร.

ดิบๆสุกๆ dìbdìb′sùgsùg′ not well-cooked, halfcooked. →Also สุกๆดิบๆ.

น้ำสุก námsùg′ N boiled water. →Also น้ำต้ม. →Opp. น้ำดิบ.

สุกก้า sùg′kàm′ 1. (gold) to be brilliant. 2. (fruit) to be fully ripe.

สุกใส sùgsǎj′ V to be bright, shining, glittering.

o ไข้สุกใส khâj′sùgsǎj′ N eleg. chicken pox.

→Syn. อีสุกอีใส colloq.

สุก ๒ in ผาสุก phǎasùg′ V to be happy.

สุกร (ตัว) sùkɔɔn′ (tua′) N eleg. hog, pig. →Syn. หมู com.

สุข sùg′, sùgɔ, sùgkhaɔ V to be happy, at ease, content. ความ-- happiness, contentment.

  ความสุขสบาย khwaamsùg′sabaaj′ N happiness, well-being.

  ความสุขสวัสดี khwaamsùg′sawàd′dii′ N well-being.

  ทุกข์สุข thúg′sùg′ N sorrow and happiness, the ups and downs of life.

  เป็นสุข pensùg′ V to be happy, content.

  o อยู่เย็นเป็นสุข jùujen′pensùg′ N elab. colloq. to live in happiness, in peace and contentment.

  ไม่มีสุข mâjmiisùg′ V to be unhappy.

  สงบสุข saŋòb′sùg′ V to be peaceful, tranquil.

  สาธารณสุข sǎa′thaaranásùg′ N public health.

  สุขกาย sùgkaaj′ V 1. to be healthy, in good health. 2. to be physically well off. ความ-- physical well-being.

  สุขใจ sùgcaj′ V to be happy.

  สุขภาพ sùgkhaphâab′ N health.

  สุขวิทยา sùg′khawídthajaa′ N hygiene.

  สุขศาลา (แห่ง) sùg′sǎalaa′ (hɛ̀ŋ′) N medical station.

สุขุม sùkhǔm′ V 1. to be gentle, delicate, careful. 2. to be profound, thoughtful.

สุโขทัย sùkhǒo′thaj′ pN Sukhothai, a township in C Thailand. →First capital of Thailand.

สุจริต sùdcarìd′ V to be upright, honest.

สุด sùd′ N 1. the end. V 2. to end, terminate. sV 3. at the extreme; utmost.

  ต่ำสุด tàm′sùd′ to be minimum, the minimum, the lowest.

  ที่สุด thîisùd′ most,-est. →See cross reference under ที่ ๓. →Comp. กว่าเพื่อน.

  o ร้อนที่สุด rɔ́ɔn′thîisùd′ hottest.

  สุดท้อง sùdthɔ́ɔŋ′ last-born, youngest.

  สุดท้าย sùdtháaj′ last, final.

  o ผลสุดท้าย phǒn′sùdtháaj′ 1. final result. 2. at last, finally.

  สุดที่จะคณานานับ sùd′thîi′-cakhananaa′náb′ lit. innumerable, countless.

สุดวิสัย sùd′wísǎj′ V to be impossible to do, be beyond human power. การ-- impossibility.

  o เหตุสุดวิสัย hèed′-sùd′wísǎj′ N unavoidable circumatances, circumstances beyond one's control.

สุดสิ้น sùdsîn′ V to end, expire, terminate.

สุดหล้าฟ้าเขียว sùdlâa′fáakhǐaw′ elab. colloq. very far away, beyond the horizon.

สุดเหวี่ยง sùdwìaŋ′ colloq. to the utmost degree; with all one's might.

สุดเอื้อม sùd?ŷam′ V to be out of reach.

สูงสุด sǔuŋsùd′ 1. to be highest, tallest. 2. to be at (its) highest; to be supreme.

สุทธิ. See entries below.

  กำไรสุทธิ kamraj′sùdthí?′ N net profit.

  ใบสุทธิ (ใบ) bajsùdthí?′ (baj′) N certificate showing level of attainment in school (given when a person leaves school before graduation).

สุนทรพจน์ sǔnthɔɔn′phód′ N eleg. speech.

สุนัข (ตัว) sunág′ (tua′) N eleg. dog. →Syn. หมา com.

  สุนัขจิ้งจอก (ตัว) sunág′cîŋcɔɔg′ (tua′) N eleg. fox. →Also หมาจิ้งจอก com.

  สุนัขป่า (ตัว) sunág′pàa′ (tua′) N eleg. wolf. →Also หมาป่า com.

สุพรรณบุรี suphan′burii′ pN Suphanburi, a township in C Thailand.

สุภาพ suphâab′ V to be polite, genteel.

  สุภาพชน (คน) suphâab′chon′ (khon′) N person(s) of good breeding, decent people.

  สุภาพบุรุษ (คน) suphâab′burùd′ (khon′) N eleg. gentleman.

  สุภาพสตรี (คน) suphâab′sàtrii′ (khon′) N eleg. lady.

  สุภาพอ่อนโยน suphâab′′ʔɔɔnjoon′ V to be gentle and polite.

สุภาษิต (บท) suphaa′sìd′ (bòd′) N proverb. คำ-- (บท) idem. →Comp. ภาษิต.

สุม sǔm′ V 1. to pile up. 2. to be piled up, be in stacks.

  มั่วสุม mûasǔm′ V (people) to assemble, congregate, gather together.

  สุมไฟ sǔmfaj′ V 1. to feed the fire. 2. to pile up wood or straw for a bonfire.

สุ่ม ๑ (ใบ) sùm/ (baj/) N 1. fish trap of bamboo strips. 2. a large framework of bamboo, covered with blankets and used as a sweathouse for mothers after childbirth. 3. short for สุ่มไก่.

สุ่มไก่ sùmkàj/ N dome-shaped chicken coop of bamboo strips, used as a protection for chicks.

สุ่ม ๒ as in สุ่มสี่สุ่มห้า sùmsìi/sùmhâa/ sV elab. colloq. at random, haphazardly, by guesswork.

สุ้ม in สุ้มเสียง sûmsǐaŋ/ N sound, voice, tone.

สุมาตรา in เกาะสุมาตรา kɔ̀ʔ/sumâad/traa/ pN the Island of Sumatra.

สุรา suraa/ N eleg. alcoholic beverage, intoxicating beverage. →Syn. เหล้า com.

คอสุรา (คน) khɔɔ/suraa/ (khon/) N eleg. a person used to drinking, a heavy drinker.

นักดื่มสุรา (คน) nágdỳym/suraa/ (khon/) N eleg. a heavy drinker. →Also นักดื่ม. →Syn. นักเลงเหล้า colloq.

โรคพิษสุรา rôog/phídsuraa/ N alcoholism.

เสพสุรา sèeb/suraa/ V eleg. to drink (liquor, alcohol).

สุราษฎร์ surâad/ pN Surat, short for สุราษฎร์ธานี.

สุราษฎร์ธานี surâad/thaanii/ pN Suratthani, a township in S Thailand.

สุรินทร surin/ pN Surin, a township in NE Thailand.

สุริย-,สุริยะ sùrijaɔ, sùrijá?/ N lit.,eleg. 1. the sun. 2. solar.

ระบบสุริยะ rabòb/sùrijá?/ N the solar system.

สุริยจักรวาล sùrijá?/càgkrawaan/ N the solar system.

สุริยุปราคา sùrijúparaa/khaa/ N solar eclipse.

สุรุ่ยสุร่าย surûj/surâaj/ V to be a spendthrift, to be wasteful.

สุสาน (แห่ง) sù?sǎan/ (hèŋ/) N eleg. cemetery. →Syn. ป่าช้า com.

สุเหร่า (แห่ง) suràw/ (hèŋ/) N mosque.

สุเอส su?èed/ pN Suez. [f. Eng.]

สู ๑ sǔu/ V to be ashamed. →Chiefly in compounds.

อดสู ?òdsǔu/ V eleg. to feel ashamed.

สู ๒ sǔu/ P lit. you (superior or older person sp. to inferior or younger person).

สู่ sùu/ sV directed toward; to, toward, into. NOTE. This word functions as a primary verb in certain combinations, in the sense of "to seek, go

for." See ไปมาหาสู่,สู่ขอ,สู่ชาย,สู่รู้ below.

o เข้ามาสู่จิตใจ khâwmaasùu/cìtdcaj/ to come to (one's) mind.

o จากสวนสู่ตลาด càagsǔan/-sùu/talàad/ from plantation to market.

o นำเงินเข้าสู่จังหวัดเชียงราย namŋən/-khâwsùu/-caŋwàd/chiaŋraaj/ (will) bring money into the township of Chiangrai.

o นำพลไปสู่ชัยชนะ namphon/-pajsùu/chajchaná?/ to lead the troops to victory.

ไปมาหาสู่ pajmaa/hǎasùu/ V to visit, pay visits.

สู่กัน sùu/kan together, sharing (something) mutually.

o เล่าสู่กันฟัง lâwsùu/kanfaŋ/ to tell each other, relate to one another.

o เอามาสู่กันกิน ?awmaasùu/kankin/ to bring (food) and eat (it) together.

สู่ขอ sùu/khɔ̌ɔ/ V to ask for a girl's hand in marriage (usually through an intermediary).

สู่ชาย usually in คบชู้สู่ชาย khóbchúu/-sùu/chaaj/ V (a woman) to have a lover or lovers, have men.

สู่รู้ sùurúu/ V 1. to think one knows it all, knows better. 2. to know more than is good for one. →Syn. 1. อวดรู้. NOTE. This expression is often used chidingly.

สู้ sûu/ V to vie with, oppose (in fighting), fight.

ต่อสู้ tɔ̀ɔsûu/ V com. 1. to resist, stand up against, combat, oppose. 2. to fight, battle. →Syn. ต่อกร lit.

o คู่ต่อสู้ (คน) khûu/tɔ̀ɔsûu/ (khon/) N opponent.

o ปืนต่อสู้อากาศยาน pyyn/-tɔ̀ɔsûu/?aakàad/sajaan/ N anti-aircraft gun. →Abbrev. ป.ต.อ.

ไม่สู้ ๑ mâjsûu/ 1. to give up, withdraw (as from competition). 2. won't fight, won't compete. คน-- weakling, coward.

ไม่สู้ ๒, --จะ mâjsûu/(caɔ) AA not very, not much, not so. →Syn. ไม่ค่อย colloq.

o ไม่สู้...นัก mâjsûu/...nág/ not so very, not exceptionally.

สู้ความ sûukhwaam/ V to fight a lawsuit, legal case.

สู้(...)ไม่ได้ sûu/(...)mâjdâaj/ can't beat, can't match, can't compete (with), can't compare (with).

สู้ยิบตา sûu/-jíb/taa/ V idiom. to fight, resist

until death.

สู้รบ sûuróp′ V to fight, battle.

สูง sǔuŋ′ V to be high, tall. ความ-- altitude,
height, tallness. →Ant. ต่ำ, เตี้ย.

กระโดดสูง kradòod′sǔuŋ′ N high jump.

ต่ำสูง tàm′sǔuŋ′ "high and low." See example.

o ความเหลื่อมล้ำต่ำสูง khwaam′-lỳamlám′tàmɔ
sǔuŋ′ N disparity, inequality.

ป่าสูง (แห่ง) pàasǔuŋ′ (hὲŋ′) N tall forest, esp.
of tall trees as found in the highlands.

ไฝ่สูง fàjsǔuŋ′ V to aim high, aspire (e.g. to
social eminence), be ambitious.

สูงตะเหลนเป็น sǔuŋ′talěenpěen′ to be extremely
tall.

สูงล้ำ sǔuŋ′lám′ to be very high, exceedingly high.

สูงลิบลิ่ว sǔuŋ′líblîw′ to be extremely high.

สูงสุด sǔuŋsùd′ 1. to be highest, tallest. 2. to
be at (its) highest; to be supreme.

o ที่บัญชาการสูงสุด thîibanchaa′kaan′-sǔuŋsùd′
N high command.

สูงอายุ sǔuŋ′ʔaajú?′ V lit. to be old, aged.

o ผู้สูงอายุ (คน) phûusǔuŋ′ʔaajú?′ (khon′) N
lit. an elderly person.

หัวสูง hǔasǔuŋ′ V idiom. to be proud or pretentious beyond one's financial or social status.

อักษรสูง (ตัว) ʔàgsɔ̌ɔnsǔuŋ′ (tua′) N a HIGH
consonant. →See อักษรคู่, p. 613.

สูจิบัตร (แผ่น, เล่ม) sǔucibàd′ (phὲn′, lêm′) N
program (list of performers, pieces to be performed, etc.).

สูญ. See ศูนย์.

สูญญากาศ. See ศูนยากาศ.

สูด sùud′ V to inhale, breathe in, suck in.

สูตร (สูตร) sùud′ (sùud′) N formula.

สูตรคูณ sùudkhuun′ N multiplication table.

เส้นศูนย์สูตร (เส้น) sên′sǔunsùud′ (sên′) N
equator.

สูบ (อัน) sùub′ (ʔan′) V 1. to draw on. 2. to pump.
N 3. pump. 4. cylinder (as in an automobile
engine). C 5. cylinder. เครื่อง-- pump.

กระบอกสูบ (กระบอก) krabɔɔg′sùub′ (krabɔɔg′)
N cylinder (of an engine).

ยาสูบ jaasùub′ N smoking tobacco.

o กล่องยาสูบ (อัน) klɔ̂ŋ′jaasùub′ (ʔan′) N

tobacco pipe.

ลูกสูบ (อัน) lûugsùub′ (ʔan′) N piston.

สูบกล้อง sùubklɔ̂ŋ′ V to smoke a pipe; to puff,
draw on a pipe.

สูบน้ำ (อัน) sùubnáam′ (ʔan′) V 1. to pump water.
N 2. water pump. เครื่อง-- water pump.

สูบบุหรี่ sùub′burìi′ V to smoke a cigar, cigarette.

สูบยา sùubjaa′ V to smoke (tobacco, opium).

เส sěe′ V to be evasive, to equivocate.

พูดเส phûud′sěe′ V to speak or answer evasively.

เสก sèeg′ V to pronounce a magical or religious
formula (as when turning smthg. into smthg.
else, or when consecrating smthg.).

เสงี่ยม as in สงบเสงี่ยม saŋòb′saŋìam′ V to be
quiet, modest, polite, well-behaved.

เสด็จ sadèd′ V roy. to go. →Often combined with
other words of motion, both royal and common.

เสด็จขึ้นครองราชสมบัติ sadèd′-khŷnkhrɔɔŋ′râadɔ
chasǒmbàd′ V roy. to begin one's reign.

เสด็จเข้าสู่ปรินิพพาน sadèd′-khâwsùu′paríníbɔ
phaan′ V roy. (Buddha) to die without rebirth.

เสด็จพระราชดำเนิน sadèd′-phrárâad′chadamɔ
nəən′ V roy. to go, proceed, travel.

เสด็จมา sadèd′maa′ V roy. to come.

เสด็จสมภพ sadèd′sǒmphób′ V roy. to be born.

เสด็จสวรรคต sadèd′sawǎnkhód′ V roy. to die.

เสถียรภาพ sathĭan′raphâab′ N eleg. stability.

เสน in ลิงเสน (ตัว) liŋsěen′ (tua′) N rufous
monkey, stump-tailed monkey.

เส้น (เส้น) sên′*(sên′) N 1. line, strand. C 2.
clf. for strands of hair, thread; for string, wire,
bracelets, automobile tires, etc. →Dist. 1. สาย.

ขีดเส้นใต้ khìid′sêntâaj′ to underline, underscore.

คงเส้นคงวา khoŋsên′khoŋwaa′ V idiom. to be
consistent.

จี้เส้น cîi′sên′ V slang to make someone
laugh; to provoke laughter.

จี้(ให้)ถูกเส้น cîi′-(hâj)thùug′sên′ fig., colloq.
to hit the right spot, touch the right chord (for
successfully evoking a desired response).

ถูกเส้นกัน thùugsên′kan′ to get along well (with
one another) because of compatibility in behavior,
character and personality.

ยาเส้น jaasên′ N prepared tobacco, pipe tobacco.

วุ้นเส้น wúnsên′ N bean thread, bean vermicelli.

เส้นขนาน (เส้น, คู่) sên′khanǎn N 1. a parallel line (sên′ for individual lines; khûu′ for pairs). 2. geog. a parallel of latitude.

เส้นด้าย (เส้น) sêndâaj′ (sên′) N cotton string, cotton thread.

เส้นดิ่ง (เส้น) sêndìŋ′ (sên′) N vertical line.

เส้นทาง (สาย) sênthaaŋ′ (sǎaj′) N line, way, course, direction.

เส้นประ (เส้น) sênprà?′ (sên′) N broken line, dotted line.

เส้นประสาท (เส้น) sên′prasàad′ (sên′) N a nerve.

o โรคเส้นประสาท rôog′sênprasàad′ N 1. a nervous disorder; neurosis. 2. nervous breakdown.

เส้นผ่าศูนย์กลาง (เส้น) sênphàa′sǔunklaaŋ′ (sên′) N diameter.

เส้นใย (เส้น) sênjaj′ (sên′) N fiber, filament.

เส้นระดับ (เส้น) sên′radàb′ (sên′) N horizontal line.

เส้นรุ้ง (เส้น) sênrúŋ′ (sên′) N geog. latitude.

เส้นโลหิต (เส้น) sên′loohìd′ (sên′) N blood-vessel. →Dist. สายโลหิต.

o เส้นโลหิตดำ sên′-loohìd′dam′ N vein.

o เส้นโลหิตแดง sên′-loohìd′dɛɛŋ′ N artery.

เส้นแวง (เส้น) sênwɛɛŋ′ (sên′) N longitude.

เส้นคูนย์สูตร (เส้น) sên′sǔunsùud′ (sên′) N equator.

เส้นเสีย sên′sǐa′ V colloq. to be nervous, upset.

เส้นเสียง sênsǐaŋ′ N vocal cords. →Also สายเสียง.

เส้นไหม (เส้น) sênmǎj′ (sên′) N silk thread.

เสน่ห์ sanèe′ N charm, glamour, attraction.

เป็นเสน่ห์ pensanèe′ V to be charming, attractive.

มีเสน่ห์ miisanèe′ V to have charm; to be charming, attractive.

เสนอ sanɔ̌ɔ′ V 1. to submit, present a proposal; to propose, propound. 2. colloq. to tattle, tell on someone. ผู้-- affirmative speaker; one who makes a motion or proposal.

ขอประทานเสนอ khɔ̌ɔprathaan′sanɔ̌ɔ′ eleg. def. (I) respectfully submit (this matter for your consideration). →Used especially in official correspondence.

ข้อเสนอ (ข้อ) khɔ̌ɔsanɔ̌ɔ′ (khɔ̌ɔ′) N proposal, offer, proposition.

ฝ่ายเสนอ fàajsanɔ̌ɔ′ N affirmative side (in a debate).

พิจารณาเสนอ phícaaranaa′sanɔ̌ɔ′ V to consider proposing, consider recommending.

เสนอข่าว sanɔ̌ɔ′khàaw′ to present the news.

เสนอขึ้น sanɔ̌ɔ′khŷn′ to propose, bring up.

เสนาธิการ (นาย, คน) sěenaa′thíkaan′ (naaj′, khon′) N milit. chief of staff.

เสนาธิการทหารผสม sěenaa′thíkaan′-thahǎan′= phasǒm′ N Joint Chiefs of Staff.

เสนาบดี (นาย, คน) sěenaa′bɔdii′ (naaj′, khon′) N obs. minister (of the government). Used before the revolution of 1932 (B. E. 2475).

เสนาะ sanɔ̌?′ V eleg. to be melodious, pleasant (to hear). →Syn. เพราะ.

เสบียง sabiaŋ′ N food supplies, provisions. →Also สะเบียง.

รถเสบียง (คัน) ród′sabiaŋ′ (khan′) N diner, dining-car.

เสบียงกรัง sabiaŋ′kraŋ′ N dried food supply.

เสพ, เสพย์ sèeb′ V eleg. to consume. →Syn. See กิน com.

ยาเสพติด jaa′sèebtìd′ N habit-forming drug, narcotic.

เสพสุรา sèeb′suraa′ V eleg. to drink liquor, alcohol.

เสเพล sěephlee′ sV dissolute, licentious, unrestrained by custom, law, or morality. คน-- a bum, dissolute person.

เสมหะ sěemhà?′ N eleg. 1. phlegm. 2. sputum. →Syn. 1. เสลด com.

เสมอ samɔ̌ɔ′ V 1. to be even, level, equal. sV 2. always, all the time, constantly. →Syn. 1. See เท่า.

ใจเสมอ caj′samɔ̌ɔ′ V to be impartial.

สม่ำเสมอ samàm′samɔ̌ɔ′ V to be constant, uniform, regular.

เสมอกัน (1) samɔ̌ɔ′kan; (2) samɔ̌ɔ′kan↓ 1. to be mutually equal, equivalent, even. 2. It's a draw.

เสมอต้นเสมอปลาย samɔ̌ɔ′tôn′-samɔ̌ɔ′plaaj′ V idiom. 1. to be consistent. sV 2. consistently.

เสมอตัว samɔ̌ɔ′tua′ V to break even.

เสมอภาค saměə'phâag' V to be equal (in legal status). ความ-- equality.

เสมอมา saměə'maa' constantly, regularly.

เสมอเหมือน saměə'mўan' V 1. to be equal and comparable (to). 2. to be just like, as if.

เสมียน (คน) samĭan' (khon') N clerk, office worker.

เสมียนพนักงาน (คน) samĭan'phanágŋaan' (khon') N employees (in general), clerks and employees.

เสมือน samўan' sV lit. eleg. just like, just the same as, virtually.

เป็นเสมือน pen'samўan' eleg. 1. to be like. 2. as if (it) were.

เสย sěəj' V to thrust, push upward (with a long object).

เสยผม sěəjphŏm' V to run one's fingers back through one's hair.

เสร็จ sèd' V 1. to be finished, ready. sV 2. finished, through (doing something)(for the time being). →Comp. สำเร็จ. →Dist. จบ,สิ้น,หมด.

o อาหารเสร็จแล้ว ʔaahăan'sèdlέεw'↓ The meal is ready.

o ทำงานเสร็จ thamŋaan'sèd' to be finished working, through working.

ใบเสร็จ (ใบ) bajsèd' (baj') N receipt (showing payment has been made).

แล้วเสร็จ lέεw'sèd' V to be finished, completed.

เสร็จธุระ sèd'thurá?' V to be finished with the business at hand.

เสร็จเรื่องกันที sèd'rŷaŋ'-kanthii'↓ Everything is settled. It's all over.

เสร็จศึก sèd'sỳg' the war is over.

เสร็จสรรพ sèd'sàb' V to finish up.

เสร็จสิ้นกันไปที sèd'sîn'-kanpajthii'↓ That's the end of that! (expression of relief).

เหมาเสร็จ măw'sèd' to contract for everything altogether; to buy or sell everything as a whole. →Sometimes best translated simply "altogether." →See also เหมาหมด.

เสริม sěəm' V to supplement, add to.

ส่งเสริม sòŋsěəm' V to enhance, encourage, promote.

เสริมความ sěəmkhwaam' V to exaggerate.

เสรี sěerii' V 1. to be free. N 2. freedom, liberty.

พรรคเสรีมนังคศิลา phág'-sěerii'manaŋ'khásilaa' nN Serimanangkhasila Party, a political party formerly headed by Phibun (Phibul) Songkhram.

เสรีภาพ sěeriiphâab' N freedom, liberty.

o เสรีภาพทางการหนังสือพิมพ์ sěeriiphâab'-thaaŋ⊃ kaan'naŋsўyphim' freedom of the press.

อิสระเสรี ʔìdsarà?'/sěerii' N freedom, liberty.

เสลด salèed' N com. phlegm. →Syn. เสมหะ.

เสวย sawŏəj' V roy. to eat. →Syn. See กิน.

เสวยราชสมบัติ sawŏəj'râadchasŏmbàd' V roy. to reign.

เสอร์ sǝ̌ə'* T Sir --. [f. Eng.]

เสา (ต้น) săw' (tôn') N 1. post, pole, pillar. C 2. clf. for compounds having เสา as initial element.

เสากระโดง (เสา) săwkradooŋ' (săw') N mast.

เสาคอนกรีต (เสา) săw'khɔɔnkrìid' (săw') N a concrete post.

เส้า as in สามเส้า săam'săw' 1. three pillars, supports. 2. having three members, tripartite.

เสาร์. See entries below.

ดาวพระเสาร์ daawphrásăw' N Saturn (the planet). →The names of the major planets are listed under ดาว.

วันเสาร์ wansăw' N Saturday. →Also เสาร์. →The days of the week are listed under วัน.

เสาะ ๑ sɔ̀?' V "to be upset," in the following entries.

ใจเสาะ cajsɔ̀?' V 1. to be afraid to face something unpleasant, feel scared, be unnerved. 2. to be unable to take it (as when teased or annoyed).

เสาะท้อง sɔ̀?'thɔ́ɔŋ' V to be stomach-upsetting; to upset the stomach.

เสาะ ๒ sɔ̀?' V to look for, search for.

เสาะหา sɔ̀?'hăa' idem.

เสือบสาน in กำเริบเสิบสาน kamrə̀əb'sə̀əbsăan', q.v. (เสิบ is used to provide a rhyme for - เริบ).

เสีย (1-3) sĭa', sĭa; (4) sía, sá V 1. to lose (beyond recovery, as money, one's estate, part of one's body). 2. to waste, pay out (money), lose (time). 3. to break down, get out of order; to get spoiled, be spoiled. sV 4. sec. vb. indicating a hortative or imperative, the completive or intensification; often best untranslated in English; see examples below. →In mng. 4 sometimes spelled ปะ reflecting the pronunciation sá.

o กิน(...)เสีย kin′(...)sĭa↓, -sá↓ Eat (it)! Go ahead and eat (it)!

o ขอเสียที khɔ̌ɔ′sĭathii′ Please don't, just this once! (requesting that something be stopped).

o เกลียดเสียจริงๆ klìad′sĭaciŋciŋ↓ (I) really hate (it). (I) hate (it) so terribly much.

o ทิ้ง(...)เสีย thíŋ′(...)sĭa to throw (something) away.

ของเสีย,ของเสียๆ khɔ̌ɔŋ′sĭa′, khɔ̌ɔŋ′sĭasĭa′ N waste matter, things that are bad, not usable, deteriorated, worn out, damaged.

ขาดเสียมิได้ khàad′sĭamídâaj′ to be indispensable.

ฆ่า(...)เสีย khâa′(...)sĭa to kill, do away with.

ใจเสีย caj′sĭa′ V to lose heart, be disheartened.

ช้าไปเสียแล้ว cháa′pajsĭalέεw↓ It is too late.

ได้เสีย dâaj′sĭa′ 1. to gain and lose, gain and spend. 2. to be common-law husband and wife. →See cross reference.

ตัด(...)เสีย tàd′(...)sĭa to cut (it) off, sever.

ถอด(...)เสีย thɔ̀ɔd′(...)sĭa to take off, remove.

ท้องเสีย thɔ́ɔŋsĭa′ 1. to have a disorder of the digestive tract, of the bowels; to have diarrhea. N 2. a disorder of the digestive tract, of the bowels; diarrhea. →Comp. ท้องเดิน.

ทำไม่รู้เสีย tham′mâjrúu′-sĭa to pretend ignorance.

ทำ(...)เสีย tham(...)sĭa′ to spoil (something).

ทิ้ง(...)เสีย thíŋ′(...)sĭa to throw (something) away. →Dist. ทิ้ง(...)ไว้.

นิสัยเสีย nísăj′sĭa′ N a bad habit.

บัตรเสีย (ใบ) bàd′sĭa′ (baj′) N void ballot.

ฟันเสีย (ซี่) fansĭa′ (sîi′) N decayed teeth.

ฟาด(...)เสีย fâad′(...)sĭa to smash up, bash in.

เมินเสียเถอะ mǝǝn′sĭathǝʔ↑↓ Not a chance! Never!

ไม่เสียไม่ได้ mâjsĭa′mâjdâaj′ to break even, neither lose or gain.

เย็บ(...)เสีย jéb′(...)sĭa to sew up.

ลมเสีย lom′sĭa′ V idiom. to be in a bad mood.

ลืมเสียเถิด lyym′sĭathǝ̀ǝd↓ Forget it! Let's forget it!

ศูนย์เสีย sŭun′sĭa′ V 1. to disappear, be lost. 2. to lose (something).

สั่งเสีย sàŋ′sĭa′ V to give one's parting instructions.

เล่นเสีย sênsĭa′ V colloq. to be nervous, upset.

เสียกล sĭa′kon′ V to be tricked, outsmarted.

เสียก่อน sĭakɔ̀ɔn′ beforehand, first.

เสียกิริยา sĭa′kirijaa′ V to show bad manners, be unmannerly, impolite.

เสียคน sĭa′khon′ V to lose one's integrity, become a bad person.

เสียเงิน sĭaŋǝn′ V to spend, use up money.

เสียจรรยา sĭa′canjaa′ V to go against etiquette; to violate the rules of proper conduct, ethics, good manners.

เสียจริง sĭaciŋ′ colloq. really, so very (much).

o เกลียดเสียจริง klìad′sĭaciŋ′ to really hate it, hate it so very much.

เสียจริต sĭa′carìd′ V 1. to lose one's mind. 2. to be insane. คน-- insane person.

เสียใจ sĭacaj′ V to be sorry, to regret. ความ-- sorrow, regret.

o น่าเสียใจ nâa′sĭacaj′ V to be regrettable.

เสียฉิบ sĭachíb′ too (e.g. easily). Here ฉิบ intensifies the completive sense of เสีย.

o ให้เขากินเสียฉิบ hâj′kháwkin′sĭachíb′↓ (We) let him win too easily!

เสียชีวิต sĭa′chiiwíd′ V lit. to lose one's life, to die.

เสียชื่อ sĭachŷy′ V to have a bad reputation, to lose one's (its) reputation or fame.

เสียดาย sĭadaaj′ V 1. to feel sorry (about something lost, about a lost opportunity); to deplore, regret. 2. to be regrettable.

o น่าเสียดาย (1) nâa′sĭadaaj′; (2) nâa′sĭadaaj′↓ V 1. to be regrettable. 2. What a pity! What a shame! It's too bad!

เสียตัว sĭatua′ V (a woman) to lose (her) virginity (by premarital relations).

เสียแต่ sĭa′tεɛ, sĭa′taɔ only, but (introducing an adverse reservation, restriction).

เสียทรง sĭasoŋ′ V 1. to lose one's shape, lose its shape. 2. to spoil the shape, the look (of something).

เสียที sĭa′thii′ V to lose the advantage to one's opponent. →Ant. ได้ที.

เสียน้ำใจ sĭa′námcaj′ V to lose heart, be discouraged, be disheartened.

เสียเปรียบ sĭaprìab′ V to be handicapped.
→Ant. ได้เปรียบ.

เสียเปล่า (1) sĭa′plàaw′; (2) sĭaplàaw′ 1. to lose
in vain, simply lose, simply waste. 2. uselessly, for nothing.

เสียภาษี sĭa′phaasĭi′ V to pay taxes. ผู้--
taxpayer.

เสียราคา sĭa′raakhaa′ V to go down in price,
decrease in value.

เสียรู้ sĭarúu′ V to be outwitted.

เสียเวลา sĭaweelaa′ V to lose time, waste time,
use up time.

เสียสละ sĭasalà?′ V to make a sacrifice.

เสียสัญญา sĭasănjaa′ V to break a promise.

เสียสัตย์ sĭasàd′ V to be untrue (to).

เสียหน้า sĭa′nâa′ V to lose face.

เสียหลัก sĭalàg′ V to lose one's footing, foothold.

เสียหาย sĭahăaj′ V 1. to lose (beyond recovery),
sustain a loss of. 2. to be damaged. 3. to be
harmful, detrimental. ความ-- damage, loss,
harm, detriment.

o ของเสียหาย khɔ̌ɔŋ′sĭahăaj′ N 1. damaged
things. 2. things that are bad or objectionable
to do.

o ค่าเสียหาย khâa′sĭahăaj′ N the damages, the
loss, the amount of the loss.

o ทำ(...)เสียหาย tham′(...)sĭahăaj′ V to
spoil, damage, ruin (something).

o ผลเสียหาย phŏn′sĭahăaj′ N damage; damaging
result.

หน้าเสีย nâa′sĭa′ V to look disappointed.

หัวเสีย hŭasĭa′ V to lose one's temper, lose
one's head, be in a bad temper.

อย่างเสียไม่ได้ jàaŋsĭa′mâjdâaj′ against one's
will, against one's better judgment (giving in
to someone's pleading).

เสียง (เสียง) sĭaŋ′ (sĭaŋ′) N 1. sound, (voice)
noise, tone. 2. gram. tone (of the Thai spoken
language). →Comp. สำเนียง.

o เสียงสามัญ sĭaŋ′săaman′ N the mid tone (of
the Thai spoken language).

กระจายเสียง kracaajsĭaŋ′ V to broadcast (by
radio).

o วิทยุกระจายเสียง wídthajú?′kracaajsĭaŋ′ N

radio broadcast.

ขยายเสียง khajăaj′sĭaŋ′ V to amplify (sound).
เครื่อง-- amplifier.

ขึ้นเสียง khŷnsĭaŋ′ V colloq. to raise one's
voice (as when provoked).

คลื่นเสียง (ลูก) khlŷynsĭaŋ′ (lûug′) N sound wave.

จานเสียง (แผ่น) caansĭaŋ′ (phèn′) N (phonograph) record.

ชื่อเสียง chŷysĭaŋ′ N fame, reputation, name.

o มีชื่อเสียง miichŷysĭaŋ′ V to be famous, famed.

ชาวเสียง saawsĭaŋ′ V to sound out (people's)
views or opinions (on an issue).

ท่อเสียง thɔ̀ɔsĭaŋ′ N vocal cords.

ทำเสียงดัง tham′sĭaŋdaŋ′ to make a loud noise,
to be noisy.

น้ำเสียง námsĭaŋ′ N tone of voice.

เบ่งเสียง bèŋ′sĭaŋ′ V to shout, talk loud; to
increase the volume of voice (as in singing).

ปากเสียง pàag′sĭaŋ′ N spokesman, mouthpiece.

o เป็นปากเสียง penpàag′sĭaŋ′ V 1. to be a
spokesman, a mouthpiece (for). 2. eleg. to
have an argument (with).

เป็นเสียงเดียวกัน pensĭaŋ′diawkan′ in one voice,
in unison.

เปล่งเสียง plèŋsĭaŋ′ V to utter, announce.

แผดเสียง phɛ̀ɛdsĭaŋ′ V to roar, scream, yell,
sing at the top of one's voice.

แผ่นเสียง (แผ่น) phɛ̀nsĭaŋ′ (phèn′) N (phonograph) record.

มีส่วนมีเสียง miisùan′miisĭaŋ′ V elab. colloq.
to have a share, a part, a voice (in).

แว่วเสียง wɛ̂w′sĭaŋ′ V to hear indistinctly.

สายเสียง săjsĭaŋ′ N vocal cords. →Also เส้นเสียง.

สุ้มเสียง sûmsĭaŋ′ N sound, voice, tone.

เส้นเสียง sênsĭaŋ′ N vocal cords.

เสียงข้างมาก sĭaŋ′khâaŋmâag′ N the majority
vote.

เสียงเขียว sĭaŋ′khĭaw′ V 1. to have an angry
voice. sV 2. in an angry voice.

เสียงแข็ง sĭaŋkhɛ̌ŋ′ V to be stern, firm, confident
(in one's manner of speaking).

เสียงจัตวา sĭaŋcàdtawaa′ N the rising tone (of
the Thai spoken language).

เสียงตรี sĭaŋtrii′ N the high tone (of the Thai

spoken language).

เสียงโท sǐaŋthoo′ N the falling tone (of the Thai spoken language). →Dist. ไม้โท, q.v. under โท.

เสียงฝีเท้า sǐaŋfíitháaw′ N the sound of footsteps.

เสียงพร่า sǐaŋphrâa′ V to have a faltering, indistinct voice.

เสียงเพราะ sǐaŋphrɔ́ʔ′ V to have a pretty voice, a pleasing tone.

เสียงลือ sǐaŋlyy′ N rumor.

เสียงสามัญ sǐaŋ′sǎaman′ N the mid tone (of the Thai spoken language).

เสียงห้าว sǐaŋhâaw′ V to have a deep voice.

เสียงแหบ sǐaŋhὲɛb′ V to have a hoarse, rasping voice.

เสียงเอก sǐaŋʔὲeg′ N the low tone (of the Thai spoken language). →Dist. ไม้เอก. q.v. under เอก.

เสียงฮา sǐaŋhaa′ N sound of laughter.

หาเสียง hǎasǐaŋ′ V to electioneer, campaign, seek votes. การ-- (election) campaign, campaigning.

หางเสียง hǎaŋsǐaŋ′ N the intonation at the end of an utterance, revealing or betraying the speaker's emotion.

หีบเสียง (เครื่อง) hìibsǐaŋ′ (khrŷaŋ′) N phonograph.

ออกเสียง ʔɔ̀ɔgsǐaŋ′ V 1. to voice, give voice to. 2. to pronounce, utter. 3. to pronounce, articulate. 4. to vote. sV 5. aloud.

o บัตรออกเสียง (ใบ) bàd′ʔɔ̀ɔgsǐaŋ′ (baj′) N ballot.

เสี่ยง ๑ sìaŋ′ C piece, part, fraction.

เสี่ยง ๒ sìaŋ′ V to risk, take a chance.

เสี่ยงโปค sìaŋchôog′ V to take a chance, try one's luck.

เสี่ยงทาย sìaŋthaaj′ V 1. to divine, practise divination. 2. to cast lots.

เสี่ยงภัย sìaŋphaj′ V to risk, venture.

เสี่ยงอันตราย sìaŋ′ʔantaraaj′ V to risk danger.

เสียด ๑ sìad′ V to pierce, thrust (into).

เบียดเสียด bìadsìad′ V 1. to be dense, congested, crowded. 2. to jostle, force one's way (into).

เสียดเคล้า sìad′khláw′ V to rub and press (against) (as a cat against the legs).

เสียดท้อง sìadthɔ́ɔŋ′ V to feel a sharp pain in the abdomen.

เสียดแทง sìadthɛɛŋ′ V to pierce, stab, sting.

o เสียดแทงหัวใจ sìadthɛɛŋ′hǔacaj′ V to cut to the quick, sting to the quick (as by sarcastic words).

เสียดสี sìadsǐi′ V 1. to rub (against). 2. to sneer, be sarcastic. 3. to satirize. การ-- abrasion; friction; sarcasm.

o พูดเสียดสี phûud′sìadsǐi′ to speak sarcastically.

เสียด ๒ in สีเสียด sǐislad′ N cutch, catechu.

เสี้ยน (อัน) sîan′ (ʔan′) N splinter, sliver.

เป็นเสี้ยนหนาม pen′sîannǎam′ to be enemies (of the state, of society): "to be splinters and thorns."

เสียบ sìab′ V to pierce, thrust, pin.

เสียม (อัน) sǐam′ (ʔan′) N spade.

เสี้ยม sîam′ V to sharpen to a point.

เสียว sǐaw′ V 1. to get a sharp sudden sensation (painful or pleasurable). 2. to feel a thrill of fear, horror.

เสียวใจ sǐawcaj′ V to feel a thrill of fear, a shiver of fear, horror. อย่าง-- in fear, with a shiver of fear.

เสียวปลาบ sǐaw′plàab′ to get a sharp sudden sensation (painful or pleasurable), to have a sudden piercing surge of sensation.

เสียวไส้ sǐawsâj′ V to feel terrified, horror-stricken.

o น่าเสียวไส้ nâa′sǐawsâj′ V 1. to be dreadful, terrifying. sV 2. in a terrifying manner.

หวาดเสียว wàadsǐaw′ V to feel a thrill of fear, horror; to have chills sent down one's spine.

เสี้ยว sîaw′ C a quarter, one fourth.

เสือ (ตัว,คน) sšǎ′ N 1. member of the tiger family, e.g. tiger, panther, jaguar (tua′). 2. bandit, outlaw (khon′).

แม่เสือ (คน) mɛ̂ɛsšǎ′ (khon′) N a tough woman, esp. one who is given to bawling people out.

ลูกเสือ (ตัว,คน) lûugsšǎ′ N 1. tiger cub (tua′). 2. boy scout (khon′).

เสือโคร่ง (ตัว) sšǎkhrôoŋ′ (tua′) N tiger.

เสือดาว (ตัว) sšǎdaaw′ (tua′) N leopard.

เสื้อดำ (ตัว) sŷadam′ (tua′) N black panther.

เสื้อผู้หญิง (คน) sŷa′phûujǐŋ′ (khon′) N slang wolf, woman-chaser.

หางเสื้อ (อัน) hǎaŋsŷa′ (ʔan′) N rudder, helm, tiller.

อ้ายเสื้อ ʔâjsŷa′ N 1. derog. bandit, outlaw. T 2. title placed before the first name of a bandit or outlaw.

เสื่อ (ผืน) sŷa′ (phɯ̌yn′) N mat.

ล้มหมอนนอนเสื่อ lómmɔ̌ɔn′nɔɔnsŷa′ V elab. colloq. to fall sick, be brought to bed because of illness.

เลี้ยงดูปูเสื่อ líaŋduu′puusŷa′ V elab. colloq. to feast.

เสื้อ (ตัว) sŷa′ (tua′) N coat, upper garment.

คอเสื้อ (อัน) khɔɔsŷa′ (ʔan′) N 1. collar (of a shirt, coat, etc.). 2. neck (of a garment).

ตัดเสื้อ tàdsŷa′ V 1. to tailor, make a coat, blouse, dress. 2. to have a coat, blouse, dress made.

o ร้านตัดเสื้อ (ร้าน,แห่ง) ráan′tàdsŷa′ (ráan′, hèŋ′) N tailor shop, dressmaker's.

ผีเสื้อ (ตัว) phǐisŷa′ (tua′) N butterfly.

ไม้แขวนเสื้อ (อัน) májkhwɛ̌ɛnsŷa′ (ʔan′) N coat hanger.

เสื้อกางเกง (ชุด) sŷa′kaaŋkeeŋ′ (chúd′) N 1. suit of clothes (for a man). 2. any ensemble of clothes that includes an upper garment and slacks or pants (e.g. women's blouse and slacks, children's coveralls, pajamas, etc.).

เสื้อคลุม (ตัว) sŷakhlum′ (tua′) N overcoat, topcoat, jacket.

เสื้อชั้นนอก (ตัว) sŷachánnɔ̂ɔg′ (tua′) N coat.

เสื้อชั้นใน (ตัว) sŷachánnaj′ (tua′) N undershirt, man's undergarment; slip, vest, woman's undergarment.

เสื้อเชิ้ต (ตัว) sŷachə́ǝd′ (tua′) N shirt. [เชิ้ต f. Eng.] →Sometimes also -เชิ้ต, -เชิร์ต, -เชิ๊ด.

เสื้อนอก (ตัว) sŷanɔ̂ɔg′ (tua′) N coat, overcoat.

เสื้อผ่าอก (ตัว) sŷa′phàaʔòg′ (tua′) N an upper garment which opens down the front.

เสื้อผ้า (ชิ้น) sŷaphâa′ (chín′) N clothes, clothing.

o ตู้เสื้อผ้า (ตู้) tûu′sŷaphâa′ (tûu′) N wardrobe, bureau.

o ร้านเสื้อผ้า (ร้าน,แห่ง) ráan′sŷaphâa′ (ráan′, hèŋ′) N clothing store.

เสื้อฝน (ตัว) sŷafǒn′ (tua′) N raincoat.

เสือก sŷag′ V 1. to push, give a shove. 2. vulg. to butt in, intrude (as when crashing a party, intruding into a conversation).

เสือกไส sŷagsǎj′ V to drive away, push away.

เสื่อม sŷam′ V to decline, deteriorate, decrease, lessen. ความ-- decline; retrogression. →Syn. โทรม. →Ant. See เจริญ.

เสื่อมเกียรติ sŷamklad′ V to be disgraced, degraded.

เสื่อมค่า sŷamkhâa′ V to devaluate, depreciate. การ-- devaluation, depreciation.

เสื่อมเสียชื่อเสียง sŷamsǐa′chŷysǐaŋ′ V to spoil one's reputation.

แส. See entries below.

เบาะแส bɔ̀ʔ′sɛ̌ɛ′ N inkling, clue, hint, trace.

o รู้เบาะแส rúu′-bɔ̀ʔ′sɛ̌ɛ′ V to have a vague knowledge of, have an inkling about.

แยแส jɛɛsɛ̌ɛ′ V colloq. to pay attention (to), mind, show interest (in).

แส่ sɛ̀ɛ′ V to look for trouble, get involved (in something which is not one's affair).

แส่หาเรื่อง sɛ̀ɛ′hǎarɯ̂aŋ′ V colloq. to take unnecessary risks, to look for trouble.

แส้ ๑ (อัน) sɛ̂ɛ′ (ʔan′) N whip.

แส้ ๒ in เป็นสาวเป็นแส้ pensǎaw′pensɛ̂ɛ′ V to be a young unmarried woman.

แสก sɛ̀ɛg′ N 1. median line. 2. middle. 3. part (of the hair). V 4. to part (the hair). →Dist. 3. ไรผม.

กลางวันแสกๆ klaaŋwan′sɛ̀ɛgsɛ̀ɛg′ in broad daylight, in the very middle of the day.

แสกกลาง sɛ̀ɛgklaaŋ′ V (hair) to be parted in the middle.

แสกหน้า sɛ̀ɛgnâa′ N forehead, esp. the part between the brows.

แสง ๑ sɛ̌ɛŋ′ N ray, beam, light.

โปร่งแสง pròoŋ′sɛ̌ɛŋ′ V to be translucent.

ยอแสง jɔɔ′sɛ̌ɛŋ′ V to be dim, become dim (of sunlight, at dusk).

ล้าแสง (ล้า) lamsɛ̌ɛŋ′ (lam′) N beam of light.

ล่องแสง sɔ̂ŋsɛ̌ɛŋ/ V (a source of light) to shine, emit light. →Dist. ล่องไฟ.

แสงจันทร์ sɛ̌ɛŋcan/ N moonlight.

แสงฉาน sɛ̌ɛŋchǎan/ bright light.

แสงดาว sɛ̌ɛŋdaaw/ N starlight.

แสงเดือน sɛ̌ɛŋdyan/ N eleg. moonlight.

แสงแดด sɛ̌ɛŋdɛ̀ɛd/ N sunlight.

แสงตะวัน sɛ̌ɛŋ/tawan/ N eleg. sunlight.

แสงพระอาทิตย์ sɛ̌ɛŋ/phráʔaathíd/ N sunlight.

แสงพร่า sɛ̌ɛŋphrâa/ N diffused light.

แสงไฟ sɛ̌ɛŋfaj/ N 1. light. 2. firelight.

o พรางแสงไฟ phraaŋ/sɛ̌ɛŋfaj/ V to have a blackout.

แสงสว่าง sɛ̌ɛŋ/sawàaŋ/ N light.

แสงอรุณ sɛ̌ɛŋ/ʔarun/ N lit., eleg. light at daybreak.

o แสงอรุณขึ้น sɛ̌ɛŋ/ʔarun/-khŷn/ it is dawning, getting lighter; the sun is rising.

แสง ๒ sɛ̌ɛŋ/ N lit., eleg. weapons.

ช่างแสง usually in โรงช่างแสง (โรง) rooŋɔ-châaŋsɛ̌ɛŋ/ (rooŋ/) N arsenal.

แสด in สีแสด sǐisɛ̀ɛd/ N 1. red-orange. V 2. to be red-orange.

แสดง sadɛɛŋ/ V 1. to show, display. 2. to put on a show, to play (act). 3. to be shown. การ-- (see below). เครื่อง-- sign, indicator. ผู้-- (see below). →Comp. ลำแดง.

การแสดง (อย่าง, รอบ) kaansadɛɛŋ/ N 1. indication, display, show (of respect, emotion, etc.) (jàaŋ/). 2. performance, show, exhibition (as on the stage, at a fair) (rɔ̂ɔb/).

o การแสดงเบ็ดเตล็ด kaansadɛɛŋ/bèdtalèd/ N skit, short revue.

o ผู้กำกับการแสดง (คน) phûukamkàb/kaansaɔ-dɛɛŋ/ (khon/) N stage director, film director.

การแสดงออก kaansadɛɛŋ/ʔɔ̀ɔg/ N expression (act of expressing).

ตัวแสดง (ตัว) tuasadɛɛŋ/ (tua/) N 1. player, actor. 2. role, part (in a play).

ผู้แสดง (คน) phûusadɛɛŋ/ (khon/) N eleg. 1. player, performer. 2. the cast.

o รายนามผู้แสดง raajnaam/phûusadɛɛŋ/ N eleg. the cast (in a performance), list of players.

แสดงกล sadɛɛŋkon/ V eleg. to do tricks, perform stunts. →Syn. เล่นกล com.

แสดงความยินดี sadɛɛŋ/-khwaam/jindii/ to congratulate.

แสดงปาฐกถา sadɛɛŋ/paathàkathǎa/ V eleg. to lecture, give a lecture.

แสดงละคร sadɛɛŋ/lakhɔɔn/ V eleg. to act, play, put on an act, a play. นัก-- actor, actress.

แสตมป์ (ดวง) satɛm/*(duaŋ/) N (postage) stamp. [f. Eng.]

ปิดแสตมป์ pìd/satɛm/ to put, stick, affix, paste a stamp (on an envelope, in an album).

อากรแสตมป์ (ดวง) ʔaakɔɔn/satɛm/ (duaŋ/) N an official revenue stamp affixed to documents to indicate legality.

แสน sɛ̌ɛn/ Nm 1. hundred thousand. C 2. idem. AA 3. greatly, extremely, awfully.

ไกลแสนไกล klaj/sɛ̌ɛnklaj/ V to be very far away.

แสนไกล sɛ̌ɛn/klaj/ V to be very far away.

แสนจะ sɛ̌ɛn/caɔ AA greatly, extremely, awfully.

แสนที่จะ sɛ̌ɛn/thîicaɔ greatly, extremely, frightfully.

แสบ sɛ̀ɛb/ V to smart, sting.

แสม. See entries below.

ปูแสม (ตัว) puu/samɛ̌ɛ/ (tua/) N small saltwater crab.

ลิงแสม (ตัว) liŋ/samɛ̌ɛ/ (tua/) N crab-eating monkey.

แสร้ง sɛ̂ɛŋ/ V eleg. to pretend.

แสลง salɛɛŋ/ V to be harmful, irritating (to the body), bad for the health.

แสวง sawɛ̌ɛŋ/ V to search, seek, pursue.

แสวงหา sawɛ̌ɛŋ/hǎa/ V to search, look for.

โส. See โสโครก, โสมม.

โสโครก sǒokhrôog/ V to be dirty, filthy.

โสด ๑ sòod/ N single, unmarried state. →Chiefly in compounds. คน-- single person, unmarried person. ชาย-- single, man, unmarried man; bachelor.

เป็นโสด pensòod/ to be single, unmarried.

หญิงโสด (คน) jĭŋsòod/ (khon/) N single woman, unmarried woman, spinster.

โสด ๒ sòod/ C 1. case, instance. 2. section, part.

โสต sòod/ N eleg. ear. →Syn. หู com.

โสตประสาท sòod/prasàad/ N 1. sense of hearing.

2. auditory nerve.

o บาดโสตประสาท bàad'-sòod'prasàad' V to offend one's sense of hearing.

โสเภณี (คน) sŏopheenii' (khon') N eleg. prostitute. →Syn. ดอกทอง colloq.

ช่องโสเภณี (คน) sɔ̂ŋ'sŏopheenii' (sɔ̂ŋ') N brothel.

นครโสเภณี (คน) nakhɔɔn'sŏopheenii' (khon') N eleg. courtesan, prostitute.

หญิงโสเภณี (คน) jǐŋ'sŏopheenii' (khon') N eleg. prostitute.

โสมม sŏomom' V eleg. 1. to be filthy. 2. to be indecent. ความ-- filthiness; indecency.

โสร่ง (ตัว) saroŋ' (tua') N sarong. [f. Malay]

โสหุ้ย sŏohûj' N colloq. expenses; overhead. [f. Chin.]

ใส sǎj' V to be clear, transparent.

แจ่มใส cɛ̀msǎj' V 1. (the weather) to be clear, fine. 2. to be bright, cheerful (in appearance, in disposition).

โปร่งใส pròoŋ'sǎj' V to be transparent.

ผ่องใส phɔ̀ŋsǎj' V 1. to be clean, pure, unclouded (as of the mind, heart). 2. to be happy, gay, cheerful (as of the face).

เลื่อมใส lŷamsǎj' V 1. to be thoroughly convinced, be impressed, believe whole-heartedly. 2. to have faith in. →Syn. ศรัทธา, เชื่อถือ.

สดใส sòdsǎj' V to be clear (as of the weather), fresh, cheerful.

สุกใส sùgsǎj' V to be bright, shining, glittering. →See cross reference.

ใสแจ๋ว sǎjcɛ̌w' to be very clear, very transparent.

ใส่ sàj' V 1. to put in, insert. 2. to put on, wear (clothing). 3. to contain, hold. sV 4. to, toward, at (see ex. below). →Syn. 2. สวม eleg.

o พูดใส่หน้า phûud'sàjnâa' to say (it) right to one's face.

กาแฟใส่นม kaafɛɛ'sàjnom' N coffee with cream.

เข้าใส่ khâwsàj' sV at, toward.

o พุ่งเข้าใส่ phûŋ'khâwsàj' 1. to throw, hurl at. 2. to move swiftly toward.

โถใส่แป้ง (ใบ, โถ) thŏo'sàjpɛ̂ɛŋ' (baj', thŏo') N powder jar.

น้ำมันใส่ผม námman'sàjphŏm' N hair oil.

เย็บ...ใส่ jébɔ...sàj' V to sew or make up (something) to wear.

ใส่กระดุม sàjkradum' V to button.

ใส่กลอน sàjklɔɔn' V to bolt, latch (a door, window).

ใส่กุญแจ sàjkuncɛɛ' V to lock.

ใส่ความ sàjkhwaam' V to calumniate, make false accusations.

ใส่ใจ sàjcaj' V to be attentive.

ใส่บาตร sàjbàad' V to give food to a priest, put food into a priest's bowl.

ใส่ร้าย sàjráaj' V to smear, calumniate, make false and defamatory accusations.

ใส่เสื้อ sàjsŷa' V to put on a coat, jacket, blouse, dress, etc.

ใส่(...)ให้เต็ม sàj'(...)hâjtem' V to fill.

เอาใจใส่ ʔawcajsàj' V 1. to pay attention. 2. to take an interest (in), put one's heart (into).

ไส sǎj' V to push, shove.

กบไสไม้ (ตัว) kòb'sǎjmáaj' (tua') N plane (carpenter's tool).

ผลักไส phlàg'sǎj' V to push away.

เสือกไส sŷagsǎj' V to drive away, push away.

ไสกบ sǎjkòb' V to plane.

ไส้ (เส้น, ขด) sâj' (sên', khòd') N 1. intestines. 2. the inside part, filling (as in a pastry, eggroll, fountain pen, etc.).

o ไส้ขนม sâjkhanŏm' N pastry filling.

คลื่นไส้ khlŷynsâj', khlŷyn'sâj' V 1. to feel nauseated (literally). 2. colloq. to feel a loathing, repugnance, disgust; to feel revolted, nauseated.

o น่าคลื่นไส้ nâakhlŷyn'sâj' V (something) to make one's stomach turn; to be nauseating, loathsome.

ลำไส้ (ขด) lamsâj' (khòd') N bowel, intestine.

เสียวไส้ sǐawsâj' V to feel terrified, horror-stricken.

ไส้กรอก (เส้น) sâjkrɔ̀ɔg' (sên') N sausage.

ไส้เดือน (ตัว) sâjdyan' (tua') N earthworm.

ไส้ติ่ง sâjtìŋ' N appendicitis.

o โรคไส้ติ่ง rôog'sâjtìŋ' N com. appendicitis.

o ไส้ติ่งอักเสบ sâjtìŋ'ʔàgsèeb' N eleg. appendicitis. →Also ไส้ติ่งอักเสบ.

ไส้ติ่ง sâjtìŋ' N appendix (body part).

o ไส้ติ่งอักเสบ sâjtìŋ'ʔàgsèeb' N eleg. appendicitis.

ไล้ศึก (คน) sâjsỳg/ (khon/) N traitor; spy (in

wartime).

หมั่นไล้ mànsâj/ V to be disgusted (with someone),

disapprove (of someone) (usually because of some

unwarranted or unreasonable action or attitude).

ไสย as in ไสยศาสตร์ sǎjjasàad/ N the magic art

(as derived from Brahmanism, and dealing esp.

with spells and incantations).

ไสว in สว่างไสว sawàaŋ/sawǎj/ V to shine

brightly all over, be bright with light.

ห

ห hɔ̌ɔ/ HIGH consonant. Pronounced h in initial posi-

tion before vowels; not pronounced in final posi-

tion. It is also placed before sonorants (nasals,

liquids, and semivowels) to convert them into high

consonants; in this event ห is not pronounced.

หก ๑ hòg/ Nm six.

สิบหก sìbhòg/ Nm sixteen.

หกสิบ hògsìb/ Nm sixty.

หกสิบเอ็ด hòg/sìb?èd/ Nm sixty-one.

หก ๒ hòg/ V 1. to spill. 2. to turn over, invert.

กระดานหก (แผ่น) kradaan/hòg/ (phèn/) N see-

saw, teeter-totter. →Syn. ไม้กระดก.

ทำ(...)หก tham(...)hòg/ to spill (something).

หกคะเมน hògkhameen/ V 1. to turn a somersault.

2. to tumble, fall down.

หกรด hògród/ V to spill, be spilled (over some-

thing).

หกล้ม hòglóm/ V to tumble over, fall over.

หัวหกก้นขวิด hǔahòg/kônkhwìd/ sV colloq.

gallivanting about, on the go.

หงส์ (ตัว) hǒŋ/ (tua/) N 1. hansa, the legendary

bird on which Brahma rode. 2. swan.

หงอก ŋɔ̀ɔg/ V to be gray (of hair).

หัวหงอก hǔaŋɔ̀ɔg/ V to have gray hair, be gray-

headed.

หงอน (หงอน,อัน) ŋɔ̌ɔn/ (ŋɔ̌ɔn/,?an/) N comb

(of fowl).

หง่อม ŋɔ̀m/ V to be very old (of people).

หงอย ŋɔ̌j/ V to be lonesome, sad and lonely, sad

and quiet, quiet and subdued.

หงาย ŋǎaj/ V 1. to lie face up, to be in a supine

position. 2. to turn face up, turn right side up.

เดือนหงาย dyanŋǎaj/ waxing moon. →Ant.

เดือนมืด.

ผงะหงาย phaŋà?/ŋǎaj/ 1. to fall over backwards.

2. to draw back suddenly, pull up short, reel back.

ล้มหงาย lómŋǎaj/ V to fall on one's back.

หงิม ŋĭm/ V to be quiet, reserved.

หงึก ๆ ŋỳgŋỳg/ a nodding of the head; with a nod.

พยักหน้าหงึกๆ phajág/nâa/-ŋỳgŋỳg/ to nod the

head up and down, nod the head several times.

หงุดหงิด ŋùdŋìd/ V to be irritable, bad-tempered,

ill-humored, moody.

หญ้า jâa/ N grass.

ดายหญ้า daajjâa/ V 1. to mow excess or unwanted

grass or weeds. 2. to weed.

ทุกหย่อมหญ้า thúgjɔ̀m/jâa/ idiom. everywhere,

all over.

ทุ่งหญ้า (แห่ง) thûŋjâa/ (hèŋ/) N 1. prairie,

grassland. 2. meadow, pasture.

ใบหญ้า (ใบ) bajjâa/ (baj/) N blade of grass.

สนามหญ้า. (สนาม) sanǎamjâa/ (sanǎam/) N

lawn, yard (of house).

หญ้ากก (ต้น) jâakòg/ (tôn/) sedge, rush, reed.

หญ้าคา (ต้น) jâakhaa/ (tôn/) N cogon, a tall, coarse

grass used for thatching (Imperata cylindrica).

หญ้าปากคอก jâa/pàagkhɔ̂ɔg/ " grass (by the barn

door," a figure used to describe something that

is easy, obvious, commonplace, ordinary, hence

so familiar as to remain unnoticed.

หญิง (คน) jĭŋ/ (khon/) N com. 1. woman. 2.

female (of people only). T 3. Princess --. Used

of various female descendants of royalty down

to the level of หม่อมราชวงศ์. →Chiefly in com-

pounds. →Opp. ชาย. →Dist. 2. ตัวเมีย

female (of animals). →Syn. สตรี. NOTE.

The usual term for "woman" is ผู้หญิง, as below.

But in special cases หญิง occurs alone, as in the

following example.

๐ ทั้งหญิงและชาย tháŋjĭŋ/lɛchaaj/ both men and

women.

ความเป็นหญิง khwaam/penjĭŋ/ N femininity.

คุณหญิง khunjĭŋ/ P 1. you, she, her (sp. to or of

the wife of a man in the conferred rank of พระยา or the wife of a premier or outstanding minister). T 2. title placed before the first name of such a lady. Hence "Lady --," "Madame --." →See เจ้าคุณ.

เจ้าฟ้าหญิง (องค์) câwfáajǐŋ/ (ʔoŋ/) N 1. princess of the highest rank, i.e. daughter of the king born by the queen. T 2. Princess --.

เจ้าหญิง (องค์) câwjǐŋ/ (ʔoŋ/) N 1. princess. Used of foreign princesses, or of any Thai princess down to the level of หม่อมเจ้า. T 2. Princess --. Used with the names of foreign princesses.

เด็กหญิง (คน) dègjǐŋ/ (khon/) N 1. girl. T 2. title placed before the first name of a girl, esp. a schoolgirl. →Comp. เด็กผู้หญิง.

นักเรียนหญิง (คน) nágrianjǐŋ/ (khon/) N schoolgirl, coed.

o นายแพทย์หญิง (คน) naajphêɛd/jǐŋ/ (khon/) N woman physician. →Syn. หมอผู้หญิง com.

บุตรหญิง (คน) bùdjǐŋ/ (khon/) N eleg. daughter. →Syn. ลูกสาว com.

ผู้หญิง (คน) phûujǐŋ/ (khon/) N com. 1. woman. 2. female (of people). →Syn. สตรี eleg. →Dist. 2. ตัวเมีย female (of animals). →Opp. ผู้ชาย.

ฝ่ายหญิง fàajjǐŋ/ N 1. the women's side. 2. (as n. mod.) woman's, female. 3. the woman (ref. to a particular woman in contrast to some man or men).

เพศหญิง phêedjǐŋ/ N female sex; feminine gender.

ลูกหญิง (คน) lûugjǐŋ/ (khon/) N daughter. →Syn. See ลูกสาว.

หญิงแก่ (คน) jǐŋkɛ̀ɛ/ (khon/) N com. old woman. →Syn. ยายแก่ colloq.

หญิงเดินโต๊ะ (คน) jǐŋ/dəəntó?/ (khon/) N waitress.

หญิงนครโสเภณี (คน) jǐŋnakhɔɔn/sǒopheenii/ (khon/) N eleg. courtesan, prostitute.

หญิงพรหมจารี (คน) jǐŋ/phrommacaa/rii/ (khon/) N virgin.

หญิงม่าย (คน) jǐŋmâaj/ (khon/) N widow. →Syn. แม่ม่าย. →Also หญิงหม้าย.

หญิงสาว jǐŋsǎaw/ N young girl, young woman.

หญิงโสด (คน) jǐŋsòod/ (khon/) N single woman, unmarried woman, spinster.

หญิงโสเภณี jǐŋ/sǒopheenii/ (khon/) N eleg. prostitute.

หญิงหม้าย (คน) jǐŋmâaj/ (khon/) N widow. →Also หญิงม่าย.

อาหญิง ʔaajǐŋ/ N younger paternal aunt.

หด hòd/ to shrink, contract, retract, draw back.

ยืดหดได้ jɯ̂ydhòd/dâaj/ V to be capable of extension, of stretching and shrinking, elastic.

หดตัว hòdtua/ V to contract, shrink.

หดมือ hòdmyy/ V to draw back one's hand.

หดหู่ hòdhùu/ V to be sad, depressed, dejected.

o ใจหดหู่,หดหู่ใจ caj/hòdhùu/, hòdhùu/caj/ V to be downhearted, despondent, depressed, heartsick.

หทย,หทัย hathaj/ N lit. heart.

บานหทัย baan/hathaj/ colloq. fully, to one's heart's content.

หน ๑ hǒn/ C time. →Syn. See คราว.

o กี่หน kìihǒn/ how many times.

o สองหน sɔ̌ɔŋhǒn/ twice, two times.

ชั่วเจ็ดที ดีเจ็ดหน chûa/cèdthii/→dii/cèdhǒn/ "bad for seven times, good for seven times," i.e. good luck is intermingled with bad.

หลายหน,หลายครั้ง-- lǎajhǒn/, lǎajkhráŋ/lǎajhǒn/ elab. several times, many a time.

หน ๒ hǒn/ N,C place. →Syn. See แห่ง.

o หนไหน hǒnnǎj/ lit. where, which place.

ต้นหน (คน) tônhǒn/ (khon/) N navigator, steersman.

ทุกหนทุกแห่ง thúghǒn/thúghɛ̀ŋ/ elab. everywhere.

ล่องหน lɔ̂ŋhǒn/ V to become invisible.

หนทาง (ทาง,สาย) hǒnthaaŋ/ (thaaŋ/, sǎaj/) N road, way.

o หนทางแก้ไข (ทาง) hǒnthaaŋ/kɛ̂ɛkhǎj/ (thaaŋ/) N remedial means; a remedy (e.g. for a difficulty).

o หมดหนทาง mòd/hǒnthaaŋ/ to have no way, no means (of doing something).

หนวก. See entries below.

หนวกหู nùaghǔu/ V to be noisy, deafening.

หูหนวก hǔunùag/ V to be deaf. →Dist. หูตึ่ง "hard of hearing."

หน่วง nùaŋ/ V to delay, hold back.

หน่วงเหนี่ยว nùaŋnìaw/ V to delay.

หนวด (เส้น) nùad/ (sên/) N 1. mustache, beard, whiskers. 2. antennae (of insects).

โกนหนวด koonnùad/ V to shave (literally, shave the beard).

หนวดเครา nùadkhraw/ N beard (including the mustache).

หน่วย ๑ nùaj/ N unit.

เลขหน่วย (ตัว) lêegnùaj/ (tua/) N cardinal number.

หน่วยดับเพลิง (หน่วย) nùaj/dàbphləəŋ/ (nùaj/) N fire department, fire-fighting unit.

หน่วยรบ (หน่วย) nùajrób/ (nùaj/) N fighting unit.

หน่วย ๒ in หน่วยก้าน nùajkâan/ N bearing, manner, manners, breeding.

หนอ nɔ̌ɔ/ Pt particle having contemplative force, used at the end of an interrogative sentence; may be rendered by "I wonder."

หน่อ (หน่อ) nɔ̀ɔ/ (nɔ̀ɔ/) N offshoot, sprout.

หน่อไม้ (หน่อ) nɔ̀ɔmáaj/ (nɔ̀ɔ/) N young bamboo shoot.

หนอง ๑ (หนอง,แห่ง) nɔ̌ɔŋ/ (nɔ̌ɔŋ/, hèŋ/) N swamp, lagoon, large pool.

หนอง ๒ nɔ̌ɔŋ/ N pus.

เป็นหนอง pennɔ̌ɔŋ/ V to produce pus, have pus.

พรรณหนอง, --ผี phan/nɔ̌ɔŋ/, phan/nɔ̌ɔŋfǐi/ N vaccine.

หนองใน, โรค-- nɔ̌ɔŋnaj/, rôog/nɔ̌ɔŋnaj/ N gonorrhea.

หนอน (ตัว) nɔ̌ɔn/ (tua/) N 1. worm. 2. caterpillar (any hairless variety). →Often ตัว--. →Dist. 2. บุ้ง. →Syn. 2. ตัวแก้ว.

ขึ้นหนอน khŷnnɔ̌ɔn/ V to get wormy.

เป็นหนอน pennɔ̌ɔn/ V to be wormy.

หน่อย nɔ̀j/* sV 1. a little, a little bit. C 2. a little bit, a little while. →Comp. น้อย.

นิดหน่อย nídnɔ̀j/ 1. little, tiny, small, wee. 2. a little bit, a wee bit.

o โตกว่า(...)นิดหน่อย too/kwàa(...)nídnɔ̀j/ a little bit bigger than.

แย่หน่อย jɛ̂ɛ/nɔ̀j/ too bad; kind of bad.

สักหน่อย ságnɔ̀j/ a little.

หน่อยหนึ่ง nɔ̀j/nyŋ for a little while; a little.

อีกหน่อย ʔìignɔ̀j/ in a little while, a little while

longer; a little more.

o ต่อมาอีกหน่อยหนึ่ง tɔ̀ɔmaa/-ʔìignɔ̀j/nyŋ a little bit later on.

หนัก nàg/ V 1. to be heavy. 2. to be hard (as of work). sV 3. heavily, severely, very, extremely. ความ-- (see below). →Ant. เบา.

กระเป๋าหนัก krapǎwnàg/ V idiom. colloq. to be rich, have loads of money.

ข้าวหนัก khâawnàg/ V a slowly maturing variety of rice. →Ant. ข้าวเบา.

ความหนัก khwaamnàg/ N heaviness. →Dist. น้ำหนัก.

ทวารหนัก (ทวารหนัก) thawaannàg/ (thawaannàg/) N anat., eleg. rectum, anus.

น้ำหนัก námnàg/ N weight. →Dist. ความหนัก.

ผ่อนหนักผ่อนเบา phɔ̀nnàg/phɔ̀nbaw/ V idiom. to ease tensions by compromise or mutual concession.

เพียบหนัก phîabnàg/ V to be in serious, critical condition, in bad shape.

ภาระหนัก phaará?/nàg/ N heavy burden.

หนักใจ nàgcaj/ V to be depressed, heavy-hearted, anxious; to have a weight upon one's mind, a burden upon one's heart. ความ-- heavy-heartedness, anxiety.

หนักแน่น nàgnɛ̂n/ V to be steady, firm (as in character, convictions, decisions).

หนักหน่วง nàgnùaŋ/ V to be strong, steady, unflinching.

หนักหนา nàgnǎa/ so very much, extremely. →Also นักหนา.

หนักอึ้ง nàg/?ŷŋ/ V to be extremely heavy.

หนัง (แผ่น,ผืน,ชิ้น,เรื่อง,ม้วน) nǎŋ/ N 1. skin, hide, leather (phɛ̀n/, phɣ̌yn/, chín/). 2. colloq. movie (rŷaŋ/, múan/). →Syn. 2. ภาพยนตร์ eleg.

ฉายหนัง chǎajnǎŋ/ V colloq. to show a movie.

ดูหนัง duunǎŋ/ V to see a movie.

ผิวหนัง phǐwnǎŋ/ N skin.

ฟอกหนัง fɔ̂ɔgnǎŋ/ V to tan hides.

โรงหนัง (โรง,แห่ง) rooŋnǎŋ/ (rooŋ/, hèŋ/) N colloq. movie (theater).

หนังตะลุง (เรื่อง,โรง) nǎŋ/taluŋ/ N 1. shadow play (rŷaŋ/). 2. shadow play establishment (rooŋ/).

หนังพูด (เรื่อง) nǎŋphûud/ (rŷaŋ/) N talking picture, sound movie.

หนังเพลง (เรื่อง) nǎŋphleeŋ/ (rŷaŋ/) N musical film.

หนังเลิก nǎŋ/lɤ̀ɤg/ the show is over.

หนังสือ (เล่ม) naŋsɯ̌y/* (lêm/) N book. →See หนัง. [สือ f. Chin.]

เขียนหนังสือ khĭannaŋsɯ̌y/ V to write.

o โต๊ะเขียนหนังสือ (ตัว) tó?/khĭannaŋsɯ̌y/ (tua/) N writing table, desk.

ดูหนังสือ duu/naŋsɯ̌y/ V to study (by oneself).

ตัวหนังสือ (ตัว) tuanaŋsɯ̌y/ (tua/) N letter (written character).

ตู้หนังสือ (ตู้) tûu/naŋsɯ̌y/ N bookcase.

โต๊ะหนังสือ (ตัว) tó?/naŋsɯ̌y/ (tua/) N desk.

ท่องหนังสือ thɔ̂ŋ/naŋsɯ̌y/ V 1. to study, do one's schoolwork. 2. to repeat (again and again in order to memorize).

พิมพ์หนังสือ phim/naŋsɯ̌y/ V 1. to print. 2. to type.

ภาษาหนังสือ phaasǎa/naŋsɯ̌y/ N literary language.

รู้หนังสือ rúu/naŋsɯ̌y/ V to be literate.

เรียนหนังสือ rian/naŋsɯ̌y/ V to study.

หนังสือเดินทาง (ฉบับ, เล่ม) naŋsɯ̌y/dəənthaaŋ/ (chabàb/, lêm/) N passport.

หนังสือพิมพ์ (ฉบับ) naŋsɯ̌yphim/ (chabàb/) N newspaper. การ-- journalism. นัก-- journalist.

o หนังสือพิมพ์รายเดือน (ฉบับ) naŋsɯ̌yphim/raajɔ dyan/ (chabàb/) N monthly magazine.

o หนังสือพิมพ์รายวัน (ฉบับ) naŋsɯ̌yphim/raajwan/ (chabàb/) N daily newspaper.

หนังสือเรียน (เล่ม) naŋsɯ̌yrian/ (lêm/) N schoolbook, textbook.

หนังสือเวียน (ฉบับ) naŋsɯ̌y/wian/ (chabàb/) N circular.

ห้องหนังสือ (ห้อง) hɔ̂ŋ/naŋsɯ̌y/ (hɔ̂ŋ/) N study, library (in a home).

หนา nǎa/ V to be thick. ความ-- thickness. →Ant. บาง.

นักหนา nágnǎa/ so very much, extremely. →Also หนักหนา. NOTE. นัก and หนา are often used in split expressions as in the following examples.

o ชอบนักชอบหนา chɔ̌ɔbnág/chɔ̌ɔbnǎa/ V elab. colloq. to favor highly, like very much.

o เป็นนักเป็นหนา pennág/pennǎa/ elab. colloq. extremely, highly, severely, roundly, unsparingly.

แน่นหนา nɛ̂nnǎa/ V 1. to be strong, tightly constructed. sV 2. strongly, securely.

หนาตา nǎa/taa/ V to get thick (in number, as of a crowd). →Ant. บางตา.

หนาเตอะ nǎa/tɤ̀?/ to be very thick.

หนาแน่น nǎa/nɛ̂n/ V to be crowded, congested, densely populated.

หน้าหนา nâanǎa/ V to be brazen, shameless. →Syn. หน้าด้าน. →Ant. หน้าบาง.

หน้า ๑ (หน้า) nâa/ (nâa/) N 1. face, front. 2. (as n. mod.) next; fore, front. Pp 3. in front of. 4. ahead, in front. C 5. page. →Opp. 2, 3. หลัง. →Occasionally coupled with ตา ๑.

o เดือนหน้า dyannâa/ next month.

o เท้าหน้า tháawnâa/ eleg. forelegs.

ก้มหน้า kômnâa/ V 1. to bow the head. 2. to knuckle down (and do something).

กระจกหน้า (แผ่น, บาน) kracòg/nâa/ N 1. windshield (phèn/); short for กระจกหน้ารถ. 2. lens of a headlight, floodlight, etc. (phèn/). 3. front mirror (baan/).

ก่อนหน้า kɔ̀ɔnnâa/ before, previously, prior to.

ก้าวหน้า kâawnâa/ V 1. to step ahead, go forward. 2. to progress, advance, develop. การ-- progress, progressing; math. progression. ความ-- progress, advancement.

o เจริญก้าวหน้า carəən/kâawnâa/ V to progress.

กู้หน้า kûu/nâa/ V to save face.

เกลียดน้ำหน้า klìad/námnâa/ V to detest; to hate the very sight of (someone).

แก้หน้า kɛ̂ɛ/nâa/ V to save face.

ข้างหน้า khâŋnâa/ in front, ahead; future; in the future; in front of.

ข้ามหน้า khâam/nâa/ V 1. to bypass (someone), go over the head (of). 2. to disrespectfully ignore the presence (of).

ขายหน้า khǎajnâa/ V to be disgraced, shamed.

ขึ้นหน้า khɯ̂nnâa/ V to get ahead (of), pass, surpass.

ขึ้นหน้าขึ้นตา khɯ̂nnâa/khɯ̂ntaa/ V elab. colloq. to be well-known, popular, outstanding.

เข้าหน้า khâw/nâa/ V 1. to face, confront. 2. to meet with, be friends with. 3. to arrange pages in proper order, insert pages.

คนแปลกหน้า (คน) khon/plὲɛgnâa/ (khon/) N a stranger.

คราวหน้า khraawnâa/ next time, on the next occasion.

คืบหน้า khŷybnâa/ V to progress, to advance.

เค้าหน้า kháwnâa/ N 1. looks, appearance (of the face). 2. facial expression.

จ่าหน้า càanâa/ V 1. to address, provide with a heading. 2. to write down, put down (a name). 3. to be addressed to (followed by ถึง).

เฉพาะหน้า chaphɔ́?/nâa/ confronting, at hand, immediate.

โฉมหน้า chɔ̌omnâa/ N face, facial features, countenance.

ชี้หน้า chíi/nâa/ V 1. to shake one's finger at (someone)(in reproach). 2. to point right at (e.g. the culprit).

เชิดหน้าชูตา chə̂ədnâa/chuutaa/ V elab. colloq. to enhance the prestige (of).

ซบหน้า sób/nâa/ V to rest one's head (on one's arms, or on the table, so that the face is hidden) (as when tired).

ต่อหน้า tɔ̀ɔnâa/ in the presence of, in front of, before.

ต่อหน้าต่อตา tɔ̀ɔnâa/tɔ̀ɔtaa/ elab. colloq. right before one's eyes.

ตั้งหน้าตั้งตา tâŋnâa/tâŋtaa/ V elab. colloq. to be determined (to), resolved (to), obsessed (with), intent.

ตีหน้า tiinâa/ V colloq. to put on an expression feigning (e.g. ignorance).

ที่หน้า thîinâaɔ in front of.

น้อยหน้า nɔ́ɔjnâa/ V to feel inferior (to); to be outdone, take second place.

นายหน้า (คน) naajnâa/ (khon/) N broker, commissioner.

บากหน้า bàagnâa/ V to swallow one's pride and turn to someone for help.

บ่ายหน้า bàaj/nâa/ V to head for, head toward, face toward.

เบื้องหน้า bŷaŋnâa/ lit. in the future.

ใบหน้า bajnâa/ N face, countenance.

ประจันหน้า pracan/nâa/ V to confront, encounter, meet face to face. →Syn. เผชิญหน้า eleg.

ปกหน้า pògnâa/ N front cover. →Comp. หน้าปก.

ผัดหน้า phàdnâa/ V to powder the face.

ผ้าเช็ดหน้า (ผืน) phâachédnâa/ (phǔyn/) N handkerchief.

เผชิญหน้า phachəən/nâa/ V eleg. to face, meet face to face. →Syn. ประจันหน้า.

พยักหน้า phajág/nâa/ V to nod in assent.

พยักหน้าหงึกๆ phajág/nâa/-ŋ̀yŋ̀yŋ̀y/ to nod the head up and down, nod the head several times.

พร้อมหน้ากัน phrɔ́ɔmnâa/kan all together.

ฟันหน้า (ซี่) fannâa/ (sîi/) N front teeth.

ภายหน้า phaajnâa/ in the future. →Also ใน--.

มอมหน้า mɔɔmnâa/ V to paint the face in order to conceal the identity.

มีหน้า (1) mii/nâa/; (2) miinâa/ V 1. to dare to, have the nerve to. 2. to have (such and such a) look; to look (thus and so); see example.

o มีหน้าเศร้า miinâa/sâw/ to have a sad look, look sad.

มีหน้ามีตา miinâa/miitaa/ V idiom. to be in a position of respect, esteem, deference.

มุ่งหน้า mûŋnâa/ V to head toward or for determinedly.

เมินหน้า məən/nâa/ V to turn the face away, to look away.

ไม่เลือกหน้า mâjlŷag/nâa/ without excepting anyone; without discrimination.

ไม่ไว้หน้า mâjwáj/nâa/ without sparing (the feelings of) anyone; without respect for anyone.

ย่อหน้า jɔ̀ɔnâa/ V to indent (as a paragraph).

เยี่ยมหน้า jîamnâa/ V to stick one's head out to see; to look out.

ล้อมหน้าล้อมหลัง lɔ́ɔmnâa/lɔ́ɔmlǎŋ/ V to surround, crowd around.

ล้างหน้า láaŋnâa/ V to wash the face.

o ที่ล้างหน้า (ที่) thîi/láaŋnâa/ (thîi/) N washbasin, washbowl.

o อ่างล้างหน้า (ใบ) ʔàaŋ/láaŋnâa/ (baj/) N washbasin.

วันหน้า wannâa/ one day, some day, some other day. →Used of future time only. →Also ใน--.

ล่ายหน้า sàajnâa/ V to shake one's head from
side to side, indicating a negative reply.

สีหน้า sǐinâa/ N facial expression.

o ฝืนสีหน้า fҳ̌yn'sǐinâa/ to force oneself to
assume a certain expression.

o มีสีหน้าสลด miisǐinâa'salòd/ to have a sad
facial expression, to look sad.

เสียหน้า sǐa/nâa/ V to lose face.

หน้ากระดาน nâakradaan/ N milit. rank, line.

o เรียงหน้ากระดาน riaŋ'nâakradaan/ V milit.
to fall in, form troops in line.

หน้ากระดาษ (หน้ากระดาษ,หน้า) nâakradàad/
(nâakradàad/,nâa/) N 1. page (of a book, newspaper, letter). C 2. page, pages (ref. to the
length of written materials such as letters,
authors' manuscripts, etc.).

หน้ากาก (หน้ากาก,อัน) nâakàag/ (nâakàag/,ʔan/)
N mask, hood, cover.

หน้าเขียว nâa/khǐaw/ V to look sick; to turn pale
(as when sick or exhausted).

หน้าแข้ง (ข้าง) nâakhêŋ/ (khâaŋ/) N shin.

หน้าแขน (ข้าง) nâa/khɛ̌ɛn/ (khâaŋ/) N "the
front of the arm," i.e. the inner part of the forearm, and the forward part of the upper arm.

หน้าเค็ม nâa/khem/ to have the face of one who
drives a hard bargain, an unfair bargain, of one
who exacts full payment (for debts owed, injuries
inflicted, etc.).

หน้างอ nâa/ŋɔɔ/ to have an angry face, look sullen.

o ทำหน้างอ thamnâa/ŋɔɔ/ to make a face expressive of anger, displeasure.

หน้าเฉยตาเฉย nâachɔ̌əj/taachɔ̌əj/ elab. colloq.
with a dead pan expression, i.e. looking expressionless, and as if nothing happened. อย่าง--
idem.

หน้าซีด nâasîid/ V to be pale (of face).

หน้าด้าน nâadâan/ V to be brazen, shameless.
→Syn. หน้าหนา. →Ant. หน้าบาง.

หน้าดำหน้าแดงอยู่กับ... nâadam'nâadɛɛŋ/-jùuⲟ
kaⲟ... colloq. to be busily engaged in (e.g.
work). Has the force of English "have one's
nose to the grindstone."

หน้าแดง nâa/dɛɛŋ/ V to blush.

หน้าตัวเมีย nâa/tuamia/ V derog. 1. to be a
sissy, be effeminate. 2. Sissy!

หน้าตา nâataa/ N countenance, look.

o หน้าตาหมดจด nâataa/mòdcòd/ V to be handsome, good-looking, have a nice, clean face.

หน้าต่าง (หน้าต่าง) nâatàaŋ/ (nâatàaŋ/) N window.

o ม่านหน้าต่าง (ผืน) mâan/nâatàaŋ/ (phҳ̌yn/)
N window curtain, window shade, drape.

หน้าทะเล้น nâa/thalén/ V 1. to have a grin, a
broad grin. 2. to be giggly. →Comp. หน้าเป็น.

หน้าที่ (อย่าง) nâathîi/ (jàaŋ/) N duty, function.

o เจ้าหน้าที่ (คน,นาย) câwnâathîi/ (khon/,naaj/)
N an official, officer, authorized person.

o ทำหน้าที่ tham/nâathîi/ to do duty (for), do the
duties (of), serve the function of.

o หน้าที่พลเมือง nâathîi/phonlamyaŋ/ N civic
duties.

หน้าบาน nâa/baan/ V idiom. to beam (with
pleasure), to be delighted.

หน้าบ้าน nâabâan/ N 1. the area in front of a
house. 2. facade of a house. 3. in front of the
house.

o ประตูหน้าบ้าน pratuu/nâabâan/ the front door.

หน้าบึ้ง nâa/bŷŋ/ V to scowl, be stern faced, have
a sulky face.

หน้าบูด nâa/bùud/ V to have a sullen face, a long
face.

หน้าปก nâapòg/ N the front of the cover. →Comp.
ปกหน้า.

o ภาพหน้าปก (ภาพ) phâab/nâapòg/ (phâab/) N
cover picture.

หน้าปัด (อัน) nâapàd/ (ʔan/) N dial, face (of a
clock).

หน้าเป็น nâa/pen/ V 1. to be given to mirth on
all occasions (suitable or unsuitable). 2. to be
all smiles. →Comp. หน้าทะเล้น.

หน้าผา (แห่ง,ลูก) nâaphǎa/ (hɛ̀ŋ/,lûug/) N cliff.

หน้าผาก nâaphàag/ N forehead.

หน้ามอย nâa/mɔj/ V 1. (one's) face to fall. 2.
to be crestfallen, have a long face.

หน้าม้า (คน) nâamáa/ (khon/) N decoy (of people
only).

หน้ามืด nâamŷyd/ V 1. to black out, have a dizzy
spell. 2. to lose control of oneself, be blind

with passion.

หน้ามุข nâamúg/ N front balcony, front porch, portico.

หน้าไม้ (คัน, อัน) nâamáaj/ (khan/, ?an/) N crossbow.

หน้าละห้อย nâa/lahɔ̂j/ V to look sad, depressed.

หน้าวัว (ต้น, ดอก) nâawua/ (tôn/, dɔ̀ɔg/) N anthurium (Anthurium), a handsome plant.

หน้าเศร้า nâa/sâw/ V to look sad.

หน้าใหญ่ใจโต nâajàj/cajtoo/ V to be lavish (e.g. in entertaining friends); to be given to lavishness.

หน้าใหม่ nâamàj/ N 1. new face, newcomer, new one. V 2. to be a newcomer, new one, stranger.

หน้าหลัง nâalăŋ/ N the last page, the back page (of a newspaper); the reverse side (of a single sheet).

หน้าอก (หน้าอก) nâa?òg/ (nâa?òg/) N chest, bust (body-part term).

หยามหน้า jăam/nâa/ V 1. to look down upon, despise. 2. to speak disparagingly or contemptuously of.

ห่วงหน้าห่วงหลัง hùaŋnâa/hùaŋlăŋ/ V to worry over two equally important things.

หัวหน้า (คน) hŭanâa/ (khon/) N head (as of a department), chief, leader.

หายหน้าหายตา hăajnâa/hăajtaa/ V elab. colloq. to be away, out of sight, not seen by others. →Also หายหน้า.

เห็นแก่หน้า hěn/kɛ̀ɛnâa/ to be partial, prejudiced.

แหงนหน้า ŋɛ̌ɛnnâa/ V to lift up one's face.

อาทิตย์หน้า ?aathíd/nâa/ next week.

หน้า ๒ (หน้า) nâa/ (nâa/) N colloq. season (of the year). →Syn. ฤดู eleg.

หน้านา nâanaa/ N colloq. rice-planting season.

หน้าฝน nâafŏn/ N colloq. rainy season.

หน้ามรสุม nâa/mɔɔrasŭm/ N colloq. monsoon season.

หน้าร้อน nâarɔ́ɔn/ N colloq. summer, the hot season.

หน้าแล้ง nâalɛ́ɛŋ/ N colloq. dry season.

หน้าหนาว nâanăaw/ N colloq. winter, the cold season.

หนาม (อัน) năam/ (?an/) N 1. thorn. 2. barb of wire.

เป็นเสี้ยนหนาม pen/sîannăam/ to be enemies (of the state, of society): "to be splinters and thorns."

ลวดหนาม (เส้น) lûadnăam/ (sên/) N barbed wire.

หน่าย. See entries below.

เบื่อหน่าย bỳanàaj/ elab. to be tired of, bored (with). ความ-- boredom.

เหนื่อยหน่าย nỳajnàaj/ to be tired of.

หนาว năaw/ V to be cold (of the weather; of personal sensation). ความ-- coldness, (the) cold. →Dist. เย็น. →Ant. ร้อน.

ขี้หนาว khîinăaw/ V to be sensitive to cold weather.

ความร้อนหนาว khwaam/rɔ́ɔnnăaw/ N heat and cold; temperature.

ฤดูหนาว (ฤดู) rýduu/năaw/ (rýduu/) N eleg. winter, the cold season.

หน้าหนาว nâanăaw/ N colloq. winter, the cold season.

หนำ in มิหนำซ้ำ mínămsám/ colloq. in addition, moreover, worse than that.

หนี nǐi/ V to flee, escape.

ขวัญหนี khwănnǐi/ V to be startled, frightened.

o ขวัญหนีดีฝ่อ khwănnǐi/diifɔ̀ɔ/ V elab. colloq. to be startled, frightened, scared out of one's wits.

ถอยหนี thɔ̌jnǐi/ V to back away (from), retreat (in order to escape, get away from).

ผละหนี phlà?/nǐi/ V to turn away from, part with, leave.

ลอบหนี lɔ̂ɔbnǐi/ V to sneak away.

วิ่งหนี wîŋnǐi/ V to run away.

หนีเอาตัวรอด nǐi/-?awtua/rɔ̀ɔd/ to flee to safety, flee saving one's own skin.

หลบหนี lòbnǐi/ V to slip away, escape (stealthily).

หนี้ nîi/ N debt.

เจ้าหนี้ (คน, เจ้า) câwnîi/ (khon/, câaw/) N creditor. →Opp. ลูกหนี้.

ใช้หนี้ chájnîi/ V to pay one's debt.

เป็นหนี้ pennîi/ V eleg. to owe, be indebted.

o เป็นหนี้เป็นสิน pennîi/pensǐn/ V elab. eleg. to be in debt.

ลูกหนี้ (คน, เจ้า) lûugnîi/ (khon/, câaw/) N debtor. →Opp. เจ้าหนี้.

หนี้สิน nîi/sǐn/ N eleg. debts, liabilities.

○ มีหนี้สินท่วมตัว miinîisǐn′-thûam′tua′ to be
deeply in debt, head over heels in debt.

หนีบ nìib′ V to nip, grip, pinch, seize with pincers
or the like.

หนึ่ง nỳŋ′, nyŋ Nm com. one. →Cf. อ้าย, เอก,
เอ็ด ๑ .   NOTE. (1) Unlike all other numerals, หนึ่ง usually follows the clf. In counting, however, หนึ่ง often (though not necessarily) precedes; see the examples below. (2) หนึ่ง
is sometimes coupled with เดียว, q.v.

○ เด็กหนึ่งคน dèg′-nỳŋ′khon′ one child.

○ เด็กคนหนึ่ง dèg′-khon′nyŋ a child, one child.

คราวหนึ่ง khraaw′nyŋ 1. once, one time. 2. once,
on one occasion.

ครู่หนึ่ง khrûu′nyŋ (for) a moment.

ขั้นหนึ่ง, ขั้นที่หนึ่ง chánnỳŋ′, chán′thîinỳŋ′ first
class (accomodations).

...ใด...หนึ่ง. See entries below.

○ ใช้คำใดคำหนึ่งก็ได้ cháj′-khamdaj′khamnỳŋ′-
kɔ̀dâaj′ You can use either word, any word.

○ ประการใดประการหนึ่ง prakaan′daj′-prakaan′ɔ
nỳŋ′ either one, any one (of a given number
of things).

○ ฝ่ายใดฝ่ายหนึ่ง fàajdaj′fàajnỳŋ′ one side or
the other; either side; any side.

พักหนึ่ง phág′nyŋ (for) one moment, a period of
time.

มือหนึ่ง myynỳŋ′ V 1. to be first rate. N 2. one
who makes the first play (as in cards, tennis).

แรมหนึ่งค่ำ rɛɛm′nỳŋkhâm′ N the first day of
the waning phase of the moon.

วันหนึ่ง wan′nyŋ one day.

วันหนึ่งๆ wan′nyŋ-wan′nyŋ 1. from day to day,
from one day to the next. 2. in any one day.

หน่อยหนึ่ง nɔ̀j′nyŋ for a little while; a little.

หนึ่งใน... nỳŋ′najɔ... one...-th (the fraction);
one of, one in (so and so many). →Use as a
fraction is restricted to a few very common
instances.

○ หนึ่งในพัน nỳŋ′najphan′ 1. "one in a thousand,"
hence extraordinary, rare, exceptional. 2.
one thousandth (the fraction).

○ หนึ่งในสี่ nỳŋ′najsìi′ 1. one of four, one in
four. 2. one fourth.

หนึ่งพันเก้าร้อยสามสิบสอง nỳŋphan′-kâawrɔ́ɔj′ɔ
sǎamsìbsɔ̌ɔŋ′ Nm one thousand nine hundred
and thirty-two; nineteen thirty-two (1932).

หนึ่งร้อย, ร้อยหนึ่ง nỳŋrɔ́ɔj′, rɔ́ɔj′nyŋ Nm one
hundred.

เหมือนหนึ่งว่า mỹan′nỳŋwâa′ as if, as though.

อย่างหนึ่งอย่างใด jàaŋnỳŋ′jàaŋdaj′ any thing, any
kind, any way (of a given number of alternatives);
either thing, either kind, either way.

อันหนึ่งอันเดียว ʔannỳŋ′ʔandiaw′ one and the same;
single, united, inseparable.

อีก...หนึ่ง ʔìig...nyŋ 1. the other one. 2.
another; one more. See อีกคนหนึ่ง and others
among the subentries of อีก.

หนืด nỳyd′ V 1. to be viscous, sticky. 2. slang
to be stingy.

หนุน nǔn′ V 1. to support, prop up. 2. to encourage.

กองหนุน (กอง) kɔɔŋnǔn′ (kɔɔŋ′) N (military)
reserves.

กำลังหนุน kamlaŋnǔn′ N reserve force, supporting
force.

หนุนน้ำใจ nǔn′námcaj′ V to encourage, give
moral support to.

หนุนเนื่อง nǔn′nŷaŋ′ V to bring up reinforcements
(troops) in a continuous stream.

หนุนหลัง nǔnlǎŋ′ V to support, back. ผู้-- backer.

อุดหนุน ʔùdnǔn′ V to patronize.

หนุ่ม nùm′ N,C 1. young man; adolescent boy. V 2.
to be young, adolescent (of men and boys). คน--
young man, a youth. ความ-- youthfulness.
→Opp. สาว, used of women.

ชายหนุ่ม (คน) chaajnùm′ (khon′) N young man,
a youth.

หนุ่มสาว (คน, คู่) nùmsǎaw′ N 1. young people,
teenagers (of both sexes) (khon′). 2. young couple (khûu′).

หนุ่มๆสาวๆ nùmnùm′sǎawsǎaw′ N colloq. young
men and women, young people; teenagers. →Also
คน-- .

หนู (ตัว) nǔu′ (tua′) N 1. mouse, rat. P 2. I, me
(used by children); you (used in sp. to children).
T 3. title used before first names of children.

ขี้หนู khîinǔu′ mouse or rat droppings. →See also
examples below.

o ขนมขี้หนู khanǒm′khîinǔu′ N a kind of sweet
food.

o พริกขี้หนู phrígkhîinǔu′ N bird pepper, a tiny,
very hot variety of chili.

คุณหนู khunnǔu′ P 1. you; he, him, she, her (sp.
to or of a child; esp. used by servants of the
household). T 2. title placed before the name
of a child; hence "Master --," "Miss --."

ผ้าขนหนู (ผืน) phâakhǒnnǔu′ (phʉ̌yn′) N 1. terry
cloth. 2. Turkish towel; washcloth.

แม่หนู (คน) mɛ̂ɛnǔu′ (khon′) N 1. you, she (sp.
to or of a little girl). T 2. title placed before
the name of a little girl; hence "Little Miss --."

สารหนู sǎannǔu′ N arsenic.

หนูตะเภา (ตัว) nǔutaphaw′ (tua′) N guinea pig.

หนูน้อย (คน) nǔunɔ́ɔj′ (khon′) N baby, little
child, little one.

หนูบ้าน (ตัว) nǔubâan′ (tua′) N house rat.

หนูพุก (ตัว) nǔuphúg′ (tua′) N field rat.

ห่ม hòm′ V to cover, cover up (with covers, with
clothing).

นุ่งลมห่มฟ้า nûŋlom′hòmfáa′ V elab. colloq.
to be naked, in the nude: "to clothe oneself with
wind and sky."

นุ่งห่ม nûŋhòm′ V 1. to dress, clothe oneself.
2. to wear. เครื่อง-- garment, clothing.

ผ้าห่ม (ผืน) phâahòm′ (phʉ̌yn′) N blanket; shawl.

ห่มผ้า hòmphâa′ V to cover with a blanket or
shawl.

หมก mòg′ V to bury, place underneath, cover over.

หมกมุ่น mògmûn′ V to be engrossed (in), preoccupied (with); to devote one's time and energy
exclusively (to).

ห่อหมก (ห่อ) hɔ̀ɔmòg′ (hɔ̀ɔ′) N a Thai dish consisting of steamed fish or chicken in coconut
cream and chili sauce.

o เออออห่อหมก ʔəəʔɔɔ′hɔ̀ɔmòg′ V elab.
colloq. to agree, approve, go along with.

หมด mòd′ V 1. to be all, be used up, exhausted
(in supply). sV 2. up, all up, completely, entirely, thoroughly. →Dist. เสร็จ. →Comp.
จบ, สิ้น.

กิน(...)หมด kin(...)mòd′ to eat (something) up,
eat (something) all up.

จ่ายหมด càajmòd′ to spend all one's money.

ทั้งหมด tháŋmòd′ com. all (of it, of them), the
whole lot. →Cf. ทั้งปวง.

o ทั้งหมดด้วยกัน tháŋmòd′dûajkan′ altogether.

o รวมทั้งหมด ruam′tháŋmòd′ altogether.

ปิดไฟฟ้าหมด pìd′fajfáa′-mòd′ to turn out all the
lights.

หมดกลิ่น mòdklìn′ V to become odorless, lose
(its) odor.

หมดกะจิตกะใจ mòd′-kacìd′kacaj′ V elab.
colloq. to lose heart, lose courage.

หมดกำลัง mòd′kamlaŋ′ V to be exhausted, all in.

หมดกำลังใจ mòd′kamlaŋcaj′ V to lose heart,
be discouraged.

หมดเขต mòdkhèed′ V (applications) to be closed;
to be past the deadline.

หมดความจำเป็น mòd′-khwaam′campen′ V to be
no longer necessary.

หมดค่า mòdkhâa′ V eleg. to become worthless,
valueless.

หมดจด mòdcòd′ V 1. to be flawless, spotless,
clean, neat. sV 2. spotlessly, neatly.

o หน้าตาหมดจด nâataa′mòdcòd′ V to be handsome, good-looking, have a nice, clean face.

o แต่งตัวหมดจด tɛ̀ŋtua′mòdcòd′ neatly dressed.

หมดด้วยกัน mòd′dûajkan′ altogether.

หมดตัว mòdtua′ V to have nothing left, be broke.

หมดน้ำอดน้ำทน mòd′-námʔòd′námthon′ V elab.
colloq. to lose patience.

หมดเนื้อหมดตัว mòdnʉ́a′mòdtua′ V elab. colloq.
to be penniless, lose everything one has.

หมดปัญญา mòd′panjaa′ V to be at one's wit's end.

หมดปัญหา mòd′panhǎa′ V to be rid of a problem;
to free (oneself) from a vexing problem; a problem to be taken care of, solved.

หมดเปลือง mòdplʉaŋ′ V 1. to consume, use up,
lose, waste (e.g. money, time, resources). 2.
to be consumed, used up, lost, wasted. NOTE.
In this expression the thing consumed need not
be expressly stated. See the following example.

o การเดินทางคราวนี้ฉันหมดเปลืองไปเยอะ kaan′ɔ
dəənthaaŋ′-khraawníi′ chán′mòdplʉaŋ′-pajjə́ʔ′↓
I spent a lot (of money) on this trip.

หมดไป mòd′paj V to be used up, consumed, out

of stock.

หมดราคา mòd'raakhaa' V com. to become
worthless, valueless.

หมดแรง mòdrɛɛŋ' V to be exhausted, lose all
one's strength or energy.

หมดแล้ว mòdléɛw' that's all (there is), it's all
gone.

หมดเวลา mòd'weelaa' the time is up.

หมดสติ mòd'satì?' V to lose consciousness.

หมดสมัย mòd'samǎj' V to be out-of-date.
→Syn. ล้าสมัย.

หมดสิ้น mòd'sîn' V 1. to be exhausted, used up,
spent. 2. to end, be over, finished.

หมดหนทาง mòd'hǒnthaaŋ' V to have no way,
no means (to do something).

หมดหวัง mòdwǎŋ' V to be hopeless; to have no
hope.

หมดอายุ mòd'?aajú?' V to expire, terminate.

หมดอาลัยตายอยาก mòd'?aalaj'-taajjàag' V
elab. colloq. to lose all hope, be in despair,
be utterly discouraged. →Also หมดอาลัย.

หมดโอกาศ mòd'?ookàad' V to have no more
opportunity.

เหมือนกันหมด mǔan'kanmòd' to be all alike, all
the same, altogether the same.

หม่น mòn' V to be dull, gray.

สีหม่น sǐimòn' N 1. dull color, gray. V 2. to be
dull-colored, gray.

หม่นหมอง mònmɔɔŋ' V to be gloomy, sad, unhappy.

หมม in หมักหมม màgmǒm' V 1. to be left to accumulate (e.g. of garbage, of dirt and perspiration
on the skin). 2. to allow (something) to accumulate.

หมวก (ใบ) mùag' (baj') N hat, cap.

เปิดหมวก pə̀ədmùag' V to remove one's hat as
a sign of respect.

หมวกกะโล่ (ใบ) mùagkalôo' (baj') N sun helmet.

หมวกแก็ป (ใบ) mùagkéb' (baj') N cap. [f. Eng.]

หมวกฟาง (ใบ) mùagfaaŋ' (baj') N straw hat.

หมวกสาน (ใบ) mùagsǎan' (baj') N plaited hat,
woven hat.

หมวด mùad' C section, group, category; platoon.

หมวดหมู่ mùadmùu' C group, category.

หมอ ๑ (คน) mɔɔ' (khon') N 1. com. doctor. 2.
slang fellow, guy. →Syn. 1. แพทย์ eleg.

มดหมอ (คน) mód'mɔɔ' (khon') N colloq.
doctor.

โรงหมอ (โรง,แห่ง) rooŋmɔɔ' (rooŋ',hɛ̀ŋ') N
hospital, clinic (usually a private one).

หมอความ (คน) mɔɔkhwaam' (khon') N colloq.
lawyer. →Also หมอถ้อยหมอความ elab.
colloq. →Syn. ทนายความ.

หมอดู (คน) mɔɔduu' (khon') N fortuneteller.

หมอตา (คน) mɔɔtaa' (khon') N com. eye doctor.

หมอตำแย (คน) mɔɔtamjɛɛ' (khon') N colloq.
midwife. →Syn. ผดุงครรภ์ eleg.

หมอถ้อยหมอความ (คน) mɔɔthɔ̂j'mɔɔkhwaam'
(khon') N elab. colloq. lawyer. →Also
หมอความ colloq.

หมอเถื่อน (คน) mɔɔthɯ̀an' (khon') N quack, i.e.
an unauthorized physician.

หมอนวด (คน) mɔɔnûad' (khon') N masseur,
masseuse.

หมอประกาศนียบัตร (คน) mɔɔ'prakàasanii'jabàd'
N certified doctor, physician.

หมอประจำบ้าน (คน) mɔɔ'pracambâan' (khon')
N family doctor.

หมอผ่าตัด (คน) mɔɔ'phàatàd' (khon') N com.
surgeon. →Syn. ศัลยแพทย์ eleg.

หมอผู้ชาย (คน,นาย) mɔɔ'phûuchaaj' (khon',naaj')
N com. (male) doctor. →Syn. นายแพทย์ eleg.

หมอผู้หญิง (คน) mɔɔ'phûujǐŋ' (khon') N com.
woman doctor. →Syn. นายแพทย์หญิง eleg.

หมอฟัน (คน) mɔɔfan' (khon') N com. dentist.
→Syn. ทันตแพทย์ eleg.

หมอยา (คน) mɔɔjaa' (khon') N colloq. medical
doctor, physician.

หมอสอนศาสนา (คน) mɔɔ'sɔ̌ɔnsàasanǎa' (khon')
N missionary.

หมอสัตว์ (คน) mɔɔsàd' (khon') N veterinarian.

หมอ ๒ in ปลาหมอ (ตัว) plaamɔɔ' (tua') N climbing fish (Anabus), a common fresh water fish.

หม้อ (ใบ) mɔ̂ɔ' (baj') N cooking pot.

หม้อเคลือบ (ใบ,ลูก) mɔ̂ɔkhlɯ̂ab' (baj',lûug') N
enamelled pot.

หม้อดิน (ลูก,ใบ) mɔ̂ɔdin' (lûug',baj') N earthen

pot.

หม้อน้ำ (หม้อ,ใบ) mɔ̌ɔnáam/ (mɔ̌ɔ/, baj/) N water pot; boiler; water heater; radiator (of a car).

หม้อไฟ (หม้อ) mɔ̌ɔfaj/ (mɔ̌ɔ/) N 1. meter for recording electrical consumption. 2. storage battery.

หมอก mɔ̀ɔg/ N fog, mist.

มีหมอก miimɔ̀ɔg/ to be foggy.

หมอกเพลิง mɔ̀ɔgphləəŋ/ N nebula.

หมอง mɔ̌ɔŋ/ V to be sad, depressed.

มัวหมอง muamɔ̌ɔŋ/ V to be tainted, stained, tarnished. →Often used in respect to one's name.

หม่นหมอง mònmɔ̌ɔŋ/ V to be gloomy, sad, unhappy.

หมองใจ mɔ̌ɔŋcaj/ V 1. to feel sad, depressed. 2. to be in dissension (with), in dispute (with), have a rift. 3. to be upset, be angry, brood (over a rift, dispute, etc.).

หมองหมาง mɔ̌ɔŋmǎaŋ/ V 1. to be flawed, marred, blemished. 2. to be in dissension (with), in dispute (with), have a rift. 3. to be upset, be angry, brood (over a rift, dispute, etc.).

หมอน (ใบ,ท่อน) mɔ̌ɔn/ N 1. pillow (baj/). 2. railroad tie, sleeper (thɔ̂ɔn/).

ปลอกหมอน (ใบ,ปลอก) plɔ̀ɔgmɔ̌ɔn/ (baj/, plɔ̀ɔg/) N pillowcase.

ไม้หมอน máajmɔ̌ɔn/ N railroad tie, sleeper.

ล้มหมอนนอนเสื่อ lómmɔ̌ɔn/nɔɔnsỳa/ V elab. colloq. to fall sick, be brought to bed because of illness.

หม่อน mɔ̀n/* N white mulberry, the leaves of which are eaten by silkworms (Morus alba).

หมอบ mɔ̀ɔb/ V to crouch, prostrate oneself.

หมอบราบคาบแก้ว mɔ̀ɔbrâab/khâabkɛ̂ɛw/ V elab. colloq. to give in, surrender, yield completely.

หมอบลาน mɔ̀ɔb/laan/ V to crouch with fear.

หม่อม mɔ̀m/* N 1. wife of a หม่อมเจ้า or a พระองค์เจ้า. T 2. title used before the name of such a person. 3. title used before the first name of a หม่อมราชวงศ์ or a หม่อมหลวง. P 4. you, she, her (sp. to or about the wife of a หม่อมเจ้า or a พระองค์เจ้า). 5. you; he, him (sp. to or about a หม่อมราชวงศ์ or a หม่อมหลวง.

หม่อมเจ้า (องค์) mɔ̀mcâaw/ (ʔoŋ/) N 1. a prince or princess who is in the grandchild generation of royal descent, or treated as such. T 2. Prince --, Princess --. →Abbrev. ม.จ.

หม่อมฉัน mɔ̀mchán/ eleg. def. w. sp. I, me (used in addr. royalty). →Comp. กระหม่อม). →Syn. See ผม ๒.

หม่อมราชวงศ์ mɔ̀mrâadchawoŋ/ N 1. great-grandchild of a king. T 2. title used before the first name of same. →Abbrev. ม.ร.ว.

หม่อมหลวง mɔ̀mlǔaŋ/ N 1. great-great-grand-child of a king. T 2. title placed before the first name of same. →Abbrev. ม.ล.

หมัก màg/ V 1. to leave (something) to ferment. 2. to let (something) stand (e.g. clothes in soapy water). 3. colloq. to let (something) accumulate or pile up. การ-- leaving (something) to ferment.

เชื้อหมัก chýamàg/ N yeast.

หมักเชื้อ màgchýa/ N 1. culture (mold, fungus, yeast, germ, bacteria, etc.). V 2. to ferment. การ-- fermenting, (the process of) fermentation.

หมักดอง màgdɔɔŋ/ V to preserve or pickle by slow fermentation.

หมักหมม màgmǒm/ V 1. to be left to accumulate (e.g. of garbage, of dirt and perspiration on the skin). 2. to allow (something) to accumulate.

หมัด ๑ (ตัว) màd/ (tua/) N flea.

หมัด ๒ (หมัด) màd/ (màd/) N 1. fist. 2. punch.

กำหมัด kammàd/ V 1. to clench one's fist. N 2. fist.

หมัดเด็ด (หมัด) màddèd/ (màd/) N decisive punch, knockout blow.

เหวี่ยงหมัด wìaŋmàd/ V to throw a punch.

หมัน in เป็นหมัน penmǎn/ to be sterile, useless, fruitless, futile.

หมั่น ๑ màn/ V to be diligent, industrious.

หมั่น ๒ in หมั่นไส้ mànsâj/ V to be disgusted (with someone), disapprove (of someone) (usually because of some unwarranted or unreasonable action or attitude).

หมั้น mân/ V to be engaged, betrothed.

คู่หมั้น khûumân/ (khon/) N fiancé, fiancée.

แหวนหมั้น (วง) wɛ̌ɛnmân/ (woŋ/) N engagement

ring.

หมับ màb′ sV colloq. with a quick, sudden motion.

คว้าหมับ khwáa′màb′ colloq. to snatch, grasp quickly and firmly.

หมา (ตัว) mǎa′ (tua′) N com. dog. →Syn. สุนัข eleg.

หมากลางถนน (ตัว) mǎa′klaaŋthanǒn′ (tua′) 1. stray dog. 2. slang derelict (person).

หมาจิ้งจอก (ตัว) mǎacîŋcɔ̀ɔg′ (tua′) N com. fox; jackal. →Syn. สุนัขจิ้งจอก eleg.

หมาบ้า (ตัว) mǎabâa′ (tua′) N mad dog, rabid dog. →Syn. สุนัขบ้า eleg.

หมาป่า (ตัว) mǎapàa′ (tua′) N com. wolf. →Syn. สุนัขป่า eleg.

หมาก ๑ (ใบ,ลูก,ผล,ต้น,คำ) màag′ N 1. areca nut (baj′,lûug′,phǒn′). 2. areca palm (tôn′). 3. betel (kham′)(essentially a combination of betel leaf, lime and areca nut for chewing). →Dist. พลู ๑.

กินหมาก kinmàag′ V to chew betel.

ขันหมาก (ใบ) khǎnmàag′ (baj′) N betel bowl or tray for presentation to the bride's parents or guardians during a wedding ceremony.

ข้าวยากหมากแพง khâawjâag′màagphɛɛŋ′ elab. famine or hard times to exist, food to be scarce.

แจกหมาก cɛ̀ɛgmàag′ V slang to punch (someone) in the mouth.

ต้นหมาก (ต้น) tônmàag′ (tôn′) N areca palm.

น้ำหมาก námmàag′ N betel saliva (i.e. chewed betel mixed with saliva, red in color).

พานหมาก (ใบ) phaanmàag′ (baj′) N betel tray.

หมากเก็บ màagkèb′ N jackstones.

หมากฝรั่ง (ห่อ,อัน,ก้อน) màag′faràŋ′ (hɔ̀ɔ′,ʔan′, kɔ̂ɔn′) N chewing gum.

หมากพลู màagphluu′ N betel: "areca and betel."

หมาก ๒ in หมากรุก (สำรับ,กระดาน) màagrúg′ N chess (sǎmráb′ for sets; kradaan′ for games).

กระดานหมากรุก (กระดาน,แผ่น) kradaan′màag⊃ rúg′ (kradaan′,phɛ̀n′) N chess board.

หมาง mǎaŋ′ V to be in disagreement, be of opposite minds.

บาดหมาง bàadmǎaŋ′ V to be in dissension (with), in dispute (with), have a rift.

หมองหมาง mɔ̌ɔŋmǎaŋ′ V 1. to be flawed, marred, blemished. 2. to be in dissension (with), in dispute (with), have a rift. 3. to be upset, be angry, brood (over a rift, dispute, etc.).

หมางใจ mǎaŋcaj′ V 1. to be in dissension (with), have a rift. 2. to be upset (over a rift, dispute).

หมาด màad′ V to be almost dry, half-dried.

หมาย (ใบ) mǎaj′ (baj′) V 1. to mean, indicate, have meaning. 2. to mark. 3. to aim at. 4. to expect. N 5. warrant, writ, summons. ความ-- meaning, sense.

กฎหมาย (ฉบับ) kòdmǎaj′ (chabàb′) N law.

คาดหมาย khâadmǎaj′ V to expect, anticipate.

เครื่องหมาย (อัน) khrŷaŋmǎaj′ (ʔan′) N sign, mark, symbol, signal.

o เครื่องหมายกากบาท (อัน) khrŷaŋmǎaj′kaaka⊃ bàad′ N a cross, an "x" mark, a plus mark (+), i.e. any mark with crossing lines (including the fourth tonal marker ✛).

o เครื่องหมายคำถาม khrŷaŋmǎaj′khamthǎam′ the question mark.

o เครื่องหมายคำพูด khrŷaŋmǎaj′khamphûud′ quotation marks.

o เครื่องหมายตกใจ khrŷaŋmǎaj′tògcaj′ the exclamation point.

จดหมาย (ฉบับ) còdmǎaj′ (chabàb′) N letter (epistle). →Abbrev. จ.ม.

o จดหมายเหตุ (ฉบับ) còdmǎajhèed′ (chabàb′) N written account, record (as of events), document.

จุดหมาย (ที่,แห่ง,อัน,จุด) cùdmǎaj′(thîi′,hɛ̀ŋ′, ʔan′,cùd′) N destination, goal, aim, end.

o จุดหมายปลายทาง (อัน,จุด) cùdmǎaj′plaajthaaŋ′ (ʔan′,cùd′) N destination, final goal, aim.

ที่หมาย (แห่ง,ที่) thîimǎaj′ (hɛ̀ŋ′,thîi′) N 1. destination. 2. target (spot aimed at). 3. goal.

o ที่หมายปลายทาง (แห่ง,ที่) thîimǎaj′plaajthaaŋ′ (hɛ̀ŋ′,thîi′) N destination.

นัดหมาย nád′mǎaj′ V to make an appointment, set a time or date.

มอบหมาย mɔ̂ɔbmǎaj′ V to assign.

o รับมอบหมาย ráb′mɔ̂ɔbmǎaj′ V 1. to accept or receive an assignment, responsibility, transaction. 2. to be in charge, have charge of.

มาดหมาย mâadmǎaj′ V to expect, anticipate, intend.

มุ่งร้ายหมายขวัญ mûŋráaj′-mǎaj′khwǎn′ V elab. to intend harm, have bad intentions, bear ill-will (toward).

มุ่งหมาย mûŋmǎaj′ V to have a definite purpose; to aim for. ความ-- purpose, aim, objective.

เลขหมาย (ตัว, จำนวน) lêegmǎaj′ (tua′, camɔ nuan′) N numeral, number.

หมายเกณฑ์ (ใบ, ฉบับ) mǎajkeen′ (baj′, chabàb′) N conscription notice.

หมายค้น (ใบ, ฉบับ) mǎajkhón′ (baj′, chabàb′) N search warrant.

หมายความ(ว่า) mǎajkhwaam′(wâaɔ) V to mean (that).

o หมายความถึง mǎajkhwaam′thʉ̌ŋɔ 1. to imply. 2. to refer to.

หมายจับ (ฉบับ) mǎajcàb′ (chabàb′) N warrant of arrest.

หมายใจ mǎajcaj′ V to have one's heart set on; to have a purpose; to intend.

หมายตา mǎaj′taa′ V to mark (something) with the eyes, take notice of.

หมายถึง mǎajthʉ̌ŋɔ to mean, have the meaning of; to imply; to refer to.

หมายประกาศ (ใบ, ฉบับ) mǎajprakàad′ (baj′, chabàb′) N written announcement, declaration, handbill.

หมายมั่นปั้นมือ mǎajmân′pânmyy′ V elab. colloq. 1. to resolve, have a strong determination (to do something). 2. to anticipate strongly.

หมายเรียก (ฉบับ) mǎajrîag′ (chabàb′) N subpoena, summons.

หมายเลข mǎajlêeg′ N number.

หมายสั่ง (ใบ, ฉบับ) mǎajsàŋ′ (baj′, chabàb′) N writ, written decree or order.

หมายเหตุ (แห่ง, ข้อ) mǎajhèed′ (hèŋ′, khɔ̂ɔ′) N note, footnote.

หม้าย. See ม่าย ๒.

หมิ่น mìn′ V 1. to insult. 2. to look down upon, despise.

ดูหมิ่น duumìn′ V 1. to insult. 2. to look down upon, despise. →Syn. ดูถูก.

หมิ่นประมาท mìn′pramàad′ V to insult, be con-

temptuous of.

หมิ่นเหม่ mìnmèe′ V to be precarious, perilous, risky.

หมี (ตัว) mǐi′ (tua′) N bear (animal).

หมี่ mìi′ N 1. a type of thin rice noodles. 2. egg noodles.

หมี่กรอบ mìikrɔ̀ɔb′ N crisp fried noodles (with meat) (a Thai dish).

หมึก mʉ̀g′ N ink.

ปลาหมึก (ตัว) plaamʉ̀g′ (tua′) N 1. cuttlefish (Sepia). 2. squid.

ปากกาหมึกซึม (ด้าม, อัน) pàagkaa′mʉ̀gsym′ (dâam′, ʔan′) N fountain pen.

หมื่น ๑ mʉ̀yn′ V slang to be impertinent, insolent.

หมื่น ๒ mʉ̀yn′ Nm 1. ten thousand. C 2. idem.

o แสนเก้าหมื่นแปดพัน sɛ̌ɛn′-kâawmʉ̀yn′-pɛ̀ɛd′phan′ Nm 198,000.

หมุด (ตัว, อัน) mùd′ (tua′, ʔan′) N tack, peg, very small screw.

เข็มหมุด (อัน, เล่ม, ตัว) khěmmùd′ (ʔan′, lêm′, tua′) N pin.

หมุน mǔn′ V to turn, rotate, spin.

พายุหมุน phaajúʔ′mǔn′ N cyclone.

หมุนติ้ว mǔntîw′ V to spin fast.

หมุนรอบ mǔnrɔ̂ɔb′ V to rotate, revolve, turn around.

หมุนเวียน mǔnwian′ V to turn, rotate, circulate.

o เงินหมุนเวียน ŋən′mǔnwian′ N currency (money in actual use, in circulation).

หัวหมุน hǔamǔn′ V to be confused, overwhelmed, overcome (as by too much work, by excessive responsibilities, etc.).

หมุบหมิบ. See มุบมิบ ๒.

หมู (ตัว) mǔu′ (tua′) N 1. com. pig, hog; pork. 2. slang fool; short for หมูโคราช. V 3. slang to be very easy, simple. →Syn. 1. สุกร eleg.

ข่มหมู khòmmǔu′ V slang to browbeat a weaker or inferior person, to bully.

ต้มหมู tômmǔu′ V slang to make a sucker out of someone, make a dupe of someone.

น้ำมันหมู námman′mǔu′ N lard.

เนื้อหมู nʉ́amǔu′ N pork.

ลมบ้าหมู lom′bâamǔu′ N 1. whirlwind. 2. epilepsy;

short for โรค-- .

o โรคลมบ้าหมู rôog/-lom/bâamŭu/ N epilepsy.

สี่เหลี่ยมคางหมู (รูป) sìilìam/khaaŋmŭu/ (rûub/)
N trapezoid.

หมูโคราช (ตัว) mŭu/khoorâad/ (tua/) N slang
fool.

หมูแดง mŭudɛɛŋ/ N Chinese-style barbecued pork.

หมูๆ mŭumŭu/ V slang to be very easy, simple.

หมูเห็ดเป็ดไก่ mŭuhèd/pèdkàj/ N colloq. meats
of various kinds.

หมู่ mùu/ C group. →Syn. See พวก .

ดาวหมู่ daawmùu/ N constellation.

เป็นหมู่เป็นเหล่า penmùu/penlàw/ elab. in groups.

เป็นหมู่ๆ penmùumùu/ in groups.

หมู่เกาะ (หมู่,หมู่เกาะ) mùukɔ́?/ (mùu/, mùukɔ́?/)
N a group of islands, archipelago.

o หมู่เกาะมะลายู mùukɔ́?/malaajuu/ pN the
Malay Archipelago.

o หมู่เกาะอินเดียตะวันตก mùukɔ́?/-?india/tawan⊃
tòg/ pN the West Indies.

หมู่นี้ mùuníi/ these days, nowadays, at present,
during this time.

หมู่บ้าน (หมู่,แห่ง) mùubâan/ (mùu/, hɛ̀ŋ/) N
village, group of houses.

หมู่ไม้ mùumáaj/ N 1. grove of trees. 2. plants
(collectively).

หยก ๑, หิน-- jòg/, hǐnjòg/ N jade.

หยก ๒ in หยกๆ jògjòg/ just now, just, recently.

หยด jòd/ C 1. drop (as of water). V 2. to drip,
drop.

หยดน้ำ (หยด) jòdnáam/ (jòd/) N drop of water.

หยดย้อย jòdjɔ́ɔj/ V to be superb, beautiful.

หยอก jɔ̀g/ V to kid, tease, play with.

ไม่หยอก mâjjɔ̀g/ colloq. quite, really, very.

หยอกล้อ jɔ̀glɔ́ɔ/ to kid, tease, play with.

หย็อกหย็อย jɔ̀gjɔ̌j/ V 1. (hair) to be thin, sparse.
2. (hair) to be tightly curled, frizzy, kinky. 3.
(foliage) to be thin, unhealthy.

หยอด jɔ̀ɔd/ V to put some drops on, into.

น้ำมันหยอดเครื่อง námman/jɔ̀ɔdkhrŷaŋ/ lubricating oil, motor oil.

หยอดน้ำมัน jɔ̀ɔd/námman/ V to oil, lubricate.

หยอดหลุม jɔ̀ɔdlǔm/ N a kind of gambling game

in which the stakes, consisting of pennies, small
cards, or marbles, are thrown or shot toward a
hole or holes.

หย่อน jɔ̀ɔn/, jɔ̀n/ V 1. to slacken, relax, loosen. 2.
to lower (something). 3. to be lax. 4. to be inadequate, short, lacking (in). →Cf. 4. ย่อม ๑.

o ราคาสามบาทหย่อนสลึง raakhaa/-sǎambàad/-
jɔ̀n/salŷŋ/ the price is 3 bahts less a quarter
(i.e. 2.75 bahts).

ยิ่งหย่อนกว่า jîŋ/jɔ̀n/-kwàa⊃ V to differ in superiority or inferiority (with respect to some quality,
as size, beauty, diligence, etc.). →See cross
reference.

ลดหย่อน lódjɔ̀n/ V to decrease, reduce, lower.

หย่อนใจ jɔ̀ncaj/ V to relax, be at leisure, take
recreation.

หย่อนเชือก jɔ̀nchŷag/ V 1. to lower a rope, let
a rope down (into). 2. to slacken a rope.

หย่อนบัตร jɔ̀nbàd/ V to drop a ballot (into a
ballot box).

หย่อนลง jɔ̀n/loŋ 1. to put down, lower. 2. to
slow down. 3. to slacken (e.g. a rope). 4. to
decrease, diminish.

o หย่อนตัวลงนั่ง jɔ̀ntua/loŋnâŋ/ to lower oneself
into a sitting position.

หย่อนอารมณ์ jɔ̀n/?aarom/ V 1. to relax. 2. to
be at leisure.

หยุดหย่อน as in ไม่หยุดหย่อน mâjjùdjɔ̀n/ without
stopping, continually, incessantly.

หย่อม in หย่อมแหยม jɔ̀mjɛ̌m/* colloq. to be
sparse, scanty, thin.

หย่อม jɔ̀m/* patch, cluster, clump.

ทุกหย่อมหญ้า thúgjɔ̀m/jâa/ idiom. everywhere,
all over.

หยอย ๑, หย็อย. See entries below.

หย็อกหย็อย jɔ̀gjɔ̌j/ V 1. (hair) to be thin, sparse.
2. (hair) to be tightly curled, frizzy, kinky. 3.
(foliage) to be thin, unhealthy.

หยิกหย็อย jìgjɔ̌j/ V (hair) to be tightly curled,
frizzy, kinky.

หยอย ๒ in หยอยๆ jɔ̌jjɔ̌j/* sV nimbly, speedily
(of walking, running).

หยัก (หยัก) jàg/ (jàg/) V 1. to be curly, wavy. 2.
to be toothed, serrated, notched, fluted, undulated

with pointed crests. N 3. tooth, point of a ser-

ration or of a wave-like design.

เป็นหยัก penjàg′ 1. to be fluted, undulated with

pointed crests. 2. to be toothed, serrated, notched.

→Dist. เป็นแฉก. →Syn. 2. เป็นจักๆ, เป็นฟัน.

หยักไปหยักมา jàgpaj′jàgmaa′ V 1. to zigzag.

2. to be zigzag, serrated, jagged.

หยักรั้ง jàgráŋ′ V to be pulled high, hiked up,

gathered up (as of a skirt, trouser legs). NOTE.

According to some speakers this expression

implies that the lower edge of the garment is

uneven, or has one portion pulled up higher

than another.

o นุ่งผ้าหยักรั้ง nûŋphâa′jàgráŋ′ to wear (an item

of) clothing pulled up high, hiked up, gathered

up.

หยักศก, หยักโศก jàgsòg′, jàgsòog′ V (hair) to be

wavy.

หยักไย่. See หยากไย่.

หยั่ง jàŋ′ V to measure, fathom, sound (the depth)

(of water; of feelings, thought).

หยั่งใจ jàŋcaj′ V to sound out one's thoughts and

feelings.

หยั่งท่าที jàŋ′thâathii′ V to sound out one's views

or attitudes.

หยัด in ยืนหยัด jyyn′jàd′ V to stand firm, be

steadfast, unyielding.

หยัน, เย้ย-- jǎn′, jɤ́ɤjjǎn′ V to mock, ridicule, jeer,

laugh at.

หยับๆ jàbjàb′ sV with an up and down motion (of

the jaws).

o เคี้ยวหยับๆ khíaw′jàbjàb′ V to chew.

o พูดหยับๆ phûud′jàbjàb′ V to jabber away.

หย่า jàa′ V 1. to divorce. 2. to withdraw (some-

thing).

ฟ้องหย่า fɔ́ɔŋjàa′ V to sue for a divorce.

หย่านม jàa′nom′ V to wean.

หย่าร้าง jàa′ráaŋ′ V to divorce.

อย่าศึก jàa′sɤ̀g′ V to cease fire, cease hostilities.

หยาก in หยากไย่ jàagjâj′ N cobweb. →Also

spelled หยักไย่.

หยาด (เม็ด) jàad′ (méd′) C 1. drop (as of water).

V 2. to drop, to drip.

หยาดเยิ้ม jàadjɤ́əm′ V 1. to look honey-sweet,

rich and sweet, meltingly sweet (as of candied

fruit, honeycomb, a woman's eyes). 2. (music)

to be rich and sweet, gorgeous, mellifluous.

หยาบ jàab′ V 1. to be rough, coarse, crude (as of

surfaces, fabrics, substances). 2. to be rude,

vulgar, crude, coarse (of action, speech).

คำหยาบ (คำ) khamjàab′ (kham′) N vulgar

word(s), vulgar speech.

พูดจาหยาบโลน phûudcaa′jàabloon′ to use vulgar

or obscene language (often with humorous intent).

หยาบคาย jàabkhaaj′ V to be crude, coarse,

vulgar, unmannerly (in speech or action).

หยาบช้า jàabcháa′ V to be rude, vulgar (in speech,

behavior).

หยาบหยาม jàabjǎam′ V to be rude and insulting

(in speech, action).

หยาม jǎam′ V 1. to despise, hold in contempt, look

down upon. 2. to speak disparagingly or con-

temptuously of.

หยาบหยาม jàabjǎam′ V to be rude and insulting

(in speech, action).

หยามหน้า jǎam′nâa′ V 1. to look down upon,

despise. 2. to speak disparagingly or contemp-

tuously of.

หยิก jìg′ V 1. to pinch, nip (with fingernail or knuck-

les). 2. to be kinky, curly. →Dist. 2. งอ, ลอน.

หยิกหยอย jìgjɔ̌j′ V to be tightly curled, frizzy,

kinky.

หยุกหยิก jùgjìg′ V 1. to fidget, wiggle; to be

fidgety, restless. 2. (handwriting) to be scrib-

bled, scrawling, unsteady, shaky. 3. to be crooked,

wiggly (as of a line).

หยิ่ง jìŋ′ V to be haughty, vain, proud.

เย่อหยิ่ง jɤ̀ɤjìŋ′ V to be haughty, vain, proud.

หยิ่งผยอง jìŋ′phajɔ̌ɔŋ′ V to be excessively proud,

arrogant, haughty.

หยิ่งยโส jìŋ′jasǒo′ V to be arrogant, impudent.

หยิบ jìb′ V to pick up, take (up) (in the hand).

หยิบมือ jìbmyy′ C small amount, pinch (e.g. of

salt).

หยิบไม่ถึง jìb′mâjthɯ̌ŋ′ can't get it, can't pick it

up (because it's beyond reach).

หยิบยก (ขึ้น) jìbjóg′(khɯ̂n⊃) V 1. to bring up,

take up, single out. 2. to be brought up, taken

up, singled out.

หยิบยื่น jìbjɯ̂ɯn′ V to give, offer, hand over.

หยิบเล็กหยิบน้อย jìblég′jìbnɔ́ɔj′ V elab. colloq. to pilfer.

หยิม. See entries below.

หยิมๆ jɪ̌mjɪ̌m′ rM sparsely, finely; used with ฝนตก "it's raining."

o ฝนตกหยิมๆ fǒntòg′jɪ̌mjɪ̌m′ it's drizzling.

หยุมหยิม jǔmjɪ̌m′ sV 1. petty, fussy, trivial. V 2. to fuss about trifles.

o เรื่องหยุมหยิม rɯ̂aŋ′jǔmjɪ̌m′ triviality, trifle.

หยี ๑ jɪ̌i′ V (eyes, eyelids) to be narrowed, squinting, partly closed.

ตาหยี taa′jɪ̌i′ V 1. to have narrow, slit eyes (as of Orientals).

ทำตาหยี thamtaa′jɪ̌i′ to squint, squint one's eyes.

หยี ๒. See entries below.

ต้นหยี tônjɪ̌i′ N a type of tree which bears a sour fruit.

ลูกหยี (พวง,ลูก,เม็ด) lûugjɪ̌i′ N the fruit of the above (phuaŋ′ for clusters; lûug′ for individual fresh fruits; méd′ for the prepared fruit). ต้น-- (ต้น) idem ต้นหยี.

หยุกหยิก jùgjìg′ V 1. to fidget, wiggle; to be fidgety, restless. 2. (handwriting) to be scribbled, scrawling, unsteady, shaky. 3. to be crooked, wiggly (as of a line).

หยุด jùd′ V 1. to stop, cease, halt. 2. to pause, take a break, take a vacation, be absent.

ป้ายหยุดรถ (ป้าย,แผ่น) pâaj′jùdród′ (pâaj′, phèn′) N 1. bus stop placard. 2. traffic stop sign.

โรงเรียนหยุด rooŋrian′jùd′ school is closed, is over, is out. →Comp. หยุดโรงเรียน.

ลาหยุด laajùd′ V to request or take leave of absence; to ask for take time off.

วันหยุด (วัน) wanjùd′ (wan′) N holiday, day off.

o วันหยุดราชการ (วัน) wanjùd′râadchakaan′ (wan′) official holiday.

หยุดกึก jùdkɯ̀g′ V to stop suddenly, stop short.

หยุดคิด jùdkhíd′ V 1. to pause (in order) to think. 2. to stop thinking.

หยุดงาน jùdŋaan′ V to stop working; to take a vacation; to absent oneself from work; to go on strike.

o วันหยุดงาน wan′jùdŋaan′ N day of rest, day off, holiday.

หยุดชะงัก jùd′chaŋág′ V to come to a sudden standstill, stop short.

หยุดเดิน jùddəən′ V 1. to stop in one's tracks. 2. to stop walking.

หยุดพัก (ครั้ง,หน) jùdphág′ (khráŋ′, hǒn′) V 1. to take a break, take time out to rest, stop to rest. N 2. time out, break, rest, recess.

o หยุดพักกลางวัน jùdphág′klaaŋwan′ 1. to take a midday break, a noon recess. 2. midday break, noon recess.

หยุดยิง jùdjiŋ′ V to cease fire.

หยุดโรงเรียน jùd′rooŋrian′ V to skip school, stay out of school. →Comp. โรงเรียนหยุด.

หยุดหย่อน as in ไม่หยุดหย่อน mâjjùdjɔ̀n′ without stopping, continually, incessantly.

หยุ่น in ยืดหยุ่น jɯ̂ɯdjùn′ V to be elastic.

หยุมหยิม jǔmjɪ̌m′ sV 1. petty, fussy, trivial. V 2. to fuss about trifles.

o เรื่องหยุมหยิม rɯ̂aŋ′jǔmjɪ̌m′ triviality, trifle.

หยูก jùug′ N medicine. →Chiefly in combination with ยา.

ยาหยูก,หยูกยา jaajùug′, jùugjaa′ N colloq. medicine.

หรดี hɔ̌ɔradii′ lit., eleg. southwest. →Syn. ตะวัน ตกเฉียงใต้ com. →The literary and the common terms for the eight chief points of the compass are listed under ทิศ.

หรอ in สึกหรอ sɯ̀grɔɔ′ V to wear out, be worn down, worn out.

หร็อก,หรอก rɔ̀g′, rɔg′, rɔ̀ɔg′, rɔɔg′ Pt com. particle often used with statements of negation, contradiction, or those correcting a misapprehension. Usually makes a statement milder, less abrupt, or expresses reassurance. →Syn. ดอก writ. NOTE. หรอก may sometimes be rendered in English by special stress or intonation somewhere in the sentence; see 1st example.

o ไม่ต้องหรอก mâjtɔ̂ŋ′rɔg↓ That's not necessary.

o ฉันเองหรอก chán?eeŋ′rɔ̀g↓ It's just me.

หร็อมแหร็ม,หรอมแหรม rɔ̌mrɛ̌m′ V to be scanty, sparse.

หรั่ง (คน) ràŋ′ (khon′) N Occidental. →Variant

of ฝรั่ง.

หรั่งจ๋า ràŋcǎa′ V to be very westernized.

หรา rǎa′ sV 1. defiantly, boldly, flauntingly. 2. gaily, in a lively manner.

เด่นหรา dèn′rǎa′ V to be conspicuously prominent, flaunted conspicuously.

เดินหรา dəən′rǎa′ V to walk boldly, defiantly.

หริ่ง in เสียงหริ่งๆ (เสียง) sǐaŋ′rìŋrìŋ′ (sǐaŋ′) N a chirping sound (as of certain kinds of insects).

หริภุญชัย in เมืองหริภุญชัย myaŋ′hàríphunchaj′ pN Hariphunchai, ancient name of Lamphun.

หรี่ rìi′ V 1. to dim, turn down (a light). 2. to squint (as from too much light). 3. (eyes) to be about to close.

ตาหรี่ taa′rìi′ the eyes are about to close (as when dozing off).

ริบหรี่ ríbrìi′ V to be dim, faint (of light).

หรี่ตา rìi′taa′ V to squint (as from too much light).

หรีด in พวงหรีด (พวง) phuaŋrìid′ (phuaŋ′) N wreath.

หรือ (1) rʏ̌y′, rý′, rɔ́′; (2) rʏ̌y′, rý′, rɔ́′, rɔ̌ə′; (3, 4) rɔ́′↓, rɔ̌ə′↓ Cj 1. or. Pt 2. interrogative particle used in a yes-or-no question. 3. Is that so? (expressing surprise at what was said). 4. Well, well. Is that so-o. ? (mildly teasing response to a child's comment or request). →The usages given under 3 and 4 are short for งั้นหรือ They are normally employed only among intimates, the deferential (short) response being หรือคะ,หรือครับ. NOTE. The common and colloquial pronunciation of this word as a conjunction is rɔ́′; the pronunciation rý′ is deferential, and rʏ̌y′ is limited to formal turns of phrase, such as หรือมิฉะนั้น (see below). For หรือ as a final particle, the common and colloquial pronunciations are rɔ́′ and, with some exaggeration in connotation, rɔ̌ə′. The pronunciation rý′ is somewhat rhetorical here, and rʏ̌y′ is a formal spelling pronunciation. In writing, rɔ́′ is sometimes rendered by เรอะ, and rɔ̌ə′ by เหรอ.

o เขาไปบ้านแล้วหรือยัง kháwpajbâan′lɛ́ɛwrýjaŋ′↓,

-rɔ́′- Has he gone home yet (or not)?

o เมื่อวานนี้คุณมาหรือเปล่า mʏawaan′níi′ khunᵓ maa′rýplàaw′↓, -rɔ́- Did you come yesterday (or not)?

o หรือมิฉะนั้น rʏ̌y′míchanán′ or else. →This is used in formal contexts; a more common wording is หรือไม่ยังงั้น rýmâj′jaŋŋán′.

o ดูเอาทีหรือ duu′-ᵓawthii′rý′↓ What is this? (rhetorical question).

o เป็นไปได้หรือนี่ pen′pajdâaj′-rýnîi′↓, -rɔ́- Is this possible? Can it be? (expressing surprise).

o งั้นหรือ ŋán′rý′↓, -rɔ́′-, -rɔ̌ə′-. Is that so? Is that it?

o หรือคะ rýkhá′↓, rɔ̌ə- w. sp. Is that so? →Also หรือครับ m. sp.

หรู, หรูหรา rǔu′, rǔurǎa′ V to be sumptuous, luxurious, splendid, gorgeous.

หฤทัย hàrýthaj′ N lit. heart.

หฤหรรษ์ hàrýhǎn′ V lit. to be joyful.

หลง lǒŋ′ V 1. to get lost, go astray. 2. to forget. 3. to misunderstand. 4. to be infatuated, fascinated.

ขี้หลงขี้ลืม khîilǒŋ′khîilyym′ V elab. colloq. to be forgetful, absent-minded.

ลุ่มหลง lûmlǒŋ′ V to be infatuated (with), madly in love (with), crazy (about).

เสียงหลง sǐaŋlǒŋ′ the voice to be shrill, distorted (as when highly excited or screaming). 2. the voice to be off tune, flat (as when singing).

หลงกล lǒŋkon′ V to be deceived, beguiled.

หลงทาง lǒŋthaaŋ′ V to lose one's way.

หลงน้ำลาย lǒŋ′námlaaj′ V slang to be fascinated by someone's words, believing them blindly.

หลงผิด lǒŋphìd′ V to err.

หลงฝูง lǒŋfǔuŋ′ V 1. to be in the wrong group. 2. to stray from one's group.

หลงรัก lǒŋrág′ V to be passionately in love, infatuated with, crazy over (someone).

หลงเล่ห์ lǒŋsanèe′ V to fall for someone's charms.

หลงหูหลงตา lǒŋhǔu′lǒŋtaa′ V elab. colloq. to escape notice.

หลงใหล lǒŋlǎj′ V to be crazy about.

หลน lǒn/ N 1. a kind of shrimp sauce served with raw vegetables. V 2. to prepare such a sauce.

หล่น lòn/ V to drop, fall (of leaves, flowers, fruit, etc.). →Syn. ร่วง.

ทำ(. . .)หล่น tham(...)lòn/ to make (something) fall off; to drop (something)(unintentionally).

หลบ lòb/ V 1. to duck in order to escape from danger. 2. to slip or sneak away. 3. to hide. 4. to avoid.

หลบตา lòbtaa/ V to avoid (someone's) eyes.

หลบมุม lòbmum/ V to hide from, evade, avoid an unpleasant encounter or situation: "to duck into a (safe) corner."

หลบหน้า lòbnâa/ V to avoid being seen, keep out of sight.

หลบหนี lòbnǐi/ V to slip away, escape (stealthily).

หลบหลีก lòblìig/ V to avoid, evade.

หลุมหลบภัยทางอากาศ (แห่ง) lǔmlòbphaj/thaaŋɔ ʔaakàad/ (hèŋ/) N air-raid shelter.

หลุม (แห่ง) lǔm/ (hèŋ/) N mud, muddy place.

ติดหล่ม tìdlòm/ V to get caught in the mud.

หล่มสัก lòmsàg/ pN Lomsak, a township in NE Thailand.

หลวง lǔaŋ/ N 1. government. 2. (as n. mod.) royal. T 3. next to the lowest conferred title for government officials, above ขุน and below พระ. 4. element used in combination with certain relationship terms to designate priests who are related to but older than the speaker; see examples below, and also the entry หลวงพ่อ which in addition has more general application. V 5. to be great (of restricted usage).

o หลวงพี่ (องค์) lǔaŋphîi/ (ʔoŋ/) N 1. a priest who is one's older brother. P 2. you; he, him (sp. to or of such a priest). T 3. title placed before the name of such a priest.

o หลวงลุง (องค์) lǔaŋluŋ/ (ʔoŋ/) N 1. a priest who is one's elder uncle. P 2. you; he, him (sp. to or of such a priest). T 3. title placed before the name of such a priest.

ข้าหลวง (คน,นาย) khâalǔaŋ/ (khon/, naaj/) N 1. royal servant (esp. female), lady in waiting. 2. governor (of a čhangwat). 3. commissioner.

เจ้าหลวง (องค์) câawlǔaŋ/ (ʔoŋ/) N king of a vassal state.

ชั่งหลวง châŋlǔaŋ/ C a unit of weight, equiv. to 600 grams.

ตลกหลวง (คน) talòg/lǔaŋ/ (khon/) N royal comedian; court jester.

ถนนหลวง (สาย) thanǒn/lǔaŋ/ (sǎaj/) N 1. public road, public highway. pN 2. Luang Road, a street in Bangkok.

ท้องสนามหลวง thɔ́ɔŋsanǎamlǔaŋ/ pN colloq. the Phra Men (Phra Meru) Grounds where official ceremonies are held. →Syn. ทุ่งพระเมรุ.

ทะเลหลวง (ทะเล,แห่ง) thalee/lǔaŋ/ (thalee/, hèŋ/) N a great sea.

ทางหลวง (สาย) thaaŋlǔaŋ/ (sǎaj/) N highway.

นครหลวง (นคร,แห่ง) nakhɔɔn/lǔaŋ/ (nakhɔɔn/, hèŋ/) N eleg. capital (of a country).

ในหลวง (องค์,พระองค์) najlǔaŋ/ (ʔoŋ/, phráʔoŋ/) N colloq. the king (short form). →See กษัตริย์.

บาทหลวง,พระ-- (องค์) bàadlǔaŋ/, phráʔ/bàadɔ lǔaŋ/ (ʔoŋ/) N 1. Roman Catholic priest or monk. 2. any robed Christian clergyman. →Also spelled บาดหลวง.

เมียหลวง (คน) mialǔaŋ/ (khon/) N lawful wife, the first wife.

เมืองหลวง (เมือง) myaŋlǔaŋ/ (myaŋ/) N com. capital (of a country). →Syn. ธานี eleg.

ยาตำราหลวง (ขนาน) jaa/-tamraa/lǔaŋ/ (khaɔ nǎan/) N drugs prepared by the Department of Public Health.

รถไฟหลวง ródfajlǔaŋ/ N Royal State Railways. →Abbrev. ร.พ.ล.

โรงเรียนหลวง (โรงเรียน,แห่ง) rooŋrian/lǔaŋ/ (rooŋrian/, hèŋ/) N colloq. government school. →Opp. โรงเรียนราษฎร์. →Syn. โรงเรียนรัฐบาล.

หมอหลวง (คน) mɔɔlǔaŋ/ (khon/) N royal doctor.

หลวงพ่อ (องค์) lǔaŋphɔ̂ɔ/ (ʔoŋ/) N 1. a venerable priest (commanding respect by virtue of high office or great age). 2. a priest who is one's father. 3. the largest Buddha image in a temple. P 4. you; he, him (sp. to or of a priest as defined above). T 5. title placed before the name of such a priest. nN 6. nickname for a person of high character, with a saintly disposition.

ใหญ่หลวง jàjlŭaŋ′ V to be tremendous, enormous, major, grave, serious.

หลวงพระบาง lŭaŋphrábaaŋ′ pN Luang Prabang, a city in Laos.

หลวม lŭam′ V to be loose, too large, baggy.

   หลวมตัว lŭamtua′ V idiom. to have gotten so deeply involved (in something) that one is unable to back out.

   หลวมโพรก lŭamphrôog′ V to be very loose, too large, very baggy (as of garments).

   หลวมๆ lŭamlŭam′ sV loose, loosely.

   หละหลวม là?lŭam′ V 1. to be careless, negligent. sV 2. carelessly, negligently.

หลอ. See entries below.

   ฟันหลอ (ซี่) fanlɔɔ′ (sîi′) N a worn-down tooth.

   เหลือหลอ lŷalɔɔ′ V to be left, remaining.

หล่อ lɔɔ′ V 1. to cast (in a mold). 2. colloq. to be handsome (of males only). 3. com. to be immersed in, covered with, surrounded by a liquid (as a means of cooling or to protect against rust or insects).

   การหล่อลื่น kaanlɔɔlŷyn′ N lubrication.

   รูปหล่อ rûublɔɔ′ V colloq. to be handsome (of males only).

   เหล็กหล่อ lèglɔɔ′ N cast iron.

หลอก lɔɔg′ V 1. to trick, deceive, fool. 2. to scare. 3. to show defiance, insubordination or ridicule (usually by making a face or defiant gesture).

   แลบลิ้นหลอก lɛɛblín′-lɔɔg′ to stick one's tongue out (at).

   หลอกลวง lɔɔgluaŋ′ V to dupe, deceive.

   หลอกหลอน,หลอนหลอก lɔɔglɔɔn′, lɔɔnlɔɔg′ V to scare, spook, haunt.

หลอด (หลอด) lɔɔd′ (lɔɔd′) N 1. tube. C 2. clf. for certain tube-like objects, spools, etc.; for substances in tubes (as of toothpaste).

   ด้ายหลอด (หลอด) dâajlɔɔd′ (lɔɔd′) N spool of thread, thread (on a spool).

   หลอดด้าย (หลอด) lɔɔddâaj′ (lɔɔd′) N spool (for thread).

   หลอดดูด (หลอด) lɔɔddùud′ N (drinking) straw.

   หลอดไฟ (หลอด) lɔɔdfaj′ (lɔɔd′) N light bulb.

   หลอดลม (หลอด) lɔɔdlom′ (lɔɔd′) N trachea.

หลอน lɔɔn′ V to scare, spook, haunt.

หล่อน lɔ̀n′/* P 1. writ. she, her. 2. you (royal person sp. to a common woman).

   เจ้าหล่อน câwlɔ̀n′ P writ. she, her.

หลอม lɔɔm′ V to melt, fuse (metal).

   จุดหลอมตัว (จุด) cùd′lɔɔmtua′ (cùd′) N melting point.

   เหล็กหลอม lèglɔɔm′ N pig iron.

หละ in หละหลวม là?lŭam′ V 1. to be careless, negligent. sV 2. carelessly, negligently.

หลัก (หลัก) làg′ (làg′) N 1. pole, pillar. 2. principle; basis. 3. (one's) footing.

   ปักหลัก pàglàg′ V 1. to drive a post or stake. 2. colloq. to dig in, settle down.

   ผู้หลักผู้ใหญ่ phûulàg′phûujàj′ N elab. colloq. (one's) superiors, elders. →See ผู้ใหญ่.

   ลงหลักปักราก loŋlàg′pàgraag′ V elab. to lay the foundation (of a building).

   เสียหลัก sĭalàg′ V to lose one's footing, foothold; to lose one's balance.

   หลักการ (หลักการ,ข้อ) làgkaan′ (làgkaan′, khɔɔ′) N principle.

   หลักเกณฑ์ (ข้อ) làgkeen′ (khɔɔ′) N rules.

   หลักชัย làgchaj′ N goal, destination.

   หลักฐาน làgthăan′ N 1. basis, foundation. 2. evidence, testimony, proof. 3. colloq. wealth.

   ○ วิชาพิสูจน์หลักฐาน wíchaa′-phísùud′làgthăan′ N criminalistics, dealing with the examination of physical evidence.

   หลักทรัพย์ (อย่าง) làgsáb′ (jàaŋ′) N property, possessions or holdings used as security.

   หลักปฏิบัติ (ข้อ) làg′pàtibàd′ (khɔɔ′) N 1. principles of conduct, of procedure. 2. practice (as opposed to theory). →Opp. 2. หลักวิชา.

   หลักประกัน làg′prakan′ N security, surety, collateral, guaranty.

   หลักวิชา làg′wíchaa′ N theory (as opposed to practice). →Opp. หลักปฏิบัติ.

   หลักสิบ làgsìb′ N arith. tens; the position occupied by numbers which are tens.

   หลักสูตร làgsùud′ N curriculum, course of study.

   หลักหน่วย làgnùaj′ N arith. units; the position occupied by units.

   หลักแหล่ง (แห่ง) làglɛ̀ŋ′ (hɛ̀ŋ′) N the place where one settles down to live.

○ เป็นหลักแหล่ง penlàglɛ̀ŋ′ 1. permanent, fixed (of a house, dwelling). 2. permanently, steadily.

หลักแหลม làglɛ̌ɛm′ V to be keen, sharp.

หลัง (หลัง) lăŋ′ (lăŋ′) N 1. back (body-part). 2. (as n. mod) back, hind, rear. C 3. clf. for houses, mosquito-nets, tents, palanquins, etc. Pp 4. back of, behind, after. ความ-- the past; past deeds, past experience. →Opp. 2, 4. หน้า ๑.

กระจกหลัง (บาน) kracòg′lăŋ′ (baan′) N rear-view mirror.

กองหลัง (กอง) kɔɔŋlăŋ′ (kɔɔŋ′) N rear guard.

ขาหลัง (ขา) khăalăŋ′ (khăa′) N hind legs.

ข้างหลัง khâŋlăŋ′ behind, (at) the rear, the back.

คล้อยหลัง khlɔ́ɔj′lăŋ′ V 1. to pass by, move past, move out of sight. 2. to turn one's back.

คิดหน้าคิดหลัง khídnâa′khídlăŋ′ V elab. colloq. to think (it) through, think over carefully.

ชักหน้าไม่ถึงหลัง chág′nâa′-mâjthŷŋlăŋ′ V idiom. to be unable to make both ends meet.

ช้างเท้าหลัง châaŋ′tháawlăŋ′ N 1. "the hind legs of the elephant," a figure used to describe one who is a follower.

ตอนหลัง tɔɔnlăŋ′ 1. the later period; later on, afterwards. 2. back part. →Ant. 1. ตอนต้น. 2. ตอนหน้า.

แต่หนหลัง tɛ̀ɛhŏn′lăŋ′ in the past.

ถอยหลัง thɔ̌jlăŋ′ V 1. to step back, back up. sV 2. backward, backwards, back.

○ ถอยหลังเข้าคลอง thɔ̌jlăŋ′khâwkhlɔɔŋ′ V idiom. (a civilization) to regress, fall into backwardness.

○ นับถอยหลัง náb′thɔ̌jlăŋ′ V to count backwards.

ทีหลัง thiilăŋ′ next time, any time after this, later.

เบื้องหลัง bŷaŋlăŋ′ behind, in the rear, in the past. →Ant. เบื้องหน้า.

ปวดหลัง pùadlăŋ′ V to have a backache.

เป็นบ้าเป็นหลัง penbâa′penlăŋ′ V elab. colloq. to be crazy.

ภายหลัง phaajlăŋ′ afterwards.

ลับหลัง láblăŋ′ behind the back of, in the absence of. →Ant. ต่อหน้า.

ล้าหลัง láalăŋ′ V to lag behind, be behind (in time or space), be backward. ความ-- backwardness.

ล้นหลัง (ล้นหลัง) sănlăŋ′ (sănlăŋ′) N back (body-part); spine; backbone.

หน้าหลัง nâalăŋ′ 1. the back page, the last page (as of a newspaper). 2. the reverse side (of a sheet).

หนุนหลัง nŭnlăŋ′ V to support, back up.

หลังโกง lăŋkooŋ′ V 1. to have a crooked back (as from a deformity). 2. to be round-shouldered, stooped over; to have one's shoulders slouched over.

○ ทำหลังโกง tham′lăŋkooŋ′ 1. to arch the back (as a cat). 2. to gather up the shoulders (as a tiger ready to spring). 3. to round one's shoulders, slouch.

หลังคา (หลังคา) lăŋkhaa′ (lăŋkhăa′) N roof.

หลังจาก lăŋ′càagɔ after.

หลังฉาก lăŋchàag′ N 1. back stage, behind the scenes. 2. the inside story or account, the real picture, the real underlying facts. NOTE. When used of people, this usually implies a shameful, hidden way of life which belies the public image.

หักหลัง hàglăŋ′ V idiom. to betray, doublecross.

เหลียวหลัง lĭawlăŋ′ V to look back.

เอนหลัง ʔeenlăŋ′ V to lean back, recline (in order to go to sleep).

หลั่ง làŋ′ V 1. to let flow, to pour, sprinkle, shed (as tears, blood). 2. to flow continuously.

ไหลหลั่ง lăjlàŋ′ V 1. to flow continuously. 2. (a crowd) to stream along, move in a mass.

หลั่น as in ลดหลั่น lódlàn′ V to be descending in regular order, to cascade.

หลับ làb′ V 1. to close (the eyes). 2. to sleep, fall asleep, be asleep. →Opp. 1. ลืม ๒. 2. ตื่น.

เครื่องหลับนอน (อย่าง, ชิ้น) khrŷaŋ′làbnɔɔn′ (jàaŋ′, chín′) N bedding.

นอนตาหลับ nɔɔn′taalàb′ V idiom. to be free of worry; to be able to sleep without worry.

นอนไม่หลับ nɔɔn′mâjlàb′ to be unable to sleep, to lie sleepless.

นอนหลับ nɔɔnlàb′ V to sleep, be asleep. →Ant. ตื่น.

นอนหลับทับสิทธิ์ nɔɔnlàb′-tháb′sìd′ V idiom. to be neglectful in exercising one's rights (as when failing to vote in an election).

หลับตา làbtaa′ V to close the eyes. →Ant. ลืมตา.

๐ หลับตาปี๋ làbtaa′pǐi′ to close the eyes tightly.

หลับนก làbnóg′ V idiom. to fall asleep, doze in a sitting position.

หลับใน làbnaj′ V idiom. to daydream.

หลับปุ๋ย làbpǔj′ V to sleep soundly.

หลับสนิท làb′sanìd′ V to be sound asleep.

หลับๆตื่นๆ làblàb′tỳyntỳyn′ V to sleep off and on, sleep fitfully.

อดตาหลับขับตานอน ?òd′taalàb′-khàb′taanɔɔn′ V elab. colloq. to deprive oneself of sleep (as when studying for exams).

หลัว ๑ (ใบ) lǔa′ (baj′) N a large tall basket.

หลัว ๒ in หลัวๆ lǔalǔa′ dim (of light); dimly.

หลา lǎa′ C yard (linear measure).

หล้า lâa′ N lit. earth, ground. →Syn. ดิน com.

สุดหล้าฟ้าเขียว sùdlâa′fáakhǐaw′ elab. colloq. very far away, beyond the horizon.

หลาก ๑ làag′ V lit. to be many; to be abundant, profuse. →Occ. cpl. with หลาย.

หลากสี làagsǐi′ V to be many-colored, variegated.

หลายหลากชะนิด lǎajlàag′chaníd′ of many different kinds.

ไหลหลาก lǎjlàag′ V to flow profusely, to overflow.

หลาก ๒ in หลากใจ làag′caj′ V to wonder, be surprised, astonished. ความ-- surprise, astonishment.

หลาน (คน) lǎan′ (khon′) N 1. grandchild. 2. nephew or niece.

ชั่วลูกชั่วหลาน chûalûug′chûalǎan′ generation after generation.

ลูกหลาน (คน) lûuglǎan′ (khon′) N descendants.

หลานเขย (คน) lǎankhɔ̌ɔj′ (khon′) N the husband of one's niece or granddaughter.

หลานชาย (คน) lǎanchaaj′ (khon′) N 1. grandson. 2. nephew.

หลานสะใภ้ (คน) lǎansapháj′ (khon′) N the wife of one's nephew or grandson.

หลานสาว (คน) lǎansǎaw′ (khon′) N 1. granddaughter. 2. niece.

หลาบ làab′ V 1. to have learned one's lesson. 2. to dread (to do something), to be afraid, esp. because of a previous bad experience.

หลาม. See entries below.

ข้าวหลาม (กระบอก) khâawlǎam′, khâwlǎam′ (krabɔ̀ɔg′) N glutinous rice with coconut cream topping stuffed in a bamboo section and roasted.

ล้นหลาม lónlǎam′ V to be overloaded, overflowing, overcrowded.

หลาย lǎaj′ Nm many, several. →Normally followed by a clf. except for certain combinations, e.g. the following entry.

ทั้งหลาย tháŋlǎaj′ all, the whole (group). →Cf. ทั้งปวง.

แพร่หลาย phrɛ̂ɛlǎaj′ V to be widespread.

มากหน้าหลายตา mâagnâa′lǎajtaa′ V elab. colloq. to be many (of people only).

รู้ไว้ไม่เสียหลาย rúu′wáj′→mâjsǐa′lǎaj′ knowledge is no burden.

หลายขนาด lǎajkhanàad′ (of) many sizes.

หลายใจ lǎajcaj′ V to have many loves (at the same time).

หลายต่อหลาย lǎaj′tɔ̀ɔlǎaj′ many many; a countless number of; so many.

หลายปีดีดัก lǎajpii′-dii′dàg′ elab. colloq. many many years.

หลายสิบ lǎajsìb′ many tens.

หลายๆ lǎajlǎaj′ Nm several.

เหลือหลาย lỷalǎaj′ sV 1. abundant, profuse; abundantly, profusely, extremely, very. V 2. to be abundant.

หลาว (อัน) lǎaw′ (?an′) N spear.

หลิม lǐm′ V to be disproportionately small and tapering, small and pointed.

หลิ่ว. See entries below.

ตาหลิ่ว taalìw′ V to be one-eyed; to have one eye open.

๐ เข้าเมืองตาหลิ่ว ต้องหลิ่วตาตาม khâwmyaŋ′ɔ taalìw′→tɔ̂ŋlìw′taataam′↓ idiom. When in Rome, do as the Romans do.

หลิ่วตา lìwtaa′ V 1. to wink (at). 2. to squint or look with one eye (the other being closed).

หลีก lìig′ V 1. to evade, avoid. 2. to get away from. 3. to step aside, move aside, move out of the way, give way to (both lit. and fig.).

หลีกทาง lìigthaaŋ′ V to step aside, move aside, give way to (both lit. and fig.).

หลีกเลี่ยง lìiglîaŋ′ V 1. to avoid. 2. to get away
from. 3. to be evasive.

หลีกหน้า lìignâa′ V colloq. to withdraw oneself.

หลีบ (หลีบ) lỳyb′ (lỳyb′) N a narrow space or
passage between cliffs, rocks, mountains,
screens, etc.

หลุกหลิก lùglìg′ V 1. to behave in an unseemly manner toward the opposite sex, distributing one's
attentions restlessly and indiscriminately. 2.
to behave in an unseemly, disorderly manner.

หลุด lùd′ V to slip loose, slip out, come loose,
come off, come out, come unfastened, become
detached.

ทำ(. . .)หลุด tham(...)lùd′ to let (something)
slip (e.g. out of one's hand).

หลุดพ้น(จาก) lùd′phón′-(càagɔ) V 1. to be
released, be free (from). 2. to escape, get
away (from).

หลุดมือ lùdmyy′ V to slip from the hand.

หลุน in เซหลุนๆ see′lŭnlŭn′ to stumble and trip,
stagger (as when pushed forcibly and unexpectedly).

หลุบ lùb′ V (the brim of a hat) to be turned down,
droop, hang down.

หลุม (หลุม) lŭm′ (lŭm′) N hole (as in the ground),
pit.

โยนหลุม joonlŭm′ N a kind of gambling game in
which the stakes, consisting of pennies, small
cards, or marbles, are thrown or shot toward
a hole or holes.

หลุมฝังศพ (หลุม) lŭm′fǎŋsòb′ (lŭm′) N grave,
tomb.

หลุมพราง (หลุม) lŭmphraaŋ′ (lŭm′) N trap,
pitfall.

หลุมหลบภัย (หลุม) lŭm′lòbphaj′ (lŭm′) N air-
raid shelter.

หลู่ in ลบหลู่ lóblùu′ V 1. to show disrespect, contempt, disdain, ungratefulness (toward parents,
guardian, teacher, or other benefactor particularly deserving of respect).

หวง hŭaŋ′ V to refuse to share or give away; to
guard, keep back, care for zealously.

หวงห้าม hŭaŋhâam′ V 1. to restrict against or
forbid public use. sV 2. restricted, forbidden.

หวงแหน hŭaŋhěεn′ V to reserve, guard, keep for
oneself, keep from falling to others.

o ขี้หวงแหน khîihŭaŋhěεn′ V to be possessive.

ห่วง ๑ (อัน,ห่วง) hùaŋ′ (ʔan′,hùaŋ′) N ring, hoop,
loop, noose. →Comp. บ่วง.

ห่วง ๒ hùaŋ′ V 1. to be worried, concerned about.
2. to think about, have one's mind occupied with.

เป็นห่วง penhùaŋ′ V to feel concern for, be worried, concerned about.

ห่วงใย hùaŋjaj′ V to be worried, anxious, concerned. ความ-- concern, care.

ห่วงหน้าห่วงหลัง hùaŋnâa′hùaŋlăŋ′ V to worry
over two equally important things.

ห้วง hûaŋ′ N 1. vastness, expanse, depth. C 2.
part, portion.

ห้วงนรก hûaŋ′naróg′ N hell (implying vastness,
depth, dreadfulness).

ห้วงน้ำ (แห่ง) hûaŋnáam′ (hὲŋ′) N a wide expanse
of water, the broad stretch of a river.

หวด ๑ (ใบ,ลูก) hùad′ (baj′,lûug′) N an earthenware steamer (for steaming food).

หวด ๒ hùad′ V to whip, lash.

หวน ๑ hŭan′ V to go back, turn back.

หวนกลับ hŭanklàb′ V to turn back, come back.

หวนคิด hŭankhíd′ V to think back, recall.

หวนนึก hŭannýg′ V to think back, recall.

หวนย้อน hŭanjɔ́ɔn′ V to go back, turn back.

หวน ๒ in โหยหวน hǒojhŭan′ V to be eerie (of
sound).

o เสียงโหยหวน sĭaŋ′hǒojhŭan′ N an eerie sound.

ห้วน hûan′ V 1. to be short, brief, curt, laconic.
sV 2. curtly, snappishly.

พูดห้วนๆ phûud′hûanhûan′ V to speak curtly.

หวย (ใบ) hŭaj′ N 1. a gambling game in which
players bet on letters or numbers. 2. colloq.
lottery; lottery ticket (baj′).

หวยเบอร์ (ใบ) hŭajbəə′ (baj′) N colloq. lottery ticket. →Syn. ลอตเตอรี่ com. สลากกิน
แบ่ง eleg.

ห่วย hùaj′ V slang to be no good, not satisfactory,
bad.

ห้วย (สาย) hûaj′ (săaj′) N brook, stream, creek.

หวอ ๑ wɔ̌ɔ′ N imit. colloq. the wail of a siren.

รถหวอ (คัน) ródwɔ̌ɔ′ (khan′) N colloq. ambulance, fire engine, police car (i.e. any vehicle with a siren).

หวอ ๒ wɔ̌ɔ/ V to be hollow, open, exposed, agape.

หวอด ๑ wɔ̀ɔd/ N foam or bubbles formed by some species of fish.

หวอด ๒ in ก่อหวอด kɔ̀ɔ/wɔ̀ɔd/ V colloq. to start, cause.

หวัง(ว่า) wǎŋ(wâa/) V to hope (that), hope for. ความ-- hope, hopes.

o มีความหวังที่จะ miikhwaamwǎŋ/thîicaʔ have hopes of (doing thus and so), be in hopes that (one) will (do thus and so).

คาดหวัง khâadwǎŋ/ V to expect, anticipate.

ผิดหวัง phìdwǎŋ/ V to be disappointed.

มีหวัง miiwǎŋ/ V to have hopes, be hopeful.

มุ่งหวัง mûŋwǎŋ/ V to anticipate, expect, intend.

สมหวัง sǒmwǎŋ/ V 1. to fulfil one's hopes. sV 2. as desired.

สิ้นหวัง sînwǎŋ/ V to despair, give up hope.

หมดหวัง mòdwǎŋ/ V to be hopeless, past hope.

หวังดี wǎŋdii/ V to have good wishes, intentions. ความ-- good wishes; good intentions. ผู้-- well-wisher.

หวัด ๑ wàd/ V to scribble, write hastily.

เขียนหวัด khǐanwàd/ V to scribble, write hastily.

หวัด ๒ wàd/ N common cold.

ไข้หวัด khâjwàd/ N fever due to a common cold.

ไข้หวัดใหญ่ khâjwàdjàj/ N influenza.

เป็นหวัด penwàd/ V to catch cold, have a cold.

โรคหวัด rôogwàd/ N common cold.

หวัดกิน wàd/kin/ V colloq. to catch a cold, have a cold.

หวัดลงคอ wàd/loŋkhɔɔ/ V to have a sore throat, a cold with phlegm.

หวั่น wàn/ V to fear, be afraid (of).

หวั่นเกรง wànkreeŋ/ V to be afraid of, apprehensive of.

หวั่นใจ wàncaj/ V to be afraid, have an apprehension.

หวั่นวิตก wàn/wítòg/ V to be worried, apprehensive.

หวั่นๆ wànwàn/ V to be somewhat afraid.

หวั่นหวาด wànwàad/ V to be afraid.

หวั่นไหว wànwǎj/ V to be moved, tremble, shake.

o สนั่นหวั่นไหว sanàn/wànwǎj/ V to be very loud, jarring, rumbling, thundering.

หวาดหวั่น wàadwàn/ V to be afraid.

หวัว in หวัวเราะ,หวัวร่อ wǔarɔ́ʔ/, hǔarɔ́ʔ/;wǔarɔ̂ɔ/, hǔarɔ̂ɔ/ V to laugh. →See หัวเราะ.

หว้า (พวง,ช่อ,ลูก) wâa/ N a kind of dark purple fruit (phuaŋ/, chɔ̂ɔ/ for clusters; lûug/ for individual fruits). ต้น-- (ต้น) the tree bearing such fruit.

หว่าง wàaŋ/ N interstice, interspace. →Cf. ระหว่าง.

หว่างขา wàaŋkhǎa/ N space between the legs.

หว่างเขา (แห่ง) wàaŋkhǎw/ (hèŋ/) N valley, esp. cultivatable depression between mountains.

หว่างอก wàaŋʔòg/ N the middle of the chest or breast.

หวาด wàad/ V to be afraid, frightened, apprehensive.

หวาดกลัว wàadklua/ V to be scared, frightened.

หวาดเกรง wàadkreeŋ/ V to be afraid; to fear.

หวาดเสียว wàadsǐaw/ V to feel a thrill of fear, horror; to have chills sent down one's spine.

หวาดหวั่น wàadwàn/ V to be afraid.

หวีดหวาด wǐidwàad/ V to scream with fear.

หวาน wǎan/ V 1. to be sweet (to the taste). 2. to be pleasing, melodious, charming. ความ-- sweetness. →Dist. หอม,เพราะ.

ขนมหวาน (อย่าง) khanǒmwǎan/ (jàaŋ/) N heavily sweetened or candied food, e.g. confections, sweetmeats.

ของหวาน (อย่าง) khɔ̌ɔŋwǎan/ (jàaŋ/) N com. dessert, sweetstuff. →Syn. อาหารหวาน eleg.

คอหวาน khɔɔwǎan/ V idiom. to have a sweet tooth.

น้ำหวาน námwǎan/ N 1. soft drink (sweetened), sweet drink. 2. flavored syrup.

ปากหวาน pàagwǎan/ V idiom. to speak nicely, throw bouquets (at someone). 2. to be suave, smooth-tongued; to be a sweet talker.

เบาหวาน bawwǎan/ N diabetes.

เปรี้ยวหวาน prîawwǎan/ N sweet and sour dish.

ผักกาดหวาน phàgkàad/wǎan/ N sugar beet.

หวานจ๋อย wǎancɔ̌j/ colloq. to be extremely sweet, sugary, sentimental.

o หน้าตาหวานจ๋อย nâataa/wǎancɔ̌j/ V to have a very sweet face, be sweet-looking.

หวานจัด wǎancàd′ to be very sweet.

หวานเจี๊ยบ wǎancíab′ to be very sweet.

หวานเจื้อย wǎancýaj′ to be melodious, dulcet, mellifluous.

หวานใจ (คน) wǎancaj′ (khon′) N sweetheart.

หวานฉ่ำ wǎanchàm′ V 1. to be sweet and juicy (as a pineapple). 2. c o l l o q. to be honeyed (of a person's eyes, speech).

หวานปะแล่มๆ wǎan′-palêm′palêm′ to be slightly sweet.

อ่อนหวาน ʔɔ̀ɔnwǎan′ V 1. to be sweet, courteous, polite, gentle and sweet. 2. to be insufficiently sweet.

อาหารหวาน ʔaahǎanwǎan′ N e l e g. dessert, sweetstuff. →S y n. ของหวาน c o m.

หว่าน wàan′ V to sow.

พูดหว่านล้อม phûud′wàanlɔ́ɔm′ V to cajole someone into doing or accepting something.

หวาม wǎam′ V to thrill with fear, be stricken with fear.

หวามๆ wǎmwǎam′* V i d e m.

หวาย (ต้น, เส้น) wǎaj′ (tôn′, sên′) N rattan.

หวิด wìd′ AA narrowly, barely, almost.

หวุดหวิด wùdwìd′ AA narrowly, almost, nearly.

หวิว wǐw′ V to be dizzy, giddy, faint.

ใจหวิว cajwǐw′ V to feel dizzy or faint, be giddy, have a dizzy spell.

หวี (เล่ม, อัน) wǐi′ V 1. to comb. N 2. comb (lêm′, ʔan′). C 3. clf. for a hand of bananas.

หวีกล้วย (หวี) wǐiklûaj′ (wǐi′) N a hand of bananas.

หวีผม wǐiphǒm′ V to comb the hair.

หวีด wìid′ N the sound of a scream, of a whistle.

นกหวีด (อัน) nógwìid′ (ʔan′) N whistle.

หวีดหวาด wìidwàad′ V to scream with fear.

หวุดหวิด wùdwìd′ AA narrowly, almost, nearly.

หวูด wùud′ N steam whistle.

หอ (หอ) hɔ̌ɔ′ (hɔ̌ɔ′) N building, structure (erected for a special purpose). →Chiefly in compounds.

กล่อมหอ klɔ̀mhɔ̌ɔ′ V to serenade bride and groom on the wedding night.

เรือนหอ (หลัง) ryanhɔ̌ɔ′ (lǎŋ′) N bridal house, a house built for a newly wedded couple.

หอการค้า hɔ̌ɔkaankháa′ N chamber of commerce.

หอคอย (หอ, หลัง) hɔ̌ɔkhɔɔj′ (hɔ̌ɔ′, lǎŋ′) N watchtower.

หอดูดาว (หอ, แห่ง) hɔ̌ɔduudaaw′ (hɔ̌ɔ′, hèŋ′) N observatory.

หอทะเบียนที่ดิน (แห่ง) hɔ̌ɔthabian′thîidin′ (hèŋ′) N land registration office.

หอนาฬิกา (หอ) hɔ̌ɔnaalikaa′ (hɔ̌ɔ′) N clock tower.

หอพัก (หลัง, แห่ง) hɔ̌ɔphág′ (lǎŋ′, hèŋ′) N boarding house, dormitory, hostel.

หอระฆัง (หอ) hɔ̌ɔrakhaŋ′ (hɔ̌ɔ′) N bell tower.

หอสมุด (แห่ง) hɔ̌ɔsamùd′ (hèŋ′) N library.

หอสินค้า (แห่ง) hɔ̌ɔsǐnkháa′ (hèŋ′) N warehouse.

ห่อ hɔ̀ɔ′ N 1. package. C 2. clf. for packages, for things wrapped in packages. V 3. to wrap, package.

ห่อของ (ห่อ) (1) hɔ̀ɔkhɔ̌ɔŋ′; (2) hɔ̀ɔ′khɔ̌ɔŋ′ N 1. package (hɔ̀ɔ′). V 2. to wrap, wrap things.

ห่อหมก (ห่อ) hɔ̀ɔmòg′ (hɔ̀ɔ′) N a Thai dish consisting of steamed fish or chicken in coconut cream and chili sauce.

ห่อหุ้ม hɔ̀ɔ′hûm′ V to wrap all around, cover, envelope.

ห่อเหี่ยว hɔ̀ɔhìaw′ V to be dejected, depressed, down-hearted.

ห้อ ๑ hɔ́ɔ′ V 1. to gallop (of horses). 2. c o l l o q. to run fast; to drive fast.

ห้อ ๒ in ห้อเลือด hɔ́ɔlýad′ V 1. to be bruised. 2. t e c h to have a hematoma. N 3. t e c h. hematoma.

หอก (ด้าม, อัน) hɔ̀ɔg′ (dâam′, ʔan′) N spear.

หอกปลายปืน (เล่ม) hɔ̀ɔg′plaajpyyn′ (lêm′) N bayonet. →S y n. ดาบปลายปืน.

ห่อง in จองหอง cɔŋhɔ̌ɔŋ′* to be haughty, proud, vain.

ห้อง (ห้อง) hɔ̌ŋ′* (hɔ̌ŋ′) N room.

ผนังห้อง (ด้าน) phanǎŋ′hɔ̌ŋ′ (dâan′) N interior wall, wall of a room (made of brick, stone, plaster, etc., but not one of wood).

ฝาห้อง (ด้าน, ฝา) fǎahɔ̌ŋ′ (dâan′, fǎa′) N interior wall, wall of a room.

มุมห้อง (มุม) mumhɔ̌ŋ′ (mum′) N corner (of a room).

ห้องกินข้าว hɔ̌ŋ′kinkhâaw′ N c o m. dining room.

ห้องเก็บของ hɔ̌ŋ′kèbkhɔ̌ɔŋ′ N storeroom.

ห้องขัง hɔ̂ŋkhǎŋ′ N cell, detention cell.

ห้องขายตั๋ว hɔ̂ŋ′khǎajtǔa′ N ticket booth, box office.

ห้องคนใช้ hɔ̂ŋ′khoncháj′ N servant's room.

ห้องครัว hɔ̂ŋkhrua′ N kitchen.

ห้องเครื่อง hɔ̂ŋkhrŷaŋ′ N engine room.

ห้องแถว (หลัง,ห้อง) hɔ̂ŋthɛ̌w′ N 1. a row of identically-constructed rooms, apartments or shops (lǎŋ′). 2. one such room, apartment or shop (hɔ̂ŋ′).

ห้องโถง hɔ̂ŋthǒoŋ′ N hai¹; large, spacious room.

ห้องทดลอง hɔ̂ŋ′thódlɔɔŋ′ N laboratory.

ห้องนอน hɔ̂ŋnɔɔn′ N bedroom.

ห้องนั่งเล่น hɔ̂ŋ′nâŋlên′ N lounge (as in a hotel or school).

ห้องน้ำ hɔ̂ŋnáam′ N bathroom.

ห้องปฏิบัติการ hɔ̂ŋ′-pàtibàd′kaan′ N eleg. laboratory.

ห้องประชุม hɔ̂ŋ′prachum′ N assembly room, meeting room, (assembly) auditorium.

ห้องปาฐกถา hɔ̂ŋ′paathàkathǎa′ N lecture room or auditorium.

ห้องพัก hɔ̂ŋphág′ N 1. waiting room, lounge, (as in a train station). 2. room where one stays temporarily (e.g. a hotel room).

ห้องภาพ (ห้อง,แห่ง) hɔ̂ŋphâab′ (hɔ̂ŋ′,hɛ̀ŋ′) N photography studio.

ห้องรับแขก hɔ̂ŋ′rábkhɛ̀ɛg′ N living room.

ห้องรับประทานอาหาร hɔ̂ŋ′-rábprathaan′ʔaahǎan′ N eleg. dining room.

ห้องเรียน hɔ̂ŋrian′ N classroom.

ห้องศิลป (ห้อง,แห่ง) hɔ̂ŋsǐn′ (hɔ̂ŋ′,hɛ̀ŋ′) N art studio.

ห้องสมุด (ห้อง,แห่ง) hɔ̂ŋ′samùd′ (hɔ̂ŋ′,hɛ̀ŋ′) N 1. study. 2. library.

ห้องส้วม hɔ̂ŋsûam′ N toilet.

ห้องหนังสือ hɔ̂ŋ′naŋsɣ̌y′ N study, library (in a home).

ห้องหับ hɔ̂ŋ′hàb′ N colloq. room.

ห้องอาหาร hɔ̂ŋ′ʔaahǎan′ N eleg. dining room.

หอน hɔ̌ɔn′ V to howl.

เห่าหอน hàwhɔ̌ɔn′ V to bark and howl; to howl.

หอบ ๑ hɔ̀ɔb′ V to pant.

เหนื่อยหอบ nỳajhɔ̀ɔb′ V to gasp for breath from fatigue.

หอบ ๒ hɔ̀ɔb′ V 1. to carry along, be carried along (as by the wind). 2. to carry an armful, to have one's arms loaded.

หอม ๑ hɔ̌ɔm′ V 1. to be fragrant, odoriferous, sweet smelling. 2. colloq. to kiss.

กล้วยหอม (ลูก,ใบ,ผล) klûajhɔ̌ɔm′ (lûug′, baj′, phǒn′) N banana (fragrant variety).

เครื่องหอม khrŷaŋhɔ̌ɔm′ N perfumes, fragrant articles.

น้ำหอม (อย่าง,ชะนิด,ขวด,หยด) námhɔ̌ɔm′ N perfume, toilet water (jàaŋ′, chaníd′ for kinds; khùad′ for bottles; jòd′ for drops). →Syn. น้ำอบ colloq.

หอมฉุย hɔ̌ɔmchǔj′ 1. to have a strong and pleasant, lingering odor. 2. to be exceedingly pleasant, sweet (in odor).

หอมระรวย hɔ̌ɔm′raruaj′ eleg. to be faintly fragrant, delightfully fragrant.

หอม ๒ (หัว) hɔ̌ɔm′ (hǔa′) N onion (the bulb). ต้น-- (ต้น) onion (the plant). →Cf. หอม ๑.

หัวหอม (หัว) hǔahɔ̌ɔm′ (hǔa′) N onion (the bulb).

หอม ๓ in เก็บหอมรอมริบ kèbhɔ̌ɔm′rɔɔmríb′ V elab. colloq. to save up.

หอม in หอมล้อม hɔ̌ɔmlɔ́ɔm′ V to surround, gather around.

หอย ๑ in คอหอย (คอหอย) khɔɔhɔ̌j′*(khɔɔhɔ̌j′) N colloq. throat.

หอย ๒ (ตัว) hɔ̌j′* (tua′) N shellfish (of all kinds). เบี้ยน้อยหอยน้อย bîanɔ́ɔj′hɔ̌jnɔ́ɔj′ elab. colloq. poor, having little money.

ลิงหอย (ตัว) liŋhɔ̌j′ (tua′) N a small species of monkey.

หอยกะพง (ตัว) hɔ̌jkaphoŋ′ (tua′) N a kind of sea mussel (Modiola senhauseni).

หอยโข่ง (ตัว) hɔ̌jkhòoŋ′ (tua′) N a kind of snail (Pila ampullacea).

หอยแครง (ตัว) hɔ̌jkhrɛɛŋ′ (tua′) N cockle (Area granosa).

หอยทาก (ตัว) hɔ̌jthâag′ (tua′) N land snail, garden snail.

หอยนางรม (ตัว) hɔ̌jnaaŋrom′ (tua′) N oyster.

หอยแมลงภู่ (ตัว) hɔ̌j′malɛɛŋphûu′ (tua′) N iridescent sea mussel. →Syn. หอยแมงภู่

colloq.

หอยสังข์ (ตัว) hɔ̌jsăŋ′ (tua′) N conch.

ห้อย ๑ hɔ̂j′* V to hang, suspend, be suspended.

ติดสร้อยห้อยตาม tìdsɔ̀j′hɔ̂jtaam′ V elab. colloq.
to follow, accompany.

ห้อยหัว hɔ̂jhŭa′ V to hang head down, be suspended head down.

ห้อยโหน hɔ̂jhŏon′ V to swing while suspended
(esp. in gymnastics).

ห้อย ๒ in หิ่งห้อย (ตัว) hìŋhɔ̂j′*(tua′) N firefly.

หัก hàg′ V 1. to break, break apart, break off, get
broken off. 2. to bend, turn. 3. to subtract,
deduct. →Dist. 1. แตก.

แตกหัก tὲɛg′hàg′ V 1. to be broken. 2. to be
critical, decisive, resolute. sV 3. decisively.

o ขั้นแตกหัก khân′tὲɛghàg′ the stage when the
final issue is decided.

ทำ(. . .)หัก tham(...)hàg′ to cause (something)
to break, break off, break apart; to break (something).

ปรักหักพัง paràg′hàgphaŋ′ V elab. eleg. to be
ruined, dilapidated.

หักกลับ hàg′klàb′ V to turn back, bend back;
to bend the other way.

หักคะแนน hàg′khanεɛn′ V to reduce the score
or grade, deduct from the score, take points
off. ถูก-- to take a deduction in one's score
or grade, to lose points.

หักใจ hàgcaj′ V to restrain one's feelings, deny
the demands of one's feelings (often in connection with separation from a loved one).

หักไปหักมา hàgpaj′hàgmaa′ V to turn this way
and that, be winding (as a road).

หักร้างถางพง hàgráaŋ′thăaŋphoŋ′ V elab.
colloq. 1. to clear land. 2. to clear a path
(e.g. through the jungle).

หักหลัง hàglăŋ′ V idiom. to double-cross,
betray.

หักห้ามใจ hàghâamcaj′ V to restrain one's emotional feelings, to exert self-control.

หักโหม hàghŏom′ V to drive oneself, push (one's
strength) to the limit, knock oneself out (doing
something).

หัก(. . .)ออก hàg(...)ʔɔ̀ɔg′ 1. to break (some-

thing) off, break (something) apart. 2. to subtract, deduct.

อกหัก ʔòghàg′ V to be broken-hearted (over a
love affair).

หัด ๑ hàd′ N measles.

เป็นหัด penhàd′ V to have the measles.

ออกหัด ʔɔ̀ɔghàd′ to break out with the measles.

หัด ๒ hàd′ V to practice; to train.

ฝึกหัด fɯ̀ghàd′ V to drill, practice; to train.

หัดพูด hàdphûud′ V to learn to speak (as a baby).

หัดให้... hàd′hâjɔ to train to (do something).

หัดใหม่ hàdmàj′ V 1. to be a beginner, newly
trained. 2. to train or practice once again.

หัตถกรรม hàdthakam′ N eleg. handicrafts. →Also
การ--.

หัน ๑ hăn′ V to turn around.

หันกลับ hănklàb′ V to turn back, turn around.

หันขวับ hănkhwàb′ V to turn around suddenly.

หันไป hănpaj′ to turn to, turn toward (away from
some point of reference).

หันมา hănmaa′ to turn to, turn toward (toward
some point of reference).

หันเห hănhĕe′ V to deviate, be deflected.

หัน ๒ in กระทันหัน krathanhăn′ V to be sudden,
abrupt.

หั่น hàn′ V to cut (into pieces), slice. →Dist. ตัด.

อย่างสะบั้นหั่นแหลก jàaŋsabân′-hàn′lὲɛg′ slang
a great deal, extremely, unsparingly.

หัว ๑ (หัว) hŭa′ (hŭa′) N com. 1. head. 2. front,
beginning. 3. bulb, tuber. C 4. clf. for heads
(as of animals, cabbages); for bulbs, tubers,
other root vegetables. →Syn. 1. ศีรษะ eleg.,
เศียร, เกล้า roy. →Ant. 2. ท้าย.

ข่าวพาดหัว (ชิ้น, เรื่อง) khàaw′phâadhŭa′ (chìn′,
rɯ̂aŋ′) N headline news.

ขี้หัว khîihŭa′ N 1. colloq. dandruff. 2. dirt
from the head or hair (such as accumulates on
a comb). →Syn. 1. ขี้รังแค com.

ตัดหัว tàdhŭa′ V to behead.

ทุกหัวระแหง thúghŭa′rahĕɛŋ′ idiom. everywhere,
every corner of the earth.

ทูนหัว (1) thuunhŭa′; (2, 3) thuun′hŭa′ V 1. to place
on the head (in order to carry). 2. to adore,
idolize. 3. to be beloved, adored. →See cross

reference.

เบนหัว beenhŭa′ V 1. to turn one's head to one
side. 2. (a vehicle) to change direction. 3. to
head (a vehicle or mount) in a different direction.

ปวดหัว pùadhŭa′ V to have a headache.

ปักหัว pàghŭa′ V to dive, plunge head first.

ปั่นหัว pànhŭa′ V to work on someone to change
his views or to incite him to action.

ผงกหัว phaŋòg′hŭa′ V to nod one's head (in
assent).

ฝังหัว făŋ′hŭa′ V to be firmly entrenched in
one's mind, in one's beliefs.

พระเจ้าอยู่หัว (พระองค์,องค์) phrácâwjùuhŭa′
(phrá?oŋ′, ?oŋ′) N king.

พาดหัวข่าว phâad′hŭakhàaw′ V to give the headline news.

โพกหัว phôoghŭa′ V to wear a turban around
one's head; to wrap a piece of cloth around
one's head.

มึนหัว mynhŭa′ V to be befuddled, dopey.

โยนหัวโยนก้อย joonhŭa′joonkɔ̀j′ V to flip a coin.

รวบหัวรวบหาง rûabhŭa′rûabhăaŋ′ V idiom.
1. to gather everything together, take the whole
kit and caboodle. 2. to sum everything up, tie
everything (e.g. facts, arguments, opinions)
together.

เวียนหัว wianhŭa′ V to feel giddy, dizzy.

ห้อยหัว hɔ̂jhŭa′ V to be suspended head down.

หัวกะทิ hŭakathí?′ N 1. concentrated coconut
cream, obtained when the coconut meat is
pressed the first time. 2. fig. the cream, i.e.
the best part (of anything). →See น้ำกะทิ,
หางกะทิ.

หัวกะโหลก (หัว) hŭakalòog′ (hŭa′) N skull.

หัวเก่า (คน) hŭakàw′ V 1. to be conservative,
traditional, old-fashioned. N 2. (a) conservative (khon′).

หัวข้อ (หัวข้อ) hŭakhɔ̂ɔ′ (hŭakhɔ̂ɔ′) N topic,
subject (as of debate); heading; outline.

หัวขั้ว (อัน,หัวขั้ว) hŭakhûa′ (?an′, hŭakhûa′) N
the point where the stem is attached to a fruit.

หัวข่าว (เรื่อง) hŭakhàaw′ (rŷaŋ′) N news
headline.

หัวเข็มขัด (หัว,อัน) hŭakhěmkhàd′ (hŭa′,?an′)
N buckle.

หัวเข่า (ข้าง) hŭakhàw′ (khâaŋ′) N knee.

หัวแข็ง hŭakhěŋ′ V to be obstinate, hard-headed.

หัวค่ำ hŭakhâm′ N dusk, the early evening.

หัวโค้ง (แห่ง) hŭakhóoŋ′ (hèŋ′) N curve (as in
a road).

หัวเงาะ hŭaŋɔ́?′ N 1. curly hair, kinky hair. 2.
Negrito mask.

หัวจุก (อัน,จุก) hŭacùg′ (?an′, cùg′) N 1. topknot.
2. certain things or parts resembling a topknot
in form or in location, e.g. the tip of an onion
bulb, the knob on a jar cover.

หัวใจ (หัวใจ,ดวง) hŭacaj′ (hŭacaj′, duaŋ′) N
1. heart (the organ). 2. fig. heart, mind.
→See ใจ.

o โรคหัวใจ rôog′hŭacaj′ N heart disease.

หัวซุกหัวซุน hŭasúg′hŭasun′ V to rush, be in a
rush. →See also following example.

o ล้มหัวซุกหัวซุน lóm′-hŭasúg′hŭasun′ V to tumble
headlong, head over heels.

หัวดื้อ hŭadŷy′ V to be bull-headed, stubborn,
obstinate.

หัวเดียวกระเทียมลีบ hŭa′diaw′-krathiam′lîib′
V idiom. to have no friends or relatives, to
be alone in the world.

หัวถนน (แห่ง) hŭathanŏn′ (hèŋ′) N the beginning
of a street. →Ant. ท้ายถนน.

หัวแถว hŭathɛ̌w′ N person at the head of a line.
→Dist. ลูกแถว. →Ant. หางแถว,ท้ายแถว.

หัวนม (อัน,หัว) hŭanom′ (?an′, hŭa′) N nipple.

หัวนอก hŭanɔ̂ɔg′ colloq. a person brought up
or educated abroad.

หัวนอนปลายตีน hŭanɔɔn′plaajtiin′ N idiom. the
background of a person (esp. as it bears upon
his social status).

หัวบันได hŭabandaj′ N eleg. the head of the stairs,
the top of a staircase.

หัวปลี (หัว) hŭaplii′ (hŭa′) N flower cluster of
the banana tree.

หัวปี hŭapii′ N 1. the early part of the year. 2.
(as n. mod) eldest, first-born. คน--,ลูก--
the first-born child. →Ant. 1. ท้ายปี. 2. สุดท้อง

หัวผักกาด (หัว) hŭaphàgkàad′ (hŭa′) N turnip.

หัวเมือง (หัวเมือง) hǔamyaŋ′ (hǔamyaŋ′) N
    1. provincial town. 2. (as n. mod.) provincial.
    →Comp. บ้านนอก.

หัวแม่มือ,นิ้ว-- (ข้าง,นิ้ว) hǔamɛ̂ɛmyy′, níwɔ
    hǔa′mɛ̂ɛmyy′ (khâaŋ′,níw′) N thumb. →Syn.
    นิ้วโป้,นิ้วโป้ง,นิ้วแม่โป้ง colloq.

หัวโยก hǔajôog′ N digging stick (for planting
    rice).

หัวรุนแรง hǔa′runrɛɛŋ′ N 1. radical mind, belief.
    V 2. to have a radical mind.

หัวเรี่ยวหัวแรง hǔarîaw′hǔarɛɛŋ′ N elab.
    colloq. mainstay, principal force.

หัวเรือ hǔarya′ N bow, prow.

หัวเรื่อง (เรื่อง,ข้อ) hǔarŷaŋ′ (rŷaŋ′,khɔ̂ɔ′) N
    title, heading, caption.

หัวแรง hǔarɛɛŋ′ N mainstay, principal force.

หัวล้าน hǔaláan′ V to be bald-headed.

หัวเลี้ยว (แห่ง) hǔalíaw′ (hɛ̀ŋ′) N a curve or
    turn (in a road, path, etc.).
o หัวเลี้ยวหัวต่อ hǔalíaw′hǔatɔ̀ɔ′ N elab.
    transition, turning point.

หัวสมัยใหม่ hǔa′samǎjmàj′ V to be modern
    minded.

หัวสูง hǔasǔuŋ′ V to be proud, pretentious, have
    pretentions beyond one's financial or social
    status.

หัวเสีย hǔasǐa′ V colloq. to lose one's temper,
    lose one's head, be in a bad temper.

หัวหกก้นขวิด hǔahòg′kônkhwìd′ sV colloq.
    gallivanting about, on the go.

หัวหงอก hǔaŋɔ̀ɔg′ V to have gray hair, be gray-
    headed.

หัวหน้า (คน) hǔanâa′ (khon′) N head, chief,
    leader.

หัวหมุน hǔamǔn′ V to be confused, overwhelmed,
    overcome (as by too much work, by excessive
    responsibilities, etc.).

หัวหอม (หัว) hǔahɔ̌ɔm′ (hǔa′) N onion (the bulb).

หัวเห็ด hǔahèd′ V colloq. to be stubborn, head-
    strong, unyielding.

หัวไหล่ (ข้าง) hǔalàj′ (khâaŋ′) N colloq.
    shoulder.

หัวอก (หัวอก) hǔaʔòg′ (hǔaʔòg′) N 1. chest,
    breast. 2. colloq. heart.

หัวอ่อน hǔaʔɔ̀ɔn′ V to be tractable, obedient,
    easy to teach. →Ant. หัวแข็ง.

หัว ๒ hǔa′ V to laugh. →Used only in special con-
    structions. The usual term is หัวเราะ.

ชวนหัว (เรื่อง) chuanhǔa′ (rŷaŋ′) N 1. humorous
    story, anecdote, comedy. V 2. to be amusing,
    comical.

เล่นหัว lênhǔa′ V to laugh and play.

หัวร่อ hǔarɔ̂ɔ′ V colloq. to laugh. →See หัวเราะ.

หัวเราะ hǔarɔ́ʔ′ V to laugh.
o เค้นหัวเราะ khén′hǔarɔ́ʔ′ V to force a laugh.
o หัวเราะแก้เก้อ hǔarɔ́ʔ/kɛ̂ɛkə̀ə′ to laugh in order
    to cover up one's embarrassment.
o หัวเราะขึ้น hǔarɔ́ʔ/khŷn′ to burst into laughter.
o หัวเราะงอหาย hǔarɔ́ʔ/ŋɔɔhǎaj′ to double up
    with (violent) laughter. →Also หัวเราะงอ.
o หัวเราะต่อกระซิก hǔarɔ́ʔ/tɔ̀ɔkrasíg′ elab.
    colloq. to giggle, laugh merrily.
o หัวเราะเยาะ hǔarɔ́ʔ/jɔ́ʔ′ V to laugh at, rid-
    icule and laugh at.
o หัวเราะร่วน hǔarɔ́ʔ/rûan′ to laugh heartily.
o หัวเราะลั่น hǔarɔ́ʔ/lân′ to roar with laughter.
o หัวเราะหึๆ hǔarɔ́ʔ/hŷʔhŷʔ′ to chuckle, laugh.

หัวลำโพง hǔalamphooŋ′ pN Hualamphong, the cen-
    tral railway station in Bangkok.

หัวหิน hǔahǐn′ pN Huahin, a popular seaside resort
    in S Thailand.

หา ๑ hǎa′ V 1. to look for, search for, seek. 2.
    to accuse. sV 3. to, toward, with a view to,
    directed toward.

กล่าวหา klàawhǎa′ V to accuse, charge, allege.
    →See cross reference.

กู่หา kùu′hǎa′ V to call out (in search of some-
    one).

ข้อหา (ข้อ,กระทง) khɔ̂ɔhǎa′ (khɔ̂ɔ′, krathoŋ′)
    N accusation, charge.

เข้าหา khâwhǎa′ V 1. to go see (someone about
    something). 2. to give oneself up, turn oneself
    in. sV 3. to, toward.

ค้นหา khónhǎa′ V to search for, look for.

คบหา(กับ) khóbhǎa′(kaɔ) V to associate (with).

ความหา khwaan′hǎa′ V to rummage around,
    feel around in search of (something).

จัดหา càdhǎa′ V to secure, provide, (try to) find.

ซ่อนหา sɔ́ɔnhǎa′ N hide-and-seek (children's game).

ซื้อหา sýyhǎa′ V to buy.

ต้องหา tɔ̂ŋhǎa′ V to be accused, charged. ผู้-- defendant; the accused.

เนื้อหา nýahǎa′ N 1. text. 2. gist, substance.

ไปมาหาสู่ pajmaa′hǎasùu′ V elab. colloq. to visit, pay visits.

ใฝ่หา fàjhǎa′ V to long for, seek for.

รนหา ronhǎa′ V to look for, go out of one's way to look for, place oneself in the way of (e.g. danger, trouble).

แสวงหา sawěɛŋ′hǎa′ V eleg. to search, look for.

หากิน hǎakin′ V 1. to make a living, earn a living. 2. to look for food.

o ทำมาหากิน thammaa′hǎakin′ V elab. colloq. to earn a living. การ-- making a living, earning a living; occupation, livelihood.

o ผู้หญิงหากิน (คน) phûujĭŋ′hǎakin′ (khon′) N prostitute, street-walker.

หาความ(ใส่) hǎakhwaam′(sàj′) V to make an allegation, accusation (against).

หาค่าบ่มิได้ hǎakhâa′bɔ̀mídâaj′ lit. to be invaluable, priceless.

หาค่ามิได้ hǎakhâa′mídâaj′ eleg. to be invaluable. May be used by some speakers in the meaning "valueless".

หาคู่ hǎakhûu′ V to seek a mate.

หาเงิน hǎaŋən′ V to earn money, earn a living.

o หาเงินหาทอง hǎaŋən′hǎathɔɔŋ′ elab. colloq. idem.

หาเช้ากินค่ำ hǎacháaw′kinkhâm′ V idiom. to live from hand to mouth.

หาที่เปรียบมิได้ hǎa′thîiprìab′-mídâaj′ eleg. incomparable.

หาประโยชน์ hǎaprajòod′ V to seek profit, gain, advantages.

หาปลา hǎaplaa′ V to fish.

หาผิด hǎaphìd′ V to find fault with.

หา(...)พบ hǎa(...)phób′ 1. to find, come upon. 2. to be able to find.

หา(...)มา hǎa(...)maa′ to find, procure.

หา(...)ไม่พบ hǎa′(...)mâjphób′ to be unable to find.

หายาก hǎajâag′ V to be scarce, rare, hard to find.

หารือ hǎaryy′ V to consult, confer. การ-- discussion, consultation. →Syn. ปรึกษา.

หาเรื่อง hǎarɣaŋ′ V colloq. 1. to look for trouble, invite trouble. 2. to start trouble, dissension.

หาเลี้ยงชีพ hǎa′líaŋchîib′ V to earn a living, seek a livelihood.

หาเลี้ยงตัว hǎa′líaŋtua′ V to earn one's living.

หาว่า hǎa′wâaɔ to accuse of, charge that, claim that.

หาเสียง hǎasǐaŋ′ V to campaign, seek votes.

หาเหตุ(กับ) hǎahèed′(kaɔ) V to find fault (with).

หุงหาอาหาร hǔŋhǎa′ʔaahǎan′ V elab. eleg. to cook, prepare food.

ให้หา hâjhǎa′ V to call for, send for.

หา ๒ hǎa′ AA adverb-auxiliary used in the following expressions.

หาไม่ hǎa′mâj′ lit. otherwise; had it been otherwise. NOTE. In certain combinations, หาไม่ expresses negation, as in the following examples. Compare also หา...ไม่ below.

o ใช่ว่า...ก็หาไม่ châj′wâa′...kɔ̂hǎa′mâj′ it is not that (such and such is the case).

o จนกว่าชีวิตจะหาไม่ conkwàa′-chiiwíd′-cahǎa′mâj′ until death, until life shall not (be).

หา...ไม่ hǎa′...mâj′ lit. not.

o หาควรไม่ hǎakhuan′mâj′ lit. ought not, should not.

o หาได้ไม่ hǎadâaj′mâj′ lit. cannot (equiv. to ไม่ได้).

o หาได้...ไม่ hǎa′dâjɔ...mâj′ lit. not, did not, has not, have not.

o หาน้อยไม่ hǎanɔ́ɔj′mâj′ lit. not little, not few.

o หาเป็นจริงไม่ hǎa′penciŋ′-mâj′ (it's) not true.

หา ๓ !hǎ* E colloq. What! Huh! (indicating surprise, disbelief).

ห่า ๑ hàa′ C eleg. clf. for a heavy rainfall. →Syn. จั๊ก com.

ห่า ๒ hàa′ N colloq. 1. a spirit believed to be responsible for cholera, plague, rinderpest, anthrax. 2. cholera; plague, rinderpest, anthrax.

แดกห่า dɛ̀ɛghàa′ V vulg. to eat: "to eat the plague."

ยัดห้า jád′hàa′ idem.

โรคห้า rôoghàa′ N colloq. 1. cholera. 2. any virulent disease which destroys large numbers of men or animals; hence also, plague, rinderpest, anthrax.

ห้า hâa′ Nm five.

แนว(ที่)ห้า (พวก,คน) nɛɛw(thîi)hâa′ N idiom. 1. fifth column, spy ring (phûag′). 2. fifth columnist, spy (khon′).

สิบห้า sìbhâa′ Nm fifteen.

ห้าแต้ม hâatɛ̂ɛm′ V 1. idiom. to commit a faux pas, make a foolish or embarrassing mistake. N 2. faux pas, foolish or embarrassing mistake.

ห้าสิบ hâa′sìb′ Nm fifty.

ห้าหก hâa′hòg′ five or six.

หาก hàag′ V 1. to be separate, apart. Cj 2. if, in case, provided that.

ตาหาก tahàag′.* Colloq. var. of ต่างหาก below.

ต่างหาก taaŋhàag′, taŋhàag′* 1. apart, separately. 2. on the contrary, contrary to what you think. →See cross reference.

ถ้าหาก(ว่า) thâahàag′(wâaɔ) if, supposing that, in the event that.

หากแต่(ว่า) hàag′tɛ̀ɔ(wâa′), -ta-* but, only.

หากว่า hàagwâa′ if, in the event that.

หาง (หาง) hǎaŋ′ (hǎaŋ′) N tail.

ดาวหาง (ดวง) daawhǎaŋ′ (duaŋ′) N comet.

รวบหัวรวบหาง rûabhǔa′rûabhǎaŋ′ V idiom. 1. to gather everything together, take the whole kit and caboodle. 2. to sum everything up, tie everything (e.g. facts, arguments, opinions) together.

หางกะทิ hǎaŋkathí?′ N dilute coconut cream obtained after the coconut meat has been pressed repeatedly. →See น้ำกะทิ,หัวกะทิ.

หางเปีย (หาง) hǎaŋpia′ (hǎaŋ′) N colloq. queue, pigtail.

หางเสียง hǎaŋsǐaŋ′ N colloq. the intonation at the end of an utterance, revealing or betraying the speaker's emotion.

หางเสือ (อัน) hǎaŋsʉ̌a′ (?an′) N rudder, helm, tiller.

ห่าง hàaŋ′ V to be separate, far apart, distant.

หางไกล(จาก) hàaŋklaj′(càagɔ) V to be far,

far away (from).

ห่างจาก hàaŋ′càagɔ to be far from.

ห่างเหิน,เหินห่าง hàaŋhǝ̌ǝn′, hǝ̌ǝnhàaŋ′ V 1. to stay away (as of a friend who no longer visits). 2. to become estranged as a result of being apart (as of husband and wife).

ออกห่าง(จาก) ?ɔ̀ɔghàaŋ′(càagɔ) V to turn away (from), stay away (from), break (relations)(with).

ห้าง ๑ (ห้าง) hâaŋ′ (hâaŋ′) N 1. scaffold (for use by a hunter). 2. temporary shed (as in an orchard or field).

ห้าง ๒ (ห้าง,แห่ง) hâaŋ′ (hâaŋ′,hɛ̀ŋ′) N (business) firm, commercial establishment, store.

ห้างร้าน (แห่ง,ห้าง,ร้าน) hâaŋráan′ (hɛ̀ŋ′,hâaŋ′, ráan′) N stores, firms, commercial establishments.

ห้าง ๓ in ไขว่ห้าง khwàjhâaŋ′ V 1. to have one's legs crossed. sV 2. cross legged; with legs crossed.

หาญ hǎan′ V 1. to dare. 2. to be brave; chiefly in compounds. →Syn. 1. กล้า.

กล้าหาญ klâahǎan′ V to be brave, bold, courageous.

อาจหาญ ?àadhǎan′ V to be bold, brave, daring.

หาด (แห่ง) hàad′ (hɛ̀ŋ′) N beach.

ชายหาด (ชายหาด,แห่ง) chaajhàad′ (chaajhàad′, hɛ̀ŋ′) N beach.

หาดทราย (แห่ง) hàadsaaj′ (hɛ̀ŋ′) N sandy beach.

ห่าน (ตัว) hàan′ (tua′) N goose.

หาบ ๑ hàab′ V to carry (something) at both ends of a pole placed on one's shoulder.

หาบเร่ (เจ้า) hàabrêe′ N 1. peddler (câaw′). V 2. to peddle, hawk.

หาบ ๒ hàab′ C unit of weight equiv. to 60 kilograms or about 132 pounds.

หาบหลวง hàablǔaŋ′ idem.

หาม hǎam′ V (two or more people) to carry, bear.

แคร่หาม (แคร่) khrɛ̂ɛhǎam′ (khrɛ̂ɛ′) N litter, palanquin.

แบกหาม bɛ̀ɛghǎam′ V to bear, carry (on the shoulder).

หามรุ่งหามค่ำ hǎamrûŋ′hǎamkhâm′ colloq. all day and all night; day and night.

ห่าม hàam′ V 1. to be almost ripe (of fruits). 2. to be a little off mentally, be a little abnormal.

ห้าม hâam′ V 1. to forbid, prohibit, stop, restrain.
2. it is forbidden (to).

o ห้ามเข้า hâamkhâw′↓ Do not enter.

o ห้ามสูบบุหรี่ hâam′sùubburìi′↓ No smoking.

ต้องห้าม tɔ̂ŋhâam′ V to be forbidden.

หวงห้าม hǔaŋhâam′ V 1. to restrict against or
forbid public use. sV 2. restricted, forbidden.

หักห้ามใจ hàghâamcaj′ V to restrain one's emotional feelings, to exert self-control.

ห้ามปราม hâampraam′ V to prohibit, forbid.

ห้ามล้อ hâamlɔ́ɔ′ V 1. to brake, put on the brakes.
N 2. brake (of vehicle, machinery). เครื่อง--
brakes.

ห้ามเลือด hâamlɯ̂ad′ V to stop the bleeding.

หาย hǎaj′ V 1. to disappear, vanish; to be missing,
be lost from sight. 2. to get well, recover, be
healed, be cured.

ขวัญหาย khwǎnhǎaj′ V to be startled, frightened.

คนหาย (คน) khonhǎaj′ (khon′) N missing person.

ใจหายใจคว่ำ,ใจหาย cajhǎaj′cajkhwâm′, cajhǎaj′
V elab. colloq. to be stunned with fear, get
scared out of one's wits.

o น่าใจหาย nâa′cajhǎaj′ V to be shocking,
frightful, frightening.

ฉิบหาย chìbhǎaj′, chíbhǎaj′, !chíbhǎaj′ V 1. to
perish, be utterly ruined, destroyed. sV 2.
m. sp. damned, darned (in the sense of very,
extremely). E 3. m. sp. Damn! Darn! →Also
2, 3. ฉิบ. →Syn. 1. See วอดวาย. NOTE.
In mngs. 2 and 3 used by men sp. to men who
are intimates; otherwise insulting. See cross
reference.

ตกหาย tòghǎaj′ V to be missing, lost (through
having been dropped).

ทำ(...)หาย tham(...)hǎaj′ V to lose, misplace (something).

เลี่ยงหายไป lîaŋhǎaj′paj′ V to sneak away.

สูนย์หาย sǔunhǎaj′ V to disappear, be lost.

เสียหาย sǐahǎaj′ V 1. to lose (beyond recovery),
sustain a loss of. 2. to be damaged. 3. to be
harmful, detrimental. ความ-- damage, loss,
harm, detriment.

o ค่าเสียหาย khâasǐahǎaj′ N the damages, the

loss, the amount of the loss.

หัวเราะงอหาย hǔarɔ́ʔ′ŋɔɔhǎaj′ V to double up
with (violent) laughter.

หายกัน hǎaj′kan to be even with each other, clear
with regard to each other (as in repaying a debt
or obligation, retaliating against an offense).

หายขาด hǎajkhàad′ V to be completely cured,
remedied.

หายเจ็บ hǎajcèb′ V to recover, get well.

หายใจ hǎajcaj′ V to breathe. การ-- breathing,
respiration.

o กลั้นหายใจ klân′hǎajcaj′ V to hold one's breath.

o ถอนหายใจ thɔ̌ɔn′hǎajcaj′ V to sigh.

o ลมหายใจ lom′hǎajcaj′ N breath.

o หายใจเข้า hǎajcaj′khâw′ V to inhale.

o หายใจไม่ทั่วท้อง hǎajcaj′mâjthûathɔ́ɔŋ′ colloq.
to breathe uneasily (as in a tense situation).

o หายใจออก hǎajcaj′ʔɔ̀ɔg′ V to exhale.

หายตัว hǎajtua′ V 1. to disappear. 2. to disappear
by supernatural power.

หายป่วย hǎajpùaj′ V to recover, get well.

หายไป hǎaj′paj′ V to disappear, vanish, be missing.

o หายไปฉิบเฉียว hǎaj′pajchíb′chiaw↓ (He) disappeared completely!

หายวันหายคืน hǎajwan′hǎajkhyyn′ V elab. colloq.
to recover quickly (from sickness); to improve
(in health) from day to day.

หายสนิท hǎaj′sanìd′ V to be completely cured,
healed; to recover completely.

หายสวย hǎajsǔaj′ V to lose beauty.

หายหน้าหายตา hǎajnâa′hǎajtaa′ V elab. colloq.
1. to disappear. 2. to be away, out of sight, not
seen by others. →Also หายหน้า.

เหือดหาย hɯ̀adhǎaj′ V to disappear gradually.

หายนะ hǎajjanáʔ′ N disaster, calamity, destruction,
ruin. →Also ความ--.

หาร hǎan′ V math. to divide.

หารด้วย hǎan′dûajɔ to divide by.

หารลงตัว hǎan′loŋtua′ to be divisible (mathe-
matically).

หารือ. See under หา ๑.

หาว ๑ hǎaw′ V to yawn.

หาวนอน hǎawnɔɔn′ V to be sleepy.

หาว ๒ in กลางหาว klaaŋhǎaw/ under the skies, in the open air.

ห้าว hâaw/ V 1. to be fully ripe, over-ripe (of coconuts only). 2. to be bold, impudent. 3. to be deep, low (of the voice).

    มะพร้าวห้าว (ลูก,ใบ,ผล) maphráawhâaw/ (lûug/, baj/,phǒn/) N fully ripe coconut.

    เสียงห้าว sǐaŋhâaw/ V to have a deep voice.

ห้ำหั่น hâmhàn/ V to hack, cut to pieces. →See หั่น.

หิ้ง (ชั้น,อัน) hîŋ (chán/,ʔan/) N shelf. →Syn. ชั้น.

หิ่งห้อย (ตัว) hìŋhɔ̂j/* (tua/) firefly.

หิด, โรค-- hìd/, rôoghìd/ N scabies (in man only).

หิน (ก้อน) hǐn/ (kɔ̂ɔn/) N stone, rock.

    ก้อนหิน (ก้อน) kɔ̂ɔnhǐn/ (kɔ̂ɔn/) N a rock (of any size).

    ถ่านหิน (ก้อน) thàanhǐn/ (kɔ̂ɔn/) N coal.

    ลูกหิน (ลูก) lûughǐn/ (lûug/) N (opaque) marble(s).

    สมัยหิน samǎj/hǐn/ N Stone Age.

    หินงอก hǐnŋɔ̂ɔg/ N stalagmite.

    หินชนวน (แผ่น) hǐn/chanuan/ (phèn/) N slate.

    หินปะการัง hǐn/-pakaa/raŋ/ N coral rock.

    หินปูน hǐnpuun/ N 1. limestone. 2. tartar calculus (i.e. incrustation on teeth).

    หินผา (ลูก) hǐnphǎa/ (lûug/) N 1. cliff. 2. rock, stone.

    หินย้อย hǐnjɔ́ɔj/ N stalactite.

    หินลับมีด (ก้อน) hǐn/lábmîid/ (kɔ̂ɔn/) N whetstone.

    หินหยก hǐnjòg/ N jade.

    หินเหล็กไฟ (ก้อน) hǐn/lègfaj/ (kɔ̂ɔn/) N flint rock.

    หินอ่อน (ก้อน,แผ่น) hǐnʔɔ̀ɔn/ (kɔ̂ɔn/, phèn/) N marble (stone).

หินยาน hǐnnajaan/ N Hinayana, the southern nontheistic form of Buddhism (prevailing in Ceylon, Burma and Thailand). →Dist. มหายาน.

หิมะ himá?/ N snow.

    พายุหิมะ phaajú?/himá?/ N snowstorm.

    หิมะตก himá?/tòg/ V 1. to snow. 2. it is snowing.

หิมาลัย himaa/laj/ pN Himalaya.

หิว hǐw/ V to be hungry. ความ-- hunger.

    หิวข้าว hǐwkhâaw/ V to be hungry.

หิวจิดๆ hǐw/-taŋìd/taŋìd/ to be slightly hungry.

หิวน้ำ hǐwnáam/ V to be thirsty.

หิวโหย hǐwhǒoj/ V to be hungry and weary.

หิ้ว hîw/ V to hold, carry (something)(by its handle, so that it hangs down from one's hand).

    กระเป๋าหิ้ว (ใบ,ลูก) krapǎwhîw/ (baj/, lûug/) N carrying bag, carrying case; handbag, pocketbook (having handles).

    o พิมพ์ดีดกระเป๋าหิ้ว phimdìid/krapǎwhîw/ portable typewriter.

หีบ ๑ (ใบ,ลูก) hìib/ (baj/,lûug/) N box.

    หีบบัตร (ใบ,ลูก) hìibbàd/ (baj/,lûug/) N ballot box.

    หีบบุหรี่ (ใบ) hìib/burìi/ (baj/) N cigarette box.

    หีบเพลง (หลัง,เครื่อง,อัน) hìibphleeŋ/ N 1. piano (lǎŋ/). 2. organ (lǎŋ/). 3. accordion (short for หีบเพลงชัก)(khrŷaŋ/). 4. mouth organ, harmonica (short for หีบเพลงปาก)(ʔan/).

    หีบเสียง (เครื่อง) hìibsǐaŋ/ (khrŷaŋ/) N phonograph.

หีบ ๒ hìib/ V to press, squeeze, crush, extract.

หึๆ in หัวเราะหึๆ hǔarɔ́?/hỳ?hỳ?/ to chuckle, laugh.

หึง hỹŋ/ V to be jealous (of husband and wife; of lovers).

    ขี้หึง khîihỹŋ/ V to be jealous, given to jealousy (of husband and wife; of lovers).

หึ่ม hỹm/ imit. 1. a humming sound, roaring sound. V 2. to make a humming sound, roaring sound.

หืด, โรค-- hỹyd/, rôoghỹyd/ N asthma.

หุง hǔŋ/ V to cook.

    หุงข้าว hǔŋkhâaw/ V to cook rice, cook a meal.

    หุงต้ม hǔŋtôm/ V to cook (in general).

    หุงหาอาหาร hǔŋhǎa/ʔaahǎan/ V elab. eleg. to cook, prepare food.

หุน hǔn/ C a Chinese unit of weight used by jewellers, equal to 375 milligrams. [f. Chin.]

หุ่น (ตัว) hùn/ (tua/) N model, puppet, mannequin, dressmaker's dummy.

    เชิดหุ่น chəədhùn/ V to make a puppet perform.

    รูปหุ่น rûubhùn/ N model, mannequin, dressmaker's dummy.

    หุ่นกระบอก (ตัว) hùnkrabɔ̀ɔg/ (tua/) N marionette, puppet.

    หุ่นยนตร์ (ตัว) hùnjon/ (tua/) N robot.

หุ้น (หุ้น) hûn/ (hûn/) N 1. share (of stock). 2.
share (as in a business). [f. Chin.]

เข้าหุ้น khâwhûn/ V to go into partnership, team
up.

หุ้นส่วน hûnsùan/ N partnership (as in a business).

หุนหัน hŭnhăn/ V to be quick-tempered, impetuous,
rash.

หุบ hùb/ V 1. to shut, close. N 2. space, depression (esp. between mountains and hills).

หุบเขา (แห่ง) hùbkhăw/ (hèŋ/) N com. valley.

หุบผา (แห่ง) hùbphăa/ (hèŋ/) N eleg. valley.

หุ้ม hûm/ V 1. to cover, wrap around, coat. 2. to
be covered, wrapped around, coated.

รถหุ้มเกราะ (คัน) ród/hûmkrɔ̀ʔ/ (khan/) N
armored car.

หู (หู, ข้าง) hŭu/ (hŭu/, khâaŋ/) N 1. ear (body-
part). 2. ear-like appendage or instrument.
NOTE. หู is often coupled with ตา ๑ "eye"
in semirepeated expressions, but the meaning
of หู is not necessarily reflected in the meaning
of the resultant combination. See ขยิบหูขยิบตา,
เปิดหูเปิดตา, ผิดหูผิดตา, and others below.

แก้วหู kɛ̂ɛwhŭu/ N eardrum.

ใกล้หูใกล้ตา klâjhŭu/klâjtaa/ elab. colloq.
right under (someone's) nose, close to (and
therefore subject to) the observation or supervision of (someone).

ขยิบหูขยิบตา khajìb/hŭu/-khajìb/taa/ V elab.
colloq. to wink, i.e. signal by a wink.

ขวางหู khwăaŋhŭu/ V to offend the ears, be
offensive to listen to.

ขัดหู, ฟัง-- khàdhŭu/, faŋ/khàdhŭu/ V to be displeasing to the ear, not sound right, be jarring.

ขี้หู khîihŭu/ N earwax.

คุ้นหู khúnhŭu/ V to sound familiar, be familiar
to the ear.

คู่หู (คน) khûuhŭu/ (khon/) N 1. (an) intimate,
(one's) trusted companion. 2. (as n. mod.) intimate, trusted, faithful.

o เพื่อนคู่หู phŷan/khûuhŭu/ intimate friend,
bosom companion.

เคยหู khəəj/hŭu/ V to sound familiar, be familiar to the ear.

เงี่ยหูฟัง ŋîahŭu/faŋ/ to cock the ears, i.e. try

hard to listen.

จอนหู (ข้าง) cɔɔnhŭu/ (khâaŋ/) 1. sideburns.
2. lock of hair growing from in front of a
woman's ear, and worn tucked up behind it.

ได้ยินกับหู dâjjin/kahŭu/ to hear with one's own
ears.

ต่างหู (คู่, อัน, ข้าง) tàaŋhŭu/ (khûu/, ʔan/, khâaŋ/)
N eleg. earring. →Syn. ตุ้มหู com.

ติดหูติดตา tìdhŭu/tìdtaa/ V elab. colloq. 1.
to see in one's mind's eye. 2. to be vivid,
striking. sV 3. vividly.

ทำหูทวนลม thamhŭu/thuanlom/ idiom. to pretend not to hear.

บาดหู bàadhŭu/ V 1. to offend one's ears, be
disagreeable to hear. 2. to hurt one's feelings
upon hearing.

ป้องหู pɔ̂ŋ/hŭu/ V to put one's hand to one's ear
in order to hear better.

เป็นหูเป็นตาแทน penhŭu/pentaa/-thɛɛn/ idiom.,
elab. colloq. to keep an eye on things, take
charge of things (for someone).

เปิดหูเปิดตา pə̀ədhŭu/pə̀ədtaa/ V elab. colloq.
to keep one's eyes and ears open in order to
learn.

แปร่งหู prɛ̀ŋ/hŭu/ V 1. to sound odd, different from
usual, not quite right. 2. to sound unlikely, not
quite believable.

ผิดหูผิดตา phìdhŭu/phìdtaa/ elab. colloq. V
to look changed; to have changed markedly in
appearance.

พูดกรอกหู(ว่า) phûud/krɔ̀ɔghŭu/-(wâa/) 1. to talk
into a person's ear. 2. to drop a hint, or make
a complaint which is intended for the ears of a
particular person present.

ฟังไม่สนิทหู faŋ/-mâjsanìd/hŭu/ to sound odd,
different from usual, not quite right; to sound
unlikely, not quite believable.

ฟังหูไว้หู faŋhŭu/wájhŭu/ V idiom. to take
(things one hears) with a grain of salt.

เย็นหู jenhŭu/ V to be pleasant to listen to.

ลืมหูลืมตา lyymhŭu/lyymtaa/ V elab. colloq.
to open one's eyes to, or become aware of what
is going on around one.

หนวกหู nùaghŭu/ V to be noisy, deafening (of

sound).

หูกระต่าย (อัน,หู) hǔukratàaj′ (ʔan′,hǔu′) 1. bow tie. 2. bowknot.

หูฉี่ hǔuchìi′ colloq. extreme, extremely: "ear-sizzling."

o แพงหูฉี่ phɛɛŋ′hǔuchìi′ to be extremely expensive.

หูช้าง (บาน) hǔucháaŋ′ (baan′) N windwing of an automobile: "elephant's ears."

หูตาสว่าง hǔutaa′sawàaŋ′ V 1. to be wide-awake. 2. to be well-informed, wide-awake about what is going on.

หูตึง hǔutyŋ′ V to be hard of hearing. →Dist. หูหนวก "deaf."

หูโทรศัพท์ (อัน) hǔu′thoorasàb′ (ʔan′) N telephone receiver.

หูเบา hǔubaw′ V to be credulous.

หูป่าตาเถื่อน hǔupàa′taathɯ̌an′ V elab. colloq. to be ignorant of what is going on, of what is happening.

หูไว hǔuwaj′ V to have keen ears, be quick in hearing things.

หูหนวก hǔunùag′ V to be deaf. →Dist. หูตึง "hard of hearing."

หู hǔu′ V to be wrinkled, shrunken, shrivelled.

หดหู hòdhǔu′ V to be sad, depressed, dejected.

o ใจหดหู caj′hòdhǔu′ V to be downhearted, despondent, depressed, heartsick.

หู in เต้าหู้ tâwhûu′ N bean cake, bean curd. [f. Chin.]

เห hěe′ V to deviate, deflect, turn off the normal course.

หันเห hǎnhěe′ V to deviate, be deflected.

เหง in ข่มเหง khòmhěeŋ′ V to bully, browbeat, abuse, mistreat, persecute.

เหงา ŋǎw′ V to be lonesome, lonely. ความ-- loneliness.

เงียบเหงา ŋîabŋǎw′ V to be quiet and lonely, quiet and lonesome.

เหงาหงอย ŋǎwŋɔ̌j′ V to be lonesome, sad and lonesome, lonesome and quiet or subdued.

เหงา. See เง่า.

เหงื่อ ŋɯ̀a′ N sweat, perspiration.

เหงื่อกาฬ ŋɯ̀akaan′ N (a) cold sweat (as from

fright).

เหงื่อออก ŋɯ̀aʔɔ̀ɔg′ V to perspire.

เหงือก (เหงือก) ŋɯ̀ag′ (ŋɯ̀ag′) N 1. gum (of teeth). 2. gills.

เห็ด ๑ (ดอก) hèd′ (dɔ̀ɔg′) N mushroom.

ดอกเห็ด dɔ̀ɔghèd′ N mushroom.

หัวเห็ด hǔahèd′ V idiom. to be stubborn, headstrong, unyielding.

เห็ด ๒ in หมูเห็ดเป็ดไก่ mǔuhèd′pèdkàj′ N elab. colloq. meats of various kinds. NOTE. เห็ด has no independent meaning in this expression, but rather has a euphonic function, rhyming with เป็ด.

เหตุ (เหตุ,ประการ,อย่าง) hèed′ (hèed′, prakaan′, jàaŋ′) N 1. cause, reason. C 2. idem.

จดหมายเหตุ (ฉบับ) còdmǎajhèed′ (chabàb′) N written account, record (as of events), document.

ด้วยเหตุนี้ dûajhèed′níi′ therefore, for this reason, because of this.

โดยใช่เหตุ doojchâjhèed′ eleg. unnecessarily, for no reason.

ต้นเหตุ (ประการ,อย่าง) tônhèed′ (prakaan′, jàaŋ′) N cause, origin.

เป็นเหตุให้ penhèed′hâjɔ to cause, be the cause of.

มูลเหตุ (อย่าง,อัน) muunhèed′ (jàaŋ′,ʔan′) N cause; original, basic cause.

สาเหตุ (อย่าง,ประการ) sǎahèed′ (jàaŋ′, prakaan′) N origin, cause. →Syn. ต้นเหตุ.

หมายเหตุ (แห่ง,ข้อ) mǎajhèed′ (hèŋ′, khɔ̂ɔ′) N note, footnote.

หาเหตุ(กับ) hǎahèed′(kaɔ) V to find fault (with).

เหตุการณ์ (อย่าง) hèedkaan′ (jàaŋ′) N 1. incident, event. 2. circumstances, situation.

o เหตุการณ์ของโลก hèedkaan′khɔ̌ɔŋlôog′ N world events, world situation.

o เหตุการณ์คับขัน hèedkaan′khábkhǎn′ an emergency situation.

เหตุขัดข้อง (เหตุ) hèed′khàdkhɔ̂ŋ′ (hèed′) N obstacle, hindrance, interference, handicap.

เหตุฉุกเฉิน hèed′chùgchɤɤn′ N emergency.

เหตุไฉน hèedchanǎj′ lit. why, for what reason.

เหตุใด hèeddaj′ eleg. why, (for) what reason, whatever reason.

เหตุที่ hèed′thîiɔ the reason why, the reasons why.

เหตุผล (ข้อ,อย่าง,ประการ) hèedphǒn′ (khɔ̌ɔ′, jàaŋ′, prakaan′) reason (for doing something).

เหตุไร hèedraj′ eleg. why, for what reason, whatever reason.

o เพราะเหตุไร phrɔ?hèed′raj′ why, for what reason.

เหตุสุดวิสัย hèed′-sùd′wísǎj′ N unavoidable circumstances, circumstances beyond one's control.

อุบัติเหตุ ?ubàd′tihèed′ N eleg. accident.

อุปัทวเหตุ ?upàd′thawahèed′ N eleg. accident.

เห็น hěn′ V to see. การ-- seeing, act of seeing. ความ-- (see below).

ความเห็น khwaamhěn′ N idea, opinion. →Syn. ทรรศนะ,ทัศนะ eleg.

คิดเห็น khídhěn′ V to think, deem. ความ-- opinion, idea.

o คุณคิดเห็นอย่างไร khun′-khídhěn′jàaŋraj′↓ What do you think? What is your opinion?

ดูเห็น duuhěn′ V to be able to see.

นึกเห็นภาพ nýg′hěnphâab′ V to picture, imagine, visualize.

เพื่อเห็นแก่ phɣ̂ahěn′kɛ̀ɛɔ for the sake of.

มองไม่เห็น mɔɔŋ′mâjhěn′ can't see (e.g. because of darkness, mental block, etc.).

มองเห็น mɔɔŋhěn′ V 1. to see, catch sight of. 2. to conceive (of). 3. to be able to see.

รู้เห็น rúuhěn′ V 1. to know, have experience. 2. to see, witness. 3. to witness (e.g. wrongdoing) with acquiescence.

รู้เห็นเป็นใจ rúuhěn′pencaj′ elab. to witness (i.e. have full knowledge of the facts) and to connive, be secretly accessory, be an accomplice. →See also เป็นใจ.

ลงความเห็น loŋ′khwaamhěn′ V to conclude, to come to a general conclusion, agreement.

เล็งเห็น leŋ′hěn′ V to foresee.

แลเห็น lɛɛhěn′ V to see, catch sight of.

สอดรู้สอดเห็น sɔ̀ɔdrúu′sɔ̀ɔdhěn′ V elab. colloq. to be inquisitive, curious, meddling, nosy. →Also สอดรู้.

เห็นแก่ hěn′kɛ̀ɔ to look out for, think (only) of.

o เพื่อเห็นแก่ phɣ̂ahěn′kɛ̀ɔ for the sake of.

o มิเห็นแก่ míhěn′kɛ̀ɔ without thinking of, with-

out regard to, without regard for.

o เห็นแก่ได้ hěn′kɛ̀dâaj′ to be acquisitive, covetous. →Syn. โลภ.

o เห็นแก่ตัว hěn′kɛ̀tua′ to think only of oneself, be selfish. ความ-- selfishness.

o เห็นแก่หน้า hěn′kɛ̀nâa′ to be partial, prejudiced.

เห็น(...)เข้า hěn(...)khâw′ to catch sight of.

เห็นควร hěnkhuan′ V to deem it proper to, see fit to.

เห็นจริง hěnciŋ′ V to be convinced.

o รู้แจ้งเห็นจริง rúucɛ̂ŋ′hěnciŋ′ V elab. colloq. to perceive and understand clearly.

o ให้เห็นจริง hâjhěn′ciŋ convincingly.

เห็นจะ hěn′caɔ AA 1. seem, appear. 2. apparently, probably.

เห็นใจ hěncaj′ V 1. to sympathize (with), be sympathetic (toward). 2. to see someone's true nature or feelings. ความ-- sympathy.

เห็นชอบ(กับ) hěnchɔ̂ɔb′(kaɔ) V to agree (with), approve, be in favor (of). →Also เห็นดีเห็นชอบ.

เห็นชีวิต hěn′chiiwíd′ V to have seen life, be experienced about life or living.

เห็นด้วย hěndûaj′ to agree (with what has been said).

เห็นดีเห็นงาม hěndii′hěnŋaam′ V elab. colloq. to agree, approve. →Also เห็นดี.

เห็นดีเห็นชอบ(กับ) hěndii′hěnchɔ̂ɔb′(kaɔ) V elab. colloq. to agree (with), approve, be in favor (of). →Also เห็นดี,เห็นชอบ.

เห็นถนัด hěn′thanàd′ V to see clearly.

เห็นท่า hěnthâa′ V to get an indication of a situation, sense a situation.

o เห็นท่าไม่ดี hěnthâa′mâjdii′ to sense a bad situation.

เห็นประจักษ์ hěn′pracàg′ V to perceive clearly.

เห็นเป็นเรื่องขัน hěn′-penrɣ̂aŋ′khǎn′ thought it was a funny story.

เห็นผิดเป็นชอบ hěnphìd′penchɔ̂ɔb′ V to mistake wrong for right, bad for good.

เห็นผิดสังเกต hěnphìd′sǎŋkèed′ V to sense something unusual happening.

เห็นพร้อมกัน hěnphrɔ́ɔm′kanɔ V to agree unanimously.

เห็นพ้อง(ด้วย) hěnphɔ́ɔŋ′(dûaj′) V to agree.

เห็นไรๆ hěn′rajraj′ to see vaguely, indistinctly

in the distance.

เห็นว่า hěn′wâaɔ to be of the opinion that, think that; to realize that; to see, perceive that.

เห็นสมควร hěn′sǒmkhuan′ to see fit to; to think it appropriate.

เห็นอกเห็นใจ hěn? òg′hěncaj′ V elab. colloq. to sympathize.

เหลือบเห็น lỳab′hěn′ V to catch a glimpse of.

ให้ความเห็น hâj′khwaamhěn′ V to give an opinion.

อยากรู้อยากเห็น jàagrúu′jàaghěn′ V elab. colloq. to be curious, inquisitive.

ออกความเห็น ?ɔ̀ɔg′khwaamhěn′ to give an idea, opinion.

เหน็ด in เหน็ดเหนื่อย nèdnỳaj′ V to be tired.

เหน็บ nèb′ V 1. to insert, stick in. N 2. numbness.

เป็นเหน็บ pennèb′ V 1. to feel numb, be numb. 2. to go to sleep (as of a limb).

เหน็บชา nèbchaa′ V 1. to be numb. 2. to have beriberi. N 3. short for โรค-- beriberi.

o โรคเหน็บชา rôog′nèbchaa′ N beriberi.

เหนอะหนะ nɔ̀?nà?′ V colloq. to be sticky.

เหนาะๆ nɔ̀?nɔ̀?′ colloq. easily, with ease.

เหนียม nĭam′ V to be shy. →Syn. อาย.

เหนียว nĭaw′ V 1. to be tough (as of fiber, membrane). 2. to be sticky, viscous.

ข้าวเหนียว khâawnĭaw′ N glutinous rice. →Opp. ข้าวเจ้า.

ขี้เหนียว khîinĭaw′ V colloq. to be stingy. →Syn. ตระหนี่ eleg., ขี้ตืด colloq.

ดินเหนียว dinnĭaw′ N clay.

เหนี่ยว nìaw′ V 1. to pull. 2. to hold back.

หน่วงเหนี่ยว nùaŋnìaw′ V to hold back, delay.

เหนือ nŷa′ sV com. 1. above. 2. north, northern, to the north, to the north of. V 3. to be superior to. →Opp. 1, 2. ใต้. →Syn. 2. อุดร lit., eleg. →The literary and the common terms for the eight chief points of the compass are listed under ทิศ.

ขั้วเหนือ khûanŷa′ N 1. north pole (of a magnet). 2. geog. North Pole.

ชาวเหนือ (คน) chaawnŷa′ (khon′) N Northerner.

ดาวเหนือ daawnŷa′ N the North Star.

ทิศเหนือ thídnŷa′ N north.

o ทางทิศเหนือ thaaŋthídnŷa′ to the north.

นอกเหนือจาก nɔ̀ɔgnŷa′càagɔ moreover, over and above, aside from (that).

ปักษ์เหนือ pàgnŷa′ N com. the north, the northern part (of the country).

ภาคเหนือ phâagnŷa′ N eleg. the north, the northern part (of the country).

รังษีเหนือม่วง raŋsĭi′-nŷa′mûaŋ′ N ultraviolet rays.

เหนือลม nŷalom′ upwind, windward, on the windward side. →Ant. ใต้ลม.

เหนื่อย nỳaj′ V to be tired, weary, fatigued. ความ-- tiredness, fatigue. →Syn. อิดโรย eleg.

เหน็ดเหนื่อย nèdnỳaj′ V to be tired.

เหนื่อยใจ nỳajcaj′ V to feel tired and discouraged.

เหนื่อยหน่าย nỳajnàaj′ V to be tired (of).

เหนื่อยหอบ nỳajhɔ̀ɔb′ V to gasp for breath from fatigue.

เห็บ ๑ (ตัว) hèb′ (tua′) N tick, i.e. woodtick. →Also ตัวเห็บ.

เห็บ ๒ in ลูกเห็บ lûughèb′ N hail.

o ลูกเห็บตก lûughèb′tòg′ to hail.

เหม่ in หมิ่นเหม่ mìnmèe′ V to be precarious, perilous, risky.

เหม็น měn′ V 1. to smell bad, stink, be foul-smelling. 2. to smell foully of.

เหม็นเขียว měnkhĭaw′ V to smell bad. According to some speakers, to have an odor of crushed green leaves.

เหม็นคาว měnkhaaw′ V to stink, smell foully of raw meat, blood, fish.

เหม็นฉุย měnchǔj′ V a bad odor to arise and be diffused suddenly.

เหม็นฉู่ měnchùu′ V to smell very bad, stink badly.

เหม็นโจ่ měnchòo′ to smell very bad, stink badly.

เหม็นตี๋, เหม็นตุ mětĭ?′, mětù?′ to have a slightly unpleasant odor.

เหม็นบูด měnbùud′ V to smell very bad (of spoiled food).

เหม็นเบื่อ měnbỳa′ V colloq. to be fed up, bored (with).

เหม็นเปรี้ยว měnprîaw′ V to smell unpleasantly sour.

เหม็นสาบ měnsàab′ V to smell, stink (as of someone who needs a bath).

เหม็นอับ mĕn²àb/ V to smell musty, stuffy.

เหม่อ mə̀ə/ V to be inattentive, have one's eyes and mind directed away from the subject at hand.

เหม่อลอย mə̀əlɔɔj/ V to be vacant, wandering aimlessly (of eyes and mind).

เหมา mǎw/ V 1. to contract for work. 2. to buy or sell as a whole (rather than by the piece). 3. to deduce, assume without evidence.

ขายเหมา khǎajmǎw/ V to sell in bulk, to sell wholesale (i.e. without allowing selection of individual or choice pieces).

รับเหมา rábmǎw/ V to contract (for work), accept a contract.

เหมาเสร็จ mǎwsèd/ to contract for everything altogether; to buy or sell everything as a whole. →Sometimes best translated simply "altogether."

เหมาหมด mǎwmòd/ idem.

เหมาเอาว่า mǎw/²awwâa/ to deduce that.

เหมาะ ๑ mɔ̀²/ V to be suitable, appropriate, fit, fitting; to fit. →Comp. สม.

พอเหมาะพอเจาะ phɔɔmɔ̀²/phɔɔcɔ̀²/ V elab. colloq. to be just right, fit exactly.

สบเหมาะ sòbmɔ̀²/ V to be opportune.

เหมาะแก่ mɔ̀²/kàɔ to be suited to.

เหมาะเจาะ mɔ̀²cɔ̀²/ V to fit perfectly, be just right.

เหมาะสม mɔ̀²sǒm/ V to be suitable, appropriate, proper.

เหมาะ ๒ in เหมาะแหมะ sV with a pattering sound.

เหมียว, เหมียวๆ mǐaw/, mǐawmǐaw/ imit. 1. meow, the sound made by a cat. 2. the sound used for calling a cat. →Cf. แมว. →Dist. ง้าว.

เหมือง (เหมือง, แห่ง) mǐaŋ/ (mǐaŋ/, hɛ̀ŋ/) N mine (of ore).

เหมืองแร่ (เหมือง) mǐaŋrɛ̂ɛ/ (mǐaŋ/) N ore-mine. →Syn. บ่อแร่.

o การทำเหมืองแร่ kaantham/mǐaŋrɛ̂ɛ/ N ore-mining.

เหมือด in สลบเหมือด salòb/mǐad/ V slang to be unconscious. →See สลบ.

เหมือน mǐan/ V 1. to be the same as (in quality). 2. to be like, resemble. Cj. 3. like, the same as. Pp 4. like, the same as. →Dist. เท่า.

→Syn. 2. See คล้าย.

ดูเหมือน duumǐan/ (it) looks as though, seems as though.

ทำท่าเหมือน thamthâa/mǐan/ to act like.

เปรียบเหมือน prìabmǐan/ V to be like, comparable to, analogous to.

เสมอเหมือน samə̀ə/mǐan/ V to be equal and comparable.

เหมือนกัน (1) mǐan/kan; (2, 3) mǐankan/ 1. to be similar, alike, the same. 2. also, too, likewise. 3. either (with negative expressions). NOTE. เหมือนกัน means "also, too" in the sense of "likewise, the same." ด้วย means "also, too" in the sense of "in addition." A similar distinction exists for the meaning "either" in negative expressions.

o ได้เหมือนกัน (1) dâaj/mǐankan/↓; (2) dâaj/-mǐan/kan 1. That's all right too. That's possible too. 2. to get the same thing, have got the same thing.

o เหมือนกันกับ mǐan/kankàɔ to be exactly the same as.

o เหมือนกันหมด mǐan/kanmòd/ to be all alike, all the same, altogether the same.

เหมือนกับว่า mǐan/kawâa/ as if, as though.

เหมือนดัง mǐan/daŋɔ as, like.

เหมือนหนึ่งว่า mǐan/nɨ̀ŋwâa/ as if, as though.

เหยอะแหยะ jə̀²jɛ̀²/ V to be mucky, gooey, slimy.

เหย่า in วิ่งเหย่าๆ wîŋ/jàwjàw/ to run slowly, trot along.

เหย้า jâw/ N home. →Chiefly in combinations with เรือน, as below.

มีเหย้ามีเรือน miijâw/miiryan/ V elab. colloq. to be married, have a family (usually of a woman).

อยู่กับเหย้าเฝ้ากับเรือน jùu/kajâw/-fâw/karyan/ V elab. colloq. to stay at home and look after things (considered a good quality for a woman).

เหยาะ ๑ jɔ̀²/ V to add, put a bit of (something) on.

o เหยาะน้ำปลาหน่อยซิ jɔ̀²/-námplaa/nɔ̀jsí↓ Put a little fish sauce on it.

เหยาะ ๒ See entries below.

วิ่งเหยาะๆ wîŋ/jɔ̀²jɔ̀²/ to run slowly, trot along.

เหยาะแหยะ jɔ̀²jɛ̀²/ sV not taking commitments or responsibilities seriously.

เหยิง in ยุ่งเหยิง jûŋjŏəŋ´ V to be in great confusion, disorder.

เหยียด ๑ jìad´ V to stretch, stretch out full length.

  นอนเหยียด nɔɔnjìad´ V to lie stretched out, lie down at full length.

  ยาวเหยียด jaawjìad´ V to be stretched long, be long and stretching.

เหยียด ๒ jìad´ V 1. to revile. 2. to despise, hold in contempt.

เหยียบ jìab´ V 1. to step on, set foot on, tread on, trample. 2. to verge on (see เหยียบร้อย below).

  ใบเหยียบย่ำ (ใบ) baj´jìabjâm´ (baj´) N land certificate (issued on the condition of use and improvement e.g. as to a homesteader).

  เหยียบ(...)ตาย jìab(...)taaj´ to trample to death.

  เหยียบร้อย jìabrɔɔj´ to be as many as a hundred, close to a hundred. NOTE. เหยียบ by itself is used in a similar sense only with the numerals พัน "thousand" and หมื่น "ten thousand."

เหยี่ยว (ตัว) jìaw´ (tua´) N hawk.

  ๐ ปากเหยี่ยวปากกา pàagjìaw´pàagkaa´ N idiom. danger, peril, hardship.

  เหยี่ยวข่าว (คน) jìawkhàaw´(khon´) N slang news reporter. [prob. tr. f. Eng. newshawk]

เหยื่อ jỳa´ N 1. bait, decoy. 2. victim, prey.

  เป็นเหยื่อกระสุน penjỳa´krasǔn´ V 1. to be cannon fodder. 2. to fall prey to a bullet.

  ออยเหยื่อ ʔɔj´jỳa´ V to bait, lure with bait.

เหยือก (ใบ) jỳag´ (baj´) N jar, jug, vessel.

เหรง. See โหรงเหรง.

เหรอ rɔ̌ə´. Colloq. variant of หรือ. →See also เรอะ.

เหรัญญิก (คน) hěeranjíg´ (khon´) N eleg. treasurer.

เหรียญ (เหรียญ,อัน) rĭan´ (rĭan´, ʔan´) N 1. coin; medal; dollar. C 2. idem.

  เหรียญตรา (อัน,เหรียญ) rĭantraa´ (ʔan´, rĭan´) N 1. medals, decorations. 2. coins.

เหรื่อ in แขกเหรื่อ (คน,ท่าน) khɛ̀ɛg´rỳa´ (khon´, thân´) N colloq. guest.

เหล่ in ตาเหล่ taalèe´ V to be cross-eyed, squint-eyed.

เหล็ก lèg´ N iron (the metal).

เครื่องเหล็ก (อย่าง) khrɯ̂aŋlèg´ (jàaŋ´) N ironware; anything made of iron or steel.

ช่างเหล็ก (คน) châaŋlèg´ (khon´) N blacksmith.

ตีเหล็ก tiilèg´ V to forge iron.

ม่านเหล็ก as in หลังม่านเหล็ก lǎŋ´mâanlèg´ behind the Iron Curtain.

แม่เหล็ก (อัน) mɛ̂ɛlèg´ (ʔan´) N magnet.

สมัยเหล็ก samǎj´lèg´ N Iron Age.

หินเหล็กไฟ (ก้อน) hǐn´lègfaj´ (kɔ̂ɔn´) N a flint rock.

เหล็กกล้า lègklâa´ N steel.

เหล็กใน (อัน) lègnaj´ (ʔan´) N sting, stinger (of an insect).

เหล็กพืด lègphɯ̂yd´ N wrought iron.

เหล็กวิลาด lèg´wílâad´ N iron plated with tin.

เหลน (คน) lěen´ (khon´) N great-grandchild.

เหลว lěew´ V to be liquid.

  ของเหลว khɔ̌ɔŋlěew´ N liquid. →Dist. ของไหล.

  ล้มเหลว lómlěew´ V to fail.

  เหลวแหลก lěewlɛ̀ɛg´ V to be dissolute, good-for-nothing.

  เหลวไหล lěewlǎj´ V 1. to be nonsense, trivial. 2. to be unreliable, undependable, dissolute.

เหลอ lɔ̌ə´ V (the face) to look blank, silly.

  เป๋อเหลอ pɔ̌əlɔ̌ə´ V (the face) to look blank, silly.

เหลา ๑ lǎw´ V to sharpen (as a pencil); to whittle, trim, smooth (as a stick).

เหลา ๒ (แห่ง) lǎw´ (hɛ̀ŋ´) N a big Chinese restaurant. [f. Chin.]

เหล่า làw´ C 1. group. 2. milit. unit. →Syn. 1. See พวก.

  ๐ คุณเป็นลูกเต้าเหล่าใคร khun´-penlûugtâw´ɔ làwkhraj´ Whose child are you?

  เป็นหมู่เป็นเหล่า penmùu´penlàw´ in groups.

  ผ่าเหล่า phàa´làw´ V idiom. 1. to be the black sheep of the family. 2. to break with family tradition.

  เหล่ากอ làwkɔɔ´ N descendants.

  เหล่าช่าง (เหล่า) làwchâaŋ´ (làw´) N engineering corps (non-technical term).

  เหล่านั้น làwnán´ those, that group.

  เหล่านี้ làwníi´ these, this group.

  เหล่าปืนใหญ่ (เหล่า) làw´pyynjàj´ (làw´) N artillery corps.

เหล่าร้าย làwráaj′ N gangsters, hoodlums.

เหล้า lâw′ N com. liquor, intoxicating beverage.
→Syn. สุรา eleg.

กินเหล้าเมายา kinlâw′mawjaa′ V elab. colloq.
to have intoxicating drinks, to drink (liquor).

แก้วเหล้า (ใบ) kɛ̂ɛwlâw′ (baj′) N glass for
liquor.

คนขี้เหล้าเมายา (คน) khon′-khîilâw′mawjaa′
(khon′) N elab. colloq. an alcoholic.

คอเหล้า (คน) khɔɔlâw′ (khon′) N a person used
to drinking, a heavy drinker.

นักเลงเหล้า (คน) nágleeŋ′lâw′ (khon′) N
colloq. a heavy drinker. →Syn. นักดื่มสุรา
eleg.

เมาเหล้า mawlâw′ V to be drunk.

เหล้ายาปลาปิ้ง (อย่าง) lâwjaa′plaapîŋ′ (jàaŋ′)
N elab. colloq. a collective term for liquor,
cigarettes, and relishes.

เหล้าโรง lâwrooŋ′ N arrack.

อดเหล้า ?òdlâw′ V to abstain from liquor.

เหลาะแหละ lɔ́ʔlɛ̀ʔ′ V colloq. 1. to be nonsense
(of speech). 2. to be unreliable, undependable,
unsettled.

เหลิง lɤ̌ɤŋ′ V 1. to forget oneself. 2. to be spoiled.
3. to carry too far beyond a proper limit (of
behavior).

เหลี่ยม (เหลี่ยม) lìam′ (lìam′) N edge, side (as
of a triangle, rectangle).

รูปสามเหลี่ยม (รูป) rûub′sǎamlìam′ (rûub′) N
triangle.

เล่ห์เหลี่ยม (อย่าง) lêelìam′ (jàaŋ′) N trick,
cunning angle or pitch (in sales).

สี่เหลี่ยม sìilìam′ quadrilateral. →See cross
reference.

เหลี่ยมคู (อย่าง) lìamkhuu′ (jàaŋ′) N artifice,
craftiness.

เหลี่ยมลูกบาศก์ lìamlûugbàad′ cubic (e.g. cubic
meters).

เหลียว lìaw′ V to turn (one's face).

เหลียวซ้ายแลขวา lìawsáaj′lɛɛkhwǎa′ V to turn
(one's face) from side to side (as when searching for something), to look this way and that.

เหลียวแล lìawlɛɛ′ V to pay attention to.

เหลียวหลัง lìawlǎŋ′ V to look back.

เหลือ lɤ̌a′ V 1. to be left over, remaining. 2. to
be surplus, in excess of what is needed.

ของเหลือใช้ (สิ่ง, อย่าง, ชิ้น) khɔ̌ɔŋ′lɤ̌acháj′ (sìŋ′,
jàaŋ′, chín′) N surplus.

ขาดเหลือ khàad′lɤ̌a′ V to be lacking (in), short
(of).

ช่วยเหลือ chûajlɤ̌a′ V to help out, assist, give
help.

ที่เหลือ thîilɤ̌a′ that which is left; that which
remains; that which is in excess.

ประหลาดเหลือ pralàad′lɤ̌a′ V to be extremely
strange.

เหลือกำลัง lɤ̌a′kamlaŋ′ V to be beyond the
strength.

เหลือเกิน lɤ̌akəən′, lɤ́akəən′ very, extremely,
exceedingly.

o ช่างเหลือเกิน châŋ′lɤ́akəən′ V 1. to be extraordinary, terrific. 2. to be awful, terrible.

เหลือขอ lɤ̌akhɔ̌ɔ′ V to be refractory, impossible,
unmanageable.

เหลือคณนา lɤ̌a′khananaa′ V lit. to be innumerable, immeasurable, countless.

เหลือใจ lɤ̌a′caj′ exceedingly, extremely, very.

เหลือเชื่อ lɤ̌achɤ̂a′ V to be unbelievable, incredible, fantastic.

เหลือทน lɤ̌athon′, lɤ̌a′thon′ V to be unbearable,
intolerable.

เหลือบ่ากว่าแรง lɤ̌abàa′kwàarɛɛŋ′ elab. colloq.
to be more than one can do, take on, shoulder.

เหลือประมาณ lɤ̌a′pramaan′ exceedingly (beyond
estimation).

เหลือเฟือ lɤ̌a′fɤa′ V colloq. 1. to be more than
necessary, more than enough, plentiful. sV 2.
more than enough, plentifully. →Also 2. อย่าง--.

เหลือล้นพ้นประมาณ lɤ̌alón′-phón′pramaan′ elab.
colloq. extremely, exceedingly, immeasurably.

เหลือวิสัย lɤ̌a′wísǎj′ V to be beyond one's ability,
beyond one's power.

เหลือแสน lɤ̌asɛ̌ɛn′ colloq. extremely, exceedingly, very.

เหลือหลอ lɤ̌alɔɔ′ V colloq. to be left, remaining.

เหลือหลาย lɤ̌alǎaj′ sV 1. abundant, profuse; abundantly, profusely, extremely, very. V 2. to be
abundant, profuse.

เหลืออด lỷa?òd′ V to be unable or scarcely able to control oneself (usually referring to anger); to lose control of one's temper.

เหลืออยู่ lỷa′jùu′, lỷa′jùuɔ to remain, be left.

เหลือก lỷag′ V to roll the eyes up.

เหลือง lỷaŋ′ V to be yellow.

ไข้เหลือง khâjlỷaŋ′ N yellow fever.

คางเหลือง khaaŋ′lỷaŋ′ V slang to be critically injured, near dead.

ชาติผิวเหลือง (ชาติ) châad′phǐwlỷaŋ′ (châad′) N the yellow race.

ถั่วเหลือง (เม็ด,ฝัก) thùalỷaŋ′ N soybean (méd′ for the seed; fàg′ for the pod). ต้น-- (ต้น) soybean plant.

ทองเหลือง thɔɔŋlỷaŋ′ N brass.

น้ำเหลือง námlỷaŋ′ N lymph.

นุ่งเหลืองห่มเหลือง nûŋlỷaŋ′hòmlỷaŋ′ V colloq. to be in the priesthood, wear the yellow robe of priesthood.

สีเหลือง sǐilỷaŋ′ N 1. yellow, the color yellow. V 2. to be yellow.

เหลืองจ๋อย lỷaŋcɔ̌j′ to be very yellow.

เหลืองจ้า lỷaŋcâa′ to be bright yellow.

เหลืองอ๋อย lỷaŋ?ɔ̌j′ to be very yellow.

เหลือบ ๑ (ตัว) lỷab′ (tua′) N horsefly; gadfly.

เหลือบ ๒ lỷab′ V to glance, look sideways.

เหลือม in งูเหลือม (ตัว) ŋuulỷam′ (tua′) N python.

เหลื่อม lỷam′ V to lap over, overlap, extend over and cover a part of.

ความเหลื่อมล้ำ khwaam′lỷamlám′ N inequality, disparity, difference.

ความเหลื่อมล้ำต่ำสูง khwaam′-lỷamlám′tàmsǔuŋ′ N disparity, inequality.

เหว (แห่ง,เหว) hěew′ (hèŋ′, hěew′) N gorge, chasm, abyss.

เหว่ in ว้าเหว่ wáawèe′ V to be lonesome, lonely and lost.

ว้าเหว่ใจ wáawèecaj′ V to be lonesome.

เหวง wěŋ′ rM intens. used with เบา "light."

เหวี่ยง wìaŋ′ V to throw, hurl, fling, cast (usually with a sidewise motion of the arm or arms).

พอพัดพอเหวี่ยง phɔɔfád′phɔɔwìaŋ′ elab. colloq. to be about the same (in strength).

สุดเหวี่ยง sùdwìaŋ′ colloq. 1. to the utmost

degree. 2. with all one's might.

เหวี่ยงหมัด wìaŋmàd′ V to throw a punch.

เหวี่ยงแห wìaŋhɛ̌ɛ′ V 1. to cast a (fishing) net. 2. slang to let go a blindly-thrown punch.

เห่อ hə̀ə′ V to be excessively proud (of something), show off (something new). ความ-- pride (of possession).

เหา (ตัว) hǎw′ (tua′) N louse.

เห่า hàw′ V 1. (a dog) to bark. 2. (a snake) to hiss.

งูเห่า (ตัว) ŋuuhàw′ (tua′) N cobra.

เห่าหอน hàwhɔ̌ɔn′ V to bark and howl; to howl.

เหาะ hɔ̀?′ V to fly through the air. →Not used of birds and insects.

เรือเหาะ (ลำ) ryahɔ̀?′ (lam′) N aircraft.

เหิน hə̌ən′ V eleg. to fly, take to the air.

เดินเหิน dəənhə̌ən′ V colloq. to walk.

ห่างเหิน, เหินห่าง hàaŋhə̌ən′, hə̌ənhàaŋ′ V 1. to stay away (as of a friend who no longer visits). 2. to become estranged as a result of being apart (as of husband and wife).

เหิม. See ฮึกเหิม.

เหี้ย (ตัว) hîa′ (tua′) N water monitor (regarded as a creature of ill omen).

อ้ายเหี้ย ?âjhîa′| derog. You ill-omened creature!

เหี้ยน hîan′ V 1. to be cut down, cut off short, razed. sV 2. until cut down, cut off short. 3. colloq. completely, all up.

เหี้ยม hîam′ V to be ruthless, pitiless.

เหี้ยมเกรียม hîamkriam′ V to be unmerciful, unrelenting.

เหี้ยมโหด hîamhòod′ V to be ruthless, brutal, cruel, heartless.

เหี่ยว hìaw′ V 1. to be wilted, withered. 2. to wrinkle.

ห่อเหี่ยว hɔ̀ɔhìaw′ V to be dejected, depressed, downhearted.

เหี่ยวแห้ง hìawhɛ̂ŋ′ V 1. to be dry, wilted. 2. to be cheerless, sad.

o เหี่ยวแห้งใจ hìawhɛ̂ŋcaj′ V to feel cheerless, mirthless.

เหื่อ hỳa′ N colloq. sweat. →Syn. เหงื่อ com.

เหื่อออก hỳa?ɔ̀ɔg′ V colloq. to sweat.

เหือด hỳad′ V to dry up, disappear, diminish.

เหือดหาย hỳadhǎaj′ V to disappear gradually.

เหือดแห้ง hỳadhɛ̂ɛŋ/ V to dry up.

แห (ปาก) hɛ̌ɛ/ (pàag/) N cast net, fish net.

แห่ hɛ̂ɛ/ N 1. parade, procession. V 2. to parade, walk in a procession.

     กระบวนแห่ (กระบวน) krabuanhɛ̂ɛ/ (krabuan/) N procession, parade.

แหก hɛ̀ɛg/ V vulg. to open widely, break open, force open.

     แหกคุก hɛ̀ɛgkhúg/ V to break out of jail.

แหง่ in ลูกแหง่ (ตัว) lûugŋɛ̀ɛ/ (tua/) N buffalo calf.

แห่ง (แห่ง) hɛ̀ŋ/* (hɛ̀ŋ/) N 1. place. C 2. place, location. Pp 3. of (esp. with places). →Dist. 1. แหล่ง . →Syn. 1. ที่ ๑. 2. แหล่ง .

     o ในเบื้องลึกแห่งหัวใจของเขา najbɨ̂ɑŋlɯ́g/hɛ̀ŋɔ- hǔacaj/-khɔ̌ŋkháw/ deep down in his heart.

     ทุกหนทุกแห่ง thúghǒnthúghɛ̀ŋ/ elab. everywhere.

     ทุกแห่ง thúghɛ̀ŋ/ everywhere, every place.

     บางแห่ง baŋhɛ̀ŋ/ (in) some places.

     หลายแห่ง lǎajhɛ̀ŋ/ various points, places.

แห้ง hɛ̂ɛŋ/ V to be dry, dried.

     เกยแห้ง kəəjhɛ̂ɛŋ/ V to run aground.

     ของแห้ง khɔ̌ŋhɛ̂ɛŋ/ N dry foods, foods which can be stored without undue spoilage (e.g. dried, pickled, bottled, and canned foods). →Also ของชำ. →Opp. ของสด .

     ซักแห้ง sághɛ̂ɛŋ/ V to be dry-cleaned.

     ปลาแห้ง plaahɛ̂ɛŋ/ N dried fish.

     ผอมแห้ง phɔ̌ɔmhɛ̂ɛŋ/ V to be gaunt, emaciated.

     o โรคผอมแห้ง rôog/phɔ̌ɔmhɛ̂ɛŋ/ N consumption, pulmonary tuberculosis.

     ยิ้มแห้งๆ jím/hɛ̂ɛŋhɛ̂ɛŋ/ to smile dryly, mirthlessly.

     เหี่ยวแห้ง hìawhɛ̂ɛŋ/ V 1. to be dry, wilted. 2. to be cheerless, sad.

     o เหี่ยวแห้งใจ hìawhɛ̂ɛŋcaj/ V to feel cheerless, mirthless.

     เหือดแห้ง hỳadhɛ̂ɛŋ/ V to dry up.

     แห้งกราก hɛ̂ɛŋkràag/ V to be completely dry.

     แห้งผาก hɛ̂ɛŋphàag/ V to be extremely dry.

     แห้งแล้ง hɛ̂ɛŋlɛ́ɛŋ/ V 1. to be dry, arid. 2. to be dreary, empty of life and freshness.

แหงน ŋɛ̌ɛn/ V to turn the face up, look up.

     แหงนคอ ŋɛ̌ɛnkhɔɔ/ V to crane one's neck (to look up).

แหงนหน้า ŋɛ̌ɛnnâa/ V to turn the face up

แหน ๑ nɛ̌ɛ/ N duckweed.

แหน ๒ in หวงแหน hǔaŋhɛ̌ɛn/ V to reserve, guard, keep for oneself, keep from falling to others.

     ขี้หวงแหน khîihǔaŋhɛ̌ɛn/ V to be possessive.

แหนง nɛ̌ɛŋ/ V to suspect, doubt, mistrust.

     กินแหนง kinnɛ̌ɛŋ/ V to be mistrustful, suspicious (of).

แหนบ (อัน) nɛ̀ɛb/ (ʔan/) N 1. tweezers. 2. leaf spring (the rear springs of a car). V 3. to pinch (with the fingers).

     แหนบจับกระดาษ (อัน) nɛ̀ɛb/-càb/kradàad/ (ʔan/) N paper clamp (i.e. a clamp type paper clip or fastener).

แหบ hɛ̀ɛb/ V to be hoarse, rasping, dry, parched (of the voice).

     เสียงแหบ sǐaŋhɛ̀ɛb/ V to have a hoarse, rasping voice.

     แหบเครือ hɛ̀ɛbkhrya/ V to be hoarse and trembly (of the voice, esp. of the elderly or the sick).

แหม mɛ̌ɛ/ E Say! Well! Oh my goodness!

แหม่ม (คน) mɛ̀m/* (khon/) N 1. an occidental woman. T 2. title used for occidental women. [f. Eng. "ma'am"]

แหย jɛ̌ɛ/ V colloq. 1. to be cowardly. sV 2. sheepishly.

     ยิ้มแหยๆ jím/jɛ̌ɛjɛ̌ɛ/ V to smile sheepishly, wryly.

แหย่ jɛ̀ɛ/ V to poke, tease by poking, annoy, provoke.

แหยม. See หยอมแหยม .

แหยะ. See เหยอะแหยะ , เหยาะแหยะ .

แหรม,แหร่ม. See หรอมแหรม,หร่อมแหร่ม .

แหล. See ตอแหล .

แหล่ ๑ lɛ̀ɛ/ sV much, many.

     ทั้งหลายแหล่ tháŋlǎaj/lɛ̀ɛ/ all those, all of.

แหล่ ๒ lɛ̀ɛ/ Pt particle having emphatic or corroborative force, used at the end of a sentence or a poem. →Var. of แล ๒.

     จะ...มิ...แหล่ caɔ...míɔ...lɛ̀ɛ/ be on the verge, on the point of.

     o กำลังจะตายมิตายแหล่ kamlaŋcataaj/mítaaj/- lɛ̀ɛ/ to be on the verge of death.

     o จะหลับมิหลับแหล่ calàb/mílàb/-lɛ̀ɛ/ to be on the verge of falling asleep.

แหลก lὲɛg/ V to be pulverized, mashed, reduced
   to a pulp, broken into small pieces.

ชั่วหมากแหลก chûamàag/lὲɛg/ idiom. (within)
   a short while (i.e. as long as it takes to chew
   betel to a pulp).

เหลวแหลก lěewlὲɛg/ V to be dissolute, good-
   for-nothing.

อย่างสะบั้นหั่นแหลก jàaŋsabân/-hàn/lὲɛg/ slang
   a great deal, extremely, unsparingly.

แหล่ง (แหล่ง) lὲŋ/*(lὲŋ/) N 1. spot, location, (specific) place. C 2. idem. →Dist. 1. ที่ ๑, แห่ง.
   →Syn. 1. สถาน eleg. 2. แห่ง.

ตั้งหลักแหล่ง tâŋ/làglὲŋ/ V 1. to settle down.
   2. to be located.

ตามแหล่งที่ taamlὲŋ/thîiɔ in places where.

แหล่งการค้า (แหล่ง, แห่ง) lὲŋ/kaankháa/ (lὲŋ/,
   hὲŋ/) N market place; business location.

แหล่งกำเนิด (แหล่ง, แห่ง) lὲŋ/kamnɔ̀ɔd/ (lὲŋ/,
   hὲŋ/) N 1. place of birth. 2. source, origin.

แหลน (อัน) lɛ̌ɛn/ (ʔan/) N javelin.

แหลม (แหลม) lɛ̌ɛm/ V 1. to be sharp-pointed,
   pointed. 2. to be high-pitched (as of the voice).
   N 3. cape, peninsula (lɛ̌ɛm/). →Dist. คม
   "sharpedged." →Ant. ทู่.

เฉียบแหลม chìablɛ̌ɛm/ V to be keen, sharp,
   shrewd (of people).

มุมแหลม (มุม) mumlɛ̌ɛm/ (mum/) N acute angle.

ล่อแหลม lɔ̂ɔlɛ̌ɛm/ V to be risky, exposed to danger.

o ยุคล่อแหลม (ยุค) júg/lɔ̂ɔlɛ̌ɛm/ (júg/) N critical period.

แหลมคม lɛ̌ɛm/khom/ V 1. to be sharp and pointed.
   2. idiom. to be quick-witted, clever, smart.

แหลมทอง lɛ̌ɛmthɔɔŋ/ N the Southeast Asian
   Peninsula.

แหลมเปี๊ยบ lɛ̌ɛmpíab/ to be very pointed.

แหลมมลายู lɛ̌ɛm/malaajuu/ N the Malay Peninsula.

แหลมอินโดจีน lɛ̌ɛm/ʔindoociin/ N the Indochinese
   Peninsula.

แหละ lὲʔ/ Pt particle used to intensify. Often
   rendered only by the exclamation point.

o เท่านั้นแหละ thâwnán/lὲʔ↓, -lὲʔ/ That's all!

o ผมก็เหมือนกันแหละ phǒm/kɔ̌mỹan/-kanlὲʔ↓
   Me too! Same here!

แหว wɛ̌ɛ/ V colloq. to scold with a loud, angry
   voice.

แหวก wὲɛg/ V to part, push aside, break through,
   wade through.

แหวกว่าย wὲɛgwâaj/ V to swim about.

แหว่ง wὲŋ/* V to be chipped, nicked.

ทำ(. . .)แหว่ง tham(. . .)wὲŋ/ V to chip, nick (smthg.).

ปากแหว่ง pàagwὲŋ/ V to have a harelip.

เว้าแหว่ง wáwwὲŋ/ V to be jagged, irregular,
   curving in and out (as of a coastline, a jaggedly
   torn hemline, a nibbled piece of bread).

แหวน (วง) wɛ̌ɛn/ (woŋ/) N (finger) ring.

วงแหวน (วง) woŋwɛ̌ɛn/ (woŋ/) N ring, gasket,
   washer.

แหวนเพชร (วง) wɛ̌ɛnphéd/ (woŋ/) N diamond
   ring.

แหวนหมั้น (วง) wɛ̌ɛnmân/ (woŋ/) N engagement
   ring.

แหวว wɛ̌w/* rM intens. used with แจ๋ว "bright."

แหวะ wὲʔ/ V to cut open.

แหะๆ hὲʔhὲʔ/ imit. the sound of laughing. →Cf. ฮึๆ.

โห่ hòo/ V 1. colloq. to boo. 2. to cheer, hail.

แต่ไก่โห่ tὲɛkàjhòo/ idiom. at cockcrow, at early
   dawn, so early.

โห่ร้อง hòorɔ́ɔŋ/ V to cheer, hail, acclaim.

โหง hǒoŋ/ N ghost, spirit. →Chiefly in compounds.

ตายโหง taajhǒoŋ/ V to die a violent death.

o ให้ตายโหงตายห่าซี hâjtaajhǒoŋ/taajhàa/-sii↓
   vulg. May the plague take me! (expression used
   to swear that one is telling the truth).

โหด. See entries below.

เหี้ยมโหด hîamhòod/ V to be ruthless, brutal,
   cruel, heartless.

โหดร้าย hòodráaj/ V to be cruel, atrocious.

โหน hǒon/ V to hang, swing from by the hands.

ห้อยโหน hɔ̂jhǒon/ V to swing while suspended
   (esp. in gymnastics).

โหม hǒom/ V to urge; to push (one's strength) to
   the limit, knock oneself out (doing something).

ลุกโหม lúg/hǒom/ V to burn intensely.

หักโหม hàghǒom/ V to drive oneself, push (one's
   strength) to the limit, knock oneself out (doing
   something).

โหมไฟ hǒomfaj/ V to coax a fire (as by fanning,
   adding fuel).

โหม่ง mòoŋ′ V to hit (a ball) with the head, bounce (a ball) off one's head.

โหย in โหยหวน hǒojhŭan′ V to be eerie (of sound).

o เสียงโหยหวน sǐaŋ′hǒojhŭan′ N an eerie sound.

โหร (คน) hǒon′ (khon′) N com. astrologer.

โหรง,--เหรง rǒoŋ′,rǒoŋrěeŋ′ V 1. to be sparse, few, small in number. sV 2. in small numbers.

ดูโหรงเหรง duu′rǒoŋrěeŋ′ to look bare, empty (because of the small number, e.g. of people in a store, leaves on a tree).

โหระพา hǒoraphaa′ N sweet basil. ต้น-- (ต้น) sweet basil (the plant).

โหรา-. See entries below.

โหราจารย์ (คน) hǒoraacaan′ (khon′) N eleg. astrologer and teacher, an astrologer who is a teacher.

โหราศาสตร์ hǒoraasàad′ N astrology.

โหล ๑ lǒo′ C dozen.

o ไข่สองโหล khàj′sɔ̌oŋlǒo′ two dozen eggs.

โหล ๒ (ใบ) lǒo′ (baj′) N 1. jar (usually of glass and with a wide mouth). V 2. (eyes) to be hollow, sunken.

ขวดโหล (ใบ) khùadlǒo′ (baj′) N wide-mouthed glass jar with glass stopper.

ตาโหล taalǒo′ V to have sunken eyes (as of a sick person).

โหล่ lǒo′ V colloq. to be last, behind.

โหว่ wòo′ V to be hollowed out, to have holes, cavities.

โหวง wǒoŋ′ rM intens. used with เบา "light."

ให้ hâj′ V 1. to give. 2. to have, let (someone do something). sV 3. to, so that. 4. for (such and such an object or person). →Syn. 1. ประทาน roy., พระราชทาน roy.

ก่อให้เกิด kɔ̀ɔ′hâjkə̀əd′ V to cause, give rise to.

ขอให้ดูตัวอย่างอันนั้น khɔ̌ɔhâjduu′-tuajàaŋ′ʔannán′↓ Let's look at that example.

ขอให้เรารู้จักเป็นเพื่อนกันดีกว่า khɔ̌ɔhâjraw′-rúuɔ càg′penphɯ̂an′-kandiikwàa′↓ Let us rather know each other as friends.

ของให้ (อย่าง,ชิ้น) khɔ̌oŋhâj′ (jàaŋ′,chín′) N gift, present.

คำให้การ (ข้อ,ฉบับ,ประการ) kham′hâjkaan′ (khɔ̂ɔ′,chabàb′,prakaan′) N testimony.

ต่อให้ tɔ̀ɔ′hâjɔ to give an advantage, a head start, a handicap to. →See cross ref.

ถลึงตาให้หยุด thalɯ̌ŋ′taa′-hâjjùd′ gave (them) a stern look to make (them) stop.

ทำร้าย(...)ให้ถึงตาย thamráaj′(...)hâjthɯ̌ŋtaaj′ to harm to the point of causing to die.

ทำให้ thamhâjɔ to cause to (do smthg.), make (do smthg.). →See Note 2 under ทำ.

o ทำให้เกิด thamhâjkə̀əd′ V to bring about, give rise to, produce, create, cause.

o ทำให้ผมตกใจ thamhâjphǒm′tògcaj′ (it) frightens me, causes me to be scared.

ทิ้งไว้ให้ thíŋ′wájhâjɔ to leave (it) until (it) becomes (e.g. hard).

ปล่อยให้ plɔ̀j′hâjɔ to let, allow.

เป็นเหตุให้ penhèed′hâjɔ to cause, be the cause of.

เพื่อจะ(...)ให้ได้ phɯ̂aca(...)hâjdâaj′ in order to be able to.

เพื่อให้ phɯ̂ahâjɔ 1. to let, allow. 2. in order to, for.

ฟังให้ซึ้ง faŋ′hâjsɯ́ŋ′ to listen with deep feeling. →Also ฟังซึ้ง.

มีมติให้ miimatì′ʔ/hâjɔ to resolve, pass a resolution, come to a decision that.

ไม่ให้ (1) mâjhâj′; (2,3) mâjhâjɔ 1. not to give. 2. not to let. 3. not to, without, so that not (followed by a verb).

o ไม่ให้จีนแดงเข้าเป็นสมาชิกยูโน mâjhâjciindɛɛŋ′-khâwpensamaachíg′juunoo′ not to allow Red China to become a member of the U.N.

o ไม่ให้มากเกินไป mâjhâjmâag′kəənpaj′ not too much.

o ครูบอกไม่ให้ทำอย่างนั้น khruu′bɔ̀ɔg′-mâjhâjɔ tham′jàaŋnán′↓ The teacher said not to do (it) that way.

o พิมพ์ไม่ให้ผิดเลยได้ไหม phim′-mâjhâjphìd′ləəj′ dâaj′máj↓ Can (you) type (it) without making any mistakes?

ยก(...)ให้ (1,2) jóg′(...)hâj′, -hâjɔ; (3,4) jóg′ɔ hâj′, jóg′hâjɔ, jóghâj′ 1. to give, offer (something)(to). 2. to lift (e.g. something heavy) for (someone). 3. to excuse, exempt. 4. to recognize (that), accept as true (that).

o ยกโทษให้ jógthôod′hâj′, -hâjɔ to forgive.

o ยกลูกสาวให้ jóg′-lûugsǎaw′hâj′, -hâjɔ to give one's daughter in marriage.

o ยอมยกให้ว่า jɔɔm′jóg′-hâjwâaɔ to concede, grant, accept as true (that).

ยอมให้ jɔɔm′hâjɔ to allow to (do).

ยัดเยียดให้ jádjîad′hâj′ to insist on giving (something) to.

ยื่น(...)ให้ jɤ̂yn′(...)hâjɔ, -hâj′ to hand over, submit (something) to.

เรียก(...)ให้มา rîag′(...)hâjmaa′ to call (someone) to come, call (someone) over.

ส่ง(...)ให้ sòŋ′(...)hâjɔ to hand (something) to, send (something) to.

สอนให้ sɔ̌ɔn′hâjɔ, sɔ̌ɔnhâj′ 1. to teach (to do something). 2. to teach (someone).

เสนอ(...)ให้ (1) sanɤ̌ə′(...)hâjɔ; (2) sanɤ̌ə′ɔ hâjɔ 1. to propose, submit (something, someone) to. 2. to propose that (such and such be done, that someone do such and such).

หัดให้ hàd′hâjɔ, hàdhâj′ 1. to train (to do something). 2. to train, teach (someone).

หันหลังให้ hǎnlǎŋ′hâjɔ, --hâj′ to turn one's back to, keep away from.

ให้การ hâjkaan′ V to give testimony, testify.

ให้(...)กิน hâj(...)kin′ fo feed, provide with food.

ให้(...)กินอยู่ hâj(...)kin′jùu′ V to provide (someone) with room and board.

ให้(...)กู้ hâj(...)kûu′ V to loan, lend to someone)(at interest).

ให้แก่ hâj′kàɔ to, for.

ให้(...)แก่ hâj(...)kɛ̀ɔ, -kaɔ to give (something) to (someone).

ให้คุณ hâjkhun′ V to do good, be beneficial, useful.

ให้เช่า hâjchâw′ V 1. to let, rent out. 2. to be for rent.

ให้ถูก hâjthùug′ 1. correctly, so as to be correct. 2. so as to hit (the target).

o จี้ให้ถูกเส้น cîi′-hâjthùug′sên′ fig., colloq. to hit the right spot, touch the right chord (for successfully evoking the desired response).

ให้ถูกต้อง hâjthùug′tɔ̂ŋ′ correctly, so as to be correct.

ให้ท่า hâjthâa′ V idiom. 1. (a woman) to encourage (a man's) advances. 2. to play Cupid, encourage or arrange for a fellow and a girl to get together.

ให้ทาน hâjthaan′ V to give alms.

ให้ท้าย hâjtháaj′ V to back, support, take sides with (usually not openly).

ให้โทษ hâjthôod′ V to do harm, be harmful.

ให้ปากคำ hâjpàag′kham′ V to testify, give testimony, make a statement.

ให้เป็นทาน hâjpenthaan′ to give as a charity.

ให้ผล hâjphǒn′ V to benefit, yield benefits, give results.

ให้พร hâjphɔɔn′ V to bless, wish (someone) happiness and good fortune. คำ-- (ข้อ,ฉบับ, ประการ) blessing.

ให้ยืม hâjjyym′ V to lend.

ให้ละเอียด hâjla?ìad′ in detail, thoroughly.

ให้สมกับ hâjsǒm′kaɔ in order to suit; so that it might suit, satisfy, make up for.

ให้สัญญา hâjsǎnjaa′ V to promise.

ให้สิ้นชีวิต hâjsîn′chiiwíd′ to terminate the life (of).

ให้หา hâjhǎa′ V to call for, send for.

ให้เห็น hâjhěn′ clearly, evidently, apparently.

o ให้เห็นจริง hâjhěn′ciŋ′ convincingly.

ให้อภัย hâj?aphaj′ V to forgive, pardon.

ให้อภัยโทษ hâj?aphaj′jathôod′ V eleg. to pardon, grant amnesty (to).

อนุมัติให้ ?ànumád′hâjɔ to grant (someone) permission to (do something).

อย่า...ให้มากไปเลย jàaɔ...hâjmâag′pajləəj′↓ Don't (do this or that) so much! Do stop (doing this or that) so much!

เอา...ให้อยู่ ?aw′(...)hâjjùu′ colloq. to get something, someone) under control, get control over, subdue, finish.

เอา(...)ออกให้ ?aw(...)?ɔɔg′hâj′ to take (something) out for (someone).

ใหญ่ jàj′ V to be large, big, main, major. ความ-- magnitude, bigness. →Ant. น้อย. →Dist. โต.

กว้างใหญ่ kwâaŋjàj′ V to be large, wide, extensive.

กองพลใหญ่ (กอง,กองพล) kɔɔŋphonjàj′ (kɔɔŋ′, kɔɔŋphon′) N milit. division.

ขนาดใหญ่ khanàad′jàj′ large-sized, of a large size.

ขนาดใหญ่ๆ khanàad′jàjjàj′ larger-sized, (of the) larger sizes.

ขนานใหญ่ khanǎn′jàj′ colloq. on a grand scale, in a big way.

ข้าหลวงใหญ่ (นาย,คน) khâalǔaŋ′jàj′ (naaj′, khon′) N high commissioner, governor general.

ไข้รากสาดใหญ่ khâjrâagsàad′jàj′ N typhus.

ไข้หวัดใหญ่ khâjwàd′jàj′ N influenza.

ครูใหญ่ (คน) khruujàj′ (khon′) N headmaster, headmistress, principal.

ครู่ใหญ่ khrûu′jàj′ (for) a long moment, a long while.

ตกจั๊กใหญ่ tòg′câgjàj′ V colloq. (rain) to pour heavily.

เติบใหญ่ tə̀əb′jàj′ V to grow up, be grown-up. →Syn. เติบโต.

ปืนใหญ่ (กระบอก) pyynjàj′ (krabɔ̀ɔg′) N cannon; artillery piece; artillery.

เป็นการใหญ่ penkaanjàj′ 1. to be on a grand scale; to be a great thing; to be overwhelming, considerable. 2. on a grand scale, to a great extent, overwhelmingly, considerably.

เป็นข้อใหญ่ penkhɔ̂ɔ′jàj′ mainly, chiefly.

เป็นใหญ่ penjàj′ to have power and authority, be head of, be a big shot. ความ-- being on top, being top man.

ผู้ใหญ่ (คน) phûujàj′ (khon′) N 1. adult. 2. (one's) superior, (one's) elder. 3. the big fellow. →Ant. 1. เด็ก. 2,3. ผู้น้อย.

o ชั้นผู้ใหญ่ chán′phûujàj′ senior, high ranking.

o ผู้ใหญ่บ้าน (คน,นาย) phûujàjbâan′ (khon′, naaj′) N elected head of a village, headman.

แผ่นดินใหญ่ (ผืน) phὲndin′jàj′ (phǔyn′) N mainland.

พักใหญ่ phág′jàj′ for a long time.

พี่ใหญ่ (คน) phîijàj′ (khon′) N eldest brother or sister.

มักใหญ่ mágjàj′ V to be ambitious. →Ant.มักน้อย.

ยิ่งใหญ่ jîŋjàj′ V to be great, powerful, important.

ส่วนใหญ่ sùanjàj′ the larger part, the major part, the majority.

o เป็นส่วนใหญ่ pensùan′jàj′ 1. to be the larger part, a large part. 2. for the most part, mostly.

หน้าใหญ่ใจโต nâajàj′cajtoo′ V to be lavish, given to lavishness (e.g. in entertaining friends).

ใหญ่โต jàjtoo′ V 1. to be big, large, immense, enormous, huge. 2. to be high (in position), great, important. sV 3. in a big way, on a large scale, immensely. ความ-- hugeness, immensity; greatness. คน-- an important person, a big shot.

ใหญ่ถนัด jàj′thanàd′ V to be very big.

ใหญ่หลวง jàjlǔaŋ′ V to be tremendous, enormous, major, grave, serious.

o ภัยอันใหญ่หลวง phaj′ʔanjàjlǔaŋ′ grave danger.

o ระเบิดอย่างใหญ่หลวง rabə̀əd′jàaŋjàjlǔaŋ′ to explode violently.

ใหม่ màj′ V 1. to be new. sV 2. anew, again.

ขึ้นใหม่ khŷnmàj′ sV again, once more, anew. May often be rendered by the English prefix re-, as in "rebuild."

น้องใหม่ (คน) nɔ́ɔŋmàj′ (khon′) N 1. newborn brother or sister. 2. freshman in a college or university. 3. new member.

ปีใหม่ piimàj′ New Year.

o งานปีใหม่ ŋaan′piimàj′ N New Year's festival.

แผนใหม่ phɛ̌ɛnmàj′ N 1. new or modern plan, project or type. 2. (as n. mod.) modern, new, new-type, of the modern plan.

พรปีใหม่ phɔɔn′piimàj′ New Year's blessing(s).

มือใหม่ (มือ,คน) myymàj′ (myy′, khon′) N idiom. beginner, a new hand (at some activity). →Opp. มือเก่า.

ยุคใหม่ júgmàj′ N the new period; the latest period; the modern age.

รุ่นใหม่ rûnmàj′ N 1. new period; new kind; new batch. 2. (as n. mod.) new, modern, of the new or present generation.

สมัยใหม่ samǎjmàj′ N 1. modern times, the present time. 2. (as n. mod.) modern, up-to-date.

หน้าใหม่ nâamàj′ N 1. new face, newcomer, new one. V 2. to be a newcomer, new one, stranger.

หัดใหม่ hàdmàj′ V 1. to be a beginner, newly trained. 2. to train or practice once again.

ใหม่จ๋า màjcǎa′ colloq. to be ultra-modern.

○ สมัยใหม่จ๋า samǎj′màjcǎa′ colloq. to be real modern, ultra-modern.

ใหม่เจี๊ยบ màjcíab′ V colloq. to be ultra-modern.

ใหม่ถอดด้าม màj′thɔ̀ɔddâam′ colloq. to be brand-new.

ใหม่ๆ màjmàj′ 1. new, brand-new. 2. just, shortly, recently.

ใหม่เอี่ยม màj?ìam′ V colloq. to be brand-new.

ใหล in หลงใหล lǒŋlǎj′ V to be crazy about.

ไห (ลูก, ใบ) hǎj′ (lûug′, baj′) N earthen crock, jar.

ไหปลาร้า (ข้าง) hǎj′plaaráa′ (khâaŋ′) N 1. the clavicle, collarbone. 2. the hollow just above the collarbone.

○ กระดูกไหปลาร้า kradùug′-hǎjplaaráa′ N the clavicle, collarbone.

ไห้ hǎj′, hâaj′ element occurring in compounds expressive of the idea of weeping.

ร้องไห้ rɔ́ɔŋhâaj′ V to cry, weep.

○ ขี้ร้องไห้ khîirɔ́ɔŋhâaj′ V com. to be a cry-baby.

ร่ำไห้ râmhâj′ V to weep and wail incessantly, lament repeatedly.

สะอื้นไห้ sa?ʔɯ̂ɯn′hâj′ V to sob.

ไหน ๑ nǎj′ iA 1. which, any (interrog.,indef.). Must be preceded by clf. 2. short for ที่ไหน where, anywhere, somewhere. →Cf. ฉน.

คนไหน khonnǎj′ which one (ref. to a person).

แค่ไหน khɛ̂ɛnǎj′ up to which point, how far, how much, to what extent.

จะไปไหนก็ลำบาก capajnǎj′kɔ̂lambàag′ it's hard to go anywhere (e.g. without a car).

ถึงไหน thɯ̌ŋnǎj′ up to where; to what extent.

ที่ไหน thîinǎj′ where, somewhere, anywhere.

ไปไหน pajnǎj′↓ Where are you going?

ไปไหนมา pajnǎjmaa↓ Where have you been?

ไปไหนมาไหน pajnǎj′maanǎj′ to get around, go hither and thither, travel about.

ไหนๆ nǎjnǎj′ anyhow, anything, any.

○ ...กว่า(...)เป็นไหนๆ ...kwàa′(...)penɔ nǎjnǎj′ far...-er (than...), far more... (than...), more...by far (than...).

○ ที่ไหนๆ thîi′nǎjnǎj′ anywhere, anywhere

whatsoever.

○ ไหนๆ(...)ก็ nǎjnǎj′(...)kɔ̀ɔ now that, since.

○○ ไหนๆมันก็แล้วไปแล้ว อย่าพูดถึงมันอีกเลย nǎjnǎj′-mankɔ̂lɛ́ɛw′pajlɛ́ɛw′→ jàaphûud′thɯ̌ŋman′-?ʔìgɔ lǝǝj↓ Now that it's over, let's not talk about it any more.

ไหน ๒ nǎj′ E Say! By the way.

ไหม ๑ mǎj′ N silk.

ตัวไหม (ตัว) tuamǎj′ (tua′) N silkworm.

ด้ายไหม (เส้น, ไจ, หลอด) dâajmǎj′ N silk thread (sên′ for strands; caj′ for skeins; lɔ̀ɔd′ for spools).

ผ้าไหม phâamǎj′ N silk cloth.

ไหม ๒ mǎj′ V to fine. →Usually in the following compound.

ปรับไหม pràbmǎj′ V to fine.

○ ค่าปรับไหม khâa′pràbmǎj′ N fine, penalty.

ไหม ๓ mǎj′, máj′, májɔ Pt part. used to convert a statement into a yes-or-no question. NOTE. In negative questions containing ไม่, หรือ must be used rather than ไหม.

ใครจะบอกได้ไหมว่า... khrajcabɔ̀ɔg′dâajmájɔ wâa′... is there anyone who can tell (me)...

○ บอกแล้วไหมล่ะ bɔ̀ɔg′lɛ́ɛwmájlâ↓ I told you so. Didn't I tell you? See, I told you.

○ รู้ไหมว่า rúu′májwâa′ do you know that (such and such is the case?).

ไหม้ mâj′ V 1. (fire) to burn. 2. to be burned, charred.

การเผาไหม้ kaan′phǎwmâj′ N combustion.

ไฟไหม้ fajmâj′ N 1. (a) fire, conflagration. V 2. to be on fire; to catch fire.

ลุกไหม้ lúgmâj′ V 1. to ignite, catch fire. 2. to be aflame, on fire. การ- - combustion.

ไหร่ ɔràj′. Var. of ไร ๑.

ไหล ๑ lǎj′ V (liquid) to flow, run.

ของไหล khɔ̌ɔŋlǎj′ N fluid. →Dist. ของเหลว.

น้ำลายไหล námlaaj′lǎj′ V to drool, salivate.

น้ำหูน้ำตาไหล námhǔu′námtaa′-lǎj′ V elab. colloq. to cry, shed tears.

รั่วไหล rûa′lǎj′ V to leak out.

เลือดไหล lɯ̂adlǎj′ V to bleed.

เหลวไหล lěewlǎj′ V 1. to be nonsense, trivial. 2. to be unreliable, undependable, dissolute.

ไหลท่วม lǎjthûam/ V to overflow, flow over.

ไหลพราก lǎjphrâag/ V to stream forth (as tears).

ไหลมาเทมา lǎjmaa/theemaa/ V elab. colloq. to pour in, stream in, flow in continuously.

ไหลริน lǎjrin/ V to flow slowly, trickle, flow in a small gentle stream.

ไหลหลั่ง lǎjlàŋ/ V 1. to flow continuously. 2. (a crowd) to stream along, move along in a mass.

ไหลหลาก lǎjlàag/ V 1. to overflow. 2. to flow profusely.

ไหล ๒ in ปลาไหล (ตัว) plaalǎj/ (tua/) N freshwater eel.

ไหล่ (ไหล่,ข้าง) làj/ (làj/,khâaŋ/) N tip of the shoulder. →Dist. บ่า.

เคียงบ่าเคียงไหล่ khiaŋbàa/khiaŋlàj/ elab. 1. shoulder to shoulder. 2. on the same level.

ยักไหล่ jáglàj/ V to shrug the shoulders.

ไหล่เขา (แห่ง) làjkhǎw/ (hèŋ/) N mountain slope, hillside.

ไหว ๑ wǎj/ V to move slightly, shake, vibrate, quiver, quake.

เคลื่อนไหว khlŷanwǎj/ V to move, move about. การ-- movement, activity, moving.

แผ่นดินไหว (ครั้ง) phèndin/wǎj/ (khráŋ/) N earthquake.

หวั่นไหว wànwǎj/ V to be moved, tremble, shake.

o สนั่นหวั่นไหว sanàn/wànwǎj/ V to be very loud, jarring, rumbling, thundering.

ไหวพริบ wǎjphríb/ N 1. alertness, astuteness, adroitness, ability to make quick judgements. V 2. to be alert, keen, astute.

ไหวเยือก wǎj/jŷag/ to be shaken, sway back and forth or up and down (as of tree branches in a strong wind).

ไหว ๒ wǎj/ sV able to, capable of (physically), can.

ไม่ไหว (1) mâjwǎj/; (2) mâjwǎj/↓ sV 1. unable to, can't, cannot, incapable of (because of lack of physical strength or energy). E 2. How impossible!

o ว่ายน้ำต่อไปไม่ไหว wâajnáam/tɔ̀ɔpaj/-mâjwǎj/ can't swim any further.

ไหว้ wâaj/ V to salute by placing the hands palm to palm and raising them toward the face (the customary Thai salute of greeting or leavetaking).

ไหว้พระเถอะ wâajphrá?/thə?/↓ phrase used by older people to acknowledge the respect paid by younger people.

ฬ

ฬ lɔɔ/ LOW consonant. Pronounced l initially, n finally. The sound l as an initial low consonant is most often written with ล. The letter ฬ is very rarely used. Examples of its noninitial occurrence are given below.

o กีฬา kiilaa/ N athletic sports.

o นาฬิกา naalikaa/ N clock, watch.

ฬ่อ FS. See ล่อ ๑.

ฬา FS. See ลา ๑.

อ

อ ?ɔɔ/ MIDDLE consonant. Pronounced ? initially; in other positions it is used as a vowel symbol, pronounced ɔɔ or sometimes ɔ. The sound ? as an initial middle consonant is always written อ. In four words (อย่า,อยาก,อย่าง,อยู่) this letter precedes ย, a low consonant, with the function of converting it into a middle consonant; in these words อ is not pronounced.

อก (อก) ? òg/ (?og/) N com. chest, breast. →Syn. ทรวง eleg. →Often coupled with ใจ in semi-repeated expressions or split expressions; see for example ดีอกดีใจ and ชื่นอกบานใจ below.

กอดอก kɔ̀ɔd?òg/ V to fold one's arms across one's chest.

คับอกคับใจ kháb?òg/khábcaj/ V elab. colloq. 1. to feel distressed, uneasy, apprehensive. 2. to feel suppressed, under restraint.

ชื่นอกชื่นใจ chŷn?òg/chŷncaj/ V elab. 1. to please, delight. 2. to be pleasant, charming, refreshing. 3. to be happy, pleased, delighted. 4. elab. colloq. to kiss, hug (one's child, lover, in order to refresh, satisfy oneself). →Also ชื่นใจ com.,colloq.

ชื่นอกบานใจ chŷn?òg/baancaj/ V elab. to be

happy, pleased, delighted.

ดีอกดีใจ dii²ᵒg'diicaj' V elab. colloq. to be happy, glad.

ทรวงอก suaŋ²ᵒg' N chest, breast.

เป็นอก(ของ) as in ถ้าเผื่อเป็นอก(ของ)คุณบ้าง thâaphỹa'-pen²ᵒg'(khɔ̌ɔŋ)khunbâaŋ' supposing it was you (instead of me).

พ้นอก phón²ᵒg' V to be rid of (e.g. one's worry), freed from; to have (something) off one's chest.

โล่งอก lôoŋ²ᵒg' V to feel relieved, free, at ease.

เสื้อผ่าอก (ตัว) sŷa'phàa²ᵒg' (tua') N an upper garment which opens down the front.

หน้าอก (หน้าอก) nâa²ᵒg' (nâa²ᵒg') N chest, bust (body-part term).

หัวอก (หัวอก) hǔa²ᵒg' (hǔa²ᵒg') N 1. chest, breast. 2. colloq. heart. →See หัวใจ.

อกตั้ง in วิ่งอกตั้ง wîŋ'²ᵒgtâŋ' V colloq. to run fast (i.e. to run like a soldier on orders).

อกสามศอก ²ᵒg'sǎamsɔ̀ɔg' V 1. (a man) to be broad-chested. 2. to be a masculine type, a he-man.

อกหัก ²ᵒghàg' V to be broken-hearted (over a love affair).

อกตัญญู ²àgkatan'juu' V to be ungrateful.

อกุศล ²àkusǒn' N 1. vice, evil. 2. (as n. mod.) bad and false (usually ref. to news).

อคติ (อย่าง) ²àkhatì²'(jàaŋ') N prejudice.

อง in องอาจ ²oŋ²àad' V 1. to be brave, valiant. 2. to be dignified, stately.

องค์ (องค์) ²oŋ' (²oŋ') N 1. body (esp. of royalty, supernatural beings, etc.). C 2. clf. for royal personages, e.g. kings, queens, princes, princesses; for supernatural beings, e.g. fairies, angels; for sacred objects, e.g. Buddha images.

พระองค์ phrá²oŋ' P 1. he, him, his (sp. of high-ranking royalty, of divine beings, of the Buddha). C 2. clf. for a king, for high-ranking royalty, divine beings, the Buddha.

o พระองค์เจ้า (องค์) phrá²oŋ'câaw', phrá²oŋ'ᵓ câwᵓ (²oŋ') N 1. roy. prince, son of the king born by a lesser concubine. T 2. Prince --. →See เจ้าฟ้า.

องค์การ (แห่ง,ประเภท,องค์การ) ²oŋkaan' (hɛ̀ŋ', praphêed', ²oŋkaan') N organization.

o องค์การกติกาแปซิฟิค ²oŋkaan'-kàtikaa'pɛɛsífìg' nN the Pacific Treaty Organization.

o องค์การรัฐบาล ²oŋkaan'rádthabaan' N a government organization.

o องค์การศึกษาวิทยาศาสตร์และวัฒนธรรมแห่งสหประชาชาติ ²oŋkaan'sỹgsǎa' wídthajaasàad' lɛwád'thanatham'-hèŋ'sahà²prachaachâad' nN the United Nations Educational, Scientific and Cultural Organization (UNESCO).

o องค์การสหประชาชาติ ²oŋkaan'sahà²prachaaᵓ châad' nN the United Nations Organization (UN, UNO). →Also ยูโน.

o องค์การเอกชน ²oŋkaan'²èegkachon' N a private organization.

องค์ประกอบ ²oŋ'prakɔ̀ɔb' N constituent part, element.

องค์ประชุม ²oŋ'prachum' N quorum.

องคมนตรี (ท่าน) ²oŋ'khamontrii' (thân') N Privy Councillor.

องครักษ์ (คน) ²oŋkharág' (khon') N 1. aide-de-camp; body-guard. 2. slang boy friend.

องศา ²oŋsǎa' C degree (of temperature; of angular measure).

องุ่น (ลูก,พวง,ช่อ) ²aŋùn' (lûug', phuaŋ', chɔ̂ɔ') N grape (lûug' for individual fruits; phuaŋ', chɔ̂ɔ' for clusters, bunches).

อณู ²ànuu' N 1. molecule. 2. (as n.mod.) molecular.

อด ²od' V 1. to starve, be starved. 2. to refrain from. AA 3. colloq. not get (to do something), lose out on, miss (getting something one expected). →Syn. 3. ปวด.

น้ำอดน้ำทน nám²òd'námthon' N elab. colloq. patience, fortitude, endurance.

เหลืออด lŷa²òd' V to be unable to, or scarcely able to control oneself (usually ref. to anger); to lose control of one's temper.

อดใจ ²òdcaj' V to restrain oneself.

อดตาหลับขับตานอน ²òd'taalàb'-khàb'taanɔɔn' V elab. colloq. to go without sleep (as when studying for examinations).

อดทน ²òdthon' V to be enduring, patient. ความ-- patience, perseverance, toughness, endurance.

อดมื้อกินมื้อ ²òdmýy'kinmýy' V colloq. to have something to eat at times and be starving at other times (because of poverty).

อด (. . .) ไม่ได้ ʔòd/(...)mâjdâaj/ cannot refrain
(from).

อดสู ʔòdsǔu/ V eleg. to feel ashamed. ความ--
shame--.

อดอยาก ʔòdjàag/ V to be starved, famished.

o ความอดอยาก khwaam/ʔòdjàag/ N starvation,
famine. →Syn. ทุพภิกขภัย eleg.

อดออม ʔòdʔɔɔm/ V to be economical, frugal.

o อดออมถนอมน้ำใจ ʔòdʔɔɔm/-thanɔɔm/námcaj/
V elab. to deny oneself in order to defer to,
humor, placate another.

อดอาหาร ʔòd/ʔaahǎan/ V 1. to starve, be
starved. 2. to diet. 3. to fast.

อดิเรก in งานอดิเรก (อย่าง) ŋaan/ʔàdirèeg/*
(jàaŋ/) N hobby.

อดีต ʔadìid/ N eleg. 1. the past. 2. (as n.mod.)
former, past. →Opp. อนาคต.

  อดีตกาล ʔadìid/takaan/ N 1. eleg. the past.
  2. gram. past tense.

อธรรม ʔàtham/ V to be evil, unrighteous.

อธิกสุรทิน ʔàthí/kàsùrathin/ N the extra day in
a leap year (February 29).

อธิการ. See entries below.

  แม่อธิการ (คน) mɛ̂ɛ/ʔàthíkaan/ (khon/) N
  Mother Superior (among Catholic nuns).

  อธิการบดี (คน) ʔàthíkaan/bɔdii/ (khon/) N
  the president of a university.

  อธิการวัด (องค์) ʔàthíkaan/wád/ (ʔoŋ/) N abbot.

อธิบดี (คน,นาย) ʔàthíbɔdii/ (khon/,naaj/) N
director-general, head of a department.

อธิบาย ʔàthíbaaj/ V to explain. คำ-- explanation.

อธิปไตย ʔàthípataj/ N eleg. sovereignty.

  อำนาจอธิปไตย ʔamnâad/ʔàthípataj/ N eleg.
  sovereign power.

อธิษฐาน ʔàthídthǎan/, ʔàthíthǎan/ V to pray; to
make a wish. คำ-- (บท,อย่าง) prayer;
wish. →Dist. สวดมนต์.

อ้น (ตัว) ʔôn/ (tua/) N bamboo rat.

อนงค์ in อนงค์นาง (คน) ʔanoŋ/naaŋ/ (khon/) N
lit. a beautiful girl.

อนันต์,อนันต- ʔanan/, ʔanan/taⵁ eleg. 1. endless,
infinite, vast. 2. numerous, countless. 3.
math. infinity. →Comp. 2. เอนก.

พระที่นั่งอนันตสมาคม phráthîinâŋ/ʔanan/tasamaaⵁ
khom/ N the Throne Hall. →Shortened form is
พระที่นั่งอนันต์.

อนันย์ ʔanan/ tech. absolute.

อนาคต ʔanaa/khód/ N eleg. the future. →Opp.
อดีต.

  อนาคตกาล ʔanaa/khódtakaan/ N 1. eleg. the
  future. 2. gram. future tense.

อนาจาร ʔanaa/caan/ N 1. immorality, immoral conduct. 2. (as n.mod.) lewd, obscene, immoral.

อนาถ in น่าอนาถ nâa/ʔanàad/ V 1. to be a pity;
to be pitiful. 2. What a pity!

อนาถา ʔanaathǎa/ poor, without means.

อนาทร in อนาทรร้อนใจ ʔanaathɔɔn/-rɔ́ɔn/caj/
V to worry about, fret about.

อนามัย ʔanaamaj/ N 1. health. 2. sanitation.

  กระดาษอนามัย kradàad/ʔanaamaj/ N eleg.
  toilet paper. →See note under กระดาษเช็ดก้น.

  ข้าวอนามัย khâaw/ʔanaamaj/ N unpolished or
  imperfectly polished rice.

  เจ้าหน้าที่อนามัย câwnâathîi/ʔanaamaj/ N health
  officer.

อนารยชน ʔànaa/rajáchon/ N barbarians, primitive
or uncivilized people. →Ant. อารยชน.

อนิจจัง ʔànídcaŋ/ N 1. transitoriness, evanescence,
uncertainty. 2. (as n. mod.) transient, transitory,
ephemeral, evanescent, uncertain.

อนิจจา ʔànídcaa↓ E lit. Alas! (excl. of sorrow,
pity, concern).

อนินทรีย์ ʔànin/sii/ tech. inorganic. →Ant. อินทรีย์.

  อนินทรีย์เคมี ʔànin/sii/kheemii/ N inorganic
  chemistry.

อนึ่ง ʔanŷŋ/ Cj lit. furthermore, for another thing.

อนุ-. Bound form meaning "lesser, minor," as in
the following derivatives.

  อนุกรรมการ (คน,ชุด) ʔànúkammakaan/ (khon/,
  chúd/) N subcommittee.

  อนุกาชาด ʔànú/kaachâad/ N Junior Red Cross.

  อนุชน (คน) ʔànúchon/ (khon/) N young people,
  the youth (in a collective sense).

  อนุปริญญา ʔànú/parin/jaa/ N university certificate (lower than a degree).

  อนุภรรยา (คน) ʔànú/phanrajaa/ (khon/) N
  eleg. minor wife. →Syn. เมียน้อย com.

อนุภาค ʔànúphâag/ N tech. particle.

อนุสัญญา (ฉบับ) ʔànú?/sănjaa/ (chabàb/) N convention (i.e. an international agreement on a specific matter).

อนุเคราะห์ ʔànúkhrɔ́?/ N eleg. 1. aid, assistance. V 2. to help, assist. ความ-- idem.

เงินอนุเคราะห์ ŋɤn/ʔànúkhrɔ́?/ N subsidy.

อนุญาต ʔànújâad/ V to permit, allow.

ใบอนุญาต (ใบ) baj/ʔànújâad/ (baj/) N permit.

อนุบาล ʔànúbaan/ V lit. to rear, take care of, look after.

โรงเรียนอนุบาล (แห่ง, โรงเรียน) rooŋrian/ʔànú⊃ baan/ (hɛ̀ŋ/, rooŋrian/) N 1. kindergarten. 2. nursery school.

อนุมัติ ʔànúmád/, ʔànumád/ N 1. approval. 2. permission. V 3. to approve. 4. to grant permission.

ขออนุมัติ khɔ̌ɔ/ʔànumád/ V to seek approval, permission, approbation. →Used chiefly in official correspondence.

อนุมัติให้ ʔànumád/hâj⊃ to grant (someone) permission to (do something).

อนุมาน ʔànumaan/, ʔànúmaan/ V lit. to guess, estimate, conclude.

อนุโมทนา ʔànúmoo/thanaa/ V 1. to express gratitude. 2. to rejoice with, rejoice for (someone).

อนุโลม ʔànúloom/ V lit. 1. to compromise, yield to expediency. 2. to follow suit. sV 3. in order, in sequence. →Ant. 3. ปฏิโลม lit.

อนุสรณ์ ʔànúsɔ̌ɔn/ N eleg. reminder, remembrance, memorial.

เป็นอนุสรณ์ pen/ʔànúsɔ̌ɔn/ 1. to be a token (of), a reminder (of). 2. in memory (of), as a memorial (to).

อนุสาวรีย์ (แห่ง) ʔànúsăa/warii/ (hɛ̀ŋ/) N monument, memorial.

อนุสาวรีย์ชัยสมรภูมิ ʔànúsăa/warii/-chaj/samɔ̌ɔ⊃ raphuum/ pN Monument of Victory (in Bangkok).

อเนก. See เอนก.

อบ ʔòb/ V 1. to bake; to roast, broil (in an oven). 2. to scent, perfume (by placing in a closed container).

เตาอบ (เตา) taw?òb/ (taw/) N 1. oven. 2. kiln.

น้ำอบ nám?òb/ N perfume; toilet water. →Syn. น้ำหอม com.

โรงอบยา (โรง) rooŋ/?òbjaa/ (rooŋ/) N tobacco curing house.

อบรม ʔòbrom/ V to bring up (with precepts); to instruct, train. การ-- training. →Syn. สั่งสอน.

อบอวล in ตลบอบอวล talòb/?òb?uan/ V to be diffused, wafted, pervading.

อบอ้าว ʔòb?âaw/ V to be close, stuffy, hot, sultry.

อบอุ่น ʔòb?ùn/ V 1. to be warm (of climate, weather). 2. to be warm, good-natured (in character, manner).

o เครื่องทำความอบอุ่น (เครื่อง) khrɣaŋ/-tham⊃ khwaam/?òb?ùn/ (khrɣaŋ/) N heater.

o แถบอบอุ่น (แถบ) thɛ̀ɛb/?òb?ùn/ (thɛ̀ɛb/) N geog. temperate zone.

อบเชย ʔòbchəəj/ N cinnamon. ต้น-- (ต้น) the cinnamon tree.

อบายมุข ʔàbaaj/jamúg/ N lit. all vices, allurements which lead to ruin.

อปกติ ʔà?/pàkatì?/ V lit. to be abnormal. →Ant. ปกติ.

อบิสซิเนีย ʔàbisinia/, ʔàbí- pN Abyssinia. [f. Eng.]

อพยพ ʔòbphajób/ V 1. to emigrate. 2. to evacuate.

อพิโธ่ ʔaphithôo/↓ E excl. expressing surprise over something simple one had overlooked. →Comp. พิโธ่.

อภัย ʔaphaj/ V eleg. to forgive, pardon.

ขออภัย khɔ̌ɔ/ʔaphaj/ V eleg. to apologize, to beg pardon.

ให้อภัย hâj/ʔaphaj/ V eleg. to forgive, pardon, excuse.

อภัยโทษ ʔaphaj/thôod/, ʔaphajjathôod/ V eleg. to forgive, pardon, excuse.

อภินันทนาการ as in ด้วยอภินันทนาการจาก dûaj/⊃ ʔàphínan/thanaakaan/-càag⊃ lit. with the compliments of.

อภินิหาร ʔàphíníhăan/ N supernatural power.

อภิบาล ʔàphíbaan/ V lit. to protect.

อภิปราย ʔàphípraaj/ V eleg. to discuss. การ-- discussion.

อภิรมย์ ʔàphírom/ V 1. eleg. to be merry, happy, delighted. 2. to rest, repose.

น่าอภิรมย์ nâa/?àphírom/ V eleg. to be delightful, enjoyable, pleasing.

อภิลักขิตสมัย ʔàphílág/khìdtàsamǎj/ N lit. the time

of a ceremony as prescribed by custom.

อภิเษก ʔàphísèeg′ V roy. to appoint ceremoniously.

พิธีอภิเษก (พิธี) phíthii′ʔàphísèeg′ (phíthii′) N
N roy. wedding ceremony.

อภิสิทธิ์ ʔàphísìd′ N special privilege, prerogative.

อม ʔom′ V to keep in the mouth.

เด็กอมมือ (คน) dèg′/ʔommyy′ (khon′) N infant,
small child (i.e. one still in the thumb-sucking
stage).

o ทำเป็นเด็กอมมือ tham′-pendèg′/ʔommyy′ to
be childish, behave like a child.

ทนหวานอมขมกลืน thon′-wǎanʔom′khǒmklyyn′
idiom. to take the bitter along with the sweet.

อมความ ʔom′khwaam′ V to keep something to
oneself.

อมพะนำ ʔomphanam′ V to keep quiet, keep
something to oneself, hold one's tongue.

อมยิ้ม ʔomjím′ V to smile knowingly, or in
mildly amused and patronizing manner (without
parting the lips).

อมโรค ʔom′rôog′ V to be sick, unhealthy.

อมเลือดอมฝาด ʔomlɯ̂ad′/ʔomfàad′ V ela b.
colloq. (the face) to have a good color, a clear,
healthy complexion.

อมนุษย์ (ตัว, ตน, องค์) ʔàʔ/manúd′ (tua′, ton′, ʔoŋ′)
N lit. supernatural being.

อมฤต in น้ำอมฤต náam′/ʔammaríd′ N 1. divine
drink, nectar of the gods. 2. slang liquor.

อเมริกัน (คน) ʔameerikan′ (khon′) N an American.
คน-- idem. [f. Eng.]

ชาวอเมริกัน (คน) chaaw′/ʔameerikan′ (khon′)
N an American.

สำนักข่าวสารอเมริกัน sǎmnág′-khàawsǎn′/ʔameeɔ
rikan′ U.S. Information Service.

อเมริกา ʔameerikaa′ N America. [f. Eng.]

สหปาลีรัฐอเมริกา sàhàʔ/paaliirád′-ʔameerikaa′
N United States of America.

อเมริกาใต้ ʔameerikaa′tâaj′ N South America.

อย่า (1) jàa′, jàaɔ; (2) jàa′↓ 1. AA do not, don't
(prohibitive). 2. Don't!

o อย่าบ่น jàabòn′↓ Don't complain.

o อย่า...เป็นอันขาด jàaɔ...-penʔankhàad′↓ Do
not (do such and such) under any circumstances.
(You) are absolutely not to (do such and such).

o อย่าไปเชื่อนักเลย jàapajchɨ̂a′/nágləəj′↓ Don't
(you) ever believe (in it)!

o อย่ารู้เจ็บรู้ไข้ jàarúucèb′/rúukhâj′↓ May you
never suffer any sickness!

o อย่า...ให้มากไปเลย jàaɔ...hâjmâag′pajləəj↓
Don't (do this or that) so much! Do stop (doing
this or that) so much!

อย่าเพ่อ (1) jàaphə̂ɔ; (2) jàaphə̂ɔ′↓ 1. AA don't
(do such and such) yet. 2. Wait!

อยาก jàag′ V 1. to want, desire. AA 2. want to,
wish to. ความ-- desire, yearning, craving.
NOTE. This word is used as a verb with noun
object in only two or three fixed expressions,
the most common being อยากน้ำ to be thirsty:
"want water."

นึกอยาก nýgjàag′ AA feel like (doing something);
feel like it.

o นึกอยากเดินเล่น nýgjàag′/dəənlên′ to feel like
taking a walk.

o ไม่นึกอยาก mâjnýgjàag′↓ (I) don't feel like it.

ไม่อยาก mâjjàag′ AA not to want to, not to wish to.

o ไม่อยากได้ mâjjàagdâaj′ not to wish to have,
not to want.

สมอยาก sǒmjàag′ V to fulfill one's craving.

สิ้นอาลัยตายอยาก sîn′-ʔaalaj′/taajjàag′ V ela b.
colloq. to lose all hope, be in despair, be
utterly discouraged.

อดอยาก ʔòdjàag′ V to starve, be famished.

อยากจะ jàagcaɔ AA want to, wish to.

o ไม่อยากจะ mâjjàagcaɔ AA not to want to,
not to wish to.

อยากได้ jàagdâaj′ to desire, wish to have. ความ--
want, desire (to get, have something).

อยากน้ำ jàagnáam′ V to be thirsty.

อยากไม่ jàag′mâjɔ to want not to.

อยากรู้ jàagrúu′ to be curious, want to know, be
anxious to know.

อยากรู้อยากเห็น jàagrúu′/jàaghěn′ to be curious,
inquisitive. ความ-- curiosity.

อย่าง jàaŋ′, jaŋɔ C 1. kind, sort, variety (hence clf.
for articles, utensils, sports, etc.). 2. like, -ly,
in ... a manner. →Syn. 1. ชนิด.

อย่างกวนๆ jàaŋkuankuan′ in an annoying manner.

อย่างกว้างขวาง jàaŋkwâaŋkhwǎaŋ′ extensively.

NOTE (1) อย่าง is often best translated as "like, the way, in the manner of," e.g. อย่างนี้ "like this," i.e. "of this kind, sort; in this way." In this sense, it is synonymous with โดย writ. See also ยัง ๕, a variant form. (2) In ordinary speech the expressions อย่างนั้น,อย่างนี้,อย่าง โน้น,อย่างไร (see below) are usually contracted to jaŋnán′, jaŋníi′, jaŋnóon′, jaŋraj′, or to jaŋᴐ ŋán′, jaŋŋíi′, etc., or even to ŋán′, ŋíi′, etc. These contractions are sometimes reflected in the spelling (e.g. ยังนั้น,ยังงั้น, งั้น, etc.) but often the full uncontracted spellings are used.

ได้อย่างเสียอย่าง dâajjàaŋ′sɪ̌ajàaŋ′ V to gain in one thing while losing in another.

ตัวอย่าง (อัน,ตัวอย่าง) tuajàaŋ′ (ʔan′, tuajàaŋ′) N 1. example. 2. sample.

o ยกตัวอย่าง jóg′tuajàaŋ′ to give an example, bring up an example.

ตามอย่าง taamjàaŋ′ V to imitate, follow (some-one's) example.

ทุกอย่าง thúgjàaŋ′ 1. everything. 2. in every way, in every respect, of every kind.

บางอย่าง baaŋjàaŋ′ 1. something; of some kind(s), of a certain kind. 2. some, certain (ones). →Also บางสิ่ง.

แบบอย่าง (แบบ,อัน) bὲεbjàaŋ′ (bὲεb′,ʔan′) N example, pattern.

เป็นอย่างๆ penjàaŋjàaŋ′ one by one, individually (ref. to kinds, varieties of things); by kinds, varieties; according to kinds, varieties.

มีอย่างหรือ miijàaŋ′rý↓ How come? What is this? (expressing indignation, reproachfulness, disappointment).

เยี่ยงอย่าง jîaŋjàaŋ′ N established example, manner, pattern.

เหมือนอย่าง mỹanjàaŋᴐ like, as.

อย่างกระดากๆ jàaŋkradàag′kradàag′ bashfully.

อย่างกันเอง jàaŋkanʔeeŋ′ informally, in a friendly, intimate manner.

อย่างกับ jàaŋkaᴐ, jaŋkaᴐ like, as if. →Syn. ดุจ lit., eleg.

อย่างขวานผ่าซาก jàaŋkhwǎan′phàasâag′ idiom. outspokenly, unreservedly (of speech).

อย่างแข็งขัน jàaŋkhɛ̌ŋkhǎn′ wholeheartedly, dili-gently, with all (one's) strength.

อย่างคร่าวๆ jàaŋkhrâawkhrâaw′ roughly, approxi-mately, sketchily.

อย่างเคย jàaŋkhəəj′ as usual.

อย่างงั้น jàaŋŋán′, jaŋŋán′ like that. →Var. of อย่างนั้น. →Also written ยังงั้น, q.v.

อย่างไง jaŋŋaj′ what, how, in what way. →Var. of อย่างไร. →Also written ยังไง, q.v.

อย่างจริงจัง jàaŋciŋcaŋ′ really, seriously, truth-fully.

อย่างใจ jàaŋcaj′ according to one's wishes.

o ถ้าไม่ได้อย่างใจ ก็ร้องไห้ thâamâjdâaj′jàaŋcaj′ →kᴐrᴐᴐŋhâaj′↓ If he doesn't have his way, he'll cry.

อย่างฉับพลัน jàaŋchàb′phlan′ instantly, promptly, at once, abruptly.

อย่างเฉียบขาด jàaŋchìab′khàad′ absolutely, strictly.

อย่างดี jàaŋdii′ 1. good, of good quality. 2. well.

o ทำอย่างดี tham′jàaŋdii′ to do (it) well.

o เป็นอย่างดี penjàaŋdii′ 1. quite well. 2. wil-lingly, gladly.

o ยาอย่างดี jaa′jàaŋdii′ tobacco of good quality, a good tobacco.

อย่างดีที่สุด jàaŋdii′thîisùd′ 1. the best, of the best kind. 2. best, in the best way. 3. at best.

อย่างเด็ดขาด jàaŋdèdkhàad′ definitely, absolutely, decidedly, unquestionably.

อย่างเดิม jàaŋdəəm′ as before, as previously; as usual.

อย่างเดียว jàaŋdiaw′ sole, solely, alone.

อย่างเดียวกัน jàaŋdiaw′kan of the same kind.

อย่างเดียวกับ jàaŋdiaw′kaᴐ 1. the same as. 2. in the same way as.

อย่างใด jàaŋdaj′ in any way.

o แต่อย่างใด tὲεjàaŋdaj′ 1. (not) at all. 2. (none) whatsoever.

อย่างใดอย่างหนึ่ง jàaŋdaj′jàaŋnỳŋ′ any kind, any way (of several alternative ways); either thing, either way.

อย่างธรรมดา jàaŋthammadaa′ 1. as usual; in the ordinary way. 2. of the ordinary kind.

อย่างน้อย jàaŋnɔ́ɔj′ at least.

อย่างนั้น jàaŋnán′, jaŋnán′, jaŋŋán′ like that, that way, of that sort. →Also ยังนั้น, ยังงั้น. →See Note 2 under main entry above.

○ ก็อย่างนั้นแหละ, ก็อย่างนั้นๆแหละ kɔ̂jaŋŋán′lɛʔ↓, kɔ̂jaŋŋán′jaŋŋán′lɛʔ↓ 1. It's so-so, fair, not too good and not too bad, indifferent. 2. It's partly true, more or less true.

○ นั่นอย่างนั้นชี nân′ jaŋŋán′sii′ colloq. There, that's it. That's the point. There you are.

○ น้ำพรรณอย่างนั้น náam′phanjaŋŋán′ that sort of liquid.

○ อย่างนั้นหรือ jaŋŋán′rə̌ə′ colloq. Oh, really? Is that right! (expressing surprise, disbelief).

○ อย่างนั้นๆ jaŋŋán′jaŋŋán′ colloq. 1. like that and that and that; this, that, and the other. 2. to be so-so, indifferent.

อย่างน่าพิศวง jàaŋnâa′phídsawɔ̌ŋ′ eleg. amazingly, astonishingly.

อย่างนี้ jàaŋníi′, jaŋníi′, jaŋŋíi′ 1. like this, this way, of this sort. 2. This is it! This is the way! →Also ยังนี้, ยังงี้. →See Note 2 under main entry above.

○ ผมอย่างนี้ phǒm′jaŋŋíi′ colloq. 1. I myself. 2. as for me.

○ รู้อย่างนี้ rúu′jaŋŋíi′ colloq. had (I) known it (before).

อย่างโน้น jàaŋnóon′, jaŋnóon′, jaŋŋóon′ like that, that way, of that sort. →Also ยังโน้น, ยังโง้น. →See Note 2 under main entry above. →Chiefly used in combinations with อย่างนี้ as in the following examples.

○ อย่างโน้นบ้างอย่างนี้บ้าง jaŋŋóon′bâŋ-jaŋŋíi′ɔ bâŋ a bit of this and a bit of that; unclearly, making little sense; hedgingly, in a roundabout manner.

○○ทำอย่างโน้นบ้างอย่างนี้บ้างเพื่อฆ่าเวลา thamɔ jaŋŋóon′bâŋ-jaŋŋíi′bâŋ phŷakhâa′weelaa′ to do a little of this and a little of that just to kill time.

○○พูดอย่างโน้นบ้างอย่างนี้บ้าง phûudjaŋŋóon′bâŋ-jaŋŋíi′bâŋ to speak in a roundabout way (showing reluctance to come to the point).

○ อย่างโน้นอย่างนี้ jaŋŋóon′jaŋŋíi′ 1. this and that; like this and like that, this way and that. 2. idiom. to complain, fuss.

อย่างเบาที่สุด jàaŋbaw′thîisùd′ most lightly, in the lightest manner.

อย่างฝืดเคือง jàaŋfŷyd′khyaŋ′ poorly, in poverty, in an impoverished manner.

อย่างมาก jàaŋmâag′ 1. at most, at the maximum. 2. very, much, highly. 3. big, great, maximum.

○ เป็นอย่างมาก penjàaŋ′mâag′ 1. at most, at the very most. 2. very much.

อย่างมีระเบียบ jàaŋmii′rablab′ in good order, in an orderly manner.

อย่างไม่มีปัญหา jàaŋmâjmii′panhǎa′ without question, unquestionably; no doubt, doubtless.

อย่างไม่ลดละ jàaŋ-mâjlódlá′ unrelentingly, relentlessly, without slackening, unceasingly, without letup, without giving in. →Also อย่างไม่ละลด.

อย่างย่อๆ jàaŋjɔ̂ɔjɔ̂ɔ′ briefly, in brief.

อย่างยิ่ง jàaŋjîŋ′ extremely, exceedingly.

○ โดยเฉพาะอย่างยิ่ง doojchaphɔʔ′jàaŋjîŋ′ in particular, especially.

○ เป็นอย่างยิ่ง penjàaŋjîŋ′ in the extreme, to the utmost.

อย่างรุนแรง jàaŋrunrɛɛŋ′ violently, with force; strong, violent (e.g. desires).

อย่างไร jàaŋraj′, jaŋraj′, jaŋŋaj′ 1. how? what? in what way? 2. how, what, in what way, in any way. 3. odd, strange, not quite right, unacceptable. →Also ยังไร, ยังไง. →See Note 2 under main entry above.

○ คุณจะว่าอย่างไร khun′-cawâa′jaŋŋaj′↓ What have you got to say for yourself? What do you wish to say?

○ จะทำอย่างไร catham′jaŋŋaj′ 1. what's to be done, what one should do; what shall (one) do? 2. no matter what (one) does.

○ จะเป็นอย่างไร capen′jaŋŋaj′ what will happen; what will happen to, what will become of.

○ ดูอย่างไรๆอยู่ duu′jaŋŋaj′jaŋŋaj′-jùu colloq. to look odd, strange, not quite right, unacceptable.

○ ถึงอย่างไร thʉ̌ŋjaŋŋaj′ however; anyhow.

○ อย่างไรก็ดี, ถึง-- jaŋŋaj′kɔ̂dii′, thʉ̌ŋjàaŋraj′ɔ kɔ̂dii′ even so, however, nevertheless, at any rate.

○ อย่างไรก็ตาม jaŋŋaj′kɔ̂taam′ however; at any rate.

○ อย่างไรๆ jaŋŋaj′jaŋŋaj′ colloq. at any rate;

no matter what.

อย่างว่า jàaŋwâa′ as stated, as said; as it is said
(e.g. in a proverb).

อย่างเสียไม่ได้ jàaŋsǐa′mâjdâaj′ against one's
will, against one's better judgment (giving in to
someone's pleading).

อย่างหนึ่ง jàaŋ′nyŋ for one thing.

o ...อย่างหนึ่ง อีกอย่างหนึ่ง... ...jàaŋ′nyŋ↓
ʔìigjàaŋ′nyŋ→... ...for one thing; for another
thing, ... (expression used when listing reasons,
examples, etc.).

อย่างหนึ่งอย่างใด jàaŋnỳŋ′jàaŋdaj′ anything, any
kind, any way (of a given number of alternatives);
either thing, either kind, either way.

อย่างไหน jàaŋnǎj′ which kind.

อีกอย่างหนึ่ง ʔìigjàaŋ′nyŋ one more thing, (and
for) another thing, also, furthermore.

เอาอย่าง ʔawjàaŋ′ to follow the example of,
imitate.

อยุติธรรม ʔàjúd′titham′ V 1. to be unjust, unfair.
N 2. injustice. ความ-- injustice.

อยุธยา ʔajúdthajaa′ pN Ayutthaya (Ayuthia), former
capital of Thailand located up the river from
Bangkok. →Also กรุงเก่า com.

อยู่ jùu′, juu V 1. to be (in such and such a location).
2. to live, stay, dwell. 3. to be nailed, i.e.
caught, seized, trapped, hit (as by a bullet),
killed; to be in the bag. sV 4. (is) in the state
of (doing). การ-- (act of) living, dwelling.
→Syn. 1. 2. ประทับ ๑ roy. NOTE. In some
expressions, อยู่ is pronounced juu (unstressed,
mid tone) by some speakers when it is at the
end of the utterance.

o ทำครัวอยู่ thamkhrua′jùu (she) is cooking.

กำลังอยู่ as in กำลังอยู่ในความนิยม kamlaŋjùu′-
najkhwaam′níjom′ is (at present) popular.

กำลัง...อยู่ kamlaŋ⊃...jùu′ to be in the process
of (doing such and such).

o กำลังทำอะไรอยู่ kamlaŋtham?araj′jùu′ What
are you doing?

o ขณะที่กำลังอ่านอยู่นั้น khanà?′-thîikamlaŋ?àan′⊃
jùunán′ while he was (in the midst of) reading.

กินอยู่ kinjùu′ V to room and board (with).

o ค่ากินอยู่ khâakinjùu′ N 1. living expenses.

2. room and board (as an expense item), the
cost of room and board.

o ให้กินอยู่ hâjkinjùu′ to provide room and board.

ขึ้นอยู่ ๑ khŷn′jùu′ to be growing, is growing.

o มีกุหลาบขึ้นอยู่สามสี่ต้น mii′kulàab′khŷn′-jùu⊃
sǎam′sìi′tôn′↓ There are three or four rose
bushes growing (there).

ขึ้นอยู่ ๒ (กับ,แก่,ที่) khŷn′jùu(ka, kɛ̀ɛ, thîi)⊃ to
depend (on), be governed (by), conditioned (by).

ค่าอยู่ khâajùu′ N lodging (as an expense item),
the cost of lodging.

จริงอยู่(ที่) ciŋjùu′(thîi⊃) it's true (that); actually,
in fact.

ดูจะกระไรอยู่ duu′cakraraj′jùu′ 1. to seem
strange, peculiar. 2. (That) looks rather odd.

ตกอยู่ในมือ tòg′jùunajmyy′ to fall into the hands of.

ตั้งอยู่ tâŋ′jùu′ to be situated, located.

ติดอยู่ tìd′jùu′ to be attached.

ทาน...อยู่ thaan′...jùu′ to be resistant to.

ที่อยู่ (แห่ง) thîijùu′ (hɛ̀ŋ′) N 1. living quarters,
residence (e.g. mailing address).

น่าอยู่ nâajùu′ V to be cozy, liveable.

บินเที่ยวอยู่ binthîaw′jùu′ to be flying around.

เป็นอยู่ penjùu′ V to be, exist, live. ความ-- way
of living; existence.

พระเจ้าอยู่หัว (องค์,พระองค์) phrácâwjùuhǔa′
(?oŋ′, phrá?oŋ′) N 1. king. T 2. King --.

มี...อยู่ mii′(...)jùu⊃ has, have; is, are in possession of; is, are in existence; is, are to be
found; there is, are.

o มีใช้อยู่ miicháj′jùu to be in force, in use; is
being used.

o มีชีวิตอยู่ miichiiwíd′jùu′ V to be alive, to
live, exist.

o มีอยู่ ๕ คน mii′-jùuhâa′khon′ there are five
people.

ไม่อยู่ as in the following entries.

o ตั้งสติไม่อยู่ tâŋ′satì?′-mâjjùu′ cannot concentrate.

o ยิงไม่อยู่ jiŋ′mâjjùu′ cannot drop (e.g. an animal)(by shooting).

ยัง(...)อยู่ jaŋ(...)jùu′ to still be in (a place,
a state of), still be there, still be around, still
be (thus and so), still be (doing such and such).

o ยังเด็กอยู่ jaŋdèg′jùu′ is still a child.

o ยังเล็กอยู่ jaŋlég′jùu′ is still small.

o ยังทำการสอบสวนอยู่ jaŋthamkaan′sɔ̀ɔbsŭan′-jùu′ is still being investigated.

o ยังมีตัวอยู่ jaŋmiitua′jùu′ is still living.

o มักจะยังอยู่ที่นี่ mág′cajaŋjùu′-thîinîi′ might still be here, might still stay here.

เหลืออยู่ lŷa′jùu′ to remain, be left.

อยู่กับที่ jùukathîi′ 1. to be fixed in place, stay in place. 2. firmly, rooted to the ground.

o ลูกรอกชนิดอยู่กับที่ lûugrɔ̂ɔg′-chaníd′jùukathîi′ a fixed pulley.

o ยืนอยู่กับที่ jyyn′jùukathîi′ 1. to stand pat, stand firm. 2. to stand in one place.

อยู่กับเหย้าเฝ้ากับเรือน jùu′kajâw′-fâw′karyan′ elab. colloq. to stay at home and look after things (considered a good quality for a woman).

อยู่กินด้วยกัน jùukin′dûajkan′ to live together, cohabit (man and woman, husband and wife).

อยู่ง่ายกินง่าย jùuŋâaj′kinŋâaj′ colloq. to be easy to please (with regard to food and accommodations).

อยู่ดีกินดี jùudii′kindii′ to live and eat well, have a fair standard of living.

อยู่ตัว jùutua′ V to be stable, maintain (its) form.

อยู่ที่ jùu′thîiɔ 1. to depend on; (something) to be up to (someone). 2. to be at, live at. →See also ขึ้นอยู่ ๒ above.

อยู่ในมือ jùunajmyy′ 1. to be in the hands (of), under the control (of). 2. to be at hand, on hand, in stock.

อยู่บ้าน jùubâan′ to be home, at home.

อยู่เป็นเพื่อน jùupenphŷan′ to keep (someone) company.

อยู่ไฟ jùufaj′ to lie by a fireplace after childbirth (a Thai custom).

อยู่มาวันหนึ่ง jùumaa′wan′nyŋ (and) then one day, one day later on.

อยู่มือ jùumyy′ V to be under control, in hand.

อยู่ยาม jùujaam′ V to be on guard (at a place).

อยู่เย็นเป็นสุข jùujen′pensùg′ V elab. to live in happiness, in peace and contentment.

อยู่แล้ว jùuléɛw′ already.

อยู่แล้วๆ jùuléɛw′-jùuléɛw′| We got it, we got it!

(e.g. an animal trapped or shot in hunting).

อาศัยอยู่ ʔaasăj′jùu′ 1. to live, dwell (regularly), inhabit. 2. to be dependent (on) (for one's living).

เอาการอยู่ ʔawkaan′jùu′ colloq. 1. to be quite a thing; that's quite a thing. 2. mighty, pretty, quite, rather.

เอา(...)ให้อยู่ ʔaw′(...)hâjjùu′ colloq. to get (something, someone) under control, get control over, subdue, finish.

อรชร ʔɔɔrachɔɔn′, ʔɔɔnchɔɔn′ V to be beautiful.

อรรถ in คำอรรถ khamʔàd′ N code, jargon, lingo, secret vocabulary of a special group.

อรรถคดี ʔàd′thakhadii′ N law case.

อรรถาธิบาย ʔàdthăa′thíbaaj′ N explanation, elucidation. →Cf. อธิบาย.

อร่อย ʔarɔ̀j′* V 1. com. to be delicious, tasty (as food). 2. slang to be fun. →Also 1. เอร็ดอร่อย colloq. →Syn. 1. โอชารส eleg.

o เที่ยวกันเสียอร่อย thîaw′kansĭaʔarɔ̀j′ 1. to have a great time, have fun in going out. 2. to go out a lot.

อร่าม ʔarâam′ V to be bright, lustrous.

อริ ʔarì′ N eleg. enemy, foe.

เป็นอริ penʔarì′ 1. to be enemies. 2. as an enemy, as enemies.

อรุณ ʔarun′ N eleg. morning; daybreak, dawn. →Syn. รุ่ง com.

รุ่งอรุณ rûŋ′ʔarun′ eleg. dawn; at dawn, in the early morning.

อล่วย. See อะลุ่มอล่วย.

อลเวง ʔonlaweeŋ′ V to be tumultuous, chaotic.

อวก ʔûag′ V com. to vomit. →Also occasionally อ้วก. →Syn. อาเจียน, สำรอก eleg., ราก vulg.

อวกาศ ʔawakàad′ N tech. space, outer space.

อวด ʔùad′ V to show, show off, display, exhibit.

อวดเก่ง ʔùadkèŋ′ V to act as though one is able to do something without trying; hence, to think oneself smart, to talk big, to brag.

อวดดี ʔùaddii′ V 1. to be impudent, bold, insolent, impertinent. 2. to be saucy, put on airs. 3. to dare, i.e. have the nerve (to do such and such). →Syn. 3. ถือดี.

อวดตัว ʔùadtua′ V to boast, brag (about oneself).

อวดรู้ ʔùadrúu/ V to think one knows it all, knows better. →Often used chidingly. →Syn. อู้รู้.

โอ้อวด ʔôoʔùad/ V to boast, brag.

อวน (ผืน,ปาก) ʔuan/ (phɯ̌yn/,pàag/) N seine.

อ้วน ʔûan/ V to be fat, stout. ความ-- fatness, obesity.

อ้วนจ้ำม่ำ ʔûan/càmmâm/ to be chubby (used esp. of children and babies).

อ้วนฉุ ʔûanchù?/ V to be fat and flabby, over- weight.

อ้วนตุ๊ ʔûantú?/ to be fat, obese (of adults), chubby (of children).

อ้วนท้วน ʔûanthúan/ 1. to be fat, plump, chubby, heavy, solid. 2. to be in good health, look healthy.

อ้วนมักขัก ʔûan/mákkhâg/ to be very fat.

อวบ ʔùab/ V to be stout, plump, well-rounded, well filled out.

อวย ๑ ʔuaj/ V to give, bestow. →Chiefly in cpds.

อวยชัยให้พร ʔuajchaj/hâjphɔɔn/ V elab. to wish (someone) happiness and good fortune.

อวยพร ʔuajphɔɔn/ V to bless, bestow a blessing; to wish (someone) well. คำ-- a blessing.

o ดื่มอวยพร dɯ̀ym/ʔuajphɔɔn/ V to toast (with a drink), to drink a toast.

เออออวย ʔəəʔuaj/ V colloq. to agree, allow, concede, go along with.

อวย ๒ (ใบ) ʔuaj/ (baj/) N a type of metal cooking pot (usually enameled), having a bail handle.

อวล in ตลบอบอวล talòb/ʔòbʔuan/ V to be diffused, wafted, pervading.

อวสาน ʔawasǎan/ N lit. 1. end. V 2. to end.

อวัยวะ (ส่วน,อย่าง) ʔawajjawá?/ (sùan/,jàaŋ/) N body part, organ (of the body).

อสรพิษ (ตัว) ʔasɔ̌ɔraphíd/ (tua/) N poisonous snake.

อสุจิ as in น้ำอสุจิ náam/ʔàsùcì?/ N semen, spermatic fluid. →Syn. น้ำกาม.

อหิวา,อหิวาต์ ʔàhiwaa/ N cholera. โรค-- idem.

อหิวาตกโรค ʔàhiwaa/tàkarôog/ N cholera.

ออ ʔɔɔ/ V to congest, crowd, gather in crowds.

ออ ๑ in ต้นออ (ต้น) tôn?ɔɔ/ (tôn/) N giant reed.

ออ ๒ ʔɔ́ɔ/ E Oh! Oh, yes! (as when one suddenly understands or remembers).

ออ ๓. See ออแอ.

ออ ʔɔ́ɔ/ E Oh (I see; I get it).

ออก (1, 2, 3) ʔɔ̀ɔg/; (4) ʔɔ̀g/ V 1. to leave. 2. to put forth, issue; to break out (as a rash). sV 3. out. 4. colloq. very (see ex.). →Ant. 1,3. เข้า.

o สวยออก sǔaj/ʔɔ̀g/ very pretty.

ขาออก khǎaʔɔ̀ɔg/ on the way out, outgoing.

เข้าใครออกใคร khâwkhraj/ʔɔ̀ɔg/khraj/ colloq. to be partial, to favor one and not another.

o ไม่เข้าใครออกใคร mâjkhâwkhraj/-ʔɔ̀ɔg/khraj/ to be neutral, impartial.

เข้าออก (1) khâw/ʔɔ̀ɔg/; (2) khâwʔɔ̀ɔg/ V 1. to go in and out. sV 2. in and out.

คัดออก khádʔɔ̀ɔg/ to weed out, eliminate by sorting out.

ฉีก(...)ออก chìig(...)ʔɔ̀ɔg/ 1. to tear (some- thing) open, tear (something) out. 2. to get torn open, torn out.

ดูออก duuʔɔ̀ɔg/ to ascertain, be able to tell just by looking.

ตะวันออก tawan/ʔɔ̀ɔg/ N com. east. →Syn. บูรพา lit.,eleg. →The literary and the com- mon terms for the eight chief points of the com- pass are listed under ทิศ.

แต่อ้อนแต่ออก tɛ̀ʔɔ́ɔn/tɛ̀ʔɔ́ɔg/ elab. colloq. from birth.

ทางออก (ทาง) thaaŋ/ʔɔ̀ɔg/ (thaaŋ/) N way out, exit, outlet.

นึกออก nýgʔɔ̀ɔg/ to recall, remember.

o นึกไม่ออก nýg/mâjʔɔ̀ɔg/ can't recall, can't think of it.

แบ่งออกเป็น bɛ̀ŋ/ʔɔ̀ɔgpenꞬ to be divided up into.

ปอก(...)ออก pɔɔg(...)ʔɔ̀ɔg/ to peel (skin, etc.) off.

แพงออก phɛɛŋ/ʔɔ̀g to be very expensive.

ฟัง(...)ออก faŋ(...)ʔɔ̀ɔg/ to make (it) out, be able to understand (something spoken).

o ฟังภาษาออก faŋ/phaasǎa/-ʔɔ̀ɔg/ to be able to understand a language (when spoken).

ไม่ออก as in คิดไม่ออก khíd/mâjʔɔ̀ɔg/ can't solve it, can't figure it out.

ลบ(...)ออก lób(...)ʔɔ̀ɔg/ 1. to subtract. 2. to erase, wipe out.

ลาออก laaʔɔ̀ɔg/ to resign.

เลือดออก lŷad'ʔɔ̀ɔg' V to bleed.

ไล่ออก lâjʔɔ̀ɔg' to dismiss, discharge, fire.

ส่ง (. . .) ออก sòŋ(...)'ʔɔ̀ɔg' 1. to send (something) out. 2. to export (something).

แสดงออก in การแสดงออก kaansadɛɛŋ'ʔɔ̀ɔg' N expression (act of expressing).

หัก (. . .) ออก hàg(...)'ʔɔ̀ɔg' 1. to break (something) off, break (something) apart. 2. to subtract, deduct.

ออกกฎหมาย ʔɔ̀ɔg'kòdmǎaj' V to promulgate a law; to pass a bill.

ออกกำลัง ʔɔ̀ɔg'kamlaŋ' V 1. to exercise, take exercise. 2. to exert strength, put forth physical effort.

ออกกำลังกาย ʔɔ̀ɔg'kamlaŋkaaj' V to exercise (one's body).

ออกไข่ ʔɔ̀ɔgkhàj' V com. to lay eggs. →Syn. ตกฟอง lit.,eleg., วางไข่,ตกไข่ eleg.

ออกความเห็น ʔɔ̀ɔg'khwaamhěn' V to express an opinion.

ออกคำสั่ง ʔɔ̀ɔg'khamsàŋ' V to issue an order, give a command.

ออกจะ ʔɔ̀ɔgcaɔ AA be rather, be likely to, tend to be.

o ออกจะตาย ʔɔ̀ɔgcataaj' colloq. extremely, very much, a lot.

ออกดอก ʔɔ̀ɔgdɔ̀ɔg' V 1. to blossom, flourish, blossom out. 2. slang to break out with a rash (from venereal disease).

ออกเดิน ʔɔ̀ɔgdəən' V to start out, set out (to walk somewhere).

ออกเดินทาง ʔɔ̀ɔg'dəənthaaŋ' V to start out, set out on a journey.

ออกตัว ʔɔ̀ɔgtua' V to put up excuses.

ออกนอกหน้า ʔɔ̀ɔg'nɔ̂ɔgnâa' openly, visibly, noticeably.

ออกแบบ ʔɔ̀ɔgbɛ̀ɛb' V to design.

ออกปาก ʔɔ̀ɔgpàag' V colloq. to utter, speak up; to mention, say, speak of.

o ออกปากขอ ʔɔ̀ɔgpàag'khɔ̌ɔ' V to ask (for something).

ออกไป (1) ʔɔ̀ɔg'paj', ʔɔ̀ɔg'pajɔ; (2) ʔɔ̀ɔgpaj', ʔɔ̀ɔgpajɔ V 1. to leave, go out. sV 2. out, away (from, to), aside.

ออกไป๊ ʔɔ̀ɔg!páj↓ Get out of here!

ออกผล ʔɔ̀ɔgphǒn' V to produce fruit, bear fruit.

ออกพรรษา ʔɔ̀ɔgphansǎa' V to be out of Lent (the Buddhist Lent). →Opp. เข้าพรรษา.

ออกมา (1) ʔɔ̀ɔg'maa', ʔɔ̀ɔg'maaɔ; (2) ʔɔ̀ɔgmaa', ʔɔ̀ɔgmaaɔ V 1. to come out. sV 2. out, forth.

o ยื่นออกมา jŷyn'ʔɔ̀ɔgmaa' to stick out, project, protrude.

ออกรส ʔɔ̀ɔgród' V 1. to be tasty. 2. to be enjoyable, zestful (as of a conversation).

ออกร้าน ʔɔ̀ɔgráan' V to set up a temporary stall or shop (esp. in a fair).

ออกเรือน ʔɔ̀ɔgryan' V (a woman) to have left (her parents') home (i.e. to have married and set up a home of her own).

ออกลูก ʔɔ̀ɔglûug' V com. to bear a child, give birth. →Syn. คลอดลูก eleg.

ออกเสียง ʔɔ̀ɔgsǐaŋ' V 1. to voice, give voice to. 2. to pronounce, utter. 3. to pronounce, articulate. 4. to vote. sV 5. aloud.

o บัตรออกเสียง (ใบ) bàd'ʔɔ̀ɔgsǐaŋ' (baj') N ballot.

ออกหนังสือพิมพ์ ʔɔ̀ɔg'naŋsɰ̌yphim' V to publish a newspaper.

ออกหน้าออกตา ʔɔ̀ɔgnâa'ʔɔ̀ɔgtaa' elab. colloq. openly. →Also อย่าง--.

ออกหัด ʔɔ̀ɔghàd' V to break out with measles.

ออกห่าง(จาก) ʔɔ̀ɔghàaŋ'(càagɔ) V to turn away (from), stay away (from), break (relations)(with).

ออกอากาศ ʔɔ̀ɔg'ʔaakàad' V to broadcast; to be on the air.

อ่านออกเขียนได้ ʔàanʔɔ̀ɔg'khǐandâaj' V to be able to read and write, be literate.

เอา(. . .)ออก ʔaw(...)'ʔɔ̀ɔg' 1. to take (something) out, get (something) out. 2. out.

o คั้นเอา(. . .)ออก khán'-ʔaw(...)'ʔɔ̀ɔg' to squeeze (e.g. the juice) out.

ออกซิเจน ʔɔ́gsicen'* N oxygen. [f. Eng.]

ออง in ชั้นออง chán'ʔɔŋ'* slang top, of the best quality, outstanding.

ออด ʔɔ̀ɔd' V to implore, beseech continuously.

ออดแอด ʔɔ̀ɔdʔɛ̀ɛd' V 1. to be sickly, delicate in health. sV 2. repeatedly, unceasingly (of complaining). 3. imit. a squeaking sound (as of a door).   4. a complaining, whining sound.

อิดออด ʔìdʔɔ̀ɔd/ V to demonstrate unwillingness
or half-heartedness.

อ่อน ʔɔ̀ɔn/ V 1. to be soft, tender.   2. to be young.
3. to be pale, light (of colors).   4. to be poor,
weak (in a subject of study).   →Comp. นวม,
นิ่ม, นุ่ม.   →Ant. แข็ง, กระด้าง.

ไก่อ่อน (คน) kàjʔɔ̀ɔn/ (khon/)   N idiom. a
naive, inexperienced person, a greenhorn.

ขนอ่อน khŏnʔɔ̀ɔn/ N 1. down (soft under feathers).
2. fuzz (body hair).

ขวัญอ่อน khwănʔɔ̀ɔn/ V 1. to be timorous, easily
frightened.   N 2. an easily frightened person;
used esp. of children, women; usually คน--.

จุดอ่อน (อัน, จุด) cùdʔɔ̀ɔn/ (ʔan/, cùd/)   N weak
point.

ใจอ่อน cajʔɔ̀ɔn/ V to be yielding, soft-hearted,
easily influenced, easily touched.

เด็กอ่อน (คน) dègʔɔ̀ɔn/ (khon/)   N infant, babe.
→Syn. ทารก eleg.

ต้นอ่อน (ต้น) tônʔɔ̀ɔn/ (tôn/)   N seedling, young
plant.

ตัวอ่อน (ตัว) tuaʔɔ̀ɔn/ (tua/)   N larva.

มะพร้าวอ่อน (ใบ, ลูก, ผล) maphráawʔɔ̀ɔn/ (baj/,
lûug/, phŏn/)   N young coconut.

ลูกอ่อน (คน, ตัว) lûugʔɔ̀ɔn/ N 1. baby, infant,
very young child (khon/).   2. very young animal
(tua/).

สีอ่อน (สี) sĭiʔɔ̀ɔn/ (sĭi/)   N pale, light color;
pastel color.

หน้าอ่อน nâaʔɔ̀ɔn/ V to be young-looking.

หัวอ่อน hŭaʔɔ̀ɔn/ V to be tractable, easy to teach.

หินอ่อน (ก้อน, แผ่น, ชนิด) hĭnʔɔ̀ɔn/ (kɔ̂ɔn/, phɛ̀n/,
chaníd/)   N marble (the stone).

อ่อนกำลัง, --ลง ʔɔ̀ɔn/kamlaŋ/, ʔɔ̀ɔn/kamlaŋ/-loŋ
V to be weakened, get softened up, become less
intense.

อ่อนเค็ม ʔɔ̀ɔnkhem/ V to be not salty enough.

อ่อนใจ(กับ, ใน) ʔɔ̀ɔncaj/ (kaɔ, najɔ)   V to feel
weary (of), discouraged (about).

อ่อนน้อม(ต่อ) ʔɔ̀ɔnnɔ́ɔm/(tɔ̀ɔ)   V 1. to submit
(e.g. to someone's authority).   2. to be respectful (toward), mindful (of)(e.g. one's elders).

อ่อนนุ่ม ʔɔ̀ɔnnûm/ V to be soft and spongy, tender.

อ่อนเปรี้ยว ʔɔ̀ɔn prîaw/ V to be not sour enough.

อ่อนเพลีย ʔɔ̀ɔnphlia/ V to be weak, weakened.

อ่อนโยน ʔɔ̀ɔnjoon/ V to be gentle, tender.

อ่อนแรง ʔɔ̀ɔnrɛɛŋ/ V to weaken, get tired.

อ่อนลง ʔɔ̀ɔn/loŋ   V to become weak, to become
milder, less intense, softer.

อ่อนละมุน ʔɔ̀ɔn/lamun/ V to be gentle, soft,
smooth, graceful.

อ่อนหวาน ʔɔ̀ɔnwăan/ V 1. to be not sweet enough.
2. to be gentle, sweet (in manner), suave.

อ่อนอกอ่อนใจ ʔɔ̀ɔnʔòg/ʔɔ̀ɔncaj/ V elab. colloq.
to become weary and discouraged; to get tired
(of), lose patience (with).

อ่อนแอ ʔɔ̀ɔnʔɛɛ/ V to be weak, frail, feeble.
ความ-- weakness.

อ้อน ʔɔ̂ɔn/ V to cry, whine, whimper.

ขี้อ้อน khîiʔɔ̂ɔn/ V to be given to crying.

อ้อนวอน ʔɔ̂ɔnwɔɔn/ V to plead, implore, beseech.

ออนซ์ ʔɔɔn/, ʔɔɔn/   C ounce. [f. Eur.]

อ้อนแอ้น ʔɔ̂ɔnʔɛ̂ɛn/* V 1. to be slender, willowy. sV
2. with slender gracefulness.

ออฟฟิศ (ออฟฟิศ) ʔɔ́ffís/, ʔɔ́ffíd/*(ʔɔ́ffis/, ʔɔ́ffid/)
N office. [f. Eng.]

ออม ʔɔɔm/ V to save, reserve, put away.

ออมสิน ʔɔɔmsĭn/ V to save money.

o คลังออมสิน (แห่ง) khlaŋ/ʔɔɔmsĭn/ (hɛ̀ŋ/)   N
(Thai) government savings bank.

อ้อม ʔɔ̂ɔm/ V 1. to go by a roundabout way, to detour.
2. to wrap around.

ทางอ้อม (ทาง) thaaŋʔɔ̂ɔm/ (thaaŋ/)   N 1. an
indirect, circuitous way; detour. 2. indirectly,
by indirect means. →Opp. ทางตรง.

ผ้าอ้อม (ผืน) phâaʔɔ̂ɔm/ (phŭyn/)   N diaper.

อ้อมกอด (อ้อมกอด) ʔɔ̂ɔmkɔ̀ɔd/ (ʔɔ̂ɔmkɔ̀ɔd/)   N
embrace.

อ้อมค้อม ʔɔ̂ɔmkhɔ́ɔm/ V to be indirect, roundabout.

o พูดอ้อมค้อม phûud/ʔɔ̂ɔmkhɔ́ɔm/ V to beat around
the bush, to speak evasively.

อ้อมแอ้ม ʔɔ̂ɔmʔɛ̂ɛm/* V 1. to mumble. sV 2. mumblingly,
indistinctly.

อ้อย ๑, อ้อยๆ ʔɔ̂j/, ʔɔ̂jʔɔ̂j/* V 1. (speech) to be soft
and slow. sV 2. slowly and easily (of speech;
of gait).

อ้อย ๒ in อ้อยเหยื่อ ʔɔ̂jjɥ̀a/* to bait, lure with bait.

อ้อย ʔɔ̂j/* N sugar cane. ต้น-- (ต้น)   the sugar
cane plant.

อ้อยควั่น (ข้อ) ʔɔ̂jkhwân/ (khɔ̂ɔ/) N sugar cane
peeled and cut into short pieces (ready to eat).

อ้อย ๑ ʔɔ̂j/* rM intens. used with เหลือง "yellow."

อ้อย ๒ ʔɔ̂j/* E excl. expressing pain, discomfort.

o ครางอ้อย khraaŋ/ʔɔ̂j/ V to moan "ʔɔ̂j."

อ้อยอิ่ง ʔɔ̂jʔìŋ/* V 1. to linger, delay, prolong the
time (e.g. before acting, making a decision). 2.
to be lingering, hanging in the air (as the threat
of war).

ออสเตรเลีย ʔɔ̀d/satreelia/, ʔɔ́ɔs/treelia/* N
Australia. [f. Eng.]

ออสเตรีย ʔɔ́ɔstria/* Austria. [f. Eng.]

อ้อแอ้ ʔɔ̂ɔʔɛ̂ɛ/ V 1. (a baby) to coo. 2. (speech) to
be unclear, indistinct (e.g. because of drunkenness). sV 3. indistinctly (of speech).

อะไร ʔaraj/ iP 1. what? 2. what, anything, something. →Cf. ไร ๑, ไง.

o ทำอะไรจะ tham/ʔaraj/cá↓ What are you doing?

o ทำอะไรไม่ได้ tham/ʔaraj/mâjdâaj/ cannot do
anything.

o หมอบอกว่าไม่ร้ายแรงอะไร mɔ̌ɔ/bɔ̀ɔgwâa/→
mâjráajrɛɛŋ/ʔaraj/↓ The doctor says it isn't
anything serious.

o เขาบอกความลับอะไรบ้างหรือเปล่าคะ kháwɔ
bɔ̀ɔg/-khwaamláb/ʔarajbâŋ/ rɯ́yplàaw/khá↓
Did she tell you any secrets?

ธุระอะไร(จะ) thúrá?/ʔaraj(caɔ) what for; what
business is it (e.g. of his, to do such and such)?

เป็นอะไร. See entries below.

o เป็นอะไรไป (1) penʔaraj/paj/, pen/ʔarajpaj/;
(2) pen/ʔarajpaj↓ 1. to have something happen
to one, have something the matter with one; what
is the matter (with you, him, etc.)? 2. It doesn't
matter!

ooเขาคงเป็นอะไรไป kháwkhoŋpen/ʔarajpaj/↓
Something must have happened to him.

o ไม่เป็นอะไร mâjpenʔaraj/ to have nothing
wrong with one; there's nothing wrong, nothing
is the matter.

มิได้อะไร (1) mídâj/ʔaraj/; (2) mídâaj/ʔaraj/ 1.
is useless. 2. (one) will not gain anything.

มีอะไร miiʔaraj/, mii/ʔaraj/ 1. what is there?;

what there is; there is something. 2. what (do
you, does he) have?; what you have, what he has;
to have something. →See examples.

o มีอะไรอยู่ในนั้น miiʔaraj/jùunajnán/ 1. what is
(there) inside it? 2. there is something inside
it. 3. to have something inside it.

o ไม่มีอะไร mâjmii/ʔaraj/ 1. there is nothing.
2. to have nothing.

o เพื่อดูว่ามีอะไรเกิดขึ้น phɯ̂aduu/wâa/→ miiʔaraj/-
kə̀ədkhɯ̂n/ in order to see what (there) was going
on.

o เรามีอะไรกินบ้าง rawmiiʔaraj/kinbâaŋ/ what
do we have to eat? what have we got to eat?

o เขามีอะไรกัน kháwmii/ʔaraj/kan what is going
on? what are they up to?

o เขาคงมีอะไรกันเป็นแน่ kháwkhoŋmii/-ʔarajkan/ɔ
pennɛ̂ɛ/ they must have something between them
(e.g. a secret, a love affair, a disagreement).

อะไรก็ได้ ʔaraj/kə̂dâaj↓ Anything will do. Anything
whatever.

อะไรกัน ʔarajkan↓ What's up? Something's up.

o เรื่องอะไรกัน rɯ̂aŋ/ʔarajkan↓ What's the matter? What's up? What for?

o อะไรกันนี่นะ ʔarajkannîi/ná?↓ What is this?
What's up?

อะไรต่อ(มิ)อะไร ʔaraj/tɔ̀ɔʔaraj/, ʔaraj/tɔ̀ɔmíɔ
ʔaraj/ various other things, (and) so on, (and)
what not; all kinds of things, lots of things.

อะไรๆ ʔaraj/ʔaraj/ anything whatever; everything;
something.

o ของอะไรๆ khɔ̌ɔŋ/-ʔaraj/ʔaraj/ various things,
anything whatsover.

อะไรอีก ʔaraj/ʔìig↓ What else? Anything else?

อะไรเอ่ย ʔaraj/ə̀əj/→ What is it? (used in introducing a riddle).

อะไร้ ʔa!ráj/, !ʔaráj/ What! (expressing reproach
and dissatisfaction).

อะลุ่มอล่วย, อะลุ่ม- ʔalúm/ʔalùaj/, ʔalûm/- V to
compromise.

อะลูมินัม ʔaluu/minam/ N aluminum. [f. Am. Eng.]
กระดาษอะลูมินัม (ม้วน, แผ่น) kradàad/ʔaluu/miɔ
nam/ (múan/, phɛ̀n/) N aluminum foil.

อะลูมิเนียม ʔaluu/miniam/ N aluminum. [f. Brit.
Eng. aluminium] →Also อาลูมิเนียม.

อะหลั่ย,อะไหล่ in เครื่องอะหลั่ย (เครื่อง,ชิ้น,อัน) khrŷaŋ/ʔalàj/ (khrŷaŋ/,chín/,ʔan/) N spare parts, replacement part.

อักษร (ตัว) ʔàgsɔ̌ɔn/ (tua/) N character, letter (of the alphabet).

ตัวอักษร (ตัว) tuaʔàgsɔ̌ɔn/ (tua/) N eleg. character, letter (of the alphabet). →Syn. ตัว หนังสือ com.

ทรงพระอักษร soŋ/phráʔàgsɔ̌ɔn/ V roy. to write.

ลายลักษณ์อักษร laajlág/ʔàgsɔ̌ɔn/ N elab. eleg. writing, script.

อักษรกลาง ʔàgsɔ̌ɔnklaaŋ/ N a MIDDLE conso- nant. The MIDDLE consonants are: ก จ ฎ ฏ ด ต บ ป อ.

อักษรคู่ ʔàgsɔ̌ɔnkhûu/ N "paired consonants," i.e. 1. any paired group of consonant symbols consisting of one or more HIGH consonants paired with one or more corresponding LOW consonants. There are seven such groups: ข paired with ค ฆ, ฉ with ช ฌ, ฐ ถ with ท ฒ ฑ ธ, ผ with พ ภ, ฝ with ฟ, ศ ษ ส with ซ, and ห with ฮ. 2. the whole set of HIGH consonants paired with the whole set of corresponding LOW consonants. 3. any one of the above consonants. →Opp. อักษรเดี่ยว.

อักษรเดี่ยว ʔàgsɔ̌ɔndìaw/ N "unpaired conso- nants," i.e. 1. any consonant symbol which has no counterpart in another tonal class; namely, any MIDDLE consonant (ก จ ฎ ฏ ด ต บ ป อ) or any LOW consonant which represents a sonorant (ง ญ ณ น ม ย ร ล ว). The sono- rants are converted from LOW to HIGH by means of a preposed ห, and rarely to MIDDLE by means of a preposed อ. 2. the whole set of consonant symbols as described above. →Opp. อักษรคู่.

อักษรต่ำ ʔàgsɔ̌ɔntàm/ N a LOW consonant. The LOW consonants are: ค ฆ ง ช ฌ ญ ฑ ฒ ณ ท ธ น พ ฟ ภ ม ย ร ว ฬ ฮ.

อักษรศาสตร์ ʔàgsɔ̌ɔnsàad/ N liberal arts.

o อักษรศาสตรบัณฑิต ʔàgsɔ̌ɔnsàad/bandìd/ N 1. holder of a Bachelor of Arts degree. 2. the Bachelor of Arts degree.

อักษรสูง ʔàgsɔ̌ɔnsǔuŋ/ N a HIGH consonant. The

HIGH consonants are: ข ฉ ฐ ถ ผ ฝ ศ ษ ส ห.

อักเสบ ʔàgsèeb/ V 1. (a wound) to be infected, inflamed. N 2. inflammation.

อัคคี in อัคคีภัย ʔagkhii/phaj/ N eleg. disaster caused by fire.

อัคร-. Bound form meaning "preeminent," as in the following entries.

อัครมเหสี (องค์) ʔàgkhamahěe/sǐi/ (ʔoŋ/) N supreme queen, queen of the highest rank.

อัครรัฐทูต in เอกอัครรัฐทูต (คน) ʔèeg/-ʔàgkhaɔ rád/thathûud/ (khon/) N ambassador (from a country which is not a monarchy). →Cf. เอก อัครราชทูต.

อัครราชทูต ʔàgkharâadchathûud/ N minister, esp. one who is the head of a legation.

o สถานอัครราชทูต (แห่ง) sathǎan/ʔàgkharâadɔ chathûud/ (hèŋ/) N legation. →Also สถานทูต.

o เอกอัครราชทูต (คน,นาย,ท่าน) ʔèeg/ʔàgkhaɔ râadchathûud/ (khon/,naaj/,thân/) N ambassador (from a monarchy). →Cf. เอกอัครรัฐทูต.

อังกฤษ ʔaŋkrìd/ N 1. England. 2. English, English- man, English person. [f. Eur.]

จักรภพอังกฤษ càgkaphób/ʔaŋkrìd/ N the British Empire.

ประเทศอังกฤษ (ประเทศ) prathêed/ʔaŋkrìd/ (prathêed/) N England.

ภาษาอังกฤษ (ภาษา) phaasǎa/ʔaŋkrìd/ (phaasǎa/) N English, the English language.

อังคาร in จันทรอังคาร can/ʔaŋkhâad/ N lunar eclipse.

อังคาร ๑. See entries below.

ดาวพระอังคาร (ดวง) daaw/phráʔaŋkhaan/ (duaŋ/) N (the planet) Mars. →The names of the major planets are listed under ดาว. →Also โลกพระ อังคาร,โลกดาวพระอังคาร.

วันอังคาร (วัน) wanʔaŋkhaan/ (wan/) N Tuesday. →Also อังคาร. →The days of the week are listed under วัน.

อังคาร ๒ ʔaŋkhaan/ N ashes.

อั้งยี่ ʔâŋjîi/ N Chinese secret society (an under- world organization). [f. Chin.]

อั้งโล่ (อัน) ʔâŋlôo/ (ʔan/) N colloq. a portable earthenware brazier for cooking. [f. Chin.] →Syn. เตา.

อัจฉริย- as in อัจฉริยภาพ ʔàd/charijaphâab/ N

unusual or marvellous quality, extraordinary
ability.

อัชฌาคัย ʔàdchaa/săj/ N character; disposition;
wish; taste. →Cf. อัธยาคัย.

อัญเชิญ ʔanchəən/ V eleg. to invite respectfully
or reverently, invoke the presence of (e.g. the
sacred virtues, a divine being, a Buddha image
when moving it from one place to another).
→Cf. เชิญ.

อัฐ ʔàd/ N 1. colloq. money. C 2. an obsolete
unit of Thai currency.

อัฐิ ʔàdthìʔ/ N eleg. 1. bones. 2. bone fragments
(after cremation).

อัฒจันทร์ (อัฒจันทร์,แห่ง) ʔàdthacan/ (ʔàdthacan/,
hὲŋ/) N semicircular grandstand, amphithea-
ter.

อัณฑะ in ลูกอัณฑะ (ลูก) lûugʔanthá/ (lûug/) N
eleg. testicles. →Syn. ลูกกระโปก com.,
vulg., ไข่ colloq.,euphem.

อัด ʔàd/ V to press, condense, compress. ความ--
compression. เครื่อง-- press; compressor.

กระดาษอัดสำเนา (แผ่น) kradàad/-ʔàd/sămnaw/
(phὲn/) N carbon paper, (mimeograph) stencil
paper, any duplicating paper.

เครื่องอัดสำเนา (เครื่อง) khrŷaŋʔàd/sămnaw/
(khrŷaŋ/) N duplicator, mimeograph.

น้ำอัดลม (ขวด,แก้ว) náam/ʔàdlom/ (khùad/,
kὲεw/) N carbonated drink.

ไม้อัด (แผ่น) májʔàd/ (phὲn/) N plywood, lami-
nated wood.

อัดใจ ʔàdcaj/ V 1. to be depressed (in spirit).
2. to hold one's breath.

อัดบุหรี่ ʔàd/burìi/ V to inhale (when smoking),
draw deeply on one's cigarette (cigar, etc.).

อัดแบตเตอรี่ ʔàd/bédtəərîi/ V to charge a battery.

อัดแผ่นเสียง ʔàd/phὲnsĭaŋ/ V to make a recording
(on a phonograph record).

อัดรูป ʔàdrûub/ V to print (a photograph).

อัดโรเนียว ʔàd/rooniaw/ V to duplicate by means
of a Roneo machine (a process similar to mimeographing).

อัดอั้นตันใจ ʔàdʔân/tancaj/ V elab. colloq. to
feel stifled, utterly helpless, depressed and
heavy at heart.

อึดอัด ʔỳdʔàd/ V to feel constricted, hemmed in,
stifled, oppressed, harassed, uncomfortable, ill
at ease (e.g. because of tight clothes, overeating,
insufficient space, a stuffy room, an awkward
situation, trying circumstances, etc.).

แออัด ʔὲεʔàd/ V to be congested, crowded (with
people).

อัตคัด ʔàdtakhád/ V to be poor, needy, in want.

อัตคัดขัดสน ʔàdtakhád/khàdsŏn/ V to be hard up
(for), short (of), hard-pressed for.

อัตตภาพ ʔàdtaphâab/ N lit. the self.

อัตโนมัติ,อัตตโนมัติ ʔàdtanoo/mád/ (as n. mod.) auto-
matic. โดย-- of its own accord, automatically.

อัตรา (อัตรา) ʔàdtraa/ (ʔàdtraa/) N rate.

อัตราค่าบำรุง ʔàdtraa/khâabamruŋ/ N 1. subscription rate. 2. membership fees.

อัตราภาษี ʔàdtraa/phaasĭi/ N tax rate.

อัตราเร่ง ʔàdtraa/rêŋ/ N acceleration.

อัตราเร็ว ʔàdtraa/rew/ N velocity.

อัตราแลกเงิน ʔàdtraa/lὲεgŋən/ N rate of (monetary) exchange.

อัตราแลกเปลี่ยน ʔàdtraa/lὲεgplìan/ N rate of
exchange.

อัตราส่วน ʔàdtraa/sùan/ N ratio.

อัธยาคัย ʔàdthajaasăj/ N disposition; character.
→Cf. อัชฌาคัย.

อัน ʔan/ C 1. a clf. used in the following ways:
(a) for small, long objects, such as toothpicks
(ไม้จิ้มฟัน), erasers (ยางลบ), hooks (ขอ),
even though the last two, and others, also have
alternate clfs. (b) loosely as a substitute for
almost any other clf. (see e.g. ไม้กวาด,กรอบ,
หิ้ง). rP 2. writ. which, that.
NOTE. อัน is also used as an invariable clf.
in a number of common fixed phrases, e.g.
เป็นอันขาด,เป็นอันตกลง,เป็นอันมาก, and others
below.

o ในเวลาอันรวดเร็ว najweelaa/ʔanrûadrew/ in
a very short time.

o ภาระอันหนัก phaará?/ʔannὰg/ a heavy burden,
a burden which is heavy.

เป็นชิ้นเป็นอัน penchín/penʔan/ V elab. colloq.
to be a good, solid piece; to be well organized,
well constructed. อย่าง-- well, solidly.

เป็นอันขาด penʔankhàad′ definitely, decidedly, positively, absolutely. →Used in negative constructions only; see under ขาด .

เป็นอันดี penʔandii′ 1. well, very well. 2. willingly, gladly.

เป็นอันตกลง penʔan′tògloŋ′ it's agreed!

เป็นอันมาก penʔanmâag′ very much; in great quantity, in great numbers.

เป็นอันว่า penʔanwâa′ this means that (such and such a result ensues, such and such a course of action is settled on).

เป็นอันหนึ่งอันเดียวกัน penʔannŷŋ′-ʔandiaw′kan to be one and the same, to be united, unified; to concur.

มีอันจะกิน miiʔancakin′ to be well-off, well-to-do.

ไม่เป็นอันกินอันนอน mâjpenʔankin′ʔannɔɔn′ colloq. to be restless, unable to eat or sleep.

สิ่งละอันพรรณละน้อย sìŋ′laʔan′-phanʔlanɔɔj′ colloq. a few things of each kind; a little of every kind, a little of everything.

อันใด ʔandaj′ what, whatever.

อันที่จริง ʔanthîiciŋ′ in fact, as a matter of fact.

อันนี้ ʔanníi′ this, this one.

อั้น ʔân′ V 1. to hold (e.g. one's breath), suppress (one's emotion), keep (something) to oneself. 2. to be dumbfounded. →Syn. 2. อึ้ง ๑ .

นิ่งอั้น nîŋʔân′ V to remain silent (as when suppressing one's anger).

ไม่อั้น mâjʔân′ colloq. 1. not to hold back, not to stint. 2. without holding back, without stint, without hesitation. →Also 2. อย่าง .

อัดอั้นตันใจ ʔàdʔân′tancaj′ V elab. colloq. to feel stifled, utterly helpless, depressed and heavy at heart.

อันดับ ʔandàb′ N 1. series, order. 2. rank, grade, level. →Syn. 1. ลำดับ . 2. ชั้น .

o อันดับห้า ʔandàb′hâa′ the fifth in order; the fifth in rank.

อันตรธาน ʔan′tarathaan′ V eleg. to disappear, vanish.

อันตราย (อย่าง) ʔantaraaj′ (jàaŋ′) N 1. danger, harm, injury. V 2. to be dangerous, harmful. →Syn. ภัย . →See also ภยันตราย , ภัยอันตราย .

ได้รับอันตราย dâajráb′ʔantaraaj′ V to be harmed, endangered.

ทำอันตราย tham′ʔantaraaj′ V to hurt, harm, injure; to do harm.

น่าอันตราย nâa′ʔantaraaj′ V to be dangerous, harmful.

เป็นอันตราย penʔantaraaj′ 1. to be harmful, dangerous. 2. to be harmed, endangered.

อับ ๑ (ใบ , อัน) ʔàb′ (baj′, ʔan′) N 1. a small flat container with a cover, e.g. for face powder, medicated wax, dentifrice in cake or powdered form, etc. C 2. clf. for specific kinds of such containers. 3. clf. for things in such containers; hence, container of (powder, etc.).

o อับสองใบ ʔàb′sɔ̌ɔŋbaj′ two containers.

o อับแป้ง (อับ , ใบ) ʔàbpɛ̂ŋ (ʔàb′, baj′) N powder box (cosmetic); compact.

o แป้งสองอับ pɛ̂ŋ′sɔ̌ɔŋʔàb′ two containers of powder.

อับ ๒ ʔàb′ V to be stuffy, unventilated.

ที่อับ (แห่ง) thîiʔàb′ (hɛ̀ŋ′) N a stuffy place, an unventilated place.

เหม็นอับ měnʔàb′ V to smell stuffy, have a stuffy odor (as a closed room).

อับ ๓. See entries below.

ตกอับ tògʔàb′ V (a person) to fall, sink into poverty, reach the depth of one's downfall; to be fallen.

อับแสง ʔàbsɛ̌ɛŋ′ V 1. to become less bright; to lack brightness. 2. tech. to be opaque. 3. idiom. to be in one's downfall, in one's decline; to lose one's glory.

อับอาย ʔàbʔaaj′ V to be ashamed.

o น่าอับอาย nâa′ʔàbʔaaj′ V to be shameful.

อับปาง ʔàbpaaŋ′ V (boat, ship) to be wrecked.

อับมงคล ʔàb′pamoŋkhon′ N eleg. 1. ill omen. 2. inauspiciousness. 3. (as n. mod.) inauspicious; defamatory, injurious (to someone's reputation).

อัปยศ ʔàbpajód′ V eleg. 1. to be disgraceful. 2. to be disgraced. →Chiefly in compounds.

อัฟริกัน ʔáffrikan′* N (as n. mod.) African. [f. Eng.]

อัฟริกา ʔáffrikaa′* N 1. Africa. 2. African. [f. Eng.] →Also อาฟริกา .

อัมพาต ʔammaphâad′ N paralysis. โรค-- idem.

อัยการ , อัยยการ (คน) ʔajjakaan′ (khon′) N public

prosecutor.

อั๊ว ʔúa/ P slang I, me. →Paired with ลื้อ "you."
→Often used among men who are intimates.
[f. Chin.]

อัศจรรย์ ʔàd/sacan/ V eleg. 1. to marvel at. sV
2. marvellous, wonderful, miraculous.

อัศเจรีย์ ʔàdsacee/rii/ N eleg., tech. the exclamation point. Used with exclamatives and exclamatory sentences. →Syn. เครื่องหมายตกใจ.

อัศวิน ʔàd/sawin/* N 1. knight. 2. courageous police
officer.

อัสดงคต, อัษฎงคต ʔàd/sadoŋkhód/ V 1. eleg. (the
sun) to set. N 2. the West.

อา (คน) ʔaa/ (khon/) N younger paternal uncle
or aunt, i.e. the younger brother or sister of
one's father. →Also written อาว. →Opp.
น้า. →Dist. ป้า, ลุง.

อ้า ʔâa/ V to open (e.g. the mouth).
อ้าแขน ʔâakhɛ̌ɛn/ V to open one's arms.
อ้าปากขึ้น ʔâapàag/khŷn/ to open up the mouth.

อากร ʔaakɔɔn/ N tax, revenue. →Syn. ภาษี ๒.
ภาษีอากร phaasʼi/ʔaakɔɔn/ N revenue, i.e. all
taxes, duties, fees collected by the government.
อากรแสตมป์ (ดวง) ʔaakɔɔn/satɛm/ (duaŋ/) N
an official revenue stamp affixed to documents
to indicate legality. [แสตมป์ f. Eng.]

อาการ (อย่าง) ʔaakaan/ (jàaŋ/) N 1. condition
(as of one's health). 2. symptom. 3. air, manner, outward expression. 4. pose, attitude, position (of the body). 5. act, action, behavior.
มีอาการปวดหัว miiʔaakaan/pùadhǔa/ to be in the
condition of having a headache.
แสดงอาการ sadɛɛŋ/ʔaakaan/ V to show symptoms.
อาการกิริยา ʔaakaan/kìrijaa/ N manner.
อาการท้องผูก ʔaakaan/thɔ́ɔŋphùug/ N constipation, constipated condition.
อาการเพียบ ʔaakaan/phîab/ N serious condition
(of illness).
อาการลังเล ʔaakaan/laŋlee/ N hesitation, hesitating manner.
อาการหนัก ʔaakaan/nàg/ N serious, grave,
critical condition.

อากาศ ʔaakàad/ N weather, air, climate.

กองทัพอากาศ (กอง) kɔɔŋtháb/ʔaakàad/ (kɔɔŋ/)
N milit. air force. →Abbrev. ทอ.
การระบายอากาศ kaanrabaaj/ʔaakàad/ N ven-
tilation.
จ่าอากาศ càa/ʔaakàad/ N designation for the
noncommissioned ranks in the air force.
ช่างอากาศ (คน) châaŋʔaakàad/ (khon/) N airplane mechanic.
ฐานทัพอากาศ (แห่ง) thǎantháb/ʔaakàad/ (hɛ̀ŋ/)
N air base.
ดินฟ้าอากาศ dinfáa/ʔaakàad/ N climate.
เดินอากาศ dəən/ʔaakàad/ V to go by air.
→Chiefly in compounds.
o บริษัทเดินอากาศ bɔɔrisàd/-dəən/ʔaakàad/ N
airlines, airline company.
ตากอากาศ tàag/ʔaakàad/ V to take an airing,
get out in the open (as when vacationing in the
country or at the seashore).
ทหารอากาศ (คน) thahǎan/ʔaakàad/ (khon/) N
airman, member of the air force. →Abbrev. ทอ.
ทางอากาศ thaaŋʔaakàad/ by air.
o กำลังทางอากาศ kamlaŋ/thaaŋʔaakàad/ milit.
air power.
o ภัยทางอากาศ phaj/thaaŋʔaakàad/ N danger
from air attacks.
นาวาอากาศ naawaa/ʔaakàad/ N designation for
the commissioned ranks of air force officers
in command of squadrons, wings, groups.
ไปรษณีย์อากาศ prajsanii/ʔaakàad/ N air mail.
พยากรณ์อากาศ phajaakɔɔn/ʔaakàad/ V 1. to give
a weather forecast. N 2. weather forecast.
→Also 2. การ--.
พลอากาศ phon/ʔaakàad/ N designation for the
highest commissioned ranks of the air force.
พันจ่าอากาศ phancàa/ʔaakàad⊃ N designation for
the warrant officer ranks of the air force.
เรืออากาศ rya/ʔaakàad/ designation for the lowest
commissioned ranks of the air force.
ลมฟ้าอากาศ lomfáa/ʔaakàad/ weather.
สายอากาศ (สาย) sǎaj/ʔaakàad/ (sǎaj/) N
antenna, aerial.
ออกอากาศ ʔɔ̀ɔg/ʔaakàad/ V to broadcast; to be
on the air.
อากาศดี ʔaakàad/dii/ the weather to be good.

อากาศแถบเส้นศูนย์สูตร ʔaakàad′-thɛ̀ɛbsên′sǔunɔ

sùud′ N equatorial climate.

อากาศทะเล ʔaakàad′thalee′ N sea air.

อากาศไปรษณีย์ ʔaakàad′prajsanii′ N air mail.

อากาศมัว ʔaakàad′mua′ the weather to be murky.

อากาศยาน (เครื่อง,ลำ) ʔaakàasajaan′ (khrŷaŋ′,

lam′) N aircraft, airplane.

อากาศสดชื่น ʔaakàad′sòdchŷyn′ the air to be

fresh.

อาคเนย์ ʔaakhanee′ lit.,eleg. southeast. →Syn.

ตะวันออกเฉียงใต้ com. →The literary and

the common terms for the eight chief points of

the compass are listed under ทิศ.

ภาคอาเซียอาคเนย์ phâag′-ʔaasia′ʔaakhanee′ N

Southeast Asia.

อาคันตุกะ (คน,ผู้) ʔaakhan′tukàʔ′ (khon′,phûu′)

N lit.,eleg. guest. →Syn. แขก com.

อาคาร (หลัง) ʔaakhaan′ (lǎŋ′) N eleg. building,

dwelling, establishment.

o อาคาร ๖ ʔaakhaan′hòg′ building no. 6.

อาคารบ้านเรือน (หลัง) ʔaakhaan′bâanryan′ N

houses and buildings.

อาฆาต ʔaakhâad′ V 1. to seek revenge, seek to

take revenge. 2. to be vengeful, vindictive,

spiteful. ความ-- revenge, vengeance; venge-

fulness. →Syn. 1, 2. จองเวร. 2. พยาบาท.

ความอาฆาตพยาบาท khwaam′-ʔaakhâad′phajaaɔ

bàad′ N revenge, vengefulness, vengeance.

อ่าง ๑ (ใบ,อ่าง) ʔàaŋ′ (baj′,ʔàaŋ′) N bowl, basin.

ชามอ่าง (ใบ) chaamʔàaŋ′ (baj′) N large bowl.

อ่างทอง ʔàaŋthɔɔŋ′ pN Angthong, a township in

C Thailand.

อ่างล้างหน้า (ใบ) ʔàaŋláaŋnâa′ (baj′) N wash

basin, wash bowl, sink.

อ่างเลี้ยงปลา (ใบ) ʔàaŋlíaŋplaa′ (baj′) N

fish-bowl.

อ่างศิลา ʔàaŋsilaa′ pN Ang Sila, a seaside resort

on the eastern shoreline of the Gulf of Thailand,

not far from Bangkok.

อ่างอาบน้ำ (ใบ) ʔàaŋʔàabnáam′ (baj′) N bath-

tub.

อ่าง ๒ in ติดอ่าง tìdʔàaŋ′, เป็นอ่าง penʔàaŋ′ V

to stammer, stutter, be stammering, stuttering.

อ่าง ๒ in อึ่งอ่าง (ตัว) ʔ`yŋʔàaŋ′ (tua′) N bullfrog.

อ้าง ๑ ʔâaŋ′ V 1. to say, assert, claim. 2. to cite,

refer to.

ข้ออ้าง (ข้อ) khɔ̂ɔʔâaŋ′ (khɔ̂ɔ′) N 1. justification.

2. supporting statement, citation, reference (to

an authority).

อ้างหลักฐาน ʔâaŋ′làgthǎan′ V to cite (the) evidence.

อ้างเหตุผล ʔâaŋ′hèedphǒn′ V to adduce reasons.

อ้างอิง ʔâaŋʔiŋ′ V to cite, refer to (an authority).

อ้าง ๒ in อ้างว้าง ʔâaŋwáaŋ′ V to feel lonely,

lonesome, empty, desolate.

อาจ ๑ ʔàad′ AA 1. might, may. 2. is supposed to.

o อาจเป็นดั่งว่า ʔàad′pendàŋwâa′ (it) might be

as (they) say.

ไม่อาจ mâjʔàadɔ AA is not supposed to.

อาจจะ ʔàadcaɔ AA might, may.

อาจไม่ ʔàad′mâjɔ AA might not, may not.

อาจ ๒ ʔàad′ V to dare (to). →Chiefly in compounds.

บังอาจ baŋʔàad′ V to dare to, to have the audacity,

have the nerve to (commit a daring deed, exceed

propriety, etc.).

องอาจ ʔoŋʔàad′ V 1. to be brave, valiant. 2. to

be dignified, stately.

อาจหาญ ʔàadhǎan′ V to be brave, bold.

อาจเอื้อม ʔàadʔŷam′ V to dare to do something

beyond one's social status.

อุกอาจ ʔùgʔàad′ V 1. to be bold, audacious. 2.

to dare (to), have the audacity (to).

อาจารย์ (คน,ท่าน) ʔaacaan′ (khon′,thân′) N 1.

teacher (who has a degree); professor. T 2.

title used with the first name of a teacher or

professor. P 3. you, he, him, she, her, Teacher

(sp. to or about a teacher). →Dist. ครู teacher

with or without a degree. →Cf. ศัลตราจารย์.

ครูอาจารย์,ครูบาอาจารย์ khruu′ʔaacaan′, khruuɔ

baa′ʔaacaan′ N teachers in general.

อาจารย์ใหญ่ ʔaacaanjàj′ N principal (of a school).

อาจิณ,อาจิณณ์,อาจินต์ ʔaacin′ sV regularly, habit-

ually, constantly.

อาเจียน ʔaacian′ V eleg. to vomit, throw up.

→Syn. See อ้วก com.

อาชญา ʔàadjaa′, ʔàadchajaa′ N law. 1. penalty,

punishment. 2. (as n. mod.) criminal. →Comp.

อาญา. →Opp. 2. แพ่ง.

กฎหมายลักษณะอาชญา (มาตรา,บท,ข้อ) kòdmǎaj′-

lágsàná?/?àadjaa/ (mǎadtraa/, bòd/, khɔ̌ɔ/) N
criminal law.

อาชญากร (คน) ?àadjaakɔɔn/ (khon/) N criminal.

o อาชญากรสงคราม ?àadjaakɔɔn/sǒŋkhraam/ N
war criminal.

อาชญากรรม (ราย) ?àadjaakam/ (raaj/) N crime.

อาชญาวิทยา ?àadjaa/wídthajaa/ N criminology.

อาชีพ ?aachîib/ N livelihood, living, occupation,
profession. →Comp. อาชีวะ.

ประกอบอาชีพ prakɔ̀ɔb/?aachîib/ V to earn a
living.

เป็นอาชีพ pen?aachîib/ 1. for a living, as an
occupation, as a profession. 2. colloq. habitually, constantly.

มีอาชีพ mii?aachîib/ V to make a living, have
a living.

โรงเรียนอาชีพ rooŋrian/?aachîib/ N vocational
school, trade school.

อาชีวศึกษา ?aachiiwá?/sỳgsǎa/ N vocational education.

อาชีวะ ?aachiiwá?/ N occupation, profession, livelihood, living. →Comp. อาชีพ.

อาเซีย ?aasia/ N Asia. →Also เอเซีย. [f. Eng.]

อาเซียน้อย ?aasia/nɔ́ɔj/ N Asia Minor.

อาญา ?aajaa/ N 1. penalty, punishment. 2. (as n.
mod.) criminal; used in legal terms. →Comp.
อาชญา. →Opp. 2. แพ่ง.

คดีอาญา (คดี) khadii/?aajaa/ (khadii/) N criminal case.

อาญาสิทธิ์ ?aajaasìd/ N absolute power, absolute
authority.

อาณัติ ?aanád/ N order, mandate.

ดินแดนในอาณัติ dindɛɛn/naj?aanád/ mandated
territory.

อาณัติสัญญาณ ?aanád/sǎnjaan/ N signal (as an
air-raid signal).

อาณา-. Bound form used in compounds such as the
following.

อาณาเขต, -เขตต์ (อาณาเขต,ส่วน) ?aanaakhèed/
(?aanaakhèed/, sùan/) N 1. territory. 2. boundary, border, frontier.

อาณาจักร (อาณาจักร,แห่ง) ?aanaacàg/ (?aanaa‐
càg/, hɛ̀ŋ/) N domain, dominion, realm; kingdom.

o ราชอาณาจักร râadcha?aanaacàg/ N kingdom.

o สหราชอาณาจักร sahàrâad/cha?aanaacàg/ N
the United Kingdom.

อาณานิคม (แห่ง) ?aanaa/níkhom/ (hɛ̀ŋ/) N
colony.

o ลัทธิอาณานิคม (ลัทธิ) ládthí?/?aanaa/níkhom/
(ládthí?/) N colonialism.

อาณาบริเวณ ?aanaa/bɔɔriween/ N area, territory.

อาด. See อืดอาด.

อาตมา ?àadtamaa/ P sacer. I, me.

อาทร ?aathɔɔn/ N interest, concern, hospitality.

อาทิ. See entries below.

เป็นอาทิ pen?aathí?/ for example, as notable
examples. NOTE. This expression follows a list,
usually of names, with examples cited in descending order of importance.

อาทิเช่น ?aathí?/chên/ notably (such and such persons). NOTE. This expression precedes a list,
usually of names, with examples cited in descending order of importance.

อาทิตย์ ?aathíd/ N 1. sun (chiefly in compounds).
2. short for วัน--. C 3. week. →The days of
the week are listed under วัน.

o ทั้งอาทิตย์ tháŋ/?aathíd/ all week.

o อาทิตย์หน้า ?aathíd/nâa/ next week.

ดวงอาทิตย์ (ดวง) duaŋ?aathíd/ (duaŋ/) N the
sun.

พระอาทิตย์ (ดวง) phrá?aathíd/ (duaŋ/) N com.
the sun. →Syn. ตะวัน eleg.

วันอาทิตย์ (วัน) wan?aathíd/ (wan/) N Sunday.
→The days of the week are listed under วัน.

อาน (อาน) ?aan/ (?aan/) N saddle.

อ่าน ?àan/ V to read. ผู้-- reader (person).

คิดอ่าน khíd?àan/ V to think, plan, use one's head
(esp. in matters of bettering one's situation).

น่าอ่าน nâa?àan/, nâa/?àan/ V to be interesting
to read, be worth reading.

ริอ่าน rí?/?àan/ V to plan; to try, attempt, initiate (as a new venture).

เรื่องอ่านเล่น (เรื่อง) rŷaŋ/?àanlên/ (rŷaŋ/) N
something which is read for pleasure, light reading (often used instead of the more specific terms
นวนิยาย "novel," เรื่องสั้น "short story," etc.).

หนังสืออ่านเล่น (เล่ม) naŋsỹy/?àanlên/ (lêm/)

N a book for light reading.

อ่าน(. . .)ข้ามๆ ʔàan′(. . .)khâamkhâam′ to skim, read (it) by skimming.

อ่านค้างไว้ ʔàankháaŋ′wáj to have left the reading unfinished, to leave off reading.

อ่านต่อหน้า ๑๐๐ ʔàantɔ̀ɔ′nâarɔ́ɔj′ continued on page 100; continue reading on page 100.

อ่านไม่ออก ʔàan′mâjʔɔ̀ɔg′ 1. can't read (it) (because of illegibility, etc.). 2. fig. can't make (it) out, can't figure (it) out.

อ่านหนังสือ ʔàan′naŋsɯ̌y′ V to read.

อ่านออกเขียนได้ ʔàanʔɔ̀ɔg′khǐandâaj′ V to be able to read and write, be literate.

อานาม in อายุอานาม ʔaajúʔ′ʔaanaam′ N colloq. age.

อานุภาพ ʔaanúphâab′ N eleg. power, might.

อาบ ʔàab′ V to bathe, bask.

   น้ำอาบ náamʔàab′ N bath water.

   อาบแดด ʔàabdɛ̀ɛd′ V to take a sunbath, bask in the sunshine.

   อาบน้ำ ʔàabnáam′ V to take a bath, to bathe.

   o ชุดอาบน้ำ (ชุด) chúd′/ʔàabnáam′ (chúd′) N bathing suit.

   o สระอาบน้ำ (สระ) sà?′/ʔàabnáam′ (sà?′) N swimming pool.

   o ห้องอาบน้ำ (ห้อง) hɔ̂ŋ′/ʔàabnáam′ (hɔ̂ŋ′) N 1. bathroom (generally for bathing only). 2. bathhouse (outdoor structure, separate from the dwelling).

   o อาบน้ำอาบท่า ʔàabnáam′/ʔàabthâa′ V elab. colloq. to take a bath, to bathe.

   อาบเลือด ʔàablɯ̂ad′ V to be soaked with blood, bathed in blood.

อาฟริกา ʔàafrikaa′* N 1. Africa. 2. African. →Also อัฟริกา, แอฟริกา. [f. Eng.]

อาภรณ์ ʔaaphɔɔn′ N lit. ornament.

อาภัพ ʔaapháb′ V to be unlucky, unfortunate.

อาย ʔaaj′ V to be shy, bashful, retiring.

   ขี้อาย khîiʔaaj′ V to be shy, bashful.

   อับอาย ʔàbʔaaj′ V to be ashamed.

   อายใจ, อายแก่ใจ ʔaajcaj′, ʔaaj′kɛ̀ɛcaj′ V to be ashamed of oneself.

   อายเหนียม ʔaajnǐam′ V to be shy, bashful.

อ้าย ๑ ʔâjɔ* T 1. derog. title used with first

names of men, esp. of criminals, but also for purposes of insult; formerly used with names of male slaves. 2. term freely used with reference to objects or persons (regardless of sex), esp. in conjunction with a demonstrative word, and without special connotation. 3. bound element in the names of a few creatures, esp. the cricket. →Also spelled ไอ้. →Also 2. อี. →Opp. 1. อี̌, used with names of w.

กับอ้าย kaʔâjɔ expression used to indicate the paltriness, insignificance, worthlessness of an object from the speaker's point of view, as in the fol. example. →Also กับอี้.

   o เขาไม่อยากได้หรอกกับอ้ายของพวกนั้น kháwmâjɔ jàag′dâaj′rɔ̀g→ kaʔâjkhɔ̌ŋ′phûagnán′↓ He doesn't care for that kind of thing.

อ้ายจั่ง ʔâjŋâŋ′↓ derog. epithet (You) fool!

อ้ายนี่ ʔâjnîi′ this one (ref. to a thing or to a person of either sex).

อ้ายถ่อย ʔâjthɔ̀j′↓ derog. epithet (You) riffraff! Scum!

อ้ายบ้า ʔâjbâa′↓ derog. epithet Crazy guy!

อ้ายเสือ ʔâjsɯ̌a′ N 1. derog. bandit, outlaw. T 2. derog. title used with the first name of a bandit.

อ้ายหนู ʔâjnǔu′ sonny boy.

อ้ายหมอนั่น ʔâjmɔ̌ɔ′nân that guy.

อ้ายแอ๊ด (ตัว) ʔâjʔɛ́d′* (tua′) N a kind of cricket often kept by children for fighting purposes.

อ้าย ๒ ʔâaj′ Nm 1. restricted one. nN 2. nickname for the first-born child. →Cf. 1. หนึ่ง, เอก, เอ็ด ๑.

   เดือนอ้าย dyanʔâaj′ N the first lunar month.

อ้าย ๓. See อุ้ยอ้าย.

อายุ ʔaajú?′ N 1. age (in years). 2. life, life span. →Syn. พระชนมพรรษา roy.

   o อายุห้าขวบ ʔaajú?′/hâakhùab′ (he) is five years old.

   ช่วงอายุ chûaŋ′/ʔaajú?′ N 1. generation. 2. life span.

   ต่ออายุ tɔ̀ɔ′/ʔaajú?′ V 1. to renew, i.e. extend the time (as of a passport). 2. to lengthen one's life.

   มีอายุ mii′/ʔaajú?′ colloq. 1. to be (so and so many years) old. 2. to be elderly, up in years.

   ผู้-- an elderly person.

o มีอายุ ๑๘ ปี mii/ʔaajúʔ/-sìbpὲɛd/pii/ (he) is eighteen years old.

สิ้นอายุ sîn/ʔaajúʔ/ V 1. to expire. 2. to die.

สูงอายุ sǔuŋ/ʔaajúʔ/ V to be old, aged.

หมดอายุ mòd/ʔaajúʔ/ V to expire, be terminated.

อายุกลางคน ʔaajúʔ/klaaŋkhon/ N 1. middle age (of people); among the Thai approx. 35-50 years of age. 2. middle-aged. →Comp. ปรา.

อายุขัย ʔaajúʔkhǎj/ N life span.

อายุความ ʔaajúʔ/khwaam/ N law limitation, the stipulated period of time after which the prosecution of a crime can no longer be initiated.

อายุยืนนาน ʔaajúʔ/jyynnaan/ V to be long-lived, to live long.

อายุสัญญา ʔaajúʔ/sǎnjaa/ N the term of a contract.

อายุอานาม ʔaajúʔ/ʔaanaam/ N colloq. age.

อาร์. ʔaa/ the English letter "R." [f. Eng.]

อารมณ์ (อารมณ์, อย่าง) ʔaarom/ (ʔaarom/, jàaŋ/) N disposition, humor, mood, spirits. →Syn. ลม.

เจ้าอารมณ์ câw/ʔaarom/ V to be temperamental, given to changes of mood.

เป็นอารมณ์ pen/ʔaarom/ sV seriously.

o ถือเป็นอารมณ์ thǔy/pen/ʔaarom/ to take (things) seriously.

o เอามาเป็นอารมณ์ ʔaw/maapen/ʔaarom/ to take (things) too hard; to worry too much, to take (things) too seriously.

ส่งบอารมณ์ saŋòb/ʔaarom/ V to calm down, calm oneself.

หย่อนอารมณ์ jɔ̀ɔn/ʔaarom/ V 1. to relax. 2. to be at leisure.

อารมณ์ขัน ʔaarom/khǎn/ N humor, sense of humor.

อารมณ์ดี ʔaarom/dii/ V 1. to be in a good humor, agreeable, good-humored. N 2. good humor.

อารย-, Bound form meaning "civilized." See entries below. →Cf. สิวิไลซ์.

อารยชน ʔaa/rajáchon/ N civilized people. →Opp. อนารยชน.

อารยธรรม ʔaa/rajátham/ N civilization.

อารยประเทศ ʔaa/rajáprathêed/ N civilized country.

อารยะ ʔaa/rajá/ N 1. civilization. 2. (as n. mod.)

civilized. →Cf. สิวิไลซ์.

อาระเบีย ʔaarabia/ N Arabia. [f. Eng.]

อารักขา ʔaarágkhǎa/ N 1. care, charge, protection. V 2. to guard, protect. ความ-- protection. ผู้-- protector, guardian.

อารัมภบท (บท) ʔaaram/phabòd/ (bòd/) N 1. introduction. V 2. introduce, give an introduction, give a preamble.

อาราธนา ʔaarâad/thanaa/ V sacer. to beg, request, invite.

อาราม ๑ ʔaaraam/ N temple buildings.

วัดวาอาราม (วัด, แห่ง) wádwaa/ʔaaraam/ (wád/, hὲŋ/) N elab. colloq. wats and temples.

อาราม ๒ ʔaaraam/ N condition, state (usually an intense emotional state).

o ขึ้นไปบนรถด้วยอารามตื่นเต้น khŷnpaj/bonród/-dûaj/ʔaaraam/-tŷyn/tên↓ (She) got into the car with excitement (excitedly, in a state of excitement).

o อารามรีบ เขาชนเด็กล้ม ʔaaraam/rîib/→ kháwᴐ chon/-dèg/lóm↓ Being in a desperate hurry, he knocked a child down.

อารี ʔaarii/ V to be kind, generous, thoughtful, hospitable. ความ-- kindness, generosity.

ใจอารี caj/ʔaarii/ V to be kind, generous.

โอบอ้อมอารี ʔòob/ʔɔ̂ɔm/ʔaarii/ V elab. to be kind, generous, thoughtful, hospitable.

อาละวาด ʔaalawâad/ V to be on the rampage; to act wild and uncontrolled; to go around picking fights, causing trouble, etc.

อาลักษณ์ (คน) ʔaalág/ (khon/) N a scribe of the royal court, the royal secretary.

อาลัย ʔaalaj/ V to long for, think about, miss.

ทอดอาลัย thɔ̂ɔd/ʔaalaj/ V to lose hope, lose interest; to despair.

ไว้อาลัย wáj/ʔaalaj/ (a ceremony, act, speech) to be in memory (of).

สิ้นอาลัยตายอยาก sîn/-ʔaalaj/taajjàag/ V elab. colloq. to lose all hope, be in despair, be utterly discouraged.

อาลูมิเนียม ʔaaluu/minîam/, ʔaaluu/miniam/ N aluminum. [f. Brit. Eng.] →Also อะลูมิเนียม.

อ้าว. See อ้า.

อ่าว (อ่าว) ʔàaw/ (ʔàaw/) N bay, gulf.

อ่าวไทย ʔàawthaj′ pN Gulf of Thailand.

อ่าวเล็ก (อ่าว) ʔàawlég′ (ʔàaw′) N inlet, cove.

อ้าว ๑ ʔâaw′ V to be sultry (of weather).

     อบอ้าว ʔòbʔâaw′ V to be close, stuffy, hot, sultry.

     อ้าวฝน ʔâawfŏn′ V (the atmosphere) to be sultry (showing definite signs of rain by high humidity and a sudden increase in temperature).

อ้าว ๒ ʔâaw′ sV quickly, hastily.

     โกยอ้าว kooj′ʔâaw′ slang to run fast.

     แจวอ้าว cɛɛw′ʔâaw′ slang to flee, run away quickly.

อ้าว ๓ ʔâaw′↓ E Oh! (excl. of surprise, dismay).

อาวรณ์ ʔaawɔɔn′ V to long for, yearn for, miss.

อาวาส (แห่ง) ʔaawâad′ (hɛ̀ŋ′) N Buddhist monastery.

     เจ้าอาวาส (องค์) câaw′ʔaawâad′ (ʔoŋ′) N abbot of a Buddhist monastery.

อาวุธ (อย่าง) ʔaawúd′ (jàaŋ′) N weapon, arms.

     ติดอาวุธเรือ tìd′-ʔaawúd′rya′ V to arm a ship, outfit a ship with weapons.

     ปลดอาวุธ plòd′ʔaawúd′ V to disarm.

     อาวุธนิวเคลีย ʔaawúd′niwkhlia′ N nuclear weapons. [นิวเคลีย f. Eng.]

     อาวุธปืน (อย่าง) ʔaawúd′pyyn′ (jàaŋ′) N firearms.

     อาวุธยุทธภัณฑ์ (อย่าง) ʔaawúd′júdthaphan′ (jàaŋ′) N arms and military equipment.

อาวุโส ʔaawúsŏo′ V 1. to be aged, senior; to have seniority. N 2. seniority.

อาศรม ʔaasŏm′ N 1. hermitage. 2. cloister, convent.

อาศัย ʔaasăj′ V 1. to live, dwell. 2. to depend on, be dependent upon; to be aided by. คน- -, ผู้- - inhabitant, tenant; dependent (one who lives in someone else's household, receiving part or all of his support there).

     ด้วยอาศัยที่ dûaj′ʔaasăj′thîiɔ by depending upon (the fact) that.

     โดยอาศัย dooj′ʔaasăj′ with the aid of, by means of.

     ถ้อยทีถ้อยอาศัยกัน thɔj′thii′-thɔj′ʔaasăj′kan V to be mutually dependent, be interdependent; to reciprocate.

     ถิ่นอาศัย (แห่ง) thìn′ʔaasăj′ (hɛ̀ŋ′) N habitat, abode, habitation.

     อาศัยใช้สอย ʔaasăj′chájsɔɔj′ V 1. to utilize, use. 2. to use (something belonging to another through his courtesy). 3. to depend on (someone to do errands, etc.).

     อาศัยอยู่ ʔaasăj′jùu′ 1. to live, dwell (regularly), inhabit. 2. to be dependent (on) (for one's living).

     o มันอาศัยอยู่ในตอนใต้ man′-ʔaasăj′jùunajtɔɔntâaj′ it inhabits the southern part.

     o เขาเป็นคนอาศัยอยู่ในบ้าน kháwpenkhon′-ʔaaɔsăj′jùunajbâan′ he lives as a dependent in the household.

อาสน์, อาสน์ ʔàadsaná′′, ʔàad′ N sacer., roy. seat.

     o ราชอาสน์ râadcha′ʔàad′ N seat for a king; throne.

อาลัญ ʔaasăn′ V lit. to die.

อาสา ʔaasăa′ V to volunteer.

     ทหารอาสา (คน) thahăan′ʔaasăa′ (khon′) N soldiers or units sent into action on a voluntary basis (esp. with reference to Thailand's participation in World War I).

     รับอาสา ráb′ʔaasăa′ V to volunteer.

อาหม ʔaahŏm′ N a Thai tribe, the Ahom of Assam.

อาหรับ ʔaaràb′ N 1. Arabia. 2. Arab; Arabian.

     ชาวอาหรับ (คน) chaaw′ʔaaràb′ (khon′) N Arab, Arabian person.

     ประเทศอาหรับ prathêed′ʔaaràb′ N Arabia.

     อาหรับราตรี ʔaaràb′raatrii′ N Arabian Nights.

อาหาร (อย่าง, มื้อ, ชะนิด) ʔaahăan′ (jàaŋ′, mýy′, chaníd′) N food, meal. →Syn. ภัตตาหาร sacer.

     กินอาหาร kin′ʔaahăan′ V com. to eat. Used of eating in general, including both snacks and regular meals. →Comp. กินข้าว. →Syn. รับประทานอาหาร eleg.

     ข้าวปลาอาหาร khâawplaa′ʔaahăan′ N elab. colloq. food.

     เจริญอาหาร carəən′ʔaahăan′ V eleg. 1. to have a great appetite. 2. (an appetizer, apéritif, etc.) to stimulate the appetite.

     ปรุงอาหาร pruŋ′ʔaahăan′ V eleg. 1. to cook. 2. to season food. →Syn. 1. ทำกับข้าว com.

     รับประทานอาหาร rábprathaan′ʔaahăan′ V eleg.

to eat. →Syn. กินอาหาร com.

o ห้องรับประทานอาหาร (ห้อง) hɔ̂ŋ′-rábpracɔ
thaan′/ʔaahăan′ (hɔ̂ŋ′) N eleg. dining room.

ร้านอาหาร (ร้าน, แห่ง) ráan′/ʔaahăan′ (ráan′,
hɛ̀ŋ′) N restaurant, food stall (selling ready-
to-eat food). →Comp. ภัตตาคาร eleg.

รายชื่ออาหาร (อย่าง, แผ่น, ใบ) raajchŷy′/ʔaahăan′
(jàaŋ′, phɛ̀n′, baj′) N menu.

เศษอาหาร sèed′/ʔaahăan′ N 1. food particles.
2. food scraps.

ห้องอาหาร (ห้อง) hɔ̂ŋ′/ʔaahăan′ (hɔ̂ŋ′) N dining
room.

อาหารกระป๋อง (อย่าง, กระป๋อง) ʔaahăan′/kracɔ
pɔ̌ŋ′ (jàaŋ′, krapɔ̌ŋ′) N canned food.

อาหารกลางวัน (มื้อ) ʔaahăan′klaaŋwan′ (mýy′)
N eleg. lunch, luncheon.

อาหารการกิน ʔaahăan′kaankin′ N nutriment,
food.

อาหารคาว (อย่าง, จาน) ʔaahăankhaaw′ (jàaŋ′,
caan′) N eleg. food of the main course (usually prepared of meat or fish).

อาหารค่ำ (มื้อ) ʔaahăankhâm′ (mýy′) N eleg.
dinner, the evening meal.

อาหารเช้า (มื้อ) ʔaahăancháaw′ (mýy′) N eleg.
breakfast.

อาหารเที่ยง (มื้อ) ʔaahăanthîaŋ′ (mýy′) N eleg.
lunch, luncheon (midday meal).

อาหารประจำ (อย่าง) ʔaahăan′pracam′ (jàaŋ′)
N eleg. staple food.

อาหารประจำวัน (อย่าง) ʔaahăan′-pracam′wan′
(jàaŋ′) N eleg. daily fare, everyday food.

อาหารเย็น (มื้อ) ʔaahăanjen′ (mýy′) N eleg.
dinner, supper.

อาหารว่าง (อย่าง, ชะนิด) ʔaahăanwâaŋ′ (jàaŋ′,
chaníd′) N eleg. snack, food taken between
meals.

อาหารสำเร็จ (อย่าง, ชะนิด) ʔaahăan′sămrèd′
(jàaŋ′, chaníd′) N prepared food, ready-to-
eat food.

อาหารหวาน (อย่าง, ชะนิด) ʔaahăanwăan′ (jàaŋ′,
chaníd′) N dessert.

อาหารแห้ง (อย่าง, ชะนิด) ʔaahăanhɛ̂ɛŋ′ (jàaŋ′,
chaníd′) N dried food.

อ้า. See entries below.

ถูกผีอ้ำ thùugphĭi/ʔam′ V to have a nightmare
(marked by a feeling of pressure or weight on
the chest, and an inability to cry out).

อำความ ʔamkhwaam′ V to conceal, suppress the
facts.

อำพราง ʔamphraaŋ′ V to conceal, suppress,
keep secret.

อ้ำ in อ้ำอึ้ง ʔâm?ŷŋ′ V to remain silent (when
confused, perplexed, etc.).

อำนวย ʔamnuaj′ V eleg. to bestow, afford.

อำนวยการ ʔamnuajkaan′ V to direct things, conduct (the) affairs. ความ-- direction, management, administration. ผู้-- director, administrator.

o ตึกอำนวยการ (ตึก, หลัง) tỳg′/ʔamnuajkaan′
(tỳg′, lăŋ′) N administration building.

อำนวยความสะดวก ʔamnuaj′khwaamsadùaŋ′ V
to accommodate.

อำนาจ ʔamnâad′ N power, influence, authority.

ดุลยภาพแห่งอำนาจ dunjaphâab′hɛ̀ŋʔamnâad′ balance of power.

ใบมอบอำนาจ (ใบ, ฉะบับ) baj′/mɔ́ɔbʔamnâad′
(baj′, chabàb′) N 1. proxy. 2. power of attorney.

มหาอำนาจ (ประเทศ) mahăa′/ʔamnâad′ (prathêed′)
N the Great Powers.

เมาอำนาจ maw′/ʔamnâad′ V colloq. to be
drunk with power.

เรืองอำนาจ ryaŋ′/ʔamnâad′ V to be very powerful,
to flourish, be at the height of one's power or
glory.

ให้อำนาจ hâjʔamnâad′ V to authorize, empower.

อย่างไว้อำนาจ jàaŋwáj′/ʔamnâad′ overbearingly,
arrogantly, domineeringly; with an authoritarian
air.

อำนาจตุลาการ ʔamnâad′-tulaa′kaan′ N judicial
power.

อำนาจทางการเมือง ʔamnâad′thaaŋkaanmyaŋ′
N political power.

อำนาจนิติบัญญัติ ʔamnâad′nítìbanjàd′ N legislative
power.

อำนาจบริหาร ʔamnâad′-bɔrihăan′ administrative
power, executive power.

อำนาจอธิปไตย ʔamnâad′/ʔàthíppataj′ N sovereign
power.

อำพัน ʔamphan⁄ N amber.

อำเภอ ๑ ʔamphəə⁄ N amphoe, a subdivision of a čhangwat. →See จังหวัด.

  กรมการอำเภอ (คณะ, ชุด, คน) krommakaan⁄ʔamɔ⁻ phəə⁄ N 1. the administrative staff of an amphoe (khaná⁄, chúd⁄). 2. a district official who is a member of this staff (khon⁄).

  นายอำเภอ (คน, นาย) naaj⁄ʔamphəə⁄ (khon⁄, naaj⁄) N head official of an amphoe.

  อำเภอพระนคร ʔamphəə⁄phránákhɔɔn⁄ pN an amphoe in Bangkok.

อำเภอ ๒ as in ตามอำเภอใจ taam⁄-ʔamphəə⁄caj⁄ according to one's own will or wish; arbitrarily, in a self-willed or high-handed manner.

อำมหิต ʔammahìd⁄ V to be cruel, wicked, savage, inhuman.

อำมาตย์ (คน) ʔammàad⁄* (khon⁄) N government official, royal attendant, courtier, councillor.

อำลาๆ ʔamlaa⁄ V eleg. to take leave, say good-bye.

อิง ʔiŋ⁄ V 1. to lean. 2. to rest against, lean against.

  นิยายอิงประวัติศาสตร์ (เรื่อง) níjaaj⁄-ʔiŋ⁄pracᵓ wàdsàad⁄ (rɯ̂aŋ⁄) N a story based on history, a historical romance.

  อ้างอิง ʔâaŋʔiŋ⁄ V to cite, refer to (an authority).

อิ่ง. See อ้อยอิ่ง.

อิจฉา ʔìdchǎa⁄ V 1. to envy. 2. to be jealous, envious. ความ-- envy, jealousy.

อิฉัน ʔichán⁄* P illit. w. s p. I, me. →Cf. ดิฉัน def. w. s p.

อิฐ (แผ่น, ก้อน) ʔìd⁄ (phɛ̀n⁄, kɔ̂ɔn⁄) N brick.

  ก้อนอิฐ (ก้อน) kɔ̂ɔnʔìd⁄ (kɔ̂ɔn⁄) N a (broken) piece of brick.

  สีอิฐ sǐiʔìd⁄ N brick color.

อิด. See the following entries.

  อิดโรย ʔìdrooj⁄ V to be weary, fatigued, tired, exhausted.

  อิดหนาระอาใจ ʔìdnǎa⁄-raʔaa⁄caj⁄ V to be tired (of), wearied (with), sick (of).

  อิดออด ʔìdʔɔ̀ɔd⁄ V to demonstrate unwillingness or half-heartedness.

  อิดเอื้อน ʔìdʔɯ̂an⁄ V to demonstrate unwillingness or half-heartedness.

อิตถี ʔìdthǐi⁄ N lit. woman. →Syn. ผู้หญิง com.

อิตาลี ʔìdtaalii⁄, ʔìtaalii⁄ N Italy. [f. Eng.]

อิตาเลียน (คน) ʔìdtaalian⁄, ʔìtaalian⁄ N 1. (as n. mod.) Italian. 2. an Italian (khon⁄). [f. Eng.]

อิทธิ ʔìdthí⁄ N power, influence, supernatural power. →Chiefly in compounds.

  อิทธิพล ʔìdthíphon⁄ N power, influence.

  อิทธิฤทธิ์ ʔìdthiríd⁄ N (supernatural) power, force (esp. of a violent, destructive nature).

  ○ สำแดงอิทธิฤทธิ์ sǎmdɛɛŋ⁄ʔìdthiríd⁄ V 1. to manifest violent supernatural power. 2. to have a violent tantrum.

อินเดีย ʔindia⁄ N 1. India. 2. (as n. mod.) Indian.

  แขกอินเดีย (คน) khɛ̀ɛg⁄ʔindia⁄ (khon⁄) N an Indian.

  ประเทศอินเดีย prathêed⁄ʔindia⁄ N India.

  มหาสมุทรอินเดีย mahǎasamùd⁄ʔindia⁄ N Indian Ocean.

  หมู่เกาะอินเดียตะวันตก mùukɔ̀ʔ⁄-ʔindia⁄tawantòg⁄ N the West Indies.

อินเดียน as in อินเดียนแดง (คน) ʔindiandɛɛŋ⁄ (khon⁄) N American Indian. [อินเดียน f. Eng.]

อินโดจีน ʔindoociin⁄ N 1. Indochina. 2. (as n. mod.) Indochinese.

  คาบสมุทรอินโดจีน khâab⁄samùd⁄ʔindoociin⁄ N the Indochinese Peninsula.

  ลาวอินโดจีน (คน) laaw⁄ʔindoociin⁄ (khon⁄) N the Indochinese Laos.

  อินโดจีนฝรั่งเศส ʔindoociin⁄faràŋsèed⁄ N French Indochina, a former Fr. colonial federation.

อินโดนีเซีย ʔindoo⁄nisia⁄ N Indonesia. [f. Eng.]

อินทนน in ดอยอินทนน dɔɔj⁄ʔin⁄thanon⁄ pN Mt. Inthanon, the highest peak in Thailand, located in the north.

อินทผลัม, อินทผาลัม (ผล, ใบ, ลูก) ʔin⁄tháphalam⁄, ʔin⁄tháphǎalam⁄ (phǒn⁄, lɯ̌ug⁄, baj⁄) N date (the fruit). ต้น-- (ต้น) the date palm.

อินทร์. See entries below.

  พระอินทร์ phráʔin⁄ N Indra.

  อินทรธนู (สาย) ʔin⁄thanuu⁄ (sǎaj⁄) N epaulet.

อินทรี in นกอินทรี (ตัว) nóg⁄ʔinsii⁄ (tua⁄) N eagle.

อินทรีย์ ʔinsii⁄ N tech. 1. (as n. mod.) organic. 2. organism (in certain cpds. only). →Ant. อนินทรีย์.

  จุลอินทรีย์ (ตัว) cun⁄laʔinsii⁄ (tua⁄) N microorganism (tr. f. Eng.).

  สารประกอบอินทรีย์ sǎanprakɔ̀ɔb⁄ʔinsii⁄ N organic

compound.

สารอินทรีย์ sǎan/ʔinsii/ N organic substance.

อินทรียเคมี ʔinsii/kheemii/ N organic chemistry.

อินทรียสาร ʔinsii/sǎan/ N organic substance.

อินัง in ไม่อินังขังขอบ mâjʔinaŋ/khǎŋkhɔ̀ɔb/ elab. colloq. to not pay attention (to), not care (about).

อิ่ม ʔìm/ V 1. to be full (from eating), satiated. 2. to be saturated (with).

แช่อิ่ม chɛ̂ɛ/ʔìm/ V (fruit) to be candied.

อิ่มใจ ʔìmcaj/ V to feel satisfied, deeply pleased, gratified.

อิ่มตัว ʔìmtua/ V tech. to be saturated.

อิ่มตื้อ ʔìmtŷy/ to be stuffed, extremely full (from eating).

อิ่มปี๋ ʔìmpǐi/ to be extremely full.

อิ่มแปร้ ʔìmprɛ̂ɛ/ to be extremely full.

อิ่มหมีพีมัน ʔìmmǐi/phiiman/ V elab. colloq. to be stuffed, extremely full (from eating).

อิ่มเอิบ ʔìmʔə̀əb/ V to be satisfied, pleased, contented.

อิระวดี in แม่น้ำอิระวดี mɛ̂ɛnáam/ʔirawadii/ pN the Irrawaddy River. →Also แม่น้ำเอราวดี.

อิรัค ʔirág/ N Iraq.

อิริยาบถ ʔìrijaabòd/ N 1. movement, action. 2. position (as of the body). →Sometimes also spelled อิริยาบท.

สำรวมอิริยาบถ sǎmruam/ʔìrijaabòd/ V to be respectfully still, quiet and respectful.

อิเล็กตรอน ʔilég/trɔɔn/ N electron. [f. Eng.]

อิสรภาพ ʔìsaraphâab/ N freedom, independence. →Also ความ--.

วันประกาศอิสรภาพ wanprakàad/ʔìsaraphâab/ N Independence Day.

อิสรภาพในการเมือง ʔìsaraphâab/najkaan/myaŋ/ N political freedom.

อิสระ ʔìsarà?/ N 1. freedom. 2. (as n. mod.) free.

กึ่งอิสระ kỳŋ/ʔìsarà?/ semi-autonomous.

เป็นอิสระ pen/ʔìsarà?/ to be free. ความ-- freedom.

อิสระภาพ. See อิสรภาพ.

อิสระเสรี ʔìsarà?/sěerii/ N freedom, liberty.

อิสราเอล ʔìd/saraa/ʔen/* N Israel.

อิสลาม ʔìsalaam/ N "Islam," as in the following entries.

ไทยอิสลาม thaj/ʔìsalaam/ N the Islamic Thai.

ศาสนาอิสลาม sàasanǎa/ʔìsalaam/ N Islam, Mohammedanism.

อิสสรภาพ. See อิสรภาพ.

อิสาน, อิสาณ ʔisǎan/ 1. lit., eleg. northeast. N 2. com. the northeast (of Thailand). →Sometimes also written อีสาน. →Syn. 1. ตะวันออกเฉียงเหนือ com. →The literary and the common terms for the eight chief points of the compass are listed under ทิศ.

ชาวอิสาน (คน) chaawʔisǎan/ (khon/) N northeastern Thai, people of NE Thailand.

ภาคอิสาน phâag/ʔisǎan/ N the northeast, the northeastern part (of Thailand).

อิโหน่อิเหน่ ʔinòo/ʔinèe/ See อีโหน่อีเหน่.

อิหร่าน ʔiràan/ N Iran.

ชาวอิหร่าน (คน) chaawʔiràan/ (khon/) N an Iranian; the Iranian people.

อี. ʔii/ the English letter "E." [f. Eng.]

อี ʔii/ T 1. derog. title used with first names of women, esp. women criminals but also for purposes of insult; formerly used with names of women slaves. 2. colloq. term freely used with reference to objects or to persons (regardless of sex), esp. in conjunction with a demonstrative word, and without special connotation. 3. bound element in names of birds and animals. A few such names are considered to be colloquial; their common counterparts have นาง in place of อี (see note 2 under นาง). →Also 2. อ้าย ๑. →Opp. 1. อ้าย ๑, used with names of men.

กับอี kaʔii⊃ expression used to indicate the paltriness, insignificance, worthlessness of an object from the speaker's point of view, as in the example below. →Also กับอ้าย.

o กับอีเงินเท่านี้ ก็ขี้เหนียวด้วย kàʔiiŋən/thâwníi/→ kɔ̀khîiniaw/dûaj↓ Even with this little bit of money he is stingy.

อีกา (ตัว) ʔiikaa/ (tua/) N com. crow. →Also กา writ. com.

อีเก้ง (ตัว) ʔiikêeŋ/ (tua/) N com. barking deer. →Also เก้ง writ. com.

อีดอก ʔiidɔ̀ɔg/ Short for อีดอกทอง.

o อีดอกทอง ʔiidɔɔg'thɔɔŋ'↓ Prostitute! Bag!
(term of abuse).

อีตา ʔiitaa' colloq. guy, fellow, mister.

o อีตาคนนี้ ʔiitaakhonníi' colloq. this guy,
this fellow.

อีนัง,อีนาง ʔiinaŋ', ʔiinaaŋɔ T derog. title
for a woman.

อีพักนี้ ʔiiphág'níi' colloq. around this time,
at present, at the moment.

อีรม in หอยอีรม (ตัว) hɔj'ʔiirom' (tua') N
colloq. oyster. →Syn. หอยนางรม com.
→See also อีร้า...อีรม as separate main entry.

อีแร้ง (ตัว) ʔiiréɛŋ' (tua') N com. vulture.
→Syn. แร้ง writ. com.

อีเห็น (ตัว) ʔiihěn' (tua') N com. palm civet.
Probably not used without อี.

อีแอ่น in นกอีแอ่น (ตัว) nóg'ʔiiʔɛ̀n' (tua') N
colloq. swallow (bird). →Syn. นกนางแอ่น
com.

อี. See อู๋อี๋.

อี !ʔíi' E exclamation expressing dislike, repulsion,
aversion.

อี ๑ ʔíi' idem.

อี ๒ ʔíi' rM intensifier used with เขียว "green."

อีก ʔìig' qM more, in addition, again; another, the
other.

o กล้วยอีกหกใบ klûaj'-ʔìighòg'baj' another six
bananas; six more bananas.

o อีก ๑๐ นาทีจะ ๘ โมง ʔìigsìb'naathii' caɔ
pɛ̀ɛd'mooŋ' colloq. it's ten minutes to eight:
"another ten minutes (and) it'll be eight."

เพิ่มขึ้นอีก phəəm'khɣ̂n'ʔìig' in addition, more.

ไม่...อีกเลย mâjɔ...ʔìigləəj' never again (do
such and such).

ยังไม่...อีก jaŋmâjɔ...ʔìig' "still not, not even
yet," as in the following examples.

o แต่งตัวยังไม่เสร็จอีกหรือ tɛ̀ŋtua'-jaŋmâjsèd'ɔ
ʔìigrɤ̌↓ Isn't she even dressed yet? Aren't
you (isn't she) ready yet?

o ยังไม่พออีกหรือ jaŋmâjphɔɔ'-ʔìigrɤ̌↓ Isn't that
enough yet? Is that still not enough?

o ยังไม่เป็นค่าจ้างพออีกหรือ jaŋmâjpenkhâacâaŋ'ɔ
phɔɔ'-ʔìigrɤ̌↓ Is that not yet sufficient pay?

ยัง...อีก jaŋɔ...ʔìig' "still more," as in the

example below.

o ยังมีต่อไปอีก jaŋmiitɔ̀ɔ'paj'ʔìig' 1. to be continued.
2. there is still more to come (as of a story).

รุ่งขึ้นอีกวันหนึ่ง rûŋkhɣ̂n'-ʔìigwan'nɣŋ the next
day, the following day.

วันแล้ววันอีก wanlɛ́ɛw'wan'ʔìig' day after day.

อะไรต่ออะไรอีก ʔaraj'tɔ̀ɔʔaraj'-ʔìig and so on;
several other things more.

อะไรอีก ʔaraj'ʔìig↓ What else? Anything else?

อีกคนหนึ่ง ʔìigkhon'nɣŋ 1. the other one (person).
2. another person, one more person.

อีกครั้งหนึ่ง ʔìigkhráŋ'nɣŋ once more, once again.

อีกต่อหนึ่ง ʔìigtɔ̀ɔ'nɣŋ colloq. in turn (as when
passing something on).

อีกทอดหนึ่ง ʔìigthɔ̂ɔd'nɣŋ colloq. in turn.

อีกทั้งยัง ʔìig'tháŋjaŋɔ furthermore, moreover.

อีกที ʔìigthii' once more, again.

อีกทีหนึ่ง ʔìigthii'nɣŋ one more time, again.

อีกนัยหนึ่ง ʔìignaj'nɣ̀ŋ' in other words; in another
sense, another way.

อีกประการหนึ่ง ʔìigprakaan'nɣŋ furthermore,
(and for) another thing.

อีกมาก ʔìigmâag' many more, plenty more.

อีกไม่ช้า ʔìigmâjcháa' soon, before long.

อีกไม่นาน ʔìigmâjnaan' soon, before long.

อีกแล้ว ʔìiglɛ́ɛw' again.

o เอาอีกแล้ว ʔaw'ʔìiglɛ́ɛw↓ What, again? Again!

อีกวาระหนึ่ง ʔìigwaará'nɣŋ eleg. once more,
once again.

อีกสักกี่หนก็ได้ ʔìigságkìihǒn'kɔ̂dâaj'↓ as many
more times as (one) wants.

อีกสักหน่อย ʔìigságnɔ̀ɔj' 1. a little later on. 2.
a little bit more.

อีกหน่อย ʔìignɔ̀ɔj' 1. in a little while, a little
while longer. 2. a little more.

อีก...หนึ่ง ʔìigɔ...nɣŋ 1. the other one. 2.
another...; one...more. See อีกคนหนึ่ง and
others among the subentries of อีก.

อีกห้องหนึ่ง ʔìighɔ̂ŋ'nɣŋ the other one (room), the
other room; another room.

อีกเหลือหลาย ʔìiglɣ̌a'lǎaj' many more.

อีกอย่างหนึ่ง ʔìigjàaŋ'nɣŋ one more thing, (and
for) another thing, also, furthermore.

อีจุ (ใบ) ʔiicǔu' (baj') N a kind of fish trap.

อีแปะ (อัน) ʔiipὲʔ/ (ʔan/) N a small Chinese coin of low value.

อียิปต์ ʔiijìb/* N Egypt. [f. Eng.]

อีร้า...อีรม in ไม่ฟังอีร้าค่าอีรม mâjfaŋ/ʔiiráa/-khâa/ʔiirom/ V colloq. to pay no attention to what others say, be unmindful of what others say. →Dist. อีรม under อี.

อีลุงตุงนัง ʔiiluŋ/tuŋnaŋ/ colloq. to be tangled up. →Also อีนุง-, อีรุง-.

อีเล็กตรอน ʔiilég/trɔɔn/ N electron. [f. Eng.]

อีสาน. See อิสาน.

อีสุกอีใส ʔiisùg/ʔiisǎj/ N colloq. chicken pox. →Syn. ไข้สุกใส eleg.

อีโหน่อีเหน่ in ไม่รู้อีโหน่อีเหน่ mâjrúu/-ʔiinòo/ʔii‐ nèe/ V colloq. to know absolutely nothing about (it).

อึก ʔỳg/ C a gulp, a swallow (liquid).

อึกทึก ʔỳgkathýg/ V to be noisy.

อึกอัก ʔỳgʔàg/ V 1. to be in turmoil, in conflict within oneself, confused. 2. to be unable to speak; to stammer (because of uneasiness, embarrassment, reluctance, confusion).

อึกอักใจ ʔỳgʔàg/caj/ V to be unable to make a decision, to feel confused, uncertain.

อึง ʔyŋ/ V to be loud, noisy.

อึงคนึง ʔyŋ/khanyŋ/ V to be noisy, tumultuous.

อึงอล ʔyŋʔon/ V to be loud, noisy.

อึ่ง (ตัว) ʔŷŋ/ (tua/) N a kind of frog.

แค่หางอึ่ง khὲε/hǎaŋʔŷŋ/ idiom. nothing, not much, very little: "as much as a frog's tail."

อึ่งอ่าง (ตัว) ʔŷŋʔàaŋ/ (tua/) N bullfrog.

อึ้ง ๑ ʔ́ŷŋ/ V to be speechless (as with perplexity, emotion), nonplussed, struck dumb. →Syn. อัน.

นิ่งอึ้ง nîŋʔŷŋ/ to be silent, speechless, struck dumb.

อ้ำอึ้ง ʔâm/ʔŷŋ/ V to remain silent (with perplexity, confusion, etc.).

อึ้ง ๒ ʔ́ŷŋ/ rM intensifier used with หนัก "heavy."

อึด ʔỳd/ V to hold, suppress. →Chiefly in compounds.

นิ่งอึด nîŋʔỳd/ V to remain silent (suppressing some kind of feeling).

อึดใจ ʔỳdcaj/ C a brief moment (i.e. as long as one can hold one's breath).

o ชั่วอึดใจ chûaʔỳdcaj/ for a brief moment, for just a few seconds.

o สักอึดใจหนึ่ง ságʔỳdcaj/nyŋ (for) just a brief moment.

อึดอัด ʔỳdʔàd/ V to feel constricted, hemmed in, stifled, oppressed, harassed, uncomfortable, ill at ease (e.g. because of tight clothes, overeating, insufficient space, a stuffy room, an awkward situation, trying circumstances, etc.).

อืด ʔ̀ŷd/ V to be swollen, distended.

อืดอาด ʔ̀ŷdʔàad/ V to be slow, inert; to be slow-moving, to move with difficulty (as a very fat person).

อื่น ʔ̀ŷn/ N other; others. ผู้-- others (ref. to people), other people.

ก่อนอื่น kɔɔnʔ̀ŷn/ first of all, before anything else.

เขาอื่น kháwʔ̀ŷn/ others, other people.

ใครอื่น khrajʔ̀ŷn/ anybody else, somebody else.

เป็นอื่น penʔ̀ŷn/ 1. to be estranged, alienated, unfaithful. 2. to be otherwise, different, something else.

o คิดเป็นอื่น khíd/penʔ̀ŷn/ colloq. to think otherwise, have one's own opinion, take (it) to mean something else.

อื่นใด ʔ̀ŷn/daj/ any other.

อื่นๆ ʔ̀ŷnʔ̀ŷn/ N other, other ones, others.

o และอื่นๆ lέʔʔ̀ŷnʔ̀ŷn/ and so on, and so forth.

อือ ʔyy/ E excl. expressing mild astonishment, interest, approval.

อื้อ ʔ́ŷy/ V 1. to be loud, noisy, tumultous. 2. (the ears) to be ringing, buzzing.

หูอื้อ hǔuʔ́ŷy/ V 1. to be nearly deaf. 2. to have a buzzing in the ears.

อื้อฉาว ʔ́ŷychǎaw/ V 1. to be talked of a lot, to be spread far and wide. sV 2. a lot, widely, far and wide.

อื้ออึง ʔ́ŷyʔyŋ/ V to be uproarious, noisy, boisterous.

อื๋อ ʔ̌ŷy/ rM modifier used with เขียว "green" to indicate a deep shade.

อุก. See the following entries.

คดีอุกฉกรรจ์ khadii/ʔùgchakan/ a serious offense, a serious case.

อุกอาจ ʔùgʔàad/ V 1. to be bold, audacious. 2. to dare (to), have the audacity (to).

อุกกาบาต ʔùgkaaʹbàad/ N meteor.

อุโฆษ as in มีนามอุโฆษ miinaam/ʹʔùkhôod/ eleg.
to be widely known, renowned.

อุ้ง (อุ้ง) ʔûŋ/ (ʔûŋʹ) N the center of the palm or
sole.

อุจจาระ (ก้อน) ʔùdcaará?/ (kɔɔnʹ) 1. eleg. fecal
matter, feces, excrement. V 2. to defecate.
การถ่าย-- evacuation of fecal matter; bowel
movement. →Also 2. ถ่ายอุจจาระ. →Syn.
ขี้ ๑ com.,vulg., ทุ่ง ๒ colloq.,euphem.
ถ่ายอุจจาระ thàaj/ʹʔùdcaará?/ eleg. to evacuate
fecal matter, have a bowel movement, defecate.
→Syn. ขี้ ๑ com.,vulg., ทุ่ง ๒ colloq.,
euphem.

อุจาด ʔucàad/ V to be obscene, disgusting, shameful, lewd.
คำอุจาดลามก (คำ) kham/-ʔucàad/laamóg/
(khamʹ) N obscene word; an obscenity.

อุณหภูมิ (องศา) ʔunhaphuum/ (ʔoŋsǎaʹ) N eleg.
temperature (in degrees).

อุณาโลม (อัน) ʔunaaʹloom/ (ʔanʹ) N insignia
(worn on a cap).

อุด ๑ ʔùd/ V 1. to stop up, plug. 2. to fill (a hole).
อุดหู ʔùdhǔu/ V to plug the ears, stop up one's
ears.
อุดอู้ ʔùdʔûu/ V 1. to be stuffy. 2. to be close,
small, narrow.

อุด ๒ in อุดหนุน ʔùdnǔn/ V to support, assist
(financially); to patronize.
เงินอุดหนุน (จำนวน,ก้อน) ŋən/ʹʔùdnǔn/ (cam⊃
nuanʹ, kɔɔnʹ) N subsidy.

อุดม ๑ ʔudom/ V 1. to be abundant, plentiful. 2.
to be prolific, productive, fertile. →Syn. 1.
มาก,บริบูรณ์,สมบูรณ์.
o พื้นที่อันอุดม phýynthîi/ʹʔanʔudom/ fertile land.
อุดมไปด้วย ʔudom/pajdûajɔ to have plenty of,
to be fertile with, to be rich in.

อุดม ๒ ʔudom/ "excellent, supreme," as in the
following compounds.
อุดมการ,อุดมการณ์ (ข้อ) ʔudom/kaan/ (khɔɔʹ)
N ideal, principle, philosophy.
อุดมคติ (อย่าง,ข้อ) ʔudom/khatì?/ (jàaŋʹ, khɔɔʹ)
N ideal.
อุดมศึกษา ʔudom/sỳgsǎa/ N higher education,

college education.

o เตรียมอุดมศึกษา triam/ʹʔudom/sỳgsǎa/ N pre-
paratory education (for college).

อุดร ʔùdɔɔn/ 1. lit.,eleg. north. pN 2. com.
Udɔn, a township in NE Thailand. →Syn. 1.
เหนือ com. →The literary and the common
terms for the eight chief points of the compass
are listed under ทิศ.

อุตรดิตถ์ ʔùd/taradìd/ pN Utaradit, a township in
N Thailand.

อุตริ ʔùdtarì?/ V to be out of the ordinary, different,
unusual.

อุตส่าห์ ʔusàa/ V to try, try hard, make a special
effort.

อุตสาหกรรม (อย่าง,ชะนิด,ประเภท) ʔùsàa/hàkam/*,
ʔùdsàa/hàkam/ (jàaŋʹ, chanídʹ, prapheedʹ) N
industry (as opposed to agriculture). การ--
industry; industrial affairs. นัก-- industrialist.
กิจการอุตสาหกรรม kìdcakaan/ʹʔùsǎa/hàkam/ N
industrialization.
เคมีอุตสาหกรรม kheemii/ʹʔùsǎa/hàkam/ N industrial chemistry.
เภสัชอุตสาหกรรม pheesàd/ʹʔùsǎa/hàkam/ N the
pharmaceutical industry.
เมืองอุตสาหกรรม (เมือง) myaŋ/ʹʔùsǎa/hàkam/
(myaŋʹ) N industrial city or town.
โรงงานอุตสาหกรรม (โรง,แห่ง) rooŋŋaan/ʹʔùɔ
sǎa/hàkam/ (rooŋʹ, hèŋʹ) N industrial plant.
อุตสาหกรรมเคมี ʔùsǎa/hakam/kheemii/ N 1. the
chemical industry. 2. industrial chemistry.

อุตสาหะ ʔùsǎa/hà?/, ʔùdsǎa/hà?/ V to be diligent,
industrious, persevering. ความ-- diligence,
industry, perseverance.

อุตุนิยม ʔùtù?/níjom/ N meteorology. →Chiefly in
compounds. นัก-- meteorologist.
กรมอุตุนิยม krom/-ʔùtù?/níjom/ N Weather
Bureau; Department of Meteorology.
อุตุนิยมวิทยา ʔùtù?/níjom/-wídthajaa/ N meteorology.

อุทกภัย ʔùthók/kaphaj/ N flood, disaster caused by
flood.

อุทธรณ์ ʔùthɔɔn/ V law to appeal.
ศาลอุทธรณ์ (แห่ง) sǎan/ʹʔùthɔɔn/ (hèŋʹ) N appellate court.

อุทัยธานี ʔùthaj/thaanii/ pN Uthaithani, a township in C Thailand.

อุทาน ʔùthaan/ V 1. to exclaim, cry out. N 2. gram. interjection. คำ-- gram. interjection.

ออกอุทาน ʔɔ̀ɔg/ʔùthaan/ V to exclaim, utter an exclamation.

อุทาหรณ์ (เรื่อง) ʔùthaa/hɔ̌ɔn/ (rɯ̂aŋ/) N eleg. example.

อุทิศ ʔùthíd/ V 1. to make an offering. 2. to dedicate, consecrate. 3. to donate on behalf of or in memory of.

อุทิศตน ʔùthíd/ton/ V to dedicate oneself (to), sacrifice oneself (for).

อุ่น ʔùn/ V 1. to be warm, lukewarm. 2. to warm (something) up, heat slowly.

อบอุ่น ʔòb²ùn/ V 1. to be warm (of climate, weather). 2. to be warm, good-natured (in character; in manner).

อุ่นขึ้น ʔùnkhŷn/ to be getting warmer.

อุ่นใจ ʔùncaj/ V to feel secure, at ease.

อุ่นหนาฝาคั่ง ʔùnnǎa/-fǎa/khâŋ/ V idiom. to be abundantly provided (with).

อุบล ʔùbon/ pN Ubon (Ubol), a township in NE Thailand. The full name is อุบลราชธานี ʔù⊃ bon/râadchathaa/nii/.

อุบ๊ะ ʔu!bá/ E excl. expressing anger, displeasure.

อุบัติ ʔubàd/, ʔubàd/tì⊃ V to happen, occur.

อุบัติเหตุ (ครั้ง,คราว,ราย) ʔubàd/tihèed/ (khráŋ/, khraaw/, raaj/) N accident. →Also อุบัติเหตุ.

อุปาทิว ʔubàad/ N 1. misery, misfortune, evil. 2. (as n. mod.) calamitous, disastrous, bad.

อุบาย (อย่าง,อัน) ʔùbaaj/ (jàaŋ/,ʔan/) N trick, device, plot.

วางอุบาย waaŋ/²ùbaaj/ V to set up a trap, prepare a stratagem.

อุบายบังหน้า (อัน,อย่าง) ʔùbaaj/-baŋ/nâa/ (ʔan/, jàaŋ/) N pretext.

อุบายคึก (อัน,อย่าง) ʔùbaaj/sŷg/ (ʔan/, jàaŋ/) N stratagem.

อุบาสก (คน) ʔùbaa/sòg/ (khon/) N a man who is a devout Buddhist.

อุบาสิกา (คน) ʔùbaa/sikaa/ (khon/) N a woman who is a devout Buddhist.

อุโบสถ, วัน-- ʔùboo/sòd/, wan/-ʔùboo/sòd/ N eleg. a Buddhist holy day.

อุปกรณ์ (อย่าง,เครื่อง) ʔùbpakɔɔn/ (jàaŋ/, khrɯ̂aŋ/) N eleg. equipment, implements, material; accessories; assistance. →Also เครื่อง--.

อุปการะ ʔùbpakaa/rá²/ V to sponsor, patronize, support. ผู้-- patron, supporter.

อุปถัมภ์ ʔùbpathǎm/ V to support, assist, help.

อุปทูต (คน,นาย) ʔùbpathûud/ (khon/,naaj/) N chargé d'affaires.

อุปโภค as in เครื่องอุปโภค (อย่าง) khrɯ̂aŋ²ùbpa⊃ phôog/ (jàaŋ/) N eleg. useful articles, things to use. →Syn. ของใช้ com.

อุปราคา ʔùbparaa/khaa/ N eclipse.

อุปสรรค (อย่าง,ประการ) ʔùbpasàg/ (jàaŋ/, pràkaan/) N obstacle, difficulties.

อุบัติเหตุ (ราย,อย่าง) ʔupàd/tihèed/ (raaj/, jàaŋ/) N accident. →Also อุบัติเหตุ.

อุปัทวเหตุ (ราย,อย่าง) ʔupàd/thawahèed/ (raaj/, jàaŋ/) N accident.

อุปาทาน ʔùpaa/thaan/ N 1. conviction, firm belief. 2. preconception. 3. colloq. misconception, illusion, imagination.

อุ้ม ʔûm/ V to hold, carry (a child, an animal) in one's arms.

อุ้มท้อง ʔûmthɔ́ɔŋ/ V 1. to be carrying a child (i.e. to be pregnant). →Cf. มีท้อง.

อุ้มน้ำ ʔûmnáam/ V (the soil) to hold water.

โอบอุ้ม ʔòob²ûm/ V 1. to carry embracing with both arms. 2. to cherish, foster; to help, support.

อุมงค์,อุโมงค์ (แห่ง) ʔumoŋ/, ʔumooŋ/ (hɛ̀ŋ/) N (underground) cave, cavity; tunnel.

อุย ʔuj/ V to be soft. Chiefly in compounds.

ขนอุย khǒnʔuj/ N down (first soft feathering).

อุย in อุยอ้าย ʔùjʔâaj/ V to be ponderous and slow-moving (as a hippopotamus, a very fat person).

อุ๊ย !ʔúj/ E 1. Ouch! Oh! (excl. of pain). 2. Oh! (excl. used by women to lend emphasis to an utterance; see examples).

o อุ๊ยน่ารักจัง !ʔúj/nâarág/caŋ↓ Oh, how absolutely lovely! How perfectly adorable! Oh, how cute!

o อุ๊ยตาย ʔújtaaj↓, !ʔújtaaj↓ E excl. expressing surprise, dismay, etc. →Sometimes written

อุย!ตาย! and pronounced !ʔúj/taaj/↓,

อุระ,อุรา ʔurá?/, ʔuraa/ N 1. lit. chest, breast.
2. colloq. heart.

อุวะ ʔuwá/ E excl. expressing anger, displeasure,
dissatisfaction.

อู่ (อู่,แห่ง) ʔùu/ (ʔùu/,hὲŋ/) N 1. place where
something is harbored, cradled, stored. Chiefly
in compounds. 2. short for such compounds,
hence dry dock, garage for repairs, etc.

พระอู่ phráʔùu/ N roy. cradle. →Syn. เปล com.

อู่ข้าวอู่น้ำ (แห่ง) ʔùukhâaw/ʔùunáam/ (hὲŋ/)
N fertile area.

อู่ต่อเรือ (อู่) ʔùu/tɔ̀ɔrya/ (ʔùu/) N shipyard.

อู่บางกอกด็อก ʔùu/baaŋkɔ̀ɔgdɔ́g/ pN Bangkok
Dock.

อู่รถ (อู่,แห่ง) ʔùuród/ (ʔùu/,hὲŋ/) N 1. garage
(for repairing motor vehicles). 2. an auto
dealer's.

อู่เรือ (อู่,แห่ง) ʔùurya/ (ʔùu/,hὲŋ/) N dry dock,
boathouse, shipyard. →Dist. ท่าเรือ.

อู้ ๑ ʔúu/ sV aloud, loudly; loud.

ครางอู้ khraaŋʔúu/ to moan loudly.

ซออู้ (คัน) sɔɔʔúu/ (khan/) N an alto stringed
instrument.

บ่นอู้ bòn/ʔúu/ 1. to mutter aloud, complain aloud.
2. to complain a lot.

อู้ ๒ in อุดอู้ ʔùdʔúu/ V 1. to be stuffy. 2. to be
close, narrow, small.

อูเครน ʔuukhreen/ N Ukraine. [f. Eng.]

อูฐ (ตัว) ʔùud/ (tua/) N camel.

อูม ʔuum/ V (the cheeks) to be full, fleshy. →Ant.
ตอบ ๒.

อูย ʔuuj/ E Ouch! (excl. expressing pain).

อู้อี้ ʔûuʔîi/ sV 1. indistinct(ly). 2. nasal(ly).

o บ่นอู้อี้ bòn/ʔûuʔîi/ to grumble, complain indistinctly.

o พูดอู้อี้ phûud/ʔûuʔîi/ to speak indistinctly or
nasally.

o เสียงอู้อี้ sǐaŋ/ʔûuʔîi/ N 1. an indistinct voice.
2. a nasal sound, a nasal twang. V 3. to have
an indistinct voice. 4. to have a nasal sound,
a nasal twang.

เอ. ʔee/ the English letter "A." [f. Eng.]

เอ ʔee/ E excl. expressing surprise, discontent.

เอ๋ in ตัวเอ๋ (ตัว) tuaʔêe/ (tua/) N colloq. the
main one (person), the responsible party, the
leader, the one to blame (used esp. when scolding children).

เอก ʔèeg/, ʔèeg/kaɔ Nm restricted 1. one.
2. first, prime, highest, leading. →Cf. หนึ่ง,
อ้าย ๒, เอ็ด ๑.

o นายพลเอก (นาย,คน) naajphonʔèeg/ (naaj/,
khon/) N 1. (full) general. T 2. General --.
→Also พลเอก. →For most other ranks in
เอก, see under นาย.

จ่าเอก càaʔèeg/ N 1. first petty officer. T 2.
title placed before first name of same.

ชั้นเอก chánʔèeg/ the first (highest) rank in civil
service.

ตัวเอก (ตัว) tuaʔèeg/ (tua/) N 1. the principal
one (person). 2. principal character in a play,
picture, etc.

นางเอก (ตัว) naaŋʔèeg/ (tua/) N 1. leading lady,
heroine (as of a play). 2. wife.

ปริญญาเอก (ปริญญา) parin/jaaʔèeg/ (parin/jaa/)
N doctor's degree.

พระเอก (ตัว) phráʔèeg/ (tua/) N 1. the hero
(as in a play). 2. husband.

พะยานเอก (คน) phajaan/ʔèeg/ (khon/) N prime
witness.

มือเอก (มือ,คน) myyʔèeg/ (myy/,khon/) N an
expert, a person with top skill and experience
(in a given field).

เมืองเอก (เมือง) myaŋʔèeg/ (myaŋ/) N principal city, province, town (esp. from the viewpoint
of strategic importance).

ไม้เอก (อัน) májʔèeg/ (ʔan/) N the first tonal
marker (`) of the Thai writing system. NOTE.
ไม้เอก should be distinguished from เสียงเอก.
The former term refers to the written symbol,
which may represent either a falling tone (when
it accompanies a low class consonant), or a low
tone (elsewhere). The term เสียงเอก, has
reference to the spoken language, and can only
mean the low tone.

เสียงเอก sǐaŋʔèeg/ N gram. the low tone.
→See note under ไม้เอก above.

เอกฉันท์ ʔèeg/kachǎn/ N 1. unanimity. 2. (as n.

mod.) unanimous.

o เป็นเอกฉันท์ pen?èeg/kachăn/ 1. to be unanimous. 2. unanimously.

เอกชน ?èeg/kachon/ N 1. an individual, a private individual. 2. (as n. mod.) individual, private.

o บริษัทเอกชน (บริษัท) bɔɔrisàd/-?èeg/kachon/
(bɔɔrisàd/) N a private enterprise.

เอกเทศ ?èeg/kathêed/ N 1. an individual part.
2. (as n. mod.) individual, separate, single.
โดย-- separately, individually.

เอกพจน์ ?èeg/kaphód/ N g r a m. singular number.

เอกภาพ ?èeg/kaphâab/ N unity.

เอกราช ?èeg/karâad/ N 1. independence. 2.
(as n. mod.) independent.

o ประเทศเอกราช (ประเทศ) prathêed/-?èeg/ɔ
karâad/ (prathêed/) N independent country.

o เป็นเอกราช pen?èeg/karâad/ to be independent.

เอกสาร (ฉะบับ) ?èeg/kasăan/ (chabàb/) N
document.

เอกสิทธิ์ ?èeg/kasìd/ N special privilege, sole
privilege.

เอกอัครรัฐทูต (คน) ?èeg/-?àgkharád/thathûud/
(khon/) N ambassador (from a country which
is not a monarchy).

เอกอัครราชทูต (คน,นาย,ท่าน) ?èeg/?àgkharâadɔ
chathûud/ (khon/, naaj/, thân/) N ambassador
(from a monarchy).

o สถานเอกอัครราชทูต (แห่ง) sathăan/-?èeg/ɔ
?àgkharâadchathûud/ (hὲŋ/) N embassy.

o เอกอัครราชทูตไทยประจำสหรัฐอเมริกา ?èeg/-
?àgkharâadchathûud/thaj/ pracam/-sahàrád/ɔ
?ameerikaa/ the Thai Ambassador to the
United States.

เอกซ์.,เอ็กซ์.,เอ็กซ์. ?ég/, ?égs/* the English
letter "X." [f. Eng.]

เอกซเรย์,เอ็กส์เรย์ ?ég/saree/* N 1. x-ray. V 2.
to x-ray, take an x-ray. 3. to have an x-ray
taken, be x-rayed. [f. Eng.]

ฟิล์มเอ็กส์เรย์ (แผ่น) fiim/-?ég/saree/ (phὲn/)
N x-ray plate.

เอ็กซิเดนท์,เอ็กสิเดนต์ ?égsiden/* N accident. [f.
Eng.] →Also แอกซิเดนท์,แอกซิเดนต์.

เอง ?eeŋ/ 1. oneself, myself, himself (see examples
of use after nominals below). 2. oneself, myself, itself (refer. to the subject, expressed or
unexpressed, as in 1st and 2nd examples of use
after verbs below); by oneself, of one's own accord, on one's own account. 3. very, downright,
just, right, etc. (see the remaining examples
below).

EXAMPLES OF USE AFTER NOMINALS
o ผมเองนั้น phǒm?eeŋ/nán/ as for me.
o ผู้เขียนเอง phûukhĭan/?eeŋ/ the writer himself.
o ส่วนตัวข้าพเจ้าเอง sùantua/khâaphacâw/-?eeŋ/
personally; as for myself; for my part.

EXAMPLES OF USE AFTER VERBS
o ทำใช้เอง thamcháj/?eeŋ/ to make for one's
own use.
o แมวไม่เคยหาปลามาเอง mɛɛw/ mâjkhəəj/ɔ
hăaplaa/maa?eeŋ/ A cat never catches fish
itself.
o จึงจำเป็นอยู่เอง cyŋ/-campen/jùu?eeŋ/ therefore it becomes downright necessary, all the
more necessary.
o เป็นธรรมดาอยู่เอง penthammadaa/jùu?eeŋ/
it is only very natural.

EXAMPLES OF USE AFTER DEMONSTRATIVES.
o แค่นี้เอง khɛ̂ɛnfi/?eeŋ/, khɛ̂ɛ/nfi?eeŋ/ only
thus far, only as far as this, only this much.
o อยู่ใกล้ ๆ นี่เอง jùuklâjklâj/nfi?eeŋ/ It's right
near here.

กันเอง ๑ kan?eeŋ/ I myself; me myself. →See
กัน ๒.

กันเอง ๒ kan?eeŋ/ N 1. an intimate, an equal.
2. intimate, familiar, informal. คน-- an acquaintance, an intimate, an equal. อย่าง-- informally; in a friendly, intimate manner. →See
กัน ๓. →Dist. the sequence กันเอง as in
ช่วยกันเอง "to help each other" (see under
กัน ๑).

ตนเอง ton?eeŋ/ oneself, one's own self. →More
emphatic than ตน alone.

o การปกครองตนเอง kaan/-pògkhrɔɔŋ/ton?eeŋ/
N self-government.

o ด้วยตนเอง dûaj/ton?eeŋ/ in person; by oneself,
as oneself, personally.

o ตามใจตนเอง taamcaj/ton?eeŋ/ to do as one
likes, follow one's own wishes.

ตัวเขาเอง tua/kháw?eeŋ/ himself, herself.

ตัวฉันเอง tuaˈchánˀeeŋ/ myself.

ตัวเอง tuaˀeeŋ/ oneself, one's own self. →More
emphatic than ตัว alone.

  o เอาแต่ใจตัวเอง ˀawtɛɛcajˈtuaˀeeŋ/ to consider only one's own interests or wishes; be
self-willed, self-centered.

นั่นเอง nânˀeeŋ/ "just, simply; the same, the
same as," in various idiomatic uses; see example.

  o ...เป็นม้าดีๆนั่นเอง ...penmáaˈdiidiiˈ-nânↄ
ˀeeŋˈↆ (What you saw there) is just an ordinary
horse, just a good old horse.

นั้นเอง nánˈ/ˀeeŋ/ that very, that very same.

  o ในวันนั้นเอง najˈwannánˈ/ˀeeŋ/ on that very
day, on that very same day.

เป็นเอง penˀeeŋ/ naturally (of itself, of one's
own accord).

มาเอง maaˀeeŋ/ 1. to come by oneself (unaccompanied). 2. to come of one's accord. 3.
to come oneself (in person).

เอ็ง ˀeŋ/ P vulg., sp. to inf. or int. you.
→Paired with ข้า ๒ "I, me."

เอช., เอ็ช. ˀéch/* the English letter "H." [f. Eng.]

เอเชีย, เอเซีย ˀeechia/, ˀeesia/ N 1. Asia. 2.
Asiatic. [f. Eng.] →Also อาเซีย.

เอ็ด ๑ ˀèd/ Nm restricted one. →Used after
tens, hundreds, etc. →Comp. หนึ่ง, อ้าย ๒, เอก.

ร้อยเอ็ด róɔjˀèd/ Nm 1. one hundred and one.
pN 2. Rɔi-et, a township in NE Thailand.

ร้อยเอ็ดเจ็ดหัวเมือง róɔjˀèd/-cèd/hǔamyaŋ/
idiom. countless provinces, all over the country. →Dist. ร้อยแปด, which is not used with
places.

ยี่สิบเอ็ด jîisìbˀèd/ Nm twenty one.

สิบเอ็ด sìbˀèd/ Nm eleven.

เอ็ด ๒ ˀèd/ V 1. to scold. 2. to be noisy, loud.

เสียงเอ็ดอึง (เสียง) sǐaŋˀèdˀyŋ/ (sǐaŋ/) N
din, loud noise.

เอ็ดตะโร ˀèdtaroo/ V 1. to scold loudly; to shout
at. 2. to make a clamor, a lot of noise.

เอน., เอ็น. ˀen/ the English letter "N." [f. Eng.]

เอน ˀeen/ V to lean.

เอนลู่ ˀeen/lûu/ V to bend, incline (as with the
wind).

เอนหลัง ˀeenlǎŋ/ V to lean back, recline, lie
down.

เอนเอียง ˀeenˀiaŋ/ V to incline toward, tend to,
have a tendency toward. ความ-- partiality,
inclination.

โอนเอน ˀoonˀeen/ V to be swaying, vacillating,
unsteady.

เอ็น (เส้น) ˀen/ (sên/) N tendon, sinew, gut.

เอนก ˀanèeg/ N 1. eleg. (as n. mod.) numerous,
innumerable. Nm 2. numerous, innumerable.
→Chiefly as in the following entries. →Also
written อเนก. →Comp. อนันต์.

เอนกประการ ˀanèeg/prakaan/ numerous or
innumerable kinds, ways.

  o มีคุณเป็นเอนกประการ miiˈkhun/-penˀanèeg/ↄ
prakaan/ to have innumerable virtues, graces.

เอนกอนันต์ ˀanèeg/ˀanan/ numerous, innumerable.

เอ็นดู ˀenduu/ V to be tender toward, have compassion and affection for. ความ-- tenderness,
affection (particularly as shown to a child or
to a pet).

น่าเอ็นดู nâaˀenduu/ V to be cute, lovely (as a
child, pet).

เอฟ., เอ็ฟ. ˀéf/ the English letter "F." [f. Eng.]

เอม., เอ็ม. ˀem/ the English letter "M." [f. Eng.]

เอมโอช ˀeemˀòod/ V to be delicious, savory.

เอย ˀəəj/ Pt lit. 1. particle used after a term of
address at the end of an utterance, serving to
suggest endearment, intimacy, affection. 2.
particle used to set off individual examples of
words or phrases when these are being listed.
3. particle used at the end of a verse for metric
reasons and without special connotation. →Comp.
เอ่ย.

ลงเอย loŋˀəəj/ V colloq. to end up, conclude,
be settled.

เอ่ย ˀə̀əj/ V colloq. 1. to mention. 2. to utter,
say something; to begin to speak. Pt 3. interrogative particle used in the introduction to a
riddle.

ใครเอ่ย khrajˀə̀əj/→ Who is it? (introducing a
riddle).

อะไรเอ่ย ˀarajˀə̀əj/→ What is it? (introducing a
riddle).

เอยขึ้น ʔðəj/khŷn to speak up, start speaking;
to say.

เอยถึง ʔðəj/thŷŋ/ to speak of, refer to.

เอยปาก ʔðəjpàag/ V 1. to open the mouth to talk.
2. to begin to talk.

เอย ๑ ʔðəj/, ʔə́j/ E excl. indicating self-cor-
rection, in the sense of "no, I mean..."

เอย ๒ in แม่เอย mɛ̂ɛ!ʔə́j/ Pt particle used by
a woman peddler at the end of her cry in which
she names her wares. →Cf. เอย.

เอย ʔðəj/, ʔə́j/*, !ʔə́j/ Pt 1. particle used after
a term of address at the beginning of an utterance serving to soften the effect and contributing
an element of endearment, intimacy, affection.
2. lit. particle used after the first word of a
verse for purposes of meter. →Comp. เอย.

โธ่เอย, พุทโธ่เอย thôo/!ʔə́j/, phûtthôo/!ʔə́j/
E What a pity! Too bad! It's a shame. (e.g.
on learning about a mishap).

เอเย่นต์ (เอเย่นต์,แห่ง,ราย) ʔeejên/*(ʔeejên/,hɛ̀ŋ/,
raaj/) N 1. agent (i.e. a firm which acts as an
agent for another firm). 2. agency. [f. Eng.]

เอร็ดอร่อย ʔarèd/ʔarɔ̀j/* V colloq. to be delicious,
delectable, very tasty. →Also อร่อย com.

เอราวดี in แม่น้ำเอราวดี mɛ̂ɛnáam/ʔeeraa/wadii/
N Irrawaddy River. →Also แม่น้ำอิระวดี.

เอล.,เอ็ล. ʔel/ the English letter "L." [f. Eng.]
→Also แอล.

เอว (เอว) ʔew/* (ʔew/) N waist (of the body; of
garments).

บั้นเอว (บั้นเอว) bân?ew/ (bân?ew/) N waist
(of the body).

ยืนเท้าเอว jyyn/tháaw?ew/ to stand arms akimbo.

เอวบาง ʔewbaaŋ/ V to have a small waist, a
slim waistline.

เอเวอเรสต์ in ยอดเอเวอเรสต์ jɔ̂ɔd/ʔeewəəréed/,
-rés/ N Mount Everest. [f. Eng.]

เอส.,เอ็ส. ʔés/ the English letter "S." [f. Eng.]

เอสกิโม (คน) ʔéskimoo/*(khon/) N Eskimo. [f.
Eng.]

เอ้หมึง ʔêemŷŋ/ N Amoy. →Also เมือง--. [f. Chin.]

เออ ʔəə E 1. excl. expressing agreement, assent,
concurrence, approval. May be variously rendered in English, e.g. "fine!" "great!" "say!"

"oh!" etc. 2. excl. similar to "oh," "say," "oh,
by the way." →In both meanings used among intimates, otherwise impolite.

เออซิวะ ʔəə/siiwá↓ Of course. (Said in ill humor.).

เออน่า ʔəənâa/ I know. OK. Yes, yes. (Used reas-
suringly).

เออออย ʔəə?uaj/ V colloq. to agree, go along
with, approve.

เออออห่อหมก ʔəə?ɔɔ/hɔ̀ɔmòg/ V elab. colloq.
to agree, approve, go along with.

เออ ʔðə/ V (water) to be on the verge of overflowing;
(tears) to well up.

เออ ʔðə/ E excl. used to express weariness, dejec-
tion.

เออระเหย ʔðərahðəj/ V 1. to dally, waste time,
sV 2. without any cares, at leisure, idly, wasting
time.

เออเฮอ ʔðəhəə/ E excl. expressing amazement.

เอะ in เอะใจ ʔè?/caj/ V colloq. to get suspicious, to sense that something is wrong.

เอะอะ ʔè?à?/ V 1. to be noisy, loud. 2. colloq.
to fuss, make a scene, object loudly, scold.

ความเอะอะกาหล khwaam?è?à?/kaahòn/ N confusion, commotion, melee, disturbance, tumult.

ความเอะอะโกลาหล khwaam?è?à?/koolaahòn/
idem.

เอะอะมะเทิ่ง ʔè?à?/má?thðəŋ/ V elab. colloq.
1. to make a loud noise. 2. to fuss loudly.

เอะ !ʔé/ E excl. expressing surprise, wonder.

เอา ʔaw/ V to take. Frequently used as the first
primary vb. in transitive expressions (1st
example). Often used at the head of a phrase
which functions as a secondary verb; in this use
it is generally not specifically rendered in English (examples 3-6).

o เอากล้วยจิ้มน้ำตาล ʔawklûaj/-cîm/námtaan/↓
Dip the banana into the sugar: "Take the banana
(and) dip into sugar."

o เก็บเอาไว้ kèb/?awwáj/ to store up, put up,
keep.

o คั้นเอาน้ำออกมา khán/-?awnáam/?ɔ̀ɔgmaa/ to
squeeze the water (or juice) out.

o ยัดเอากลับเข้าไป jád/-?awklàb/khâwpaj/ to
stuff (it) back in.

○ ยึดเอาไป jýd/ʔawpaj/ to take away (by force).

○ หนีเอาตัวรอด nɯ̃i-ʔawtua/rɔ̂ɔd/ to flee to safety.

ถือเอา thɯ̃y/ʔawɔ to regard, take (it) to be.

เล่นเอา lên/ʔawɔ colloq. to make, cause to.

เลือกเอา (1) lɯ̂ag/ʔawɔ; (2) lɯ̂ag/ʔaw↓ 1. to choose, select. 2. Take your choice.

เอาการ (อยู่) ʔawkaan/(jùu/) V colloq. 1. to be quite a thing; that's quite a thing. sV 2. mighty, pretty, quite, rather.

เอาการเอางาน ʔawkaan/ʔawŋaan/ V elab. to take one's work seriously, be in earnest about one's work.

เอาแก้ว as in ถามเอาแก้วเอาวิมานอะไร thǎam/-ʔawkɛ̂ɛw/ʔawwímaan/-ʔaraj↓ idiom. Why in the world (do you, should I, etc.) ask?

เอาคืน ʔawkhyyn/ V to take back; to win back.

เอาไงก็เอา ʔawŋaj/kɔ̂ʔaw↓ colloq. 1. to take it as it comes. 2. no matter what, regardless of what others think, whatever others might say.

เอาจริง ʔawciŋ/ V to be serious, earnest; to take things seriously.

เอาใจ ʔawcaj/ V to please, humor.

เอาใจกลางออก ʔaw/cajklaaŋ/-ʔɔɔg/ to remove the central part of something, e.g. to core (an apple).

เอาใจช่วย ʔawcaj/chûaj/ V to give moral support (to), root (for).

เอาใจใส่ ʔawcajsàj/ V 1. to pay attention. 2. to take an interest (in), put one's heart (into). ความ-- attention.

○ ด้วยความเอาใจใส่ dûajkhwaam/ʔawcajsàj/ attentively.

เอาใจออกห่าง ʔawcaj/ʔɔ̀ɔghàaŋ/ V to betray, break one's faith, break away (from).

เอาชนะ ʔaw/chaná/ V to strive to win or win out, strive to overcome.

เอาชีวิต ʔaw/chiiwíd/ V to take a life, kill.

เอาชีวิตรอด ʔaw/-chiiwíd/rɔ̂ɔd/ V to save one's life.

เอาซี ʔawsɯ̂↓ Yes. All right. Go ahead.

เอาตัวรอด ʔawtua/rɔ̂ɔd/ V 1. to save oneself, get oneself to safety, save one's own skin. 2.

to manage to live; to make something of one's life.

○ หนีเอาตัวรอด nɯ̃i/-ʔawtua/rɔ̂ɔd/ to flee to safety, flee saving one's own skin.

เอาแต่ใจตัวเอง ʔaw/-tɛcaj/tuaʔeeŋ/ to consider only one's own interests or wishes; to be self-willed, self-centered.

เอาแต่สะดวกเข้าว่า ʔaw/-tɛsadùag/khâwwâa/ colloq. to think only in terms of one's own convenience.

เอาถ่าน ʔawthàan/ V idiom. to be serious, earnest, industrious, to take things with due seriousness.

เอาเถอะ (1) ʔawthə?/; (2) ʔaw/thə?/↓ 1. Okay,... (e.g. I'll help you). All right. So be it. Let's agree on that. 2. Get it! Take it! NOTE. The spelling เถอะ is used to render the usual pronunciation, which is thə?. A more formal spelling is เถิด.

เอาเถิด (1) ʔawthə?/; (2) ʔawthə̀əd/ 1. All right. So be it. Let's agree on that. N 2. a kind of tag (children's game). →See Note under the entry above.

เอาเป็นนิยมนิยาย ʔaw/-penníjom/níjaaj/ to take (it) seriously; to consider (it); to count on (it).

เอาเปรียบ ʔawprìab/ V to take advantage of.

เอา(...)ไป ʔaw(...)paj/ 1. to take away, take (something) away (somewhere). 2. away.

○ เอาจดหมายไปส่งที่ไปรษณีย์ ʔawcòdmǎaj/-pajɔ sòŋ/thîiprajsanii/ to take the mail to the post office.

○ ฉวยเอาไป chǔaj/ʔawpaj/ to snatch away.

เอา(...)มา ʔaw(...)maa/ 1. to bring. 2. hither, along, up.

○ ฉุดเอาคุณแม่มาด้วย chùd/-ʔawkhunmɛ̂ɛ/maadûaj↓ Bring your mother along!

○ เอามาสู่กันกิน ʔawmaasùu/kankin/ to bring (food) and share (it) together.

○ เอามาเป็นอารมย์ ʔaw/maapenʔaarom/ V to take (things) too hard, too seriously; to worry too much.

○ ฉวยเอามา chǔaj/ʔawmaa/ to snatch up, snatch to oneself.

เอาเรื่อง ʔawrɯ̂aŋ/ V 1. to be strict, severe,

stern. 2. to cause trouble; to make an issue
(of something). sV 3. colloq. mighty, quite,
quite a bit.

เอาละ ʔaw/laʔↆ, ʔawlaʔ⁄ↆ All right. Okay.
Ready.

เอา(...)ไว้ (1) ʔaw(...)wáj⁄, -wájↄ; (2, 3) ʔawↄ
wáj⁄, -wájↄ 1. to take (and keep), keep, put
aside, put away. 2. to put off, postpone. 3. up,
away (as in "store up, put away."); in this sense
cf. ไว้.

o กาเอาไว้ kaa/ʔawwáj⁄ V to mark, mark off
(as with an x, check mark, etc.).

o เก็บเอาไว้ kèb/ʔawwáj⁄ to store up, put up,
keep.

o วางหม้อน้ำเอาไว้ให้คนดื่มแก้กระหาย waaŋ/ↄ
mɔ́ↄnáam/-ʔawwáj⁄ hâjkhondỳym/-kɛ̀ɛ/kraↄ
hǎajↆ (They) put out a jar of water for travel-
lers to quench their thirst.

o เอาไว้จวนๆวัน ʔawwájcuancuan/wan⁄ to delay
or put (it) off until almost the day.

o เอาเสือไว้อยู่มือ ʔawsǔa/-wájjùu/myy⁄ to get
the tiger under control.

เอาหน้า ʔawnâa⁄ V to do (something) in order
to win compliments, approval, glory.

เอา(...)ให้อยู่ ʔaw/(...)hâjjùu⁄ V colloq.
to get (something, someone) under control, get
control over, subdue, finish.

เอาอกเอาใจกัน ʔawʔòg/ʔawcaj⁄/-kan⁄ V to
attend to and please each other.

เอาอย่าง ʔawjàaŋ⁄ to follow the example of; to
imitate.

เอา(...)ออก ʔaw(...)ʔↄ̀ↄg⁄ 1. to take (something) out, get (something) out. 2. out.

o คั้นเอา(...)ออก khán/-ʔaw(...)ʔↄ̀ↄg⁄ to
squeeze (e.g. the juice) out.

o เอาออกไป้ ʔaw/ʔↄ̀ↄg!páj⁄ↆ Get it out of here!

o เอา(...)ออกให้ ʔaw(...)ʔↄ̀ↄg/hâj⁄ to take
(something) out for (someone).

เอาอีกแล้ว ʔaw/ʔìiglɛ́ɛwↆ What, again? Again!

เอ้า ʔâw⁄ E excl. used in expressions such as
those below.

o เอ้า นี่ของคุณ ʔâw/→ nîi/khɔ̌ↄŋkhun/ↆ Here,
this is yours.

o เอ้า เอาเข้าไป ʔâw/→ ʔaw/khâwpaj/ↆ Again!

There it is again! Another one! (as when watching contestants striking each other in a fight; also
expressing impatience with one's constantly recurring mistakes, as when typing).

เอิ๊ก ʔə́ↄg⁄ imit. the sound of laughter.

เอิ๊กเกริก ʔə́ↄg/karə̀ↄg⁄ V 1. to be clamorous, uproarious, hilarious. 2. to be bruited about,
noised abroad.

เอิบ in อิ่มเอิบ ʔìm?ə̀ↄb⁄ V to be satisfied, pleased,
contented.

เอียง ʔiaŋ⁄ V to bend, slant, incline; to be inclined,
tilted, slanting.

ลำเอียง lam?iaŋ⁄ V to be inclined toward someone; to be partial.

o ความไม่ลำเอียง khwaam/mâjlam?iaŋ⁄ N impartiality.

เอียงอาย ʔiaŋ?aaj⁄ V to be shy, bashful. →Also
อายเอียง.

เอนเอียง ʔeen?iaŋ⁄ V to incline toward, tend to,
have a tendency toward.

เอียงหู ʔiaŋhǔu⁄ V to turn the ear (toward)(in
order to listen).

เอี้ยง in นกเอี้ยง (ตัว) nóg?îaŋ⁄ (tua⁄) N singing
myna. →Resembles นกขุนทอง.

เอี่ยม ʔìam⁄ rM intens. used with ใหม่ "new."

เอี๊ยม (ตัว) ʔíam⁄ (tua⁄) N 1. an apron-like garment
used to keep the chest and abdomen of a baby
warm. 2. colloq. dickey (for women). [f. Chin.]

เอี้ยว ʔîaw⁄ V to turn, twist (esp. the body); to
swerve.

เอื้อ ʔŷa⁄ V to be obliging.

เอื้อเฟื้อ ʔŷafýa⁄ V 1. to be obliging, generous.
2. to help, support (with kindness); to be charitable to. ความ-- generosity, obligingness.

o มีใจเอื้อเฟื้อ miicaj/ʔŷafýa⁄ V to be obliging,
generous.

o เอื้อเฟื้อเผื่อแผ่ ʔŷafýa/phỳaphɛ̀ɛ⁄ V elab. to
be generous, liberal.

เอื้อก ʔŷag⁄ imit. 1. the sound of swallowing saliva
or water (in big gulps). C 2. gulp, swallow.

เอื้อง in เคี้ยวเอื้อง khíaw?ŷaŋ⁄ V to chew the cud,
ruminate.

เอื้อน in อิดเอื้อน ʔìd?ŷan⁄ V to demonstrate unwillingness or half-heartedness.

เอือม ʔɯ̂am/ V to be tired of, fed up with, sick of.

  เอือมระอา ʔɯ̂am/raʔaa/ V to be tired, wearied, fed up.

เอื้อม ʔɯ̂am/ V to reach for, stretch one's hand out (to get).

  แค่เอื้อม khɛ̂εʔɯ̂am/ V to be near, within reach.

  สุดเอื้อม sùdʔɯ̂am/ V to be out of reach, beyond reach.

  อาจเอื้อม ʔàadʔɯ̂am/ V to dare to do something beyond one's social status.

  เอื้อมมือ ʔɯ̂ammyy/ V to reach out (for), stretch out one's hand (in order to reach something).

  เอื้อมไม่ถึง ʔɯ̂am/mâjthɯ̌ŋ/ can't reach, can't be reached.

เอื่อย, เอื่อยๆ ʔɯ̀aj/, ʔɯ̀ajʔɯ̀aj/ sV slowly, unhurriedly, in a leisurely manner; gently, softly (as of a wind blowing).

แอ ๑ in อ่อนแอ ʔɔ̀ɔnʔεε/ V to be weak, frail, feeble.

แอ ๒ in แออัด ʔεεʔàd/ V to be congested, crowded (with people).

  แออัดยัดเยียด ʔεεʔàd/jádjîad/ V to be overcrowded, congested.

แอ๊. See อ้อแอ้.

แอก (อัน) ʔεεg/ (ʔan/) N yoke.

แอ๊กซิเดนท์, แอ๊กซิเดนต์ ʔέgsiden/* N accident. [f. Eng.] →Also เอ๊กซิเดนท์, เอ๊กซิเดนต์.

แอ่ง (แอ่ง) ʔὲŋ/* (ʔέŋ/) N depression (in the ground), basin.

  แอ่งน้ำ (แอ่ง) ʔὲŋnáam/ (ʔέŋ/) N water hole, pond, puddle.

แอด. See ออดแอด under ออด.

แอ๊ด in อ๊ายแอ๊ด (ตัว) ʔâjʔέd/*(tua/) N a kind of cricket kept by children for fighting purposes.

แอตแลนติก ʔεεdlεεntìg/ N 1. the Atlantic (Ocean). 2. (as n. mod.) Atlantic. [f. Eng.]

แอ่น ๑ ʔὲn/* V 1. to curve, bend out, curve out. (esp. of a person's chest). 2. to push out (e.g. the chest).

แอ่น ๒ in นกนางแอ่น (ตัว) nógnaaŋʔὲn/*(tua/) N com. swallow (the bird). →Syn. นกอีแอ่น colloq.

แอ้น. See อ้อนแอ้น.

แอบ ʔεεb/ V 1. to lie in wait, lie in hiding; to hide (in ambush, out of sight). 2. to sneak (through, in, out). 3. to do secretly. →Syn. 2,3. ลอบ.

แอบดู ʔεεbduu/ V to watch from a hiding place; to peep (at), peek (at).

แอบได้ยิน ʔεεb/dâjjin/ V to overhear (unintentionally).

แอบฟัง ʔεεbfaŋ/ V to eavesdrop, listen secretly.

แอบเห็น ʔεεbhěn/ V to happen to see (unintentionally).

แอ๊ปเปิ้ล (ใบ,ลูก,ผล) ʔέbpə̂n/, ʔέbpə̂l*(baj/, lûug/, phǒn/) N apple. ต้น-- (ต้น) apple tree. [f. Eng.]

แอฟริกา ʔέf/frikaa/* N Africa. [f. Eng.] →Also อัฟริกา, อาฟริกา.

แอม ๑ ʔέm/* V slang to get, obtain, take.

แอม ๒. See อ้อมแอม.

แอมโมเนีย ʔεmmoonia/* N ammonia. [f. Eng.]

แอล. ʔεl/* the English letter "L." [f. Eng.] →Also เอล.

แอลกอฮอล์ ʔεl/kɔɔhɔɔ/* N alcohol. [f. Eng.]

โอ. ʔoo/ the English letter "O." [f. Eng.]

โอ ๑ (ใบ,ลูก) ʔoo/ (baj/, lûug/) N a woven bowl-shaped vessel (usually lacquered, and used for drinking water).

โอ ๒ ʔoo/ E Oh! (excl. of surprise, dismay).

โอ ๓ in ส้มโอ (ลูก,ใบ,ผล) sômʔoo/ (lûug/, baj/, phǒn/) N pomelo. ต้น-- (ต้น) pomelo tree.

โอ่ ʔòo/ V to boast. →Chiefly in compounds.

  ขี้โอ่ khîiʔòo/ V to be a dandy.

  โอ่โถง ʔòothǒoŋ/ V to be splendid, magnificent, luxurious.

  โอ่อวด ʔòoʔùad/ V to brag, boast.

  โอ่อ่า ʔòoʔàa/ V 1. to be splendid, luxurious, grand. 2. to be ostentatious. ความ-- gorgeousness, splendor.

โอ้ ๑ ʔôo/ E Oh! (excl. of sorrow).

โอ้ ๒ ʔôo/ sV loudly, openly.

  คุยโอ้ khuj/ʔôo/ colloq. to brag loudly, openly.

  โอ้อวด ʔôoʔùad/ V to boast, brag.

โอ๋ ʔǒo/ E 1. com. excl. expressing solace, esp. to small children. V 2. colloq. to console, comfort. 3. to indulge, pamper, humor.

โอ๊ก ʔóog/ N oak. ต้น-- (ต้น) oak tree. [f. Eng.]

โอกาส (หน,ครั้ง) ʔookàad/ (hǒn/, khráŋ/) N,C opportunity, chance, occasion. →Sometimes also spelled โอกาศ.

ฉวยโอกาส chǔaj/ˀookàad/ V to seize the opportunity. ผู้- -,นัก- - opportunist.

ได้โอกาส dâjˀookàad/ V to have a chance, get a chance.

ถือโอกาส thǔyˀookàad/ V to take the opportunity.

ในโอกาส najˀookàad/ on the occasion of.

บางโอกาส baaŋ/ˀookàad/ on some occasions.

เปิดโอกาส pòədˀookàad/ V to give an opportunity.

มีโอกาสครึ่งต่อครึ่ง miiˀookàad/-khrŷŋ/tɔ̀ɔkhrŷŋ/ V to have a 50-50 chance.

หมดโอกาส mòdˀookàad/ V to lose an opportunity; to have no more opportunity.

โอ่ง (ใบ) ˀòoŋ/ (baj/) N big jar for water.

โอ่งต่อขา ˀòoŋ/tɔ̀ɔkhǎa/ V slang to be very fat (of people): "jar with legs."

โองการ ˀooŋkaan/ as in พระบรมราชโองการ (ฉะ บับ) phrábɔrommaraad/chaˀooŋ/kaan/ (chaɔ bàb/) N roy. royal command, royal decree.

โอช in เอมโอช ˀeemˀòod/ V to be delicious, savory.

โอชะ,โอชา ˀoochá?/, ˀoochaa/ V eleg. to be delicious. →Syn. อร่อย com.

โอชารส ˀoochaaród/ V eleg. to be delicious.

โอด ˀòod/ V to cry, lament, complain in a pathetic manner.

โอดครวญ ˀòodkhruan/ V 1. to lament, moan, cry. 2. slang to squawk, complain.

โอเดียน ˀoodîan/* nN Odeon, name of a movie house in Bangkok.

โอน ๑ ˀoon/ V to transfer (ownership, control, etc.).

โอนกรรมสิทธิ์ ˀoon/kammasìd/ V to transfer ownership.

โอนชาติ ˀoonchâad/ V to become naturalized, to change one's citizenship.

โอนทะเบียนรถ ˀoon/thabianród/ V to transfer the registered ownership of a car.

โอนเป็นของชาติ ˀoon/penkhɔ̌ɔŋchâad/ to nationalize.

โอน ๒ ˀoon/ V to bend, incline. →Chiefly in compounds.

โอนอ่อน ˀoonˀɔ̀ɔn/ V to comply, acquiesce.

o โอนอ่อนผ่อนตาม ˀoonˀɔ̀ɔn/phɔ̀ɔntaam/ V elab. colloq. to yield to; to be compliant; to comply with, acquiesce.

โอนเอน ˀoonˀeen/ V to be swaying, vacillating, unsteady.

โอนเอียง ˀoonˀiaŋ/ V to be inclined.

โอบ ˀòob/ V 1. to put an arm around, to embrace. 2. to encircle, surround.

ตีโอบหลังข้าศึก tii/-ˀòoblǎŋ/khâasỳg/ V to outflank the enemy and attack from behind.

โอบปีกกาล้อม ˀòob-plìgkaa/lɔ́ɔm/ V to flank and encircle.

โอบไหล่ ˀòoblàj/ V to put one's arm around the shoulders (of).

โอบอ้อมอารี ˀòobˀɔ́ɔm/ˀaarii/ V to be generous, hospitable, thoughtful, kind.

โอบอุ้ม ˀòobˀûm/ V 1. to carry embracing with both arms. 2. to cherish, foster; to help, support.

โอภา in โอภาปราศรัย ˀoophaa/praasǎj/ V elab. eleg. to greet cordially, converse cordially.

โอย,โอ๊ย ˀooj/↓, !ˀóoj/↓ E Ouch! Oh! (excl. of pain).

โอยตาย !ˀóojtaaj/↓ E excl. expressing fear, dismay.

โอ๊ยโย่ !ˀóojjôo/↓ E excl. expressing surprise, fear.

โอรส (องค์) ˀooród/ (ˀoŋ/) N roy. son.

โอเลี้ยง ˀoolíaŋ/ N slang black iced coffee. [f. Chin.] →Syn. ดำเย็น colloq.

โอวาท ˀoowâad/ N eleg. teaching, instruction, admonition, advice (esp. dealing with moral conduct).

ให้โอวาท hâj/ˀoowâad/ V eleg. to admonish, to deliver an admonitory speech.

อยู่ในโอวาท jùu/najˀoowâad/ eleg. to be obedient.

โอษฐ์ in พระโอษฐ์ phráˀòod/ N roy. mouth, lips, →Syn. ปาก com.

โอสถ (ขนาน) ˀoosòd/ (khanǎan/) N eleg. medicine, drug.

โอสถศาลา (แห่ง) ˀoosòd/sǎalaa/ (hὲŋ/) N obsolesc. 1. pharmacy. 2. medical station.

โอหัง ˀoohǎŋ/ V to be arrogant, haughty, disdainful,

proud, daring.

โอฬาร ʔoolaan′ V eleg. to be great, spacious.

โอ้เอ้ ʔôoʔêe′ V to linger, delay, waste time.

มัวโอ้เอ้ mua′ʔôoʔêe′ to linger, loiter, waste time unnecessarily.

โอ้โฮ ʔôohoo′→ E Gosh! Oh! (excl. expressing surprise, excitement).

ไอ. ʔaj′ the English letter "I." [f. Eng.]

ไอ ๑ ʔaj′ N vapor, steam.

กลายเป็นไอ klaaj′penʔaj′ to become steam, vaporize, evaporate.

กลิ่นไอ klìnʔaj′ N 1. smell, odor. 2. idiom. atmosphere.

ท่อไอเสีย (ท่อ) thɔɔ′ʔajsĭa′ (thɔɔ′) N exhaust pipe.

ไอตัว ʔajtua′ N body warmth.

ไอน้ำ ʔajnáam′ N steam, vapor.

o เครื่องจักรไอน้ำ (เครื่อง) khrŷaŋcàg′ʔajnáam′ (khrŷaŋ′) N steam engine.

ไอพ่น ʔajphôn′ N jet (as of heated gases). Used in compounds such as the following.

o เครื่องบินไอพ่น (เครื่อง,ลำ) khrŷaŋbin′ʔajɔ- phôn′ (khrŷaŋ′, lam′) N jet plane.

o เครื่องไอพ่น (เครื่อง) khrŷaŋ′ʔajphôn′ (khrŷaŋ′) N jet engine.

ไอพิษ ʔajphíd′ N poisonous gas.

o เครื่องป้องกันไอพิษ (เครื่อง,อัน) khrŷaŋ′- pɔŋkan′ʔajphíd′ (khrŷaŋ′, ʔan′) N gas mask.

ไอ ๒ ʔaj′ V to cough.

ไอ้. See อ้าย.

ไอติม ʔajtim′ N colloq. ice cream. [f. Eng.] →See also ไอสกรีม.

ไอย่า ʔájjâa′→ E excl. expressing fright, dismay. [f. Chin.]

ไอสกรีม ʔajsakriim′ N ice cream. [f. Eng.] →See also ไอติม.

ไอโอดีน ʔajʔoodiin′ N iodine. [f. Eng.]

ฮ

ฮ hɔɔ′ LOW consonant. Pronounced h and used only initially. This consonant is rare, and is found especially in onomatopoetic words, loanwords,

and words of the northern dialect of Thai which has ฮ for Bangkok ร.

ฮก. Abbrev. for เฮกโตกรัม hectogram.

ฮ่องกง hɔŋkoŋ′* N Hong Kong. [f. Chin.]

ฮอลันดา hɔɔlandaa′ N Holland. [f. Eur.]

ฮะ ๑ (1) há?′; (2) há′ Pt 1. def. m. sp. Variant of ครับ, q.v. Pt 2. def. w. sp. Variant of คะ, q.v.

ฮะ ๒ !há′ E excl. expressing contempt, irritation.

ฮะ ๆ hâhâ′ imit. the sound of a laugh.

ฮักๆ hâghâg′ imit. the sound of sobbing.

ฮังการี haŋkaarii′ N Hungary. [f. Eng.]

ฮัน hân′ N Hun. [f. Eng.]

ฮัลโหล hanlŏo′, halŏo′ Hello! [f. Eng.]

ฮา haa′ imit. 1. the sound of laughter. V 2. to laugh loudly. 3. to express approval (with the voice, by clapping, etc.).

เสียงฮา sĭaŋhaa′ N laughter, the sound of laughter.

ฮาป่า haapàa′ (a group of people) to laugh and hoot, give a roar of laughter (i.e. to give a loud "ha," indicating either amusement, or derision).

ฮาฮา haahaa′ imit. the sound of laughing.

ฮาๆ hâahâa′ imit. the sound of laughing.

ฮานอย haanɔɔj′ N Hanoi. [f. Viet.]

ฮาวาย haawaaj′ N 1. Hawaii. 2. Hawaiian.

ฮินดู hinduu′ N Hindu. [f. Hind.]

ฮี hý′, !hý′ E Hm! Huh! (excl. expressing surprise, displeasure, bemused contempt).

ฮึกเหิม hýghšƏm′ V to be bold, daring.

ฮึดฮัด hýdhád′ V to grunt or expel the breath with exasperation, fury.

ฮือ ๑, ฮือๆ hyy′, hyyhyy′ imit. a crying or groaning sound.

ฮือ ๒ hyy′ V imit. 1. to burst suddenly into flame, flare up all at once (of a fire). 2. to act all at once, suddenly and all together (as of a mob).

ลุกฮือ lúghyy′ V 1. to flare up all at once (of a fire). 2. to rise up all at once, suddenly and all together (as of a mob).

ฮือ. A spelling used to indicate an utterance pronounced variously hŷy′ (with nasalized vowel) hm̂m′, hm̂n′, hm̂ŋ′ and signifying "yes."

ฮุบ húb′ V 1. (a fish) to strike, snatch at, snap up. 2. fig. to snap up, swallow up.

ฮูก in นกฮูก (ตัว) nóghûug′ (tua′) N owl.

เฮ hee′ imit. 1. the hubbub of a crowd. V 2. (a
crowd) to make a hubbub. 3. to flock (together,
in large numbers).

  เฮโล heeloo′ V 1. to throng, go in large numbers.
E. 2. excl. used by a group of people dragging
a heavy load; similar to "heave ho" but not restricted to nautical usage.

  เฮฮา heehaa′ imit. 1. the sound of hearty
laughter. V 2. laugh heartily, uproariously.

เฮ́ hée′ E Say! Hey! (used to call attention, sometimes indicating displeasure, irritation).

เฮกโตกรัม hég′tookram′ C hectogram. [f. Eur.]
  →Abbrev. ฮก.

เฮ้ย hə́j′* E exclamative. Often used to express
reluctance about going along with what has been
said.

เฮ̌ย hə̌j′* E vulg. Hey! (used to call attention;
used when sp. to inferior, also among men and
sometimes among women who are intimates,
otherwise considered impolite).

เฮ้อ hə́ə′ E 1. excl. expressing relief. 2. excl.
expressing strong dissatisfaction, boredom.

เฮี้ยว híaw′ V colloq. 1. to bully. 2. to be un-
cooperative, recalcitrant, contrary.

เฮือ hya′ N boat. →Northern dialect form for เรือ.

เฮือก hŷag′ imit. 1. the sound of sighing. 2. the
sound of a gasp. C 3. an occurrence of any
such sound. sV 4. suddenly, with a gasp.

  ถอนใจเฮือกใหญ่ thɔɔncaj′-hŷag′jàj′ to heave a
big sigh.

  สะดุ้งเฮือก sadûŋ′hŷag′ V to start suddenly,
start with a gasp, be startled.

แฮม hɛɛm′ N ham. [f. Eng.]

แฮะ hɛ́′ Pt particle used with the force of an exclamative, often expressing an element of surprise.

  o สวยจริงแฮะวันนี้ sŭaj′ciŋhɛ́′-wanníi′↑ Gee,
you sure are prettied up today!

โฮ ๑, โฮ́ๆ hoo′, hoohoo′ imit. the sound of weeping, crying.

โฮ ๒ in โอ̂โฮ ʔôohoo′ E Wow! Oh! (excl. expressing surprise, excitement).

โฮกฮาก, กระโฮก-- hôoghâag′, krachôog′hôoghâag′
V 1. to be harsh, rough, crude, brusque (in
manner, esp. of speaking). sV 2. harshly,
brusquely.

โฮเต็ล (แห่ง) hooten′, hootel′ (hὲŋ′) N hotel. [f.
Eur.]

ไฮโดรเจน,ไฮโดรเยน hajdroocên′*, hajdroojên′* N
hydrogen. [f. Eng.]